BRITISH NATIONAL FORMULARY

March 1991

BRITISH NATIONAL FORMULARY

Number 21
(March 1991)

British Medical Association
and
Royal Pharmaceutical Society of Great Britain

Copyright 1991 © by the British Medical Association and the Royal Pharmaceutical Society of Great Britain

Copies may be obtained through any bookseller or, in any case of difficulty, direct from the publishers:

British Medical Association
Tavistock Square
London WC1H 9JP, England

The Pharmaceutical Press
1 Lambeth High Street
London SE1 7JN, England

ISBN: 0 85369 251 3. ISSN: 0260–535X

All rights reserved. No part of this publication may be reproduced, stored in a retrieval system, or transmitted in any form or by any means—electronic, mechanical, photocopying, recording or otherwise—without the prior written permission of the joint copyright holders.

Typeset in Great Britain by Page Bros, Norwich, Norfolk NR6 6SA and printed and bound by The Bath Press, Bath, Avon BA2 3BL.

Joint Formulary Committee 1990–91

Chairman

C. F. George, BSc, MD, FRCP

Deputy Chairman

C. R. Hitchings, BPharm, MSc, FRPharmS, MCPP

Committee Members

Alison Blenkinsopp, PhD, BPharm, MRPharmS

M. Goodman, MRCS, LRCP, FRCGP, DObstRCOG

P. E. Green, BSc, MSc, LLM, MRPharmS

K. H. Jones, MD, MB, BCh

P. A. Leech, MRCS, LRCP, DMJ(clin)

F. P. Marsh, MA, MB, BChir, FRCP

G. M. Mitchell, KStJ, MB, ChB, FRPharmS

P. C. Waller, MD, MRCP (alternate to K. H. Jones)

N. L. Wood, BPharm, MRPharmS

Joint Secretaries

Natalie-Jane Macdonald, MB, ChB, MRCP

A. Wade, BPharm, MPhil, FRPharmS

Executive Editor

Anne B. Prasad, FRPharmS

Assistant Editor

Sheenagh M. Townsend-Smith, BSc, DipLib

Editorial Staff

A. G. Desson, BPharm, MSc, MRPharmS

Pamela M. Mason, BSc, PhD, MRPharmS

D. K. Mehta, BPharm, MSc, MRPharmS

Anjana Patel, BPharm, MSc, PhD, MRPharmS

Executive Secretary

Susan M. Thomas, BSc(Econ), MA

Contents

APPENDIXES AND INDEXES

Arrangement of Information

Guidance on prescribing
This part includes information on prescription writing, prescribing for children and elderly patients, and prescribing in terminal care. Information is also given on adverse reactions, controlled drugs, and dependence.

Emergency treatment of poisoning
The main intention of this chapter is to provide information on the management of acute poisoning when first seen in the home, although aspects of hospital-based treatment are mentioned.

Classified notes on drugs and preparations
The main text consists of classified notes on drugs and preparations used in the treatment of diseases and conditions. These notes are divided into 15 chapters, each of which is related to a particular system of the human body or to another main subject. Each chapter is then divided into sections which begin with appropriate *notes for prescribers*. These notes are intended to provide information to doctors, pharmacists, nurses etc. to facilitate the selection of suitable treatment. The notes are followed by details of relevant drugs and preparations.

DRUGS appear under pharmacopoeial or other non-proprietary titles. When there is an *appropriate current monograph* (Medicines Act 1968, Section 65) preference is given to a name at the head of that monograph; otherwise a British Approved Name, if available, is used. If there is an acknowledged reference drug, information on it is usually given first; otherwise the drugs are arranged alphabetically.

PREPARATIONS usually follow immediately after the drug which is their main ingredient. They are printed in text-sized type but those considered by the Committee to be less suitable for prescribing are described in smaller type. Small type is also used for the entries describing foods for special diets, preparations for stoma care, and wound management products. Preparations are included under a non-proprietary title only if:

(a) they are marketed under such a title,
(b) they are not otherwise prescribable under the NHS, or
(c) they may be prepared extemporaneously.

If proprietary preparations are of a distinctive colour this is stated, but flavour is not usually mentioned.

In the case of compound preparations the indications, cautions, contra-indications, side-effects, and drug interactions of all constituents should be taken into account in prescribing; usually the ingredients should be looked up separately.

PREPARATIONS NOT AVAILABLE FOR NHS PRESCRIPTION. The symbol NHS has been placed against those preparations included in the BNF that are not prescribable under the NHS. Those prescribable only for specific disorders have a foot-note specifying the condition(s) for which the preparation remains available. Prescribers are reminded that although some preparations are not *prescribable* by brand name under the NHS the brand in question may nevertheless be *dispensed* if no non-proprietary preparation is marketed.

PRESCRIPTION-ONLY MEDICINES. The symbol PoM has been placed against those preparations that are available only on medical or dental prescription. For more detailed information see *Medicines, Ethics and Practice*, No. 5, London, Pharmaceutical Press, 1990 (and subsequent editions as available). The symbol **CD** indicates that the preparation is subject to the prescription requirements of the Misuse of Drugs Act. For regulations governing prescriptions for such preparations see pages 7–9.

PRICES (see p. 1) have been calculated whenever possible from the basic cost used in pricing NHS prescriptions dispensed in August 1990, see p. 1 for further details.

DILUENTS indicated in the entries for certain creams, ointments, elixirs, and mixtures are intended to be used when lower strengths or doses are ordered, as indicated under 'General Guidance'.

Appendixes and indexes
The appendixes include information on interactions, liver disease, renal impairment, pregnancy, breast-feeding, intravenous additives, borderline substances, and cautionary and advisory labels for dispensed medicines. Where relevant they are designed for use in association with the main body of the text.

The Dental Practitioners' List is also included in this section. The indexes consist of the Index of Manufacturers and the Main Index.

Preface

The present format of the British National Formulary was introduced in February 1981. Information is included on most products available to prescribers in the United Kingdom. The product entries, are preceded by relevant notes to help in the choice of appropriate treatment.

Basic net prices are included to provide better indications of relative cost. Where there is a choice of suitable preparations for a particular disease or condition the relative cost may be used in making a selection. It should be emphasised, however, that cost-effective prescribing must take into account other factors (such as dose frequency and duration of treatment) that affect the total cost. The use of more expensive drugs is justified if it will result in better treatment of the patient or a reduction of the length of an illness or the time spent in hospital.

The BNF is intended to be a pocket book for rapid reference and so cannot contain all the information necessary for prescribing and dispensing. It should be supplemented as necessary from specialised publications. Manufacturers' data sheets prepared in accordance with the Medicines (Data Sheet) Regulations 1972 are available for most proprietary medicines and these should also be consulted. Less detail is given in the chapters on malignant disease and immunosuppression, and anaesthesia, as it is expected that those undertaking treatment will have specialised knowledge and will consult specialist literature. Supplementary information may be available from local drug information services.

The Joint Formulary Committee acknowledges the help of individuals and organisations that provided information or advised on specific matters. The principal contributors for this edition were J. M. Aitken, S. P. Allison, D. G. Arkell, R. S. Atkinson, C. G. Barnes, L. Beeley, R. H. Behrens, D. R. Bell, M. J. Brodie, I. Burgess, C. M. Castleden, D. A. Chamberlain, J. F. Davidson, S. I. Davidson, C. Diamond, R. Dinwiddie, A. J. Duxbury, H. M. Elliston, A. M. Geddes, A. H. Ghodse, J. Guillebaud, C. H. Hawkes, A. V. Hoffbrand, M. J. S. Langman, T. H. Lee, P. N. Leigh, R. Levinsky, R. Marks, M. W. McNicol, G. M. Mead, M. R. Moore, D. J. Oliver, L. E. Ramsay, P. A. Routledge, P. C. Rubin, R. S. Sawers, M. C. Sheppard, S. D. Shorvon, M. Tarr, A. Tattersfield, G. R. Thompson, V. R. Tindall, D. G. Waller, D. A. Warrell, P. Watkins, K. Watson, J. Wilson. The Committee also wishes to express its thanks to correspondents in the pharmaceutical industry who provided information and made numerous comments on points of detail, to colleagues who have advised members of the committee and the editorial staff on specific matters, and to J. Holmes and T. M. Roberts for clerical assistance. Finally, the Committee would like to thank those doctors, pharmacists, nurses, and others who sent comments and suggestions.

Comments and constructive criticism will be welcome, and should be sent to:
Executive Editor,
British National Formulary,
1 Lambeth High Street,
London SE1 7JN.

Changes

The BNF is revised twice yearly and numerous changes are made between issues. All copies of BNF No. 20 (September 1990) should therefore be withdrawn and replaced by BNF No. 21 (March 1991).

Significant changes have been made in the following sections for BNF No. 21:

Antihypertensive therapy (section 2.5)
Antimanic drugs (section 4.2.3)
Summary of antibacterial prophylaxis (section 5.1)
Prostaglandins and oxytocics (section 7.1.1)
Progestogens (section 6.4.1.2)
Pituitary hormones (section 6.5)
Hypercalcaemia (section 9.5.1.2)
Drugs which may affect the rheumatic disease process (section 10.1.3)
Otitis externa (section 12.1.1)
Otitis media (12.1.2)
Parasiticidal preparations (section 13.10.4)
Immunoglobulins (section 14.5)
General anaesthesia (surgery and long-term medication) (section 15.1)
Muscle relaxants (section 15.1.5)
Appendix 1 (potentially hazardous interactions now highlighted)
Appendix 6 (presentation)
Appendix 8 (cautionary label changes)

ADDITIVES. Oral liquid preparations in the BNF that do not contain *fructose*, *glucose* or *sucrose* are labelled "sugar-free".

Where the presence of *gluten* or of *tartrazine* is specified on a data sheet this is indicated in the BNF against the preparation in question; not all data sheets provide details of additives therefore if it is essential to know whether a preparation is free of gluten or of tartrazine the manufacturer should be contacted.

Information is provided on *preservatives* in eye-drops.

Information is provided on *selected additives* in skin preparations (for details see section 13.1)

Dose Changes

Preparations affected by changes in dose statements introduced into BNF No. 21:

Aminoglutethimide, p. 290
Bendrofluazide [hypertension], p. 54
Benzylpenicillin [meningitis], p. 186
Bleomycin [potency **only** in units], p. 281
Carbenoxolone [elderly], p. 36
Carisoprodol, p. 337
Ceftazidime [elderly], p. 195
Cyclizine [child], p. 153
Desferrioxamine [poisoning], p. 19
DHC Continus, p. 164
Doxycycline, p. 199
Edrophonium, p. 335
Ethamsylate, p. 95
Fenfluramine, p. 151
Fletchers Phosphate Enema [child], p. 46
Haloperidol [nausea and vomiting], p. 135
Hydralazine, p. 72
Imipramine, p. 145
Isoniazid, pp. 208 [text], 210
Karvol [avoid in infants], p. 118
MST Continus, p. 162
Neostigmine, p. 335
Nifedipine, p. 83
Paracetamol, pp. 158, 407
Pemoline, p. 149
Pimozide, p. 136
Pregaday, p. 294
Rifampicin, p. 208 [text]
Sinemet-Plus, p. 177
Sulphadiazine, p. 207
Tubocurarine, p. 431
Zidovudine, p. 219

Classification Changes

4.4.1	no longer exists
4.4.2	no longer exists
9.1.3	Drugs used in hypoplastic, haemolytic and renal anaemias [title change]
12.2.1	*Rinatec* now in 12.2.2
12.3.3	Antiseptic lozenges, sprays and gels [title change]
13.3	Local anaesthetics and antipruritics [title change]
13.8	Sunscreens and camouflagers [title change]
13.9	Shampoos and some other scalp preparations [title change]
13.14	Topical circulatory preparations [title change]

New Preparations

PoM **Burinex A®** (Leo)
Tablets, ivory, scored, amiloride hydrochloride 5 mg, bumetanide 1 mg. Net price 28-tab pack = £3.20. BNF section 2.2.4
Dose: 1–2 tablets daily

Capasal® (Dermal)
Shampoo, coal tar 1%, coconut oil 1%, salicylic acid 0.5%. Net price 250 mL = £4.95. For dry, scaly scalp conditions. BNF section 13.9

▼ PoM **Clexane®** (Rhône-Poulenc Rorer)
Injection, enoxaparin 100 mg/mL. Net price 0.2-mL syringe (20 mg) = £4.90; 0.4-mL syringe (40 mg) = £8.82. BNF section 2.8.1
For prophylaxis of deep-vein thrombosis and prevention of clotting in extracorporeal circulation
Consult data sheet for details of administration

PoM **Dalacin T®** (Upjohn)
Topical lotion, clindamycin (as phosphate) 1% in an aqueous basis. Net price 30 mL = £6.65. BNF section 13.6
Administration: acne, apply twice daily

▼ PoM **Dimetriose®** (Roussel)
Capsules, gestrinone 2.5 mg, net price 8-cap pack = £75.00. BNF section 6.7.3
Cautions; Contra-indications; Side-effects: as for Danazol, p. 259 (including barrier contraception); interactions: antiepileptics, rifampicin
Dose: endometriosis, 2.5 mg twice weekly starting on first day of menstrual cycle with second dose 3 days later; repeated on same two days, preferably at same time, each week, duration of treatment usually 6 months
MISSED DOSES, one missed dose—2.5 mg as soon as possible and maintain original sequence; two or more missed doses—discontinue, re-start on first day of new cycle (following negative pregnancy test)

PoM **Frumil®** (Rhône-Poulenc Rorer)
Forte tablets, orange, scored, co-amilofruse 10/80 (amiloride hydrochloride 10 mg, frusemide 80 mg). Net price 28-tab pack = £7.38. BNF section 2.2.4
Dose: 1 tablet daily in the morning

▼ PoM **Lustral®** (Invicta)
Tablets, sertraline (as hydrochloride) 50 mg, net price 28-tab pack = £26.51; 100 mg, 28-tab pack = £39.77. Label: 21, counselling, driving. BNF section 4.3.4
Cautions: epilepsy (avoid if unstable); avoid in hepatic and renal impairment, and in electroconvulsive therapy; pregnancy and breast-feeding; interactions: lithium
DRIVING. May affect performance of skilled tasks
Side-effects: dry mouth, nausea, diarrhoea, delayed ejaculation, tremor, sweating, dyspepsia; rarely, increase in liver enzymes
Dose: depressive illness, initially 50 mg daily, increased if necessary by increments of 50 mg over several weeks to max. 200 mg daily, then reduced to usual maintenance of 50–100 mg daily; doses of 150 mg daily or greater should not be used for more than 8 weeks

▼ PoM **Oxivent®** (Boehringer Ingelheim)
Aerosol inhalation, oxitropium bromide 100 micrograms/metered inhalation. Net price 200-dose unit = £12.98. BNF section 3.1.2
Cautions; Contra-indications; Side-effects: as for Ipratropium Bromide, p. 104
COUNSELLING. Advise not to exceed prescribed dose and to follow manufacturer's directions
Dose: reversible airways obstruction, *by aerosol inhalation*, 200 micrograms (2 puffs) 2–3 times daily

PEC High Compression Bandage (Drug Tariff). Polyamide, elastane, and cotton compression (high) extensible bandage. 3 m unstretched (both): 7.5 cm, net price = £1.89; 10 cm = £2.44. (Seton—*Setopress®*). BNF section 13.13.1
Uses: high compression for varicose ulcers

▼ PoM **Prostap SR®** (Lederle)
Injection (aqueous suspension), leuprorelin acetate, net price 3.75-mg vial microcapsule powder for reconstitution with 2-mL vehicle-filled syringe, needles and swabs = £125.40. BNF section 8.3.4
Cautions; Side-effects: see under Buserelin, p. 290; also, infrequently, peripheral oedema, fatigue, nausea, irritation at injection site; rotate injection site periodically
Dose: by subcutaneous or by intramuscular injection, 3.75 mg every 4 weeks; start anti-androgen 3 days before initial leuprorelin acetate injection if combination given

▼ PoM **Serevent®** (A&H)
Aerosol inhalation, salmeterol (as hydroxynaphthoate) 25 micrograms/metered inhalation, net price 120-dose unit = £28.60.
Powder for inhalation, disks containing 4 blisters of salmeterol (as hydroxynaphthoate) 50 micrograms/blister, net price pack of 14 disks with Diskhaler® = £29.97; 14-disk refill = £29.40. BNF section 3.1.1.1
Cautions; Side-effects: as for Salbutamol, p. 101
Dose: asthma and other conditions associated with reversible airways obstruction, 50 micrograms twice daily; up to 100 micrograms twice daily in more severe airways obstruction

▼ PoM **Staril®** (Squibb)
Tablets, fosinopril sodium 10 mg, net price 28-tab pack = £12.04; 20 mg, 28-tab pack = £21.00. BNF section 2.5.5
Cautions; Contra-indications; Side-effects: as for ACE inhibitors, p. 76
Dose: hypertension where standard therapy ineffective or inappropriate, initially 10 mg daily; usual maintenance 20 mg daily; max. 40 mg daily
Note: If used in addition to diuretic, discontinue diuretic several days before and resume after about 4 weeks if blood pressure inadequately controlled (if diuretic therapy cannot be stopped careful medical supervision for several hours)

CD **Temgesic®** (R&C)
Tablets (sublingual), buprenorphine 400 micrograms (as hydrochloride). Net price 50 = £12.00. Label: 2, 26. BNF section 4.7.2

New Preparations (*continued*)

Trifyba® (Sanofi)

Powder, wheat fibre 80%. Net price 56 × 3.5-g sachets = £3.36. Label: 27, counselling, see below. BNF section 1.6.1

Indications; Cautions; Contra-indications; Side-effects: see Bulk-forming drugs, p. 41

COUNSELLING. Preparations that swell in contact with liquid should always be carefully swallowed with water and should not be taken immediately before going to bed

Dose: 1 sachet mixed with food or liquid 2–3 times daily; CHILD half to one sachet 1–2 times daily

PoM **Vagifem®** (Novo Nordisk)

Vaginal tablets, controlled-release, oestradiol 25 micrograms in disposable applicators, net price 15-applicator pack = £14.99. BNF section 7.2.1

Cautions; Contra-indications; Side-effects: as for Ethinyloestradiol, p. 246

Dose: menopausal vaginitis, insert 1 tablet daily for 2 weeks then reduce to 2 tablets each week; discontinue after 3 months to assess need for further treatment

PEAK FLOW METERS

Mini-Wright® (Clement Clarke)

Peak flow meter, standard (60 to 800 litres/minute), net price = £6.39, low range (30 to 370 litres/minute) = £6.39, replacement mouthpiece adult = 38p, small = 38p, adaptor to fit small mouthpiece = 38p

Vitalograph® (Vitalograph)

Peak flow meter, standard (50 to 750 litres/minute), net price = £5.99, low range (25 to 280 litres/minute) = £5.99, replacement mouthpiece = 40p

Preparations included in appropriate sections of BNF No. 21

Discontinued Preparations

Preparations discontinued during the compilation of BNF No. 21

Akrotherm
Anaflex Aerosol Spray, Dusting Powder, Lozenges, Paste
Anaflex
Asilone gel
Asilone for Infants
Attenuvax
Aventyl Liquid
Bactrim Intramuscular Injection
Benoxyl with Sulphur
Betadren
Bismodyne
Bronchodil Respirator Solution
Broxil
Decaserpyl preparations
Dispray 1 Quick Prep
Duo-Autohaler
Eczederm with Hydrocortisone
Emetrol
Epodyl
Erycen Suspension
Erymax Sprinkle Capsules
Erythrolar
Forane [name only]
Gastrese LA
Haelan-X
H-B-Vax
Ipral Paediatric Suspension
Iso-Autohaler
Isoket
Koate HT
Lejfibre
Maxtrex
Medised Tablets
Meruvax II
Metoros preparations
Monovent Tablets
Nystan Dusting Powder and Triple pack
Nystavescent
Orbenin Syrup
Paynocil
Pharmorubicin [replaced by Pharmorubicin Rapid Dissolution]
Pimafucin Vaginal Tablets
PK Aid 1 [replaced by PK Aid 3]
Prostin F2 Alpha Intravenous Solution
Salicylic Acid Adhesive Plaster
Somatonorm
Staphlipen
Stesolid Injection
Sulphamezathine
Tedral
Tenavoid
Unimycin
Uromide
Uticillin
Vira-A preparations

Drug Information Services

Information on any aspect of drug therapy can be obtained, free of charge, from Regional and District Drug Information Services. Details regarding the *local* services provided within your Region can be obtained by telephoning the following numbers.

England		
Birmingham	021-378 2211	Extn 2296/2297
Bristol	0272 282867	Direct Line
Guildford	0483 504312	Direct Line
Ipswich	0473 704430	Direct Line
	or 0473 704431	Direct Line
Leeds	0532 430715	Direct Line
Leicester	0533 555779	Direct Line
Liverpool	051-236 4620	Extn 2126/2127/2128
London (Guy's Hospital)	071-955 5000	Extn 3594/5892
	or 071-378 0023	Direct Line
London (London Hospital)	071-377 7487	Direct Line
	or 071-377 7488	Direct Line
London (Northwick Park)	081-869 2761	Direct Line
Manchester	061-225 2063	Direct Line
	or 061-276 6270	Direct Line
Newcastle	091-232 1525	Direct Line
Oxford	0865 742424	Direct Line
Southampton	0703 796908	Direct Line
	or 0703 796909	Direct Line
Northern Ireland		
Belfast	0232 248095	Direct Line
Londonderry	0504 45171	Extn 3262
Scotland		
Aberdeen	0224 681818	Extn 52316
Dundee	0382 60111	Extn 2351
Edinburgh	031-229 2477	Extn 2094/2416/2443
	or 031-229 3901	Direct Line
Glasgow	041-552 4726	Direct Line
Inverness	0463 234151	Extn 288
	or 0463 220157	Direct Line
Wales		
Cardiff	0222 759541	Direct Line

Poisons Information Services

Belfast	0232 240503
Birmingham	021-554 3801
Cardiff	0222 709901
Dublin	0001 379964 *or* 0001 379966
Edinburgh	031-229 2477
	031-228 2441 (Viewdata)
Leeds	0532 430715 *or* 0532 432799
London	071-635 9191 *or* 071-955 5095
Newcastle	091-232 5131

Note. Some of these centres also advise on laboratory analytical services which may be of help in the diagnosis and management of a small number of cases.

Guidance on Prescribing

Prices in the BNF

Basic **net prices** have been introduced into the BNF in order to provide better indications of relative cost. Whenever possible they have been calculated from the basic cost used in pricing NHS prescriptions dispensed in August 1990; unless an original pack is available these prices are based on the largest pack size of the preparation in use in community pharmacies. The price for an extemporaneously prepared preparation has been omitted where the net cost of the ingredients used to make it would give a misleadingly low impression of the final price.

The unit of 20 is still used as a basis for comparison, but where suitable original packs are available these are priced instead.

Gross prices vary as follows:

1. Costs to the NHS are greater than the net prices quoted and include professional fees and overhead allowances;
2. Private prescription charges are calculated on a separate basis;
3. Over-the-counter sales are at retail price, as opposed to basic net price, and include VAT.

BNF prices are NOT, therefore, suitable for quoting to patients seeking private prescriptions or contemplating over-the-counter purchases.

A fuller explanation of costs to the NHS may be obtained from the Drug Tariff.

PACT

PACT (Prescribing Analysis and Costs) automatically provides general practitioners with information about their prescribing. The information is sent on a quarterly basis direct from the Prescription Pricing Authority. It is available at three levels of complexity:

Level 1 reports compare practice prescribing with that of the local Family Health Services Authority (FHSA) and England and Wales as a whole—they are produced once a quarter for each general practitioner;

Level 2 reports are produced for general practitioners with above average costs—they can also be requested;

Level 3 reports are available only on request—they are effectively a list of all items prescribed by the general practitioner, grouped into the BNF therapeutic categories, giving detailed cost information.

General Guidance

Medicines should be prescribed only when they are essential, and in all cases the benefit of administering the medicine should be considered in relation to the risk involved. This is particularly important during pregnancy where the risk to both mother and fetus must be considered (for further details see Prescribing in Pregnancy, Appendix 4).

ABBREVIATION OF TITLES. In general, titles of drugs and preparations should be written *in full*. Unofficial abbreviations should not be used as they may be misinterpreted; obsolete titles, such as Mist. Expect. and Mist. Tussis should not be used.

NON-PROPRIETARY TITLES. Where non-proprietary ('generic') titles are given, they should be used in prescribing. This will enable any suitable product to be dispensed, thereby saving delay to the patient and sometimes expense to the health service. The only exception is where bioavailability problems are so important that the patient should always receive the same brand; in such cases, the brand name or the manufacturer should be stated.

Titles used as headings for monographs may be used freely in Great Britain and Northern Ireland but in other countries may be subject to restriction.

Many of the non-proprietary titles used in this book are titles of monographs in the European Pharmacopoeia, British Pharmacopoeia or British Pharmaceutical Codex 1973. In such cases the preparations must comply with the standard (if any) in the appropriate publication, as required by the Medicines Act (section 65).

PROPRIETARY TITLES. Names followed by the symbol® are or have been used as proprietary names in the United Kingdom. These names may in general be applied only to products supplied by the owners of the trade marks.

DOSES. The doses stated in the BNF are intended for general guidance and represent, unless otherwise stated, the usual range of doses that are generally regarded as being suitable for adults; unless otherwise indicated the quantities are those generally suitable for administration on one occasion.

DILUTIONS. When fractional doses are prescribed *liquid preparations for oral use* will be diluted with a suitable vehicle to dose-volumes of 5 mL or a multiple thereof, unless otherwise directed in the text. Dilution should be effected at the time of dispensing and such diluted preparations may be less stable than the original undiluted preparations. Where a complete formula is given the diluent is the specified vehicle, otherwise the diluent specified should be used.

In the case of *creams, ointments etc.*, where a complete recipe is available the diluent is the specified vehicle, otherwise only diluents specified should be used.

STRENGTHS AND QUANTITIES. The strength or quantity to be contained in capsules, lozenges, tablets, etc. should be stated by the prescriber.

If a pharmacist receives an incomplete prescription for a systemically administered preparation other than a prescription for a controlled drug and considers it would not be appropriate for the patient to return to the doctor, the following procedures will apply:

(a) an attempt must always be made to contact the prescriber to ascertain the intention;
(b) if the attempt is successful the pharmacist must, where practicable, subsequently arrange for details of quantity, strength where applicable, and dosage to be inserted by the prescriber on the incomplete form;
(c) where, although the prescriber has been contacted, it has not proved possible to obtain the written intention regarding an incomplete prescription, the pharmacist may endorse the form 'p.c.' (prescriber contacted) and add details of the quantity and strength where applicable of the preparation supplied, and of the dose indicated. The endorsement should be initialled and dated by the pharmacist;
(d) where the prescriber cannot be contacted and the pharmacist has sufficient information to make a professional judgment a sufficient quantity of the preparation may be dispensed to complete up to 5 days' treatment; except that where a combination pack (i.e., a proprietary pack containing more than one medicinal product) or oral contraceptive is prescribed by name only, the smallest pack shall be dispensed. In all cases the prescription must be endorsed 'p.n.c.' (prescriber not contacted) the quantity, the dose, and the strength (where applicable) of the preparation supplied must be indicated, and the endorsement must be initialled and dated;
(e) if the pharmacist has any doubt about exercising discretion, an incomplete prescription must be referred back to the prescriber.

ADDITIVES. Oral liquid preparations in the BNF that do not contain *fructose*, *glucose* or *sucrose* are labelled "sugar-free".

Where the presence of *gluten* or of *tartrazine* is specified on a data sheet this is indicated in the BNF against the preparation in question; not all data sheets provide details of additives therefore if it is essential to know whether a preparation is free of gluten or of tartrazine the manufacturer should be contacted.

Information is provided on *preservatives* in eye-drops.

Information is provided on *selected additives* in skin preparations (for details see section 13.1).

EXTEMPORANEOUS PREPARATION. The BP direction that a preparation must be *freshly prepared* indicates that it must be made not more than 24 hours before it is issued for use. The direction that a preparation should be *recently prepared* indicates that deterioration is likely if the preparation is stored for longer than about 4 weeks at 15° to 25°.

APPLIANCES AND CHEMICAL REAGENTS. A limited selection of appliances (including elastic hosiery, and trusses) and chemical reagents is available for prescribing by general medical practitioners in the NHS; dressings are included in BNF section 13.13. For full details the Drug Tariff should be consulted.

DRUGS AND DRIVING. Prescribers should advise patients if treatment is likely to affect their ability to drive motor vehicles. This applies particularly to drugs with sedative effects and patients should be warned that these effects are increased by alcohol. See also Appendix 8.

NOTICE CONCERNING PATENTS. In the BNF certain drugs have been included notwithstanding the existence of actual or potential patent rights. In so far as such substances are protected by Letters Patent, their inclusion in this Formulary neither conveys, nor implies, licence to manufacture.

HEALTH AND SAFETY. When handling chemical or biological materials particular attention should be given to the possibility of allergy, fire, explosion, radiation, or poisoning. Some substances, including corticosteroids, antibiotics, phenothiazines, and many cytotoxics, are irritant or very potent and should be handled with caution. Contact with the skin and inhalation of dust should be avoided.

SAFETY IN THE HOME. Patients must be warned to keep all medicines out of the reach of children. All solid dose oral medicines should be dispensed either in reclosable *child-resistant containers* complying with the British Standard or in unit packaging of strip or blister type unless:

(i) they are in manufacturers' original packs so designed that transfer to a reclosable child-resistant container would be a retrograde or unnecessary procedure;
(ii) the patient is elderly or handicapped and would have difficulty in opening a child-resistant container;
(iii) the patient specifically requests otherwise.

In cases (ii) and (iii) the pharmacist should make a particular point of advising that the medicines be kept well out of the reach of children.

All patients should be advised to dispose of *unwanted medicines* by flushing them down a WC or returning them to a supplier for destruction.

NAME OF MEDICINE. The name of the medicine should appear on the label unless the prescriber indicates otherwise.

1. Subject to the conditions of paragraphs 4 and 6 below, the name of the prescribed medicine is stated on the label unless the prescriber deletes the letters 'NP' which appear on NHS prescription forms.
2. The strength is also stated on the label in the case of tablets, capsules, and similar preparations that are available in different strengths.
3. If it is the wish of the prescriber that a description such as 'The Sedative Tablets' should appear on the label, the prescriber should write the desired description on the prescription form.
4. The arrangement will extend to approved names, proprietary names or titles given in the BP, BPC, BNF, or DPF. The arrangement does not apply when a prescription is written so that several ingredients are given.
5. The name written on the label is that used by the prescriber on the prescription.
6. If more than one item is prescribed on one form and the prescriber does not delete the letters 'NP', each dispensed medicine is named on the label, subject to the conditions given above in paragraph 4. If the prescriber wants only selected items on such a prescription to be so labelled this should be indicated by deleting the letters 'NP' on the form and writing 'NP' alongside the medicines to be labelled.
7. When a prescription is written other than on an NHS prescription form the name of the prescribed preparation will be stated on the label of the dispensed medicine unless the prescriber indicates otherwise.
8. The Council of the Royal Pharmaceutical Society advises that the labels of dispensed medicines should indicate the total quantity of the product dispensed in the container to which the label refers. This requirement applies equally to solid, liquid, internal, and external preparations. If a product is dispensed in more than one container, the reference should be to the amount in each container.

SCOPE OF THE BNF. The BNF is intended for the guidance of medical practitioners, pharmacists, dentists, nurses, and other workers who have the necessary training and experience to interpret the information it provides. It is intended as a reference book for the pocket, and should be supplemented by a study of more detailed publications when required.

Security and validity of prescriptions

The Councils of the British Medical Association and the Royal Pharmaceutical Society have issued a joint statement on the security and validity of prescriptions.

In particular, prescription forms should:
(i) not be left unattended at reception desks;
(ii) not be left in a car where they may be visible; and
(iii) when not in use, be kept in a locked drawer within the surgery and at home.

Where there is any doubt about the authenticity of a prescription, the pharmacist should contact the prescriber. If this is done by telephone, the number should be obtained from the directory rather than relying on the prescription form information, which may be false.

Prescription Writing

The following recommendations are acceptable for prescription-only medicines (PoM). For items marked **CD** see Controlled Drugs and Drug Dependence p. 7.

Prescriptions should be written legibly in ink or otherwise as to be indelible[1], should be dated, should state the full name and address of the patient, and should be signed in ink by the prescriber. The age of the patient should preferably be stated, and is a legal requirement in the case of prescription-only medicines for children under 12 years of age. In general practice the following should be noted:

(a) For solids, quantities of 1 gram or more should be written as 1 g etc.

Quantities less than 1 gram should be written in milligrams, e.g. 500 mg, not 0.5 g.

Quantities less than 1 mg should be written in micrograms, e.g. 100 micrograms, not 0.1 mg.

When decimals are unavoidable a zero should be written in front of the decimal point where there is no other figure, e.g. 0.5 mL, not .5 mL.

Use of the decimal point is acceptable to express a range, e.g. 0.5 to 1 g.

(b) 'Micrograms' and 'nanograms' should **not** be abbreviated. Similarly 'units' should **not** be abbreviated.

(c) The term 'millilitre' (ml or mL)[2] is used in medicine and pharmacy, and cubic centimetre, c.c., or cm³ should not be used.

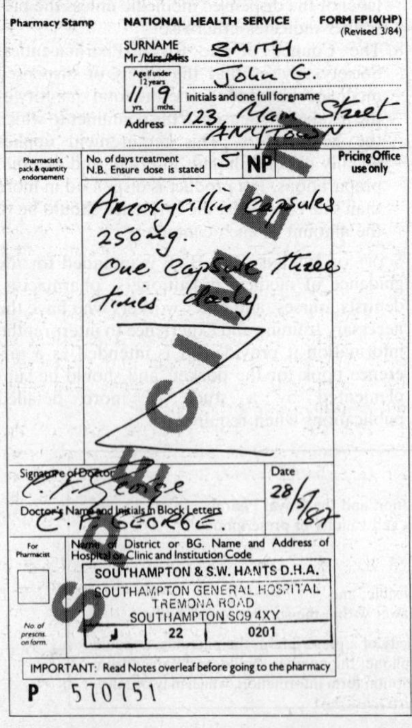

Pharmacy Stamp | NATIONAL HEALTH SERVICE | FORM FP10(HP) (Revised 3/84)

SURNAME Mr/~~Mrs/Miss~~ SMITH

Age if under 12 years: 11 yrs. 9 mths. | John G. (initials and one full forename)

Address 123, Main Street ANYTOWN

Pharmacist's pack & quantity endorsement | No. of days treatment N.B. Ensure dose is stated: 5 | NP | Pricing Office use only

Amoxycillin Capsules 250mg.
One capsule three times daily

Signature of Doctor: C. F. George | Date 28/5/87

Doctor's Name and Initials in Block Letters: C. F. GEORGE.

For Pharmacist | Name of District or BG. Name and Address of Hospital or Clinic and Institution Code

SOUTHAMPTON & S.W. HANTS D.H.A.
SOUTHAMPTON GENERAL HOSPITAL
TREMONA ROAD
SOUTHAMPTON SO9 4XY

No. of prescns. on form | J | 22 | 0201

IMPORTANT: Read Notes overleaf before going to the pharmacy

P 570751

SPECIMEN

(d) Dose and dose frequency should be stated.

For oral liquid preparations of the *linctus* or *elixir* type and for *preparations for children*, doses should preferably be stated in terms of 5-mL spoonfuls.

For *mixtures for adults*, doses should preferably be stated in 10-mL quantities; unless the prescription states otherwise, the patient will be directed to take the dose with water.

When doses other than 5 or 10 mL are prescribed the dose-volume will be diluted to 5 or 10 mL or a multiple thereof (except for preparations intended to be measured with a pipette).

The volume of liquid preparations should normally be 50, 100, 150, 200, 300, or 500 mL. Suitable quantities of liquid preparations:

Elixirs, Linctuses, and Paediatric Mixtures (5-mL dose), 50, 100, or 150 mL
Adult Mixtures (10-mL dose), 200 or 300 mL
Ear Drops, Eye-drops, and Nasal Drops, 10 mL (or the manufacturer's pack)
Eye Lotions, Gargles, and Mouth-washes, 200 mL
Liniments, 100 mL

(e) Quantities of solids prescribed should normally be 15, 25, 50, 100, 200, 300, or 500 grams (or the manufacturer's appropriate pack).

For suitable quantities of dermatological preparations, see section 13.1.

(f) The names of drugs and preparations should be written clearly and **not** abbreviated.

(g) The symbol 'NP' on NHS forms should be deleted if it is required that the name of the preparation should not appear on the label. For full details see p. 3.

(h) The quantity to be supplied may be stated by indicating the number of days of treatment required in the box provided on NHS forms. In most cases the exact amount will be supplied. This does not apply to items directed to be used as required; if the dose and frequency are not given the quantity to be supplied should be stated.

When several items are ordered on one form the box can be marked with the number of days of treatment providing the quantity is added for any item for which the amount cannot be calculated.

(i) Although directions should preferably be in **English without abbreviation**, it is recognised that some Latin abbreviations are used (for details see Inside Back Cover).

(j) A prescription for a preparation that has been withdrawn or needs to be specially imported for a named patient should be handwritten. The name of the preparation should be endorsed with the prescriber's signature and the letters 'WD' (withdrawn or specially-imported drug); this will be a valuable indication to the pharmacist of the prescriber's intentions. There may be considerable delay in obtaining a withdrawn medicine.

1. It is permissible to issue carbon copies of NHS prescriptions as long as they are signed in ink.
2. The use of capital 'L' in mL is a printing convention throughout the BNF; both mL and ml are recognised abbreviations for SI units.

Hospital Prescriptions

In hospitals the following should also be noted:

1. There should be a prescription sheet on which prescriptions and a record of dispensing and administration *only* are written.
2. Not more than one prescription sheet should be in use at any one time for any one patient.
3. Frequency of administration of 'as required' medicines should be indicated by clear and definitely stated intervals.
4. The route of administration should be clearly shown.
5. The prescription sheet should show signed and dated cancellations of any prescriptions no longer current.

Arrangements should be made for doses to be given at special times when intervals are critical.

Computer-issued Prescriptions

For computer-issued prescriptions the following should also be noted:

1. The computer must print out the date, the patient's surname, one forename, other initials, and address, and may also print out the patient's title. The age of children under 12 years must be printed in the box available; a facility may exist to print out the age of older children and adults as well.

2. The doctor's name[1] must be printed at the bottom of the prescription form; this will be the name of the doctor responsible for the prescription (who will normally sign it). The doctor's surgery address, reference number, and Family Health Services Authority (FHSA)[2] are also necessary. In addition, the surgery telephone number should be printed.

3. When prescriptions are to be signed by trainees, assistants, locums, or deputising doctors, the name of the doctor printed at the bottom of the form must still be that of the responsible principal. To avoid difficulties for the pharmacist checking the prescription, the name of the signing doctor may be printed in the signature box, to be signed over on prescribing.

4. Names of medicines must come from a dictionary held in the computer memory, to provide a check on the spelling and ensure that the name is written in full. The computer can be programmed to recognise both the non-proprietary and the proprietary name of a particular drug and to print out the preferred choice, but must not print out both names. For medicines not in the dictionary, separate checking mechanisms are required—the user must be warned that no check was possible and the entire prescription must be entered in the lexicon.

5. The dictionary may contain information on the usual doses, formulations, and (where relevant) pack sizes to produce standard predetermined prescriptions for common preparations, and to provide a check on the validity of an individual prescription on entry.

6. The prescription must be printed in English without abbreviation, see (i) above; information may be entered or stored in abbreviated form. The dose must be in numbers, the frequency in words, and the quantity in numbers in brackets, thus:

40 mg four times daily (112)

It must also be possible to prescribe by indicating the length of treatment required, see (h) above.

7. The BNF recommendations should be followed as in (a), (b), (c), (d), and (e) above.

8. Checks may be incorporated to ensure that all the information required for dispensing a particular drug has been filled in. Instructions such as 'as directed' should be avoided. For the instruction 'when required' the maximum daily dose should normally be specified.

9. Numbers and codes used in the system for organising and retrieving data must never appear on the form.

10. Supplementary warnings or advice should be written in full, should not interfere with the clarity of the prescription itself, and should be in line with any warnings or advice in the BNF; numerical codes should not be used.

11. A mechanism (such as printing a series of non-specific characters) may be incorporated to cancel out unused space, or wording such as 'no more items on this prescription' may be added after the last item. Otherwise the doctor should delete the space manually.

12. To avoid forgery the computer may print on the form the number of items to be dispensed (somewhere separate from the box for the pharmacist). The number of items per form need be limited only by the ability of the printer to produce clear and well-demarcated instructions with sufficient space for each item and a spacer line before each fresh item.

13. Handwritten alterations should only be made in exceptional circumstances—it is preferable to print out a new prescription. Any alterations that are made must be written in the doctor's own handwriting and countersigned.

14. Prescriptions for controlled drugs cannot be produced by a printer[3]. If there is a record of such a prescription in the computer, it must not be printed. Instead the computer may print out a blank form with the doctor's name[1] and other details printed at the bottom.

15. The strip of paper on the side of the FP10[4](Comp) may be used for various purposes but care should be taken to avoid including confidential information. It may be advisable for the patient's name to appear at the top, but this should be preceded by 'confidential'.

16. In rural dispensing practices prescription requests (or details of medicines dispensed) will normally be entered in one surgery. The prescriptions (or dispensed medicines) may then need to be delivered to another surgery or location; if possible the computer should hold up to 10 alternatives.

---

1. Except in Scotland where it does not appear.
2. Health Board in Scotland.
3. Except in the case of phenobarbitone or where the prescriber has been exempted from handwriting requirements, for details see Controlled Drugs and Drug Dependence.
4. GP10 in Scotland.

Emergency Supply of PoM at Patient's Request[1]

The Medicines (Products Other Than Veterinary Drugs) (Prescription Only) Order 1983, as amended, allows exemptions from the Prescription Only requirements for emergency supply to be made by a person lawfully conducting a retail pharmacy business provided:

(a) that the pharmacist has interviewed the person requesting the prescription-only medicine and is satisfied:

(i) that there is immediate need for the prescription-only medicine and that it is impracticable in the circumstances to obtain a prescription without undue delay;

(ii) that treatment with the prescription-only medicine has on a previous occasion been prescribed by a doctor[2] for the person requesting it;

(iii) as to the dose which it would be appropriate for the person to take;

(b) that no greater quantity shall be supplied than will provide five days' treatment except when the prescription-only medicine is:

(i) an ointment, cream, or preparation for the relief of asthma in an aerosol dispenser when the smallest pack can be supplied;

(ii) an oral contraceptive when a full cycle may be supplied;

(iii) an antibiotic in liquid form for oral adminstration when the smallest quantity that will provide a full course of treatment can be supplied;

(c) that an entry shall be made in the prescription book stating:

(i) the date of supply;

(ii) the name, quantity and, where appropriate, the pharmaceutical form and strength;

(iii) the name and address of the patient;

(iv) the nature of the emergency;

(d) that the container or package must be labelled to show:

(i) the date of supply;

(ii) the name, quantity and, where appropriate, the pharmaceutical form and strength;

(iii) the name of the patient;

(iv) the name and address of the pharmacy;

(v) the words "Emergency supply".

(e) that the prescription-only medicine is not a substance specifically excluded from the emergency supply provision, and does not contain a Controlled Drug specified in schedules 1, 2, or 3 to the Misuse of Drugs Regulations 1985 except for phenobarbitone or phenobarbitone sodium for the treatment of epilepsy: for details see *Medicines, Ethics and Practice*, No. 5, London, Pharmaceutical Press, 1990 (and subsequent editions as available).

ROYAL PHARMACEUTICAL SOCIETY'S GUIDELINES

(1) The pharmacist should consider the medical consequences, if any, of **not** supplying.

(2) The pharmacist should identify the patient by means of documentary evidence and/or personal knowledge.

(3) The doctor who prescribed on a previous occasion should be identified and contacted, if possible.

(4) The patient should be asked whether the doctor has stopped the treatment.

(5) The patient should be asked whether any other medicine is being taken at the same time to check drug interactions.

(6) An emergency supply should not be made if the item requested was prescribed previously more than six months prior to the request. Variations may be made in the case of illnesses which occur infrequently, e.g. hay fever, asthma attack, or migraine.

(7) Consideration should be given to providing less than five days' supply if this is justified.

(8) Labelling should be clear and legible and there should be some suitable identification of emergency supply entries in the prescription book.

1. For emergency supply at the request of a doctor see *Medicines, Ethics and Practice*, No. 5, London, Pharmaceutical Press, 1990 (and subsequent editions as available).
2. The doctor must be a UK-registered doctor.

Plasma concentrations in the BNF are expressed in mass units per litre (e.g. mg/litre). The approximate equivalent in terms of amount of substance units (e.g. micromol/litre) is given in brackets.

Approximate Conversions and Units

lb	*kg*	*stones*	*kg*	*mL*	*fl. oz*
1	0.45	1	6.35	50	1.8
2	0.91	2	12.70	100	3.5
3	1.36	3	19.05	150	5.3
4	1.81	4	25.40	200	7.0
5	2.27	5	31.75	500	17.6
6	2.72	6	38.10	1000	35.2
7	3.18	7	44.45		
8	3.63	8	50.80		
9	4.08	9	57.15		
10	4.54	10	63.50		
11	4.99	11	69.85		
12	5.44	12	76.20		
13	5.90	13	82.55		
14	6.35	14	88.90		
		15	95.25		

Mass

1 kilogram (kg)	= 1000 grams (g)
1 gram (g)	= 1000 milligrams (mg)
1 milligram (mg)	= 1000 micrograms
1 microgram	= 1000 nanograms
1 nanogram	= 1000 picograms

Volume

1 litre	= 1000 millilitres (mL)
1 millilitre	= 1000 microlitres
1 pint	≈ 568 mL

Other units

1 kilocalorie (kcal)	= 4186.8 joules (J)
1000 kilocalories (kcal)	= 4.1868 megajoules (MJ)
1 megajoule (MJ)	= 238.8 kilocalories (kcal)
1 millimetre of mercury (mmHg)	= 133.3 pascals (Pa)
1 kilopascal (kPa)	= 7.5 mmHg (pressure)

Controlled Drugs and Drug Dependence

PRESCRIPTIONS. Preparations which are subject to the prescription requirements of the Misuse of Drugs Regulations 1985, i.e. preparations specified in schedules 2 and 3, are distinguished throughout the BNF by the symbol **CD** (Controlled Drugs). The principal legal requirements relating to medical prescriptions are listed below.

Prescriptions ordering Controlled Drugs subject to prescription requirements must be *signed* and *dated*[1] by the prescriber and specify the prescriber's *address*. The prescription must always state *in the prescriber's own handwriting*[2] in ink or otherwise so as to be indelible:

1. The name and address of the patient;
2. In the case of a preparation, the form[3] and where appropriate the strength of the preparation;
3. The total quantity of the preparation, or the number of dose units, *in both words and figures;*
4. The dose.

A prescription may order a Controlled Drug to be dispensed by instalments; the amount of the instalments and the intervals to be observed must be specified.[4] Prescriptions ordering 'repeats' on the same form are **not** permitted.

Pharmacy Stamp | NATIONAL HEALTH SERVICE | FORM FP10(HP) (Revised 3/84)

SURNAME Mr./Mrs./Miss JONES
Age if under 12 years (yrs. mths.) Jane M
initials and one full forename
Address 23, Wide Road ELSEWHERE.

Pharmacist's pack & quantity endorsement | No. of days treatment N.B. Ensure dose is stated | NP | Pricing Office use only

Morphine hydrochloride 15mg.
Chloroform water to 5ml.
Supply: 100ml (one hundred millilitres)
5ml every four hours.

SPECIMEN

Signature of Doctor C. F. George | Date 28/5/87
Doctor's Name and Initials in Block Letters C. F. GEORGE.

For Pharmacist | Name of District or BG. Name and Address of Hospital or Clinic and Institution Code
SOUTHAMPTON & S.W. HANTS D.H.A.
SOUTHAMPTON GENERAL HOSPITAL
TREMONA ROAD
SOUTHAMPTON SO9 4XY
No. of prescns. on form. | J | 22 | 0201

IMPORTANT: Read Notes overleaf before going to the pharmacy

P 570752

It is an offence for a doctor to issue an incomplete prescription and a pharmacist is **not** allowed to dispense a Controlled Drug unless all the information required by law is given on the prescription. Failure to comply with the regulations concerning the writing of prescriptions will result in inconvenience to patients and delay in supplying the necessary medicine.

DEPENDENCE AND MISUSE. The prevalence of drug dependence and misuse in Great Britain, particularly amongst young people, continues to give cause for concern to teachers, social workers, and the police, as well as doctors.

The most serious drugs of addiction are **diamorphine** (heroin), **morphine,** and the **synthetic opioids**; illicit **cocaine** is now also a problem.

Although a campaign by doctors led to marked reduction in the prescribing of **amphetamines** there is concern that abuse of illicitly produced amphetamine and related compounds is widespread.

The principal **barbiturates** are now Controlled Drugs, but phenobarbitone and phenobarbitone sodium or a preparation containing either of these are exempt from the handwriting requirement; moreover, for the treatment of epilepsy phenobarbitone and phenobarbitone sodium are available under the emergency supply regulations (p. 6).

Cannabis (Indian hemp) has no approved medicinal use and cannot be prescribed by doctors (except under licence from the Home Secretary). Its use is illegal but has become widespread in certain sections of society. Cannabis is a mild hallucinogen seldom accompanied by a desire to increase the dose; withdrawal symptoms are unusual. **Lysergide** (lysergic acid diethylamide, LSD) is a much more potent hallucinogen; its use can lead to severe psychotic states in which life may be at risk.

---

1. A prescription is valid for 13 weeks from the date stated thereon.
2. Unless the prescriber has been specifically exempted from this requirement or unless the prescription contains no controlled drug other than phenobarbitone or phenobarbitone sodium or a preparation containing either of these. The exemption does **not** apply to the date; a computer-generated date need not be deleted but the date must also be added by hand.
3. The dosage form (e.g. tablets) must be included on a Controlled Drugs prescription irrespective of whether it is implicit in the proprietary name (e.g. Tenuate Dospan®) or of whether only one form is available.
4. A special form, FP10(HP)(ad), in Scotland HBP(A), is available to certain doctors in the NHS for prescribing cocaine, dextromoramide, diamorphine, dipipanone, methadone, morphine, or pethidine by instalments. In Scotland general practitioners can prescribe by instalments on form GP10. In England and Wales forms FP10 and FP10(HP) are not suitable for this purpose but a new form FP10(MDA) is now available (**important:** a special licence is still necessary, however, to prescribe cocaine, diamorphine, or dipipanone).

PRESCRIBING DRUGS LIKELY TO CAUSE DEPENDENCE OR MISUSE. The prescriber has three main responsibilities:

1. To avoid creating dependence by introducing drugs to patients without sufficient reason. In this context, the proper use of the morphine-like drugs is well understood. The dangers of other controlled drugs are less clear because recognition of dependence is not easy and its effects, and those of withdrawal, are less obvious. Perhaps the most notable result of uninhibited prescribing is that a very large number of patients in the country take tablets which do them neither much good nor much harm, but are committed to them indefinitely because they cannot readily be stopped.
2. To see that the patient does not gradually increase the dose of a drug, given for good medical reasons, to the point where dependence becomes more likely. This tendency is seen especially with hypnotics and anxiolytics (for CSM advice see section 4.1). The prescriber should keep a close eye on the amount prescribed to prevent patients from accumulating stocks that would enable them to arrange their own dosage or even that of their families and friends. A minimal amount should be prescribed in the first instance, or when seeing a new patient for the first time.
3. To avoid being used as an unwitting source of supply for addicts. Methods include visiting more than one doctor, fabricating stories, and forging prescriptions. A doctor should therefore be wary of prescribing for strangers and may be able to get information about suspected opioid addicts from the Home Office (for details see p. 9).

Patients under temporary care should be given only small supplies of drugs unless they present an unequivocal letter from their own doctors. Doctors should also remember that their own patients may be doing a collecting round with other doctors, especially in hospitals. It is sensible to decrease dosages steadily or to issue weekly or even daily prescriptions for small amounts if it is apparent that dependence is occurring.

The stealing and misuse of prescription forms could be minimised by the following precautions:

(a) do not leave unattended if called away from the consulting room or at reception desks; do not leave in a car where they may be visible; when not in use, keep in a locked drawer within the surgery and at home;
(b) draw a diagonal line across the blank part of the form under the prescription;
(c) write the quantity in words and figures when prescribing drugs prone to abuse; this is obligatory for controlled drugs (see Prescriptions, above);
(d) alterations are best avoided but if any are made they should be clear and unambiguous; add initials against altered items;
(e) if prescriptions are left for collection they should be left in a safe place in a sealed envelope.

TRAVELLING ABROAD. Prescribed drugs listed in schedules 4 and 5 to the Misuse of Drugs Regulations 1985 are not subject to import or export licensing but doctors are advised that patients travelling abroad may only carry 15 days' supply of any schedule 2 or 3 prescribed controlled drug without a licence. If especially high doses are prescribed, however, or if prescriptions are for a longer period, an import or export licence may be required. Licences are issued by the Home Secretary, Home Office, Drugs Branch, Queen Anne's Gate, London SW1H 9AT, telephone 071-273 3806.

There is no standard application form but applications must be supported by a letter from a doctor giving details of:

the patient's name and current address;
the quantities of drugs to be carried;
the strength and form in which the drugs will be dispensed;
the dates of travel to and from the United Kingdom.

Ten days should be allowed for processing the application.

Individual doctors who wish to take Controlled Drugs abroad while accompanying patients, may similarly be issued with licences. Licences are not normally issued to doctors who wish to take Controlled Drugs abroad solely in case a family emergency should arise.

These import/export licences for named individuals do not have any legal status outside the UK and are only issued to comply with the Misuse of Drugs Act and facilitate passage through UK Customs control. For clearance in the country to be visited it would be necessary to approach that country's embassy or High Commission in the UK.

The Misuse of Drugs Act, 1971

This Act was passed in 1971 to provide more flexible and more comprehensive control over the misuse of drugs of all kinds than was possible under the earlier Dangerous Drugs Act. The Act as amended prohibits certain activities in relation to 'Controlled Drugs', in particular their manufacture, supply, and possession. The penalties applicable to offences involving the different drugs are graded broadly according to the *harmfulness attributable to a drug when it is misused* and for this purpose the drugs are defined in the following three classes:

Class A includes: alfentanil, cocaine, dextromoramide, diamorphine (heroin), dipipanone, lysergide (LSD), methadone, morphine, opium, pethidine, phencyclidine, and class B substances when prepared for injection

Class B includes: oral amphetamines, barbiturates, cannabis, cannabis resin, codeine, ethylmorphine, glutethimide, pentazocine, phenmetrazine, and pholcodine

Class C includes: certain drugs related to the amphetamines such as benzphetamine and chlorphentermine, buprenorphine, diethylpropion, mazindol, meprobamate, pemoline, pipradrol, and most benzodiazepines

The Misuse of Drugs Regulations 1985 define the classes of person who are authorised to supply and possess controlled drugs while acting in their professional capacities and lay down the conditions under which these activities may be carried out. In the regulations drugs are divided into five schedules each specifying the requirements governing such activities as import, export, production, supply, possession, prescribing, and record keeping which apply to them.

Schedule 1 includes drugs such as cannabis and lysergide which are not used medicinally. Possession and supply are prohibited except in accordance with Home Office authority.

Schedule 2 includes drugs such as diamorphine (heroin), morphine, pethidine, quinalbarbitone, glutethimide, amphetamine, and cocaine and are subject to the full controlled drug requirements relating to prescriptions, safe custody, the need to keep registers, etc. (unless exempted in schedule 5).

Schedule 3 includes the barbiturates (except quinalbarbitone, now schedule 2), buprenorphine, diethylpropion, mazindol, meprobamate, pentazocine, and phentermine. They are subject to the special prescription requirements (except for phenobarbitone, see p. 7) but not to the safe custody requirements (except for buprenorphine and diethylpropion) nor to the need to keep registers (although there are requirements for the retention of invoices for 2 years).

Schedule 4 includes 34 benzodiazepines and pemoline which are subject to minimal control. In particular, controlled drug prescription requirements do not apply and they are not subject to safe custody.

Schedule 5 includes those preparations which, because of their strength, are exempt from virtually all Controlled Drug requirements other than retention of invoices for two years.

Notification of Addicts

The Misuse of Drugs (Notification of and Supply to Addicts) Regulations 1973 require that any doctor who attends a person who the doctor considers or has reasonable grounds to suspect, is addicted to any drug shall, within seven days of the attendance, furnish in writing particulars of that person to:

Chief Medical Officer,
Home Office, Drugs Branch,
Queen Anne's Gate, London SW1H 9AT.

The drugs commonly in use to which the Regulations apply are:

Cocaine	Methadone
Dextromoramide	Morphine
Diamorphine	Opium
Dipipanone	Oxycodone
Hydrocodone	Pethidine
Hydromorphone	Phenazocine
Levorphanol	Piritramide

Note. Dipipanone is only legally available as Diconal® Tablets. These have been much misused by opiate addicts in recent years; only medical practitioners with a special licence may now prescribe them for addicts to treat addiction. Doctors and others should be suspicious of young people who ask for them, especially as temporary residents.

Particulars[1] to be notified to the Chief Medical Officer are:

- Name and address
- Sex
- Date of birth
- National Health Service number
- Date of attendance
- Name of drugs of addiction
- Whether patient injects any drug (whether or not notifiable)

Notification must be confirmed annually in writing if the patient is still being treated by the practitioner. Notified information is incorporated in an Index of Addicts which is maintained in the Home Office and information from this is available on a confidential basis to doctors; in fact, it is good medical practice to check all new cases of addiction or suspected addiction with the Index before prescribing or supplying controlled drugs since this is a safeguard against addicts obtaining supplies simultaneously from two or more doctors. Enquiries can be made either in writing to the Chief Medical Officer or, preferably, by telephoning 071-273 2213. To keep notified information confidential, such enquiries are normally answered by means of a return telephone call. The reply will come from lay staff who are not qualified to give guidance on the clinical handling of cases; a recorded telephone service is available for out-of-office hours.

The preceding paragraph applies only to medical practitioners in England, Scotland, and Wales. In Northern Ireland notification should be sent to:

Chief Medical Officer,
Department of Health and Social Services,
Dundonald House,
Belfast BT4 3SF.

Enquiries should also be made to that Department, telephone number 0232 63939 extension 2867.

Prescribing of diamorphine (heroin), dipipanone, and cocaine for addicts

The Misuse of Drugs (Notification of and Supply to Addicts) Regulations 1973 also provide that only medical practitioners who hold a special licence issued by the Home Secretary may prescribe diamorphine, dipipanone (Diconal®), or cocaine for addicts; other practitioners must refer any addict who requires these drugs to a treatment centre. General practitioners and other doctors may still prescribe diamorphine, dipipanone, and cocaine for patients (including addicts) for relief of pain due to organic disease or injury without a special licence. Whenever possible the addict will be introduced by a member of staff from the treatment centre to a pharmacist whose agreement has been obtained and whose pharmacy is conveniently sited for the patient. Prescriptions for weekly supplies will be sent to the pharmacy by post and will be dispensed on a daily basis as indicated by the doctor. If any alterations of the arrangements are requested by the addict, the portion of the prescription affected must be represcribed and not merely altered.

1. Only the particulars of which the doctor has knowledge need be notified immediately; the remainder may be notified at a later date. General practitioners may obtain forms HSA2/1(rev) for notification from their Family Health Services Authority (FHSA); hospitals and treatment centres may obtain them from the district health authority.

Adverse Reactions to Drugs

Any drug may produce unwanted or unexpected adverse reactions. Detection and recording of these is of vital importance. Doctors are urged to help by reporting adverse reactions to:

CSM
Freepost
London SW8 5BR
(071-720 2188)

Yellow prepaid lettercards for reporting are available from the above address or by dialling 100 and asking for 'CSM Freefone'; also, forms are bound in this book (inside back cover).

A 24-hour Freefone service is now available to all parts of the United Kingdom, for doctors seeking advice and information on adverse reactions; it may be obtained by dialling 100 and asking for 'CSM Freefone'. Outside office hours a telephone-answering machine will take messages.

The following regional centres also collect data:

CSM Mersey Freepost Liverpool L3 3AB (051-236 4620 Extn 2126)	CSM Northern Freepost 1085 Newcastle upon Tyne NE1 1BR (0632 321525 Direct Line)
CSM Wales Freepost Cardiff CF4 1ZZ (0222 759541 Direct Line)	CSM West Midlands Freepost Birmingham B15 1BR (021-472 1311 Extn 4516)

Suspected adverse reactions to *any* therapeutic agent should be reported, including drugs, blood products, vaccines, X-ray contrast media, dental or surgical materials, intra-uterine devices, and contact lens fluids.

NEWER DRUGS. These are indicated by the sign ▼. Doctors are asked to report *all* suspected reactions (i.e. any adverse or any unexpected event, however minor, which could conceivably be attributed to the drug). Reports should be made despite uncertainty about a causal relationship, irrespective of whether the reaction is well recognized, and even if other drugs have been given concurrently.

ESTABLISHED DRUGS. Doctors are asked to report *all* serious suspected reactions, including those that are fatal, life-threatening, disabling, incapacitating, or which result in or prolong hospitalisation; they should be reported even if the effect is well recognised.

Examples include anaphylaxis, blood disorders, endocrine disturbances, effects on fertility, haemorrhage from any site, renal impairment, jaundice, ophthalmic disorders, severe CNS effects, severe skin reactions, reactions in pregnant women, and any drug interactions. Reports of serious adverse reactions are required to enable risk/benefit ratios to be compared with other drugs of a similar class. For established drugs doctors are asked not to report well-known, relatively minor side-effects, such as dry mouth with tricyclic antidepressants, constipation with opioids, or nausea with digoxin.

Special problems

Delayed drug effects. Some reactions (e.g. cancers, chloroquine retinopathy, and retroperitoneal fibrosis) may become manifest months or years after exposure. Any suspicion of such an association should be reported.

The elderly. Doctors are asked to be particularly alert to adverse reactions in the elderly.

Congenital abnormalities. When an infant is born with a congenital abnormality or there is a malformed aborted fetus doctors are asked to consider whether this might be an adverse reaction to a drug and to report all drugs (including self-medication) taken during pregnancy.

Vaccines. Doctors are asked to report all suspected reactions to both new and established vaccines. The balance between risks and benefits needs to be kept under continuous review.

Prevention of adverse reactions

Adverse reactions may be prevented as follows:

1. Never use any drug unless there is a good indication. If the patient is pregnant do not use a drug unless the need for it is imperative.
2. It is very important to recognise allergy and idiosyncrasy as causes of adverse drug reactions. Ask if the patient had previous reactions.
3. Ask if the patient is already taking other drugs *including self-medication*; remember that interactions may occur.
4. Age and hepatic or renal disease may alter the metabolism or excretion of drugs, so that much smaller doses may need to be prescribed. Pharmacogenetic factors may also be responsible for variations in the rate of metabolism, notably of isoniazid and the tricyclic antidepressants.
5. Prescribe as few drugs as possible and give very clear instructions to the elderly or any patient likely to misunderstand complicated instructions.
6. When possible use a familiar drug. With a new drug be particularly alert for adverse reactions or unexpected events.
7. If serious adverse reactions are liable to occur warn the patient.

Defective Medicines

During the manufacture or distribution of a medicine an error or accident may occur whereby the finished product does not conform to its specification. While such a defect may impair the therapeutic effect of the product and could adversely affect the health of a patient, it should **not** be confused with an Adverse Drug Reaction where the product conforms to its specification.

The Defect Medicines Report Centre operates a 24-hour service to assist with the investigation of problems arising from licensed medicinal products thought to be defective, and to co-ordinate any necessary protective action. Reports on suspect defective medicinal products should include the brand or the non-proprietary name, the name of the manufacturer or supplier, the strength and dosage form of the product, the product licence number, the batch number or numbers of the product, the nature of the defect, and an account of any action already taken in consequence. The Centre can be contacted at:

The Defect Medicines Report Centre
Department of Health
Room 1801, Market Towers
1 Nine Elms Lane
London SW8 5NQ
071-627 1513 (weekdays 8.30 am–5.30 pm)
or 071-210 5368 or 5371 (any other time)

Prescribing for Children

All children, and particularly neonates, differ from adults in their response to drugs. Special care is needed in the neonatal period (first 30 days of life) and doses should always be calculated according to weight. At this age, the risk of toxicity is increased by inefficient renal filtration, relative enzyme deficiencies, differing target organ sensitivity, and inadequate detoxifying systems causing delayed excretion. In childhood dosage should be adjusted for weight until 50 kg or puberty is reached.

PRESCRIPTION WRITING. Prescriptions should be written according to the guidelines in Prescription Writing (p. 4). Inclusion of age is a legal requirement in the case of prescription-only medicines for children under 12 years of age, but it is preferable to state the age for **all** prescriptions for children.

It is particularly important to state the strengths of capsules or tablets. Although liquid preparations are particularly suitable for children, many contain sucrose which encourages dental decay. When taken over a long period, sugar-free tablets, liquid medicines, and diluents should be used when possible.

When a prescription for a liquid oral preparation is written and the dose ordered is smaller than 5 mL, the preparation will normally be diluted so that the required dose is contained in 5 mL. Parents must be instructed to use the standard 5-mL spoon to measure the dose and not to heap up a viscous preparation. They should also be advised not to add any medicines to the contents of the infant's feeding bottle, since the drug may interact with the milk or other liquid in it; moreover the ingested dosage may be reduced, if the child does not drink all the contents.

See also General Guidance, Safety in the Home, p. 3.

Dosage in Children

Children's doses in the BNF are stated in the individual drug entries as far as possible, except where paediatric use is not recommended or there are special hazards.

Doses are generally based on body-weight (in kilograms) or the following age ranges:

first month (neonate)
up to 1 year (infant)
1–5 years
6–12 years

Where a single dose is quoted for a given range, it applies to the middle of the age range and some extrapolation may be necessary to obtain doses for ages at the lower and upper limits of the stated range.

DOSE CALCULATION. Children's doses may be calculated from adult doses by using age, body-weight, or body-surface area, or by a combination of these factors. The most reliable methods are those based on body-surface area.

Body-weight may be used to calculate doses expressed in mg/kg. Young children may require a higher dose per kilogram than adults because of their higher metabolic rates. Other problems need to be considered. For example, calculation by body-weight in the obese child would result in much higher doses being administered than necessary; in such cases, dose should be calculated from an ideal weight, related to height and age.

Body-surface area (BSA) estimates are more accurate for calculation of paediatric doses than body-weight since many physical phenomena are more closely related to body-surface area. The average body-surface area of a 70-kilogram human is about 1.8 m^2. Thus, to calculate the dose for a child the following formula may be used:

$$\text{Approximate dose for patient} = \frac{\text{surface area of patient } (m^2)}{1.8} \times \text{adult dose}$$

The **percentage method** below may be used to calculate paediatric doses of commonly prescribed drugs that have a wide margin between the therapeutic and the toxic dose.

Age	Ideal body-weight kg	lb	Height cm	in	Body-surface m^2	Percentage of adult dose
Newborn*	3.4	7.5	50	20	0.23	12.5
1 month*	4.2	9	55	22	0.26	14.5
3 months*	5.6	12	59	23	0.32	18
6 months	7.7	17	67	26	0.40	22
1 year	10	22	76	30	0.47	25
3 years	14	31	94	37	0.62	33
5 years	18	40	108	42	0.73	40
7 years	23	51	120	47	0.88	50
12 years	37	81	148	58	1.25	75
Adult						
Male	68	150	173	68	1.8	100
Female	56	123	163	64	1.6	100

* The figures relate to full term and not preterm infants who may need reduced dosage according to their clinical condition.

More precise body-surface values may be calculated from height and weight by means of a table (e.g. *Martindale: The Extra Pharmacopoeia*, 29th Edition, London, Pharmaceutical Press, 1989) or a nomogram (e.g. J. Insley and B. Wood, *A Paediatric Vademecum*, 11th Edition, London, Lloyd Luke, 1986).

DOSE FREQUENCY. Doses for antibiotics are usually stated as every 6 hours. Some flexibility should be allowed in children to avoid waking them during the night. For example, the night-time dose may be given at the parent's bedtime.

Where new or potentially toxic drugs are used, the manufacturers' recommended doses should be carefully followed.

Prescribing in Terminal Care

In recent years there has been increased interest in providing better treatment and support for patients with terminal illness. The aim is to keep them as comfortable, alert, and free of pain as possible. If patients are to end their days in serenity it may also be necessary to direct attention to emotional, financial, social, or family problems. The patient's minister or the hospital chaplain may give invaluable help.

DOMICILIARY TREATMENT. Whenever possible patients should end their days in their own homes with their families. Although families may at first be afraid of caring for the patient at home, they will usually do so if extra support from district nursing services and social services is provided. Families may be reassured if an assurance is given that the patient will be admitted to hospital if they cannot cope.

HOSPITAL TREATMENT. The most important lesson to be drawn from the experience of hospices is that both doctors and nurses must give time to listen to the patient. This gives great support and comfort to a patient who may otherwise suffer intolerable loneliness. Often problems come to light that can easily be dealt with—adjusting a blind in the late afternoon, an irritating noise to be avoided, drinks to be placed in easier reach, someone to read the newspaper, or the TV to be replaced by radio. The staff should not exclude the family from contributing to the patient's care; if prevented they may be resentful or subsequently suffer a feeling of guilt.

DRUG TREATMENT. The number of drugs should be as few as possible, for even the taking of medicine may be an effort. Oral medication is usually satisfactory unless there is severe nausea and vomiting, dysphagia, weakness, or coma, in which case parenteral medication may be necessary.

PAIN

Analgesics are always more effective in preventing the development of pain than in the relief of established pain. The non-opioid analgesics **aspirin** or **paracetamol** given regularly will often make the use of opioids unnecessary.

Morphine is the most useful of the opioid analgesics. It is given by mouth regularly every 4 hours as an oral solution, the initial dose depending largely on the patient's previous treatment. A dose of 5–10 mg is enough to replace a weaker analgesic (such as paracetamol or co-proxamol), but 10–20 mg or more is required to replace a strong one (comparable to morphine itself). If the first dose of morphine is no more effective than the previous analgesic it should be increased by 50%, the aim being to choose the lowest dose which prevents pain. Although a dose of 5–20 mg is usually adequate there should be no hesitation in increasing it to 30–60 mg or occasionally to 90–150 mg or higher if necessary. If breakthrough pain occurs between doses the next dose due is increased; in the interim an additional dose is given.

Slow-release tablets of morphine (MST Continus® tablets) are an alternative to the oral solution; they have the advantage that they need only be taken every 12 hours. The starting dose of MST Continus® tablets is usually 10–20 mg every 12 hours if no other analgesic (or only paracetamol) has previously been taken, but to replace a weaker opioid analgesic (such as co-proxamol) the starting dose is usually 20–30 mg every 12 hours.

Increments should be made to the dose, not to the frequency of administration, which should remain at every 12 hours. The effective dose of MST Continus® tablets can alternatively be found by giving the oral solution of morphine every 4 hours in increasing doses until the pain has been controlled, and then transferring the patient to the same total 24-hour dose of morphine given as MST Continus® tablets (divided into two portions for 12-hourly administration). The first dose of MST Continus® tablets is usually given 4 hours after the last dose of the oral solution.

If the patient becomes unable to swallow, the equivalent intramuscular dose of morphine is half the oral solution dose; in the case of MST Continus® tablets it is half the total 24-hour dose (which is then divided into 6 portions to be given every 4 hours). **Diamorphine** is preferred for injection[1] because being more soluble it can be given in a smaller dose-volume. The equivalent intramuscular dose of diamorphine is only about a quarter to a third of the oral dose of morphine.

Morphine is also available as suppositories; alternatively **oxycodone** suppositories can be obtained on special order.

Nausea and vomiting may occur in the initial stages of morphine therapy and can be prevented by giving an anti-emetic such as haloperidol or prochlorperazine. An anti-emetic is usually only necessary for the first 4 or 5 days therefore fixed-combination opioid preparations containing an anti-emetic are not recommended since they lead to unnecessary anti-emetic therapy (often with undesirable drowsiness).

Constipation is almost invariable and should be prevented by the regular administration of a laxative (see next page).

BONE PAIN. Aspirin (or other NSAIDs if preferred) may control the pain of bone secondaries. Naproxen, flurbiprofen, and indomethacin (see section 10.1.1) are valuable and if necessary can be given rectally. Corticosteroids or radiotherapy are often useful for pain due to bone metastasis.

GASTRO-INTESTINAL PAIN. The pain of *intestinal colic* may be reduced by loperamide 2–4 mg 4 times daily. Hyoscine hydrobromide may also be

1. Diamorphine is also preferred for subcutaneous injection via syringe driver.

helpful, given sublingually at a dose of 300 micrograms 3 times daily as Kwells® (Nicholas) tablets, or as a continuous subcutaneous infusion of 0.6–2.4 mg over 24 hours using a syringe driver.

Gastric distension pain due to pressure on the stomach may be helped by a preparation incorporating an antacid with an antiflatulent (see section 1.1.1.1) and by domperidone 10 mg 3 times daily before meals.

HEADACHE. See under Raised Intracranial Pressure, below.

MUSCLE SPASM. The pain of muscle spasm can be helped by a muscle relaxant such as diazepam 5–10 mg daily or baclofen 5–10 mg 3 times daily.

NERVE PAIN. Pain due to *nerve compression* may be reduced by a corticosteroid such as dexamethasone 8 mg daily, which reduces oedema around the tumour, thus reducing compression.

Dysaesthetic or stabbing pain resulting from *nerve irritation* may be reduced by amitriptyline 25–75 mg at night, or by carbamazepine 200 mg 3 times daily.

MISCELLANEOUS CONDITIONS

RAISED INTRACRANIAL PRESSURE. Headache due to raised intracranial pressure often responds to a high dose of a corticosteroid, such as dexamethasone 16 mg daily for 4 to 5 days, subsequently reduced to 4 to 6 mg daily if possible.

INTRACTABLE COUGH. Intractable cough may be relieved by moist inhalations or may require regular administration of an oral morphine hydrochloride solution in an initial dose of 5 mg every 4 hours. Methadone linctus should be avoided as it has a long duration of action and tends to accumulate.

DYSPNOEA. Dyspnoea may be relieved by regular oral morphine hydrochloride solution in carefully titrated doses, starting at 5 mg every 4 hours. Diazepam 5–10 mg daily may be helpful; a corticosteroid, such as dexamethasone 4 to 8 mg daily, may also be helpful if there is bronchospasm or partial obstruction.

EXCESSIVE RESPIRATORY SECRETION. Excessive respiratory secretion (death rattle) may be reduced by subcutaneous injection of hyoscine hydrobromide 400 to 600 micrograms every 4 to 8 hours.

RESTLESSNESS AND CONFUSION. Restlessness and confusion may require treatment with haloperidol 1 to 3 mg by mouth every 8 hours. Chlorpromazine 25–50 mg by mouth every 8 hours is an alternative, but causes more sedation. Methotrimeprazine is also used occasionally for restlessness.

HICCUP. Hiccup due to gastric distension may be helped by a preparation incorporating an antacid with an antiflatulent (see section 1.1.1.1). If this fails, metoclopramide 10 mg every 6 to 8 hours by mouth or by intramuscular injection can be added; if this also fails, chlorpromazine 10 to 25 mg every 6 to 8 hours can be tried.

ANOREXIA. Anorexia may be helped by prednisolone 15 to 30 mg daily or dexamethasone 2 to 4 mg daily.

CONSTIPATION. Constipation is a very common cause of distress and should be prevented if possible by the regular administration of laxatives; a faecal softener with a peristaltic stimulant (e.g. co-danthramer), or lactulose solution with a senna preparation should be used.

FUNGATING GROWTH. Fungating growth may be treated by cleansing with a mixture of 1 part of 4% povidone-iodine skin cleanser solution and 4 parts of liquid paraffin. Oral administration of metronidazole may eradicate the anaerobic bacteria responsible for the odour of fungating tumours; topical application is also used but may increase the likelihood of resistance.

CAPILLARY BLEEDING. Capillary bleeding may be reduced by applying gauze soaked in adrenaline solution (1 in 1000).

DRY MOUTH. Dry mouth may be due to candidiasis which can be treated by nystatin oral suspension or amphotericin lozenges after food; alternatively, fluconazole can be given by mouth (see section 5.2). Dry mouth can also be a side-effect of morphine.

PRURITUS. Pruritus, even when associated with obstructive jaundice, often responds to simple measures such as emollients. In the case of obstructive jaundice, further measures include administration of cholestyramine or an anabolic steroid, such as stanozolol 5–10 mg daily; antihistamines can be helpful but are not usually necessary (see section 3.4.1).

CONVULSIONS. Patients with cerebral tumours or uraemia may be susceptible to convulsions. Prophylactic treatment with phenytoin or carbamazepine (see section 4.8.1) should be considered. When oral medication is no longer possible, diazepam as suppositories 10–20 mg every 4 to 8 hours (see section 4.8.2), or phenobarbitone by injection 50–200 mg twice daily is continued as prophylaxis.

DYSPHAGIA. A corticosteroid such as dexamethasone 8 mg daily may help, temporarily, if there is an obstruction due to tumour. See also under Dry Mouth.

INSOMNIA. Patients with advanced cancer may not sleep because of discomfort, cramps, night sweats, joint stiffness, or fear. There should be appropriate treatment of these problems before hypnotics are used. Benzodiazepines, such as temazepam, may be useful (see section 4.1.1).

NAUSEA AND VOMITING. Nausea and vomiting are very common in patients with advanced cancer. The cause should be diagnosed before treatment with anti-emetics (see section 4.6) is started.

Prescribing for the Elderly

Old people, especially the very old, require special care and consideration from prescribers.

Elderly patients are apt to receive multiple drugs for their multiple diseases. This greatly increases the risk of drug interactions as well as other adverse reactions. Moreover, symptoms such as headache, sleeplessness, and lightheadedness which may be associated with social stress, as in widowhood, loneliness, and family dispersal can lead to further prescribing, especially of psychotropics. The use of drugs in such cases can at best be a poor substitute for effective social measures and at worst pose a serious threat from adverse reactions.

In very old subjects, manifestations of normal ageing may be mistaken for disease and lead to inappropriate prescribing. For example, drugs such as prochlorperazine are commonly misprescribed for giddiness due to age-related loss of postural stability. Not only is such treatment ineffective but the patient may experience serious side-effects such as drug-induced parkinsonism, postural hypotension, and mental confusion.

Self-medication with over-the-counter products or with drugs prescribed for a previous illness (or even for another person) may be an added complication. Discussion with relatives and a home visit may be needed to establish exactly what is being taken.

The ageing nervous system shows increased *susceptibility* to many commonly used drugs, such as opioid analgesics, benzodiazepines, and antiparkinsonian drugs, all of which must be used with caution.

PHARMACOKINETICS. While drug distribution and metabolism may be significantly altered, the most important effect of age is reduction in renal clearance, frequently aggravated by the effects of prostatism, nephrosclerosis, or chronic urinary tract infection. Many aged patients thus possess only limited reserves of renal function, excrete drugs slowly, and are highly susceptible to nephrotoxic drugs. Acute illness may lead to rapid reduction in renal clearance, especially if accompanied by dehydration. Hence, a patient stabilised on a drug with a narrow margin between the therapeutic and the toxic dose (e.g. digoxin) may rapidly develop adverse effects in the aftermath of a myocardial infarction or a respiratory tract infection.

The net result of pharmacokinetic changes is that tissue concentrations are commonly increased by over 50%, and aged and debilitated patients may show even larger changes.

COMMON ADVERSE REACTIONS. Adverse reactions often present in the elderly in a vague and non-specific fashion. *Mental confusion* is often the presenting symptom (caused by almost any of the commonly used drugs). Other common manifestations are *constipation* (with antimuscarinics and many tranquillisers) and postural *hypotension* and *falls* (with diuretics and many psychotropics).

Many hypnotics with long half-lives have serious hangover effects of drowsiness, unsteady gait, and even slurred speech and confusion. Those with short half-lives should be used but they too can present problems (see section 4.1.1). Short courses of hypnotics are occasionally useful for helping a patient through an acute illness or some other crisis but every effort must be made to avoid dependence.

Diuretics are overprescribed in old age and should not be used on a long-term basis to treat simple gravitational oedema which will usually respond to increased movement, raising the legs, and support stockings. A few days of diuretic treatment may speed the clearing of the oedema but it should rarely need continued drug therapy.

Other drugs which commonly cause adverse reactions are antiparkinsonian drugs, antihypertensives, psychotropics, and digoxin; the usual maintenance dose of digoxin in very old patients is 125 micrograms daily (62.5 micrograms is often inadequate, and toxicity is common in those given 250 micrograms).

Drug-induced blood disorders are much more common in the elderly. Therefore drugs with a tendency to cause bone marrow depression (e.g. co-trimoxazole) should be avoided unless there is no acceptable alternative.

Bleeding associated with aspirin and other NSAIDs is more common in the elderly, and the outcome tends to be more serious.

GUIDELINES. First one must always pose the question of whether a drug is indicated at all.

It is a sensible policy to prescribe from a limited range of drugs and to be thoroughly familiar with their effects in the elderly.

Dosage should generally be substantially lower than for younger patients and it is common to start with about 50% of the adult dose. Some drugs (e.g. chlorpropamide) should be avoided altogether.

Review repeat prescriptions regularly. It may be possible to stop the drug (e.g. digoxin can often be withdrawn) or it may be necessary to reduce the dose to match diminishing renal function.

Simplify regimens. Elderly patients cannot normally cope with more than three different drugs and, ideally, these should not be given more than twice daily. In particular, regimens which call for a confusing array of dosage intervals should be avoided.

Write full instructions on every prescription (*including* repeat prescriptions) so that containers can be properly labelled with full directions. Avoid imprecisions like 'as directed'. Child-resistant containers may be unsuitable.

Instruct patients what to do when drugs run out, and also how to dispose of any that are no longer necessary.

If these guidelines are followed most elderly people will cope adequately with their own medicines. If not then it is essential to enrol the help of a third party, usually a relative but sometimes a home help, neighbour, or a sheltered-housing warden.

Emergency Treatment of Poisoning

Poisons Information Services

Belfast	0232 240503
Birmingham	021-554 3801
Cardiff	0222 709901
Dublin	0001 379964
	or 0001 379966
Edinburgh	031-229 2477
	031-228 2441
	(Viewdata)
Leeds	0532 430715
	or 0532 432799
London	071-635 9191
	or 071-955 5095
Newcastle	091-232 5131

Note. Some of these centres also advise on laboratory analytical services which may be of help in the diagnosis and management of a small number of cases.

CONSULT POISONS
INFORMATION CENTRES
DAY AND NIGHT

These notes deal with the initial management of acute poisoning in the home; brief mention only is given of hospital-based treatment. The notes are only guidelines and it is strongly recommended that **poisons information services** (see previous page) be consulted in cases where there is doubt about the degree of risk or about appropriate management.

Hospital admission. All patients who show features of poisoning should generally be admitted to hospital. Patients who have taken poisons with delayed actions should also be admitted, even if they appear well; delayed-action poisons include aspirin, iron, paracetamol, tricyclic antidepressants, co-phenotrope (diphenoxylate with atropine, *Lomotil*®), and paraquat, also sustained-release capsules or tablets. A note should be sent of what is known and what treatment has been given.

It is often impossible to establish with certainty the identity of the poison and the size of the dose. Fortunately this is not usually important because only a few poisons (such as opioids, paracetamol, and iron) have specific antidotes and few patients require active removal of the poison. Most patients must be treated symptomatically. Nevertheless, knowledge of the type of poisoning does help in anticipating the course of events. Patients' reports may be of little help, as they may be confused or may only be able to say that they have taken an undefined amount, possibly of mixed drugs. Parents may think a child has taken something which could be poisonous and may exaggerate or underplay the risks out of anxiety or guilt. Sometimes symptoms are due to an illness such as appendicitis. Accidents can arise from a number of domestic and industrial products (the contents of which are not generally known).

> The **poisons information services** (see p. 15) will provide advice on all aspects of poisoning day and night.

General care

RESPIRATION

Respiration is often impaired in unconscious patients. An obstructed airway requires immediate attention. Pull the tongue forward, remove dentures and oral secretions, hold the jaw forward, insert an oropharyngeal airway if one is available, and turn the patient semiprone. The risk of inhaling vomit is minimised with the patient positioned semiprone and head down.

Most poisons that impair consciousness also depress respiration. Assisted ventilation by mouth-to-mouth or Ambu bag inflation may be needed. Oxygen is not a substitute for adequate ventilation, though it should be given in the highest concentration possible in poisoning with carbon monoxide and irritant gases.

Respiratory stimulants do not help and are **potentially dangerous**.

BLOOD PRESSURE

Hypotension is common in severe poisoning with central nervous system depressants. A systolic blood pressure of less than 70 mmHg may lead to irreversible brain damage or renal tubular necrosis. The patient should be carried head downwards on a stretcher and nursed in this position in the ambulance. Oxygen should be given to correct hypoxia and an intravenous infusion should be set up if at all practicable. Vasopressor drugs should **not** be used.

Fluid depletion without hypotension is common after prolonged coma and after aspirin poisoning due to vomiting, sweating, and hyperpnoea.

HEART

Cardiac conduction defects and arrhythmias may occur in acute poisoning, notably with tricyclic antidepressants. Arrhythmias often respond to correction of underlying hypoxia or acidosis. Ventricular arrhythmias that have been confirmed by emergency ECG and which are causing serious hypotension may require treatment with lignocaine 50–100 mg by slow intravenous injection. Supraventricular arrhythmias are seldom life-threatening and drug treatment is best withheld until the patient reaches hospital.

BODY TEMPERATURE

Hypothermia may develop in patients of any age who have been deeply unconscious for some hours particularly following overdose with barbiturates or phenothiazines. It may be missed unless temperature is measured rectally using a low-reading rectal thermometer. It is best treated by wrapping the patient in blankets to conserve body heat. Hot-water bottles are of little value and may cause burns.

CONVULSIONS

Single short-lived convulsions do not require treatment. Diazepam, up to 10 mg by slow intravenous injection, preferably in emulsion form, should be given if convulsions are protracted or recur frequently; it should not be given intramuscularly.

> CONSULT POISONS INFORMATION CENTRES DAY AND NIGHT—see p. 15

Removal and elimination

REMOVAL FROM THE STOMACH

The dangers of attempting to empty the stomach have to be balanced against the toxicity of the ingested poison, as assessed by the quantity ingested, the inherent toxicity of the poison, and the time since ingestion. Gastric emptying is clearly unnecessary if the risk of toxicity is small or if the patient presents too late.

Emptying the stomach by **gastric lavage** or **emesis** is of doubtful value if attempted more than 4 hours after ingestion. However, a worthwhile recovery of salicylates can be achieved up to 24 hours after ingestion and of tricyclic antidepressants (which delay gastric emptying) up to 8 hours after ingestion. The chief danger of gastric aspiration and lavage is inhalation of stomach contents, and it should **not** be attempted in drowsy or comatose patients unless there is a good enough cough reflex or the airway can be protected by a cuffed endotracheal tube. Stomach tubes should **not** be passed after corrosive poisoning.

Petroleum products are more dangerous in the lungs than in the stomach and therefore removal from the stomach is **not** advised because of the risk of inhalation.

On balance gastric lavage is seldom practicable or desirable before the patient reaches hospital.

Emesis induced by using **ipecacuanha** (Paediatric Ipecacuanha Emetic Mixture BP[1]) is favoured in children and is also effective in adults. It may be given safely in the home providing that the patient is fully conscious and that the poison ingested is neither a corrosive nor a petroleum distillate.

Salt solutions, copper sulphate, apomorphine, and mustard are dangerous and should **not** be used.

IPECACUANHA

Indications: induction of emesis in selected patients, see notes above

Cautions: avoid in poisoning with corrosive compounds or petroleum products (risk of aspiration); shock; history of convulsions; cardiovascular disease

Side-effects: excessive vomiting and mucosal damage; cardiac effects if absorbed

Dose: see under preparation below

Ipecacuanha Emetic Mixture, Paediatric[1] (BP)
Paediatric Ipecacuanha Emetic
Mixture, ipecacuanha liquid extract 0.7 mL, hydrochloric acid 0.025 mL, glycerol 1 mL, syrup to 10 mL
Dose: ADULT 30 mL; CHILD 6–18 months 10 mL, older children 15 mL; the dose is followed by a tumblerful of water and repeated after 20 minutes if necessary

PREVENTION OF ABSORPTION

Given by mouth, **activated charcoal** can bind many poisons in the stomach, thereby *reducing their absorption*, but it is only effective if given within 1–2 hours of ingestion. It is safe and is particularly useful for the prevention of absorption of poisons which are toxic in small amounts, e.g. antidepressants.

For the use of charcoal in active elimination techniques, see below.

1. Equivalent in strength to Ipecac Syrup USP

Carbomix® (Penn)
Powder, activated charcoal. Net price 50-g bottle = £10.93
Dose: reduction of absorption, 50 g; CHILD, 25 g (50 g in severe poisoning)
Active elimination, see below

Medicoal® (Torbet)
Granules, effervescent, activated charcoal 5 g/sachet. Net price 5-sachet pack = £3.05; 30-sachet pack = £15.35
Caution: povidone (present as suspending agent) may cause pneumonitis after aspiration
Dose: Dose excluded because product not recommended

ACTIVE ELIMINATION TECHNIQUES

Repeated doses of **activated charcoal** by mouth *enhance the elimination* of some drugs after they have been absorbed; repeated doses are given after overdosage with aspirin, carbamazepine, digoxin, phenobarbitone and other barbiturates, phenytoin, quinine, and theophylline. The usual adult dose is 50 g every 4 hours or 25 g every 2 hours.

Other techniques intended to enhance the elimination of poisons after absorption are only practicable in hospital and are only suitable for a small number of severely poisoned patients. Moreover, they only apply to a limited number of poisons. Examples include:

Forced alkaline diuresis for salicylates and phenobarbitone
Haemodialysis for salicylates, phenobarbitone, methyl alcohol (methanol), ethylene glycol, and lithium
Haemoperfusion for medium- and short-acting barbiturates, chloral hydrate, meprobamate, and theophylline.

Specific drugs

ALCOHOL

Acute intoxication with alcohol (ethanol) is common in adults but also occurs in children. The features include ataxia, dysarthria, nystagmus, and drowsiness, which may progress to coma, with hypotension and acidosis. Aspiration of vomit is a special hazard and hypoglycaemia may occur in children and some adults. Patients are managed supportively with particular attention to maintaining a clear airway and measures to reduce the risk of aspiration of gastric contents. The blood glucose is measured and glucose given if indicated.

ANALGESICS (NON-OPIOID)

ASPIRIN. Absorption of aspirin and other salicylates may be delayed, especially if enteric-coated tablets have been taken; blood concentrations taken within the first 6 hours may therefore be misleadingly low.

The chief features of poisoning are hyperventilation, tinnitus, deafness, vasodilatation, and sweating. Coma is uncommon but indicates very severe poisoning. The associated acid-base disturbances are complex.

Gastric emptying is carried out in all cases; a worthwhile recovery of salicylates can be achieved up to 24 hours after ingestion.

Treatment must be in hospital where plasma salicylate, pH, and electrolytes can be measured. Fluid losses are replaced and forced alkaline diuresis is considered when the plasma-salicylate concentration is greater than

500 mg/litre (3.6 mmol/litre) in adults *or*
300 mg/litre (2.2 mmol/litre) in children.

NSAIDs. Mefenamic acid is the most significant member of this group encountered in overdosage. Convulsions are the only important feature of toxicity and are treated with diazepam.

Ibuprofen may cause nausea, vomiting, and tinnitus, but more serious toxicity is very uncommon. Gastric emptying is indicated if more than 10 tablets have been ingested within the preceding 4 hours, followed by symptomatic measures.

PARACETAMOL. As little as 10–15 g (20–30 tablets) of paracetamol may cause severe hepatocellular necrosis and, less frequently, renal tubular necrosis. Nausea and vomiting, the only early features of poisoning, usually settle within 24 hours. Persistence beyond this time, often associated with the onset of right subcostal pain and tenderness, usually indicates development of hepatic necrosis. Liver damage is maximal 3–4 days after ingestion and may lead to encephalopathy, haemorrhage, hypoglycaemia, cerebral oedema, and death.

Therefore, despite a lack of significant early symptoms, patients who have taken an overdose of paracetamol should be transferred to hospital urgently.

Gastric emptying is carried out if the overdose was taken within 4 hours of admission.

Antidotes such as **acetylcysteine** and **methionine** protect the liver if given within 10–12 hours of ingestion; acetylcysteine may also be effective up to and beyond 15 hours but expert advice is **essential**.

Patients at risk of liver damage and therefore requiring treatment can be identified from a single measurement of the plasma-paracetamol concentration, related to the time from ingestion, provided this time interval is not less than 4 hours; earlier samples may be misleading. The concentration is compared against a reference line joining plots of 200 mg/litre (1.32 mmol/litre) at 4 hours and 30 mg/litre (0.2 mmol/litre) at 15 hours, on a semi-logarithmic graph. Those whose concentrations are above that line are treated either with acetylcysteine intravenously or with methionine by mouth. Patients on enzyme-inducing drugs (e.g. carbamazepine) may develop toxicity at **lower** plasma-paracetamol concentrations; they should be treated with acetylcysteine if their plasma-paracetamol concentrations are 50% or more of the standard reference line.

In remote areas, emesis should be induced if the patient presents within 4 hours of the overdose. Methionine (2.5 g) should be given by mouth once vomiting has occurred; it is seldom practicable to give acetylcysteine outside hospital. Once the patient reaches hospital the need to continue treatment with the antidote will be assessed from the plasma-paracetamol concentration (related to the time from ingestion).

See also Co-proxamol, under Analgesics (opioid).

ACETYLCYSTEINE

Indications: paracetamol overdosage (see notes above)
Cautions: asthma
Side-effects: rashes, anaphylaxis
Dose: *by intravenous infusion,* in glucose intravenous infusion 5%, initially 150 mg/kg in 200 mL over 15 minutes, followed by 50 mg/kg in 500 mL over 4 hours, then 100 mg/kg in 1000 mL over 16 hours

PoM **Parvolex®** (DF)
Injection, acetylcysteine 200 mg/mL. Net price course of 12 amps of 10 mL = £31.75

METHIONINE

Indications: paracetamol overdosage, see notes above
Dose: *by mouth,* 2.5 g initially, followed by 3 further doses of 2.5 g every 4 hours

Methionine Tablets (Evans), DL-methionine 250 mg. Net price course of 40 tabs = £5.21

ANALGESICS (OPIOID)

Opioids (narcotic analgesics) cause varying degrees of coma, respiratory depression, and pinpoint pupils. The specific antidote **naloxone** is indicated if there is coma or bradypnoea. Since naloxone is short-acting repeated injections are necessary according to the respiratory rate and depth of coma. Alternatively, it may be given by continuous intravenous infusion, the rate of administration being adjusted according to response.

CO-PROXAMOL. Combinations of dextropropoxyphene and paracetamol (co-proxamol) are frequently taken in overdosage. The initial features are those of acute opioid overdosage with coma, respiratory depression, and pinpoint pupils. Patients may die of acute cardiovascular collapse before reaching hospital (particularly if alcohol has also been consumed) unless adequately resuscitated or given **naloxone** as antidote to the dextropropoxyphene. Paracetamol hepatotoxicity may develop later and should be anticipated and treated as indicated above.

NALOXONE HYDROCHLORIDE

Indications: overdosage with opioids; for postoperative respiratory depression, see section 15.1.7
Cautions: physical dependence on opioids; cardiac irritability; naloxone is short-acting, see notes above
Dose: *by intravenous injection,* 0.8–2 mg repeated at intervals of 2–3 minutes to a max. of 10 mg if respiratory function does not improve (then question diagnosis); CHILD 10 micrograms/kg; subsequent dose of 100 micrograms/kg if no response
By subcutaneous or intramuscular injection, as intravenous injection but only if intravenous route not feasible (onset of action slower)
By continuous intravenous infusion, 2 mg diluted in 500 mL intravenous infusion solution at a rate adjusted according to the response

PoM **Naloxone** (Non-proprietary)
Injection, naloxone hydrochloride 400 micrograms/mL. Net price 1-mL amp = £4.92
PoM **Min-I-Jet® Naloxone** (IMS)
Injection, naloxone hydrochloride 400 micrograms/mL. Net price 1-mL disposable syringe = £5.17; 2-mL disposable syringe = £9.66
PoM **Narcan®** (Du Pont)
Injection, naloxone hydrochloride 400 micrograms/mL, net price 1-mL amp = £4.92, 1-mL disposable syringe = £5.44; 1 mg/mL, 2-mL amp = £22.00
Neonatal preparations —see section 15.1.7

ANTIDEPRESSANTS

Tricyclic and related antidepressants cause dry mouth, coma of varying degree, hypotension, hypothermia, hyperreflexia, extensor plantar responses, convulsions, respiratory failure, cardiac conduction defects, and arrhythmias. Dilated pupils and urinary retention also occur. Metabolic acidosis may complicate severe poisoning; delirium with confusion, agitation, and visual and auditory hallucinations, is common during recovery.

Symptomatic treatment and activated charcoal by mouth may reasonably be given in the home before transfer but hospital admission is strongly advised, and supportive measures to ensure a patent airway and adequate ventilation during transfer are mandatory. Intravenous diazepam may be required for control of convulsions (preferably in emulsion form). Although arrhythmias are worrying, the use of anti-arrhythmic drugs is best avoided. Diazepam given by mouth is usually adequate to sedate delirious patients but large doses may be required.

HYPNOTICS AND ANXIOLYTICS

Barbiturates. These cause drowsiness, coma, respiratory depression, hypotension, and hypothermia. The duration and depth of cerebral depression vary greatly with the drug, the dose, and the tolerance of the patient. The severity of poisoning is often greater with a large dose of barbiturate hypnotics than with the longer-acting phenobarbitone. The majority of patients survive with supportive measures alone. Forced alkaline diuresis may be considered in severe phenobarbitone poisoning. Charcoal haemoperfusion is the treatment of choice for the small minority of patients with very severe barbiturate poisoning who fail to improve, or who deteriorate despite good supportive care.

Benzodiazepines. Benzodiazepines taken alone cause drowsiness, ataxia, dysarthria, and occasionally minor and short-lived depression of consciousness. They potentiate the effects of other central nervous system depressants taken concomitantly. Flumazenil, a benzodiazepine antagonist, may be used in the *differential diagnosis* of unclear cases of multiple drug overdose but expert advice is **essential**.

IRON SALTS

Iron poisoning is commonest in childhood and is usually accidental. The symptoms are nausea, vomiting, abdominal pain, diarrhoea, haematemesis, and rectal bleeding. Hypotension, coma, and hepatocellular necrosis occur later. Mortality is reduced with intensive and specific therapy with **desferrioxamine**, which chelates iron. The stomach should be emptied at once, preferably by inducing vomiting as this is quickest. Gastric lavage in hospital should follow as soon as possible, leaving a solution of 5–10 g of desferrioxamine mesylate in 50–100 mL water in the stomach. The serum-iron concentration is measured as an emergency and parenteral desferrioxamine given to chelate absorbed iron in excess of the expected iron binding capacity.

DESFERRIOXAMINE MESYLATE

Indications: removal of iron from the body in poisoning; for use in chronic iron overload, see section 9.1.3
Cautions: avoid prochlorperazine
Side-effects: pain at site of intramuscular injection, anaphylactic reactions, and hypotension when given too rapidly by intravenous injection
Dose: *by mouth* after gastric lavage, see notes above
By intramuscular injection, 1–2 g in 10–20 mL of water for injections every 3–12 hours; max. in 24 hours 6 g
By continuous intravenous infusion, up to 15 mg/kg/hour; max. in 24 hours 80 mg/kg

PoM **Desferal®** (Ciba)
Injection, powder for reconstitution, desferrioxamine mesylate. Net price 500-mg vial = £2.53

LITHIUM

Most cases of lithium intoxication occur as a complication of long-term therapy and are caused by reduced excretion of the drug due to a variety of factors including deterioration of renal function, infections, dehydration, and co-adminstration of diuretics. Acute deliberate overdoses may also occur with delayed onset of symptoms (12 hours or more) due to slow entry of lithium into the tissues and continuing absorption from sustained-release formulations.

The early clinical features are non-specific and may include apathy and restlessness which could be confused with mental changes due to the patient's depressive illness. Vomiting, diarrhoea, ataxia, weakness, dysarthria, muscle twitching, and tremor may follow. Severe poisoning is associated with convulsions, coma, renal failure, electrolyte imbalance, and hypotension.

Therapeutic lithium concentrations are within the range of 0.4–1.0 mmol/litre; concentrations in excess of 2.0 mmol/litre are usually associated with serious toxicity and such cases may need treatment with forced diuresis or dialysis (if there is renal failure). In acute overdosage much higher serum concentrations may be present without features of toxicity and measures to increase urine production are usually all that are necessary.

Otherwise treatment is supportive with special regard to electrolyte balance, renal function, and control of convulsions.

PHENOTHIAZINES AND RELATED DRUGS

Phenothiazines cause less depression of consciousness and respiration than other sedatives. Hypotension, hypothermia, sinus tachycardia, and arrhythmias (particularly with thioridazine) may complicate poisoning. Dystonic reactions can occur with therapeutic doses, (particularly with prochlorperazine and trifluoperazine) and convulsions may occur in severe cases. Drugs to control arrhythmias and convulsions may be needed. Dystonic reactions are rapidly abolished by injection of drugs such as benztropine or procyclidine (see section 4.9.2).

STIMULANTS

AMPHETAMINES. These cause wakefulness, excessive activity, paranoia, hallucinations, and hypertension followed by exhaustion, convulsions, hyperthermia, and coma. The early stages can be controlled by chlorpromazine and, if necessary, beta-blockers. Later, tepid sponging, anticonvulsants, and artificial respiration may be needed. Amphetamine excretion can be increased by forced acid diuresis but this is seldom necessary.

COCAINE. Cocaine can be smoked, sniffed, or injected. It stimulates the central nervous system causing agitation, dilated pupils, tachycardia, hypertension, hallucinations, hypertonia, and hyperreflexia. Convulsions, coma and metabolic acidosis may develop in the worst cases. Sedation, with intravenous diazepam, may be all that is necessary but intravenous propranolol may be indicated for severe intoxication.

THEOPHYLLINE

Theophylline and related drugs are often prescribed as sustained-release formulations and toxicity may therefore be delayed. They cause vomiting (which may be severe and intractable), agitation, restlessness, dilated pupils, and sinus tachycardia. More serious effects are haematemesis, convulsions, and supraventricular and ventricular arrhythmias. Profound hypokalaemia may develop rapidly.

The stomach should be emptied as early as possible. Elimination of theophylline may be enhanced by repeated doses of activated charcoal by mouth (see also under Active Elimination Techniques). Hypokalaemia is corrected by intravenous infusion of potassium chloride and may be so severe as to require 60 mmol/hour (high doses under ECG monitoring). Convulsions should be controlled by intravenous administration of diazepam (emulsion preferred). Sedation with chlorpromazine or diazepam may be necessary in agitated patients. In non-asthmatic patients extreme tachycardia, hypokalaemia, and hyperglycaemia may be reversed by intravenous administration of propranolol (see section 2.4).

Other poisons

CONSULT POISONS INFORMATION CENTRES DAY AND NIGHT—see p. 15

CYANIDES

Cyanide antidotes include dicobalt edetate, given alone, and sodium nitrite, followed by sodium thiosulphate. These antidotes are held for emergency use in hospitals as well as in centres where cyanide poisoning is a risk such as factories and laboratories.

DICOBALT EDETATE

Indications: acute poisoning with cyanides
Cautions: owing to toxicity to be used only when patient tending to lose, or has lost, consciousness; not to be used as a precautionary measure
Side-effects: transient hypotension, tachycardia, and vomiting
Dose: by intravenous injection, 300 mg (20 mL) over 1 minute, followed by 50 mL of glucose intravenous infusion 50%, both repeated once or twice if necessary

PoM **Kelocyanor®** (Lipha)
Injection, dicobalt edetate 300 mg/20 mL. Net price 20-mL amp = £2.66

SODIUM NITRITE

Indications: poisoning with cyanides in conjunction with sodium thiosulphate
Side-effects: flushing and headache due to vasodilatation

PoM **Sodium Nitrite Injection**
Injection, sodium nitrite 3% (30 mg/mL) in water for injections
Dose: 10 mL by intravenous injection over 3 minutes, followed by 25 mL of sodium thiosulphate injection 50%, by intravenous injection over 10 minutes
Available from Macarthys, Penn, etc. (special order)

SODIUM THIOSULPHATE

Indications: poisoning with cyanides in conjunction with sodium nitrite

PoM **Sodium Thiosulphate Injection**
Injection, sodium thiosulphate 50% (500 mg/mL) in water for injections
Dose: see above under Sodium Nitrite Injection
Available from Macarthys, Penn, etc. (special order)

HEAVY METALS

Heavy metal antidotes include dimercaprol, penicillamine, and sodium calciumedetate.

DIMERCAPROL
(BAL)

Indications: poisoning by antimony, arsenic, bismuth, gold, mercury, thallium; adjunct (with sodium calciumedetate) in lead poisoning
Cautions: hypertension
Contra-indications: not indicated for iron or cadmium poisoning; severe hepatic impairment
Side-effects: hypertension, tachycardia, malaise, nausea, vomiting, lachrymation, sweating, burning sensation (mouth and eyes), constriction of throat and chest, headache, muscle spasm, abdominal pain, tingling of extremities; pyrexia in children; pain on injection
Dose: *by intramuscular injection*, 2.5–3 mg/kg every 4 hours for 2 days, 2–4 times on the 3rd day, then 1–2 times daily for 10 days or until recovery

PoM **Dimercaprol Injection** (Boots), dimercaprol 50 mg/mL. Net price 2-mL amp = 70p

PENICILLAMINE

Indications: poisoning by certain toxic metal ions, particularly by copper and lead
Cautions; Contra-indications; Side-effects: see section 10.1.3
Dose: 1–2 g daily in divided doses before food until urinary lead is stabilised at less than 500 micrograms/day; CHILD 20 mg/kg daily

Preparations
See section 10.1.3

SODIUM CALCIUMEDETATE

Indications: poisoning by heavy metals, especially lead
Cautions: renal impairment
Side-effects: nausea, cramp; in overdosage renal damage
Dose: *by intravenous infusion*, adults and children, up to 40 mg/kg twice daily in sodium chloride intravenous infusion 0.9% or glucose intravenous infusion 5% for up to 5 days, repeated if necessary after 48 hours

PoM **Ledclair**® (Sinclair)
Injection, sodium calciumedetate 200 mg/mL. Net price 5-mL amp = £3.05

NOXIOUS GASES

CARBON MONOXIDE. Carbon monoxide poisoning is now usually due to inhalation of smoke, car exhaust, or fumes caused by blocked flues or incomplete combustion of fuel gases in confined spaces. Its toxic effects are entirely due to hypoxia.

Immediate treatment is essential. The person should be removed into the fresh air, the airway cleared, and **oxygen** 100% administered as soon as available. Artificial respiration should be given as necessary and continued until adequate spontaneous breathing starts, or stopped only after persistent and efficient treatment of cardiac arrest has failed. Admission to hospital is desirable because complications may arise after a delay of hours or days. Cerebral oedema should be anticipated in severe poisoning and is treated with an intravenous infusion of mannitol (see section 2.2.5). Referral for hyperbaric oxygen treatment should be discussed with the poisons information services if the victim is or has been unconscious or has a blood carboxyhaemoglobin concentration of more than 40%.

SULPHUR DIOXIDE, CHLORINE, PHOSGENE, AMMONIA. The immediate effect of all except phosgene is coughing and choking. Pulmonary oedema, with severe breathlessness and cyanosis may develop suddenly up to 36 hours after exposure. Death may occur. Patients are kept under observation and those who develop pulmonary oedema are given corticosteroids and oxygen. Assisted ventilation may be necessary in the most serious cases.

PESTICIDES

PARAQUAT. Concentrated liquid paraquat preparations (e.g. Gramoxone®), available to farmers and horticulturists, contain 10–20% paraquat and are extremely toxic. Granular preparations, for garden use, contain only 2.5% paraquat and have caused few deaths.

Paraquat has local and systemic effects. Splashes in the eyes irritate and ulcerate the cornea and conjunctiva. Copious washing of the eye and instillation of antibacterial eye-drops, should aid healing but it may be a long process. Skin irritation, blistering, and ulceration can occur from prolonged contact both with the concentrated and dilute forms. Inhalation of spray, mist, or dust containing paraquat may cause nose bleeding and sore throat but not systemic toxicity.

Ingestion of concentrated paraquat solutions is followed by nausea, vomiting, and diarrhoea. Painful ulceration of the tongue, lips, and fauces may appear after 36 to 48 hours together with renal failure. Some days later there may be dyspnoea with pulmonary fibrosis due to proliferative alveolitis and bronchiolitis.

Treatment should be started immediately. The single most useful measure is oral administration of either **Fuller's earth** or **bentonite** to adsorb paraquat and reduce absorption. The stomach is then emptied by careful gastric lavage and 300 mL of a suspension containing 30 g of Fuller's earth and 15 g of magnesium sulphate should be left in the stomach. Further quantities of 300 mL of a 30% Fuller's earth suspension are given after 2 and after 4 hours; magnesium sulphate or mannitol is given as required to produce diarrhoea and empty the gut. Some authorities prefer regimens employing 15% Fuller's earth suspensions. Intravenous fluids and analgesics are given as necessary. Oxygen therapy should be avoided if possible since this may exacerbate damage to the lungs. Measures to enhance elimination of absorbed paraquat are probably valueless but should be discussed with the poisons information services who will also give guidance on predicting the likely outcome from plasma concentrations. Paraquat absorption can be confirmed by a simple qualitative urine test.

ORGANOPHOSPHORUS INSECTICIDES. Organophosphorus insecticides are usually supplied as powders or dissolved in organic solvents. All are absorbed through the bronchi and intact skin as well as through the gut and inhibit cholinesterase activity thereby prolonging and intensifying the effects of acetylcholine. Toxicity between different organophosphorus compounds varies considerably, and onset may be delayed after skin exposure.

Anxiety, restlessness, dizziness, headache, miosis, nausea, hypersalivation, vomiting, abdominal colic, diarrhoea, bradycardia, and sweating are common. Muscle weakness and fasciculation may develop and progress to generalised flaccid paralysis including the ocular and respiratory muscles. Convulsions, coma, pulmonary oedema with copious bronchial secretions, hypoxia, and arrhythmias occur in severe cases. Hyperglycaemia and glycosuria without ketonuria may also be present.

Further absorption should be prevented by emptying the stomach, removing the patient to fresh air, or removing soiled clothing and washing contaminated skin as appropriate. In severe poisoning it is vital to ensure a clear airway, frequent removal of bronchial secretions, and adequate ventilation and oxygenation. **Atropine** will reverse the muscarinic effects of acetylcholine and is given in a dose of 2 mg as atropine sulphate injection (intramuscularly or intravenously according to the severity of poisoning) every 20 to 30 minutes until the skin becomes flushed and dry, the pupils dilate, and tachycardia develops.

Pralidoxime mesylate (P2S), a cholinesterase reactivator, is indicated, as an adjunct to atropine, in moderate or severe poisoning but is only effective if given within 24 hours. It may be obtained from designated centres, the names of which are held by the poisons information services (see p. 15). A dose of 1 g by intramuscular injection or, diluted with 10–15 mL water for injections, by slow intravenous injection should produce improvement in muscle power within 30 minutes but repeated doses or, in severe cases, an intravenous infusion of up to 500 mg/hour may be required.

PRALIDOXIME MESYLATE

Indications: adjunct to atropine in the treatment of organophosphorus poisoning

Cautions: renal impairment, myasthenia gravis

Contra-indications: poisoning due to carbamates and to organophosphorus compounds without anticholinesterase activity

Side-effects: drowsiness, dizziness, disturbances of vision, nausea, tachycardia, headache, hyperventilation, and muscular weakness

Dose: by intramuscular injection, 1 g initially followed by 1–2 further doses if necessary; in very severe poisoning the initial dose can be doubled; usual max. 12 g in 24 hours

By slow intravenous injection (diluted to 10–15 mL with water for injections and given over 5–10 minutes), 1 g initially followed by 1–2 further doses if necessary; in very severe poisoning the initial dose can be doubled; usual max. 12 g in 24 hours

CHILD 20–60 mg/kg as required depending on severity of poisoning and response

PoM **Pralidoxime Mesylate Injection,** pralidoxime mesylate 200 mg/mL. Available as 5-mL amps (from designated centres)

SNAKE AND INSECT BITES

SNAKE BITE. Acute poisoning due to venomous snakes is extremely rare in the United Kingdom and the only indigenous venomous snake is the adder. The bite may cause local and systemic effects. The local effects include pain and swelling. Systemic effects include agitation, restlessness, abdominal colic, diarrhoea, and vomiting. Death is unlikely except in the case of a very weak debilitated person who receives a large amount of venom.

Only patients with persistent or recurrent hypotension, polymorphonuclear leucocytosis, electrocardiographic abnormalities, or extensive limb swelling within 4 hours of the bite should be given antivenom. Two ampoules of **Zagreb antivenom** (Regent) diluted with 2–3 volumes of sodium chloride intravenous infusion 0.9% are given intravenously and repeated in 1–2 hours if there is no clinical improvement (the dose is the same for adults and children). Adrenaline injection should be immediately to hand for treatment of serum hypersensitivity reactions (for full details see section 3.4.3).

For slight or moderate poisoning (local pain and swelling, possibly vomiting and diarrhoea), symptomatic treatment only is required. The site should be cleaned, covered with a dry dressing, and immobilised. An antihistamine may be given by injection.

Antivenom is available for certain foreign snakes and spiders. Information on supply, telephone:

London (also identification and management)	071-635 9191
Liverpool (Walton Hospital Pharmacy) (supply only)	051-525 3611

INSECT BITES. Stings from ants, wasps, bees, and hornets cause local pain and swelling but seldom cause severe toxicity. If the bite is in the mouth or on the tongue marked swelling may cause respiratory distress. The stings from these insects are usually treated by cleansing the area, applying a cooling lotion (such as a calamine preparation), and giving an antihistamine by mouth. Bee stings should be removed by scraping them off with a finger nail or knife before cleansing the area. Anaphylactic reactions require treatment with **adrenaline**. Inhalation of adrenaline (Medihaler-epi®, see section 3.4.3) is sufficient for mild attacks and is convenient for patients at risk to carry. A dose of 0.5–1 mL of adrenaline injection 1 in 1000 (1 mg/mL) should be given intramuscularly in more severe cases (for full details see section 3.4.3).

Classified Notes on Drugs and Preparations

1: Drugs acting on the GASTRO-INTESTINAL SYSTEM

The drugs and preparations in this chapter are described under the following sections:

1.1 Antacids

Antacids are still useful for treating gastro-intestinal disease; they can often relieve symptoms in both *ulcer* and *non-ulcer dyspepsia*, and in *reflux oesophagitis*. They are best given when symptoms occur or are expected, usually between meals and at bedtime, four or more times daily; additional doses may be required up to once an hour. Conventional doses e.g. 10 mL three or four times daily of liquid magnesium–aluminium antacids promote ulcer healing, possibly less well than antisecretory agents (section 1.3); proof of a relationship between healing and neutralising capacity is lacking. Liquid preparations are more effective than solids.

Antacids should not be taken at the same time as other drugs as they may impair their absorption. Antacids may also damage enteric coatings designed to prevent dissolution in the stomach.

1.1.1 Aluminium- and magnesium-containing antacids

Aluminium- and **magnesium-containing** antacids, such as magnesium carbonate, hydroxide and trisilicate, and aluminium glycinate and hydroxide, being relatively insoluble in water, are long-acting if retained in the stomach. They are suitable for most antacid purposes. Magnesium-containing antacids tend to be laxative whereas aluminium-containing antacids may be constipating. Aluminium accumulation does not appear to be a risk if renal function is normal.

Compound preparations have no clear advantages over simpler preparations: neutralising capacity may be the same.

Complexes, such as **alexitol sodium**, **almasilate**, and **hydrotalcite**, confer no special advantage.

ALUMINIUM HYDROXIDE

Indications: dyspepsia; for use in hyperphosphataemia, see section 9.5.2.2

Cautions: see notes above; porphyria, see section 9.8.2; **interactions:** Appendix 1 (antacids and adsorbents)

Contra-indications: hypophosphataemia

Aluminium-only preparations

Aluminium Hydroxide (Non-proprietary)

Tablets, dried aluminium hydroxide 500 mg. Net price 20 = 29p

Dose: 1–2 tablets chewed 4 times daily and at bedtime or as required

Mixture (gel), about 4% w/w Al_2O_3 in water, with a peppermint flavour. Net price 200 mL = 37p

Dose: antacid, 5–10 mL 4 times daily between meals and at bedtime or as required; CHILD 6–12 years, up to 5 mL 3 times daily

Note. The brand name NHS Aludrox® (Charwell) is used for aluminium hydroxide mixture; net price 200 mL = 58p. For NHS Aludrox® tablets see preparations with magnesium, below.

Alu-Cap® (3M)

Capsules, green/red, dried aluminium hydroxide 475 mg (low Na^+). Net price 120-cap pack = £3.84

Dose: antacid, 1 capsule 4 times daily and at bedtime

With magnesium

NHS **Aludrox®** (Charwell)

Tablets, aluminium hydroxide-magnesium carbonate co-dried gel 282 mg, magnesium hydroxide 85 mg. Net price 60 = £1.52

Dose: 1 or 2 tablets chewed 4 times daily between meals and at bedtime when required

NHS **Dijex®** (Crookes)

Tablets, pink, aluminium hydroxide-magnesium carbonate co-dried gel 400 mg (low Na^+). Net price 30 = 55p

Dose: 1–2 tablets chewed every 2–4 hours when required

Liquid, aluminium hydroxide mixture 98%, magnesium hydroxide 1.7%. Net price 200 mL = £1.04

Dose: 5–10 mL every 2–4 hours when required

NHS **Gastrils®** (Jackson)

Pastilles, green (mint-flavoured) or yellow (fruit-flavoured), s/c, aluminium hydroxide-magnesium carbonate co-dried gel 500 mg. Net price 40 g = 54p

Dose: 1–2 pastilles sucked when required; CHILD 1 pastille 3 times daily

NHS **Gelusil®** (W-L)

Tablets, dried aluminium hydroxide 250 mg, magnesium trisilicate 500 mg (low Na^+). Net price 50 = £1.71

Dose: 1–2 tablets chewed or sucked after meals or when required; CHILD half adult dose

Maalox® (Rhône-Poulenc Rorer)
Tablets, dried aluminium hydroxide 400 mg, magnesium hydroxide 400 mg (low Na^+). Net price 20 = 28p
Dose: 1–2 tablets chewed 20 minutes–1 hour after meals and at bedtime or when required
Suspension, sugar-free, dried aluminium hydroxide 220 mg, magnesium hydroxide 195 mg/5 mL (low Na^+). Net price 100 mL = 39p; 20 × 10-mL sachets = 78p
Dose: 10–20 mL 20 minutes–1 hour after meals and at bedtime or when required

[1]**Maalox TC®** (Rhône-Poulenc Rorer)
Tablets, dried aluminium hydroxide 600 mg, magnesium hydroxide 300 mg (low Na^+). Net price 100 = £3.60
Suspension, sugar-free, dried aluminium hydroxide 600 mg, magnesium hydroxide 300 mg/5 mL (low Na^+). Net price 500 mL = £3.60
Dose: antacid, 1–2 tablets or 5–10 mL suspension 4 times daily 20 minutes–1 hour after meals and at bedtime; duodenal ulcer, 3 tablets or 15 mL suspension 4 times daily (treatment) *or* twice daily (prevention of recurrence)

[1]formerly Maalox Concentrate

Mucogel® (Pharmax)
Tablets, dried aluminium hydroxide 400 mg, magnesium hydroxide 400 mg (low Na^+). Net price 100 = £1.36
Dose: 1–2 tablets to be chewed 20 minutes–1 hour after meals and at bedtime or as required
Suspension, sugar-free, dried aluminium hydroxide 220 mg, magnesium hydroxide 195 mg/5 mL (low Na^+). Net price 500 mL = £1.96
Dose: 10–20 mL 3 times daily, preferably 20 minutes–1 hour after meals, and at bedtime or when required

ALEXITOL SODIUM

Sodium poly(hydroxyaluminium) carbonate-hexitol complex

Indications: dyspepsia

Cautions: see notes above; **interactions:** Appendix 1 (antacids and adsorbents)

NHS **Alexitol Sodium** (Non-proprietary)
Tablets, alexitol sodium 360 mg. Net price 20 = 40p
Dose: 1–2 tablets chewed or sucked when required

MAGNESIUM CARBONATE

Indications: dyspepsia

Cautions: renal impairment; see also notes above; **interactions:** Appendix 1 (antacids and adsorbents)

Contra-indications: hypophosphataemia

Side-effects: diarrhoea; belching due to liberated carbon dioxide

Aromatic Magnesium Carbonate Mixture (BP) (Aromatic Magnesium Carbonate Oral Suspension)
Oral suspension, light magnesium carbonate 3%, sodium bicarbonate 5%, in a suitable vehicle containing aromatic cardamom tincture. Extemporaneous preparations should be recently prepared according to the following formula: light magnesium carbonate 300 mg, sodium bicarbonate 500 mg, aromatic cardamom tincture 0.3 mL, double-strength chloroform water 5 mL, water to 10 mL. Contains about 6 mmol Na^+/10 mL. Net price 200 mL = 30p
Dose: 10 mL 3 times daily in water

For compound preparations with aluminium, see under Aluminium Hydroxide (previous page)

MAGNESIUM TRISILICATE

Indications: dyspepsia

Cautions; Contra-indications: see under Magnesium Carbonate

Side-effects: diarrhoea

Magnesium Trisilicate Tablets, Compound (BP)
Tablets, magnesium trisilicate 250 mg, dried aluminium hydroxide 120 mg. Net price 20 = 20p
Dose: 1–2 tablets chewed when required

Magnesium Trisilicate Mixture (BP) (Magnesium Trisilicate Oral Suspension)
Oral Suspension, 5% each of magnesium trisilicate, light magnesium carbonate, and sodium bicarbonate in a suitable vehicle with a peppermint flavour. Extemporaneous preparations should be recently prepared according to the following formula: magnesium trisilicate 500 mg, light magnesium carbonate 500 mg, sodium bicarbonate 500 mg, concentrated peppermint emulsion 0.25 mL, double-strength chloroform water 5 mL, water to 10 mL. Contains about 6 mmol Na^+/10 mL. Net price 200 mL = 22p
Dose: 10 mL 3 times daily in water

Magnesium Trisilicate Oral Powder, Compound (BP)
Oral Powder, magnesium trisilicate 250 mg, chalk 250 mg, heavy magnesium carbonate 250 mg, sodium bicarbonate 250 mg/g. Contains about 3 mmol Na^+/g. Net price 20 g = 16p. Label: 13
Dose: 1–5 g in liquid when required

For compound preparations with aluminium, see under Aluminium Hydroxide (previous page)

ALUMINIUM-MAGNESIUM COMPLEXES

ALMASILATE

Aluminium magnesium silicate hydrate (artificial)

Indications: dyspepsia

Cautions: see notes above; **interactions:** Appendix 1 (antacids and adsorbents)

Almasilate (Non-proprietary)
Suspension, almasilate 500 mg/5 mL. Net price 200 mL = 76p
Dose: 10 mL with meals and at bedtime or when required
Note. The brand name NHS Malinal® (Wyeth) is used for almasilate suspension.

HYDROTALCITE

Aluminium magnesium carbonate hydroxide hydrate
Indications: dyspepsia
Cautions: see notes above; **interactions:** Appendix 1 (antacids and adsorbents)

Hydrotalcite (Non-proprietary)
Tablets, hydrotalcite 500 mg. Net price 56 = 82p
Dose: 2 tablets chewed between meals and at bedtime; CHILD 6–12 years 1 tablet
Suspension, hydrotalcite 500 mg/5 mL. Net price 100 mL = 39p
Dose: 10 mL between meals and at bedtime; CHILD 6–12 years 5 mL
Note. The brand name NHS Altacite® (Roussel) is used for hydrotalcite suspension and tablets; see section 1.1.1.1 for Altacite Plus® preparations.

MAGALDRATE

A synthetic combination of aluminium and magnesium hydroxides and sulphuric acid
Indications: dyspepsia
Cautions: see notes above; **interactions:** Appendix 1 (antacids and adsorbents)

Magaldrate (Non-proprietary)
Suspension, magaldrate 800 mg/5 mL. Net price 100 mL = 38p
Dose: 5–10 mL after meals and at bedtime; CHILD 6–12 years 2.5–5 mL
Note. The brand name NHS Dynese® (Galen) is used for magaldrate suspension; it is sugar-free and low Na^+.

1.1.1.1 Aluminium- and magnesium-containing antacids with additional ingredients

Activated dimethicone (simethicone), given alone or added to an antacid as an antifoaming agent to relieve flatulence, is of uncertain value. Alginates added as protectants against *reflux oesophagitis* may be useful, but surface anaesthetics (e.g. oxethazaine) added to improve symptom relief are of doubtful efficacy. The amount of additional ingredient or antacid in individual preparations varies widely, as does their sodium content, so that preparations may not be freely interchangeable.

Preparations containing activated dimethicone with an antacid may be useful for the relief of hiccup in terminal care.

NHS **Actonorm®** (Wallace Mfg)
Gel, dried aluminium hydroxide 220 mg, activated dimethicone 25 mg, magnesium hydroxide 200 mg/5 mL (low Na^+). Net price 200 mL = £1.70
Dose: 5–20 mL when required

Algicon® (Rorer)
Tablets, aluminium hydroxide-magnesium carbonate co-dried gel 360 mg, magnesium alginate 500 mg, magnesium carbonate 320 mg, potassium bicarbonate 100 mg, sucrose 1.5 g (low Na^+). Net price 60 = £2.40
Dose: 1–2 tablets chewed after meals and at bedtime
Suspension, yellow, aluminium hydroxide-magnesium carbonate co-dried gel 140 mg, magnesium alginate 250 mg, magnesium carbonate 175 mg, potassium bicarbonate 50 mg/5 mL (low Na^+). Net price 500 mL = £2.88
Dose: 10–20 mL after meals and at bedtime

Altacite Plus® (Roussel)
NHS *Tablets*, co-simalcite 250/500 (activated dimethicone 250 mg, hydrotalcite 500 mg) (low Na^+). Net price 20 = £1.04
Dose: 2 tablets chewed between meals and at bedtime when required; CHILD 8–12 years 1 tablet
Suspension, sugar-free, co-simalcite 125/500 (activated dimethicone 125 mg, hydrotalcite 500 mg)/5 mL (low Na^+). Net price 500 mL = £1.85
Dose: 10 mL between meals and at bedtime when required; CHILD 8–12 years 5 mL

NHS **Andursil®** (Ciba Consumer)
Tablets, aluminium hydroxide-magnesium carbonate co-dried gel 750 mg, activated dimethicone 250 mg. Contains about 1 mmol Na^+/tablet. Net price 20 = 86p
Dose: 1–2 tablets 3 or 4 times daily and at bedtime when required
Suspension, sugar-free, Al_2O_3 200 mg (as aluminium hydroxide mixture), magnesium hydroxide 200 mg, aluminium hydroxide-magnesium carbonate co-dried gel 200 mg, activated dimethicone 150 mg/5 mL (low Na^+). Net price 100 mL = 77p
Dose: 5–10 mL 3 or 4 times daily and at bedtime

Asilone® (Boots)
NHS *Tablets*, dried aluminium hydroxide 500 mg, activated dimethicone 270 mg (low Na^+). Net price 30-tab pack = £1.27
Dose: 1–2 tablets chewed or sucked before meals and at bedtime
Suspension, sugar-free, dried aluminium hydroxide 420 mg, activated dimethicone 135 mg, light magnesium oxide 70 mg/5 mL (low Na^+). Diluent purified water, freshly boiled and cooled, life of diluted suspension 14 days. Net price 500 mL = £1.90
Dose: 5–10 mL before meals and at bedtime

Diovol® (Pharmax)
Suspension, sugar-free, aluminium hydroxide 200 mg, dimethicone 25 mg, magnesium hydroxide 200 mg/5 mL (low Na^+). Net price 300 mL = £1.16
Dose: 5–10 mL when required

Gastrocote® (Boehringer Mannheim)
Tablets, alginic acid 200 mg, dried aluminium hydroxide 80 mg, magnesium trisilicate 40 mg, sodium bicarbonate 70 mg. Contains about 1 mmol Na^+/tablet. Net price 100 = £3.76
Dose: 1–2 tablets chewed 4 times daily, after meals and at bedtime.
Liquid, sugar-free, peach-coloured, dried aluminium hydroxide 80 mg, magnesium trisilicate 40 mg, sodium alginate 220 mg, sodium bicarbonate 70 mg/5 mL. Contains 1.8 mmol Na^+/5 mL. Net price 500 mL = £2.86
Dose: 5–15 mL 4 times daily, after meals and at bedtime.

Gastron® (Sterling-Winthrop)
Tablets, alginic acid 600 mg, dried aluminium hydroxide 240 mg, magnesium trisilicate 60 mg, sodium bicarbonate 210 mg. Contains about 2.5 mmol Na^+/tablet. Net price 20 = 78p
Dose: 1–2 tablets chewed 3 times daily after meals and 2 tablets at bedtime

Gaviscon® (R&C)
Tablets, alginic acid 500 mg, dried aluminium hydroxide 100 mg, magnesium trisilicate 25 mg, sodium bicarbonate 170 mg. Contains 2 mmol Na^+/tablet. Net price 60 = £2.25
Dose: 1–2 tablets chewed after meals and at bedtime, followed by water; CHILD 1 tablet
Liquid, pink, sugar-free, sodium alginate 250 mg, sodium bicarbonate 133.5 mg, calcium carbonate 80 mg/5 mL. Contains about 3 mmol Na^+/5 mL. Net price 100 mL = 54p
Dose: 10–20 mL after meals and at bedtime; CHILD 5–10 mL

Infant Gaviscon® (R&C) [New formulation]
Oral powder, sugar-free, sodium alginate 225 mg, magnesium alginate 87.5 mg, dried aluminium hydroxide 112.5 mg with colloidal silica and mannitol/dose (half dual-sachet). Contains 0.92 mmol Na^+/dose. Net price 15 dual-sachets (30 doses) = £2.46
Dose: INFANT under 4.5 kg 1 dose (half dual-sachet) mixed with feeds (or water in breast-fed infants) when required; over 4.5 kg 2 doses (1 dual-sachet); CHILD 2 doses (1 dual-sachet) in water after each meal
Note. Not to be used in premature infants, or where excessive water loss likely (e.g. fever, diarrhoea, vomiting, high room temperature)
IMPORTANT. This is a new formulation; each half of the dual-sachet is identified as 'one dose'. To avoid errors prescribe as 'dual-sachet' with directions in terms of 'dose'

Infacol® (Pharmax)
Liquid, sugar-free, activated dimethicone 40 mg/mL (low Na^+). Net price 50 mL = £1.42. Counselling, use of dropper
Dose: gripes, colic or wind pains, INFANT 0.5–1 mL before feeds

Maalox Plus® (Rhône-Poulenc Rorer)
NHS *Tablets*, white/yellow, dried aluminium hydroxide 200 mg, activated dimethicone 25 mg, magnesium hydroxide 200 mg (low Na^+). Net price 50 = £1.54
Dose: 1–2 tablets chewed 4 times daily after meals and at bedtime or when required
Suspension, sugar-free, dried aluminium hydroxide 220 mg, activated dimethicone 25 mg, magnesium hydroxide 195 mg/5 mL (low Na^+). Net price 500 mL = £1.95
Dose: 5–10 mL 4 times daily after meals and at bedtime or when required

PoM **Mucaine**® (Wyeth)
Suspension, sugar-free, aluminium hydroxide mixture 4.75 mL, magnesium hydroxide 100 mg, oxethazaine 10 mg/5 mL. Net price 200-mL pack = 76p
Dose: 5–10 mL (without fluid) 3–4 times daily 15 minutes before meals and at bedtime or when required

Polycrol® (Nicholas)
Tablets, green/white, aluminium hydroxide-magnesium carbonate co-dried gel 275 mg, activated dimethicone 25 mg, magnesium hydroxide 100 mg (low Na^+). Net price 20-tab pack = 46p; 200-tab pack = £2.71
Dose: 1–2 tablets chewed between meals and at bedtime or when required; CHILD 5–12 years 1 tablet 2–3 times daily
Gel, sugar-free, aluminium hydroxide mixture 4.75 mL, activated dimethicone 25 mg, magnesium hydroxide 100 mg/5 mL (low Na^+). Net price 300 mL = £1.16
Dose: 5–10 mL between meals and at bedtime or when required; CHILD 5–12 years 5 mL up to six times daily

Polycrol Forte® (Nicholas)
Tablets, aluminium hydroxide-magnesium carbonate co-dried gel 275 mg, activated dimethicone 250 mg, magnesium hydroxide 100 mg (low Na^+). Net price 12-tab pack = 46p; 120-tab pack = £1.63
Dose: 1–2 tablets chewed between meals and at bedtime or when required
Gel, sugar-free, aluminium hydroxide mixture 4.75 mL, activated dimethicone 125 mg, magnesium hydroxide 100 mg/5 mL (low Na^+). Net price 300 mL = £1.16
Dose: 5–10 mL between meals and at bedtime or when required; CHILD 5–12 years 5 mL, up to six times daily

NHS **Siloxyl**® (Martindale)
Tablets, dried aluminium hydroxide 500 mg, activated dimethicone 250 mg (low Na^+). Net price 60 = £1.80; 120 = £3.18
Dose: 1–2 tablets chewed or sucked when required
Suspension, dried aluminium hydroxide 420 mg, activated dimethicone 125 mg, light magnesium oxide 70 mg/5 mL (low Na^+). Net price 300 mL = £1.61
Dose: 5–10 mL when required; CHILD 7–12 years 5 mL

NHS **Simeco**® (Wyeth)
Tablets, pink/white, aluminium hydroxide–magnesium carbonate co-dried gel 282 mg, activated dimethicone 25 mg, magnesium hydroxide 85 mg. Net price 60-tab pack = £3.15
Dose: 2 tablets to be chewed after or between meals and at bedtime
Suspension, aluminium hydroxide 215 mg, activated dimethicone 25 mg, magnesium hydroxide 80 mg/5 mL. Net price 200 mL = £1.35
Dose: 10 mL after or between meals and at bedtime; CHILD 6–12 years, up to 5 mL 3 times daily

Topal® (ICI)
Tablets, alginic acid 200 mg, dried aluminium hydroxide 30 mg, light magnesium carbonate 40 mg with lactose 220 mg, sucrose 880 mg (low Na^+). Net price 42 = £1.67
Dose: 1–3 tablets chewed 4 times daily after meals and at bedtime; CHILD half adult dose

NHS **Unigest**® (Unigreg)
Tablets, dried aluminium hydroxide 450 mg, dimethicone 400 mg (low Na^+). Net price 12 = 89p
Dose: 1–2 tablets chewed or sucked after meals and at bedtime or when required

1.1.2 Sodium bicarbonate

Sodium bicarbonate, being soluble in water, is rapid-acting, but absorbed bicarbonate can cause alkalosis in excessive doses. Like other carbonate-containing antacids it liberates carbon dioxide which causes belching. Sodium bicarbonate and antacid preparations with a high sodium content, such as magnesium trisilicate mixture, should be avoided in patients on salt-restricted diets (in heart failure, and hepatic and renal impairment).

SODIUM BICARBONATE

Indications: rapid relief of dyspepsia
Cautions: renal impairment; patients on a sodium-restricted diet; avoid prolonged use; **interactions:** Appendix 1 (antacids and adsorbents)
Side-effects: belching due to liberated carbon dioxide and, with prolonged use, alkalosis

Sodium Bicarbonate (BP). Label: 13
Dose: 1–5 g in water when required

Sodium Bicarbonate Tablets, Compound (BP) (Soda Mint Tablets), sodium bicarbonate 300 mg. Contains about 4 mmol Na^+/tab. Net price 20 = 7p
Dose: 2–6 tablets sucked when required

1.1.3 Calcium- and bismuth-containing antacids

Bismuth-containing antacids (unless chelates) are best avoided because absorbed bismuth can be neurotoxic, causing encephalopathy; they tend to be constipating. Calcium-containing antacids can induce rebound acid secretion: with modest doses the clinical significance is doubtful, but prolonged high doses also cause hypercalcaemia and alkalosis, and can precipitate the milk alkali syndrome. **Interactions:** Appendix 1 (antacids and adsorbents).

NHS **Nulacin**® (Bencard)
Tablets, calcium carbonate 130 mg, heavy magnesium carbonate 30 mg, heavy magnesium oxide 130 mg, magnesium trisilicate 230 mg, with milk solids, dextrins and maltose (low Na^+). Net price 25 = 82p
Additives: include gluten
Dose: 1 tablet chewed or sucked when required between meals and at bedtime; max. 8 tablets daily

NHS **Roter**® (Roterpharma)
Tablets, pink, bismuth subnitrate 300 mg, frangula 25 mg, magnesium carbonate 400 mg, sodium bicarbonate 200 mg. Net price 20 = 48p
Dose: 1–2 tablets dispersed in warm water 3 times daily after meals

1.2 Antispasmodics and other drugs altering gut motility

The smooth muscle relaxant properties of antimuscarinic and other antispasmodic drugs may be useful as adjunctive treatment in *non-ulcer dyspepsia*, in the *irritable bowel syndrome*, and in *diverticular disease*. The gastric antisecretory effects of conventional antimuscarinic drugs are of little practical significance since dosage is limited by atropine-like side-effects. Moreover, they have been superseded by more powerful and specific antisecretory drugs, including the histamine H_2-receptor antagonists and the selective antimuscarinic pirenzepine.

The dopamine-receptor antagonists metoclopramide and domperidone have different properties, tending to stimulate transit in the gut.

ANTIMUSCARINICS

The antimuscarinics (less correctly termed 'anticholinergics') can be divided into atropine and its related alkaloids (including the belladonna alkaloids), and synthetic antimuscarinics. The synthetic antimuscarinics can, in turn, be divided into **tertiary amine** (dicyclomine hydrochloride) and **quaternary ammonium compounds** (ambutonium bromide, mepenzolate bromide, pipenzolate bromide, poldine methylsulphate, and propantheline bromide). The tertiary amine dicyclomine hydrochloride has a much less marked antimuscarinic action than atropine and may also have some direct action on smooth muscle.

Quaternary ammonium compounds are less lipid soluble than atropine and so may be less likely to cross the blood–brain barrier; they are also less well absorbed. Although central atropine-like side-effects, such as confusion, are thereby reduced, peripheral atropine-like side-

 Prices are **net**, see p. 1

effects remain common with dry mouth, difficult visual accommodation, hesitant micturition, and constipation at doses which act as gut neuromuscular relaxants or inhibitors of acid secretion. The elderly are particularly susceptible; glaucoma and urinary retention may occur.

Antimuscarinics tend to relax the oesophageal sphincter and should be avoided in patients with symptomatic reflux; all antispasmodics should be avoided in paralytic ileus. Despite these side-effects antimuscarinics are nevertheless useful in some *dyspeptics*, in the *irritable bowel syndrome*, and in *diverticular disease*. A dose at night will delay gastric emptying and prolong the gastric retention of antacids, thus helping to reduce nocturnal acidity; side-effects are also better tolerated then.

The quaternary ammonium compound, **hyoscine butylbromide** is advocated as a gastro-intestinal antispasmodic, but it is poorly absorbed and its action is brief; the injection is a useful anti-spasmodic in endoscopy and radiology.

ATROPINE SULPHATE and BELLADONNA ALKALOIDS

Indications: see notes above; see also section 15.1.3

Cautions: elderly; urinary retention, prostatic enlargement, tachycardia, cardiac insufficiency, paralytic ileus, ulcerative colitis, and pyloric stenosis; may aggravate gastro-oesophageal reflux; pregnancy and breast-feeding; **interactions:** Appendix 1 (antimuscarinics)

Contra-indications: glaucoma

Side-effects: dry mouth with difficulty in swallowing and thirst, dilatation of the pupils with loss of accommodation and sensitivity to light, increased intra-ocular pressure, flushing, dry skin, bradycardia followed by tachycardia, palpitations and arrhythmias, difficulty with micturition, and constipation; rarely fever, confusional states and rashes

Dose and **Preparations**

See section 15.1.3

Compound preparations

NHS **Actonorm**® (Wallace Mfg)

Powder, atropine sulphate 100 micrograms, aluminium hydroxide gel 50 mg, calcium carbonate 145 mg, magnesium carbonate 381.4 mg, magnesium trisilicate 50 mg, sodium bicarbonate 373 mg, peppermint oil 500 micrograms/g. Net price 85 g = £1.86. Label: 13

Dose: one level 5-mL spoonful (2 g) in liquid 3–4 times daily; elderly, initially 5 mL twice daily

NHS **Alka-Donna**® (Carlton)

Suspension, belladonna alkaloids 60 micrograms (calc. as hyoscyamine), aluminium hydroxide mixture 2.15 mL, magnesium trisilicate 342.5 mg/5 mL. Net price 100 mL = 13p

Dose: 5–10 mL 3 times daily between meals

NHS **Aluhyde**® (Sinclair)

Tablets, scored, belladonna liquid extract 7.8 mg, dried aluminium hydroxide 245 mg, magnesium trisilicate 245 mg. Net price 50-tab pack = £3.20

Dose: 2 tablets 3 times daily

NHS **Bellocarb**® (Sinclair)

Tablets, beige, scored, belladonna dry extract 10 mg (equivalent to 100 micrograms of hyoscyamine), magnesium carbonate 300 mg, magnesium trisilicate 300 mg. Net price 50-tab pack = £3.20

Dose: 1–2 tablets 4 times daily

NHS **Carbellon**® (Torbet)

Tablets, black, belladonna dry extract 6 mg (equivalent to 60 micrograms hyoscyamine), charcoal 100 mg, magnesium hydroxide 100 mg, peppermint oil 0.003 mL. Net price 20 = 36p

Dose: flatulence and abdominal distension, 2–4 tablets 3 times daily

AMBUTONIUM BROMIDE

Indications: adjunct in gastro-intestinal disorders characterised by smooth muscle spasm

Cautions; Contra-indications; Side-effects: see under Atropine Sulphate and notes above

NHS PoM **Aludrox SA**® (Charwell)

Suspension, sugar-free, green, ambutonium bromide 2.5 mg, aluminium hydroxide mixture 4.75 mL, magnesium hydroxide 100 mg/5 mL. Net price 100 mL = 34p

Dose: 5–10 mL 3–4 times daily between meals and at bedtime

DICYCLOMINE HYDROCHLORIDE

Indications: adjunct in gastro-intestinal disorders characterised by smooth muscle spasm

Cautions; Contra-indications; Side-effects: see under Atropine Sulphate. Contra-indicated in infants under 6 months

Dose: 10–20 mg 3 times daily; CHILD 6–24 months 5–10 mg up to 3–4 times daily, 15 minutes before feeds, 2–12 years 10 mg 3 times daily

PoM **Merbentyl**® (Merrell)

Tablets, dicyclomine hydrochloride 10 mg. Net price 20 = 58p

Syrup, dicyclomine hydrochloride 10 mg/5 mL. Diluent syrup, life of diluted preparation 14 days. Net price 100 mL = 88p

PoM **Merbentyl 20**® (Merrell)

Tablets, dicyclomine hydrochloride 20 mg. Net price 84-tab pack = £4.89

Compound preparations

Kolanticon® (Merrell)

Gel, sugar-free, dicyclomine hydrochloride 2.5 mg, dried aluminium hydroxide 200 mg, light magnesium oxide 100 mg, activated dimethicone (simethicone USP) 20 mg/5 mL. Net price 200 mL = £1.24; 500 mL = £1.90

Dose: 10–20 mL every 4 hours when required

HYOSCINE BUTYLBROMIDE

Indications: adjunct in gastro-intestinal disorders characterised by smooth muscle spasm

Cautions; Contra-indications; Side-effects: see under Atropine Sulphate and notes above; avoid in porphyria

Dose: by mouth, 20 mg 4 times daily; CHILD 6–12 years, 10 mg 3 times daily
By intramuscular or intravenous injection (acute spasm), 20 mg, repeated after 30 minutes if necessary

PoM **Buscopan®** (Boehringer Ingelheim)
Tablets, coated, hyoscine butylbromide 10 mg. Net price 20 = 81p (not recommended, see notes above)
Injection, hyoscine butylbromide 20 mg/mL. Net price 1-mL amp = 19p

MEPENZOLATE BROMIDE

Indications: adjunct in gastro-intestinal disorders characterised by smooth muscle spasm
Cautions; Contra-indications; Side-effects: see under Atropine Sulphate and notes above
Dose: 25–50 mg 3–4 times daily

PoM **Cantil®** (Boehringer Mannheim)
Tablets, yellow, scored, mepenzolate bromide 25 mg. Net price 20 = £1.10
Additives: include tartrazine

PIPENZOLATE BROMIDE

Indications: adjunct in gastro-intestinal disorders characterised by smooth muscle spasm
Cautions; Contra-indications; Side-effects: see under Atropine Sulphate and notes above
Dose: 5 mg 3 times daily and 5–10 mg at night

PoM **Piptal®** (Boehringer Mannheim)
Tablets, peach, pipenzolate bromide 5 mg. Net price 50 = £1.14

Compound preparations
PoM **Piptalin®** (Boehringer Mannheim)
Suspension, orange, sugar-free, pipenzolate bromide 4 mg, activated dimethicone 40 mg/5 mL. Diluent syrup or water, life of diluted suspension 14 days. Net price 100 mL = £1.03
Dose: 10 mL 3–4 times daily before meals; CHILD up to 10 kg 2.5 mL, 10–20 kg 2.5–5 mL, 20–40 kg 5 mL, 3–4 times daily 15 minutes before meals (or feeds)

POLDINE METHYLSULPHATE

Indications: adjunct in gastro-intestinal disorders characterised by smooth muscle spasm
Cautions; Contra-indications; Side-effects: see under Atropine Sulphate and notes above
Dose: 2–4 mg 4 times daily

PoM **Nacton®** (Bencard)
Tablets, scored, poldine methylsulphate 2 mg. Net price 112-tab pack = £1.89
Tablets forte, orange, scored, poldine methylsulphate 4 mg. Net price 112-tab pack = £3.61

PROPANTHELINE BROMIDE

Indications: adjunct in gastro-intestinal disorders characterised by smooth muscle spasm; for use in urinary frequency, see section 7.4.2
Cautions; Contra-indications; Side-effects: see under Atropine Sulphate and notes above
Dose: 15 mg 3 times daily at least 1 hour before meals and 30 mg at night, max. 120 mg daily

PoM **Pro-Banthine®** (Gold Cross)
Tablets, pink, s/c, propantheline bromide 15 mg. Net price 100 = £2.34. Label: 23

OTHER ANTISPASMODICS

Alverine citrate, mebeverine hydrochloride, and peppermint oil are believed to be direct relaxants of intestinal smooth muscle and may relieve pain in the *irritable bowel syndrome* and *diverticular disease*. They have no serious adverse effects but, like all antispasmodics, should be avoided in paralytic ileus. Peppermint oil occasionally causes heartburn.

ALVERINE CITRATE

Indications: adjunct in gastro-intestinal disorders characterised by smooth muscle spasm
Cautions: paralytic ileus
Dose: 60–120 mg 1–3 times daily

Spasmonal® (Norgine)
Capsules, blue/grey, alverine citrate 60 mg. Net price 20 = £2.09

Compound preparations
[1]**Alvercol®** (Norgine)
Granules, beige, coated, sterculia 62%, alverine citrate 0.5%. Net price 500 g = £12.50. Label: 25, 27, counselling, see below
Dose: 1–2 heaped 5-mL spoonfuls swallowed without chewing with water once or twice daily after meals; CHILD 6–12 years, half adult dose
COUNSELLING. Preparations that swell in contact with liquid should always be carefully swallowed with water and should not be taken immediately before going to bed

1. Formerly Normacol Antispasmodic

MEBEVERINE HYDROCHLORIDE

Indications: adjunct in gastro-intestinal disorders characterised by smooth muscle spasm
Cautions: paralytic ileus; avoid in porphyria

PoM **Colofac®** (Duphar)
Tablets, s/c, mebeverine hydrochloride 135 mg. Net price 20 = £1.67. Label: 22
Dose: 1 tablet 3 times daily preferably 20 minutes before meals
Liquid, yellow, sugar-free, mebeverine hydrochloride 50 mg (as embonate)/5 mL. Net price 300 mL = £3.50. Label: 22
Dose: adults and children over 10 years, 15 mL 3 times daily, preferably 20 minutes before food

Compound preparations

PoM **Colven®** (R&C)

Granules, yellowish-brown, effervescent, ispaghula husk 3.5 g, mebeverine hydrochloride 135 mg/sachet. Contains 6.1 mmol Na^+/sachet; caution in renal impairment. Net price 60 sachets = £15.00. Label: 13, 22, counselling, see below

Dose: irritable bowel syndrome, 1 sachet in water morning and night 30 minutes before food; an additional sachet may also be taken before the midday meal if necessary

COUNSELLING. Preparations that swell in contact with liquid should always be carefully swallowed with water and should not be taken immediately before going to bed

PEPPERMINT OIL

Indications: relief of abdominal colic and distension, particularly in irritable bowel syndrome

Cautions: ulcerative colitis, paralytic ileus, rarely sensitivity to menthol

Side-effects: heartburn, rarely, allergy

LOCAL IRRITATION. Capsules should not be broken or chewed because this would release peppermint oil causing irritation of mouth or oesophagus

Colpermin® (Tillotts)

Capsules, e/c, light blue/dark blue, green band, peppermint oil 0.2 mL. Net price 100-cap pack = £12.15. Label: 5, 22, 25

Dose: 1–2 capsules, swallowed whole with water, 3 times daily before meals for up to 2–3 months if necessary

Mintec® (Innovex)

Capsules, e/c, green/ivory, peppermint oil 0.2 mL. Net price 100-cap pack = £12.80. Label: 5, 22, 25

Dose: 1–2 capsules, swallowed whole with water, 3 times daily before meals for up to 2–3 months if necessary

MOTILITY STIMULANTS

Metoclopramide and **domperidone** are dopamine antagonists which stimulate gastric emptying and small intestinal transit, and enhance the strength of oesophageal sphincter contraction. Metoclopramide is used in some patients with *non-ulcer dyspepsia*, for speeding the transit of barium during intestinal follow-through examination, and as accessory treatment for *oesophageal reflux*. Both metoclopramide and domperidone are useful in nonspecific or cytotoxic-induced *nausea and vomiting* (section 4.6).

Metoclopramide and, occasionally, domperidone induce extrapyramidal reactions with facial and skeletal muscle spasms and oculogyric crises. These are more common in the young (especially girls and young women) and the very old, usually occur shortly after starting treatment, and subside within 24 hours of stopping the drug. Injection of an antiparkinsonian agent such as procyclidine (see section 4.9.2) will abort attacks. Other side-effects include gynaecomastia and galactorrhoea; diarrhoea can occur. Dosage of both should be reduced in renal impairment and both should be avoided in the period immediately after abdominal surgery.

Cisapride is a newly introduced motility stimulant believed to promote release of acetylcholine in the gut wall; it does not have dopamine-antagonist properties. It is of use in treating *oesophageal reflux and gastric stasis*.

CISAPRIDE

Indications: see under dose

Cautions: halve dose initially in hepatic and renal impairment; elderly; **interactions:** Appendix 1 (cisapride)

Contra-indications: where gastro-intestinal stimulation dangerous; pregnancy

Side-effects: abdominal cramps and diarrhoea, occasional headaches and lightheadedness; convulsions and extrapyramidal effects reported

Dose: ADULTS and CHILDREN over 12 years

Symptoms and mucosal lesions associated with gastro-oesophageal reflux, 10 mg 3–4 times daily; 12-week course recommended

Symptoms of impaired gastric motility secondary to disturbed and delayed gastric emptying associated with diabetes, systemic sclerosis and autonomic neuropathy, 10 mg 3–4 times daily initially for 6 weeks (but longer treatment may be necessary)

Symptoms of dyspepsia (peptic ulcer or other lesions excluded), 10 mg 3 times daily (usual course 4 weeks)

COUNSELLING. Advise patient to take 15–30 minutes before meals and at bedtime (to control night symptoms)

▼ PoM **Alimix®** (Cilag)

Tablets, scored, cisapride (as monohydrate) 10 mg, net price 112-tab pack = £36.00. Counselling, administration, see above

▼ PoM **Prepulsid®** (Janssen)

Tablets, scored, cisapride (as monohydrate) 10 mg, net price 120-tab pack = £38.57. Counselling, administration, see above

DOMPERIDONE

See section 4.6

METOCLOPRAMIDE HYDROCHLORIDE

Indications: see notes above; for use in nausea and vomiting, see section 4.6

PATIENTS UNDER 20 YEARS. Use restricted to severe intractable vomiting of known cause, vomiting of radiotherapy and cytotoxics, aid to gastro-intestinal intubation, pre-medication

Cautions; Side-effects; Dose: see notes above and section 4.6

Preparations

See section 4.6

1.2.1 Compound antispasmodic preparations

These preparations should be **avoided**, especially where they contain barbiturates. Sedatives should only be used in gastro-intestinal disease on their own individual merits.

NHS CD **Alka-Donna-P**® (Carlton)
Tablets, belladonna dry extract 8 mg, phenobarbitone 8 mg, dried aluminium hydroxide 250 mg, magnesium trisilicate 500 mg. Net price 20 = 7p
Dose: 1–2 tablets sucked before meals when required

NHS PoM **APP Stomach Tablets**® (Consolidated)
Tablets, homatropine methylbromide 1.5 mg, papaverine hydrochloride 3 mg, aluminium hydroxide mixture 15 mg, bismuth carbonate 12.5 mg, calcium carbonate 180.5 mg, magnesium carbonate 195 mg, magnesium trisilicate 92.5 mg. Net price 20 = 27p
Dose: 1–2 tablets 3–4 times daily after meals

NHS PoM **APP Stomach Powder**® (Consolidated)
Powder, homatropine methylbromide 1 mg, papaverine hydrochloride 1 mg, aluminium hydroxide mixture 30 mg, bismuth carbonate 20 mg, calcium carbonate 378 mg, magnesium carbonate 375 mg, magnesium trisilicate 195 mg/g. Net price 100 g = 95p. Label: 13
Dose: 5-mL spoonful in liquid 3–4 times daily

1.3 Ulcer-healing drugs

Peptic ulceration commonly involves the stomach, duodenum, and lower oesophagus; after gastric surgery it involves the gastro-enterostomy stoma.

General measures, including stopping smoking and taking **antacids**, promote healing as do the use of a wide variety of antisecretory and other treatments. **H_2-receptor antagonists** (cimetidine, famotidine, nizatidine, ranitidine) are all very effective in gastric and duodenal ulcer and to a lesser extent in oesophageal disease. Relapse is common when treatment ceases, and can be managed by further short courses of treatment or by maintenance H_2-receptor antagonist therapy. **Pirenzepine** (a selective antimuscarinic) and **misoprostol** (a prostaglandin analogue) also inhibit acid secretion; **bismuth chelate** and **sucralfate** act by as yet poorly understood means. **Carbenoxolone**, a liquorice derivative, causes fluid retention too commonly for routine use; a **deglycyrrhizinised liquorice** preparation is of doubtful efficacy.

Resistant ulcers and erosive oesophagitis respond to the proton pump inhibitor **omeprazole**.

NSAID-associated peptic ulceration can be treated with the conventional range of drugs. Short-term treatment in patients taking NSAIDs may prevent the development of peptic ulcers but has not been shown to prevent complications of bleeding or perforation.

1.3.1 H_2-receptor antagonists

All H_2-receptor antagonists heal *gastric and duodenal ulcers* by reducing gastric acid output as a result of H_2-receptor blockade; like cimetidine and ranitidine, the newer ones (famotidine and nizatidine) can also be expected to relieve *peptic oesophagitis* and, in high doses, to reduce gastric acid output in the *Zollinger–Ellison syndrome*.

Maintenance treatment with half doses prevents *ulcer relapse*, but does not modify the natural course of the disease when treatment has ceased; it is probably best given in courses of 4–6 weeks with further short courses if symptoms recur. Maintenance treatment is best suited to those with frequent severe recurrences who cannot be treated surgically because of age or concomitant disease.

Treatment of *undiagnosed dyspepsia* may be acceptable in younger patients but is undesirable in older people because the diagnosis of gastric cancer may be delayed.

Therapy can promote healing of NSAID-associated ulcers but there is no proof that the ulcer complications are prevented.

Clear proof that treatment is beneficial in *haematemesis* and *melaena* is lacking, but prophylactic use reduces the frequency of bleeding from gastroduodenal erosions in *hepatic coma*, and possibly in other conditions requiring *intensive care*. Treatment also reduces the frequency of *acid aspiration* in obstetric patients at delivery (Mendelson's syndrome).

SIDE-EFFECTS. H_2-receptor antagonists are well tolerated and side-effects are uncommon with few significant differences between available drugs (see under individual entries below), except that cimetidine is associated with occasional gynaecomastia and rare reports of impotence.

INTERACTIONS. Cimetidine retards oxidative hepatic drug metabolism by binding to microsomal cytochrome P450. It should be avoided in patients stabilised on warfarin, phenytoin, and theophylline (or aminophylline), but other interactions (see **Appendix 1**) may be of less clinical relevance. Famotidine, nizatidine, and ranitidine do not share the drug metabolism inhibitory properties of cimetidine.

CIMETIDINE

Indications: benign gastric and duodenal ulceration, stomal ulcer, reflux oesophagitis, Zollinger-Ellison syndrome, other conditions where gastric acid reduction is beneficial (see notes above and section 1.9.4)

Cautions: see notes above; renal and hepatic impairment (reduce dose); pregnancy and breast-feeding. Avoid intravenous injection in high dosage (may rarely cause arrhythmias) and in cardiovascular impairment; **interactions:** Appendix 1 (histamine H_2-antagonists) and notes above

Side-effects: altered bowel habit, dizziness, rash,

tiredness; occasionally, gynaecomastia (cimetidine only, and usually only in high dosage), reversible confusional states, reversible liver damage, headache; rarely, decreased blood counts, alopecia, muscle or joint pain, bradycardia and AV block; interstitial nephritis and acute pancreatitis (both cimetidine); see also notes above

Dose: *by mouth*, 400 mg twice daily (with breakfast and at night) *or* 800 mg as a single daily dose at night (benign gastric and duodenal ulceration). Doses should be taken for at least 4 weeks (6 weeks in gastric ulceration, 8 weeks in NSAID-associated ulceration); when necessary the dose may be increased to 400 mg 4 times daily or rarely (e.g. as in stress ulceration) to a max. of 2.4 g daily in divided doses; CHILD 20–30 mg/kg daily in divided doses

Maintenance, 400 mg at night *or* 400 mg morning and night

Reflux oesophagitis, 400 mg 4 times daily for 4–8 weeks, Zollinger-Ellison syndrome, 400 mg 4 times daily or more

Gastric acid reduction (prophylaxis of acid aspiration; do not use syrup), obstetrics 400 mg at start of labour, then up to 400 mg every 4 hours if required (max. of 2.4 g daily); surgical procedures 400 mg 90–120 minutes before induction of general anaesthesia

Short-bowel syndrome, 400 mg twice daily (with breakfast and at bedtime) adjusted according to response

To reduce degradation of pancreatic enzyme supplements, 0.8–1.6 g daily in 4 divided doses according to response 1–1½ hours before meals

By intramuscular injection, 200 mg every 4–6 hours; max. 2.4 g daily

By slow intravenous injection, 200 mg given over at least 2 minutes; may be repeated every 4–6 hours; if a larger dose is needed or there is cardiovascular impairment, the dose should be diluted and given over at least 10 minutes (infusion is preferable); max. 2.4 g daily

By intravenous infusion, 400 mg in 100 mL of sodium chloride 0.9% intravenous infusion infused over ½–1 hour (may be repeated every 4–6 hours) *or* by continuous infusion at an average rate of 50–100 mg/hour over 24 hours, max. 2.4 g daily; CHILD, *by intramuscular injection or slow intravenous injection or infusion*, 20–30 mg/kg daily in divided doses

PoM **Cimetidine** (Non-proprietary)
Tablets, cimetidine 200 mg, net price 120-tab pack = £17.70; 400 mg, 60-tab pack = £18.61; 800 mg, 30-tab pack = £17.72

PoM **Dyspamet®** (Bridge)
Chewtab® (chewable tablets), sugar-free, cimetidine 200 mg. Net price 120-tab pack = £16.73. Counselling, chew thoroughly before swallowing
Suspension, sugar-free, cimetidine 200 mg/5 mL. Contains sorbitol 2.79 g/5 mL. Net price 600 mL = £21.89

PoM **Tagamet®** (SK&F)
Tablets, all green, f/c, cimetidine 200 mg, net price 120-tab pack = £17.80; 400 mg, 60-tab pack = £18.69; 800 mg, 30-tab pack = £17.76
Syrup, orange, cimetidine 200 mg/5 mL. Diluent syrup, life of diluted syrup 28 days. Net price 600 mL = £25.90
Injection, cimetidine 100 mg/mL. Net price 2-mL amp = 30p
Intravenous infusion, cimetidine 4 mg/mL in sodium chloride intravenous infusion 0.9%. Net price 100-mL infusion bag = £1.86

Cimetidine with alginate

PoM **Algitec®** (SK&F)
Chewtab® (chewable tablets), off-white, cimetidine 200 mg, alginic acid 500 mg. Contains 2.05 mmol Na^+/tablet. Net price 120-tab pack = £22.49. Counselling, chew thoroughly before swallowing
Suspension, cimetidine 100 mg, sodium alginate 250 mg/5 mL. Contains 1.43 mmol Na^+/5 mL. Net price 600 mL = £15.41
Dose: gastro-oesophageal reflux disease, 1 tablet chewed or 10 mL suspension 4 times daily (after meals and at bedtime), increased if necessary to 2 tablets or 20 mL suspension 4 times daily
To be taken for 4–8 weeks

FAMOTIDINE

Indications: see under Dose

Cautions: see under Cimetidine; does not inhibit hepatic microsomal drug metabolism

Side-effects: see under Cimetidine; dry mouth and anorexia also reported

Dose: benign gastric and duodenal ulceration, treatment, 40 mg at night for 4–8 weeks; maintenance, 20 mg at night

Zollinger–Ellison syndrome, 20 mg every 6 hours (higher dose in those who have previously been receiving another H_2-antagonist)

PoM **Pepcid PM®** (Morson)
Tablets, famotidine 20 mg (beige), net price 28-tab pack = £14.00; 40 mg (brown), 28-tab pack = £26.60

NIZATIDINE

Indications: see under Dose

Cautions: see under Cimetidine; does not inhibit hepatic microsomal drug metabolism

Side-effects: reported, headache, asthenia, chest pain, myalgia, abnormal dreams, somnolence, rhinitis, pharyngitis, cough, pruritus, and sweating; reversible increases in liver enzymes also reported

Dose: benign gastric and duodenal ulceration, treatment, 300 mg at night *or* 150 mg twice daily for 4–8 weeks; maintenance, 150 mg at night for up to 1 year

PoM **Axid®** (Lilly)
Capsules, nizatidine 150 mg (pale yellow/dark yellow), net price 28-cap pack = £14.11; 300 mg (pale yellow/brown), 28-cap pack = £27.05

RANITIDINE

Indications: benign gastric and duodenal ulceration, stomal ulcer, reflux oesophagitis, Zollinger–Ellison syndrome, other conditions where reduction of gastric acidity is beneficial (see notes above and section 1.9.4)
Cautions: see under Cimetidine; does not significantly inhibit hepatic microsomal drug metabolism
Side-effects: see under Cimetidine; rare reports of breast swelling and tenderness in men; also rare reports of bradycardia, AV block, and asystole
Dose: by mouth, 150 mg twice daily (morning and night), or for patients with gastric and duodenal ulceration 300 mg as a single daily dose at night, for 4 to 8 weeks, up to 6 weeks in chronic episodic dyspepsia, and up to 8 weeks in reflux oesophagitis and NSAID-associated ulceration; Zollinger–Ellison syndrome, 150 mg 3 times daily increased if necessary to 6 g daily in divided doses
Maintenance, 150 mg at night
CHILD 8–18 years up to 150 mg twice daily
Gastric acid reduction (prophylaxis of acid aspiration) in obstetrics, *by mouth*, 150 mg at onset of labour, then every 6 hours; surgical procedures, *by intramuscular or slow intravenous injection*, 50 mg 45–60 minutes before induction (intravenous injection diluted to 20 mL and given over at least 2 minutes), or *by mouth*, 150 mg 2 hours before induction, and also, when possible on the preceding evening
By intramuscular injection, 50 mg every 6–8 hours
By slow intravenous injection, 50 mg diluted to 20 mL and given over at least 2 minutes; may be repeated every 6–8 hours
By intravenous infusion, 25 mg/hour for 2 hours; may be repeated every 6–8 hours

PoM **Zantac®** (Glaxo)
Tablets, f/c, ranitidine (as hydrochloride) 150 mg, net price 60-tab pack = £29.76; 300 mg, 30-tab pack = £27.43
Dispersible tablets, f/c, scored, sugar-free, ranitidine 150 mg (as hydrochloride). Net price 60-tab pack = £31.25. Label: 13
Syrup, sugar-free, ranitidine (as hydrochloride) 75 mg/5 mL. Net price 300 mL = £22.32
Injection, ranitidine 25 mg (as hydrochloride)/mL. Net price 2-mL amp = 64p

1.3.2 Selective antimuscarinics

Pirenzepine is a selective antimuscarinic drug which inhibits gastric acid and pepsin secretion with fewer peripheral side-effects than the drugs in section 1.2. As it does not cross the blood-brain barrier it is unlikely to have central effects. It is as effective as H_2-receptor antagonists in healing *gastric and duodenal ulcers* and may also be useful in maintenance treatment. It has also been used in conjunction with H_2-receptor antagonists in resistant cases.

PIRENZEPINE

Indications: benign gastric and duodenal ulceration
Side-effects: occasionally dry mouth and visual disturbances; agranulocytosis and thrombocytopenia have been reported
Dose: 50 mg twice daily, increased if necessary to a max. of 150 mg daily in 3 divided doses, for 4–6 weeks, or in resistant cases for up to 3 months. Doses should preferably be taken 30 minutes before meals

PoM **Gastrozepin®** (Boots)
Tablets, scored, pirenzepine hydrochloride, equivalent to anhydrous pirenzepine hydrochloride, 50 mg. Net price 60 = £20.50. Label: 22

1.3.3 Chelates and complexes

Tripotassium dicitratobismuthate is a bismuth chelate effective in healing *gastric and duodenal ulcers*. Its mechanism of action is unclear, but it may coat the ulcer or stimulate mucosal bicarbonate secretion; ulcer healing may also be related to eradication of gastric *Helicobacter (Campylobacter) pylori*. The healing tends to be longer lasting but relapse still occurs. The bismuth content is low but absorption has been reported; encephalopathy (described with older high-dose bismuth preparations) has not been reported. As the elixir, which has a pungent ammoniacal odour, is likely to adhere to food rather than to the surface of the ulcer, patients should be advised to avoid food, antacids, and large quantities of milk when taking doses. Tablets are as effective as the liquid and more palatable.

Sucralfate is another effective treatment for *gastric and duodenal ulcers* and may act by protecting the mucosa from acid-pepsin attack. It is a complex of aluminium hydroxide and sulphated sucrose but has minimal antacid properties. Long-term use needs further assessment because some aluminium may be absorbed.

BISMUTH CHELATE

Indications: benign gastric and duodenal ulceration
Cautions: avoid in severe renal impairment; see also notes above; ***interactions:*** Appendix 1 (bismuth chelate)
Side-effects: may darken tongue and blacken faeces; nausea and vomiting reported

De-Nol® (Brocades)
Liquid, red, tripotassium dicitratobismuthate 120 mg/5 mL. Net price 560 mL = £14.65. Label: 14, counselling, see below
Dose: adults, 10 mL twice daily *or* 5 mL 4 times daily; taken for 28 days, followed by further 28 days if necessary; maintenance not indicated but course may be repeated after interval of 1 month; CHILDREN, no longer recommended

COUNSELLING. Each dose to be diluted with 15 mL of water; twice daily dosage to be taken 30 minutes before breakfast and main evening meal; four times daily dosage to be taken as follows: one dose 30 minutes before breakfast, midday meal and main evening meal, and one dose 2 hours after main evening meal; milk should not be drunk by itself during treatment but small quantities may be taken in tea or coffee or on cereal; antacids should not be taken half an hour before or after a dose

De-Noltab® (Brocades)
Tablets, white, tripotassium dicitratobismuthate 120 mg. Net price 112-tab pack = £20.98. Label: 14, counselling, see below
Dose: adults 2 tablets twice daily *or* 1 tablet 4 times daily; taken for 28 days followed by further 28 days if necessary; maintenance not indicated but course may be repeated after interval of 1 month; CHILD, not recommended
COUNSELLING. Each dose to be swallowed with a tumblerful of water then as above under De-Nol

SUCRALFATE

Indications: benign gastric and duodenal ulceration; chronic gastritis
Cautions: renal disease; **interactions:** Appendix 1 (sucralfate)
Side-effects: constipation; diarrhoea, nausea, indigestion, dry mouth, rash, pruritus, back pain, dizziness, insomnia, and vertigo; also gastric discomfort reported
Dose: 2 g twice daily (on rising and at bedtime) *or* 1 g 4 times daily 1 hour before meals and at bedtime, taken for up to 6 weeks or in resistant cases 12 weeks; max. 8 g daily
Prophylaxis of stress ulceration (suspension), 1 g 6 times daily (max. 8 g daily)
COUNSELLING. Tablets may be dispersed in 10–15 mL of water; antacids should not be taken half an hour before or after a dose

PoM **Antepsin®** (Wyeth)
Tablets, scored, sucralfate 1 g. Net price 20 = £2.50. Label: 5, counselling, see dose above
Suspension, sucralfate, 1 g/5 mL. Net price 560 mL = £14.00. Label: 5, counselling, antacids

1.3.4 Prostaglandin analogues

Misoprostol, a synthetic analogue of prostaglandin E_1 (alprostadil) inhibits gastric acid secretion promoting *gastric and duodenal ulcer* healing. It can protect against *NSAID-associated gastric ulcers* but not dyspepsia.

MISOPROSTOL

Indications: see notes above and under Dose
Cautions: conditions where hypotension might precipitate severe complications (e.g. cerebrovascular disease, cardiovascular disease)
Contra-indications: pregnancy or planning pregnancy (increases uterine tone)
Side-effects: diarrhoea (may be severe, reduced by giving single doses not exceeding 200 micrograms and by avoiding magnesium-containing antacids); also reported: abdominal pain, dyspepsia, flatulence, nausea and vomiting, abnormal vaginal bleeding (including intermenstrual bleeding, menorrhagia, and postmenopausal bleeding)
Dose: benign gastric and duodenal ulceration and NSAID-associated ulceration, 800 micrograms daily (in 2–4 divided doses) with breakfast (or main meals) and at bedtime; treatment should be continued for at least 4 weeks and may be continued for up to 8 weeks if required
Prophylaxis of NSAID-induced gastric ulcer, 200 micrograms 2–4 times daily according to condition of patient

▼ PoM **Cytotec®** (Searle)
Tablets, scored, misoprostol 200 micrograms. Net price 56-tab pack = £13.00; 112-tab pack = £26.00

1.3.5 Proton pump inhibitors

Omeprazole inhibits gastric acid by blocking the hydrogen-potassium adenosine triphosphatase enzyme system (the 'proton pump') of the gastric parietal cell. It is indicated for *resistant ulcers* and *erosive oesophagitis*.

OMEPRAZOLE

Indications: see under Dose
Cautions: exclude malignancy; avoid in pregnancy and breast-feeding; **interactions:** Appendix 1 (omeprazole)
Side-effects: nausea; occasional headache, diarrhoea, constipation, flatulence, and rashes
Dose: benign gastric and duodenal ulcers unresponsive to conventional therapy (including those complicating NSAID therapy) 20 mg daily for 4 weeks in duodenal ulceration or 8 weeks in gastric ulceration; in severe cases increase to 40 mg daily; long-term use not recommended
Zollinger–Ellison syndrome, initially 60 mg once daily; usual range 20–120 mg daily (above 80 mg in 2 divided doses)
Healing of erosive reflux oesophagitis, 20 mg daily for 4 weeks, followed by a further 4 weeks if not fully healed; 40 mg daily has been given for 8 weeks in reflux oesophagitis refractory to other treatment

▼ PoM **Losec®** (Astra)
Capsules, pink/brown, enclosing e/c granules, omeprazole 20 mg, net price 28-cap pack = £36.36 (also 5-cap pack, hosp. only). Label: 25

1.3.6 Other ulcer-healing drugs

Carbenoxolone, a synthetic derivative of glycyrrhizinic acid (a constituent of liquorice) is effective in *gastric ulcer*; it is also effective in *duodenal ulcer* if released at the site of the lesion. However, side-effects (commonly sodium and water retention and occasionally hypokalaemia) may cause or exacerbate hypertension, oedema, cardiac failure, and muscle weakness. For these reasons other drugs are preferred; if used regular monitoring of weight, blood pressure, and electrolytes is advisable during treatment. Carbenoxolone may act by protecting the mucosal barrier from acid–pepsin attack and increasing mucosal mucin production.

Deglycyrrhizinised liquorice is free from the above side-effects but is of doubtful efficacy.

CARBENOXOLONE SODIUM

Indications: benign gastric and duodenal ulceration in young and middle-aged patients

Cautions: elderly, cardiac disease, hypertension, impaired hepatic and renal function. See also notes above. Potassium supplements and thiazides may be necessary; **interactions:** Appendix 1 (carbenoxolone)

ELDERLY. Reduce dose in elderly; not recommended in those over 65 years of age.

Contra-indications: hypokalaemia, pregnancy; avoid use with spironolactone and amiloride

Side-effects: sodium and water retention leading to oedema, alkalosis, hypertension, hypokalaemia

PoM **Biogastrone**® (Sterling-Winthrop)

Tablets, scored, carbenoxolone sodium 50 mg. Net price 20 = £4.55. Label: 21

Dose: for gastric ulceration, 2 tablets 3 times daily after meals for 1 week, then 1 tablet 3 times daily until the ulcer is healed (4–6 weeks)

PoM **Duogastrone**® (Sterling-Winthrop)

Capsules (for duodenal release), carbenoxolone sodium 50 mg. Net price 28-tab pack = £12.80. Label: 22, 25

Dose: for duodenal ulceration, 1 capsule with liquid 4 times daily 15–30 minutes before meals for 6–12 weeks

Compound preparation

PoM **Pyrogastrone**® (Sterling-Winthrop)

Tablets, chewable, carbenoxolone sodium 20 mg, alginic acid 600 mg, dried aluminium hydroxide 240 mg, magnesium trisilicate 60 mg, sodium bicarbonate 210 mg (Na^+ 2.6 mmol/tablet). Net price 100-tab pack = £24.28. Label: 21, 24

Dose: for oesophageal inflammation and ulceration, 1 tablet, chewed, 3 times daily immediately after meals, and 2 at night, for 6–12 weeks

Liquid, carbenoxolone sodium 10 mg, dried aluminium hydroxide 150 mg (Na^+ 0.85 mmol, K^+ 1.5 mmol)/5 mL when reconstituted with water. Net price 500 mL = £12.10. Label: 21

Dose: 10 mL 3 times daily after meals and 20 mL at night, for 6–12 weeks

LIQUORICE, DEGLYCYRRHIZINISED

Indications: benign gastric and duodenal ulceration

Caved-S® (Tillotts)

Tablets, brown, deglycyrrhizinised liquorice 380 mg, aluminium hydroxide mixture 100 mg, bismuth subnitrate 100 mg, magnesium carbonate 200 mg, sodium bicarbonate 100 mg. Net price 20 = £1.25. Label: 24

Dose: benign gastric and duodenal ulceration, treatment, 2 tablets chewed 3 times daily (for duodenal ulceration increased if necessary to 6 times daily); maintenance, 1 tablet chewed 3 times daily (gastric ulceration), 2 tablets chewed 3 times daily (duodenal ulceration); CHILD no longer recommended

Note. Caved-S® tablets now contain bismuth subnitrate; long-term use should be avoided, see also section 1.1.3.

Rabro® (Sinclair)

Tablets, brown, deglycyrrhizinised liquorice 400 mg, calcium carbonate 500 mg, frangula 25 mg, magnesium oxide 100 mg. Net price 20 = £1.22. Label: 21, 24

Dose: 1–2 tablets chewed and swallowed with liquid 3 times daily after meals for 1–2 months

1.4 Antidiarrhoeal drugs

1.4.1 Adsorbents
1.4.2 Antimotility drugs

The **first line** of treatment in acute diarrhoea, as in gastro-enteritis, is prevention or treatment of fluid and electrolyte depletion. This is particularly important in infants and in frail and elderly patients. Clinical signs of severe dehydration require immediate admission to hospital and urgent replacement of fluid, sodium, potassium, and chloride deficits. For details of **oral rehydration therapy** and of preparations available, see section 9.2.1.2.

Antidiarrhoeal drugs are of secondary value in the treatment of diarrhoea, may have undesirable side-effects, and may distract from giving fluids.

Antispasmodics (section 1.2) are occasionally of value in treating abdominal cramp associated with diarrhoea but they should not be used for primary treatment. Antispasmodics and anti-emetics should be **avoided** in young children with gastro-enteritis as they are rarely effective and have troublesome side-effects.

Antibiotics and sulphonamides are generally unnecessary in simple gastro-enteritis, even when a bacterial cause is suspected, because the complaint will usually resolve quickly without such treatment, and infective diarrhoeas in the UK are often caused by viral infections. Systemic bacterial infection does, however, need appropriate systemic treatment. **Erythromycin** (see section 5.1.5) is the drug of choice for treating enteritis caused by *Campylobacter* spp. For drugs for shigellosis and salmonellosis, see section 5.1, table 1. The general use of sulphonamides in treating diarrhoea of travellers is inadvisable because of the risks of rash and agranulocytosis.

Poorly absorbed drugs such as dihydrostreptomycin, neomycin, and sulphaguanidine should be **avoided** altogether in gastro-intestinal infection. They prolong rather than shorten the time taken to control diarrhoea by causing masked bacterial diarrhoea, carrier states, or pseudomembranous colitis. Clioquinol should be avoided as it is neurotoxic; both it and lactobacillus preparations are valueless.

1.4.1 Adsorbents

Mixtures containing **kaolin** may be effective particularly in mild chronic diarrhoea but fluid replacement is of prime importance in acute disease, especially in children (see Oral Rehydration, section 9.2.1.2). **Methylcellulose** is used in diarrhoea and is also useful in controlling faecal consistency in ileostomy and colostomy.

KAOLIN, LIGHT

Indications: diarrhoea but see notes above

Cautions: **interactions:** Appendix 1 (antacids and adsorbents)

Kaolin Mixture (BP)
(Kaolin Oral Suspension)
Oral suspension, light kaolin or light kaolin (natural) 20%, and 5% each of light magnesium carbonate and sodium bicarbonate in a suitable vehicle with a peppermint flavour. Extemporaneous preparations should be prepared according to the following formula: light kaolin or light kaolin (natural) 2 g, light magnesium carbonate 500 mg, sodium bicarbonate 500 mg, concentrated peppermint emulsion 0.25 mL, double-strength chloroform water 5 mL, water to 10 mL. It should be recently prepared, unless the kaolin has been sterilised. Net price 200 mL = 57p
Dose: 10–20 mL every 4 hours

Kaopectate® (Upjohn)
Mixture, sugar-free, kaolin 1.03 g/5 mL. Diluent water, life of diluted mixture 14 days. Net price 100 mL = 94p
Dose: 10–30 mL every 4 hours; CHILD up to 1 year 5 mL, 1–5 years 10 mL every 4 hours but see notes above

KLN® (Ashe)
Mixture, kaolin 1.15 g, pectin 57.5 mg, sodium citrate 17.25 mg/5 mL. Net price 100 mL = 97p
Dose: CHILD 6 months–1 year 5 mL, 1–3 years 10 mL, 3–10 years 20 mL every 4 hours but see notes above

CERATONIA

Indications: diarrhoea

Arobon® (Nestlé)
Powder, sugar-free, ceratonia 80%, starch 15%, cocoa 5%. Net price 150 g (with measure) = £1.49
Dose: adults and children 20–40 g, in liquid, daily; infants 2–10%, premature infants 1%, added to feeds

ISPAGHULA HUSK

Indications: diarrhoea (also constipation, section 1.6.1)
Side-effects: flatulence, abdominal distension
Note. For diarrhoea the dose given in section 1.6.1 should be taken with a minimum of water.

Preparations: section 1.6.1

METHYLCELLULOSE

Indications: diarrhoea (also ileostomy, colostomy control, and constipation, section 1.6.1)
Note. For diarrhoea the dose given in section 1.6.1 should be taken with a minimum of water.

Preparations: section 1.6.1

STERCULIA

Indications: diarrhoea (also ileostomy and colostomy control and constipation, section 1.6.1)
Note. For diarrhoea the dose given in section 1.6.1 should be taken with a minimum of water.

Preparations: section 1.6.1

1.4.2 Antimotility drugs

In *acute diarrhoeas* fluid and electrolyte replacement are the prime requirements, especially in children (see section 1.4). In *chronic diarrhoeas* **opioids** (such as codeine, diphenoxylate, and mixtures containing morphine or opium) are useful symptomatic treatments, but **loperamide** may be preferable as it is unlikely to cause dependence.

There are few side-effects associated with these drugs but excessive sedation may occur in children and in patients with chronic liver disease. They should be used with caution in colitic attacks as they may possibly increase the risk of toxic megacolon. Prolonged use could possibly aggravate irritable bowel syndrome.

They should be used with caution in the elderly as they may induce faecal impaction, producing incontinence, spurious diarrhoea, abdominal pain, and rarely colonic obstruction.

In acute gastro-enteritis, fluid and electrolyte replacement are the vital measures (see Oral Rehydration, section 9.2.1.2).

CODEINE PHOSPHATE

Indications: see notes above
Cautions; Contra-indications; Side-effects: see notes above and section 4.7.2; caution in children (respiratory depression); tolerance and dependence may occur with prolonged use; **interactions:** Appendix 1 (opioid analgesics)
Dose: 10–60 mg every 4–6 hours; CHILD over 4 years 1–3 mg/kg daily in divided doses but see cautions and notes above

PoM **Codeine Phosphate Tablets,** codeine phosphate 15 mg, net price 20 = 38p; 30 mg, 20 = 39p; 60 mg, 20 = £1.21. Label: 2
Note. Travellers needing to take codeine phosphate tablets abroad may require a doctor's letter explaining why they are necessary.

PoM **Diarrest®** (Galen)
Liquid, yellow, codeine phosphate 5 mg, dicyclomine hydrochloride 2.5 mg, potassium chloride 40 mg, sodium chloride 50 mg, sodium citrate 50 mg/5 mL. For diarrhoea, vomiting, and cramp. Net price 200 mL = £3.34
Dose: 20 mL; CHILD 4–5 years 5 mL, 6–9 years 10 mL, 10–13 years 15 mL but see cautions and notes above. Doses should be taken with water 4 times daily

Kaodene® (Boots)
Mixture, codeine phosphate 10 mg, light kaolin 3 g/10 mL. Net price 250 mL = 89p
Dose: 20 mL 3–4 times daily; CHILD over 5 years 10 mL but see cautions and notes above

CO-PHENOTROPE

A mixture of diphenoxylate hydrochloride and atropine sulphate in the mass proportions 100 parts to 1 part respectively

Indications: adjunct to rehydration in acute diarrhoea (but see notes above); chronic mild ulcerative colitis
Cautions; Contra-indications; Side-effects: see notes above and under Codeine Phosphate; young children are particularly susceptible to

OVERDOSAGE and symptoms may be delayed so that observation is needed for at least 48 hours after ingestion; in addition the presence of subclinical doses of atropine may give rise to the side-effects of atropine in susceptible individuals or in overdosage

PoM **Lomotil®** (Gold Cross)

Tablets, co-phenotrope 2.5/0.025 (diphenoxylate hydrochloride 2.5 mg, atropine sulphate 25 micrograms). Net price 20 = £1.96

Dose: initially 4 tablets, followed by 2 tablets every 6 hours until diarrhoea controlled; CHILD 4–8 years 1 tablet 3 times daily, 9–12 years 1 tablet 4 times daily, 13–16 years 2 tablets 3 times daily, but see also notes above

Liquid, red, sugar-free, co-phenotrope 2.5/0.025 (diphenoxylate hydrochloride 2.5 mg, atropine sulphate 25 micrograms)/5 mL. Diluent glycerol, life of diluted preparation 14 days. Net price 100 mL = £3.73

Dose: initially 20 mL, followed by 10 mL every 6 hours until diarrhoea controlled; CHILD 4–8 years 5 mL 3 times daily, 9–12 years 5 mL 4 times daily, 13–16 years 10 mL 3 times daily, but see also notes above

Non-proprietary versions are also available

LOPERAMIDE HYDROCHLORIDE

Indications: adjunct to rehydration in acute diarrhoea in adults and children over 4 years (but see notes above); chronic diarrhoea in adults only

Cautions; Contra-indications: see notes above and under Codeine Phosphate (except dependence)

Side-effects: abdominal cramps and skin reactions, including urticaria reported; paralytic ileus and abdominal bloating also reported

Dose: acute diarrhoea, 4 mg initially followed by 2 mg after each loose stool for up to 5 days; usual dose 6–8 mg daily; max. 16 mg daily; CHILD 4–8 years 1 mg 4 times daily for up to *3 days only*, 9–12 years 2 mg 4 times daily for up to 5 days

Chronic diarrhoea in adults, initially, 4–8 mg daily in divided doses, subsequently adjusted according to response and given in 2 divided doses for maintenance

PoM[1] **Loperamide** (Non-proprietary)

Capsules, loperamide hydrochloride 2 mg. Net price 30 = £3.32

PoM[1] **Imodium®** (Janssen)

Capsules, green/grey, loperamide hydrochloride 2 mg. Net price 30 = £2.17

Syrup, red, sugar-free, loperamide hydrochloride 1 mg/5 mL. Diluent water, life of diluted preparation 14 days. Net price 100 mL = £1.90

[1]*Note.* Loperamide capsules can be sold to the public, for adults and children over 12 years, provided they are licensed and labelled for the treatment of acute diarrhoea; a proprietary brand (Arret® capsules and adult syrup) is also on sale to the public

OPIUM AND MORPHINE

Indications: see notes above

Cautions; Contra-indications; Side-effects: see notes above and under Codeine Phosphate, sedation and the risk of dependence are greater

Kaolin and Morphine Mixture (BP)
(Kaolin and Morphine Oral Suspension)

Oral Suspension, light kaolin or light kaolin (natural) 20%, sodium bicarbonate 5%, and chloroform and morphine tincture 4% in a suitable vehicle. Extemporaneous preparations should be prepared according to the following formula: light kaolin or light kaolin (natural) 2 g, sodium bicarbonate 500 mg, chloroform and morphine tincture 0.4 mL, water to 10 mL. It should be recently prepared, unless the kaolin has been sterilised. Contains 550 to 800 micrograms of anhydrous morphine/10 mL.

Dose: 10 mL every 4 hours in water

1.5 Treatment of chronic diarrhoeas

Once tumours are ruled out individual complaints need specific treatment including dietary manipulation as well as drug treatment and the maintenance of a liberal fluid intake.

IRRITABLE BOWEL SYNDROME. This can present with pain, constipation, or diarrhoea, all of which may benefit from a high-fibre diet with bran or other agents which increase stool bulk (section 1.6.1) if necessary. In some patients there may be important psychological aggravating factors which respond to reassurance. Antidiarrhoeal drugs such as **loperamide** may sometimes be necessary but prolonged use may aggravate the condition (section 1.4.2). Antispasmodics (section 1.2) may relieve the pain.

MALABSORPTION SYNDROMES. Individual conditions need specific treatment and also general nutritional consideration. Thus coeliac disease (gluten enteropathy) usually needs a gluten-free diet (Appendix 7) and pancreatic insufficiency needs pancreatin supplements (section 1.9.4).

ULCERATIVE COLITIS. For *acute attacks* topical **corticosteroid** treatment such as prednisolone enemas or suppositories for localised rectal disease will induce remission; foam preparations are especially useful where patients have difficulty retaining liquid enemas. More extensive disease requires oral corticosteroid treatment and severe extensive or fulminant disease needs hospital admission and intravenous corticosteroid administration.

Sulphasalazine, a chemical combination of sulphapyridine and 5-aminosalicylic acid ('5-ASA') is useful in mild symptomatic disease requiring oral treatment; it is also available as suppositories for rectal disease. Activity resides in the 5-aminosalicylic acid moiety; sulphapyridine acts only as a carrier to the colonic site of action (but it still causes side-effects). Newer alternatives include **olsalazine** (2 molecules of 5-aminosalicylic acid bonded together, separating in the lower bowel) and **mesalazine** (5-aminosalicylic acid itself) in a slow-release formulation. Olsalazine is active in mild symptomatic disease; like mesalazine it does not have sulphasalazine's sulphonamide-related side-effects, but each has its own side-effect profile which includes watery diarrhoea and (as with sulphasalazine) salicylate hypersensitivity. By contrast, the sulphapyridine-related side-effects of sulphasalazine include sulphonamide-related rashes and blood disorders, azoospermia, and lupoid syndromes.

Corticosteroids are unsuitable for *maintenance treatment* because of side-effects. Sulphasalazine, mesalazine, and olsalazine all have value in preventing relapse and choice is related in part to their different side-effects. In resistant cases **azathioprine** (see section 8.2.1), 2 mg/kg daily, given under close supervision may be helpful.

Laxatives are required to facilitate bowel movement when proctitis is present but a high-fibre diet and bulk-forming drugs such as **methylcellulose** are more useful in adjusting faecal consistency (section 1.6.1).

Symptoms of mild ulcerative colitis may be relieved with antidiarrhoeal drugs such as **codeine** or **loperamide** but they should be used with caution in severe cases as paralytic ileus and toxic megacolon may be precipitated. For similar reasons antispasmodics should **not** be used in ulcerative colitis.

CROHN'S DISEASE. Treatment particularly of colonic disease is similar to that for ulcerative colitis. In small bowel disease **sulphasalazine** is of doubtful value. **Oral corticosteroids** (e.g. prednisolone) suppress inflammation, and **metronidazole** may be beneficial possibly through antibacterial activity. Other antibacterials should be given if specifically indicated and for managing bacterial overgrowth in the small bowel.

In both colitis and Crohn's disease general nutritional care and appropriate supplements are essential.

Cholestyramine and **aluminium hydroxide mixture** (section 1.1.1), bind unabsorbed bile salts and provide symptomatic relief of diarrhoea following ileal disease or resection, in bacterial colonisation of the small bowel, and in post-vagotomy diarrhoea.

PSEUDOMEMBRANOUS COLITIS. This is due to colonisation of the colon with *Clostridium difficile* which may develop after antibiotic therapy. It is usually of acute onset, but may run a chronic course; it is a particular hazard of clindamycin and lincomycin but few antibiotics are free of this side-effect. Oral **vancomycin** (see section 5.1.7) or **metronidazole** (see section 5.1.11) are used as specific treatment.

DIVERTICULAR DISEASE. This is treated with a high-fibre diet, **bran supplements**, and **bulk-forming laxatives. Antispasmodics** may provide symptomatic relief when colic is a problem (section 1.2). **Antibiotics** should be used only when the diverticula in the intestinal wall become infected. **Antidiarrhoeal** drugs which slow intestinal motility, for example codeine, diphenoxylate, and loperamide could possibly exacerbate the symptoms of diverticular disease and are therefore **contra-indicated**.

AMINOSALICYLATES

SULPHASALAZINE

Indications: induction and maintenance of remission in ulcerative colitis; treatment of active Crohn's disease (for use in rheumatoid arthritis see section 10.1.3)

Cautions: pregnancy; hepatic and renal disease; G6PD deficiency (including breast-feeding of affected infants); slow acetylator status; withdraw treatment if blood disorders, hypersensitivity reactions, or other serious disorders occur; upper gastro-intestinal side-effects become common with doses over 4 g daily; blood counts, liver-function tests, and rheumatoid arthritis, see section 10.1.3

Contra-indications: salicylate and sulphonamide hypersensitivity; porphyria

Side-effects: nausea, vomiting, epigastric discomfort, headache, rashes; *occasionally:* fever, minor haematological abnormalities such as Heinz-body anaemia, reversible neutropenia, folate deficiency; reversible azoospermia; *rarely:* pancreatitis, hepatitis, exacerbation of colitis, thrombocytopenia, agranulocytosis, Stevens–Johnson syndrome, neurotoxicity, photosensitisation, lupus erythematosus-like syndrome, and pneumonitis; proteinuria, crystalluria and nephrotic syndrome; urine may be coloured orange; some soft contact lenses may be stained

Dose: *by mouth*, acute attack 1–2 g 4 times daily (but see **cautions**) until remission occurs (if necessary corticosteroids may also be given), reducing to a maintenance dose of 500 mg 4 times daily; CHILD over 2 years, acute attack 40–60 mg/kg daily, maintenance dose 20–30 mg/kg daily

By rectum, in suppositories, alone or in conjunction with oral treatment 0.5–1 g morning and night after a bowel movement. As an enema, 3 g at night, retained for at least 1 hour

PoM **Sulphasalazine** (Non-proprietary)

Tablets, sulphasalazine 500 mg. Net price 100 = £6.80. Label: 14, counselling, lenses see above

PoM **Salazopyrin®** (Pharmacia)

Tablets, orange-brown, scored, sulphasalazine 500 mg. Net price 20 = £1.41. Label: 14, counselling, lenses see above

EN-tablets® (= tablets e/c), yellow, f/c, sulphasalazine 500 mg. Net price 125-tab pack =

£12.75. Label: 5, 14, 25, counselling, lenses see above
Suspension, yellow, sulphasalazine 250 mg/5 mL. Net price 473 mL = £15.95. Label: 14, counselling, lenses see above
Suppositories, brown, sulphasalazine 500 mg. Net price 10 = £2.95; 50 = £14.02. Label: 14, counselling, lenses see above
Retention enema, sulphasalazine 3 g in 100-mL single-dose disposable packs fitted with a nozzle. Net price 7 × 100 mL = £12.75. Label: 14, counselling, lenses see above

MESALAZINE

Indications: maintenance of remission in ulcerative colitis and treatment of mild to moderate exacerbations
Cautions: elderly; renal impairment; pregnancy and breast-feeding; avoid administration with lactulose
Contra-indications: salicylate hypersensitivity; severe renal impairment
Side-effects: nausea, diarrhoea, and abdominal pain; headache; exacerbation of symptoms of colitis; rarely reversible pancreatitis, hepatitis, and interstitial nephritis; reversible myocarditis also reported
Dose: *by mouth*, 1.2–2.4 g daily in divided doses
By rectum, see under preparations

PoM **Asacol®** (SK&F)
Tablets, red, coated with an acrylic-based resin, mesalazine 400 mg. Net price 120-tab pack = £28.58. Label: 25
Suppositories, mesalazine 250 mg, net price 20 = £6.50; 500 mg, 10 = £6.50
Dose: 3–6 suppositories of 250 mg (max. 3 suppositories of 500 mg) daily in divided doses, with last dose at bedtime

PoM **Pentasa®** (Nordic)
Tablets, s/r, enclosing coated granules, mesalazine 250 mg. Net price 200-tab pack = £32.28. Label: 25
Dose: maintenance of remission 2 tablets 3 times daily
Retention enema, mesalazine 1 g in 100-mL single-dose bottle. Net price 7 × 100 mL = £19.45
Dose: 100 mL enema at bedtime

OLSALAZINE SODIUM

Indications: treatment of acute mild ulcerative colitis and maintenance of remission
Cautions; Contra-indications; Side-effects: see under Mesalazine; also arthralgia, rash
Dose: acute attack, 1 g daily in divided doses increased if necessary over 1 week to max. 3 g daily (max. single dose 1 g)
Maintenance, 500 mg twice daily

PoM **Dipentum®** (Pharmacia)
Capsules, brown, olsalazine sodium 250 mg. Net price 20 = £4.78. Label: 21

ANION-EXCHANGE RESINS

CHOLESTYRAMINE

Indications: diarrhoea associated with Crohn's disease, ileal resection, vagotomy, diabetic vagal neuropathy, and radiation; pruritus in liver disease, and hypercholesterolaemia, see section 2.12
Cautions; Contra-indications; Side-effects: see section 2.12
Dose: diarrhoea, 12–24 g daily mixed with water, in single or divided doses, subsequently adjusted as required; max. 36 g daily
COUNSELLING. Other drugs should be taken at least 1 hour before or 4–6 hours after cholestyramine to reduce possible interference with absorption

Preparations: Section 2.12

CORTICOSTEROIDS

HYDROCORTISONE

Indications: inflammation associated with colitis, proctitis
Cautions; Contra-indications; Side-effects: systemic absorption may occur, see section 6.3.3; prolonged use should be avoided; avoid use of enemas and rectal foams in obstruction, bowel perforation, and extensive fistulas; contra-indicated in untreated infection
Dose: rectal, see under Preparations

PoM **Hydrocortisone Suppositories,** hydrocortisone or hydrocortisone acetate 25 mg in theobroma oil or other suitable basis. Net price 6 = £2.15
Dose: proctitis, 1 suppository inserted night and morning after a bowel movement

PoM **Colifoam®** (Stafford-Miller)
Foam in aerosol pack, hydrocortisone acetate 10%. Net price 25 g (= 14 applications) with applicator = £7.25
Dose: initially 1 metered application (125 mg hydrocortisone acetate) inserted into the rectum once or twice daily for 2–3 weeks, then once on alternate days

PREDNISOLONE

Indications: induction and maintenance of remission in ulcerative colitis, and Crohn's disease
Cautions; Contra-indications; Side-effects: see under Hydrocortisone and section 6.3.3
Dose: *by mouth*, initial dose 40 mg daily, in single or divided doses, until remission occurs, followed by reducing doses
By rectum, see under Preparations

Oral preparations, see section 6.3.4

Rectal preparations

PoM **Predenema®** (Pharmax)
Retention enema, prednisolone 20 mg (as sodium metasulphobenzoate) in 100-mL single-dose

disposable pack. Net price 10 (standard tube) = £7.72, 7 (long tube) = £9.26
Dose: initially 1 enema at bedtime for 2–4 weeks, extending course if good response obtained

PoM **Predfoam®** (Pharmax)
Foam in aerosol pack, prednisolone 20 mg (as metasulphobenzoate sodium)/metered application. Net price 25 g (14 applications) with disposable applicators = £7.25
Dose: 1 metered application (20 mg prednisolone) inserted into the rectum once or twice daily for 2 weeks, continued for further 2 weeks if good response

PoM **Predsol®** (Glaxo)
Retention enema, prednisolone 20 mg (as sodium phosphate) in 100-mL single-dose disposable packs fitted with a nozzle. Net price 7 = £5.24
Dose: initially 1 enema at bedtime for 2–4 weeks, extending course if good response obtained
Suppositories, prednisolone 5 mg (as sodium phosphate). Net price 10 = £1.00
Dose: proctitis and rectal complications of Crohn's disease, 1 suppository inserted night and morning after a bowel movement

CROMOGLYCATE

SODIUM CROMOGLYCATE

Indications: food allergy (in conjunction with dietary restriction)
Side-effects: occasional nausea, rashes, and joint pain
Dose: 200 mg 4 times daily before meals; CHILD 2–14 years 100 mg; capsules may be swallowed whole or the contents dissolved in hot water and diluted with cold water before taking. May be increased if necessary after 2–3 weeks to a max. of 40 mg/kg daily and then reduced according to the response

PoM **Nalcrom®** (Fisons)
Capsules, sodium cromoglycate 100 mg. Net price 100 = £13.73. Label: 22, counselling, see dose above

1.6 Laxatives

Misconceptions about bowel habits have led to excessive laxative use. Abuse may lead to hypokalaemia and an atonic non-functioning colon. Simple constipation is usually relieved by increasing the intake of dietary fibre. The use of laxatives in children is undesirable and the introduction of fruit purée into the diet may be sufficient to regulate bowel action. In infants constipation is often remedied by adjustment of the diet.

Laxatives should generally be **avoided** except where straining will exacerbate a condition (such as angina) or increase the risk of rectal bleeding as in haemorrhoids. Laxatives are also of value in *drug-induced constipation*, for the expulsion of *parasites* after anthelmintic treatment, and to clear the alimentary tract before *surgery and radiological procedures*.

The laxatives that follow have been divided into 4 main groups (sections 1.6.1–1.6.4). This simple classification disguises the fact that some laxatives have a complex action.

1.6.1 Bulk-forming drugs

These relieve constipation by increasing faecal mass which stimulates peristalsis, but patients should be told that the full effect may take some days to develop. They are useful in the management of patients with colostomy, ileostomy, haemorrhoids, anal fissure, chronic diarrhoea associated with diverticular disease, irritable bowel syndrome, and ulcerative colitis (section 1.5). Adequate fluid intake must be maintained to avoid intestinal obstruction. Unprocessed wheat **bran**, taken with food or fruit juice, is a most effective bulk-forming preparation. Finely ground bran, though more palatable, has poorer water-retaining properties, but can be taken as bran bread or biscuits in appropriately increased quantities. Oat bran is also used.

Methylcellulose, **ispaghula**, and **sterculia** are useful in patients who cannot tolerate bran. Methylcellulose also acts as a faecal softener.

BRAN

Indications: see notes above
Cautions; Contra-indications; Side-effects: see under Ispaghula Husk. Calcium and iron absorption may be impaired. Avoid in gluten enteropathies and coeliac disease
Dose: see preparations below
COUNSELLING. Preparations that swell in contact with liquid should always be carefully swallowed with water and should not be taken immediately before going to bed

NHS **Fybranta®** (Norgine)
Tablets, brown, bran 2 g. Net price 20 = 46p. Label: 24, 27, counselling, see above
Dose: 1–3 tablets chewed and swallowed with water 3–4 times daily, preferably with meals

NHS **Proctofibe®** (Roussel)
Tablets, beige, f/c, fibrous grain extract 375 mg, fibrous citrus extract 94 mg. Net price 20 = 56p. Counselling, see above
Dose: adults and children over 3 years 4–12 tablets daily in divided doses swallowed with plenty of water *or* crushed and dispersed in water

ISPAGHULA HUSK

Indications: see notes above

Cautions: adequate fluid intake should be maintained to avoid intestinal obstruction

Contra-indications: intestinal obstruction, colonic atony, faecal impaction

Side-effects: flatulence, abdominal distension

Dose: see preparations below

COUNSELLING. Preparations that swell in contact with liquid should always be carefully swallowed with water and should not be taken immediately before going to bed

Fybogel® (R&C)

Granules, buff or orange, effervescent, sugar- and gluten-free, ispaghula husk 3.5 g/sachet. Net price 60 sachets (plain or orange flavoured) = £4.24. Label: 13, counselling, see above

Note. Contains potassium approx. 7 mmol/sachet

Dose: 1 sachet in water twice daily preferably after meals; CHILD ½–1 level 5-mL spoonful

Isogel® (A&H)

Granules, pink, sugar-free, ispaghula husk 90%. Net price 200 g = 97p. Label: 13, counselling, see above

Dose: constipation, 2 teaspoonfuls in water once or twice daily, preferably at mealtimes; CHILD 1 teaspoonful

Diarrhoea (section 1.4.1), 1 teaspoonful 3 times daily

Metamucil® (Searle)

Powder, buff, ispaghula husk 49%, gluten-free. Net price 200 g = 96p. Label: 13, counselling, see above

Dose: one 5-mL spoonful 1–3 times daily in 150 mL water; CHILD 6–12 years 2.5–5 mL

Regulan® (Gold Cross)

Powder, beige, effervescent, ispaghula husk 3.6 g/6.4-g sachet (gluten-free). Net price 10 sachets = 71p. Label: 13, counselling, see above

Note. Contains potassium 6.4 mmol/sachet

Dose: 1 sachet in 150 mL water 1–3 times daily; CHILD 6–12 years 2.5–5 mL

METHYLCELLULOSE

Indications: see notes above

Cautions; Contra-indications; Side-effects: see under Ispaghula Husk

Dose: see preparations below

COUNSELLING. Preparations that swell in contact with liquid should always be carefully swallowed with water and should not be taken immediately before going to bed

Methylcellulose Mixture, methylcellulose '450' 900 mg/10 mL. Diluent water, life of diluted mixture 14 days. Net price 500 mL = £3.42. Counselling, see above and dose

Dose: constipation, 5–15 mL taken with a tumblerful of water preferably after meals 3 times daily initially, reducing to a maintenance dose of 5–15 mL daily

Note. The brand name NHS Cologel® (Lilly) is used for methylcellulose mixture, net price 500 mL = £3.42 (sugar-free)

Celevac® (Boehringer Ingelheim)

Tablets, pink, methylcellulose '450' 500 mg. Net price 112-tab pack = 93p. Counselling, see above and dose

Dose: 3–6 tablets twice daily. In constipation the dose should be taken with at least 300 mL of water. In diarrhoea, ileostomy, and colostomy control, minimise liquid intake for 30 minutes before and after the dose

STERCULIA

Indications: see notes above

Cautions; Contra-indications; Side-effects: see under Ispaghula Husk

COUNSELLING. Preparations that swell in contact with liquid should always be carefully swallowed with water and should not be taken immediately before going to bed

[1]Normacol® (Norgine)

Granules, coated, sterculia 62%. Net price 100 g = £1.13; 60 × 7-g sachets = £4.77. Label: 25, 27, counselling, see above

Dose: 1–2 heaped 5-mL spoonfuls, or the contents of 1–2 sachets, washed down without chewing with plenty of liquid once or twice daily after meals; CHILD 6–12 years half adult dose

1. formerly Normacol Special

[2]Normacol Plus® (Norgine)

Granules, brown, coated, sterculia 62%, frangula (standardised) 8%. Net price 200 g = £2.43; 10 × 7-g sachets = 96p; 60 sachets = £5.11. Label: 25, 27, counselling, see above

Dose: constipation and after haemorrhoidectomy, 1–2 heaped 5-mL spoonfuls or the contents of 1–2 sachets washed down without chewing with plenty of liquid once or twice daily after meals

2. formerly Normacol Standard

1.6.2 Stimulant laxatives

The recognised stimulant laxatives include **bisacodyl** and members of the **anthraquinone** group, e.g. senna. **Docusate** sodium probably acts both as a stimulant and as a softening agent. **Danthron** has limited indications (see below) because *rodent* studies indicate potential carcinogenic risk. Powerful stimulants such as **cascara** and **castor oil** are seldom needed at all.

Stimulant laxatives increase intestinal motility and often cause abdominal cramp. They should not be used in intestinal obstruction, and prolonged use can precipitate the onset of an atonic non-functioning colon and hypokalaemia. They should preferably be avoided in children.

Glycerol suppositories act as a rectal stimulant by virtue of the mildly irritant action of glycerol.

Soft soap is a more severe irritant; the use of soft soap enema should be **avoided**, expecially in pregnancy, as it may inflame the colonic mucosa.

The **parasympathomimetics** bethanechol, distigmine, neostigmine, and pyridostigmine (see sections 7.4.1 and 10.2.1) enhance parasympathetic activity in the gut and increase intestinal motility. They are rarely used for their gastro-intestinal effects but may be needed in cases of paralytic ileus, for example postoperatively. Organic obstruction of the gut must first be excluded and they should be used with caution in bowel anastomosis.

Oxyphenisatin is indicated for diagnostic procedures or surgery only, since it causes hepatitis in chronic use.

BISACODYL

Indications: see under Dose; tablets act in 10–12 hours; suppositories act in 20–60 minutes
Cautions; Contra-indications; Side-effects: see notes on stimulant laxatives; tablets, griping; suppositories, local irritation
Dose: by mouth for constipation, 10 mg at night; occasionally necessary to increase to 15–20 mg; CHILD 5 mg
By rectum in suppositories for constipation, 10 mg in the morning; CHILD 5 mg
Before radiological procedures and surgery, 10 mg by mouth at bedtime for 2 days before examination and, if necessary, a 10-mg suppository 1 hour before examination.

Oral preparations

Bisacodyl Tablets, e/c, s/c, bisacodyl 5 mg. Net price 20 = 26p. Label: 5, 25

Dulcolax® (Boehringer Ingelheim)
NHS *Tablets*, yellow, e/c, s/c, bisacodyl 5 mg. Net price 20 = 38p. Label: 5, 25

Rectal preparations

Bisacodyl Suppositories, bisacodyl 10 mg, net price 12 = 99p; 5 mg (paediatric), 12 = 96p

Dulcolax® (Boehringer Ingelheim)
NHS *Suppositories*, bisacodyl 10 mg. Net price 20 = £1.83
Paediatric suppositories, bisacodyl 5 mg. Net price 12 = 96p

CASCARA

Indications: constipation; acts in 6–8 hours
Cautions; Contra-indications; Side-effects: see notes on stimulant laxatives, urine may be coloured red; avoid in breast-feeding

NHS **Cascara Tablets,** coated, 20 mg total hydroxyanthracene derivatives of which not less than 40% consists of cascarosides. Net price 20 = 18p. Label: 14
Dose: 1–2 tablets, usually at bedtime

CASTOR OIL

Indications: constipation; bowel evacuation before radiological procedures, endoscopy, surgery; acts in 2–8 hours
Cautions: menstruation, pregnancy; see also notes on stimulant laxatives
Contra-indications: intestinal obstruction
Side-effects: nausea, vomiting
Dose: 5–20 mL when required (best given in milk or fruit juice)
Net price 100 mL = 63p

DANTHRON

Indications: only for: constipation in geriatric practice; analgesic-induced constipation in terminally ill patients of all ages; constipation in cardiac failure and coronary thrombosis (conditions in which bowel movement must be free of strain); acts within 6–12 hours
Cautions; Contra-indications; Side-effects: see notes on stimulant laxatives; urine may be coloured red; avoid prolonged contact with skin (as in incontinent patients) since irritation and excoriation may occur; avoid in pregnancy and breast-feeding; *rodent* studies indicate potential carcinogenic risk
Dose: see below

Co-danthramer

PoM **Co-danthramer** (Non-proprietary)
Suspension, co-danthramer 25/200 in 5 mL (danthron 25 mg, poloxamer '188' 200 mg/5 mL). Diluent tragacanth mucilage or syrup, life of diluted suspension 14 days. Label: 14 (urine red)
Dose: 5–10 mL; CHILD 2.5–5 mL (restricted indications, see notes above)
Note. The brand name NHS Codalax® (Napp) is used for co-danthramer 25/200 in 5 mL suspension, net price 100 mL = £2.16, 1 litre = £18.36
Strong suspension, co-danthramer 75/1000 in 5 mL (danthron 75 mg, poloxamer '188' 1 g/5 mL). Diluent as above. Label: 14 (urine red)
Dose: 2.5–5 mL (restricted indications, see notes above)
Note. The brand name NHS Codalax Forte® (Napp) is used for co-danthramer 75/1000 in 5 mL suspension, net price 100 mL = £3.00, 1 litre = £25.50

Co-danthrusate

PoM **Co-danthrusate** (Non-proprietary)
Capsules, co-danthrusate 50/60 (danthron 50 mg, docusate sodium 60 mg). Label: 14 (urine red)
Dose: 1–3 capsules, usually at bedtime; CHILD 6–12 years 1 capsule
Note. The brand name NHS Normax® (Innovex) is used for co-danthrusate 50/60 capsules, net price 63-cap pack = £4.91

DOCUSATE SODIUM

(Dioctyl Sodium Sulphosuccinate)

Indications: constipation (acts within 1–2 days); adjunct in abdominal radiological procedures
Cautions; Contra-indications; Side-effects: see notes on stimulant laxatives
Dose: by mouth, constipation, up to 500 mg daily in divided doses; initial doses should be large and gradually reduced; CHILD over 6 months 12.5–25 mg 3 times daily
With barium meal, 400 mg

Dioctyl® (Medo)
Tablets, yellow, f/c, docusate sodium 100 mg. Net price 30-tab pack = 83p
Solution 1%, sugar-free, docusate sodium 50 mg/5 mL. Diluent as above. Net price 300-mL pack = £2.25
Paediatric solution, yellow, sugar-free, docusate sodium 12.5 mg/5 mL. Net price 125-mL pack = 73p

Fletchers' Enemette® (Pharmax)
Enema, docusate sodium 90 mg, glycerol 3.78 g, macrogol 2.25 g, sorbic acid 5 mg/5 mL. Net price 5-mL unit = 31p
Dose: adults and children over 3 years, 5 mL when required

GLYCEROL

(Glycerin)
Indications: constipation
Dose: see below

Glycerol Suppositories (BP) (Glycerin Suppositories)
Suppositories, gelatin 140 mg, glycerol 700 mg, purified water to 1 g. Net price 12 = 42p (infant), 47p (child), 54p (adult)
Dose: 1 suppository moistened with water before use. The usual sizes are for *infants* small (1-g mould), *children* medium (2-g mould), *adults* large (4-g mould)

OXYPHENISATIN

Indications: see under Dose
Cautions; Contra-indications; Side-effects: see notes on stimulant laxatives; avoid repeated use owing to liver toxicity

Veripaque® (Sterling-Winthrop)
Enema, powder for reconstitution, oxyphenisatin 50 mg in 3 g. Net price 1 vial = £1.89
Dose: before diagnostic procedures or surgery, oxyphenisatin 50 mg dissolved in 2 litres of water given over 5–8 minutes
Adjuvant to barium enema, oxyphenisatin 50 mg mixed thoroughly with 2 litres of barium sulphate enema

SENNA

Indications: constipation; bowel evacuation before abdominal radiological procedures, endoscopy, and surgery; acts in 8–12 hours
Cautions; Contra-indications; Side-effects: see notes on stimulant laxatives

Senna Tablets, ≡ total sennosides 7.5 mg. Net price 20 = 26p
Dose: 2–4 tablets, usually at night; initial dose should be low then gradually increased; CHILD over 6 years, half adult dose
Note. The brand name NHS Senokot® (see below) is used for Senna tablets

[1]**Manevac**® (Galen)
Granules, coated, senna fruit 12.4%, ispaghula 54.2%. Net price 250 g = £2.82. Label: 25, 27, counselling, see Ispaghula Husk
Dose: 1–2 level 5-mL spoonfuls with water or warm drink after supper and, if necessary, before breakfast *or* every 6 hours in resistant cases for 1–3 days; CHILD 5–12 years 1 level 5-mL spoonful daily
1. formerly Agiolax®

Senokot® (R&C)
NHS *Tablets*, brown, ≡ total sennosides (calculated as sennoside B) 7.5 mg. Net price 20 = 28p
Dose: 2–4 tablets, usually at bedtime; initial dose should be low then gradually increased; CHILD over 6 years, half adult dose
Note. For Senokot tablets on general sale to the public the maximum recommended dose is 2 tablets.
Granules, brown, total sennosides (calculated as sennoside B) 15 mg/5 mL or 5.5 mg/g (one 5-mL spoonful = 2.7 g). Net price 100 g = £1.79
Dose: 5–10 mL, usually at bedtime; CHILD over 6 years 2.5–5 mL
Syrup, brown, ≡ total sennosides (calculated as sennoside B) 7.5 mg/5 mL. Diluent syrup, life of diluted syrup 14 days. Net price 100 mL = £1.30
Dose: 10–20 mL, usually at bedtime; CHILD 2–6 years 2.5–5 mL, over 6 years 5–10 mL

X-Prep® (Napp)
Liquid, brown, total sennosides 72 mg/72 mL bottle (also contains 47.52 g sucrose). For bowel evacuation before radiological procedures
Dose: 72 kg or more, 72 mL on day before (in 2 divided doses between 2 and 4 p.m. with 1 hour between doses); each dose followed by 2 tumblerfuls of water and further 2 tumblerfuls every hour throughout afternoon and evening; lighter patients, 1 mL/kg
Acts within 6–8 hours

SODIUM PICOSULPHATE

Indications: constipation, bowel evacuation before abdominal radiological procedures, endoscopy, and surgery
Cautions; Contra-indications; Side-effects: see notes on stimulant laxatives
Dose: see below

Sodium Picosulphate Elixir, sodium picosulphate 5 mg/5 mL. Diluent purified water, freshly boiled and cooled, life of diluted elixir 14 days. Acts within 10–14 hours. Net price 100 mL = £1.38
Dose: 5–15 mL at night; CHILD 2–5 years 2.5 mL, 5–10 years 2.5–5 mL
Note. The brand name NHS Laxoberal® (Windsor) is used for sodium picosulphate elixir 5 mg/5 mL

Picolax® (Nordic)
Oral powder, sugar-free, sodium picosulphate 10 mg/sachet, with magnesium citrate (for bowel evacuation before radiological procedures, endoscopy, and surgery). Net price 2 sachets = 59p. Label: 13, counselling, see below
Dose: adults and children over 9 years, 1 sachet in water in morning and a second in afternoon of day preceding procedures; CHILD 1–2 years quarter sachet morning and afternoon, 2–4 years half sachet morning and afternoon, 4–9 years 1 sachet morning and half sachet afternoon
Acts within 3 hours of first dose
COUNSELLING. Patients should be warned that heat is generated on addition to water; for this reason the powder should be added initially to 30 mL (2 tablespoonfuls) of water; after 5 minutes (when reaction complete) the solution should be further diluted to 150 mL (about a tumblerful)

OTHER STIMULANT LAXATIVES

Unstandardised preparations of cascara, frangula, rhubarb, and senna should be **avoided** as their laxative action is unpredictable. Aloes, colocynth, and jalap should be **avoided** as they have a drastic purgative action. Phenolphthalein should be **avoided** as it may cause rashes. Its laxative effects may continue for several days because of enterohepatic recycling; alkaline urine may be coloured pink.

NHS **Alophen®** (W-L)
Pills, brown, f/c, aloin 15 mg, belladonna dry extract 5 mg, ipecacuanha 4 mg, phenolphthalein 30 mg. Net price 50 pills = £1.25. Label: 14 (urine pink)
Dose: 1–3 pills, usually at bedtime

NHS **Kest®** (Torbet)
Tablets, magnesium sulphate 300 mg, phenolphthalein 50 mg. Net price 50 = 70p. Label: 14 (urine pink)
Dose: 1 tablet with water at bedtime and 2 tablets in the morning

1.6.3 Faecal softeners

Liquid paraffin, the classical lubricating agent, has disadvantages (see below). Bulk laxatives (section 1.6.1), non-ionic surfactant 'wetting' agents e.g. docusate sodium, and glycerol suppositories (both section 1.6.2) also have softening properties. Such drugs are useful in the management of haemorrhoids and anal fissure.

Enemas containing **arachis oil** lubricate and soften impacted faeces and promote a bowel movement.

CSM recommendations

Preparations containing liquid paraffin for use as laxatives should no longer be available directly to the public and restrictions should be placed on over-the-counter sales through pharmacies:
pack size be limited to 160 mL;
be indicated only for symptomatic relief of constipation;
be contra-indicated for children under 3 years of age; prolonged used not advised;
package labels to state 'repeated use is not recommended' and 'consult your doctor if laxatives are needed every day, if you have persistent abdominal pain or have a condition which makes swallowing difficult'.

ARACHIS OIL

Indications: see notes above
Dose: see below

Fletchers' Arachis Oil Retention Enema® (Pharmax)
Enema, arachis oil in 130-mL single-dose disposable packs. Net price 130 mL = £1.04
Dose: to soften impacted faeces, 130 mL; the enema should be warmed before use

LIQUID PARAFFIN

Indications: constipation but see CSM warning above
Cautions: avoid prolonged use
Side-effects: anal seepage of paraffin and consequent anal irritation after prolonged use, granulomatous reactions caused by absorption of small quantities of liquid paraffin (especially from the emulsion), lipoid pneumonia, and interference with the absorption of fat-soluble vitamins
Dose: 10–30 mL but see CSM warning above

Liquid Paraffin Oral Emulsion (BP)
(Liquid Paraffin Emulsion)
Oral emulsion, liquid paraffin 5 mL, vanillin 5 mg, chloroform 0.025 mL, benzoic acid solution 0.2 mL, methylcellulose-20 200 mg, saccharin sodium 500 micrograms, water to 10 mL
Dose: 10–30 mL at night when required

NHS **Petrolagar®** (Whitehall)
Emulsion, sugar-free, liquid paraffin 7%, light liquid paraffin 18%. Net price 100 mL = 38p
Dose: 10 mL morning and night or after meals

With phenolphthalein

NHS **Agarol®** (W-L)
Mixture, sugar-free, phenolphthalein 66 mg, liquid paraffin 1.6 mL, agar 10 mg/5 mL. Net price 100 mL = 59p. Label: 14 (urine pink)
Dose: 5–15 mL, usually at bedtime; CHILD under 5 years contra-indicated; 5–12 years 5 mL

1.6.4 Osmotic laxatives

These act by retaining fluid in the bowel by osmosis or by changing the pattern of water distribution in the faeces.

Saline purgatives are commonly abused but are satisfactory for occasional use. Adequate fluid intake should be maintained. **Magnesium sulphate** is useful where rapid bowel evacuation is required; a dose taken before breakfast or on an empty stomach and followed by a tumblerful of warm fluid usually causes evacuation within 2 hours. Sodium salts should be avoided as they may give rise to sodium and water retention in susceptible individuals. **Phosphate enemas** are useful in bowel clearance before radiological procedures, endoscopy, and surgery.

Lactulose is a semi-synthetic disaccharide which is not absorbed from the gastro-intestinal tract. It produces an osmotic diarrhoea of low faecal pH, and discourages the proliferation of ammonia-producing organisms. It is therefore useful in the treatment of hepatic encephalopathy.

LACTULOSE

Indications: constipation (may take up to 48 hours to act), hepatic encephalopathy
Contra-indications: galactosaemia, intestinal obstruction
Side-effects: flatulence, cramps, and abdominal discomfort
Dose: expressed in terms of the elixir containing lactulose 3.35 g/5 mL
Constipation, initially 15 mL twice daily, gradually reduced according to patient's needs; CHILD under 1 year 2.5 mL, 1–5 years 5 mL, 6–12 years 10 mL twice daily, gradually reduced
Hepatic encephalopathy, 30–50 mL 3 times daily, subsequently adjusted to produce 2–3 soft stools daily

Lactulose (Non-proprietary)
Solution, lactulose 3.35 g/5 mL with other ketoses. Net price 100 mL = 77p
Note. The brand name NHS Duphalac® (Duphar) is used for Lactulose solution; net price 100 mL = 77p

MAGNESIUM HYDROXIDE

Indications: mild constipation (acts in 2–4 hours)

Cautions: use only occasionally; the elderly, in renal impairment; **interactions:** Appendix 1 (antacids and adsorbents)

Contra-indications: intestinal obstruction

Dose: see below

Liquid Paraffin and Magnesium Hydroxide Emulsion (BP)

Oral emulsion, 25% dispersion of liquid paraffin in an aqueous suspension containing 6% of hydrated magnesium oxide

Dose: 5–20 mL when required

See also **CSM recommendations** (previous page)

Magnesium Hydroxide Mixture (BP)

(Cream of Magnesia). An aqueous suspension containing about 8% of hydrated magnesium oxide. Do not store in a cold place

Dose: 25–50 mL when required

MAGNESIUM SULPHATE

Indications: rapid bowel evacuation (acts in 2–4 hours when given by mouth)

Cautions; Contra-indications: see under Magnesium Hydroxide; hepatic impairment (see table); enema should be used in hospital only (as an adjunct to neurosurgery)

Side-effects: colic

Dose: see below

Magnesium Sulphate (Epsom salts). Label: 13, 23

Dose: 5–10 g in a tumblerful of water preferably before breakfast

Fletchers' Magnesium Sulphate Retention Enema® (Pharmax)

Enema, magnesium sulphate 50%, in 130-mL single-dose disposable packs. Net price 130 mL = 56p (hosp. only)

Dose: 130 mL, as an adjunct in neurosurgery to lower cerebrospinal fluid pressure

PHOSPHATES (RECTAL)

Indications: rectal use in constipation; bowel evacuation before abdominal radiological procedures, endoscopy, and surgery

Cautions: see notes above

Contra-indications: acute gastro-intestinal conditions

Dose: see below

[1]**Carbalax®** (Pharmax)

Suppositories, sodium acid phosphate 1.72 g in an effervescent basis. Net price 12 = £2.30

Dose: constipation, 1 suppository, inserted 30 minutes before evacuation is required; moisten with water before use; CHILD, not recommended

1. formerly Beogex

Fletchers' Phosphate Enema® (Pharmax)

Enema, sodium acid phosphate 12.8 g, sodium phosphate 10.24 g, purified water, freshly boiled and cooled, to 128 mL (corresponds to Phosphates Enema Formula B). Net price 128 mL with standard tube = 44p, with long rectal tube = 62p

Dose: 128 mL; CHILD, over 3 years, reduced according to body weight (under 3 years not recommended)

SODIUM CITRATE (RECTAL)

Indications: rectal use in constipation

Cautions: see notes above

Contra-indications: acute gastro-intestinal conditions

Dose: see below

Micolette Micro-enema® (Cusi)

Enema, sodium citrate 450 mg, sodium lauryl sulphoacetate 45 mg, glycerol 625 mg, together with citric acid, potassium sorbate, and sorbitol in a viscous solution, in 5-mL single-dose disposable packs with nozzle. Net price 5 mL = 33p

Dose: adults and children over 3 years, 5–10 mL

Micralax Micro-enema® (Evans)

Enema, sodium citrate 450 mg, sodium alkylsulphoacetate 45 mg, sorbic acid 5 mg, together with glycerol and sorbitol in a viscous solution in 5-mL single-dose disposable packs with nozzle. Net price 5 mL = 45p

Dose: adults and children over 3 years, 5 mL

Relaxit Micro-enema® (Pharmacia)

Enema, sodium citrate 450 mg, sodium lauryl sulphate 75 mg, sorbic acid 5 mg, together with glycerol and sorbitol in a viscous solution in 5-mL single-dose disposable packs with nozzle. Net price 5 mL = 30p

Dose: adults and children over 3 years, 5 mL

BOWEL CLEANSING SOLUTIONS

Bowel cleansing solutions are used prior to colonic surgery, colonoscopy, or barium enema to ensure the bowel is free of solid contents. They are **not** treatments for constipation.

Indications: see preparations below

Cautions: pregnancy; ulcerative colitis; impaired gag reflex; unconscious or semiconscious or possibility of regurgitation or aspiration; prevent absorption of oral medication

Contra-indications: gastro-intestinal obstruction, gastric retention, perforated bowel; toxic colitis, toxic megacolon or ileus; body-weight less than 20 kg

Side-effects: nausea, bloating, abdominal cramps (usually transient—reduced by taking more slowly); rarely vomiting, anal irritation; urticaria, rhinorrhoea and dermatitis reported

Dose: see below

PoM **Bowel Cleansing Solutions**

Provide: macrogol 3350 or 4000 (polyethylene glycol 3350 or 4000) 236 g, sodium sulphate 22.74 g, sodium bicarbonate 6.74 g, sodium chloride 5.86 g, potassium chloride 2.97 g/4 litres

Available from Norgine (*Klean-Prep®*), net price 4 sachets = £8.60; and Seward (*Golytely®*), net price 4-litre unit with disposable jug = £7.50. Label: 10, counselling

When reconstituted with water to 4 litres provides an iso-osmotic solution for bowel cleansing before surgery, colonoscopy or radiological procedures

Dose: by mouth, 240 mL (1 tumblerful) of reconstituted solution every 10–15 minutes, or by nasogastric tube 20–30 mL/minute, until 4 litres have been consumed or watery stools are free of solid matter (usually 3 litres). First bowel movement occurs after approximately 1 hour

COUNSELLING. Advise patient to take at least 2 hours after and preferably 3–4 hours after food; more palatable if chilled; do not add flavouring or other ingredients; drink each portion as rapidly as possible

After reconstitution the solution should be kept in a refrigerator and discarded if unused after 48 hours

1.7 Preparations for haemorrhoids

1.7.1 Soothing preparations
1.7.2 Compound preparations with corticosteroids
1.7.3 Rectal sclerosants

Anal and perianal pruritus, soreness, and excoriation are best treated by application of bland ointments, suppositories, and dusting-powders (section 1.7.1). These conditions occur commonly in patients suffering from haemorrhoids, fistulas, and proctitis. Careful local toilet as well as adjustment of the diet to avoid hard stools, and bulk-forming materials such as bran (section 1.6.1) and a high residue diet are also helpful. In proctitis these measures may supplement treatment with corticosteroids or sulphasalazine (see section 1.5).

When necessary topical preparations containing **local anaesthetics** (section 1.7.1) or **corticosteroids** (section 1.7.2) are used provided perianal thrush has been excluded. Perianal thrush is best treated with **nystatin** by mouth and by local application (see sections 5.2, 7.2.2, and 13.10.2).

1.7.1 Soothing preparations

Bland soothing preparations containing mild astringents such as bismuth subgallate, zinc oxide, and hamamelis may give symptomatic relief in haemorrhoids. Many proprietary preparations also contain lubricants, vasoconstrictors, or mild antiseptics.

Prolonged application of preparations containing **resorcinol** should be **avoided** because it may interfere with thyroid function. Heparinoids are claimed to promote the resorption of local oedema and extravasated blood.

Local anaesthetics are used to relieve pain associated with *haemorrhoids*, and *pruritus ani* but good evidence is lacking. Lignocaine ointment (see section 15.2) is used prior to emptying the bowel to relieve pain associated with *anal fissure*. Alternative local anaesthetics include amethocaine, cinchocaine, and pramoxine, but they are more irritant.

Local anaesthetics should be used for short periods only (no longer than 2 weeks) since they may cause sensitisation of the anal skin.

ADMINISTRATION. Unless otherwise indicated a suppository is usually inserted into the rectum night and morning and after a bowel movement. Rectal ointments and creams are applied night and morning and after a bowel movement, externally or by rectum using a rectal nozzle.

Note. Local anaesthetic ointments can be absorbed through the rectal mucosa therefore excessive application should be avoided, particularly in infants and children.

Bismuth Subgallate Suppositories, Compound, bismuth subgallate 200 mg, castor oil 60 mg, resorcinol 60 mg, zinc oxide 120 mg, in theobroma oil or other suitable basis. Net price 12 = £1.44

Hamamelis and Zinc Oxide Suppositories. Usual strength hamamelis dry extract 200 mg, zinc oxide 600 mg. Net price 12 = £2.35

Anodesyn® (Crookes)
Ointment, ephedrine hydrochloride 0.25%, lignocaine hydrochloride 0.5%, allantoin 0.5%. Net price 25 g = £1.04
Suppositories, ephedrine hydrochloride 5.1 mg, lignocaine hydrochloride 10.25 mg, allantoin 10.25 mg. Net price 12 = £1.16

Anusol® (W-L)
Cream, bismuth oxide 2.14%, Peru balsam 1.8%, zinc oxide 10.75%. Net price 23 g (with rectal nozzle) = £1.16
Ointment, bismuth oxide 0.875%, bismuth subgallate 2.25%, zinc oxide 10.75%, Peru balsam 1.875%. Net price 25 g (with rectal nozzle) = £1.12
Suppositories, bismuth oxide 24 mg, bismuth subgallate 59 mg, Peru balsam 49 mg, zinc oxide 296 mg. Net price 12 = £1.18

Lasonil® (Bayer)
Ointment, hyaluronidase 150 units, heparinoid 50 units/g. Net price 14 g = 38p; 40 g = £1.08 (both with applicator)

1.7.2 Compound preparations with corticosteroids

Corticosteroids are often combined with antibiotics, local anaesthetics, and soothing agents. They are suitable for occasional short-term use after exclusion of infections, such as herpes simplex; see section 13.4 for general comments on topical corticosteroids.

Antibiotics may do little more than encourage the growth of resistant bacteria and should be avoided. See section 1.7.1 for comment on local anaesthetics.

PoM **Anacal®** (Panpharma)
Rectal ointment, hexachlorophane 0.5%, laureth '9' 5%, heparinoid 0.2%, prednisolone 0.15%. Net price 30 g (with rectal nozzle) = £3.04
Apply 1–4 times daily
Suppositories, hexachlorophane 5 mg, laureth '9' 50 mg, a heparinoid 4 mg, prednisolone 1 mg. Net price 10 = £1.70
Insert 1 suppository once or twice daily

PoM **Anugesic-HC®** (P-D)
Cream, benzyl benzoate 1.2%, bismuth oxide 0.875%, hydrocortisone acetate 0.5%, Peru balsam 1.85%, pramoxine hydrochloride 1%,

zinc oxide 12.35%. Net price 30 g (with rectal nozzle) = £6.19
Apply night and morning and after a bowel movement; do not use for longer than 7 days
Suppositories, benzyl benzoate 33 mg, bismuth oxide 24 mg, bismuth subgallate 59 mg, hydrocortisone acetate 5 mg, Peru balsam 49 mg, pramoxine hydrochloride 27 mg, zinc oxide 296 mg. Net price 12 = £2.64
Insert 1 suppository night and morning and after a bowel movement; do not use for longer than 7 days

PoM **Anusol-HC**® (P-D)
Ointment, benzyl benzoate 1.25%, bismuth oxide 0.875%, bismuth subgallate 2.25%, hydrocortisone acetate 0.25%, Peru balsam 1.875%, zinc oxide 10.75%. Net price 30 g (with rectal nozzle) = £5.81
Apply night and morning and after a bowel movement; do not use for longer than 7 days
Suppositories, benzyl benzoate 33 mg, bismuth oxide 24 mg, bismuth subgallate 59 mg, hydrocortisone acetate 10 mg, Peru balsam 49 mg, zinc oxide 296 mg. Net price 12 = £2.64
Additives: include tartrazine lake
Insert 1 suppository night and morning and after a bowel movement; do not use for longer than 7 days

PoM **Betnovate**® (Glaxo)
Rectal ointment, betamethasone valerate 0.05%, lignocaine hydrochloride 2.5%, phenylephrine hydrochloride 0.1%. Net price 30 g (with applicator) = £1.50
Apply 2–3 times daily until inflammation subsides then once daily, externally or by rectum; do not use for longer than 7 days

PoM **Proctofoam HC**® (Stafford-Miller)
Foam in aerosol pack, hydrocortisone acetate 1%, pramoxine hydrochloride 1%. Net price 24-g pack (approx. 40 applications) with applicator = £4.83
Dose: haemorrhoids and proctitis, 1 applicatorful (4–6 mg hydrocortisone acetate, 4–6 mg pramoxine hydrochloride) by rectum 2–3 times daily and after a bowel movement

PoM **Proctosedyl**® (Roussel)
Ointment, cinchocaine hydrochloride 0.5%, hydrocortisone 0.5%. Net price 30 g = £6.65 (with cannula)
Apply morning and night and after a bowel movement, externally or by rectum
Suppositories, cinchocaine hydrochloride 5 mg, hydrocortisone 5 mg. Net price 12 = £3.00
Insert 1 suppository night and morning and after a bowel movement

PoM **Scheriproct**® (Schering Health Care)
Ointment, cinchocaine hydrochloride 0.5%, prednisolone hexanoate 0.19%. Net price 30 g = £4.41
Apply twice daily for 5–7 days (3–4 times daily on 1st day if necessary), then once daily for few days after symptoms have cleared
Suppositories, cinchocaine hydrochloride 1 mg, prednisolone hexanoate 1.3 mg. Net price 12 = £2.08
Insert 1 suppository daily after a bowel movement, for 5–7 days (in severe cases initially 2–3 times daily)

PoM **Ultraproct**® (Schering Health Care)
Ointment, cinchocaine hydrochloride 0.5%, fluocortolone hexanoate 0.095%, fluocortolone pivalate 0.092%. Net price 30 g (with rectal nozzle) = £4.57
Apply twice daily for 5–7 days (3–4 times daily on 1st day if necessary), then once daily for few days after symptoms have cleared
Suppositories, cinchocaine hydrochloride 1 mg, fluocortolone hexanoate 630 micrograms, fluocortolone pivalate 610 micrograms. Net price 12 = £2.15
Insert 1 suppository daily after a bowel movement, for 5–7 days (in severe cases initially 2–3 times daily) then 1 suppository every other day for 1 week

PoM **Uniroid**® (Unigreg)
Ointment, cinchocaine hydrochloride 0.5%, hydrocortisone 0.5%, neomycin sulphate 3400 units, polymyxin B sulphate 6250 units/g. Net price 15 g (with applicator) = £2.77
Apply 3 times daily, preferably after a bowel movement, externally or by rectum; do not use for longer than 7 days
Suppositories, cinchocaine hydrochloride 5 mg, hydrocortisone 5 mg, neomycin sulphate 6800 units, polymyxin B sulphate 12 500 units. Net price 10 = £2.09
Insert 1 suppository 3 times daily, preferably after a bowel movement; do not use for longer than 7 days

PoM **Xyloproct**® (Astra)
Ointment (water-miscible), aluminium acetate 3.5%, hydrocortisone acetate 0.275%, lignocaine 5%, zinc oxide 18%. Net price 30 g (with applicator) = £3.48
Apply several times daily
Suppositories, aluminium acetate 50 mg, hydrocortisone acetate 5 mg, lignocaine 60 mg, zinc oxide 400 mg. Net price 10 = £1.63
Insert 1 suppository at night and after a bowel movement

1.7.3 Rectal sclerosants

Oily phenol injection is used to inject haemorrhoids particularly when unprolapsed.

PHENOL

Indications: injection of haemorrhoidal veins
Side-effects: irritation, tissue necrosis
Dose: 2–3 mL of oily phenol injection into the submucosal layer at the base of the pile; several injections may be given at different sites, max. total injected 10 mL at any one time

Oily Phenol Injection, phenol 5% in almond oil or other suitable oil. Net price 2-mL amp = 59p; 5-mL amp = £1.11; 25-mL vial = £3.83

1.8 Stoma care

1.8.1 Local care of stoma

Patients are usually given advice about the use of cleansing agents, protective creams, lotions, deodorants, or sealants whilst in hospital, either by the surgeon or by the health authority stoma care nurses. Voluntary organisations offer help and support to patients with stoma.

Items in the following list are prescribable as drugs or as accessories to stoma appliances (see Drug Tariff).

Adhesives

Aquadry® (Thackraycare)
Medical adhesive. Net price 20 mL (with brush) = £3.00

Dow Corning DC 355® (Dow Corning)
Medical adhesive brushable. Net price 20-mL bottle (with brush) = £2.72

Dow Corning B Spray® (Dow Corning)
Spray adhesive. Net price 206-g aerosol spray = £8.97

Hollister® (Hollister)
Medical adhesive spray (with silicones). Net price 170-g aerosol spray = £10.65

Latex adhesive solution (Salt)
Net price per tube = £1.51
Caution: flammable

Adhesive removers

Dow Corning Remover® (Dow Corning)
Adhesive remover spray. Net price 227-g aerosol spray = £7.06

Hollister® (Hollister)
Adhesive remover spray. Net price 170-g spray = £9.00

Salts 'SPR' Plaster Remover (Rezolve®) (Salt)
Adhesive remover spray. Net price 70-g aerosol spray = £2.31. *Caution:* flammable

Deodorants

Atmocol® is used as a deodorising spray when emptying the appliance. The other deodorants listed are placed in the appliance.

Atmocol® (Thackraycare)
Aerosol deodorant. Net price 1 unit (400 sprays) = £1.80

Chironair Odour Control Liquid® (Simcare)
Deodorant solution. Net price 113 g = £4.48

Colostomy Plus® (Shannon)
Deodorant. Net price 1 unit = £2.28

Dor® (Simpla)
Deodorant solution. Net price 7 mL = £1.37

Forest Breeze® (Shaw)
Deodorant. Net price 1 unit = £2.55

Limone® (CliniMed)
Deodorant spray. Net price 50 mL = £3.40

Nilodor® (Loxley)
Deodorant solution. Net price (with dropper) 7.5 mL = £1.46; 15 mL = £2.82

Ostobon® (Coloplast)
Deodorant powder. Net price 22 g = £2.96

Saltair No-Roma® (Salt)
Deodorant solution. Net price 30 mL = £1.85; 300 mL = £6.01

Stomogel® (Thackraycare)
Deodorant gel. Net price 50 g = £2.60

Sween® (Francol)
Deodorant. Net price 15 mL = £3.40

Translet Plus One® (Warne-Franklin)
Deodorant solution for men. Net price 7 mL = £2.43

Translet Plus Two® (Warne-Franklin)
Deodorant solution for women. Net price 7 mL = £2.43

Skin protectives, fillers, and cleansers

Bullen Karaya Gum Powder® (Bullen)
Powder. Net price 70 g = £3.80

Chiron® (Simcare)
Barrier cream (with antiseptic). Net price 52 g = £3.85

Clinimed Barrier Wipes® (Clinimed)
Barrier wipes. Net price 50 = £8.90

Comfeel® (Coloplast)
Barrier cream. Net price 60 g = £2.88
Protective film. Net price 30 sachets = £6.90; applicator = £3.18

Derma-gard® (Simcare)
Protective skin wipes. Net price 50 = £11.28

Hollister® (Hollister)
Karaya paste. Net price 128 g = £5.33
Do not apply to severely excoriated skin
Karaya powder. Net price 71 g = £6.35
Skin gel. Net price 28 g = £6.33. *Caution:* flammable
Do not apply to severely excoriated skin

Orabase® (ConvaTec)
Paste, see section 12.3.1

Orahesive® (ConvaTec)
Powder (with adherent properties), see section 12.3.1

Saltair® (Salt)
Karaya gum powder. Net price per puffer pack = £3.47
Ostomy cleansing soap (soap spirit). Net price 110-mL = £2.09
'Protect' Friar's Balsam Spray (compound benzoin tincture). Net price 150 g aerosol spray = £5.50
Skin prep wipes. Net price 50 = £11.29

Simcare® (Simcare)
Karaya gel. Net price 35 g = £4.62
Karaya gum powder. Net price 100 g = £5.43
Karaya gum sheet. Net price 1 = £5.06
Ostomy seal protective paste. Net price 52 g = £4.65

Simpla Sassco® (Simpla)
Gel. Net price 35 g = £4.84

Stomahesive® (ConvaTec)
Paste. Net price 60 g = £5.41. For filling and sealing skin creases

Stomobar® (Thackraycare)
Barrier cream. Net price 20 g = £1.80

Stomosol® (Thackraycare)
Antiseptic liquid. Dilute before use. Net price 200 mL = £4.12

Translet® (Warne-Franklin)
Barrier cream. Net price 51 g = £2.11
Wipes. Net price 30 = £4.58

United Skin Barrier Paste® (Salt)
Paste. Net price 70 g = £5.08

1.8.2 Prescribing for patients with stoma

Enteric-coated and *sustained-release* preparations are **unsuitable**, particularly in patients with ileostomies, as there may not be sufficient release of the active ingredient.

Laxatives. Enemas and washouts should **not** be prescribed for patients with ileostomies as they may cause rapid and severe dehydration.

Colostomy patients may suffer from constipation and whenever possible should be treated by increasing fluid intake or dietary fibre. **Bulk-forming laxatives** (section 1.6.1) should be tried. If they are insufficient, as small a dose as possible of senna (section 1.6.2) should be used. Preparations such as X-Prep® should be avoided when preparing patients for radiological procedures as they may cause severe dehydration with nausea, vomiting, and griping.

Antidiarrhoeals. Drugs such as **loperamide**, **codeine phosphate**, or **co-phenotrope** (diphenoxylate with atropine) are effective. Bulk-forming drugs (section 1.6.1) may be tried but it is often difficult to adjust the dose appropriately.

Antibiotics should **not** be given for an episode of acute diarrhoea.

Antacids. The tendency to diarrhoea from magnesium salts or constipation from aluminium salts may be increased in these patients.

Diuretics should be used with caution in patients with ileostomies as they may become excessively dehydrated and potassium depletion may easily occur. It is usually advisable to use a **potassium-sparing** diuretic (see section 2.2.3).

Digoxin. Patients with a stoma are particularly susceptible to hypokalaemia if on digoxin therapy and potassium supplements or a potassium-sparing diuretic may be advisable (for comment see section 9.2.1.1).

Potassium supplements. Liquid formulations are preferred to sustained-release formulations (see above).

Analgesics. Opioid analgesics (see section 4.7.2) may cause troublesome constipation in colostomy patients. When a non-opioid analgesic is required **paracetamol** is usually suitable but anti-inflammatory analgesics may cause gastric irritation and bleeding.

Iron preparations may cause loose stools and sore skin in these patients. If this is troublesome and if iron is definitely indicated one of the intramuscular iron preparations (see section 9.1.1.2) should be used. Sustained-release preparations should be **avoided** for the reasons given above.

1.9 Drugs affecting intestinal secretions

1.9.1 Drugs acting on the gall bladder
1.9.2 Drugs which increase gastric acidity
1.9.3 Aprotinin
1.9.4 Pancreatin

1.9.1 Drugs acting on the gall bladder

The bile acids **chenodeoxycholic** or **ursodeoxycholic acid** are used in selected patients to dissolve cholesterol gallstones as an alternative to surgery. They are only suitable for patients who have mild symptoms, unimpaired gall bladder function, and small or medium sized radiolucent stones; they are not suitable for radio-opaque stones, which are unlikely to be dissolved. Patients should preferably be supervised in hospital because radiological monitoring is required. Long-term prophylaxis may be needed after complete dissolution of the gallstones has been confirmed (preferably with cholecystograms and ultrasound on two separate occasions) as gallstones may recur in up to 25% of patients within one year of stopping treatment.

Dehydrocholic acid is used to improve biliary drainage by stimulating the secretion of thin watery bile. It is given after surgery of the biliary tract to flush the common duct and drainage tube and wash away small calculi obstructing flow through the common bile duct but its value has not been established.

A **terpene** mixture (Rowachol®) also raises biliary cholesterol solubility. It is less effective than the bile acids but may be a useful adjunct.

CHENODEOXYCHOLIC ACID

Indications; Cautions: see notes above

Contra-indications: do not use when stones are radio-opaque, in pregnancy, in non-functioning gall bladders, in chronic liver disease, and inflammatory diseases of the small intestine and colon

Side-effects: diarrhoea particularly initially with high dosage (reduce dose for few days), pruritus, minor hepatic abnormalities and transient rise in serum transaminases

Dose: 10–15 mg/kg daily as a single dose at bedtime *or* in divided doses for 3–24 months, depending on size of stone; treatment is continued for 3 months after stones dissolve

PoM **Chendol®** (CP)
Capsules, orange/white, chenodeoxycholic acid 125 mg. Net price 224-cap pack = £48.50
Tablets, orange, f/c, scored, chenodeoxycholic acid 250 mg. Net price 112-tab pack = £47.50

PoM **Chenofalk®** (Thames)
Capsules, chenodeoxycholic acid 250 mg. Net price 60 = £18.00
Additives: include gluten

DEHYDROCHOLIC ACID

Indications: see notes above

Contra-indications: complete mechanical biliary obstruction and occlusive hepatitis, chronic liver disease

Dose: 250–750 mg, 3 times daily
Cholecystography, 500–750 mg every 4 hours for 12 hours before and after the examination

Dehydrocholic Acid (Non-proprietary)
Tablets, dehydrocholic acid 250 mg. Net price 20 = £5.36

URSODEOXYCHOLIC ACID

Indications; Cautions; Contra-indications: see under Chenodeoxycholic Acid

Side-effects: see under Chenodeoxycholic Acid; diarrhoea occurs rarely; liver changes have not been reported

Dose: 8–12 mg/kg (obese patients up to 15 mg/kg) daily as a single dose at bedtime or in divided doses, for up to 2 years; treatment is continued for 3–4 months after stones dissolve

PoM **Destolit®** (Merrell)
Tablets, scored, ursodeoxycholic acid 150 mg. Net price 60 = £19.40. Label: 21

PoM **Ursofalk®** (Thames)
Capsules, ursodeoxycholic acid 250 mg. Net price 60 = £31.50. Label: 21
Additives: include gluten

OTHER PREPARATIONS FOR BILIARY DISORDERS

Rowachol® (Monmouth)
PoM *Capsules*, green, e/c, borneol 5 mg, camphene 5 mg, cineole 2 mg, menthol 32 mg, menthone 6 mg, pinene 17 mg in olive oil. Net price 20 = £2.50. Label: 22
Dose: 1–2 capsules 3 times daily before food
Liquid, yellow, borneol 50 mg, camphene 50 mg, cineole 20 mg, menthol 320 mg, menthone 60 mg, pinene

170 mg/g in olive oil. Net price 10-mL dropper bottle = £6.60. Label: 22
Dose: 3–5 drops 4–5 times daily before food
Interactions: Appendix 1 (*Rowachol®*)

1.9.2 Drugs which increase gastric acidity

Muripsin® is used in achlorhydria and hypochlorhydria but is of uncertain value; it replaced dilute hydrochloric acid.

Muripsin® (Norgine)
Tablets, orange, f/c, glutamic acid hydrochloride 500 mg, pepsin 35 mg: 1 tablet ≈ 1 mL dilute hydrochloric acid. Net price 50 = £4.75. Label: 21
Dose: 1–2 tablets with meals

1.9.3 Aprotinin

Aprotinin is a proteolytic enzyme inhibitor formerly used in the treatment of acute pancreatitis. It is now indicated for the treatment of life-threatening haemorrhage due to hyperplasminaemia, see section 2.11.

1.9.4 Pancreatin

Supplements of pancreatin are given by mouth to compensate for reduced or absent exocrine secretion in cystic fibrosis, and following pancreatectomy, total gastrectomy, or chronic pancreatitis. They assist the digestion of starch, fat, and protein.

Pancreatin is inactivated by gastric acid therefore pancreatin preparations are best taken with food (or immediately before or after food). Gastric acid secretion may be reduced by giving cimetidine or ranitidine an hour beforehand (section 1.3). Concurrent use of antacids also reduces gastric acidity. The newer enteric-coated preparations such as Creon®, Nutrizym GR®, and Pancrease® deliver a higher enzyme concentration in the duodenum (providing the granules are swallowed whole without chewing).

Since pancreatin is also inactivated by heat, excessive heat should be avoided if preparations are mixed with liquids or food; the resulting mixtures should not be kept for more than one hour.

Dosage is adjusted according to size, number, and consistency of stools, so that the patient thrives; extra allowance may be needed if snacks are taken between meals.

Pancreatin may irritate the skin around mouth and anus, particularly if preparations are retained in the mouth or dosage is excessive. Hypersensitivity reactions occur occasionally and may affect those handling the powder.

For reference to acetylcysteine in cystic fibrosis, see Acetylcysteine Granules (section 3.7).

PANCREATIN

Indications; Cautions; Side-effects: see above
Dose: see below

Pancreatin, BP (Non-proprietary)
Powder, pancreatin, providing minimum of: protease 1400 units, lipase 20000 units, amylase 24000 units/g

Cotazym® (Organon)
Capsules, green, pancreatin, providing minimum of: protease 450 units, lipase 13000 units, amylase 9000 units. Net price 100 = £3.33. Counselling, see dose
Dose: 6 capsules daily in divided doses; contents sprinkled on food

Creon® (Duphar)
Capsules, brown/yellow, enclosing buff-coloured e/c granules of pancreatin, providing: protease 210 units, lipase 8000 units, amylase 9000 units. Net price 100 = £13.33. Counselling, see dose
Dose: initially 1–2 capsules with meals either taken whole or contents mixed with fluid or soft food (then swallowed immediately without chewing); usual range 5–15 capsules daily

Nutrizym® GR (Merck)
Capsules, green/orange, enclosing e/c pellets of pancreatin, providing minimum of: protease 650 units, lipase 10000 units, amylase 10000 units. Net price 100 = £12.52. Counselling, see dose
Dose: 1–2 capsules with meals swallowed whole or contents sprinkled on soft food (then swallowed immediately without chewing); dosage may be increased in severe cases

Pancrease® (Cilag)
Capsules, enclosing e/c beads of pancreatin, providing minimum of: protease 330 units, lipase 5000 units, amylase 2900 units. Net price 100 = £15.98. Counselling, see dose
Dose: 1–2 (occasionally 3) capsules during each meal and 1 capsule with snacks swallowed whole or contents sprinkled on liquid or soft food (then swallowed immediately without chewing)

Pancrex® (Paines & Byrne)
Granules, pancreatin, providing minimum of: protease 300 units, lipase 5000 units, amylase 4000 units/g. Net price 100 g = £7.15, 500 g = £28.61. Label: 25, counselling, see dose
Dose: 5–10 g 4 times daily with meals washed down or mixed with liquid

Pancrex V® (Paines & Byrne)
Capsules, pancreatin, providing minimum of: protease 430 units, lipase 8000 units, amylase 9000 units. Net price 100 = £4.29. Counselling, see dose
Dose: up to 1 year 1–2 capsules mixed with feeds; adults and children over 1 year 2–6 capsules 4 times daily with meals, swallowed whole or sprinkled on food
Capsules '125', pancreatin, providing minimum of: protease 160 units, lipase 2950 units, amylase 3000 units. Net price 50 = £1.63. Counselling, see dose
Dose: NEONATE 1–2 capsules with feeds
Tablets, e/c, s/c, pancreatin, providing minimum of: protease 110 units, lipase 1900 units, amylase 1700 units. Net price 100 = £1.43. Label: 5, 25, counselling, see dose
Dose: 5–15 tablets 4 times daily before meals
Tablets forte, e/c, s/c, pancreatin, providing minimum of: protease 330 units, lipase 5600 units, amylase 5000 units. Net price 100 = £3.72. Label: 5, 25, counselling, see dose
Dose: 6–10 tablets 4 times daily before meals
Powder, pancreatin, providing minimum of: protease 1400 units, lipase 25000 units, amylase 30000 units/g. Net price 100 g = £9.75, 250 g = £20.76. Counselling, see dose
Dose: 0.5–2 g 4 times daily washed down or mixed with liquid

2: Drugs used in the treatment of diseases of the CARDIOVASCULAR SYSTEM

In this chapter, drug treatment is discussed under the following headings:

2.1 Positive inotropic drugs

Positive inotropic drugs increase the force of contraction of the myocardium; for sympathomimetics with inotropic activity see section 2.7.1.

2.1.1 Cardiac glycosides

The principal actions of the cardiac glycosides are an increase in the force of myocardial contraction and a reduction in the conductivity of the heart. They are most useful in the treatment of *supraventricular tachycardias*, especially for controlling ventricular response in atrial fibrillation. *Heart failure* may also be improved, even in patients in sinus rhythm, because of changes in the availability of intracellular calcium; this action is relatively unimportant, however, compared with effects that can be achieved with diuretics and vasodilators. Except when needed to maintain satisfactory rhythm, cardiac glycosides can often be withdrawn from patients with heart failure that is well controlled, without clinical deterioration. Their use for heart failure alone is therefore best avoided in the elderly who are particularly susceptible to digitalis toxicity.

Loss of appetite, nausea, and vomiting are common toxic effects; sinus bradycardia, atrioventricular block, ventricular extrasystoles, and sometimes ventricular tachycardia or atrial tachycardia with block also occur—especially in the presence of underlying conducting system defects or myocardial disease. These unwanted effects depend both on the plasma concentrations of the drugs and on the sensitivity of the conducting system or myocardium, which is often increased in heart disease. Thus, no one plasma concentration can indicate toxicity reliably but the likelihood increases progressively through the range 1.5 to 3 micrograms/litre for digoxin; higher steady-state concentrations must certainly be avoided. Measurements of plasma concentration are not necessary, however, unless problems occur during maintenance treatment. Hypokalaemia predisposes to toxicity, therefore diuretics used with digoxin should either be potassium sparing or should be given with potassium supplements.

Renal function is the most important determinant of digoxin dosage, whereas elimination of digitoxin depends on metabolism by the liver. Toxicity can often be managed by discontinuing therapy and correcting hypokalaemia if appropriate; serious manifestations require urgent specialist management. Digoxin-specific antibody fragments are available for reversal of life-threatening overdosage (see next page).

Digoxin is the glycoside most commonly used. In patients with *mild failure* a loading dose is not required, and a satisfactory plasma concentration can be achieved over a period of about a week, using a dose of 125 to 250 micrograms twice a day which may then be reduced having special regard to renal function. Because it has a long half-life maintenance doses need only be given once daily (but higher doses should be divided to avoid nausea). For management of *atrial fibrillation* the maintenance dose can usually be governed by ventricular response which should not be allowed to fall below 60 beats per minute except in special and recognised circumstances, e.g. with the concomitant administration of beta-blockers.

When *very rapid control* is needed, digoxin may be given intravenously in a digitalising dose of 0.75 to 1 mg, preferably as an infusion (suggested volume 50 mL) over two or more hours, followed by normal maintenance therapy. The intramuscular route is not recommended, except when other methods of administration are not available.

Lanatoside C is less well absorbed than digoxin. Most is converted to digoxin after ingestion. The maintenance dose is about twice that of digoxin, and depends in part on renal function.

Digitoxin has a long half-life and maintenance doses, again, need only be given once daily.

CHILDREN. The dose is based on body-weight; they require a relatively larger dose of digoxin than adults.

DIGOXIN

Indications: heart failure, supraventricular arrhythmias (particularly atrial fibrillation)

Cautions: recent infarction, hypothyroidism; reduce dose in the elderly and in renal impairment; avoid hypokalaemia; **interactions:** Appendix 1 (cardiac glycosides)

Contra-indications: supraventricular arrhythmias caused by Wolff-Parkinson-White syndrome

Side-effects: anorexia, nausea, vomiting, visual disturbances, arrhythmias, heart block; see also notes above

Dose: *by mouth*, rapid digitalisation, 1–1.5 mg in divided doses over 24 hours; less urgent digitalisation, 250–500 micrograms daily (higher dose divided)
Maintenance, 62.5–500 micrograms daily (higher dose divided) according to renal function and, in atrial fibrillation, on heart-rate response; usual range, 125–250 micrograms daily (elderly 125 micrograms)
For intravenous doses, see notes above
Note. For plasma concentration monitoring blood should ideally be taken at least 6 hours after a dose

PoM **Digoxin** (Non-proprietary)
Tablets, digoxin 62.5 micrograms, net price 20 = 9p; 125 micrograms, 20 = 6p; 250 micrograms, 20 = 9p
Injection, digoxin 250 micrograms/mL, see Lanoxin®
Paediatric injection, digoxin 100 micrograms/mL (hosp. only, available from Boots)

PoM **Lanoxin®** (Wellcome)
Tablets, digoxin 125 micrograms, net price 20 = 28p; 250 micrograms, 20 = 25p
Injection, digoxin 250 micrograms/mL. Net price 2-mL amp = 56p

PoM **Lanoxin-PG®** (Wellcome)
Tablets, blue, digoxin 62.5 micrograms. Net price 20 = 28p
Elixir, yellow, digoxin 50 micrograms/mL. Do not dilute, measure with pipette. Net price 60 mL = £4.55. Counselling, use of pipette

DIGITOXIN

Indications: heart failure, supraventricular arrhythmias (particularly atrial fibrillation)
Cautions; Contra-indications; Side-effects: see under Digoxin
Dose: 50–200 micrograms daily

PoM **Digitoxin** (Evans)
Tablets, digitoxin 100 micrograms, net price 20 = 43p

LANATOSIDE C

Indications: heart failure, supraventricular arrhythmias (particularly atrial fibrillation)
Cautions; Contra-indications; Side-effects: see under Digoxin
Dose: slow digitalisation 1.5–2 mg daily for 3–5 days; maintenance 0.25–1 mg daily

PoM **Cedilanid®** (Sandoz)
Tablets, scored, lanatoside C 250 micrograms. Net price 20 = 30p

DIGOXIN-SPECIFIC ANTIBODY

PoM **Digibind®** (Wellcome)
Injection, powder for preparation of infusion, digoxin-specific antibody fragments (F(ab)) 40 mg. Net price per vial = £87.44
For reversal of life-threatening manifestations of intoxication by digoxin; although designed specifically to treat digoxin overdose has successfully reversed digitoxin overdose

2.1.2 Phosphodiesterase inhibitors

Enoximone and milrinone are selective phosphodiesterase inhibitors which exert most of their effect on the myocardium. Sustained haemodynamic benefit has been observed after administration, but as yet there is no conclusive evidence of any beneficial effect on survival.

ENOXIMONE

Indications: congestive heart failure where cardiac output reduced and filling pressures increased
Cautions: heart failure associated with hypertrophic cardiomyopathy, stenotic or obstructive valvular disease or other outlet obstruction; monitor blood pressure, heart rate, ECG, central venous pressure, fluid and electrolyte status, platelet count, hepatic enzymes; reduce dose in renal impairment; avoid extravasation
Side-effects: ectopic beats; less frequently ventricular tachycardia or supraventricular arrhythmias (more likely in patients with pre-existing arrhythmias); hypotension; also headache, insomnia, nausea and vomiting, diarrhoea; occasionally, chills, oliguria, fever, urinary retention; upper and lower limb pain
Dose: *by slow intravenous injection* (rate not exceeding 12.5 mg/minute), diluted before use, initially 0.5–1 mg/kg, then 500 micrograms/kg every 30 minutes until satisfactory response or total of 3 mg/kg given; maintenance, initial dose of up to 3 mg/kg may be repeated every 3–6 hours as required
By intravenous infusion, initially 90 micrograms/kg/minute over 10–30 minutes, followed by continuous or intermittent infusion of 5–20 micrograms/kg/minute
Total dose over 24 hours should not normally exceed 24 mg/kg

▼ PoM **Perfan®** (Merrell)
Injection, enoximone 5 mg/mL. For dilution before use. Net price 20-mL amp = £15.40
Note. Plastic apparatus should be used; crystal formation if glass used

MILRINONE

Indications: short-term treatment of severe congestive heart failure unresponsive to conventional maintenance therapy (not immediately after myocardial infarction)
Cautions; Side-effects: see under Enoximone; also correct hypokalaemia, monitor renal function, chest pain reported
Dose: *by slow intravenous injection* (over 10 minutes), 50 micrograms/kg followed by *intravenous infusion* at a rate of 375–750 nanograms/kg/minute (usually 500 nanograms/kg/minute), usually for 48–72 hours; max. daily dose 1.13 mg/kg

▼ PoM **Primacor®** (Sterling-Winthrop)
Injection, milrinone (as lactate) 1 mg/mL. For dilution before use. Net price 10-mL amp = £14.74

2.2 Diuretics

Thiazides (section 2.2.1) are used to relieve oedema due to *heart failure* and, in lower doses, to reduce *blood pressure.*

Loop diuretics (section 2.2.2) are used in pulmonary oedema due to *left ventricular failure* and in patients with *longstanding heart failure* who no longer respond to thiazides.

Combination diuretic therapy may be effective in patients with oedema resistant to treatment with one diuretic. For example, a loop diuretic may be combined with a potassium-sparing diuretic (section 2.2.3).

The combination of a thiazide with spironolactone is of value in *less severe heart failure* when hypokalaemia is difficult to counter or when any degree of hypokalaemia should be avoided, as in patients with a continuing tendency to life-threatening ventricular arrhythmias.

THE ELDERLY. Diuretics are overprescribed in old age and the elderly are particularly susceptible to many of their side-effects. They should not be used on a long-term basis to treat simple gravitational oedema (which will usually respond to increased movement, raising the legs, and support stockings).

POTASSIUM LOSS. Hypokalaemia may occur with both thiazide and loop diuretics. It is dangerous in severe coronary artery disease and in patients also being treated with cardiac glycosides. Often the use of potassium-sparing diuretics (section 2.2.3) avoids the need to take potassium supplements.

In hepatic failure hypokalaemia caused by diuretics can precipitate encephalopathy, particularly in alcoholic cirrhosis; diuretics may also increase the risk of hypomagnesaemia in alcoholic cirrhosis, leading to arrhythmias.

Potassium supplements are seldom necessary when thiazides are used in routine treatment of hypertension. For further comment see section 9.2.1.1.

2.2.1 Thiazides and related diuretics

Thiazides and related compounds are moderately potent diuretics; they inhibit sodium reabsorption at the beginning of the distal convoluted tubule. They act within 1 to 2 hours of oral administration and most have a duration of action of 12 to 24 hours; they are usually administered early in the day so that the diuresis does not interfere with sleep.

In the management of *hypertension* a low dose of a thiazide, e.g. bendrofluazide 2.5 mg daily, produces a maximal or near-maximal blood pressure lowering effect, with very little biochemical disturbance. Higher doses cause more marked changes in plasma potassium, uric acid, glucose, and lipids, with no advantage in blood pressure control, and should not be used. Optimum doses for the control of *heart failure* may be larger, and long-term effects are of less importance.

Bendrofluazide is widely used for mild or moderate heart failure when the patient is not desperately ill and severe pulmonary oedema is not present. It is also used for hypertension—alone in the treatment of mild hypertension or with other drugs in more severe hypertension.

Chlorthalidone, a thiazide-related compound, has a longer duration of action than the thiazides and may be given on alternate days to control oedema. It is also useful if acute retention is liable to be precipitated by a more rapid diuresis or if patients dislike the altered pattern of micturition promoted by diuretics.

Other thiazides do not offer any significant advantage over those mentioned.

Metolazone is particularly effective when combined with a loop diuretic (even in renal failure); profound diuresis may occur therefore the patient should be monitored carefully.

Xipamide resembles chlorthalidone structurally, and is more potent than the other thiazides.

Indapamide is also chemically related to chlorthalidone. It is claimed to lower blood pressure with less metabolic disturbance, particularly less aggravation of diabetes mellitus. Any advantage of these agents, which are more expensive than the longer-established thiazides, has not been shown.

BENDROFLUAZIDE

Indications: oedema, hypertension

Cautions: may cause hypokalaemia, aggravates diabetes and gout; pregnancy (see also Appendix 4) and breast-feeding; renal and hepatic impairment; see also notes above; **interactions:** Appendix 1 (diuretics)

Contra-indications: hypercalcaemia, renal failure, Addison's disease, porphyria

Side-effects: impotence (reversible on withdrawal of treatment), hypokalaemia (see also notes above), hypomagnesaemia, hyponatraemia, hypercalcaemia, hypochloraemic alkalosis, hyperuricaemia, gout, hyperglycaemia, and increases in plasma cholesterol concentration; less commonly rashes, photosensitivity, neutropenia, and thrombocytopenia (when given in late pregnancy neonatal thrombocytopenia has been reported)

Dose: oedema, initially 5–10 mg in the morning, daily *or* on alternate days; maintenance 2.5–10 mg 1–3 times weekly

Hypertension, 2.5 mg in the morning; higher doses rarely necessary (see notes above)

PoM **Bendrofluazide** (Non-proprietary)
Tablets, bendrofluazide 2.5 mg, net price 20 = 14p; 5 mg, 20 = 5p
PoM **Aprinox®** (Boots)
Tablets, bendrofluazide 2.5 mg, net price 20 = 8p; 5 mg, 20 = 13p
PoM **Berkozide®** (Berk)
Tablets, bendrofluazide 2.5 mg, net price 20 = 8p; 5 mg (scored), 20 = 11p
PoM **Centyl®** (Leo)
Tablets, bendrofluazide 2.5 mg, net price 20 = 38p; 5 mg (scored), 20 = 57p
PoM **Neo-NaClex®** (DF)
Tablets, scored, bendrofluazide 5 mg, net price 20 = 20p

BENZTHIAZIDE

Cautions; Contra-indications; Side-effects: see under Bendrofluazide

Preparation

Ingredient of Dytide® (section 2.2.4)

CHLOROTHIAZIDE

Indications: oedema, hypertension
Cautions; Contra-indications; Side-effects: see under Bendrofluazide
Dose: oedema, initially 0.5–1 g 1–2 times daily; maintenance 0.5–1 g daily, on alternate days, or less frequently
Hypertension, 0.5–1 g daily in single or divided doses

PoM **Saluric®** (MSD)
Tablets, scored, chlorothiazide 500 mg. Net price 20 = 38p

CHLORTHALIDONE

Indications: oedema, hypertension; diabetes insipidus (see section 6.5.2)
Cautions; Contra-indications; Side-effects: see under Bendrofluazide
Dose: oedema, initially 50 mg in the morning *or* 100–200 mg on alternate days, reduced for maintenance if possible
Hypertension, 25 mg, increased to 50 mg if necessary, in the morning

PoM **Hygroton®** (Geigy)
Tablets, both scored, chlorthalidone 50 mg (yellow), net price 20 = 82p; 100 mg, 20 = £1.58

CLOPAMIDE

Cautions; Contra-indications; Side-effects: see under Bendrofluazide

Preparation

Ingredient of Viskaldix® (see Pindolol, section 2.4)

CYCLOPENTHIAZIDE

Indications: oedema, hypertension
Cautions; Contra-indications; Side-effects: see under Bendrofluazide
Dose: oedema, initially 0.5–1 mg in the morning; maintenance 500 micrograms on alternate days
Hypertension, 250–500 micrograms in the morning
Max. 1.5 mg daily

PoM **Navidrex®** (Ciba)
Tablets, scored, cyclopenthiazide 500 micrograms. Net price 20 = 35p
Additives: include gluten

HYDROCHLOROTHIAZIDE

Indications: oedema, hypertension
Cautions; Contra-indications; Side-effects: see under Bendrofluazide
Dose: oedema, initially 50–100 mg daily; maintenance 25–50 mg on alternate days
Hypertension, 25 mg daily, can be increased to 50–100 mg daily if necessary

PoM **Esidrex®** (Ciba)
Tablets, both scored, hydrochlorothiazide 25 mg, net price 20 = 57p; 50 mg, 20 = £1.05
Additives: include gluten
PoM **HydroSaluric®** (MSD)
Tablets, both scored, hydrochlorothiazide 25 mg, net price 20 = 29p; 50 mg, 20 = 54p

HYDROFLUMETHIAZIDE

Indications: oedema, hypertension
Cautions; Contra-indications; Side-effects: see under Bendrofluazide
Dose: oedema, initially 50–200 mg in the morning; maintenance 25–50 mg on alternate days
Hypertension, 25–50 mg daily

PoM **Hydrenox®** (Boots)
Tablets, hydroflumethiazide 50 mg. Net price 20 = 32p

INDAPAMIDE

Indications: hypertension
Cautions: severe hepatic or renal impairment; avoid diuretics liable to induce hypokalaemia; **interactions:** Appendix 1 (diuretics)
Side-effects: nausea, headache, rashes, slight weight loss; diuresis with doses above 2.5 mg daily
Dose: 2.5 mg in the morning

PoM **Natrilix®** (Servier)
Tablets, pink, s/c, indapamide 2.5 mg. Net price 30-tab pack = £5.96

MEFRUSIDE

Indications: oedema, hypertension
Cautions; Contra-indications; Side-effects: see under Bendrofluazide
Dose: initially 25–50 mg in the morning, increased to 75–100 mg for oedema; maintenance 25 mg daily *or* on alternate days

PoM **Baycaron®** (Bayer)
Tablets, scored, mefruside 25 mg. Net price 20 = £1.41

METHYCLOTHIAZIDE

Indications: oedema, hypertension
Cautions; Contra-indications; Side-effects: see under Bendrofluazide
Dose: 2.5–5 mg in the morning, increased to 10 mg daily if required

PoM **Enduron®** (Abbott)
Tablets, pink, scored, methyclothiazide 5 mg. Net price 20 = 41p

METOLAZONE

Indications: oedema, hypertension
Cautions; Contra-indications; Side-effects: see under Bendrofluazide; also profound diuresis on concomitant administration with frusemide (monitor patient carefully)
Dose: oedema, 5–10 mg in the morning, increased if necessary; max. 80 mg daily
Hypertension, initially 5 mg in the morning; maintenance 5 mg on alternate days

PoM **Metenix 5®** (Hoechst)
Tablets, blue, metolazone 5 mg. Net price 20 = £1.75

POLYTHIAZIDE

Indications: oedema, hypertension
Cautions; Contra-indications; Side-effects: see under Bendrofluazide
Dose: usually 1–4 mg daily; in hypertension 500 micrograms daily may be adequate

PoM **Nephril®** (Pfizer)
Tablets, scored, polythiazide 1 mg. Net price 28-tab pack = 79p

XIPAMIDE

Indications: oedema, hypertension
Cautions; Contra-indications: see under Bendrofluazide
Side-effects: slight gastro-intestinal disturbances; mild dizziness
Dose: oedema, initially 40 mg in the morning, increased to 80 mg in resistant cases; maintenance 20 mg in the morning
Hypertension, usual dose 20 mg in the morning (may be increased to 40 mg if necessary, but not if other antihypertensive therapy being given)

PoM **Diurexan®** (Degussa)
Tablets, scored, xipamide 20 mg. Net price strip of 14 = £1.83

2.2.2 Loop diuretics

These drugs inhibit resorption from the ascending loop of Henle in the renal tubule and are powerful diuretics. Hypokalaemia may develop, and care is needed to avoid hypotension. If there is an enlarged prostate, urinary retention may occur; this is less likely if small doses and less potent diuretics are used initially.

Frusemide and **bumetanide** are similar in activity; both act within 1 hour of oral administration and diuresis is complete within 6 hours so that, if necessary, they can be given twice in one day without interfering with sleep. Following intravenous administration they have a peak effect within 30 minutes. The degree of diuresis associated with these drugs is dose related. In patients with impaired renal function very large doses may occasionally be needed; in such doses both drugs can cause deafness and bumetanide can cause myalgia.

Ethacrynic acid has a similar onset and duration of action. Gastro-intestinal side-effects are more severe and deafness may occur in patients with renal failure, especially when it is given intravenously.

Piretanide is the newest member of this group; it has properties similar to those of frusemide and bumetanide, but is promoted for the treatment of hypertension.

FRUSEMIDE

Indications: oedema, oliguria due to renal failure
Cautions: pregnancy (see also Appendix 4); may cause hypokalaemia and hyponatraemia; aggravates diabetes and gout; liver failure, prostatism; **interactions:** Appendix 1 (diuretics)
Contra-indications: precomatose states associated with liver cirrhosis; porphyria
Side-effects: hyponatraemia, hypokalaemia (see also section 2.2), hypochloraemic alkalosis, increased calcium excretion, hypotension; less commonly nausea, gastro-intestinal disturbances, hyperuricaemia and gout; hyperglycaemia (less common than with thiazides); temporary increase in plasma cholesterol and triglyceride concentrations; rarely rashes and bone marrow depression (withdraw treatment), pancreatitis (with large parenteral doses), tinnitus and deafness (usually with large parenteral doses and rapid administration and in renal impairment)
Dose: by mouth, oedema, initially 40 mg in the morning; maintenance 20 mg daily *or* 40 mg on alternate days, increased in resistant oedema to 80 mg daily; CHILD 1–3 mg/kg daily
Oliguria, initially 250 mg daily; if necessary larger doses, increasing in steps of 250 mg, may be given every 4–6 hours to a max. of a single dose of 2 g
By intramuscular injection or slow intravenous injection (rate not exceeding 4 mg/minute), initially 20–50 mg; CHILD 0.5–1.5 mg/kg to a max. daily dose of 20 mg
By intravenous infusion (by syringe pump if necessary), in oliguria, initially 250 mg over 1 hour (rate not exceeding 4 mg/minute), if satisfactory urine output not obtained in the subsequent hour further 500 mg over 2 hours, then if no satisfactory response within subsequent hour, further 1 g over 4 hours, if no response obtained dialysis probably required; effective dose (up to 1 g) can be repeated every 24 hours

PoM **Frusemide** (Non-proprietary)
Tablets, frusemide 20 mg, net price 20 = 29p; 40 mg, 20 = 8p; 500 mg, 20 = £6.00
Available from APS (20 mg, 40 mg, 500 mg), Berk (Dryptal® 40 mg, 500 mg), CP (Rusyde® 20 mg, 40 mg), Evans (20 mg, 40 mg), Kerfoot (20 mg, 40 mg), Steinhard (Aluzine® 20 mg, 40 mg, 500 mg)
Oral solutions, sugar-free, frusemide 1 mg/mL available as Lasix® paediatric liquid; frusemide 4, 8, and 10 mg/mL available from RP Drugs (special order)
Injection, frusemide 10 mg/mL, net price 2-mL amp = 26p

PoM **Diuresal®** (Lagap)
Injection, frusemide 10 mg/mL. Net price 2-mL amp = 22p

PoM **Lasix®** (Hoechst)
Tablets, all scored, frusemide 20 mg, net price 28-tab pack = 84p; 40 mg, 28-tab pack = £1.22; 500 mg (yellow), 20 = £11.74
Paediatric liquid, sugar-free, frusemide 1 mg/mL when reconstituted with purified water, freshly boiled and cooled, net price 150 mL = £1.13
Injection, frusemide 10 mg/mL, net price 2-mL amp = 26p; 5-mL amp = 54p; 25-mL amp = £2.27

BUMETANIDE

Indications: oedema, oliguria due to renal failure
Cautions; Contra-indications: see under Frusemide (but has been used in porphyria)
Side-effects: see under Frusemide; also myalgia
Dose: *by mouth*, 1 mg in the morning, repeated after 6–8 hours if necessary; severe cases, increased up to 5 mg or more daily
ELDERLY, 500 micrograms daily may be sufficient
By intravenous injection, 1–2 mg, repeated after 20 minutes; when *intramuscular injection* considered necessary, 1 mg initially then adjusted according to response
By intravenous infusion, 2–5 mg over 30–60 minutes

PoM **Burinex®** (Leo)
Tablets, both scored, bumetanide 1 mg, net price 20 = £1.14; 5 mg, 20 = £5.72
Liquid, green, sugar-free, bumetanide 1 mg/5 mL. Net price 150 mL = £3.41
Injection, bumetanide 500 micrograms/mL. Net price 2-mL amp = 41p; 4-mL amp = 71p; 10-mL amp = £1.49

ETHACRYNIC ACID

Indications: oedema, oliguria due to renal failure
Cautions; Contra-indications; Side-effects: see under Frusemide and notes above; gastro-intestinal disturbances more severe; also pain on injection
Dose: *by mouth*, initially 50 mg daily after breakfast; effective initial range of 50–150 mg daily (max. 400 mg) can often be reduced for maintenance and given on alternate days (daily doses above 50 mg divided)
By slow intravenous injection or infusion, 50 mg, increased to 100 mg if necessary

PoM **Edecrin®** (MSD)
Tablets, scored, ethacrynic acid 50 mg. Net price 20 = 75p. Label: 21
Injection, powder for reconstitution, ethacrynic acid (as sodium salt). Net price 50-mg vial = £1.05

PIRETANIDE

Indications: hypertension
Cautions: causes hypokalaemia, monitor plasma electrolytes in hepatic and renal impairment; prostatism; **interactions:** Appendix 1 (diuretics)
Contra-indications: severe electrolyte imbalance, hypovolaemia
Side-effects: rarely nausea, vomiting, diarrhoea, rashes; myalgia after high doses
Dose: 6–12 mg in the morning with food

PoM **Arelix®** (Hoechst)
Capsules, s/r, green/orange, enclosing yellow pellets, piretanide 6 mg. Net price 28-cap pack = £3.70. Label: 21

2.2.3 Potassium-sparing diuretics

Amiloride and **triamterene** on their own are weak diuretics. They cause retention of potassium and are therefore used as an alternative to giving potassium supplements with thiazide or loop diuretics. (See section 2.2.4 for compound preparations with thiazides or loop diuretics.)

Spironolactone is also a potassium-sparing diuretic, and potentiates thiazide or loop diuretics by antagonising aldosterone. It is of value in the treatment of the oedema of cirrhosis of the liver and is effective in oedema of heart failure, particularly when congestion has caused hepatic engorgement.

Spironolactone is also used in primary hyperaldosteronism (Conn's syndrome).

Potassium canrenoate has similar uses to spironolactone, but can be given parenterally. It is metabolised to canrenone, which is also a metabolite of spironolactone.

Potassium supplements must **not** be given with potassium-sparing diuretics.

AMILORIDE HYDROCHLORIDE

Indications: oedema, potassium conservation with thiazide and loop diuretics
Cautions: pregnancy; diabetes mellitus; **interactions:** Appendix 1 (diuretics)
Contra-indications: hyperkalaemia, renal failure
Side-effects: rashes, mental confusion
Dose: alone, initially 10 mg daily *or* 5 mg twice daily, adjusted according to response; max. 20 mg daily
With other diuretics, congestive heart failure and hypertension, initially 5–10 mg daily
Cirrhosis with ascites, initially 5 mg daily

Prices are **net**, see p. 1

PoM **Amiloride** (Non-proprietary)
Tablets, amiloride hydrochloride 5 mg, net price 20 = £1.36
Oral solution, sugar-free, amiloride hydrochloride 5 mg/5 mL available from RP Drugs (special order)

PoM **Midamor®** (Morson)
Tablets, yellow, amiloride hydrochloride 5 mg. Net price 20 = £1.46

TRIAMTERENE

Indications: oedema, potassium conservation with thiazide and loop diuretics
Cautions; Contra-indications: see under Amiloride Hydrochloride; monitor plasma urea and potassium, particularly in the elderly and in renal impairment; also may cause blue fluorescence of urine
Side-effects: gastro-intestinal disturbances, dry mouth, rashes; triamterene found in kidney stones
Dose: initially 150–250 mg daily, reducing to alternate days after 1 week; taken in divided doses after breakfast and lunch; lower initial dose when given with other diuretics
COUNSELLING. Urine may look slightly blue in some lights

PoM **Dytac®** (Bridge)
Capsules, maroon, triamterene 50 mg. Net price 30-cap pack = £1.94. Label: 14 (see above), 21

ALDOSTERONE ANTAGONISTS

POTASSIUM CANRENOATE

Indications: oedema associated with secondary aldosteronism, liver failure, chronic decompensated heart disease
Cautions; Contra-indications: see under Spironolactone; also contra-indicated in hyponatraemia
Side-effects: nausea and vomiting, particularly after high doses; pain and irritation at injection site
Dose: *by slow intravenous injection or intravenous infusion*, 200–400 mg daily (exceptionally 800 mg)

PoM **Spiroctan-M®** (Boehringer Mannheim)
Injection, potassium canrenoate 20 mg/mL. Net price 10-mL amp = 72p

SPIRONOLACTONE

Indications: oedema in cirrhosis of the liver, nephrotic syndrome, congestive heart failure; primary aldosteronism
Cautions: potential human metabolic products carcinogenic in *rodents*; **interactions:** Appendix 1 (diuretics)
Contra-indications: hyperkalaemia, renal failure; pregnancy and breast-feeding; Addison's disease; porphyria
Side-effects: gastro-intestinal disturbances, gynaecomastia
Dose: 100–200 mg daily, increased to 400 mg if required; CHILD 3 mg/kg daily in divided doses

PoM **Spironolactone** (Non-proprietary)
Tablets, spironolactone 25 mg, net price 20 = 54p; 50 mg, 20 = £2.40; 100 mg, 20 = £2.20
Oral suspensions, sugar-free, spironolactone 5, 10, 25, and 50 mg/5 mL available from RP Drugs (special order)

PoM **Aldactone®** (Searle)
Tablets, all f/c, spironolactone 25 mg (buff), net price 20 = £1.80; 50 mg (off-white), 20 = £3.59; 100 mg (buff), 20 = £7.18

PoM **Diatensec®** (Gold Cross)
Tablets, off-white, f/c, spironolactone 50 mg. Net price 20 = £3.59

PoM **Laractone®** (Lagap)
Tablets, both f/c, spironolactone 25 mg, net price 20 = 54p; 50 mg, 20 = £2.40; 100 mg, 20 = £2.20

PoM **Spiroctan®** (Boehringer Mannheim)
Tablets, both s/c, spironolactone 25 mg (blue, contains tartrazine), net price 20 = £1.48; 50 mg (green), 20 = £2.84
Capsules, green, spironolactone 100 mg. Net price 28-cap pack = £7.75

PoM **Spirolone®** (Berk)
Tablets, all s/c, spironolactone 25 mg, net price 20 = £1.25; 50 mg, 20 = £2.48; 100 mg, 20 = £5.02

2.2.4 Potassium-sparing diuretics with other diuretics

Although it is preferable to prescribe thiazides and potassium-sparing diuretics separately, the use of fixed combinations may be justified if compliance is a problem. There is an increased risk of hyponatraemia if these are given with chlorpropamide (Appendix 1, diuretics).

Amiloride with thiazides

PoM **Co-amilozide** (Non-proprietary)
Tablets, co-amilozide 5/50 (amiloride hydrochloride 5 mg, hydrochlorothiazide 50 mg). Net price 20 = £1.34
Available from Abbott (Normetic®), APS, Cox, Kerfoot, Norton (Amilco®), Schwarz (Hypertane 50®), Shire (Vasetic®)
Dose: 1–2 tablets, increased if necessary to max. of 4, daily
Tablets, co-amilozide 2.5/25 available as Moduret 25®

PoM **Moduret 25®** (Morson)
Tablets, off-white, co-amilozide 2.5/25 (amiloride hydrochloride 2.5 mg, hydrochlorothiazide 25 mg). Net price 28-tab pack = £2.08
Dose: 1–4 tablets, increased if necessary to a max. of 8, daily

PoM **Moduretic®** (MSD)
Tablets, peach, scored, co-amilozide 5/50 (amiloride hydrochloride 5 mg, hydrochlorothiazide 50 mg). Net price 20 = £1.80
Dose: 1–2 tablets, increased if necessary to a max. of 4, daily
Oral solution, co-amilozide 5/50 (amiloride hydrochloride 5 mg, hydrochlorothiazide 50 mg/5 mL). Do not dilute. Net price 200 mL = £4.95
Dose: as for tablets above (5 mL = 1 tablet)

PoM **Navispare**® (Ciba)
Tablets, f/c, orange, amiloride 2.5 mg, cyclopenthiazide 250 micrograms. Net price 28-tab pack = £1.79
Dose: 1–2 tablets in the morning

Amiloride with loop diuretics
PoM **Frumil**® (Rhône-Poulenc Rorer)
Tablets, orange, scored, co-amilofruse 5/40 (amiloride hydrochloride 5 mg, frusemide 40 mg). Net price 28-tab pack = £3.97; 56-tab pack = £7.77
Dose: 1–2 tablets in the morning
LS tablets, orange, co-amilofruse 2.5/20 (amiloride hydrochloride 2.5 mg, frusemide 20 mg). Net price 28-tab pack = £3.25
Dose: 1 tablet in the morning
PoM **Lasoride**® (Hoechst)
Tablets, yellow, co-amilofruse 5/40 (amiloride hydrochloride 5 mg, frusemide 40 mg). Net price 28-tab pack = £3.33
Dose: 1–2 tablets in the morning

Triamterene with thiazides
COUNSELLING. Urine may look slightly blue in some lights
PoM **Dyazide**® (Bridge)
Tablets, peach, scored, triamterene 50 mg, hydrochlorothiazide 25 mg. Net price 30-tab pack = £2.15. Label: 14 (see above), 21
Dose: hypertension, 1 tablet daily after breakfast; oedema, 2 tablets daily (1 after breakfast and 1 after midday meal) increased to 3 daily if necessary (2 after breakfast and 1 after midday meal); usual maintenance, 1 daily or 2 on alternate days; max. 4 daily
PoM **Dytide**® (Bridge)
Capsules, clear/maroon, triamterene 50 mg, benzthiazide 25 mg. Net price 30-cap pack = £2.08. Label: 14 (see above), 21
Dose: oedema, initially 3 capsules daily (2 after breakfast and 1 after midday meal) for 1 week then 1 or 2 on alternate days
PoM **Kalspare**® (Cusi)
Tablets, orange, f/c, scored, triamterene 50 mg, chlorthalidone 50 mg. Net price 28-tab pack = £3.27. Label: 14 (see above), 21
Dose: 1–2 tablets in the morning
PoM **Triamco**® (Norton)
Tablets, peach, scored, triamterene 50 mg, hydrochlorothiazide 25 mg. Net price 20 = £1.19. Label: 14 (see above), 21
Dose: hypertension, 1 tablet daily after breakfast; oedema, 2 tablets daily (1 after breakfast and 1 after midday meal) increased to 3 daily if necessary (2 after breakfast and 1 after midday meal); usual maintenance, 1 daily or 2 on alternate days; max. 4 daily

Triamterene with loop diuretics
COUNSELLING. Urine may look slightly blue in some lights
PoM **Frusene**® (Fisons)
Tablets, yellow, scored, triamterene 50 mg, frusemide 40 mg. Net price 56-tab pack = £4.90. Label: 14 (see above), 21
Dose: 1–2 tablets daily

Spironolactone with thiazides
PoM **Aldactide 25**® (Gold Cross)
Tablets, buff, f/c, co-flumactone 25/25 (hydroflumethiazide 25 mg, spironolactone 25 mg). Net price 20 = £3.07
Dose: congestive heart failure, initially 4 tablets daily; range 1–8 daily
PoM **Aldactide 50**® (Gold Cross)
Tablets, buff, f/c, co-flumactone 50/50 (hydroflumethiazide 50 mg, spironolactone 50 mg). Net price 20 = £5.79
Dose: congestive heart failure, initially 2 tablets daily; range 1–4 daily

Spironolactone with loop diuretics
PoM **Lasilactone**® (Hoechst)
Capsules, blue/white, spironolactone 50 mg, frusemide 20 mg. Net price 28-cap pack = £5.04
Dose: resistant oedema, 1–4 capsules daily

2.2.5 Osmotic diuretics

Osmotic diuretics are rarely used in heart failure as they may acutely expand the blood volume. **Mannitol** is used in cerebral oedema—a typical dose is 1 g/kg as a 20% solution given by rapid intravenous infusion.

MANNITOL

Indications: see notes above
Cautions: extravasation causes inflammation and thrombophlebitis
Contra-indications: congestive cardiac failure, pulmonary oedema
Side-effects: chills, fever
Dose: by intravenous infusion, diuresis, 50–200 g over 24 hours, preceded by a test dose of 200 mg/kg by slow intravenous injection
Cerebral oedema, see notes above

PoM **Mannitol** (Non-proprietary)
Intravenous infusion, mannitol 10%, 15%, 20%, and 25%
Available from Baxter (10% and 20%) and IMS (25%)

2.2.6 Mercurial diuretics

They are effective diuretics but are now little used because of their nephrotoxicity. Mersalyl **must** be given by intramuscular injection; intravenous use may cause severe hypotension and sudden death.

MERSALYL

Indications: oedema unresponsive to other diuretics
Cautions: recent myocardial infarction, treatment with cardiac glycosides, frequent extrasystoles
Contra-indications: renal impairment; pregnancy; porphyria
Side-effects: gastro-intestinal disturbances, allergic reactions

PoM **Mersalyl Injection,** mersalyl sodium 100 mg, theophylline 50 mg/mL
Dose: by deep intramuscular injection, 0.5–2 mL

2.2.7 Carbonic anhydrase inhibitors

Acetazolamide and dichlorphenamide are weak diuretics, and are little used for their diuretic effect. They inhibit the formation of aqueous fluid, and are used in glaucoma (see section 11.6). Although acetazolamide is used as a prophylactic measure for mountain sickness it is not a substitute for acclimatisation.

2.2.8 Diuretics with potassium

Many patients on diuretics do not need potassium supplements (see section 9.2.1.1). For many of those who do, the amount of potassium ion in combined preparations may not be enough, and for this reason their use is to be discouraged.

Diuretics with potassium and potassium-sparing diuretics should **not** usually be given together.

COUNSELLING. Sustained-release potassium tablets should be swallowed whole with plenty of fluid during meals while sitting or standing

PoM **Burinex K**® (Leo)
Tablets, bumetanide 500 micrograms, potassium 7.7 mmol for sustained release. Net price 20 = 85p. Label: 25, 27, counselling, see above

PoM **Centyl K**® (Leo)
Tablets, green, bendrofluazide 2.5 mg, potassium 7.7 mmol for sustained release. Net price 20 = 58p. Label: 25, 27, counselling, see above

PoM **Diumide-K Continus**® (Degussa)
Tablets, white/orange, frusemide 40 mg, potassium 8 mmol for sustained release. Net price 30-tab pack = £2.14. Label: 25, 27, counselling, see above

PoM **Hygroton-K**® (Geigy)
Tablets, red, s/c, chlorthalidone 25 mg, potassium 6.7 mmol for sustained release. Net price 20 = 48p. Label: 25, 27, counselling, see above
Additives: include gluten and azo dyes

PoM **Lasikal**® (Hoechst)
Tablets, white/yellow, f/c, frusemide 20 mg, potassium 10 mmol for sustained release. Net price 20 = £1.09. Label: 25, 27, counselling, see above

PoM **Lasix + K**® (Hoechst)
Calendar pack, 30 white scored tablets, frusemide 40 mg; 60 s/r yellow tablets, potassium chloride (potassium 10 mmol). Net price = £3.05. Label: 25, 27, counselling, see above

PoM **Navidrex-K**® (Ciba)
Tablets, yellow, s/c, cyclopenthiazide 250 micrograms, potassium 8.1 mmol for sustained release. Net price 20 = 23p. Label: 25, 27, counselling, see above

PoM **Neo-NaClex-K**® (DF)
Tablets, pink/white, f/c, bendrofluazide 2.5 mg, potassium 8.4 mmol for sustained release. Net price 20 = 24p. Label: 25, 27, counselling, see above

2.3 Anti-arrhythmic drugs

2.3.1 Management of arrhythmias

Management of an arrhythmia, apart from the treatment of associated heart failure, requires precise diagnosis of the type of arrhythmia, and electrocardiography is essential.

Ectopic beats. If spontaneous with a normal heart, these rarely require treatment beyond reassurance. If they are particularly troublesome, beta-blockers are sometimes effective and may be safer than other suppressant drugs.

Atrial fibrillation. The ventricular rate can be controlled with digoxin (section 2.1.1).

Atrial flutter. The ventricular rate can often be controlled with digoxin. Reversion to sinus rhythm (if indicated) is best achieved by appropriately synchronised d.c. shock, rather than by drug therapy. If the arrhythmia is long-standing a period of treatment with anticoagulants should be considered before cardioversion to avoid the complication of emboli.

Paroxysmal supraventricular tachycardia. In most patients this remits spontaneously or can be returned to sinus rhythm by reflex vagal stimulation with respiratory manoeuvres, prompt squatting, or pressure over one carotid sinus (**important:** pressure over carotid sinus should be restricted to monitored patients, it can be dangerous in recent ischaemia, digitalis toxicity, or the elderly).

If vagal stimulation fails, digitalisation or intravenous administration of a beta-blocker may be effective. Intravenous administration of verapamil is useful for patients without myocardial or valvular disease (**important:** never in patients recently treated with beta-blockers, see section 2.3.2). For arrhythmias that are poorly tolerated, synchronised d.c. shock usually provides rapid relief.

In cases of paroxysmal supraventricular tachycardia with block, digitalis toxicity should be suspected. In addition to stopping administration of the cardiac glycoside and giving potassium supplements, intravenous administration of a beta-blocker or phenytoin may be useful. Specific digoxin antibody is available if the toxicity is considered life-threatening (section 2.1.1).

Acute arrhythmias after myocardial infarction. It is best to do nothing in patients with a paroxysmal tachycardia or rapid irregularity of the pulse until an ECG record is obtainable. If the condition of the patient is such that death due to the arrhythmia seems possible 100 mg of lignocaine should be given intravenously. Bradycardia, particularly if complicated by hypotension, should be treated with atropine sulphate (section 15.1.3) in an initial dose of 300 micrograms, increasing to 1 mg if necessary.

Ventricular tachycardia. Drug treatment is used both for the treatment of ventricular tachycardia and for prophylaxis of recurrent attacks that merit suppression. Ventricular tachycardia requires treatment most commonly in the acute stage of myocardial infarction, but the likelihood of this and other life-threatening arrhythmias diminishes sharply over the first 24 hours after the attack, especially in patients without heart failure or shock. Lignocaine is the preferred drug for emergency use. Other drugs are best administered under specialist supervision. Very rapid ventricular tachycardia causes profound circulatory collapse and should be treated urgently with d.c. shock.

2.3.2 Drugs for arrhythmias

Anti-arrhythmic drugs can be classified clinically into those that act on supraventricular arrhythmias (e.g. verapamil), those that act on both supraventricular and ventricular arrhythmias (e.g. quinidine), and those that act on ventricular arrhythmias (e.g. lignocaine).

They can also be classified according to their effects on the electrical behaviour of myocardial cells during activity (termed 'action potential'):

Class Ia, b, c	Membrane stabilising drugs (e.g. quinidine, lignocaine, flecainide respectively)
Class II	Beta-blockers
Class III	Amiodarone, Bretylium, and Sotalol (also Class II)
Class IV	Calcium-channel blockers (includes verapamil but not the nifedipine group)

This latter classification (the Vaughan Williams classification) is of less clinical significance.

CAUTIONS. The negative inotropic effects of anti-arrhythmic drugs tend to be additive therefore special care should be taken if two or more are used, especially in impaired myocardial function. Most or all drugs that are effective in countering arrhythmias can also provoke them in some circumstances; moreover, hypokalaemia enhances the pro-arrhythmic effect of many drugs.

SUPRAVENTRICULAR ARRHYTHMIAS

Oral administration of a **cardiac glycoside** (such as digoxin, section 2.1.1) is the treatment of choice in slowing ventricular response in cases of atrial fibrillation and atrial flutter. Intravenous digoxin, preferably infused slowly, is occasionally required if the ventricular rate needs rapid control. Ouabain acts more quickly but may be difficult to obtain since it is not on the UK market.

Verapamil (section 2.6.2) is usually effective for supraventricular tachycardias. An initial intravenous dose may be followed by oral treatment; hypotension may occur with larger doses. It should not be used for tachyarrhythmias where the QRS complex is wide (i.e. broad complex) unless a supraventricular origin has been established beyond reasonable doubt. It is also contra-indicated in atrial fibrillation with pre-excitation (e.g. Wolff-Parkinson-White syndrome). It should not be used in children with arrhythmias without specialist advice; some supraventricular arrhythmias in childhood can be accelerated by verapamil with dangerous consequences.

> **Verapamil** should not be injected into patients recently treated with **beta-blockers** because of the risk of hypotension and asystole. It has been suggested that when verapamil injection has been given first, an interval of 30 minutes before giving a beta-blocker is sufficient but this too is open to doubt.
>
> It may even be hazardous to give verapamil and a beta-blocker together by mouth (should only be contemplated if myocardial function well preserved).

CARDIAC GLYCOSIDES
Section 2.1.1

VERAPAMIL
Section 2.6.2

SUPRAVENTRICULAR AND VENTRICULAR ARRHYTHMIAS

Amiodarone is used in the treatment of the Wolff-Parkinson-White syndrome. It may only be used for the treatment of other arrhythmias when other drugs are ineffective or contra-indicated. These include supraventricular and ventricular tachycardias, atrial fibrillation and flutter, and recurrent ventricular fibrillation. Since amiodarone has a very long half-life it only needs to be given once daily (but high doses may cause nausea unless divided). It may be given by intravenous infusion as well as by mouth, and has the advantage of causing little or no myocardial depression. Unlike oral amiodarone, intravenous amiodarone may act relatively rapidly.

Most patients taking amiodarone develop corneal microdeposits (reversible on withdrawal of treatment); these rarely interfere with vision, but drivers may be dazzled by headlights at night. Because of the possibility of phototoxic reactions, patients should be advised to shield the skin from light and to use a wide-spectrum sunscreen such as RoC Total Sunblock® (section 13.8.1) to protect against both long ultraviolet and visible light.

Amiodarone contains iodine and can cause disorders of thyroid function; both hypothyroidism and hyperthyroidism may occur. Thyroid function tests which rely on plasma concentrations of thyroxine alone, rather than on both thyroxine and triiodothyronine, may be spuriously elevated, but where doubt exists amiodarone should be withdrawn.

Beta-blockers (section 2.4) act as anti-arrhythmic drugs principally by attenuating the effects of the sympathetic system on automaticity and conductivity within the heart. Some have additional anti-arrhythmic effects. They may be used in conjunction with digoxin to control the ventricular response in atrial fibrillation, especially in patients with thyrotoxicosis. Beta-blockers are also useful in the management of supraventricular tachycardias.

Evidence is now available that at least some **beta-blockers** (such as metoprolol) can reduce the incidence of life-threatening arrhythmias in the acute stage of myocardial infarction.

Disopyramide may be given by intravenous injection to control arrhythmias after myocardial infarction (including those not responding to lignocaine), but it impairs cardiac contractility. Oral administration of disopyramide is useful but it has an antimuscarinic effect which limits its use in patients with glaucoma or prostatic hypertrophy.

Flecainide is a newer drug in the same general class as lignocaine. It may be of value for serious symptomatic ventricular arrhythmias. It may also be indicated for junctional re-entry tachycardias. Preliminary results with paroxysmal atrial fibrillation are promising.

Procainamide can be given by intravenous injection to control ventricular arrhythmias, but prolonged oral use can cause a syndrome resembling systemic lupus erythematosus.

Quinidine may be effective in suppressing supraventricular and ventricular arrhythmias. It may itself precipitate rhythm disorders, and is best used on specialist advice; it can cause hypersensitivity reactions and gastro-intestinal upsets.

AMIODARONE HYDROCHLORIDE

Indications: see notes above

Cautions: liver-function and thyroid-function tests required in long-term therapy; interferes with tests of thyroid function; heart failure; renal impairment; severe bradycardia and conduction disturbances in excessive dosage; **interactions:** Appendix 1 (amiodarone)

Contra-indications: sinus bradycardia, atrioventricular block, thyroid dysfunction; pregnancy and breast-feeding; iodine sensitivity; porphyria

Side-effects: reversible corneal microdeposits (sometimes with night glare), peripheral neuropathy, phototoxicity and rarely persistent slate-grey skin discoloration (see also notes above); hypothyroidism, hyperthyroidism, diffuse pulmonary alveolitis, hepatitis; rarely nausea, vomiting, metallic taste, tremor, nightmares, vertigo, headache, sleeplessness, fatigue; epididymitis with higher doses; ataxia, rashes, blood disorders, and increased prothrombin time reported

Dose: by mouth, 200 mg 3 times daily for 1 week reduced to 200 mg twice daily for a further week; maintenance, usually 200 mg daily or the minimum required to control the arrhythmia

By intravenous infusion via caval catheter, up to 5 mg/kg over 20–120 minutes with ECG monitoring; max. 1.2 g in 24 hours

PoM **Cordarone X®** (Sanofi)

Tablets, both scored, amiodarone hydrochloride 100 mg, net price 28-tab pack = £5.13; 200 mg, 28-tab pack = £8.40. Label: 11

Injection, amiodarone hydrochloride 50 mg/mL. Net price 3-mL amp = £1.54. For dilution and use as an infusion

DISOPYRAMIDE

Indications: ventricular arrhythmias, especially after myocardial infarction; supraventricular arrhythmias

Cautions: glaucoma; heart failure or diminished cardiac output; prostatic enlargement; reduce dose in renal impairment; pregnancy; **interactions:** Appendix 1 (disopyramide)

Side-effects: myocardial depression, hypotension, atrioventricular block; antimuscarinic effects include dry mouth, blurred vision, urinary retention

Dose: by mouth, 300–800 mg daily in divided doses

By slow intravenous injection, 2 mg/kg over at least 5 minutes to a max. of 150 mg, with ECG monitoring, followed immediately *either* by 200 mg *by mouth*, then 200 mg every 8 hours for 24 hours *or* 400 micrograms/kg/hour *by intravenous infusion*; max. 300 mg in first hour and 800 mg daily

PoM **Disopyramide** (Non-proprietary)

Capsules, disopyramide 100 mg, net price 20 = £1.59; 150 mg, 20 = £2.53

PoM **Rythmodan®** (Roussel)

Capsules, disopyramide 100 mg (green/beige), net price 84-cap pack = £7.52; 150 mg, 84-cap pack = £11.27

Injection, disopyramide 10 mg (as phosphate)/mL, net price 5-mL amp = 70p

Sustained release

PoM **Dirythmin SA®** (Astra)

Durules® (= tablets, s/r), f/c, disopyramide 150 mg (as phosphate). Net price 20 = £2.53. Label: 25

Dose: 300 mg every 12 hours; max. 900 mg daily

PoM **Rythmodan Retard®** (Roussel)

Tablets, s/r, scored, f/c, disopyramide 250 mg (as phosphate). Net price 56-tab pack = £16.24. Label: 25

Dose: 250–375 mg every 12 hours

FLECAINIDE ACETATE

Indications: tablets and injection: AV nodal reciprocating tachycardia, Wolff-Parkinson-White syndrome and similar conditions with accessory pathway and anterograde or retrograde conduction; *tablets only:* symptomatic sustained ventricular tachycardia, premature ventricular contractions and/or non-sustained ventricular tachycardia causing disabling symptoms in patients resistant to or intolerant of other therapy; *injection only:* ventricular tachyarrhythmias resistant to other treatment

Cautions: patients with pacemakers; avoid in sino-atrial disorders or AV block unless pacing rescue available; elderly; reduce dose in hepatic and renal impairment; pregnancy (toxicity in *animal* studies); **interactions:** Appendix 1 (flecainide)

Contra-indications: heart failure; history of myocardial infarction and either asymptomatic ventricular ectopics or asymptomatic non-sustained ventricular tachycardia

Side-effects: dizziness, visual disturbances; rarely nausea and vomiting

Dose: by mouth, 100 mg twice daily; max. 400 mg daily, reduced after 3–5 days if possible; elderly 100 mg twice daily, reduced after 1 week if possible

By slow intravenous injection, 2 mg/kg over 10–30 minutes, max. 150 mg, with ECG monitoring; followed if required by *infusion* at a rate of 1.5 mg/kg/hour for 1 hour, subsequently reduced to 100–250 micrograms/kg/hour for up to 24 hours; max. cumulative dose in first 24 hours, 600 mg; transfer to *oral* treatment, as above

PoM **Tambocor®** (3M)

Tablets, scored, flecainide acetate 100 mg. Net price 60-tab pack = £19.98

Injection, flecainide acetate 10 mg/mL. Net price 15-mL amp = £4.25

PROCAINAMIDE HYDROCHLORIDE

Indications: ventricular arrhythmias, especially after myocardial infarction; atrial tachycardia

Cautions: elderly; renal impairment, asthma, myasthenia gravis; **interactions:** Appendix 1 (procainamide)

Contra-indications: heart block, heart failure, hypotension

Side-effects: nausea, diarrhoea, rashes, fever, myocardial depression, heart failure, lupus erythematosus-like syndrome, agranulocytosis after prolonged treatment

Dose: by mouth, ventricular arrhythmias, up to 50 mg/kg daily in divided doses, preferably controlled by measurement of plasma concentration (dosage intervals can range from 3–6 hours); atrial arrhythmias, higher doses may be required

By slow intravenous injection, rate not exceeding 50 mg/minute, 100 mg with ECG monitoring, repeated at 5-minute intervals until arrhythmia controlled; max. 1 g

By intravenous infusion, 500–600 mg over 25–30 minutes with ECG monitoring, followed by maintenance at rate of 2–6 mg/minute, then if necessary oral treatment as above, starting 3–4 hours after infusion

PoM **Pronestyl®** (Squibb)

Tablets, scored, procainamide hydrochloride 250 mg. Net price 20 = 94p

Injection, procainamide hydrochloride 100 mg/mL. Net price 10-mL vial = £1.90

Sustained release

PoM **Procainamide Durules®** (Astra)

Tablets, s/r, yellow, procainamide hydrochloride 500 mg. Net price 20 = £1.46. Label: 25

Dose: 1–1.5 g every 8 hours

QUINIDINE

Indications: suppression of supraventricular tachycardias and ventricular arrhythmias (see notes above)

Cautions: 200-mg test dose to detect hypersensitivity reactions; **interactions:** Appendix 1 (quinidine)

Contra-indications: heart block

Side-effects: see under Procainamide Hydrochloride; also ventricular arrhythmias, thrombocytopenia, haemolytic anaemia; rarely granulomatous hepatitis; also cinchonism (see Quinine, section 5.4.1) with tinnitus, visual disturbances, headache, hot and flushed skin, confusion, vertigo, vomiting, and abdominal pain

Dose: by mouth, quinidine sulphate 200–400 mg 3–4 times daily

Note. Quinidine sulphate 200 mg ≡ quinidine bisulphate 250 mg

PoM **Quinidine Sulphate** (Non-proprietary)

Tablets, quinidine sulphate 200 mg, net price 20 = £1.31; 300 mg, 20 = £1.76

Sustained release

PoM **Kiditard®** (Delandale)

Capsules, s/r, blue, quinidine bisulphate 250 mg. Net price 20 = £2.43. Label: 25

Dose: 500 mg every 12 hours, adjusted as required

PoM **Kinidin Durules®** (Astra)

Tablets, s/r, f/c, quinidine bisulphate 250 mg. Net price 20 = £2.15. Label: 25

Dose: 500 mg every 12 hours, adjusted as required

VENTRICULAR ARRHYTHMIAS

Bretylium is only used as an anti-arrhythmic drug in resuscitation. It is given both intramuscularly and intravenously but can cause severe hypotension, particularly after intravenous administration; nausea and vomiting can occur with either route. The intravenous route should only be used in emergency when there is doubt about absorption because of inadequate circulation.

Lignocaine is relatively safe when used by slow intravenous injection and should be considered first for emergency use. Though effective in suppressing ventricular tachycardia and reducing the risk of ventricular fibrillation following myocardial infarction, it has not been shown convincingly to reduce mortality when used prophylactically in this condition. In patients with cardiac or hepatic failure doses may need to be reduced to avoid convulsions, depression of the central nervous system, or depression of the cardiovascular system.

Mexiletine may be given as a slow intravenous injection if lignocaine is ineffective; it has a similar action. Adverse cardiovascular and central nervous system effects may limit the dose tolerated; nausea and vomiting may prevent an effective dose being given by mouth.

Phenytoin by slow intravenous injection is sometimes useful in ventricular arrhythmias particularly those caused by cardiac glycosides.

Propafenone is a newer drug in the same general class as lignocaine. It is indicated in the prophylaxis and treatment of ventricular arrhythmias and is undergoing evaluation in some supraventricular arrhythmias. CSM advice on avoidance in obstructive airways disease, see next page.

Tocainide is an analogue of lignocaine; because of a high incidence of blood disorders its use is limited to treatment of life-threatening symptomatic ventricular tachyarrhythmias associated with severely compromised left ventricular function in patients who do not respond to other therapy or for whom other therapy is contra-indicated.

BRETYLIUM TOSYLATE

Indications: ventricular arrhythmias resistant to other treatment

Cautions: do not give noradrenaline or other sympathomimetic amines; may exacerbate ventricular arrhythmias due to cardiac glycosides; **interactions:** Appendix 1 (bretylium)

Contra-indications: phaeochromocytoma

Side-effects: hypotension, nausea and vomiting

Dose: by intramuscular injection, 5 mg/kg repeated after 6–8 hours if necessary

By slow intravenous injection, 5–10 mg/kg over 8–10 minutes with blood pressure and ECG monitoring; may be repeated after 1–2 hours to a total dosage of 30 mg/kg (initial dose being diluted to 10 mg/mL in glucose 5% or sodium chloride intravenous infusion)

Maintenance 5–10 mg/kg *by intramuscular injection* every 6–8 hours *or* 1–2 mg/minute *by intravenous infusion*

PoM **Bretylate®** (Wellcome)

Injection, bretylium tosylate 50 mg/mL. Net price 10-mL amp = £19.81

LIGNOCAINE HYDROCHLORIDE

Indications: ventricular arrhythmias, especially after myocardial infarction

Cautions: lower doses in congestive cardiac failure, in hepatic failure, and following cardiac surgery; **interactions:** Appendix 1 (lignocaine)

Contra-indications: sino-atrial disorders, all grades of atrioventricular block, severe myocardial depression; porphyria

Side-effects: confusion, convulsions

Dose: by intravenous injection, in patients without gross circulatory impairment, 100 mg as a bolus over a few minutes, followed by *infusion* of 2–4 mg/minute

PoM **Lignocaine in Glucose Injection,** lignocaine hydrochloride 0.1% (1 mg/mL) and 0.2% (2 mg/mL) in glucose intravenous infusion 5%. 500-mL containers

Available from Baxter

PoM **Min-I-Jet® Lignocaine** (IMS)

Injection, lignocaine hydrochloride 1% (10 mg/mL), net price 10-mL disposable syringe = £2.89; 2% (20 mg/mL), 5-mL disposable syringe = £2.64

PoM **Select-A-Jet® Lignocaine** (IMS)

Injection, lignocaine hydrochloride 20% (200 mg/mL). To be diluted before use. Net price 5-mL vial = £3.88

PoM **Xylocard®** (Astra)

Injection 100 mg, lignocaine hydrochloride (anhydrous) 20 mg/mL. Net price 5-mL syringe = £1.65

Intravenous infusion, lignocaine hydrochloride (anhydrous) 200 mg/mL. To be diluted before use. Net price 5-mL syringe (1 g) = £2.01; 10-mL syringe (2 g) = £2.35

MEXILETINE HYDROCHLORIDE

Indications: ventricular arrhythmias, especially after myocardial infarction

Cautions: hepatic impairment; close monitoring on initiation of therapy (including ECG, blood pressure, etc.); **interactions:** Appendix 1 (mexiletine)

Contra-indications: bradycardia, heart block

Side-effects: bradycardia, hypotension, confusion, convulsions, psychiatric disorders, dysarthria; nystagmus, tremor; jaundice, hepatitis, and blood disorders reported

Dose: by mouth, initial dose 400 mg (may be increased to 600 mg if opioid analgesics also given), followed after 2 hours by 200–250 mg 3–4 times daily

By intravenous injection, 100–250 mg at a rate of 25 mg/minute with ECG monitoring followed by *infusion* of 250 mg as a 0.1% solution over 1 hour, 125 mg/hour for 2 hours, then 500 micrograms/minute

PoM **Mexitil®** (Boehringer Ingelheim)

Capsules, mexiletine hydrochloride 50 mg (purple/red), net price 20 = 91p; 200 mg (red), 20 = £2.18

Injection, mexiletine hydrochloride 25 mg/mL. Net price 10-mL amp = £1.36

Sustained release

PoM **Mexitil PL®** (Boehringer Ingelheim)

Perlongets® (= capsules, s/r, each enclosing 5 miniature tablets), turquoise/scarlet, mexiletine hydrochloride 360 mg. Net price 56-cap pack = £10.98. Label: 25

Dose: 1 capsule twice daily

PHENYTOIN SODIUM

Indications: arrhythmias, see notes above; for use in epilepsy, see section 4.8.1

Cautions; Contra-indications; Side-effects: see section 4.8.2

Dose: arrhythmias, *by intravenous injection* via caval catheter, 3.5–5 mg/kg at a rate not exceeding 50 mg/minute, with blood pressure and ECG monitoring; repeat once if necessary

Preparations

See section 4.8.2

PROPAFENONE HYDROCHLORIDE

Indications: ventricular arrhythmias

Cautions: heart failure; hepatic and renal impairment; elderly; pacemaker patients; pregnancy; **CSM** advises great caution in obstructive airways disease owing to beta-blocking activity (contra-indicated if severe); **interactions:** Appendix 1 (propafenone)

Contra-indications: uncontrolled congestive heart failure, cardiogenic shock (except arrhythmia induced), severe bradycardia, uncontrolled electrolyte disturbances, severe obstructive pulmonary disease, marked hypotension; myasthenia gravis; unless adequately paced avoid in sinus node dysfunction, atrial conduction defects, second degree or greater atrioventricular block, bundle branch block or distal block

Side-effects: constipation, blurred vision, dry mouth (due to antimuscarinic action); dizziness, nausea and vomiting, fatigue, bitter taste, diarrhoea, headache, and allergic skin reactions reported; postural hypotension, particularly in elderly; bradycardia, sino-atrial, atrioventricular, or intraventricular blocks;

proarrhythmic effect; rarely cholestasis, blood disorders, lupus syndrome, seizures

Dose: 70 kg and over, initially 150 mg 3 times daily after food under direct hospital supervision with ECG monitoring and blood pressure control, increased at intervals of at least 3 days to 300 mg twice daily and, if necessary, to max. 300 mg 3 times daily; under 70 kg, reduce dose ELDERLY may respond to lower doses

▼ PoM **Arythmol®** (Knoll)

Tablets, both f/c, propafenone hydrochloride 150 mg, net price 90-tab pack = £19.98; 300 mg (scored), 60-tab pack = £19.98. Label: 21, 25

TOCAINIDE HYDROCHLORIDE

Indications: ventricular arrhythmias (restricted use—see notes above)

Cautions: weekly blood counts essential for first 12 weeks, then monthly; severe hepatic or renal impairment, uncompensated heart failure, pregnancy (toxicity in *animal* studies); **interactions:** Appendix 1 (tocainide)

Contra-indications: see under Lignocaine Hydrochloride

Side-effects: CNS effects including tremor, dizziness, convulsions, paraesthesia; gastro-intestinal effects including nausea and vomiting; bradycardia and hypotension after injection; rash and fever; lupus erythematosus-like syndrome, fibrosing alveolitis, agranulocytosis, aplastic anaemia, and thrombocytopenia—see also notes above; psychiatric disorders reported

Dose: chronic arrhythmias, *by mouth*, 1.2 g daily in 2–3 divided doses; max. 2.4 g daily

Acute treatment, *by slow intravenous injection or infusion*, 500–750 mg over 15–30 minutes with ECG monitoring, followed immediately by 600–800 mg by mouth.

Maintenance, *by mouth*, 1.2 g daily, in 2–3 divided doses

PoM **Tonocard®** (Astra)

Tablets, both yellow, f/c, tocainide hydrochloride 400 mg, net price 20 = £3.35; 600 mg, 20 = £4.50

Injection, tocainide hydrochloride 50 mg/mL. Net price 15-mL vial = £5.80

2.4 Beta-adrenoceptor blocking drugs

Beta-adrenoceptor blocking drugs (beta-blockers) block the beta-adrenoreceptors in the heart, peripheral vasculature, bronchi, pancreas, and liver.

Many beta-blockers are now available and in general they are all equally effective. There are, however, differences between them which may affect choice in treating particular diseases or individual patients.

Intrinsic sympathomimetic activity (ISA, partial agonist activity) represents the capacity of beta-blockers to stimulate as well as to block adrenergic receptors. Oxprenolol, pindolol, and acebutolol have intrinsic sympathomimetic activity; they tend to cause less bradycardia than the other beta-blockers and may also cause less coldness of the extremities.

Some beta-blockers are lipid soluble and some are water soluble. Atenolol, nadolol, and sotalol are the most water-soluble; they are less likely to enter the brain, and may therefore cause less sleep disturbance and nightmares. Water-soluble beta-blockers are excreted by the kidneys; they accumulate in renal impairment and dosage reduction is therefore often necessary.

Some beta-blockers have a relatively short duration of action and have to be given twice or three times daily. Many of these are, however, available in slow-release formulations so that in general it is not necessary to give beta-blockers more often than once daily for hypertension (for angina twice-daily treatment may sometimes be needed even with a slow-release formulation).

All beta-blockers slow the heart and may induce myocardial depression and precipitate heart failure. They should not therefore be given to patients who have incipient cardiac failure or those with second- or third-degree heart block. Sotalol may prolong the QT interval, and has occasionally caused life-threatening ventricular arrhythmias. Particular care should be taken to avoid hypokalaemia in patients taking sotalol.

Beta-blockers may precipitate asthma and this effect can be dangerous. Some, such as atenolol, betaxolol, metoprolol, and (to a lesser extent) acebutolol, have less effect on the $beta_2$ (bronchial) receptors and are, therefore, relatively cardioselective, but they are not cardiospecific. They have a lesser effect on airways resistance but are not free of this side-effect. Patients who have a tendency towards obstructive airways disease must be treated with great caution and may require to take increased doses of their $beta_2$-stimulants (e.g. salbutamol) to overcome the effect of blockade of the bronchial adrenoceptors.

CSM advice. Beta-blockers, even those with apparent cardioselectivity, should not be used in patients with asthma or a history of obstructive airways disease, unless no alternative treatment is available. In such cases the risk of inducing bronchospasm should be appreciated and appropriate precautions taken.

Beta-blockers may occasionally aggravate intermittent claudication.

Beta-blockers can lead to a small deterioration of glucose tolerance in diabetics; they also interfere with metabolic and autonomic responses to hypoglycaemia. Their use is not contra-indicated in diabetics, but cardioselective beta-blockers may be preferable and they should be avoided altogether in those with frequent episodes of hypoglycaemia.

Labetalol combines alpha- and beta-receptor blocking activity. Alpha-blocking activity in the peripheral vessels lowers peripheral resistance. There is no evidence that labetalol has an important advantage over other beta-blockers as regards reduction of blood pressure. The alpha-blocking properties tend to offset the lack of cardioselectivity of the beta blockade, with the net effect that labetalol and atenolol have roughly similar effects on airways resistance.

HYPERTENSION

Beta-blockers are effective antihypertensive drugs but their mode of action is not understood; they reduce cardiac output, alter baroceptor reflex sensitivity, and block peripheral adrenoceptors. Some beta-blockers depress plasma renin secretion. It is possible that a central effect may also explain their mode of action. Despite the many contra-indications blood pressure can usually be controlled with relatively few side-effects. In general the dose of beta-blocker does not have to be as high as originally thought. The maximum dose of oxprenolol and propranolol necessary is probably 320 mg daily. Atenolol can usually be given in a dose of 50 mg daily and it is only rarely necessary to increase to 100 mg.

Combined thiazide/beta-blocker preparations are now available. These may help compliance with treatment regimens but combined preparations should only be used when blood pressure is uncontrolled by thiazide or beta-blocker alone. Beta-blockers reduce, but do not abolish, the tendency for diuretics to cause hypokalaemia.

Beta-blockers can be used to control the pulse rate in patients with *phaeochromocytoma.* However, they should never be used alone as beta-blockade without concurrent alpha-blockade may lead to a hypertensive crisis. For this reason phenoxybenzamine should always be used together with the beta-blocker.

ANGINA

Beta-blockers improve exercise tolerance and relieve symptoms in patients with angina; this effect is caused by their reduction of cardiac work. As with hypertension there is no good evidence of the superiority of any one drug, although occasionally a patient will respond better to one beta-blocker than to another. There is some evidence that sudden withdrawal may cause an exacerbation of angina therefore gradual reduction of dose is preferable when beta-blockers are to be stopped. There is a risk of precipitating heart failure when beta-blockers and verapamil are used together in established ischaemic heart disease (**important**: see section 2.3.2).

MYOCARDIAL INFARCTION

Several studies have now shown that some beta-blockers can cause a reduction in the recurrence rate of myocardial infarction. However, pre-existing heart failure, hypotension, bradyarrhythmias, and obstructive airways disease render this group of drugs unsuitable in some patients who have recovered from a myocardial infarction. Atenolol and metoprolol may reduce early mortality after intravenous and subsequent oral administration in the acute phase, while timolol and propranolol have protective value when started in the early convalescent phase. Acebutolol may also be useful in patients judged to be at high risk. The evidence relating to other beta-blockers is less convincing; some have not been tested in trials of secondary protection. It is also not known whether the protective effect of beta-blockers continues after two years; it is possible that sudden cessation may cause a rebound worsening of myocardial ischaemia.

ARRHYTHMIAS

Beta-blockers are used to control supraventricular tachycardia following myocardial infarction, see above.

THYROTOXICOSIS

Beta-blockers are used in pre-operative preparation for thyroidectomy. Administration of propranolol can reverse clinical features of thyrotoxicosis within 4 days. Routine tests of increased thyroid function remain unaltered. The thyroid gland is rendered less vascular thus making surgery easier (see section 6.2.2).

OTHER USES

Beta-blockers have been used to alleviate some symptoms of anxiety; probably patients with palpitations, tremor, and tachycardia respond best. (See also sections 4.1.2 and 4.9.3.) Beta-blockers are also used in the prophylaxis of migraine (section 4.7.4.2). Beta-blockers are used topically in the management of glaucoma (section 11.6).

PROPRANOLOL HYDROCHLORIDE

Indications: see under Dose

Cautions: late pregnancy and breast-feeding (see also Appendices 4 and 5); avoid abrupt withdrawal in angina; reduce oral dose of propranolol in liver disease; liver function deteriorates in portal hypertension; reduce initial dose in renal impairment; diabetes; myasthenia gravis; see also notes above; **interactions:** Appendix 1 (beta-blockers), **important:** verapamil interaction, see also section 2.3.2

Contra-indications: asthma or history of obstructive airways disease (see CSM advice on previous page), heart failure, second or third degree heart block, cardiogenic shock, after prolonged fasting, metabolic acidosis

Side-effects: bradycardia, heart failure, bronchospasm, peripheral vasoconstriction, gastro-intestinal disturbances, fatigue, sleep disturbances; rare reports of rashes and dry eyes (reversible on withdrawal)

Dose: *by mouth*, hypertension, initially 80 mg twice daily, increased at weekly intervals as required; maintenance 160–320 mg daily

Portal hypertension, initially 40 mg twice daily, increased to 80 mg twice daily according to heart-rate; max. 160 mg twice daily

Phaeochromocytoma (only with an alpha-blocker), 60 mg daily for 3 days before surgery; 30 mg daily in patients unsuitable for surgery
Angina, initially 40 mg 2–3 times daily; maintenance 120–240 mg daily
Arrhythmias, hypertrophic obstructive cardiomyopathy, anxiety tachycardia, and thyrotoxicosis, 10–40 mg 3–4 times daily
Prophylaxis after infarction, 40 mg 4 times daily for 2–3 days, then 80 mg twice daily, beginning 5 to 21 days after infarction
Migraine prophylaxis and essential tremor, initially 40 mg 2–3 times daily; maintenance 80–160 mg daily
By intravenous injection, arrhythmias and thyrotoxic crisis, 1 mg over 1 minute; if necessary repeat at 2-minute intervals; max. 10 mg (5 mg in anaesthesia)
Note. Excessive bradycardia can be countered with intravenous injection of atropine 0.6–2.4 mg in divided doses of 600 micrograms

PoM **Propranolol** (Non-proprietary)
Tablets, propranolol hydrochloride 10 mg, net price 20 = 5p; 40 mg, 20 = 8p; 80 mg, 20 = 15p; 160 mg, 20 = 26p. Label: 8
Available from APS (Apsolol®), Berk (Berkolol®), Cox, CP (Cardinol®), DDSA (Angilol®), Evans, Kerfoot
Oral suspensions, propranolol hydrochloride 5 mg/5 mL and 50 mg/5 mL available from RP Drugs (special order)
PoM **Inderal®** (ICI)
Tablets, all pink, f/c, propranolol hydrochloride 10 mg, net price 20 = 20p; 40 mg, 20 = 54p; 80 mg, 20 = 88p; 160 mg, 20 = £1.56. Label: 8
Injection, propranolol hydrochloride 1 mg/mL, net price 1-mL amp = 24p

Sustained release
PoM **Bedranol S.R.®** (Lagap)
Capsules, s/r, white/pink, propranolol hydrochloride 160 mg. Net price 20 = £5.24. Label: 8, 25
PoM **Half-Inderal LA®** (ICI)
Capsules, s/r, lavender/pink, propranolol hydrochloride 80 mg. Net price 28-cap pack = £5.04. Label: 8, 25
PoM **Inderal-LA®** (ICI)
Capsules, s/r, lavender/pink, propranolol hydrochloride 160 mg. Net price 28-cap pack = £7.49. Label: 8, 25
PoM **Sloprolol®** (CP)
Capsules, s/r, green/clear enclosing off-white pellets, propranolol hydrochloride 160 mg. Net price 20 = £3.65. Label: 8, 25

With diuretic
PoM **Inderetic®** (ICI)
Capsules, propranolol hydrochloride 80 mg, bendrofluazide 2.5 mg. Net price 20 = £2.19. Label: 8
Dose: hypertension, 1 capsule twice daily
PoM **Inderex®** (ICI)
Capsules, pink/grey, propranolol hydrochloride 160 mg (s/r), bendrofluazide 5 mg. Net price28-cap pack = £8.37. Label: 8, 25
Dose: hypertension, 1 capsule daily

ACEBUTOLOL

Indications: see under Dose
Cautions; Contra-indications; Side-effects: see under Propranolol Hydrochloride
Dose: hypertension, initially 400 mg once daily *or* 200 mg twice daily, increased after 2 weeks to 400 mg twice daily if necessary
Angina, initially 400 mg once daily *or* 200 mg twice daily; 300 mg 3 times daily in severe angina; up to 1.2 g daily has been used
Arrhythmias, 0.4–1.2 g daily in 2–3 divided doses

PoM **Sectral®** (Rhône-Poulenc Rorer)
Capsules, acebutolol (as hydrochloride) 100 mg (buff/white), net price 84-cap pack = £7.14; 200 mg (buff/pink), 56-cap pack = £9.16. Label: 8
Tablets, f/c, acebutolol 400 mg (as hydrochloride). Net price 28 tab = £8.88. Label: 8

With diuretic
PoM **Secadrex®** (Rhône-Poulenc Rorer)
Tablets, f/c, acebutolol 200 mg (as hydrochloride), hydrochlorothiazide 12.5 mg. Net price 28-tab pack = £8.39. Label: 8
Dose: hypertension, 1 tablet daily, increased to 2 daily as a single dose if necessary

ATENOLOL

Indications: see under Dose
Cautions; Contra-indications; Side-effects: see under Propranolol Hydrochloride; reduce dose in renal impairment (25-mg tablets available)
Dose: *by mouth*, hypertension, 50–100 mg daily
Angina, 100 mg daily in 1 or 2 doses
Arrhythmias, 50–100 mg daily
By intravenous injection, arrhythmias, 2.5 mg at a rate of 1 mg/minute, repeated at 5-minute intervals to a max. of 10 mg
Note. Excessive bradycardia can be countered with intravenous injection of atropine 0.6–2.4 mg in divided doses of 600 micrograms
By intravenous infusion, 150 micrograms/kg over 20 minutes, repeated every 12 hours if required
Early intervention within 12 hours of infarction, 5–10 mg *by slow intravenous injection*, then *by mouth* 50 mg after 15 minutes, 50 mg after 12 hours, then 100 mg daily

PoM **Atenolol** (Non-proprietary)
Tablets, atenolol 50 mg, net price 28-tab pack = £4.77; 100 mg, 28-tab pack = £6.74. Label: 8
Available from APS, Berk (Antipressan®), Cox, CP (Totamol®), Evans, Kerfoot, Shire (Vasaten®)
PoM **Tenormin®** (Stuart)
'25' tablets, f/c, atenolol 25 mg. Net price 28-tab pack = £4.31. Label: 8
LS tablets, orange, f/c, scored, atenolol 50 mg. Net price 28-tab pack = £5.49. Label: 8
Tablets, orange, f/c, scored, atenolol 100 mg. Net price 28-tab pack = £6.98. Label: 8
Syrup, sugar-free, atenolol 25 mg/5 mL. Net price 300 mL = £8.35. Label: 8
Injection, atenolol 500 micrograms/mL. Net price 10-mL amp = 90p (hosp. only)

With diuretic

PoM **Co-tenidone** (Non-proprietary)

Tablets, co-tenidone 50/12.5 (atenolol 50 mg, chlorthalidone 12.5 mg), net price 28-tab pack = £5.27; co-tenidone 100/25 (atenolol 100 mg, chlorthalidone 25 mg), 28-tab pack = £7.50. Label: 8

Available from Kerfoot

Dose: hypertension, 1 tablet daily

PoM **Kalten®** (Stuart)

Capsules, red/ivory, atenolol 50 mg, co-amilozide 2.5/25 (anhydrous amiloride hydrochloride 2.5 mg, hydrochlorothiazide 25 mg). Net price 28-cap pack = £7.49. Label: 8

Dose: hypertension, 1 capsule daily

PoM **Tenoret 50®** (Stuart)

Tablets, brown, f/c, co-tenidone 50/12.5 (atenolol 50 mg, chlorthalidone 12.5 mg). Net price 28-tab pack = £5.85. Label: 8

Dose: hypertension, 1 tablet daily

PoM **Tenoretic®** (Stuart)

Tablets, brown, f/c, co-tenidone 100/25 (atenolol 100 mg, chlorthalidone 25 mg). Net price 28-tab pack = £8.33. Label: 8

Dose: hypertension, 1 tablet daily

With calcium-channel blocker

Note. Only indicated when calcium-channel blocker or beta-blocker alone proves inadequate

PoM **Beta-Adalat®** (Bayer)

Capsules, reddish-brown, atenolol 50 mg, nifedipine 20 mg (s/r). Net price 28-cap pack = £10.90. Label: 8, 25

Dose: hypertension, 1 capsule daily, increased if necessary to twice daily; elderly, 1 daily

Angina, 1 capsule twice daily

PoM **Tenif®** (Stuart)

Capsules, reddish-brown, atenolol 50 mg, nifedipine 20 mg (s/r). Net price 28-cap pack = £10.90. Label: 8, 25

Dose: hypertension, 1 capsule daily, increased if necessary to twice daily; elderly, 1 daily

Angina, 1 capsule twice daily

BETAXOLOL HYDROCHLORIDE

Indications: hypertension

Cautions; Contra-indications; Side-effects: see under Propranolol Hydrochloride; reduce dose in renal impairment

Dose: 20 mg daily (elderly patients 10 mg), increased to 40 mg if required

PoM **Kerlone®** (Lorex)

Tablets, f/c, scored, betaxolol hydrochloride 20 mg. Net price 28-tab pack = £7.70. Label: 8

BISOPROLOL FUMARATE

Indications: hypertension, angina

Cautions; Contra-indications; Side-effects: see under Propranolol Hydrochloride; reduce dose in hepatic and renal impairment

Dose: usual dose 10 mg daily (5 mg may be adequate in some patients); max. recommended dose 20 mg daily

PoM **Emcor®** (Merck)

LS Tablets, yellow, f/c, scored, bisoprolol fumarate 5 mg. Net price 28-tab pack = £7.98. Label: 8

Tablets, orange, f/c, scored, bisoprolol fumarate 10 mg. Net price 28-tab pack = £8.96. Label: 8

PoM **Monocor®** (Cyanamid)

Tablets, both f/c, bisoprolol fumarate 5 mg (pink), net price 28-tab pack = £7.98; 10 mg, 28-tab pack = £8.96. Label: 8

CARTEOLOL HYDROCHLORIDE

Indications: angina

Cautions; Contra-indications; Side-effects: see under Propranolol Hydrochloride

Dose: 10 mg daily; if necessary increased gradually to 30 mg daily

▼ PoM **Cartrol®** (Sanofi)

Tablets, carteolol hydrochloride 10 mg. Net price 28-tab pack = £5.60. Label: 8

LABETALOL HYDROCHLORIDE

Indications: hypertension (including hypertension in pregnancy, hypertension with angina, and hypertension following acute myocardial infarction); hypertensive crisis; controlled hypotension in surgery

Cautions: late pregnancy, breast-feeding; avoid abrupt withdrawal; reduce oral dose in liver disease; interferes with laboratory tests for catecholamines; **interactions:** Appendix 1 (beta-blockers)

Contra-indications: as for Propranolol Hydrochloride

Side-effects: postural hypotension, tiredness, weakness, headache, rashes, scalp tingling, difficulty in micturition, epigastric pain, nausea, vomiting; rarely lichenoid rash

Dose: *by mouth*, initially 100 mg (50 mg in elderly) twice daily with food, increased at intervals of 14 days to usual dose of 200 mg twice daily; up to 800 mg daily in 2 divided doses (3–4 divided doses if higher); max. 2.4 g daily

By intravenous injection, 50 mg over 1 minute, repeated after 5 minutes if necessary; max. 200 mg

Note. Excessive bradycardia can be countered with intravenous injection of atropine 0.6–2.4 mg in divided doses of 600 micrograms

By intravenous infusion, 2 mg/minute to a max. of 200 mg

Hypertension of pregnancy, 20 mg/hour, doubled every 30 minutes; max. 160 mg/hour

Hypertension following infarction, 15 mg/hour, gradually increased to max. 120 mg/hour

PoM **Labetalol Hydrochloride** (Non-proprietary)

Tablets, all f/c, labetalol hydrochloride 100 mg, net price 20 = £1.43; 200 mg, 20 = £2.27; 400 mg, 20 = £3.58. Label: 8, 21

Available from APS, Cox, Evans, Kerfoot, Lagap (Labrocol®)

PoM **Trandate**® (DF)
Tablets, all orange, f/c, labetalol hydrochloride 50 mg, net price 56-tab pack = £5.05; 100 mg, 56-tab pack = £5.56; 200 mg, 56-tab pack = £9.02; 400 mg, 20 = £4.26. Label: 8, 21
Injection, labetalol hydrochloride 5 mg/mL. Net price 20-mL amp = £2.83

METOPROLOL TARTRATE

Indications: see under Dose
Cautions; Contra-indications; Side-effects: see under Propranolol Hydrochloride. Reduce dose in hepatic and renal impairment
Dose: *by mouth*, hypertension, initially 100 mg daily, maintenance 100–400 mg daily in 1–2 doses
Angina, 50–100 mg 2–3 times daily
Arrhythmias, usually 50 mg 2–3 times daily; up to 300 mg daily in divided doses if necessary
Migraine prophylaxis, 100–200 mg daily in divided doses
Thyrotoxicosis, 50 mg 4 times daily
By intravenous injection, up to 5 mg at rate 1–2 mg/minute, repeated after 5 minutes if necessary, total dose 10–15 mg
Note. Excessive bradycardia can be countered with intravenous injection of atropine 0.6–2.4 mg in divided doses of 600 micrograms
In surgery, 2–4 mg *by slow intravenous injection* at induction or to control arrhythmias developing during anaesthesia; 2-mg doses may be repeated to a max. of 10 mg
Early intervention within 12 hours of infarction, 5 mg *by intravenous injection* every 2 minutes to a max. of 15 mg, followed after 15 minutes by 50 mg *by mouth* every 6 hours for 48 hours; maintenance 200 mg daily

PoM **Metoprolol Tartrate** (Non-proprietary)
Tablets, metoprolol tartrate 50 mg, net price 20 = 94p; 100 mg, 20 = £1.75. Label: 8
Available from APS, Cox, Kerfoot

PoM **Betaloc**® (Astra)
Tablets, both scored, metoprolol tartrate 50 mg, net price 20 = 92p, 56-tab pack = £2.90; 100 mg, 20 = £1.71. Label: 8
Injection, metoprolol tartrate 1 mg/mL. Net price 5-mL amp = 45p

PoM **Lopresor**® (Geigy)
Tablets, both f/c, scored, metoprolol tartrate 50 mg (pink), net price 20 = £1.16; 100 mg (blue), 56-tab pack = £6.06. Label: 8

Sustained release

PoM **Betaloc-SA**® (Astra)
Durules® (= tablets, s/r), metoprolol tartrate 200 mg. Net price 28-tab pack = £6.51. Label: 8, 25
Dose: 200–400 mg daily

PoM **Lopresor SR**® (Geigy)
Tablets, s/r, yellow, f/c, metoprolol tartrate 200 mg. Net price 28-tab pack = £7.42. Label: 8, 25
Dose: 200–400 mg daily

With diuretic

PoM **Co-Betaloc**® (Astra)
Tablets, scored, metoprolol tartrate 100 mg, hydrochlorothiazide 12.5 mg. Net price 28-tab pack = £6.65. Label: 8
Dose: hypertension, 1–3 tablets daily in single or divided doses

PoM **Co-Betaloc SA**® (Astra)
Tablets, yellow, f/c, metoprolol tartrate 200 mg (s/r), hydrochlorothiazide 25 mg. Net price 28-tab pack = £8.20. Label: 8, 25
Dose: hypertension, 1 tablet daily

PoM **Lopresoretic**® (Geigy)
Tablets, f/c, scored, metoprolol tartrate 100 mg, chlorthalidone 12.5 mg. Net price 56-tab pack = £7.47. Label: 8
Dose: hypertension, 1–2 tablets in the morning; max. 3–4 daily in single or divided doses

NADOLOL

Indications: see under Dose
Cautions; Contra-indications; Side-effects: see under Propranolol Hydrochloride; reduce dose in renal impairment
Dose: hypertension, 80 mg daily, increased at weekly intervals if required; max. 240 mg daily
Angina, 40 mg daily, increased at weekly intervals if required; usual max. 160 mg daily
Arrhythmias, initially 40 mg daily, increased to 160 mg if required; reduce to 40 mg if bradycardia occurs
Migraine prophylaxis, initially 40 mg daily, increased by 40 mg at weekly intervals; usual maintenance dose 80–160 mg daily
Thyrotoxicosis, 80–160 mg daily

PoM **Corgard**® (Squibb)
Tablets, both blue, nadolol 40 mg, net price 28-tab pack = £5.22; 80 mg, 28-tab pack = £7.55. Label: 8

With diuretic

PoM **Corgaretic 40**® (Squibb)
Tablets, scored, nadolol 40 mg, bendrofluazide 5 mg. Net price 28-tab pack = £6.07. Label: 8
Dose: hypertension, 1–2 tablets daily

PoM **Corgaretic 80**® (Squibb)
Tablets, scored, nadolol 80 mg, bendrofluazide 5 mg. Net price 28-tab pack = £8.69. Label: 8
Dose: hypertension, 1–2 tablets daily

OXPRENOLOL HYDROCHLORIDE

Indications: see under Dose
Cautions; Contra-indications; Side-effects: see under Propranolol Hydrochloride
Dose: hypertension, initially 80 mg twice daily, increased as required at weekly intervals; max. 480 mg daily
Angina, 40–160 mg 3 times daily
Arrhythmias, initially 20–40 mg 3 times daily, increased as necessary
Anxiety symptoms (short-term use), initially 40 mg twice daily, increased if necessary to 160 mg daily in divided doses

PoM **Oxprenolol** (Non-proprietary)
Tablets, all coated, oxprenolol hydrochloride 20 mg, net price 20 = 30p; 40 mg, 20 = 43p; 80 mg, 20 = 71p; 160 mg, 20 = £1.38. Label: 8
Available from APS (Apsolox®, 80-mg tablets contain tartrazine), Cox, Evans, Kerfoot

PoM **Trasicor®** (Ciba)
Tablets, all f/c, oxprenolol hydrochloride 20 mg (contain gluten), net price 20 = 58p; 40 mg (contain gluten), 20 = 96p; 80 mg (beige), 20 = £1.46; 160 mg (orange), 20 = £2.64. Label: 8

Sustained release
PoM **Slow-Pren®** (Norton)
Tablets, s/r, f/c, oxprenolol hydrochloride 160 mg. Net price 28-tab pack = £6.10. Label: 8, 25
Dose: 160–480 mg daily

PoM **Slow-Trasicor®** (Ciba)
Tablets, s/r, f/c, oxprenolol hydrochloride 160 mg. Net price 28-tab pack = £6.50. Label: 8, 25
Dose: 160–480 mg daily

With diuretic
PoM **Trasidrex®** (Ciba)
Tablets, red, s/c, co-prenozide 160/0.25 (oxprenolol hydrochloride 160 mg (s/r), cyclopenthiazide 250 micrograms). Net price 28-tab pack = £6.73. Label: 8
Dose: hypertension, 1 tablet daily, increased to 2 daily as a single dose if necessary

PENBUTOLOL SULPHATE

Indications: hypertension
Cautions; Contra-indications; Side-effects: see under Propranolol Hydrochloride
Dose: see below

With diuretic
PoM **Lasipressin®** (Hoechst)
Tablets, yellow-white, f/c, scored, penbutolol sulphate 40 mg, frusemide 20 mg. Net price 30-tab pack = £8.49. Label: 8
Dose: hypertension, 1 tablet daily, increased to twice daily if necessary

PINDOLOL

Indications: see under Dose
Cautions; Contra-indications; Side-effects: see under Propranolol Hydrochloride; reduce dose in renal impairment
Dose: hypertension, initially 5 mg 2–3 times daily *or* 15 mg once daily, increased as required at weekly intervals; max. 45 mg daily
Angina, 2.5–5 mg up to 3 times daily

PoM **Visken®** (Sandoz)
Tablets, both scored, pindolol 5 mg, net price 100-tab pack = £7.46; 15 mg, 30-tab pack = £6.71. Label: 8

With diuretic
PoM **Viskaldix®** (Sandoz)
Tablets, scored, pindolol 10 mg, clopamide 5 mg. Net price 28-tab pack = £5.72. Label: 8
Dose: hypertension, 1 tablet daily in the morning, increased to 2 daily if necessary; max. 3 daily

SOTALOL HYDROCHLORIDE

Indications: see under Dose
Cautions; Contra-indications; Side-effects: see under Propranolol Hydrochloride; reduce dose in renal impairment; occasionally causes atypical ventricular arrhythmias (torsade de pointes)—special need to avoid hypokalaemia (stop if severe or persistent diarrhoea etc.)
Dose: *by mouth*, hypertension and angina, initially 80 mg twice daily *or* 160 mg once daily; maintenance 160 mg daily, increased to 400–600 mg daily if necessary
Arrhythmias, 120–240 mg daily in single or divided doses
Thyrotoxicosis, 120–240 mg daily in single or divided doses
Prophylaxis after infarction, 320 mg daily, starting 5–14 days after infarction
By slow intravenous injection, 20–60 mg over 2–3 minutes with ECG monitoring, repeated if necessary with 10-minute intervals between injections; up to 100 mg over 3 minutes or longer
Note. Excessive bradycardia can be countered with intravenous injection of atropine 0.6–2.4 mg in divided doses of 600 micrograms

PoM **Beta-Cardone®** (DF)
Tablets, all scored, sotalol hydrochloride 40 mg (green), net price 20 = 79p; 80 mg (pink), 20 = £1.17; 200 mg, 30-tab pack = £4.15. Label: 8

PoM **Sotacor®** (Bristol-Myers)
Tablets, sotalol hydrochloride 80 mg (pink), net price 28-tab pack = £2.05; 160 mg (blue), 28-tab pack = £4.05. Label: 8
Injection, sotalol hydrochloride 10 mg/mL. Net price 4-mL amp = £1.76

With diuretic
PoM **Sotazide®** (Bristol-Myers)
Tablets, blue, sotalol hydrochloride 160 mg, hydrochlorothiazide 25 mg. Net price 28-tab pack = £7.12. Label: 8
Dose: hypertension, 1 tablet daily, increased to 2 daily if necessary

PoM **Tolerzide®** (Bristol-Myers)
Tablets, lilac, sotalol hydrochloride 80 mg, hydrochlorothiazide 12.5 mg. Net price 28-tab pack = £4.05. Label: 8
Dose: hypertension, 1 tablet daily

TIMOLOL MALEATE

Indications: see under Dose
Cautions; Contra-indications; Side-effects: see under Propranolol Hydrochloride
Dose: hypertension, initially 5 mg twice daily *or* 10 mg once daily; max. 60 mg daily

Angina, initially 5 mg 2–3 times daily, maintenance 15–45 mg daily
Prophylaxis after infarction, initially 5 mg twice daily, increased after 2 days to 10 mg twice daily, starting 7 to 28 days after infarction
Migraine prophylaxis, 10–20 mg daily

PoM **Betim®** (Leo)
Tablets, scored, timolol maleate 10 mg. Net price 20 = £1.75. Label: 8

PoM **Blocadren®** (MSD)
Tablets, blue, scored, timolol maleate 10 mg. Net price 20 = £2.12. Label: 8

With diuretic

PoM **Moducren®** (Morson)
Tablets, blue, scored, timolol maleate 10 mg, co-amilozide 2.5/25 (amiloride hydrochloride 2.5 mg, hydrochlorothiazide 25 mg). Net price 28-tab pack = £8.00. Label: 8
Dose: hypertension, 1–2 tablets daily as a single dose

PoM **Prestim®** (Leo)
Tablets, scored, timolol maleate 10 mg, bendrofluazide 2.5 mg. Net price 20 = £2.79. Label: 8
Dose: hypertension, 1–2 tablets daily; max. 4 daily

PoM **Prestim Forte®** (Leo)
Tablets, scored, timolol maleate 20 mg, bendrofluazide 5 mg. Net price 20 = £5.88. Label: 8
Dose: hypertension, ½–2 tablets daily in single or divided doses

2.5 Antihypertensive therapy

Antihypertensive therapy has improved the outlook for patients with high blood pressure by decreasing the frequency of stroke, heart failure, and renal failure. The recommendations of the British Hypertension Society are that, in general, patients whose diastolic pressure averages 110 mmHg or higher when measured on three separate occasions, or 100 to 109 mmHg when measured repeatedly over 4 to 6 months, should receive antihypertensive therapy. Below that level the benefits of therapy are unproven. The usual aim should be to reduce the diastolic blood pressure preferably to below 90 mmHg and certainly below 100 mmHg. The quality of control of blood pressure at follow-up is an important predictor of outcome, and efficient long-term care is necessary.

Malignant (or accelerated) hypertension or very severe hypertension (diastolic blood pressure >140 mmHg) requires urgent treatment in hospital but is not an indication for parenteral antihypertensive therapy. Normally treatment should be by mouth with a beta-blocker (atenolol or labetalol) or a calcium-channel blocker (nifedipine). Within the first 24 hours the diastolic blood pressure should be reduced to 100–110 mmHg. Over the next two or three days blood pressure should be normalised by using beta-blockers, calcium-channel blockers, diuretics, vasodilators, or angiotensin-converting enzyme inhibitors. Very rapid falls in blood pressure can cause reduced cerebral perfusion leading to cerebral infarction, a reduction in renal perfusion causing a deterioration in renal function, and myocardial ischaemia. Parenteral antihypertensive drugs are, therefore, hardly ever necessary.

Sodium nitroprusside by infusion is the parenteral antihypertensive drug of choice. Small doses of diazoxide by slow intravenous injection, labetalol by infusion, or hydralazine by slow intravenous injection may also be used, but again precipitate falls in blood pressure should be carefully avoided.

In moderate to severe hypertension (diastolic blood pressure >110 mmHg) or in patients with vascular complications, antihypertensive drugs are best added 'stepwise' until control has been achieved; an attempt can then be made to 'step down' treatment under supervision. In mild uncomplicated hypertension (diastolic blood pressure <110 mmHg), drugs may be substituted rather than added. The strategy for reducing blood pressure is probably best as follows:

1. *Non-drug treatment*—obesity, high alcohol intake, and high salt intake may elevate blood pressure and these should be corrected.
2. *Diuretic therapy*—any thiazide will be effective, e.g. bendrofluazide 2.5 mg/day (section 2.2.1). The optimum dose of a thiazide used to treat hypertension is the lowest possible dose; higher doses do not have a major additional anti-hypertensive effect, but do cause more metabolic side-effects. Potassium supplements are seldom necessary but plasma potassium concentration should be checked 3 to 4 weeks after starting treatment. Potassium-sparing diuretics (amiloride or triamterene) are usually not necessary in the routine treatment of hypertension, unless hypokalaemia develops.
3. *Beta-adrenoceptor blocking drugs* (section 2.4) should be used in combination with a thiazide where they are not effective alone.

4(a). *Calcium-channel blockers*—nifedipine, nicardipine, and verapamil have antihypertensive efficacy broadly similar to that of thiazides or beta-blockers. Minor side-effects are more common, and their safety during long-term treatment is less well established; they should therefore be considered for hypertension only when thiazides and beta-blockers are contra-indicated, not tolerated, or fail to control blood pressure. There are important differences between verapamil and the dihydropyridine calcium-channel blockers, nifedipine and nicardipine (see section 2.6.2).

4(b). *ACE inhibitors* (section 2.5.5)—all ACE inhibitors may cause a precipitate drop in blood

pressure in patients with renal impairment and/or receiving diuretic therapy; they should be given in low initial doses and where possible diuretic therapy should be omitted for a few days before starting. About 20% of women and 10% of men receiving an ACE inhibitor develop a persistent dry cough.
5. *Other drugs*—Vasodilators (hydralazine, minoxidil, diazoxide), alpha-adrenoceptor blocking drugs (prazosin, terazosin, doxazosin), and centrally acting drugs (methyldopa, reserpine) are generally reserved for patients whose blood pressure is not controlled by, or who have contra-indications to, the drugs already mentioned.

SYSTOLIC HYPERTENSION. High systolic blood pressure carries a poor prognosis. This may be because the height of the systolic blood pressure reflects evidence of end-organ damage caused by the hypertension itself. The quality of control of systolic blood pressure may have some importance in determining the outcome in patients with antihypertensive treatment.

HYPERTENSION IN PREGNANCY. It is important to control blood pressure in pregnancy. High blood pressure may be due to pre-existing essential hypertension or to pre-eclampsia. Oral methyldopa or atenolol or labetalol are safe in pregnancy. Hydralazine by mouth is useful as second-line therapy; intravenous injection can be used to control hypertensive crises associated with *eclampsia*.

HYPERTENSION IN THE ELDERLY. There is evidence that treating hypertension in patients up to the age of 80 years is worthwhile provided treatment is carefully supervised. Little or no benefit has been shown in those over 80.

2.5.1 Vasodilator antihypertensive drugs

These are potent drugs, especially when used in combination with a beta-blocker and a thiazide.

Diazoxide is diabetogenic and is not used by mouth, except in very severe hypertension; it can be used by intravenous injection in hypertensive emergencies.

Hydralazine given by mouth is a useful adjunct to other treatment, but when used alone causes tachycardia and fluid retention. Side-effects can be few if the dose is kept below 100 mg daily.

Sodium nitroprusside is given by intravenous infusion to control severe hypertensive crises.

Minoxidil should be reserved for the treatment of severe hypertension resistant to other drugs. Vasodilatation is accompanied by increased cardiac output and tachycardia and the patients develop fluid retention. For this reason a beta-blocker and a diuretic (usually frusemide, in high dosage) are mandatory. Hypertrichosis is troublesome and renders this drug unsuitable for women.

Prazosin and terazosin (section 2.5.4) have alpha-blocking and vasodilator properties.

DIAZOXIDE

Indications: hypertensive crisis (but see section 2.5); hypoglycaemia, section 6.1.4

Cautions: ischaemic heart disease, pregnancy, labour, impaired renal function; **interactions:** Appendix 1 (diazoxide)

Side-effects: tachycardia, hyperglycaemia, fluid retention

Dose: *by rapid intravenous injection* (less than 30 seconds), 1–3 mg/kg to max. single dose of 150 mg (see below); may be repeated after 5–15 minutes if required

Note. Single doses of 300 mg have been associated with angina and with myocardial and cerebral infarction

PoM **Eudemine**® (A&H)
Injection, diazoxide 15 mg/mL. Net price 20-mL amp = £2.70

HYDRALAZINE HYDROCHLORIDE

Indications: moderate to severe hypertension, with beta-blocker and thiazide; hypertensive crisis (but see section 2.5)

Cautions: reduce initial dose in renal impairment; coronary artery disease, cerebrovascular disease; over-rapid blood pressure reduction is occasionally encountered even with low parenteral doses; pregnancy, breast-feeding; **interactions:** Appendix 1 (hydralazine)

Contra-indications: idiopathic systemic lupus erythematosus, severe tachycardia, high output heart failure, myocardial insufficiency due to mechanical obstruction, cor pulmonale, dissecting aortic aneurysm; porphyria

Side-effects: tachycardia, fluid retention, nausea, and vomiting; systemic lupus erythematosus-like syndrome after long-term therapy with over 100 mg daily (or less in women)

Dose: *by mouth*, 25 mg twice daily, increased to a max. of 50 mg twice daily (see notes above)

By slow intravenous injection, 5–10 mg over 20 minutes; may be repeated after 20–30 minutes (see Cautions)

By intravenous infusion, initially 200–300 micrograms/minute; maintenance usually 50–150 micrograms/minute

PoM **Hydralazine** (Non-proprietary)
Tablets, hydralazine hydrochloride 25 mg, net price 20 = 27p; 50 mg, 20 = 55p

PoM **Apresoline**® (Ciba)
Tablets, both s/c, hydralazine hydrochloride 25 mg (yellow), net price 20 = 36p; 50 mg (violet), 20 = 70p
Additives: include gluten, azo dye (50-mg tabs)
Injection, powder for reconstitution, hydralazine hydrochloride. Net price 20-mg amp = 32p

MINOXIDIL

Indications: severe hypertension, in addition to a diuretic and a beta-blocker

Cautions: see notes above; lower doses in dialysis patients; pregnancy; **interactions:** Appendix 1 (minoxidil)

Contra-indications: phaeochromocytoma; porphyria

Side-effects: weight gain, peripheral oedema, tachycardia, hypertrichosis; occasionally, gastro-intestinal disturbances, breast tenderness, rashes
Dose: initially 5 mg daily, in 1–2 doses, increased by 5–10 mg every 3 or more days; max. usually 50 mg daily

PoM **Loniten®** (Upjohn)
Tablets, all scored, minoxidil 2.5 mg, net price 20 = £2.47; 5 mg, 20 = £4.40; 10 mg, 20 = £8.52

SODIUM NITROPRUSSIDE

Indications: hypertensive crisis (but see section 2.5); controlled hypotension in surgery; acute or chronic heart failure
Cautions: hypothyroidism, severe renal impairment, impaired cerebral circulation, elderly patients; monitor plasma-cyanide concentration; **interactions:** Appendix 1 (nitroprusside)
Contra-indications: severe hepatic impairment; vitamin B_{12} deficiency; Leber's optic atrophy; compensatory hypertension
Side-effects: headache, dizziness, nausea, retching, abdominal pain, perspiration, palpitations, apprehension, retrosternal discomfort—reduce infusion rate
Dose: hypertensive crisis, in patients not already receiving antihypertensives, *by intravenous infusion*, 0.3–1 micrograms/kg/minute initially, then adjusted; usual range 0.5–6 micrograms/kg/minute (usual range 20–400 micrograms/minute; max. 8 micrograms/kg/minute); lower doses for patients already being treated with antihypertensives
Lower doses should also be employed for controlled hypotension in surgery (max. 1.5 micrograms/kg/minute)
Heart failure, *by intravenous infusion*, initially 10–15 micrograms/minute, increased every 5–10 minutes as necessary; usual range 10–200 micrograms/minute; max. 400 micrograms/minute (6 micrograms/kg/minute)

PoM **Sodium Nitroprusside** (Non-proprietary)
Intravenous solution, sodium nitroprusside 10 mg/mL. For dilution and use as an infusion. Net price 5-mL vial = £3.65
PoM **Nipride®** (Roche)
Infusion, sodium nitroprusside 50-mg amp (with solvent for reconstitution). Net price = £4.00

2.5.2 Centrally acting antihypertensive drugs

This group includes methyldopa and clonidine and is largely falling from use.

Methyldopa, however, has the advantage of being safe in asthmatics, in heart failure, and in pregnancy. Side-effects are minimised if the daily dose is kept below 1 g.

Clonidine has the disadvantage that sudden withdrawal may cause a hypertensive crisis. Reserpine and rauwolfia are not used much in Britain but if their dose is kept low and they are taken at night, blood pressure control can be achieved with few side-effects in mild hypertension.

CLONIDINE HYDROCHLORIDE

Indications: hypertension (for use in migraine, see section 4.7.4.2)
Cautions: must be withdrawn gradually to avoid hypertensive crisis; Raynaud's syndrome or other occlusive peripheral vascular disease; history of depression; avoid in porphyria; **interactions:** Appendix 1 (clonidine)
Side-effects: dry mouth, sedation, depression, fluid retention, bradycardia, Raynaud's phenomenon, headache, dizziness, euphoria, nocturnal unrest, rash, nausea, constipation, rarely impotence
Dose: by mouth, 50–100 micrograms 3 times daily, increased every second or third day; max. daily dose usually 1.2 mg
By slow intravenous injection, 150–300 micrograms; max. 750 micrograms in 24 hours

PoM **Catapres®** (Boehringer Ingelheim)
Tablets, both scored, clonidine hydrochloride 100 micrograms, net price 84-tab pack = £5.39; 300 micrograms, 84 tab = £12.56. Label: 3, 8
Injection, clonidine hydrochloride 150 micrograms/mL. Net price 1-mL amp = 27p
PoM **Dixarit®** (migraine), see section 4.7.4.2

Sustained release
PoM **Catapres® Perlongets** (Boehringer Ingelheim)
Capsules, s/r, red/yellow, clonidine hydrochloride 250 micrograms. Net price 56-cap pack = £12.74. Label: 3, 8, 25
Dose: usually 1 capsule in the evening; 2–3 capsules daily (1 morning and 1–2 evening) if necessary

METHYLDOPA

Indications: hypertension, in conjunction with diuretic; hypertensive crisis when immediate effect not necessary
Cautions: positive direct Coombs' test in 20% of patients (may affect blood cross-matching); interference with laboratory tests; reduce initial dose in renal impairment; blood counts and liver-function tests advised; **interactions:** Appendix 1 (methyldopa)
Contra-indications: history of depression, active liver disease, phaeochromocytoma; porphyria
Side-effects: dry mouth, sedation, depression, drowsiness, diarrhoea, fluid retention, failure of ejaculation, liver damage, haemolytic anaemia, systemic lupus erythematosus-like syndrome, parkinsonism, rashes, nasal stuffiness
Dose: by mouth, 250 mg 2–3 times daily, gradually increased; max. daily dose 3 g
ELDERLY 125 mg twice daily initially, gradually increased; max. daily dose 2 g
By intravenous infusion, methyldopate hydrochloride 250–500 mg, repeated after 6 hours if required

PoM **Methyldopa** (Non-proprietary)
Tablets, coated, methyldopa (anhydrous) 125 mg, net price 20 = 43p; 250 mg, 20 = 68p; 500 mg, 20 = £1.38. Label: 3, 8

PoM **Aldomet®** (MSD)
Tablets, all yellow, f/c, methyldopa (anhydrous) 125 mg, net price 20 = 77p; 250 mg, 20 = £1.19; 500 mg, 20 = £2.34. Label: 3, 8
Suspension, methyldopa 250 mg/5 mL. Do not dilute. Net price 200 mL = £3.96. Label: 3, 8
Injection, methyldopate hydrochloride 50 mg/mL. Net price 5-mL amp = £2.31

PoM **Dopamet®** (Berk)
Tablets, all yellow, f/c, methyldopa (anhydrous) 125 mg, net price 20 = 43p; 250 mg, 20 = 73p; 500 mg, 20 = £1.46. Label: 3, 8
Additives: include tartrazine

With diuretic

PoM **Hydromet®** (MSD)
Tablets, pink, f/c, methyldopa (anhydrous) 250 mg, hydrochlorothiazide 15 mg. Net price 20 = £1.52. Label: 3, 8

RESERPINE AND RAUWOLFIA ALKALOIDS

Indications: hypertension
Cautions: heart failure, pregnancy, breast-feeding; **interactions:** Appendix 1 (reserpine and rauwolfia alkaloids)
Contra-indications: history of depression, phaeochromocytoma, peptic ulcer, Parkinson's disease, ulcerative colitis, thyrotoxicosis, renal impairment, epilepsy
Side-effects: dry mouth, nasal congestion, sedation, depression, postural hypotension, bradycardia, fluid retention

PoM **Hypercal®** (Carlton)
Tablets, rauwolfia alkaloids 2 mg. Net price 20 = 10p. Label: 3

PoM **Serpasil®** (Ciba)
Tablets, blue, scored, reserpine 250 micrograms, net price 20 = 19p. Label: 3
Additives: include gluten

With diuretic

PoM **Serpasil-Esidrex®** (Ciba)
Tablets, scored, reserpine 150 micrograms, hydrochlorothiazide 10 mg. Net price 20 = 38p. Label: 3
Additives: include gluten

With barbiturate

Note. There is no justification for the use of barbiturates in the treatment of hypertension

CD **Hypercal-B®** (Carlton)
Tablets, rauwolfia alkaloids 2 mg, amylobarbitone 15 mg. Net price 20 = 10p. Label: 2

2.5.3 Adrenergic neurone blocking drugs

These drugs prevent the release of noradrenaline from postganglionic adrenergic neurones. Guanethidine also depletes the nerve endings of noradrenaline. These drugs do not control supine blood pressure and may cause postural hypotension. For this reason they have largely fallen from use, but they may be necessary in combination with other therapy in resistant hypertension.

GUANETHIDINE MONOSULPHATE

Indications: moderate to severe hypertension that has failed to respond adequately to other antihypertensives, in conjunction with a diuretic or a vasodilator antihypertensive
Cautions: postural hypotension may cause falls in elderly; pregnancy; **interactions:** Appendix 1 (adrenergic neurone blockers)
Contra-indications: phaeochromocytoma, renal failure
Side-effects: postural hypotension, failure of ejaculation, fluid retention, nasal congestion, diarrhoea, drowsiness
Dose: *by mouth*, 10 mg daily, increased by 10 mg at weekly intervals; usual daily dose 25–50 mg
By intramuscular injection, 10–20 mg, repeated after 3 hours if required

PoM **Ismelin®** (Ciba)
Tablets, guanethidine monosulphate 10 mg, net price 20 = 46p; 25 mg (pink), 20 = £1.03
Additives: include gluten
Injection, guanethidine monosulphate 10 mg/mL. Net price 1-mL amp = 23p

BETHANIDINE SULPHATE

Indications; Cautions; Contra-indications; Side-effects: see under Guanethidine Monosulphate (except diarrhoea)
Dose: 10 mg 3 times daily after food, increased by 5 mg at intervals; max. daily dose 200 mg

PoM **Bendogen®** (Lagap)
Tablets, scored, bethanidine sulphate 10 mg, net price 20 = 95p; 50 mg, 20 = £4.20. Label: 21

PoM **Esbatal®** (Calmic)
Tablets, peach, scored, bethanidine sulphate 10 mg, net price 20 = £2.11; 50 mg, 20 = £9.51. Label: 21

DEBRISOQUINE

Indications; Cautions; Contra-indications; Side-effects: see under Guanethidine Monosulphate (except diarrhoea)
Dose: 10 mg 1–2 times daily, increased by 10 mg every 3 days; max. daily dose usually 120 mg

PoM **Declinax®** (Roche)
Tablets, both scored, debrisoquine (as sulphate) 10 mg, net price 20 = 77p; 20 mg (blue), 20 = £1.12

2.5.4 Alpha-adrenoceptor blocking drugs

Prazosin has post-synaptic alpha-blocking and vasodilator properties and rarely causes tachycardia. It may, however, cause a rapid reduction in blood pressure after the first dose and should be introduced with caution. **Doxazosin** and **terazosin** have properties similar to those of prazosin.

Phenoxybenzamine and **indoramin** are alpha-blockers which are effective agents, but have many side-effects. They can be used in conjunction with beta-blockers and/or diuretics. Phenoxybenzamine is used with a beta-blocker in the short-term management of severe hypertensive episodes associated with phaeochromocytoma.

Phentolamine is used rarely as a suppression test for phaeochromocytoma.

PROSTATIC HYPERTROPHY. Both prazosin and indoramin are also indicated for prostatic hypertrophy (see below and also section 7.4.1).

DOXAZOSIN

Indications: hypertension, if necessary in conjunction with thiazide or beta-blocker

Cautions: care with initial dose (postural hypotension); **interactions:** Appendix 1 (alpha-blockers)

Side-effects: postural hypotension (rarely associated with fainting); dizziness, vertigo, headache, fatigue, asthenia, oedema

Dose: 1 mg daily, increased after 1–2 weeks to 2 mg daily, if necessary, and thereafter to 4 mg daily, if necessary; max. 16 mg daily

▼ PoM **Cardura**® (Invicta)

Tablets, doxazosin (as mesylate) 1 mg, net price 28-tab pack = £9.60; 2 mg, 28-tab pack = £12.80; 4 mg, 28-tab pack = £16.00

INDORAMIN

Indications: see preparations below

Cautions: patient's ability to drive or operate machinery may be impaired; avoid alcohol (enhances rate and extent of absorption); control incipient heart failure with diuretics and digoxin; hepatic or renal impairment; elderly patients; Parkinson's disease; epilepsy (convulsions in *animal* studies); history of depression; **interactions:** Appendix 1 (alpha-blockers)

Contra-indications: established heart failure; patients receiving MAOIs

Side-effects: sedation; also dizziness, depression, failure of ejaculation, dry mouth, nasal congestion, extrapyramidal effects

PoM **Baratol**® (Wyeth)

Tablets, both f/c, indoramin (as hydrochloride) 25 mg (blue), net price 20 = £2.15; 50 mg (green), scored, 20 = £3.80. Label: 2

Dose: hypertension, usually in conjunction with thiazide or beta-blocker, initially 25 mg twice daily, increased by 25–50 mg daily at intervals of 2 weeks; max. daily dose 200 mg in 2–3 divided doses

Prostatic hypertrophy

PoM **Doralese**® (Bridge)

Tablets, yellow, f/c, indoramin 20 mg. Net price 60-tab pack = £8.40. Label: 2

Dose: benign prostatic hypertrophy, 20 mg twice daily; increased if necessary by 20 mg every 2 weeks to max. 100 mg daily in divided doses; ELDERLY, 20 mg at night may be adequate

Note. Not licensed for treatment of hypertension

PHENOXYBENZAMINE HYDROCHLORIDE

Indications: phaeochromocytoma only (see notes above)

Cautions: elderly patients; congestive heart failure; ischaemic heart disease, marked arteriosclerosis; renal impairment; carcinogenic in *animals*

Contra-indications: porphyria

Side-effects: postural hypotension with dizziness and marked tachycardia, lassitude, nasal congestion, miosis, retrograde ejaculation; rarely gastro-intestinal disturbances

Dose: by mouth, phaeochromocytoma, 10 mg daily, increased by 10 mg daily; usual dose 1–2 mg/kg daily in 2 divided doses

PoM **Dibenyline**® (SK&F)

Capsules, red/white, phenoxybenzamine hydrochloride 10 mg. Net price 30-cap pack = £3.19

Injection, phenoxybenzamine hydrochloride 50 mg/mL. To be diluted before use. 2-mL amp (hosp. only)

PHENTOLAMINE MESYLATE

Indications: hypertensive crises due to phaeochromocytoma or interaction of foods with MAOIs, diagnosis of phaeochromocytoma; clonidine withdrawal; acute left ventricular failure

Cautions: monitor blood pressure, heart rate

Side-effects: hypotension, tachycardia, dizziness; nausea, diarrhoea, nasal congestion

Dose: by intravenous injection, 5–10 mg repeated if necessary

By intravenous infusion, 5–60 mg over 10–30 minutes at a rate of 0.2–2 mg/minute

PoM **Rogitine**® (Ciba)

Injection, phentolamine mesylate 10 mg/mL. Net price 1-mL amp = 27p

PRAZOSIN HYDROCHLORIDE

Indications: see under Dose

Cautions: first dose may cause collapse due to hypotension (therefore should be taken on retiring to bed); reduce initial dose in renal failure; **interactions:** Appendix 1 (alpha-blockers)

Side-effects: postural hypotension, drowsiness, weakness

 Prices are **net**, see p. 1

Dose: hypertension, 500 micrograms 2–3 times daily, the initial dose on retiring to bed at night (to avoid collapse, see Cautions); increased to a max. of 20 mg daily
Congestive heart failure, 500 micrograms initially (at bedtime, see above), then 1 mg 3–4 times daily; maintenance 4–20 mg daily
Raynaud's syndrome, initially 500 micrograms twice daily (initial dose at bedtime, see above); maintenance 1–2 mg twice daily
Benign prostatic hypertrophy, initially 500 micrograms twice daily for 3–7 days (initial dose at bedtime, see above), dose subsequently adjusted according to response; usual maintenance (and max.) 2 mg twice daily

PoM **Hypovase®** (Invicta)
Tablets, prazosin hydrochloride 500 micrograms, net price 56-tab pack = £2.41; 1 mg (orange, scored), 56-tab pack = £3.10; 2 mg (scored), 56-tab pack = £4.21; 5 mg (scored), 56-tab pack = £9.07; starter pack of 8 × 500-microgram tabs and 32 × 1-mg tabs = £2.90. Label: 3, counselling, see dose above

TERAZOSIN

Indications: mild to moderate hypertension
Cautions: first dose may cause collapse due to hypotension (within 30–90 minutes, therefore should be taken on retiring to bed) (may also occur with rapid dose increase); **interactions:** Appendix 1 (alpha-blockers)
Side-effects: dizziness, lack of energy, peripheral oedema
Dose: 1 mg at bedtime (compliance with bedtime dose important to avoid collapse, see Cautions); dose doubled after 7 days if necessary; usual maintenance dose 2–10 mg daily; more than 20 mg daily rarely improves efficacy

PoM **Hytrin®** (Abbott)
Tablets, terazosin (as hydrochloride) 2 mg (yellow), net price 28-tab pack = £12.32; 5 mg (tan), 28-tab pack = £16.63; 10 mg (blue), 28-tab pack = £23.41; starter pack of 7 × 1-mg tabs and 21 × 2-mg tabs = £12.95. Label: 3, counselling, see dose above

2.5.5 Angiotensin-converting enzyme inhibitors (ACE inhibitors)

Angiotensin-converting enzyme inhibitors inhibit the conversion of angiotensin I to angiotensin II. They are effective and generally well tolerated, but experience is limited as regards long-term use.

They should therefore be considered for *hypertension* only when thiazides and beta-blockers are contra-indicated, not tolerated, or fail to control blood pressure. All may cause very rapid falls of blood pressure in some patients. Therefore where possible diuretic therapy should be stopped for a few days before initiating therapy and the first dose should preferably be given at bedtime.

Some ACE inhibitors are also used in *heart failure*, as adjuncts to diuretics and, where appropriate, digoxin. Since it may not be possible to suspend diuretics in heart failure, treatment should be initiated under close hospital supervision.

RENAL IMPAIRMENT. ACE inhibitors occasionally cause impairment of renal function which may progress and become severe. At particular risk are those with pre-existing renal disease or impairment, the elderly, and those with bilateral renal artery stenosis (or stenosis of the artery supplying a single functioning kidney). Concomitant treatment with NSAIDs or potassium-sparing diuretics, and use of potassium-containing salt substitutes, may increase the risk. Renal function and electrolytes should be checked before starting an ACE inhibitor, and monitored during treatment.

ACE inhibitors should be used with **particular caution** in patients with peripheral vascular disease or generalised atherosclerosis, as such patients may have clinically silent renovascular disease.

CAPTOPRIL

Indications: mild to moderate essential hypertension alone or with thiazide therapy and severe hypertension resistant to other treatment (but see cautions and notes above); congestive heart failure (adjunct)
Cautions: diuretics (**important:** see notes above); first doses may cause hypotension especially in patients taking diuretics, on a low-sodium diet, on dialysis, or dehydrated; monitor renal function before and during treatment; reduce dose or **avoid** in renal impairment (white cell counts and urinary protein estimations needed); see also notes above; **interactions:** Appendix 1 (ACE inhibitors)
Contra-indications: hypersensitivity to ACE inhibitors; known or suspected renovascular disease, aortic stenosis or outflow tract obstruction; pregnancy; porphyria
Side-effects: persistent dry cough; loss of taste, sore mouth, abdominal pain, rash, angioedema, hypotension (see Cautions); proteinuria, thrombocytopenia, neutropenia, agranulocytosis, hyperkalaemia (all more common in renal impairment); renal impairment, see notes above
Dose: hypertension, used alone, initially 12.5 mg twice daily; if used in addition to diuretic (see notes), in elderly, or in renal impairment, initially 6.25 mg twice daily (first dose at bedtime); usual maintenance dose 25 mg twice daily; max. 50 mg twice daily (rarely 3 times daily in severe hypertension)
Heart failure (adjunct), initially 6.25–12.5 mg under close hospital supervision; usual maintenance dose 25 mg 2–3 times daily

PoM **Capoten®** (Squibb)
Tablets, captopril 12.5 mg (scored), net price 100 = £18.86; 25 mg, 56-tab pack = £12.03, 90-tab pack = £19.34; 50 mg (scored), 56-tab pack = £20.50, 90-tab pack = £32.95
Note. Also available as Acepril® (Squibb)

With diuretic

PoM **Capozide**® (Squibb)

Tablets, scored, captopril 50 mg, hydrochlorothiazide 25 mg. Net price 28 tab = £16.07

Note. Also available as Acezide® (Squibb)

ENALAPRIL MALEATE

Indications: all grades of essential hypertension (but see cautions and notes above); congestive heart failure (adjunct)

Cautions; Contra-indications: see under Captopril and notes above

Side-effects: persistent dry cough; dizziness, headache, fatigue, weakness, hypotension (see Cautions), change of taste, nausea, diarrhoea, muscle cramps, rash, and angioedema; renal impairment, see notes above

Dose: hypertension, used alone, initially 5 mg daily; if used in addition to diuretic (see notes), in elderly patients, or in renal impairment, initially 2.5 mg daily; usual maintenance dose 10–20 mg daily; max. 40 mg daily

Heart failure (adjunct), initially 2.5 mg daily under close hospital supervision; usual maintenance 10–20 mg daily

PoM **Innovace**® (MSD)

Tablets, enalapril maleate 2.5 mg, net price 50 = £10.00; 5 mg (scored), 28-tab pack = £7.86, 50 = £14.03; 10 mg (red), 28-tab pack = £11.03, 50 = £19.69; 20 mg (peach), 28-tab pack = £13.10, 50 = £23.40

LISINOPRIL

Indications: all grades of essential hypertension (but see cautions and notes above); congestive heart failure (adjunct)

Cautions; Contra-indications: see under Captopril and notes above

Side-effects: see under Enalapril; palpitations and chest pain also reported

Dose: hypertension, initially 2.5 mg daily; usual maintenance dose 10–20 mg daily; max. 40 mg daily

Note. In hypertension discontinue diuretic for 2–3 days beforehand and resume later if required (see also notes above)

Heart failure (adjunct), initially 2.5 mg daily under close hospital supervision; usual maintenance dose 5–20 mg daily

PoM **Carace**® (Morson)

Tablets, lisinopril 2.5 mg (blue), net price 50 = £15.30; 5 mg (scored), 28-tab pack = £10.14; 10 mg (yellow, scored), 28-tab pack = £12.13; 20 mg (orange, scored), 28-tab pack = £20.30

PoM **Zestril**® (ICI)

Tablets, lisinopril (as dihydrate) 2.5 mg, net price 28-tab pack = £7.84; 5 mg (pink, scored), 28-tab pack = £9.83; 10 mg (pink), 28-tab pack = £12.13; 20 mg (red), 28-tab pack = £20.96

PERINDOPRIL

Indications: essential hypertension where standard therapy is ineffective or inappropriate because of adverse effects (but see cautions and notes above)

Cautions; Contra-indications: see under Captopril and notes above

Side-effects: see under Enalapril; abdominal pain, mood and sleep disturbances also reported

Dose: initially 2 mg daily; usual maintenance dose 4–8 mg daily; max. 8 mg daily

Note. Discontinue diuretic 3 days beforehand and resume later if required (see also notes above)

▼ PoM **Coversyl**® (Servier)

Tablets, perindopril tert-butylamine 2 mg, net price 30-tab pack = £9.45; 4 mg (scored), 30-tab pack = £13.00. Label: 22

QUINAPRIL

Indications: all grades of essential hypertension where standard therapy ineffective or inappropriate because of adverse effects (but see cautions and notes above); congestive heart failure (adjunct)

Cautions; Contra-indications: see under Captopril and notes above

Side-effects: see under Enalapril; rhinitus, sinusitus, pharyngitis, dyspepsia, abdominal pain, back pain, vomiting, chest pain, insomnia, paraesthesia, nervousness also reported

Dose: hypertension, initially 5 mg daily; with a diuretic, in elderly, or in renal impairment initially 2.5 mg daily; usual maintenance dose 20–40 mg daily in single or 2 divided doses; up to 80 mg daily has been given

Heart failure (adjunct), initial dose 2.5 mg under close hospital supervision; usual maintenance 10–20 mg daily in 2 divided doses; max. 40 mg daily

▼ PoM **Accupro**® (P-D)

Tablets, all brown, f/c, quinapril 5 mg, net price 28-tab pack = £8.40; 10 mg, 28-tab pack = £11.48; 20 mg, 28-tab pack = £13.10

RAMIPRIL

Indications: mild to moderate essential hypertension where standard therapy ineffective or inappropriate because of adverse effects (but see cautions and notes above)

Cautions; Contra-indications: see under Captopril and notes above

Side-effects: see under Enalapril; also abdominal pain, vomiting; increases in blood urea nitrogen and serum creatinine (particularly in renal impairment)

Dose: initially 1.25 mg daily, increased at intervals of 1–2 weeks; usual range 2.5–5 mg daily; max. 10 mg daily

Note. Discontinue diuretic for 2–3 days beforehand and resume later if required (see also notes above)

▼ PoM **Tritace**® (Astra, Hoechst)

Capsules, ramipril 1.25 mg (yellow/white), net price 28-cap pack = £5.44; 2.5 mg (orange/white), 28-cap pack = £7.70; 5 mg (red/white), 28-cap pack = £9.79

Prices are **net**, see p. 1

2.5.6 Ganglion-blocking drugs

Trimetaphan is used to provide controlled hypotension in surgery.

TRIMETAPHAN CAMSYLATE

Indications: see notes above
Cautions: hepatic or renal impairment, diabetes mellitus, Addison's disease, CNS degenerative disease
Contra-indications: severe arteriosclerosis, severe cardiac disease, pyloric stenosis
Side-effects: tachycardia and respiratory depression (particularly with muscle relaxants); pupillary dilatation
Dose: by intravenous infusion, 3–4 mg/minute initially, then adjusted according to response

PoM **Arfonad**® (Roche)
Injection, trimetaphan camsylate 50 mg/mL. Net price 5-mL amp = £3.12. For dilution and use as an infusion

2.5.7 Tyrosine hydroxylase inhibitor

Metirosine inhibits the enzyme tyrosine hydroxylase, and hence the synthesis of catecholamines. It is used in the pre-operative management of phaeochromocytoma, and long term in patients unsuitable for surgery; an alpha-adrenoceptor blocking drug (e.g. phenoxybenzamine) may also be required. Metirosine should **not** be used to treat essential hypertension.

METIROSINE

Indications: see notes above
Cautions: maintain high fluid intake and adequate blood volume; may impair ability to drive or operate machinery; **interactions:** Appendix 1 (metirosine)
Side-effects: sedation; extrapyramidal symptoms; diarrhoea (may be severe); hypersensitivity
Dose: initially 250 mg 4 times daily, increased to 2–3 g daily should be given for 5–7 days before surgery

PoM **Demser**® (MSD)
Capsules, blue, metirosine 250 mg (hosp. only). Label: 2

2.6 Nitrates and other vasodilators, and calcium-channel blockers

Most patients with *angina pectoris* are treated with beta-blockers (section 2.4) or calcium-channel blockers (section 2.6.2). However, short-acting nitrates (section 2.6.1) retain an important role both for prophylactic use before exertion and for chest pain occurring at rest. Nitrates are sometimes used as sole therapy, especially in elderly patients with infrequent symptoms.

Vasodilators are known to act in *heart failure* either by:

arteriolar dilatation which reduces both peripheral vascular resistance and left ventricular pressure at systole and results in improved cardiac output, *or*

venous dilatation which results in dilatation of capacitance vessels, increase of venous pooling, and diminution of venous return to the heart (decreasing left ventricular end-diastolic pressure).

Three groups of drugs should be considered—nitrates (section 2.6.1) which act predominantly by venous dilatation; ACE inhibitors (section 2.5.5) and hydralazine (section 2.5.1) which act predominantly by arteriolar dilatation; and phentolamine and prazosin (section 2.5.4) and sodium nitroprusside (section 2.5.1) which produce both arteriolar and venous dilatation. Combinations of drugs with different effects can be tried. Abrupt withdrawal may be hazardous.

Other drugs used in the treatment of heart failure include positive inotropics (sections 2.1 and 2.7.1) and diuretics (section 2.2).

2.6.1 Nitrates

Sublingual **glyceryl trinitrate** is one of the most effective drugs for providing rapid symptomatic relief of angina, but its effect lasts only for 20 to 30 minutes. Though a potent coronary vasodilator, its principal benefit follows from a reduction in venous return which reduces left ventricular work. Unwanted effects such as flushing, headache, and postural hypotension may limit therapy, especially when angina is severe or when patients are unusually sensitive to the effects of nitrates. The 300-microgram tablet is often appropriate when glyceryl trinitrate is first used and tolerance to the unwanted effects has not developed. Duration of action may be prolonged by *slow-release* preparations. The *aerosol spray* provides an alternative method of rapid relief of symptoms for those who find difficulty in dissolving sublingual preparations. The *percutaneous* preparations may be useful in the prophylaxis of angina for patients who suffer attacks at rest, especially at night.

Isosorbide dinitrate is active *sublingually* and is a more stable preparation for those who only require nitrates infrequently. It is also effective by mouth for prophylaxis; although the effect is slower in onset, it may persist for several hours. Duration of action of up to 12 hours is claimed for *sustained-release* preparations. The activity of isosorbide dinitrate may depend on the production of active metabolites, the most important of which is isosorbide mononitrate. **Isosorbide mononitrate** itself is also available for angina prophylaxis, though the advantages over isosorbide dinitrate have not yet been firmly established.

Glyceryl trinitrate or isosorbide dinitrate may be tried by *intravenous injection* when the sublingual form is ineffective in patients with chest pain due to myocardial infarction or severe ischaemia. Intravenous injections are also useful in the treatment of acute left ventricular failure.

TOLERANCE. Some patients on long-acting or transdermal nitrates rapidly develop tolerance (with reduced therapeutic effects). Reduction of blood-nitrate concentrations to low levels for 4 to 8 hours each day usually maintains effectiveness in such patients. If tolerance is suspected after the use of transdermal patches they should be removed for several consecutive hours in each 24 hours; in the case of sustained-release tablets, the second of the two daily doses can be given after about 8 hours rather than after 12 hours.

GLYCERYL TRINITRATE

Indications: prophylaxis and treatment of angina; left ventricular failure

Cautions: hypotensive conditions (avoid intravenous); tolerance (see notes above); **interactions:** Appendix 1 (glyceryl trinitrate)

Contra-indications: marked anaemia, head trauma, cerebral haemorrhage, closed-angle glaucoma

Side-effects: throbbing headache, flushing, dizziness, postural hypotension, tachycardia

Dose: *sublingually*, 0.3–1 mg, repeated as required

By mouth, 2.6–6.4 mg as sustained-release tablets, 2–3 times daily

By intravenous infusion, 10–200 micrograms/minute

Short-acting tablets and sprays

Glyceryl Trinitrate (Non-proprietary)

Tablets, glyceryl trinitrate 300 micrograms, net price 100 = £1.05; 500 micrograms, 100 = 44p; 600 micrograms, 100 = 65p. Label: 16

Note. Glyceryl trinitrate tablets should be supplied in glass containers of not more than 100 tablets, closed with a foil-lined cap, and containing no cotton wool wadding; they should be discarded after 8 weeks in use

Coro-Nitro Spray® (Boehringer Mannheim)

Aerosol spray, glyceryl trinitrate 400 micrograms/metered dose. Net price 200-dose unit = £3.36

Dose: treatment or prophylaxis of angina, spray 1–2 doses under tongue and then close mouth

Caution: flammable

GTN 300 mcg (Martindale)

Tablets, glyceryl trinitrate 300 micrograms. Net price 100 = 95p. Label: 16

Nitrolingual Spray® (Lipha)

Aerosol spray, glyceryl trinitrate 400 micrograms/metered dose. Net price 200-dose unit = £4.36

Dose: treatment or prophylaxis of angina, spray 1–2 doses under tongue and then close mouth

Note. No need to shake canister; caution flammable

Sustained-release tablets

Nitrocontin Continus® (Degussa)

Tablets, s/r, both pink, glyceryl trinitrate 2.6 mg, net price 20 = 67p; 6.4 mg, 20 = 88p. Label: 25

Suscard® (Pharmax)

Buccal tablets, s/r, glyceryl trinitrate 1 mg, net price 20 = £1.95; 2 mg, 20 = £2.91; 3 mg, 20 = £4.08; 5 mg, 20 = £5.72. Counselling, see administration below

Dose: treatment of angina, 1–2 mg as required; prophylaxis 1–2 mg 3 times daily; 5 mg in severe angina

Congestive heart failure, 5 mg 3 times daily, increased to 10 mg 3 times daily in severe cases

Acute heart failure, 5 mg repeated until symptoms abate

ADMINISTRATION. Tablets are placed between upper lip and gum, and left to dissolve

Sustac® (Pharmax)

Tablets, s/r, all pink, glyceryl trinitrate 2.6 mg, net price 20 = £1.21; 6.4 mg, 20 = £1.74; 10 mg, 20 = £2.43. Label: 25

Dose: severe angina, 10 mg 3 times daily

Parenteral preparations

Note. Glass or polyethylene apparatus is preferable; loss of potency will occur if PVC is used

PoM **Glyceryl Trinitrate** (Non-proprietary)

Injection, glyceryl trinitrate 5 mg/mL. To be diluted before use. Net price 5-mL amp = £6.00; 10-mL amp = £12.00

PoM **Nitrocine®** (Schwarz)

Injection, glyceryl trinitrate 1 mg/mL. To be diluted before use or given undiluted with syringe pump. Net price 10-mL amp = £9.45; 50-mL bottle = £22.15

PoM **Nitronal®** (Lipha)

Injection, glyceryl trinitrate 1 mg/mL. To be diluted before use or given undiluted with syringe pump. Net price 5-mL vial = £2.20; 50-mL vial = £18.00

PoM **Tridil®** (Du Pont)

Injection, glyceryl trinitrate 500 micrograms/mL. To be diluted before use. Net price 10-mL amp = £4.50

Injection, glyceryl trinitrate 5 mg/mL. To be diluted before use. Net price 10-mL amp = £21.88; 10-mL amp with polyethylene giving set = £24.98

Transdermal preparations

Deponit® (Schwarz)

'5' dressing, self-adhesive, transparent, releasing glyceryl trinitrate approx. 5 mg/24 hours when in contact with skin. Net price 30 = £19.25. Counselling, see administration below

'10' dressing, self-adhesive, peach-coloured, releasing glyceryl trinitrate approx. 10 mg/24 hours when in contact with skin. Net price 30 = £21.19. Counselling, see administration below

ADMINISTRATION: prophylaxis of angina, apply one '5' or one '10' dressing to lateral chest wall; replace every 24 hours, siting replacement dressing on different area

Percutol® (Cusi)

Ointment, glyceryl trinitrate 2%. Net price 30 g = £6.14. Counselling, see administration below

ADMINISTRATION: prophylaxis of angina, ½–2 inches of ointment measured on to Applirule, which is applied to body (usually chest, arm, or thigh) without rubbing in, and secured with a dressing; repeat every 3–4 hours or as required

Note. 1 inch of ointment contains glyceryl trinitrate 16.64 mg

Transiderm-Nitro® (Geigy)

'5' dressing, self-adhesive, pink, releasing glyceryl trinitrate approx. 5 mg/24 hours when in contact with skin. Net price 30 = £15.95. Counselling, see administration below

'10' dressing, self-adhesive, pink, releasing glyceryl trinitrate approx. 10 mg/24 hours when in contact with skin. Net price 30 = £17.54. Counselling, see administration below

ADMINISTRATION: prophylaxis of angina, apply one '5' or one '10' dressing to lateral chest wall; replace every 24 hours, siting replacement dressing on different area; max. two '10' dressings daily; see also notes above

Prophylaxis of phlebitis and extravasation ('5' dressing only), see literature

ISOSORBIDE DINITRATE

Indications: prophylaxis and treatment of angina; left ventricular failure

Cautions; Contra-indications; Side-effects: see under Glyceryl Trinitrate

Dose: *sublingually*, 5–10 mg

By mouth, daily in divided doses, angina 30–120 mg, left ventricular failure 40–160 mg, up to 240 mg if required

By intravenous infusion, 2–10 mg/hour

Short-acting tablets

Isosorbide Dinitrate (Non-proprietary)

Tablets, isosorbide dinitrate 10 mg, net price 20 = 24p; 20 mg, 20 = 44p

Cedocard® (Tillotts)

Cedocard-5 tablets (sublingual), scored, isosorbide dinitrate 5 mg. Net price 20 = 46p

Cedocard-10 tablets, pink, scored, isosorbide dinitrate 10 mg. Net price 20 = 38p

Cedocard-20 tablets, blue, scored, isosorbide dinitrate 20 mg. Net price 20 = 73p

Cedocard-40 tablets, green, scored, isosorbide dinitrate 40 mg. Net price 20 = £1.51

Isordil® (Wyeth)

Tablets (sublingual), pink, isosorbide dinitrate 5 mg. Net price 20 = 23p. Label: 26

Tablets, both scored, isosorbide dinitrate 10 mg, net price 20 = 23p; 30 mg, 20 = 54p

Sorbichew® (Stuart)

Tablets (chewable), green, scored, isosorbide dinitrate 5 mg. Net price 20 = 31p. Label: 24

Sorbitrate® (Stuart)

Tablets, both scored, isosorbide dinitrate 10 mg (yellow), net price 20 = 29p; 20 mg (blue), 20 = 43p

Vascardin® (Nicholas)

Tablets, both scored, isosorbide dinitrate 10 mg (as diluted isosorbide dinitrate), net price 20 = 28p; 30 mg, 20 = 54p

Sustained-release preparations

Cedocard Retard® (Tillotts)

Retard-20 tablets, s/r, yellow, scored, isosorbide dinitrate 20 mg. Net price 20 = £1.92. Label: 25

Dose: prophylaxis of angina, 1 tablet every 12 hours

Retard-40 tablets, s/r, orange-red, scored, isosorbide dinitrate 40 mg. Net price 60-tab pack = £10.63. Label: 25

Dose: prophylaxis of angina, 1–2 tablets every 12 hours

Isoket Retard® (Schwarz)

Retard-20 tablets, s/r, yellow, scored, isosorbide dinitrate 20 mg. Net price 50-tab pack = £3.24. Label: 25

Retard-40 tablets, s/r, orange, scored, isosorbide dinitrate 40 mg. Net price 50-tab pack = £7.99. Label: 25

Dose: prophylaxis of angina, 20–40 mg every 12 hours

Isordil Tembids® (Wyeth)

Capsules, s/r, blue/clear, isosorbide dinitrate 40 mg. Net price 20 = £1.28. Label: 25

Dose: prophylaxis of angina, 1 capsule 2–3 times daily

Soni-Slo® (Lipha)

Capsules, s/r, pink/clear, enclosing off-white pellets, isosorbide dinitrate 20 mg. Net price 20 = £1.19. Label: 25

Capsules, s/r, red/clear, enclosing off-white pellets, isosorbide dinitrate 40 mg. Net price 20 = £1.40. Label: 25

Dose: prophylaxis of angina, 40–120 mg daily in divided doses

Sorbid-20 SA® (Stuart)

Capsules, s/r, red/yellow, isosorbide dinitrate 20 mg. Net price 56-cap pack = £3.59. Label: 25

Dose: prophylaxis of angina, 1–2 twice daily

Sorbid-40 SA® (Stuart)

Capsules, s/r, red/clear, isosorbide dinitrate 40 mg. Net price 56-cap pack = £5.13. Label: 25

Dose: prophylaxis of angina, 1–2 twice daily

Parenteral preparations

PoM **Cedocard IV**® (Tillotts)

Injection, isosorbide dinitrate 1 mg/mL. To be diluted before use. Net price 10-mL amp = £4.33; 50-mL infusion bottle = £21.50; 100-mL infusion bottle = £29.69

Note. Glass or polyethylene infusion apparatus is preferable; loss of potency if PVC used

PoM **Isoket**® (Schwarz)

Injection 0.05%, isosorbide dinitrate 500 micrograms/mL. To be diluted before use or given undiluted with syringe pump. Net price 50-mL bottle = £11.50

Injection 0.1%, isosorbide dinitrate 1 mg/mL. To be diluted before use. Net price 10-mL amp = £4.33; 50-mL bottle = £21.50; 100-mL bottle = £29.69

Note. Glass or polyethylene infusion apparatus is preferable; loss of potency if PVC used

ISOSORBIDE MONONITRATE

Indications: prophylaxis and treatment of angina; adjunct in congestive heart failure

Cautions; Contra-indications; Side-effects: see under Glyceryl Trinitrate

Dose: initially 20 mg 2–3 times daily *or* 40 mg twice daily (10 mg twice daily in those who have not previously received nitrates); up to 120 mg daily in divided doses if required

PoM **Isosorbide Mononitrate** (Non-proprietary)
Tablets, isosorbide mononitrate 20 mg, net price 20 = £1.40; 40 mg, 20 = £2.69. Label: 25

Elantan® (Schwarz)
Elantan 10 tablets, scored, isosorbide mononitrate 10 mg. Net price 50-tab pack 2= £3.33. Label: 25
PoM *Elantan 20 tablets*, scored, isosorbide mononitrate 20 mg. Net price 50-tab pack = £4.34. Label: 25
PoM *Elantan 40 tablets*, scored, isosorbide mononitrate 40 mg. Net price 50-tab pack = £7.07. Label: 25

PoM **Ismo®** (Boehringer Mannheim)
Ismo 10 tablets, isosorbide mononitrate 10 mg. Net price 20 = £1.16. Label: 25
Ismo 20 tablets, isosorbide mononitrate 20 mg. Net price 56-tab pack = £4.76. Label: 25
Starter pack, 8 tablets, isosorbide mononitrate 10 mg; 60 tablets, scored, isosorbide mononitrate 20 mg. Net price = £5.18. Label: 25
Ismo 40 tablets, isosorbide mononitrate 40 mg. Net price 20 = £2.79. Label: 25

PoM **Isotrate®** (Thames)
Tablets, isosorbide mononitrate 20 mg. Net price 60-tab pack = £4.32. Label: 25

PoM **Monit®** (Stuart)
Tablets, scored, isosorbide mononitrate 20 mg. Net price 56-tab pack = £4.78. Label: 25

Monit LS® (Stuart)
Tablets, isosorbide mononitrate 10 mg. Net price 56-tab pack = £3.74. Label: 25

Mono-Cedocard® (Tillotts)
Mono-Cedocard 10 tablets, orange, scored, isosorbide mononitrate 10 mg. Net price 60-tab pack = £3.77. Label: 25
Mono-Cedocard 20 tablets, scored, isosorbide mononitrate 20 mg. Net price 20 = £2.06. Label: 25
Mono-Cedocard 40 tablets, scored, isosorbide mononitrate 40 mg. Net price 60-tab pack = £9.35. Label: 25

Sustained-release preparations

PoM **Elantan LA50®** (Schwarz)
Capsules s/r, pink/dark pink, enclosing white micropellets, isosorbide mononitrate 50 mg. Net price 28-cap pack = £11.30. Label: 25
Dose: prophylaxis of angina, 1 capsule daily in the morning

PoM **Imdur®** (Astra)
Durules® (= tablets s/r), yellow, f/c, scored, isosorbide mononitrate 60 mg. Net price 28-tab pack = £11.43. Label: 25
Dose: prophylaxis of angina, 1 tablet in the morning (half a tablet if headache occurs), increased to 2 tablets if required

Ismo Retard® (Boehringer Mannheim)
Tablets, s/r, s/c, isosorbide mononitrate 40 mg. Net price 28-tab pack = £10.50. Label: 25
Dose: prophylaxis of angina, 1 tablet daily in the morning

[1]**MCR-50®** (Tillotts)
Capsules, s/r, containing white micropellets, isosorbide mononitrate 50 mg. Net price 28-cap pack = £11.37. Label: 25
Dose: prophylaxis of angina, 1 capsule in the morning, increased to 2 capsules if required

1. Full product name Mono Cedocard Retard-50

PoM **Monit SR®** (Stuart)
Tablets, s/r, s/c, isosorbide mononitrate 40 mg. Net price 28-tab pack = £10.50. Label: 25
Dose: prophylaxis of angina, 1 tablet daily in the morning

PENTAERYTHRITOL TETRANITRATE

Indications: prophylaxis of angina

Cautions; Contra-indications; Side-effects: see under Glyceryl Trinitrate

Dose: see below

Cardiacap® (Consolidated)
Capsules, s/r, blue/yellow, pentaerythritol tetranitrate 30 mg. Net price 20 = 74p. Label: 22, 25
Dose: prophylaxis of angina, 30 mg every 12 hours

Mycardol® (Sterling-Winthrop)
Tablets, scored, pentaerythritol tetranitrate 30 mg. Net price 20 = 89p. Label: 22
Dose: 2 tablets 3–4 times daily

2.6.2 Calcium-channel blockers

Calcium-channel blockers interfere with the inward displacement of calcium ions through the slow channels of active cell membranes. They influence the myocardial cells, the cells within the specialised conducting system of the heart, and the cells of vascular smooth muscle. Thus, myocardial contractility may be reduced, the formation and propagation of electrical impulses within the heart may be depressed, and coronary or systemic vascular tone may be diminished.

Calcium-channel blockers differ in their predeliction for the various possible sites of action therefore their therapeutic effects are disparate, with much greater variation than those of beta-blockers. There are important differences between verapamil and the dihydropyridine calcium-channel blockers, nifedipine, nicardipine and isradipine.

Verapamil is used for the treatment of *angina*, *hypertension*, and *arrhythmias* (section 2.3.2). It reduces cardiac output, slows the heart rate, and may impair atrioventricular conduction. It may precipitate heart failure, exacerbate conduction disorders, and cause hypotension at high doses and should **not** be used with beta-blockers (see section 2.3.2). Constipation is the most common side-effect.

Nifedipine relaxes vascular smooth muscle and dilates coronary and peripheral arteries. It has more influence on vessels and less on the myocardium than does verapamil, and unlike verapamil has no anti-arrhythmic activity. It rarely precipitates heart failure because any negative inotropic effect is offset by a reduction in left ventricular work. **Nicardipine** has similar effects to those of nifedipine; it does not reduce myocardial contractility. Both nifedipine and nicardipine are valuable in forms of *angina associated with coronary vasospasm*; they are useful as adjuncts to beta-blockers for patients with severe symptoms, and as alternative treatment for those who are intolerant of beta-blockers. Side-effects associated with vasodilatation such as flushing and headache (which become less obtrusive after a few days), and ankle swelling (which does not respond to diuretics) are common. Nifedipine (as tablets) in a dose of 10 or 20 mg twice daily, increasing to 40 mg twice daily, is useful in managing *hypertensive* patients, especially in conjunction with beta-blockers.

Isradipine has similar effects to those of nifedipine and nicardipine; it is only indicated for *hypertension*. **Amlodipine** also resembles nifedipine and nicardipine in its effects. It has a longer duration of action and can be given once daily for *hypertension* or *angina*.

Nimodipine is related to nifedipine but the smooth muscle relaxant effect preferentially acts on cerebral arteries. Its use if confined to prevention of *vascular spasm following subarachnoid haemorrhage*.

Diltiazem is effective in most forms of *angina*. It may be used in patients for whom beta-blockers are contra-indicated or ineffective; although it has a less depressant effect on the myocardium than verapamil and significant myocardial depression occurs rarely, but nevertheless because of the risk of bradycardia it should be used with caution in association with beta-blockers.

WITHDRAWAL. There is some evidence that sudden withdrawal of calcium-channel blockers may be associated with an exacerbation of angina.

AMLODIPINE BESYLATE

Indications: hypertension, prophylaxis of angina
Cautions: pregnancy; hepatic impairment; **interactions:** Appendix 1 (calcium-channel blockers)
Side-effects: headache, oedema, fatigue, nausea, flushing, dizziness
Dose: hypertension or angina, initially 5 mg once daily; max. 10 mg daily

▼ PoM **Istin**® (Pfizer)
Tablets, amlodipine (as besylate) 5 mg. Net price 28-tab pack = £11.85; 10 mg, 28-tab pack = £17.70

DILTIAZEM HYDROCHLORIDE

Indications: prophylaxis and treatment of angina
Cautions: reduce dose in hepatic and renal impairment; reduced left ventricular function, mild bradycardia, first degree AV block, or prolonged PR interval; **interactions:** Appendix 1 (calcium-channel blockers)
Contra-indications: severe bradycardia, second- or third-degree heart block, sick sinus syndrome; pregnancy (toxicity in *animal* studies), left ventricular failure; porphyria
Side-effects: bradycardia and first-degree heart block, hypotension, ankle oedema; rarely headache, nausea, rashes (toxic erythema reported); depression reported
Dose: 60 mg 3 times daily (elderly twice daily); max. 480 mg daily

PoM **Diltiazem** (Non-proprietary)
Tablets, diltiazem hydrochloride 60 mg. Net price 100 = £15.00. Label: 25

PoM **Adizem-60**® (Napp)
Tablets, f/c, diltiazem hydrochloride 60 mg. Net price 100-tab pack = £15.77. Label: 25

PoM **Britiazim**® (Thames)
Tablets, diltiazem hydrochloride 60 mg. Net price 100 = £16.49. Label: 25

PoM **Tildiem**® (Lorex)
Tablets, off-white, diltiazem hydrochloride 60 mg. Net price 100 = £15.00. Label: 25

Sustained release

PoM [1]**Adizem-SR**® (Napp)
Tablets, controlled-release, f/c, diltiazem hydrochloride 120 mg. Net price 56-tab pack = £18.60. Label: 25
Dose: 1 tablet twice daily; max. 2 twice daily
Note. Not appropriate for the elderly or those with hepatic or renal impairment
1. Formerly Adizem Continus

ISRADIPINE

Indications: hypertension
Cautions: tight aortic stenosis, sick sinus syndrome (if pacemaker not fitted); reduce dose in hepatic or renal impairment; pregnancy (may prolong labour); **interactions:** Appendix 1 (calcium-channel blockers)
Side-effects: headache, flushing, dizziness, tachycardia and palpitations, localised peripheral oedema; hypotension uncommon; rarely weight gain, fatigue, abdominal discomfort, rashes
Dose: 2.5 mg twice daily (1.25 mg twice daily in elderly, hepatic or renal impairment); increased if necessary after 3–4 weeks to 5 mg twice daily (exceptionally up to 10 mg twice daily); maintenance 2.5 or 5 mg once daily may be sufficient

▼ PoM **Prescal**® (Ciba)
Tablets, yellow, scored, isradipine 2.5 mg. Net price 56-tab pack = £11.39

NICARDIPINE HYDROCHLORIDE

Indications: prophylaxis and treatment of angina; mild to moderate hypertension
Cautions: withdraw if ischaemic pain occurs or existing pain worsens within 30 minutes of initiating treatment or increasing dose; hepatic or

 Prices are **net**, see p. 1

renal impairment; **interactions:** Appendix 1 (calcium-channel blockers)
Contra-indications: advanced aortic stenosis; pregnancy
Side-effects: dizziness, headache, peripheral oedema, flushing, palpitations, nausea; also gastro-intestinal disturbances, drowsiness, hypotension, rashes, salivation, frequency of micturition
Dose: initially 20 mg 3 times daily, increased to 30 mg 3 times daily (usual range 60–120 mg daily); patients with hypertension controlled on 20–30 mg 3 times daily can be given 30–40 mg twice daily

PoM **Cardene**® (Syntex)
Capsules, nicardipine hydrochloride 20 mg (blue/white), net price 20 = £2.87; 30 mg (blue/pale blue), 20 = £3.43

NIFEDIPINE

Indications: prophylaxis and treatment of angina; hypertension; Raynaud's phenomenon
Cautions: withdraw if ischaemic pain occurs or existing pain worsens shortly after initiating treatment; poor cardiac reserve; severe hypotension; reduce dose in hepatic impairment; diabetes mellitus; may inhibit labour; breast-feeding; **interactions:** Appendix 1 (calcium-channel blockers)
Contra-indications: cardiogenic shock; pregnancy (toxicity in *animal* studies); porphyria
Side-effects: headache, flushing, dizziness, lethargy; also gravitational oedema, rash, nausea, increased frequency of micturition, eye pain, gum hyperplasia; depression reported
Dose: by mouth, angina and Raynaud's phenomenon, *capsules*, initially 10 mg (elderly 5 mg) 3 times daily with or after food; usual maintenance 5–20 mg 3 times daily; for immediate effect in angina bite into capsule and retain liquid in mouth or swallow (evidence points to more rapid action if contents swallowed)
Hypertension and angina prophylaxis, *tablets*, 20 mg twice daily with or after food (initial titration 10 mg twice daily); usual maintenance 10–40 mg twice daily
By intracoronary injection, see preparation below

PoM **Nifedipine** (Non-proprietary)
Capsules, nifedipine 5 mg, net price 100 = £7.95; 10 mg, 100 = £12.70. Label: 21, counselling, see dose
Available from APS, Evans, Kerfoot, Shire (Vasad®)

PoM **Adalat**® (Bayer)
Capsules, both orange, nifedipine 5 mg, net price 20 = £1.63; 10 mg, 20 = £2.44. Label: 21, counselling, see dose

PoM **Adalat**® **Retard** (Bayer)
Tablets, pink, nifedipine 20 mg. Net price 20 = £3.86. Label: 21, 25

PoM **Adalat**® **Retard 10** (Bayer)
Tablets, pink, nifedipine 10 mg. Net price 56-tab pack = £8.34. Label: 21, 25

PoM **Adalat**® **IC** (Bayer)
Coronary injection, nifedipine 100 micrograms/mL. Net price 2-mL pre-filled syringe = £7.43
Note. Use polyethylene catheters only
Dose: for treatment of coronary spasm during coronary angiography and balloon angioplasty, 100–200 micrograms via coronary catheter over 90–120 seconds (with monitoring of blood pressure and pulse); reduce dose in severe stenosis; lasts 15 minutes; do not exceed total of six 200-microgram injections in 3 hours

Sustained release
PoM **Coracten**® (Evans)
Capsules, s/r, brown/red, enclosing yellow pellets, nifedipine 20 mg. Net price 20 = £3.48. Label: 25
Dose: hypertension and angina prophylaxis, 1 capsule every 12 hours; increased if necessary to 2 capsules every 12 hours

With atenolol
Section 2.4

NIMODIPINE

Indications: prevention and treatment of ischaemic neurological deficits following subarachnoid haemorrhage
Cautions: cerebral oedema or severely raised intracranial pressure; avoid concomitant administration of nimodipine tablets and infusion, other calcium-channel blockers, or beta-blockers; impaired renal function or nephrotoxic drugs; pregnancy; **interactions:** Appendix 1 (calcium-channel blockers)
Side-effects: hypotension, variation in heart-rate, flushing, headache, gastro-intestinal disorders, nausea, and feeling of warmth; transient increase in liver enzymes after intravenous administration
Dose: prevention, *by mouth*, 60 mg every 4 hours (total daily dose 360 mg), starting within 4 days of subarachnoid haemorrhage and continued for 21 days
Treatment, *by intravenous infusion* via central catheter, 1 mg/hour initially, increased after 2 hours to 2 mg/hour, providing no severe decrease in blood pressure; patients with unstable blood pressure or weighing less than 70 kg, 500 micrograms/hour initially or less if necessary; treatment should start as soon as possible and should continue for 5 days; in the event of surgical intervention during treatment continue for at least 5 days after

PoM **Nimotop**® (Bayer)
Tablets, yellow, f/c, nimodipine 30 mg. Net price 100-tab pack = £35.30
Intravenous infusion, nimodipine 200 micrograms/mL; also contains ethanol 20% and macrogol '400' 17%. Net price 50-mL vial (with polyethylene infusion catheter) = £13.24
Note. Polyethylene, or polypropylene apparatus should be used; PVC should be avoided

VERAPAMIL HYDROCHLORIDE

Indications: see under Dose

Cautions: first-degree heart block; acute phase of myocardial infarction (avoid if bradycardia, hypotension, left ventricular failure); patients taking beta-blockers (**important:** see section 2.3.2—both oral and intravenous routes); reduce dose in hepatic impairment; children, specialist advice only (see section 2.3.2); pregnancy and breast-feeding; **interactions:** Appendix 1 (calcium-channel blockers)

Contra-indications: hypotension, bradycardia, second- and third-degree heart block, sick sinus syndrome, cardiogenic shock, sino-atrial block, heart failure; atrial flutter or fibrillation complicating Wolff-Parkinson-White syndrome; porphyria

Side-effects: constipation; less commonly nausea, vomiting, flushing, headache, dizziness, fatigue, ankle oedema; rarely reversible impairment of liver function; rarely gynaecomastia and gingival hyperplasia after long-term treatment; after intravenous administration, hypotension, bradycardia, heart block, ventricular fibrillation, and asystole

Dose: by mouth, supraventricular arrhythmias, 40–120 mg 3 times daily
Angina, 80–120 mg 3 times daily
Hypertension, 240–480 mg daily in 2–3 divided doses
By slow intravenous injection over 2 minutes (3 minutes in elderly), 5–10 mg (preferably with ECG monitoring); in paroxysmal tachyarrhythmias a further 5 mg after 5–10 minutes if required

PoM **Verapamil** (Non-proprietary)
Tablets, coated, verapamil hydrochloride 40 mg, net price 20 = 89p; 80 mg, 20 = £1.78; 120 mg, 20 = £2.72; 160 mg, 20 = £3.28

PoM **Berkatens**® (Berk)
Tablets, all yellow, f/c, verapamil hydrochloride 40 mg, net price 20 = 90p; 80 mg, 20 = £1.80; 120 mg, 20 = £2.59; 160 mg, 20 = £3.27

PoM **Cordilox**® (Abbott)
Tablets, all yellow, f/c, verapamil hydrochloride 40 mg, net price 20 = 89p; 80 mg, 20 = £1.78; 120 mg, 20 = £2.72; 160 mg, 56-tab pack = £13.10
Injection, verapamil hydrochloride 2.5 mg/mL, net price 2-mL amp = £1.11

PoM **Securon**® (Knoll)
Tablets, f/c, verapamil hydrochloride 40 mg, net price 100 = £4.69; 80 mg, 100 = £9.38; 120 mg, 56-tab pack = £7.87, 100 = £14.05; 160 mg, 56-tab pack = £10.49, 100 = £18.73
Injection, verapamil hydrochloride 2.5 mg/mL. Net price 2-mL syringe = £1.11

Sustained release
PoM **Securon SR**® (Knoll)
Tablets, s/r, pale green, f/c, verapamil hydrochloride 240 mg. Net price 28-tab pack = £10.92. Label: 25
Dose: hypertension, 1 tablet daily, increased to twice daily if necessary (new patients, initial dose ½ tablet); angina, 1 tablet twice daily (may sometimes be reduced to once daily)

PoM **Univer**® (Rorer)
Capsules, all s/r, verapamil hydrochloride 120 mg (yellow/dark blue), net price 28-cap pack = £7.00; 180 mg (yellow), 56-cap pack = £16.92; 240 mg (yellow/dark blue), 28-cap pack = £11.42. Label: 25
Dose: hypertension, 240 mg daily, max. 480 mg daily (new patients, initial dose 120 mg); angina, 360 mg daily, max. 480 mg daily

2.6.3 Peripheral vasodilators and related drugs

Most serious peripheral disorders, such as *intermittent claudication*, are now known to be due to occlusion of vessels, either by spasm or sclerotic plaques; use of vasodilators may increase blood flow at rest, but no controlled studies have shown any improvement in walking distance or sustained increase in muscle blood flow during exercise. Rest pain is rarely affected.

Management of *Raynaud's syndrome* includes avoidance of exposure to cold and stopping smoking. More severe symptoms may require vasodilator treatment, which is most often successful in primary Raynaud's syndrome. Nifedipine (section 2.6.2), prazosin (section 2.5.4) and thymoxamine have all been shown to be beneficial; cyclandelate, naftidrofuryl, nicotinic acid derivatives, and oxpentifylline are not established as being effective.

CHILBLAINS. Vasodilator therapy is not recommended for chilblains (see section 13.14).

CINNARIZINE

Indications: peripheral vascular disease, Raynaud's syndrome

Cautions; Side-effects: see section 4.6

Dose: initially, 75 mg 3 times daily; maintenance, 75 mg 2–3 times daily

Stugeron Forte® (Janssen)
Capsules, orange/ivory, cinnarizine 75 mg. Net price 20 = £1.61. Label: 2

Stugeron® see section 4.6

NICOTINIC ACID DERIVATIVES

Indications: peripheral vascular disease (for hyperlipidaemia, see section 2.12)
Side-effects: flushing, dizziness, nausea, vomiting, hypotension (more frequent with nicotinic acid than derivatives); occasional diabetogenic effect reported with nicotinic acid

Bradilan® see section 2.12
Hexopal® (Sterling-Winthrop)
Tablets, scored, inositol nicotinate 500 mg. Net price 20 = £3.88
Dose: 0.5–1 g 3 times daily, increased to 4 g daily if required
Tablets forte, scored, inositol nicotinate 750 mg. Net price 112-tab pack = £32.46
Dose: 1.5–3 g daily
Suspension, sugar-free, inositol nicotinate 1 g/5 mL. Diluent syrup, life of diluted suspension 14 days. Net price 300 mL = £19.90
Dose: as for tablets (above)
Ronicol® (Roche)
Tablets, scored, nicotinyl alcohol 25 mg (as tartrate). Net price 20 = 37p
Dose: 25–50 mg 4 times daily
Timespan® (= tablets s/r), red, s/c, nicotinyl alcohol 150 mg (as tartrate). Net price 20 = £1.58. Label: 25
Dose: 150–300 mg twice daily

OXPENTIFYLLINE

Indications: peripheral vascular disease
Cautions: hypotension
Side-effects: nausea, dizziness, flushing
Dose: 400 mg 2–3 times daily

PoM **Trental®** (Hoechst)
Tablets, s/r, pink, s/c, oxpentifylline 400 mg. Net price 90-tab pack = £17.24. Label: 21, 25

THYMOXAMINE

Indications: primary Raynaud's syndrome (short-term treatment)
Cautions: diabetes mellitus
Side-effects: nausea, diarrhoea, flushing, headache, dizziness
Dose: 40–80 mg 4 times daily; discontinue after 2 weeks if no response

PoM **Opilon®** (P-D)
Tablets, yellow, f/c, thymoxamine 40 mg (as hydrochloride). Net price 120-tab pack = £27.48. Label: 21

OTHER PREPARATION USED IN PERIPHERAL VASCULAR DISEASE

Rutosides (oxerutins, Paroven®) are not vasodilators and are not generally regarded as effective preparations as capillary sealants or for the treatment of cramps.

Paroven® (Zyma)
Capsules, yellow, oxerutins 250 mg. Net price 20 = £2.34. Label: 21

2.6.4 Cerebral vasodilators

These drugs are claimed to improve mental function. Some improvements in performance of psychological tests have been reported but the drugs have not been shown clinically to be of much benefit in dementia.

CO-DERGOCRINE MESYLATE

A mixture in equal proportions of dihydroergocornine mesylate, dihydroergocristine mesylate, and (in the ratio 2:1) α- and β-dihydroergocryptine mesylates
Indications: adjunct in elderly patients with mild to moderate dementia
Cautions: severe bradycardia
Side-effects: nausea, vomiting, flushing, headache, rash, nasal congestion, postural hypotension in hypertensive patients
Dose: 1.5 mg 3 times daily *or* 4.5 mg once daily

PoM **Hydergine®** (Sandoz)
Tablets, co-dergocrine mesylate 1.5 mg (scored), net price 20 = £2.21; 4.5 mg, 28-tab pack = £11.06. Label: 22

CYCLANDELATE

Indications: cerebral and peripheral vascular disease
Contra-indications: acute phase of cerebrovascular accident
Side-effects: nausea, flushing, dizziness with high doses
Dose: 1.2–1.6 g daily in 2–4 divided doses

Cyclobral® (Norgine)
Capsules, pink/brown, cyclandelate 400 mg. Net price 20 = £2.36
Cyclospasmol® (Brocades)
Capsules, pink/grey, cyclandelate 400 mg. Net price 20 = £2.40
Tablets, pink, s/c, cyclandelate 400 mg. Net price 112-tab pack = £15.91
Suspension, cyclandelate 400 mg/5 mL when reconstituted with freshly boiled and cooled purified water. Net price 450-mL pack = £11.87

NAFTIDROFURYL OXALATE

Indications: cerebral and peripheral vascular disease
Contra-indications: parenteral administration in atrioventricular block
Side-effects: nausea, epigastric pain
Dose: see below

PoM **Praxilene®** (L:pha)
Capsules, pink, naftidrofuryl oxalate 100 mg. Net price 84-cap pack = £8.60
Dose: peripheral vascular disease, 100–200 mg 3 times daily; cerebral vascular disease, 100 mg 3 times daily
Injection forte, naftidrofuryl oxalate 20 mg/mL. Net price 10-mL amp = £1.10
Dose: peripheral vascular disease only, by intravenous or intra-arterial infusion, 200 mg over at least 90 minutes, twice daily

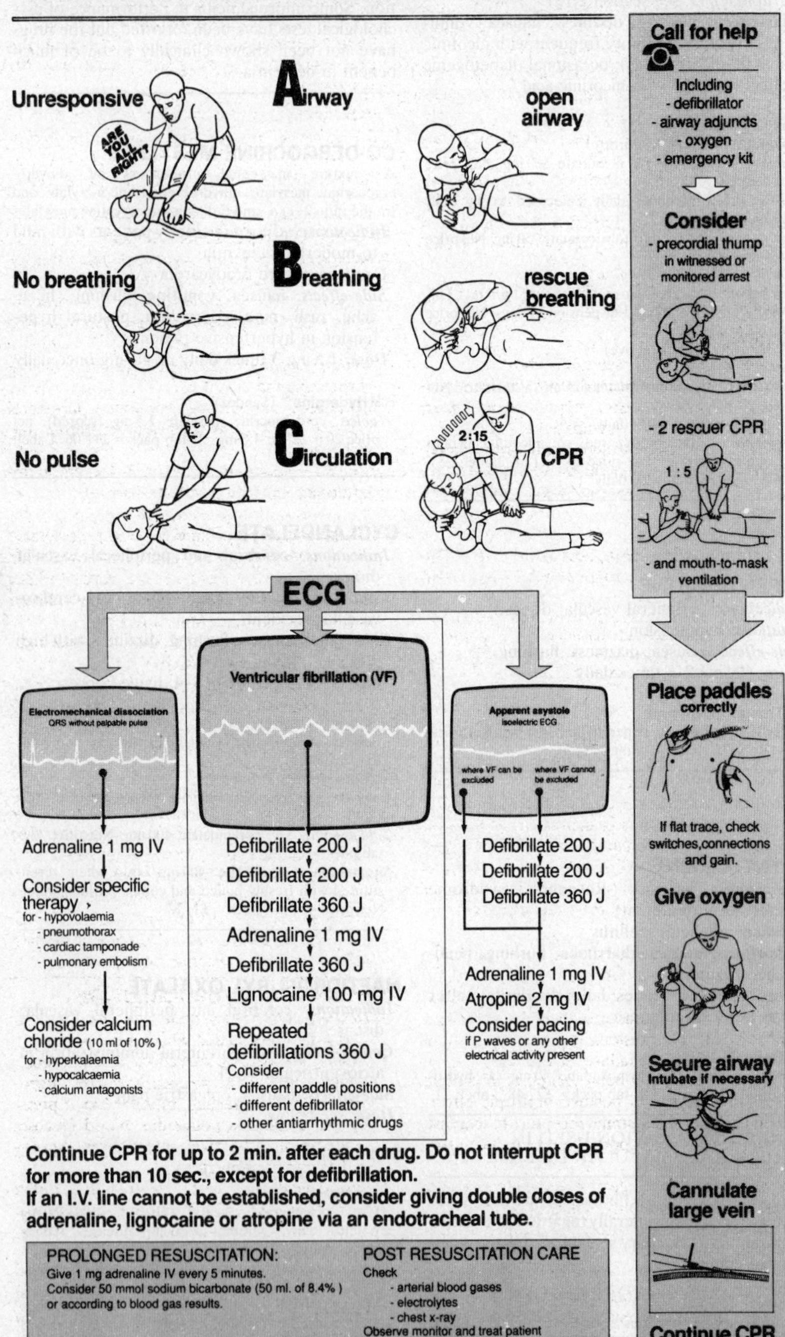

Reproduced with permission of the Resuscitation Council (UK), charts available from Laerdal Medical Ltd

2.7 Sympathomimetics

The properties of sympathomimetics vary according to whether they act on alpha or on beta adrenergic receptors. Adrenaline acts on both alpha and beta receptors and increases both heart rate and contractility (beta$_1$ effects); it can cause peripheral vasodilation (a beta$_2$ effect) or vasoconstriction (an alpha effect).

In *cardiac arrest* adrenaline 1 in 10 000 (1 mg per 10 mL) is recommended in a dose of 10 mL by central intravenous injection. The procedure for cardiopulmonary resuscitation is given in the algorithm (see opposite) which reflects the revised recommendations of the Resuscitation Council (UK).

IMPORTANT. For *acute anaphylaxis* use **intramuscular route** (for dose, see p. 116).

ADRENALINE

Indications and Dose: see notes above

Cautions: ischaemic heart disease, diabetes mellitus, hyperthyroidism, hypertension; **interactions:** Appendix 1 (sympathomimetics)

Side-effects: anxiety, tremor, tachycardia, headache, cold extremities; in overdosage arrhythmias, cerebral haemorrhage, pulmonary oedema

PoM **Adrenaline Injection,** adrenaline 1 in 10000 (adrenaline 100 micrograms/mL as acid tartrate). 10-mL amp.

Available from Macarthys and Penn (special order); also from IMS (Min-I-Jet® Adrenaline)

Note. Adrenaline Injection BP is 1 in 1000 (adrenaline 1 mg/mL, as acid tartrate), see p. 116

2.7.1 Inotropic sympathomimetics

The cardiac stimulants **dobutamine** and **dopamine** act on beta$_1$ receptors in cardiac muscle, and increase contractility with little effect on rate; they are used in cardiogenic shock. Dosage of dopamine is critical since although low doses induce vasodilatation and increase renal perfusion, higher doses (more than 5 micrograms per kg per minute) lead to vasoconstriction and may exacerbate heart failure.

Xamoterol also acts on beta$_1$ receptors but being a partial agonist it provokes only a modest stimulatory response at rest. **Important:** for CSM restriction limiting xamoterol to **mild heart failure only**, owing to deterioration in patients with moderate to severe heart failure, see p. 88.

Dopexamine acts on beta$_2$ receptors in cardiac muscle to produce its positive inotropic effect; and on peripheral dopamine receptors to increase renal perfusion; it is reported not to induce vasoconstriction.

Isoprenaline is less selective and increases both heart rate and contractility; it may prevent Stokes-Adams attacks, but insertion of a pacemaker is preferable.

DOBUTAMINE HYDROCHLORIDE

Indications: inotropic support in infarction, cardiac surgery, cardiomyopathies, septic shock, and cardiogenic shock

Cautions: severe hypotension complicating cardiogenic shock

Side-effects: tachycardia and marked increase in systolic blood pressure indicate overdosage

Dose: *by intravenous infusion*, 2.5–10 micrograms/kg/minute, adjusted according to response

PoM **Dobutrex®** (Lilly)

Strong sterile solution, dobutamine (as hydrochloride) 12.5 mg/mL. For dilution and use as an intravenous infusion. Net price 20-mL vial = £13.92

DOPAMINE HYDROCHLORIDE

Indications: cardiogenic shock in infarction or cardiac surgery

Cautions: correct hypovolaemia; low dose in shock due to acute myocardial infarction—see notes above

Contra-indications: tachyarrhythmia, phaeochromocytoma

Side-effects: nausea and vomiting, peripheral vasoconstriction, hypotension, hypertension, tachycardia

Dose: *by intravenous infusion*, 2–5 micrograms/kg/minute initially (see notes above)

PoM **Dopamine Hydrochloride** (Non-proprietary)

Strong sterile solution, dopamine hydrochloride 40 mg/mL, net price 5-mL amp = £4.30; 160 mg/mL, 5-mL amp = £17.25. For dilution and use as an intravenous infusion

PoM **Dopamine Hydrochloride in Dextrose (Glucose) Injection** (Abbott)

Intravenous infusions (in glucose 5% intravenous infusion), dopamine hydrochloride 800 micrograms/mL, 1.6 mg/mL, and 3.2 mg/mL. 250-mL containers (all hosp. only)

PoM **Intropin®** (Du Pont)

Strong sterile solution, dopamine hydrochloride 40 mg/mL, net price 5-mL amp or syringe = £4.80; 160 mg/mL, 5-mL amp = £19.20. For dilution and use as an intravenous infusion

PoM **Select-A-Jet® Dopamine** (IMS)

Strong sterile solution, dopamine hydrochloride 40 mg/mL. Net price 5-mL vial = £3.88; 10-mL vial = £7.75; 20-mL vial = £11.63. For dilution and use as an intravenous infusion.

DOPEXAMINE HYDROCHLORIDE

Indications: inotropic support and vasodilator in heart failure associated with cardiac surgery

Cautions: myocardial infarction, recent angina, hypokalaemia, hyperglycaemia; correct hypovolaemia before starting, monitor blood pressure, pulse, plasma potassium, blood glucose; avoid abrupt withdrawal; interactions: Appendix 1 (sympathomimetics)

Contra-indications: left ventricular outlet obstruction such as hypertrophic cardiomyopathy or aortic stenosis; phaeochromocytoma, thrombocytopenia

Side-effects: increased heart rate (occasionally excessive tachycardia, particularly in atrial fibrillation), ventricular ectopic beats; also reported: nausea, vomiting, anginal pain, tremor

Dose: *by intravenous infusion* via caval catheter, 500 nanograms/kg/minute, may be increased to 1 microgram/kg/minute and further increased up to 6 micrograms/kg/minute in increments of 1 microgram/kg/minute at intervals of 10–15 minutes

▼ PoM **Dopacard®** (Fisons)
Strong sterile solution, dopexamine hydrochloride 10 mg/mL (1%). For dilution and use as an intravenous infusion. Net price 5-mL amp = £19.42
Note. Contact with metal in infusion apparatus should be minimised

ISOPRENALINE HYDROCHLORIDE

Indications: heart block, severe bradycardia
Cautions: ischaemic heart disease, diabetes mellitus, hyperthyroidism; **interactions:** Appendix 1 (sympathomimetics)
Side-effects: tachycardia, arrhythmias, hypotension, sweating, tremor, headache
Dose: *by mouth*, 30 mg every 8 hours, then increased; max. daily dose usually 840 mg
By intravenous infusion, 0.5–10 micrograms/minute

PoM **Min-I-Jet® Isoprenaline** (IMS)
Injection, isoprenaline hydrochloride 20 micrograms/mL. Net price 10-mL disposable syringe = £2.95 and £3.46 (longer needle)

PoM **Saventrine®** (Pharmax)
Tablets, isoprenaline hydrochloride 30 mg. Net price 20 = £1.72

PoM **Saventrine IV®** (Pharmax)
Strong sterile solution, isoprenaline hydrochloride 1 mg/mL. For dilution and use as an intravenous infusion. Net price 2-mL amp = 45p

XAMOTEROL

Indications: restricted by CSM to chronic mild heart failure (in patients not breathless at rest but limited by symptoms on exertion)
Cautions: withdraw if heart failure deteriorates; cardiac outflow obstruction, arrhythmias (maintain concurrent digoxin in atrial fibrillation), obstructive airways disease (withdraw if worsening, and reverse bronchospasm with inhaled bronchodilator such as salbutamol), reduce dose in renal impairment; pregnancy (toxicity in *animal* studies)
Contra-indications: moderate to severe heart failure; breast-feeding

HEART FAILURE. Patients in whom xamoterol is contra-indicated are those:
- who are short of breath or fatigued at rest or limited on minimal exercise;
- with resting tachycardia (>90 beats per minute) or hypotension (systolic BP<100 mmHg);
- with peripheral oedema, raised jugular venous pressure, enlarged liver, or third heart sound;
- with (or with history of) acute pulmonary oedema;
- who require treatment with frusemide in dose in excess of 40 mg daily (or equivalent);
- who require ACE inhibitor treatment

Side-effects: gastro-intestinal disturbances, headache, dizziness, bronchospasm, hypotension; also reported: chest pain, palpitations, muscle cramp, rashes
Dose: 200 mg daily for 1 week, then 200 mg twice daily
IMPORTANT. Treatment should be started in hospital after full assessment of severity of heart failure by exercise test

▼ PoM **Corwin®** (Stuart)
Tablets, yellow, f/c, xamoterol (as fumarate) 200 mg. Net price 56-tab pack = £26.60

2.7.2 Vasoconstrictor sympathomimetics

Vasoconstrictors raise blood pressure transiently by constricting peripheral vessels. They are sometimes used as an emergency method of elevating blood pressure while preparations are being made for more effective therapy such as transfusion. They may also be used in general and spinal anaesthesia to control blood pressure.

The danger of vasoconstrictors is that although they raise blood pressure they do so at the expense of perfusion of vital organs such as the kidney. Further, in many patients with shock the peripheral resistance is already high, and to raise it further is unhelpful. Thus the use of vasoconstrictors in the treatment of shock is to be generally **deprecated**. The use of volume expanders such as blood or plasma, or of the inotropic agents dopamine, dobutamine, or isoprenaline is more appropriate (section 2.7.1). Treatment of the underlying condition, e.g. with antibiotics, in septic shock, is obviously important.

METARAMINOL

Indications: acute hypotension
Cautions; Contra-indications: see under Noradrenaline Acid Tartrate
Side-effects: tachycardia, arrhythmias, reduced renal blood flow
Dose: *by subcutaneous or intramuscular injection*, 2–10 mg
By intravenous infusion, 15–100 mg in 500 mL, adjusted according to response

PoM **Aramine®** (MSD)
Injection, metaraminol 10 mg (as tartrate)/mL. Net price 1-mL amp = 48p

METHOXAMINE HYDROCHLORIDE

Indications: hypotension in anaesthesia
Cautions: hyperthyroidism; pregnancy; **interactions:** Appendix 1 (sympathomimetics)
Contra-indications: severe coronary or cardiovascular disease
Side-effects: headache, hypertension, bradycardia
Dose: *by intramuscular injection*, 5–20 mg
By slow intravenous injection, 5–10 mg (rate 1 mg/minute)

PoM **Vasoxine®** (Calmic)
Injection, methoxamine hydrochloride 20 mg/mL. Net price 1-mL amp = 45p

NORADRENALINE ACID TARTRATE

Indications: acute hypotension, cardiac arrest
Cautions: extravasation at injection site may cause necrosis; **interactions:** Appendix 1 (sympathomimetics)
Contra-indications: myocardial infarction, pregnancy
Side-effects: headache, palpitations, bradycardia
Dose: *by intravenous infusion*, of a solution containing noradrenaline acid tartrate 8 micrograms/mL (equivalent to noradrenaline base 4 micrograms/mL) at an initial rate of 2 to 3 mL/minute, adjusted according to response
By rapid intravenous or intracardiac injection, 0.5 to 0.75 mL of a solution containing noradrenaline acid tartrate 200 micrograms/mL (equivalent to noradrenaline base 100 micrograms/mL)

PoM **Levophed®** (Sterling-Winthrop)
Strong sterile solution, noradrenaline acid tartrate 2 mg/mL. For dilution and use as an intravenous infusion. Net price 2-mL amp = 86p; 4-mL amp = £1.27
Special injection, noradrenaline acid tartrate 200 micrograms/mL. Net price 2-mL amp = 83p

PHENYLEPHRINE HYDROCHLORIDE

Indications: acute hypotension
Cautions; Contra-indications: see under Noradrenaline Acid Tartrate; also contra-indicated in severe hypertension and hyperthyroidism
Side-effects: hypertension with headache, palpitations, vomiting; tachycardia or reflex bradycardia; tingling and coolness of skin
Dose: *by subcutaneous or intramuscular injection*, 5 mg
By slow intravenous injection, 100–500 micrograms
By intravenous infusion, 5–20 mg in 500 mL, adjusted according to response

PoM **Phenylephrine Injection 1%** (Boots)
Injection, phenylephrine hydrochloride 10 mg/mL. 1-mL amp

2.8 Anticoagulants and protamine

The main use of anticoagulants is to prevent thrombus formation or extension of an existing thrombus in the slower-moving venous side of the circulation, where the thrombus consists of a fibrin web enmeshed with platelets and red cells. They are therefore widely used in the prevention and treatment of *deep-vein thrombosis in the legs*.

Anticoagulants are of less use in preventing thrombus formation in arteries, for in faster-flowing vessels thrombi are composed mainly of platelets with little fibrin. They are used to prevent thrombi forming on *prosthetic heart valves*.

2.8.1 Parenteral anticoagulants

Heparin is given to initiate anticoagulation and is rapidly effective. As its effects are short-lived it is best given by continuous infusion; if given by intermittent intravenous injection, the interval between doses must not exceed 6 hours. Oral anticoagulants are started at the same time, and the heparin infusion withdrawn after 3 days.

If oral anticoagulants cannot be given and heparin is continued, its dose is adjusted after determination of the activated partial thromboplastin time.

If haemorrhage occurs it is usually sufficient to withdraw heparin, but if rapid reversal of the effects of heparin is required, protamine sulphate is a specific antidote (section 2.8.3).

For the prophylaxis of thrombosis in patients undergoing heart surgery or renal dialysis full therapeutic doses of heparin are given for the duration of the procedure. Low-dose heparin by subcutaneous injection is widely advocated to prevent postoperative deep-vein thrombosis and pulmonary embolism in 'high risk' patients, i.e. those with obesity, malignant disease, or previous history of thrombosis. Laboratory monitoring is not required with this regimen.

CSM advice. Platelet counts should be measured in patients under heparin treatment for longer than 5 days and the treatment should be stopped immediately in those who develop thrombocytopenia.

HEPARIN

Indications: deep-vein thrombosis, disseminated intravascular coagulation, prevention of postoperative thrombosis
Cautions: pregnancy; **interactions:** Appendix 1 (heparin)
Contra-indications: haemophilia and other haemorrhagic disorders, peptic ulcer, cerebral aneurysm, severe hypertension, severe liver disease, recent surgery of eye or nervous system, hypersensitivity to heparin
Side-effects: haemorrhage, thrombocytopenia (see CSM advice above), hypersensitivity reactions; osteoporosis after prolonged use, alopecia
Dose: *by intravenous injection*, loading dose of 5000 units followed by continuous *infusion* of 1000–2000 units/hour (approx. 14–28 units/kg/hour) adjusted daily by laboratory monitoring *or* 5000–10 000 units by *intravenous injection* every 4 hours
By subcutaneous injection, prophylaxis of deep-vein thrombosis, 5000 units 2 hours before surgery, then every 8–12 hours until patient is ambulant; in pregnancy, 10 000 units every 12 hours
Treatment of deep-vein thrombosis, initially 10000–20000 units every 12 hours *or* 250 units/kg (2500 units/10 kg) every 12 hours, adjusted daily by laboratory monitoring

Intravenous preparations

PoM **Heparin Injection** (heparin sodium)

1000 units/mL, net price 1-mL amp = 21p; 5-mL amp = 69p; 5-mL vial = 54p

5000 units/mL, net price 1-mL amp = 33p; 5-mL amp = 98p; 5-mL vial = £1.46

10 000 units/mL, net price 1-mL amp = 45p

25 000 units/mL, net price 1-mL amp = 86p; 5-mL vial = £6.43

PoM **Monoparin®** (CP)

Injection, heparin sodium (mucous) 1000 units/mL, net price 1-mL amp = 16p; 5-mL amp = 46p; 10-mL amp = 66p; 5000 units/mL, 1-mL amp = 32p; 5-mL amp = 98p; 25 000 units/mL, 1-mL amp = £1.27

PoM **Multiparin®** (CP)

Injection, heparin sodium (mucous) 1000 units/mL, net price 5-mL vial = 45p; 5000 units/mL, 5-mL vial = £1.32; 25 000 units/mL, 5-mL vial = £5.41

PoM **Pump-Hep®** (Leo)

Intravenous infusion, heparin sodium (mucous) 1000 units/mL. Net price 5-mL amp = 40p; 10-mL amp = 66p; 20-mL amp = 98p

Dose: by continuous infusion pump, 20 000–40 000 units daily

PoM **Unihep®** (Leo)

Injection, heparin sodium (mucous) 1000 units/mL, net price 1-mL amp = 14p; 5000 units/mL, 1-mL amp = 27p; 10 000 units/mL, 1-mL amp = 45p; 25 000 units/mL, 1-mL amp = £1.07

Subcutaneous preparations

PoM **Heparin Injection** (heparin sodium or heparin calcium)

25 000 units/mL (subcutaneous). Net price 0.2-mL amp = 54p

PoM **Calciparine®** (Sanofi)

Injection (subcutaneous), heparin calcium 25 000 units/mL. Net price 0.2-mL syringe = 70p; 0.5-mL amp = £1.50; 0.8-mL amp = £1.80

PoM **Minihep®** (Leo)

Injection (subcutaneous), heparin sodium 25 000 units/mL. Net price 0.2-mL amp = 42p

PoM **Minihep Calcium®** (Leo)

Injection (subcutaneous), heparin calcium 25 000 units/mL. Net price 0.2-mL amp = 45p

PoM **Monoparin®** (CP)

Injection (subcutaneous), heparin sodium (mucous) 25 000 units/mL. Net price 0.2-mL amp = 37p

PoM **Monoparin Calcium®** (CP)

Injection (subcutaneous), heparin calcium 25 000 units/mL. Net price 0.2 mL amp = 52p

PoM **Uniparin®** (CP)

Injection (subcutaneous), heparin sodium 25 000 units/mL. Net price 0.2-mL syringe = 60p; 0.4-mL syringe (Uniparin Forte) = £1.30

PoM **Uniparin Calcium®** (CP)

Injection (subcutaneous), heparin calcium 25 000 units/mL. Net price 0.2-mL syringe = 60p; 0.5-mL syringe = £1.45

Low molecular weight heparin

For the prevention of clotting in extracorporeal circulation during haemodialysis or haemofiltration in patients with chronic renal insufficiency or acute renal failure.

▼ PoM **Fragmin®** (Kabi)

Injection, low molecular weight heparin 2500 units/mL, net price 4-mL amp = £5.50; 10000 units/mL, 1-mL amp = £5.50

For prevention of clotting in extracorporeal circulation (consult data sheet)

Heparin flushes

For maintaining catheter patency sodium chloride injection 0.9% is as effective as heparin flushes for up to 48 hours, and is therefore recommended for cannulas intended to be in place for 48 hours or less. Heparin flushes are recommended for cannulas intended to be in place for longer than 48 hours.

PoM **Heparinised Saline** (Paines & Byrne)

Solution, heparin sodium (mucous) 10 units/mL. Net price 5-mL amp = 22p

To maintain patency of catheters, cannulas, etc., 50 units flushed through every 4 hours or as required. Not for therapeutic use

PoM **Hep-Flush®** (Leo)

Solution, heparin sodium 100 units/mL. Net price 2-mL amp = 26p

To maintain patency of catheters, cannulas, etc., 200 units flushed through every 4–8 hours. Not for therapeutic use

PoM **Heplok®** (Leo)

Solution, heparin sodium 10 units/mL. Net price 5-mL amp = 30p

To maintain patency of catheters, cannulas, etc., 10–50 units flushed through every 4 hours. Not for therapeutic use

PoM **Hepsal®** (CP)

Solution, heparin sodium 10 units/mL. Net price 5-mL amp = 22p

To maintain patency of catheters, cannulas, etc., 50 units flushed through every 4 hours or as required. Not for therapeutic use

Ancrod reduces plasma fibrinogen by cleavage of fibrin. It has been shown to be as effective as heparin in the resolution of deep-vein thromboses, but some patients develop resistance.

Ancrod has been used subcutaneously for prophylaxis in patients likely to develop deep-vein thrombosis, but is not in common use.

ANCROD

Indications: deep-vein thrombosis, prevention of postoperative thrombosis

Cautions; Contra-indications; Side-effects: see under Heparin; resistance may develop; avoid administration with dextrans

Dose: *by intravenous infusion*, 2–3 units/kg over 4–12 hours (usually 6–8 hours), then *by infusion or slow intravenous injection*, 2 units/kg every 12 hours

By subcutaneous injection, prophylaxis of deep-vein thrombosis, 280 units immediately after surgery, then 70 units daily for 4 days (fractured femur) or 8 days (hip replacement)

Note. The initial infusion must be given slowly, as there is a risk of massive intravascular formation of unstable fibrin. Response can be monitored by observing clot size after the blood has been allowed to stand for about 2 hours, the aim being to predict a dose that produces a 2–3 mm clot. Alternatively, plasma-fibrinogen concentrations can be measured directly.

The major complication of ancrod is haemorrhage, and since it takes 12 to 24 hours for haemostatic fibrinogen concentrations to be restored after stopping administration it may be necessary to give ancrod antivenom (Arvin® Antidote, available from Armour) as an antidote (0.2-mL test dose subcutaneously followed by 0.8 mL intramuscularly, and 30 minutes later 1 mL intravenously). The antivenom may cause anaphylaxis (adrenaline etc. should be available, for details see Allergic Emergencies, section 3.4.3). As an alternative to the antivenom reconstituted freeze-dried fibrinogen may be given, or if this is not available one litre of fresh frozen plasma.

PoM **Arvin®** (Armour)
Injection, ancrod 70 units/mL. Net price 1-mL amp = £9.25 (hosp. only)

Epoprostenol (prostacyclin) can be given to inhibit platelet aggregation during renal dialysis either alone or with heparin. Since its half-life is only about 3 minutes it must be given by continuous intravenous infusion. It is a potent vasodilator and therefore its side-effects include flushing, headache, and hypotension.

EPOPROSTENOL

Indications: see notes above
Cautions: anticoagulant monitoring required when given with heparin
Side-effects: see notes above; also bradycardia, pallor, sweating with higher doses
Dose: see manufacturer's literature

PoM **Flolan®** (Wellcome)
Infusion, powder for reconstitution, epoprostenol (as sodium salt). Net price 500-microgram vial (with diluent) = £103.86

2.8.2 Oral anticoagulants

Oral anticoagulants antagonise the effects of vitamin K, and take at least 36 to 48 hours for the anticoagulant effect to develop; if an immediate effect is required, heparin must be given concomitantly.

The main indication for oral anticoagulant therapy is *deep-vein thrombosis*. Patients with poorly controlled *atrial fibrillation who are at risk of embolisation* should also be treated, as should patients with *mechanical heart valve prostheses*, to prevent emboli developing on the valves; antiplatelet drugs may also be useful in these patients.

Oral anticoagulants should not be used in cerebral thrombosis or peripheral arterial occlusion, but may be of value in patients with *transient brain ischaemic attacks* whether due to carotid or vertebrobasilar arterial disease; if these patients also have severe hypertension anticoagulants are contra-indicated, and antiplatelet drugs are an alternative (section 2.9).

Warfarin and other coumarins are the drugs of choice, as they are less likely to cause sensitivity reactions than **phenindione**.

Whenever possible, the base-line prothrombin time should be determined before the initial dose is given.

A typical induction dose of warfarin is 10 mg[1] daily for 2 days (but this should be tailored to individual requirement). The subsequent maintenance dose depends upon the prothrombin time (reported as INR[2]); the currently recommended therapeutic ranges are:

INR 2–2.5 for prophylactic therapy of deep-vein thrombosis including high-risk surgery;
INR 2–3 for prophylactic therapy in hip surgery and fractured femur operations, for treatment of deep-vein thrombosis, pulmonary embolism, and transient ischaemic attacks;
INR 3–4.5 for recurrent deep-vein thrombosis and pulmonary embolism, arterial disease including myocardial infarction, and mechanical prosthetic heart valves.

It is essential that the INR be determined:
daily or on alternate days in early days of treatment, *then*
at longer intervals (depending on response) *then*
up to every 8 weeks

The daily maintenance dose[3] of warfarin is usually 3 to 9 mg (taken at the **same time** each day).

The main adverse effect of all oral anti-coagulants is haemorrhage. Omission of dosage with checking of the INR is essential. The following recommendations of the British Society for Haematology are based on the result of the INR and the clinical state:

Life-threatening haemorrhage—immediately give phytomenadione (vitamin K_1) 5 mg by slow intravenous injection and a concentrate of factors II, IX, X (with factor VII concentrate if available). If no concentrate is available, fresh frozen plasma should be infused (approximately 1 litre for an adult) but this may not be as effective
Less severe haemorrhage e.g. haematuria and epistaxis—withhold warfarin for one or more days and consider giving phytomenadione (vitamin K_1) 0.5–2 mg[4] by slow intravenous injection
INR 4.5–7 without haemorrhage—withhold warfarin for 1 or 2 days then review
INR > 7 without haemorrhage—withhold warfarin and consider giving phytomenadione (vitamin K_1) 500 micrograms by slow intravenous injection
Unexpected bleeding at therapeutic levels[5]—investigate possibility of underlying cause e.g. unexpected renal or alimentary tract pathology

---

1. Less than 10 mg if base-line prothrombin time prolonged, if liver-function tests abnormal, or if patient in cardiac failure, on parenteral feeding, or over 80 years of age.
2. The International Normalised Ratio (INR) has now replaced the British Ratio (BR).
3. Change in patient's clinical condition, particularly associated with liver disease or drug administration, necessitates more frequent testing. See also **interactions**, Appendix 1 (warfarin). Major changes in diet may also affect warfarin control.
4. Usually 1 mg adequate and should be given if INR greater than desired.
5. Should always be investigated regardless of INR since even if patients over-anticoagulated bleeding generally has an additional underlying cause.

Phytomenadione will take up to 12 hours to act and will prevent oral anticoagulants from acting for several days or even weeks.

PREGNANCY. Oral anticoagulants are weakly teratogenic and should not be given in the first trimester of pregnancy. Women at risk of pregnancy should be warned of this danger. Also, oral anticoagulants cross the placenta with risk of placental or fetal haemorrhage; they should therefore not be given during the last few weeks of pregnancy.

Anticoagulant treatment cards must be carried by patients, and are available from:

DHSS Store	SHHD (Div IIID)
No. 2 Site	Room 9
Manchester Rd	St. Andrew's House
Heywood	Edinburgh EH1 3DE
Lancs OL10 2PZ	

Cards giving advice for patients on anticoagulant treatment may be given to patients at the discretion of the doctor or pharmacist.

WARFARIN SODIUM

Indications: prophylaxis of embolisation in rheumatic heart disease and atrial fibrillation; prophylaxis after insertion of prosthetic heart valve; prophylaxis and treatment of venous thrombosis and pulmonary embolism; transient ischaemic attacks
Cautions: hepatic or renal disease, recent surgery; **interactions:** Appendix 1 (warfarin)
Contra-indications: pregnancy (see notes above), peptic ulcer, severe hypertension, bacterial endocarditis
Side-effects: haemorrhage
Dose: see notes above

PoM **Marevan**® (DF)
Tablets, brown, scored, warfarin sodium 1 mg. Net price 20 = 9p. Label: 10 anticoagulant card
Tablets, blue, scored, warfarin sodium 3 mg. Net price 20 = 10p. Label: 10 anticoagulant card
Tablets, pink, scored, warfarin sodium 5 mg. Net price 20 = 16p. Label: 10 anticoagulant card

PoM **Warfarin WBP** (Boehringer Ingelheim)
Tablets, brown, scored, warfarin sodium 1 mg. Net price 20 = 9p. Label: 10 anticoagulant card
Tablets, blue, scored, warfarin sodium 3 mg. Net price 20 = 10p. Label: 10 anticoagulant card
Tablets, pink, scored, warfarin sodium 5 mg. Net price 20 = 16p. Label: 10 anticoagulant card

NICOUMALONE

Indications: prophylaxis of embolisation in rheumatic heart disease and atrial fibrillation; prophylaxis after insertion of prosthetic heart valve; prophylaxis and treatment of venous thrombosis and pulmonary embolism; transient ischaemic attacks
Cautions; Contra-indications; Side-effects: see under Warfarin Sodium; avoid breast-feeding
Dose: 8–12 mg on 1st day; 4–8 mg on 2nd day; maintenance dose usually 1–8 mg daily

PoM **Sinthrome**® (Geigy)
Tablets, pink, nicoumalone 1 mg. Net price 20 = 15p. Label: 10 anticoagulant card
Tablets, scored, nicoumalone 4 mg. Net price 20 = 31p. Label: 10 anticoagulant card

PHENINDIONE

Indications: prophylaxis of embolisation in rheumatic heart disease and atrial fibrillation; prophylaxis after insertion of prosthetic heart valve; prophylaxis and treatment of venous thrombosis and pulmonary embolism
Cautions; Contra-indications; Side-effects: see under Warfarin Sodium; also hypersensitivity reactions including rashes, fever, leucopenia, agranulocytosis, diarrhoea, renal and hepatic damage; urine coloured pink; avoid breast-feeding; **interactions:** Appendix 1 (phenindione)
Dose: 200 mg on 1st day; 100 mg on 2nd day; maintenance dose usually 50–150 mg daily

COUNSELLING. It should be made clear to patient that it is urine that may be coloured, not stools

PoM **Dindevan**® (DF)
Tablets, phenindione 10 mg, net price 20 = 26p; 25 mg (green), 20 = 36p; 50 mg, 20 = 46p. Label: 10 anticoagulant card, counselling, urine pink, see above

2.8.3 Protamine sulphate

Although protamine sulphate is used to counteract overdosage with heparin, if used in excess it has an anticoagulant effect.

PROTAMINE SULPHATE

Indications; Cautions: see above
Side-effects: flushing, hypotension, bradycardia
Dose: *by slow intravenous injection*, 1 mg neutralises 100 units heparin (mucous) or 80 units heparin (lung) when given within 15 minutes; if longer time, less protamine required as heparin rapidly excreted; max. 50 mg

PoM **Protamine Sulphate**
Injection, protamine sulphate 10 mg/mL. Net price 5-mL amp = 98p; 10-mL amp = 84p
Available from CP (Prosulf®)

2.9 Antiplatelet drugs

By decreasing platelet adhesiveness, these drugs may inhibit thrombus formation on the arterial side of the circulation, where thrombi are formed by platelet aggregation and anticoagulants have little effect. Antiplatelet drugs have little effect in venous thromboembolism. **Dipyridamole** is used with anticoagulants to prevent thrombus formation on prosthetic valves.

Encouraging results have been obtained using **aspirin** 300 mg daily for the *secondary* prevention of cerebrovascular or cardiovascular disease;

studies are still needed to determine whether lower doses (such as 75 mg daily or 300 mg on alternate days) might not be equally (or more) effective. Aspirin has also been shown to reduce mortality when given in a dose of 150 mg daily for a month after myocardial infarction. Physicians in the USA have demonstrated that 325 mg on alternate days can have a *primary* preventive action for myocardial infarction but further analysis is awaited before aspirin can be recommended for routine use in primary prevention.

For use of epoprostenol, see section 2.8.1.

ASPIRIN (antiplatelet)

Indications: prophylaxis of cerebrovascular disease or myocardial infarction (see notes above)

Cautions: asthma; uncontrolled hypertension; pregnancy; **interactions:** Appendix 1 (aspirin)

Contra-indications: children under 12 years and in breast-feeding (Reye's syndrome, see section 4.7.1); active peptic ulceration; haemophilia and other bleeding disorders

Side-effects: bronchospasm; gastro-intestinal haemorrhage (occasionally major)

Dose: see below

Aspirin (Non-proprietary)

Dispersible tablets, aspirin 75 mg, net price 20 = 10p; 300 mg, see section 4.7.1. Label: 13, 21

Angettes 75® (Bristol-Myers)

Tablets, aspirin 75 mg. Net price 56-tab pack = £1.88

Dose: prophylaxis after myocardial infarction, 2 tablets daily as a single dose; unstable angina, 4 tablets daily as a single dose

Nu-Seals Aspirin 300 mg: see section 4.7.1

Platet® (Nicholas)

Tablets, effervescent, aspirin 100 mg. Net price 30-tab pack = 90p. Label: 13

Dose: antiplatelet, following bypass surgery, 1 tablet daily

300 Tablets, effervescent, aspirin 300 mg. Net price 30-tab pack = £1.03. Label: 13

Dose: to reduce risk of myocardial infarction in patients with unstable angina or following a previous myocardial infarction and to reduce risk of occlusive stroke and recurrent transient cerebral ischaemic attacks in patients with history of such attacks, 1 tablet daily

DIPYRIDAMOLE

Indications: see notes above

Cautions: rapidly worsening angina, aortic stenosis, recent myocardial infarction; may exacerbate migraine, hypotension; **interactions:** Appendix 1 (dipyridamole)

Side-effects: nausea, diarrhoea, throbbing headache, hypotension

Dose: by mouth, 300–600 mg daily in 3–4 divided doses before food

By intravenous injection, diagnostic only, see manufacturer's literature

PoM **Dipyridamole** (Non-proprietary)

Tablets, coated, dipyridamole 25 mg, net price 20 = 74p; 100 mg, 20 = £1.89. Label: 22

Available from APS, Cox, Kerfoot, Shire (Vasyrol®)

PoM **Persantin®** (Boehringer Ingelheim)

Tablets, both s/c, dipyridamole 25 mg (orange), net price 84-tab pack = £3.17; 100 mg, 84-tab pack = £8.84. Label: 22

Injection, dipyridamole 5 mg/mL. Net price 2-mL amp = 10p

2.10 Fibrinolytic drugs

Fibrinolytic drugs act as thrombolytics by activating plasminogen to form plasmin, which degrades fibrin and so breaks up thrombi.

Streptokinase is used in the treatment of *life-threatening venous thrombosis*, and in *pulmonary embolism*, but treatment must be started rapidly.

Urokinase is currently used for *thrombolysis in the eye* and in *arteriovenous shunts*. It has the advantage of being non-immunogenic.

The value of thrombolytic drugs for the treatment of *myocardial infarction* has recently been established. **Streptokinase, alteplase,** and **anistreplase** have all been shown to reduce mortality when given by the intravenous route; evidence on comparative efficacy is incomplete. The potential for benefit lessens as the delay from the onset of major symptoms increases, but the value of treatment within the first 12 hours is reasonably well established. Knowledge of the role of adjuvant therapy is also incomplete, but in the case of streptokinase the reduction in mortality by aspirin has been shown to be additive whilst immediate heparin is necessary to obtain full efficacy from alteplase. Thrombolytic drugs are indicated for any patient with acute myocardial infarction for whom the benefit is believed to outweigh the risk of treatment. Trials have shown that the benefit is greatest in those with ECG changes that include ST segment elevation and in those with anterior infarction. Patients should not be excluded on account of age alone because mortality in this group is high and the percentage reduction in mortality is the same as in younger patients.

CAUTIONS. Risk of bleeding from venepuncture or invasive procedures, any external chest compression, pregnancy, possibility of pre-existing thrombus as in abdominal aneurysm or enlarged left atrium with atrial fibrillation (risk of dissolution of clot and subsequent embolisation), recent or concurrent anticoagulant therapy.

CONTRA-INDICATIONS. Recent haemorrhage, trauma, or surgery (including dental extraction), coagulation defects, bleeding diatheses, history of cerebrovascular disease especially recent events or with any residual disability, recent symptoms of possible peptic ulceration, heavy vaginal bleeding, severe hypertension, pulmonary disease with cavitation, acute pancreatitis, diabetic retinopathy, severe liver disease, oesophageal varices. In the case of streptokinase or anistreplase, previous allergic reactions to either drug, or therapy with either drug from 5 days to 12 months previously.

SIDE-EFFECTS. Side-effects of thrombolytics are mainly nausea and vomiting and bleeding. Bleeding is usually limited to the site of injection, but intracerebral haemorrhage or bleeding from other sites may occur. Serious bleeding calls for discontinuation of the thrombolytic and may require administration of coagulation factors and antifibrinolytic drugs (aprotinin or tranexamic acid). Streptokinase and anistreplase may cause allergic reactions and anaphylaxis has been reported (for details of management see Allergic Emergencies, section 3.4.3).

ALTEPLASE

(rt-PA, tissue-type plasminogen activator)

Indications: acute myocardial infarction (see notes above)

Cautions; Contra-indications; Side-effects: see notes above

Dose: by intravenous injection, 10 mg over 1–2 minutes, followed by *intravenous infusion* of 50 mg over 1 hour, then 40 mg over the subsequent 2 hours (total dose 100 mg over 3 hours); treatment should be initiated within 6 hours; patients weighing less than 67 kg should receive a total dose of 1.5 mg/kg according to the above schedule

PoM **Actilyse®** (Boehringer Ingelheim)

Injection, powder for reconstitution, alteplase 20 mg (11.6 mega units)/vial, net price per vial (with diluent and transfer device) = £200.00; 50 mg (29 mega units)/vial, pack of 2 vials (with diluent, transfer device, and infusion bag) = £816.00

ANISTREPLASE

(APSAC)

Indications: acute myocardial infarction (see notes above)

Cautions; Contra-indications; Side-effects: see notes above

Dose: by intravenous injection, 30 units over 4–5 minutes; treatment should be initiated as soon as possible and preferably within 6 hours

▼ PoM **Eminase®** (Beecham)

Injection, powder for reconstitution, anistreplase. Net price 30-unit vial = £495.00

STREPTOKINASE

Indications: deep-vein thrombosis, pulmonary embolism, acute arterial thromboembolism, thrombosed arteriovenous shunts; acute myocardial infarction (see notes above)

Cautions; Contra-indications; Side-effects: see notes above

Dose: by intravenous infusion, 250 000 units over 30 minutes, then 100 000 units every hour for up to 24–72 hours according to condition (see data sheet)

Myocardial infarction, 1 500 000 units over 60 minutes followed by aspirin 150 mg daily *by mouth* for at least 4 weeks (see data sheet)

PoM **Kabikinase®** (Kabi)

Injection, powder for reconstitution, streptokinase; net price 100 000-unit vial = £7.50; 250 000-unit vial = £15.00; 600 000-unit vial = £34.20; 1.5 million-unit vial = £85.00

PoM **Streptase®** (Hoechst)

Injection, powder for reconstitution, streptokinase; net price 100 000-unit vial = £7.66; 250 000-unit vial = £15.36; 750 000-unit vial = £40.26; 1.5 million-unit vial = £80.52 (hosp. only)

UROKINASE

Indications: thrombosed arteriovenous shunts and intravenous cannulas; thrombolysis in the eye; deep-vein thrombosis, pulmonary embolism, peripheral vascular occlusion

Cautions; Contra-indications; Side-effects: see notes above

Dose: by instillation into arteriovenous shunt, 5000–37 500 International units in 2–3 mL sodium chloride intravenous infusion 0.9%

By intravenous infusion, 4400 International units/kg over 10 minutes, then 4400 units/kg/hour for 12 hours in pulmonary embolism or 12–24 hours in deep-vein thrombosis; for bolus injection for pulmonary embolism consult data sheet

Peripheral vascular occlusion, consult data sheet

Intra-ocular administration, 5000–37 500 International units in 2 mL sodium chloride intravenous infusion 0.9%

Note. 1.5 International units ≈ 1 Ploug unit

PoM **Ukidan®** (Serono)

Injection, powder for reconstitution, urokinase; net price 5000 International unit vial = £6.71; 25 000 International unit vial = £23.58; 100 000 International unit vial = £60.00

PoM **Urokinase** (Leo)

Injection, powder for reconstitution, urokinase; net price 7500 International unit (5000 Ploug unit) amp = £9.75; 37 500 International unit (25 000 Ploug unit) amp = £27.79

2.11 Antifibrinolytic drugs and haemostatics

Fibrin dissolution can be impaired by the administration of **tranexamic acid**, which inhibits plasminogen activation and fibrinolysis. It may be useful when haemorrhage cannot be staunched, e.g. in prostatectomy, dental extraction in haemophiliacs, or menorrhagia; it may also be used in hereditary angioedema and in streptokinase overdose.

Aprotinin is a proteolytic enzyme inhibitor acting on plasmin and kallidinogenase (kallikrein). It is indicated for the treatment of life-threatening haemorrhage due to hyperplasminaemia (occasionally observed during the mobilisation and dissection of malignant tumours, in acute promyelocytic leukaemia, and following thrombolytic therapy).

Ethamsylate reduces capillary bleeding in the presence of a normal number of platelets. It does not act by fibrin stabilisation, but probably by correcting abnormal platelet adhesion.

APROTININ

Indications: life-threatening haemorrhage due to hyperplasminaemia (see notes above)
Side-effects: occasionally hypersensitivity reactions and localised thrombophlebitis
Dose: by slow intravenous injection or infusion (max. rate 5 mL/minute), initially 500000–1000000 kallikrein inactivator units, if necessary followed by 200000 units every hour until bleeding stops

PoM **Trasylol®** (Bayer)
Injection, aprotinin 10000 kallikrein inactivator units/mL. Net price 50-mL vial = £20.53

ETHAMSYLATE

Indications: see under preparations
Contra-indications: porphyria
Side-effects: nausea, headache, rashes
Dose: see below

PoM **Dicynene®** (Delandale)
Tablets, scored, ethamsylate 500 mg, net price 100-tab pack = £20.12
Dose: short-term treatment of blood loss in menorrhagia, 500 mg 4 times daily during menstruation
Injection, ethamsylate 125 mg/mL. Net price 2-mL amp = 74p
Dose: prophylaxis and treatment of periventricular haemorrhage in low birth-weight infants, by intramuscular or intravenous injection, 12.5 mg/kg every 6 hours
IMPORTANT. The ampoules currently available contain a total of 250 mg in 2 mL volume therefore **small fraction only** required for neonatal use

TRANEXAMIC ACID

Indications: see notes above
Cautions: reduce dose in renal impairment; massive haematuria (ureteric obstruction); regular eye examinations and liver function tests in long-term treatment of hereditary angioedema
Contra-indications: thromboembolic disease
Side-effects: nausea, vomiting, diarrhoea (reduce dose); giddiness on rapid intravenous injection
Dose: by mouth, 1–1.5 g 2–4 times daily
By slow intravenous injection, 1 g 3 times daily

PoM **Cyklokapron®** (Kabi)
Tablets, f/c, scored, tranexamic acid 500 mg. Net price 60-tab pack = £12.96
Syrup, tranexamic acid 500 mg/5 mL. Diluent syrup, life of diluted syrup 14 days. Net price 300 mL = £15.60
Injection, tranexamic acid 100 mg/mL. Net price 5-mL amp = £1.35

BLOOD PRODUCTS

FACTOR VIII FRACTION, DRIED

(Human Antihaemophilic Fraction, Dried)
A concentrate prepared from pooled plasma from suitable human donors
Indications: control of haemorrhage in haemophilia A
Cautions: intravascular haemolysis after large or frequently repeated doses in patients with blood groups A, B, or AB
Side-effects: allergic reactions including chills, fever; hyperfibrinogenaemia occurred after massive doses with earlier products but less likely since fibrinogen content has now been substantially reduced
Available as: *Dried Factor VIII Fraction, High purity, Heat-treated* (BPL); *Human Antihaemophilic Factor* (SNBTS); *Profilate-SD®* (Alpha); *Hemofil®* HT (Baxter); *Kryobulin®* (Immuno); ▼ *Monoclate-P®* (Armour)

FACTOR VIII INHIBITOR BYPASSING FRACTION

Preparations with factor VIII inhibitor bypassing activity are prepared from human plasma

Human Factor VIII Inhibitor Bypassing Fraction (*Anti-inhibitor Coagulant Complex*, Baxter; *Feiba Immuno*, Immuno) is used in patients with factor VIII inhibitors

FACTOR IX FRACTION, DRIED

Factor IX fraction is prepared from pooled human plasma and may also contain clotting factors II, VII, and X.
Indications: congenital factor IX deficiency (haemophilia B)
Cautions: risk of thrombosis
Contra-indications: disseminated intravascular coagulation
Side-effects: allergic reactions, including chills, fever
Available as: *Dried Factor IX Fraction, Heat-Treated* (BPL); *Human Factor IX Concentrate* (SNBTS); *Proplex® Factor IX Complex* (Baxter)

FRESH FROZEN PLASMA

Fresh frozen plasma is prepared from the supernatant liquid obtained by centrifugation of one donation of whole blood.
Indications: to replace coagulation factors or other plasma proteins where their concentration or functional activity is critically reduced, e.g. haemorrhage due to anticoagulant therapy
Cautions: avoid in circulatory overload
Side-effects: allergic reactions including chills, fever, bronchospasm
Available from SNBTS

2.12 Lipid-lowering drugs

There are a number of common conditions, some familial, in which there are very high plasma concentrations of cholesterol, or triglycerides, or both. There is evidence that therapy which lowers low density lipoprotein (LDL) cholesterol and raises high density lipoprotein (HDL) cholesterol reduces the progression of coronary atherosclerosis and may even induce regression. Lipid-lowering drugs should be reserved for patients in whom severe hyperlipidaemia is inadequately controlled by a modified fat diet. Any drug therapy must be combined with strict adherence to diet, maintenance of near-ideal body weight and, if appropriate, reduction of blood pressure and cessation of smoking.

ANION-EXCHANGE RESINS

Cholestyramine and **colestipol** are anion-exchange resins used in the management of hypercholesterolaemia. They act by binding bile acids, preventing their reabsorption; this promotes hepatic conversion of cholesterol into bile acids; the resultant increased LDL-receptor activity of liver cells increases the breakdown of LDL-cholesterol. Thus both compounds effectively reduce LDL-cholesterol but can aggravate hypertriglyceridaemia.

COUNSELLING. Other drugs should be taken at least 1 hour before or 4–6 hours after cholestyramine or colestipol to reduce possible interference with absorption

CHOLESTYRAMINE

Indications: hyperlipidaemias, particularly type IIa, in patients who have not responded adequately to diet and other appropriate measures; primary prevention of coronary heart disease in men aged 35–59 years with primary hypercholesterolaemia who have not responded to diet and other appropriate measures; pruritus associated with partial biliary obstruction and primary biliary cirrhosis; diarrhoeal disorders, see section 1.5

Cautions: supplements of fat-soluble vitamins and of folic acid may be required with high doses, particularly in children; pregnancy and breast-feeding; **interactions:** Appendix 1 (cholestyramine and colestipol)

Contra-indications: complete biliary obstruction

Side-effects: nausea, constipation or diarrhoea, heartburn, flatulence, abdominal discomfort; on prolonged use, increased bleeding tendency (due to hypoprothrombinaemia associated with vitamin K deficiency)

Dose: lipid reduction (after initial introduction over 3–4 weeks) 12–24 g daily in water in single or divided doses; up to 36 g daily if necessary

Pruritus, 4–8 g daily in water

PoM **Questran**® (Bristol-Myers)

Powder, orange, cholestyramine (anhydrous) 4 g/sachet. Net price 168-sachet pack = £70.21. Label: 13, counselling, avoid other drugs at same time (see notes above)

PoM **Questran A**® (Bristol-Myers)

Powder, orange, cholestyramine (anhydrous) 4 g/sachet, with aspartame. Net price 168-sachet pack = £73.72. Label: 13, counselling, avoid other drugs at same time (see notes above)

COLESTIPOL HYDROCHLORIDE

Indications: hyperlipidaemias, particularly type IIa, in patients who have not responded adequately to diet and other appropriate measures

Cautions; Contra-indications; Side-effects: see under Cholestyramine; **interactions:** Appendix 1 (cholestyramine and colestipol)

Dose: 5 g 1–2 times daily in liquid increased if necessary at intervals of 1–2 months to max. of 30 g daily (in single or 2 divided doses)

PoM **Colestid**® (Upjohn)

Granules, yellow, colestipol hydrochloride. Net price 30 × 5-g sachets = £12.54. Label: 13, counselling, avoid other drugs at same time (see notes above)

CLOFIBRATE GROUP

Clofibrate, **bezafibrate**, **fenofibrate**, and **gemfibrozil** can be regarded as broad-spectrum lipid-modulating agents in that although their main action is to decrease serum triglycerides they also tend to reduce LDL-cholesterol and to raise HDL-cholesterol.

All can cause a myositis-like syndrome, especially in patients with impaired renal function. In addition, clofibrate predisposes to gallstones by increasing biliary cholesterol excretion; it is therefore only indicated in patients who have had a cholecystectomy.

BEZAFIBRATE

Indications: hyperlipidaemias of types IIa, IIb, III, IV and V in patients who have not responded adequately to diet and other appropriate measures

Cautions: renal impairment (avoid if severe); **interactions:** Appendix 1 (clofibrate group)

Contra-indications: severe renal or hepatic impairment, hypoalbuminaemia, primary biliary cirrhosis, gall bladder disease, nephrotic syndrome, pregnancy

Side-effects: nausea, abdominal discomfort; rarely myositis-like syndrome, pruritus, urticaria, impotence; headache reported

Dose: 200 mg 3 times daily with or after food; may be reduced to 200 mg twice daily in hypertriglyceridaemia

PoM **Bezalip**® (Boehringer Mannheim)

Tablets, f/c, bezafibrate 200 mg. Net price 20 = £2.05. Label: 21

PoM **Bezalip-Mono**® (Boehringer Mannheim)

Tablets, f/c, bezafibrate 400 mg. Net price 28-tab pack = £8.72. Label: 21, 25

Dose: 1 tablet daily in the evening

CLOFIBRATE

Indications: hyperlipidaemias of types IIb, III, IV and V in patients who have not responded adequately to diet and other appropriate measures (but see also notes above)

Cautions; Contra-indications: see under Bezafibrate; **interactions:** Appendix 1 (clofibrate group)
Side-effects: see under Bezafibrate; also cholesterol cholelithiasis
Dose: over 65 kg, 2 g daily in 2 or 3 divided doses (50–65 kg, 1.5 g daily)

PoM **Atromid-S®** (ICI)
Capsules, red, clofibrate 500 mg. Net price 100-cap pack = £4.18. Label: 21

FENOFIBRATE

Indications: hyperlipidaemias of types IIa, IIb, III, IV, and V in patients who have not responded adequately to diet and other appropriate measures
Cautions: see under Bezafibrate; **interactions:** Appendix 1 (clofibrate group)
Contra-indications: severe renal or hepatic impairment, existing gall bladder disease, pregnancy
Side-effects: see under Bezafibrate
Dose: initially 300 mg daily in divided doses with food, adjusted according to response to 200–400 mg daily; CHILD 5 mg/kg daily

▼ PoM **Lipantil®** (Fournier)
Capsules, fenofibrate 100 mg. Net price 84-cap pack = £19.80. Label: 21

GEMFIBROZIL

Indications: hyperlipidaemias of types IIa, IIb, III, IV and V in patients who have not responded adequately to diet and other appropriate measures; primary prevention of coronary heart disease in men aged 40–55 years with hyperlipidaemias that have not responded to diet and other appropriate measures
Cautions: lipid profile, blood counts, and liver-function tests before initiating long-term treatment; renal impairment; annual eye examinations; **interactions:** Appendix 1 (clofibrate group)
Contra-indications: alcoholism, hepatic impairment, gallstones; pregnancy
Side-effects: gastro-intestinal disturbances; pruritus, rash, headache, dizziness, blurred vision, painful extremities; rarely myalgia; impotence reported
Dose: 1.2 g daily, usually in 2 divided doses; range 0.9–1.5 g daily

PoM **Lopid®** (P-D)
Capsules, white/maroon, gemfibrozil 300 mg. Net price 20 = £4.80

NICOTINIC ACID GROUP

The value of nicotinic acid and nicofuranose is limited by their side-effects, especially vasodilatation. In doses of 1.5 to 3 g daily they lower both cholesterol and triglyceride concentrations by inhibiting synthesis; they also increase HDL-cholesterol.

ACIPIMOX

Indications: hyperlipidaemias of types IIa, IIb, and IV in patients who have not responded adequately to diet and other appropriate measures
Contra-indications: peptic ulcer
Side-effects: vasodilatation, flushing, itching, rashes, erythema; occasionally, heartburn, epigastric pain, nausea, diarrhoea, headache, malaise
Dose: usually 500–750 mg daily in divided doses

PoM **Olbetam®** (Farmitalia Carlo Erba)
Capsules, brown/pink, acipimox 250 mg. Net price 100-cap pack = £44.00. Label: 21

NICOFURANOSE

Indications: see notes above (for use in peripheral vascular disease, see section 2.6.3)
Cautions; Side-effects: see under Nicotinic Acid, but prostaglandin-mediated symptoms less severe
Dose: 0.5–1 g 3 times daily

Bradilan® (Napp)
Tablets, e/c and s/c, nicofuranose 250 mg. Net price 20 = £1.55. Label: 5, 25

NICOTINIC ACID

Indications: see notes above
Cautions: diabetes mellitus, gout, liver disease, peptic ulcer
Contra-indications: pregnancy, breast-feeding
Side-effects: flushing, dizziness, palpitations, pruritus (prostaglandin-mediated symptoms can be reduced by low initial doses taken with meals, or by taking aspirin 300 mg 30 minutes before the dose—needed in only a very small proportion of patients); nausea, vomiting; rarely impaired liver function and rashes
Dose: initially 100–200 mg 3 times daily (see above), gradually increased over 2–4 weeks to 1–2 g 3 times daily

Nicotinic Acid Tablets, nicotinic acid 50 mg, net price 20 = 13p. Label: 21

FISH OILS

A fish-oil preparation (Maxepa®), rich in omega-3 marine triglycerides, is useful in the treatment of severe hypertriglyceridaemia; however, it can sometimes aggravate hypercholesterolaemia.

OMEGA-3 MARINE TRIGLYCERIDES

Indications: reduction of plasma triglycerides in patients with severe hypertriglyceridaemia judged to be at special risk of ischaemic heart disease and/or pancreatitis, in conjunction with dietary and other methods (see notes above)
Side-effects: occasional nausea and belching
Dose: see under preparations below

Maxepa® (DF)
Capsules, 1 g (approx. 1.1 mL) concentrated fish oils of composition below. Net price 200-cap pack = £28.57. Label: 21
Dose: 5 capsules twice daily with food
Liquid, golden-coloured, concentrated fish oils containing, as percentage of total fatty acid composition, eicosapentaenoic acid 18% w/w, docosahexaenoic acid 12% w/w. Vitamin A content less than 100 units/g, vitamin D content less than 10 units/g. Net price 150 mL = £21.43. Label: 21
Dose: 5 mL twice daily with food

OTHER DRUGS

Probucol decreases both LDL- and HDL-cholesterol; despite the latter effect it appears to promote resolution of xanthomata.

Simvastatin and **pravastatin** belong to a new class of drugs which competitively inhibit 3-hydroxy-3-methylglutaryl coenzyme A (HMG CoA) reductase, an enzyme that catalyses a step in cholesterol synthesis, especially in the liver. They are more potent than anion-exchange resins in lowering LDL-cholesterol but less effective than the clofibrate group in reducing triglycerides and raising HDL-cholesterol. The main side-effect is reversible myositis, which is rare except in patients on cyclosporin, nicotinic acid, or gemfibrozil (careful monitoring of liver function and creatine phosphokinase should be performed if these drugs are used with an HMG CoA reductase inhibitor).

PROBUCOL

Indications: see notes above
Cautions: ECG before treatment in patients with recent myocardial damage, ventricular arrhythmias; avoid pregnancy during and for 6 months after stopping treatment
Contra-indications: breast-feeding
Side-effects: generally mild and transient and mainly consist of gastro-intestinal effects such as nausea, vomiting, flatulence, diarrhoea, abdominal pain; ventricular arrhythmias and angioedema rarely reported
Dose: 500 mg twice daily with food

PoM **Lurselle**® (Merrell)
Tablets, probucol 250 mg. Net price 120-tab pack = £13.40. Label: 21

PRAVASTATIN

Indications: primary hypercholesterolaemia (hyperlipidaemia type IIa) in patients intolerant of or not responsive to other therapy
Cautions; Contra-indications; Side-effects: as for Simvastatin
Dose: usual range 10–40 mg once daily at night, adjusted at intervals of not less than 4 weeks

▼ PoM **Lipostat**® (Squibb)
Tablets, both pink, pravastatin sodium 10 mg, net price 28-tab pack = £16.18; 20 mg, 28-tab pack = £31.09

SIMVASTATIN

Indications: primary hypercholesterolaemia (hyperlipidaemia type IIa) in patients intolerant of or not responsive to other therapy
Cautions: monitor liver function; avoid pregnancy during and for 1 month after treatment; advise patients to report muscle pain; **interactions:** Appendix 1 (simvastatin)
Contra-indications: active liver disease; pregnancy (toxicity in *animal* studies) and breast-feeding; porphyria
Side-effects: constipation, flatulence, headache, nausea, dyspepsia, abdominal pain, diarrhoea, fatigue, insomnia, rash reported; raised creatine phosphokinase concentrations (discontinue if markedly raised or myopathy diagnosed); transient hypotension reported
Dose: 10 mg daily at night, adjusted at intervals of not less than 4 weeks; usual range 10–40 mg once daily at night

▼ PoM **Zocor**® (MSD)
Tablets, both f/c, simvastatin 10 mg (peach), net price 28-tab pack = £18.29; 20 mg (tan), 28-tab pack = £31.09

2.13 Local sclerosants

Ethanolamine oleate and sodium tetradecyl sulphate are used in sclerotherapy of varicose veins, and phenol is used in haemorrhoids (see section 1.7.3).

ETHANOLAMINE OLEATE

Indications: sclerotherapy of varicose veins
Cautions: extravasation may cause necrosis of tissues
Contra-indications: inability to walk, acute phlebitis, oral contraceptive use, obese legs
Side-effects: allergic reactions

PoM **Ethanolamine Oleate Injection,** ethanolamine oleate 5%. Net price 2-mL amp = 70p; 5-mL amp = 65p
Dose: by intravenous injection, 2–5 mL divided between 3–4 sites; repeated at weekly intervals

SODIUM TETRADECYL SULPHATE

Indications: sclerotherapy of varicose veins
Cautions; Contra-indications; Side-effects: see under Ethanolamine Oleate

PoM **STD**® (STD Pharmaceutical)
Injection, sodium tetradecyl sulphate 3%. Net price 1-mL amp = 64p; 30-mL vial = £12.50
Dose: by intravenous injection, 0.5–1 mL at up to 4 sites

3: Drugs used in the treatment of diseases of the RESPIRATORY SYSTEM

In this chapter, drug treatment is described under the following headings:

The initial treatment of exacerbations of chronic bronchitis and bacterial pneumonia is indicated in section 5.1 (Table 1) and the treatment of tuberculosis is discussed in section 5.1.9.

3.1 Bronchodilators

3.1.1 Adrenoceptor stimulants (sympathomimetics)

Most mild to moderate attacks of asthma respond rapidly to aerosol administration of a selective beta$_2$-adrenoceptor stimulant such as salbutamol or terbutaline (section 3.1.1.1). In frequently occurring moderate asthma the introduction of a corticosteroid by inhalation (section 3.2), sodium cromoglycate (section 3.3), or oral theophylline (section 3.1.3) may stabilise the asthma and avoid the use of oral corticosteroids. However in more severe attacks a short course of an oral corticosteroid may be necessary to bring the asthma under control (section 3.2).

Treatment of patients with severe acute asthma or airways obstruction (see also below) is safer in hospital where oxygen and resuscitation facilities are immediately available.

Patients with chronic bronchitis and emphysema are often described as having irreversible airways obstruction, but they usually respond partially to the beta$_2$-adrenoceptor stimulant drugs or to the antimuscarinic drug ipratropium (section 3.1.2).

CHOICE OF DRUG. The **selective beta$_2$-adrenoceptor stimulants** (selective beta$_2$-agonists) (section 3.1.1.1) such as salbutamol or terbutaline (preferably given by aerosol inhalation) are the safest and most effective preparations. The drugs described in section 3.1.1.2 should be avoided whenever possible.

There are some differences between the various selective beta$_2$-adrenoceptor stimulant drugs. **Salbutamol** and **terbutaline** are available in the widest range of formulations. **Rimiterol** has a shorter duration of action than salbutamol, terbutaline and fenoterol. **Fenoterol** may be less beta$_2$-selective than salbutamol. The dose or frequency of administration of beta$_2$-adrenoceptor stimulants can often be reduced by concurrent treatment with prophylactic drugs such as corticosteroid inhalations (section 3.2) or sodium cromoglycate (section 3.3).

CHOICE OF FORMULATION. The *pressurised aerosol inhaler* is an effective and convenient method of administration for mild to moderate airways obstruction. Aerosol inhalers usually act for about 3 to 5 hours (rimiterol less than the others) but this depends to some extent on the severity of the asthma and on the dose administered. Aerosol inhalation is preferred because it provides relief more rapidly and causes fewer side-effects (such as tremor and nervous tension) than tablets; the drug is delivered directly to the bronchi and is therefore effective in smaller doses.

Patients should be given careful instruction on the use of their pressurised aerosol inhalers and it is important to check that they continue to use them correctly as inadequate technique may be mistaken for drug failure. In particular, it should be emphasised that they must inhale slowly and hold their breath for 10 seconds after inhalation. Most patients can be successfully taught to use pressurised aerosol inhalers but some patients, particularly the elderly, the arthritic, and small children are unable to use them; some patients are unable to synchronise their breathing with the administration of aerosol.

The dose should be stated explicitly in terms of the number of inhalations at one time, the frequency, and the maximum number of inhalations allowed in 24 hours. Very high doses of beta$_2$-stimulants can be dangerous in some patients. Excessive use is usually an indication of inadequately treated asthma. Patients should be advised to seek medical advice when they fail to obtain their usual degree of symptomatic relief as this usually indicates a worsening of the asthma and may require alternative medication. When patients with asthma are not adequately controlled with 2 to 4 puffs daily, addition of a prophylactic drug such as a corticosteroid inhalation should be considered; this is more convenient for the patient than higher doses of beta$_2$-stimulants and usually provides better overall control.

Dry powder inhalers are actuated by the patient's inspiration and hence are of particular value in subjects who cannot use pressurised aerosol inhalers correctly. Some dry powder inhalations occasionally cause coughing.

A variety of spacing devices are now available for use with metered dose inhalers. By providing a space between inhaler and mouth, they reduce the velocity of the aerosol and subsequent impaction on the oropharynx; in addition they allow more time for evaporation of the propellent so that a larger proportion of the particles can be inhaled and deposited in the lungs; also co-ordination of inspiration with actuation of the aerosol is less important. They range from the Bricanyl Spacer® (for terbutaline), a collapsible extended mouthpiece, to larger spacing devices with a one-way valve (Nebuhaler®, Rondo®, Volumatic®). Spacing devices are particularly useful for patients with poor inhalation technique, for children, for patients requiring higher doses, for nocturnal asthma, and for patients prone to develop candidiasis with inhaled corticosteroids.

Respirator solutions of salbutamol and terbutaline are increasingly used for the treatment of acute asthma both in hospital and in general practice; more recently a respirator solution of fenoterol has been made available. Respirator solutions are usually administered over a period of about 15 minutes from a nebuliser, usually driven from an oxygen cylinder in hospital. An electrical compressor is most suitable for domiciliary use but these are costly and not currently prescribable under the NHS. Patients with a severe attack of asthma should have oxygen during nebulisation since beta-adrenoceptor stimulants can cause an increase in arterial hypoxaemia. For patients with chronic bronchitis and hypercapnia, however, oxygen can be dangerous, and the nebuliser should be driven by air. The dose prescribed by nebuliser is substantially higher than that prescribed by metered dose inhaler. For example, a 2.5-mL Ventolin Nebule® contains 2.5 mg of salbutamol, which is equivalent to 25 puffs from the aerosol inhaler. Patients should therefore be warned that it is dangerous to exceed the stated dose and that if they fail to respond to the usual dose of beta$_2$-adrenoceptor stimulant they should call for help.

Oral preparations are available for patients who cannot manage the inhaled route. They are sometimes used for children, though the inhaled route is better and most children can use one or other of the inhalation devices available. They have a slower onset but slightly more prolonged action than the aerosol inhalers. The *sustained-release* preparations may be of value in patients with nocturnal asthma as an alternative to the sustained-release theophylline preparations (section 3.1.3).

Intravenous, and occasionally *subcutaneous*, injections of salbutamol and terbutaline are given for severe acute asthma.

EMERGENCY TREATMENT OF SEVERE ACUTE ASTHMA. Severe asthma can be fatal and **must** be treated promptly and energetically. It is characterised by persistent dyspnoea poorly relieved by bronchodilators, restlessness, exhaustion, a high pulse rate (usually over 110/minute), often pulsus paradoxus of over 10 mmHg, and a very low peak expiratory flow. The respiration is so shallow that wheezing may be absent. Such patients should be given a large dose of a **corticosteroid** (see section 6.3.4)—for adults hydrocortisone 200 mg (preferably as sodium succinate) intravenously or prednisolone 40 mg by mouth, children half these doses. They should also be given a beta$_2$-selective adrenoceptor stimulant such as **salbutamol** or **terbutaline** by nebuliser.

If there is little response the following additional treatment should be considered: **ipratropium** by nebuliser (section 3.1.2), **aminophylline** by slow intravenous injection, if the patient has not already been receiving theophylline (section 3.1.3), or change of administration of the beta$_2$-selective adrenoceptor stimulant to the intravenous route.

Further treatment of these patients is safer in hospital where oxygen therapy and resuscitation facilities are immediately available. Treatment should **never** be delayed for investigations, patients should **never** be sedated, and the possibility of a pneumothorax should also be remembered.

If the patient deteriorates despite appropriate pharmacological treatment, intermittent positive pressure ventilation may be needed temporarily.

CSM advice. Potentially serious hypokalaemia may result from beta$_2$-adrenoceptor stimulant therapy. Particular caution is required in severe asthma, as this effect may be potentiated by concomitant treatment with theophylline and its derivatives, corticosteroids, and diuretics, and by hypoxia. Plasma potassium concentrations should therefore be monitored in severe asthma.

CHILDREN. Selective beta$_2$-adrenoceptor stimulants are useful even in children under the age of 18 months. They are most effective by the inhaled route, but an inhalation device may be needed (with the technique carefully checked). They are also effective by mouth. In severe attacks nebulisation using a selective beta$_2$-adrenoceptor stimulant or ipratropium is advisable.

PREGNANCY AND BREAST-FEEDING. It is particularly important that asthma should be well-controlled during pregnancy; where this is achieved asthma has no important effects on pregnancy, labour, or the fetus.

Inhalation has particular advantages as a means of drug administration during pregnancy because the therapeutic action can be achieved without the need for plasma concentrations liable to have a pharmacological effect on the fetus.

Severe exacerbations of asthma can have an adverse effect on pregnancy and should be treated promptly with conventional therapy, including oral or parenteral administration of corticosteroids and nebulisation of a selective beta$_2$-adrenoceptor stimulant; prednisolone is the preferred corticosteroid for oral administration since placental transfer is slower than with some others.

Although theophylline has been given without

adverse effects during pregnancy or breast-feeding there have been occasional reports of toxicity in the fetus and neonate.

See also under Prescribing in Pregnancy (Appendix 4) and Prescribing during Breast-feeding (Appendix 5).

3.1.1.1 SELECTIVE BETA$_2$-ADRENOCEPTOR STIMULANTS

SALBUTAMOL

Indications: asthma and other conditions associated with reversible airways obstruction; premature labour, see section 7.1.2

Cautions: hyperthyroidism, ischaemic heart disease, hypertension, pregnancy (but appropriate to use, see notes above), elderly patients; intravenous administration to diabetics (monitor blood glucose; ketoacidosis reported); see also notes above; **interactions:** Appendix 1 (sympathomimetics)

Side-effects: fine tremor (usually hands), nervous tension, headache, peripheral vasodilatation, tachycardia (seldom troublesome when given by aerosol inhalation); hypokalaemia after high doses (**CSM** recommends monitor plasma-potassium in severe asthma); slight pain on intramuscular injection

Dose: by mouth, 4 mg (elderly and sensitive patients initially 2 mg) 3–4 times daily; max. 8 mg (but unlikely to be tolerated); CHILD under 2 years 100 micrograms/kg 4 times daily; 2–6 years 1–2 mg 3–4 times daily, 6–12 years 2 mg

By subcutaneous or intramuscular injection, 500 micrograms, repeated every 4 hours if necessary

By slow intravenous injection, 250 micrograms, repeated if necessary

By intravenous infusion, initially 5 micrograms/minute, adjusted according to response and heart-rate usually in range 3–20 micrograms/minute, or more if necessary

By aerosol inhalation, acute and intermittent episodes of wheezing and asthma, 100–200 micrograms (1–2 puffs); CHILD 100 micrograms (1 puff)

Prophylaxis in exercise-induced bronchospasm, 200 micrograms (2 puffs); CHILD 100 micrograms (1 puff)

Chronic maintenance therapy, 200 micrograms (2 puffs) 3–4 times daily; CHILD 100 micrograms (1 puff) 3–4 times daily, increased to 200 micrograms (2 puffs) if necessary

By inhalation of a powder (Rotacaps®, Ventodisks®), acute and intermittent episodes of wheezing and asthma, 200–400 micrograms; CHILD 200 micrograms

Prophylaxis in exercise-induced bronchospasm, 400 micrograms; CHILD 200 micrograms

Chronic maintenance therapy, 400 micrograms 3–4 times daily; CHILD 200 micrograms 3–4 times daily

Note. Bioavailability appears to be lower, so recommended doses for dry powder inhalers are twice those in a metered inhaler

By inhalation of nebulised solution, chronic bronchospasm unresponsive to conventional therapy and severe acute asthma, 2.5 mg, repeated up to 4 times daily, increased to 5 mg if necessary; in refractory patients with severe acute asthma up to 10 mg if side-effects permit; CHILD 2.5 mg, increased to 5 mg if required

Oral

PoM **Salbutamol** (Non-proprietary)

Tablets, salbutamol (as sulphate) 2 mg, net price 20 = 17p; 4 mg, 20 = 33p

Syrup, salbutamol (as sulphate) 2 mg/5 mL, net price 150 mL = 68p

PoM **Asmaven®** (APS)

Tablets, both pink, salbutamol (as sulphate), 2 mg, net price 20 = 23p; 4 mg, 20 = 42p

PoM **Salbulin®** (3M)

Tablets, pink, salbutamol (as sulphate), 4 mg, net price 120-tab pack = £1.20

PoM **Salbuvent®** (Tillotts)

Tablets, both scored, salbutamol (as sulphate) 2 mg, net price 90-tab pack = £1.06; 4 mg, 90-tab pack = £2.03

Syrup, salbutamol (as sulphate) 2 mg/5 mL. Net price 150 mL = 67p

PoM **Ventolin®** (A&H)

Tablets, both pink, scored, salbutamol (as sulphate), 2 mg, net price 20 = 22p; 4 mg, 20 = 43p

CR Tablets, controlled-release, salbutamol (as sulphate) 4 mg, net price 56-tab pack = £10.00; 8 mg, 56-tab pack = £12.00. Label: 25, 27

Dose: 8 mg twice daily; CHILD 3–12 years 4 mg twice daily

Syrup, sugar-free, salbutamol 2 mg (as sulphate)/5 mL. Diluent purified water, freshly boiled and cooled, life of diluted syrup 28 days. Net price 150 mL = 67p

PoM **Volmax®** (DF)

Tablets, controlled-release, salbutamol (as sulphate) 4 mg, net price 56-tab pack = £10.00; 8 mg, 56-tab pack = £12.00. Label: 25

Dose: 8 mg twice daily; CHILD 3–12 years 4 mg twice daily

Parenteral

PoM **Salbuvent®** (Tillotts)

Injection, salbutamol (as sulphate) 50 micrograms/mL. Net price 5-mL amp = 57p

Injection, salbutamol (as sulphate) 500 micrograms/mL. Net price 1-mL amp = 43p

Solution for intravenous infusion, salbutamol (as sulphate) 1 mg/mL. Dilute before use. Net price 5-mL amp = £3.08

PoM **Ventolin®** (A&H)

Injection, salbutamol 50 micrograms (as sulphate)/mL. Net price 5-mL amp = 57p

Injection, salbutamol 500 micrograms (as sulphate)/mL. Net price 1-mL amp = 43p

Solution for intravenous infusion, salbutamol 1 mg (as sulphate)/mL. Dilute before use. Net price 5-mL amp = £3.08

Inhalation

COUNSELLING. Advise patients not to exceed prescribed dose and to follow manufacturer's directions

PoM **Salbutamol** (Non-proprietary)

Aerosol inhalation, salbutamol 100 micrograms/metered inhalation, net price 200-dose unit = £2.08

PoM **Aerolin 400®** (3M)

Aerosol inhalation, salbutamol 100 micrograms (as sulphate)/metered inhalation. Net price 400-dose unit = £4.98

PoM **Aerolin® Autohaler**[1] (3M)

Aerosol inhalation, salbutamol 100 micrograms (as sulphate)/metered inhalation. Net price 200-dose breath-actuated unit = £10.50; also 100-dose unit = £5.25 (hosp. only)

[1]replaces *Aerolin Auto*

PoM **Asmaven®** (APS)

Aerosol inhalation, salbutamol 100 micrograms/metered inhalation. Net price 200-dose unit = £2.20

PoM **Salbulin®** (3M)

Aerosol inhalation, salbutamol 100 micrograms/metered inhalation. Net price 200-dose unit = £1.87

PoM **Salbuvent®** (Tillotts)

Aerosol inhalation, salbutamol 100 micrograms/metered inhalation. Net price 200-dose unit = £2.62

Respirator solution (for use with a nebuliser or ventilator), salbutamol (as sulphate) 0.5% (5 mg/mL). Net price 20 mL = £2.71

PoM **Ventodisks®** (A&H)

Powder for inhalation, disks containing 8 blisters of salbutamol (as sulphate) 200 micrograms/blister, net price pack of 14 disks with Diskhaler® = £7.11; 14-disk refill = £6.54; 400 micrograms/blister, pack of 14 disks with Diskhaler® = £12.02; 14-disk refill = £11.45

PoM **Ventolin®** (A&H)

Aerosol inhalation, salbutamol 100 micrograms/metered inhalation. Net price 200-dose unit = £2.62

Nebules® (for use with nebuliser), salbutamol 0.1% (1 mg/mL, as sulphate), net price 2.5 mL (2.5 mg) = 19p; 0.2% (2 mg/mL), 2.5 mL (5 mg) = 38p. May be diluted with physiological saline

Respirator solution (for use with a nebuliser or ventilator), salbutamol 0.5% (5 mg/mL, as sulphate). Net price 20 mL = £2.71. May be diluted with physiological saline

Rotacaps® (powder for inhalation), light-blue/clear, salbutamol 200 micrograms (as sulphate). Net price 20 = £1.06

Rotacaps® (powder for inhalation), dark-blue/clear, salbutamol 400 micrograms (as sulphate). Net price 20 = £1.79

Devices

NHS **Haleraid®** (Glaxo)

Device to place over standard inhalers as aid to operation by patients with impaired strength in hands (e.g. with arthritis). Net price = 80p

Rondo® (Tillotts)

Spacer device for use with Salbuvent. Net price = £2.75

Rotahaler® (A&H)

Breath actuated inhaler for use with Rotacaps. Net price = 78p

Volumatic® (A&H)

Inhaler, large-volume spacer device. For use with Ventolin, Becotide, Becloforte, and Ventide inhalers. Net price = £2.75

TERBUTALINE SULPHATE

Indications; Cautions; Side-effects: see under Salbutamol; premature labour, see section 7.1.2

Dose: *by mouth*, 5 mg 2–3 times daily; CHILD under 3 years 750 micrograms 3 times daily, 3–7 years 0.75–1.5 mg 3 times daily, 7–15 years 1.5–3 mg 3 times daily (as syrup) *or* 2.5 mg 2–3 times daily (as tablets)

By subcutaneous, intramuscular, or slow intravenous injection, 250–500 micrograms up to 4 times daily; CHILD 2–15 years 10 micrograms/kg to a max. of 300 micrograms

By continuous intravenous infusion as a solution containing 3–5 micrograms/mL, 1.5–5 micrograms/minute for 8–10 hours; reduce dose for children

By aerosol inhalation, prophylaxis, adults and children 250–500 micrograms (1–2 puffs) repeated after 4 hours if necessary; not more than 8 inhalations should be necessary in any 24 hours

By inhalation of powder (Turbohaler®), 500 micrograms (1 inhalation) as required; not more than 4 inhalations in any 24 hours

By inhalation of nebulised solution, 5–10 mg 2–4 times daily; additional doses may be necessary in severe acute asthma; CHILD, up to 3 years 2 mg, 3–6 years 3 mg; 6–8 years 4 mg, over 8 years 5 mg, 2–4 times daily

Oral and parenteral

PoM **Bricanyl®** (Astra)

Tablets, scored, terbutaline sulphate 5 mg. Net price 20 = 71p

Syrup, sugar-free, terbutaline sulphate 1.5 mg/5 mL. Diluent water, life of diluted syrup 14 days. Net price 300 mL = £2.24

Injection, terbutaline sulphate 500 micrograms/mL. Net price 1-mL amp = 28p; 5-mL amp = £1.30

PoM **Bricanyl SA®** (Astra)

Tablets, s/r, terbutaline sulphate 7.5 mg. Net price 20 = £1.59. Label: 25

Dose: 7.5 mg twice daily

PoM **Monovent®** (Lagap)

Syrup, terbutaline sulphate 1.5 mg/5 mL. Diluent water, life of diluted syrup 14 days. Net price 300 mL = £2.20

PoM **Monovent SA®** (Lagap)

Tablets, s/r, terbutaline sulphate 7.5 mg. Net price 20 = £1.43. Label: 25

Dose: 7.5 mg twice daily

Inhalation

PoM **Bricanyl®** (Astra)

COUNSELLING. Advise patients not to exceed prescribed dose and to follow manufacturer's directions; little sensation associated with use of Turbohaler®

Aerosol inhalation, terbutaline sulphate 250 micrograms/metered inhalation. Net price 400-dose unit = £5.31; 400-dose unit with Spacer inhaler (collapsible extended mouthpiece) = £7.21; 400-dose refill cannister for use with Nebuhaler or Spacer inhaler = £5.21

Turbohaler® (= breath-actuated dry powder inhaler), terbutaline sulphate 500 micrograms/inhalation. Net price 100-dose unit = £8.94

Respules® (= single-dose units for nebulisation), terbutaline sulphate 2.5 mg/mL. Net price 20 × 2-mL units = £3.76

Respirator solution (for use with a nebuliser or ventilator), terbutaline sulphate 10 mg/mL. Net price 10 mL = £1.35. Before use dilute with sterile physiological saline

Devices

Nebuhaler® (Astra), see p. 110

FENOTEROL HYDROBROMIDE

Indications; Cautions; Side-effects: see under Salbutamol

Note. Preparations below contain relatively **higher** dose-equivalences than corresponding salbutamol preparations and may cause more side-effects

Dose: *by aerosol inhalation*, chronic maintenance therapy, 200–400 micrograms (1–2 puffs) 3 times daily, if necessary increased to every 4 hours; CHILD 6–12 years 200 micrograms (1 puff)

By inhalation of nebulised solution, 0.5–2.5 mg (increased in severe cases to a max. of 5 mg) up to 4 times daily, dilution adjusted to equipment and length of administration; CHILD 6–14 years, up to 1 mg up to 3 times daily

PoM **Berotec®** (Boehringer Ingelheim)

COUNSELLING. Advise patients not to exceed prescribed dose and to follow manufacturer's directions

Aerosol inhalation, fenoterol hydrobromide 200 micrograms/metered inhalation. Net price 200-dose unit = £2.78 (extension tube also available)

Nebuliser solution, fenoterol hydrobromide 0.5% (5 mg/mL, 20 drops ≈1 mL). Net price 20 mL (with dropper) = £1.76. For use with nebuliser or ventilator; if dilution is necessary, use only sterile sodium chloride 0.9% solution

PIRBUTEROL

Indications: reversible airways obstruction

Cautions; Side-effects: see under Salbutamol

Dose: *by mouth*, 10–15 mg 3–4 times daily

By aerosol inhalation, intermittent episodes, prophylaxis in exercise-induced bronchospasm, 200–400 micrograms (1–2 puffs) repeated after 4 hours if necessary; max. 2.4 mg (12 puffs) daily

Chronic maintenance therapy, 400 micrograms (2 puffs) 3–4 times daily or in severe bronchospasm every 4 hours; max. 2.4 mg (12 puffs) daily

PoM **Exirel®** (3M)

Capsules, pirbuterol (as hydrochloride) 10 mg (turquoise/olive), net price 20 = 48p; 15 mg (turquoise/beige), 20 = 71p

Aerosol inhalation, pirbuterol 200 micrograms (as acetate)/metered inhalation. Net price 200-dose unit = £2.86

COUNSELLING. Advise patients not to exceed prescribed dose and to follow manufacturer's directions

REPROTEROL HYDROCHLORIDE

Indications: reversible airways obstruction

Cautions; Side-effects: see under Salbutamol

Dose: *by mouth*, 10–20 mg 3 times daily; CHILD 6–12 years 10 mg 3 times daily

By aerosol inhalation, intermittent episodes and prophylaxis in exercise-induced bronchospasm, 0.5–1 mg (1–2 puffs) repeated after 3–6 hours if necessary; CHILD 6–12 years 500 micrograms (1 puff)

Chronic maintenance therapy, 1 mg (2 puffs) 3 times daily or in severe bronchospasm every 3–6 hours; CHILD 6–12 years 500 micrograms (1 puff) 3 times daily

PoM **Bronchodil®** (Degussa)

Tablets, scored, reproterol hydrochloride 20 mg. Net price 20 = 68p

Aerosol inhalation, reproterol hydrochloride 500 micrograms/metered inhalation. Net price 400-dose unit = £6.84

COUNSELLING. Advise patients not to exceed prescribed dose and to follow manufacturer's directions

RIMITEROL HYDROBROMIDE

Indications: reversible airways obstruction (particularly when short action required)

Cautions; Side-effects: see under Salbutamol

Dose: *by aerosol inhalation*, adults and children 200–600 micrograms (1–3 puffs); should not be repeated in less than 30 minutes; max. 8 doses daily

PoM **Pulmadil®** (3M)

COUNSELLING. Advise patients not to exceed prescribed dose and to follow manufacturer's directions

Aerosol inhalation, rimiterol hydrobromide 200 micrograms/metered inhalation. Net price 300-dose unit = £6.32

Auto aerosol inhalation, rimiterol hydrobromide 200 micrograms/metered inhalation. Net price 300-dose cartridge in breath-actuated unit = £7.93; replacement cartridge = £6.32

3.1.1.2 OTHER ADRENOCEPTOR STIMULANTS

These preparations (including the partially selective orciprenaline) are now regarded as less suitable and less safe for use as bronchodilators than the selective beta$_2$-adrenoceptor stimulants, as they are more likely to cause arrhythmias and other side-effects. They should be avoided whenever possible. For use as nasal decongestants see section 3.10.

Adrenaline injection (1 in 1000) is used in the emergency treatment of acute allergic and anaphylactic reactions (section 3.4.3).

ADRENALINE

See section 3.4.3

EPHEDRINE HYDROCHLORIDE

Indications: reversible airways obstruction, but see notes above

Cautions; Side-effects: see under Adrenaline (section 3.4.3); incidence of tachycardia lower; anxiety, restlessness, and insomnia common; may cause acute retention in prostatic hypertrophy; interaction with MAOIs a disadvantage; **interactions:** Appendix 1 (sympathomimetics)

Dose: 3 times daily, 15–60 mg; CHILD 3 times daily, up to 1 year 7.5 mg, 1–5 years 15 mg, 6–12 years 30 mg (but not recommended, see notes above)

PoM [1]**Ephedrine Hydrochloride** (Non-proprietary)

Tablets, ephedrine hydrochloride 15 mg, net price 20 = 6p; 30 mg, 20 = 8p; 60 mg, 20 = 27p

Elixir, ephedrine hydrochloride 15 mg/5 mL in a suitable flavoured vehicle, containing alcohol 12%. Net price 100 mL = 49p

1. For exemptions see *Medicines, Ethics and Practice*, No. 5, London, Pharmaceutical Press, 1990 (and subsequent editions as available)

CAM® (Rybar)

Mixture, sugar-free, ephedrine hydrochloride 4 mg/5 mL. Diluent sorbitol solution, life of diluted mixture 28 days. Net price 100 mL = 89p

Dose: 20 mL 3–4 times daily; CHILD 3 months–2 years 2.5 mL, 2–4 years 5 mL, 5–12 years 10 mL, 3 times daily

Note. The dose of ephedrine in this preparation is inadequate for the relief of bronchospasm and is therefore not recommended

ISOETHARINE HYDROCHLORIDE

Indications: reversible airways obstruction, but see notes above

Cautions; Side-effects: see under Salbutamol (section 3.1.1.1) and notes above

PoM **Numotac®** (3M)

Tablets, s/r, isoetharine hydrochloride 10 mg. Net price 90-tab pack = £2.48. Label: 25

Dose: 10–20 mg 3–4 times daily (but not recommended, see notes above)

ISOPRENALINE SULPHATE

Indications: reversible airways obstruction, but see notes above

Cautions; Side-effects: see under Salbutamol (section 3.1.1.1) and notes above

PoM **Medihaler-iso®** (3M)

Aerosol inhalation, isoprenaline sulphate 80 micrograms/metered inhalation. Net price 400-dose vial = £2.73

Note. Not recommended therefore no dose stated

PoM **Medihaler-iso Forte®** (3M)

Aerosol inhalation, isoprenaline sulphate 400 micrograms/metered inhalation. Net price 400-dose vial = £3.17

Note. Not recommended therefore no dose stated

ORCIPRENALINE SULPHATE

Indications: reversible airways obstruction, but see notes above

Cautions; Side-effects: see under Salbutamol (section 3.1.1.1) and notes above

Dose: by mouth, 20 mg 4 times daily; CHILD up to 1 year 5–10 mg 3 times daily, 1–3 years 5–10 mg 4 times daily, 3–12 years 40–60 mg daily in divided doses (but not recommended, see notes above)

By aerosol inhalation, 750–1500 micrograms (1–2 puffs) repeated if necessary after not less than 30 minutes to a max. of 9 mg (12 puffs) daily; CHILD up to 6 years 750 micrograms (1 puff) up to 4 times daily, 6–12 years 750–1500 micrograms (1–2 puffs) up to 4 times daily (but not recommended, see notes above)

PoM **Alupent®** (Boehringer Ingelheim)

Tablets, scored, orciprenaline sulphate 20 mg. Net price 112-tab pack = £4.26

Syrup, sugar-free, orciprenaline sulphate 10 mg/5 mL. Diluents syrup or sorbitol solution, life of diluted syrup 14 days. Net price 100 mL = 69p

Aerosol inhalation, orciprenaline sulphate 750 micrograms/metered inhalation. Net price 300-dose vial with mouthpiece = £3.22; refill vial = £2.66

COUNSELLING. Advise patients not to exceed prescribed dose and to follow manufacturer's directions

3.1.2 Antimuscarinic bronchodilators

These drugs have traditionally been regarded as more effective in relieving bronchoconstriction associated with chronic bronchitis. Of this group, **ipratropium** may provide some bronchodilation in patients with chronic bronchitis who fail to respond to the selective $beta_2$-adrenoceptor stimulants (section 3.1.1.1). Unlike the other antimuscarinic drugs, side-effects are rare and it does not increase sputum viscosity or affect mucociliary clearance of sputum. The aerosol inhalation has a slower onset of action than that of the $beta_2$-adrenoceptor stimulants, with a maximum effect 30–60 minutes after use; its duration of action is longer than that of $beta_2$-adrenoceptor stimulants following inhalation and bronchodilatation can usually be maintained with treatment three times a day.

The other atropine-like bronchodilators are now rarely used and often have unpleasant side-effects which limit their usefulness. They should be avoided, particularly in children, because although they reduce bronchial secretions, sputum viscosity may be increased and this can lead to blockage of the smaller airways.

IPRATROPIUM BROMIDE

Indications: reversible airways obstruction, particularly in chronic bronchitis

Cautions: glaucoma (standard doses unlikely to be harmful); prostatic hypertrophy

Side-effects: dry mouth occasionally reported; rarely urinary retention, constipation

Dose: see below

PoM **Atrovent®** (Boehringer Ingelheim)

COUNSELLING. Advise patient not to exceed prescribed dose and to follow manufacturer's directions

Aerosol inhalation, ipratropium bromide 20 micrograms/metered inhalation. Net price 200-dose unit = £4.21

Dose: by aerosol inhalation, 20–40 micrograms (1–2 puffs), in early treatment up to 80 micrograms (4 puffs) at a time, 3–4 times daily; CHILD up to 6 years 20 micrograms (1 puff) 3 times daily, 6–12 years 20–40 micrograms (1–2 puffs) 3 times daily

Forte aerosol inhalation, ipratropium bromide 40 micrograms/metered inhalation. Net price 200-dose unit = £4.91

Dose: by aerosol inhalation 40 micrograms (1 puff), in early treatment 80 micrograms (2 puffs), 3–4 times daily; CHILD 6–12 years 40 micrograms (1 puff) 3 times daily

Nebuliser solution, isotonic, ipratropium bromide 250 micrograms/mL (0.025%); net price 10 × 1-mL unit-dose vials (preservative-free) = £3.20; 10 × 2-mL vials = £3.76. If dilution is necessary use only sterile sodium chloride solution 0.9%

Dose: reversible airways obstruction, *by inhalation of nebulised solution*, 100–500 micrograms (0.4–2 mL of a 0.025% solution) up to 4 times daily; CHILD 3–14 years 100–500 micrograms up to 3 times daily. Dilution of solution is adjusted according to equipment and length of administration

Note. Because paradoxical bronchospasm has occurred, first dose should be inhaled under medical supervision. Bottles of nebuliser solution (which contained preservative) have been discontinued to reduce the risk; unit-dose vials are preservative-free

PoM **Rinatec®** nasal spray, see section 12.2.2

3.1.3 Theophylline

Theophylline and its derivatives are used primarily for the relief of bronchospasm. With the introduction of the beta$_2$-adrenoceptor stimulants (section 3.1.1.1), the use of *rapid-release* oral aminophylline and theophylline preparations declined because of the high incidence of side-effects associated with rapid absorption. However, there has been a revival of interest in these drugs since the introduction of *sustained-release* preparations which are usually able to produce adequate plasma concentrations for up to 12 hours. These sustained-release preparations are all equally effective but due to different pharmacokinetic profiles are not interchangeable without retitration of dosage.

Theophylline is metabolised in the liver and there is considerable variation in its half-life in healthy non-smokers, which is even more marked in smokers, in patients with hepatic impairment or heart failure, or if other drugs are taken concurrently. The half-life is *increased* in heart failure, cirrhosis, viral infections, and by drugs such as cimetidine, ciprofloxacin, erythromycin, and oral contraceptives. The half-life is *decreased* in smokers and in heavy drinkers, and by drugs such as phenytoin, carbamazepine, rifampicin, and barbiturates.

These differences in half-life are important because theophylline has a narrow margin between the therapeutic and toxic dose. In most subjects *plasma concentrations* of between 10 and 20 mg/litre are required for satisfactory bronchodilatation. Side-effects can occur with concentrations below 20 mg/litre and are common at concentrations above 30–40 mg/litre.

Theophylline *sustained-release* preparations when given as a single dose at night have a useful role in controlling nocturnal asthma and early morning wheezing. They have replaced aminophylline suppositories which cause proctitis and can show an unpredictable response. Recent studies suggest that theophylline may have an additive effect when used in conjunction with small doses of beta$_2$-adrenoceptor stimulants; the combination may increase the risk of side-effects, including arrhythmias.

Choline theophyllinate is a modification of theophylline. There is no evidence that it is better tolerated than the sustained-release preparations.

Aminophylline, a mixture of theophylline with ethylenediamine, is 20 times more soluble than theophylline alone, which is an advantage for the injection but not for the tablets.

The use of aminophylline *injection*, given intravenously, is of established value in the treatment of severe attacks of asthma and is still preferred by many prescribers to intravenous treatment with the selective beta$_2$-adrenoceptor stimulants (section 3.1.1.1). Measurement of *plasma concentrations* may be helpful, and is **essential** if aminophylline is to be given to patients who have been taking oral theophylline preparations, as serious side-effects such as convulsions and arrhythmias can occasionally occur before the appearance of other symptoms of toxicity. For **CSM** advice on hypokalaemia risk, see p. 100.

Aminophylline *suppositories* cause proctitis and show an unpredictable response; they are no longer used. See also under Children (below).

Aminophylline injection was formerly used in the treatment of left ventricular failure but has been superseded by diuretics (see sections 2.2.1 and 2.2.2) and the opioid analgesics (see section 4.7.2) for this purpose. However, it may have a role in patients with heart failure who are also suffering from asthma and bronchitis, where opioids are contra-indicated, though care is needed in using aminophylline in patients with increased myocardial excitability.

CHILDREN. Aminophylline suppositories should **not** be used in children; there have been reports of severe toxicity when adult suppositories have been given to young children. There is no good evidence that theophylline benefits the wheezy infant (unless due to ventilator-induced bronchopulmonary dysplasia); it is indicated for recurrent apnoeic attacks but can be given by mouth.

THEOPHYLLINE

Indications: reversible airways obstruction, severe acute asthma

Cautions: see notes above; also liver disease, epilepsy, pregnancy and breast-feeding, cardiac disease, elderly, fever; **CSM** advice on hypokalaemia risk, p. 100; avoid in porphyria; **interactions:** Appendix 1 (theophylline)

Side-effects: tachycardia, palpitations, nausea, gastro-intestinal disturbances, headache, insomnia, arrhythmias, and convulsions especially if given rapidly by intravenous injection; intramuscular injection is painful (this route is therefore not used)

Dose: see below

Note. Plasma theophylline concentration for optimum response 10–20 mg/litre (55–110 micromol/litre); narrow margin between therapeutic and toxic dose, see also notes above

Biophylline® (Delandale)

Syrup, yellow, sugar-free, theophylline hydrate 125 mg (as sodium glycinate)/5 mL. Net price 250 mL = £3.77 (includes 2.5-mL measure). Label: 21

Dose: 125–250 mg 3–4 times daily; CHILD 2–6 years 62.5 mg, 7–12 years 62.5–125 mg, 3–4 times daily

PoM **Labophylline®** (LAB)

Injection, theophylline 20 mg/mL, lysine 12.2 mg/mL. Net price 10-mL amp = 26p

Dose: in patients not previously treated with xanthines, *by slow intravenous injection* (over 20 minutes) initially 200 mg, *or by intravenous infusion* 4 mg/kg; maintenance if required, 500 micrograms/kg/hour for 12 hours, then 400 micrograms/kg/hour; CHILD *by slow intravenous injection* (over 20 minutes) 4 mg/kg initially

Nuelin® (3M)

Tablets, scored, theophylline 125 mg. Net price 90-tab pack = £3.39. Label: 21

Dose: 125 mg 3–4 times daily after food, increased to 250 mg if required; CHILD 7–12 years 62.5–125 mg 3–4 times daily

Liquid, brown, theophylline 60 mg (as sodium glycinate)/5 mL. Diluent syrup, life of diluted liquid 14 days. Net price 200 mL = £2.02. Label: 21

Dose: 120–240 mg 3–4 times daily after food; CHILD 2–6 years 60–90 mg, 7–12 years 90–120 mg, 3–4 times daily

Sustained release

Note. The Council of the Royal Pharmaceutical Society of Great Britain advises pharmacists that if a general practitioner prescribes a sustained-release, oral theophylline preparation without specifying a brand name, the pharmacist should contact the prescriber and agree the brand to be dispensed. Additionally, it is essential that a patient discharged from hospital should be maintained on the brand on which that patient was stabilised as an in-patient.

Biophylline® (Delandale)

Tablets, s/r, both scored, theophylline 350 mg, net price 56-tab pack = £5.44; 500 mg, 56-tab pack = £7.44. Label: 25

Dose: over 70 kg, 500 mg every 12 hours; under 70 kg and elderly, 350 mg every 12 hours

Lasma® (Pharmax)

Tablets, s/r, scored, theophylline 300 mg. Net price 20 = £1.94. Label: 25

Dose: 300 mg every 12 hours (increased after 1 week to 450 mg every 12 hours in patients over 70 kg); adjust dose by 150-mg increments as required

Total daily dose may be given as single dose at night when nocturnal symptoms predominate (daytime symptoms then controlled with inhaled bronchodilators)

Nuelin SA® (3M)

Tablets, s/r, theophylline 175 mg. Net price 60-tab pack = £3.13. Label: 25

Dose: 175–350 mg every 12 hours; CHILD over 6 years 175 mg every 12 hours

Nuelin SA 250® (3M)

Tablets, s/r, scored, theophylline 250 mg. Net price 60-tab pack = £4.39. Label: 25

Dose: 250–500 mg every 12 hours; CHILD over 6 years 125–250 mg every 12 hours

Pro-Vent® (Wellcome)

Capsules, s/r, white/clear, theophylline 300 mg. Net price 20 = £2.13. Label: 25

Dose: 300 mg every 12 hours, an additional 300 mg may be taken daily (night *or* morning) if plasma concentrations inadequate

Slo-Phyllin® (Lipha)

Capsules, s/r, white/clear, enclosing white pellets, theophylline 60 mg. Net price 56-cap pack = £2.02. Label: 25 *or* counselling, see below

Capsules, s/r, brown/clear, enclosing white pellets, theophylline 125 mg. Net price 56-cap pack = £2.55. Label: 25 *or* counselling, see below

Capsules, s/r, blue/clear, enclosing white pellets, theophylline 250 mg. Net price 56-cap pack = £3.18. Label: 25 *or* counselling, see below

Dose: 250–500 mg every 12 hours; CHILD, every 12 hours, 2–6 years 60–120 mg, 7–12 years 125–250 mg

COUNSELLING. Swallow whole with fluid *or* swallow enclosed granules with soft food (e.g. yoghurt)

Theo-Dur® (Astra)

Tablets, s/r, both scored, theophylline 200 mg, net price 20 = £1.24; 300 mg, 20 = £1.80. Label: 25

Dose: every 12 hours; CHILD up to 35 kg 100 mg, over 35 kg 200 mg, every 12 hours

Uniphyllin Continus® (Napp)

Tablets, s/r, both scored, theophylline 300 mg, net price 56-tab pack = £5.50; 400 mg, 56-tab pack = £7.51. Label: 25

Dose: 200 mg every 12 hours increased after 1 week to 300 mg every 12 hours; over 70 kg 300 mg every 12 hours increased after 1 week to 400 mg every 12 hours

May be appropriate to give larger evening or morning dose to achieve optimum therapeutic effect when symptoms most severe; in patients whose night- or daytime symptoms persist despite other therapy, who are not currently receiving theophylline, total daily requirement may be added as single evening or morning dose

Paediatric tablets, s/r, scored, theophylline 200 mg. Net price 56-tab pack = £3.61. Label: 25

Dose: CHILD over 5 years, maintenance, 9 mg/kg twice daily

AMINOPHYLLINE

Note: Aminophylline is a stable mixture or combination of theophylline and ethylenediamine; the ethylenediamine confers greater solubility in water

Indications: reversible airways obstruction, severe acute asthma

Cautions; Side-effects: see under Theophylline; also allergy to ethylenediamine can cause urticaria, erythema, and exfoliative dermatitis

Dose: see below

Note. Plasma theophylline concentration for optimum response 10–20 mg/litre (55–110 micromol/litre); narrow margin between therapeutic and toxic dose, see also notes above

Aminophylline (Non-proprietary)

Tablets, aminophylline 100 mg, net price 20 = 34p. Label: 21

Dose: by mouth, 100–300 mg, 3–4 times daily, after food

PoM *Injection*, aminophylline 25 mg/mL, net price 10-mL amp = 53p; 250 mg/mL, 2 mL = 29p

Dose: by slow intravenous injection (over 20 minutes), 250–500 mg (5 mg/kg) when necessary; maintenance, if required, in patients not previously treated with theophylline, 500 micrograms/kg/hour *by slow intravenous infusion*

CHILD, *by slow intravenous injection* (over 20 minutes), 5 mg/kg; maintenance, if required, in patients not previously treated with theophylline, 6 months–9 years 1 mg/kg/hour, 10–16 years 800 micrograms/kg/hour *by slow intravenous infusion*

Suppositories—all discontinued

With antacid

Theodrox® (3M)

Tablets, aminophylline 195 mg, dried aluminium hydroxide gel 260 mg. Net price 120-tab pack = £1.88. Label: 21

Dose: 1 tablet 3 times daily, after food; max. 1–2 tablets 4 times daily.

Sustained release

(see advice on p. 106)

Pecram® (Zyma)

Tablets, s/r, yellow, aminophylline hydrate 225 mg. Net price 20 = £1.02. Label: 25

Dose: 1 tablet twice daily initially, increased if necessary to 2 tablets twice daily (steady-state concentrations usually reached after 3–4 days)

Phyllocontin Continus® (Napp)

Tablets, s/r, yellow, f/c, aminophylline 225 mg. Net price 60-tab pack = £3.61. Label: 25

Dose: 1 tablet twice daily initially, increased after 1 week to 2 tablets twice daily

Forte tablets, s/r, yellow, f/c, aminophylline 350 mg. Net price 60-tab pack = £6.00. Label: 25

Note. Forte tablets are for smokers and other patients with decreased theophylline half-life (see notes above)

Paediatric tablets, s/r, yellow, aminophylline 100 mg. Net price 50-tab pack = £1.94. Label: 25

Dose: CHILD over 3 years, 6 mg/kg twice daily initially, increased after 1 week to 12 mg/kg twice daily

CHOLINE THEOPHYLLINATE

Indications: reversible airways obstruction

Cautions; Side-effects: see under Theophylline

Dose: *by mouth*, 100–400 mg 2–4 times daily preferably after food; CHILD, 3 times daily, 3–5 years 62.5–125 mg, 6–12 years 100 mg

Note. Plasma theophylline concentration for optimum response 10–20 mg/litre (55–110 micromol/litre); narrow margin between therapeutic and toxic dose, see also notes above

Choledyl® (P-D)

Tablets, both compression coated, choline theophyllinate 100 mg (pink), net price 20 = 44p; 200 mg (yellow), 20 = 54p

Syrup, yellow, choline theophyllinate 62.5 mg/5 mL. Net price 100 mL = £1.15

Sustained release

(see advice on p. 106)

Sabidal SR 270® (Zyma)

Tablets, s/r, light yellow, choline theophyllinate 424 mg. Net price 20 = £1.54. Label: 25

Dose: 1 tablet twice daily initially, increased after 3 days to 1 in the morning and 2 at night

3.1.4 Compound bronchodilator preparations

Most compound bronchodilator preparations have no place in the management of patients with airways obstruction.

In general, patients are best treated with single-ingredient preparations, such as a selective beta$_2$-adrenoceptor stimulant (section 3.1.1.1) or ipratropium bromide (section 3.1.2), so that the dose of each drug can be adjusted. This flexibility is lost with combinations, although those in which both components are effective may occasionally have a role when compliance is a problem.

PoM **Bricanyl Expectorant®** (Astra)

Elixir, sugar-free, guaiphenesin 66.5 mg, terbutaline sulphate 1.5 mg/5 mL. Diluent water, life of diluted elixir 14 days. Net price 300 mL = £2.88

Dose: 10–15 mL 3 times daily

PoM **Bronchilator®** (Sterling-Winthrop)

Aerosol inhalation, isoetharine mesylate 350 micrograms, phenylephrine hydrochloride 70 micrograms/metered dose. Net price 250-dose unit = £11.71

Dose: 1–2 puffs repeated after 30 minutes if necessary; max. 8 puffs daily

PoM **Duovent®** (Boehringer Ingelheim)

Aerosol inhalation, fenoterol hydrobromide 90 micrograms, ipratropium bromide 36 micrograms/metered inhalation. Net price 200-dose unit with mouthpiece = £5.28 (extension tube also available)

Dose: 1–2 puffs 3–4 times daily; CHILD over 6 years 1 puff 3 times daily

PoM **Franol®** (Sterling-Winthrop)
Tablets, ephedrine hydrochloride 11 mg, theophylline 120 mg. Net price 100-tab pack = £5.11. Label: 21
Dose: 1 tablet 3 times daily; an additional tablet may be taken at bedtime for nocturnal attacks

PoM **Franol Plus®** (Sterling-Winthrop)
Tablets, ephedrine sulphate 15 mg, theophylline 120 mg. Net price 50-tab pack = £4.15. Label: 21
Dose: 1 tablet 3 times daily; an additional tablet may be taken at bedtime for nocturnal attacks

PoM **Medihaler-duo®** (3M)
Aerosol inhalation, isoprenaline hydrochloride 160 micrograms, phenylephrine bitartrate 240 micrograms/metered inhalation. Net price 400-dose unit = £3.25
Note. Not recommended therefore no dose stated

3.2 Corticosteroids

Corticosteroids have been used in the treatment of asthma for many years. In recent years, with the introduction of corticosteroid inhalations, their use has increased and has been extended to the treatment of less severe and more chronic asthma, as the side-effects associated with systemic administration (see section 6.3.3) are much reduced. Corticosteroids are usually of no benefit in patients with chronic bronchitis and emphysema; some patients with asthma, however, may be clinically indistinguishable from those with chronic bronchitis except that they will respond to a trial course of corticosteroids.

The action of corticosteroids is not fully understood but it is probable that they provide relief by reducing bronchial mucosal inflammatory reactions such as oedema and hypersecretion of mucus.

INHALATION. Corticosteroid aerosol inhalations must be used regularly to obtain maximum benefit; alleviation of symptoms usually occurs 3 to 7 days after initiation. **Beclomethasone dipropionate** and **budesonide** appear to be equally effective. *High-dose inhalers* are available for patients who only have a partial response to *standard inhalers*.

The maximum doses for high-dose corticosteroid inhalers are associated with some adrenal suppression (see section 6.3.3), therefore patients on high doses should be given a steroid card and may need corticosteroid cover during an episode of stress (e.g. an operation). Systemic therapy may also be necessary during episodes of infection or increased bronchoconstriction where higher doses are needed and access of inhaled drug to small airways may be reduced; patients may need a reserve supply of tablets.

Corticosteroids are better inhaled using spacing devices (e.g. Nebuhaler® or Volumatic®). These increase airway deposition and reduce oropharyngeal deposition, resulting in a marked reduction in the incidence of candidiasis and reducing systemic absorption (so that there is less adrenal suppression); these devices are bulky, but most patients only need to use them morning and night.

Dry powder inhalers (Becotide Rotacaps®) (see section 3.1.1 for description) may be tried in patients who are unable to use the aerosol inhalers.

Beclomethasone dipropionate *suspension for nebulisation* is relatively inefficient because of its poor solubility; only a small amount is nebulised in 15 minutes. A spacing device will allow a larger amount to be administered more effectively and can be used by some children as young as 2 years.

Maximum penetration of inhaled corticosteroid is facilitated if a beta$_2$-adrenoceptor stimulant drug such as salbutamol is inhaled beforehand; this is usual practice even in patients with only a mild degree of bronchospasm.

Patients who have been taking long-term oral corticosteroids can often be transferred to inhalation but the transfer must be done slowly, with gradual reduction in dose of oral corticosteroid, and at a time when the asthma is well controlled.

ORAL. *Acute attacks* of asthma should be treated with short courses of oral corticosteroids starting with a high dose, e.g. prednisolone 30 to 40 mg daily for a few days, gradually reduced once the attack has been controlled. Patients whose asthma has deteriorated rapidly usually respond quickly to corticosteroids, which can then be tailed down over a few days; more gradual reduction is necessary in those whose asthma has deteriorated gradually.

For use of corticosteroids in the emergency treatment of *severe acute asthma* see section 3.1.1.

In *chronic continuing asthma*, when the response to other anti-asthma drugs has been relatively small, continued administration of oral corticosteroids may be necessary; in such cases high doses of inhaled corticosteroids should be continued so that oral requirements are reduced to a minimum. Oral corticosteroids should normally be taken as a single dose in the morning to reduce the disturbance to circadian cortisol secretion. Dosage should always be titrated to the lowest dose which controls symptoms. Regular monitored peak flow measurements often help both patient and doctor to adjust the dose optimally. Prednisolone is available as tablets of 1 mg as well as 5 mg, and the smaller tablets may conveniently be used to adjust the maintenance dosage to the minimum necessary.

Alternate-day administration has not been very successful in the management of asthma and patients tend to deteriorate during the second 24 hours. If an attempt is made to introduce this pulmonary function should be monitored carefully over the 48 hours.

Corticotrophin and **tetracosactrin** (see section 6.5.1) were formerly used instead of the corticosteroids; their value was limited by the variable and unpredictable therapeutic response and the waning of their effect with time.

BECLOMETHASONE DIPROPIONATE

Indications: prophylaxis of asthma especially if not fully controlled by bronchodilators or cromoglycate

Cautions: see notes above; also active or quiescent tuberculosis; may need to reinstate systemic therapy during periods of stress or when airways obstruction or mucus prevent drug access to smaller airways

Side-effects: hoarseness; candidiasis of mouth or throat, usually only with large doses (reduced by using spacer, see notes above; responds to antifungal lozenges, see section 12.3.2, without discontinuation of therapy; rinsing the mouth with water after inhalation of a dose may also be helpful)

Dose: see preparations below

Standard-dose inhalers

PoM **Becodisks**® (A&H)

Powder for inhalation, disks containing 8 blisters of beclomethasone dipropionate 100 micrograms/blister, net price pack of 14 disks with Diskhaler® = £10.99, 14-disk refill = £10.42; 200 micrograms/blister, pack of 14 disks with Diskhaler® = £20.90, 14-disk refill = £20.33; 400 micrograms/blister, pack of 7 disks with Diskhaler® = £20.90, 7-disk refill = £20.33. Label: 8, counselling, dose

Dose: by inhalation of powder, 400 micrograms twice daily *or* 200 micrograms 3–4 times daily; CHILD 100 micrograms 2–4 times daily

PoM **Becotide**® (A&H)

Rotacaps®, buff/clear, beclomethasone dipropionate 100 micrograms. Net price 100-cap pack = £7.56. Label: 8, counselling, dose

Rotacaps®, brown/clear, beclomethasone dipropionate 200 micrograms. Net price 100-cap pack = £14.35. Label: 8, counselling, dose

Rotacaps®, dark brown/clear, beclomethasone dipropionate 400 micrograms. Net price 100-cap pack = £27.27. Label: 8, counselling, dose

Dose: by inhalation of powder, 200 micrograms 3–4 times daily or 400 micrograms twice daily; max. 1 mg daily; CHILD 100 micrograms 2–4 times daily

Suspension for nebulisation, beclomethasone dipropionate 50 micrograms/mL. Net price 10 mL = £2.50. For use with respirator or nebuliser. May be diluted up to 50% with sterile physiological saline

Dose: by inhalation of nebulised suspension, CHILD up to 1 year 50 micrograms 2–4 times daily; 1–12 years 100 micrograms 2–4 times daily, adjusted according to response

Note. Unsuitable for adults because of large volumes required.

PoM **Becotide 50**® (A&H)

Aerosol inhalation, beclomethasone dipropionate 50 micrograms/metered inhalation. Net price 200-dose unit = £5.56. Label: 8, counselling, dose

Dose: by aerosol inhalation, 200 micrograms (4 puffs) twice daily *or* 100 micrograms (2 puffs) 3–4 times daily (in more severe cases initially 600–800 micrograms daily); CHILD 50–100 micrograms (1–2 puffs) 2–4 times daily

PoM **Becotide 100**® (A&H)

Aerosol inhalation, beclomethasone dipropionate 100 micrograms/metered inhalation. Net price 200-dose unit = £10.56. Label: 8, counselling, dose

Dose: by aerosol inhalation, 200 micrograms (2 puffs) twice daily *or* 100 micrograms (1 puff) 3–4 times daily (in more severe cases initially 600–800 micrograms daily)

High-dose inhalers

PoM **Becloforte**® (A&H)

Aerosol inhalation, beclomethasone dipropionate 250 micrograms/metered inhalation. Net price 200-dose unit = £23.10; net price Becloforte® VM (2 Becloforte® inhalers with Volumatic®) = £46.20. Label: 8, counselling, dose, 10 steroid card

Dose: by aerosol inhalation, 500 micrograms (2 puffs) twice daily *or* 250 micrograms (1 puff) 4 times daily; if necessary may be increased to 500 micrograms 3–4 times daily

Note. Not indicated for children

Compound preparations

Not recommended, see section 3.3

PoM **Ventide**® (A&H)

Aerosol inhalation, beclomethasone dipropionate 50 micrograms, salbutamol 100 micrograms/metered inhalation. Net price 200-dose unit = £8.02. Label: 8, counselling, dose

Dose: maintenance, 2 puffs 3–4 times daily; CHILD 1–2 puffs 2–4 times daily

Paediatric Rotacaps®, light grey/clear, beclomethasone dipropionate 100 micrograms, salbutamol (as sulphate) 200 micrograms. Net price 100 = £12.59. Label: 8, counselling, dose

Dose: by inhalation of powder, 1 Rotacap® 2–4 times daily

Rotacaps®, dark grey/clear, beclomethasone dipropionate 200 micrograms, salbutamol (as sulphate) 400 micrograms. Net price 100 = £22.83. Label: 8, counselling, dose

Dose: by inhalation of powder, 1 Rotacap® 2–4 times daily

Devices

Rotahaler® (A&H)

Breath actuated inhaler for use with Rotacaps. Net price = 78p

Volumatic® (A&H)

Inhaler, large-volume spacer device. For use with Ventolin, Becotide, Becloforte, and Ventide inhalers. Net price = £2.75

BUDESONIDE

Indications; Cautions; Side-effects: see under Beclomethasone Dipropionate

Dose: by aerosol inhalation, 200 micrograms twice daily; may be reduced in well-controlled asthma to not less than 200 micrograms daily; in severe asthma dose may be increased to 1.6 mg daily; CHILD 50–200 micrograms twice daily; may be increased to 400 micrograms twice daily

Standard-dose inhalers

PoM **Pulmicort LS®** (Astra)

Aerosol inhalation, budesonide 50 micrograms/metered inhalation. Net price 200-dose unit with standard or Spacer inhaler = £6.66; 200-dose refill for use with Nebuhaler or Spacer inhaler = £4.66. Label: 8, counselling, dose

High-dose inhalers

PoM **Pulmicort®** (Astra)

Aerosol inhalation, budesonide 200 micrograms/metered inhalation. Net price 200-dose unit with standard or Spacer inhaler = £19.00; 200-dose refill for use with Nebuhaler or Spacer inhaler = £17.00; 100-dose unit with standard and Spacer inhaler = £10.16 (hosp. only); 100-dose refill = £8.66 (hosp. only). Label: 8, counselling, dose, 10 steroid card

Turbohaler® (= breath-actuated dry powder inhaler), budesonide 200 micrograms/inhalation, net price 100-dose unit = £18.50; 400 micrograms/inhalation, 50-dose unit = £18.50. Label: 8, counselling, dose, 10 steroid card

Devices

Nebuhaler® (Astra)

Inhaler, fitted with plastic cone and one-way valve. For use with Bricanyl and Pulmicort refill canisters. Net price = £4.75

3.3 Prophylaxis of asthma

Regular administration of prophylactic drugs such as sodium cromoglycate and inhaled corticosteroids can reduce the incidence of attacks of asthma and allow dosage reduction of bronchodilators and oral corticosteroids. Prophylactic drugs are of no value in the treatment of acute attacks as their effects take some time to develop.

Evidence that selective beta$_2$-adrenoceptor stimulants such as salbutamol and terbutaline may be used on a regular basis for prophylaxis rather than just for bronchodilatation has led to marketing of aerosols which contain both a beta$_2$-adrenoceptor stimulant and a corticosteroid or ipratropium. Although convenient and cheaper for the patient, they do not provide flexibility in dosage, and patient education is more difficult.

Sodium cromoglycate is administered by inhalation; its mode of action is not completely understood but it prevents release of pharmacological mediators of bronchospasm by stabilising mast-cell membranes.

Sodium cromoglycate is of particular value in asthma with an allergic basis, but, in practice, it is difficult to predict who will benefit, therefore it is reasonable to try it for a 4-week period in any patient whose asthma is poorly controlled with bronchodilators. Children seem to respond better than adults. Dose frequency is adjusted according to response but is usually 4 times a day initially; this may subsequently be reduced.

Sodium cromoglycate is also of value in the prevention of exercise-induced asthma, a single dose being inhaled half-an-hour beforehand.

If inhalation of the dry powder form of sodium cromoglycate causes bronchospasm a selective beta$_2$-adrenoceptor stimulant such as salbutamol or terbutaline should be inhaled a few minutes beforehand. The nebuliser solution is useful for patients who cannot manage the dry powder inhaler or the aerosol.

Nedocromil has a pharmacological action similar to that of sodium cromoglycate.

Ketotifen is an antihistamine with an action said to resemble that of sodium cromoglycate. It has not fulfilled its early promise.

SODIUM CROMOGLYCATE

Indications: prophylaxis of asthma

Side-effects: coughing, transient bronchospasm, and throat irritation due to inhalation of powder (see also notes above)

Dose: see below

COUNSELLING. Regular use is necessary

PoM **Intal®** (Fisons)

Aerosol inhalation, sodium cromoglycate 5 mg/metered inhalation. Net price 112-dose unit = £14.52. Label: 8

Dose: by aerosol inhalation, adults and children, 10 mg (2 puffs) 4 times daily initially, increased in severe cases or during periods of risk to 6–8 times daily; additional doses may also be taken before exercise; maintenance 5 mg (1 puff) 4 times daily

Note. Formerly Intal 5®

Autohaler® (= breath-actuated inhaler), sodium cromoglycate 5 mg/metered inhalation. Net price 112-dose unit = £18.99. Label: 8

Dose: as for Aerosol inhalation above

Spincaps®, yellow/clear, sodium cromoglycate 20 mg. Net price 112-cap pack = £11.59. Label: 8

Dose: by inhalation of powder, adults and children, 20 mg 4 times daily, increased in severe cases to 8 times daily

Spinhaler insufflator® (for use with Intal and Intal Compound Spincaps). Net price = £1.80

Nebuliser solution, sodium cromoglycate 10 mg/mL. Net price 2-mL amp = 25p. For use with power-operated nebuliser

Dose: by inhalation of nebulised solution, adults and children, 20 mg 4 times daily, increased in severe cases to 6 times daily

PoM **Intal Compound®** (Fisons)

Spincaps®, orange/clear, isoprenaline sulphate 100 micrograms, sodium cromoglycate 20 mg. Net price 112-cap pack = £9.17. Label: 8

Note. The compound inhalation of sodium cromoglycate with isoprenaline is not recommended; not only has isoprenaline a less selective action but it is liable to be used inappropriately for relief of bronchospasm rather than for its prophylactic effect

KETOTIFEN

Indications: see notes above

Cautions: may affect ability to drive or operate machinery and increase effects of alcohol; previous anti-asthmatic treatment should be continued for a minimum of 2 weeks after initiation of ketotifen treatment; **interactions:** Appendix 1 (antihistamines)

Side-effects: dry mouth, sedation
Dose: 1–2 mg twice daily with food; initial treatment in readily sedated patients 0.5–1 mg at night; CHILD over 2 years 1 mg twice daily

PoM **Zaditen®** (Sandoz)
Capsules, ketotifen 1 mg (as hydrogen fumarate). Net price 60-cap pack = £8.35. Label: 2, 8, 21
Tablets, off-white, scored, ketotifen 1 mg (as hydrogen fumarate). Net price 60-tab pack = £8.35. Label: 2, 8, 21
Elixir, sugar-free, ketotifen 1 mg (as hydrogen fumarate)/5 mL. Net price 150 mL = £4.94. Label: 2, 8, 21

NEDOCROMIL SODIUM

Indications: prophylaxis of asthma
Side-effects: see under Sodium Cromoglycate; also headache, nausea (both mild and transient); bitter taste
Dose: by aerosol inhalation, 4 mg (2 puffs) twice daily, increased to 4 times daily if necessary; CHILD under 12 years, not yet recommended

PoM **Tilade®** (Fisons)
Aerosol inhalation, nedocromil sodium 2 mg/metered inhalation. Net price 112-dose unit = £17.76. Label: 8

3.4 Allergic disorders

Drugs modifying allergic disorders are discussed under the following headings:

3.4.1 Antihistamines
3.4.2 Hyposensitisation
3.4.3 Allergic emergencies

For the treatment of asthma see sections 3.1.1 and 3.2. For the treatment of hay fever by nasal application of corticosteroids and prophylaxis with sodium cromoglycate see section 12.2. For eye preparations see section 11.4. For the treatment of allergic skin conditions with topical corticosteroid preparations see section 13.4.

3.4.1 Antihistamines

All antihistamines are of potential value in the treatment of *nasal allergies*, particularly seasonal (hay fever), and may be of some value in *vasomotor rhinitis*. They reduce rhinorrhoea and sneezing but are usually less effective for nasal congestion.

Oral antihistamines are also of some value in preventing *urticaria* and are used to treat *allergic rashes, pruritus,* and *insect bites and stings*; they are also used in *drug allergies*. Injections of chlorpheniramine or promethazine are used as an adjunct to adrenaline in the emergency treatment of *angioedema* and *anaphylaxis* (section 3.4.3).

There is no evidence that any one of the older antihistamines is superior to any other and patients vary widely in their responses. Antihistamines differ somewhat in duration of action and incidence of side-effects (drowsiness and antimuscarinic effects). Most are relatively short-acting but some, (e.g. promethazine) act for up to 12 hours. They all cause sedation but **promethazine**, **trimeprazine**, and **dimenhydrinate** may be more sedating whereas **chlorpheniramine**, **cyclizine**, and **mequitazine** may be less so.

Acrivastine, **astemizole**, **cetirizine**, **loratadine**, and **terfenadine** are newer antihistamines; they are a very major advance over the older antihistamines. They cause less sedation and psychomotor impairment because they only penetrate the blood brain barrier to a slight extent (and for this reason do not alleviate pruritus of non-allergic origin). Astemizole has a relatively slow onset of action and is more appropriate for use on a regular basis than when symptoms occur. The drug interactions described in Appendix 1 apply to a lesser extent to the non-sedative antihistamines, and they do not appear to potentiate the effects of alcohol.

DISADVANTAGES OF ANTIHISTAMINES. With most antihistamines drowsiness is a serious disadvantage; patients should be warned that their ability to drive or operate machinery may be impaired, and that the effects of alcohol may be increased. Other side-effects include headache, psychomotor impairment, antimuscarinic effects such as urinary retention, dry mouth, blurred vision, and gastro-intestinal disturbances; occasional rashes and photosensitivity reactions have been reported; paradoxical stimulation may rarely occur, especially in high dosage or in children. Antihistamines should be used with caution in epilepsy, prostatic hypertrophy, glaucoma, and hepatic disease. Most antihistamines should be avoided in **porphyria**, but chlorpheniramine and cyclizine have been used (see section 9.8.2).
Interactions: Appendix 1 (antihistamines). **Pregnancy** and **breast-feeding:** Appendixes 4 and 5 (antihistamines)

NON-SEDATIVE ANTIHISTAMINES

DRIVING. Although drowsiness is rare, nevertheless patients should be advised that it can occur and may affect performance of skilled tasks (e.g. driving); excess alcohol should be avoided.

ACRIVASTINE

Indications: symptomatic relief of allergy such as hay fever, urticaria
Cautions: see notes above; pending specific studies avoid in renal impairment
Side-effects: see notes above; incidence of sedation and antimuscarinic effects low
Dose: 8 mg 3 times daily; CHILD under 12 years, not yet recommended

PoM **Semprex®** (Calmic)
Capsules, acrivastine 8 mg. Net price 84-cap pack = £5.38. Counselling, driving, see above

ASTEMIZOLE

Indications: symptomatic relief of allergy such as hay fever, urticaria
Cautions: see notes above; pregnancy (toxicity at high doses in *animal* studies)
Side-effects: see notes above; weight gain occurs infrequently; incidence of sedation is low; antimuscarinic effects and psychomotor impairment have not been reported; ventricular arrhythmias have followed excessive dosage
Dose: 10 mg daily (must **not** be exceeded); CHILD 6–12 years, 5 mg daily (must **not** be exceeded)

PoM [1]**Hismanal®** (Janssen)
Tablets, scored, astemizole 10 mg. Net price 30 tab = £5.70. Counselling, driving, see above
Suspension, sugar-free, astemizole 5 mg/5 mL. Net price 100 mL = £2.90; 200 mL = £5.80. Counselling, driving, see above

1. Can be sold to the public provided it is licensed and labelled for the treatment of hay fever in adults and children over 12 years; a proprietary brand of astemizole tablets (Pollon-eze®) is on sale to the public

CETIRIZINE

Indications: symptomatic relief of allergy such as hay fever, urticaria
Cautions: see notes above; halve dose in renal impairment; incidence of sedation and antimuscarinic effects low
Side-effects: see notes above
Dose: 10 mg daily *or* 5 mg twice daily; CHILD under 12 years, not yet recommended

PoM **Zirtek®** (A&H)
Tablets, f/c, scored, cetirizine hydrochloride 10 mg. Net price 30-tab pack = £8.95. Counselling, driving, see above

LORATADINE

Indications: symptomatic relief of allergy such as hay fever; urticaria
Cautions; Side-effects: see notes above; incidence of sedation and antimuscarinic effects low; pregnancy (toxicity at high doses in *animals*)
Dose: 10 mg daily; CHILD under 12 years and ELDERLY, not yet recommended

▼ PoM **Clarityn®** (Schering-Plough)
Tablets, scored, loratadine 10 mg. Net price 30-tab pack = £6.90. Counselling, driving, see above

TERFENADINE

Indications: symptomatic relief of allergy such as hay fever, urticaria
Cautions: hepatic impairment; **interactions:** Appendix 1 (antihistamines)
Side-effects: see notes above; incidence of sedation is low; antimuscarinic effects and psychomotor impairment have not been reported; possibly associated with hair loss
Dose: 60 mg twice daily *or* 120 mg in the morning; CHILD 3–6 years 15 mg twice daily; 6–12 years 30 mg twice daily

Triludan® (Merrell)
Tablets, scored, terfenadine 60 mg. Net price 60-tab pack = £5.80. Counselling, driving, see above
Forte tablets, terfenadine 120 mg. Net price 7-tab pack = £1.91; 30-tab pack = £5.80. Counselling, driving, see above
Suspension, sugar-free, terfenadine 30 mg/5 mL. Net price 120 mL = £2.54; 200 mL = £4.24. Counselling, driving, see above

Note. A proprietary brand of terfenadine (Seldane®) is on sale to the public

SEDATIVE ANTIHISTAMINES

DRIVING. Drowsiness may affect performance of skilled tasks (e.g. driving): effects of alcohol enhanced.

AZATADINE MALEATE

Indications: symptomatic relief of allergy such as hay fever, urticaria
Cautions; Side-effects: see notes above
Dose: 1 mg, increased if necessary to 2 mg, twice daily; CHILD 1–6 years 250 micrograms twice daily, 6–12 years 0.5–1 mg twice daily

Optimine® (Schering-Plough)
Tablets, scored, azatadine maleate 1 mg. Net price 56-tab pack = £4.48. Label: 2
Syrup, azatadine maleate 500 micrograms/5 mL. Diluent syrup, life of diluted syrup 28 days. Net price 120 mL = £1.43. Label: 2

BROMPHENIRAMINE MALEATE

Indications: symptomatic relief of allergy such as hay fever, urticaria
Cautions; Side-effects: see notes above
Dose: 4–8 mg 3–4 times daily; CHILD up to 3 years 0.4–1 mg/kg daily in 4 divided doses, 3–6 years 2 mg 3–4 times daily, 6–12 years 2–4 mg 3–4 times daily

Dimotane® (Wyeth)
Tablets, peach, scored, brompheniramine maleate 4 mg. Net price 20 = 70p. Label: 2
Elixir, yellow-green, brompheniramine maleate 2 mg/5 mL. Diluent syrup, life of diluted elixir 14 days. Net price 100 mL = 84p. Label: 2

Dimotane LA® (Wyeth)
Tablets, s/r, peach, s/c, brompheniramine maleate 12 mg. Net price 20 = £1.05. Label: 2, 25
Dose: 12–24 mg twice daily; CHILD 6–12 years 12 mg at bedtime, increased if necessary to 12 mg twice daily

CHLORPHENIRAMINE MALEATE

Indications: symptomatic relief of allergy such as hay fever, urticaria; emergency treatment of anaphylactic reactions (section 3.4.3)
Cautions; Side-effects: see notes above. Injections may be irritant and cause transitory hypotension or CNS stimulation

Dose: by mouth, 4 mg every 4–6 hours, max. 24 mg daily; CHILD 1–2 years 1 mg twice daily, 2–5 years 1 mg every 4–6 hours, max. 6 mg daily, 6–12 years 2 mg every 4–6 hours, max. 12 mg daily
By subcutaneous or intramuscular injection, 10–20 mg, repeated if required; max. 40 mg in 24 hours
By slow intravenous injection over 1 minute, 10–20 mg diluted in syringe with 5–10 mL blood

Chlorpheniramine Tablets, chlorpheniramine maleate 4 mg. Net price 20 = 18p. Label: 2

Alunex® (Steinhard)
Tablets, yellow, scored, chlorpheniramine maleate 4 mg. Net price 20 = 16p. Label: 2

Piriton® (A&H)
Tablets, ivory, chlorpheniramine maleate 4 mg. Net price 20 = 19p. Label: 2
Spandets® (= tablets s/r), ivory/white, chlorpheniramine maleate 12 mg. Net price 20 = 53p. Label: 2, 25
Dose: 12 mg every 8–12 hours, max. 24 mg daily; CHILD over 12 years 12 mg daily
Syrup, chlorpheniramine maleate 2 mg/5 mL. Diluent syrup (without preservative), life of diluted syrup 14 days. Net price 150 mL = 29p. Label: 2
PoM *Injection*, chlorpheniramine maleate 10 mg/mL. Net price 1-mL amp = 12p

CINNARIZINE
See section 4.6

CLEMASTINE
Indications: symptomatic relief of allergy such as hay fever, urticaria
Cautions; Side-effects: see notes above
Dose: 1 mg twice daily; CHILD up to 12 years 0.5–1 mg twice daily

Tavegil® (Sandoz)
Tablets, scored, clemastine 1 mg (as hydrogen fumarate). Net price 50-tab pack = £2.10. Label: 2
Elixir, sugar-free, clemastine 500 micrograms (as hydrogen fumarate)/5 mL. Diluent syrup or sorbitol solution 70%, life of diluted elixir 14 days. Net price 150 mL = 98p. Label: 2
Note. A proprietary brand of clemastine hydrogen fumarate (Aller-eze®) is on sale to the public

CYCLIZINE
See section 4.6

CYPROHEPTADINE HYDROCHLORIDE
Indications: symptomatic relief of allergy such as hay fever, urticaria
Cautions; Side-effects: see notes above; may cause weight gain
Dose: allergy, usual dose 4 mg 3–4 times daily; usual range 4–20 mg daily, max. 32 mg daily; CHILD 2–6 years 2 mg 2–3 times daily, max. 12 mg daily; 7–14 years 4 mg 2–3 times daily, max. 16 mg daily
Migraine, 4 mg with a further 4 mg after 30 minutes if necessary; maintenance, 4 mg every 4–6 hours
Stimulation of appetite—not recommended therefore no dose stated

Periactin® (MSD)
Tablets, scored, cyproheptadine hydrochloride 4 mg. Net price 20 = 57p. Label: 2
Syrup, yellow, cyproheptadine hydrochloride 2 mg/5 mL. Diluent syrup, life of diluted syrup 14 days. Net price 200 mL = £1.27. Label: 2

DIMENHYDRINATE
See section 4.6

DIMETHINDENE MALEATE
Indications: symptomatic relief of allergy such as hay fever, urticaria
Cautions; Side-effects: see notes above

Fenostil Retard® (Zyma)
Tablets, s/r, greyish-white, dimethindene maleate 2.5 mg. Net price 20 = 57p. Label: 2, 25
Dose: 2.5 mg twice daily

DIPHENHYDRAMINE HYDROCHLORIDE
Indications: symptomatic relief of allergy such as hay fever
Cautions; Side-effects: see notes above

Preparations
Ingredient of compound cough preparations (section 3.9.2)

DIPHENYLPYRALINE HYDROCHLORIDE
Indications: symptomatic relief of allergy such as hay fever, urticaria
Cautions; Side-effects: see notes above

Histryl® (SK&F)
Spansule® (= capsules s/r), pink/clear, enclosing pink and white pellets, diphenylpyraline hydrochloride 5 mg. Net price 30-cap pack = £1.62. Label: 2, 25
Dose: 5–10 mg twice daily
Paediatric Spansule® (= capsules s/r), pink/clear, enclosing pink and white pellets, diphenylpyraline hydrochloride 2.5 mg. Net price 30-cap pack = £1.23. Label: 1, 25
Dose: CHILD over 7 years 2.5 mg twice daily

Lergoban® (3M)
Tablets, s/r, diphenylpyraline hydrochloride 5 mg. Net price 60-tab pack = £2.22. Label: 2, 25
Dose: 5–10 mg twice daily; CHILD over 10 years 5 mg twice daily

HYDROXYZINE HYDROCHLORIDE
See section 4.1.2

KETOTIFEN
See section 3.3

MEBHYDROLIN

Indications: symptomatic relief of allergy such as hay fever, urticaria
Cautions: see notes above
Side-effects: see notes above; also very rarely granulocytopenia or agranulocytosis
Dose: ADULT and CHILD over 10 years, 50–100 mg 3 times daily

PoM **Fabahistin®** (Bayer)
Tablets, orange, s/c, mebhydrolin 50 mg. Net price 20 = 68p. Label: 2

MEQUITAZINE

Indications: symptomatic relief of allergy such as hay fever, urticaria
Cautions; Side-effects: see notes above
Dose: 5 mg twice daily; CHILD under 12 years, not yet recommended

PoM **Primalan®** (Rhône-Poulenc Rorer)
Tablets, mequitazine 5 mg. Net price 56-tab pack = £5.00. Label: 2

OXATOMIDE

Indications: symptomatic relief of allergy such as hay fever, food allergy, urticaria
Cautions; Side-effects: see notes above; drowsiness most common; increased appetite with weight gain may occur above 120 mg daily
Dose: 30 mg twice daily after food, increased if necessary to 60 mg twice daily; ELDERLY 30 mg twice daily; CHILD 5–14 years 15–30 mg twice daily

PoM **Tinset®** (Janssen)
Tablets, scored, oxatomide 30 mg. Net price 25-tab pack = £4.90. Label: 2, 21

PHENINDAMINE TARTRATE

Indications: symptomatic relief of allergy such as hay fever, urticaria
Cautions; Side-effects: see notes above; may cause mild CNS stimulation
Dose: 25–50 mg 1–3 times daily; CHILD over 10 years 25 mg 1–3 times daily

Thephorin® (Sinclair)
Tablets, s/c, phenindamine tartrate 25 mg. Net price 20 = 91p. Label: 2

PHENIRAMINE MALEATE

Indications: symptomatic relief of allergy such as hay fever, urticaria
Cautions; Side-effects: see notes above

Daneral SA® (Hoechst)
Tablets, s/r, pink, s/c, pheniramine maleate 75 mg. Net price 30-tab pack = £2.61. Label: 2, 25
Dose: 75–150 mg at night or 75 mg night and morning

PROMETHAZINE HYDROCHLORIDE

Indications: symptomatic relief of allergy such as hay fever, urticaria, emergency treatment of anaphylactic reactions (section 3.4.3)
For use in premedication see section 15.1.4.2; sedation see section 4.1.1
Cautions; Side-effects: see notes above; intramuscular injection may be painful
Dose: by mouth, 25 mg at night increased to 50 mg if necessary *or* 10–20 mg 2–3 times daily; CHILD 1–5 years 5–15 mg daily, 5–10 years 10–25 mg daily
By deep intramuscular injection, 25–50 mg; max. 100 mg; CHILD 5–10 years 6.25–12.5 mg
By slow intravenous injection in emergencies, 25–50 mg, max. 100 mg, as a solution containing 2.5 mg/mL in water for injections

Phenergan® (Rhône-Poulenc Rorer)
Tablets, both blue, f/c, promethazine hydrochloride 10 mg, net price 56-tab pack = £1.03; 25 mg, 56-tab pack = £1.53. Label: 2
Elixir, golden, promethazine hydrochloride 5 mg/5 mL. Diluent syrup, life of diluted elixir 14 days. Net price 100 mL = £1.15. Label: 2
PoM *Injection*, promethazine hydrochloride 25 mg/mL. Net price 1-mL amp = 28p; 2-mL amp = 34p
Note. A proprietary brand of promethazine hydrochloride tablets 20 mg (Sominex®) is on sale to the public for the treatment of occasional insomnia in adults

PROMETHAZINE THEOCLATE

See section 4.6

TRIMEPRAZINE TARTRATE

Indications: urticaria and pruritus; premedication, see section 15.1.4.2
Cautions; Side-effects: see notes above
Dose: 10 mg 2–3 times daily, in severe cases up to max. 100 mg daily has been used; ELDERLY 10 mg 1–2 times daily; CHILD over 2 years 2.5–5 mg 3–4 times daily

PoM **Vallergan®** (Rhône-Poulenc Rorer)
Tablets, blue, f/c, trimeprazine tartrate 10 mg. Net price 28-tab pack = £1.06. Label: 2
Syrup, straw coloured, trimeprazine tartrate 7.5 mg/5 mL. Diluent syrup (without preservatives), life of diluted syrup 14 days. Net price 100 mL = £1.20. Label: 2
Syrup forte, pale yellow, trimeprazine tartrate 30 mg/5 mL. Diluent as above. Net price 100 mL = £2.48. Label: 2
Note. For use of Forte Syrup see section 15.1.4.2

TRIPROLIDINE HYDROCHLORIDE

Indications: symptomatic relief of allergy such as hay fever, urticaria
Cautions; Side-effects: see notes above
Dose: 2.5–5 mg 3 times daily; CHILD, 3 times daily, up to 1 year 1 mg, 1–5 years 2 mg, 6–12 years 2–3 mg

Actidil® (Wellcome)
Tablets, scored, triprolidine hydrochloride 2.5 mg. Net price 20 = £1.53. Label: 2
Elixir, orange, triprolidine hydrochloride 2 mg/5 mL. Diluent syrup, life of diluted elixir 14 days. Net price 100 mL = £1.27. Label: 2

Pro-Actidil® (Wellcome)
Tablets, s/r, white/pink/blue, triprolidine hydrochloride 10 mg. Net price 20 = £4.76. Label: 2, 25
Dose: 10 mg early evening or 5–6 hours before retiring increased to 20 mg daily if symptoms very severe; CHILD under 12 years not recommended

3.4.2 Hyposensitisation

Except for wasp and bee sting allergy the value of specific hyposensitisation is uncertain; administration of allergen extract desensitising vaccines is associated with a significant risk of anaphylaxis, see CSM warning below. Most atopic (allergic) patients are sensitive to a wide range of allergens hence hyposensitisation with an extract of a single allergen is usually no more than partially successful.

Diagnostic skin tests are unreliable and can only be used in conjunction with a detailed history of allergen exposure.

CSM Warning. The CSM has warned that since 1980, in the UK alone, 11 patients, most of whom were young, have died from anaphylaxis caused by allergen extract desensitising vaccines; patients with asthma appear to be particularly susceptible. The CSM is not aware of such problems when these allergens are used for diagnostic purposes (skin testing). Although some vaccines can prevent anaphylactic reactions (e.g. to bee stings) the effectiveness of the others is controversial. The CSM therefore recommends that it is important for doctors to balance carefully the known risks of desensitising vaccines against potential benefits before embarking on treatment. *Such treatment should only be carried out where facilities for full cardiorespiratory resuscitation are immediately available, and patients should be kept under medical observation for at least 2 hours after treatment.*

For details of the management of anaphylactic shock, see section 3.4.3.

ALLERGEN EXTRACT VACCINES

Each set usually contains vials for the administration of graded amounts to patients undergoing hyposensitisation. Maintenance sets containing vials at the highest strength are also available. Manufacturer's literature must be consulted for details of allergens, vial strengths, and administration

Indications: hypersensitivity to one or more common allergens (see notes above)

Cautions: see notes above including CSM warning; manufacturers recommend that patients should be warned not to eat a heavy meal before the injection

Contra-indications: pregnancy, febrile conditions, acute asthma

Side-effects: allergic reactions, especially in small children

Dose: by subcutaneous injection, see manufacturer's literature; very sensitive patients may be given an antihistamine tablet one hour before the injection

Pollen allergy (hay fever) preparations

PoM **Spectralgen Single Species®** (Pharmacia)
Prepared from Timothy grass. Net price treatment set = £59.29

PoM **Spectralgen 4 Grass Mix®** (Pharmacia)
Prepared from 4 varieties of common grasses. Net price treatment set = £64.99

PoM **Spectralgen 3 Tree Mix®** (Pharmacia)
Prepared from 3 varieties of common trees. Net price treatment set = £63.06

Wasp and bee venom allergy preparations

PoM **Pharmalgen®** (Pharmacia)
Bee venom extract (*Apis mellifera*) or wasp venom extract (*Vespula* spp.). Net price treatment set = £44.14 (bee), £56.76 (wasp)

3.4.3 Allergic emergencies

Anaphylactic shock requires prompt energetic treatment of laryngeal oedema, bronchospasm, and hypotension. It is relatively uncommon and is usually precipitated by blood products, vaccines, insect stings, and certain drugs such as antibiotics, iron injections, anti-inflammatory analgesics, heparin, hyposensitising (allergen) preparations, and neuromuscular blocking drugs. It is more likely to occur after parenteral administration and atopic individuals are particularly susceptible.

First-line treatment includes restoration of blood pressure, laying the patient flat, raising the feet, and administration of **adrenaline**[1] injection. This is given intramuscularly in a dose of 0.5–1 mg (0.5–1 mL adrenaline injection 1 in 1000), repeated every 10 minutes, according to blood pressure and pulse, until improvement occurs. Antihistamines, e.g. **chlorpheniramine**, given by slow intravenous injection (section 3.4.1), are a useful adjunctive treatment. This is given after adrenaline injection and continued for 24 to 48 hours to prevent relapse.

Continuing deterioration requires further treatment including intravenous fluids (see section 9.2.2), intravenous aminophylline (section 3.1.3) or a nebulised beta$_2$-adrenoceptor stimulant (such as salbutamol or terbutaline, section 3.1.1.1), oxygen, assisted respiration, and possibly emergency tracheotomy.

Intravenous **corticosteroids** are of secondary value in anaphylatic shock as their onset of action is delayed for several hours but they should be used to prevent further deterioration in severely affected patients (see section 6.3.4).

Some patients with severe allergy to insect stings are encouraged to carry pre-filled adrenaline syringes for emergency administration during periods of risk; adrenaline inhalations (Medihaler-epi®) are much less effective.

1. In patients on non-cardioselective beta-blockers severe anaphylaxis may not respond to adrenaline injection, calling for addition of salbutamol injection

Angioedema is dangerous when it affects respiration. If obstruction is present, adrenaline injection should be given as described above; antihistamine injections are also helpful but corticosteroids are of secondary value (see also above). Tracheal intubation as well as other measures may be necessary.

ADRENALINE

Indications: emergency treatment of acute anaphylaxis; cardiopulmonary resuscitation, section 2.7

Cautions: hyperthyroidism, diabetes mellitus, ischaemic heart disease, hypertension, elderly patients; **interactions:** Appendix 1 (sympathomimetics)

Side-effects: anxiety, tremor, tachycardia, arrhythmias, dry mouth, cold extremities (seldom troublesome when given by aerosol inhalation, but tolerance and increased viscosity of bronchial secretions occur)

Dose: acute anaphylaxis, *by intramuscular injection*, see table below:

IMPORTANT. Intravenous route is for cardiac resuscitation **only** (see section 2.7)

Volume of adrenaline injection 1 in 1000 (1 mg/mL) for intramuscular injection in anaphylactic shock

Age	Volume of adrenaline 1 in 1000
Under 1 year	0.05 mL
1 year	0.1 mL
2 years	0.2 mL[1]
3–4 years	0.3 mL[1]
5 years	0.4 mL[1]
6–12 years	0.5 mL[1]
Adult	0.5–1 mL

These doses may be repeated every 10 minutes, according to blood pressure and pulse, until improvement occurs (may be repeated several times).

1. Suitable for robust children in these age groups; for underweight children use half these doses.

PoM **Adrenaline Injection, BP,** adrenaline 1 in 1000 (adrenaline 1 mg/mL as acid tartrate). Net price 0.5-mL amp = 31p; 1-mL amp = 30p

Available from Boots, Evans, Macarthys

Note. For 1 in 10000 strength, see section 2.7

PoM **Min-I-Jet® Adrenaline** (IMS)

Injection, adrenaline 1 in 1000 (1 mg/mL as hydrochloride). Net price 0.5-mL = £3.00; 1-mL = £2.64 (both disposable syringe)

Injection, adrenaline 1 in 10000, see section 2.7

Inhalation

PoM **Medihaler-epi®** (3M)

Aerosol inhalation, adrenaline acid tartrate 280 micrograms/metered inhalation. Net price 400-dose unit = £2.73

Dose: by aerosol inhalation, adjunct to anaphylaxis treatment only, min. of 20 puffs

3.5 Respiratory stimulants

Respiratory stimulants (analeptic drugs) have a limited place in the treatment of ventilatory failure in patients with chronic obstructive airways disease. They are effective only when given by intravenous injection or infusion and have a short duration of action. Their use has largely been replaced by ventilatory support. However, occasionally when the latter is contra-indicated and in patients with hypercapnic respiratory failure who are becoming drowsy or comatose, respiratory stimulants in the short term may arouse patients sufficiently to co-operate and clear their secretions.

Respiratory stimulants may be harmful in respiratory failure since they stimulate non-respiratory as well as respiratory muscles. They should only be given under **expert supervision** in hospital and must be combined with active physiotherapy. There is at present no oral respiratory stimulant available for long-term use in chronic respiratory failure.

Doxapram is given by continuous intravenous infusion in a dosage of 2 mg per minute. Frequent arterial blood gas studies and pH measurements are necessary during treatment to ensure the correct dosage.

Nikethamide and ethamivan were formerly used as respiratory stimulants but are no longer recommended; the effective doses were close to those causing toxic effects, especially convulsions. Respiratory stimulants such as ethamivan and nikethamide have no place whatsoever in the management of asphyxia in the newborn.

DOXAPRAM HYDROCHLORIDE

Indications: ventilatory failure (see notes above); postoperative respiratory depression

Cautions: epilepsy, hepatic impairment; see also notes above; **interactions:** Appendix 1 (doxapram)

Contra-indications: severe hypertension, status asthmaticus, coronary artery disease, thyrotoxicosis

Side-effects: increase in blood pressure and heart rate, dizziness, perineal warmth

Dose: by intravenous infusion, 1.5–4 mg per minute according to patient's response

By intravenous injection over at least 30 seconds, 1–1.5 mg/kg repeated if necessary at intervals of 1 hour

PoM **Dopram®** (Wyeth)

Injection, doxapram hydrochloride 20 mg/mL. Net price 5-mL amp = £2.14

Intravenous infusion, doxapram hydrochloride 2 mg/mL in glucose 5%. Net price 500-mL bottle = £22.34

NIKETHAMIDE

Indications: specialist hospital use only (see notes above)

Cautions: see notes above, severe hypertension

Contra-indications: respiratory failure due to neurological disease or drug overdose; status asthmaticus, coronary artery disease, thyrotoxicosis; porphyria

Side-effects: nausea, restlessness, convulsions, dizziness, tremor, vasoconstriction, arrhythmias

Dose: by slow intravenous injection, 0.5–1 g but not recommended see notes above

PoM **Nikethamide Injection,** nikethamide 250 mg/mL. Net price 2-mL amp = 68p (hosp. only)

ETHAMIVAN

Indications; Cautions; Contra-indications; Side-effects: see under Nikethamide and notes above

Dose: *by intravenous injection*, 100 mg, but not recommended see notes above

PoM **Clairvan**® (Sinclair)

Oral solution, ethamivan 50 mg/mL (5%) in ethyl alcohol 25%. Net price 5-mL dropper bottle = £5.71

Note. Use of this paediatric preparation is not recommended (see notes above)

Injection, ethamivan 50 mg/mL (5%). Net price 2-mL amp = £2.67

3.6 Oxygen

Oxygen should be regarded as a drug. It is prescribed for hypoxaemic patients to increase alveolar oxygen tension and decrease the work of breathing necessary to maintain a given arterial oxygen tension. The concentration depends on the condition being treated; an inappropriate concentration may have serious or even lethal effects.

High concentration oxygen therapy, with concentrations of up to 60% for short periods, is safe in conditions such as pneumonia, pulmonary thromboembolism, and fibrosing alveolitis. In such conditions low arterial oxygen (P_aO_2) is usually associated with low or normal arterial carbon dioxide (P_aCO_2), therefore there is little risk of hypoventilation and carbon dioxide retention.

In severe acute asthma, the arterial carbon dioxide (P_aCO_2) is usually subnormal but as asthma deteriorates may rise steeply (particularly in children). These patients usually require high concentrations of oxygen and if the arterial carbon dioxide (P_aCO_2) remains high despite other treatment intermittent positive pressure ventilation needs to be considered urgently. Where facilities for blood gas measurements are not immediately available, for example while transferring the patient to hospital, 35% to 50% oxygen delivered through a conventional mask is recommended. Exceptionally, asthma is diagnosed in patients with a long history of chronic bronchitis and probable respiratory failure; in these patients a lower concentration (24% to 28%) may be needed to limit oxygen-induced reduction of respiratory drive.

Low concentration oxygen therapy (controlled oxygen therapy) is reserved for patients with ventilatory failure due to chronic obstructive airways disease or other causes. The concentration should not exceed 28% and in some patients a concentration above 24% may be excessive. The aim is to provide the patient with just enough oxygen to improve hypoxaemia without worsening pre-existing carbon dioxide retention and respiratory acidosis. Treatment should be initiated in hospital as repeated blood gas measurements are required to estimate the correct concentration.

DOMICILIARY OXYGEN. Oxygen should only be prescribed for patients in the home after careful evaluation in hospital by respiratory experts; it should never be prescribed on a placebo basis.

Oxygen is occasionally prescribed for *intermittent* use for episodes of hypoxaemia of short duration, for example asthma. It is important, however, that the patient does not rely on oxygen instead of obtaining medical help or taking more specific treatment.

Alternatively, intermittent oxygen may be prescribed for patients with advanced irreversible respiratory disorders to increase mobility and capacity for exercise and to ease discomfort, for example in chronic obstructive bronchitis, emphysema, widespread fibrosis, and primary or thromboembolic pulmonary hypertension. These patients may be prescribed portable equipment through the hospital service, refillable from cylinders in the home.

Long-term administration of oxygen (at least 15 hours daily) may be prescribed on an elective basis in an attempt to prolong survival in patients with severe chronic obstructive airways disease with cor pulmonale.

Department of Health guidelines suggest that this treatment should be reserved for patients who fulfil the following criteria:

$P_aO_2 < 7.3$ kPa; $P_aCO_2 > 6$ kPa;
$FEV_1 < 1.5$ litre and $FVC < 2$ litre

The measurements should be stable on two occasions at least three weeks apart after the patient has received appropriate bronchodilator therapy.

Less information is available on long-term oxygen in patients with a similar degree of hypoxaemia and airflow obstruction but no hypercapnia; the Department of Health suggests that these patients should not be denied this form of treatment but the effects of long-term therapy have not yet been assessed completely.

Increased respiratory depression from low concentrations of oxygen is seldom a problem in patients with stable respiratory failure although it may occur during exacerbations; patients and relatives should be warned to call for medical help if drowsiness or confusion occur.

Patients should be advised of the fire risks when receiving therapy.

To provide oxygen for 15 hours a day at a rate of 2 litres per minute requires ten 'F' size oxygen cylinders a week. The Department of Health recommends that patients prescribed long-term oxygen should be provided with a concentrator. Oxygen concentrators are more economical for patients requiring oxygen for long periods, and in England and Wales are now prescribable on the NHS on a regional tendering basis.

Long-term oxygen treatment is very demanding. Before a concentrator is installed patients must be prepared to take oxygen for 15 hours a day.

Under the NHS oxygen may be supplied by chemist contractors as cylinders. Oxygen flow can be adjusted as the cylinders are equipped with an oxygen flow meter with 'medium' (2 litres/minute) and 'high' (4 litres/minute) settings. Patients are supplied with either constant or variable performance masks. The Intersurgical 010 28% or

Ventimask Mk III 28% are constant performance masks and provide a nearly constant supply of oxygen (28%) over a wide range irrespective of the patient's breathing pattern. The variable performance masks include the Intersurgical 005 Mask and the MC Mask; the concentration of oxygen supplied to the patient varies with the rate of flow of oxygen and also with the patient's breathing pattern.

3.7 Mucolytics

Mucolytics are often prescribed to facilitate expectoration by reducing sputum viscosity in chronic asthma and bronchitis. Few patients, however, have been shown to derive much benefit from them although they do render sputum less viscid. Steam inhalation with postural drainage, is good expectorant therapy in bronchiectasis and some chronic bronchitics.

ACETYLCYSTEINE

Indications: reduction of sputum viscosity
Side-effects: occasional gastro-intestinal irritation, headache, urticaria, tinnitus, and sensitivity
Dose: adults and children over 6 years, 200 mg in water 3 times daily, usually for 5–10 days but if necessary may be extended to 6 months or longer; CHILD up to 2 years 200 mg daily, 2–6 years 200 mg twice daily

NHS * PoM **Acetylcysteine Granules,** acetylcysteine 200 mg/sachet. Net price 30 sachets = £5.74. Label: 13
* except for abdominal complications associated with cystic fibrosis and endorsed 'S3B' ('S2B' in Scotland)
Note. The brand name NHS Fabrol® (Zyma) is used for acetylcysteine granules

CARBOCISTEINE

Indications: reduction of sputum viscosity
Side-effects: occasional gastro-intestinal irritation, rashes
Dose: 750 mg 3 times daily initially, then 1.5 g daily in divided doses; CHILD 2–5 years 62.5–125 mg 4 times daily, 6–12 years 250 mg 3 times daily

NHS *PoM **Carbocisteine Capsules,** carbocisteine 375 mg. Net price 30-cap pack = £3.20
NHS *PoM **Carbocisteine Syrup,** carbocisteine 125 mg/5 mL. Diluent syrup, life of diluted syrup 14 days, net price 300 mL = £3.51; 250 mg/5 mL, 300 mL = £4.50
* except, for patients under the age of 18 years, any condition which, through damage or disease, affects the airways and has required a tracheostomy and endorsed 'S3B' ('S2B' in Scotland)
Note. The brand name NHS Mucodyne® (Rorer) is used for carbocisteine preparations; capsules and 250 mg/5 mL strength of syrup contain tartrazine

METHYLCYSTEINE HYDROCHLORIDE

Indications: reduction of sputum viscosity
Dose: 100–200 mg 3–4 times daily before meals reduced to 200 mg twice daily after 6 weeks; CHILD over 5 years 100 mg 3 times daily
Prophylaxis, 100–200 mg 2–3 times every other day during winter months

NHS **Visclair®** (Sinclair)
Tablets, yellow, s/c, e/c, methylcysteine hydrochloride 100 mg. Net price 20 = £3.20. Label: 5, 22, 25

3.8 Aromatic inhalations

Inhalations containing volatile substances such as eucalyptus oil are traditionally used and although the vapour may contain little of the additive it encourages deliberate inspiration of warm moist air which is often comforting in bronchitis; boiling water should not be used owing to the risk of scalding. Inhalations are also used for the relief of nasal obstruction in acute rhinitis or sinusitis.

CHILDREN. The use of strong aromatic decongestants (applied as rubs or to pillows) could be hazardous to infants less than one month of age, since in certain circumstances, apnoea could be induced. Mothers with young infants in whom nasal obstruction with mucus is a problem can readily be taught appropriate techniques of suction aspiration.

Benzoin Tincture, Compound, balsamic acids approx. 4.5%. Net price 50 mL = 28p. Label: 15
Directions for use: add one teaspoonful to a pint of hot, **not** boiling, water and inhale the vapour

NHS **Menthol and Benzoin Inhalation, BP,** menthol 2 g, benzoin inhalation to 100 mL. Net price 50 mL = 36p. Label: 15
Directions for use: add one teaspoonful to a pint of hot, **not** boiling, water and inhale the vapour

Menthol and Eucalyptus Inhalation, BP 1980, menthol 2 g, eucalyptus oil 10 mL, light magnesium carbonate 7 g, water to 100 mL. Net price 50 mL = 20p
Directions for use: add one teaspoonful to a pint of hot, **not** boiling, water and inhale the vapour

NHS **Karvol®** (Crookes)
Inhalation capsules, menthol 35.33 mg, with chlorbutol, pine oils, terpineol, and thymol. Net price 10 = 90p
Directions for use: inhale vapour from contents of 1 capsule expressed into handkerchief or a pint of hot, **not** boiling, water; avoid in infants under 3 months

3.9 Antitussives

3.9.1 Cough suppressants

The drawbacks of prescribing cough suppressants are rarely outweighed by the benefits of treatment and only occasionally are they useful, as, for example, if sleep is disturbed by a dry cough. Cough suppressants may cause sputum retention and this may be harmful in patients with chronic bronchitis and bronchiectasis. Though commonly used in acute bronchitis and pneumonia they can be harmful; such conditions are best treated by prompt administration of antibacterial drugs (see section 5.1, Table 1).

Cough suppressants such as codeine, dextromethorphan, and pholcodine are seldom sufficiently potent to be effective and all tend to cause constipation.

CHILDREN. The use of cough suppressants containing codeine or similar opioid analgesics is not generally recommended in children and should be avoided altogether in those under 1 year of age.

CODEINE PHOSPHATE

Indications: dry or painful cough
Cautions: asthma; hepatic and renal impairment; history of drug abuse; see also notes above and section 4.7.2; **interactions:** Appendix 1 (opioid analgesics)
Contra-indications: liver disease, ventilatory failure
Side-effects: constipation, in large doses respiratory depression

Codeine Linctus, codeine phosphate 15 mg/5 mL. Net price 100 mL = 35p (diabetic, 68p)
Dose: 5–10 mL 3–4 times daily; CHILD 5–12 years, 2.5–5 mL
Available from APS, Evans, Galen (Galcodine®, sugar-free), Kerfoot
The title 'Diabetic Codeine Linctus' may be used for a preparation that complies with the requirements of the BP monograph for Codeine Linctus and that is formulated with a vehicle appropriate for administration to diabetics.

Codeine Linctus, Paediatric, codeine phosphate 3 mg/5 mL. Net price 100 mL = 19p
Dose: CHILD 1–5 years 5 mL 3–4 times daily
Available from Evans, Galen (Galcodine®, sugar-free)
Note. Sugar-free versions are available
Paediatric Codeine Linctus may be prepared extemporaneously by diluting Codeine Linctus with a suitable vehicle in accordance with the manufacturer's instructions

---

DEXTROMETHORPHAN

Indications: dry or painful cough
Cautions; Contra-indications; Side-effects: see under Codeine Phosphate; avoid in porphyria

Preparations
Ingredient of compound cough preparations (section 3.9.2)
Note. A proprietary brand of dextromethorphan sustained-release capsules (Coughcaps®) is on sale to the public

ISOAMINILE CITRATE

Indications: dry or painful cough
Cautions: see notes above
Side-effects: occasionally constipation, dizziness, nausea
Dose: see below

PoM **Isoaminile Linctus,** isoaminile citrate 40 mg/5 mL. Diluent syrup, life of diluted linctus 14 days. Net price 150 mL = £1.88
Dose: 5 mL 3–5 times daily; CHILD, 2.5–5 mL
The brand name NHS Dimyril® (Fisons) is used for isoaminile linctus

---

PHOLCODINE

Indications: dry or painful cough
Cautions; Contra-indications; Side-effects: see under Codeine Phosphate

Pholcodine Linctus, pholcodine 5 mg/5 mL in a suitable flavoured vehicle, containing citric acid monohydrate 1%. Net price 100 mL = 29p
Dose: 5–10 mL 3–4 times daily; CHILD 5–12 years 2.5–5 mL
Available from APS, Boehringer Ingelheim (Pavacol-D®, sugar-free), Evans, Galen (Galenphol®, sugar-free), Kerfoot, Medo (NHS Pholcomed D®, sugar-free)

Pholcodine Linctus, Strong, pholcodine 10 mg/5 mL in a suitable flavoured vehicle, containing citric acid monohydrate 2%. Net price 100 mL = 47p
Dose: 5 mL 3–4 times daily
Available from APS, Evans, Kerfoot, Medo (NHS Pholcomed Diabetic Forte®, sugar-free)

Galenphol® (Galen)
Paediatric linctus, orange, sugar-free, pholcodine 2 mg/5 mL. Diluent as above. Net price 100 mL = 17p
Dose: CHILD 1–5 years 5 mL 3 times daily; 6–12 years 5–10 mL
Note. A proprietary brand of pholcodine pastilles (NHS Pholcomed®) is on sale to the public

---

TERMINAL CARE

Diamorphine and methadone are effective cough suppressants; they are given in linctuses to control distressful cough in terminal lung cancer although morphine is now preferred (see Terminal Care, p. 12). In other circumstances they are contra-indicated because they induce sputum retention and ventilatory failure as well as causing opioid dependence.

DIAMORPHINE HYDROCHLORIDE

Indications: cough in terminal disease
Cautions; Contra-indications; Side-effects: see notes in section 4.7.2; more potent than morphine
Dose: see below

CD **Diamorphine Linctus, BPC 1973,** diamorphine hydrochloride 3 mg, oxymel 1.25 mL, glycerol 1.25 mL, compound tartrazine solution 0.06 mL, syrup to 5 mL. It should be recently prepared. Net price 100 mL = 76p. Label: 2
Dose: 2.5–10 mL every 4 hours

METHADONE HYDROCHLORIDE

Indications: cough in terminal disease
Cautions; Contra-indications; Side-effects: see notes in section 4.7.2; longer-acting than morphine therefore effects may be cumulative
Dose: see below

CD **Methadone Linctus,** methadone hydrochloride 2 mg/5 mL in a suitable vehicle with a tolu flavour. Net price 100 mL = 94p. Label: 2
Dose: 2.5–5 mL every 4–6 hours, reduced to twice daily on prolonged use

MORPHINE HYDROCHLORIDE

Indications: cough in terminal disease (see also p. 12)
Cautions; Contra-indications; Side-effects: see notes in section 4.7.2
Dose: initially 5 mg every 4 hours

Preparations
See section 4.7.2

3.9.2 Expectorant, demulcent, and compound cough preparations

Although there is no scientific basis for prescribing any of the preparations listed in this section, it may be that a harmless expectorant such as ammonia and ipecacuanha mixture or a demulcent such as simple linctus has a useful placebo role in minor respiratory disorders. Certainly this is preferable to the indiscriminate prescribing of antibiotics.

Expectorants are claimed to promote expulsion of bronchial secretions but there is no evidence that any drug can specifically facilitate expectoration.

The assumption that sub-emetic doses of expectorants, such as ammonium chloride, ipecacuanha, and squill promote expectoration is a myth. However, a simple expectorant mixture may serve a useful placebo function and has the advantage of being inexpensive.

Demulcent cough preparations contain soothing substances such as syrup or glycerol and certainly some patients believe that such preparations relieve a dry irritating cough. Preparations such as **simple linctus** have the advantage of being harmless and inexpensive and **paediatric simple linctus** is particularly useful in children.

Compound cough preparations have no place in the treatment of respiratory disorders. Many contain an unnecessarily large number of ingredients, often in individually subtherapeutic doses, and often with similar therapeutic properties. Others incorporate ingredients with opposing effects such as expectorants and cough suppressants, and claim dual benefits. All such preparations are to be **deprecated** not only as irrational but also for leading to patients receiving inappropriate drugs; for example, the sedative effect of antihistamines may lead to carbon dioxide retention in patients with chronic bronchitis or emphysema. It is therefore best to prescribe one of the simple cough mixtures recommended above; if any other component is needed it may then be prescribed separately, tailored to the needs of the patient.

CHILDREN. The use of cough suppressants containing codeine or similar opioid analgesics is not generally recommended in children and should be avoided altogether in those under 1 year of age.

NHS **Ammonia and Ipecacuanha Mixture, BP,** ammonium bicarbonate 200 mg, liquorice liquid extract 0.5 mL, ipecacuanha tincture 0.3 mL, concentrated camphor water 0.1 mL, concentrated anise water 0.05 mL, double-strength chloroform water 5 mL, water to 10 mL. It should be recently prepared
Dose: 10–20 mL 3–4 times daily

NHS **Ammonium Chloride and Morphine Mixture, BP,** ammonium chloride 300 mg, ammonium bicarbonate 200 mg, chloroform and morphine tincture 0.3 mL, liquorice liquid extract 0.5 mL, water to 10 mL. It should be recently prepared. Contains 500 micrograms of anhydrous morphine in 10 mL
Dose: 10–20 mL 3–4 times daily

NHS **Ipecacuanha and Morphine Mixture BP, 1980,** ipecacuanha tincture 0.2 mL, chloroform and morphine tincture 0.4 mL, liquorice liquid extract 1 mL, water to 10 mL. It should be recently prepared. 10 mL contains 700 micrograms of anhydrous morphine
Dose: 10 mL 3–4 times daily

Simple Linctus, BP, citric acid monohydrate 125 mg, concentrated anise water 0.05 mL, chloroform spirit 0.3 mL, amaranth solution 0.075 mL, syrup to 5 mL. Net price 100 mL = 16p
Dose: 5 mL 3–4 times daily

Simple Linctus, Paediatric, BP, simple linctus 1.25 mL, syrup to 5 mL. Net price 100 mL = 17p
Dose: CHILD, 5–10 mL 3–4 times daily

NHS **Squill Linctus, Opiate, BP,** Gee's Linctus, equal volumes of camphorated opium tincture, squill oxymel, and tolu syrup. It contains 800 micrograms of anhydrous morphine in 5 mL. Net price 100 mL = 27p
Dose: 5 mL 3–4 times daily

NHS **Tolu Linctus, Compound, Paediatric,** citric acid monohydrate 30 mg/5 mL in a suitable vehicle with a tolu flavour. Net price 100 mL = 58p
Dose: CHILD, 5–10 mL 3–4 times daily

NHS **Actifed Compound Linctus®** (Wellcome)
Linctus, dextromethorphan hydrobromide, pseudoephedrine hydrochloride, triprolidine hydrochloride. Net price 100 mL = £1.14; 200 mL = £1.85. Label: 2

NHS **Actifed Expectorant®** (Wellcome)
Elixir, guaiphenesin, pseudoephedrine hydrochloride, triprolidine hydrochloride. Net price 100 mL = £1.14; 200 mL = £1.85. Label: 2

NHS **Benylin Chesty Cough Linctus**[1]® (W-L)
Syrup, diphenhydramine hydrochloride, menthol. Net price 125 mL = £1.22; 300 mL = £2.42. Label: 2
1. Has replaced Benylin Expectorant

NHS **Benylin Childrens Cough Linctus**[2]® (W-L)
Syrup, diphenhydramine hydrochloride, menthol. Net price 125 mL = £1.10. Label: 1
2. Has replaced Benylin Paediatric

NHS **Benylin with Codeine®** (W-L)
Syrup, codeine phosphate, diphenhydramine hydro-

chloride, menthol, sodium citrate. Net price 300 mL = £2.89. Label: 2

NHS **Benylin Dry Cough Linctus**[3]® (W-L)
Syrup, diphenhydramine hydrochloride, dextromethorphan hydrobromide, menthol. Net price 125 mL = £1.22. Label: 2

3. Has replaced Benylin Fortified

NHS **Benylin Mentholated Linctus**® (W-L)
Syrup, diphenhydramine hydrochloride, dextromethorphan hydrobromide, pseudoephedrine hydrochloride, menthol. Net price 125 mL = £1.22. Label: 2

NHS **Copholco**® (Fisons)
Linctus, pholcodine, cineole, menthol, terpin hydrate. Net price 100 mL = 90p

NHS **Davenol**® (Whitehall)
Linctus, carbinoxamine maleate, ephedrine hydrochloride, pholcodine. Net price 100 mL = 46p. Label: 2

NHS **Dimotane Expectorant**® (Whitehall)
Elixir, brompheniramine maleate, guaiphenesin, pseudoephedrine hydrochloride. Net price 100 mL = £1.19. Label: 2

NHS **Dimotane Co**® (Whitehall)
Elixir, brompheniramine maleate, codeine phosphate, pseudoephedrine hydrochloride. Net price 100 mL = £1.19. Label: 2

NHS **Dimotane Co Paediatric**® (Whitehall)
Elixir, brompheniramine maleate, codeine phosphate, pseudoephedrine hydrochloride. Net price 100 mL = £1.16. Label: 1

NHS **Expulin**® (Galen)
Linctus, chlorpheniramine maleate, pseudoephedrine hydrochloride, pholcodine, menthol. Net price 100 mL = £1.08. Label: 2
Paediatric linctus, chlorpheniramine maleate, pholcodine, menthol. Net price 100 mL = £1.04. Label: 1

NHS **Guanor Expectorant**® (RP Drugs)
Syrup, ammonium chloride, diphenhydramine hydrochloride, menthol, sodium citrate. Net price 200 mL = 57p. Label: 2

NHS **Histalix**® (Wallace Mfg)
Syrup, ammonium chloride, diphenhydramine hydrochloride, menthol, sodium citrate. Net price 150 mL = £1.14. Label: 2

NHS **Lotussin**® (Searle)
Linctus, dextromethorphan hydrobromide, diphenhydramine hydrochloride. Net price 100 mL = 98p. Label: 2

NHS **Noradran**® (Norma)
Syrup, diphenhydramine hydrochloride, diprophylline, ephedrine hydrochloride, guaiphenesin. Net price 150 mL = 95p. Label: 2

NHS **Phensedyl**® (Rhône-Poulenc Rorer)
Linctus, codeine phosphate, promethazine hydrochloride. Net price 100 mL = £1.43. Label: 2

NHS **Sudafed Expectorant**® (Calmic)
Syrup, guaiphenesin, pseudoephedrine hydrochloride. Net price 100 mL = £1.14

NHS **Sudafed Linctus**® (Calmic)
Linctus, dextromethorphan hydrobromide, pseudoephedrine hydrochloride. Net price 100 mL = £1.14. Label: 2

NHS **Tancolin**® (Ashe)
Linctus (paediatric), ascorbic acid, citric acid, dextromethorphan hydrobromide, glycerol, sodium citrate. Net price 100 mL = £1.07

NHS **Tercoda**® (Sinclair)
Elixir, codeine phosphate, terpin hydrate. Net price 100 mL = £1.07

NHS **Terpoin**® (Hough)
Elixir, codeine phosphate with cineole and menthol. Net price 225 mL = £3.28

NHS **Tixylix**® (Intercare)
Linctus, pholcodine (as citrate), promethazine hydrochloride. Net price 100 mL = £1.09. Label: 1 *or* 2

3.10 Systemic nasal decongestants

These preparations are of doubtful value but unlike the preparations for local application (see section 12.2.2) they do not give rise to rebound nasal congestion. They contain sympathomimetics, and should therefore be **avoided** in patients with hypertension, hyperthyroidism, coronary heart disease, or diabetes, and in patients taking monoamine-oxidase inhibitors; **interactions:** Appendix 1 (sympathomimetics). Many of the preparations also contain antihistamines which may cause drowsiness and affect ability to drive or operate machinery.

NHS **Actifed**® (Wellcome)
Tablets, pseudoephedrine hydrochloride, triprolidine hydrochloride. Net price 12-tab pack = 85p. Label: 2
Syrup, pseudoephedrine hydrochloride, triprolidine hydrochloride. Net price 100 mL = £1.11. Label: 2

Congesteze® (Schering-Plough)
PoM *Tablets*, s/c, azatadine maleate 1 mg, pseudoephedrine sulphate 60 mg in outer layer, pseudoephedrine sulphate 60 mg in s/r core. Net price 28-tab pack = £2.60. Label: 2, 25
Dose: 1 tablet twice daily
Syrup, yellow, azatadine maleate 1 mg, pseudoephedrine sulphate 30 mg/5 mL. Diluent syrup, life of diluted syrup 28 days. Price 120 mL = £1.26. Label: 2
Dose: 5–10 mL twice daily; CHILD 1–5 years 1.25 mL, 6–12 years 2.5–5 mL
Paediatric syrup, azatadine maleate 250 micrograms, pseudoephedrine sulphate 7.5 mg/5 mL. Price 120 mL = £1.26. Label: 1
Dose: CHILD 1–6 years 5 mL twice daily, 7–12 years 10–20 mL

Dimotane Plus® (Wyeth)
Liquid, brown, sugar-free, brompheniramine maleate 4 mg, pseudoephedrine hydrochloride 30 mg/5 mL. Diluent glycerol 70%, life of diluted liquid 14 days. Net price 100 mL = 81p. Label: 2
Dose: 10 mL 3 times daily; CHILD 2–6 years 2.5 mL, 6–12 years 5 mL
Paediatric liquid, brown, sugar-free, brompheniramine maleate 2 mg, pseudoephedrine hydrochloride 15 mg/5 mL. Diluent as above. Net price 100 mL = 74p. Label: 1
Dose: CHILD 2–6 years 5 mL, 6–12 years 10 mL, 3 times daily

PoM **Dimotane® Plus LA** (Wyeth)
Tablets, s/r, f/c, brompheniramine maleate 12 mg, pseudoephedrine hydrochloride 120 mg. Net price 14-tab pack = 91p. Label: 2, 25
Dose: 1 tablet twice daily

NHS **Dimotapp**® (Whitehall)
Elixir, brompheniramine maleate, phenylephrine hydrochloride, phenylpropanolamine hydrochloride. Net price 100 mL = £1.10. Label: 2
Paediatric elixir, brompheniramine maleate, phenylephrine hydrochloride, phenylpropanolamine hydrochloride. Net price 100 mL = £1.04. Label: 1

NHS **Dimotapp LA**® (Whitehall)
Tablets, brompheniramine maleate, phenylephrine hydrochloride, phenylpropanolamine hydrochloride. Net price 30 = £2.15. Label: 2, 25, counselling, gluten

NHS **Eskornade**® (SK&F)
Spansule® (= capsules s/r), diphenylpyraline hydrochloride, phenylpropanolamine hydrochloride. Net price 30-cap pack = £2.32. Label: 2, 25
Syrup, diphenylpyraline hydrochloride, phenylpropanolamine hydrochloride. Net price 150 mL = £2.39. Label: 2

NHS **Expurhin®** (Galen)
Paediatric linctus, chlorpheniramine maleate, ephedrine hydrochloride, menthol. Net price 100 mL = 98p. Label: 1

Galpseud® (Galen)
Tablets, pseudoephedrine hydrochloride 60 mg. Net price 20 = 63p
Dose: 1 tablet 3 times daily
Linctus, orange, sugar-free, pseudoephedrine hydrochloride 30 mg/5 mL. Diluent water, life of diluted linctus 14 days. Net price 100 mL = 49p
Dose: 10 mL 3 times daily; CHILD 2–6 years 2.5 mL, 6–12 years 5 mL

Haymine® (Pharmax)
Tablets, s/r, yellow, chlorpheniramine maleate 10 mg, ephedrine hydrochloride 15 mg. Net price 30-tab pack = £2.23. Label: 2, 25
Dose: 1 tablet 1–2 times daily

Sudafed® (Calmic)
Tablets, red, f/c, pseudoephedrine hydrochloride 60 mg. Net price 20 = £1.17
Dose: 1 tablet 3 times daily
Elixir, pink, pseudoephedrine hydrochloride 30 mg/5 mL. Diluent syrup, life of diluted elixir 14 days. Net price 100 mL = 94p
Dose: 10 mL 3 times daily; CHILD 2–5 years 2.5 mL, 6–12 years 5 mL

Sudafed Plus® (Calmic)
Tablets, pseudoephedrine hydrochloride 60 mg, triprolidine hydrochloride 2.5 mg. Net price 100-tab pack = £6.49. Label: 2
Dose: 1 tablet 3 times daily
Syrup, yellow, pseudoephedrine hydrochloride 30 mg, triprolidine hydrochloride 1.25 mg/5 mL. Diluent syrup, life of diluted syrup 28 days. Net price 100 mL = £1·06. Label: 2
Dose: 10 mL 3 times daily; CHILD 2–5 years 2.5 mL 3 times daily, 6–12 years 5 mL 3 times daily

PoM **Sudafed SA®** (Calmic)
Capsules, s/r, red/clear, pseudoephedrine hydrochloride 120 mg. Net price 20 = £1.44. Label: 25
Dose: 1 capsule every 12 hours

NHS **Sudafed-Co®** (Calmic)
Tablets, paracetamol, pseudoephedrine hydrochloride. Net price 12-tab pack = 91p

NHS **Triogesic®** (Beecham)
Tablets, paracetamol, phenylpropanolamine hydrochloride. Net price 30-tab pack = £1.43
Elixir, paracetamol, phenylpropanolamine hydrochloride. Net price 100 mL = £1.09

NHS **Triominic®** (Beecham)
Tablets, pheniramine maleate, phenylpropanolamine hydrochloride. Net price 30-tab pack = £1.43. Label: 2
Syrup, pheniramine maleate, phenylpropanolamine hydrochloride. Net price 100 mL = £1.09. Label: 2

NHS **Uniflu with Gregovite C®** (Unigreg)
Tablets, composite pack of pairs of tablets: Uniflu *tablets*, caffeine, codeine phosphate, diphenhydramine hydrochloride, paracetamol, phenylephrine hydrochloride; Gregovite C *tablets*, ascorbic acid. Net price 6 of each tablet = £1.25; or 12 of each tablet = £2.09. Label: 2
Dose: 1 of each tablet every 6 hours

4: Drugs acting on the CENTRAL NERVOUS SYSTEM

In this chapter, drug treatments are discussed under the following headings:

4.1 Hypnotics and anxiolytics

Most anxiolytics ('sedatives') will induce sleep when given in large doses at night and most hypnotics will sedate when given in divided doses during the day. Prescribing of these drugs is widespread but dependence (either physical or psychological) and tolerance to their effects occurs. This may lead to difficulty in withdrawing the drug after the patient has been taking it regularly for more than a few weeks (see Dependence and Withdrawal, below). Hypnotics and anxiolytics should not therefore be prescribed indiscriminately and should, instead, be reserved for short courses to alleviate acute conditions after causal factors have been established.

Prescribing of more than one anxiolytic or hypnotic at the same time is **not** recommended. It may constitute a hazard and there is no evidence that side-effects are minimised.

Benzodiazepines are the most commonly used anxiolytics and hypnotics; barbiturates (section 4.1.3) are no longer recommended.

Benzodiazepines have fewer side-effects than barbiturates and are much less dangerous in overdosage. They are also less likely to interact with other drugs because, unlike barbiturates, they do not induce liver microsomal enzymes.

Side-effects of benzodiazepines are generally mild and include drowsiness and ataxia (particularly in the elderly).

A paradoxical increase in hostility and aggression may be reported by patients taking benzodiazepines. The effects range from talkativeness and excitement, to aggressive and antisocial acts. Adjustment of the dose (up or down) usually attenuates the impulses. Increased anxiety and perceptual disorders are other paradoxical effects. Increased hostility and aggression after barbiturates and alcohol usually indicates intoxication.

DEPENDENCE AND WITHDRAWAL. Compared with other anxiolytics and hypnotics, especially the barbiturates, the benzodiazepine withdrawal syndrome may be delayed in onset (but less so with those that are short-acting); it may also last longer. It is characterised by insomnia, anxiety, loss of appetite and body weight, tremor, perspiration, and perceptual disturbances. These symptoms may be similar to the original complaint and encourage further prescribing; some symptoms may continue for weeks or months.

Withdrawal of a benzodiazepine should be gradual as abrupt withdrawal may produce confusion, toxic psychosis, convulsions, or a condition resembling delirium tremens.

DRIVING. Hypnotics and anxiolytics may impair judgement and increase reaction time, and so affect ability to drive or operate machinery; they increase the effects of alcohol. Moreover the hangover effects of a night dose may impair driving on the following day.

BENZODIAZEPINE WITHDRAWAL

A suggested protocol for patients unable to reduce existing benzodiazepine[1]:

1. Transfer patient to equivalent daily dose of diazepam[2] preferably taken at night
2. Reduce diazepam dose in fortnightly steps of 2 or 2.5 mg; if withdrawal symptoms occur, maintain this dose until symptoms improve
3. Reduce dose further, if necessary in smaller fortnightly steps[3]; it is better to reduce too slowly rather than too quickly
4. Stop completely; time needed for withdrawal can vary from about 4 weeks to several months; withdrawal symptoms may persist for a year or more

Counselling may help; beta-blockers should **only** be tried if other measures fail; antidepressants should **only** be used if clinical depression present; **avoid** antipsychotics and buspirone (which may aggravate withdrawal symptoms)

1. Generally, existing benzodiazepines can be withdrawn in steps of about $\frac{1}{8}$ (range $\frac{1}{10}$–$\frac{1}{4}$) of daily dose every fortnight
2. Approximate equivalent doses, diazepam 5 mg
≡ chlordiazepoxide 15 mg
≡ lorazepam 500 micrograms
≡ nitrazepam 5 mg
≡ oxazepam 15 mg
≡ temazepam 10 mg
≡ triazolam 250 micrograms
3. Steps may be adjusted according to initial dose and duration of treatment and can range from diazepam 500 micrograms ($\frac{1}{4}$ of a 2-mg tablet) to 2.5 mg

CSM advice.
1. Benzodiazepines are indicated for the short-term relief (two to four weeks only) of anxiety that is severe, disabling or subjecting the individual to unacceptable distress, occurring alone or in association with insomnia or short-term psychosomatic, organic or psychotic illness.
2. The use of benzodiazepines to treat short-term 'mild' anxiety is inappropriate and unsuitable.
3. Benzodiazepines should be used to treat insomnia only when it is severe, disabling, or subjecting the individual to extreme distress.

4.1.1 Hypnotics

Before a hypnotic is prescribed the cause of the insomnia should be established and, where possible, underlying factors should be treated. However, it should be noted that some patients have unrealistic sleep expectations, and others understate their alcohol consumption which is often the cause of the insomnia.

Transient insomnia may occur in those who normally sleep well and may be due to extraneous factors such as noise, shift work, and jet lag. If a hypnotic is indicated one that is rapidly eliminated should be chosen, and only one or two doses should be given.

Short-term insomnia is usually related to an emotional problem or serious medical illness. It may last for a few weeks, and may recur; a hypnotic can be useful but should not be given for more than three weeks (preferably only one week). Intermittent use is desirable with omission of some doses. A rapidly eliminated drug is generally appropriate.

Chronic insomnia is rarely benefited by hypnotics and is more often due to mild dependence caused by injudicious prescribing. Psychiatric disorders such as anxiety, depression, and abuse of drugs and alcohol are common causes. Sleep disturbance is very common in depressive illness and early wakening is often a useful pointer. The underlying psychiatric complaint should be treated, adapting the drug regimen to alleviate insomnia. For example, amitriptyline, prescribed for depression, will also help to promote sleep if it is taken at night. Other causes of insomnia include daytime cat-napping and physical causes such as pain, pruritus, and dyspnoea.

Hypnotics should **not** be prescribed indiscriminately and routine prescribing is undesirable. Ideally, they should be reserved for short courses in the acutely distressed. Tolerance to their effects develops within 3 to 14 days of continuous use and long-term efficacy cannot be assured. A major drawback of long-term use is that withdrawal causes rebound insomnia and precipitates a withdrawal syndrome (section 4.1).

Where prolonged administration is unavoidable hypnotics should be discontinued as soon as feasible and the patient warned that sleep may be disturbed for a few days before normal rhythm is re-established; broken sleep with vivid dreams and increased REM (rapid eye movement) may persist for several weeks. This represents a mild form of dependence even if clinical doses are used.

CHILDREN. The prescribing of hypnotics to children, except for occasional use such as for night terrors and somnambulism, is not justified.

ELDERLY. Hypnotics should be avoided in the elderly, who are at risk of becoming ataxic and confused and so liable to fall and injure themselves.

BENZODIAZEPINES

Benzodiazepines used as hypnotics include **nitrazepam**, **flunitrazepam**, and **flurazepam** which have a prolonged action and may give rise to residual effects on the following day; repeated doses tend to be cumulative.

Loprazolam, **lormetazepam**, **temazepam**, and **triazolam** act for a shorter time and they have little or no hangover effect. Withdrawal phenomena however are more common with the short-acting benzodiazepines.

Benzodiazepine anxiolytics such as **diazepam** given as a single dose at night may also be used as hypnotics.

For general guidelines on benzodiazepine prescribing see section 4.1.2 and for benzodiazepine withdrawal see section 4.1.

NITRAZEPAM

Indications: insomnia (short-term use)
Cautions: respiratory disease, muscle weakness, history of drug abuse, marked personality disorder, pregnancy, breast-feeding; reduce dose in elderly and debilitated, and in hepatic and renal impairment; avoid prolonged use (and abrupt withdrawal thereafter); **interactions:** Appendix 1 (benzodiazepines)

DRIVING. Drowsiness may persist the next day and affect performance of skilled tasks (e.g. driving); effects of alcohol enhanced

Contra-indications: respiratory depression; acute pulmonary insufficiency; phobic or obsessional states, chronic psychosis; porphyria
Side-effects: drowsiness and lightheadedness the next day; confusion and ataxia (especially in the elderly); dependence. See also under Diazepam (section 4.1.2)
Dose: 5–10 mg at bedtime; ELDERLY (or debilitated) 2.5–5 mg

PoM **Nitrazepam** (Non-proprietary)
Tablets, nitrazepam 5 mg, net price 20 = 7p. Label: 19
Available from APS, Cox, DDSA (NHS Remnos®), Evans, Kerfoot, Unigreg (NHS Unisomnia®)
Mixture, nitrazepam 2.5 mg/5 mL. Diluent syrup, life of diluted mixture 14 days. Net price 150 mL = £3.36. Label: 19

NHS PoM **Mogadon®** (Roche)
Capsules, purple/black, nitrazepam 5 mg. Net price 20 = 96p. Label: 19
Tablets, scored, nitrazepam 5 mg. Net price 20 = 96p. Label: 19

NHS PoM **Somnite**® (Norgine)
Suspension, off-white, nitrazepam 2.5 mg/5 mL. Diluent syrup, life of diluted suspension 14 days. Net price 150-mL pack = £3.36. Label: 19
NHS PoM **Surem**® (Galen)
Capsules, mauve/grey, nitrazepam 5 mg. Net price 20 = 26p. Label: 19

FLUNITRAZEPAM

Indications: insomnia (short-term use)
Cautions; Contra-indications; Side-effects: see under Nitrazepam
Dose: 0.5–1 mg at bedtime; max. 2 mg; ELDERLY (or debilitated) 500 micrograms (max. 1 mg)

NHS PoM **Rohypnol**® (Roche)
Tablets, purple, f/c, scored, flunitrazepam 1 mg. Net price 30-tab pack = £3.39. Label: 19

FLURAZEPAM

Indications: insomnia (short-term use)
Cautions; Contra-indications; Side-effects: see under Nitrazepam
Dose: 15–30 mg at bedtime; ELDERLY (or debilitated) 15 mg

NHS PoM **Dalmane**® (Roche)
Capsules, flurazepam (as hydrochloride), 15 mg (grey/yellow), net price 30-cap pack = £2.24; 30 mg (black/grey), 30-cap pack = £2.89. Label: 19
NHS PoM **Paxane**® (Mercury)
Capsules, flurazepam (as hydrochloride), 15 mg (green/grey), net price 20 = 82p; 30 mg (green/black), 20 = £1.10. Label: 19

LOPRAZOLAM

Indications: insomnia (short-term use)
Cautions; Contra-indications; Side-effects: see under Nitrazepam
Dose: 1 mg at bedtime, increased to 1.5 or 2 mg if required; ELDERLY (or debilitated) 0.5–1 mg

PoM **Loprazolam** (Non-proprietary)
Tablets, loprazolam 1 mg (as mesylate). Net price 28-tab pack = £1.68. Label: 19
Available from Roussel (previously known as NHS Dormonoct®)

LORMETAZEPAM

Indications: insomnia (short-term use)
Cautions; Contra-indications; Side-effects: see under Nitrazepam; shorter acting, hence preferable in elderly and less drowsiness next day, but withdrawal phenomena more common with short-acting benzodiazepines
Dose: 0.5–1.5 mg at bedtime; ELDERLY (or debilitated) 500 micrograms

PoM **Lormetazepam** (Non-proprietary)
Tablets, lormetazepam 500 micrograms, net price 20 = 84p; 1 mg, 20 = £1.09. Label: 19

TEMAZEPAM

Indications: insomnia (short-term use); see also section 15.1.4 for peri-operative use
Cautions; Contra-indications; Side-effects: see under Nitrazepam; shorter acting, hence preferable in elderly and less drowsiness next day, but withdrawal phenomena more common with short-acting benzodiazepines
Dose: 10–30 mg (severe insomnia, up to 40–60 mg) at bedtime; ELDERLY (or debilitated) 5–15 mg

PoM **Temazepam** (Non-proprietary)
Gel-filled capsules (soft gelatin), temazepam 10 mg, net price 20 = 48p; 15 mg, 20 = 62p; 20 mg, 20 = 84p; 30 mg, 20 = £1.24. Label: 19
Available from APS, Berk, Cox, CP, Evans, Farmitalia Carlo Erba, Kerfoot, Wyeth
Note. The name NHS Temazepam Gelthix® is used for some gel-filled capsules
Capsules (hard gelatin), temazepam 10 mg, net price 20 = 36p; 20 mg, 20 = 58p. Label: 19
Tablets, temazepam 10 mg, net price 20 = 48p; 20 mg, 20 = 84p. Label: 19
Oral solution, temazepam 10 mg/5 mL; diluent glycerol, life of diluted solution 14 days; net price 100 mL = £2.65. Label: 19
NHS PoM **Temazepam Planpak**® (Farmitalia Carlo Erba)
Capsules (soft gelatin), all green, 14 capsules each of temazepam 2 mg, 5 mg, and 10 mg. Net price per pack = £8.57. Label: 19
Dose: withdrawal, 1 capsule at bedtime, commencing with highest strength and finishing with lowest

TRIAZOLAM

Indications: insomnia (short-term use)
Cautions; Contra-indications; Side-effects: see under Nitrazepam; shorter acting, less drowsiness next day, but withdrawal phenomena more common with short-acting benzodiazepines; amnesia, sometimes with inappropriate behaviour, reported; paradoxical anxiety may develop after prolonged treatment at high doses
Dose: 125–250 micrograms at bedtime; ELDERLY (or debilitated) initially 125 micrograms

PoM **Triazolam** (Non-proprietary)
Tablets, triazolam 125 micrograms, net price 20 = £1.15; 250 micrograms, 20 = £1.55. Label: 19
NHS PoM **Halcion**® (Upjohn)
Tablets, triazolam 125 micrograms (lavender), net price 30-tab pack = £1.72; 250 micrograms (blue, scored), 30-tab pack = £2.32. Label: 19

CHLORAL AND DERIVATIVES

Chloral hydrate and chloral derivatives are useful hypnotics for children (but see notes above). There is no convincing evidence that they are particularly useful in the elderly. **Triclofos sodium** causes fewer gastro-intestinal upsets than chloral hydrate.

CHLORAL HYDRATE

Indications: insomnia (short-term use)

Cautions: respiratory disease, history of drug abuse, marked personality disorder, pregnancy, breast-feeding; reduce dose in elderly and debilitated; avoid prolonged use (and abrupt withdrawal thereafter); avoid contact with skin and mucous membranes; **interactions:** Appendix 1 (chloral)

DRIVING. Drowsiness may persist the next day and affect performance of skilled tasks (e.g. driving); effects of alcohol enhanced

Contra-indications: severe cardiac disease, gastritis, marked hepatic or renal impairment

Side-effects: gastric irritation; *occasionally:* rashes, headache, ketonuria, excitement, delirium; dependence and renal damage on prolonged use

Dose: insomnia, 0.5–1 g (max. 2 g) with plenty of water at bedtime; CHILD 30–50 mg/kg up to a max. single dose of 1 g

PoM **Chloral Mixture** (BP)
(Chloral Oral Solution)

Mixture, chloral hydrate 10% in a suitable vehicle. Extemporaneous preparations should be recently prepared according to the following formula: chloral hydrate 1 g, syrup 2 mL, water to 10 mL. Net price 100 mL = 15p. Label: 19, 27

Dose: 5–20 mL; CHILD 1–5 years 2.5–5 mL, 6–12 years 5–10 mL, taken well diluted with water at bedtime

PoM **Chloral Elixir, Paediatric** (BP)
(Chloral Oral Solution, Paediatric)

Elixir, chloral hydrate 4% in a suitable vehicle with a blackcurrant flavour. Extemporaneous preparations should be recently prepared according to the following formula: chloral hydrate 200 mg, water 0.1 mL, blackcurrant syrup 1 mL, syrup to 5 mL. Net price 100 mL = 49p. Label: 1, 27

Dose: up to 1 year 5 mL, well diluted with water

PoM **Noctec®** (Squibb)

Capsules, red, chloral hydrate 500 mg. Net price 50-cap pack = £1.90. Label: 19, 27

Dose: 1–2 capsules with plenty of water at bedtime (max. 4 capsules); CHILD not recommended

PoM **Welldorm®** (S&N Pharm.)

Tablets, blue-purple, f/c, chloral betaine 707 mg (≡chloral hydrate 414 mg). Net price 30-tab pack = £2.27. Label: 19, 27

Dose: 1–2 tablets with water or milk at bedtime, max. 5 tablets (2 g chloral hydrate) daily.

Elixir, red, chloral hydrate 143 mg/5 mL. Diluent syrup, life of diluted elixir 28 days. Net price 150-mL pack = £2.50. Label: 19, 27

Dose: 15–45 mL (0.4–1.3 g chloral hydrate) with water or milk, at bedtime, max. 70 mL (2 g chloral hydrate) daily; CHILD 1–1.75 mL/kg (30–50 mg/kg chloral hydrate), max. 35 mL (1 g chloral hydrate) daily

Note. Previous formulations of Welldorm® Tablets and Elixir contained dichloralphenazone

TRICLOFOS SODIUM

Indications: insomnia (short-term use)

Cautions; Contra-indications; Side-effects: see under Chloral Hydrate; less gastric irritation

Dose: see under preparation below

PoM **Triclofos** (Non-proprietary)

Elixir, triclofos sodium 500 mg/5 mL. Net price 100 mL = £4.40. Label: 19

Dose: 10–20 mL (1–2 g triclofos sodium) at bedtime; CHILD up to 1 year 1–2.5 mL (100–250 mg triclofos sodium), 1–5 years 2.5–5 mL (250–500 mg triclofos sodium), 6–12 years 5–10 mL (0.5–1 g triclofos sodium)

OTHER HYPNOTICS

Chlormethiazole may be a useful hypnotic for elderly patients because of its freedom from hangover but, as with all hypnotics, routine administration is undesirable and dependence occurs occasionally. It is used in the treatment of acute withdrawal symptoms in alcoholics but to minimise the risk of dependence administration should be limited to 9 days under inpatient supervision.

Promethazine is popular for use in children (but see notes above).

Zopiclone is a newly introduced hypnotic; although not a benzodiazepine it acts on the same receptors as benzodiazepines. As with other hypnotics it should not be used for long-term treatment.

Alcohol is a poor hypnotic as its diuretic action interferes with sleep during the latter part of the night. With chronic use, alcohol disturbs sleep patterns and causes insomnia; **interactions:** Appendix 1 (alcohol).

CHLORMETHIAZOLE

Indications: see under Dose

Cautions: cardiac and respiratory disease, history of drug abuse, marked personality disorder, pregnancy, breast-feeding; reduce dose in elderly and debilitated, and in hepatic and renal impairment; avoid prolonged use (and abrupt withdrawal thereafter); during intravenous infusion the sleep induced may quickly lapse into deep unconsciousness and patients must be observed constantly; see also section 4.8.2; **interactions:** Appendix 1 (chlormethiazole)

DRIVING. Drowsiness may persist the next day and affect performance of skilled tasks (e.g. driving); effects of alcohol enhanced

Contra-indications: acute pulmonary insufficiency; alcoholics who continue to drink

Side-effects: sneezing, conjunctival irritation, headache, gastro-intestinal disturbances; rarely, confusion, dependence. Localised thrombophlebitis on intravenous infusion, and at rapid infusion rates cardiovascular and respiratory depression

Dose: by mouth, severe insomnia in the elderly, 1–2 capsules at bedtime

Restlessness and agitation in the elderly, 1 capsule 3 times daily

Alcohol withdrawal, initially 2–4 capsules, if necessary repeated after some hours;
day 1 (first 24 hours), 9–12 capsules in 3–4 divided doses;
day 2, 6–8 capsules in 3–4 divided doses;
day 3, 4–6 capsules in 3–4 divided doses; then gradually reduced over days 4–6; total treatment for not more than 9 days

Note. For an equivalent therapeutic effect 1 capsule ≡ 5 mL elixir

By intravenous infusion, acute alcohol withdrawal, 40–100 mL (320–800 mg) initially as 0.8% solution over 5–10 minutes, then continued if necessary at a reduced rate adjusted according to the patient's condition

Note. Special care on prolonged intravenous administration since accumulation may occur; also, contains no electrolytes

PoM **Heminevrin®** (Astra)
Capsules, grey-brown, chlormethiazole base 192 mg in an oily basis. Net price 60 = £4.45. Label: 19
Syrup, sugar-free, chlormethiazole edisylate 250 mg/5 mL. Diluent water, life of diluted syrup 14 days. Net price 300-mL pack = £3.72. Label: 19
Intravenous infusion 0.8%, chlormethiazole edisylate 8 mg/mL. Net price 500-mL bottle = £5.25

PROMETHAZINE HYDROCHLORIDE

Indications: insomnia (short-term use); other indications, see sections 3.4.1, 4.6, 15.1.4.2
Cautions; Side-effects: see section 3.4.1
Dose: *by mouth*, 25 mg at bedtime increased to 50 mg if necessary; CHILD 1–5 years 15–20 mg, 5–10 years 20–25 mg, at bedtime

Preparations
See section 3.4.1

ZOPICLONE

Indications: insomnia (short-term use)
Cautions: hepatic impairment; pregnancy and breast-feeding; elderly; history of drug abuse, psychiatric illness; avoid prolonged use (and abrupt withdrawal thereafter); **interactions:** Appendix 1 (zopiclone)

DRIVING. Drowsiness may persist the next day and affect performance of skilled tasks (e.g. driving); effects of alcohol enhanced

Side-effects: bitter or metallic taste; gastro-intestinal disturbances including nausea and vomiting; irritability, confusion, depressed mood; drowsiness, dizziness, lightheadedness, and incoordination on the next day; dependence; rarely urticaria and rashes; hallucinations, amnesia, and behavioural disturbances (including aggression) reported
Dose: 7.5 mg at bedtime increased to 15 mg in severe insomnia; ELDERLY initially 3.75 mg at bedtime

▼ PoM **Zimovane®** (Rhône-Poulenc)
Tablets, f/c, scored, zopiclone 7.5 mg. Net price 28-tab pack = £27.44. Label: 19

4.1.2 Anxiolytics

Benzodiazepine anxiolytics can be effective in alleviating definite anxiety states and they are widely prescribed. Although there has been a tendency to prescribe these drugs to almost anyone with stress-related symptoms, unhappiness, or minor physical disease, their use in many situations is unjustified. In particular, they should not be used to treat depression, phobic or obsessional states, or chronic psychosis. In bereavement, psychological adjustment may be inhibited by benzodiazepines. In children anxiolytic treatment should be used only to relieve acute anxiety (and related insomnia) caused by fear e.g. before surgery.

Anxiolytic treatment should be limited to the lowest possible dose for the shortest possible time (see CSM advice, section 4.1). Dependence is particularly likely in patients with a history of alcoholism or drug abuse and in patients with marked personality disorders.

Anxiolytics, particularly the benzodiazepines, have been termed 'minor tranquillisers'. This term is misleading because not only do they differ markedly from the antipsychotic drugs ('major tranquillisers') but their use is by no means minor. Antipsychotics, in low doses, are also sometimes used in severe anxiety for their sedative action but long-term use should be avoided in view of a possible risk of tardive dyskinesia (section 4.2.1).

BENZODIAZEPINES

Benzodiazepines are indicated for the short-term relief of severe anxiety but long-term use should be avoided (see notes above). Diazepam, alprazolam, bromazepam, chlordiazepoxide, clobazam, clorazepate, and medazepam have a sustained action. Shorter-acting compounds such as **lorazepam** and **oxazepam** may be preferred in patients with hepatic impairment but they carry a greater risk of withdrawal symptoms.

Diazepam or lorazepam are very occasionally administered intravenously for the control of severe panic. This route is the most rapid but the procedure is not without risk (section 4.8.2) and should be used only when alternative measures have failed. The intramuscular route has no advantage over the oral route.

For guidelines on benzodiazepine withdrawal, see section 4.1.

DIAZEPAM

Indications: short-term use in anxiety or insomnia, adjunct in acute alcohol withdrawal; epilepsy (section 4.8); muscle spasm see section 10.2.2; peri-operative use see section 15.1.4.2
Cautions: respiratory disease, muscle weakness, history of drug abuse, marked personality disorder, pregnancy, breast-feeding; reduce dose in elderly and debilitated, and in hepatic and renal impairment; avoid prolonged use (and abrupt withdrawal thereafter); special precautions for intravenous injection (section

4.8.2); **interactions:** Appendix 1 (benzodiazepines)

DRIVING. Drowsiness may affect performance of skilled tasks (e.g. driving); effects of alcohol enhanced

Contra-indications: respiratory depression; acute pulmonary insufficiency; phobic or obsessional states, chronic psychosis; porphyria (but see section 9.8.2)

Side-effects: drowsiness and lightheadedness the next day; confusion and ataxia (especially in the elderly); amnesia may occur; dependence; *occasionally:* headache, vertigo, hypotension, salivation changes, gastro-intestinal disturbances, rashes, visual disturbances, changes in libido, urinary retention; blood disorders and jaundice reported; on intravenous injection, pain, thrombophlebitis

Dose: *by mouth*, anxiety, 2 mg 3 times daily increased if necessary to 15–30 mg daily in divided doses; ELDERLY (or debilitated) half adult dose

Insomnia associated with anxiety, 5–15 mg at bedtime

CHILD night terrors and somnambulism, 1–5 mg at bedtime

By intramuscular injection or slow intravenous injection (at a rate of not more than 5 mg/minute), for severe anxiety, control of acute panic attacks, and acute alcohol withdrawal, 10 mg, repeated if necessary after 4 hours

Note. Only use intramuscular route when oral and intravenous routes not possible

By intravenous infusion—section 4.8.2

By rectum as rectal solution, for acute anxiety and agitation, adults and children over 3 years 10 mg (elderly 5 mg), repeated after 5 minutes if necessary; CHILD 1–3 years, 5 mg

PoM **Diazepam** (Non-proprietary)

Capsules, diazepam 2 mg, net price 20 = 12p; 5 mg, 20 = 18p. Label: 2 *or* 19

Available from Galen (NHS Solis®)

Tablets, diazepam 2 and 5 mg, net price (both), 20 = 2p; 10 mg, 20 = 5p. Label: 2 *or* 19

Available from APS, Berk (NHS Atensine®), Cox, DDSA (NHS Tensium®), Evans, Kerfoot, Steinhard (NHS Alupram®)

Oral solution, diazepam 2 mg/5 mL. Diluent syrup or sorbitol solution, life of diluted solution 14 days. Net price 100 mL = £1.43. Label: 2 *or* 19

Injection (solution), diazepam 5 mg/mL. Do not dilute (except for intravenous infusion). Net price 2-mL amp = 25p

Available from CP

PoM **Diazemuls®** (Dumex)

Injection (emulsion), diazepam 5 mg/mL. For intravenous injection or infusion. Net price 2-mL amp = 63p

PoM **Stesolid®** (CP)

Rectal tubes (= rectal solution), diazepam 2 mg/mL, net price 5 × 2.5-mL (5 mg) tubes = £5.25; 4 mg/mL, 5 × 2.5-mL (10 mg) tubes = £6.70

PoM **Valium®** (Roche)

NHS *Tablets*, all scored, diazepam 2 mg, net price 20 = 31p; 5 mg (yellow), 20 = 47p; 10 mg (blue), 20 = 95p. Label: 2 *or* 19

NHS *Syrup*, pink, sugar-free, diazepam 2 mg/5 mL. Diluent sorbitol solution, life of diluted syrup 14 days. Net price 100-mL pack = £1.43. Label: 2 *or* 19

Injection, diazepam 5 mg/mL. Do not dilute (except for intravenous infusion). Net price 2-mL amp = 28p

Suppositories, diazepam 10 mg, net price 5 = £1.08. Label: 2 *or* 19

ALPRAZOLAM

Indications: anxiety (short-term use)

Cautions; Contra-indications; Side-effects: see under Diazepam

Dose: 250–500 micrograms 3 times daily (elderly or debilitated 250 micrograms 2–3 times daily), increased if necessary to a total of 3 mg daily

NHS PoM **Xanax®** (Upjohn)

Tablets, both scored, alprazolam 250 micrograms, net price 60-tab pack = £2.39; 500 micrograms (pink), 60-tab pack = £4.58. Label: 2

BROMAZEPAM

Indications: anxiety (short-term use)

Cautions; Contra-indications; Side-effects: see under Diazepam

Dose: 3–18 mg daily in divided doses; ELDERLY (or debilitated) half adult dose; max. (in exceptional circumstances in hospitalised patients) 60 mg daily in divided doses

NHS PoM **Lexotan®** (Roche)

Tablets, both scored, bromazepam 1.5 mg (lilac), net price 60-tab pack = £4.54; 3 mg (pink), 60-tab pack = £5.76. Label: 2

CHLORDIAZEPOXIDE

Indications: anxiety (short-term use), adjunct in acute alcohol withdrawal

Cautions; Contra-indications; Side-effects: see under Diazepam

Dose: anxiety, 10 mg 3 times daily increased if necessary to 60–100 mg daily in divided doses; ELDERLY (or debilitated) half adult dose

Note. The doses stated above refer equally to chlordiazepoxide and to its hydrochloride

PoM **Chlordiazepoxide Capsules,** chlordiazepoxide hydrochloride 5 mg, net price 20 = 28p; 10 mg, 20 = 35p. Label: 2

Available from APS, Cox, DDSA (NHS Tropium®), Kerfoot

PoM **Chlordiazepoxide Hydrochloride Tablets,** chlordiazepoxide hydrochloride 5 mg, net price 20 = 20p; 10 mg, 20 = 22p; 25 mg, 20 = 44p. Label: 2

PoM **Chlordiazepoxide Tablets,** chlordiazepoxide 5 mg, net price 20 = 28p; 10 mg, 20 = 35p; 25 mg, 20 = 71p. Label: 2

NHS PoM **Librium®** (Roche)

Capsules, chlordiazepoxide hydrochloride 5 mg (green/yellow), net price 20 = 28p; 10 mg (green/black), 20 = 35p. Label: 2

Tablets, all green, f/c, chlordiazepoxide 5 mg, net price 20 = 28p; 10 mg, 20 = 35p; 25 mg, 20 = 78p. Label: 2

CLOBAZAM

Indications: anxiety (short-term use); adjunct in epilepsy

Cautions; Contra-indications; Side-effects: see under Diazepam

Dose: anxiety, 20–30 mg daily in divided doses or as a single dose at bedtime, increased in severe anxiety (in hospital patients) to a max. of 60 mg daily in divided doses; ELDERLY (or debilitated) 10–20 mg daily

Epilepsy, 20–30 mg daily; max. 60 mg daily; CHILD over 3 years, not more than half adult dose

NHS [1]PoM **Clobazam** (Non-proprietary)
Capsules, clobazam 10 mg. Net price 30-cap pack = £2.42. Label: 2 *or* 19
1. except for epilepsy and endorsed 'S3B' ('S2B'in Scotland)
Note. The brand name NHS Frisium® (Hoechst) is used for clobazam capsules

CLORAZEPATE DIPOTASSIUM

Indications: anxiety (short-term use)

Cautions; Contra-indications; Side-effects: see under Diazepam

Dose: 7.5–22.5 mg daily in 2–3 divided doses *or* a single dose of 15 mg at bedtime; ELDERLY (or debilitated) half adult dose

NHS PoM **Tranxene®** (Boehringer Ingelheim)
Capsules, clorazepate dipotassium 7.5 mg (maroon/grey), net price 20-cap pack = £1.50; 15 mg (pink/grey), 20-cap pack = £1.62. Label: 2 *or* 19

LORAZEPAM

Indications: short-term use in anxiety or insomnia; status epilepticus (section 4.8.2); peri-operative (section 15.1.4.2)

Cautions; Contra-indications; Side-effects: see under Diazepam; short acting hence preferable in elderly and less drowsiness next day, but withdrawal phenomena more common with short-acting benzodiazepines

Dose: *by mouth*, anxiety, 1–4 mg daily in divided doses; ELDERLY (or debilitated) half adult dose

Insomnia associated with anxiety, 1–2 mg at bedtime

By intramuscular or slow intravenous injection, for the control of acute panic attacks, 25–30 micrograms/kg every 6 hours if necessary

Note. Only use intramuscular route when oral and intravenous routes not possible

PoM **Lorazepam** (Non-proprietary)
Tablets, lorazepam 1 mg, net price 20 = 23p; 2.5 mg, 20 = 37p. Label: 2 *or* 19
Available from Cox, Steinhard (NHS Almazine®)

PoM **Ativan®** (Wyeth)
NHS *Tablets*, both scored, lorazepam 1 mg (blue), net price 20 = 48p; 2.5 mg (yellow), 20 = 77p. Label: 2 *or* 19
Injection, lorazepam 4 mg/mL. Net price 1-mL amp = 40p. For intramuscular injection it should be diluted with an equal volume of water for injections or sodium chloride intravenous infusion 0.9%

MEDAZEPAM

Indications: anxiety (short-term use)

Cautions; Contra-indications; Side-effects: see under Diazepam

Dose: anxiety, 15–30 mg daily in divided doses, increased in severe anxiety to max. 40 mg daily in divided doses; ELDERLY (or debilitated) half adult dose

NHS PoM **Nobrium®** (Roche)
Capsules, medazepam 5 mg (orange/yellow), net price 20 = 58p; 10 mg (orange/black), 20 = 87p. Label: 2

OXAZEPAM

Indications: anxiety (short-term use)

Cautions; Contra-indications; Side-effects: see under Diazepam; short acting hence preferable in elderly and less drowsiness next day, but withdrawal phenomena more common with short-acting benzodiazepines

Dose: anxiety, 15–30 mg (elderly or debilitated 10–20 mg) 3–4 times daily

Insomnia associated with anxiety, 15–25 mg (max. 50 mg) at bedtime

PoM **Oxazepam** (Non-proprietary)
Capsules, oxazepam 30 mg, net price 20 = 33p. Label: 2
Tablets, oxazepam 10 mg, net price 20 = 24p; 15 mg, 20 = 27p; 30 mg, 20 = 33p. Label: 2
Various strengths available from Steinhard (NHS Oxanid®), Wyeth

OTHER DRUGS FOR ANXIETY

Buspirone is a new drug for the treatment of anxiety; its mode of action is not fully understood and response to treatment may take up to 2 weeks. It does not alleviate the symptoms of benzodiazepine withdrawal. Therefore a patient taking a benzodiazepine should not be transferred directly to buspirone but must first have the benzodiazepine withdrawn gradually. The dependence and abuse liability of buspirone has not yet been established.

Meprobamate is **less effective** than the benzodiazepines, more hazardous in overdosage, and can also induce dependence.

Beta-blockers (e.g. propranolol, oxprenolol) (see section 2.4) do not affect psychological symptoms, such as worry, tension, and fear, but they do reduce autonomic symptoms, such as palpitations, sweating, and tremor; they do not reduce non-autonomic symptoms, such as muscle tension.

Beta-blockers are therefore indicated for patients with predominantly somatic symptoms; this, in turn, may prevent the onset of worry and fear. Patients with predominantly psychological symptoms may obtain no benefit.

BUSPIRONE HYDROCHLORIDE

Indications: anxiety (short-term use)

Cautions: does not alleviate benzodiazepine withdrawal (see notes above); history of hepatic or renal impairment; **interactions:** Appendix 1 (buspirone)

DRIVING. May affect performance of skilled tasks (e.g. driving); effects of alcohol may be enhanced

Contra-indications: epilepsy, severe hepatic or renal impairment, pregnancy and breast-feeding

Side-effects: nausea, dizziness, headache, nervousness, lightheadedness, excitement; rarely tachycardia, palpitations, chest pain, drowsiness, confusion, dry mouth, fatigue, and sweating

Dose: initially 5 mg 2–3 times daily, increased as necessary every 2–3 days; usual range 15–30 mg daily in divided doses; max. 45 mg daily (30 mg in elderly)

PoM **Buspar®** (Bristol-Myers)

Tablets, buspirone hydrochloride 5 mg, net price 126-tab pack = £40.32; 10 mg, 100-tab pack = £48.00. Counselling, driving

CHLORMEZANONE

Indications: short-term use in anxiety or insomnia; muscle spasm (but see section 10.2.2)

Cautions: respiratory disease, muscle weakness, history of drug abuse, marked personality disorder, pregnancy, breast-feeding; reduce dose in elderly and debilitated, and in hepatic and renal impairment; avoid prolonged use (and abrupt withdrawal thereafter); **interactions:** Appendix 1 (chlormezanone)

DRIVING. Drowsiness may persist the next day and affect performance of skilled tasks (e.g. driving); effects of alcohol enhanced

Contra-indications: acute pulmonary insufficiency; respiratory depression; porphyria

Side-effects: drowsiness and lethargy, dizziness, nausea, headache, dry mouth, rashes, dependence; cholestatic jaundice reported

Dose: 200 mg 3–4 times daily *or* 400 mg at bedtime; elderly patients half adult dose

PoM **Trancopal®** (Sterling-Winthrop)

Tablets, yellow, chlormezanone 200 mg. Net price 60 = £5.73. Label: 2 *or* 19

HYDROXYZINE HYDROCHLORIDE

Indications: anxiety (short-term use)

Cautions; Side-effects: see under Antihistamines (section 3.4.1)

Dose: 50–100 mg 4 times daily

PoM **Atarax®** (Pfizer)

Tablets, both s/c, hydroxyzine hydrochloride 10 mg (orange), net price 84-tab pack = £1.52; 25 mg (green), 28-tab pack = £1.02. Label: 2

Syrup, hydroxyzine hydrochloride 10 mg/5 mL. Diluent syrup, life of diluted syrup 14 days. Net price 150-mL pack = 85p. Label: 2

MEPROBAMATE

Indications: short-term use in anxiety, but see notes above

Cautions: respiratory disease, muscle weakness, epilepsy (may induce seizures), history of drug abuse, marked personality disorder, pregnancy; reduce dose in elderly and debilitated, and in hepatic and renal impairment; avoid prolonged use, abrupt withdrawal may precipitate convulsions; **interactions:** Appendix 1 (meprobamate)

DRIVING. Drowsiness may affect performance of skilled tasks (e.g. driving); effects of alcohol enhanced

Contra-indications: acute pulmonary insufficiency; respiratory depression; porphyria; breast-feeding

Side-effects: see under Diazepam, but the incidence is greater and drowsiness is the most common side-effect. Also gastro-intestinal disturbances, hypotension, paraesthesia, weakness, CNS effects which include headache, paradoxical excitement, disturbances of vision; rarely agranulocytosis and rashes

Dose: 400 mg 3–4 times daily; elderly patients half adult dose or less

CD **Equanil®** (Wyeth)

Tablets, meprobamate 200 mg, net price 20 = 15p; 400 mg (scored), 20 = 22p. Label: 2

4.1.3 Barbiturates

The intermediate-acting **barbiturates** only have a place in the treatment of severe intractable insomnia in patients already taking barbiturates; they should be avoided in the elderly. The long-acting barbiturates, phenobarbitone and methylphenobarbitone, are of value in epilepsy (section 4.8.1) but their use as sedatives is unjustified. The very short-acting barbiturates, methohexitone and thiopentone, are used in anaesthesia (see section 15.1.1).

BARBITURATES

Indications: severe intractable insomnia in patients already taking barbiturates

Cautions: avoid use where possible; dependence and tolerance readily occur; abrupt withdrawal may precipitate a serious withdrawal syndrome (rebound insomnia, anxiety, tremor, dizziness, nausea, convulsions, delirium, and death); repeated doses are cumulative and may lead to excessive sedation; caution in respiratory disease, renal disease, hepatic impairment; **interactions:** Appendix 1 (barbiturates and primidone)

DRIVING. Drowsiness may persist the next day and affect performance of skilled tasks (e.g. driving); effects of alcohol enhanced

Contra-indications: insomnia caused by pain; porphyria, pregnancy, breast-feeding; avoid in children, young adults, elderly and debilitated patients, also patients with a history of drug or alcohol abuse

Side-effects: hangover with drowsiness, dizziness, ataxia, respiratory depression, hypersensitivity reactions, headache, particularly in elderly; paradoxical excitement and confusion occasionally precede sleep

CD Amytal ® (Lilly)
Tablets, amylobarbitone 15 mg, net price 20 = 17p; 30 mg, 20 = 22p; 50 mg, 20 = 28p; 100 mg, 20 = 49p; 200 mg (scored), 20 = £1.01. Label: 19
Dose: 100–200 mg at bedtime

CD Sodium Amytal ® (Lilly)
Capsules, both blue, amylobarbitone sodium 60 mg, net price 20 = 43p; 200 mg, 20 = 90p. Label: 19
Tablets, amylobarbitone sodium 60 mg, net price 20 = 49p; 200 mg, 20 = 81p. Label: 19
Dose: 60–200 mg at bedtime
Injection, powder for reconstitution, amylobarbitone sodium. Net price 250-mg vial = £3.41.
Dose: by intramuscular or slow intravenous injection, status epilepticus, 0.25–1 g daily; max. single dose, intramuscular 500 mg, intravenous 1 g

CD Soneryl ® (M&B)
Tablets, pink, scored, butobarbitone 100 mg. Net price 20 = 26p. Label: 19
Dose: 100–200 mg at bedtime

Quinalbarbitone
Note. Quinalbarbitone has been transferred from schedule 3 to schedule 2 of the Misuse of Drugs Regulations 1985; receipt and supply must therefore be recorded in the CD register.

CD Seconal Sodium ® (Lilly)
Capsules, both orange, quinalbarbitone sodium 50 mg, net price 20 = 85p; 100 mg, 20 = £1.22. Label: 19
Dose: 50–100 mg at bedtime

CD Tuinal ® (Lilly)
Capsules, orange/blue, amylobarbitone sodium 50 mg, quinalbarbitone sodium 50 mg. Net price 20 = 54p. Label: 19
Dose: 1–2 capsules at bedtime

4.2 Drugs used in psychoses and related disorders

4.2.1 Antipsychotic drugs

Antipsychotic drugs are also known as 'neuroleptics' and (misleadingly) as 'major tranquillisers'. Antipsychotic drugs generally tranquillise without impairing consciousness and without causing paradoxical excitement but they should not be regarded merely as tranquillisers. For conditions such as schizophrenia the tranquillising effect is of secondary importance.

In the short term they are used to quieten disturbed patients whatever the underlying psychopathology, which may be brain damage, mania, toxic delirium, agitated depression, or acute behavioural disturbance.

They are used to alleviate severe anxiety but this too should be a short-term measure. Some antipsychotic drugs (e.g. chlorpromazine, thioridazine, flupenthixol) also have an antidepressant effect while others may exacerbate depression (e.g. fluphenazine, pimozide, pipothiazine).

SCHIZOPHRENIA. Antipsychotic drugs relieve florid psychotic symptoms such as thought disorder, hallucinations, and delusions, and prevent relapse. Although they are usually less effective in apathetic withdrawn patients, they sometimes appear to have an activating influence. For example, chlorpromazine may restore an acutely ill schizophrenic to normal activity and social behaviour who was previously withdrawn or even mute and akinetic. Patients with acute schizophrenia generally respond better than those with chronic symptoms.

Long-term treatment of a patient with a definite diagnosis of schizophrenia may be necessary even after the first episode of illness in order to prevent the manifest illness from becoming chronic. Withdrawal of drug treatment requires careful surveillance because the patient who appears well on medication may suffer a disastrous relapse if treatment is withdrawn inappropriately. In addition the need for continuation of treatment may not become immediately evident because relapse is often delayed for several weeks after cessation of treatment.

Antipsychotic drugs are considered to act by interfering with dopaminergic transmission in the brain by blocking dopamine receptors and may give rise to the extrapyramidal effects described below, and also to hyperprolactinaemia. Antipsychotic drugs also affect cholinergic, alpha-adrenergic, histaminergic, and tryptaminergic (serotonergic) receptors.

SIDE-EFFECTS. Extrapyramidal symptoms are the most troublesome. They are caused most frequently by the piperazine phenothiazines (fluphenazine, perphenazine, prochlorperazine, and trifluoperazine), the butyrophenones (benperidol, droperidol, haloperidol, and trifluperidol), and the depot preparations. They are easy to recognise but cannot be accurately predicted because they depend partly on the dose and partly on the type of drug, and on patient susceptibility. They consist of parkinsonian symptoms (including tremor) which may occur gradually, dystonia (abnormal face and body movements) which may appear after only a few doses, akathisia (restlessness) which may resemble an exacerbation of the condition being treated, and tardive dyskinesia (which usually takes longer to develop).

Parkinsonian symptoms remit if the drug is withdrawn and may be suppressed by the administration of **antimuscarinic** drugs (section 4.9.2). Routine administration of such drugs is **not** justified as not all patients are affected and because tardive dyskinesia may be unmasked or worsened by them. Furthermore, these drugs are sometimes abused for their mood-altering effects. Tardive dyskinesia is of particular concern because it may be irreversible on withdrawing therapy and treatment may be ineffective. It occurs fairly frequently in patients (especially the elderly) on long-term therapy and with high dosage, and the treatment of such patients must be carefully and regularly reviewed. Tardive dyskinesia may also occur occasionally after short-term treatment with low dosage.

Hypotension and interference with temperature regulation are dose-related side-effects and are liable to cause dangerous falls and hypothermia in the elderly; very serious consideration should be given before prescribing these drugs for patients over 70 years of age.

Neuroleptic malignant syndrome (hyperthermia, fluctuating level of consciousness, muscular rigidity and autonomic dysfunction with pallor, tachycardia, labile blood pressure, sweating, and urinary incontinence) is a rare but potentially fatal side-effect of some drugs. Drugs for which it has been reported in the UK include haloperidol, chlorpromazine, and flupenthixol decanoate. Discontinuation of drug therapy is essential as there is no proven effective treatment but bromocriptine and dantrolene have been used. The syndrome, which usually lasts for 5–10 days after drug discontinuation, may be unduly prolonged if depot preparations have been used.

CLASSIFICATION OF ANTIPSYCHOTICS. The **phenothiazine** derivatives can be divided into 3 main groups.

Group 1: chlorpromazine, methotrimeprazine, and promazine, generally characterised by pronounced sedative effects and moderate antimuscarinic and extrapyramidal side-effects.

Group 2: pericyazine, pipothiazine, and thioridazine, generally characterised by moderate sedative effects, marked antimuscarinic effects, but fewer extrapyramidal side-effects than groups 1 or 3.

Group 3: fluphenazine, perphenazine, prochlorperazine, and trifluoperazine, generally characterised by fewer sedative effects, fewer antimuscarinic effects, but more pronounced extrapyramidal side-effects than groups 1 and 2.

Drugs of other chemical groups tend to resemble the phenothiazines of *group 3*. They include the **butyrophenones** (benperidol, droperidol, haloperidol, and trifluperidol); **diphenylbutylpiperidines** (fluspirilene and pimozide); **thioxanthenes** (flupenthixol and zuclopenthixol); **oxypertine**; and **loxapine. Clozapine** differs in that it is sedative with fewer extrapyramidal effects.

CHOICE. As indicated above, the various drugs differ somewhat in predominant actions and side-effects. Selection is influenced by the degree of sedation required and the patient's susceptibility to extrapyramidal side-effects. However, the differences between antipsychotic drugs are less important than the great variability in patient response; moreover, tolerance to these secondary effects usually develops.

Prescribing of more than one antipsychotic at the same time is **not** recommended; it may constitute a hazard and there is no significant evidence that side-effects are minimised.

Chlorpromazine is widely used. It has a marked sedating effect and is particularly useful for treating violent patients without causing stupor. Agitated states in the elderly can be controlled without confusion, a dose of 25 mg usually being adequate.

Flupenthixol and **pimozide** (see CSM recommendations, p. 136) are less sedating than chlorpromazine.

Sulpiride is structurally distinct from other antipsychotic drugs. In high doses it controls florid positive symptoms, but in lower doses it has an alerting effect on apathetic withdrawn schizophrenics; further reductions in dosage increase this alerting effect.

Fluphenazine, haloperidol, and **trifluoperazine** are also of value but their use is limited by the high incidence of extrapyramidal symptoms. Haloperidol may be preferred for the rapid control of hyperactive psychotic states.

Thioridazine is popular for treating the elderly as there is a reduced incidence of extrapyramidal symptoms.

Promazine is not sufficiently active by mouth to be used as an antipsychotic drug

Clozapine is indicated only for the treatment of schizophrenia in patients unresponsive to, or intolerant of, conventional antipsychotic drugs. As it can cause agranulocytosis, its use is restricted to patients registered with the Clozaril Patient Monitoring Service (see under Clozapine, below).

Loxapine causes relatively little sedation; in overdosage it has a high potential for serious neurological and cardiac toxicity.

OTHER USES. Nausea and vomiting (section 4.6), choreas, motor tics (section 4.9.3), and intractable hiccup (see under Chlorpromazine Hydrochloride and under Haloperidol). **Benperidol** is used in deviant antisocial sexual behaviour but its value is not established.

WITHDRAWAL. Withdrawal of antipsychotic drugs after long-term therapy should always be gradual and closely monitored to avoid the risk of acute withdrawal syndromes or rapid relapse.

DOSAGE. In some patients it is necessary to raise the dose of an antipsychotic drug above that which is normally recommended. This should be done with caution and under specialist supervision.

Once-daily dose. After an initial period of stabilisation, in most patients, the long half-life of antipsychotic drugs allows the total daily dose to be given as a single dose.

CHLORPROMAZINE HYDROCHLORIDE

WARNING. Owing to the risk of contact sensitisation, pharmacists, nurses, and other health workers should avoid direct contact with chlorpromazine; tablets should not be crushed and solutions should be handled with care

Indications: see under Dose; antiemetic (in terminal illness), section 4.6; peri-operative use, see section 15.1.4.2

Cautions: cardiovascular and cerebrovascular disease, respiratory disease, phaeochromocytoma, parkinsonism, epilepsy, acute infections, pregnancy, breast-feeding, renal and hepatic impairment, history of jaundice, leucopenia (blood counts if unexplained infections); hypothyroidism, myasthenia gravis, prostatic hypertrophy; caution in elderly particularly in very hot or very cold weather. On prolonged use examinations for eye defects and abnormal skin pigmentation are required. Avoid abrupt withdrawal. Patients should remain supine for 30 minutes after intramuscular injection; **interactions:** Appendix 1 (phenothiazines and other antipsychotics)

DRIVING. Drowsiness may affect performance of skilled tasks (e.g. driving); effects of alcohol enhanced

Contra-indications: coma caused by CNS depressants; bone-marrow depression; closed-angle glaucoma

Side-effects: extrapyramidal symptoms (reversed by dose reduction or antimuscarinic drugs) and, on prolonged administration, occasionally tardive dyskinesia; hypothermia (occasionally pyrexia), drowsiness, apathy, pallor, nightmares, insomnia, depression, and, more rarely, agitation. Antimuscarinic symptoms such as dry mouth, nasal congestion, constipation, difficulty with micturition, and blurred vision; cardiovascular symptoms such as hypotension and arrhythmias; endocrine effects such as menstrual disturbances, galactorrhoea, gynaecomastia, impotence, and weight gain; sensitivity reactions such as agranulocytosis, leucopenia, leucocytosis, and haemolytic anaemia, photosensitisation (more common with chlorpromazine than with other antipsychotics), contact sensitisation, rashes, and jaundice; lupus erythematosus-like syndrome reported. With prolonged high dosage, corneal and lens opacities and purplish pigmentation of the skin, cornea, conjunctiva, and retina. Intramuscular injection may be painful, cause hypotension and tachycardia (see Cautions), and give rise to nodule formation

Dose: *by mouth*,

Schizophrenia and other psychoses, mania, short-term adjunctive management of severe anxiety, psychomotor agitation, excitement, and violent or dangerously impulsive behaviour initially 25 mg 3 times daily (*or* 75 mg at night), adjusted according to response, to usual maintenance dose of 75–300 mg daily (but up to 1 g daily may be required in psychoses);

CHILD 1–5 years 500 micrograms/kg every 4–6 hours (max. 40 mg daily); 6–12 years third to half adult dose (max. 75 mg daily)

ELDERLY (or debilitated) third to half adult dose

Intractable hiccup, 25–50 mg 3–4 times daily

By deep intramuscular injection, (for relief of acute symptoms), 25–50 mg every 6–8 hours; CHILD, as dose by mouth

By rectum in suppositories, chlorpromazine 100 mg every 6–8 hours

Note. For equivalent therapeutic effect 100 mg chlorpromazine base given *rectally* as a suppository ≡ 20–25 mg chlorpromazine hydrochloride *by intramuscular injection* ≡ 40–50 mg of chlorpromazine base or hydrochloride *by mouth*

PoM **Chlorpromazine** (Non-proprietary)

Tablets, coated, chlorpromazine hydrochloride 10 mg, net price 20 = 12p; 25 mg, 20 = 8p; 50 mg, 20 = 33p; 100 mg, 20 = 62p. Label: 2

Available from APS, DDSA (Chloractil®)

Elixir, chlorpromazine hydrochloride 25 mg/5 mL. Net price 100 mL = 26p. Label: 2

Injection, chlorpromazine hydrochloride 25 mg/mL, net price 1-mL amp = 21p; 2-mL amp = 27p

Suppositories, chlorpromazine 100 mg. Net price 10 = £1.91. Label: 2

Available from Penn (special order)

PoM **Largactil®** (Rhône-Poulenc Rorer)

Tablets, all off-white, f/c, chlorpromazine hydrochloride 10 mg. Net price 56-tab pack = 33p; 25 mg, 56-tab pack = 50p; 50 mg, 56-tab pack = £1.56; 100 mg, 56-tab pack = £2.16. Label: 2

Syrup, brown, chlorpromazine hydrochloride 25 mg/5 mL. Diluent syrup (without preservative), life of diluted syrup 14 days. Net price 100-mL pack = 59p. Label: 2

Suspension forte, orange, sugar-free, chlorpromazine hydrochloride 100 mg (as embonate)/5 mL. Diluent syrup (without preservative), life of diluted suspension 7 days. Net price 100-mL pack = £1.19. Label: 2

Injection, chlorpromazine hydrochloride 25 mg/mL. Net price 2-mL amp = 28p

BENPERIDOL

Indications: control of deviant antisocial sexual behaviour (but see notes above)

Cautions; Contra-indications; Side-effects: see under Haloperidol; avoid in children

Dose: 0.25–1.5 mg daily in divided doses, adjusted according to the response; ELDERLY (or debilitated) initially half adult dose

PoM **Anquil®** (Janssen)

Tablets, benperidol 250 micrograms. Net price 20 = £5.36. Label: 2

CLOZAPINE

Indications: schizophrenia in patients unresponsive to, or intolerant of, conventional antipsychotic drugs

Cautions: leucocyte and differential blood counts must be normal before treatment and must be monitored weekly for first 18 weeks then fortnightly; avoid drugs which depress leucopoiesis; withdraw treatment if leucocyte count falls below 3000/mm^3 or absolute neutrophil count falls below 1500/mm^3; patients should report any infections; hepatic or renal impairment (avoid if severe); epilepsy; cardiovascular disorders; prostatic enlargement, glaucoma, paralytic ileus; avoid abrupt withdrawal; avoid in children; **interactions**: Appendix 1 (clozapine)

DRIVING. Drowsiness may affect performance of skilled tasks (e.g. driving); effects of alcohol enhanced

Contra-indications: history of drug-induced neutropenia/agranulocytosis; bone marrow disorders; alcoholic and toxic psychoses; drug intoxication; coma or severe CNS depression; pregnancy and breast-feeding

Side-effects: neutropenia and potentially fatal agranulocytosis; drowsiness, hypersalivation, tachycardia, fatigue; transient dry mouth, accommodation disturbances, postural hypotension, hyperthermia; extrapyramidal symptoms, EEG changes, reduced seizure threshold, gastro-intestinal disturbances, and ECG changes reported; rarely arrhythmias, delirium, hepatic dysfunction, neuroleptic malignant syndrome

Dose: initially 25–50 mg daily (elderly 25 mg), increased as necessary by 25–50 mg daily (elderly 25 mg) over 7–14 days to 300 mg daily in divided doses (larger dose at night; up to 200 mg daily may be given as a single dose at bedtime); usual antipsychotic dose 200–450 mg daily (max. 900 mg daily), and subsequently adjusted to usual maintenance of 150–300 mg daily

▼ PoM **Clozaril®** (Sandoz)

Tablets, both yellow, scored, clozapine 25 mg, net price 84-tab pack = £38.50; 100 mg, 84-tab pack = £154.00 (hosp. only, patient, prescriber, and supplying pharmacist must be registered with the Sandoz Clozaril Patient Monitoring Service). Label: 2

DROPERIDOL

Indications: see under Dose; peri-operative use, see section 15.1.4.2

Cautions; Contra-indications; Side-effects: see under Haloperidol

Dose: by mouth, tranquillisation and emergency control in mania, 5–20 mg repeated every 4–8 hours if necessary (elderly, initially half adult dose); CHILD, 0.5–1 mg daily

By intramuscular injection, up to 10 mg repeated every 4–6 hours if necessary (elderly, initially half adult dose); CHILD, 0.5–1 mg daily

By intravenous injection, 5–15 mg repeated every 4–6 hours if necessary (elderly, initially half adult dose)

Cancer chemotherapy-induced nausea and vomiting, *by intramuscular or intravenous injection*, 1–10 mg 30 minutes before starting therapy, followed by *continuous intravenous infusion* of 1–3 mg/hour *or* 1–5 mg *by intramuscular or intravenous injection* every 1–6 hours as necessary; CHILD *by intramuscular or intravenous injection*, 20–75 micrograms/kg

PoM **Droleptan®** (Janssen)

Tablets, yellow, scored, droperidol 10 mg. Net price 50-tab pack = £12.62. Label: 2

Oral liquid, sugar-free, droperidol 1 mg/mL. Diluent purified water, freshly boiled and cooled, life of diluted liquid 14 days. Net price 100-mL pack (with graduated cap) = £4.59; 500-mL pack = £21.79. Label: 2

Injection, droperidol 5 mg/mL. Net price 2-mL amp = 84p

FLUPENTHIXOL

Indications: schizophrenia and other psychoses, particularly with apathy and withdrawal but not mania or psychomotor hyperactivity; depression, section 4.3.4

Cautions; Contra-indications; Side-effects: see under Chlorpromazine Hydrochloride but less sedating; extrapyramidal symptoms more frequent (25% of patients); avoid in children, senile confusional states, excitable and overactive patients; avoid in porphyria

Dose: initially 3–9 mg twice daily adjusted according to the response; max. 18 mg daily

PoM **Depixol®** (Lundbeck)

Tablets, yellow, s/c, flupenthixol 3 mg (as dihydrochloride). Net price 20 = £2.59. Label: 2

Depot injection (flupenthixol decanoate): section 4.2.2

PoM **Fluanxol®** (depression), see section 4.3.4

FLUPHENAZINE HYDROCHLORIDE

Indications: see under Dose

Cautions; Contra-indications; Side-effects: see under Chlorpromazine Hydrochloride, but less sedating and fewer antimuscarinic or hypotensive symptoms; extrapyramidal symptoms, particularly dystonic reactions and akathisia, are more frequent; avoid in depression; avoid in children

Dose: schizophrenia and other psychoses, mania, initially 2.5–10 mg daily in 2–3 divided doses, adjusted according to response to 20 mg daily; doses above 20 mg daily (10 mg in elderly) only with special caution

Short-term adjunctive management of severe anxiety, psychomotor agitation, excitement, and violent or dangerously impulsive behaviour, initially 1 mg twice daily, increased as necessary to 2 mg twice daily

PoM **Moditen®** (Squibb)

Tablets, all s/c, fluphenazine hydrochloride 1 mg (pink), net price 20 = £1.09; 2.5 mg (yellow), 20 = £1.36; 5 mg, 20 = £1.82. Label: 2

Depot injections (fluphenazine decanoate): section 4.2.2

HALOPERIDOL

Indications: see under Dose; motor tics, section 4.9.3

Cautions; Contra-indications; Side-effects: see under Chlorpromazine Hydrochloride but less sedating, and fewer antimuscarinic or hypotensive symptoms; pigmentation and photosensitivity reactions rare. Extrapyramidal symptoms, particularly dystonic reactions and akathisia are more frequent especially in thyrotoxic patients. Rarely, alterations in liver function, gastro-intestinal disturbances, and weight loss. Caution in depression. Avoid in basal ganglia disease

Dose: by mouth

Schizophrenia and other psychoses, mania, short-term adjunctive management of psychomotor agitation, excitement, and violent or dangerously impulsive behaviour, initially 1.5–20 mg daily in divided doses, gradually increased to 100 mg (and occasionally 200 mg) daily in severely disturbed patients; ELDERLY (or debilitated) initially half adult dose; CHILD initially 25–50 micrograms/kg daily to a max. of 10 mg; adolescents up to 30 mg daily (exceptionally 60 mg)

Short-term adjunctive management of severe anxiety, adults 500 micrograms twice daily

Intractable hiccup, 1.5 mg 3 times daily adjusted according to response

By intramuscular injection, 2–10 mg (increasing to 30 mg for emergency control) then 5 mg up to every hour if necessary (intervals of 4–8 hours may be satisfactory)

Nausea and vomiting, 1–2 mg

PoM **Haloperidol** (Non-proprietary)

Tablets, haloperidol 1.5 mg, net price 20 = 44p; 5 mg, 20 = 84p; 10 mg, 20 = £1.98; 20 mg, 20 = £3.29. Label: 2

PoM **Dozic®** (RP Drugs)

Oral liquid, sugar-free, haloperidol 1 mg/mL. Net price 100-mL pack (with pipette) = £5.00. Label: 2

Oral liquid, sugar-free, haloperidol 2 mg/mL. Net price 100-mL pack (with pipette) = £5.50. Label: 2

PoM **Fortunan®** (Mercury)

Tablets, haloperidol 500 micrograms, net price 20 = 44p; 1.5 mg (scored), 20 = 83p; 5 mg (green, scored), 20 = £2.25; 10 mg (pink, scored), 20 = £3.80; 20 mg (scored), 20 = £7.47. Label: 2

PoM **Haldol®** (Janssen)

Tablets, both scored, haloperidol 5 mg (blue), net price 20 = £1.69; 10 mg (yellow), 20 = £3.30. Label: 2

Oral liquid, sugar-free, haloperidol 2 mg/mL. Net price 100-mL pack (with pipette) = £5.21. Label: 2

Oral liquid concentrate, sugar-free, haloperidol 10 mg/mL. Net price 100-mL pack = £22.84. Label: 2

Diluent purified water, freshly boiled and cooled, life of diluted concentrate 14 days. Alternatively, purified water, freshly boiled and cooled, containing 0.05% of methyl hydroxybenzoate and 0.005% of propyl hydroxybenzoate, life of diluted concentrate 2 months.

Injection, haloperidol 5 mg/mL. Net price 1-mL amp = 33p; 2-mL amp = 63p

Depot injection (haloperidol decanoate): section 4.2.2

PoM **Serenace®** (Searle)

Capsules, green, haloperidol 500 micrograms. Net price 20 = 67p. Label: 2

Tablets, all scored, haloperidol 1.5 mg, net price 20 = £1.19; 5 mg (pink), 20 = £3.36; 10 mg (pale pink), 20 = £6.02; 20 mg (dark pink), 20 = £10.85. Label: 2

Oral liquid, sugar-free, haloperidol 2 mg/mL. Diluent syrup or purified water, freshly boiled and cooled, or syrup for dilutions containing 1% or less of the elixir, life of diluted elixir 2 months. Net price 100-mL pack = £8.99. Label: 2

Injection, haloperidol 5 mg/mL, net price 1-mL amp = 59p; 10 mg/mL, 2-mL amp = £2.03

LOXAPINE

Indications: acute and chronic psychoses

Cautions; Contra-indications: see under Chlorpromazine Hydrochloride

Side-effects: see under Chlorpromazine Hydrochloride; nausea and vomiting, weight gain or loss, dyspnoea, ptosis, hyperpyrexia, flushing and headache, paraesthesia, and polydipsia also reported; no endocrine effects yet reported; avoid in porphyria

Dose: initially 20–50 mg daily in 2 divided doses, increased as necessary over 7–10 days to 60–100 mg daily (max. 250 mg) in 2–4 divided doses, then adjusted to usual maintenance dose of 20–100 mg daily

▼ PoM **Loxapac®** (Lederle)

Capsules, loxapine (as succinate) 10 mg (yellow/green), net price 20 = £1.90; 25 mg (light green/dark green), 20 = £3.81; 50 mg (blue/dark green), 20 = £6.85. Label: 2

METHOTRIMEPRAZINE

Indications: see under Dose

Cautions; Contra-indications; Side-effects: see under Chlorpromazine Hydrochloride but more sedating; risk of postural hypotension particularly in patients over 50 years

Dose: *by mouth*, schizophrenia, initially 25–50 mg daily in divided doses increased as necessary; bedpatients initially 100–200 mg daily in 3 divided doses, increased if necessary to 1 g daily

Adjunctive treatment in terminal care (including management of pain and associated restlessness, distress, or vomiting), 12.5–50 mg every 4–8 hours

By intramuscular injection or by intravenous injection (after dilution with an equal volume of sodium chloride injection), adjunct in terminal care, 12.5–25 mg (severe agitation up to 50 mg) every 6–8 hours if necessary

By continuous subcutaneous infusion, adjunct in terminal care (via syringe driver), 25–200 mg daily (over 24-hour period), diluted in a suitable volume of sodium chloride 0.9% injection

PoM **Nozinan®** (Rhône-Poulenc Rorer)

Tablets[1], scored, methotrimeprazine maleate 25 mg. Net price 20 = £2.11. Label: 2

Injection, methotrimeprazine hydrochloride 25 mg/mL. Net price 1-mL amp = £1.23

1. Formerly named Veractil®

OXYPERTINE

Indications: see under Dose

Cautions; Contra-indications; Side-effects: see under Chlorpromazine Hydrochloride, but extrapyramidal symptoms may occur less frequently. With low doses agitation and hyperactivity occur and with high doses sedation. Occasionally gastro-intestinal disturbances, photophobia, and rashes may occur

Dose: schizophrenia and other psychoses, mania, short-term adjunctive management of psychomotor agitation, excitement, and violent or dangerously impulsive behaviour, initially 80–120 mg daily in divided doses adjusted according to the response; max. 300 mg daily

Short-term adjunctive management of severe anxiety, initially 10 mg 3–4 times daily preferably after food; max. 60 mg daily

PoM **Integrin**® (Sterling-Winthrop)

Capsules, oxypertine 10 mg. Net price 20 = £1.68. Label: 2

Tablets, scored, oxypertine 40 mg. Net price 20 = £5.25. Label: 2

PERICYAZINE

Indications: see under Dose

Cautions; Contra-indications; Side-effects: see under Chlorpromazine Hydrochloride, but more sedating; hypotension commonly occurs when treatment initiated

Dose: schizophrenia and other psychoses, initially 75 mg daily in divided doses increased at weekly intervals by steps of 25 mg according to response; usual max. 300 mg daily (elderly initially 15–30 mg daily).

Short-term adjunctive management of severe anxiety, psychomotor agitation, and violent or dangerously impulsive behaviour, initially 15–30 mg (elderly 5–10 mg) daily divided into 2 doses, taking the larger dose at bedtime, adjusted according to response

CHILD (severe mental or behavioural disorders only), initially, 500 micrograms daily for 10-kg child, increased by 1 mg for each additional 5 kg to max. total daily dose of 10 mg; dose may be gradually increased according to response but maintenance should not exceed twice initial dose

PoM **Neulactil**® (Rhône-Poulenc Rorer)

Tablets, all yellow, scored, pericyazine 2.5 mg, net price 20 = 44p; 10 mg, 84-tab pack = £5.04; 25 mg, 50-tab pack = £8.29. Label: 2

Syrup forte, brown, pericyazine 10 mg/5 mL. Diluent syrup, life of diluted syrup 14 days. Net price 100-mL pack = £2.35. Label: 2

PERPHENAZINE

Indications: see under Dose; anti-emetic, section 4.6

Cautions; Contra-indications; Side-effects: see under Chlorpromazine Hydrochloride, but less sedating; extrapyramidal symptoms, especially dystonia, more frequent, particularly at high dosage; avoid in children under 14 years; not indicated for agitation and restlessness in the elderly

Dose: schizophrenia and other psychoses, mania, short-term adjunctive management of severe anxiety, psychomotor agitation, excitement, and violent or dangerously impulsive behaviour, initially 4 mg 3 times daily adjusted according to the response; max. 24 mg daily; elderly quarter to half adult dose (but see Cautions)

PoM **Fentazin**® (A&H)

Tablets, both s/c, perphenazine 2 mg, net price 20 = 52p; 4 mg, 20 = 62p. Label: 2

PIMOZIDE

Indications: see under Dose

Cautions; Contra-indications; Side-effects: see under Chlorpromazine Hydrochloride, but less sedating; avoid in children; contra-indicated in breast-feeding; serious arrhythmias reported (contra-indicated if history of arrhythmias or pre-existing congenital QT prolongation); following reports of sudden unexplained death, the CSM recommends ECG before treatment in all patients, periodic ECGs at doses over 16 mg daily and review of need for pimozide if repolarisation changes or arrhythmias develop (close supervision and preferably dose reduction advised); concucrrent cardioactive or antipsychotic drugs, or electrolyte disturbances (notably hypokalaemia) may predispose to cardiotoxicity

Dose: schizophrenia, initially 10 mg daily in acute conditions, adjusted according to response in increments of 2–4 mg at intervals of not less than 1 week; max. 20 mg daily; prevention of relapse, initially 2 mg daily (range 2–20 mg daily)

Monosymptomatic hypochondriacal psychosis, paranoid psychoses, initially 4 mg daily, adjusted according to response in increments of 2–4 mg at intervals of not less than 1 week; max. 16 mg daily

Mania, hypomania, short-term adjunctive management of excitement and psychomotor agitation, initially 10 mg daily adjusted according to response in increments of 2–4 mg at intervals of not less than 1 week; max. 20 mg daily

ELDERLY half usual starting dose

PoM **Orap**® (Janssen)

Tablets, all scored, pimozide 2 mg, net price 20 = £2.96; 4 mg (green), 20 = £5.72; 10 mg, 20 = £10.97. Label: 2

PROCHLORPERAZINE

Indications: see under Dose; anti-emetic, section 4.6

Cautions; Contra-indications; Side-effects: see under Chlorpromazine Hydrochloride, but less sedating; extrapyramidal symptoms, particularly dystonic reactions, more frequent; avoid in children (but see section 4.6 for use as anti-emetic)

Dose: by mouth, schizophrenia and other psychoses, mania, prochlorperazine maleate or mesylate, 12.5 mg twice daily for 7 days adjusted to 75–100 mg daily according to response
Short-term adjunctive management of severe anxiety, 15–20 mg daily in divided doses; max. 40 mg daily
By deep intramuscular injection, psychoses, mania, prochlorperazine mesylate 12.5–25 mg 2–3 times daily
By rectum in suppositories, psychoses, mania, the equivalent of prochlorperazine maleate 25 mg 2–3 times daily

Preparations
Section 4.6

PROMAZINE HYDROCHLORIDE

Indications: see under Dose
Cautions; Contra-indications; Side-effects: see under Chlorpromazine Hydrochloride
Dose: by intramuscular injection, short-term adjunctive management of psychomotor agitation, 50 mg (25 mg in elderly or debilitated), repeated if necessary after 6–8 hours

PoM **Sparine®** (Wyeth)
Tablets—discontinued
Suspension, yellow, promazine hydrochloride 50 mg (as embonate)/5 mL. Diluent syrup, life of diluted suspension 14 days. Net price 150-mL pack = £1.72. Label: 2. *Note*. Unsuitable for children
Dose: by mouth, short-term adjunctive management of psychomotor agitation, 100–200 mg 4 times daily
Agitation and restlessness in elderly, 25–50 mg 4 times daily
Injection, promazine hydrochloride 50 mg/mL. Net price 1-mL amp = 26p

SULPIRIDE

Indications: schizophrenia
Cautions; Contra-indications; Side-effects: see under Chlorpromazine Hydrochloride, but less sedating; structurally distinct from chlorpromazine hence not associated with jaundice or skin reactions; avoid in phaeochromocytoma, porphyria, and breast-feeding; reduce dose (preferably avoid) in renal impairment
Dose: 200–400 mg twice daily; max. 800 mg daily in patients with predominantly negative symptoms, and 2.4 g daily in patients with mainly positive symptoms; ELDERLY, initially 100–200 mg

PoM **Dolmatil®** (Squibb)
Tablets, scored, sulpiride 200 mg. Net price 20 = £4.20. Label: 2

PoM **Sulpitil®** (Tillotts)
Tablets, scored, sulpiride 200 mg. Net price 28-tab pack = £5.75; 112-tab pack = £23.00. Label: 2

THIORIDAZINE

Indications: see under Dose
Cautions; Contra-indications; Side-effects: see under Chlorpromazine Hydrochloride, but less sedating and extrapyramidal symptoms and hypothermia rarely occur; more likely to induce hypotension. Caution in depression. Pigmentary retinopathy (with reduced visual acuity, brownish colouring of vision, and impaired night vision) occurs rarely with high doses. Sexual dysfunction, particularly retrograde ejaculation, may occur; avoid in porphyria
Dose: schizophrenia and other psychoses, mania, 150–600 mg daily (initially in divided doses); max. 800 mg daily (hospital patients only) for up to 4 weeks
Short-term adjunctive management of psychomotor agitation, excitement, violent or dangerously impulsive behaviour, 75–200 mg daily
Short-term adjunctive management of severe anxiety, and agitation and restlessness in the elderly, 30–100 mg daily
CHILD (severe mental or behavioural problems only) under 5 years 1 mg/kg daily, 5–12 years 75–150 mg daily (in severe cases, up to 300 mg daily)

PoM **Thioridazine** (Non-proprietary)
Tablets, coated, thioridazine hydrochloride 25 mg, net price 20 = 32p; 50 mg, 20 = 61p; 100 mg, 20 = £1.16. Label: 2

PoM **Melleril®** (Sandoz)
Tablets, all f/c, thioridazine hydrochloride 10 mg, net price 20 = 23p; 25 mg, 20 = 32p; 50 mg, 20 = 61p; 100 mg, 20 = £1.16. Label: 2
Suspension 25 mg/5 mL, thioridazine 25 mg/5 mL. Net price 100 mL = 58p. Label: 2
Suspension 100 mg/5 mL, thioridazine 100 mg/5 mL. Net price 100 mL = £2.13. Label: 2
Note. These suspensions should not be diluted but the two preparations may be mixed with each other to provide intermediate doses
Syrup, orange, thioridazine 25 mg (as hydrochloride)/5 mL. Diluent syrup or sorbitol solution 70%, life of diluted syrup 14 days. Net price 100-mL pack = 78p. Label: 2

TRIFLUOPERAZINE

Indications: see under Dose; anti-emetic, section 4.6
Cautions; Contra-indications; Side-effects: see under Chlorpromazine Hydrochloride but less sedating, and hypotension, hypothermia, and antimuscarinic side-effects occur less frequently; extrapyramidal symptoms, particularly dystonic reactions and akathisia, are more frequent (particularly when the daily dose exceeds 6 mg); caution in children
Dose: by mouth
Schizophrenia and other psychoses, short-term adjunctive management of psychomotor agitation, excitement, and violent or dangerously impulsive behaviour, initially 5 mg twice daily, *or* 10 mg daily in slow-release form, increased by 5 mg after 1 week, then at intervals of 3 days, according to the response; CHILD up to 12 years, initially up to 5 mg daily in divided doses, adjusted according to response, age, and bodyweight

Short-term adjunctive management of severe anxiety, 2–4 mg daily in divided doses *or* 2–4 mg daily in slow-release form, increased if necessary to 6 mg daily; CHILD 3–5 years up to 1 mg daily, 6–12 years up to 4 mg daily, in divided doses
By deep intramuscular injection 1–3 mg daily in divided doses to a max. of 6 mg daily; CHILD 50 micrograms/kg daily in divided doses

PoM **Trifluoperazine** (Non-proprietary)
Tablets, coated, trifluoperazine (as hydrochloride) 1 mg, net price 20 = 30p; 5 mg; 20 = 39p. Label: 2

PoM **Stelazine®** (SK&F)
Tablets, both blue, s/c, trifluoperazine (as hydrochloride) 1 mg, net price 20 = 38p; 5 mg, 20 = 54p. Label: 2
Spansule® (=capsules s/r), all clear/yellow, enclosing dark blue, light blue, and white pellets, trifluoperazine (as hydrochloride) 2 mg, net price 60-cap pack = £2.46; 10 mg, 30-cap pack = £1.61; 15 mg, 30-cap pack = £2.42. Label: 2, 25
Syrup, yellow, sugar-free, trifluoperazine 1 mg (as hydrochloride)/5 mL. Diluent sorbitol solution (70%), life of diluted syrup 28 days. Net price 200-mL pack = £1.50. Label: 2
Liquid concentrate, yellow, sugar-free, trifluoperazine 10 mg (as hydrochloride)/mL for dilution before use. Diluent sorbitol solution (70%) or water containing benzoic acid 0.1%, life of diluted liquid 12 weeks. Net price 100 mL = £3.37 (hosp. only)
Injection, trifluoperazine 1 mg (as hydrochloride)/mL. Net price 1-mL amp = 42p

TRIFLUPERIDOL

Indications: schizophrenia and other psychoses, particularly those with manic features
Cautions; Contra-indications; Side-effects: see under Haloperidol
Dose: initially 500 micrograms daily, adjusted by 500 micrograms every 3–4 days according to response; max. 6–8 mg daily; CHILD 5–12 years initially 250 micrograms daily, adjusted according to response; max. 2 mg daily; usual maintenance 1 mg daily

PoM **Triperidol®** (Lagap)
Tablets, both scored, trifluperidol 500 micrograms, net price 20 = £1.36; 1 mg, 20 = £2.00. Label: 2

ZUCLOPENTHIXOL ACETATE

Indications: short-term management of acute psychosis, mania, or exacerbations of chronic psychosis
Cautions; Contra-indications; Side-effects: see under Chlorpromazine Hydrochloride; avoid in porphyria; treatment duration should not exceed 2 weeks
Dose: *by deep intramuscular injection*, 50–150 mg (elderly 50–100 mg), if necessary repeated after 2–3 days (1 additional dose may be needed 1–2 days after the first injection); max. cumulative dose 400 mg per course and max. 4 injections; if maintenance treatment necessary change to an oral antipsychotic 2–3 days after last injection, *or* to a longer acting antipsychotic depot injection given concomitantly with last injection of zuclopenthixol acetate

PoM **Cloxipol Acuphase®** (Lundbeck)
Injection (oily), zuclopenthixol acetate 50 mg/mL. Net price 1-mL amp = £4.50; 2-mL amp = £9.01

ZUCLOPENTHIXOL DIHYDROCHLORIDE

Indications: schizophrenia and other psychoses, particularly when associated with agitated, aggressive, or hostile behaviour
Cautions; Contra-indications; Side-effects: see under Chlorpromazine Hydrochloride; should not be used in apathetic or withdrawn states; avoid in children and in porphyria
Dose: initially 20–30 mg daily in divided doses, increasing to a max. of 150 mg daily if necessary; usual maintenance dose 20–50 mg daily

PoM **Clopixol®** (Lundbeck)
Tablets, all f/c, zuclopenthixol (as dihydrochloride) 2 mg (pink), net price 20 = 61p; 10 mg (light brown), 20 = £1.50; 25 mg (brown), 20 = £3.00. Label: 2
Depot injection (zuclopenthixol decanoate): section 4.2.2

4.2.2 Antipsychotic depot injections

For maintenance therapy, long-acting depot injections of antipsychotic drugs are used because they are more convenient than oral preparations and ensure better patient compliance. However, they may give rise to a higher incidence of extrapyramidal reactions than oral preparations.

ADMINISTRATION. Depot antipsychotics are administered by deep intramuscular injection at intervals of 1 to 4 weeks. Patients should first be given a small test-dose as undesirable side-effects are prolonged. In general not more than 2–3 mL of oily injection should be administered at any one site.

Individual responses to neuroleptic drugs are very variable and to achieve optimum effect, dosage and dosage interval must be titrated according to the patient's response.

CHOICE. There is no clear-cut division in the use of these drugs, but **zuclopenthixol** may be suitable for the treatment of agitated or aggressive patients whereas **flupenthixol** can cause over-excitement in such patients. **Fluspirilene** has a shorter duration of action than the other depot injections. The incidence of extrapyramidal reactions is similar for all these drugs.

CAUTIONS. Treatment requires careful monitoring for optimum effect; extrapyramidal symptoms occur frequently. When transferring from oral to depot therapy, dosage by mouth should be gradually phased out. Caution in arteriosclerosis.

CONTRA-INDICATIONS. Do not use in children, confusional states, coma caused by CNS depressants, parkinsonism, intolerance to antipsychotics.

SIDE-EFFECTS. Pain may occur at injection site and occasionally erythema, swelling, and nodules. For side-effects of specific antipsychotics see under the relevant monograph.

FLUPENTHIXOL DECANOATE

Indications: maintenance in schizophrenia and other psychoses

Cautions; Contra-indications; Side-effects: see under Chlorpromazine Hydrochloride (section 4.2.1) and notes above, but it may have a mood elevating effect; extrapyramidal symptoms usually appear 1–3 days after administration and continue for about 5 days but may be delayed; an alternative antipsychotic may be necessary if symptoms such as aggression or agitation appear; avoid in porphyria

Dose: *by deep intramuscular injection* into the gluteal muscle, test dose 20 mg, then after 5–10 days 20–40 mg repeated at intervals of 2–4 weeks, adjusted according to response; max. 400 mg weekly; usual maintenance dose 50 mg every 4 weeks to 300 mg every 2 weeks

ELDERLY initially quarter to half adult dose

PoM **Depixol®** (Lundbeck)

Injection (oily), flupenthixol decanoate 20 mg/mL. Net price 1-mL amp = £1.55; 1-mL syringe = £1.70; 2-mL amp = £2.60; 2-mL syringe = £2.75; 10-mL vial = £14.74

PoM **Depixol Conc.®** (Lundbeck)

Injection (oily), flupenthixol decanoate 100 mg/mL. Net price 0.5-mL amp = £3.25; 1-mL amp = £5.95; 5-mL vial = £28.27

FLUPHENAZINE DECANOATE

Indications: maintenance in schizophrenia and other psychoses

Cautions; Contra-indications; Side-effects: see under Chlorpromazine Hydrochloride (section 4.2.1) and notes above. Extrapyramidal symptoms usually appear a few hours after the dose has been administered and continue for about 2 days but may be delayed. Contra-indicated in severely depressed states

Dose: *by deep intramuscular injection* into the gluteal muscle, test dose 12.5 mg (6.25 mg in elderly), then after 4–7 days 12.5–100 mg repeated at intervals of 14–35 days, adjusted according to response

PoM **Modecate®** (Squibb)

Injection (oily), fluphenazine decanoate 25 mg/mL. Net price 0.5-mL amp = £1.45; 1-mL amp = £2.52; 1-mL syringe = £2.79; 2-mL amp = £4.97; 2-mL syringe = £5.05; 10-mL vial = £24.05

PoM **Modecate Concentrate®** (Squibb)

Injection (oily), fluphenazine decanoate 100 mg/mL. Net price 0.5-mL amp = £5.00; 1-mL amp = £9.77

FLUPHENAZINE ENANTHATE

Indications; Cautions; Contra-indications; Side-effects: see under Fluphenazine Decanoate but it has less prolonged effect and higher incidence of extrapyramidal symptoms

Dose: *by deep intramuscular injection* into the gluteal muscle, test dose 12.5 mg (6.25 mg in elderly patients), then after 4–7 days 12.5–100 mg repeated at intervals of 10–21 days, adjusted according to the response

PoM **Moditen Enanthate®** (Squibb)

Injection (oily), fluphenazine enanthate 25 mg/mL. Net price 1-mL amp = £3.00

FLUSPIRILENE

Indications: maintenance in schizophrenia

Cautions; Contra-indications; Side-effects: see under Chlorpromazine Hydrochloride (section 4.2.1) and notes above, but less sedating. Extrapyramidal symptoms usually appear 6–12 hours after the dose and continue for about 48 hours but may be delayed. Common side-effects are restlessness and sweating. With prolonged use, tissue damage (subcutaneous nodules) may occur at injection site

Dose: *by deep intramuscular injection*, 2 mg, increased by 2 mg at weekly intervals, according to response; usual maintenance dose 2–8 mg weekly; max. 20 mg weekly

ELDERLY initially quarter to half adult dose

PoM **Redeptin®** (SK&F)

Injection (aqueous suspension), fluspirilene 2 mg/mL. Net price 1-mL amp = 90p; 3-mL amp = £1.59; 6-mL vial = £2.76

HALOPERIDOL DECANOATE

Indications: maintenance in schizophrenia and other psychoses

Cautions; Contra-indications; Side-effects: see Haloperidol (section 4.2.1) and notes above

Dose: *by deep intramuscular injection* into the gluteal muscle, initially 50 mg every 4 weeks, if necessary increasing after 2 weeks by 50-mg increments to 300 mg every 4 weeks; higher doses may be needed in some patients; elderly, initially 12.5–25 mg every 4 weeks

PoM **Haldol Decanoate®** (Janssen)

Injection (oily), haloperidol (as decanoate) 50 mg/mL, net price 1-mL amp = £4.66; 100 mg/mL, 1-mL amp = £5.91

PIPOTHIAZINE PALMITATE

Indications: maintenance in schizophrenia and other psychoses

Cautions; Contra-indications; Side-effects: see under Chlorpromazine Hydrochloride (section 4.2.1) and notes above

Dose: by *deep intramuscular injection* into the gluteal muscle, test dose 25 mg, then a further 25–50 mg after 4–7 days, then adjusted according to response at intervals of 4 weeks; usual maintenance range 50–100 mg (max. 200 mg) every 4 weeks
ELDERLY initially 5–10 mg

PoM **Piportil Depot®** (Rhône-Poulenc Rorer)
Injection (oily), pipothiazine palmitate 50 mg/mL. Net price 1-mL amp = £6.28; 2-mL amp = £10.27

ZUCLOPENTHIXOL DECANOATE

Indications: maintenance in schizophrenia and other psychoses, particularly with aggression and agitation
Cautions; Contra-indications; Side-effects: see under Chlorpromazine Hydrochloride (section 4.2.1) and notes above, but it is less sedating; avoid in porphyria
Dose: *by deep intramuscular injection* into the gluteal muscle, test dose 100 mg, then after 7–28 days 100–200 mg or more, followed by 200–400 mg repeated at intervals of 2–4 weeks, adjusted according to the response; max. 600 mg weekly

PoM **Clopixol®** (Lundbeck)
Injection (oily), zuclopenthixol decanoate 200 mg/mL. Net price 1-mL amp = £3.01; 10-mL vial = £28.63

PoM **Clopixol Conc.®** (Lundbeck)
Injection (oily), zuclopenthixol decanoate 500 mg/mL. Net price 1-mL amp with needle = £7.25

4.2.3 Antimanic drugs

Drugs are used in mania both to control acute attacks and also to prevent their recurrence.

ANTIPSYCHOTIC DRUGS

In an acute attack of mania, treatment with antipsychotic drugs (section 4.2.1) is usually required because it may take a few days for lithium to exert its antimanic effect. Lithium may be given concurrently with the antipsychotic drug, and treatment with the antipsychotic gradually tailed off as lithium becomes effective. Alternatively, lithium therapy may be commenced once the patient's mood has been stabilised with the antipsychotic. Haloperidol may be preferred for rapid control of acute mania. However, high doses of haloperidol, fluphenazine, or flupenthixol may be hazardous when used with lithium; irreversible toxic encephalopathy has been reported.

LITHIUM

Lithium salts are used in the *prophylaxis and treatment of mania*, in the *prophylaxis of manic-depressive illness* (bipolar illness or bipolar depression) and in the *prophylaxis of recurrent depression* (unipolar illness or unipolar depression). Lithium is unsuitable for children.

The decision to give prophylactic lithium usually requires specialist advice, and must be based on careful consideration of the likelihood of recurrence in the individual patient, and the benefit weighed against the risks. In long-term use, therapeutic concentrations have been thought to cause histological and functional changes in the kidney. The significance of such changes is not clear but is of sufficient concern to discourage long-term use of lithium unless it is definitely indicated. Patients should therefore be maintained on lithium after 3–5 years only if, on assessment, benefit persists.

PLASMA CONCENTRATIONS. Lithium salts have a narrow therapeutic/toxic ratio and should therefore not be prescribed unless facilities for monitoring plasma concentrations are available. There seem few if any reasons for preferring one or other of the salts of lithium available. Doses are adjusted to achieve plasma concentrations of 0.4 to 1.0 mmol Li^+/litre (lower end of the range for maintenance therapy and elderly patients) on samples taken 12 hours after the preceding dose. It is important to determine the optimum range for each individual patient.

Overdosage, usually with plasma concentrations over 1.5 mmol Li^+/ litre, may be fatal and toxic effects include tremor, ataxia, dysarthria, nystagmus, renal impairment, and convulsions. If these potentially hazardous signs occur, treatment should be stopped, plasma-lithium concentrations redetermined, and steps taken to reverse lithium toxicity. In mild cases withdrawal of lithium and administration of generous amounts of sodium and fluid will reverse the toxicity. Plasma concentrations in excess of 2.0 mmol Li^+/litre require emergency treatment as indicated under Emergency Treatment of Poisoning. When toxic concentrations are reached there may be a delay of 1 or 2 days before maximum toxicity occurs.

INTERACTIONS. Lithium toxicity is made worse by sodium depletion, therefore concurrent use of diuretics (particularly thiazides) is hazardous and should be avoided. For other interactions with lithium, see Appendix 1 (lithium).

LITHIUM CARDS. A lithium treatment card available from pharmacies tells patients how to take lithium preparations, what to do if a dose is missed, and what side-effects to expect. It also explains why regular blood tests are important and warns that some medicines and illnesses can change lithium plasma concentrations.

The cards are available from the Royal Pharmaceutical Society of Great Britain.

LITHIUM CARBONATE

Indications: treatment and prophylaxis of mania, manic-depressive illness, and recurrent depression (see also notes above); aggressive or self-mutilating behaviour
Cautions: plasma concentrations must be measured regularly (every month on stabilised regimens), and thyroid function monitored; maintain adequate sodium and fluid intake. Avoid in renal impairment, cardiac disease, and conditions with sodium imbalance such as

Addison's disease (dose adjustment may be necessary in diarrhoea, vomiting, and heavy sweating). Caution in pregnancy, breast-feeding, elderly patients (reduce dose), diuretic treatment, myasthenia gravis; **interactions:** Appendix 1 (lithium)

Side-effects: gastro-intestinal disturbances, fine tremor, polyuria and polydipsia; also weight gain and oedema (may respond to dose reduction). Signs of lithium intoxication are blurred vision, increasing gastro-intestinal disturbances (anorexia, vomiting, diarrhoea), muscle weakness, increasing CNS disturbances (mild drowsiness and sluggishness increasing to giddiness with ataxia, coarse tremor, lack of co-ordination, dysarthria), and require withdrawal of treatment. With severe overdosage (plasma concentrations above 2 mmol/litre) hyperreflexia and hyperextension of limbs, convulsions, toxic psychoses, syncope, oliguria, circulatory failure, coma, and occasionally, death. Goitre, raised antidiuretic hormone concentration, hypothyroidism, hypokalaemia, ECG changes, exacerbation of psoriasis, and kidney changes may also occur

Dose: see under preparations below, adjusted to achieve a plasma concentration of 0.4–1.0 mmol Li^+/litre 12 hours after the preceding dose on the fourth or seventh day of treatment, then every week until dosage has remained constant for 4 weeks and every 3 months thereafter

COUNSELLING. Patients should maintain an adequate fluid intake and should avoid dietary changes which might reduce or increase sodium intake; lithium treatment cards are available from pharmacies (see above)

Note. **Different preparations vary widely in bioavailability**; a change in the preparation used requires the same precautions as initiation of treatment.

PoM **Camcolit®** (Norgine)

Camcolit 250® tablets, f/c, scored, lithium carbonate 250 mg (6.8 mmol Li^+). Net price 20 = 59p. Label: 10 lithium card, counselling, see above

Camcolit 400® tablets, s/r, f/c, scored, lithium carbonate 400 mg (10.8 mmol Li^+). Net price 20 = 79p. Label: 10 lithium card, 25, counselling, see above

Dose (plasma monitoring, see above):

Treatment, initially 1.5–2 g daily (elderly, 0.5–1 g daily)

Prophylaxis, initially 0.5–1.2 g daily (elderly, 0.5–1 g daily)

Camcolit 250® should be given in divided doses, whereas Camcolit 400® may be given in single or divided doses

PoM **Liskonum®** (SK&F)

Tablets, s/r, f/c, scored, lithium carbonate 450 mg (12.2 mmol Li^+). Net price 60-tab pack = £2.82. Label: 10 lithium card, 25, counselling, see above

Dose (plasma monitoring, see above):

Treatment, initially 450–675 mg twice daily (elderly, initially 225 mg twice daily)

Prophylaxis, initially 450 mg twice daily (elderly, 225 mg twice daily)

PoM **Phasal®** (Lagap)

Tablets, s/r, lithium carbonate 300 mg (8.1 mmol Li^+). Net price 60-tab pack = £2.90. Label: 10 lithium card, 25, counselling, see above

Dose (plasma monitoring, see above):

Treatment, initially 600 mg twice daily (elderly, 0.5–1 g daily in divided doses)

Prophylaxis, initially 600 mg daily

PoM **Priadel®** (Delandale)

Tablets, both s/r, scored, lithium carbonate 200 mg (5.4 mmol Li^+), net price 20 = 42p; 400 mg (10.8 mmol Li^+), 20 = 62p. Label: 10 lithium card, 25, counselling, see above

Dose (plasma monitoring, see above):

Treatment and prophylaxis, initially 0.4–1.2 g daily as a single dose or in 2 divided doses (elderly or patients less than 50 kg, 400 mg daily)

Liquid, see under Lithium Citrate, below

LITHIUM CITRATE

Indications; Cautions; Side-effects: see under Lithium Carbonate and notes above

Dose: see under preparations below, adjusted to achieve plasma concentrations of 0.4–1.0 mmol Li^+/litre as described under Lithium Carbonate

PoM **Litarex®** (CP)

Tablets, s/r, lithium citrate 564 mg (6 mmol Li^+). Net price 20 = 72p. Label: 10 lithium card, 25, counselling, see under Lithium Carbonate

Dose (plasma monitoring, see above):

Treatment and prophylaxis, initially 564 mg twice daily

PoM **Priadel®** (Delandale)

Liquid, yellow, sugar-free, lithium citrate 520 mg/5 mL (5.4 mmol Li^+/5 mL). Net price 150-mL pack = £6.75. Label: 10 lithium card, counselling, see under Lithium Carbonate

Dose (plasma monitoring, see above):

Treatment and prophylaxis, initially 1.04–3.12 g daily in 2 divided doses (elderly or patients less than 50 kg, 520 mg twice daily)

CARBAMAZEPINE

Carbamazepine may be used for the prophylaxis of manic-depressive illness in patients unresponsive to lithium; it seems to be particularly effective in patients with rapid cycling manic-depressive illness (4 or more affective episodes per year).

CARBAMAZEPINE

Indications: prophylaxis of manic-depressive illness unresponsive to lithium; for use in epilepsy see section 4.8.1

Cautions; Contra-indications; Side-effects: see section 4.8.1

Dose: initially 400 mg daily in divided doses increased until symptoms controlled; usual range 400–600 mg daily; max. 1.6 g daily

Preparations: section 4.8.1

4.3 Antidepressant drugs

Tricyclic and related antidepressants (antidepressives) are the drugs of choice in the treatment of depressive illness, unless it is so severe that electroconvulsive therapy is immediately indicated. They are preferred to MAOIs because they are more effective antidepressants and do not show the dangerous interactions with some foods and drugs that are characteristic of the MAOIs. **Lithium** (section 4.2.3) has a mood-regulating action and is used in the treatment and prophylaxis of mania, manic depressive illness, and recurrent depression.

Prescribing more than one antidepressant of the tricyclic type is **not** recommended. It may constitute a hazard and there is no evidence that side-effects are minimised.

Mixtures of antidepressants with tranquillisers are in section 4.3.3; they are **not** recommended.

Other drugs used to treat depression are in section 4.3.4.

It should be noted that although anxiety is often present in depressive illness and may be the presenting symptom, the use of antipsychotics or anxiolytics may mask the true diagnosis. They should therefore be used with caution though they are useful adjuncts in agitated depression.

4.3.1 Tricyclic and related antidepressant drugs

The term 'tricyclic' is misleading as there are now 1-, 2-, and 4-ring structured drugs with broadly similar properties.

These drugs are most effective for treating moderate to severe *endogenous depression* associated with psychomotor and physiological changes such as loss of appetite and sleep disturbances; improvement in sleep is usually the first benefit of therapy. Since there may be an interval of 2 to 4 weeks before the antidepressant action takes place electroconvulsive treatment may be required in severe depression when delay is hazardous or intolerable.

Tricyclic antidepressants are also effective in the management of *panic disorder*.

Oral and facial pain may respond to a tricyclic antidepressant, particularly if associated with depression.

Some tricyclic antidepressants are used for the treatment of *nocturnal enuresis* in children, see section 7.4.2.

DOSAGE. About 10 to 20% of patients fail to respond to tricyclic and related antidepressant drugs and inadequate plasma concentrations may account for some of these failures. It is important to achieve plasma concentrations which are sufficiently high for effective treatment but not high enough to cause toxic effects. Low doses should be used for initial treatment in the **elderly** (see under Side-effects, below).

In most patients the long half-life of tricyclic antidepressant drugs allows **once-daily** administration, usually at night; the use of sustained-release preparations is therefore unnecessary.

MANAGEMENT. The patient's condition must be checked frequently, especially in the early weeks of treatment, to detect any suicidal tendencies. Limited quantities of antidepressant drugs should be prescribed at any one time as they are dangerous in overdosage. Some of the newer drugs, for example mianserin and trazodone, seem less dangerous in overdose than the older tricyclics.

Treatment should be continued for 2 to 4 weeks before suppression of symptoms can be expected and thereafter should be maintained at the optimum level for at least another month before any attempt is made at dose reduction. Treatment should not be withdrawn prematurely, otherwise symptoms are likely to recur. The natural history of depressive illness suggests that remission usually occurs after 3 months to a year or more and some patients appear to benefit from maintenance therapy with about half the therapeutic dosage for several months to prevent relapse. In recurrent depression, prophylactic maintenance therapy may need to be continued for several years.

In patients who do not respond to antidepressants, the diagnosis, dosage, compliance, and possible continuation of psychosocial or physical aggravating causes should all be carefully reviewed; other drug treatment may be successful. The patient may respond to low-dose **flupenthixol** (Fluanxol®, section 4.3.4) or to MAOIs (section 4.3.2), but see **Interactions**, below.

WITHDRAWAL. Gastro-intestinal symptoms of nausea, vomiting, and anorexia, accompanied by headache, giddiness, 'chills', and insomnia, and sometimes by hypomania, panic-anxiety, and extreme motor restlessness may occur if an antidepressant (particularly an MAOI) is stopped suddenly after regular administration for 8 weeks or more. Reduction in dosage should preferably be carried out gradually over a period of about 4 weeks.

CHOICE. Antidepressant drugs can be roughly divided into those with additional sedative properties, for example **amitriptyline**, and those with less, for example **imipramine**. Agitated and anxious patients tend to respond best to the sedative compounds whereas withdrawn and apathetic patients will often obtain most benefit from less sedating compounds.

Amitriptyline may be given in divided doses or the entire daily dose may be given at night to promote sleep and avoid daytime drowsiness. **Imipramine** can also be given once daily but as it has a much less sedative action there is less need.

Imipramine and amitriptyline are well established and relatively safe and effective, but nevertheless have more marked antimuscarinic or cardiac side-effects than some of the newer compounds (**doxepin, lofepramine, mianserin, trazodone**, and **viloxazine**); this may be important in individual patients.

Amoxapine is related to the antipsychotic loxapine and its side-effects include tardive dyskinesia; overdosage has been associated with seizures.

Antidepressants with **sedative** properties include amitriptyline, dothiepin, doxepin, maprotiline, mianserin, trazodone, and trimipramine.

Less sedative antidepressants include butriptyline, clomipramine, desipramine, imipramine, iprindole, lofepramine, nortriptyline, and viloxazine. Protriptyline has a **stimulant** action.

SIDE-EFFECTS. Arrhythmias and heart block occasionally follow the use of tricyclic antidepressants, particularly amitriptyline, and may be a factor in the sudden death of patients with cardiac disease. Although the use of the older tricyclic antidepressants has been associated with reports of convulsions and of hepatic and haematological reactions, the frequency of these side-effects appears to be much higher, and deaths have been reported, with the newer non-tricyclic antidepressants. In particular, mianserin has been associated with haematological and hepatic reactions and maprotiline has been associated with convulsions. Patients being treated with these drugs therefore require careful supervision. In the case of **mianserin** a full **blood count** is recommended every 4 weeks during the first 3 months of treatment; subsequent clinical monitoring should continue and treatment should be stopped and a full blood count obtained if fever, sore throat, stomatitis, or other signs of infection develop.

Other side-effects of tricyclic and related antidepressants include drowsiness, dry mouth, blurred vision, constipation, urinary retention, and sweating, attributed to antimuscarinic activity. The patient should be encouraged to persist with treatment as some tolerance to these side-effects seems to develop. They are further reduced if low doses are given initially and then gradually increased.

This gradual introduction of treatment is particularly important in the elderly, who, because of the hypotensive effects of these drugs, are prone to attacks of dizziness or even syncope. The tricyclic and related antidepressants should be prescribed with caution in epilepsy as they lower the convulsive threshold.

Neuroleptic malignant syndrome (section 4.2.1) may, very rarely, arise in the course of antidepressant treatment.

INTERACTIONS. MAOIs should preferably not be started until at least a week after tricyclics have been stopped; they should not be started until 5 weeks after fluoxetine has been stopped. For other tricyclic interactions, see Appendix 1 (antidepressants, tricyclic).

TRICYCLIC ANTIDEPRESSANTS

AMITRIPTYLINE HYDROCHLORIDE

Indications: depressive illness, particularly where sedation is required; nocturnal enuresis in children (see section 7.4.2)

Cautions: diabetes, cardiac disease (particularly with arrhythmias, see contra-indications below), epilepsy, pregnancy and breast-feeding, hepatic impairment, thyroid disease, psychoses (may aggravate mania), glaucoma, urinary retention. Avoid abrupt cessation of therapy. Also caution in anaesthesia (increased risk of arrhythmias). See notes above for nocturnal enuresis; **interactions:** Appendix 1 (antidepressants, tricyclic)

DRIVING. Drowsiness may affect performance of skilled tasks (e.g. driving); effects of alcohol enhanced

Contra-indications: recent myocardial infarction, heart block, mania; porphyria

Side-effects: dry mouth, sedation, blurred vision, constipation, nausea, difficulty with micturition (due to antimuscarinic action). Other common side-effects are cardiovascular (arrhythmias, postural hypotension, tachycardia, syncope, particularly with high doses), sweating, tremor, rashes, behavioural disturbances (particularly children), hypomania, confusion (particularly elderly), interference with sexual function, blood sugar and weight changes. Less common, black tongue, paralytic ileus, convulsions, agranulocytosis, leucopenia, eosinophilia, purpura, thrombocytopenia, and jaundice

Dose: *by mouth*, initially 50–75 mg (elderly and adolescents 25–50 mg) daily in divided doses *or* as a single dose at bedtime increased gradually as necessary to a max. of 150–200 mg; usual maintenance 50–100 mg daily

Nocturnal enuresis, CHILD 7–10 years 10–20 mg, 11–16 years 25–50 mg at night; max. period of treatment (including gradual withdrawal) should not exceed 3 months

By intramuscular or intravenous injection, 10–20 mg 4 times daily

PoM **Amitriptyline** (Non-proprietary)

Tablets, coated, amitriptyline hydrochloride 10 mg, net price 20 = 22p; 25 mg, 20 = 8p; 50 mg, 20 = 48p. Label: 2

Available from APS, Berk (Domical®), Cox, DDSA (Elavil®), Evans, Kerfoot

PoM **Lentizol®** (P-D)

Capsules, s/r, both enclosing white pellets, amitriptyline hydrochloride 25 mg (pink), net price 20 = 87p; 50 mg (pink/red), 20 = £1.63. Label: 2, 25

PoM **Tryptizol**® (Morson)

Tablets, all f/c, amitriptyline hydrochloride 10 mg (blue), net price 20 = 22p; 25 mg (yellow), 20 = 46p; 50 mg (brown), 20 = 95p. Label: 2

Capsules, s/r, orange, amitriptyline hydrochloride 75 mg. Net price 20 = £1.78. Label: 2, 25

Mixture, pink, sugar-free, amitriptyline 10 mg (as embonate)/5 mL. Diluent syrup, life of diluted mixture 14 days. Net price 200-mL pack = £1.87. Label: 2

Injection, amitriptyline hydrochloride 10 mg/mL. Net price 10-mL vial = 47p

AMOXAPINE

Indications: depressive illness

Cautions; Contra-indications; Side-effects: see under Amitriptyline Hydrochloride; tardive dyskinesia reported; menstrual irregularities, breast enlargement, and galactorrhoea reported in women

Dose: initially 100–150 mg daily in divided doses *or* as a single dose at bedtime increased as necessary to max. 300 mg daily; usual maintenance 150–250 mg daily

ELDERLY initially 25 mg twice daily increased as necessary after 5–7 days to max. 50 mg 3 times daily

▼ PoM **Asendis**® (Lederle)

Tablets, amoxapine 25 mg, net price 20 = £2.18; 50 mg (orange, scored), 20 = £3.63; 100 mg (blue, scored), 20 = £6.05; 150 mg (scored), 20 = £9.02. Label: 2

BUTRIPTYLINE

Indications: depressive illness

Cautions; Contra-indications; Side-effects: see under Amitriptyline Hydrochloride, but less sedating

Dose: 25 mg 3 times daily, increased gradually as necessary to a max. of 150 mg; usual maintenance dose 25 mg 3 times daily

PoM **Evadyne**® (Wyeth)

Tablets, both f/c, butriptyline (as hydrochloride) 25 mg (orange), net price 20 = 77p; 50 mg (pink), 20 = £1.35. Label: 2

CLOMIPRAMINE HYDROCHLORIDE

Indications: depressive illness, adjunctive treatment of phobic and obsessional states; cataplexy associated with narcolepsy

Cautions; Contra-indications; Side-effects: see under Amitriptyline Hydrochloride. Postural hypotension may occur on intravenous infusion

Dose: *by mouth*, initially 10 mg daily, increased gradually as necessary to 30–150 mg (elderly 75 mg) in divided doses *or* as a single dose at bedtime; usual maintenance 30–50 mg daily

By intramuscular injection, up to 150 mg daily

By intravenous infusion, initially to assess tolerance, 25–50 mg, then usually about 100 mg daily for 7–10 days

PoM **Anafranil**® (Geigy)

Capsules, clomipramine hydrochloride 10 mg (yellow/caramel), net price 20 = 66p; 25 mg (orange/caramel), 20 = £1.29; 50 mg (blue/caramel), 20 = £2.46. Label: 2

Syrup, orange, clomipramine hydrochloride 25 mg/5 mL. Diluent purified water, freshly boiled and cooled; for dilutions below 15 mg/5 mL equal parts of syrup and tragacanth mucilage (freshly prepared), life of diluted syrup 7 days. Net price 150-mL pack = £6.18. Label: 2

Injection, clomipramine hydrochloride 12.5 mg/mL. Net price 2-mL amp = 40p

PoM **Anafranil SR**® (Geigy)

Tablets, s/r, pink, f/c, clomipramine hydrochloride 75 mg. Net price 20 = £4.90. Label: 2, 25

DESIPRAMINE HYDROCHLORIDE

Indications: depressive illness

Cautions; Contra-indications; Side-effects: see under Amitriptyline Hydrochloride, but less sedating

Dose: 75 mg (elderly 25 mg) daily in divided doses *or* as a single dose at bedtime, increased as necessary to a max. of 200 mg

PoM **Pertofran**® (Ciba)

Tablets, pink, s/c, desipramine hydrochloride 25 mg. Net price 20 = 71p. Label: 2

DOTHIEPIN HYDROCHLORIDE

Indications: depressive illness, particularly where sedation is required

Cautions; Contra-indications; Side-effects: see under Amitriptyline Hydrochloride

Dose: initially 75 mg (elderly 50–75 mg) daily in divided doses *or* as a single dose at bedtime, increased gradually as necessary to 150 mg daily (elderly 75 mg); up to 225 mg daily in hospital patients

PoM **Prothiaden**® (Boots)

Capsules, red/brown, dothiepin hydrochloride 25 mg. Net price 20 = 96p. Label: 2

Tablets, red, s/c, dothiepin hydrochloride 75 mg. Net price 28 = £4.00. Label: 2

DOXEPIN

Indications: depressive illness, particularly where sedation is required

Cautions; Contra-indications; Side-effects: see under Amitriptyline Hydrochloride; avoid in breast-feeding (see Appendix 5)

Dose: initially 75 mg (elderly 10– 50 mg) daily in 3 divided doses, increased gradually to a max. of 300 mg daily in divided doses; range 30–300 mg daily; up to 100 mg may be given as a single dose at bedtime

PoM **Sinequan**® (Pfizer)

Capsules, doxepin (as hydrochloride) 10 mg (orange), net price 56-cap pack = £1.10; 25 mg (orange/blue), 28-cap pack = 79p; 50 mg (blue), 28-cap pack = £1.30; 75 mg (yellow/blue), 28-cap pack = £2.06. Label: 2

IMIPRAMINE HYDROCHLORIDE

Indications: depressive illness; nocturnal enuresis in children (see section 7.4.2)

Cautions; Contra-indications; Side-effects: see under Amitriptyline Hydrochloride, but less sedating

Dose: initially up to 75 mg daily in divided doses increased gradually to 150–200 mg (up to 300 mg in hospital patients); up to 150 mg may be given as a single dose at bedtime; usual maintenance 50–100 mg daily; elderly initially 10 mg daily, increased gradually to 30–50 mg daily

Nocturnal enuresis, CHILD 7 years 25 mg, 8–11 years 25–50 mg, over 11 years 50–75 mg at bedtime; max. period of treatment (including gradual withdrawal) not to exceed 3 months

PoM **Imipramine** (Non-proprietary)

Tablets, coated, imipramine hydrochloride 10 mg, net price 20 = 15p; 25 mg, 20 = 14p. Label: 2

PoM **Tofranil®** (Geigy)

Tablets, both red-brown, s/c, imipramine hydrochloride 10 mg, net price 20 = 33p; 25 mg, 20 = 63p. Label: 2

Syrup, imipramine hydrochloride 25 mg/5 mL. Diluent purified water, freshly boiled and cooled; for dilutions below 15 mg/5 mL equal parts of syrup and tragacanth mucilage (freshly prepared), life of diluted syrup 14 days. Net price 150-mL pack = £2.70. Label: 2

LOFEPRAMINE

Indications: depressive illness

Cautions; Contra-indications; Side-effects: see under Amitriptyline Hydrochloride, but less sedating; hepatic disorders reported; avoid in hepatic and severe renal impairment

Dose: 140–210 mg daily in divided doses

PoM **Gamanil®** (Merck)

Tablets, lacquer-coated, brown-violet, lofepramine 70 mg (as hydrochloride). Net price 56-tab pack = £9.97. Label: 2

NORTRIPTYLINE

Indications: depressive illness; nocturnal enuresis in children (see section 7.4.2)

Cautions; Contra-indications; Side-effects: see under Amitriptyline Hydrochloride but less sedating

Dose: initially 20–40 mg (elderly 30 mg) daily in single *or* divided doses, increased gradually as necessary to a max. of 100 mg daily; usual maintenance dose 30–75 mg daily

Nocturnal enuresis, CHILD 7 years 10 mg, 8–11 years 10–20 mg, over 11 years 25–35 mg, at night; max period of treatment (including gradual withdrawal) should not exceed 3 months

PoM **Allegron®** (Dista)

Tablets, nortriptyline (as hydrochloride) 10 mg, net price 20 = 67p; 25 mg (orange, scored), 20 = £1.36. Label: 2

PoM **Aventyl®** (Lilly)

Capsules, both yellow/white, nortriptyline (as hydrochloride) 10 mg, net price 20 = 67p; 25 mg, 20 = £1.36. Label: 2

PROTRIPTYLINE HYDROCHLORIDE

Indications: depressive illness, particularly with apathy and withdrawal

Cautions; Contra-indications; Side-effects: see under Amitriptyline Hydrochloride but less sedating; anxiety, agitation, tachycardia, and hypotension more common; rashes associated with photosensitisation (avoid direct sunlight); daily dose above 20 mg in elderly (increased risk of cardiovascular side-effects)

Dose: initially 10 mg 3–4 times daily (elderly 5 mg 3 times daily initially) if insomnia, last dose not after 4 p.m.; usual range 15–60 mg daily

PoM **Concordin®** (MSD)

Tablets, both f/c, protriptyline hydrochloride 5 mg (pink), net price 20 = 37p; 10 mg, 20 = 54p. Label: 2, 11

TRIMIPRAMINE

Indications: depressive illness, particularly where sedation is required

Cautions; Contra-indications; Side-effects: see under Amitriptyline Hydrochloride

Dose: 50–75 mg daily as a single dose 2 hours before bedtime *or* as 25 mg midday and 50 mg evening, increased as necessary to max. of 300 mg daily; usual maintenance dose 75–150 mg daily

ELDERLY 10–25 mg 3 times daily initially, half adult maintenance dose may be sufficient

PoM **Surmontil®** (Rorer)

Capsules, green/white, trimipramine 50 mg (as maleate). Net price 28-tab pack = £4.63. Label: 2

Tablets, trimipramine (as maleate) 10 mg, net price 50 = £2.49; 25 mg, 50 = £4.12. Label: 2

RELATED ANTIDEPRESSANTS

IPRINDOLE

Indications: depressive illness

Cautions; Contra-indications; Side-effects: see under Amitriptyline Hydrochloride, but less sedating. Caution in liver disease; jaundice, although rare, may develop, usually in the first 14 days

Dose: initially 15–30 mg 3 times daily, increased gradually to max. of 60 mg 3 times daily; usual maintenance 30 mg 3 times daily

PoM **Prondol®** (Wyeth)

Tablets, both yellow, iprindole (as hydrochloride), 15 mg, net price 20 = 42p; 30 mg, 20 = 82p. Label: 2

MAPROTILINE HYDROCHLORIDE

Indications: depressive illness, particularly where sedation is required

Cautions; Contra-indications; Side-effects: see under Amitriptyline Hydrochloride, antimuscarinic effects may occur less frequently but rashes common and increased risk of convulsions at higher dosage

Dose: initially 25–75 mg (elderly 30 mg) daily in 3 divided doses *or* as a single dose at bedtime, increased gradually as necessary to a max. of 150 mg daily

PoM **Ludiomil®** (Ciba)

Tablets, all f/c, maprotiline hydrochloride 10 mg (pale orange), net price 20 = 60p; 25 mg (greyish-red), 20 = £1.10; 50 mg (light orange), 20 = £2.15; 75 mg (brownish-orange), 28-tab pack = £4.40. Label: 2

Additives: include gluten

MIANSERIN HYDROCHLORIDE

Indications: depressive illness, particularly where sedation is required

Cautions; Contra-indications; Side-effects: see under Amitriptyline; leucopenia, agranulocytosis and aplastic anaemia (particularly in the elderly); jaundice; arthritis, arthralgia; influenza-like syndrome may occur; **blood counts needed, p. 143**

Fewer and milder antimuscarinic and cardiovascular effects; **interactions:** Appendix 1 (mianserin)

Dose: initially 30–40 mg (elderly 30 mg) daily in divided doses *or* as a single dose at bedtime, increased gradually as necessary; usual dose range 30–90 mg

PoM **Mianserin** (Non-proprietary)

Tablets, mianserin hydrochloride 10 mg, net price 20 = £1.33; 20 mg, 20 = £2.68; 30 mg, 20 = £4.00. Label: 2, 25

PoM **Bolvidon®** (Organon)

Tablets, all f/c, mianserin hydrochloride 10 mg, net price 90-tab pack = £5.30; 20 mg, 56-tab pack = £6.59; 30 mg, 28-tab pack = £4.94. Label: 2, 25

PoM **Norval®** (Bencard)

Tablets, all orange, f/c, mianserin hydrochloride 10 mg, net price 84-tab pack = £5.50; 20 mg, 28-tab pack = £3.66; 30 mg, 28-tab pack = £5.50. Label: 2, 25

TRAZODONE HYDROCHLORIDE

Indications: depressive illness, particularly where sedation is required

Cautions; Contra-indications; Side-effects: see under Amitriptyline Hydrochloride but fewer antimuscarinic and cardiovascular effects; rarely priapism; **interactions:** Appendix 1 (trazodone)

Dose: initially 150 mg (elderly 100 mg) daily in divided doses after food *or* as a single dose at bedtime; may be increased to 300 mg daily; hospital patients up to max. 600 mg daily in divided doses

PoM **Molipaxin®** (Roussel)

Capsules, trazodone hydrochloride 50 mg (violet/green), net price 84-cap pack = £15.04; 100 mg (violet/fawn), 56-cap pack = £17.72. Label: 2, 21

Tablets, pink, f/c, trazodone hydrochloride 150 mg. Net price 28-tab pack = £10.10. Label: 2, 21

Liquid, sugar-free, trazodone hydrochloride 50 mg/5 mL. Net price 150-mL pack = £6.73. Label: 2, 21

VILOXAZINE HYDROCHLORIDE

Indications: depressive illness

Cautions; Contra-indications; Side-effects: see under Amitriptyline Hydrochloride, but less sedating and antimuscarinic and cardiovascular side-effects are fewer and milder; nausea and headache may occur; **interactions:** Appendix 1 (viloxazine)

Dose: 300 mg daily (preferably as 200 mg in the morning and 100 mg at midday), increased gradually as necessary; max. 400 mg daily; last dose not later than 6 p.m.

ELDERLY 100 mg daily initially, half adult maintenance dose may be sufficient

PoM **Vivalan®** (ICI)

Tablets, f/c, viloxazine 50 mg (as hydrochloride). Net price 20 = £1.27. Label: 2

4.3.2 Monoamine-oxidase inhibitors (MAOIs)

Monoamine-oxidase inhibitors are used much less frequently than tricyclic and related antidepressants because of the dangers of dietary and drug interactions and the fact that it is easier to prescribe MAOIs when tricyclic antidepressants have been unsuccessful than vice versa. **Tranylcypromine**, is the most **hazardous** of the MAOIs because of its stimulant action. The drugs of choice are **phenelzine** or **isocarboxazid** which are less stimulant and therefore safer.

Phobic patients and depressed patients with atypical, hypochondriacal, or hysterical features are said to respond best to MAOIs. However, MAOIs should be tried in any patients who are refractory to treatment with other antidepressants as there is occasionally a dramatic response. Response to treatment may be delayed for 3 weeks or more and may take an additional 1 or 2 weeks to become maximal.

WITHDRAWAL. See section 4.3.1

INTERACTIONS. MAOIs inhibit monoamine oxidase, thereby causing an accumulation of amine neurotransmitters. The metabolism of some amine drugs such as sympathomimetics is also inhibited and their pressor action may be potentiated; the pressor effect of the tyramine (in some foods) may also be dangerously potentiated.

Sympathomimetics are present in many proprietary cough mixtures and decongestant nasal drops. See Appendix 1 (MAOIs) and Treatment Card. These interactions may cause a dangerous rise in blood pressure. An early warning symptom may be a throbbing headache. The danger of interaction persists for up to 14 days after treatment with MAOIs is discontinued. Treatment cards which list the necessary precautions are distributed by the Royal Pharmaceutical Society and given to patients at pharmacies etc.

Tricyclic and related antidepressants should **not** be given to patients for 14 days after treatment with MAOIs has been discontinued. Some psychiatrists use selected tricyclics in conjunction with MAOIs but this is hazardous, indeed potentially lethal, except in experienced hands and there is no evidence that the combination is more effective than when either constituent is used alone. The combination of tranylcypromine with clomipramine is particularly **dangerous**.

For other interactions with monoamine-oxidase inhibitors including those with opioid analgesics (notably pethidine), see Appendix 1 (MAOIs).

Other MAOIs. Discontinue first MAOI for at least a week before starting another.

TREATMENT CARD

Carry this card with you at all times. Show it to any doctor who may treat you other than the doctor who prescribed this medicine, and to your dentist if you require dental treatment.

INSTRUCTIONS TO PATIENTS

Please read carefully

While taking this medicine and for 14 days after your treatment finishes you must observe the following simple instructions:-

1 Do not eat CHEESE, PICKLED HERRING OR BROAD BEAN PODS.

2 Do not eat or drink BOVRIL, OXO, MARMITE or ANY SIMILAR MEAT OR YEAST EXTRACT.

3 Eat only FRESH foods and avoid food that you suspect could be stale or 'going off'. This is especially important with meat, fish, poultry or offal. Avoid game.

4 Do not take any other MEDICINES (including tablets, capsules, nose drops, inhalations or suppositories) whether purchased by you or previously prescribed by your doctor, without first consulting your doctor or your pharmacist.

NB *Treatment for coughs and colds, pain relievers, tonics and laxatives are medicines.*

5 Avoid alcoholic drinks and de-alcoholised (low alcohol)drinks.

Keep a careful note of any food or drink that disagrees with you, avoid it and tell your doctor.

Report any unusual or severe symptoms to your doctor and follow any other advice given by him.

M.A.O.I. Prepared by The Pharmaceutical Society and the British Medical Association on behalf of the Health Departments of the United Kingdom.

Printed in the UK for HMSO 8217411/150M/9.89/45292
Revised Sep. 1989

PHENELZINE

Indications: depressive illness

Cautions: diabetes mellitus, cardiovascular disease, epilepsy, and blood disorders; avoid abrupt discontinuation of treatment; severe hypertensive reactions to certain drugs and foods (see Treatment Card); avoid in elderly and agitated patients; pregnancy and breast-feeding; **interactions:** Appendix 1 (MAOIs)

DRIVING. Drowsiness may affect performance of skilled tasks (e.g. driving)

Contra-indications: hepatic, cerebrovascular disease, phaeochromocytoma, porphyria, children

Side-effects: Adverse effects commonly associated with phenelzine and other MAOIs include postural hypotension and dizziness; other common side-effects include drowsiness, headache, weakness and fatigue, dryness of mouth, constipation and other gastro-intestinal disturbances, and oedema; agitation and tremors, nervousness, blurred vision, difficulty in micturition, sweating, convulsions, rashes, leucopenia, sexual disturbances, and weight gain with inappropriate appetite may also occur; psychotic episodes with hypomanic behaviour, confusion, and hallucinations, may be induced in susceptible persons; jaundice has been reported and, on rare occasions, fatal progressive hepatocellular necrosis; peripheral neuropathy may be due to pyridoxine deficiency

Dose: 15 mg 3 times daily, increased if necessary to 4 times daily after 2 weeks (hospital patients, max. 30 mg 3 times daily), then reduced gradually to lowest possible maintenance dose (15 mg on alternate days may be adequate)

PoM **Nardil**® (P-D)

Tablets, orange, f/c, phenelzine 15 mg (as sulphate). Net price 20 = £1.33. Label: 3, 10 MAOI card

ISOCARBOXAZID

Indications: depressive illness

Cautions; Contra-indications; Side-effects: see under Phenelzine

Dose: initially up to 30 mg daily in single or divided doses increased after 4 weeks if necessary to max. 60 mg daily for up to 6 weeks under close supervision only; then reduced to usual maintenance dose 10–20 mg daily (but up to 40 mg daily may be required)

PoM **Marplan**® (Roche)

Tablets, pink, scored, isocarboxazid 10 mg. Net price 50 = 98p. Label: 3, 10 MAOI card

TRANYLCYPROMINE

Indications: depressive illness

Cautions; Contra-indications: see under Phenelzine; also contra-indicated in hyperthyroidism

Side-effects: see under Phenelzine; insomnia if given in evening; hypertensive crises with throbbing headache requiring discontinuation of treatment occur more frequently than with

Prices are **net**, see p. 1

other MAOIs; liver damage occurs less frequently than with phenelzine
Dose: initially 10 mg twice daily not later than 3 p.m., increasing the second daily dose to 20 mg after 1 week if necessary; doses above 30 mg daily under close supervision only; usual maintenance dose 10 mg daily

PoM **Parnate®** (SK&F)
Tablets, red, s/c, tranylcypromine 10 mg (as sulphate). Net price 20 = 91p. Label: 3, 10 MAOI card

4.3.3 Compound antidepressant preparations

The use of preparations listed below is **not** recommended because the dosage of the individual components should be adjusted separately. Whereas antidepressants are given continuously over several months, anxiolytics are prescribed on a short-term basis.

NHS PoM **Limbitrol 5®** (Roche)
Capsules, pink/green, amitriptyline 12.5 mg (as hydrochloride), chlordiazepoxide 5 mg. Net price 20 = £1.06. Label: 2

NHS PoM **Limbitrol 10®** (Roche)
Capsules, pink/dark green, amitriptyline 25 mg (as hydrochloride), chlordiazepoxide 10 mg. Net price 20 = £1.55. Label: 2

PoM **Motipress®** (Squibb)
Tablets, yellow, s/c, fluphenazine hydrochloride 1.5 mg, nortriptyline 30 mg (as hydrochloride). Net price 28-tab pack = £2.90. Label: 2

PoM **Motival®** (Squibb)
Tablets, pink, s/c, fluphenazine hydrochloride 500 micrograms, nortriptyline 10 mg (as hydrochloride). Net price 20 = 70p. Label: 2

PoM **Parstelin®** (SK&F)
Tablets, green, s/c, tranylcypromine 10 mg (as sulphate), trifluoperazine 1 mg (as hydrochloride). Net price 20 = 93p. Label: 3, 10 MAOI card
Caution: contains MAOI

PoM **Triptafen®** (A&H)
Tablets, pink, s/c, amitriptyline hydrochloride 25 mg, perphenazine 2 mg. Net price 20 = 54p. Label: 2

PoM **Triptafen-M®** (A&H)
Tablets, pink, s/c, amitriptyline hydrochloride 10 mg, perphenazine 2 mg. Net price 20 = 48p. Label: 2

4.3.4 Other antidepressant drugs

Flupenthixol (Fluanxol®) has antidepressant properties, and low doses (1 to 3 mg daily) are given by mouth for this purpose. Its advantage over the tricyclic and related antidepressants is that, with the low doses employed, side-effects are fewer and overdosage less toxic.

Tryptophan appears to benefit some patients when given alone or as adjunctive therapy. Its antidepressant effect may take up to 4 weeks to develop. **Important:** the tryptophan products Optimax®, Optimax WV®, and Pacitron® have been withdrawn following evidence of an association with the eosinophilia-myalgia syndrome; they remain available on a named-patient basis for patients for whom no alternative treatment is suitable.

Fluvoxamine is a non-sedative antidepressant which selectively inhibits the re-uptake of serotonin (5-hydroxytryptamine, 5-HT). It has few antimuscarinic effects and low cardiotoxicity, but it has a high incidence of gastro-intestinal side-effects (nausea and vomiting) and may exacerbate agitation and insomnia. **Fluoxetine** is also a selective inhibitor of serotonin re-uptake.

CSM Warning.
Combination therapy with other antidepressants including MAOIs, lithium, or tryptophan, may enhance the serotonin-related effects of **fluvoxamine** or **fluoxetine**. While potentially beneficial in some selected cases, these combinations can increase severity of serotonin-related side-effects; in the most severe cases a life-threatening serotonin syndrome of hyperthermia, tremor, and convulsions may develop. Such combination therapy should be used with care.

FLUOXETINE HYDROCHLORIDE

Indications: see under Dose
Cautions: hepatic impairment, renal impairment (avoid if severe), epilepsy (avoid if poorly controlled), diabetes mellitus, pregnancy; long half-life (delayed response to dose change or cessation); do not give an MAOI until at least 5 weeks after discontinuing fluoxetine; rare reports of prolonged seizures with electroconvulsive therapy; **interactions:** Appendix 1 (fluoxetine)
DRIVING. May impair performance of skilled tasks (e.g. driving)
Contra-indications: breast-feeding
Side-effects: rash (discontinue treatment, may be associated with vasculitis, anaphylaxis, and pulmonary inflammation or fibrosis), nausea, vomiting, diarrhoea, anorexia with weight loss, headache, nervousness, insomnia, anxiety, tremor, dry mouth, dizziness, hypomania, drowsiness, convulsions, fever, sexual dysfunction, sweating; less common, raised serum transaminases, depressed leucocyte counts; other side-effects reported are vaginal bleeding on withdrawal, hyperprolactinaemia, thrombocytopenia, altered platelet function and abnormal bleeding, confusion, suicidal ideation and violent behaviour; rarely hyponatraemia
Dose: depressive illness, usually 20 mg daily
Bulimia nervosa, 60 mg daily
Max. for either indication 80 mg daily (elderly, 60 mg daily)

▼ PoM **Prozac®** (Dista)
Capsules, green/off-white, fluoxetine hydrochloride 20 mg. Net price 28-cap pack = £27.44. Counselling, driving

FLUPENTHIXOL

Indications: depressive illness (short-term use). For use in psychoses, see section 4.2.1
Cautions: cardiovascular disease (including cardiac disorders and cerebral arteriosclerosis), senile confusional states, parkinsonism, renal and hepatic disease; avoid in excitable and overactive patients; avoid in porphyria; **interactions**:

Appendix 1 (phenothiazines and other antipsychotics)

DRIVING. Drowsiness may affect performance of skilled tasks (e.g. driving); effects of alcohol enhanced

Side-effects: restlessness, insomnia; hypomania reported; rarely dizziness, tremor, visual disturbances, headache, hyperprolactinaemia, extrapyramidal symptoms

Dose: initially 1 mg (elderly 500 micrograms) in the morning, increased after 1 week to 2 mg (elderly 1 mg) if necessary. Max. 3 mg (elderly 2 mg) daily, doses above 2 mg (elderly 1 mg) being divided in 2 portions, second dose not after 4 p.m.

Discontinue if no response after 1 week at maximum dosage

COUNSELLING. Although drowsiness may occur, can also have an alerting effect so should not be taken in the evening

PoM **Depixol®** (psychoses), see section 4.2.1

PoM **Fluanxol®** (Lundbeck)

Tablets, both red, s/c, flupenthixol (as dihydrochloride) 500 micrograms, net price 20 = £1.18; 1 mg, 60-tab pack = £7.16. Label: 2, counselling, administration

FLUVOXAMINE MALEATE

Indications: depressive illness

Cautions: renal and hepatic impairment; pregnancy and breast-feeding; **interactions:** Appendix 1 (fluvoxamine)

DRIVING. May impair performance of skilled tasks (e.g. driving); effects of alcohol enhanced

Contra-indications: history of epilepsy

Side-effects: nausea and vomiting, diarrhoea, drowsiness, dizziness, agitation, anxiety, headache, tremor; bradycardia; convulsions

Dose: 100–200 mg daily (up to 100 mg as single dose in evening); max. 300 mg daily

▼ PoM **Faverin®** (Duphar)

Tablets, both yellow, e/c, fluvoxamine maleate 50 mg, net price 60-tab pack = £25.00; 100 mg, 30-tab pack = £25.00. Label: 5, 25, counselling, driving

4.4 Central nervous stimulants

Central nervous system stimulants have very few indications and in particular, should **not** be used to treat depression, obesity, senility, debility, or for relief of fatigue.

Caffeine is a weak stimulant present in tea and coffee. It is included in many analgesic preparations (section 4.7.1.1) but does not contribute to their analgesic or anti-inflammatory effect. Over-indulgence may lead to a state of anxiety.

The **amphetamines** have a limited field of usefulness and their use should be **discouraged** as they may cause dependence and psychotic states.

Patients with narcolepsy may derive benefit from treatment with amphetamines.

Amphetamines have been advocated for the management of hyperactive children; beneficial effects have been described. However, they must be used very selectively as they retard growth and the effect of long-term therapy has not been evaluated.

Amphetamines have **no place** in the management of **depression** or **obesity**.

Pemoline is a weak central nervous system stimulant that has been advocated for the management of hyperactive children. The same general reservations apply as for amphetamines and treatment should be carried out only under specialist supervision.

DEXAMPHETAMINE SULPHATE

Indications: narcolepsy, adjunct in the management of hyperkinesia in children (under specialist supervision)

Cautions: mild hypertension (contra-indicated if moderate or severe); monitor growth in children; avoid abrupt withdrawal; **interactions:** Appendix 1 (sympathomimetics)

Contra-indications: cardiovascular disease or moderate to severe hypertension (caution if mild), hyperexcitable states, hyperthyroidism, history of drug abuse, glaucoma, extrapyramidal disorders, pregnancy and breast-feeding, porphyria

DRIVING. May affect performance of skilled tasks (e.g. driving); effects of alcohol unpredictable

Side-effects: insomnia, restlessness, irritability, nervousness, night terrors, euphoria, tremor, dizziness, headache; dependence, tolerance, sometimes psychosis; anorexia, gastro-intestinal symptoms, growth retardation in children; dry mouth, sweating, tachycardia, palpitations, increased blood pressure; rarely cardiomyopathy reported with chronic use

Dose: narcolepsy, 10 mg (elderly, 5 mg) daily in divided doses increased by 10 mg (elderly, 5 mg) daily at intervals of 1 week to a max. of 60 mg daily

Hyperkinesia, CHILD over 6 years 5–10 mg in the morning, increased by 5 mg at intervals of 1 week to a max. of 40 mg daily

CD **Dexedrine®** (SK&F)

Tablets, scored, dexamphetamine sulphate 5 mg. Net price 20 = 15p. Counselling, driving

PEMOLINE

Indications: adjunct in the management of hyperkinesia in children (under specialist supervision)

Cautions; Contra-indications; Side-effects: see under Dexamphetamine Sulphate; chorea, tics, mania, depression, neutropenia, and liver enzyme abnormalities also reported

Dose: CHILD over 6 years, initially 20 mg every morning increased by increments of 20 mg at intervals of 1 week to 60 mg every morning, followed, if no improvement, by gradual increase to max. 120 mg every morning

PoM **Volital®** (LAB)

Tablets, scored, pemoline 20 mg. Net price 25-tab pack = 95p

STIMULANT WITH VITAMINS

Prolintane is contained in a preparation with vitamins; it is **not** recommended and is specifically **contra-indicated** in epilepsy and hyperthyroidism.

NHS PoM **Villescon**® (Boehringer Ingelheim)
Liquid, red, prolintane hydrochloride 2.5 mg/5 mL with vitamins B group and C. Net price 150-mL pack = 85p
Dose: 10 mL twice daily before 4 p.m. for 1–2 weeks but see notes above.

COCAINE

Cocaine is a drug of addiction which causes central nervous stimulation. Its clinical use is mainly as a topical local anaesthetic (see sections 11.7 and 15.2). It has been included in analgesic elixirs for the relief of pain in terminal care but this use is obsolete.

4.5 Appetite suppressants

4.5.1 Bulk-forming drugs
4.5.2 Centrally acting appetite suppressants

The development of obesity appears to be multifactorial. Aggravating factors may be depression or other psychosocial problems or drug treatment.

The main treatment of the obese patient is an appropriate diet, carefully explained to the patient, with support and encouragement from the doctor. Attendance at groups (for example 'weight-watchers') helps some individuals. Drugs can play only a limited role and should never be used as the sole element of treatment; their effects tend to be disappointing.

The use of diuretics is **not** appropriate for weight reduction.

4.5.1 Bulk-forming drugs

The most commonly used bulk-forming drug is **methylcellulose.** It is claimed to reduce intake by producing feelings of satiety but there is little evidence to support this claim.

METHYLCELLULOSE

Indications: obesity; other indications, see section 1.6.1
Cautions: maintain adequate fluid intake
Contra-indications: gastro-intestinal obstruction
Side-effects: flatulence, abdominal distension, intestinal obstruction
Dose: see under preparations

COUNSELLING. Preparations that swell in contact with liquid should always be carefully swallowed with water and should not be taken immediately before going to bed

Celevac® (Boehringer Ingelheim)
Tablets, pink, methylcellulose '450' 500 mg. Net price 112-tab pack = 93p. Counselling, see above
Dose: 3 tablets, chewed or crushed, with a tumblerful of liquid half an hour before food or when hungry

Nilstim® (De Witt)
Tablets, green, cellulose (microcrystalline) 220 mg, methylcellulose '2500' 400 mg. Net price 20 = 23p. Counselling, see above
Dose: 2 tablets, chewed or crushed, with a tumblerful of liquid 15 minutes before the 2 main meals or when hungry

STERCULIA

Indications; Cautions; Side-effects: see under Methylcellulose

Prefil® (Norgine)
Granules, brown, coated, sterculia 55%. Net price 200 g = £1.92. Label: 22, 27, counselling, administration
Dose: two 5-mL spoonfuls followed by a tumblerful of liquid ½–1 hour before food, reduced in patients accustomed to a low-residue diet

4.5.2 Centrally acting appetite suppressants

Centrally acting appetite suppressants are of no real value in the treatment of obesity since they do not improve the long-term outlook. They are sympathomimetics and most have a pronounced stimulant effect on the central nervous system.

Use of the amphetamine-like drugs **diethylpropion, mazindol,** and **phentermine** is **not** justified as any possible benefits are outweighed by the risks involved; abuse, particularly of diethylpropion, is an increasing problem.

Although **fenfluramine** is also related to amphetamine, in standard doses it has a sedative rather than a stimulant effect. Nevertheless, abuse has occurred and abrupt withdrawal may induce depression. It should preferably be avoided but may be considered for short-term adjunctive treatment in selected patients with severe obesity, given close support and supervision. It should **not** be given to patients with a past history of epilepsy, drug abuse or psychiatric illness and is **not recommended** for periods of treatment beyond 3 months. It should **not** be used for cosmetic reasons in mild to moderate obesity.

Dexfenfluramine is the dextro isomer of fenfluramine.

Thyroid hormones have no place in the treatment of obesity except in hypothyroid patients.

CHILDREN. These drugs should be avoided in children because of the possibility of growth suppression.

DEXFENFLURAMINE HYDROCHLORIDE

Indications: see notes above
Cautions; Contra-indications; Side-effects: see under Fenfluramine Hydrochloride; so far, no reports of schizophrenia-like reactions
Dose: 15 mg morning and evening, at mealtimes; max. period of treatment should not exceed 3 months

▼ PoM **Adifax**® (Servier)
Capsules, dexfenfluramine hydrochloride 15 mg, net price 60-cap pack = £8.29. Label: 2

DIETHYLPROPION HYDROCHLORIDE

Indications: see notes above

Cautions: cardiovascular disease (avoid if severe), peptic ulceration, depression; **interactions:** Appendix 1 (sympathomimetics)

DRIVING. May impair performance of skilled tasks (e.g. driving); effects of alcohol unpredictable

Contra-indications: glaucoma, hyperthyroidism, epilepsy, unstable personality, severe hypertension, history of drug abuse, porphyria; pregnancy (congenital malformations reported) and breast-feeding; avoid in children and elderly

Side-effects: headache, rashes, dependence; less common, insomnia, increased nervousness, psychosis, hallucinations, tachycardia, constipation; rarely, gynaecomastia

CD Apisate® (Wyeth)

Tablets, s/r, yellow, diethylpropion hydrochloride 75 mg, thiamine hydrochloride 5 mg, pyridoxine hydrochloride 2 mg, riboflavine 4 mg, nicotinamide 30 mg. Net price 20 = 52p. Label: 25, counselling, driving

Dose: 1 tablet mid-morning; to reduce risk of dependence max. continuous period of treatment should not exceed 4–8 weeks (followed by similar period without treatment)

CD Tenuate Dospan® (Merrell)

Tablets, s/r, scored, diethylpropion hydrochloride 75 mg. Net price 30-tab pack = 96p. Label: 25, counselling, driving

Dose: 1 tablet mid-morning; to reduce risk of dependence max. continuous period of treatment should not exceed 8 weeks (followed by similar period without treatment)

Note. Brand name prescriptions for Tenuate Dospan must also specify the word 'tablets' (i.e. 'Tenuate Dospan Tablets').

FENFLURAMINE HYDROCHLORIDE

Indications: see notes above

Cautions: dependence reported, depression on sudden withdrawal; elderly; **interactions:** Appendix 1 (sympathomimetics)

DRIVING. Drowsiness may affect performance of skilled tasks (e.g. driving); effects of alcohol enhanced

Contra-indications: history of depressive illness, drug or alcohol abuse; personality disorders; epilepsy; pregnancy and breast-feeding; avoid in children

Side-effects: diarrhoea and other gastro-intestinal disturbances; drowsiness, dizziness, and lethargy; also dry mouth, headache, nervousness, irritability, sleep disturbances, depression, visual disorders, hypotension, urinary frequency, impotence and loss of libido; rarely rashes, blood disorders, reversible pulmonary hypertension, schizophrenia-like reactions; neurotoxicity reported in *animal* studies

Dose: see below

PoM **Ponderax**® (Servier)

Pacaps® (= capsules s/r), clear/blue, enclosing white pellets, fenfluramine hydrochloride 60 mg. Net price 60-cap pack = £7.26. Label: 2, 25

Dose: 1 capsule daily; max. period of treatment should not exceed 3 months (see also notes above)

MAZINDOL

Indications: see notes above

Cautions; Contra-indications; Side-effects: see under Diethylpropion Hydrochloride. Avoid in peptic ulceration; **interactions:** Appendix 1 (sympathomimetics)

Dose: 2 mg after breakfast; to reduce the risk of dependence max. continuous period of treatment should not exceed 4–8 weeks (followed by similar period without treatment)

CD Teronac ® (Sandoz)

Tablets, scored, mazindol 2 mg. Net price 30-tab pack = £3.02. Counselling, driving

PHENTERMINE

Indications: see notes above

Cautions; Contra-indications; Side-effects: see under Diethylpropion Hydrochloride

Dose: 15–30 mg before breakfast; to reduce the risk of dependence max. continuous period of treatment should not exceed 4–8 weeks (followed by similar period without treatment)

CD Duromine ® (3M)

Capsules, both s/r, phentermine (as resin complex) 15 mg (green/grey), net price 30-cap pack = £1.31; 30 mg (maroon/grey), 30-cap pack = £1.72. Label: 25, counselling, driving

CD Ionamin ® (Lipha)

Capsules, both s/r, phentermine (as resin complex) 15 mg (grey/yellow), net price 20 = 99p; 30 mg (yellow), 20 = £1.26. Label: 25, counselling, driving

4.6 Drugs used in nausea and vertigo

Drug treatment of nausea and vertigo is discussed under the following headings:

- Vestibular disorders
- Vomiting of pregnancy
- Symptomatic relief of nausea from underlying disease

Anti-emetics should be prescribed only when the cause of vomiting is known, particularly in children, otherwise the symptomatic relief that they produce may delay diagnosis. Anti-emetics are unnecessary and sometimes harmful when the cause can be treated, e.g. as in diabetic keto-acidosis, or in excessive digoxin or antiepileptic dosage.

If antinauseant drug treatment is indicated the choice of drug depends on the aetiology of vomiting.

VESTIBULAR DISORDERS

Anti-emetics may be required in motion sickness, Ménière's disease, positional vertigo, labyrinthitis, and operative manipulation of the otovestibular apparatus. **Hyoscine** and the **antihistamines**, which act on the vomiting centre, are the drugs of choice. If possible they should be administered prophylactically at least 30 minutes before the emetic stimulus. Patients should be **warned** that these compounds may cause drowsiness, impair driving performance, and enhance the effects of alcohol and central nervous depressants.

MOTION SICKNESS. The most effective drug for the prevention of motion sickness is **hyoscine**. Adverse effects (drowsiness, blurred vision, dry mouth, urinary retention) are more frequent than with the **antihistamines** but are not generally prominent at the doses employed.

Antihistamines such as **cinnarizine, cyclizine, dimenhydrinate**, and **promethazine** are slightly less effective but generally better tolerated. There is no evidence that one antihistamine is superior to another but their duration of action and incidence of adverse effects (drowsiness and antimuscarinic effects) differ. If a sedative effect is desired promethazine and dimenhydrinate are useful, but generally a less sedating antihistamine like cyclizine or cinnarizine is preferred. To prevent motion sickness the first dose is usually taken half an hour (2 hours for cinnarizine) before the start of the journey. Metoclopramide and the phenothiazines (except promethazine), which act selectively on the chemoreceptor trigger zone, are ineffective in motion sickness.

OTHER LABYRINTHINE DISORDERS. Vertigo and nausea associated with Ménière's disease and middle-ear surgery disorders may be difficult to treat. **Hyoscine, antihistamines**, and **phenothiazines** (such as prochlorperazine and thiethylperazine) are effective in the prophylaxis and treatment of such conditions. **Betahistine** and **cinnarizine** have been promoted as specific treatment for Ménière's disease. In the acute attack **cyclizine, prochlorperazine**, or **thiethylperazine** may be given rectally or by intramuscular injection.

Treatment of vertigo in its chronic forms is seldom fully effective but antihistamines (such as dimenhydrinate) or phenothiazines (such as prochlorperazine) may help.

For advice to avoid the inappropriate prescribing of drugs (notably phenothiazines) for dizziness in the elderly, see Prescribing for the Elderly, p. 14.

VOMITING OF PREGNANCY

Nausea in the first trimester of pregnancy does **not** require drug therapy. On rare occasions if vomiting is severe, an antihistamine or a phenothiazine (promethazine or thiethylperazine) may be required. If symptoms have not settled in 24 to 48 hours then a specialist opinion should be sought.

SYMPTOMATIC RELIEF OF NAUSEA FROM UNDERLYING DISEASE

The **phenothiazines** are dopamine antagonists and act centrally by blocking the chemoreceptor trigger zone. In low doses they are the drugs of choice for the prophylaxis and treatment of nausea and vomiting associated with uraemia, diffuse neoplastic disease, radiation sickness, and the emesis caused by drugs such as opioid analgesics, general anaesthetics, and cytotoxic drugs. Rectal or parenteral administration is required if the vomiting has already started. **Prochlorperazine, perphenazine, trifluoperazine**, and **thiethylperazine** are less sedating than chlorpromazine but severe dystonic reactions sometimes occur, especially in children.

Metoclopramide is an effective anti-emetic with a spectrum of activity closely resembling that of the phenothiazines but it has a peripheral action on the gut in addition to its central effect and therefore may be superior to the phenothiazines in the emesis associated with gastroduodenal, hepatic, and biliary disease. The high-dose preparation is of value in the prevention of nausea and vomiting associated with cytotoxic drug therapy. Acute dystonic reactions may occur, particularly with children and young women, but they are less frequent than with phenothiazines.

Domperidone is used for the relief of nausea and vomiting, especially when associated with cytotoxic drug therapy. It has the advantage over metoclopramide and the phenothiazines of being less likely to cause central effects such as sedation and dystonic reactions because it does not readily cross the blood-brain barrier. It may be given for the treatment of levodopa- and bromocriptine-induced vomiting in parkinsonism (section 4.9.1). Domperidone acts at the chemoreceptor trigger zone and so is unlikely to be effective in motion sickness and other vestibular disorders.

Antihistamines are active in most of these conditions, but are not usually drugs of choice.

Nabilone is a synthetic cannabinoid with anti-emetic properties, reported to be superior to prochlorperazine. It is beneficial in the relief of nausea and vomiting associated with cytotoxic drug therapy. Side-effects (more frequent than with prochlorperazine) occur in about half of patients given standard doses.

Ondansetron may have a valuable role in the management of nausea and vomiting in patients receiving cytotoxics who are unable to tolerate, or whose nausea and vomiting is not controlled by, less expensive drugs.

BETAHISTINE HYDROCHLORIDE

Indications: vertigo and hearing disturbances in Ménière's disease
Cautions: asthma; **interactions:** Appendix 1 (betahistine)
Contra-indications: phaeochromocytoma
Side-effects: nausea; rarely headache, rashes
Dose: initially 16 mg 3 times daily, preferably with food; maintenance 24–48 mg daily

PoM **Serc®** (Duphar)
Tablets, scored, betahistine hydrochloride 8 mg, net price 20 = £2.15; 16 mg (Serc®-16), 84-tab pack = £18.03. Label: 21

CHLORPROMAZINE HYDROCHLORIDE

Indications: nausea and vomiting of terminal illness (where other drugs have failed or are not available); other indications, see sections 4.2.1, 15.1.4.2

Cautions; Contra-indications; Side-effects: see section 4.2.1

Dose: by mouth, 10–25 mg every 4–6 hours

By deep intramuscular injection 25 mg initially then 25–50 mg every 3–4 hours until vomiting stops

By rectum in suppositories, chlorpromazine 100 mg every 6–8 hours

Preparations

Section 4.2.1

CINNARIZINE

Indications: vestibular disorders, such as vertigo, tinnitus, nausea, and vomiting in Ménière's disease; motion sickness; vascular disease, see section 2.6.3

Cautions; Side-effects: see under Cyclizine; also allergic skin reactions and fatigue; caution in hypotension (high doses); rarely, extrapyramidal symptoms in elderly on prolonged therapy; avoid in porphyria

Dose: vestibular disorders, 30 mg 3 times daily; CHILD 5–12 years half adult dose

Motion sickness, 30 mg 2 hours before travel then 15 mg every 8 hours during journey if necessary; CHILD 5–12 years half adult dose

Cinnarizine (Non-proprietary)

Tablets, cinnarizine 15 mg, net price 20 = £1.10. Label: 2

Stugeron® (Janssen)

Tablets, scored, cinnarizine 15 mg. Net price 20 = 98p. Label: 2

Note. A proprietary brand of cinnarizine 15 mg tablets (Marzine RF®) is on sale to the public for travel sickness

Stugeron Forte®: see section 2.6.3

CYCLIZINE

Indications: nausea, vomiting, vertigo, motion sickness, labyrinthine disorders

Cautions; Side-effects: drowsiness, occasional dry mouth and blurred vision; see also section 3.4.1 (Disadvantages of Antihistamines); cyclizine may aggravate severe heart failure and counteract the haemodynamic benefits of opioids; **interactions:** Appendix 1 (antihistamines)

DRIVING. Drowsiness may affect performance of skilled tasks (e.g. driving); effects of alcohol enhanced

Dose: by mouth, cyclizine hydrochloride 50 mg 3 times daily; CHILD 6–12 years 25 mg 3 times daily

By intramuscular or intravenous injection, cyclizine lactate 50 mg 3 times daily

Valoid® (Calmic)

Tablets, scored, cyclizine hydrochloride 50 mg. Net price 20 = 86p. Label: 2

PoM *Injection*, cyclizine lactate 50 mg/mL. Net price 1-mL amp = 49p

DIMENHYDRINATE

Indications: nausea, vomiting, vertigo, motion sickness, labyrinthine disorders

Cautions; Side-effects: see under Cyclizine; avoid in porphyria

Dose: 50–100 mg 2–3 times daily; CHILD 1–6 years 12.5–25 mg, 7–12 years 25–50 mg 2–3 times daily

Motion sickness, first dose 30 minutes before journey

Dramamine® (Searle)

Tablets, scored, dimenhydrinate 50 mg. Net price 20 = 93p. Label: 2

DOMPERIDONE

Indications: see under Dose

Cautions: renal impairment; pregnancy and breast-feeding; not recommended for chronic administration; **interactions:** Appendix 1 (domperidone)

Side-effects: raised prolactin concentrations (possible galactorrhoea and gynaecomastia); acute dystonic reactions reported

Dose: by mouth, acute nausea and vomiting, (including nausea and vomiting induced by levodopa and bromocriptine), 10–20 mg every 4–8 hours, max. period of treatment 3 months; CHILD, nausea and vomiting following cytotoxic therapy or radiotherapy only, 200–400 micrograms/kg

By rectum, 30–60 mg every 4–8 hours; CHILD, 2–12 years 30–120 mg daily according to bodyweight (approximately 4 mg/kg)

PoM **Motilium®** (Sterling-Winthrop)

Tablets, f/c, domperidone 10 mg (as maleate). Net price 30-tab pack = £2.45; 100-tab pack = £8.17

Suspension, sugar-free, domperidone 5 mg/5 mL. Net price 200-mL pack = £1.80

Suppositories, domperidone 30 mg. Net price 10 = £2.64

DROPERIDOL

Section 4.2.1

HALOPERIDOL

Section 4.2.1

HYOSCINE HYDROBROMIDE

(Scopolamine)

Indications: nausea, vomiting, vertigo, labyrinthine disorders, motion sickness; pre-medication, see section 15.1.3

Cautions: elderly, urinary retention, cardiovascular disease, paralytic ileus, pyloric stenosis; pregnancy and breast-feeding; **interactions:** Appendix 1 (antimuscarinics)

DRIVING. Drowsiness may affect performance of skilled tasks (e.g. driving): effects of alcohol enhanced

Contra-indications: glaucoma
Side-effects: drowsiness, dry mouth, dizziness, blurred vision, difficulty with micturition
Dose: motion sickness, *by mouth*, 300 micrograms 30 minutes before start of journey followed by 300 micrograms every 6 hours if required; max. 3 doses in 24 hours; CHILD 4–10 years 75–150 micrograms, over 10 years 150–300 micrograms
By subcutaneous or intramuscular injection, 200 micrograms

PoM **Hyoscine** (Non-proprietary)
Tablets, hyoscine hydrobromide 300 micrograms, net price 20 = 23p; 600 micrograms, 20 = 41p. Label: 2
Injection, hyoscine hydrobromide 400 micrograms/mL, net price 1-mL amp = £1.11; 600 micrograms/mL, 1-mL amp = 90p

PoM **Scopoderm TTS®** (Ciba)
Dressing, self-adhesive, pink, releasing hyoscine approx. 500 micrograms/72 hours when in contact with skin. Net price 2 = £2.84. Label: 2, counselling, see below
Administration: motion sickness prevention, apply 1 dressing to hairless area of skin behind ear 5–6 hours before journey; replace if necessary after 72 hours, siting replacement dressing behind other ear
COUNSELLING. Explain accompanying instructions to patient and in particular emphasise advice to wash hands after handling and to wash application site after removing, and to use one at a time

METHOTRIMEPRAZINE
Section 4.2.1

METOCLOPRAMIDE HYDROCHLORIDE
Indications: adults, nausea and vomiting, particularly in gastro-intestinal disorders and treatment with cytotoxics or radiotherapy; gastro-intestinal—section 1.2; migraine—section 4.7.4.1

PATIENTS UNDER 20 YEARS. Use restricted to severe intractable vomiting of known cause, vomiting of radiotherapy and cytotoxics, aid to gastro-intestinal intubation, pre-medication

Cautions: hepatic and renal impairment; elderly, young adults, and children (measure dose accurately, preferably with a pipette); may mask underlying disorders such as cerebral irritation; avoid for 3–4 days following gastro-intestinal surgery, may cause acute hypertensive response in phaeochromocytoma; pregnancy and breast-feeding; avoid in porphyria; **interactions:** Appendix 1 (metoclopramide)
Side-effects: extrapyramidal effects (especially in children/young adults), hyperprolactinaemia, occasionally tardive dyskinesia on prolonged administration; also reported, drowsiness, restlessness, diarrhoea
Dose: *by mouth, or by intramuscular or intravenous injection*, 10 mg (5 mg in young adults 15–19 years under 60 kg) 3 times daily; CHILD up to 1 year (up to 10 kg) 1 mg twice daily, 1–3 years (10–14 kg) 1 mg 2–3 times daily, 3–5 years (15–19 kg) 2 mg 2–3 times daily, 5–9 years (20–29 kg) 2.5 mg 3 times daily, 9–14 years (30 kg and over) 5 mg 3 times daily
Note. Daily dose of metoclopramide should not normally exceed 500 micrograms/kg, particularly for children and young adults (restricted use, see above)
For radiological examinations, as a single dose *by intramuscular or intravenous injection* 5–10 minutes before examination, 10–20 mg (10 mg in young adults 15–19 years); CHILD under 3 years 1 mg, 3–5 years 2 mg, 5–9 years 2.5 mg, 9–14 years 5 mg
By continuous intravenous infusion (preferred method), initially (before starting chemotherapy), 2–4 mg/kg over 15–30 minutes, then 3–5 mg/kg over 8–12 hours; max. in 24 hours, 10 mg/kg
By intermittent intravenous infusion, initially (before starting chemotherapy), up to 2 mg/kg over at least 15 minutes then up to 2 mg/kg over at least 15 minutes every 2 hours; max. in 24 hours, 10 mg/kg

PoM **Metoclopramide** (Non-proprietary)
Tablets, metoclopramide hydrochloride 10 mg, net price 20 = 45p
Injection, metoclopramide hydrochloride 5 mg/mL, net price 2-mL amp = 24p

PoM **Maxolon®** (Beecham)
Tablets, scored, metoclopramide hydrochloride 10 mg. Net price 21-tab pack = £1.91
Syrup, yellow, sugar-free, metoclopramide hydrochloride 5 mg/5 mL. Diluent purified water, freshly boiled and cooled, life of diluted syrup 14 days. Net price 200-mL pack = £3.03
Paediatric liquid, yellow, sugar-free, metoclopramide hydrochloride 1 mg/mL. Diluent as above. Net price 15-mL pack with pipette = £1.37. Counselling, use of pipette
Injection, metoclopramide hydrochloride 5 mg/mL. Net price 2-mL amp = 24p

PoM **Maxolon High Dose®** (Beecham)
Injection, metoclopramide hydrochloride 5 mg/mL. Net price 20-mL amp = £2.43.
For dilution and use as an intravenous infusion in nausea and vomiting associated with cytotoxic chemotherapy only

PoM **Metox®** (Mercury)
Tablets, scored, metoclopramide hydrochloride 10 mg. Net price 20 = £1.71

PoM **Metramid®** (Nicholas)
Tablets, scored, metoclopramide hydrochloride 10 mg. Net price 20 = £1.03

PoM **Parmid®** (Lagap)
Tablets, scored, metoclopramide hydrochloride 10 mg. Net price 20 = 45p
Syrup, metoclopramide hydrochloride 5 mg/5 mL. Net price 100-mL pack = £1.05

PoM **Primperan®** (Berk)
Tablets, scored, metoclopramide hydrochloride 10 mg. Net price 20 = 97p
Syrup, lime, sugar-free, metoclopramide hydrochloride 5 mg/5 mL. Diluent syrup, life of diluted syrup 14 days. Net price 100-mL pack = £1.05

Injection, metoclopramide hydrochloride 5 mg/mL. Net price 2-mL amp = 17p

Sustained-release preparations
Note. All unsuitable for patients under 20 years.

PoM **Gastrobid Continus®** (Napp)
Tablets, s/r, metoclopramide hydrochloride 15 mg. Net price 56-tab pack = £8.06. Label: 25
Dose: patients over 20 years, 1 tablet twice daily

PoM **Gastromax®** (Farmitalia Carlo Erba)
Capsules, s/r, orange/yellow, enclosing white to light beige pellets, metoclopramide hydrochloride 30 mg. Net price 28-tab pack = £11.85. Label: 22, 25
Dose: patients over 20 years, 1 capsule daily

PoM **Maxolon SR®** (Beecham)
Capsules, s/r, clear, enclosing white granules, metoclopramide hydrochloride 15 mg. Net price 56-tab pack = £8.50. Label: 25
Dose: patients over 20 years, 1 capsule twice daily

Antimigraine preparations, section 4.7.4.1

NABILONE

Indications: nausea and vomiting caused by cytotoxic drugs
Cautions: severe hepatic impairment; history of psychosis
DRIVING. Drowsiness may affect performance of skilled tasks (e.g. driving); effects of alcohol enhanced
Side-effects: drowsiness, postural hypotension, tachycardia, dry mouth, decreased appetite, abdominal cramps; also confusion, disorientation, euphoria, dizziness, hallucinations, psychosis, depression, headache, blurred vision, tremors, decreased concentration and co-ordination
Dose: 1–2 mg twice daily throughout each cycle of cytotoxic therapy and, if necessary, for 24 hours after the last dose of each cycle; max. 6 mg daily. The first dose should be taken the night before initiation of cytotoxic treatment, and the second dose 1–3 hours before the first dose of cytotoxic drug

PoM **Cesamet®** (Lilly)
Capsules, blue/white, nabilone 1 mg. Net price 20 = £42.35 (hosp. only). Label: 2

ONDANSETRON

Indications: nausea and vomiting induced by cytotoxic chemotherapy or by radiotherapy
Cautions: pregnancy and breast-feeding
Side-effects: constipation; headache, sensation of warmth or flushing in head and over stomach; occasional alterations in liver enzymes; hypersensitivity reactions reported
Dose: moderately emetogenic chemotherapy, *by mouth*, 8 mg 1–2 hours before chemotherapy *or, by slow intravenous injection or by intravenous infusion over 15 minutes*, 8 mg immediately before chemotherapy, *then* 8 mg *by mouth* every 8 hours for up to 5 days
Severely emetogenic chemotherapy, *by slow intravenous injection or by intravenous infusion over 15 minutes*, 8 mg immediately before chemotherapy, followed by 8 mg at intervals of 4 hours for 2 further doses *or* by 1 mg/hour *by continuous intravenous infusion* for up to 24 hours *then* 8 mg *by mouth* every 8 hours for up to 5 days
Radiotherapy-induced, *by mouth*, 8 mg every 8 hours, first dose 1–2 hours before starting radiotherapy
ELDERLY as for younger adults
CHILD over 4 years, *by slow intravenous injection or by intravenous infusion over 15 minutes*, 5 mg/m² then, 4 mg *by mouth* every 8 hours for up to 5 days

▼ PoM **Zofran®** (Glaxo)
Tablets, both yellow, f/c, ondansetron (as hydrochloride) 4 mg, net price 30-tab pack = £187.50; 8 mg, 30-tab pack = £270.00
Injection, ondansetron (as hydrochloride) 2 mg/mL, net price 2-mL amp = £10.50; 4-mL amp = £15.00

PERPHENAZINE

Indications: severe nausea, vomiting (see notes above); other indications, section 4.2.1
Cautions; Contra-indications; Side-effects: see section 4.2.1; extrapyramidal symptoms may occur, particularly in children, elderly, and debilitated; avoid in children under 14 years
Dose: 4 mg 3 times daily, adjusted according to response; max. 24 mg daily (chemotherapy-induced); ELDERLY quarter to half adult dose

Preparations
Section 4.2.1

PROCHLORPERAZINE

Indications: severe nausea, vomiting, vertigo, labyrinthine disorders (see notes above); other indications, section 4.2.1
Cautions; Contra-indications: see under Chlorpromazine Hydrochloride (section 4.2.1). Oral route only for children (avoid if less than 10 kg); elderly (see notes above)
Side-effects: see under Chlorpromazine Hydrochloride; extrapyramidal symptoms may occur, particularly in children, elderly, and debilitated
Dose: *by mouth*, nausea and vomiting, prochlorperazine maleate or mesylate, acute attack, 20 mg initially then 10 mg after 2 hours; prevention 5–10 mg 2–3 times daily; CHILD (over 10 kg only) 250 micrograms/kg 2–3 times daily
Labyrinthine disorders, 5 mg 3 times daily, gradually increased if necessary to 30 mg daily in divided doses, then reduced after several weeks to 5–10 mg daily
By deep intramuscular injection, nausea and vomiting, 12.5 mg when required followed if

necessary after 6 hours by an oral dose, as above; CHILD not recommended
By rectum in suppositories, nausea and vomiting, 25 mg followed if necessary after 6 hours by oral dose, as above; CHILD not recommended

PoM **Prochlorperazine** (Non-proprietary)
Tablets, prochlorperazine maleate 5 mg, net price 20 = 71p. Label: 2

PoM **Stemetil®** (Rhône-Poulenc Rorer)
Tablets, prochlorperazine maleate 5 mg (off-white), net price 84-tab pack = £2.95; 25 mg (scored), 56-tab pack = £5.19. Label: 2
Syrup, straw-coloured, prochlorperazine mesylate 5 mg/5 mL. Diluent syrup, life of diluted syrup 14 days. Net price 100-mL pack = £1.66. Label: 2
Eff sachets, granules, effervescent, sugar-free, prochlorperazine mesylate 5 mg/sachet. Net price 21-sachet pack = £3.09. Label: 2, 13
Injection, prochlorperazine mesylate 12.5 mg/mL. Net price 1-mL amp = 32p; 2-mL amp = 41p
Suppositories, prochlorperazine maleate (as prochlorperazine), 5 mg, net price 10 = £4.16; 25 mg, 10 = £5.47. Label: 2

PoM **Vertigon®** (SK&F)
Spansule® (= capsules s/r), both clear/purple, enclosing yellowish-green and white pellets, prochlorperazine (as maleate), 10 mg, net price 60-cap pack = £2.24; 15 mg, 60-cap pack = £2.74. Label: 2, 25
Dose: initially 10–15 mg once or twice daily (elderly 10 mg daily). Maintenance 10–15 mg daily

Buccal preparation

PoM **Buccastem®** (R&C)
Tablets (buccal), pale yellow, prochlorperazine maleate 3 mg. Net price 4 × 15-tab pack = £6.90. Label: 2, counselling, administration, see under Dose below
Dose: 1–2 tablets twice daily; tablets are placed high between upper lip and gum and left to dissolve

PROMETHAZINE HYDROCHLORIDE

Indications: nausea, vomiting, vertigo, labyrinthine disorders, motion sickness; other indications, see sections 3.4.1, 4.1.1, 15.1.4.2
Cautions; Side-effects: see under Cyclizine but more sedating; intramuscular injection may be painful; avoid in porphyria
Dose: *by mouth*, 25–50 mg daily in single or divided doses; max. 75 mg
CHILD, motion sickness prevention, 1–5 years, 5 mg at night and following morning; 5–10 years, 10 mg at night and following morning
By deep intramuscular injection, 25–50 mg when necessary; CHILD 5–10 years 6.25–12.5 mg
By slow intravenous injection, section 3.4.1

Preparations
See section 3.4.1

PROMETHAZINE THEOCLATE

Indications: nausea, vertigo, labyrinthine disorders, motion sickness (acts longer than the hydrochloride)
Cautions; Side-effects: see under Promethazine Hydrochloride
Dose: 25–75 mg, max. 100 mg, daily; CHILD 5–10 years, 12.5–37.5 mg daily
Motion sickness prevention, 25 mg at bedtime on night before travelling *or* 25 mg 1–2 hours before travelling; CHILD 5–10 years, half adult dose
For severe vomiting in pregnancy, 25 mg at bedtime, increased if necessary to a max. of 100 mg daily (but see also Vomiting of Pregnancy in notes above)

Avomine® (Rhône-Poulenc Rorer)
Tablets, scored, promethazine theoclate 25 mg. Net price 10-tab pack = 80p; 30-tab pack = 99p. Label: 2

THIETHYLPERAZINE

Indications: severe nausea, vomiting, vertigo, labyrinthine disorders
Cautions; Contra-indications; Side-effects: see under Chlorpromazine Hydrochloride (section 4.2.1); young adults, elderly, and debilitated particularly susceptible to extrapyramidal effects; avoid in children under 15 years
Dose: *by mouth*, thiethylperazine maleate 10 mg 2–3 times daily
By intramuscular injection, thiethylperazine [base] 6.5 mg
By rectum in suppositories, thiethylperazine [base] 6.5 mg night and morning
Note: Thiethylperazine 6.5 mg ≡ thiethylperazine malate 10.86 mg ≡ thiethylperazine maleate 10.28 mg

PoM **Torecan®** (Sandoz)
Tablets, s/c, thiethylperazine *maleate* 10 mg. Net price 50 = £1.42. Label: 2
Injection, thiethylperazine 6.5 mg (as *malate*)/mL. Net price 1-mL amp = 18p
Suppositories, thiethylperazine 6.5 mg (as *maleate*). Net price 5 = 91p. Label: 2

TRIFLUOPERAZINE

Indications: severe nausea and vomiting (see notes above); other indications, section 4.2.1
Cautions; Contra-indications; Side-effects: see section 4.2.1; extrapyramidal symptoms may occur, particularly in children, elderly, and debilitated
Dose: *by mouth*, 2–4 mg daily in divided doses *or* as a single dose of a sustained-release preparation; max. 6 mg daily; CHILD 3–5 years up to 1 mg daily, 6–12 years up to 4 mg daily
By deep intramuscular injection, 1–3 mg daily in divided doses, max. 6 mg daily

Preparations
Section 4.2.1

4.7 Analgesics

Analgesic requirements may be profoundly affected by the attitude of both the patient and the prescriber to the pain; in many cases where analgesics might normally have been given, a placebo has provided substantial relief. For advice on pain relief in terminal care see Prescribing in Terminal Care, p. 12.

4.7.1 Non-opioid analgesics

The non-opioid drugs, aspirin and paracetamol, are particularly suited to the relief of pain in musculoskeletal conditions, whereas the opioid analgesics are more suited for the relief of severe pain of visceral origin.

Aspirin is the analgesic of choice for headache, transient musculoskeletal pain, and dysmenorrhoea. It also has anti-inflammatory properties which may be useful, and is an antipyretic. Aspirin tablets or dispersible aspirin tablets are adequate for most purposes as they act rapidly and are inexpensive.

Gastric irritation may be a problem; it is minimised by taking the dose after food. Numerous formulations are available which improve gastric tolerance, e.g. the buffered aspirin preparations such as aloxiprin (Palaprin Forte®) and enteric-coated aspirin. Some of these preparations have a slow onset of action and are therefore unsuitable for single-dose analgesic use though their prolonged action may be useful for the relief of night pain.

Paracetamol is similar in efficacy to aspirin, but has no demonstrable anti-inflammatory activity; it is less irritant to the stomach. Overdosage with paracetamol is particularly dangerous as it may cause hepatic damage which is sometimes not apparent for 4 to 6 days. **Benorylate** is an aspirin–paracetamol ester which releases paracetamol slowly and so hepatotoxicity in overdosage may be reduced.

Nefopam may have a place in the relief of persistent pain unresponsive to other non-opioid analgesics. It causes little or no respiratory depression, but sympathomimetic and antimuscarinic side-effects may be troublesome.

Anti-inflammatory analgesics (see section 10.1.1) are particularly useful for the treatment of patients with chronic disease accompanied by pain and inflammation. Some of them are also used in the short-term treatment of mild to moderate pain including transient musculoskeletal pain. They are also suitable for the relief of pain in *dysmenorrhoea* and to treat pain caused by *secondary bone tumours*, many of which produce lysis of bone and release prostaglandins (see Prescribing in Terminal Care, p. 12).

CSM advice.
The CSM has considered available evidence on possible links between Reye's syndrome and aspirin use by feverish children, and recommends that aspirin should no longer be given to children aged under 12 years, unless specifically indicated, e.g. for juvenile rheumatoid arthritis. It is therefore important to advise families that aspirin is not, on the evidence now available, a suitable medicine for children with minor illnesses. Paracetamol (see below) is an effective alternative treatment for fever in children.

ASPIRIN

Indications: mild to moderate pain, pyrexia (see notes above); see also section 10.1.1; antiplatelet, see section 2.9

Cautions: asthma, allergic disease, impaired renal or hepatic function (avoid if severe), dehydration, pregnancy; **interactions:** Appendix 1 (aspirin)

Contra-indications: children under 12 years and in breast-feeding (Reye's syndrome, see notes above); gastro-intestinal ulceration, gout, haemophilia

Side-effects: generally mild and infrequent but high incidence of gastro-intestinal irritation with slight asymptomatic blood loss, increased bleeding time, bronchospasm and skin reactions in hypersensitive patients. Prolonged administration, see section 10.1.1

Dose: 300–900 mg every 4–6 hours when necessary; max. 4 g daily

Aspirin (Non-proprietary)
Tablets, aspirin 300 mg. Net price 20 = 9p. Label: 21
Tablets, Dispersible, aspirin 300 mg. Net price 20 = 9p. Label: 13, 21
Note. Addendum 1989 to BP 1988 directs that when soluble aspirin tablets are prescribed, dispersible aspirin tablets shall be dispensed.

NHS **Laboprin®** (LAB)
Tablets, mottled white/brown, aspirin 300 mg with lysine 245 mg. Net price 20 = £1.25. Label: 21

Palaprin Forte® (Nicholas)
Tablets, orange, scored, aloxiprin[1] 600 mg ≡ aspirin 500 mg. To be taken dispersed in water, chewed, sucked, or swallowed whole. Net price 20 = 50p. Label: 12, 21
Dose: ½–2 tablets up to 4 times daily; max. 8 daily

[1] Aloxiprin is a polymeric condensation product of aluminium oxide and aspirin

NHS **Solprin®** (R&C)
Tablets, dispersible, aspirin 300 mg. Net price 20 = 8p. Label: 13, 21

Preparations for intestinal release
Caprin® (Sinclair)
Tablets, s/r, pink, aspirin 324 mg (for intestinal release). Net price 20 = 69p. Label: 25
Dose: 1–4 tablets 3–4 times daily

Nu-Seals® Aspirin (Lilly)
Tablets, both red, e/c, aspirin 300 mg, net price 20 = 76p; 600 mg, 20 = £1.30. Label: 5, 25
Note. Nu-Seals® Aspirin 300 mg daily now also indicated for antithrombotic effect following myocardial infarction and in unstable angina

Compound preparations, section 4.7.1.1

PARACETAMOL

Indications: mild to moderate pain, pyrexia
Cautions: hepatic and renal impairment, alcoholism; **interactions:** Appendix 1 (paracetamol)
Side-effects: side-effects rare, but rashes, blood disorders, and acute pancreatitis reported; **important:** liver damage (and less frequently renal damage) following overdosage, see under Emergency Treatment of Poisoning
Dose: 0.5–1 g every 4–6 hours to a max. of 4 g daily; CHILD under 3 months (on doctor's advice only) 10 mg/kg (5 mg/kg if jaundiced); 3 months–1 year 60–120 mg, 1–5 years 120–250 mg, 6–12 years 250–500 mg; these doses may be repeated every 4–6 hours when necessary (max. of 4 doses in 24 hours)
Post-immunisation pyrexia, CHILD under 3 months 60 mg; for further advice see p. 407

Paracetamol (Non-proprietary)
Tablets, paracetamol 500 mg. Net price 20 = 8p. Label: 29
Soluble tablets (= Dispersible tablets), paracetamol 500 mg. Net price 60 = £1.29. Label: 13, 29
Paediatric Oral Solution (= Paediatric Elixir), paracetamol 120 mg/5 mL. Net price 100 mL = 46p
Note. Sugar-free versions are available and can be ordered by specifying 'sugar-free' on the prescription.
Oral Suspension 120 mg/5 mL (= Paediatric Mixture), paracetamol 120 mg/5 mL. Net price 100 mL = 43p
Note. BP directs that when Paediatric Paracetamol Oral Suspension or Paediatric Paracetamol Mixture is prescribed Paracetamol Oral Suspension 120 mg/5 mL should be dispensed.
Oral Suspension 250 mg/5 mL (= Mixture), paracetamol 250 mg/5 mL. Net price 100 mL = £1.16

Calpol® (Calmic)
Infant suspension, pink, paracetamol 120 mg/5 mL. Net price 70-mL pack = 64p; 140-mL pack = £1.16
Sugar-free infant suspension, pink, sugar-free, paracetamol 120 mg/5 mL. Net price 140-mL pack = £1.16
NHS *Six plus suspension*, orange, paracetamol 250 mg/5 mL. Net price 100-mL pack = £1.16

Disprol® (R&C)
Paediatric suspension, yellow, sugar-free, paracetamol 120 mg/5 mL. Net price 100 mL = 43p

Paldesic® (RP Drugs)
Syrup, paracetamol 120 mg/5 mL. Net price 60-mL pack = 44p

Panadol® (Sterling-Winthrop)
NHS *Tablets*, paracetamol 500 mg. Net price 12-tab pack = 46p. Label: 29
Elixir, red, sugar-free, paracetamol 120 mg/5 mL. Net price 100-mL pack = 97p

NHS **Panadol Soluble®** (Sterling-Winthrop)
Tablets, effervescent, scored, paracetamol 500 mg. Net price 60-tab pack = £1.25. Label: 13, 29

Panaleve® (Leo)
Elixir, yellow, sugar-free, paracetamol 120 mg/5 mL. Net price 100-mL pack = 92p

NHS **Salzone®** (Wallace Mfg)
Syrup, paracetamol 120 mg/5 mL. Diluent syrup, life of diluted syrup 14 days. Net price 75-mL pack = 91p

With methionine

NHS **Pameton®** (Sterling-Winthrop)
Tablets, paracetamol 500 mg, DL-methionine 250 mg. Net price 60-tab pack = £2.77. Label: 29
Dose: 2 tablets when required up to 4 times daily; CHILD 6–12 years ½–1 tablet when required; not more often than every 4 hours and max. of 4 doses in 24 hours

Compound preparations, section 4.7.1.1

BENORYLATE

(Aspirin-paracetamol ester; 2 g benorylate is equivalent to approximately 1.15 g aspirin and 970 mg paracetamol)
Indications: mild to moderate pain; pyrexia; see also section 10.1.1
Cautions; Contra-indications; Side-effects: see under Aspirin and under Paracetamol; patients should be advised against taking analgesics containing aspirin or paracetamol
Note. Preparations containing aspirin are now contra-indicated in children under 12 years of age owing to an association with Reye's syndrome, see notes above
Dose: 2 g twice daily, preferably after food

Preparations
See section 10.1.1

DICLOFENAC SODIUM

See section 10.1.1

DIFLUNISAL

Indications: mild to moderate pain; see also section 10.1.1
Cautions; Contra-indications; Side-effects: see section 10.1.1
Dose: 250–500 mg twice daily preferably after food

Preparations
See section 10.1.1

FENOPROFEN

Indications: mild to moderate pain, pyrexia; see also section 10.1.1
Cautions; Contra-indications; Side-effects: See section 10.1.1

Dose: 200–600 mg 3–4 times daily, after food; max. 3 g daily

PoM **Progesic**® (Lilly)
Tablets, yellow, fenoprofen 200 mg (as calcium salt). Net price 20 = £2.20. Label: 21
PoM **Fenopron**®: see section 10.1.1

IBUPROFEN

Indications: mild to moderate pain; see also section 10.1.1
Cautions; Contra-indications; Side-effects: see section 10.1.1
Dose: 1.2–1.8 g daily in divided doses, preferably after food, increased if necessary to a max. of 2.4 g daily; CHILD, see section 10.1.1

Preparations: See section 10.1.1

Fever and pain in children
▼ PoM **Junifen**® (Boots)
Suspension, ibuprofen 100 mg/5 mL, net price 150-mL pack = £2.40. Label: 21
Dose: fever and pain in children, under 1 year, not recommended, 1–12 years 20 mg/kg daily in divided doses *or* 1–2 years 2.5 mL 3–4 times daily, 3–7 years 5 mL, 8–12 years 10 mL

MEFENAMIC ACID

Indications: mild to moderate pain, pyrexia in children; menorrhagia; see also section 10.1.1
Cautions; Contra-indications; Side-effects: see section 10.1.1; exclude pathological conditions before treating menorrhagia
Dose: 500 mg 3 times daily after food; CHILD over 6 months 25 mg/kg daily in divided doses for not longer than 7 days, except in juvenile arthritis (Still's disease)

Preparations
See section 10.1.1

NAPROXEN SODIUM

Indications: mild to moderate pain; rheumatic disease, see Naproxen, section 10.1.1
Cautions; Contra-indications; Side-effects: see section 10.1.1
Dose: 550 mg twice daily when necessary, preferably after food
Note. 275 mg naproxen sodium ≡ 250 mg naproxen but the sodium salt has a more rapid action.

PoM **Synflex**® (Syntex)
Tablets, orange, naproxen sodium 275 mg. Net price 20 = £2.59. Label: 21

NEFOPAM HYDROCHLORIDE

Indications: moderate pain
Cautions: hepatic disease, elderly, urinary retention; **interactions:** Appendix 1 (nefopam)
Contra-indications: convulsive disorders; not indicated for myocardial infarction
Side-effects: nausea, nervousness, urinary retention, dry mouth; less frequently blurred vision, drowsiness, sweating, insomnia, tachycardia, headache; confusion and hallucinations also reported; may colour urine (pink)
Dose: by mouth, initially 60 mg (elderly, 30 mg) 3 times daily, adjusted according to response; usual range 30–90 mg 3 times daily
By intramuscular injection, 20 mg every 6 hours
Note. Nefopam hydrochloride 20 mg by injection ≡ 60 mg by mouth

PoM **Acupan**® (3M)
Tablets, f/c, nefopam hydrochloride 30 mg. Net price 90-tab pack = £11.73. Label: 14
Injection, nefopam hydrochloride 20 mg/mL. Net price 1-mL amp = 74p

4.7.1.1 COMPOUND ANALGESIC PREPARATIONS

Compound analgesic preparations of, for example, aspirin, paracetamol, and codeine are **not** recommended. Single-ingredient preparations should be prescribed in preference because compound preparations rarely have any advantage and complicate the treatment of overdosage. The dangers of co-proxamol (dextropropoxyphene-paracetamol) overdosage call for rapid treatment as described in Emergency Treatment of Poisoning, p. 18.

It is even more desirable to **avoid** mixtures of analgesics with antihistamines or muscle relaxants; the individual components should be prescribed separately so that the dose of each can be adjusted as appropriate.

Caffeine is a weak stimulant that is often included, in small doses, in analgesic preparations. It does not contribute to the analgesic or anti-inflammatory effect of the preparation and may possibly aggravate the gastric irritation caused by aspirin. Moreover, in excessive dosage or on withdrawal caffeine may itself induce headache.

> Patients should be warned when compound analgesics contain paracetamol so that they can avoid other paracetamol-containing preparations.

Co-codamol
Co-codamol (Non-proprietary)
Tablets, co-codamol 8/500 (codeine phosphate 8 mg, paracetamol 500 mg). Net price 20 = 28p. Label: 29
Dose: 1–2 tablets every 4–6 hours; max. 8 tablets daily; CHILD 6–12 years ½–1 tablet
Available from APS, Cox, Evans, Galen (NHS Parake®), Kerfoot, Sterling-Winthrop (NHS Panadeine®)
Effervescent tablets, co-codamol 8/500 (paracetamol 500 mg, codeine phosphate 8 mg). Net price 20 = 49p. Label: 13, 29
Dose: 1–2 tablets in water every 4–6 hours, max. 8 tablets daily; CHILD 6–12 years ½–1 tablet, max. 4 tablets daily
Available from Fisons (NHS Paracodol®)
Capsules, co-codamol 8/500 (paracetamol 500 mg, codeine phosphate 8 mg). Net price 20 = 87p. Label: 29
Dose: 1–2 capsules every 4 hours; max. 8 capsules daily
Available from Fisons (NHS Paracodol®)
When co-codamol tablets, dispersible tablets, or capsules are prescribed and no strength is stated tablets,

dispersible tablets, or capsules, respectively, containing codeine phosphate 8 mg and paracetamol 500 mg should be dispensed.

Co-codaprin

Co-codaprin (Non-proprietary)
Tablets, co-codaprin 8/400 (codeine phosphate 8 mg, aspirin 400 mg). Net price 20 = 24p. Label: 21
Dose: 1–2 tablets every 4–6 hours when necessary; max. 8 tablets daily
Available from Cox
Dispersible tablets, co-codaprin 8/400 (codeine phosphate 8 mg, aspirin 400 mg). Net price 20 = 31p. Label: 13, 21
Dose: 1–2 tablets in water every 4–6 hours; max. 8 tablets daily
Available from Cox, R & C (NHS Codis®)
When co-codaprin tablets or dispersible tablets are prescribed and no strength is stated tablets, or dispersible tablets, respectively, containing codeine phosphate 8 mg and aspirin 400 mg should be dispensed.

Co-dydramol

PoM **Co-dydramol** (Non-proprietary)
Tablets, scored, co-dydramol 10/500 (dihydrocodeine tartrate 10 mg, paracetamol 500 mg). Net price 20 = 33p. Label: 21, 29
Dose: 1–2 tablets every 4–6 hours; max. 8 tablets daily
Available from APS, Cox, Macfarlan Smith (NHS Paramol®), Evans, Kerfoot
When co-dydramol tablets are prescribed and no strength is stated tablets containing dihydrocodeine tartrate 10 mg and paracetamol 500 mg should be dispensed.

Co-proxamol

PoM **Co-proxamol** (Non-proprietary)
Tablets, co-proxamol 32.5/325 (dextropropoxyphene hydrochloride 32.5 mg, paracetamol 325 mg). Net price 20 = 28p. Label: 2, 10 patient information leaflet (if available), 29
Dose: 2 tablets 3–4 times daily; max. 8 tablets daily
Available from APS, Cox (NHS Cosalgesic®), Dista (NHS Distalgesic®), Evans, Kerfoot, Mercury (NHS Paxalgesic®)
When co-proxamol tablets are prescribed and no strength is stated tablets containing dextropropoxyphene hydrochloride 32.5 mg and paracetamol 325 mg should be dispensed.

Other compound analgesic preparations

NHS **Antoin®** (Cox Pharmaceuticals)
Dispersible tablets, scored, aspirin 400 mg, codeine phosphate 5 mg, caffeine citrate 15 mg. Net price 50 = £1.33. Label: 13, 21
Dose: 1–2 tablets in water 3–4 times daily; max. 10 tablets daily

NHS **Cafadol®** (Typharm)
Tablets, yellow, scored, paracetamol 500 mg, caffeine 30 mg. Net price 20 = 60p. Label: 29
Dose: 2 tablets every 4 hours; max. 8 tablets daily; CHILD not recommended in view of caffeine content

NHS CD **Equagesic®** (Wyeth)
Tablets, pink/white/yellow, ethoheptazine citrate 75 mg, meprobamate 150 mg, aspirin 250 mg. Net price 20 = 60p. Label: 2, 21
Dose: muscle pain, 1–2 tablets 3–4 times daily

NHS **Hypon®** (Calmic)
Tablets, yellow, aspirin 325 mg, caffeine 10 mg, codeine phosphate 5 mg. Net price 20 = 51p. Label: 21
Dose: 2 tablets every 4 hours; max. 12 tablets daily

NHS PoM **Lobak®** (Sterling-Winthrop)
Tablets, scored, chlormezanone 100 mg, paracetamol 450 mg. Net price 50 = £6.97. Label: 2, 29
Dose: muscle pain, 1–2 tablets 3 times daily; max. 8 tablets daily

NHS **Medised®** (Panpharma)
Suspension, paracetamol 120 mg, promethazine hydrochloride 2.5 mg/5 mL. Net price 140-mL pack = £1.14. Label: 1
Note. Dose excluded because combination not recommended

NHS **Parahypon®** (Calmic)
Tablets, pink, scored, paracetamol 500 mg, codeine phosphate 5 mg, caffeine 10 mg. Net price 20 = 83p. Label: 29
Dose: 2 tablets up to 4 times daily; CHILD not recommended in view of caffeine content

NHS **Pardale®** (Martindale)
Tablets, scored, paracetamol 400 mg, codeine phosphate 9 mg, caffeine 10 mg. Net price 20 = 79p. Label: 29
Dose: 1–2 tablets 3–4 times daily; max. 8 tablets daily

NHS **Propain®** (Panpharma)
Tablets, yellow, scored, codeine phosphate 10 mg, diphenhydramine hydrochloride 5 mg, paracetamol 400 mg, caffeine 50 mg. Net price 12-tab pack = 74p. Label: 2, 29
Dose: 1–2 tablets every 4 hours; max. 8 tablets daily

NHS PoM **Robaxisal Forte®** (Wyeth)
Tablets, pink/white, scored, methocarbamol 400 mg, aspirin 325 mg. Net price 20 = £1.90. Label: 2, 21
Dose: muscle pain, 2 tablets 4 times daily

NHS **Solpadeine®** (Sterling-Winthrop)
Effervescent tablets, paracetamol 500 mg, codeine phosphate 8 mg, caffeine 30 mg. Contains 18.5 mmol Na^+/tablet; avoid in renal impairment. Net price 24-tab pack = £1.34. Label: 13, 29
Dose: 2 tablets in water 3–4 times daily; CHILD not recommended in view of caffeine content
Capsules, ingredients as for Effervescent Tablets. Net price 24-cap pack = £1.28. Label: 29
Dose: 2 capsules up to 4 times daily

NHS **Syndol®** (Merrell)
Tablets, yellow, scored, paracetamol 450 mg, codeine phosphate 10 mg, doxylamine succinate 5 mg, caffeine 30 mg. Net price 20 = £1.22. Label: 2, 29
Dose: 1–2 tablets every 4–6 hours; max. 8 tablets daily

NHS **Veganin®** (W-L)
Tablets, scored, aspirin 250 mg, paracetamol 250 mg, codeine phosphate 6.8 mg. Net price 20 = 75p. Label: 21, 29
Dose: 1–2 tablets every 4 hours; max. 8 tablets daily

HIGHER OPIOID CONTENT

The following preparations have a higher opioid analgesic content than most compound analgesic preparations. For cautions and side-effects, see section 4.7.2.

PoM **Aspav®** (Roussel)
Dispersible tablets, aspirin 500 mg, papaveretum 10 mg. Net price 20 = £1.35. Label: 2, 13, 21
Dose: 1–2 tablets in water every 4–6 hours if necessary; max. 8 tablets daily

NHS PoM **Doloxene Compound®** (Lilly)
Capsules, grey/red, dextropropoxyphene napsylate 100 mg, aspirin 375 mg, caffeine 30 mg. Net price 20 = £1.34. Label: 2, 21
Dose: 1 capsule 3–4 times daily; max. 4 capsules daily

PoM **Solpadol®** (Sterling-Winthrop)
Effervescent tablets, paracetamol 500 mg, codeine phosphate 30 mg. Contains 18.6 mmol Na^+/tablet; avoid in renal impairment. Net price 60-tab pack = £5.30. Label: 2, 13
Dose: 2 tablets in water every 4 hours; max. 6 daily

PoM **Tylex®** (Cilag)
Capsules, paracetamol 500 mg, codeine phosphate 30 mg. Net price 100 = £7.96. Label: 2
Dose: 1–2 capsules every 4 hours; max. 6 daily

Paediatric
NHS PoM **Formulix®** (Cilag)

Elixir, paracetamol 120 mg, codeine phosphate 12 mg/5 mL. Net price 100 mL = £1.20. Label: 3
Dose: CHILD 3–6 years 5 mL, 7–12 years 10 mL 3–4 times daily
Caution: high codeine content

4.7.2 Opioid analgesics

Opioid analgesics are used to relieve moderate to severe pain particularly of visceral origin. Repeated administration may cause dependence and tolerance, but this is no deterrent in the control of pain in terminal illness, for guidelines see Prescribing in Terminal Care, p. 12.

SIDE-EFFECTS. Opioid analgesics share many side-effects though qualitative and quantitative differences exist. The most common include nausea, vomiting, constipation, and drowsiness. Larger doses produce respiratory depression and hypotension.

INTERACTIONS. See Appendix 1 (opioid analgesics) (**important**: special hazard with *pethidine and possibly other opioids* and MAOIs).

DRIVING. Drowsiness may affect performance of skilled tasks (e.g. driving); effects of alcohol enhanced.

CHOICE. **Morphine** remains the most valuable opioid analgesic for severe pain although it frequently causes nausea and vomiting. It is the standard against which other opioid analgesics are compared. In addition to relief of pain, morphine also confers a state of euphoria and mental detachment.

Morphine is the opioid of choice for the oral treatment of *severe pain in terminal care*. It is given regularly every 4 hours as an oral solution, or every 12 hours as slow-release tablets. For guidelines on dosage adjustment in terminal care, see p. 12.

Buprenorphine has both opioid agonist and antagonist properties and may precipitate withdrawal symptoms, including pain, in patients dependent on other opioids. It has a much longer duration of action than morphine and sublingually is an effective analgesic for 8 to 12 hours. Vomiting may be a problem but it is thought to have a low dependence potential. Unlike most opioid analgesics its effects are only partially reversed by naloxone.

Codeine is effective for the relief of mild to mode..e pain but is too constipating for long-term use.

Dextromoramide is less sedating than morphine and has a short duration of action.

Dipipanone used alone is less sedating than morphine but the only preparation available contains an anti-emetic and is therefore not suitable for regular regimens in terminal care (see p. 12).

Dextropropoxyphene given alone is a very mild analgesic somewhat less potent than codeine. Combinations of dextropropoxyphene with paracetamol or aspirin have little more analgesic effect than paracetamol or aspirin alone. An important disadvantage of combinations with paracetamol is that overdosage (which may be combined with alcohol) is complicated by respiratory depression and acute heart failure due to the dextropropoxyphene and by hepatotoxicity due to the paracetamol. Rapid treatment is essential (see Emergency Treatment of Poisoning, p. 18).

Diamorphine (heroin) is a powerful opioid analgesic. It may cause less nausea and hypotension than morphine. In *terminal care* the greater solubility of diamorphine allows effective doses to be injected in smaller volumes and this is important in the emaciated patient.

Dihydrocodeine is similar in potency to codeine. It is suitable for use in ambulant patients with moderate pain but may cause dizziness and constipation.

Meptazinol is claimed to have a low incidence of respiratory depression. It has a reported length of action of 2 to 7 hours with onset within 15 minutes, but there is an incidence of nausea and vomiting.

Methadone is less sedating than morphine and acts for longer periods. In prolonged use, methadone should not be administered more often than twice daily to avoid the risk of accumulation and opioid overdosage.

Nalbuphine is equipotent with morphine for pain relief, but may have fewer side-effects and less abuse potential. Nausea and vomiting occur less than with other opioids but respiratory depression is similar to that with morphine.

Oxycodone is used as the pectinate in suppositories (special order, Boots) for the control of *pain in terminal care*.

Pentazocine has both agonist and antagonist properties and precipitates withdrawal symptoms, including pain in patients dependent on other opioids. By injection it is more potent than dihydrocodeine or codeine, but hallucinations and thought disturbances may occur. It is not recommended and, in particular, should be avoided after myocardial infarction as it may increase pulmonary and aortic blood pressure as well as cardiac work.

Pethidine produces a prompt but short-lasting analgesia and even in high doses it is a less potent analgesic than morphine. It is not suitable for the relief of pain in terminal care. It is used for analgesia in labour and in the neonate is associated with less respiratory depression than other opioid analgesics (probably because its action is weaker). See also section 15.1.4.1 (peri-operative use).

Phenazocine is effective in severe pain and has less tendency to increase biliary pressure than other opioid analgesics. It can be administered sublingually if nausea and vomiting are a problem.

ADDICTS. Although caution is necessary addicts (and ex-addicts) may be treated with analgesics in the same way as other people when there is a real clinical need. Doctors are reminded that they do not require a special licence to prescribe opioid analgesics for addicts for relief of pain due to organic disease or injury. For details, see p. 7.

MORPHINE SALTS

Indications: see notes above; acute pulmonary oedema; see also section 15.1.4 for peri-operative use

Cautions: hypotension, hypothyroidism, asthma, and decreased respiratory reserve; pregnancy and breast-feeding; may precipitate coma in hepatic impairment (but many such patients tolerate morphine well); reduce dose in renal impairment, elderly and debilitated; dependence (severe withdrawal symptoms if withdrawn abruptly); use of cough suppressants containing opioid analgesics not generally recommended in children and should be avoided altogether in those under 1 year; **interactions:** Appendix 1 (opioid analgesics)

TERMINAL CARE. In the control of pain in terminal illness these cautions should not necessarily be a deterrent to the use of opioid analgesics

Contra-indications: avoid in raised intracranial pressure or head injury (in addition to interfering with respiration, affect pupillary responses vital for neurological assessment)

Side-effects: nausea and vomiting (particularly in initial stages), constipation, and drowsiness; larger doses produce respiratory depression and hypotension; other side-effects include difficulty with micturition, ureteric or biliary spasm, dry mouth, sweating, facial flushing, vertigo, bradycardia, palpitations, postural hypotension, hypothermia, hallucinations, mood changes, dependence, miosis, urticaria and pruritus

Dose: acute pain, *by subcutaneous or intramuscular injection*, 10 mg every 4 hours if necessary (15 mg for heavier well-muscled patients); CHILD up to 1 month 150 micrograms/kg, 1–12 months 200 micrograms/kg, 1–5 years 2.5–5 mg, 6–12 years 5–10 mg

By slow intravenous injection, quarter to half corresponding intramuscular dose

Myocardial infarction, *by slow intravenous injection* (2 mg/minute), 10 mg followed by a further 5–10 mg if necessary; elderly or frail patients, reduce dose by half

Acute pulmonary oedema, *by slow intravenous injection* (2 mg/minute) 5–10 mg

Chronic pain, *by mouth or by subcutaneous or intramuscular injection*, 5–20 mg regularly every 4 hours; dose may be increased according to needs; oral dose should be approximately double corresponding intramuscular dose and triple to quadruple corresponding intramuscular *diamorphine* dose (see also Prescribing in Terminal Care, p. 12); *by rectum*, as suppositories, 15–30 mg regularly every 4 hours

Note. The doses stated above refer equally to morphine hydrochloride, sulphate, and tartrate.

Oral solutions

PoM or **CD Morphine Oral Solutions**

Oral solutions of morphine can be prescribed by writing the formula:

Morphine hydrochloride 5 mg
Chloroform water to 5 mL

Note. The proportion of morphine hydrochloride may be altered when specified by the prescriber; if above 13 mg per 5 mL the solution becomes **CD**. For sample prescription see Controlled Drugs and Drug Dependence, p. 7. It is usual to adjust the strength so that the dose volume is 5 or 10 mL.

Oramorph® (Boehringer Ingelheim)

PoM *Oral solution*, morphine sulphate 10 mg/5 mL. Net price 100-mL pack = £2.31; 250-mL pack = £5.10; 500-mL pack = £9.24. Label: 2

Diluent freshly boiled and cooled purified water, life of diluted solution 14 days.

CD *Concentrated oral solution*, sugar-free, morphine sulphate 100 mg/5 mL. Net price 30-mL pack = £6.16; 120-mL pack = £23.00 (both with calibrated dropper). Label: 2

Tablets

CD Sevredol® (Napp)

Tablets, both f/c, scored, morphine sulphate 10 mg (blue), net price 56-tab pack = £6.47; 20 mg (pink), 56-tab pack = £12.94. Label: 2

Sustained-release tablets

CD MST Continus® (Napp)

Tablets, s/r, f/c, morphine sulphate 10 mg (brown), net price 60-tab pack = £7.70; 30 mg (purple), 60-tab pack = £18.49; 60 mg (orange), 60-tab pack = £36.06; 100 mg (grey), 60-tab pack = £57.10. Label: 2, 25

Dose: Severe pain uncontrolled by weaker opioids, 30 mg every 12 hours, increased to 60 mg every 12 hours when required, then further increments of 30–50% if necessary. For lower initial doses in patients who have not received other opioids, see Prescribing in Terminal Care, p. 12

CHILD severe, intractable pain in cancer, initially 200–800 micrograms/kg every 12 hours, then further increments of 30–50% if necessary

Note. Brand name prescriptions for MST Continus must also specify the word 'tablets' (i.e. 'MST Continus Tablets').

Parenteral

CD Morphine Sulphate Injection, morphine sulphate 10, 15, and 30 mg/mL, net price 1- and 2-mL amp (all) = 37–66p

CD Min-I-Jet® Morphine Sulphate (IMS)

Injection, morphine sulphate 10 mg/mL, net price 2-mL disposable syringe = £5.50

CD Morphine and Atropine Injection

See section 15.1.4.1

Parenteral with anti-emetic

CAUTION. In myocardial infarction cyclizine may aggravate severe heart failure and counteract the haemodynamic benefits of opioids, see section 4.6. **Not recommended** in terminal care, see p. 12

CD Cyclimorph® (Calmic)

Cyclimorph-10® Injection, morphine tartrate 10 mg, cyclizine tartrate 50 mg/mL. Net price 1-mL amp = £1.01

Dose: by subcutaneous, intramuscular, or intravenous injection, 1 mL, repeated not more often than 4-hourly, with not more than 3 doses in any 24-hour period; CHILD 1–5 years 0.25–0.5 mL as a single dose, 6–12 years 0.5–1 mL as a single dose

Cyclimorph-15® *Injection*, morphine tartrate 15 mg, cyclizine tartrate 50 mg/mL. Net price 1-mL amp = £1.05

Dose: by subcutaneous, intramuscular, or intravenous injection, 1 mL, repeated not more often than 4-hourly, with not more than 3 doses in any 24-hour period

Rectal

CD Morphine Suppositories, morphine hydrochloride or sulphate 15 mg, net price 12 = £3.52; 30 mg, 12 = £5.51. Label: 2.

Note. Both the strength of the suppositories and the morphine salt contained in them must be specified by the prescriber

Mixed opium alkaloids

Mixed opium alkaloids do not have any advantage over morphine alone; alcoholic solutions are liable to evaporation and are **not** recommended.

CD Nepenthe (Evans)

Oral solution (= elixir), brown, anhydrous morphine 8.4 mg/mL (500 micrograms from opium tincture, 7.9 mg from morphine). Diluent syrup, life of diluted elixir 4 weeks. Net price 100-mL pack = £22.45. Label: 2

Dose: 1–2 mL, repeated not more often than every 4 hours when necessary; CHILD 6–12 years 0.5–1 mL, as a single dose

Note. This product must always be diluted when being dispensed.

CAUTION. *Nepenthe Oral Solution may become concentrated through evaporation of the solvent. It should be stored in a cool place in the original airtight container. If evaporation occurs during storage the solution should not be used because of risk of overdosage.*

Injection, anhydrous morphine 8.4 mg/mL (500 micrograms from papaveretum, 7.9 mg from morphine hydrochloride). Net price 0.5-mL amp = £1.45

Dose: by subcutaneous or intramuscular injection, 1–2 mL, repeated not more often than every 4 hours when necessary; CHILD 6–12 years 0.5–1 mL as a single dose

ALFENTANIL: See section 15.1.4.1

BUPRENORPHINE

Indications: moderate to severe pain

Cautions; Contra-indications; Side-effects: see under Morphine Salts, but side-effects less marked; can give rise to mild withdrawal symptoms in patients dependent on opioids; effects only partially reversed by naloxone; **interactions:** Appendix 1 (opioid analgesics)

Dose: by sublingual administration, initially 200–400 micrograms every 8 hours, increasing if necessary to 200–400 micrograms every 6–8 hours; CHILD over 6 months, 16–25 kg, 100 micrograms; 25–37.5 kg, 100–200 micrograms; 37.5–50 kg, 200–300 micrograms

By intramuscular or slow intravenous injection, 300–600 micrograms every 6–8 hours; CHILD over 6 months 3–6 micrograms/kg every 6–8 hours; max. 9 micrograms/kg

CD Temgesic® (R&C)

Tablets (sublingual), buprenorphine 200 micrograms (as hydrochloride). Net price 50 = £6.00. Label: 2, 26

Injection, buprenorphine 300 micrograms (as hydrochloride)/mL. Net price 1-mL amp = 55p; 2-mL amp = 99p

CODEINE PHOSPHATE

Indications: mild to moderate pain

Cautions; Contra-indications; Side-effects: see under Morphine Salts but side-effects less marked; use of cough suppressants containing codeine or similar opioid analgesics not generally recommended in children and should be avoided altogether in those under 1 year; **interactions:** Appendix 1 (opioid analgesics)

Dose: by mouth, 30–60 mg every 4 hours when necessary, to a max. of 180 mg daily; CHILD 1–12 years, 3 mg/kg daily in divided doses

By intramuscular injection, 30–60 mg every 4 hours when necessary

Codeine Phosphate (Non-proprietary)

PoM *Tablets*, codeine phosphate 15 mg, net price 20 = 38p; 30 mg, 20 = 39p; 60 mg, 20 = £1.21. Label: 2

Note. As for schedule 2 controlled drugs, travellers needing to take codeine phosphate preparations abroad may require a doctor's letter explaining why they are necessary.

CD *Injection*, codeine phosphate 60 mg/mL. Net price 1-mL amp = £1.18

Codeine Linctuses

See section 3.9.1

Compound preparations, section 4.7.1.1

DEXTROMORAMIDE

Indications: severe pain

Cautions; Contra-indications; Side-effects: see under Morphine Salts, but less sedating than morphine; only short duration of action (2–3 hours); avoid in obstetric analgesia (increased risk of neonatal depression); **interactions:** Appendix 1 (opioid analgesics)

Dose: by mouth, 5 mg increasing to 20 mg, when required

By subcutaneous or intramuscular injection, 5 mg increasing to 15 mg, when required

By rectum in suppositories, 10 mg when required

CD Palfium® (Boehringer Mannheim)

Tablets, both scored, dextromoramide (as tartrate) 5 mg, net price 60-tab pack = £4.78; 10 mg (peach), 60-tab pack = £9.45. Label: 2

Injection, dextromoramide 5 mg (as tartrate)/mL. Net price 1-mL amp = 20p

Injection, dextromoramide 10 mg (as tartrate)/mL. Net price 1-mL amp = 24p

Suppositories, dextromoramide 10 mg (as tartrate). Net price 10 = £2.35. Label: 2

DEXTROPROPOXYPHENE HYDROCHLORIDE

Indications: mild to moderate pain

Cautions; Contra-indications; Side effects: see under Morphine Salts but side-effects less marked; occasional hepatotoxicity; avoid in porphyria; compound preparations special hazard in overdose, see notes above; convulsions reported in overdose

Dose: 65 mg every 6–8 hours when necessary

Note. 65 mg dextropropoxyphene hydrochloride ≡ 100 mg dextropropoxyphene napsylate

PoM **Dextropropoxyphene Capsules,** the equivalent of dextropropoxyphene hydrochloride 65 mg (as napsylate). Net price 20 = £1.19. Label: 2

Note. The brand name NHS Doloxene®(Lilly) is used for dextropropoxyphene capsules, net price 20 = £1.19

Compound preparations, section 4.7.1.1

DIAMORPHINE HYDROCHLORIDE

Indications: see notes above; acute pulmonary oedema

Cautions; Contra-indications; Side-effects: see under Morphine Salts; **interactions:** Appendix 1 (opioid analgesics)

Dose: acute pain, *by subcutaneous or intramuscular injection*, 5 mg repeated every 4 hours if necessary (up to 10 mg for heavier well-muscled patients)

By slow intravenous injection, quarter to half corresponding intramuscular dose

Myocardial infarction, *by slow intravenous injection* (1 mg/minute), 5 mg followed by a further 2.5–5 mg if necessary; elderly or frail patients, reduce dose by half

Acute pulmonary oedema, *by slow intravenous injection* (1 mg/minute) 2.5–5 mg

Chronic pain, *by mouth or by subcutaneous or intramuscular injection*, 5–10 mg regularly every 4 hours; dose may be increased according to needs; intramuscular dose should be approximately half corresponding oral dose, and quarter to third corresponding oral *morphine* dose; see also Prescribing in Terminal Care, p. 12

CD **Diamorphine** (Non-proprietary)

Tablets, diamorphine hydrochloride 10 mg. Net price 20 = 91p. Label: 2

Injection, powder for reconstitution, diamorphine hydrochloride. Net price 5-mg amp = £1.03, 10-mg amp = £1.18, 30-mg amp = £1.42, 100-mg amp = £3.96, 500-mg amp = £18.83

CD **Diamorphine Linctus**

See section 3.9.1

DIHYDROCODEINE TARTRATE

Indications: moderate to severe pain

Cautions; Contra-indications; Side-effects: see under Morphine Salts

Dose: by mouth, 30 mg every 4–6 hours when necessary, preferably after food; CHILD over 4 years 0.5–1 mg/kg every 4–6 hours

By deep subcutaneous or intramuscular injection, up to 50 mg every 4–6 hours

Dihydrocodeine (Non-proprietary)

PoM *Tablets*, dihydrocodeine tartrate 30 mg. Net price 20 = 62p. Label: 2, 21

PoM *Elixir*, dihydrocodeine tartrate 10 mg/5 mL. Net price 150 mL = £1.28. Label: 2, 21

CD *Injection*, dihydrocodeine tartrate 50 mg/mL. Net price 1-mL amp = 30p

NHS **DF 118®** (Macfarlan Smith)

PoM *Tablets*, dihydrocodeine tartrate 30 mg. Net price 20 = 62p. Label: 2, 21

PoM *Elixir*, brown, dihydrocodeine tartrate 10 mg/5 mL. Diluent syrup (without preservative or preserved with *p*-hydroxybenzoic acid), life of diluted elixir 14 days. Net price 150-mL pack = £1.28. Label: 2, 21

CD *Injection*, dihydrocodeine tartrate 50 mg/mL. Net price 1-mL amp = 30p

PoM **DHC Continus®** (Napp)

Tablets, s/r, dihydrocodeine tartrate 60 mg (scored), net price 56-tab pack = £6.75; 90 mg, 56-tab pack = £10.63; 120 mg, 56-tab pack = £14.18. Label: 2, 25

Dose: chronic severe pain, 60–120 mg every 12 hours

Compound preparations, section 4.7.1.1

DIPHENOXYLATE

See Co-phenotrope, section 1.4.2

DIPIPANONE HYDROCHLORIDE

Indications: moderate to severe pain

Cautions; Contra-indications; Side-effects: see under Morphine Salts; **interactions:** Appendix 1 (opioid analgesics)

CD **Diconal®** (Calmic)

Tablets, pink, scored, dipipanone hydrochloride 10 mg, cyclizine hydrochloride 30 mg. Net price 50 = £6.00. Label: 2

Dose: 1 tablet gradually increased to 3 tablets every 6 hours

CAUTION. **Not recommended** in terminal care, see p. 12.

FENTANYL

See section 15.1.4.1

MEPTAZINOL

Indications: moderate to severe pain, including postoperative and obstetric pain and renal colic; peri-operative analgesia, see section 15.1.4.1

Cautions; Contra-indications; Side-effects: see under Morphine Salts

Dose: by mouth, 200 mg every 3–6 hours as required

By intramuscular injection, 75–100 mg every 2–4 hours if necessary; obstetric analgesia, 100–150 mg according to patient's weight (2 mg/kg)

By slow intravenous injection, 50–100 mg every 2–4 hours if necessary

PoM **Meptid®** (Wyeth)

Tablets, orange, f/c, meptazinol 200 mg. Net price 20 = £1.80. Label: 2

Injection, meptazinol 100 mg (as hydrochloride)/mL. Net price 1-mL amp = 79p

METHADONE HYDROCHLORIDE

Indications: severe pain, see notes above; adjunct in treatment of opioid dependence, section 4.10

Cautions; Contra-indications; Side-effects: see under Morphine Salts, but less sedating than morphine; **interactions:** Appendix 1 (opioid analgesics)

Dose: by mouth or by subcutaneous or intramuscular injection, 5–10 mg every 6–8 hours, adjusted according to response

CD **Methadone Linctus,** see section 3.9.1

CD **Methadone Mixture 1 mg/mL,** section 4.10

CD **Physeptone®** (Calmic)

Tablets, scored, methadone hydrochloride 5 mg. Net price 50 = £2.46. Label: 2

Injection, methadone hydrochloride 10 mg/mL. Net price 1-mL amp = 68p

NALBUPHINE HYDROCHLORIDE

Indications: moderate to severe pain; peri-operative analgesia, see section 15.1.4.1

Cautions; Contra-indications; Side-effects: see under Morphine Salts; **interactions:** Appendix 1 (opioid analgesics)

Dose: by subcutaneous, intramuscular, or intravenous injection, 10–20 mg for 70-kg patient every 3–6 hours, adjusted as required; CHILD 300 micrograms/kg repeated once or twice as necessary

Myocardial infarction, *by slow intravenous injection*, 10–20 mg repeated after 30 minutes if necessary

PoM **Nubain®** (Du Pont)

Injection, nalbuphine hydrochloride 10 mg/mL. Net price 1-mL amp = 75p; 2-mL amp = £1.16

PAPAVERETUM

See section 15.1.4.1

PENTAZOCINE

Indications: moderate to severe pain, but see notes above

Cautions; Contra-indications; Side-effects: see under Morphine Salts; occasional hallucinations; avoid in patients dependent on opioids and in arterial or pulmonary hypertension and heart failure; avoid in porphyria

Dose: by mouth, pentazocine hydrochloride 50 mg every 3–4 hours preferably after food (range 25–100 mg); CHILD 6–12 years 25 mg

By subcutaneous, intramuscular, or intravenous injection, moderate pain, pentazocine 30 mg, severe pain 45–60 mg every 3–4 hours when necessary; CHILD over 1 year, *by subcutaneous or intramuscular injection*, up to 1 mg/kg, *by intravenous injection* up to 500 micrograms/kg

By rectum in suppositories, pentazocine 50 mg up to 4 times daily

CD **Pentazocine** (Non-proprietary)

Capsules, pentazocine hydrochloride 50 mg. Net price 20 = £3.66. Label: 2, 21

Tablets, pentazocine hydrochloride 25 mg. Net price 20 = £1.65. Label: 2, 21

Injection, pentazocine 30 mg (as lactate)/mL. Net price 1-mL amp = 70p; 2-mL amp = £1.34

Suppositories, pentazocine 50 mg (as lactate). Net price 20 = £8.40. Label: 2

NHS CD **Fortral®** (Sterling-Winthrop)

Capsules, grey/yellow, pentazocine hydrochloride 50 mg. Net price 20 = £3.66. Label: 2, 21

Tablets, f/c, pentazocine hydrochloride 25 mg. Net price 20 = £1.65. Label: 2, 21

Injection, pentazocine 30 mg (as lactate)/mL. Net price 1-mL amp = 70p; 2-mL amp = £1.34

Suppositories, pentazocine 50 mg (as lactate). Net price 20 = £8.30. Label: 2

PETHIDINE HYDROCHLORIDE

Indications: moderate to severe pain, obstetric analgesia; peri-operative analgesia, see section 15.1.4.1

Cautions; Contra-indications; Side-effects: see under Morphine Salts, but less constipating than morphine; avoid in severe renal impairment; convulsions reported in overdosage; **interactions:** Appendix 1 (opioid analgesics)

Dose: by mouth, 50–150 mg every 4 hours; CHILD 0.5–2 mg/kg

By subcutaneous or intramuscular injection, 25–100 mg, repeated after 4 hours; CHILD, *by intramuscular injection*, 0.5–2 mg/kg

By slow intravenous injection, 25–50 mg, repeated after 4 hours

Obstetric analgesia, *by subcutaneous or intramuscular injection*, 50–100 mg, repeated 1–3 hours later if necessary; max. 400 mg in 24 hours

CD **Pethidine** (Roche)

Tablets, pethidine hydrochloride 50 mg, net price 20 = 39p. Label: 2

Injection, pethidine hydrochloride 50 mg/mL. Net price 1-mL amp = 11p; 2-mL amp = 14p. 10 mg/mL see section 15.1.4.1

CD **Pamergan P100®** (Martindale)

Injection, pethidine hydrochloride 50 mg, promethazine hydrochloride 25 mg/mL. Net price 2-mL amp = 45p

Dose: by intramuscular injection, for obstetric analgesia, 1–2 mL every 4 hours if necessary; severe pain, 1–2 mL every 4–6 hours if necessary; premedication, see section 15.1.4.1

PHENAZOCINE HYDROBROMIDE

Indications: severe pain

Cautions; Contra-indications; Side-effects: see under Mophine Salts, but less sedating than morphine; **interactions:** Appendix 1 (opioid analgesics)

Dose: by mouth or sublingually, 5 mg every 4–6 hours when necessary; single doses may be increased to 20 mg

CD **Narphen®** (S&N Pharm.)

Tablets, scored, phenazocine hydrobromide 5 mg. Net price 100-tab pack = £18.15. Label: 2

PHENOPERIDINE
See section 15.1.4.1

4.7.3 Trigeminal neuralgia

Carbamazepine (section 4.8.1), taken during the acute stages of trigeminal neuralgia, reduces the frequency and severity of attacks if given continuously. It has no effect on other forms of headache. A dose of 100 mg once or twice a day should be given initially and the dose slowly increased until the best response is obtained; most patients require 200 mg 3–4 times daily but a few may require an increased total daily dosage of up to 1.6 g. Plasma concentrations should be monitored when high doses are given. Occasionally extreme dizziness is encountered which is a further reason for starting treatment with a small dose and increasing it slowly.

Some cases of trigeminal neuralgia respond to **phenytoin** (section 4.8.1) given alone or in conjunction with carbamazepine. A combination of phenytoin and carbamazepine is only required in very refractory cases or in those unable to tolerate high doses of carbamazepine.

4.7.4 Antimigraine drugs

These drugs are discussed under treatment of the acute migraine attack (section 4.7.4.1) and prophylaxis of migraine (section 4.7.4.2).

4.7.4.1 TREATMENT OF THE ACUTE MIGRAINE ATTACK

Most migraine headaches respond to analgesics such as **aspirin** or **paracetamol** (section 4.7.1) but as peristalsis is often reduced during migraine attacks the medication may not be sufficiently well absorbed to be effective; dispersible or effervescent preparations should therefore preferably be used.

Ergotamine is used in patients who do not respond to analgesics. It relieves migraine headache by constricting cranial arteries but visual and other prodromal symptoms are not affected and vomiting may be made worse. This can be relieved by the addition of an **anti-emetic** (see below).

The value of ergotamine is limited by difficulties in absorption and by its side-effects, particularly nausea, vomiting, abdominal pain, and muscular cramps. In some patients repeated administration may cause habituation. Rarely headache may be provoked, either by chronic overdosage or by rapid withdrawal of the drug. Doses of 6 to 8 mg per attack and 10 to 12 mg per week should **not** be exceeded. Ergotamine treatment should **not** be repeated at intervals of less than 4 days and it should **never** be prescribed prophylactically[1]; it should not be given to patients with hemiplegic migraine.

1. In the management of cluster headache, a low dose of ergotamine is occasionally given on a daily basis for 1–2 weeks; ergotamine is not licensed for this purpose.

There are various ergotamine preparations designed to improve absorption and best results are obtained when the dose is given early in an attack. An aerosol form (Medihaler-Ergotamine®) is acceptable to some patients. Sublingual ergotamine (Lingraine®) probably has no advantage over oral treatment.

Dihydroergotamine is of doubtful value.

Anti-emetics (section 4.6), such as **metoclopramide** by mouth or, if vomiting is likely, by intramuscular injection, or the phenothiazine and antihistamine anti-emetics, relieve the nausea associated with migraine attacks. Prochlorperazine may be given rectally if vomiting is a problem. Metoclopramide has the added advantage of promoting gastric emptying and normal peristalsis. A single dose should be given at the onset of symptoms. Oral analgesic preparations containing metoclopramide are available.

ANALGESICS
Section 4.7.1

ANALGESICS WITH ANTI-EMETICS

Migraleve® (Charwell)
Tablets, all f/c, *pink tablets*, buclizine hydrochloride 6.25 mg, paracetamol 500 mg, codeine phosphate 8 mg; *yellow tablets*, paracetamol 500 mg, codeine phosphate 8 mg. Net price 16 tabs (pink) + 8 tabs (yellow) = £2.48; 24 pink = £2.74; 24 yellow = £2.27. Label: 2, 17
Dose: 2 pink tablets at onset of attack, or if it is imminent then 2 yellow tablets every 4 hours if necessary; max. in 24 hours 2 pink and 6 yellow; CHILD 10–14 years, half adult dose

PoM **Migravess®** (Bayer)
Tablets, effervescent, scored, metoclopramide hydrochloride 5 mg, aspirin 325 mg. Net price 30-tab pack = £3.60. Label: 13, 17
Forte tablets, effervescent, scored, metoclopramide hydrochloride 5 mg, aspirin 450 mg. Net price 30-tab pack = £4.94. Label: 13, 17
Dose: tablets or Forte tablets, 2 dissolved in water at onset of attack then every 4 hours when necessary; max. 6 tablets in 24 hours; CHILD 12–15 years, half adult dose

PoM **Paramax®** (Bencard)
Tablets, scored, paracetamol 500 mg, metoclopramide hydrochloride 5 mg. Net price 42-tab pack = £3.63. Label: 17
Sachets, effervescent powder, sugar-free, the contents of 1 sachet = 1 tablet; to be dissolved in ¼ tumblerful of liquid before administration. Net price 42-sachet pack = £4.79. Label: 13, 17
Dose: (tablets or sachets): 2 at onset of attack then every 4 hours when necessary to max. of 6 in 24 hours (young adult 15–19 years, over 60 kg, max. of 5 in 24 hours); ADOLESCENT and YOUNG ADULT 12–19 years, 30–59 kg, 1 at onset of attack then 1 every 4 hours when necessary to max. of 3 in 24 hours

ERGOTAMINE TARTRATE
Indications: acute attacks of migraine and migraine variants unresponsive to analgesics

Cautions: withdraw treatment immediately if numbness or tingling of extremities develops; should not be used for migraine prophylaxis; **interactions:** Appendix 1 (ergotamine)

Contra-indications: peripheral vascular disease, coronary heart disease, obliterative vascular disease and Raynaud's syndrome, hepatic or renal impairment, sepsis, severe or inadequately controlled hypertension, hyperthyroidism, pregnancy and breast-feeding, porphyria

Side-effects: headache, nausea, vomiting, and abdominal pain; repeated high dosage may cause ergotism with gangrene and confusion; pleural and peritoneal fibrosis may occur with excessive use

Dose: see under preparations below

PoM **Cafergot®** (Sandoz)

Tablets, ergotamine tartrate 1 mg, caffeine 100 mg. Net price 20 = 91p. Label: 18, counselling, dosage

Dose: 1–2 tablets at onset; max. 4 tablets in 24 hours; not to be repeated at intervals of less than 4 days; max. 10 tablets weekly

Suppositories, ergotamine tartrate 2 mg, caffeine 100 mg. Net price 6 = £1.06; 30 = £4.99. Label: 18, counselling, dosage

Dose: 1 suppository at onset; max. 2 in 24 hours; not to be repeated at intervals of less than 4 days; max. 5 suppositories weekly

PoM **Lingraine®** (Sterling-Winthrop)

Tablets (for sublingual use), green, ergotamine tartrate 2 mg. Net price 12 = £6.93. Label: 18, 26, counselling, dosage

Dose: 1 tablet at onset repeated after 30 minutes if necessary; max. 3 in 24 hours and 6 weekly

PoM **Medihaler-Ergotamine®** (3M)

Aerosol inhalation (oral), ergotamine tartrate 360 micrograms/metered inhalation. Net price 75-dose unit = £3.44. Label: 18, counselling, dosage

Dose: 360 micrograms (1 puff) repeated if necessary after 5 minutes; max. 6 inhalations in 24 hours and 15 inhalations weekly

PoM **Migril®** (Wellcome)

Tablets, scored, ergotamine tartrate 2 mg, cyclizine hydrochloride 50 mg, caffeine hydrate 100 mg. Net price 20 = £9.22. Label: 2, 18, counselling, dosage

Dose: 1 tablet at onset, followed after 30 minutes by ½–1 tablet, repeated every 30 minutes if necessary; max. 4 tablets per attack and 6 tablets weekly

DIHYDROERGOTAMINE MESYLATE

Indications: migraine attack unresponsive to analgesics

Cautions; Contra-indications; Side-effects: see under Ergotamine Tartrate, as well as numbness and tingling of extremities, precordial pain reported; also contra-indicated in shock; avoid intra-arterial injection

Dose: by subcutaneous or intramuscular injection, 1 mg repeated once after 30–60 minutes if necessary; max. 3 mg daily and 6 mg weekly

PoM **Dihydergot®** (Sandoz)

Injection, dihydroergotamine mesylate 1 mg/mL. Net price 1-mL amp = 21p

ISOMETHEPTENE MUCATE

Indications: migraine attack

Cautions: cardiovascular disease; **interactions:** Appendix 1 (sympathomimetics)

Contra-indications: glaucoma; porphyria

Side-effects: dizziness, circulatory disturbances

Midrid® (Shire)

Capsules, red, isometheptene mucate 65 mg, paracetamol 325 mg. Net price 20 = £2.72. Label: 17

Dose: migraine, 2 capsules at onset of attack, followed by 1 capsule every hour if necessary; max. 5 capsules in 12 hours

4.7.4.2 PROPHYLAXIS OF MIGRAINE

Where attacks are frequent, search should be made for provocative factors such as stress or diet (chocolate, cheese, alcohol, etc.). Benzodiazepines should be avoided because of the risk of dependence. In patients with more than one attack a month, one of three prophylactic agents may be tried: pizotifen, beta-blockers, or tricyclic antidepressants (even when the patient is not obviously depressed). Oral contraceptives may precipitate or worsen migraine; patients reporting a sharp increase in frequency of migraine or focal features should be recommended alternative contraceptive measures.

Pizotifen is an antihistamine and antiserotonergic drug structurally related to the tricyclic antidepressants. It affords good prophylaxis but may cause weight gain. To avoid undue drowsiness treatment may be started at 500 micrograms at night and gradually increased to 3 mg; it is rarely necessary to exceed this dose.

Beta-blockers. Propranolol, metoprolol, nadolol, and timolol (see section 2.4) are all effective. Propranolol is the most commonly used in an initial dose of 40 mg 2 to 3 times daily by mouth. Beta-blockers may also be given as a single dose of a long-acting preparation. The value of beta-blockers is limited by their contra-indications (see section 2.4) and by interaction with ergotamine (see Appendix 1, beta-blockers).

Tricyclic antidepressants may usefully be prescribed in a dose, for example, of amitriptyline 10 mg at night, increasing to a maintenance dose of 50 to 75 mg at night.

There is recent evidence that the **calcium-channel blockers** (see section 2.6.2), e.g. verapamil and nifedipine may be useful in migraine prophylaxis.

Cyproheptadine, an antihistamine with serotonin-antagonist and calcium channel-blocking properties, may also be tried in refractory cases.

Clonidine (Dixarit®) is probably little better than placebo and may aggravate depression or produce insomnia. **Methysergide** has dangerous side-effects (retroperitoneal fibrosis and fibrosis of the heart valves and pleura); **important:** it should only be administered under hospital supervision.

CLONIDINE HYDROCHLORIDE

Indications: prevention of recurrent migraine (but see notes above), vascular headache, menopausal flushing
Cautions: depressive illness, concurrent antihypertensive therapy; **interactions:** Appendix 1 (clonidine)
Side-effects: dry mouth, sedation, dizziness, nausea, nocturnal restlessness; occasionally rashes
Dose: 50 micrograms twice daily, increased after 2 weeks to 75 micrograms twice daily if necessary

PoM **Dixarit®** (Boehringer Ingelheim)
Tablets, blue, s/c, clonidine hydrochloride 25 micrograms. Net price 112-tab pack = £6.13
PoM **Catapres®** (hypertension), see section 2.5.2

METHYSERGIDE

Indications: prevention of severe recurrent migraine and cluster headache in patients who are refractory to other treatment and whose lives are seriously disrupted (**important:** hospital supervision only, see notes above)
Cautions: history of peptic ulceration; avoid abrupt withdrawal of treatment; after 6 months withdraw for reassessment for at least 1 month (see also notes above)
Contra-indications: renal, hepatic, pulmonary, and cardiovascular disease, collagen disease, cellulitis, urinary tract disorders, cachectic or septic conditions, pregnancy, breast-feeding
Side-effects: nausea, vomiting, heartburn, abdominal discomfort, drowsiness, and dizziness occur frequently in initial treatment; psychic reactions, insomnia, oedema, weight gain, rashes, loss of scalp hair, cramps, arterial spasm, paraesthesias of extremities, postural hypotension, and tachycardia also occur. Retroperitoneal and other abnormal fibrotic reactions may occur on prolonged administration, requiring immediate withdrawal of treatment
Dose: 1 mg at bedtime, gradually increased to 1–2 mg 2–3 times daily with food (see notes above)
Carcinoid syndrome, usual range, 12–20 mg daily (hospital supervision)

PoM **Deseril®** (Sandoz)
Tablets, s/c, methysergide 1 mg (as maleate). Net price 50 = £4.58. Label: 2, 21

PIZOTIFEN

Indications: prevention of vascular headache including classical migraine, common migraine, and cluster headache
Cautions: urinary retention; closed-angle glaucoma, renal impairment; pregnancy and breast-feeding; **interactions:** Appendix 1 (pizotifen)
DRIVING. Drowsiness may affect performance of skilled tasks (e.g. driving); effects of alcohol enhanced
Side-effects: antimuscarinic effects, drowsiness, increased appetite and weight gain; occasionally nausea, dizziness
Dose: 1.5 mg at night *or* 500 micrograms 3 times daily (but see also notes above), adjusted according to response within the usual range 0.5–3 mg daily; max. single dose 3 mg, max. daily dose 6 mg; CHILD up to 1.5 mg daily; max. single dose at night 1 mg

PoM **Sanomigran®** (Sandoz)
Tablets, both ivory-yellow, s/c, pizotifen (as hydrogen malate), 500 micrograms, net price 20 = £1.60; 1.5 mg, 28-tab pack = £7.98. Label: 2
Elixir, sugar-free, pizotifen 250 micrograms (as hydrogen malate)/5 mL. Net price 300-mL pack = £4.23. Label: 2

4.8 Antiepileptics

In this section drugs are discussed under the following subsections:

4.8.1 Control of epilepsy
4.8.2 Drugs used in status epilepticus
4.8.3 Febrile convulsions

4.8.1 Control of epilepsy

The object of treatment is to prevent the occurrence of seizures by maintaining an effective plasma concentration of the drug. Careful adjustment of doses is necessary, starting with low doses and increasing gradually until seizures are controlled or there are overdose effects.

The frequency of administration is determined by the plasma half-life, and should be kept as low as possible to encourage better patient compliance. Most antiepileptics, when used in average dosage, may be given twice daily. Phenobarbitone and sometimes phenytoin, which have long half-lives, may often be given as a daily dose at bedtime. However, with large doses, some antiepileptics may need to be administered 3 times daily to avoid adverse effects associated with high peak plasma concentrations. Young children metabolise antiepileptics more rapidly than adults and therefore require more frequent doses and a higher amount per kilogram body-weight.

Therapy with several drugs concurrently should be avoided. Patients are best controlled with one antiepileptic. Combinations of drugs have been used on the grounds that their therapeutic effects were additive while their individual toxicity was reduced but there is no evidence for this. In fact, toxicity may be enhanced with combination therapy. A second drug should only be added to the regimen if seizures continue despite high plasma concentrations or toxic effects. The use of more than two antiepileptics is rarely justified.

Another disadvantage of multiple therapy is that drug interactions occur between the various antiepileptics (see Appendix 1, antiepileptics) and other drugs. Because of liver enzyme induction, phenobarbitone, phenytoin, primidone, and carbamazepine may increase each other's metabolism and reduce plasma concentrations. The reduction of carbamazepine concentration by concurrent phenytoin administration is a most important example. Moreover, it is illogical to combine primidone and phenobarbitone as the former is largely metabolised to phenobarbitone in the liver, which is responsible for most, if not all, of its antiepileptic action.

Abrupt withdrawal of antiepileptics, particularly the barbiturates and benzodiazepines, should be avoided, as this may precipitate severe rebound seizures. Reduction in dosage should be carried out in stages and, in the case of the barbiturates, the withdrawal process may take months. The changeover from one antiepileptic drug regimen to another should be made cautiously, withdrawing the first drug only when the new regimen has been largely established.

The decision to withdraw all antiepileptics from a seizure-free patient, and its timing, is often difficult and may depend on individual patient factors.

DRIVING. Patients suffering from epilepsy may drive a motor vehicle (but not a heavy goods or public service vehicle) provided that they have had a seizure-free period of two years or, if subject to attacks only while asleep, have established a three-year period of asleep attacks without awake attacks. Patients affected by drowsiness should not drive or operate machinery.

PREGNANCY AND BREAST-FEEDING. During pregnancy, plasma concentrations of antiepileptics should be frequently monitored as they may fall, particularly in the later stages. There is an increased risk of teratogenicity associated with the use of anticonvulsant drugs but, generally, prescribing in pregnancy should follow the same principles as that in non-pregnant patients. Breast-feeding is acceptable with all antiepileptic drugs, taken in normal doses, with the possible exception of the barbiturates.

Important see also under Prescribing in Pregnancy (Appendix 4) and Prescribing during Breast-feeding (Appendix 5).

Drug treatment is usually independent of the aetiology but does vary according to the type of seizure. It is discussed under the headings tonic-clonic (grand mal) seizures; partial (focal) seizures; absence seizures (petit mal); myoclonic seizures (myoclonic jerks), atypical absence, atonic and tonic seizures (all in section 4.8.1); status epilepticus (section 4.8.2); and febrile convulsions (section 4.8.3).

TONIC-CLONIC (GRAND MAL) AND PARTIAL (FOCAL) SEIZURES

The drugs of choice for *tonic-clonic seizures* occurring as part of a syndrome of *primary generalised epilepsy* are carbamazepine, phenytoin, and sodium valproate. Phenobarbitone and primidone are also effective but may be more sedating.

Partial epilepsy is more difficult to control. Carbamazepine and phenytoin are the drugs of choice for secondary generalised tonic-clonic seizures and for partial seizures themselves; controlled trials with sodium valproate suggest similar efficacy but more evidence is awaited. Phenobarbitone and primidone are also effective but, once again, are likely to be more sedating. Second-line drugs for both tonic-clonic and partial seizures include clonazepam, clobazam, and acetazolamide.

Phenytoin is effective in tonic-clonic and partial seizures. It has a narrow therapeutic index and the relationship between dose and plasma concentration is non-linear; small dosage increases in some patients may produce large rises in plasma concentrations with acute toxic side-effects. Monitoring of plasma concentration greatly assists dosage adjustment. A few missed doses or a small change in drug absorption may result in a marked change in plasma concentration.

Phenytoin may cause coarse facies, acne, hirsutism, and gingival hyperplasia and so may be particularly undesirable in adolescent patients.

Carbamazepine is a drug of choice for simple and complex partial seizures and for tonic-clonic seizures regardless of whether they are primary or secondary to a focal discharge. It has a wider therapeutic index than phenytoin and the relationship between dose and plasma concentration is linear, but monitoring of plasma concentrations may be helpful in determining optimum dosage. It has generally fewer side-effects than phenytoin or the barbiturates, but reversible blurring of vision, dizziness, and unsteadiness are dose-related, and may be dose-limiting. These side-effects may be reduced by altering the timing of medication. It is essential to initiate carbamazepine therapy at a low dose and build this up over one or two weeks.

Phenobarbitone is an effective drug but may be sedative in adults and cause behavioural disturbances and hyperkinesia in children. Rebound seizures may be a problem on withdrawal. Monitoring plasma concentrations is less useful than with other drugs because tolerance occurs. **Methylphenobarbitone** is largely converted to phenobarbitone in the liver and has no advantages. **Primidone** is largely converted to phenobarbitone in the body and this is probably responsible for its antiepileptic action. A small starting dose (125 mg) is essential, and the drug should be introduced over several weeks.

Sodium valproate is effective in controlling tonic-clonic seizures, particularly in primary generalised epilepsy. Plasma concentrations are not a useful index of efficacy, therefore routine monitoring is unhelpful. The drug has widespread metabolic effects, and may have dose-related side-effects. There has been recent concern over severe hepatic or pancreatic toxicity, although these effects are rare.

Vigabatrin is a new antiepileptic for use in chronic epilepsy not satisfactorily controlled by other antiepileptics. It is useful in tonic-clonic and partial seizures but has prominent behavioural side-effects in some patients.

Clonazepam is occasionally used in tonic-clonic or partial seizures, but its sedative side-effects may be prominent. **Clobazam** may be used as adjunctive therapy in the treatment of epilepsy (section 4.1.2), but the effectiveness of these and other **benzodiazepines** may wane considerably after weeks or months of continuous therapy.

ABSENCE SEIZURES (PETIT MAL)

Ethosuximide and **sodium valproate** are the drugs of choice in simple absence seizures. Sodium valproate is also highly effective in treating the tonic-clonic seizures which may co-exist with absence seizures in primary generalised epilepsy. Monitoring plasma-ethosuximide concentrations is helpful in determining optimum dosage.

MYOCLONIC SEIZURES (MYOCLONIC JERKS)

Myoclonic seizures occur in a variety of syndromes, and response to treatment varies considerably. **Sodium valproate** is the drug of choice and **clonazepam**, **ethosuximide**, and other antiepileptic drugs may be used.

ATYPICAL ABSENCE, ATONIC, AND TONIC SEIZURES

These seizure types are usually seen in childhood, in specific epileptic syndromes, or associated with cerebral damage or mental retardation. They may respond poorly to the traditional drugs. **Phenytoin**, **sodium valproate**, **clonazepam**, **ethosuximide**, and **phenobarbitone** may be tried. Other second-line antiepileptic drugs are occasionally helpful, including acetazolamide and corticosteroids.

ACETAZOLAMIDE

Indications: see notes above
Cautions; Side-effects: see section 11.6
Dose: 0.25–1 g daily in divided doses; CHILD 125–750 mg daily

Preparations: See section 11.6

CARBAMAZEPINE

Indications: all forms of epilepsy except absence seizures; trigeminal neuralgia (section 4.7.3); prophylaxis in manic-depressive illness (section 4.2.3)
Cautions: see notes above; hepatic impairment; pregnancy and breast-feeding (see notes above); avoid sudden withdrawal; **interactions:** Appendix 1 (carbamazepine)
Contra-indications: atrioventricular conduction abnormalities (unless paced); porphyria; patients on MAOIs or within 2 weeks of MAOI therapy (theoretical grounds only)
Side-effects: gastro-intestinal disturbances, dizziness, drowsiness, headache, ataxia, confusion and agitation (elderly), visual disturbances (especially double vision and often associated with peak plasma concentrations); constipation, anorexia; generalised erythematous rash may occur in about 3% of patients; leucopenia and other blood disorders have occurred rarely; cholestatic jaundice, acute renal failure, Stevens-Johnson syndrome, toxic epidermal necrolysis, alopecia, thromboembolism, fever, proteinuria, lymph node enlargement, cardiac conduction disturbances, and hepatitis reported; hyponatraemia and oedema also reported (with higher doses)
Dose: epilepsy, initially, 100–200 mg 1–2 times daily, increased slowly to usual dose of 0.8–1.2 g daily in divided doses; in some cases 1.6 g daily may be needed; CHILD daily in divided doses, up to 1 year 100–200 mg, 1–5 years 200–400 mg, 5–10 years 400–600 mg, 10–15 years 0.6–1 g

Note. Plasma concentration for optimum response 4–12 mg/litre (20–50 micromol/litre)

PoM **Carbamazepine** (Non-proprietary)
Tablets, carbamazepine 100 mg, net price 20 = 62p; 200 mg, 20 = £1.15; 400 mg, 20 = £2.34

PoM **Tegretol®** (Geigy)
Tablets, all scored, carbamazepine 100 mg, net price 20 = 62p; 200 mg, 20 = £1.15; 400 mg, 20 = £2.34
Chewtabs, orange, carbamazepine 100 mg, net price 20 = £1.05; 200 mg, 20 = £1.96. Label: 21, 24
Liquid, sugar-free, carbamazepine 100 mg/5 mL. Diluent tragacanth mucilage for 1 + 1 dilution, life of diluted liquid 14 days. Net price 300-mL pack = £5.72

PoM **Tegretol® Retard** (Geigy)
Tablets, controlled-release, both scored, carbamazepine 200 mg (beige-orange), net price 20 = £1.50; 400 mg (brown-orange), 20 = £2.94. Label: 25
Dose: epilepsy (ADULT and CHILD over 5 years), as above; trigeminal neuralgia, as section 4.7.3; total daily dose given in 2 divided doses

CLOBAZAM: Section 4.1.2

CLONAZEPAM

Indications: all forms of epilepsy; myoclonus; status epilepticus, section 4.8.2
Cautions: see notes above; respiratory disease; hepatic and renal impairment; elderly and debilitated; pregnancy and breast-feeding (see notes above); avoid sudden withdrawal; **interactions:** Appendix 1 (clonazepam)

DRIVING. Drowsiness may affect the performance of skilled tasks (e.g. driving); effects of alcohol enhanced

Contra-indications: respiratory depression; acute pulmonary insufficiency; porphyria
Side-effects: drowsiness, fatigue, dizziness, muscle hypotonia, coordination disturbances; hypersalivation in infants, paradoxical aggression, irritability and mental changes; rarely, blood disorders, abnormal liver-function tests
Dose: 1 mg (elderly, 500 micrograms), initially at night for 4 nights, increased over 2–4 weeks to a usual maintenance dose of 4–8 mg daily in divided doses; CHILD up to 1 year 250 micrograms increased as above to 0.5–1 mg, 1–5 years 250 micrograms increased to 1–3 mg, 5–12 years 500 micrograms increased to 3–6 mg

PoM **Rivotril®** (Roche)
Tablets, both scored, clonazepam 500 micro-

grams (beige), net price 20 = 88p; 2 mg, 20 = £1.84. Label: 2

ETHOSUXIMIDE

Indications: absence seizures

Cautions: see notes above; hepatic and renal impairment; pregnancy and breast-feeding (see notes above); avoid sudden withdrawal; avoid in porphyria; **interactions:** Appendix 1 (ethosuximide)

Side-effects: gastro-intestinal disturbances, drowsiness, dizziness, ataxia, dyskinesia, hiccup, photophobia, headache, depression, and mild euphoria. Psychotic states, rashes, liver changes, and haematological disorders such as leucopenia and agranulocytosis occur rarely; systemic lupus erythematosus reported

Dose: initially, 500 mg daily, increased by 250 mg at intervals of 4–7 days to usual dose of 1–1.5 g daily; occasionally up to 2 g daily may be needed; CHILD up to 6 years 250 mg daily, over 6 years 500 mg, increased gradually to a max. of 1 g daily

Note. Plasma concentration for optimum response 40–100 mg/litre (300–700 micromol/litre)

PoM **Emeside®** (LAB)

Capsules, orange, ethosuximide 250 mg. Net price 112-cap pack = £8.32

Syrup (elixir), black currant or orange, ethosuximide 250 mg/5 mL. Diluent syrup, life of diluted syrup 14 days. Net price 200-mL pack = £4.50

PoM **Zarontin®** (P-D)

Capsules, orange, ethosuximide 250 mg. Net price 50 = £3.82

Syrup, red, ethosuximide 250 mg/5 mL. Diluent syrup, life of diluted syrup 14 days. Net price 250-mL pack = £4.67

METHYLPHENOBARBITONE

Indications; Cautions; Side-effects: see under Phenobarbitone

Dose: 100–600 mg daily

CD **Prominal®** (Sterling-Winthrop)

Tablets, methylphenobarbitone 30 mg, net price 20 = 72p; 60 mg, 20 = 96p; 200 mg, 20 = £2.05. Label: 2

PHENOBARBITONE

Indications: all forms of epilepsy except absence seizures; status epilepticus, section 4.8.2

Cautions: elderly, debilitated, children, impaired renal or hepatic function, respiratory depression (avoid if severe), pregnancy and breast-feeding (see notes above); avoid sudden withdrawal; avoid in porphyria; see also notes above; **interactions:** Appendix 1 (barbiturates and primidone)

Side-effects: drowsiness, lethargy, mental depression, ataxia and allergic skin reactions; paradoxical excitement, restlessness and confusion in the elderly and hyperkinesia in children; megaloblastic anaemia (may be treated with folic acid)

Dose: by mouth, 60–180 mg at night; CHILD 5–8 mg/kg daily (febrile convulsions, see 4.8.3)

By intramuscular or intravenous injection, 50–200 mg, repeated after 6 hours if necessary; max. 600 mg daily

Note. For therapeutic purposes phenobarbitone and phenobarbitone sodium may be considered equivalent in effect. Plasma concentration for optimum response 15–40 mg/litre (60–180 micromol/litre)

CD [1]**Phenobarbitone Tablets,** phenobarbitone 15 mg, net price 20 = 6p; 30 mg, 20 = 7p; 60 mg, 20 = 10p; 100 mg, 20 = 18p. Label: 2

CD [1]**Phenobarbitone Sodium Tablets,** phenobarbitone sodium 30 mg, net price 20 = 13p; 60 mg, 20 = 29p. Label: 2

CD [1]**Phenobarbitone Elixir,** phenobarbitone 15 mg/5 mL in a suitable flavoured vehicle, containing alcohol 38%. Net price 100 mL = 53p. Label: 2

CD [1]**Phenobarbitone Injection,** phenobarbitone sodium 200 mg/mL in propylene glycol 90% and water for injections 10%. Net price 1-mL amp = 58p

CD [1]**Gardenal Sodium®** (Rhône-Poulenc Rorer)

Injection, phenobarbitone sodium 200 mg/mL. Net price 1-mL amp = 47p

1. See p. 7 for prescribing requirements for phenobarbitone

PHENYTOIN

Indications: all forms of epilepsy except absence seizures; trigeminal neuralgia (see also section 4.7.3)

Cautions: hepatic impairment (reduce dose), pregnancy and breast-feeding (see notes above); change-over from other drugs should be made cautiously; avoid sudden withdrawal; avoid in porphyria; see also notes above; **interactions:** Appendix 1 (phenytoin)

Side-effects: nausea, vomiting, mental confusion, dizziness, headache, tremor, transient nervousness, insomnia occur commonly; rarely dyskinesias, peripheral neuropathy; ataxia, slurred speech, nystagmus and blurred vision are signs of overdosage; rashes (discontinue, if mild re-introduce cautiously but discontinue immediately if recurrence), coarse facies, acne and hirsutism, fever and hepatitis; lupus erythematosus, erythema multiforme (Stevens–Johnson syndrome), toxic epidermal necrolysis, polyarteritis nodosa; lymphadenopathy; gingival hypertrophy and tenderness; rarely haematological effects, including megaloblastic anaemia (may be treated with folic acid), leucopenia, thrombocytopenia, agranulocytosis, and aplastic anaemia; plasma calcium may be lowered (rickets and osteomalacia)

Dose: by mouth, initially 3–4 mg/kg daily *or* 150–300 mg daily (as a single dose *or* in two divided doses) increased gradually as necessary (plasma monitoring, see notes above); usual dose 300–400 mg daily; max. 600 mg daily; CHILD 5–8 mg/kg daily (in 1 or 2 doses)

By intravenous injection—section 4.8.2

Note. Plasma concentration for optimum response 10–20 mg/litre (40–80 micromol/litre)

Note. Phenytoin 100 mg ≡ phenytoin sodium 108 mg
COUNSELLING. Take preferably with or after food

PoM **Phenytoin** (Non-proprietary)
Tablets, coated, phenytoin sodium 50 mg, net price 20 = 14p; 100 mg, 20 = 14p. Label: 27, counselling, administration

Note. Owing to variation in bioavailability different brands of phenytoin tablets may not be interchangeable with one another.

PoM **Epanutin®** (P-D)
Capsules, phenytoin sodium 25 mg (white/purple), net price 20 = 39p; 50 mg (white/pink), 20 = 40p; 100 mg (white/orange), 20 = 43p. Label: 27, counselling, administration
Infatabs® (= tablets, chewable), yellow, scored, phenytoin 50 mg. Net price 20 = £1.10. Label: 24
Suspension, red, phenytoin 30 mg/5 mL. Diluent syrup, life of diluted suspension 14 days. Net price 100 mL = 71p. Counselling, administration
Note. For an equivalent therapeutic effect, phenytoin 90 mg as phenytoin suspension 90 mg in 15 mL ≡ phenytoin sodium 100 mg as tablets or capsules
Injection, section 4.8.2

PRIMIDONE

Indications: all forms of epilepsy except absence seizures; essential tremor (section 4.9.3)
Cautions; Side-effects: see under Phenobarbitone. Drowsiness, ataxia, nausea, visual disturbances, and rashes, particularly at first, usually reversible on continued administration; **interactions:** Appendix 1 (barbiturates and primidone)
Dose: epilepsy, initially, 125 mg daily at bedtime, increased by 125 mg every 3 days to 500 mg daily in 2 divided doses then increased by 250 mg every 3 days to a max. of 1.5 g daily in divided doses; CHILD 20–30 mg/kg daily in 2 divided doses
Note. Monitor plasma concentrations of derived phenobarbitone. Optimum range as for phenobarbitone.

PoM **Mysoline®** (ICI)
Tablets, scored, primidone 250 mg. Net price 20 = 36p. Label: 2
Oral suspension, primidone 250 mg/5 mL. Diluent propyl hydroxybenzoate 0.015%, methyl hydroxybenzoate 0.15%, carmellose sodium '50' 1%, sucrose 20%, in freshly boiled and cooled purified water. Net price 250-mL pack = £1.04. Label: 2

SODIUM VALPROATE

Indications: all forms of epilepsy
Cautions: in patients most at risk (e.g. children and those with history of liver disease) monitor liver function in first 6 months; pregnancy (**important** see notes above and Appendix 4 (neural tube screening)); breast-feeding; monitor platelet function before major surgery; may give false-positive urine tests for ketones in diabetes mellitus; avoid sudden withdrawal; see also notes above; **interactions:** Appendix 1 (valproate)
Contra-indications: active liver disease
Side-effects: gastric irritation, nausea, ataxia and tremor; hyperammonaemia, increased appetite and weight gain; transient hair loss (regrowth may be curly), oedema, thrombocytopenia, and inhibition of platelet aggregation; impaired hepatic function leading rarely to fatal hepatic failure (see Cautions—withdraw treatment immediately if vomiting, anorexia, jaundice, drowsiness, or loss of seizure control occurs); amenorrhoea, rashes; rarely pancreatitis (measure plasma amylase in acute abdominal pain), leucopenia, red cell hypoplasia
Dose: *by mouth*, initially, 600 mg daily in divided doses, preferably after food, increasing by 200 mg/day at 3-day intervals to a max. of 2.5 g daily in divided doses, usual maintenance 1–2 g daily (20–30 mg/kg daily); CHILD up to 20 kg (about 4 years), initially 20 mg/kg daily in divided doses, may be increased gradually providing plasma concentrations monitored to 40 mg/kg daily; over 20 kg, initially 400 mg daily in divided doses increased gradually to 20–30 mg/kg daily; max. 35 mg/kg daily
By intravenous injection (over 3–5 minutes) or *by intravenous infusion*, continuation of valproate treatment when oral therapy not possible, same as current dose by oral route
Initiation of valproate therapy (when oral valproate not possible), *by intravenous injection* (over 3–5 minutes), 400–800 mg (up to 10 mg/kg) followed by *intravenous infusion* up to max. 2.5 g daily
CHILD, usually 20–30 mg/kg daily

PoM **Epilim®** (Sanofi)
Tablets (crushable), scored, sodium valproate 100 mg. Net price 20 = 80p
Tablets, both e/c, lilac, sodium valproate 200 mg, net price 20 = £1.32; 500 mg, 20 = £3.29. Label: 5, 25
Liquid, red, sugar-free, sodium valproate 200 mg/5 mL. Net price 300-mL pack = £6.04
Syrup, red, sodium valproate 200 mg/5 mL. Diluent syrup (without preservative), life of diluted syrup 14 days. Net price 300-mL pack = £6.04

PoM **Epilim® Intravenous** (Sanofi)
Injection, powder for reconstitution, sodium valproate. Net price 400-mg vial (with 4-mL amp water for injections) = £9.00

VIGABATRIN

Indications: epilepsy not satisfactorily controlled by other antiepileptics
Cautions: renal impairment; closely monitor neurological function; avoid sudden withdrawal; history of psychosis or behavioural problems; **interactions:** Appendix 1 (vigabatrin)
Contra-indications: pregnancy (high doses teratogenic in *animals*) and breast-feeding
Side-effects: drowsiness, fatigue, dizziness, nervousness, irritability, depression, headache; less commonly confusion, aggression, psychosis, memory disturbance, visual dis-

turbance (e.g. diplopia); weight gain and gastro-intestinal disturbances reported; excitation and agitation in children

Dose: with current antiepileptic therapy, initially 2 g daily in single or 2 divided doses then increased or decreased according to response in steps of 0.5–1 g; usual max. 4 g daily; CHILD 3–9 years initially 1 g daily

▼ PoM **Sabril®** (Merrell)
Tablets, scored, vigabatrin 500 mg, net price 100-tab pack = £46.00. Label: 3

4.8.2 Drugs used in status epilepticus

Major status epilepticus should be treated first with intravenous **diazepam** or **clonazepam** but they should be used with caution because of the risk of respiratory depression; in situations where facilities for resuscitation are not immediately available, *small doses* of diazepam can be given intravenously or the drug can be administered as a rectal solution (Stesolid®). Intramuscular injection is unsatisfactory as the drugs are too slowly absorbed. When diazepam is given intravenously there may be a high risk of venous thrombophlebitis which is minimised by using an emulsion (Diazemuls®). Absorption from suppositories is too slow for treatment of status epilepticus.

If status epilepticus continues or returns, **chlormethiazole** may be given by intravenous infusion. Chlormethiazole has a short half-life, and the rate of infusion can be titrated against the patient's clinical condition. It does, however, cause respiratory depression. Alternatively **phenytoin sodium** may be given by slow intravenous injection, with ECG monitoring at a rate of not more than 50 mg/minute (in adults) to a maximum of 1 g followed by the maintenance dosage. Intramuscular use of phenytoin is not recommended (absorption is slow and erratic) and intravenous infusion is not recommended (precipitates).

Paraldehyde also remains a valuable drug. It is usually given by deep intramuscular injection but may be given rectally. In some specialist centres, with intensive care facilities, it is also given, with caution, by intravenous injection diluted with sodium chloride intravenous infusion. When given by intramuscular injection, paraldehyde causes little respiratory depression and is therefore useful where facilities for resuscitation are poor.

Phenobarbitone sodium (section 4.8.1) is occasionally used but it is less satisfactory for urgent treatment because of its slow metabolism.

Lorazepam is rarely used for status epilepticus.

DIAZEPAM

Indications: status epilepticus; convulsions due to poisoning (see Emergency Treatment of Poisoning); other indications, see sections 4.1.2, 10.2.2, 15.1.4.2

Cautions; Contra-indications; Side-effects: see section 4.1.2. When given intravenously facilities for reversing respiratory depression with mechanical ventilation should be at hand (see also notes above)

Dose: by slow intravenous injection, 10–20 mg at a rate of 0.5 mL (2.5 mg) per 30 seconds, repeated if necessary after 30–60 minutes; may be followed by *slow intravenous infusion* to a max. of 3 mg/kg over 24 hours; CHILD 200–300 micrograms/kg

By rectum as rectal solution, ADULT and CHILD over 3 years 10 mg; CHILD 1–3 years and ELDERLY 5 mg; repeat after 5 minutes if necessary

PoM **Diazepam** (Non-proprietary)
Injection (solution), diazepam 5 mg/mL. See Appendix 6. Net price 2-mL amp = 25p
Available from CP

PoM **Diazemuls®** (Dumex)
Injection (emulsion), diazepam 5 mg/mL (0.5%). See Appendix 6. Net price 2-mL amp = 63p

PoM **Stesolid®** (CP)
Rectal tubes (= rectal solution), diazepam 2 mg/mL. Net price 5 × 2.5-mL (5 mg) tubes = £5.25; 4 mg/mL, 5 × 2.5-mL (10 mg) tubes = £6.70

PoM **Valium®** (Roche)
Injection (solution), diazepam 5 mg/mL. See Appendix 6. Net price 2-mL amp = 28p

Oral preparations, section 4.1.2

CLONAZEPAM

Indications: status epilepticus; other forms of epilepsy, and myoclonus, section 4.8.1

Cautions; Contra-indications; Side-effects: see section 4.8.1. Hypotension and apnoea may occur and resuscitation facilities must be available

Dose: by slow intravenous injection or infusion, 1 mg over 30 seconds; CHILD all ages, 500 micrograms

PoM **Rivotril®** (Roche)
Injection, clonazepam 1 mg/mL in solvent, for dilution with 1 mL water for injections immediately before injection or as described in Appendix 6. Net price 1-mL amp (with 1 mL water for injections) = 71p

Oral preparations, section 4.8.1

CHLORMETHIAZOLE EDISYLATE

Indications: status epilepticus; other indications, see sections 4.1.1, 15.1.4.2

Cautions: obstructive pulmonary disease; during continuous infusion the sleep induced may quickly lapse into deep unconsciousness and patients must be observed constantly; see also section 4.1.1

Contra-indications: acute pulmonary insufficiency

Side-effects: tingling in the nose, sneezing, conjunctival irritation, headache, slight hypotension, respiratory depression, local thrombophlebitis at site of continuous infusion and at rapid infusion rates cardiovascular and respiratory depression; see also section 4.1.1

Dose: by intravenous infusion, as a 0.8% solution, initially, 40–100 mL (320–800 mg) over 5–10 minutes then continued if necessary at a reduced rate adjusted according to the patient's condition (see notes above)

Note. Special care on prolonged administration since accumulation may occur; also, contains no electrolytes

PoM **Heminevrin**® (Astra)

Intravenous infusion 0.8%, chlormethiazole edisylate 8 mg/mL. Net price 500-mL bottle = £5.25

Oral preparations, section 4.1.1

LORAZEPAM

Indications: status epilepticus; other indications, section 4.1.2

Cautions; Contra-indications; Side-effects: see section 4.1.2

Dose: *by intravenous injection*, 4 mg; CHILD 2 mg

Preparations

Section 4.1.2

PARALDEHYDE

Indications: status epilepticus

Cautions: bronchopulmonary disease, hepatic impairment; avoid intramuscular injection near sciatic nerve (causes severe causalgia)

Side-effects: rashes; intramuscular injection, pain and sterile abscess; enema, rectal irritation

Dose: *by deep intramuscular injection*, as a single dose, 5–10 mL; usual max. 20 mL daily with not more than 5 mL at any one site; CHILD up to 3 months 0.5 mL, 3–6 months 1 mL, 6–12 months 1.5 mL, 1–2 years 2 mL, 3–5 years 3–4 mL, 6–12 years 5–6 mL

By slow intravenous injection, diluted with several times its volume of sodium chloride intravenous infusion 0.9%, up to 4–5 mL (specialist centres only, see notes above)

By rectum, 5–10 mL, administered as a 10% enema in physiological saline; CHILD as for intramuscular dose

Note. Do not use paraldehyde if it has a brownish colour or an odour of acetic acid. Avoid contact with rubber and plastics.

PoM **Paraldehyde** (Non-proprietary)

Injection, sterile paraldehyde. Net price 5-mL amp = £2.15; 10-mL amp = £2.77

PHENYTOIN SODIUM

Indications: status epilepticus; seizures in neurosurgery; arrhythmias, see section 2.3.2

Cautions: hypotension and heart failure; resuscitation facilities must be available; injection solutions alkaline (irritant to tissues); see also section 4.8.1; **interactions:** Appendix 1 (phenytoin)

Contra-indications: sinus bradycardia, sino-atrial block, and second- and third-degree heart block; Stokes-Adams syndrome; porphyria

Side-effects: intravenous injection may cause cardiovascular and CNS depression (particularly if injection too rapid) with arrhythmias, hypotension, and cardiovascular collapse; alterations in respiratory function (including respiratory arrest)

Dose: *by slow intravenous injection* (with blood pressure and ECG monitoring), status epilepticus, 10–15 mg/kg at a rate not exceeding 50 mg per minute, as a loading dose (see also notes above). Maintenance doses of about 100 mg should be given thereafter at intervals of every 6 hours, monitored by measurement of plasma concentrations; rate and dose reduced according to weight

By intramuscular injection, not recommended (see notes above)

PoM **Epanutin Ready Mixed Parenteral**® (P-D)

Injection, phenytoin sodium 50 mg/mL with propylene glycol 40% and alcohol 10% in water for injections. Net price 5-mL amp = £4.07

Oral preparations, section 4.8.1

4.8.3 Febrile convulsions

Brief febrile convulsions need only simple treatment such as tepid sponging or bathing, or antipyretic medication, e.g. **paracetamol** (section 4.7.1). *Prolonged febrile convulsions* (those lasting 15 minutes or longer), *recurrent convulsions*, or those occurring in a child at known risk must be treated more actively, as there is the possibility of resulting brain damage. **Diazepam** is the drug of choice given either by slow intravenous injection in a dose of 250 micrograms/kg (as Diazemuls®, section 4.8.2) or preferably rectally in solution (Stesolid®, section 4.8.2) in a dose of 500 micrograms/kg, repeated if necessary. The rectal route is preferred as satisfactory absorption is achieved within minutes and administration is much easier. Suppositories are not suitable because absorption is too slow.

Intermittent prophylaxis (i.e. the anticonvulsant administered at the onset of fever) is possible in only a small proportion of children. Again **diazepam** is the treatment of choice, orally or rectally.

The exact role of continuous prophylaxis in children at risk from prolonged or complex febrile convulsions is controversial. It is probably indicated in only a small proportion of children, including those whose first seizure occurred at under 14 months or who have pre-existing neurological abnormalities or who have had previous prolonged or focal convulsions. Either **phenobarbitone** (3 to 4 mg/kg daily) or **sodium valproate** (20 mg/kg daily) (section 4.8.1) may be given (but sodium valproate is associated very rarely with hepatitis or pancreatitis).

4.9 Drugs used in parkinsonism and related disorders

4.9.1 Dopaminergic drugs used in parkinsonism
4.9.2 Antimuscarinic drugs used in parkinsonism
4.9.3 Drugs used in essential tremor, chorea, tics, and related disorders

In idiopathic Parkinson's disease, progressive degeneration of pigment-containing cells of the substantia nigra leads to deficiency of the neurotransmitter dopamine. This, in turn, results in a neurohumoral imbalance in the basal ganglia, causing the characteristic signs and symptoms of the illness to appear. The pathogenesis of this process is still obscure and current therapy aims simply to correct the imbalance. Although this approach fails to prevent the progression of the disease, it greatly improves the quality and expectancy of life of most patients.

Levodopa, used in conjunction with **dopa-decarboxylase inhibitors** (section 4.9.1), is the treatment of choice for patients disabled by idiopathic Parkinson's disease. It is less effective in patients with post-encephalitic parkinsonism and should be avoided in neuroleptic-induced parkinsonism.

Parkinsonism caused by generalised degenerative brain disease does not normally respond to levodopa.

Antimuscarinic drugs (section 4.9.2) are the other main class of drugs used in Parkinson's disease. They are less effective than levodopa in idiopathic Parkinson's disease although they often usefully supplement its action. Patients with mild symptoms, particularly where tremor predominates, may be treated initially with antimuscarinic drugs; levodopa is added or substituted as symptoms progress. Antimuscarinic drugs have value in treating drug-induced parkinsonism or in patients with post-encephalitic parkinsonism.

Other antiparkinsonian drugs include amantadine and bromocriptine (section 4.9.1).

The patient should be advised at the outset of the limitations of treatment and possible side-effects. About 10 to 20% of patients are unresponsive to treatment.

ELDERLY. Antiparkinsonian drugs carry a special risk of inducing confusion in the elderly. It is particularly important to initiate treatment with low doses and to use small increments.

4.9.1 Dopaminergic drugs used in parkinsonism

Levodopa is the treatment of choice for disabled patients. It is least valuable in elderly patients and in those with long-standing disease who may not tolerate a dose large enough to overcome their deficit. It is also less valuable in patients with post-encephalitic disease who are particularly susceptible to the side-effects.

Levodopa, the amino-acid precursor of dopamine, acts mainly by replenishing depleted striatal dopamine. It improves bradykinesia and rigidity more than tremor. It is generally administered in conjunction with an extra-cerebral dopa-decarboxylase inhibitor (**carbidopa**, as in co-careldopa preparations or **benserazide**, as in co-beneldopa preparations) which prevents the peripheral degradation of levodopa to dopamine.

The presence of the inhibitor enables the effective dose of levodopa to be greatly reduced, while peripheral side-effects such as nausea and vomiting and cardiovascular effects are minimised. There is less delay in onset of therapeutic effect and a smoother clinical response is obtained. A disadvantage is that there is an increased incidence of abnormal involuntary movements. When co-careldopa 10/100 (containing 10 mg of carbidopa for each 100 mg of levodopa) is used the dose of carbidopa may be insufficient to achieve full inhibition of extracerebral dopa-decarboxylase; co-careldopa 25/100 (containing 25 mg of carbidopa for each 100 mg of levodopa) should then be used so that the daily dose of carbidopa is at least 75 mg. This will ensure maximum effectiveness of the levodopa with a minimum of adverse peripheral effects. A sustained-release preparation of co-beneldopa 25/100 (Madopar® CR) may help with 'end-of-dose' deterioration or nocturnal immobility and rigidity.

Levodopa therapy should be initiated with low doses and gradually increased, by small increments, at intervals of 2 to 3 days. (It is rarely necessary to exceed a daily dose of 1 gram when levodopa is used in conjunction with a dopa-decarboxylase inhibitor.) When titrated in this way the final dose is usually a compromise between increased mobility and dose-limiting side-effects. Intervals between doses may be critical and should be chosen to suit the needs of the individual patient. Nausea and vomiting are rarely dose-limiting if levodopa is given in this way but doses should be taken after meals. Domperidone may be useful in controlling vomiting (section 4.6). The most frequent dose-limiting side-effects of levodopa are involuntary movements and psychiatric complications.

Levodopa therapy should not be discontinued abruptly. As the patient ages, the maintenance dose may need to be reduced. When substituting the combined levodopa-decarboxylase inhibitor preparations for levodopa alone, treatment should be discontinued for 12 hours before starting therapy with the combined preparation.

During the first 6 to 18 months of levodopa therapy there may be a slow improvement in the response of the patient which is maintained for 1½ to 2 years; thereafter a slow decline may occur. Particularly troublesome is the 'on-off' effect the incidence of which increases as the treatment progresses. This is characterised by fluctuations in performance with normal performance during the 'on' period and weakness and akinesia lasting for 2 to 4 hours during the 'off' period.

Monoamine-oxidase inhibitors must be withdrawn at least 14 days before treatment. Close observation is especially necessary in patients with dementia or with a past history of psychiatric illness, open-angle glaucoma, or skin melanoma. Antipsychotic drugs should not be administered concurrently.

Selegiline is a monoamine-oxidase-B inhibitor used in severe parkinsonism in conjunction with levodopa to reduce 'end-of-dose' deterioration. Unlike other monoamine-oxidase inhibitors, it does not cause episodes of hypertension. Early treatment with selegiline may delay the need for levodopa therapy and possibly slow the rate of progression of the disease.

Bromocriptine acts by direct stimulation of surviving dopamine receptors. Although effective, it has no advantages over levodopa. Its use should be restricted to the treatment of those for whom levodopa alone is no longer adequate or who despite careful titration cannot tolerate levodopa. Its use is often restricted by its side-effects and when used with levodopa, abnormal involuntary movements and confusional states are common. The doses of the two drugs should be balanced for optimum effect.

Lysuride is a newly introduced drug for parkinsonism; it is similar to bromocriptine in its action.

Amantadine has modest antiparkinsonian effects. It improves mild bradykinetic disabilities as well as tremor and rigidity. Unfortunately only a small proportion of patients derive much benefit from this drug and tolerance to its effects occurs. However it has the advantage of being relatively free from side-effects.

LEVODOPA

Indications: parkinsonism (but not drug-induced extrapyramidal symptoms), see notes above

Cautions: pulmonary disease, peptic ulceration, cardiovascular disease, diabetes mellitus, open-angle glaucoma, skin melanoma, psychiatric illness (avoid if severe). In prolonged therapy, psychiatric, hepatic, haematological, renal, and cardiovascular surveillance is advisable. Warn patients who benefit from therapy to resume normal activities gradually; avoid abrupt withdrawal; **interactions:** Appendix 1 (levodopa)

Contra-indications: closed-angle glaucoma

Side-effects: anorexia, nausea, insomnia, agitation, postural hypotension (rarely labile hypertension), dizziness, tachycardia, arrhythmias, reddish discoloration of urine and other body fluids, rarely hypersensitivity; abnormal involuntary movements and psychiatric symptoms which include hypomania and psychosis may be dose-limiting; occasionally depression, drowsiness, and rarely headache, peripheral neuropathy reported

Dose: initially 125–500 mg daily in divided doses after meals, increased according to response (see notes above)

PoM **Brocadopa®** (Brocades)

Capsules, levodopa 125 mg, net price 20 = 71p; 250 mg, 20 = 85p; 500 mg, 20 = £1.52. Label: 14, 21

PoM **Larodopa®** (Roche)

Tablets, scored, levodopa 500 mg. Net price 20 = £1.34. Label: 14, 21

CO-BENELDOPA

A mixture of benserazide hydrochloride and levodopa in mass proportions corresponding to 1 part of benserazide and 4 parts of levodopa

Indications; Cautions; Contra-indications; Side-effects: see under Levodopa and notes above

Dose: expressed as levodopa, initially 50–100 mg twice daily, adjusted according to response; usual maintenance dose 400–800 mg daily in divided doses after meals

Note. When transferring patients from levodopa, 3 capsules co-beneldopa 25/100 (Madopar 125®) should be substituted for 2 g levodopa; the levodopa should be discontinued 12 hours beforehand

PoM **Madopar®** (Roche)

Capsules 62.5, blue/grey, co-beneldopa 12.5/50 (benserazide 12.5 mg (as hydrochloride), levodopa 50 mg). Net price 100-cap pack = £7.76. Label: 14, 21

Capsules 125, blue/pink, co-beneldopa 25/100 (benserazide 25 mg (as hydrochloride), levodopa 100 mg). Net price 100-cap pack = £13.51. Label: 14, 21

Capsules 250, blue/caramel, co-beneldopa 50/200 (benserazide 50 mg (as hydrochloride), levodopa 200 mg). Net price 100-cap pack = £22.46. Label: 14, 21

Dispersible tablets 62.5, scored, co-beneldopa 12.5/50 (benserazide 12.5 mg (as hydrochloride), levodopa 50 mg). Net price 100-tab pack = £8.29. Label: 14, 21, counselling, administration, see below

Dispersible tablets 125, scored, co-beneldopa 25/100 (benserazide 25 mg (as hydrochloride) levodopa 100 mg). Net price 100-tab pack = £14.70. Label: 14, 21, counselling, administration, see below

Note. The tablets may be dispersed in water or orange squash or swallowed whole

PoM **Madopar® CR** (Roche)

Capsules 125, s/r, dark green/light blue, co-beneldopa 25/100 (benserazide 25 mg (as hydrochloride), levodopa 100 mg). Net price 100-cap pack = £17.97. Label: 5, 14, 25

Dose: fluctuations in response to conventional levodopa/decarboxylase inhibitor preparations, initially 1 capsule substituted for every 100 mg of levodopa and given at same dosage frequency, subsequently increased every 2–3 days according to response; average increase of 50% needed over previous levodopa dose and titration may take up to 4 weeks; supplementary dose of conventional Madopar® may be needed with first morning dose; if response still poor to total daily dose of Madopar® CR plus Madopar® corresponding to 1.2 g levodopa, consider alternative therapy

CO-CARELDOPA

A mixture of carbidopa and levodopa; the proportions are expressed in the form x/y where x and y are the strengths in milligrams of carbidopa and levodopa respectively

Indications; Cautions; Contra-indications; Side-effects: see under Levodopa and notes above

Dose: expressed as levodopa, initially 100–125 mg 3–4 times daily adjusted according to response; usual maintenance dose 0.75–1.5 g daily in divided doses after food. See also under Sinemet-Plus®

Note. When transferring patients from levodopa, 3 tablets co-careldopa 25/250 (Sinemet-275®) should be substituted for 4 g levodopa; the levodopa should be discontinued 12 hours beforehand

PoM **Sinemet®** (MSD)

Tablets (Sinemet-110), blue, scored, co-careldopa 10/100 (carbidopa 10 mg (as monohydrate), levodopa 100 mg). Net price 20 = £1.71. Label: 14, 21

Tablets (Sinemet-275), blue, scored, co-careldopa 25/250 (carbidopa 25 mg (as monohydrate), levodopa 250 mg). Net price 20 = £3.57. Label: 14, 21

PoM **Sinemet LS®** (MSD)

Tablets, yellow, scored, co-careldopa 12.5/50 (carbidopa 12.5 mg (as monohydrate), levodopa 50 mg). Net price 84-tab pack = £6.87. Label: 14, 21

Dose: initially 1 tablet 3 times daily, adjusted according to response; see also Sinemet Plus®, 2 tablets Sinemet LS® ≡ 1 tablet Sinemet Plus®

PoM **Sinemet-Plus®** (MSD)

Tablets, yellow, scored, co-careldopa 25/100 (carbidopa 25 mg (as monohydrate), levodopa 100 mg). Net price 20 = £2.52. Label: 14, 21

Dose: initially 1 tablet 3 times daily, adjusted according to response to 8 daily in divided doses; larger doses by gradual substitution of Sinemet® for Sinemet-Plus®

AMANTADINE HYDROCHLORIDE

Indications: parkinsonism (but not drug-induced extrapyramidal symptoms); antiviral, see section 5.3

Cautions: cardiovascular, hepatic, or renal disease (avoid if severe), recurrent eczema, psychosis, elderly patients, breast-feeding. Avoid abrupt discontinuation of treatment; **interactions:** Appendix 1 (amantadine)

DRIVING. May affect performance of skilled tasks (e.g. driving)

Contra-indications: epilepsy, gastric ulceration

Side-effects: nervousness, inability to concentrate, insomnia, dizziness, convulsions, hallucinations, gastro-intestinal disturbances, skin discoloration, dry mouth, peripheral oedema; rarely leucopenia

Dose: 100 mg daily increased if necessary to 100 mg twice daily (not later than 4 p.m.), usually in conjunction with other treatment; max. 400 mg daily (with close supervision)

PoM **Mantadine®** (Du Pont)

Capsules, red, amantadine hydrochloride 100 mg. Net price 14-cap pack = £2.05; 100 = £14.70. Counselling, driving

PoM **Symmetrel®** (Geigy)

Capsules, brownish-red, amantadine hydrochloride 100 mg. Net price 20 = £3.38. Counselling, driving

Syrup, amantadine hydrochloride 50 mg/5 mL. Diluent syrup, life of diluted syrup 4 weeks. Net price 150-mL pack = £3.17. Counselling, driving

BROMOCRIPTINE

Indications: parkinsonism (but not drug-induced extrapyramidal symptoms); endocrine disorders, see section 6.7.1

Cautions; Side-effects: see section 6.7.1

HYPOTENSIVE REACTIONS. Hypotensive reactions may be disturbing in some patients during the first few days of treatment and particular care should be exercised when driving or operating machinery; tolerance to bromocriptine reduced by alcohol

Dose: first week 1–1.25 mg at night, second week 2–2.5 mg at night, third week 2.5 mg twice daily, then 3 times daily increasing by 2.5 mg every 3–14 days according to response to a usual range of 10–40 mg daily; taken with food

PoM **Bromocriptine** (Non-proprietary)

Tablets, bromocriptine (as mesylate), 2.5 mg, net price 20 = £5.13. Label: 21, counselling, hypotensive reactions

PoM **Parlodel®** (Sandoz)

Tablets, both scored, bromocriptine (as mesylate), 1 mg, net price 20 = £1.86; 2.5 mg, 20 = £3.61. Label: 21, counselling, hypotensive reactions

Capsules, bromocriptine (as mesylate), 5 mg (blue/white), net price 20 = £7.04; 10 mg, 20 = £13.03. Label: 21, counselling, hypotensive reactions

LYSURIDE MALEATE

Indications: Parkinson's disease

Cautions: history of pituitary tumour; psychotic disturbance; **interactions:** Appendix 1 (lysuride)

HYPOTENSIVE REACTIONS. Hypotensive reactions may be disturbing in some patients during the first few days of treatment and particular care should be exercised when driving or operating machinery

Contra-indications: severe disturbances of peripheral circulation; coronary insufficiency, porphyria

Side-effects: nausea and vomiting; dizziness; headache, lethargy, malaise, drowsiness, psychotic reactions (including hallucinations); occasionally severe hypotension, rashes; rarely abdominal pain and constipation; Raynaud's phenomenon reported

Dose: initially 200 micrograms at bedtime with food increased as necessary at weekly intervals to 200 micrograms twice daily (midday and bedtime) then to 200 micrograms 3 times daily (morning, midday, and bedtime); further increases made by adding 200 micrograms each week first to the bedtime dose, then to the midday dose and finally to the morning dose; max. 5 mg daily in 3 divided doses after food

▼ PoM **Revanil®** (Roche)

Tablets, scored, lysuride maleate 200 micrograms. Net price 100-tab pack = £24.00. Label: 21, counselling, hypotensive reactions

SELEGILINE

Indications: Parkinson's disease or symptomatic parkinsonism (but not drug-induced extrapyramidal symptoms), either used alone (in early disease) or as an adjunct to levodopa therapy

Cautions: side-effects of levodopa may be increased, concurrent levodopa dosage may need to be reduced by 20–50%

Side-effects: hypotension, nausea and vomiting, confusion, agitation

Dose: 10 mg in the morning, or 5 mg at breakfast and midday

PoM **Eldepryl®** (Britannia)
Tablets, scored, selegiline hydrochloride 5 mg. Net price 20 = £9.30

4.9.2 Antimuscarinic drugs used in parkinsonism

These drugs exert their antiparkinsonian effect by correcting the relative central cholinergic excess thought to occur in parkinsonism as a result of dopamine deficiency. In most patients their effects are only moderate, reducing tremor and rigidity to some effect but without significant action on bradykinesia. Antimuscarinics (less correctly termed 'anticholinergics') exert a synergistic effect when used with levodopa and are also useful in reducing sialorrhoea.

They may be used as first-line drugs in mild cases, particularly with tremor or rigidity, or as adjunctive therapy with levodopa. The antimuscarinic drugs also reduce the symptoms of drug-induced parkinsonism as seen, for example, with antipsychotic drugs (section 4.2.1) but there is no justification for giving them simultaneously with antipsychotics unless parkinsonian side-effects occur. Tardive dyskinesia is not improved by the antimuscarinic drugs and may be made worse.

No important differences exist between the many synthetic drugs available but certain patients appear to tolerate one preparation better than another. Doses may be taken before food if dry mouth is troublesome, or after food if gastro-intestinal symptoms predominate.

The most commonly used drugs are **orphenadrine** and **benzhexol; benztropine** and **procyclidine** are also used. Benztropine is similar to benzhexol but is excreted more slowly; changes in dose therefore need to be carried out very gradually. Both procyclidine and benztropine may be given parenterally and are effective emergency treatment for acute drug-induced dystonic reactions which may be severe.

BENZHEXOL HYDROCHLORIDE

Indications: parkinsonism; drug-induced extrapyramidal symptoms (but not tardive dyskinesia, see notes above)

Cautions: urinary retention, closed-angle glaucoma, cardiovascular disease, hepatic or renal impairment; gastro-intestinal obstruction; avoid abrupt discontinuation of treatment; drugs of this type liable to abuse; **interactions:** Appendix 1 (antimuscarinics)

DRIVING. May affect performance of skilled tasks (e.g. driving)

Side-effects: dry mouth, gastro-intestinal disturbances, dizziness, blurred vision; less commonly urinary retention, tachycardia, hypersensitivity, nervousness, and with high doses in susceptible patients, mental confusion, excitement, and psychiatric disturbances which may necessitate discontinuation of treatment

Dose: 1 mg daily, gradually increased; usual maintenance dose 5–15 mg daily in 3–4 divided doses

PoM **Benzhexol** (Non-proprietary)
Tablets, benzhexol hydrochloride 2 mg, net price 20 = 31p; 5 mg, 20 = 63p. Counselling, before or after food (see notes above), driving

PoM **Artane®** (Lederle)
Tablets, both scored, benzhexol hydrochloride 2 mg, net price 20 = 32p; 5 mg, 20 = 65p. Counselling, before or after food (see notes above), driving

PoM **Bentex®** (Steinhard)
Tablets, both scored, benzhexol hydrochloride 2 mg, net price 20 = 31p; 5 mg, 20 = 63p. Counselling, before or after food (see notes above), driving

PoM **Broflex®** (Bioglan)
Syrup, pink, benzhexol hydrochloride 5 mg/5 mL. Diluent syrup, life of diluted syrup 14 days. Net price 200-mL pack = £3.80. Counselling, before or after food (see notes above), driving

BENZTROPINE MESYLATE

Indications; Cautions; Side-effects: see under Benzhexol Hydrochloride, but causes sedation rather than stimulation; avoid in children under 3 years

Dose: by mouth, 0.5–1 mg daily usually at bedtime, gradually increased; max. 6 mg daily; usual maintenance dose 1–4 mg daily in single or divided doses

By intramuscular or intravenous injection, 1–2 mg, repeated if symptoms reappear

PoM **Cogentin®** (MSD)
Tablets, scored, benztropine mesylate 2 mg. Net price 20 = 29p. Label: 2
Injection, benztropine mesylate 1 mg/mL. Net price 2-mL amp = 77p

BIPERIDEN

Indications; Cautions; Side-effects: see under Benzhexol Hydrochloride, but may cause drowsiness; injection may cause hypotension

Dose: by mouth, biperiden hydrochloride 1 mg twice daily, gradually increased to 2 mg 3 times daily; usual maintenance dose 3–12 mg daily in divided doses

By intramuscular or slow intravenous injection, biperiden lactate 2.5–5 mg up to 4 times daily

PoM **Akineton®** (Knoll)
Tablets, scored, biperiden hydrochloride 2 mg. Net price 100-tab pack = £4·72. Label: 2
Injection, biperiden lactate 5 mg/mL. Net price 1-mL amp = 70p

METHIXENE HYDROCHLORIDE

Indications; Cautions; Side-effects: see under Benzhexol Hydrochloride
Dose: 2.5 mg 3 times daily gradually increased; usual maintenance dose 15–60 mg (elderly 15–30 mg) daily in divided doses

PoM **Tremonil®** (Sandoz)
Tablets, scored, methixene hydrochloride 5 mg. Net price 50 = £1.71. Label: 2

ORPHENADRINE HYDROCHLORIDE

Indications; Cautions; Side-effects: see under Benzhexol Hydrochloride, but more euphoric; may cause insomnia; avoid in porphyria
Dose: *by mouth*, 150 mg daily in divided doses, gradually increased; max. 400 mg daily

PoM **Biorphen®** (Bioglan)
Elixir, sugar-free, orphenadrine hydrochloride 25 mg/5 mL. Net price 200-mL pack = £4.50. Counselling, driving
PoM **Disipal®** (Brocades)
Tablets, yellow, s/c, orphenadrine hydrochloride 50 mg. Net price 20 = 30p. Counselling, driving
Additives: include tartrazine

PROCYCLIDINE HYDROCHLORIDE

Indications; Cautions; Side-effects: see under Benzhexol Hydrochloride
Dose: *by mouth*, 2.5 mg 3 times daily, gradually increased if necessary; usual max. 30 mg daily (60 mg daily in exceptional circumstances)
Acute dystonia, *by intramuscular injection*, 5–10 mg repeated if necessary after 20 minutes; max. 20 mg daily; *by intravenous injection*, 5 mg (usually effective within 5 minutes); an occasional patient may need 10 mg or more and may require up to half an hour to obtain relief

PoM **Procyclidine** (Non-proprietary)
Tablets, procyclidine hydrochloride 5 mg. Net price 20 = £1.00. Counselling, driving
PoM **Arpicolin®** (RP Drugs)
Syrup, procyclidine hydrochloride 2.5 mg/5 mL, net price 200-mL pack = £2.80; 5 mg/5 mL, 200-mL pack = £5.00. Counselling, driving
PoM **Kemadrin®** (Wellcome)
Tablets, scored, procyclidine hydrochloride 5 mg. Net price 20 = £1.39. Counselling, driving
Injection, procyclidine hydrochloride 5 mg/mL. Net price 2-mL amp = £1.49

4.9.3 Drugs used in essential tremor, chorea, tics, and related disorders

Tetrabenazine is mainly used to control movement disorders in Huntington's chorea and related disorders. It may act by depleting nerve endings of dopamine. It has useful action in only a proportion of patients and its use may be limited by the development of depression.

Haloperidol may be useful in improving motor tics and symptoms of Gilles de la Tourette syndrome and related choreas. **Pimozide** (see section 4.2.1 for CSM warning) and more recently clonidine (section 4.7.4.2) and sulpiride (section 4.2.1), are also used in Gilles de la Tourette syndrome. **Benzhexol** (section 4.9.2) at high dosage may also improve some movement disorders. It is sometimes necessary to build the dose up over many weeks, to 20 to 30 mg daily or higher. Other antipsychotic drugs including **chlorpromazine** and **haloperidol** are used to relieve intractable hiccup (section 4.2.1).

Propranolol or another beta-adrenoceptor blocking drug (see section 2.4) may be useful in treating essential tremor or tremors associated with anxiety or thyrotoxicosis. Propranolol is given in a dosage of 40 mg 2 or 3 times daily, increased if necessary; 80 to 160 mg daily is usually required for maintenance.

Primidone in some cases provides relief from benign essential tremor; the dose is increased slowly to reduce side-effects.

HALOPERIDOL

Indications: motor tics, adjunctive treatment in choreas and Gilles de la Tourette syndrome; other indications, section 4.2.1
Cautions; Contra-indications; Side-effects: see section 4.2.1
Dose: *by mouth*, 0.5–1.5 mg 3 times daily adjusted according to the response; 10 mg daily or more may occasionally be necessary in Gilles de la Tourette syndrome; CHILD, Gilles de la Tourette syndrome up to 10 mg daily

Preparations: Section 4.2.1

PRIMIDONE

Indications: essential tremor; epilepsy, see section 4.8.1
Cautions; Contra-indications; Side-effects: see section 4.8.1
Dose: essential tremor, initially 50 mg daily increased gradually over 2–3 weeks according to response; max. 750 mg daily

Preparations: Section 4.8.1

TETRABENAZINE

Indications: movement disorders due to Huntington's chorea, senile chorea, and related neurological conditions
Cautions: pregnancy; avoid in breast-feeding; **interactions:** Appendix 1 (tetrabenazine)
Side-effects: drowsiness, gastro-intestinal disturbances, depression, extrapyramidal dysfunction, hypotension
Dose: initially 12.5 mg twice daily (elderly 12.5 mg daily) gradually increased to 12.5–25 mg 3 times daily; max. 200 mg daily

PoM **Nitoman**® (Roche)
Tablets, pale yellow-buff, scored, tetrabenazine 25 mg. Net price 120-tab pack = £5·59. Label: 2

4.10 Drugs used in substance dependence

This section includes drugs used in alcoholism, cigarette smoking, and opioid addiction.

ALCOHOLISM

Disulfiram (Antabuse®) is used as an adjunct to the treatment of alcoholism. It gives rise to extremely unpleasant systemic reactions after the ingestion of even small amounts of alcohol because it leads to accumulation of acetaldehyde in the body. Reactions include flushing of the face, throbbing headache, palpitations, tachycardia, nausea, vomiting, and, with large doses of alcohol, arrhythmias, hypotension, and collapse. Even the small amounts of alcohol included in many oral medicines may be sufficient to precipitate a reaction. It may be advisable for patients to carry a card warning of the danger of administration of alcohol.

Chlormethiazole (section 4.1.1) and benzodiazepines (section 4.1.2) are used to attenuate withdrawal symptoms but themselves have a dependence potential (section 4.1).

DISULFIRAM

Indications: adjunct in the treatment of chronic alcoholism (under specialist supervision)
Cautions: ensure that alcohol not consumed for at least 12 hours before initiating treatment; see also notes above; variable and occasionally severe reactions on alcohol challenge; hepatic or renal impairment, respiratory disease, diabetes mellitus, epilepsy; **interactions:** Appendix 1 (disulfiram)

ALCOHOL REACTION. Patients should be warned of unpredictable and occasionally severe nature of disulfiram-alcohol interactions. Reactions can occur in 10 minutes and last several hours (may require intensive supportive therapy). Patients should not ingest alcohol at all and should be warned of possible presence of alcohol in liquid medicines

Contra-indications: cardiac failure, coronary artery disease, psychosis and drug addiction, pregnancy
Side-effects: initially drowsiness and fatigue; nausea, vomiting, halitosis, reduced libido; rarely psychotic reactions (depression, paranoia, schizophrenia, mania), allergic dermatitis, peripheral neuritis, hepatic cell damage
Dose: 800 mg as a single dose on first day, reducing over 5 days to 100–200 mg daily; may be continued for up to 1 year

PoM **Antabuse 200**® (CP)
Tablets, scored, disulfiram 200 mg. Net price 50 = £17.50. Label: 2

CIGARETTE SMOKING

Nicotine chewing gum may be prescribed as an adjunct to counselling; it is not available on the NHS.

NHS PoM **Nicorette**® (Lundbeck)
Chewing gum, sugar-free, nicotine (as resin) 2 mg, net price, pack of 105 = £6.12; 4 mg, 105 = £9.39.
Cautions: angina, coronary artery disease; exacerbation of gastritis or peptic ulcer if swallowed
Contra-indications: pregnancy
Dose: nicotine replacement, initially one 2-mg piece to be chewed slowly for approx. 30 minutes, when urge to smoke occurs; patients needing more than 15 2-mg pieces daily may need the 4-mg strength; max. 15 pieces of 4-mg strength daily

OPIOID DEPENDENCE

Methadone is an opioid *agonist*. It can be substituted for opioids such as diamorphine, preventing the onset of withdrawal symptoms; it is itself addictive and should only be prescribed for those who are physically dependent on opioids. It is administered in a single daily dose usually as methadone mixture 1 mg/mL. The dose is adjusted according to the degree of dependence with the aim of gradual reduction.

Naltrexone is an opioid *antagonist*. It blocks the action of opioids such as diamorphine and precipitates withdrawal symptoms in opioid-dependent subjects. Since the euphoric action of opioid agonists is blocked by naltrexone it is given to former addicts to prevent readdiction. Naltrexone should be initiated in specialist clinics only.

METHADONE HYDROCHLORIDE

Indications: adjunct in treatment of opioid dependence, see notes above; analgesia, section 4.7.2
Cautions; Contra-indications; Side-effects: section 4.7.2
Dose: initially 10–20 mg daily, increased by 10–20 mg daily until no signs of withdrawal or intoxication; usual dose 40–60 mg daily

CD **Methadone Mixture 1 mg/mL** (Drug Tariff Formula)
Net price 500 mL = £5.66. Label: 2
Available from Macarthys, Penn (special order)

This preparation is 2½ times the strength of Methadone Linctus and is intended only for drug dependent persons for whom treatment is normally ordered on form FP10(H.P.)(ad) or FP10(MDA)
The title includes the strength and prescriptions should be written accordingly
Syrup preserved with hydroxybenzoate esters may be incompatible with methadone hydrochloride.

NALTREXONE HYDROCHLORIDE

Indications: adjunct to prevent relapse in detoxified formerly opioid-dependent patients

Cautions: hepatic and renal impairment; liver function tests needed before and during treatment; test for opioid dependence with naloxone; avoid concomitant use of opioids but increased dose of opioid analgesic may be required for pain (monitor for opioid intoxication)

Contra-indications: patients currently dependent on opioids; acute hepatitis or liver failure

Side-effects: nausea, vomiting, abdominal pain; anxiety, nervousness, sleeping difficulty, headache, reduced energy; joint and muscle pain; less frequently, loss of appetite, diarrhoea, constipation, increased thirst; chest pain; increased sweating and lachrymation; increased energy, 'feeling down', irritability, dizziness, chills; delayed ejaculation, decreased potency; rash; occasionally, liver function abnormalities; reversible idiopathic thrombocytopenia reported

Dose: 25 mg initially then 50 mg daily; the total weekly dose may be divided and given on 3 days of the week for improved compliance (e.g. 100 mg on Monday and Wednesday, and 150 mg on Friday)

PoM **Nalorex**® (Du Pont)

Tablets, orange, scored, naltrexone hydrochloride 50 mg. Net price 50-tab pack = £79.49

5: Drugs used in the treatment of INFECTIONS

In this chapter, drug treatment is discussed under the following headings:

5.1 Antibacterial drugs

CHOICE OF A SUITABLE DRUG. Before selecting an antibiotic the clinician must first consider two factors—the patient and the known or likely causative organism. Factors related to the patient which must be considered include history of allergy, renal and hepatic function, resistance to infection (i.e. whether immunocompromised), ability to tolerate drugs by mouth, severity of illness, ethnic origin, age and, if female, whether pregnant, breast-feeding or taking an oral contraceptive.

The known or likely organism and its antibiotic sensitivity, in association with the above factors, will suggest one or more antibiotics, the final choice depending on the microbiological, pharmacological, and toxicological properties.

An example of a rational approach to the selection of an antibiotic is treatment of a urinary-tract infection in a patient complaining of nausea in early pregnancy. The organism is reported as being resistant to ampicillin but sensitive to nitrofurantoin (can cause nausea), gentamicin (can only be given by injection and best avoided in pregnancy), tetracycline and co-trimoxazole (both contra-indicated in pregnancy), and cephalexin. The safest antibiotics in pregnancy are the penicillins and cephalosporins; therefore, cephalexin would be indicated for this patient.

The principles involved in selection of an antibiotic must allow for a number of variables including changing renal and hepatic function, increasing bacterial resistance, and new information on side-effects. Duration of therapy, dosage, and route of administration depend on site, type and severity of infection.

ANTIBIOTIC POLICIES. Many health authorities now place limits on the antibiotics that may be used in their hospitals, to achieve reasonable economy consistent with adequate cover, and to reduce the development of resistant organisms. An authority may indicate a range of drugs for general use, and permit treatment with other drugs only on the advice of the microbiologist or physician responsible for the control of infectious diseases.

BEFORE STARTING THERAPY. The following precepts should be considered before starting:

Viral infections should not be treated with antibiotics.

Samples should be taken for culture and sensitivity testing; **'blind'** prescribing of an antibiotic for a patient ill with unexplained pyrexia usually leads to further difficulty in establishing the diagnosis.

An up-to-date knowledge of **prevalent organisms** and their current sensitivity is of great help in choosing an antibiotic before bacteriological confirmation is available.

The **dose** of an antibiotic will vary according to a number of factors including age, weight, renal function, and severity of infection. The prescribing of the so-called 'standard' dose in serious infections may result in failure of treatment or even death of the patient. Most antibiotics are rapidly excreted from the body and should be administered every 6 hours for the treatment of serious infections. Less severe infections as seen in general practice usually respond to administration every 8 hours. Agents with prolonged plasma half-lives such as trimethoprim need only be given every 12 hours. The aminoglycoside antibiotics should not be given more frequently than every 8 hours and the interval between doses must be increased in patients with renal failure.

The **route** of administration of an antibiotic will often depend on the severity of the infection. Life-threatening infections require intravenous therapy. Whenever possible painful intramuscular injections should be avoided in children.

Duration of therapy depends on the nature of the infection and the response to treatment. Courses should not be unduly prolonged as they are wasteful and may lead to side-effects. However, in certain infections such as endocarditis or tuberculosis it is necessary to continue treatment for relatively long periods. Conversely a single dose of an antibiotic may cure uncomplicated urinary-tract infections.

Suggested treatment is shown in Table 1. When the pathogen has been isolated treatment may be changed to a more appropriate antibiotic if necessary. If no bacterium is cultured the antibiotic can be continued or stopped on clinical grounds. Infections for which prophylaxis is useful are listed in Table 2.

Table 1. Summary of antibacterial therapy

Infection	Suggested antibacterial	Comment
1: Gastro-intestinal system		
Gastro-enteritis	Antibiotic not usually indicated	Frequently nonbacterial aetiology
Campylobacter enteritis	Erythromycin *or* ciprofloxacin	
Invasive salmonellosis	Amoxycillin[1] *or* trimethoprim *or* ciprofloxacin	Includes severe infections which may be invasive
Shigellosis	Amoxycillin *or* trimethoprim *or* ciprofloxacin	Antibiotic not indicated for mild cases
Typhoid fever	Chloramphenicol *or* ciprofloxacin *or* amoxycillin[1]	
Biliary-tract infection	Gentamicin *or* a cephalosporin	
Peritonitis	Gentamicin (*or* a cephalosporin) + metronidazole (*or* clindamycin)	
Peritoneal dialysis-associated peritonitis	Vancomycin + gentamicin added to dialysis fluid	Discontinue either gentamicin or vancomycin when sensitivity known; treat for 5–10 days
2: Cardiovascular system		
Endocarditis caused by:		
Penicillin-sensitive streptococci (e.g. viridans streptococci)	Benzylpenicillin (*or* vancomycin if penicillin-allergic) + low-dose gentamicin (i.e. 60–80 mg twice daily)	Treat for 4 weeks; stop gentamicin after 2 weeks if organism fully sensitive to penicillin. Oral amoxycillin[1] may be substituted for benzylpenicillin after 2 weeks
Streptococci with reduced sensitivity to penicillin e.g. *Streptococcus faecalis*	Benzylpenicillin (*or* vancomycin if penicillin-allergic) + low-dose gentamicin (i.e. 60–80 mg twice daily)	Treat for at least 4 weeks
Staphylococcus aureus (and *Staphylococcus epidermidis*)	Flucloxacillin[2] + *either* gentamicin *or* fusidic acid (*or* vancomycin alone if penicillin-allergic)	Treat for at least 4 weeks; stop gentamicin after 2 weeks
3: Respiratory system		
Haemophilus epiglottitis	Chloramphenicol	Give intravenously
Exacerbations of chronic bronchitis	Amoxycillin[1] *or* trimethoprim *or* erythromycin *or* tetracycline	Note that 20% of pneumococci and some *Haemophilus influenzae* strains are tetracycline-resistant
Pneumonia:		
Previously healthy chest	Benzylpenicillin *or* amoxycillin[1]	Add flucloxacillin[2] if *Staphylococcus* suspected e.g. in influenza or measles; use erythromycin if *Legionella* infection is suspected (severe *Legionella* infections may require rifampicin)
Previously unhealthy chest	Flucloxacillin[2] + amoxycillin[1] (*or* trimethoprim *or* erythromycin)	Substitute erythromycin (*or* rifampicin, see above) for flucloxacillin if *Legionella* infection is suspected
4: Central nervous system		
Meningitis caused by:		
Meningococcus	Benzylpenicillin	Give rifampicin for 2 days before hospital discharge
Pneumococcus	Benzylpenicillin	
Haemophilus influenzae	Chloramphenicol	For *H. influenzae* type b give rifampicin for 4 days before hospital discharge
Listeria	Amoxycillin[1] + gentamicin	
7: Urinary tract		
Acute pyelonephritis or prostatitis	Trimethoprim *or* gentamicin *or* cephalosporin *or* ciprofloxacin	Do not give trimethoprim in pregnancy. Treat prostatitis with trimethoprim for 4 weeks
'Lower' UTI	Trimethoprim *or* amoxycillin[1] *or* nitrofurantoin *or* oral cephalosporin	

1. Where amoxycillin is suggested ampicillin or an ester of ampicillin (see section 5.1.1.3) may be used.
2. Where flucloxacillin is suggested cloxacillin may be used.

Table 1. Summary of antibacterial therapy (*continued*)

Infection	Suggested antibacterial	Comment
7: Genital system		
Syphilis	Procaine penicillin (*or* tetracycline *or* erythromycin if penicillin-allergic)	Treat for 10–21 days
Gonorrhoea	Amoxycillin[1] with probenecid (*or* spectinomycin, *or* ciprofloxacin if penicillin-allergic)	Single-dose treatment in uncomplicated infection; choice depends on locality where infection acquired; contact-tracing advised; remember chlamydia
Non-gonococcal urethritis	Tetracycline	Treat for 7–21 days; contact-tracing advised
Pelvic inflammatory disease	Metronidazole + doxycycline	Not active against all causative organisms; remember gonorrhoea and chlamydia
9: Blood		
Septicaemia		
Initial 'blind' therapy	Aminoglycoside + a penicillin *or* a cephalosporin alone *In immunocompromised*, aminoglycoside + a broad-spectrum penicillin *or* a 'third generation' cephalosporin alone	Choice depends on local resistance patterns and clinical presentation; add metronidazole if anaerobic infection suspected; add flucloxacillin *or* vancomycin if Gram-positive infection suspected
10: Musculoskeletal system		
Osteomyelitis and septic arthritis	Clindamycin *or* flucloxacillin[2] + fusidic acid. If *Haemophilus influenzae* give amoxycillin[1] *or* co-trimoxazole	Under 5 years of age may be *H. influenzae* Treat acute disease for at least 6 weeks and chronic infection for at least 12 weeks
11: Eye		
Purulent conjunctivitis	Chloramphenicol *or* gentamicin eye-drops	
12: Ear, nose, and oropharynx		
Dental infections	Phenoxymethylpenicillin (*or* amoxycillin[1]) *or* erythromycin *or* metronidazole	Tetracycline for chronic destructive forms of periodontal disease
Sinusitis	Amoxycillin[1] *or* doxycycline	
Otitis media	Benzylpenicillin Phenoxymethylpenicillin	Initial i/m therapy (if possible) with benzylpenicillin, then oral therapy with phenoxymethylpenicillin
	Amoxycillin[1] if under 5 years (*or* erythromycin if penicillin-allergic)	Under 5 years of age may be *Haemophilus influenzae*
Tonsillitis	Benzylpenicillin Phenoxymethylpenicillin (*or* erythromycin if penicillin-allergic)	Initial i/m therapy (in severe infection) with benzylpenicillin, then oral therapy with phenoxymethylpenicillin. Most infections are caused by viruses
13: Skin		
Impetigo	Topical chlortetracycline *or* oral flucloxacillin[2] if systemic toxicity	
Erysipelas	Benzylpenicillin Phenoxymethylpenicillin	Initial i/m therapy (if possible) with benzylpenicillin, then oral therapy with phenoxymethylpenicillin
Cellulitis	Flucloxacillin[2] (*or* erythromycin if penicillin-allergic)	
Acne	Tetracycline	Treat for at least 3–4 months

1. Where amoxycillin is suggested ampicillin or an ester of ampicillin (see section 5.1.1.3) may be used.
2. Where flucloxacillin is suggested cloxacillin may be used.

Table 2. Summary of antibacterial prophylaxis

Infection	Antibacterial and dose
Prevention of recurrence of rheumatic fever	Phenoxymethylpenicillin 500 mg daily *or* sulphadimidine 500 mg daily (250 mg for children)
Prevention of secondary case of meningococcal meningitis	Rifampicin 600 mg every 12 hours for 2 days; CHILD 10 mg/kg (3 months–1 year, 5 mg/kg) every 12 hours for 2 days *or* sulphadimidine (if strain known to be sensitive) 1 g every 12 hours for 2 days; CHILD 500 mg (3 months–1 year, 250 mg) every 12 hours for 2 days
Prevention of secondary case of *Haemophilus influenzae* type b disease	Rifampicin 600 mg once daily for 4 days (optimum regimen for adults); CHILD over 3 months 20 mg/kg once daily for 4 days (max. 600 mg daily)
Prevention of secondary case of diphtheria in non-immune patient	Erythromycin 500 mg every 6 hours for 5 days
Prevention of endocarditis in patients with heart-valve lesion, septal defect, patent ductus, or prosthetic valve Note. High-dose 3-g amoxycillin regimens are now considered suitable for patients who have received a penicillin not more than once in the previous month	*Dental procedures under local or no anaesthesia*, patients who have not received a penicillin more than once in the previous month, including those with a prosthetic heart valve (but not those who have had endocarditis), oral amoxycillin 3 g 1 hour before procedure; CHILD under 5 years quarter adult dose; 5–10 years half adult dose patients who are penicillin-allergic or have received a penicillin more than once in the previous month, *either* oral erythromycin 1.5 g (as stearate) 1–2 hours before procedure, then 500 mg 6 hours later; CHILD under 5 years quarter adult dose; 5–10 years half adult dose *or* oral clindamycin 600 mg 1 hour before procedure; CHILD under 10 years 6 mg/kg patients who have had endocarditis, amoxycillin + gentamicin, as under general anaesthesia *Dental procedures under general anaesthesia*, no special risk, *either* i/m amoxycillin 1 g just before induction, then oral amoxycillin 500 mg 6 hours later; CHILD under 10 years half adult dose *or* oral amoxycillin 3 g 4 hours before induction then oral amoxycillin 3 g as soon as possible after procedure; CHILD under 5 years quarter adult dose; 5–10 years half adult dose *or* oral amoxycillin 3 g + oral probenecid 1 g 4 hours before procedure; *special risk* (patients with a prosthetic heart valve or who have had endocarditis), i/m amoxycillin 1 g + i/m gentamicin 120 mg just before induction, then oral amoxycillin 500 mg 6 hours later; CHILD under 10 years amoxycillin half adult dose, gentamicin 2 mg/kg patients who are penicillin-allergic or who have received a penicillin more than once in the previous month, i/v vancomycin 1 g over 60 minutes then i/v gentamicin 120 mg just before induction or 15 minutes before procedure; CHILD under 10 years vancomycin 20 mg/kg, gentamicin 2 mg/kg *Upper respiratory-tract procedures*, as for dental procedures; post-operative dose may be given parenterally if swallowing is painful *Genito-urinary procedures*, as for special risk patients undergoing dental procedures under general anaesthesia, see above; if urine infected, prophylaxis should cover infective organism *Obstetric, gynaecological and gastro-intestinal procedures* (prophylaxis required for patients with prosthetic valves only), as for genito-urinary procedures
Prevention of gas-gangrene in high lower-limb amputations or following major trauma	Benzylpenicillin 300–600 mg every 6 hours for 5 days *or* if penicillin-allergic give metronidazole 500 mg every 8 hours
Prevention of tuberculosis in susceptible close contacts	Isoniazid 300 mg daily for 6 months; CHILD, isoniazid 5–10 mg/kg daily *or* isoniazid 300 mg daily + rifampicin 600 mg daily (450 mg if less than 50 kg) for 3 months; CHILD isoniazid 5–10 mg/kg daily + rifampicin 10 mg/kg daily
Prevention of infection in abdominal surgery	
Operations on stomach or oesophagus for carcinoma, or cholecystectomy in patients with possibly infected bile	Single immediate pre-operative dose of gentamicin *or* a cephalosporin
Resections of colon and rectum for carcinoma, and resections in inflammatory bowel disease	Single immediate pre-operative dose of *either* gentamicin + metronidazole *or* cefuroxime + metronidazole
Hysterectomy	Metronidazole as suppository *or* single i/v dose

5.1.1 Penicillins

The penicillins are bactericidal and act by interfering with bacterial cell wall synthesis. They diffuse well into body tissues and fluids, but penetration into the cerebrospinal fluid is poor except when the meninges are inflamed. They are excreted in the urine in therapeutic concentrations. Probenecid blocks the renal tubular excretion of the penicillins, producing higher and more prolonged plasma concentrations (see section 10.1.4); it is not recommended in children under 2 years of age.

The most important side-effect of the penicillins is hypersensitivity, which causes rashes and, occasionally, anaphylaxis, which can be fatal. Patients who are allergic to one penicillin will be allergic to all as the hypersensitivity is related to the basic penicillin structure. A rare but serious toxic effect of the penicillins is encephalopathy due to cerebral irritation. This may result from excessively high doses but can also develop with normal doses given to patients with renal failure. The penicillins should **not** be given by intrathecal injection as they can cause encephalopathy which may be fatal.

A second problem relating to high doses of penicillin, or normal doses given to patients with renal failure, is the accumulation of electrolyte since most injectable penicillins contain either sodium or potassium.

Diarrhoea frequently occurs during oral penicillin therapy. It is most common with ampicillin and its derivatives, which can also cause pseudomembranous colitis.

5.1.1.1 BENZYLPENICILLIN AND PHENOXYMETHYLPENICILLIN

Benzylpenicillin (Penicillin G), the first of the penicillins, remains an important and useful antibiotic; it is inactivated by bacterial penicillinases (beta-lactamases). It is the drug of choice for streptococcal, pneumococcal, gonococcal, and meningococcal infections and also for actinomycosis, anthrax, diphtheria, gas-gangrene, syphilis, tetanus, yaws, and treatment of Lyme disease in children. Pneumococci, meningococci, and gonococci have recently been isolated which have decreased sensitivity to penicillin. Benzylpenicillin is inactivated by gastric acid and absorption from the gut is low; therefore it is best given by injection. Benzylpenicillin may cause convulsions after high doses by intravenous injection or in renal failure.

Procaine penicillin is a sparingly soluble salt of benzylpenicillin. It is used in intramuscular depot preparations which provide therapeutic tissue concentrations for up to 24 hours. It is the preferred choice for the treatment of syphilis; neurosyphilis requires special consideration.

Benethamine penicillin is a benzylpenicillin salt with very low solubility giving a prolonged action after intramuscular injection, though producing low plasma concentrations; it is used, with soluble and procaine penicillin, in Triplopen® (which is effective for syphilis).

Phenoxymethylpenicillin (Penicillin V) has a similar antibacterial spectrum to benzylpenicillin, but is less active. It is gastric acid-stable, so is suitable for oral administration. It should not be used for serious infections because absorption can be unpredictable and plasma concentrations variable. It is indicated principally for respiratory-tract infections in children, for streptococcal tonsillitis, and for continuing treatment after one or more injections of benzylpenicillin when clinical response has begun. It should not be used for meningococcal or gonococcal infections. Phenoxymethylpenicillin is used for prophylaxis against streptococcal infections following rheumatic fever.

Phenethicillin has similar antibacterial activity, but is no more effective than phenoxymethylpenicillin.

BENZYLPENICILLIN

(Penicillin G)

Indications: tonsillitis, otitis media, erysipelas, streptococcal endocarditis, meningococcal and pneumococcal meningitis, prophylaxis in limb amputation

Cautions: history of allergy; renal impairment

Contra-indications: penicillin hypersensitivity

Side-effects: sensitivity reactions including urticaria, fever, joint pains; angioedema; anaphylactic shock in hypersensitive patients; diarrhoea after administration by mouth

Dose: by intramuscular or by slow intravenous injection or by infusion, 0.6–1.2 g daily in 2–4 divided doses, increased if necessary to 2.4 g daily; NEONATE, 30 mg/kg daily (in 2 divided doses in the first few days of life then in 3–4 divided doses); CHILD 1 month–12 years, 10–20 mg/kg daily in 4 divided doses

Bacterial endocarditis, *by slow intravenous injection or by infusion*, 7.2 g daily in divided doses

Meningitis, *by slow intravenous injection or by infusion*, 2.4 g every 4–6 hours; CHILD 1 month–12 years, 180–300 mg/kg daily in 4–6 divided doses

Prophylaxis in limb amputation, section 5.1, Table 2

By intrathecal injection, **not** recommended, see section 5.1.1

PoM **Crystapen**® (Glaxo)

Injection, powder for reconstitution, benzylpenicillin sodium (unbuffered). Net price 600-mg vial = 12p

BENETHAMINE PENICILLIN

Indications: penicillin-sensitive infections; prophylaxis

Cautions; Contra-indications; Side-effects: see under Benzylpenicillin

PoM **Triplopen®** (Glaxo)

Injection, powder for reconstitution, benethamine penicillin 475 mg, procaine penicillin 250 mg, benzylpenicillin sodium 300 mg. Net price per vial = 40p

Dose: by deep intramuscular injection, 1 vial every 2–3 days

BENZATHINE PENICILLIN

Indications: penicillin-sensitive infections

Cautions; Contra-indications; Side-effects: see under Benzylpenicillin

Dose: see below

PoM **Penidural®** (Wyeth)

Suspension, pink, benzathine penicillin 229 mg/5 mL. Diluent syrup, life of diluted suspension 14 days. Net price 100 mL = £1.49. Label: 9

Dose: 10 mL 3–4 times daily; CHILD 5 mL 3–4 times daily

Paediatric drops, pink, benzathine penicillin 115 mg/mL. Net price 10 mL = £1.63. Label: 9, counselling, use of pipette

Dose: CHILD up to 5 years, 1–2 dropperfuls (approx. 77–154 mg) 3–4 times daily

PHENETHICILLIN

Indications: penicillin-sensitive infections

Cautions; Contra-indications; Side-effects: see under Benzylpenicillin

Dose: 250 mg every 6 hours, at least 30 minutes before food; CHILD, under 2 years quarter adult dose, 2–10 years half adult dose

PoM **Broxil®** (Beecham)

Product discontinued.

PHENOXYMETHYLPENICILLIN

(Penicillin V)

Indiccations: tonsillitis, otitis media, erysipelas, rheumatic fever prophylaxis

Cautions; Contra-indications; Side-effects: see under Benzylpenicillin; **interactions:** Appendix 1 (penicillins)

Dose: 250–500 mg every 6 hours, at least 30 minutes before food; CHILD, every 6 hours, up to 1 year 62.5 mg, 1–5 years 125 mg, 6–12 years 250 mg

PoM **Phenoxymethylpenicillin** (Non-proprietary)

Capsules, phenoxymethylpenicillin (as potassium salt) 250 mg, net price 20 = 51p. Label: 9, 23

Tablets, phenoxymethylpenicillin (as potassium salt) 250 mg, net price 20 = 33p. Label: 9, 23

Oral solution, phenoxymethylpenicillin (as potassium salt) for reconstitution with water, 125 mg/5 mL, net price 100 mL = 53p; 250 mg/5 mL, 100 mL = 82p. Label: 9, 23

PoM **Apsin VK®** (APS)

Tablets, f/c, scored, phenoxymethylpenicillin 250 mg (as potassium salt). Net price 20 = 41p. Label: 9, 23

Syrup, both orange, phenoxymethylpenicillin (as potassium salt) for reconstitution with water, 125 mg/5 mL, net price 100 mL = 66p; 250 mg/5 mL, 100 mL = £1.01. Diluent syrup, life of diluted syrup 7 days. Label: 9, 23

PoM **Distaquaine V-K®** (Dista)

Tablets, scored, phenoxymethylpenicillin (as potassium salt) 250 mg, net price 20 = 38p. Label: 9, 23

Syrup, orange, phenoxymethylpenicillin (as potassium salt) for reconstitution with water, 125 mg/5 mL, net price 100 mL = 58p. Diluent syrup, life of diluted syrup 7 days. Label: 9, 23

PoM **Stabillin V-K®** (Boots)

Tablets, phenoxymethylpenicillin 250 mg (as potassium salt). Net price 20 = 22p. Label: 9, 23

Elixir, phenoxymethylpenicillin (as potassium salt) for reconstitution with water, 62.5 mg/5 mL, net price 100 mL = 40p; 125 mg/5 mL, 100 mL = 50p; 250 mg/5 mL 100 mL = 80p. Diluent syrup, life of diluted elixir 7 days. Label: 9, 23

PoM **V-Cil-K®** (Lilly)

Capsules, pink, phenoxymethylpenicillin 250 mg (as potassium salt). Net price 20 = 51p. Label: 9, 23

Tablets, phenoxymethylpenicillin (as potassium salt) 250 mg, net price 20 = 36p. Label: 9, 23

Paediatric syrup, phenoxymethylpenicillin (as potassium salt) for reconstitution with water, 125 mg/5 mL, net price 100 mL = 58p. Diluent syrup, life of diluted syrup 7 days. Label: 9, 23

PROCAINE PENICILLIN

Indications: penicillin-sensitive infections

Cautions; Contra-indications; Side-effects: see under Benzylpenicillin; **not** for intravenous administration

Dose: see below

PoM **Bicillin®** (Brocades)

Injection, powder for reconstitution, procaine penicillin 1.8 g, benzylpenicillin sodium 360 mg. Net price 6-mL multidose vial = £1.93

Dose: when reconstituted with 4.6 mL water for injections, 1 mL (procaine penicillin 300 mg, benzylpenicillin sodium 60 mg) every 12–24 hours by intramuscular injection

Early syphilis, by intramuscular injection, 3 mL (4 mL in heavier patients) daily for 10 days

Note. Reconstitution with 4.6 mL water for injections produces 6 mL

5.1.1.2 PENICILLINASE-RESISTANT PENICILLINS

Most staphylococci are now resistant to benzylpenicillin because they produce penicillinases. **Cloxacillin** and **flucloxacillin**, however, are not inactivated by these enzymes and are thus effective in infections caused by penicillin-resistant staphylococci, which is the sole indication for their use. They are acid-stable and can, therefore, be given by mouth as well as by injection.

Flucloxacillin is better absorbed from the gut than cloxacillin and is, therefore, to be preferred for oral therapy.

Methicillin is also effective against penicillin-resistant *Staph. aureus*, but can only be given by injection because it is not acid-stable and is now seldom used.

Staph. aureus strains resistant to methicillin and cloxacillin have emerged in some hospitals; some of these organisms are only sensitive to vancomycin (section 5.1.7).

Temocillin is a new penicillin with activity against penicillinase-producing Gram-negative bacteria (except *Pseudomonas aeruginosa*); it is not active against Gram-positive bacteria.

CLOXACILLIN

Indications: infections due to penicillinase-producing staphylococci

Cautions; Contra-indications; Side-effects: see under Benzylpenicillin (section 5.1.1.1)

Dose: by mouth, 500 mg every 6 hours, at least 30 minutes before food

By intramuscular injection, 250 mg every 4–6 hours

By slow intravenous injection or by infusion, 500 mg every 4–6 hours

Doses may be doubled in severe infections

CHILD, any route, under 2 years quarter adult dose; 2–10 years half adult dose

PoM **Cloxacillin** (Non-proprietary)

Capsules, cloxacillin (as sodium salt) 250 mg, net price 20 = £3.64; 500 mg, 20 = £7.29. Label: 9, 23

PoM **Orbenin®** (Beecham)

Capsules, both orange/black, cloxacillin (as sodium salt) 250 mg, net price 20 = £3.64; 500 mg, 20 = £7.29. Label: 9, 23

Injection, powder for reconstitution, cloxacillin (as sodium salt). Net price 250-mg vial = 93p; 500-mg vial = £1.86; also available as 1-g vial

FLUCLOXACILLIN

Indications: infections due to penicillinase-producing staphylococci

Cautions; Contra-indications; Side-effects: see under Benzylpenicillin (section 5.1.1.1); hepatitis and cholestatic jaundice reported rarely; avoid in porphyria

Dose: by mouth, 250 mg every 6 hours, at least 30 minutes before food

By intramuscular injection, 250 mg every 6 hours

By slow intravenous injection or by infusion, 0.25–1 g every 6 hours

Doses may be doubled in severe infections

CHILD, any route, under 2 years ¼ adult dose; 2–10 years ½ adult dose

PoM **Flucloxacillin** (Non-proprietary)

Capsules, flucloxacillin (as sodium salt) 250 mg, net price 20 = £2.70; 500 mg, 20 = £5.60. Label: 9, 23

Available from APS, Ashbourne (Fluclomix®), Berk (Ladropen®), Brocades (Stafoxil®), Cox, Evans, Kerfoot

Oral solution (= elixir or syrup), flucloxacillin (as sodium salt) for reconstitution with water, 125 mg/5 mL. Net price 100 mL = £3.22. Label: 9, 23

Available from APS, Cox

Oral suspension (= mixture), flucloxacillin (as magnesium salt) for reconstitution with water, 125 mg/5 mL, net price 100 mL = £3.32; 250 mg/5 mL, 100 mL = £6.64. Label: 9, 23

PoM **Floxapen®** (Beecham)

Capsules, both black/caramel, flucloxacillin (as sodium salt) 250 mg, net price 28-cap pack = £5.63; 500 mg, 28-cap pack = £11.26. Label: 9, 23

Syrup, flucloxacillin 125 mg (as magnesium salt)/5 mL when reconstituted with water. Diluent syrup, life of diluted syrup 14 days. Net price 100 mL = £3.32. Label: 9, 23

Syrup forte, flucloxacillin 250 mg (as magnesium salt)/5 mL when reconstituted with water. Diluent as above. Net price 100 mL = £6.64. Label: 9, 23

Injection, powder for reconstitution, flucloxacillin (as sodium salt). Net price 250-mg vial = 93p; 500-mg vial = £1.86; 1-g vial = £3.71

PoM **Ladropen®** (Berk)

Injection, powder for reconstitution, flucloxacillin (as sodium salt). Net price 250-mg vial = 77p; 500-mg vial = £1.53

METHICILLIN SODIUM

Indications: infections due to penicillinase-producing staphylococci

Cautions; Contra-indications; Side-effects: see under Benzylpenicillin (section 5.1.1.1)

Dose: by intramuscular injection or slow intravenous injection or infusion, 1 g every 4–6 hours

PoM **Celbenin®** (Beecham)

Injection, powder for reconstitution, methicillin sodium. Net price 1-g vial = £1.88

TEMOCILLIN

Indications: infections due to penicillinase-producing Gram-negative bacteria except pseudomonas.

Cautions; Contra-indications; Side-effects: see under Benzylpenicillin (section 5.1.1.1)

Prices are **net**, see p. 1

Dose: by intramuscular injection or by intravenous injection (over 3–4 minutes) *or by intravenous infusion*, 1–2 g every 12 hours
Acute uncomplicated urinary-tract infections, 1 g daily as a single dose or in divided doses

▼ PoM **Temopen**® (Bencard)
Injection, powder for reconstitution, temocillin (as sodium salt). Net price 500-mg vial = £7.50; 1-g vial = £15.00

5.1.1.3 BROAD-SPECTRUM PENICILLINS

Ampicillin is active against certain Gram-positive and Gram-negative organisms but is inactivated by penicillinases including those produced by *Staphylococcus aureus* and by common Gram-negative bacilli such as *Escherichia coli.* Almost all staphylococci, 40% of *E. coli* strains and up to one-tenth of *Haemophilus influenzae* strains are now resistant. The likelihood of resistance should therefore be considered before using ampicillin for the 'blind' treatment of infections; in particular, it should not be used for hospital patients without checking sensitivity.

Ampicillin is well excreted in the bile and urine. It is principally indicated for the treatment of exacerbations of chronic bronchitis and middle ear infections, both of which are usually due to *Streptococcus pneumoniae* and *H. influenzae*, and for urinary-tract infections (section 5.1.13) and gonorrhoea.

Ampicillin can be given by mouth but less than half the dose is absorbed, and absorption is further decreased by the presence of food in the gut. Higher plasma concentrations are obtained with the ampicillin esters **bacampicillin, pivampicillin** and **talampicillin**; their absorption is little affected by the presence of food, and the incidence of diarrhoea is less than with ampicillin. These antibiotics should be given every 8 hours for moderate or severe infections, especially outside the renal tract.

Maculopapular rashes commonly occur with ampicillin (and amoxycillin) but are not usually related to true penicillin allergy. They almost always occur in patients with glandular fever; broad-spectrum penicillins should not therefore be used for 'blind' treatment of a sore throat. Rashes are also common in patients with chronic lymphatic leukaemia and in patients infected with the human immunodeficiency virus (HIV).

Amoxycillin is a derivative of ampicillin which differs by only one hydroxyl group and has a similar antibacterial spectrum. It is, however, better absorbed when given by mouth, producing higher plasma and tissue concentrations; unlike ampicillin, absorption is not affected by the presence of food in the stomach.

Co-amoxiclav consists of amoxycillin with the beta-lactamase inhibitor clavulanic acid. Clavulanic acid itself has no significant antibacterial activity but, by inactivating penicillinases, it makes the combination active against penicillinase-producing bacteria that are resistant to amoxycillin. These include most *Staph. aureus*, 40% of *E. coli* strains, and up to 10% of *H. influenzae* strains, as well as many *Bacteroides* and *Klebsiella* spp. **Sulbactam** is another beta-lactamase inhibitor which is available in combination with ampicillin as Dicapen®.

Combinations of ampicillin with flucloxacillin (as co-fluampicil) and ampicillin with cloxacillin (Ampiclox®) are available.

Mezlocillin is a ureidopenicillin which is active against certain ampicillin-resistant bacteria. However, like ampicillin, it is inactivated by beta-lactamases. It possesses anti-pseudomonal activity.

AMOXYCILLIN

Indications: see under Ampicillin; also typhoid fever and dental prophylaxis
Cautions; Contra-indications; Side-effects: see under Ampicillin
Dose: *by mouth*, 250 mg every 8 hours, doubled in severe infections; CHILD up to 10 years, 125 mg every 8 hours, doubled in severe infections
Severe or recurrent purulent respiratory infection, 3 g every 12 hours
Dental prophylaxis, section 5.1, Table 2

Short-course oral therapy
Dental abscess, 3 g repeated after 8 hours
Urinary-tract infections, 3 g repeated after 10–12 hours
Gonorrhoea, single dose of 3 g with probenecid 1 g
Otitis media, CHILD 3–10 years, 750 mg twice daily for 2 days
By intramuscular injection, 500 mg every 8 hours; CHILD, 50–100 mg/kg daily in divided doses
By intravenous injection or infusion. 500 mg every 8 hours increased to 1 g every 6 hours; CHILD, 50–100 mg/kg daily in divided doses

PoM **Amoxycillin** (Non-proprietary)
Capsules, amoxycillin (as trihydrate) 250 mg, net price 20 = £2.78; 500 mg, 20 = £5.60. Label: 9
Available from APS, Ashbourne (Amix®), Berk (Almodan®), Cox, Eastern (Amoram®), Evans, Galen (Galenamox®), Kerfoot, Rima (Rimoxallin®)
Oral suspension, amoxycillin (as trihydrate) for reconstitution with water, 125 mg/5 mL, net price 100 mL = £1.75; 250 mg/5 mL, 100 mL = £3.26. Label: 9.
Available from APS, Berk (Almodan®), Cox, Eastern (Amoram®), Evans, Galen (Galenamox®), Kerfoot, Rima (Rimoxallin®)

PoM **Almodan**® (Berk)
Injection, powder for reconstitution, amoxycillin (as sodium salt), 250-mg vial, net price = 39p; 500-mg vial = 71p

PoM **Amoxil**® (Bencard)
Capsules, both maroon/gold, amoxycillin (as trihydrate), 250 mg, net price 21-cap pack = £3.34; 500 mg, 21-cap pack = £6.68. Label: 9
Dispersible tablets, sugar-free, amoxycillin 500 mg (as trihydrate). Net price 21-tab pack = £7.71. Label: 9, 13
Syrup SF, both sugar-free, amoxycillin (as trihydrate) for reconstitution with water, 125 mg/

5 mL, net price 100 mL = £2.00; 250 mg/5 mL, 100 mL = £4.00. Diluent water, life of diluted preparation 14 days. Label: 9

Paediatric suspension, amoxycillin 125 mg (as trihydrate)/1.25 mL when reconstituted with water. Net price 20 mL = £3.00. Label: 9, counselling, use of pipette

Sachets SF, powder, sugar-free, amoxycillin 750 mg (as trihydrate)/sachet, net price 4 sachets = £2.60. 3 g/sachet, 2 sachets = £4.30. Label: 9, 13

Injection, powder for reconstitution, amoxycillin (as sodium salt). Net price 250-mg vial = 36p; 500-mg vial = 66p; 1-g vial = £1.31

AMPICILLIN

Indications: urinary-tract infections, otitis media, chronic bronchitis, invasive salmonellosis, gonorrhoea

Cautions: history of allergy; renal impairment; erythematous rashes common in glandular fever and in chronic lymphatic leukaemia; **interactions:** Appendix 1 (penicillins)

Contra-indications: penicillin hypersensitivity

Side-effects: nausea, diarrhoea; rashes (discontinue treatment); rarely, pseudomembranous colitis; see also under Benzylpenicillin (section 5.1.1.1)

Dose: *by mouth*, 0.25–1 g every 6 hours, at least 30 minutes before food

Gonorrhoea, 2 g as a single dose with probenecid 1 g

Urinary-tract infections, 500 mg every 8 hours

By intramuscular injection or intravenous injection or infusion, 500 mg every 4–6 hours; higher doses in meningitis

CHILD under 10 years, any route, half adult dose

PoM **Ampicillin** (Non-proprietary)

Capsules, ampicillin 250 mg, net price 20 = 67p; 500 mg, 20 = £1.40. Label: 9, 23

Available from APS, Berk (Vidopen®), Brocades (Amfipen®), Cox, Evans, Kerfoot, Rima (Rimacillin®)

Oral suspension, ampicillin 125 mg/5 mL when reconstituted with water. Diluent syrup, life of diluted suspension 7 days, net price 100 mL = 76p; 250 mg/5 mL, 100 mL = £1.23. Label: 9, 23

Available from APS, Berk (Vidopen®), Brocades (Amfipen®), Cox, Evans, Kerfoot, Rima (Rimacillin®)

PoM **Amfipen®** (Brocades)

Injection, powder for reconstitution, ampicillin (as sodium salt). Net price 250-mg vial = 31p; 500-mg vial = 62p

PoM **Penbritin®** (Beecham)

Capsules, both black/red, ampicillin (as trihydrate) 250 mg, net price 28-cap pack = £2.05; 500 mg, 28-cap pack = £4.10. Label: 9, 23

Syrup, ampicillin 125 mg (as trihydrate)/5 mL when reconstituted with water. Diluent syrup, life of diluted syrup 7 days. Net price 100 mL = £1.09. Label: 9, 23

Syrup forte, ampicillin 250 mg (as trihydrate)/5 mL when reconstituted with water. Diluent as above. Net price 100 mL = £2.17. Label: 9, 23

Paediatric suspension, pink, ampicillin 125 mg (as trihydrate)/1.25 mL. Net price 25 mL = £2.03. Label: 9, 23, counselling, use of pipette

Injection, powder for reconstitution, ampicillin (as sodium salt). Net price 250-mg vial = 33p; 500-mg vial = 67p

PoM **Vidopen®** (Berk)

Injection, powder for reconstitution, ampicillin (as sodium salt). Net price 250-mg vial = 33p; 500-mg vial = 67p.

With cloxacillin

PoM **Ampiclox®** (Beecham)

Injection, ampicillin 250 mg (as sodium salt), cloxacillin 250 mg (as sodium salt). Net price per vial = £1.36

Dose: by intramuscular injection or intravenous injection or infusion, 1–2 vials every 4–6 hours; CHILD up to 2 years quarter adult dose, 2–10 years half adult dose

PoM **Ampiclox Neonatal®** (Beecham)

Suspension, sugar-free, ampicillin 60 mg (as trihydrate), cloxacillin 30 mg (as sodium salt)/0.6 mL when reconstituted with water. Net price 10 mL = £2.06. Label: 9, counselling, use of pipette

Dose: 0.6 mL every 4 hours

With flucloxacillin

See Co-fluampicil

AMPICILLIN WITH SULBACTAM

Indications: infections due to beta-lactamase producing organisms; prophylaxis in abdominal and obstetric procedures

Cautions; Contra-indications; Side-effects: see under Ampicillin

Dose: *by intramuscular injection or by intravenous injection* over 3 minutes *or by intravenous infusion*, expressed as ampicillin, 1 g every 6–8 hours, doubled for severe infections (max. 8 g daily); CHILD, expressed as ampicillin, 100 mg/kg in 3–4 divided doses (2 divided doses in neonates)

Surgical prophylaxis, expressed as ampicillin, 1–2 g at induction; may be repeated every 6–8 hours for up to 24 hours

▼ PoM **Dicapen®** (Leo)

Injection 750 mg, powder for reconstitution, ampicillin (as sodium salt) 500 mg, sulbactam (as sodium salt) 250 mg. Net price per vial = £1.23

Injection 1.5 g, powder for reconstitution, ampicillin (as sodium salt) 1 g, sulbactam (as sodium salt) 500 mg. Net price per vial = £2.46

Injection 3 g, powder for reconstitution, ampicillin (as sodium salt) 2 g, sulbactam (as sodium salt) 1 g. Net price per vial = £4.92

BACAMPICILLIN HYDROCHLORIDE

Indications; Cautions; Contra-indications; Side-effects: see under Ampicillin

Dose: 400 mg 2–3 times daily, doubled in severe infections; CHILD over 5 years, 200 mg 3 times daily

Uncomplicated gonorrhoea, 1.6 g as a single dose with probenecid 1 g

PoM **Ambaxin®** (Upjohn)

Tablets, scored, bacampicillin hydrochloride 400 mg. Net price 20 = £6.34. Label: 9

CO-AMOXICLAV

A mixture of amoxycillin (as the trihydrate or as the sodium salt) and clavulanic acid (as potassium clavulanate); the proportions are expressed in the form *x*/*y* where *x* and *y* are the strengths in milligrams of amoxycillin and clavulanic acid respectively

Indications: see under Ampicillin and notes above

Cautions; Contra-indications; Side-effects: see under Ampicillin; also caution in severe hepatic impairment; hepatitis, cholestatic jaundice, and erythema multiforme (including Stevens-Johnson syndrome) reported; phlebitis at injection site also reported

Dose: *by mouth*, expressed as amoxycillin, 250 mg every 8 hours, dose doubled in severe infections; CHILD see under preparations below (3 months–6 years Augmentin® Paediatric suspension; 6–12 years Augmentin® Junior suspension)

By intravenous injection or infusion, expressed as amoxycillin, 1 g every 8 hours increased to 1 g every 6 hours in more serious infections; INFANTS up to 3 months 25 mg/kg every 8 hours (every 12 hours in the perinatal period and in premature infants); CHILD 3 months–12 years, 25 mg/kg every 8 hours increased to 25 mg/kg every 6 hours in more serious infections

PoM **Augmentin®** (Beecham)

Tablets, f/c, co-amoxiclav 250/125 (amoxycillin 250 mg as trihydrate, clavulanic acid 125 mg as potassium salt). Net price 21-tab pack = £6.67; 30-tab pack = £9.65. Label: 9

Dispersible tablets, sugar-free, co-amoxiclav 250/125 (amoxycillin 250 mg as trihydrate, clavulanic acid 125 mg as potassium salt). Net price 21-tab pack = £7.49. Label: 9, 13

Junior suspension, sugar-free, co-amoxiclav 125/62 (amoxycillin 125 mg as trihydrate, clavulanic acid 62 mg as potassium salt)/5 mL when reconstituted with water. Net price 100 mL = £3.93. Label: 9

Dose: CHILD 6–12 years, 5 mL every 8 hours, increased to 10 mL in severe infections

Paediatric suspension, sugar-free, co-amoxiclav 125/31 (amoxycillin 125 mg as trihydrate, clavulanic acid 31 mg as potassium salt)/5 mL when reconstituted with water. Diluent not more than an equal volume of water, life of diluted suspension 7 days. Net price 100 mL = £3.12. Label: 9

Dose: CHILD 3–8 months, 1.25 mL every 8 hours; 9 months–2 years, 2.5 mL every 8 hours; 3–6 years, 5 mL every 8 hours, increased to 10 mL in severe infections

Injection 600 mg, powder for preparing intravenous injections, co-amoxiclav 500/100 (amoxycillin 500 mg as sodium salt, clavulanic acid 100 mg as potassium salt). Net price per vial = £1.35

Injection 1.2 g, powder for preparing intravenous injections, co-amoxiclav 1000/200 (amoxycillin 1 g as sodium salt, clavulanic acid 200 mg as potassium salt). Net price per vial = £2.70

CO-FLUAMPICIL

A mixture of equal parts by mass of flucloxacillin and ampicillin

Indications: mixed infections involving penicillinase-producing staphylococci

Cautions; Contra-indications; Side-effects: see under Ampicillin and Flucloxacillin

Dose: *by mouth*, co-fluampicil, 250/250 every 6 hours, dose doubled in severe infections; CHILD under 10 years half adult dose, dose doubled in severe infections

By intramuscular or slow intravenous injection or by intravenous infusion, co-fluampicil 250/250 every 6 hours, dose doubled in severe infections; CHILD under 2 years quarter adult dose, 2–10 years half adult dose, dose doubled in severe infections

PoM **Co-fluampicil** (Non-proprietary)

Capsules, co-fluampicil 250/250 (flucloxacillin 250 mg as sodium salt, ampicillin 250 mg as trihydrate). Net price 20 = £4.00. Label: 9, 23

Available from Generics (Flu-Amp®), Norton

PoM **Magnapen®** (Beecham)

Capsules, black/turquoise, co-fluampicil 250/250 (flucloxacillin 250 mg as sodium salt, ampicillin 250 mg as trihydrate). Net price 20 = £4.23. Label: 9, 23

Syrup, co-fluampicil 125/125 (flucloxacillin 125 mg as magnesium salt, ampicillin 125 mg as trihydrate)/5 mL when reconstituted with water. Diluent syrup, life of diluted syrup 14 days. Net price 100 mL = £3.44. Label: 9, 23

Injection 500 mg, powder for reconstitution, co-fluampicil 250/250 (flucloxacillin 250 mg as sodium salt, ampicillin 250 mg as sodium salt). Net price per vial = £1.10

Injection 1 g, powder for reconstitution, co-fluampicil 500/500 (flucloxacillin 500 mg as sodium salt, ampicillin 500 mg as sodium salt). Net price per vial = £2.20

MEZLOCILLIN

Indications: Gram-positive and Gram-negative infections (including enteric bacilli); see also notes above.

Cautions; Contra-indications; Side-effects: see under Benzylpenicillin (section 5.1.1.1)

Dose: *by deep intramuscular injection*, 0.5–2 g every 6–8 hours

By intravenous injection, over 2–4 minutes, 2 g every 6–8 hours

Serious infections, *by intravenous infusion*, 5 g every 6–8 hours; NEONATE and PREMATURE INFANT, *by prolonged intravenous infusion*, 75 mg/kg every 12 hours; INFANT and CHILD, *by intravenous injection or infusion*, 75 mg/kg every 8 hours

 Prices are **net**, see p. 1

Gonorrhoea, *by deep intramuscular injection*, 1 g as a single dose

PoM **Baypen**® (Bayer)
Injection, powder for reconstitution, mezlocillin (as sodium salt). Net price 500-mg vial = £1.20; 1-g vial = £1.85; 2-g vial = £3.36
Infusion, powder for reconstitution, mezlocillin (as sodium salt). Net price 5-g vial = £7.64 (also available with 50 mL water for injections, transfer needle, and infusion bag)

PIVAMPICILLIN

Indications: see under Ampicillin
Cautions; Contra-indications; Side-effects: see under Ampicillin; liver- and kidney-function tests required in long-term use; avoid in porphyria
Dose: 500 mg every 12 hours, doubled in severe infections; CHILD up to 1 year 40–60 mg/kg daily in 2–3 divided doses; 1–5 years 350–525 mg daily; 6–10 years 525–700 mg daily; doses can be doubled in severe infections

PoM **Pondocillin**® (Leo)
Tablets, f/c, pivampicillin 500 mg. Net price 20 = £4.22. Label: 5, 9, 21
Suspension, sugar-free, pivampicillin 175 mg/5 mL when reconstituted with water. Net price 50 mL = £1.76; 100 mL = £2.84. Label: 5, 9, 21
Sachets, granules, off-white, pivampicillin 175 mg/sachet. Net price 10-sachet pack = £1.98. Label: 5, 9, 13, 21

With pivmecillinam
PoM **Miraxid**® (Fisons)
Tablets, f/c, pivampicillin 125 mg, pivmecillinam hydrochloride 100 mg. Net price 20 = £2.59. Label: 9, 21, 27, counselling, posture (see below)
Dose: 2 tablets twice daily, increased to 3 tablets twice daily for severe infections; CHILD 6–10 years 1 tablet twice daily
450 Tablets, f/c, pivampicillin 250 mg, pivmecillinam hydrochloride 200 mg. Net price 20 = £5.06. Label: 9, 21, 27, counselling, posture (see below)
Dose: 1 tablet twice daily, increased to 2 tablets twice daily for severe infections
COUNSELLING. Tablets should be swallowed whole with plenty of fluid during meals while sitting or standing
Paediatric suspension, pivampicillin 62.5 mg, pivmecillinam 46.2 mg/unit-dose sachet. Net price 10-sachet pack = £2.70. Label: 9, 13, 21
Dose: under 6 years 1 sachet twice daily increased to 2 sachets twice daily for severe infections, 6–10 years 2 sachets twice daily increased to 3 sachets twice daily for severe infections

PoM **Pondocillin Plus**® (Leo)
Tablets, f/c, pivampicillin 250 mg, pivmecillinam hydrochloride 200 mg. Net price 20 = £5.98. Label: 9, 21, 27, counselling, posture (see below)
Dose: 1 tablet twice daily, increased to 2 tablets twice daily for severe infections
COUNSELLING. Tablets should be swallowed whole with plenty of fluid during meals while sitting or standing

TALAMPICILLIN HYDROCHLORIDE

Indications: see under Ampicillin
Cautions; Contra-indications; Side-effects: see under Ampicillin; avoid in severe hepatic or renal impairment
Dose: 250–500 mg every 8 hours

PoM **Talpen**® (Beecham)
Tablets, f/c, talampicillin hydrochloride 250 mg. Net price 20 = £2.99. Label: 9
Syrup, talampicillin hydrochloride 125 mg (as napsylate)/5 mL when reconstituted with water. Diluent syrup, life of diluted syrup 7 days. Net price 100 mL = £2.13. Label: 9

5.1.1.4 ANTIPSEUDOMONAL PENICILLINS

The carboxypenicillins, **carbenicillin** and **ticarcillin**, are principally indicated for the treatment of serious infections caused by *Pseudomonas aeruginosa* although they also have activity against certain other Gram-negative bacilli including *Proteus* spp. and *Bacteroides fragilis*. Carbenicillin has been replaced by ticarcillin which is more active against these organisms.

Timentin®, which consists of ticarcillin and clavulanic acid (section 5.1.1.3), is active against penicillinase-producing bacteria that are resistant to ticarcillin.

The ureidopenicillins, **azlocillin** and **piperacillin**, have a broad spectrum of activity and are both more active than ticarcillin against *Ps. aeruginosa*.

For pseudomonas septicaemias (especially in neutropenic patients or those with endocarditis) these antipseudomonal penicillins should be given with an aminoglycoside (e.g. gentamicin or tobramycin, section 5.1.4) as there is a synergistic effect. Penicillins and aminoglycosides must not, however, be mixed in the same syringe or infusion.

AZLOCILLIN

Indications: infections due to *Pseudomonas aeruginosa*, see notes above
Cautions; Contra-indications; Side-effects: see under Benzylpenicillin (section 5.1.1.1)
Dose: *by intravenous injection*, 2 g every 8 hours
Serious infections, *by intravenous infusion*, 5 g every 8 hours; PREMATURE INFANT 50 mg/kg every 12 hours; NEONATE 100 mg/kg every 12 hours; INFANT 7 days–1 year 100 mg/kg every 8 hours; CHILD 1–14 years 75 mg/kg every 8 hours

PoM **Securopen**® (Bayer)

Injection, powder for reconstitution, azlocillin (as sodium salt). Net price 500-mg vial = £1.62; 1-g vial = £3.21; 2-g vial = £5.02

Infusion, powder for reconstitution, azlocillin (as sodium salt). Net price 5-g vial = £11·80 (also available with 50 mL water for injections, transfer needle, and infusion bag)

CARBENICILLIN

Indications: infections due to *Pseudomonas aeruginosa* and *Proteus* spp., see notes above

Cautions; Contra-indications: see under Benzylpenicillin (section 5.1.1.1)

Side-effects: see under Benzylpenicillin (section 5.1.1.1); also hypokalaemia, alteration in platelet function

Dose: *by slow intravenous injection or rapid infusion*, severe systemic infections, 5 g every 4–6 hours; CHILD 250–400 mg/kg daily in divided doses

By intramuscular injection, urinary-tract infections, 2 g every 6 hours; CHILD 50–100 mg/kg daily in divided doses

PoM **Pyopen**® (Beecham)

Injection, powder for reconstitution, carbenicillin (as sodium salt). Net price 1-g vial = £1.54; 5-g vial = £7.50

CARFECILLIN SODIUM

Indications: urinary-tract infections due to *Pseudomonas* and *Proteus* spp.

Cautions; Contra-indications; Side-effects: see under Benzylpenicillin (section 5.1.1.1)

Dose: 0.5–1 g 3 times daily

PoM **Uticillin**® (Beecham)

Product discontinued

PIPERACILLIN

Indications: infections due to *Pseudomonas aeruginosa*, see notes above

Cautions; Contra-indications; Side-effects: see under Benzylpenicillin (section 5.1.1.1)

Dose: *by intramuscular or by slow intravenous injection or by intravenous infusion*, 100–150 mg/kg daily (in divided doses), increased to 200–300 mg/kg daily in severe infections, and to at least 16 g daily in life-threatening infections; single doses over 2 g intravenous route only

PoM **Pipril**® (Lederle)

Injection, powder for reconstitution, piperacillin (as sodium salt). Net price 1-g vial = £3.07; 2-g vial = £6.08; 4-g vial = £12.01

Infusion, powder for reconstitution, piperacillin 4 g (as sodium salt), with 50-mL bottle water for injections and transfer needle. Net price complete unit = £12.80

TICARCILLIN

Indications: infections due to *Pseudomonas* and *Proteus* spp, see notes above.

Cautions; Contra-indications; Side-effects: see under Benzylpenicillin (section 5.1.1.1)

Dose: *by slow intravenous injection* over 3–4 minutes *or by intravenous infusion*, 15–20 g daily in divided doses; CHILD 200–300 mg/kg daily in divided doses

Urinary-tract infections, *by intramuscular or slow intravenous injection*, 3–4 g daily in divided doses; CHILD 50–100 mg/kg daily in divided doses

PoM **Ticar**® (Beecham)

Injection, powder for reconstitution, ticarcillin (as sodium salt). Net price 1-g vial = £1.68; 5-g vial = £6.84

Infusion, powder for reconstitution, ticarcillin 5 g (as sodium salt) in infusion bottle, with transfer needle and diluent. Net price complete unit = £8.03

With clavulanic acid

PoM **Timentin**® (Beecham)

Injection 1.6 g, powder for reconstitution, ticarcillin 1.5 g (as sodium salt), clavulanic acid 100 mg (as potassium salt). Net price per vial = £2.65

Injection 3.2 g, powder for reconstitution, ticarcillin 3 g (as sodium salt), clavulanic acid 200 mg (as potassium salt). Net price per vial = £5.29

Dose: by intravenous infusion, 3.2 g every 6–8 hours increased to every 4 hours in more severe infections; CHILD 80 mg/kg every 6–8 hours (every 12 hours in neonates)

5.1.1.5 MECILLINAMS

Mecillinam and **pivmecillinam** have significant activity against many Gram-negative bacteria including salmonellae, but excluding *Ps. aeruginosa*. Pivmecillinam is given by mouth and subsequently hydrolysed to mecillinam, which is the active drug and must itself be given by injection.

MECILLINAM

Indications: severe infections due to Gram-negative enteric bacteria

Cautions; Contra-indications; Side-effects: see under Benzylpenicillin (section 5.1.1.1); liver and renal function tests on long-term use

Dose: *by intramuscular or by slow intravenous injection or by intravenous infusion*, 5–15 mg/kg every 6–8 hours

PoM **Selexidin**® (Leo)

Injection, powder for reconstitution, mecillinam. Net price 200-mg vial = 61p; 400-mg vial = £1.22

PIVMECILLINAM

Indications: see under Dose below

Cautions; Contra-indications; Side-effects: see under Benzylpenicillin (section 5.1.1.1); also liver and renal function tests required in long-term use

Dose: acute uncomplicated cystitis, 400 mg initially, then 200 mg every 8 hours for 3 days (10-tab pack)

Chronic or recurrent bacteriuria, 400 mg every 6–8 hours

Salmonellosis, 1.2–2.4 g daily for 14 days (14–28 days for carriers)

COUNSELLING. Tablets should be swallowed whole with plenty of fluid during meals while sitting or standing

PoM **Selexid®** (Leo)

Tablets, f/c, pivmecillinam hydrochloride 200 mg. Net price 10-tab pack = £2.32, 20 = £4.48. Label: 9, 21, 27, counselling, posture (see Dose above)

Suspension, granules, pivmecillinam 100 mg/single-dose sachet. Net price 20 sachets = £4.03. Label: 9, 13, 21

With pivampicillin

see under Pivampicillin (section 5.1.1.3)

5.1.2 Cephalosporins, cephamycins and other beta-lactam antibiotics

Antibiotics discussed in this section include the **cephalosporins**, such as cefotaxime, ceftazidime, cefuroxime, cephalexin and cephradine, the **cephamycin**, cefoxitin, the **monobactam**, aztreonam, and the **carbapenem** imipenem (a thienamycin derivative).

CEPHALOSPORINS AND CEPHAMYCINS

The cephalosporins are broad-spectrum antibiotics but in spite of the number of cephalosporins currently available there are few absolute indications for their use. All have a similar antibacterial spectrum although individual agents have differing activity against certain organisms. The pharmacology of the cephalosporins is similar to that of the penicillins, excretion being principally renal and blocked by probenecid.

The principal side-effect of the cephalosporins is hypersensitivity and about 10% of penicillin-sensitive patients will also be allergic to the cephalosporins. Haemorrhage due to interference with blood clotting factors has been associated with several cephalosporins.

One of the first cephalosporins was **cephalothin** which is less active and less stable than the newer cephalosporins. It has been replaced by the newer cephalosporins, **cephradine**, **cephazolin**.

Cefuroxime and **cephamandole** are 'second generation' cephalosporins and are less susceptible than the other cephalosporins to inactivation by penicillinases. They are, therefore, active against certain bacteria which are resistant to the other drugs and have greater activity against *H. influenzae* and *Neisseria gonorrhoeae*.

Cefotaxime, **ceftazidime**, and **ceftizoxime** are 'third generation' cephalosporins with greater activity than the 'second generation' cephalosporins against certain Gram-negative bacteria. However, they are less active than cefuroxime and cephamandole against Gram-positive bacteria, most notably *Staphylococcus aureus*. Their broad antibacterial spectrum may encourage superinfection with resistant bacteria or fungi.

Cefsulodin and **ceftazidime** have good activity against pseudomonas. Ceftazidime is also active against other Gram-negative bacteria. Cefsulodin has a very much narrower spectrum and should be used only for pseudomonal infections.

Cefoxitin, a cephamycin antibiotic, is active against bowel flora including *Bacteroides fragilis* and because of this it has been recommended for abdominal sepsis such as peritonitis.

ORALLY ACTIVE CEPHALOSPORINS. The orally active 'first generation' cephalosporins, **cephalexin**, **cephradine**, and **cefadroxil** and the 'second generation' cephalosporin, **cefaclor** have a similar antimicrobial spectrum. They are useful for urinary-tract infections which do not respond to other drugs or which occur in pregnancy. Cefaclor has good activity against *Haemophilus influenzae*, but is associated with protracted skin reactions especially in children. Cefadroxil has a longer duration of action but it has poor activity against *H. influenzae*. **Cefuroxime axetil**, an ester of the 'second generation' cephalosporin cefuroxime, has the same antibacterial spectrum as the parent compound; gastro-intestinal side-effects are quite common.

Cefixime, a 'third generation' cephalosporin, has a longer duration of action than the other cephalosporins that are active by mouth. It is presently only indicated for acute infections.

CEFACLOR

Indications: infections due to sensitive Gram-positive and Gram-negative bacteria, but see notes above

Cautions: penicillin sensitivity; renal impairment; pregnancy and breast-feeding; false positive urinary glucose (if tested for reducing substances) and false positive Coombs' test; **interactions:** Appendix 1 (cephalosporins)

Contra-indications: cephalosporin hypersensitivity; porphyria

Side-effects: diarrhoea, colitis (rarely pseudomembranous colitis reported), nausea and vomiting; allergic reactions including rashes, pruritus, urticaria, serum sickness-like reactions with rashes, fever and arthralgia, and anaphylaxis; erythema multiforme, toxic epidermal necrolysis reported; eosinophilia and rarely thrombocytopenia or neutropenia; disturbances in liver enzymes, transient hepatitis and cholestatic jaundice; other side-effects reported include reversible interstitial nephritis, hyperactivity, nervousness, sleep disturbances, confusion, hypertonia, and dizziness.

Dose: 250 mg every 8 hours, doubled for severe infections; max. 4 g daily; CHILD over 1 month, 20 mg/kg daily in 3 divided doses, doubled for severe infections, max. 1 g daily; *or* 1 month–1 year, 62.5 mg every 8 hours; 1–5 years, 125 mg; over 5 years, 250 mg; doses doubled for severe infections

PoM **Distaclor®** (Dista)

Capsules, cefaclor 250 mg (violet/white), net price 20-cap pack = £9.46; 500 mg (violet/grey), 20 = £17.36. Label: 9

Suspension, both pink, cefaclor for reconstitution with water, 125 mg/5 mL, net price 100 mL = £4.60; 250 mg/5 mL, 100 mL = £8.58. Diluent syrup, life of diluted suspension 14 days. Label: 9

CEFADROXIL

Indications: see under Cefaclor; see also notes above

Cautions; Contra-indications; Side-effects: see under Cefaclor

Dose: patients over 40 kg, 0.5–1 g twice daily; skin, soft tissue, and simple urinary-tract infections, 1 g daily; CHILD under 1 year, 25 mg/kg daily in divided doses; 1–6 years, 250 mg twice daily; over 6 years, 500 mg twice daily

PoM **Baxan®** (Bristol-Myers)

Capsules, cefadroxil 500 mg (as monohydrate). Net price 20 = £6.63. Label: 9

Suspension, cefadroxil (as monohydrate) for reconstitution with water, 125 mg/5 mL, net price 60 mL = £1.75; 250 mg/5 mL, 60 mL = £3.48; 500 mg/5 mL, 60 mL = £5.21. Label: 9

CEFIXIME

Indications: see Cefaclor and notes above

Cautions; Contra-indications; Side-effects: see under Cefaclor

Dose: 200–400 mg daily as a single dose or in 2 divided doses; CHILD 8 mg/kg daily as a single dose or in 2 divided doses *or* 6 months–1 year 75 mg; 1–4 years 100 mg; 5–10 years 200 mg; 11–12 years 300 mg

▼ PoM **Suprax®** (Lederle)

Tablets, f/c, scored, cefixime 200 mg. Net price 20 = £25.60. Label: 9

Paediatric oral suspension, cefixime 100 mg/5 mL when reconstituted with water. Net price 37.5 mL (with double-ended spoon for measuring 3.75 mL or 5 mL since dilution not recommended) = £6.10; 75 mL = £10.95. Label: 9

CEFOTAXIME

Indications: see under Cefaclor; surgical prophylaxis; see also notes above

Cautions; Contra-indications; Side-effects: see under Cefaclor

Dose: by intramuscular or intravenous injection, moderate to serious infection, 1 g every 8 hours; life-threatening infection, 2 g every 8 hours; exceptionally, for life-threatening infections due to organisms less sensitive to cefotaxime, up to 12 g daily

Urinary-tract and mild to moderate infections, 1 g every 12 hours

Gonorrhoea 1 g as a single dose

In severe renal impairment, doses to be halved after initial dose of 1 g. NEONATE, 50 mg/kg daily in 2–4 divided doses; in severe infections 150–200 mg/kg daily. CHILD, 100–150 mg/kg daily in 2–4 divided doses; in severe infections, up to 200 mg/kg daily

By intravenous infusion, 1–2 g over 20–60 minutes

PoM **Claforan®** (Roussel)

Injection, powder for reconstitution, cefotaxime (as sodium salt). Net price 500-mg vial = £2.48; 1-g vial = £4.95; 2-g vial = £9.90

CEFOXITIN

Indications: see under Cefaclor; surgical prophylaxis; more active against Gram-negative bacteria

Cautions; Contra-indications; Side-effects: see under Cefaclor

Dose: by intramuscular or by slow intravenous injection or by infusion, 1–2 g every 6–8 hours, increased in severe infections; max. 12 g daily; CHILD up to 1 week 20–40 mg/kg every 12 hours; 1–4 weeks 20–40 mg/kg every 8 hours; over 1 month 20–40 mg/kg every 6–8 hours

PoM **Mefoxin®** (MSD)

Injection, powder for reconstitution, cefoxitin (as sodium salt). Net price 1-g vial = £4.92; 2-g vial = £9.84

CEFSULODIN SODIUM

Indications: infections due to sensitive strains of *Ps. aeruginosa*; surgical prophylaxis

Cautions; Contra-indications; Side-effects: see under Cefaclor

Dose: by intramuscular or intravenous injection, 1–4 g daily in 2–4 divided doses; CHILD 20–50 mg/kg daily

PoM **Monaspor®** (Ciba)

Injection, powder for reconstitution, cefsulodin sodium. Net price 500-mg vial = £5.65; 1-g vial = £11.30

CEFTAZIDIME

Indications: see under Cefaclor; see also notes above

Cautions; Contra-indications; Side-effects: see under Cefaclor

Dose: by intramuscular injection or intravenous injection or infusion, 1 g every 8 hours *or* 2 g every 12 hours; 2 g every 8–12 hours in severe infections; elderly usual max. 3 g; single doses over 1 g intravenous route only; CHILD, up to 2

months 25–60 mg/kg daily in 2 divided doses, over 2 months 30–100 mg/kg daily in 2–3 divided doses; up to 150 mg/kg daily if immunocompromised or meningitis; intravenous route recommended for children
Urinary-tract and less serious infections, 0.5–1 g every 12 hours
Pseudomonal lung infection in cystic fibrosis, ADULT with normal renal function 100–150 mg/kg daily in 3 divided doses; CHILD up to 150 mg/kg daily; intravenous route recommended for children

PoM **Fortum®** (Glaxo)
Injection, powder for reconstitution, ceftazidime (as pentahydrate), with sodium carbonate. Net price 250-mg vial = £2.48; 500-mg vial = £4.95; 1-g vial = £9.90; 2-g vial (for injection and for infusion) = £19.80

CEFTIZOXIME

Indications: see under Cefaclor; also notes above
Cautions; Contra-indications; Side-effects: see under Cefaclor
Dose: *by deep intramuscular or slow intravenous injection or by intravenous infusion*, 1–2 g every 8–12 hours increased in severe infections up to 8 g daily, in 3 divided doses; CHILD over 3 months 30–60 mg/kg daily in 2–4 divided doses, increased to 100–150 mg/kg daily for severe infections
Gonorrhoea, *by intramuscular injection*, 1 g as a single dose
Urinary-tract infections, *by deep intramuscular or slow intravenous injection or by infusion*, 0.5–1 g every 12 hours

PoM **Cefizox®** (Wellcome)
Injection, powder for reconstitution, ceftizoxime (as sodium salt). Net price 500-mg vial = £2.76; 1-g vial = £5.50; 2-g vial = £11.00

CEFUROXIME

Indications: see under Cefaclor; surgical prophylaxis; more active against *H. influenzae* and *N. gonorrhoeae*
Cautions; Contra-indications; Side-effects: see under Cefaclor
Dose: *by mouth* (as cefuroxime axetil), 250 mg twice daily, doubled in bronchitis and pneumonia
Urinary-tract infection, 125 mg twice daily, doubled in pyelonephritis
Gonorrhoea, 1 g as a single dose
CHILD over 5 years, 125 mg twice daily, if necessary doubled in otitis media
By intramuscular injection or intravenous injection or infusion, 750 mg every 6–8 hours; 1.5 g every 6–8 hours in severe infections; single doses over 750 mg intravenous route only
CHILD usual dose 60 mg/kg daily (range 30–100 mg/kg daily) in 3–4 divided doses (2–3 divided doses in neonates)
Gonorrhoea, 1.5 g as a single dose by intramuscular injection (divided between 2 sites)
Surgical prophylaxis, 1.5 g by intravenous injection at induction; may be supplemented with 750 mg intramuscularly 8 and 16 hours later (abdominal, pelvic, and orthopaedic operations) *or* followed by 750 mg intramuscularly every 8 hours for further 24–48 hours (cardiac, pulmonary, oesophageal, and vascular operations)
Meningitis, 3 g intravenously every 8 hours; CHILD, 200–240 mg/kg daily (in 3–4 divided doses) reduced to 100 mg/kg daily after 3 days or on clinical improvement; NEONATE, 100 mg/kg daily reduced to 50 mg/kg daily

PoM **Zinacef®** (Glaxo)
Injection, powder for reconstitution, cefuroxime (as sodium salt). Net price 250-mg vial = 88p; 750-mg vial = £2.64; 1.5-g vial = £5.29

PoM **Zinnat®** (Glaxo)
Tablets, both f/c, cefuroxime 125 mg (as cefuroxime axetil), net price 14-tab pack = £6.30; 250 mg, 14-tab pack = £12.60. Label: 9, 21, 25

CEPHALEXIN

Indications: see under Cefaclor
Cautions; Contra-indications; Side-effects: see under Cefaclor
Dose: 250 mg every 6 hours *or* 500 mg every 8–12 hours increased to 1–1.5 g every 6–8 hours for severe infections; CHILD, 25 mg/kg daily in divided doses, doubled for severe infections, max. 100 mg/kg daily; *or* under 1 year, 125 mg every 12 hours; 1–5 years, 125 mg every 8 hours; 6–12 years, 250 mg every 8 hours

PoM **Cephalexin** (Non-proprietary)
Capsules, cephalexin 250 mg, net price 20 = £3.22; 500 mg, 20 = £6.40. Label: 9
Tablets, cephalexin 250 mg, net price 20 = £3.23; 500 mg, 20 = £6.40. Label: 9
Oral suspension, cephalexin for reconstitution with water, 125 mg/5 mL, net price 100 mL = £1.59; 250 mg/5 mL, 100 mL = £3.19. Label: 9

PoM **Ceporex®** (Glaxo)
Capsules, both caramel/grey, cephalexin 250 mg, net price 20 = £3.00, 28-cap pack = £4.47; 500 mg, 20 = £5.88, 28-cap pack = £8.72. Label: 9
Tablets, both pink, f/c, cephalexin 250 mg, net price 20 = £3.00, 28-tab pack = £4.47; 500 mg, 20 = £5.88, 28-tab pack = £8.72; 1 g (scored), 14-tab pack = £8.72. Label: 9
Paediatric drops, orange, cephalexin 125 mg/1.25 mL when reconstituted with water. Net price 10 mL = £1.52. Label: 9, counselling, use of pipette
Suspension, both yellow, cephalexin 125 mg/5 mL, net price 100 mL = £1.59; 250 mg/5 mL, 100 mL = £3.19. Do not dilute. Label: 9
Syrup, all orange, cephalexin for reconstitution with water, 125 mg/5 mL, net price 100 mL = £1.59; 250 mg/5 mL, 100 mL = £3.19; 500 mg/5 mL, 100 mL = £6.19. Diluent water, life of diluted syrup 7 days. Label: 9

 Prices are **net**, see p. 1

PoM **Keflex®** (Lilly)

Capsules, cephalexin 250 mg (green/white), net price 20-cap pack = £3.19; 500 mg (pale green/dark green), 20-cap pack = £6.23. Label: 9

Tablets, both peach, cephalexin 250 mg, net price 20-tab pack = £3.19; 500 mg (scored), 20-tab pack = £6.23. Label: 9

Suspension, cephalexin for reconstitution with water, 125 mg/5 mL (pink), net price 100 mL = £1.59; 250 mg/5 mL (orange), 100 mL = £3.19. Diluent syrup, life of diluted suspension 10 days. Label: 9

CEPHALOTHIN

Indications: see under Cefaclor; surgical prophylaxis

Cautions; Contra-indications; Side-effects: see under Cefaclor.

Dose: *by intravenous injection or infusion*, 1 g every 4–6 hours; max. 12 g daily; CHILD, 80–160 mg/kg daily in divided doses

PoM **Keflin®** (Lilly)

Injection, powder for reconstitution, cephalothin (as sodium salt). Net price 1-g vial = £2.28

CEPHAMANDOLE

Indications: see under Cefaclor; surgical prophylaxis

Cautions; Contra-indications; Side-effects: see under Cefaclor

Dose: *by deep intramuscular injection or intravenous injection or infusion*, 0.5–2 g every 4–8 hours; CHILD, 50–100 mg/kg daily in divided doses

PoM **Kefadol®** (Dista)

Injection, powder for reconstitution, cephamandole (as nafate) with sodium carbonate. Net price 500-mg vial = £2.05; 1-g vial = £3.91; 2-g vial = £7.51 (hosp. only)

CEPHAZOLIN

Indications: see under Cefaclor; surgical prophylaxis

Cautions; Contra-indications; Side-effects: see under Cefaclor

Dose: *by intramuscular injection or intravenous injection or infusion*, 0.5–1 g every 6–12 hours; CHILD, 25–50 mg/kg daily (in divided doses), increased to 100 mg/kg daily in severe infections

PoM **Kefzol®** (Lilly)

Injection, powder for reconstitution, cephazolin (as sodium salt). Net price 500-mg vial = £2.45; 1-g vial = £4.63

CEPHRADINE

Indications: see under Cefaclor; surgical prophylaxis

Cautions; Contra-indications; Side-effects: see under Cefaclor

Dose: *by mouth*, 250–500 mg every 6 hours *or* 0.5–1 g every 12 hours; CHILD, 25–50 mg/kg daily in divided doses

By intramuscular injection or intravenous injection or infusion, 0.5–1 g every 6 hours, increased to 8 g daily in severe infections; CHILD, 50–100 mg/kg daily in 4 divided doses

PoM **Velosef®** (Squibb)

Capsules, cephradine 250 mg (orange/blue), net price 20-cap pack = £3.55; 500 mg, 20-cap pack = £7.00. Label: 9

Syrup, cephradine 250 mg/5 mL when reconstituted with water. Diluent syrup, life of diluted syrup 7 days. Net price 100 mL = £4.22. Label: 9

Injection, powder for reconstitution, cephradine. Net price 500-mg vial = 99p; 1-g vial = £1.95

OTHER BETA-LACTAM ANTIBIOTICS

Aztreonam is a monocyclic beta-lactam ('monobactam') antibiotic with an antibacterial spectrum limited to Gram-negative aerobic bacteria including *Pseudomonas aeruginosa*, *Neisseria meningitidis*, and *Haemophilus influenzae*; it should not be used alone for 'blind' treatment since it is not active against Gram-positive organisms. Aztreonam is also effective against *Neisseria gonorrhoea* (but not against concurrent chlamydial infection). Side-effects are similar to those of the other beta-lactams although aztreonam may be less likely to cause hypersensitivity in penicillin-sensitive patients.

Imipenem, a carbapenem, is the first thienamycin beta-lactam antibiotic; it has a very broad spectrum of activity which includes aerobic and anaerobic Gram-positive and Gram-negative bacteria. Imipenem is partially inactivated in the kidney by enzymatic activity and is therefore administered in combination with **cilastatin**, a specific enzyme inhibitor, which blocks its renal metabolism. Side-effects are similar to those of other beta-lactam antibiotics; neurotoxicity has been observed at very high dosage or in renal failure.

AZTREONAM

Indications: Gram-negative infections including *Pseudomonas aeruginosa*, *Haemophilus influenzae*, and *Neisseria meningitidis*

Cautions: hypersensitivity to beta-lactam antibiotics; hepatic impairment; reduce dose in renal impairment; **interactions:** Appendix 1 (aztreonam)

Contra-indications: aztreonam hypersensitivity; pregnancy and breast-feeding

Side-effects: nausea, vomiting, diarrhoea, abdominal cramps; mouth ulcers, altered taste; jaundice and hepatitis; blood disorders (including thrombocytopenia and neutropenia); urticaria and rashes

Dose: *by intramuscular injection or intravenous injection or infusion:* 1 g every 8 hours *or* 2 g every 12 hours; 2 g every 6–8 hours for severe infections (including systemic *Pseudomonas aeruginosa* and lung infections in cystic fibrosis); single doses over 1 g intravenous route only

CHILD over 1 week, *by intravenous injection or infusion*, 30 mg/kg every 6–8 hours increased in severe infections for child of 2 years or older to 50 mg/kg every 6–8 hours; max. 8 g daily

Urinary-tract infections, 0.5–1 g every 8–12 hours

Gonorrhoea/cystitis, *by intramuscular injection*, 1 g as a single dose

PoM **Azactam**® (Squibb)

Injection, powder for reconstitution, aztreonam. Net price 500-mg vial = £4.48; 1-g vial = £8.95; 2-g vial and 2-g bottle (for preparing infusion) (both) = £17.90

IMIPENEM WITH CILASTATIN

Indications: aerobic and anaerobic Gram-positive and Gram-negative infections

Cautions: hypersensitivity to penicillins, cephalosporins and other beta-lactam antibiotics; renal impairment; CNS disorders (e.g. epilepsy)

Contra-indications: hypersensitivity to imipenem or cilastatin; breast-feeding

Side-effects: nausea, vomiting, diarrhoea (pseudomembraneous colitis reported), blood disorders, positive Coombs test; allergic reactions (with rash, pruritus, urticaria, fever, anaphylactic reactions); myoclonic activity, convulsions, confusion and mental disturbances reported; slight increases in liver enzymes and bilirubin reported; local reactions: erythema, local pain and induration, and thrombophlebitis

Dose: *by intravenous infusion*, in terms of imipenem, 1–2 g daily in 3–4 divided doses; less sensitive organisms, up to 50 mg/kg daily (to max. 4 g daily); CHILD 3 months and older, 60 mg/kg (up to max. of 2 g) daily in 4 divided doses

▼ PoM **Primaxin**® (MSD)

Intravenous infusion, powder for reconstitution, imipenem (as monohydrate) 250 mg with cilastatin (as sodium salt) 250 mg. Net price 60-mL vial = £9.00

Intravenous infusion, powder for reconstitution, imipenem (as monohydrate) 500 mg with cilastatin (as sodium salt) 500 mg. Net price 120-mL vial = £15.00

5.1.3 Tetracyclines

The tetracyclines are broad-spectrum antibiotics whose usefulness has decreased as a result of increasing bacterial resistance. They remain, however, the treatment of choice for infections caused by chlamydia (causing trachoma, psittacosis, salpingitis, urethritis, and lymphogranuloma venereum), rickettsia (including Q-fever), mycoplasma (respiratory and genital tract infections), brucella, and the spirochaete, *Borrelia burgdorferi* (Lyme disease). They are also used for the treatment of exacerbations of chronic bronchitis because of their activity against *Haemophilus influenzae*. They are also used in acne and in destructive (refractory) periodontal disease.

Microbiologically, there is little to choose between the various tetracyclines, the only exception being **minocycline** which has a broader spectrum, is active against *Neisseria meningitidis* and has been used for meningococcal prophylaxis; however it may cause dizziness and vertigo.

The tetracyclines are deposited in growing bone and teeth (being bound to calcium) causing staining and occasionally dental hypoplasia, and should **not** be given to children under 12 years or to pregnant women. With the exception of **doxycycline** and **minocycline** the tetracyclines may exacerbate renal failure and should **not** be given to patients with kidney disease. Absorption of tetracyclines is decreased by milk (except doxycycline and minocycline), antacids, and calcium, iron, and magnesium salts.

TETRACYCLINE

Indications: exacerbations of chronic bronchitis; infections due to brucella, chlamydia, mycoplasma, and rickettsia; acne vulgaris; pleural effusions due to malignancy or cirrhosis

Cautions: breast-feeding; hepatic impairment (avoid intravenous administration); renal impairment (avoid if severe); rarely causes photosensitivity; **interactions:** Appendix 1 (tetracyclines)

Contra-indications: severe renal impairment, pregnancy (see also Appendix 4), children under 12 years of age, systemic lupus erythematosus

Side-effects: nausea, vomiting, diarrhoea; erythema (discontinue treatment); headache and visual disturbances may indicate benign intracranial hypertension; pseudomembranous colitis reported

Dose: *by mouth*, 250 mg every 6 hours, increased in severe infections to 500 mg every 6–8 hours

Acne, see section 13.6

Early syphilis, 500 mg every 6 hours for 15 days

Non-gonococcal urethritis, 500 mg every 6 hours for 7–21 days

By intramuscular injection, 100 mg every 8–12 hours, or every 4–6 hours in severe infections

By intravenous infusion, 500 mg every 12 hours; max. 2 g daily

Pleural effusions, see under Achromycin® intravenous infusion

COUNSELLING. Tablets or capsules should be swallowed whole with plenty of fluid while sitting or standing

PoM **Tetracycline Tablets,** coated, tetracycline hydrochloride 250 mg. Net price 20 = 30p. Label: 7, 9, 23, counselling, posture, see above

PoM **Achromycin**® (Lederle)

Capsules, orange, tetracycline hydrochloride 250 mg. Net price 20 = 95p. Label: 7, 9, 23, counselling, posture, see above

Tablets, orange, f/c, tetracycline hydrochloride 250 mg. Net price 20 = 67p. Label: 7, 9, 23, counselling, posture, see above

Syrup, red, tetracycline hydrochloride 125 mg (as tetracycline)/5 mL. Net price 100 mL = £1.66. Diluent syrup, life of diluted syrup 14 days. Label: 7, 9, 23

Note. Stains teeth; avoid in children under 12 years

Intramuscular injection, powder for reconstitution, tetracycline hydrochloride 100 mg, procaine hydrochloride 40 mg. Net price per vial = £1.09

Intravenous infusion, powder for reconstitution, tetracycline hydrochloride. Net price 250-mg vial = £1.27; 500-mg vial = £2.03

Dose: infections, see above

Recurrent pleural effusions, by intrapleural instillation, 500 mg in 30–50 mL sodium chloride intravenous infusion 0.9%

PoM **Achromycin V®** (Lederle)

Capsules, pink, tetracycline hydrochloride 250 mg (as tetracycline) with buffer. Net price 20 = £2.27. Label: 7, 9, 23, counselling, posture, see above

PoM **Panmycin®** (Upjohn)

Capsules, grey/yellow, tetracycline hydrochloride 250 mg. Net price 20 = 80p. Label: 7, 9, 23, counselling, posture, see above

Syrup, yellow, tetracycline 125 mg/5 mL. Net price 100 mL = £4.18. Label: 7, 9, 23

Note. Stains teeth; avoid in children under 12 years

PoM **Sustamycin®** (Boehringer Mannheim)

Capsules, s/r, light blue/dark blue, tetracycline hydrochloride 250 mg. Net price 20 = £2.12. Label: 7, 9, 23, 25

Dose: 2 capsules initially, then 1 every 12 hours

PoM **Tetrabid-Organon®** (Organon)

Capsules, s/r, purple/yellow, tetracycline hydrochloride 250 mg. Net price 20 = £1.70. Label: 7, 9, 23, 25

Dose: 2 capsules initially, then 1 every 12 hours; acne, 1 daily

PoM **Tetrachel®** (Berk)

Capsules, orange, tetracycline hydrochloride 250 mg. Net price 20 = 29p. Label: 7, 9, 23, counselling, posture, see above

Tablets, orange, f/c, tetracycline hydrochloride 250 mg. Net price 20 = 27p. Label: 7, 9, 23, counselling, posture, see above

PoM **Tetrex®** (Bristol-Myers)

Capsules, yellow/orange, tetracycline 250 mg (as phosphate complex). Net price 20 = £1.82. Label: 7, 9, 23, counselling, posture, see above

Compound preparations

PoM **Deteclo®** (Lederle)

Tablets, blue, f/c, tetracycline hydrochloride 115.4 mg, chlortetracycline hydrochloride 115.4 mg, demeclocycline hydrochloride 69.2 mg. Net price 20 = £2.54. Label: 7, 9, 11, 23, counselling, posture, see above

Dose: 1 tablet every 12 hours; 3–4 tablets daily in more severe infections

PoM **Mysteclin®** (Squibb)

Tablets, orange, s/c, tetracycline hydrochloride 250 mg, nystatin 250 000 units. Net price 20 = £1.34. Label: 7, 9, 23, counselling, posture, see above

CHLORTETRACYCLINE HYDROCHLORIDE

Indications: see under Tetracycline

Cautions; Contra-indications; Side-effects: see under Tetracycline

Dose: 250–500 mg every 6 hours

PoM **Aureomycin®** (Lederle)

Capsules, yellow, chlortetracycline hydrochloride 250 mg. Net price 20 = £2.36. Label: 7, 9, 23

CLOMOCYCLINE SODIUM

Indications: see under Tetracycline

Cautions; Contra-indications; Side-effects: see under Tetracycline

Dose: 170–340 mg every 6–8 hours

PoM **Megaclor®** (Pharmax)

Capsules, red, clomocycline sodium 170 mg. Net price 20 = £1.96. Label: 7, 9

DEMECLOCYCLINE HYDROCHLORIDE

Indications: see under Tetracycline; also inappropriate secretion of antidiuretic hormone, section 6.5.2

Cautions; Contra-indications; Side-effects: see under Tetracycline, but photosensitivity is more common

Dose: 150 mg every 6 hours *or* 300 mg every 12 hours

PoM **Ledermycin®** (Lederle)

Capsules, red, demeclocycline hydrochloride 150 mg. Net price 20 = £4.24. Label: 7, 9, 11, 23

Tablets, red, f/c, demeclocycline hydrochloride 300 mg. Net price 20 = £8.43. Label: 7, 9, 11, 23

DOXYCYCLINE

Indications: see under Tetracycline; also chronic prostatitis and sinusitis

Cautions; Contra-indications; Side-effects: see under Tetracycline, but may be used in renal impairment; avoid in porphyria

Dose: 200 mg on first day, then 100 mg daily; severe infections (including chronic urinary-tract infections), 200 mg daily

Acne, 50 mg daily for 6–12 weeks or longer

COUNSELLING. Capsules should be swallowed whole with plenty of fluid during meals while sitting or standing

PoM **Doxycycline** (Non-proprietary)

Capsules, doxycycline 100 mg (as hydrochloride). Net price 20 = £8.40. Label: 6, 9, 27, counselling, posture, see above

PoM **Nordox®** (Panpharma)

Capsules, green, doxycycline 100 mg (as hydrochloride). Net price 10-cap pack = £4.66. Label: 6, 9, 27, counselling, posture, see above

PoM **Vibramycin®** (Invicta)

Capsules, doxycycline (as hydrochloride) 50 mg (green/ivory), net price 28-cap pack = £7.74; 100 mg (green), 8-cap pack = £4.18. Label: 6, 9, 27, counselling, posture, see above

Syrup, sugar-free, red, doxycycline 50 mg (as calcium chelate)/5 mL. Diluent syrup, life of diluted preparation 14 days. Net price 30 mL = £1.55. Label: 6, 9

Note. Stains teeth; avoid in children under 12 years

PoM **Vibramycin-D**® (Invicta)
Dispersible tablets, off-white, doxycycline 100 mg. Net price 8-tab pack = £4.91. Label: 6, 9, 13

LYMECYCLINE

Indications: see under Tetracycline
Cautions; Contra-indications; Side-effects: see under Tetracycline
Dose: 408 mg every 12 hours

PoM **Tetralysal 300**® (Farmitalia Carlo Erba)
Capsules, lymecycline 408 mg (≡ tetracycline 300 mg). Net price 20 = £3.03. Label: 6, 9

MINOCYCLINE

Indications: see under Tetracycline; also meningococcal carrier state
Cautions; Contra-indications: see under Tetracycline, but may be used in renal impairment
Side-effects: see under Tetracycline; also dizziness and vertigo (more common in women); severe exfoliative rashes and liver damage reported
Dose: 100 mg twice daily
Acne, 50 mg twice daily (minimum course of 6 weeks)

PoM **Minocin**® (Lederle)
Tablets, both f/c, minocycline (as hydrochloride) 50 mg (beige), net price 84-tab pack = £24.94; 100 mg (orange), 20-tab pack = £11.86. Label: 6, 9

OXYTETRACYCLINE

Indications: see under Tetracycline
Cautions; Contra-indications; Side-effects: see under Tetracycline; avoid in porphyria
Dose: 250–500 mg every 6 hours

PoM **Oxytetracycline** (Non-proprietary)
Tablets, coated, oxytetracycline dihydrate 250 mg, net price 20 = 24p. Label: 7, 9, 23
Available from APS, Berk (Berkmycen®, contain tartrazine), Cox, DDSA (Oxymycin®), Evans, Kerfoot
Mixture, oxytetracycline (as calcium salt) 125 mg/5 mL. Net price 100 mL = £1.32. Label: 7, 9, 23
Note. Stains teeth; avoid in children under 12 years of age

PoM **Imperacin**® (ICI)
Tablets, yellow, f/c, oxytetracycline dihydrate 250 mg. Net price 20 = 49p. Label: 7, 9, 23
Additives: include tartrazine

PoM **Terramycin**® (Pfizer)
Capsules, yellow, oxytetracycline 250 mg (as hydrochloride). Net price 28-cap pack = 96p. Label: 7, 9, 23
Tablets, yellow, s/c, oxytetracycline 250 mg (as dihydrate). Net price 28-tab pack = 96p. Label: 7, 9, 23

5.1.4 Aminoglycosides

This group includes amikacin, gentamicin, kanamycin, neomycin, netilmicin, streptomycin, and tobramycin. All are bactericidal and active against some Gram-positive and many Gram-negative organisms. Amikacin, gentamicin, and tobramycin are also active against *Pseudomonas aeruginosa*; streptomycin is active against *Mycobacterium tuberculosis* and is now almost entirely reserved for tuberculosis (section 5.1.9).

The aminoglycosides are not absorbed from the gut (although there is a risk of absorption in inflammatory bowel disease and liver failure) and must therefore be given by injection to treat systemic infections.

Excretion is principally via the kidney and accumulation occurs in renal impairment.

Most side-effects of this group of antibiotics are dose-related therefore care must be taken with dosage and whenever possible treatment should not exceed 7 days. The important side-effects are ototoxicity, and to a lesser degree nephrotoxicity; they occur most commonly in the elderly and in patients with renal failure.

If there is impairment of renal function (or high pre-dose plasma concentrations) the interval between doses must be increased; if the renal impairment is severe the dose itself should be reduced as well.

Aminoglycosides may impair neuromuscular transmission and should not be given to patients with myasthenia gravis; large doses given during surgery have been responsible for a transient myasthenic syndrome in patients with normal neuromuscular function.

Aminoglycosides should not be given with potentially ototoxic diuretics (e.g. frusemide and ethacrynic acid); if concurrent use is unavoidable administration of the aminoglycoside and of the diuretic should be separated by as long a period as practicable.

PLASMA CONCENTRATIONS. Plasma concentration monitoring avoids both excessive and subtherapeutic concentrations, thus preventing toxicity and, at the same time, ensuring efficacy.

If possible plasma concentrations of aminoglycosides should be measured in all patients and **must** be determined in infants *or* if high doses are being given, *or* if there is renal impairment, *or* if treatment lasts longer than 7 days.

Note. Plasma concentrations should be measured approximately one hour after intravenous or intramuscular injection, and also just before the next dose.

Gentamicin is the most important of the aminoglycosides and is widely used for the treatment of serious infections. It is the aminoglycoside of choice in the UK. It has a broad spectrum but is inactive against anaerobes and has poor activity against haemolytic streptococci and pneumococci. When used for the 'blind' therapy of undiagnosed serious infections it is usually given in conjunction with a penicillin and/or metronidazole.

The daily dose is up to 5 mg/kg given in divided doses every 8 hours (if renal function is normal); whenever possible treatment should not exceed 7

 Prices are **net**, see p. 1

days. Higher doses are occasionally indicated for serious infections, especially in the neonate or the compromised host. A lower dose of 80 mg twice daily (60 mg for lighter or elderly patients) in association with benzylpenicillin is sufficient for endocarditis due to oral streptococci (often termed *Streptococcus viridans*) and gut streptococci.

Amikacin is a derivative of kanamycin and has one important advantage over gentamicin in that it is stable to 8 of the 9 classified aminoglycoside-inactivating enzymes whereas gentamicin is inactivated by 5. It is principally indicated for the treatment of serious infections caused by Gram-negative bacilli resistant to gentamicin, and is given by intramuscular or intravenous injection.

Kanamycin has been superseded by other aminoglycosides.

Netilmicin has similar activity to gentamicin, but may cause less ototoxicity in those needing treatment for longer than 10 days. Netilmicin is active against a number of gentamicin-resistant Gram-negative bacilli but is less active against *Ps. aeruginosa* than gentamicin or tobramycin.

Tobramycin is similar to gentamicin. It is slightly more active against *Ps. aeruginosa* but shows less activity against certain other Gram-negative bacteria.

Neomycin is too toxic for parenteral administration and can only be used for infections of the skin or mucous membranes or to reduce the bacterial population of the colon prior to bowel surgery or in hepatic failure. Oral administration may lead to malabsorption. Small amounts of neomycin may be absorbed from the gut in patients with hepatic failure and, as these patients may also be uraemic, cumulation may occur with resultant ototoxicity. **Framycetin** is almost identical with neomycin in its actions and uses.

PREGNANCY. Where possible, the aminoglycosides should be avoided in pregnancy as they cross the placenta and can cause fetal eighth nerve damage.

GENTAMICIN

Indications: septicaemia and neonatal sepsis; meningitis and other CNS infections; biliary tract infection, acute pyelonephritis or prostatitis, endocarditis caused by *Strep. viridans* or *faecalis* (with a penicillin)

Cautions: renal impairment, infants and elderly (adjust dose and monitor renal, auditory and vestibular function together with plasma gentamicin concentrations); avoid prolonged use; **interactions:** Appendix 1 (aminoglycosides)

Contra-indications: pregnancy, myasthenia gravis

Side-effects: vestibular damage, reversible nephrotoxicity; rarely, hypomagnesaemia on prolonged therapy, pseudomembranous colitis; see also notes above

Dose: *by intramuscular or by slow intravenous injection over at least 3 minutes or by intravenous infusion*, 2–5 mg/kg daily (in divided doses every 8 hours). In renal impairment the interval between successive doses should be increased to 12 hours when the creatinine clearance is 30–70 mL/minute, 24 hours for 10–30 mL/minute, 48 hours for 5–10 mL/minute, and after twice-weekly dialysis for less than 5 mL/minute

CHILD up to 2 weeks, 3 mg/kg every 12 hours; 2 weeks–12 years, 2 mg/kg every 8 hours

By intrathecal injection, 1 mg daily (increased if necessary to 5 mg daily), with 2–4 mg/kg daily *by intramuscular injection* (in divided doses every 8 hours)

Endocarditis prophylaxis in dentistry, see section 5.1, table 2

Note. One-hour ('peak') concentration should not exceed 10 mg/litre; pre-dose ('trough') concentration should be less than 2 mg/litre

PoM **Cidomycin®** (Roussel)
Injection, gentamicin 40 mg (as sulphate)/mL. Net price 2-mL amp or vial = £1.59
Paediatric injection, gentamicin 10 mg (as sulphate)/mL. Net price 2-mL vial = 67p
Intrathecal injection, gentamicin 5 mg (as sulphate)/mL. Net price 1-mL amp = 79p

PoM **Genticin®** (Nicholas)
Injection, gentamicin 40 mg (as sulphate)/mL. Net price 2-mL amp or vial = £1.58

PoM **Isotonic Gentamicin Injection** (Baxter)
Intravenous infusion, gentamicin 800 micrograms (as sulphate)/mL in sodium chloride intravenous infusion 0.9%. Net price 100-mL (80-mg) Viaflex® bag = £1.50

AMIKACIN

Indications: serious Gram-negative infections resistant to gentamicin

Cautions; Contra-indications; Side-effects: see under Gentamicin

Dose: *by intramuscular or by slow intravenous injection or by infusion*, 15 mg/kg daily in 2 divided doses

Note. One-hour ('peak') concentration should not exceed 30 mg/litre; pre-dose ('trough') concentration should be less than 10 mg/litre

PoM **Amikin®** (Bristol-Myers)
Injection, amikacin 250 mg (as sulphate)/mL. Net price 2-mL vial = £10.14
Paediatric injection, amikacin 50 mg (as sulphate)/mL. Net price 2-mL vial = £2.36

FRAMYCETIN SULPHATE

Indications; Cautions; Contra-indications; Side-effects: see under Neomycin Sulphate

Dose: *by mouth*, bowel sterilisation, 2–4 g daily

PoM **Soframycin®** (Roussel)
Tablets, scored, framycetin sulphate 250 mg. Net price 20-tab pack = £6.01

KANAMYCIN

Indications: superseded by other aminoglycosides (see notes above)

Cautions; Contra-indications; Side-effects: see under Gentamicin

Dose: by intramuscular injection, 250 mg every 6 hours *or* 500 mg every 12 hours
By slow intravenous infusion, 15–30 mg/kg daily in divided doses every 8–12 hours
Note. One-hour ('peak') concentration should not exceed 30 mg/litre; pre-dose ('trough') concentration should be less than 10 mg/litre

PoM **Kannasyn**® (Sterling-Winthrop)
Powder (for preparing injections), kanamycin (as acid sulphate). Net price 1-g vial = £22.16

NEOMYCIN SULPHATE

Indications: bowel sterilisation prior to surgery, see also notes above
Cautions; Contra-indications; Side-effects: see under Gentamicin but too toxic for systemic use, see notes above; avoid in renal impairment
Dose: *by mouth*, bowel sterilisation, 1 g every 4 hours

PoM **Neomycin Elixir,** neomycin sulphate 100 mg/5 mL. Net price 100 mL = 60p
PoM **Mycifradin**® (Upjohn)
Tablets, neomycin sulphate 500 mg. Net price 20 = £3.60
PoM **Nivemycin**® (Boots)
Tablets, neomycin sulphate 500 mg. Net price 20 = £1.88
Elixir, neomycin sulphate 100 mg/5 mL. Net price 100 mL = 60p

NETILMICIN

Indications: serious Gram-negative infections resistant to gentamicin
Cautions; Contra-indications; Side-effects: see under Gentamicin
Dose: *by intramuscular injection or intravenous injection or infusion*, 4–6 mg/kg daily, in divided doses every 8 or 12 hours; in severe infections, up to 7.5 mg/kg daily in divided doses every 8 hours (usually for 48 hours)
INFANT age up to 1 week, 3 mg/kg every 12 hours; age over 1 week, 2.5–3 mg/kg every 8 hours; CHILD 2–2.5 mg/kg every 8 hours
Note. One-hour ('peak') concentration should not exceed 12 mg/litre; pre-dose ('trough') concentration should be less than 2 mg/litre

PoM **Netillin**® (Schering-Plough)
Injection, netilmicin 10 mg (as sulphate)/mL. Net price 1.5-mL amp = £1.49
Injection, netilmicin 50 mg (as sulphate)/mL. Net price 1-mL amp = £2.21
Injection, netilmicin 100 mg (as sulphate)/mL. Net price 1-mL amp = £2.88; 1.5-mL amp or vial = £4.11; 2-mL amp = £5.33

TOBRAMYCIN

Indications: see under Gentamicin and notes above
Cautions; Contra-indications; Side-effects: see under Gentamicin
Dose: *by intramuscular injection or intravenous injection or infusion*, 3–5 mg/kg daily in divided doses every 8 hours; INFANT age up to 1 week 2 mg/kg every 12 hours; age over 1 week 2–2.5 mg/kg every 8 hours
Note. One-hour ('peak') concentration should not exceed 10 mg/litre; pre-dose ('trough') concentration should be less than 2 mg/litre

PoM **Nebcin**® (Lilly)
Injection, tobramycin 10 mg (as sulphate)/mL. Net price 2-mL vial = £1.08
Injection, tobramycin 40 mg (as sulphate)/mL. Net price 1-mL vial = £1.46; 2-mL vial = £2.63

5.1.5 Erythromycin

Erythromycin has a similar, although not identical, antibacterial spectrum to that of penicillin and is thus an alternative in penicillin-allergic patients.

Indications for erythromycin include respiratory infections in children, whooping-cough, legionnaires' disease, and campylobacter enteritis. It has activity against gut anaerobes and has been used with neomycin for prophylaxis prior to bowel surgery. It is active against many penicillin-resistant staphylococci, and also chlamydia and mycoplasmas.

Erythromycin, if given for more than 14 days, may occasionally cause cholestatic jaundice.

Erythromycin causes nausea in some patients; in mild to moderate infections this can be avoided by giving a lower dose (250 mg 4 times daily) but if a more serious infection, such as Legionella pneumonia, is suspected higher doses are needed.

ERYTHROMYCIN

Indications: alternative to penicillin in hypersensitive patients; sinusitis, diphtheria and whooping cough prophylaxis; legionnaires' disease; chronic prostatitis; acne vulgaris (see section 13.6)
Cautions: hepatic impairment; **interactions:** Appendix 1 (erythromycin)
Contra-indications: porphyria; estolate contra-indicated in liver disease
Side-effects: nausea, vomiting, diarrhoea after large doses
Dose: *by mouth*, 250–500 mg every 6 hours *or* 0.5–1 g every 12 hours (see notes above); up to 4 g daily in severe infections; CHILD up to 2 years 125 mg every 6 hours, 2–8 years 250 mg every 6 hours, doses doubled for severe infections
Dental prophylaxis, section 5.1, Table 2
Acne, see section 13.6
Early syphilis, 500 mg 4 times daily for 14 days
By intravenous infusion, ADULT and CHILD severe infections, 50 mg/kg daily by continuous infusion *or* in divided doses every 6 hours; mild infections (oral treatment not possible), 25 mg/kg daily
Bolus injection not recommended

PoM **Erythromycin** (Non-proprietary)
Tablets, e/c, erythromycin 250 mg, net price 20 = 86p; 500 mg, 20 = £2.01. Label: 5, 9, 25
Note. Erythromycin Tablets are not recommended for the dental prophylaxis of bacterial endocarditis; a Working Party of the British Society for Antimicrobial Chemotherapy has recommended that Erythromycin Stearate Tablets should be specified
Mixture, erythromycin (as ethyl succinate) 125 mg/5 mL, net price 100 mL = £1.47; 250 mg/5 mL, 100 mL = £2.17; 500 mg/5 mL, 100 mL = £3.59. Label: 9

PoM **Erythromycin Stearate** (Non-proprietary)
Tablets, erythromycin 250 and 500 mg (both as stearate). Label: 9

PoM **Arpimycin®** (RP Drugs)
Mixture, all pink, erythromycin (as ethyl succinate) for reconstitution with water, 125 mg/5 mL, net price 100 mL = £1.36; 250 mg/5 mL, 100 mL = £2.03; 500 mg/5 mL, 100 mL = £3.85. Label: 9

PoM **Erycen®** (Berk)
Tablets, both orange, e/c, f/c, erythromycin 250 mg, net price 20 = 97p; 500 mg, 20 = £2.41. Label: 5, 9, 25

PoM **Erymax®** (P-D)
Capsules, opaque orange/clear orange, enclosing orange and white e/c pellets, erythromycin 250 mg. Net price 20 = £4.04. Label: 5, 9, 25
Dose: 1 every 6 hours *or* 2 every 12 hours; acne, 1 twice daily then 1 daily after 1 month

PoM **Erythrocin®** (Abbott)
Tablets, both f/c, erythromycin (as stearate), 250 mg, net price 20 = £2.13; 500 mg, 20 = £4.48, 56-tab 'acne pack' = £12.54. Label: 9
Intravenous infusion, powder for reconstitution, erythromycin (as lactobionate). Net price 1-g vial = £8.03

PoM **Erythromid®** (Abbott)
Tablets, orange, e/c, f/c, erythromycin 250 mg. Net price 20 = 86p. Label: 5, 9, 25

PoM **Erythromid DS®** (Abbott)
Tablets, e/c, f/c, erythromycin 500 mg. Net price 20 = £1.94. Label: 5, 9, 25

PoM **Erythroped®** (Abbott)
Suspension PI, erythromycin 125 mg (as ethyl succinate)/5 mL when reconstituted with water. Net price 140 mL = £2.07. Label: 9
Granules PI, erythromycin (as ethyl succinate) 125 mg/sachet. Net price 28-sachet pack = £2.91. Label: 9, 13
Suspension, erythromycin 250 mg (as ethyl succinate)/5 mL when reconstituted with water. Net price 140 mL = £3.36. Label: 9
Granules, erythromycin (as ethyl succinate) 250 mg/sachet. Net price 28-sachet pack = £4.20. Label: 9, 13
Sugar-free granules, erythromycin 250 mg (as ethyl succinate)/sachet. Net price 20 sachets = £5.60. Label: 9, 13
Suspension forte, erythromycin 500 mg (as ethyl succinate)/5 mL when reconstituted with water. Net price 140 mL = £5.96. Label: 9
Granules forte, erythromycin (as ethyl succinate) 500 mg/sachet. Net price 28-sachet pack = £6.80. Label: 9, 13

PoM **Erythroped A®** (Abbott)
Tablets, yellow, f/c, erythromycin 500 mg (as ethyl succinate). Net price 28-tab pack = £5.88. Label: 9
Granules, erythromycin 1 g (as ethyl succinate)/sachet. Net price 14-sachet pack = £6.82. Label: 9, 13

PoM **Ilosone®** (Dista)
Capsules, ivory/red, erythromycin 250 mg (as estolate). Net price 20 = £4.05. Label: 9
Tablets, pink, erythromycin 500 mg (as estolate). Net price 12-tab pack = £4.96. Label: 9
Suspension, orange, erythromycin 125 mg (as estolate)/5 mL. Diluent syrup, life of diluted suspension 14 days. Net price 100 mL = £2.51. Label: 9
Suspension forte, orange, erythromycin 250 mg (as estolate)/5 mL. Diluent as above. Net price 100 mL = £4.89. Label: 9

5.1.6 Clindamycin and lincomycin

These antibiotics have only a limited use because of their serious side-effects.

Clindamycin, which is more active and better absorbed from the gut, has generally replaced **lincomycin**.

They are active against Gram-positive cocci, including penicillin-resistant staphylococci and also against many anaerobes, especially *Bacteroides fragilis*. They are well concentrated in bone and excreted in bile and urine.

Clindamycin is recommended for staphylococcal joint and bone infections such as osteomyelitis, and intra-abdominal sepsis.

The most serious toxic effect of clindamycin and lincomycin is pseudomembranous colitis which may be fatal and is most common in middle-aged and elderly females, especially following operation. This complication may occur with most antibiotics but is more frequently seen with clindamycin and is due to a toxin produced by *Clostridium difficile*, an anaerobic organism resistant to many antibiotics including clindamycin. It is sensitive to vancomycin (section 5.1.7) and metronidazole (section 5.1.11) administered by mouth.

CLINDAMYCIN

Indications: staphylococcal bone and joint infections, peritonitis; dental prophylaxis, section 5.1, Table 2
Cautions: discontinue immediately if diarrhoea or colitis develops; impaired hepatic or renal function; **interactions:** Appendix 1 (clindamycin)

 Prices are **net**, see p. 1

Contra-indications: diarrhoeal states
Side-effects: diarrhoea (discontinue treatment), nausea, vomiting, pseudomembranous colitis
Dose: by mouth, 150–300 mg every 6 hours; up to 450 mg every 6 hours in severe infections; CHILD, 3–6 mg/kg every 6 hours
Dental prophylaxis, section 5.1, Table 2
COUNSELLING. Patients should discontinue immediately and contact doctor if diarrhoea develops; capsules should be swallowed with a glass of water.
By intramuscular injection or slow intravenous infusion, 0.6–2.7 g daily in 2–4 divided doses; CHILD, 15–40 mg/kg daily in 3–4 divided doses

PoM **Dalacin C®** (Upjohn)
Capsules, clindamycin (as hydrochloride) 75 mg (lavender), net price 20 = £4.92; 150 mg, (lavender/maroon), 20 = £9.07. Label: 9, 27, counselling, see above (diarrhoea)
Paediatric suspension, pink, clindamycin 75 mg (as palmitate hydrochloride)/5 mL when reconstituted with purified water (freshly boiled and cooled). Diluent purified water (freshly boiled and cooled), life of diluted suspension 14 days. Net price 100 mL = £6.62. Label: 9, 27, counselling, see above (diarrhoea)
Injection, clindamycin 150 mg (as phosphate)/mL. Net price 2-mL amp = £5.17; 4-mL amp = £10.29

LINCOMYCIN

Indications: see under Clindamycin, also notes above
Cautions; Contra-indications; Side-effects: see under Clindamycin; **interactions:** Appendix 1 (lincomycin)
Dose: by mouth, 500 mg every 6–8 hours
COUNSELLING. Patients should discontinue immediately and contact doctor if diarrhoea develops
By intramuscular injection, 600 mg every 12–24 hours
By slow intravenous infusion, 600 mg every 8–12 hours

PoM **Lincocin®** (Upjohn)
Capsules, blue, lincomycin 500 mg (as hydrochloride). Net price 12-cap pack = £7.21. Label: 9, 23, counselling, see above (diarrhoea)
Syrup, red, lincomycin 250 mg (as hydrochloride)/5 mL. Diluent syrup, life of diluted syrup 14 days. Net price 100 mL = £7.55. Label: 9, 23, counselling, see above (diarrhoea)
Injection, lincomycin 300 mg (as hydrochloride)/mL. Net price 2-mL amp = £2.64

5.1.7 Some other antibiotics

Antibacterials discussed in this section include chloramphenicol, fusidic acid, spectinomycin, glycopeptide antibiotics (vancomycin and teicoplanin), and the polymyxins (colistin and polymyxin B).

Chloramphenicol is a potent, potentially toxic, broad-spectrum antibiotic which should be reserved for the treatment of life-threatening infections, particularly those caused by *Haemophilus influenzae*, and also for typhoid fever.

Its toxicity renders it unsuitable for systemic use except in the circumstances indicated above.

Eye-drops of chloramphenicol (see section 11.3.1) are useful for bacterial conjunctivitis.

CHLORAMPHENICOL

Indications: see notes above
Cautions: avoid repeated courses and prolonged treatment; reduce doses in hepatic or renal impairment; blood counts required before and periodically during treatment; may cause 'grey syndrome' in neonates (monitor plasma concentrations); **interactions:** Appendix 1 (chloramphenicol)
Contra-indications: pregnancy (see also Appendix 4), breast-feeding, porphyria
Side-effects: blood disorders including irreversible aplastic anaemia (aplastic anaemia attributed to chloramphenicol has terminated in leukaemia), peripheral neuritis, optic neuritis, erythema multiforme, nausea, vomiting, diarrhoea; nocturnal haemoglobinuria reported)
Dose: by mouth or by intravenous injection or infusion, 50 mg/kg daily in 4 divided doses; CHILD, haemophilus epiglottitis and pyogenic meningitis, 50–100 mg/kg daily in divided doses (high dosages decreased as soon as clinically indicated); INFANTS under 2 weeks 25 mg/kg daily in divided doses, under 1 year 50 mg/kg daily in divided doses
Note. Plasma concentration monitoring required in neonates and preferred also in those under 4 years of age; recommended plasma concentration 15–25 mg/litre

PoM **Chloromycetin®** (P-D)
Capsules, white/grey, chloramphenicol 250 mg. Net price 20 = £1.64
Suspension, chloramphenicol 125 mg (as palmitate)/5 mL. Diluent syrup, life of diluted suspension 14 days. Net price 100 mL = £3.85
Injection, powder for reconstitution, chloramphenicol (as sodium succinate). Net price 300 mg vial = £5.16; 1.2-g vial = £5.03

PoM **Kemicetine®** (Farmitalia Carlo Erba)
Injection, powder for reconstitution, chloramphenicol (as sodium succinate). Net price l-g vial = 79p

Fusidic acid and its salts are narrow-spectrum antibiotics. The only indication for their use is in infections caused by penicillin-resistant staphylococci, especially osteomyelitis, as they are well concentrated in bone; a second antistaphylococcal antibiotic is usually required to prevent emergence of resistance.

SODIUM FUSIDATE

Indications: see notes above
Cautions: liver-function tests required
Side-effects: nausea, vomiting, rashes, reversible

jaundice, especially after high dosage or rapid infusion (withdraw therapy if persistent)
Dose: by mouth, 500 mg every 8 hours, doubled for severe infections
By slow intravenous infusion, 500 mg 3 times daily

PoM **Fucidin**® (Leo)
Tablets, f/c, sodium fusidate 250 mg. Net price 20 = £13.89. Label: 9
Suspension, orange, fusidic acid 250 mg (≡ sodium fusidate 175 mg)/5 mL. Do not dilute. Net price 50 mL = £7.77. Label: 9, 21
Intravenous infusion, powder for reconstitution, diethanolamine fusidate 580 mg (≡ sodium fusidate 500 mg), with buffer. Net price per vial (with diluent) = £4.65

Spectinomycin is active against Gram-negative organisms, including *N. gonorrhoeae*. Its only indication is the treatment of gonorrhoea caused by penicillin-resistant organisms or in a penicillin-allergic patient.

SPECTINOMYCIN

Indications: see notes above
Side-effects: nausea, dizziness, urticaria, fever
Dose: *by deep intramuscular injection*, 2 g; up to 4 g in difficult-to-treat cases and in geographical areas of resistance

PoM **Trobicin**® (Upjohn)
Injection, powder for reconstitution, spectinomycin (as hydrochloride). Net price 2-g vial (with diluent) = £8.16

VANCOMYCIN AND TEICOPLANIN

The glycopeptide antibiotics vancomycin and teicoplanin have bactericidal activity against aerobic and anaerobic Gram-positive bacteria.

Vancomycin is the drug of choice for antibiotic-associated pseudomembranous colitis, for which it is given by mouth; a dose of 125 mg every 6 hours for 7 to 10 days is considered to be adequate; it is not absorbed by mouth. It has a limited use by the intravenous route in the prophylaxis and treatment of endocarditis and other serious infections caused by Gram-positive cocci including multi-resistant staphylococci. It has a relatively long duration of action therefore administration every 12 hours is usually adequate; plasma concentrations should be monitored (especially in patients with renal impairment in whom the dose may need marked reduction). It is ototoxic and nephrotoxic.

Teicoplanin is very similar to vancomycin but has a significantly longer duration of action allowing once daily administration. Unlike vancomycin, teicoplanin can be given by intramuscular as well as intravenous injection.

VANCOMYCIN

Indications: see notes above
Cautions: extravasation at injection site may cause necrosis and thrombophlebitis, blood counts and liver- and kidney-function tests required; reduce dose in elderly; **interactions:** Appendix 1 (vancomycin)
Contra-indications: if possible avoid parenteral administration in patients with renal impairment or a history of deafness
Side-effects: after parenteral administration nausea, chills, fever, urticaria, rashes, 'red man' syndrome (on rapid intravenous injection), eosinophilia, tinnitus (discontinue use), renal impairment
Dose: *by mouth*, 125 mg every 6 hours for 7–10 days, see notes above; CHILD, half adult dose
By intravenous infusion, 500 mg over at least 60 minutes every 6 hours *or* 1 g every 12 hours; NEONATE up to 1 week, 15 mg/kg initially then 10 mg/kg every 12 hours; INFANT 1–4 weeks, 15 mg/kg initially then 10 mg/kg every 8 hours; CHILD over 1 month, 44 mg/kg daily in divided doses
Note. Plasma concentration monitoring required
Endocarditis prophylaxis in dentistry, see section 5.1, table 2

PoM **Vancocin**® (Lilly)
Matrigel capsules, vancomycin hydrochloride 125 mg (blue/peach), net price 20 = £63.08; 250 mg (blue/grey), 20 = £126.16
Injection, powder for reconstitution, vancomycin (as hydrochloride). Net price 500-mg vial = £13.36

TEICOPLANIN

Indications: potentially serious Gram-positive infections including endocarditis, dialysis-associated peritonitis, and serious infections due to *Staphylococcus aureus*
Cautions: blood counts and liver and kidney function tests required; reduce dose in renal impairment (and monitor renal and auditory function on prolonged administration or if other nephrotoxic drugs given); reduce dose in elderly
Side-effects: nausea, vomiting, diarrhoea; rash, fever, bronchospasm, anaphylactic reactions; dizziness, headache; blood disorders including eosinophilia, leucopenia, and thrombocytopenia; disturbances in liver enzymes, transient increase of serum creatinine; tinnitus, mild hearing loss, and vestibular disorders also reported; local reactions include erythema, pain, and thrombophlebitis
Dose: *by intravenous injection or infusion*, 400 mg initially, subsequently 200 mg daily; severe infections, 400 mg every 12 hours for 3 doses initially, subsequently 400 mg daily; the subsequent doses can alternatively be given by intramuscular injection
CHILD *by intravenous injection or infusion*, initially 6 mg/kg every 12 hours for 3 doses, subsequently 3 mg/kg daily (severe infections, 6 mg/kg daily)

▼ PoM **Targocid**® (Merrell)
Injection, powder for reconstitution, teicoplanin, net price 200-mg vial (with diluent) = £26.72; 400-mg vial (with diluent) = £53.44

POLYMYXINS

The polymyxin antibiotics, colistin and polymyxin B, are active against Gram-negative organisms, including *Pseudomonas aeruginosa*. They are **not** absorbed by mouth and thus need to be given by injection to obtain a systemic effect; however, they are toxic and have few, if any, indications for systemic use.

Colistin is used in bowel sterilisation regimens in neutropenic patients; it is **not** recommended for gastro-intestinal infections.

Both colistin and polymyxin B are included in some preparations for topical application. For reference to use as a bladder irrigation see section 7.4.4.

COLISTIN

Indications: see notes above

Cautions: reduce dose in renal impairment; **interactions:** Appendix 1 (polymyxins)

Contra-indications: myasthenia gravis

Side-effects: perioral and peripheral paraesthesia, vertigo, muscle weakness, apnoea, nephrotoxicity

Dose: by mouth, bowel sterilisation, 1.5–3 million units every 8 hours

By intramuscular injection or intravenous injection or infusion, 2 million units every 8 hours (but see notes above)

PoM **Colomycin®** (Pharmax)

Tablets, scored, colistin sulphate 1.5 million units. Net price 50 = £63.60

Syrup, pink, colistin sulphate 250 000 units/5 mL when reconstituted with water. Diluent syrup, life of diluted syrup 14 days. Net price 80 mL = £3.79

Injection, powder for reconstitution, colistin sulphomethate sodium. Net price 500 000-unit vial = £1.25; 1 million-unit vial = £1.83

POLYMYXIN B SULPHATE

Indications; Cautions; Contra-indications; Side-effects: see under Colistin

Dose: by slow intravenous infusion, 15 000–25 000 units/kg daily in divided doses

PoM **Aerosporin®** (Calmic)

Injection, powder for reconstitution, polymyxin B sulphate. Net price 500 000-unit vial = £12.01

PoM **Polybactrin®** (Calmic)

Soluble GU, powder for reconstitution, polymyxin B sulphate 75 000 units, neomycin sulphate 20 000 units, bacitracin 1000 units. For bladder irrigation. Net price per vial = £5.76

5.1.8 Sulphonamides and trimethoprim

The importance of the sulphonamides as chemotherapeutic agents has decreased as a result of increasing bacterial resistance and their replacement by antibiotics which are generally more active and less toxic.

The principal indication for sulphonamides used alone is urinary-tract infections caused by sensitive organisms.

Sulphamethoxazole and trimethoprim have been used in combination (as co-trimoxazole) because of their synergistic activity. Increasing bacterial resistance to sulphonamides and the high incidence of sulphonamide-related side-effects have however diminished the value of co-trimoxazole.

Indications for **co-trimoxazole** include urinary-tract infections, prostatitis, exacerbations of chronic bronchitis, invasive salmonella infections, and brucellosis but trimethoprim alone is now preferred. High doses of co-trimoxazole are used for *Pneumocystis carinii* infections. Co-trimoxazole is no longer recommended for gonorrhoea.

Trimethoprim can be used alone for the treatment of urinary- and respiratory-tract infections and for prostatitis and invasive salmonella infections. Side-effects are less than with co-trimoxazole especially in older patients.

Side-effects of the sulphonamides include rashes, which are common, the Stevens-Johnson syndrome (erythema multiforme), renal failure (especially with the less soluble preparations), and blood dyscrasias, notably marrow depression and agranulocytosis.

Side-effects of co-trimoxazole are similar to those of the sulphonamides but a particular watch should be kept for haematological effects and special care should be taken in patients who may be folate deficient such as the elderly and chronic sick. There have been recent reports of deaths in patients over the age of 65 years being treated with co-trimoxazole and almost certainly associated with the sulphonamide component. For this reason co-trimoxazole should be used with care in the elderly and preferably only if there is no acceptable alternative. The effect on the fetus is unknown and the drugs should not be used in pregnancy.

The **longer-acting sulphonamide**, sulfametopyrazine which is highly bound to plasma proteins, has the advantage of requiring less frequent administration, but toxic effects due to accumulation are more likely to occur.

The **poorly-absorbed sulphonamides** (calcium sulphaloxate is now the only one remaining on the UK market) have been widely used for the treatment of intestinal infections and pre-operative bowel preparation but can no longer be recommended for these indications.

For *topical preparations* of sulphonamides used in the treatment of burns see section 13.10.1.1.

CO-TRIMOXAZOLE

A mixture of trimethoprim and sulphamethoxazole in the proportions of 1 part to 5 parts

Indications: invasive salmonellosis, typhoid fever, bone and joint infections due to *Haemophilus influenzae*, urinary-tract infections, sinusitis, exacerbations of chronic bronchitis, gonorrhoea in penicillin-allergic patients

Cautions: blood counts in prolonged treatment,

maintain adequate fluid intake, renal impairment, breast-feeding; photosensitivity; elderly patients (**important:** see notes above); **interactions:** Appendix 1 (co-trimoxazole)

Contra-indications: pregnancy, infants under 6 weeks (risk of kernicterus), renal or hepatic failure, jaundice, blood disorders

Side-effects: nausea, vomiting, glossitis, rashes, erythema multiforme (includes Stevens-Johnson syndrome), epidermal necrolysis, eosinophilia, agranulocytosis, granulocytopenia, purpura, leucopenia; megaloblastic anaemia due to trimethoprim

Dose: *by mouth*, 960 mg every 12 hours, increased to 1.44 g in severe infections; 480 mg every 12 hours if treated for more than 14 days; CHILD, every 12 hours, 6 weeks to 5 months, 120 mg; 6 months to 5 years, 240 mg; 6–12 years, 480 mg

Prophylaxis of recurrent urinary-tract infection, 480 mg at night; CHILD 6–12 mg/kg at night

Gonorrhoea, 1.92 g every 12 hours for 2 days, or 2.4 g followed by a further dose of 2.4 g after 8 hours but see notes above

High-dose therapy for *Pneumocystis carinii* infections, 120 mg/kg daily in divided doses for 14 days

By intramuscular injection or intravenous infusion, 960 mg every 12 hours

Note. 480 mg of co-trimoxazole consists of sulphamethoxazole 400 mg and trimethoprim 80 mg

PoM **Co-trimoxazole** (Non-proprietary)

Tablets, co-trimoxazole 480 mg; net price 20 = 97p; 960 mg, 20 = £3.14. Label 9

Available from APS, Cox (480 mg), DDSA (Fectrim®, Fectrim® Forte), Evans (480 mg), Kerfoot (960 mg), Lagap (Laratrim® 960 mg), Norton (Comox®)

Dispersible tablets, co-trimoxazole 480 mg. Net price 20 = £1.31. Label: 9, 13

Available from APS, Kerfoot, Norton (Comox®)

Paediatric oral suspension, co-trimoxazole 240 mg/5 mL. Net price 100 mL = £2.09. Label: 9

Available from APS, Evans, Kerfoot, Lagap (Laratrim®), Norton (Comox®), RP Drugs (Chemotrim®)

Oral suspension, co-trimoxazole 480 mg/5 mL. Net price 100 mL = £3·00. Label: 9

Available from APS, Evans, Kerfoot, Lagap (Laratrim®)

PoM **Bactrim**® (Roche)

Drapsules®(= tablets), orange, f/c, co-trimoxazole 480 mg. Net price 20 = £2.26. Label: 9

Tablets (dispersible), yellow, scored, co-trimoxazole 480 mg. Net price 20 = £2.49. Label: 9, 13

Double-strength tablets, scored, co-trimoxazole 960 mg. Net price 20 = £3.54. Label: 9

Paediatric tablets, co-trimoxazole 120 mg. Net price 20 = 64p. Label: 9

Adult suspension, yellow, co-trimoxazole 480 mg/5 mL. Net price 100 mL = £3.00. Label: 9

Paediatric syrup, sugar-free, yellow, co-trimoxazole 240 mg/5 mL. Net price 100 mL = £2.09. Label: 9

Intravenous infusion, co-trimoxazole 96 mg/mL. To be diluted before use. Net price 5-mL amp = £1.12 (hosp. only)

PoM **Septrin**® (Wellcome)

Tablets, co-trimoxazole 480 mg. Net price 20 = £3.03. Label: 9

Dispersible tablets, orange, sugar-free, co-trimoxazole 480 mg. Net price 20 = £3.22. Label: 9, 13

Forte tablets, scored, co-trimoxazole 960 mg. Net price 20 = £5.05. Label: 9

Paediatric dispersible tablets, orange, sugar-free, co-trimoxazole 120 mg. Net price 20 = £1.01. Label: 9, 13

Adult suspension, co-trimoxazole 480 mg/5 mL. Diluent syrup, life of diluted suspension 14 days. Net price 100 mL = £4.74. Label: 9

Paediatric suspension, sugar-free, co-trimoxazole 240 mg/5 mL. Diluent syrup or sorbitol solution 70%, life of diluted suspension 14 days. Net price 100 mL = £2.63. Label: 9

Intramuscular injection, co-trimoxazole 320 mg/mL. Net price 3-mL amp = £2.71

Intravenous infusion, co-trimoxazole 96 mg/mL. To be diluted before use. Net price 5-mL amp = £1.59

CALCIUM SULPHALOXATE

Indications: see notes on poorly-absorbed sulphonamides

Cautions; Contra-indications; Side-effects: see under Co-trimoxazole; side-effects less common because of limited absorption

Dose: 1 g every 8 hours

PoM **Enteromide**® (Consolidated)

Tablets, calcium sulphaloxate 500 mg. Net price 20 = £1.06

SULFAMETOPYRAZINE

Indications: urinary-tract infections, chronic bronchitis

Cautions; Contra-indications; Side-effects: see under Co-trimoxazole

Dose: 2 g once weekly

PoM **Kelfizine W**® (Farmitalia Carlo Erba)

Tablets, sulfametopyrazine 2 g. Tablets to be taken in water. Net price 1 = £1.25. Label: 9, 13

SULPHADIAZINE

Indications: meningococcal meningitis

Cautions; Contra-indications; Side-effects: see under Co-trimoxazole; avoid in severe renal impairment

Dose: *by deep intramuscular injection or intravenous infusion*, 2 g initially then 1 g every 6 hours for 2 days, followed by oral treatment for a further 5 days

PoM **Sulphadiazine** (Non-proprietary)

Tablets, sulphadiazine 500 mg. Net price 20 = £1.36. Label: 9, 27

Injection, sulphadiazine 250 mg (as sodium salt)/mL. Net price 4-mL amp = 94p

SULPHADIMIDINE

Indications: urinary-tract infections; meningococcal meningitis

Cautions; Contra-indications; Side-effects: see under Co-trimoxazole

Dose: by mouth, 2 g initially, then 0.5–1 g every 6–8 hours

Meningitis prophylaxis, see section 5.1, table 2

PoM **Sulphadimidine** (Non-proprietary)

Tablets, sulphadimidine 500 mg. Net price 20 = £1.17. Label: 9, 27

Paediatric oral suspension, sulphadimidine 500 mg/5 mL. Net price 100 mL = 66p. Label: 9, 27

TRIMETHOPRIM

Indications: urinary-tract infections, acute and chronic bronchitis

Cautions: renal impairment, breast-feeding, predisposition to folate deficiency, blood counts required on long-term therapy; **interactions:** Appendix 1 (trimethoprim)

Contra-indications: severe renal impairment, pregnancy, neonates

Side-effects: gastro-intestinal disturbances including nausea and vomiting, pruritus, rashes, depression of haemopoiesis

Dose: by mouth, acute infections, 200 mg every 12 hours; urinary-tract infections, 300 mg daily *or* 200 mg twice daily; CHILD, twice daily, 2–5 months 25 mg, 6 months–5 years 50 mg, 6–12 years 100 mg

Chronic infections and prophylaxis, 100 mg at night; CHILD 1–2 mg/kg at night

By slow intravenous injection or infusion, 150–250 mg every 12 hours; CHILD under 12 years, 6–9 mg/kg daily in 2–3 divided doses

PoM **Trimethoprim** (Non-proprietary)

Tablets, trimethoprim 100 mg, net price 20 = 62p; 200 mg, 20 = 91p. Label: 9

PoM **Ipral®** (Squibb)

Tablets, trimethoprim 100 mg, net price 20 = 80p; 200 mg, 20 = £1.71. Label: 9

PoM **Monotrim®** (Duphar)

Tablets, both scored, trimethoprim 100 mg, net price 20 = 82p; 200 mg, 20 = £1.44. Label: 9

Suspension, sugar-free, trimethoprim 50 mg/5 mL. Diluents sorbitol solution or water, life of diluted suspension 14 days. Net price 100 mL = £1.36. Label: 9

Injection, trimethoprim 20 mg (as lactate)/mL. Net price 5-mL amp = 68p

PoM **Syraprim®** (Wellcome)

Tablets, both scored, trimethoprim 100 mg, net price 20 = £3.84; 300 mg, 20 = £11.34. Label: 9

Injection, trimethoprim 20 mg (as lactate)/mL. Net price 5-mL amp = £1.62

PoM **Trimogal®** (Lagap)

Tablets, trimethoprim 100 mg, net price 20 = 61p; 200 mg, 20 = 91p. Label: 9

PoM **Trimopan®** (Berk)

Tablets, both scored, trimethoprim 100 mg, net price 20 = 97p; 200 mg, 20 = £1.75. Label: 9

Suspension, sugar-free, trimethoprim 50 mg/5 mL. Diluent syrup, life of diluted suspension 14 days. Net price 100 mL = £1.37. Label: 9

5.1.9 Antituberculous drugs

The treatment of tuberculosis has two phases—an *initial phase* using at least three drugs and a *continuation phase* with two drugs.

Treatment requires specialised knowledge, particularly where the disease involves resistant organisms or non-respiratory organs.

The treatment outlined below reflects current practice in the UK; variations occur in other countries

INITIAL PHASE. The concurrent use of at least three drugs during the initial phase is designed to reduce the population of viable bacteria as rapidly as possible and to minimise the risk of ineffective treatment in those patients infected by drug-resistant bacteria. Treatment of choice for the initial phase is the daily use of isoniazid, rifampicin, and pyrazinamide; either ethambutol or streptomycin should be added if drug resistance is thought likely. The initial phase drugs should be continued for 8 weeks.

CONTINUATION PHASE. After the initial phase, treatment is continued with isoniazid and rifampicin (in the absence of contra-indications). Pyrazinamide is ineffective after the first two or three months and should be stopped after that time. Ethambutol can be used in the continuation phase with either isoniazid or rifampicin but requires a more prolonged course and particular care to avoid ophthalmic toxicity. Streptomycin should only be used in the continuation phase under exceptional circumstances because of its cumulative toxicity. Treatment under full supervision with high-dose isoniazid (15 mg/kg) and rifampicin (600–900 mg) three times weekly is as effective as unsupervised therapy.

DURATION OF TREATMENT. The duration of treatment depends on the combination of drugs used in the initial phase. Where isoniazid and rifampicin are given daily throughout treatment a *9-month course* is sufficient for patients with respiratory disease regardless of its extent. If in the initial phase pyrazinamide is included with isoniazid and rifampicin, which are then used in the continuation phase, a total of *6 months treatment* gives equally good results.

> Major causes of treatment failure are incorrect prescribing by the physician and inadequate compliance by the patient. It is important to avoid both excessive and inadequate dosage.

Isoniazid is cheap and highly effective. Its only common side-effect is peripheral neuropathy which is more likely to occur when high dosage is used (as in meningitis) or where there are pre-existing risk factors. In these circumstances pyridoxine 10 mg daily should be given prophylactically from the start of treatment. Other side-effects such as hepatitis and psychosis are rare.

Rifampicin is an essential component of any short-course regimen. It should be given in a single daily dose of 450 mg in adults of less than 50 kg and 600 mg in those above that weight.

During the first two months of rifampicin administration transient disturbance of liver function with elevated serum transaminases is common but generally does not require interruption of treatment. Occasionally more serious liver toxicity requires a change of treatment particularly in those with pre-existing liver disease.

On intermittent treatment six toxicity syndromes have been recognised—influenzal, abdominal, and respiratory symptoms, shock, renal failure, and thrombocytopenic purpura—and can occur in 20 to 30% of patients.

Rifampicin induces hepatic enzymes which accelerate the metabolism of several drugs including oestrogens, corticosteroids, phenytoin, sulphonylureas, and anticoagulants. The effectiveness of oral contraceptives is reduced and alternative family planning advice should be offered.

Pyrazinamide is a bactericidal drug only active against intracellular dividing forms of *Mycobacterium tuberculosis*; it exerts its main effect only in the first two or three months. It is particularly useful in tuberculous meningitis because of good meningeal penetration. It is not active against *M. bovis*.

Ethambutol is used in conjunction with isoniazid or rifampicin. Side-effects are largely confined to visual disturbances in the form of loss of acuity, colour blindness, and restriction of visual fields. These toxic effects are more common where excessive dosage is used or the patient's renal function is impaired, in which case the drug should be **avoided**. The earliest features of ocular toxicity are subjective and patients should be advised to discontinue therapy immediately if they develop deterioration in vision and promptly seek further advice. Early discontinuation of the drug is almost always followed by recovery of eyesight. Patients who cannot understand warnings about visual side-effects should, if possible, be given an alternative drug. In particular, ethambutol should be **avoided** in children until they are at least 6 years old and capable of reporting symptomatic visual changes accurately.

Ophthalmic examination should be performed prior to treatment and at intervals during treatment.

Streptomycin is given intramuscularly in a standard dose of 1 g daily, reduced to 500 to 750 mg in small patients or those over the age of 40 years. Measurement of plasma drug concentrations should be performed, particularly in patients with impaired renal function in whom streptomycin must be used with great care. Side-effects increase after a cumulative dose of 100 g, which should only be exceeded in exceptional circumstances.

Second-line drugs available for infections caused by resistant organisms, or when first-line drugs cause unacceptable side-effects, include capreomycin, cycloserine, and prothionamide (no longer on UK market).

CAPREOMYCIN

Indications: tuberculosis resistant to first-line drugs
Cautions: renal, hepatic, or auditory impairment; breast-feeding; do not give with streptomycin or other ototoxic drugs
Contra-indications: pregnancy
Side-effects: hypersensitivity reactions including urticaria and rashes, changes in liver function, renal damage, hearing loss with tinnitus and vertigo, pain and induration at injection site
Dose: *by intramuscular injection*, 1 g daily (not more than 20 mg/kg)

PoM **Capastat**® (Dista)
Injection, powder for reconstitution, capreomycin sulphate 1 million units (capreomycin approx. 1 g). Net price per vial = £2.28

CYCLOSERINE

Indications: tuberculosis resistant to first-line drugs
Cautions: reduce dose in renal impairment
Contra-indications: epilepsy, depression, severe anxiety, psychotic states, alcoholism
Side-effects: mainly neurological, including headache, dizziness, vertigo, drowsiness, convulsions; allergic rashes
Dose: usually 250 mg every 12 hours; max. 1 g daily

PoM **Cycloserine** (Lilly)
Capsules, cycloserine 250 mg, net price 20 = £11.35. Label: 2, 8

ETHAMBUTOL HYDROCHLORIDE

Indications: tuberculosis, in combination with other drugs
Cautions: warn patients to report visual changes—see notes above
Contra-indications: renal impairment; young children (see notes), elderly patients, optic neuritis, poor vision
Side-effects: optic neuritis, red/green colour blindness, peripheral neuritis
Dose: ADULT and CHILD over 6 years, 15 mg/kg daily

PoM **Myambutol**® (Lederle)
Tablets, ethambutol hydrochloride 100 mg (yellow), net price 20 = £1.45; 400 mg (grey), 20 = £5.23. Label: 8

PoM **Mynah**® (Lederle)
Mynah 200 tablets, ethambutol hydrochloride 200 mg, isoniazid 100 mg. Net price 84-tab pack = £13.27. Label: 8, 23

Mynah 250 tablets, yellow, ethambutol hydrochloride 250 mg, isoniazid 100 mg. Net price 84-tab pack = £16.45. Label: 8, 23
Mynah 300 tablets, orange, ethambutol hydrochloride 300 mg, isoniazid 100 mg. Net price 84-tab pack = £19.66. Label: 8, 23
Mynah 365 tablets, pink, ethambutol hydrochloride 365 mg, isoniazid 100 mg. Net price 84-tab pack = £23.83. Label: 8, 23

ISONIAZID

Indications: tuberculosis, in combination with other drugs; prophylaxis—section 5.1, Table 2
Cautions: impaired liver and kidney function, epilepsy, history of psychosis, alcoholism, breast-feeding; **interactions:** Appendix 1 (isoniazid)
Contra-indications: drug-induced liver disease, porphyria
Side-effects: nausea, vomiting, hypersensitivity reactions including rashes, peripheral neuritis with high doses (pyridoxine prophylaxis, see notes above), convulsions, psychotic episodes, agranulocytosis; hepatitis (especially over age of 35); systemic lupus erythematosus-like syndrome reported
Dose: *by mouth or by intramuscular or intravenous injection*, pulmonary tuberculosis, 300 mg daily (*or* up to 1 g (15 mg/kg) three times weekly); CHILD 6 mg/kg daily
Tuberculous meningitis, 10 mg/kg daily

PoM **Isoniazid Tablets,** isoniazid 50 mg, net price 20 = 28p; 100 mg, 20 = 33p. Label: 8, 22
PoM **Isoniazid Elixir** (BPC)
(Isoniazid Syrup)
Elixir, isoniazid 50 mg, citric acid monohydrate 12.5 mg, sodium citrate 60 mg, concentrated anise water 0.05 mL, compound tartrazine solution 0.05 mL, glycerol 1 mL, double-strength chloroform water 2 mL, water to 5 mL. Diluent chloroform water, life of diluted elixir 14 days. Label: 8, 22
Isoniazid Syrup (isoniazid 50 mg/5 mL) available from Penn, RP Drugs (both special order)
PoM **Rimifon**® (Roche)
Injection, isoniazid 25 mg/mL. Net price 2-mL amp = 9p

PYRAZINAMIDE

Indications: tuberculosis in combination with other drugs
Cautions: impaired renal function, diabetes, gout; **interactions:** Appendix 1 (pyrazinamide)
Contra-indications: liver damage, porphyria
Side-effects: hepatotoxicity including fever, anorexia, hepatomegaly, jaundice, liver failure; nausea, vomiting, arthralgia, sideroblastic anaemia, urticaria
Dose: 20–35 mg/kg daily in 3–4 divided doses; max. 3 g daily

PoM **Zinamide**® (MSD)
Tablets, scored, pyrazinamide 500 mg. Net price 20 = £1.44. Label: 8

RIFAMPICIN

Indications: tuberculosis, in combination with other drugs; leprosy (section 5.1.10); meningococcal meningitis and *H. influenzae* (type b) prophylaxis—section 5.1, Table 2
Cautions: reduce dose in hepatic impairment; alcoholism, pregnancy; advise patients on oral contraceptives to use additional means; discolours soft contact lenses; see also notes above; **interactions:** Appendix 1 (rifampicin)
Contra-indications: jaundice, porphyria
Side-effects: gastro-intestinal symptoms including anorexia, nausea, vomiting, diarrhoea; those occurring mainly on intermittent therapy include influenzal syndrome (with chills, fever, dizziness, bone pain), respiratory symptoms including shortness of breath, collapse and shock, acute renal failure, and thrombocytopenic purpura; alterations of liver function, jaundice; urticaria and rashes; urine, saliva, and other body secretions coloured orange-red; pseudomembranous colitis reported
Dose: *by mouth or by intravenous infusion*, 450–600 mg (about 10 mg/kg) daily (oral doses preferably before breakfast); CHILD up to 20 mg/kg daily to a max. of 600 mg
Note. If treatment interrupted re-introduce with low dosage

PoM **Rifadin**® (Merrell)
Capsules, rifampicin 150 mg (blue/red), net price 20 = £3.82; 300 mg (red), 20 = £7.64. Label: 8, 14, 22, counselling, see lenses above
Syrup, red, rifampicin 100 mg/5 mL. Do not dilute. Net price 120 mL = £3.71. Label: 8, 14, 22, counselling, see lenses above
Intravenous infusion, powder for reconstitution, rifampicin. Net price 600-mg vial (with solvent) = £8.00
PoM **Rimactane**® (Ciba)
Capsules, rifampicin 150 mg (red), net price 20 = £3.44; 300 mg (red/brown), 20 = £6.88. Label: 8, 14, 22, counselling, see lenses above
Syrup, red, rifampicin 100 mg/5 mL. Do not dilute. Net price 100 mL = £2.78. Label: 8, 14, 22, counselling, see lenses above
Intravenous infusion, powder for reconstitution, rifampicin. Net price 300-mg vial (with diluent) = £7.28
Note. Owing to risk of contact sensitisation care must be taken to avoid contact during preparation and infusion

Combined preparations
PoM **Rifater**® (Merrell)
Tablets, pink-beige, s/c, rifampicin 120 mg, isoniazid 50 mg, pyrazinamide 300 mg. Net price 20 = £4.40. Label: 8, 14, 22, counselling, see lenses above
Dose: initial treatment of pulmonary tuberculosis, patients up to 40 kg 3 tablets daily preferably before breakfast, 40–49 kg 4 tablets daily, 50–64 kg 5 tablets daily, 65 kg or more, 6 tablets daily; not suitable for use in children
PoM **Rifinah 150**® (Merrell)
Tablets, pink, rifampicin 150 mg, isoniazid

100 mg. Net price 84-tab pack = £16.59. Label: 8, 14, 22, counselling, see lenses above
Dose: ADULT under 50 kg, 3 tablets daily, preferably before breakfast

PoM **Rifinah 300®** (Merrell)
Tablets, orange, rifampicin 300 mg, isoniazid 150 mg. Net price 56-tab pack = £21.93. Label: 8, 14, 22, counselling, see lenses above
Dose: ADULT 50 kg and over, 2 tablets daily, preferably before breakfast

PoM **Rimactazid 150®** (Ciba)
Tablets, pink, s/c, rifampicin 150 mg, isoniazid 100 mg. Net price 84-tab pack = £14.93. Label: 8, 14, 22, counselling, see lenses above
Additives: include gluten
Dose: ADULT under 50 kg, 3 tablets daily, preferably before breakfast

PoM **Rimactazid 300®** (Ciba)
Tablets, orange, s/c, rifampicin 300 mg, isoniazid 150 mg. Net price 56-tab pack = £19.74. Label: 8, 14, 22, counselling, see lenses above
Additives: include gluten
Dose: ADULT 50 kg and over, 2 tablets daily, preferably before breakfast

STREPTOMYCIN

Indications: tuberculosis, in combination with other drugs
Cautions; Contra-indications; Side-effects: see under Aminoglycosides, section 5.1.4; also hypersensitivity reactions, paraesthesia of mouth
Dose: *by intramuscular injection*, 1 g daily; in patients over 40 years, 750 mg; in small patients, 500 mg; cumulative dose should not normally exceed 100 g, see notes above

PoM **Streptomycin Sulphate** (Evans)
Injection, powder for reconstitution, streptomycin (as sulphate). Net price 1-g vial = £1.69

5.1.10 Antileprotic drugs

Advice from a member of the Panel of Leprosy Opinion is essential for the treatment of leprosy (Hansen's disease). Details of the Panel can be obtained from the Department of Health telephone 071-972 3272.

For over twenty years the mainstay of leprosy treatment was dapsone monotherapy but resistance to dapsone became an increasing concern. The World Health Organization has made recommendations to overcome this problem of dapsone resistance and to prevent the emergence of resistance to other antileprotic drugs. These recommendations are based on the same principles as for the chemotherapy of tuberculosis. Drugs recommended are **dapsone**, **rifampicin,** and **clofazimine** and, secondarily ethionamide or prothionamide (which are not marketed in the UK).

A three-drug regimen is recommended for *multibacillary leprosy* (lepromatous, borderline-lepromatous, and borderline leprosy) and a two-drug regimen for those suffering from *paucibacillary leprosy* (borderline-tuberculoid, tuberculoid, and indeterminate). These regimens, which are widely applicable throughout the world (with minor local variations), are as follows:

Multibacillary leprosy (*3-drug regimen*)

Rifampicin	600 mg once-monthly, supervised (450 mg for those weighing less than 35 kg)
Dapsone	100 mg daily, self-administered
Clofazimine	300 mg once-monthly, supervised, *and* 50 mg daily, self-administered

(*or*, if clofazimine unacceptable, ethionamide or prothionamide 250–375 mg daily, self-administered).

Treatment should be given for at least 2 years and be continued, wherever possible, up to smear negativity. It should be continued unchanged during both type I (reversal) or type II (erythema nodosum leprosum) reactions which, if severe, should receive their own specific treatment (e.g. prednisolone or increased clofazimine dosage).

Paucibacillary leprosy (*2-drug regimen*)

Rifampicin	600 mg once-monthly, supervised (450 mg for those weighing less than 35 kg)
Dapsone	100 mg daily, self-administered

Treatment should be given for 6 months. If treatment is interrupted the regimen should be recommenced where it was left off to complete the full course.

Neither the multibacillary nor the paucibacillary antileprosy regimen is sufficient to treat tuberculosis, therefore patients who also have tuberculosis should be given appropriate antituberculous drugs in addition to the antileprosy regimen.

DAPSONE

Indications: leprosy, dermatitis herpetiformis
Cautions: cardiac or pulmonary disease; anaemia (treat severe anaemia before starting); G6PD-deficiency (including breast-feeding of affected children); pregnancy; avoid in porphyria; **interactions:** Appendix 1 (dapsone)
Side-effects: (dose-related and uncommon at doses used for leprosy), neuropathy, allergic dermatitis, anorexia, nausea, vomiting, headache, insomnia, tachycardia, anaemia, hepatitis, agranulocytosis
Dose: leprosy, 1–2 mg/kg daily, see notes above
Dermatitis herpetiformis, see specialist literature

PoM **Dapsone Tablets,** dapsone 50 mg, net price 20 = 41p; 100 mg, 20 = 58p. Label: 8

CLOFAZIMINE

Indications: leprosy
Cautions: hepatic and renal impairment—function tests required
Side-effects: nausea, giddiness, headache, and diarrhoea with high doses, skin and urine coloured (red), lesions discoloured (blue-black)
Dose: leprosy, see notes above
Lepromatous lepra reactions, dosage increased to 300 mg daily for max. of 3 months

PoM **Lamprene®** (Geigy)
Capsules, brown, clofazimine 100 mg. Net price 20 = £1.65. Label: 8, 14, 21

RIFAMPICIN

Section 5.1.9

5.1.11 Metronidazole and tinidazole

Metronidazole is an antimicrobial drug with high activity against anaerobic bacteria and protozoa. Indications for metronidazole include trichomonal vaginitis (section 5.4.3), bacterial vaginosis (notably *Gardnerella vaginalis* infections), and *Entamoeba histolytica* and *Giardia lamblia* infections (section 5.4.2). It is also used for surgical and gynaecological sepsis in which its activity against colonic anaerobes, especially *Bacteroides fragilis*, is important. Metronidazole is effective in the treatment of pseudomembranous colitis in a dose of 400 mg by mouth three times daily. Side-effects are uncommon but neuropathy can occur during prolonged therapy. Gastro-intestinal disturbances may be minimised by taking tablets with or after food, but the mixture (which contains metronidazole benzoate) should be taken at least 1 hour before food.

Tinidazole is similar to metronidazole but has a longer duration of action.

METRONIDAZOLE

Indications: see under Dose below; protozoal infections, section 5.4.2

Cautions: disulfiram-like reaction with alcohol, hepatic impairment; pregnancy and breast-feeding (manufacturer advises avoidance of high-dose regimens); avoid in porphyria; **interactions:** Appendix 1 (metronidazole)

Side-effects: nausea, vomiting, unpleasant taste, furred tongue, and gastro-intestinal disturbances, rashes, urticaria and angioedema; rarely drowsiness, headache, dizziness, ataxia, and darkening of urine; on prolonged or intensive therapy peripheral neuropathy, transient epileptiform seizures, and leucopenia

Dose: anaerobic infections (usually treated for 7 days), *by mouth*, 800 mg initially then 400 mg every 8 hours; *by rectum*, 1 g every 8 hours for 3 days, then 1 g every 12 hours; *by intravenous infusion*, 500 mg every 8 hours; CHILD, any route, 7.5 mg/kg every 8 hours

Leg ulcers and pressure sores, *by mouth*, 400 mg every 8 hours for 7 days

Bacterial vaginosis, *by mouth*, 400 mg twice daily for 7 days *or* 2 g as a single dose

Acute ulcerative gingivitis, *by mouth*, 200 mg every 8 hours for 3 days; CHILD 1–3 years 50 mg every 8 hours for 3 days; 3–7 years 100 mg every 12 hours; 7–10 years 100 mg every 8 hours

Acute dental infections, *by mouth*, 200 mg every 8 hours for 3–7 days

Surgical prophylaxis, *by mouth*, 400 mg every 8 hours during 24 hours before surgery; CHILD 7.5 mg/kg every 8 hours, then until oral administration can be resumed *either by rectum*, 1 g every 8 hours; CHILD 125–250 mg every 8 hours *or by intravenous infusion*, 500 mg shortly before surgery then every 8 hours; CHILD 7.5 mg/kg every 8 hours

PoM **Metronidazole** (Non-proprietary)
Tablets, metronidazole 200 mg, net price 20 = 58p; 400 mg, 20 = £1.45. Label: 4, 9, 21, 25, 27
Available from APS (200 mg, 400 mg), Cox (200 mg, 400 mg), DDSA (Vaginyl® 200 mg, 400 mg), Evans (200 mg), Kerfoot (200 mg, 400 mg), Lagap (Metrolyl® 200 mg, 400 mg), Lederle (Zadstat® 200 mg), Mercury (Nidazol® 200 mg)

PoM **Elyzol®** (CP)
Suppositories, metronidazole 500 mg, net price 10 = £4.50; 1 g, 10 = £7.00. Label: 4

PoM **Flagyl®** (Rhône-Poulenc Rorer)
Tablets, both f/c, ivory, metronidazole 200 mg, net price 21-tab pack = £2.19; 400 mg, 14-tab pack = £3.11. Label: 4, 9, 21, 25, 27
Intravenous infusion, metronidazole 5 mg/mL. Net price 20-mL amp = £2.06; 100-mL bottle = £4.34; 100-mL Viaflex® bag = £4.78
Suppositories, metronidazole 500 mg, net price 10 = £6.77; 1 g, 10 = £10.28. Label: 4, 9

PoM **Flagyl S®** (Rhône-Poulenc Rorer)
Suspension, metronidazole 200 mg (as benzoate)/5 mL. Diluent syrup, life of diluted suspension 14 days. Net price 50 mL = £2.36; 100 mL = £4.53. Label: 4, 9, 23

PoM **Metrolyl®** (Lagap)
Intravenous infusion, metronidazole 5 mg/mL. Net price 100-mL Steriflex® bag = £4.05
Suppositories, metronidazole 500 mg, net price 10 = £4.25; 1 g, 10 = £6.80. Label: 4, 9

PoM **Zadstat®** (Lederle)
Intravenous infusion, metronidazole 5 mg/mL. Net price 100-mL Steriflex Minipack® = £4.62
Suppositories, metronidazole 500 mg, net price 10 = £4.25; 1 g, 10 = £6.80. Label: 4, 9

With antifungal

PoM **Flagyl Compak®** (Rhône-Poulenc Rorer)
Treatment pack, tablets, off-white, f/c, metronidazole 400 mg, with pessaries, yellow, nystatin 100000 units. Net price 14 tablets and 14 pessaries (with applicator) = £4.24
Dose: for mixed trichomonal and candidal infections, 1 tablet twice daily for 7 days and 1 pessary inserted twice daily for 7 days *or* 1 at night for 14 nights

TINIDAZOLE

Indications: anaerobic bacterial and protozoal infections

Cautions; Side-effects: see under Metronidazole; pregnancy (manufacturer advises avoidance in first trimester)

Dose: anaerobic infections *by mouth*, 2 g initially, followed by 1 g daily *or* 500 mg twice daily, usually for 5–6 days
Bacterial vaginosis, trichomoniasis, giardiasis and acute ulcerative gingivitis, a single 2-g dose; CHILD single dose of 50–75 mg/kg
Intestinal amoebiasis, 2 g daily for 2–3 days; CHILD 50–60 mg/kg daily for 3 days

Amoebic involvement of liver, 1.5–2 g daily for 3–5 days; CHILD 50–60 mg/kg daily for 5 days
Abdominal surgery prophylaxis, a single 2-g dose approximately 12 hours before surgery

PoM **Fasigyn**® (Pfizer)
Tablets, f/c, tinidazole 500 mg. Net price 20 = £11.50. Label: 4, 9, 21, 25

5.1.12 4-Quinolones

Antibacterials discussed in this section include acrosoxacin, ciprofloxacin, enoxacin, ofloxacin, and the urinary antiseptics cinoxacin, nalidixic acid, and norfloxacin.

Acrosoxacin is used only in the treatment of gonorrhoea in patients allergic to penicillins or who have strains resistant to penicillins and other antibiotics.

Nalidixic acid and **cinoxacin** are effective in uncomplicated urinary-tract infections.

Ciprofloxacin is active against both Gram-positive and Gram-negative bacteria. It is particularly active against Gram-negative bacteria, including salmonella, shigella, campylobacter, neisseria, and pseudomonas. It only has moderate activity against Gram-positive bacteria such as *Streptococcus pneumoniae* and *Streptococcus faecalis*. It is active against chlamydia and some mycobacteria. Most anaerobic organisms are not susceptible. Uses for ciprofloxacin include infections of the respiratory and urinary tracts, and of the gastro-intestinal system, and gonorrhoea and septicaemia caused by sensitive organisms. Whenever possible, ciprofloxacin should be reserved for the treatment of infections caused by organisms resistant to standard drugs.

Enoxacin is used for urinary-tract infections, skin and soft-tissue infection, gonorrhoea, and shigellosis.

Ofloxacin is used for urinary-tract infections, lower respiratory-tract infections, gonorrhoea, and non-gonococcal urethritis and cervicitis.

CSM warning. Ciprofloxacin increases plasma theophylline concentrations. If concomitant use is essential, the dose of theophylline should be reduced and plasma concentrations should be closely monitored to avoid toxicity.

CIPROFLOXACIN

Indications: Gram-negative and Gram-positive infections, see notes above
Cautions: epilepsy and history of CNS disorders; excessive alkalinity of urine, inadequate fluid intake (risk of crystalluria with ciprofloxacin); renal impairment; pregnancy and breast-feeding (arthropathy in *animal* studies); not recommended in children or growing adolescents; G6PD deficiency; anaphylaxis has been reported, particularly in patients with AIDS; **interactions:** Appendix 1 (4-quinolones)
DRIVING. May impair performance of skilled tasks (e.g, driving); effects of alcohol enhanced
Side-effects: nausea, vomiting, diarrhoea, dyspepsia, abdominal pain; dizziness, headache, restlessness; rash, pruritus; also tremor, confusion, convulsions, hallucinations, somnolence, blurred vision, muscle and joint pain, photosensitivity, disturbances in liver function (particularly if previous liver damage) including jaundice and hepatitis with necrosis; increase in urea or creatinine, renal failure, nephritis, blood disorders including eosinophilia, leucopenia, thrombocytopenia, thrombocytosis; psuedomembanous colitis, vasculitis, Stevens-Johnson syndrome and tachycardia reported
Dose: *by mouth*, 250–750 mg twice daily
Urinary-tract infections, 250–500 mg twice daily
Gonorrhoea, 250 mg as a single dose
By intravenous infusion (over 30–60 minutes), 200 mg twice daily
Urinary-tract infections, 100 mg twice daily
Gonorrhoea, 100 mg as a single dose
CHILD not recommended (see Cautions) but where benefit outweighs risk, *by mouth*, 7.5–15 mg/kg daily in 2 divided doses *or by intravenous infusion*, 5–10 mg/kg daily in 2 divided doses

PoM **Ciproxin**® (Baypharm)
Tablets, f/c, scored, ciprofloxacin (as hydrochloride) 250 mg. Net price 20 = £15.00. Label: 5, 9, 25, counselling, driving
Intravenous infusion, ciprofloxacin 2 mg (as lactate)/mL. Net price 50-mL bottle = £12.00; 100-mL bottle = £24.00

ACROSOXACIN

(Rosoxacin)
Indications: gonorrhoea
Cautions; Side-effects: see under Ciprofloxacin; caution in hepatic impairment; avoid frequent repeat doses in patients under 18 years
DRIVING. May impair performance of skilled tasks (e.g, driving)
Dose: 300 mg as a single dose on an empty stomach

PoM **Eradacin**® (Sterling-Winthrop)
Capsules, red/yellow, acrosoxacin 150 mg. Net price 20-cap pack = £29.04. Label: 2, 23

CINOXACIN

Indications: urinary-tract infections
Cautions; Side-effects: see under Ciprofloxacin; history of hepatic disease; avoid in severe renal impairment; other side-effects reported, peripheral and oral oedema, tinnitus, perineal burning, thrombocytopenia
Dose: 500 mg every 12 hours; prophylaxis, 500 mg at night

PoM **Cinobac**® (Lilly)
Capsules, green/orange, cinoxacin 500 mg. Net price 14-cap pack = £9.17. Label: 9

ENOXACIN

Indications: urinary-tract and skin infections, gonorrhoea, shigellosis

Cautions; Side-effects: see under Ciprofloxacin; other side-effects reported, dry mouth and throat, altered taste, stomatitis, palpitation and tachycardia, oedema, tremor, nervousness, amblyopia, and tinnitus

Dose: urinary-tract infections, 200 mg twice daily for 3 days; complicated infections, 400 mg (elderly 200 mg) twice daily for 7–14 days

Skin infections, 400 mg (elderly 200 mg) twice daily for 7–14 days

Chancroid, 400 mg (elderly 200 mg) every 12 hours for 3 doses

Gonorrhoea, 400 mg as a single dose

Shigellosis, 400 mg (elderly 200 mg) twice daily for 5 days

▼ PoM **Comprecin®** (P-D)

Tablets, f/c, blue, enoxacin 200 mg. Net price 6-tab pack = £5.40. Label: 9

NALIDIXIC ACID

Indications: urinary-tract infections

Cautions; Side-effects: see under Ciprofloxacin; caution in hepatic impairment, avoid strong sunlight, false positive urinary glucose (if tested for reducing substances); other side-effects reported, haemolysis in G6PD deficiency, eosinophilia, myalgia, muscle weakness, jaundice and visual disturbances

Contra-indications: history of convulsive disorders, porphyria

Dose: 1 g every 6 hours for 7 days, reducing to 500 mg every 6 hours

PoM **Nalidixic Acid** (Non-proprietary)

Tablets, nalidixic acid 500 mg. Net price 56-tab pack = £10.34. Label: 9, 11

PoM **Mictral®** (Sterling-Winthrop)

Granules, effervescent, nalidixic acid 660 mg, sodium citrate (as sodium citrate and citric acid) 4.1 g/sachet (Na^+ 41 mmol/sachet). Net price 9 sachets = £4.87. Label: 9, 11, 13

Dose: 1 sachet in water 3 times daily for 3 days

PoM **Negram®** (Sterling-Winthrop)

Tablets, beige, nalidixic acid 500 mg. Net price 56-tab pack = £11.39. Label: 9, 11

Suspension, pink, sugar-free, nalidixic acid 300 mg/5 mL. Diluent syrup, life of diluted suspension 14 days. Net price 150 mL = £11.41. Label: 9, 11

PoM **Uriben®** (RP Drugs)

Suspension, pink, nalidixic acid 300 mg/5 mL. Diluent syrup, life of diluted suspension 14 days. Net price 200 mL = £16.00; 500 mL = £32.00. Label: 9, 11

NORFLOXACIN

Indications: see under Dose

Cautions; Side-effects: see under Ciprofloxacin; other side-effects reported include anorexia, sleep disturbances, depression, anxiety, irritability, hallucinations, epiphora, tinnitus, toxic epidermal necrolysis

Dose: urinary-tract infections, 400 mg twice daily for 7–10 days (for 3 days in uncomplicated lower urinary-tract infections)

Chronic relapsing urinary-tract infections, 400 mg twice daily for 12 weeks; may be reduced to 400 mg once daily if adequate suppression within first 4 weeks

▼ PoM **Utinor®** (MSD)

Tablets, norfloxacin 400 mg. Net price 6-tab pack = £2.88, 14-tab pack = £6.72. Label: 5, 9

OFLOXACIN

Indications: see under Dose

Cautions: see under Ciprofloxacin; history of psychiatric illness; avoid strong sunlight

DRIVING. May affect performance of skilled tasks (e.g. driving)

Side-effects: see under Ciprofloxacin; also sleep disturbances, unsteady gait and tremor, paraesthesia, visual disturbances, disturbances of taste and smell; hallucinations and psychotic reactions (discontinue treatment); bone marrow depression

Dose: urinary-tract infections, 200–400 mg daily preferably in the morning, increased if necessary in upper urinary-tract infections to 400 mg twice daily

Lower respiratory-tract infections, 400 mg daily preferably in the morning, increased if necessary to 400 mg twice daily

Uncomplicated gonorrhoea, 400 mg as a single dose

Non-gonococcal urethritis and cervicitis, 400 mg daily in single or divided doses

▼ PoM **Tarivid®** (Hoechst, Roussel)

Tablets, scored, yellow-white, ofloxacin 200 mg, net price 10-tab pack = £7.38, 20-tab pack = £14.75. Label: 5, 9, counselling, driving

5.1.13 Urinary-tract infections

Urinary-tract infection is more common in women than in men; when it occurs in men there is frequently an underlying abnormality of the renal tract. Recurrent episodes of infection are an indication for radiological investigation especially in children in whom untreated pyelonephritis may lead to permanent kidney damage.

Escherichia coli is the most common cause of urinary-tract infection. Less common causes include Proteus and Klebsiella spp. *Pseudomonas aeruginosa* infections are almost invariably associated with functional or anatomical abnormalities of the renal tract. *Staphylococcus epidermidis* and *Enterococcus faecalis* infection may complicate catheterisation or instrumentation. Whenever possible a specimen of urine should be collected for culture and sensitivity testing before starting antibiotic therapy.

Uncomplicated lower urinary-tract infections usually respond to ampicillin, nalidixic acid, nitrofurantoin, or trimethoprim given for 5–7 days; those caused by fully sensitive bacteria respond to two 3-g doses of amoxycillin (section 5.1.1.3). Bacterial resistance, however, especially to ampicillin (to which approximately 40% of *E. coli* are now resistant), has increased the importance of urine culture prior to therapy. Alternatives for resistant organisms include co-amoxiclav (amoxycillin with clavulanic acid) and ciprofloxacin. Hexamine should **not** be used as it is only bacteriostatic, requires acid urine, and frequently causes side-effects.

Long-term low dose therapy may be required in selected patients to prevent *recurrence of infection*; indications include frequent relapses and significant kidney damage. Trimethoprim and nitrofurantoin have been recommended for long-term therapy.

Acute pyelonephritis can be associated with septicaemia and is best treated initially by injection of a broad-spectrum antibiotic such as cefuroxime or gentamicin especially if the patient is vomiting or severely ill.

Prostatitis can be difficult to cure and requires treatment for several weeks with an antibiotic which penetrates prostatic tissue such as trimethoprim, erythromycin, or ciprofloxacin.

Where infection is localised and associated with an indwelling *catheter* a bladder instillation is often effective (see section 7.4.4).

Patients with *heart-valve lesions* undergoing instrumentation of the urinary tract should be given a parenteral antibiotic to prevent bacteraemia and endocarditis (section 5.1, Table 2).

Urinary-tract infection in *pregnancy* may be asymptomatic and requires prompt treatment to prevent progression to acute pyelonephritis. Penicillins and cephalosporins can be given in pregnancy but trimethoprim, sulphonamides, 4-quinolones, and tetracyclines should be avoided.

In *renal failure* antibiotics normally excreted by the kidney accumulate with resultant toxicity unless the dose is reduced. This applies especially to the aminoglycosides which should be used with great caution; tetracyclines, hexamine, and nitrofurantoin should be avoided altogether.

NITROFURANTOIN

Indications: urinary-tract infections

Cautions: monitor lung and liver function on long-term therapy, especially in the elderly; susceptibility to peripheral neuropathy; false positive urinary glucose (if tested for reducing substances); urine may be coloured yellow or brown; **interactions:** Appendix 1 (nitrofurantoin)

Contra-indications: impaired renal function, infants less than 1 month old, G6PD deficiency (including late pregnancy, and breast-feeding of affected infants), porphyria

Side-effects: anorexia, nausea, vomiting, and diarrhoea; acute and chronic pulmonary reactions; peripheral neuropathy; also reported, angioedema, urticaria, rash and pruritus; rarely, cholestatic jaundice, hepatitis, exfoliative dermatitis, erythema multiforme, pancreatitis, arthralgia, blood disorders (including agranulocytosis, thrombocytopenia, and aplastic anaemia), and transient alopecia

Dose: 50–100 mg every 6 hours with food; CHILD 3 mg/kg daily in 4 divided doses

Prophylaxis (but see Cautions), 50–100 mg at night; CHILD 1 mg/kg at night

PoM **Nitrofurantoin** (Non-proprietary)

Tablets, nitrofurantoin 50 mg, net price 20 = 75p. Label: 9, 14, 21

PoM **Furadantin®** (Norwich Eaton)

Tablets, all yellow, scored, nitrofurantoin 50 mg, net price 20 = £1.96; 100 mg, 20 = £3.29. Label: 9, 14, 21

Suspension, yellow, sugar-free, nitrofurantoin 25 mg/5 mL. Do not dilute. Net price 300 mL = £4.50. Label: 9, 14, 21

PoM **Macrodantin®** (Norwich Eaton)

Capsules, nitrofurantoin 50 mg (yellow/white), net price 28-cap pack = £3.05; 100 mg (yellow), 20 = £3.49. Label: 9, 14, 21

HEXAMINE HIPPURATE

(Methenamine hippurate)

Indications: prophylaxis and long-term treatment of recurrent urinary-tract infections

Cautions: pregnancy; **interactions:** Appendix 1 (hexamine)

Contra-indications: severe renal impairment, dehydration, metabolic acidosis

Side-effects: gastro-intestinal disturbances, bladder irritation, rash

Dose: 1 g every 12 hours (may be increased in patients with catheters to 1 g every 8 hours); CHILD 6–12 years 500 mg every 12 hours

Hiprex® (3M)

Tablets, scored, hexamine hippurate 1 g. Net price 60-tab pack = £4.64. Label: 9

5.2 Antifungal drugs

Fungal infections are frequently associated with a defect in host resistance which should, if possible, be corrected otherwise drug therapy may fail. Similarly, treatment of dermatophyte infection may be unsuccessful until the animal source has been removed or controlled.

Amphotericin is not absorbed from the gut and is the only polyene antibiotic which can be given parenterally. It is used for the treatment of systemic fungal infections and is active against most fungi and yeasts. It is highly protein bound and penetrates poorly into body fluids and tissues. Amphotericin is toxic and side-effects are common.

Flucytosine is a synthetic antifungal drug which is only active against yeasts and has been used for the treatment of systemic candidiasis, cryptococcosis, and torulopsosis. It is well absorbed from the gut and distributed widely in the body. Side-effects are uncommon but bone-marrow depression can occur and weekly blood counts are necessary during prolonged therapy. Synergy has been demonstrated with amphotericin. Resistance to flucytosine is not uncommon and can develop during therapy; sensitivity testing is, therefore, essential before treatment.

Griseofulvin is selectively concentrated in keratin and is the drug of choice for widespread or intractable dermatophyte infections. It is well absorbed from the gut but is inactive when applied topically. It is more effective in skin than in nail infections and treatment must be continued for several weeks or even months. Side-effects are uncommon.

The imidazole group includes clotrimazole, econazole, ketoconazole, and miconazole; they are active against a wide range of fungi and yeasts (excluding aspergillosis). Their main indications are vaginal candidiasis and dermatophyte infections.

Econazole is used for local treatment. **Miconazole** is used for local treatment and can be given by mouth for oral and intestinal infection; it can also be given parenterally for systemic infections but the injection contains polyethoxylated castor oil which may give rise to hypersensitivity reactions.

Ketoconazole is significantly better absorbed after oral administration than the other imidazoles, but has been associated with fatal hepatotoxicity. The CSM has advised that prescribers should weigh the potential benefits of ketoconazole treatment against the liver damage risk and should carefully monitor patients both clinically and biochemically. It should **not** be given for superficial fungal infections.

Fluconazole is an oral triazole antifungal indicated for local and systemic candidiasis and cryptococcal infections. **Itraconazole** is a new oral triazole antifungal indicated for vulvovaginal candidiasis, pityriasis versicolor, and tinea corporis and pedis; it is metabolised in the liver and should not be given to patients with a history of liver disease.

Nystatin is a polyene antibiotic which is not absorbed when given by mouth and is too toxic for parenteral use. It is active against a number of yeasts and fungi but is principally used for *Candida albicans* infections of skin and mucous membranes. It is also used in the treatment of intestinal candidiasis.

See also sections 7.2.2 (genital), 13.10.2 (skin), 7.4.4 (bladder).

AMPHOTERICIN

Indications: See under Dose

Cautions: when given parenterally, toxicity common (close supervision necessary); hepatic and renal-function tests, blood counts, and plasma electrolyte monitoring required; other nephrotoxic drugs, corticosteroids (avoid except to control reactions), antineoplastics; frequent change of injection site (irritant); **interactions:** Appendix 1 (amphotericin)

Side-effects: when given parenterally, anorexia, nausea and vomiting, diarrhoea, epigastric pain; febrile reactions, headache, muscle and joint pain; anaemia; disturbances in renal function (including hypokalaemia and hypomagnesaemia) and renal toxicity; also cardiovascular toxicity (including arrhythmias), blood disorders, neurological disorders (including hearing loss, diplopia, convulsions, peripheral neuropathy), abnormal liver function (discontinue treatment), rash, anaphylactoid reactions

Dose: by mouth, intestinal candidiasis, 100–200 mg every 6 hours

By slow intravenous infusion, systemic fungal infections, 250 micrograms/kg daily, gradually increased if tolerated to 1 mg/kg daily; max. (severe infection) 1.5 mg/kg daily or on alternate days

Note. Prolonged treatment usually necessary; if interrupted for longer than 7 days recommence at 250 micrograms/kg daily and increase gradually

PoM **Fungilin®** (Squibb)

Tablets, yellow, scored, amphotericin 100 mg. Net price 56-tab pack = £8.32. Label: 9

Lozenges—see section 12.3.2

Suspension, yellow, sugar-free, amphotericin 100 mg/mL. Net price 12 mL = £2.31. Label: 9, counselling, use of pipette

PoM **Fungizone®** (Squibb)

Intravenous infusion, powder for reconstitution, amphotericin (as sodium deoxycholate complex). Net price 50-mg vial = £3.70

FLUCONAZOLE

Indications: see under Dose

Cautions: renal impairment; pregnancy (toxicity at high doses in *animal* studies); children (use only if imperative and if no alternative treatment; not recommended under 1 year); **interactions:** Appendix 1 (fluconazole)

Side-effects: nausea, abdominal discomfort, diarrhoea, and flatulence; occasionally abnormalities of liver enzymes; rarely rash (discontinue treatment)

Dose: acute or recurrent vaginal candidiasis, *by mouth*, a single dose of 150 mg

Mucosal candidiasis (except vaginal), *by mouth*, 50 mg daily (100 mg daily in unusually difficult infections) given for 7–14 days in oropharyngeal candidiasis (max. 14 days except in severely immunocompromised patients); for 14 days in atrophic oral candidiasis associated with dentures; for 14–30 days in other mucosal infections (e.g. oesophagitis, candiduria)

Systemic candidiasis and cryptococcal infections (including meningitis), *by mouth or intravenous infusion*, 400 mg initially then 200 mg daily, increased if necessary to 400 mg daily; treatment continued according to response (at least 6–8 weeks for cryptococcal meningitis)

Prevention of relapse of cryptococcal meningitis in AIDS patients after completion of primary therapy, at least 100 mg daily

CHILD over 1 year (see Cautions), *by mouth or by intravenous infusion*, superficial candidal

Prices are **net**, see p. 1

infections, 1–2 mg/kg daily; systemic candidiasis and cryptococcal infections, 3–6 mg/kg daily

PoM **Diflucan®** (Pfizer)

Capsules, fluconazole 50 mg (blue/white), net price 7-cap pack = £16.61; 150 mg (blue), single-capsule pack = £7.12; 200 mg (purple/white), 7-cap pack = £66.42. Label: 50 and 200 mg, 9

Intravenous infusion, fluconazole 2 mg/mL in sodium chloride intravenous infusion 0.9%, net price 25-mL bottle = £7.32; 100-mL bottle = £29.28

FLUCYTOSINE

Indications: systemic yeast infections

Cautions: hepatic impairment, renal impairment (reduce dose and monitor plasma concentrations), blood disorders, liver-function tests and blood counts required; pregnancy, breast-feeding

Side-effects: nausea, vomiting, diarrhoea, rashes, thrombocytopenia, leucopenia

Dose: *by mouth or intravenous infusion*, 200 mg/kg daily in 4 divided doses; extremely sensitive organisms, 100–150 mg/kg daily may be sufficient

Note. Plasma concentration for optimum response 25–50 mg/litre (200–400 micromol/litre)

PoM **Alcobon®** (Roche)

Tablets, scored, flucytosine 500 mg. Net price 20 = £9.43 (hosp. only)

Intravenous infusion, flucytosine 10 mg/mL. Net price 250-mL infusion bottle and giving set = £16.56 (hosp. only)

GRISEOFULVIN

Indications: dermatophyte infections of the skin, scalp, hair and nails, where topical therapy has failed or is inappropriate

Cautions: rarely aggravation or precipitation of systemic lupus erythematosus; **interactions:** Appendix 1 (griseofulvin)

Contra-indications: liver failure, porphyria; pregnancy

Side-effects: headache, nausea, vomiting, rashes, photosensitivity

Dose: 0.5–1 g daily, in divided doses or as a single dose; CHILD, 10 mg/kg daily in divided doses or as a single dose

PoM **Fulcin®** (ICI)

Tablets, griseofulvin 125 mg (scored), net price 20 = 63p; 500 mg (f/c), 20 = £2.35. Label: 9, 21

Suspension, brown, griseofulvin 125 mg/5 mL. Diluent syrup, life of diluted suspension 14 days. Net price 100 mL = £1.13. Label: 9, 21

PoM **Grisovin®** (Glaxo)

Tablets, both f/c, griseofulvin 125 mg, net price 20 = 47p; 500 mg, 20 = £1.75. Label: 9, 21

ITRACONAZOLE

Indications: vulvovaginal candidiasis; pityriasis versicolor and other dermatophyte infections

Cautions: avoid if history of liver disease; pregnancy (toxicity in *animal* studies) and breast-feeding; **interactions:** Appendix 1 (itraconazole)

Side-effects: nausea, abdominal pain, dyspepsia, headache

Dose: vulvovaginal candidiasis, 200 mg twice daily for 1 day

Pityriasis versicolor, 200 mg daily for 7 days

Tinea corporis and tinea cruris, 100 mg daily for 15 days

Tinea pedis and tinea manuum, 100 mg daily for 30 days

Max. period of treatment, 30 days

▼ PoM **Sporanox®** (Janssen)

Capsules, blue/pink, enclosing coated beads, itraconazole 100 mg. Net price 4-cap pack = £5.99; 15-cap pack = £22.46. Label: 5, 9, 21, 25

KETOCONAZOLE

Indications: systemic mycoses, serious chronic resistant mucocutaneous candidiasis, serious resistant gastro-intestinal mycoses, chronic resistant vaginal candidiasis, resistant dermatophyte infections of skin or finger nails (not toe nails); prophylaxis of mycoses in immunosuppressed patients

Cautions: **important:** monitor liver function clinically and biochemically—for details see data sheet; pregnancy (teratogenicity in *animal* studies); avoid in porphyria; **interactions:** Appendix 1 (ketoconazole)

Contra-indications: hepatic impairment

Side-effects: nausea, vomiting, abdominal pain; headache; rashes, urticaria, pruritus; rarely thrombocytopenia, gynaecomastia; fatal liver damage—for CSM advice see notes above, risk of developing hepatitis greater if given for longer than 14 days

Dose: 200 mg once daily with food, usually for 14 days; if response inadequate after 14 days continue until at least 1 week after symptoms have cleared and cultures become negative; max. 400 mg daily.

CHILD, 3 mg/kg daily

Chronic resistant vaginal candidiasis, 400 mg daily with food for 5 days

PoM **Nizoral®** (Janssen)

Tablets, scored, ketoconazole 200 mg. Net price 30-tab pack = £15.69. Label: 5, 9, 21

Suspension, pink, ketoconazole 100 mg/5 mL. Net price 100 mL = £7.16. Label: 5, 9, 21

MICONAZOLE

Indications: see under Dose

Cautions: change infusion site to avoid phlebitis; pregnancy; avoid in porphyria; **interactions:** Appendix 1 (miconazole)

Side-effects: nausea and vomiting, pruritus, rashes

Dose: by mouth as tablets, oral and intestinal fungal infections, 250 mg every 6 hours for 10 days or up to 2 days after symptoms clear; as oral gel, see under Daktarin® oral gel

By intravenous infusion, systemic fungal infections, initially, 600 mg every 8 hours; CHILD, max. 15 mg/kg every 8 hours up to 40 mg/kg/day

Daktarin® (Janssen)

PoM *Tablets*, scored, miconazole 250 mg. Net price 20 = £14.89. Label: 9, 21

Note. Can be sucked for oral treatment

PoM[1] *Oral gel*, sugar-free, miconazole 25 mg/mL. Net price 80 g = £5.00. Label: 9, counselling advised, hold in mouth, after food

Dose: oral and intestinal fungal infections, 5–10 mL in the mouth after food 4 times daily; retain near lesions before swallowing; CHILD under 2 years, 2.5 mL twice daily, 2–6 years, 5 mL twice daily, over 6 years, 5 mL 4 times daily

Localised lesions, smear affected area with clean finger; a 15-g tube (net price £1.39) also available

1. 15-g tube can be sold to public

PoM *Intravenous solution*, miconazole 10 mg/mL. For dilution and use as an infusion. Net price 20-mL amp = £1.47 (hosp. only)

Note. Contains polyethoxylated castor oil which has been associated with anaphylaxis

NYSTATIN

Indications: candidiasis

Side-effects: nausea, vomiting, diarrhoea at high doses

Dose: by mouth, intestinal candidiasis 500 000 units every 6 hours, doubled in severe infections; CHILD 100 000 units 4 times daily

For use as a mouthwash in oral candidiasis, see section 12.3.2

PoM **Nystatin** (Non-proprietary)

Oral suspension, nystatin 100 000 units/mL. Net price 30 mL with pipette = £2.50. Label: 9, counselling, use of pipette

PoM **Nystan®** (Squibb)

Tablets, brown, s/c, nystatin 500 000 units. Net price 56-tab pack = £4.70. Label: 9

Pastilles—see section 12.3.2

Suspension, yellow, nystatin 100 000 units/mL. Net price 30 mL with pipette = £2.50. Label: 9, counselling, use of pipette

Suspension, gluten-, lactose-, and sugar-free, nystatin 100 000 units/mL when reconstituted with water. Measure with pipette. Net price 24 mL with pipette = £1.67. Label: 9, counselling, use of pipette

PoM **Nystatin-Dome®** (Lagap)

Suspension, yellow, nystatin 100 000 units/mL. Net price 30 mL with 1-mL spoon = £2.86. Label: 9, counselling, use of 1-mL spoon

5.3 Antiviral drugs

The specific therapy of virus infections is generally unsatisfactory and treatment is, therefore, primarily symptomatic. Fortunately, the majority of infections resolve spontaneously.

HERPES SIMPLEX AND VARICELLA–ZOSTER

Acyclovir is active against herpes viruses but does not eradicate them. It is effective only if started at the onset of infection. Uses of acyclovir include the systemic treatment of varicella–zoster and the systemic and topical treatment of herpes simplex infections of the skin and mucous membranes (including initial and recurrent genital herpes); it is also used topically in the eye. It can be life-saving in herpes simplex and varicella–zoster infections in the immunocompromised, and is also used in the immunocompromised for prevention of recurrence and prophylaxis. See also 11.3.3 (eye) and 13.10.3 (skin, including herpes labialis).

Idoxuridine is also only effective if started at the onset of infection; it is too toxic for systemic use. It has been used topically in the treatment of herpes simplex lesions of the skin and external genitalia with variable results; it has also been used topically in the treatment of zoster, but evidence of its value is dubious. See also 11.3.3 (eye) and 13.10.3 (skin, including herpes labialis).

Inosine pranobex has been used by mouth for herpes simplex infections; its effectiveness has not been established. **Amantadine** has also been used by mouth but, again, its effectiveness has not been established; it has also been used for the prophylaxis of influenza A infections.

ACYCLOVIR

Indications: herpes simplex and varicella–zoster

Cautions: maintain adequate hydration; reduce dose in renal impairment; pregnancy; **interactions:** Appendix 1 (acyclovir)

Side-effects: rashes; gastro-intestinal disturbances; rises in bilirubin and liver-related enzymes, increases in blood urea and creatinine, decreases in haematological indices, headache, neurological reactions, fatigue

Dose: by mouth,

Herpes simplex, treatment, 200 mg (400 mg in the immunocompromised) 5 times daily, usually for 5 days; CHILD under 2 years, half adult dose, over 2 years, adult dose

Herpes simplex, prevention of recurrence, 200 mg 4 times daily *or* 400 mg twice daily possibly reduced to 200 mg 2 or 3 times daily and interrupted every 6–12 months

Herpes simplex, prophylaxis in the immunocompromised, 200–400 mg 4 times daily; CHILD under 2 years, half adult dose, over 2 years, adult dose

Herpes zoster, 800 mg 5 times daily for 7 days

By slow intravenous infusion, herpes simplex or zoster 5 mg/kg over 1 hour, repeated every 8 hours; doubled in zoster in the immunocompromised, and in simplex encephalitis;

CHILD 3 months–12 years, 250 mg/m² doubled in the immunocompromised and in simplex encephalitis

By topical application, herpes simplex (*cream* or *eye ointment* as appropriate) every 4 hours (5 times daily), see sections 13.10.3 and 11.3.3

PoM **Zovirax®** (Wellcome)

Tablets, acyclovir 200 mg (blue), net price 25-tab pack = £28.89; 400 mg (pink), 56-tab pack = £105.95; 800 mg (blue, scored), 35-tab pack = £113.00. Label: 9

Suspension, off-white, sugar-free, acyclovir 200 mg/5 mL. Diluent syrup or sorbitol solution for 1 + 1 dilution, life of diluted mixture 28 days. Net price 125 mL = £28.89. Label: 9

Intravenous infusion, powder for reconstitution, acyclovir (as sodium salt). Net price 250-mg vial = £10.80; 500-mg vial = £19.44

Cream, see section 13.10.3

Eye ointment, see section 11.3.3

AMANTADINE HYDROCHLORIDE

Indications: see under Dose; parkinsonism, see section 4.9.1

Cautions; Contra-indications; Side-effects: see section 4.9.1

Dose: herpes zoster, 100 mg twice daily for 14 days, if necessary extended for a further 14 days for post-herpetic neuralgia

Influenza A_2, treatment, 100 mg twice daily for 5–7 days; prophylaxis 100 mg twice daily for as long as required (usually 7–10 days); CHILD 10–15 years, 100 mg daily

Preparations: see section 4.9.1

IDOXURIDINE

See sections 11.3.3 (eye) and 13.10.3 (skin including herpes labialis)

INOSINE PRANOBEX

Indications: see under Dose

Cautions: avoid in renal impairment; history of gout or hyperuricaemia

Side-effects: reversible increases in serum and urinary uric acid

Dose: mucocutaneous herpes simplex, 1 g 4 times daily for 7–14 days

Adjunctive treatment of genital warts, 1 g 3 times daily for 14–28 days

PoM **Imunovir®** (Leo)

Tablets, inosine pranobex 500 mg. Net price 100 = £37.24. Label: 9

HUMAN IMMUNODEFICIENCY VIRUS

Zidovudine inhibits the human immunodeficiency virus (HIV) but does not eradicate it from the body; it is not therefore a cure for AIDS but may delay progression of the disease. It is now also being recommended for asymptomatic HIV antibody positive individuals.

Zidovudine is toxic and expensive and should only be prescribed by those experienced in its use.

ZIDOVUDINE

(Azidothymidine, AZT)

Indications: management of advanced human immunodeficiency virus (HIV) disease such as acquired immunodeficiency syndrome (AIDS) or AIDS-related complex; early symptomatic or asymptomatic HIV infection with markers indicating risk of disease progression

Cautions: haematological toxicity (blood tests at least every 2 weeks for first 3 months then at least once a month, early disease with good bone marrow reserves may require less frequent tests e.g. every 1–3 months); adjust dose according to data sheet if anaemia or myelosuppression; renal and hepatic impairment; elderly; pregnancy; avoid in breast-feeding; **interactions:** Appendix 1 (zidovudine)

Contra-indications: abnormally low neutrophil counts or haemoglobin values (see data sheet)

Side-effects: anaemia (often requiring transfusion), neutropenia, and leucopenia (all more frequent with high dose and advanced disease); also include, nausea and vomiting, anorexia, abdominal pain, headache, rash, fever, myalgia, paraesthesia, insomnia, malaise, and asthenia

Dose: symptomatic disease, 200 mg every 4 hours (total 1.2 g daily) for 70-kg patient; for advanced disease with poorer tolerance dose may be reduced to maintenance of 100 mg every 4 hours (total 600 mg daily); daily dosage can be given in 4–5 divided doses

Asymptomatic disease, initially 500 mg daily increased if disease progresses to 1.5 g daily

PoM **Retrovir®** (Wellcome)

Capsules, white/blue band, zidovudine 100 mg, net price 100 = £91.68; 250 mg (blue/white), 40-cap pack = £91.68

CYTOMEGALOVIRUS (CMV)

Ganciclovir is related to acyclovir but with enhanced activity against cytomegalovirus; it is much more toxic than acyclovir and indicated only for life- or sight-threatening *cytomegalovirus infections in immunocompromised* patients. It can cause leucopenia and thrombocytopenia and is also a potential carcinogen. It should therefore only be prescribed when the potential benefit outweighs the risks of adverse reactions. Ganciclovir causes profound myelosuppression when given with zidovudine; the two should not normally be given together particularly during initial ganciclovir therapy.

Foscarnet is also active against cytomegalovirus and is indicated for cytomegalovirus retinitis in patients with AIDS in whom ganciclovir is contra-indicated or is inappropriate. It is not recommended for the treatment of CMV infections other than retinitis or for use in non-AIDS patients. Foscarnet is a toxic drug which can cause impairment of renal function in up to 50% of patients.

GANCICLOVIR

Indications: life-threatening or sight-threatening cytomegalovirus infections in immunocompromised patients only (consult manufacturer's literature)

Cautions: haematological toxicity (blood counts required every 1–2 days for first 14 days—see literature); renal impairment; concomitant administration of drugs that inhibit replication of rapidly dividing cells (e.g. pentamidine, co-trimoxazole); history of exposure to irradiation or to drugs toxic to bone marrow (avoid concomitant zidovudine during induction); increased risk of seizures with imipenem; potential carcinogen; ensure adequate hydration after administration; vesicant—infuse only into veins with adequate blood flow; **not** for neonatal or congenital cytomegalovirus; **interactions:** Appendix 1 (ganciclovir)

Contra-indications: pregnancy (includes effective contraception during treatment and barrier contraception for men for 90 days after treatment); breast-feeding (until 72 hours after last dose); hypersensitivity to ganciclovir or acyclovir; abnormally low neutrophil counts (see literature)

Side-effects: most frequent, neutropenia and thrombocytopenia; anaemia and eosinophilia; fever, rash, abnormal liver function tests; raised blood urea nitrogen or serum creatinine; also sepsis, facial oedema, sore throat, epistaxis, malaise; other side-effects reported have included all body systems, including cardiovascular, CNS and special senses, gastro-intestinal, metabolic, musculoskeletal, respiratory, dermatological, urogenital (see literature); local reactions at injection site

Dose: *by intravenous infusion* over 1 hour, initially 5 mg/kg every 12 hours for 14–21 days; maintenance (for patients at risk of relapse of retinitis) 6 mg/kg daily on 5 days per week *or* 5 mg/kg daily every day

In renal impairment, consult manufacturers' literature for dosage reduction

PoM **Cymevene®** (Syntex)

Intravenous infusion, powder for reconstitution, ganciclovir (as sodium salt). Net price 500-mg vial = £28.34

CAUTION IN HANDLING. Wear polythene gloves and safety glasses when reconstituting; if solution contacts skin or mucosa immediately wash with soap and water

FOSCARNET SODIUM

Indications: cytomegalovirus retinitis in patients with AIDS in whom ganciclovir is inappropriate

Cautions: renal impairment (avoid if severe), hypocalcaemia, monitor serum creatinine and serum calcium concentrations every second day; ensure adequate hydration

Contra-indications: pregnancy, breast-feeding

Side-effects: nausea, vomiting, headache, fatigue, rash; impairment of renal function including acute renal failure, symptomatic hypocalcaemia; decreased haemoglobin concentration; rarely hypoglycaemia, convulsions; thrombophlebitis if given undiluted by peripheral vein

Dose: *by intravenous infusion*, 20 mg/kg over 30 minutes then 21–200 mg/kg daily according to renal function for 2–3 weeks

▼ PoM **Foscavir®** (Astra)

Intravenous infusion, foscarnet sodium hexahydrate 24 mg/mL. Net price 500-mL bottle = £53.58

RESPIRATORY SYNCYTIAL VIRUS

Tribavirin inhibits a wide range of DNA and RNA viruses. It is given by inhalation for the treatment of severe bronchiolitis caused by the respiratory syncytial virus in infants, especially when they have other serious diseases.

TRIBAVIRIN

(Ribavirin)

Indications: severe respiratory syncytial virus bronchiolitis in infants and children

Cautions: maintain standard supportive respiratory and fluid management therapy; monitor equipment for precipitation

Contra-indications: pregnancy

Side-effects: reticulocytosis; also worsening respiration, bacterial pneumonia, and pneumothorax reported

Dose: *by aerosol inhalation or nebulisation* (via small particle aerosol generator) of solution containing 20 mg/mL for 12–18 hours for at least 3 days; max. 7 days

PoM **Virazid®** (Britannia)

Inhalation, tribavirin 6 g for reconstitution with 300 mL water for injections. Net price 3 × 6-g vials = £585.00

5.4 Antiprotozoal drugs

Advice on specific problems available from:

Birmingham	021-772 4311
Glasgow	041-946 7120 (travel prophylaxis)
	041-946 7120 Extn 277 (treatment)
Liverpool	051-708 9393
London	071-387 4411 (treatment)
	071-388 9600 (travel prophylaxis)
	071-636 8636 (travel prophylaxis)
	071-636 7921 (recorded advice)
Oxford	(0865) 225570

5.4.1 Antimalarials

Recommendations on the prophylaxis and treatment of malaria reflect guidelines agreed by UK malaria specialists.

The centres listed above should be consulted for advice on special problems.

TREATMENT OF MALARIA

If the infective species is **not known** or if the infection is **mixed** initial treatment should be with quinine or mefloquine as for *falciparum malaria* (below).

FALCIPARUM MALARIA

Falciparum malaria (malignant malaria) is caused by *Plasmodium falciparum*. In most parts of the world *P. falciparum* is now resistant to chloroquine which should not therefore be given for treatment[1].

Quinine or **mefloquine** should be given *by mouth* if the patient can swallow tablets and there are no serious manifestations (e.g. impaired consciousness); quinine should be given *by intravenous infusion* (see below) if the patient is seriously ill or unable to take tablets.

The adult dosage regimen for **quinine** *by mouth* is:

600 mg (of quinine salt[2]) every 8 hours for 7 days
either followed by **Fansidar®** 3 tablets as a single dose
or (if Fansidar®-resistant) *given with* **tetracycline** 250 mg every 6 hours for 7 days.

Alternatively **mefloquine** may be given instead of quinine; the adult dosage regimen for **mefloquine** *by mouth* is:

20 mg/kg (of mefloquine base) as a single dose *or preferably* as 2 divided doses 6–8 hours apart; it is **not** necessary to give Fansidar® or tetracycline after mefloquine treatment.

If the patient is seriously ill, **quinine**[3] should be given *by intravenous infusion*. The adult dosage regimen for quinine *by infusion* is:

loading dose[4] of 20 mg/kg[5] (up to maximum 1.4 g) of quinine salt[2] infused over 4 hours *then after 8 hours* maintenance dose of 10 mg/kg[6] (up to maximum 700 mg) of quinine salt[2] infused over 4 hours every 8 hours (until patient can swallow tablets or complete the 7-day course) *either followed by* Fansidar® *or given with* tetracycline as above.

CHILDREN.
Oral. Quinine is well tolerated by children although the salts are bitter. The dosage regimen for quinine *by mouth* for children is:

10 mg/kg (of quinine salt[2]) every 8 hours for 7 days *then*
Fansidar® as a single dose: up to 4 years ½ tablet, 5–6 years 1 tablet, 7–9 years 1½ tablets, 10–14 years 2 tablets.

Alternatively mefloquine may be given instead of quinine. The dosage regimen for mefloquine *by mouth* for children is calculated on a mg/kg basis as for adults (see above); it is not necessary to give Fansidar® after mefloquine treatment.
Parenteral. The dosage regimen for quinine *by intravenous infusion* for children is calculated on a mg/kg basis as for adults (see above).

BENIGN MALARIAS

Benign malaria is usually caused by *Plasmodium vivax* and less commonly by *P. ovale* and *P. malariae*. **Chloroquine** is the drug of choice for the treatment of benign malarias.

The adult dosage regimen for **chloroquine** *by mouth* is:

initial dose of 600 mg (of base) *then*
a single dose of 300 mg after 6 to 8 hours *then*
a single dose of 300 mg daily for 2 days
(approximate total cumulative dose of 25 mg/kg of base)

Chloroquine alone is adequate for *P. malariae* infections but in the case of *P. vivax* and *P. ovale*, a *radical cure* (to destroy parasites in the liver and thus prevent relapses) is required. This is achieved with **primaquine**[7] in an adult dosage of 15 mg daily for 14 to 21 days given after the chloroquine; a double dose (*or* twice the length of treatment) is recommended for Chesson-type strains of *P. vivax* from south-east Asia and western Pacific.

CHILDREN. The dosage regimen of chloroquine for benign malaria in children is:

initial dose of 10 mg/kg (of base) *then*
a single dose of 5 mg/kg after 6–8 hours *then*
a single dose of 5 mg/kg daily for 2 days

For a *radical cure* children are then given primaquine[7] in a dose of 250 micrograms/kg daily.

1. For chloroquine-sensitive strains of falciparum malaria chloroquine is effective *by mouth* in the dosage schedule outlined under benign malarias but it should **not** be used unless there is an **unambiguous exposure history** in one of the few remaining areas of chloroquine sensitivity.
   If the patient with a *chloroquine-sensitive infection* is seriously ill, chloroquine is given by *continuous intravenous infusion*. The dosage (for adults and children) is chloroquine 10 mg/kg (of base) infused over 8 hours, followed by three 8-hour infusions of 5 mg/kg (of base) each. *Oral therapy* is instituted as soon as possible to complete the course; the total cumulative dose for the course should be 25 mg/kg of base.
2. Valid for quinine hydrochloride, dihydrochloride, and sulphate; not valid for quinine bisulphate which contains a correspondingly smaller amount of quinine.
3. If quinine is not available quinidine may be given by intravenous infusion in a dose of 7.5 mg/kg (of base) but cardiotoxicity is more likely (ECG monitoring).
4. In intensive care units the loading dose can alternatively be given as quinine salt[2] 7 mg/kg infused over 30 minutes followed immediately by 10 mg/kg over 4 hours then (after 8 hours) maintenance dose as described.
5. **Important:** the loading dose of 20 mg/kg should **not** be used if the patient has received quinine (or quinidine) or mefloquine or possibly chloroquine during the previous 24 hours
6. Maintenance dose should be reduced to 5–7 mg/kg of salt if parenteral treatment is required for more than 72 hours.
7. Before starting primaquine the blood should be tested for glucose-6-phosphate dehydrogenase (G6PD) activity as the drug can cause haemolysis in patients who are deficient in the enzyme. If the patient is G6PD deficient primaquine, in a dose for adults of 30 mg once a week for 8 weeks, has been found useful and without undue harmful effects.

PROPHYLAXIS AGAINST MALARIA

The recommendations on prophylaxis reflect guidelines agreed by UK malaria specialists; the advice is aimed at residents of the UK who travel to endemic areas for short stays. The choice of drug takes account of:

- risk of exposure to malaria;
- extent of drug resistance;
- efficacy of the recommended drugs;
- side-effects of the drugs;
- patient-related criteria (e.g. age, pregnancy, renal or hepatic impairment).

NETS AND REPELLENTS. The most important point to remember is that **prophylaxis is relative and not absolute**, and that breakthrough can occur with any of the drugs recommended anywhere in the world. Personal protection against being bitten, e.g. use of mosquito nets, repellents etc. is **very important**.

LENGTH OF PROPHYLAXIS. Prophylaxis should be started one week before travel into an endemic area (or if not possible at earliest opportunity up to 1 or 2 days before travel); it should be continued for at least 4 weeks after leaving (except for mefloquine).

CHILDREN. Prophylactic doses are reduced as follows:

		Fraction of adult dose	
Age	Weight (kg)	Chloroquine Proguanil	Maloprim®
0–5 weeks		$\frac{1}{8}$	—
6 weeks–11 months		$\frac{1}{4}$	—
1–5 years	10–19	$\frac{1}{2}$	$\frac{1}{4}$
6–11 years	20–39	$\frac{3}{4}$	$\frac{1}{2}$
12 years	40	adult dose	adult dose

Note. Weight is a better guide than age for children over 6 months old. Specialist advice should be obtained for use of Maloprim® in children under 1 year of age.

Prophylaxis is required in **breast-fed infants**; although antimalarials are excreted in milk, the amounts are too variable to give reliable protection.

PREGNANCY. Chloroquine and proguanil may be given in usual doses in areas where *P. falciparum* strains are sensitive; in the case of proguanil folate supplements should be given. Maloprim® is contra-indicated in the first trimester; folate supplements should be given if Maloprim® is prescribed in the second and third trimester. The centres listed in section 5.4 should be consulted for advice on prophylaxis in resistant areas.

SPECIFIC RECOMMENDATIONS. Specific recommendations by geographical regions are given below.

North Africa and the Middle East

(risk: generally low; transmission confined to rural areas and may be seasonal)

chloroquine 300 mg (as base) once weekly

or

proguanil hydrochloride 200 mg once daily

Above recommendations apply to some areas of Turkey (south coast and border with Syria) and also to Mauritius. No chemoprophylaxis needed for Algeria, Libya, Morocco, Tunisia, or tourist areas of Egypt; *both* chloroquine *and* proguanil needed for Afghanistan and Iran.

Sub-Saharan Africa (includes East, Central and West Africa and also Madagascar) (risk: very high)

both

chloroquine 300 mg (as base) once weekly

and

proguanil hydrochloride 200 mg once daily

Mefloquine alone is an option for short-term travellers (max. 3 weeks abroad) to Cameroon, Kenya, Malawi, Tanzania, Uganda, Zaire, and Zambia; see Mefloquine p. 224 for details of regimen.

South Asia (Bangladesh, Bhutan, India, Nepal, Pakistan, and Sri Lanka) (risk: variable)

both

chloroquine 300 mg (as base) once weekly

and

proguanil hydrochloride 200 mg once daily

South-East Asia

(risk: varies from very low to substantial)

both

chloroquine 300 mg (as base) once weekly

and

proguanil hydrochloride 200 mg once daily

Mefloquine alone is an option for short-term travellers (max. 3 weeks abroad); see Mefloquine p. 224 for details of regimen.

No chemoprophylaxis needed for tourist areas and cities of Brunei, China, Hong Kong, peninsular west Malaysia, Philippines, Sarawak, Singapore, and Thailand (all very low risk).

Oceania (Papua New Guinea, Solomon Islands, Vanuatu) (risk: very high)

both
Maloprim® 1 tablet once weekly
and
chloroquine 300 mg (as base) once weekly

Mefloquine alone is an option for short-term travellers (max. 3 weeks abroad); see Mefloquine p. 224 for details of regimen.

Latin America
(risk: variable to high)

Variable risk areas:

chloroquine 300 mg (as base) once weekly

or

proguanil hydrochloride 200 mg once daily

Used for variable risk areas which include Argentina (a few areas), Belize, rural Costa Rica, Dominican Republic, El Salvador, Guatemala, Haiti, Honduras, rural Mexico, Nicaragua, rural Paraguay, and Peru (below 1500 m)

Variable to high risk areas:

both
chloroquine 300 mg (as base) once weekly
and
proguanil hydrochloride 200 mg once daily

Used for variable to high risk areas which include Bolivia (below 2500 m), rural Brazil, Colombia, Equador, French Guiana, Guyana, Panama, Suriname, and rural Venezuela.
Mefloquine alone is an option for short-term travellers (max. 3 weeks abroad) to the Amazonas region of Brazil; see Mefloquine p. 224 for details of regimen.

Advice on specific problems available from:

Birmingham	021-772 4311
Glasgow	041-946 7120 (travel prophylaxis)
	041-946 7120 Extn 277 (treatment)
Liverpool	051-708 9393
London	071-387 4411 (treatment)
	071-388 9600 (travel prophylaxis)
	071-636 8636 (travel prophylaxis)
	071-636 7921 (recorded advice)
Oxford	(0865) 225570

TREATMENT COURSES. Adults travelling to areas of chloroquine-resistance who are unlikely to have easy access to medical care should carry a treatment course of 3 tablets of Fansidar® which should be taken (in a single dose) at the first sign of fever. Travellers to chloroquine-resistant areas such as East Africa, South-east Asia, Western Pacific, and Oceania should preferably carry a treatment course of quinine[1] tablets, 600 mg (of salt[2]) every 8 hours for 5 to 7 days[3]. Self-medication should be **avoided** if medical help is accessible; prophylaxis should be continued during and after the attack.

1. Quinine should **not** be used if mefloquine has been taken for prophylaxis
2. Valid for quinine hydrochloride, dihydrochloride, and sulphate; not valid for quinine bisulphate which contains a correspondingly smaller amount of quinine
3. Alternatively a single dose of mefloquine 750 mg (3 tablets of 250 mg) has been recommended

CHLOROQUINE

Indications: chemoprophylaxis and treatment of malaria; rheumatoid arthritis and lupus erythematosus—see section 10.1.3

Cautions: hepatic and renal impairment, pregnancy (but for malaria benefit outweighs risk, see Appendix 4, Antimalarials), porphyria, may exacerbate psoriasis, neurological disorders (especially history of epilepsy), severe gastro-intestinal disorders, G6PD deficiency (see section 9.1.5); elderly; regular ophthalmic examinations if prophylaxis treatment given for more than 3 years; avoid concurrent therapy with hepatotoxic drugs—other **interactions**: Appendix 1 (chloroquine)

Side-effects: gastro-intestinal disturbances, headache, visual disturbances, irreversible retinal damage, corneal opacities, depigmentation or loss of hair, skin reactions; rarely blood disorders (thrombocytopenia, agranulocytosis, and aplastic anaemia)

Dose: see notes above

PoM* **Avloclor®** (ICI)
Tablets, scored, chloroquine phosphate 250 mg (≡chloroquine base 150 mg). Net price 20-tab pack = 70p. Label: 5
* Can be sold to the public provided it is licensed and labelled for the prophylaxis of malaria

Nivaquine® (Rhône-Poulenc Rorer)
PoM* *Tablets*, f/c, yellow, chloroquine sulphate 200 mg (≡chloroquine base 150 mg). Net price 30-tab pack = £1.12. Label: 5
* Can be sold to the public provided it is licensed and labelled for the prophylaxis of malaria
PoM* *Syrup*, golden, chloroquine sulphate 68 mg/5 mL (≡chloroquine base 50 mg/5 mL). Net price 60 mL = £1.31. Label: 5
* Can be sold to the public provided it is licensed and labelled for the prophylaxis of malaria
PoM *Injection*, chloroquine sulphate 54.5 mg/mL (≡chloroquine base 40 mg/mL). Net price 5-mL amp = 52p

MEFLOQUINE

Indications: chemoprophylaxis and treatment of chloroquine-resistant falciparum malaria, see also notes above

Cautions: avoid for chemoprophylaxis in severe hepatic and in renal impairment; avoid frequent or prolonged administration (accumulation occurs due to long half-life); not recommended in young children (under 15 kg); **interactions:** Appendix 1 (mefloquine)

COUNSELLING. May affect performance of skilled tasks

Contra-indications: chemoprophylaxis in pregnancy (teratogenic in *animals*, avoid pregnancy during and for 3 months after), breast-feeding, and history of psychiatric disturbances or convulsions

Side-effects: nausea, vomiting, diarrhoea, abdominal pain, anorexia; dizziness and loss of balance; rarely bradycardia, headache, neuropsychiatric disturbances (discontinue treatment), weakness, rash, pruritus, and disturbances in liver function tests

Dose: short-term chemoprophylaxis (max. 3 weeks in endemic area), 250 mg each week for 6 weeks starting 1 week before departure; CHILD 15–19 kg (2–5 years) ¼ adult dose, 20–30 kg (6–8 years) ½ adult dose, 31–45 kg (9–11 years) ¾ adult dose

Longer chemoprophylaxis (more than 3 weeks in endemic area), not recommended by UK experts

Treatment, see notes above

▼ PoM **Lariam**® (Roche)

Tablets, scored, mefloquine 250 mg (as hydrochloride). Net price 6-tab pack = £10.90. Label: 21, 25, 27

PRIMAQUINE

Indications: eradication of benign malaria

Cautions: see notes above; pregnancy; **interactions:** Appendix 1 (primaquine)

Side-effects: higher-doses are associated with anorexia, nausea and vomiting; abdominal pain (especially if given on empty stomach); less commonly bone-marrow depression, methaemoglobinaemia, haemolytic anaemia especially in G6PD deficiency

Dose: see notes above

Primaquine Tablets, coated, primaquine 7.5 mg (as phosphate). Net price 20 = 12p

PROGUANIL HYDROCHLORIDE

Indications: chemoprophylaxis of malaria

Cautions: renal impairment; pregnancy (folate supplements needed)

Side-effects: mild gastric intolerance; mouth ulcers

Dose: see notes above

Paludrine® (ICI)

Tablets, scored, proguanil hydrochloride 100 mg. Net price 20 = 48p. Label: 21

PYRIMETHAMINE

Indications: malaria (but used only in combination with dapsone or sulphadoxine); toxoplasmosis (section 5.4.7)

Cautions: hepatic or renal impairment, folate supplements in pregnancy, blood counts required with prolonged treatment; **interactions:** Appendix 1 (pyrimethamine)

Side-effects: depression of haemopoiesis with high doses, rashes, insomnia

Daraprim® (Wellcome)

Tablets, scored, pyrimethamine 25 mg. Net price 30-tab pack = £1.93

Dose: not recommended alone

With sulfadoxine

ADDITIONAL CAUTIONS: Severe adverse reactions on long-term use therefore not for prophylaxis; pregnancy (see also Appendix 4) and breast-feeding (see also Appendix 5); **interactions**: Appendix 1

PoM **Fansidar**® (Roche)

Tablets, scored, pyrimethamine 25 mg, sulfadoxine 500 mg. Net price 10-tab pack = £2.52

Dose: treatment, see notes above

Chemoprophylaxis, not recommended by UK experts.

With dapsone

ADDITIONAL CAUTIONS: G6PD deficiency; pregnancy (see also Appendix 4) and breast-feeding (see also Appendix 5); **interactions**: Appendix 1

PoM **Maloprim**® (Wellcome)

Tablets, scored, pyrimethamine 12.5 mg, dapsone 100 mg. Net price 30-tab pack = £2.40

Dose: limited use, see Chemoprophylaxis

QUININE

Indications: falciparum malaria

Cautions: atrial fibrillation, conduction defects, heart block, pregnancy; **interactions:** Appendix 1 (quinine)

Contra-indications: haemoglobinuria, optic neuritis

Side-effects: cinchonism, including tinnitus, headache, nausea, abdominal pain, rashes, visual disturbances (including temporary blindness), confusion; hypersensitivity reactions including angioedema; hypoglycaemia (especially after parenteral administration); **important:** toxicity in overdosage (including blindness and fatalities)

Dose: see notes above

Note. Quinine (anhydrous base) 100 mg ≡ quinine bisulphate 169 mg ≡ quinine dihydrochloride 122 mg ≡ quinine hydrochloride 122 mg ≡ quinine sulphate 121 mg. Quinine bisulphate 300-mg are available but provide smaller amounts of quinine than the dihydrochloride, hydrochloride, or sulphate

PoM **Quinine Dihydrochloride Tablets,** quinine dihydrochloride 300 mg. Net price 20 = £2.01

PoM **Quinine Hydrochloride Tablets,** quinine hydrochloride 300 mg. Net price 20 = £2.01

PoM **Quinine Sulphate Tablets,** coated, quinine sulphate 125 mg, net price 20 = 50p; 200 mg, 20 = 74p; 300 mg, 20 = 72p

PoM **Quinine Dihydrochloride Injection,** quinine dihydrochloride 300 mg/mL. For dilution with physiological saline and use as an infusion. 1- and 2-mL amps

Injection available from Macarthys and Penn (both special order) or from specialist centres (see p. 220)

Note. Intravenous injection of quinine is so hazardous that it has been superseded by infusion

5.4.2 Amoebicides

Metronidazole is the drug of choice for *acute invasive amoebic dysentery* for it is very effective against vegetative amoebae in ulcers at a dosage of 800 mg three times daily for 5 days; it is also effective against amoebae which may have migrated to the liver. It is given either for 10 days, or for 5 days followed by a 10-day course of diloxanide furoate. **Tinidazole** (section 5.1.11) is also effective.

Diloxanide furoate is the drug of choice in *chronic intestinal amoebiasis* in which only cysts and not vegetative forms of *Entamoeba histolytica* are present in the faeces; metronidazole and tinidazole are relatively ineffective. Diloxanide furoate is relatively free from toxic effects in therapeutic doses and the usual course is of 10 days, given alone for chronic infections or following 5 days of metronidazole in acute dysenteric infections.

For *amoebic abscesses* of the liver **metronidazole** is effective in doses of 400 mg 3 times daily for 5–10 days; the course may be repeated after 2 weeks if necessary. Aspiration of the abscess is indicated where it is suspected that it may rupture or where there is no improvement after 72 hours of metronidazole; the aspiration may need to be repeated. Aspiration aids penetration of metronidazole and, for abscesses with more than 100 mL of pus, if carried out in conjunction with drug therapy, may reduce the period of disability.

If metronidazole or tinidazole are not available emetine may be used but its side-effects are much more marked. Diloxanide is not effective against hepatic amoebiasis, but a 10-day course should be given at the completion of metronidazole or tinidazole treatment to destroy any amoebae in the gut.

DILOXANIDE FUROATE

Indications: chronic amoebiasis—see notes
Side-effects: flatulence, vomiting, urticaria, pruritus
Dose: 500 mg every 8 hours for 10 days; CHILD 20 mg/kg daily in divided doses—see notes

PoM **Furamide**® (Boots)
Tablets, scored, diloxanide furoate 500 mg. Available only on direct order from Boots. Label: 9

PoM **Entamizole**® (Boots)
Tablets, off-white, diloxanide furoate 250 mg, metronidazole 200 mg. Available only on direct order from Boots. Label: 4, 9, 21, 25
Dose: amoebiasis, 2 tablets 3 times daily for 5 days; CHILD 5–12 years ½–1 tablet, according to age, for 5 days
Treatment may be extended to 10 days in refractory cases; not suitable for prolonged (e.g. prophylactic) use

METRONIDAZOLE

Indications: see under Dose below; anaerobic infections, section 5.1.11
Cautions; Side-effects: section 5.1.11
Dose: by mouth, invasive intestinal amoebiasis, 800 mg every 8 hours for 5 days; CHILD 1–3 years 200 mg every 8 hours; 3–7 years 200 mg every 6 hours; 7–10 years 400 mg every 8 hours

Intestinal amoebiasis in less susceptible subjects, chronic amoebic hepatitis, and extra-intestinal amoebiasis (including liver abscess), 400 mg every 8 hours for 5–10 days (5 days for extra-intestinal disease); CHILD 1–3 years 100 mg every 8 hours; 3–7 years 100 mg every 6 hours; 7–10 years 200 mg every 8 hours

Symptomless amoebic cyst passers, 400–800 mg every 8 hours for 5–10 days; CHILD 1–3 years 100–200 mg every 8 hours; 3–7 years 100–200 mg every 6 hours; 7–10 years 200–400 mg every 8 hours

Urogenital trichomoniasis, 200 mg every 8 hours *or* 400 mg every 12 hours for 7 days, *or* 800 mg in the morning and 1.2 g at night for 2 days, *or* 2 g as a single dose; CHILD 1–3 years 50 mg every 8 hours for 7 days; 3–7 years 100 mg every 12 hours; 7–10 years 100 mg every 8 hours

Giardiasis, 2 g daily for 3 days; CHILD 1–3 years 500 mg daily; 3–7 years 600–800 mg daily; 7–10 years 1 g daily

Preparations
Section 5.1.11

5.4.3 Trichomonacides

Metronidazole (section 5.4.2) is the treatment of choice for *Trichomonas vaginalis* infection.

If metronidazole is ineffective, **nimorazole** may be tried; it is usually given as a single 2-g dose, with food. A further 2-g dose may be given if there is no clinical improvement.

Alcohol should be avoided during treatment with both metronidazole and nimorazole.

NIMORAZOLE

Indications: trichomoniasis (acute ulcerative gingivitis, see section 12.3.2)
Contra-indications: active CNS disease, severe renal failure
Side-effects: nausea, vomiting, rashes, vertigo, drowsiness, ataxia (discontinue treatment), intolerance to alcohol
Dose: see notes above

Naxogin 500® (Farmitalia Carlo Erba)
Tablets, scored, nimorazole 500 mg. Net price 8-tab pack = £1.45. Label: 4, 21

5.4.4 Antigiardial drugs

Metronidazole (section 5.4.2) is the treatment of choice for *Giardia lamblia* infections, given by mouth in a dosage of 2 g daily for 3 days or 400 mg every 8 hours for 5 days.

Alternative treatments are **tinidazole** (section 5.1.11) 2 g as a single dose or **mepacrine hydrochloride** 100 mg every 8 hours for 5–7 days.

MEPACRINE HYDROCHLORIDE

Indications: giardiasis

Cautions: hepatic impairment, elderly, history of psychosis; avoid in psoriasis; **interactions:** Appendix 1 (mepacrine)

Side-effects: gastro-intestinal disturbances; dizziness, headache; with large doses nausea, vomiting and occasionally transient acute toxic psychosis and CNS stimulation; on prolonged treatment yellow discoloration of skin and urine, chronic dermatoses (including severe exfoliative dermatitis), hepatitis, aplastic anaemia; also reported blue/black discoloration of palate and nails and corneal deposits with visual disturbances

Dose: 100 mg every 8 hours for 5–7 days; CHILD 2 mg/kg every 8 hours

Mepacrine Hydrochloride

Tablets, mepacrine hydrochloride 100 mg. Net price 20 = 28p. Label: 4, 9, 14, 21

Available from Boots (special order)

5.4.5 Leishmaniacides

Cutaneous leishmaniasis frequently heals spontaneously without specific treatment. If the skin lesions are extensive or unsightly, treatment is indicated, as it is in visceral leishmaniasis (kala-azar).

Sodium stibogluconate, an organic pentavalent antimony compound, is the treatment of choice for visceral leishmaniasis. The dose is 10 mg/kg daily for 30 days by intramuscular or intravenous injection; the dosage varies with different geographical regions and expert advice should be obtained. Skin lesions are treated for 10 days.

Pentamidine isethionate (section 5.4.8) has been used in antimony-resistant visceral leishmaniasis, but although the initial response is often good, the relapse rate is high; it is associated with serious side-effects.

SODIUM STIBOGLUCONATE

Indications: leishmaniasis

Cautions: intravenous injections must be given slowly and stopped if coughing or substernal pain develops; intramuscular injection painful

Contra-indications: pneumonia, myocarditis, nephritis, hepatitis

Side-effects: anorexia, vomiting, coughing, substernal pain

Dose: see notes above

PoM **Pentostam**® (Wellcome)

Injection, sodium stibogluconate equivalent to pentavalent antimony 100 mg/mL. Net price 100-mL bottle = £59.14

5.4.6 Trypanocides

The prophylaxis and treatment of trypanosomiasis is difficult and differs according to the strain of organism. Expert advice should therefore be obtained.

5.4.7 Drugs for toxoplasmosis

Most infections caused by *Toxoplasma gondii* are self-limiting, and treatment is not necessary. Exceptions are patients with eye involvement (toxoplasma choroidoretinitis), and those who are immunosuppressed. The treatment of choice is a combination of pyrimethamine and sulphadiazine, given for several weeks. Pyrimethamine is a folate antagonist, and adverse reactions to this combination are relatively common.

If toxoplasmosis is acquired in pregnancy, transplacental infection may lead to severe disease in the fetus. The pyrimethamine and sulphadiazine combination is best avoided in pregnancy but there are encouraging reports with spiramycin.

5.4.8 Drugs for Pneumocystis pneumonia

Pneumonia caused by *Pneumocystis carinii* occurs in immunosuppressed or severely debilitated patients. It is the commonest cause of pneumonia in AIDS. **Co-trimoxazole** (section 5.1.8) in high dosage is the drug of choice for the treatment of pneumocystis pneumonia. **Pentamidine isethionate** is an alternative to co-trimoxazole and is particularly indicated for patients with a history of adverse reactions to, or who have not responded to, co-trimoxazole. Pentamidine isethionate is a potentially toxic drug that can cause severe hypotension during or immediately after administration; it should only be administered by those experienced in its use. Pentamidine isethionate is given by intravenous infusion but can also be administered by inhalation which reduces side-effects (although systemic absorption may still occur); intermittent prophylactic inhalation may prevent relapse.

PENTAMIDINE ISETHIONATE

Indications: see under Dose (should only be given by specialists)

Cautions: risk of severe hypotension following administration (establish baseline blood pressure and administer with patient lying down; monitor blood pressure closely during administration, and at regular intervals, until treatment concluded); hepatic and renal impairment; hypertension or hypotension; hyperglycaemia or hypoglycaemia; leucopenia, thrombocytopenia, or anaemia; carry out laboratory monitoring for all functions according to data sheet

Side-effects: severe reactions, sometimes fatal, due to hypotension, hypoglycaemia, pancreatitis, and arrhythmias; also. leucopenia, thrombocytopenia, acute renal failure, hypocalcaemia; also reported: azotaemia, abnormal liver-function tests, leucopenia, anaemia, hyperkalaemia, nausea and vomiting, dizziness, syncope, flushing, hyperglycaemia, rash, and taste disturbances; bronchoconstriction reported on inhalation; discomfort, pain, induration, abscess formation, and muscle necrosis at injection site

Dose: Pneumocystis carinii pneumonia, *by intravenous infusion*, 4 mg/kg daily for at least 14 days (reduced according to manufacturer's literature in renal impairment)
By inhalation of nebulised solution (using suitable equipment—see data sheet) 600 mg pentamidine isethionate in 6 mL water for injections daily for 3 weeks; secondary prevention, 300 mg in 4–6 mL as a single inhalation every 4 weeks
Visceral leishmaniasis (Kala-azar), *by deep intramuscular injection*, 3–4 mg/kg on alternate days to max. total of 10 injections; course may be repeated if necessary
Cutaneous leishmaniasis, *by deep intramuscular injection*, 3–4 mg/kg once or twice weekly until condition resolves (but see also section 5.4.5)
Trypanosomiasis, *by deep intramuscular injection or intravenous infusion*, 4 mg/kg daily or on alternate days to total of 7–10 injections
Note. Direct bolus intravenous injection should be avoided whenever possible and **never** given rapidly; intramuscular injections should be deep and preferably given into the buttock

PoM **Pentacarinat®** (Rhône-Poulenc Rorer)
Injection, powder for reconstitution, pentamidine isethionate. Net price 300-mg vial = £15.98

5.5 Anthelmintics

Advice on prophylaxis and treatment of helminth infections is available from:

Birmingham	021-772 4311
Glasgow	041-946 7120 Extn 277
Liverpool	051-708 9393
London	071-387 4411 (treatment)

5.5.1 Drugs for threadworms

(pinworms, *Enterobius vermicularis*)

Anthelmintics are relatively ineffective in threadworm infections, and their use should be combined with hygienic measures to break the cycle of auto-infection. All members of the family require treatment.

Adult threadworms do not live for longer than 6 weeks and for development of fresh worms, ova must be swallowed and exposed to the action of digestive juices in the upper intestinal tract. Direct multiplication of worms does not take place in the large bowel. Adult female worms lay ova on the peri-anal skin which causes pruritus; scratching the area then leads to ova being transmitted on fingers to the mouth, often via food eaten with unwashed hands. Washing hands and scrubbing nails before each meal and after each visit to the toilet is essential. A bath taken immediately after rising will remove ova laid during the night.

Mebendazole is the drug of choice for patients of all ages over 2 years. It is given as a single dose; if reinfection occurs, a second dose may be given after 2–3 weeks.

Piperazine salts are preferably given daily for 7 days; a further 7-day course may be given if necessary after an interval of 1 week. Single-dose preparations are also available.

Pyrantel is equally effective. It is given as a single dose; cure-rates are improved if one or two further doses are given at intervals of 2 weeks.

MEBENDAZOLE

Indications: threadworm, roundworm, whipworm, and hookworm infections
Cautions: pregnancy (toxicity in *rats*)
Note. The package insert in the Vermox® pack includes the statement that it is not suitable for women known to be pregnant or children under 2 years
Contra-indications: children under 2 years
Side-effects: rarely abdominal pain, diarrhoea
Dose: threadworms, ADULT and CHILD over 2 years, 100 mg as a single dose; if reinfection occurs second dose may be needed after 2–3 weeks
Roundworms—section 5.5.2

[1]PoM **Vermox®** (Janssen)
Tablets, pink, scored, chewable, mebendazole 100 mg. Net price 6-tab pack = £1.57
Suspension mebendazole 100 mg/5 mL. Net price 30 mL = £1.82

1. Can be sold to the public if supplied for the oral treatment of enterobiasis in a container or package containing only a single dose of not more than 100 mg of mebendazole; a proprietary brand (Ovex®) is also on sale to the public.

PIPERAZINE

Indications: threadworm and roundworm infections
Cautions: renal impairment (avoid if severe), neurological disease
Contra-indications: epilepsy, liver disease
Side-effects: nausea, vomiting, colic, diarrhoea, allergic reactions including urticaria, bronchospasm, and rare reports of Stevens-Johnson syndrome and angioedema; rarely dizziness, muscular incoordination ('worm wobble'); drowsiness, confusion and clonic contractions in patients with neurological or renal abnormalities
Dose: threadworms, as piperazine hydrate, 2 g once daily for 7 days; CHILD under 2 years 50–75 mg/kg once daily for 7 days, 2–4 years 750 mg once daily for 7 days, 5–12 years 1.5 g once daily for 7 days; repeat course after 1 week if necessary

Roundworms—section 5.5.2
Note. 100 mg piperazine hydrate ≡ 125 mg piperazine citrate ≡ 104 mg piperazine phosphate

Antepar® (Wellcome)
Tablets, yellow, scored, piperazine hydrate 500 mg (as phosphate). Net price 28-tab pack = £2.86. Label: 24
Elixir, orange, piperazine hydrate 750 mg/5 mL (as hydrate and citrate). Diluent syrup, life of diluted elixir 14 days. Net price 100-mL pack = £2.89

Pripsen® (R&C)
Oral powder, cream, piperazine phosphate 4 g and sennosides 15.3 mg/sachet. Net price two-dose sachet pack = £1.16. Label: 13
Dose: threadworms, stirred into a small glass of milk or water and drunk immediately, ADULT and CHILD over 6 years, 1 sachet, repeat after 14 days; INFANTS 3 months–1 year, one-third sachet (2.5 mL powder); CHILD 1–6 years, two-thirds sachet (5 mL powder), repeat after 14 days
Roundworms, first dose as for threadworms; repeat at monthly intervals if reinfection risk

5.5.2 Ascaricides

(common roundworm infections)

Levamisole (not on UK market) is very effective against ascaris and is generally considered to be the drug of choice. It is very well tolerated; mild nausea or vomiting has been reported in about 1% of treated patients; it is given as a single dose of 120–150 mg in adults.

Mebendazole (section 5.5.1) is also active against *Ascaris lumbricoides*; the usual dose is 100 mg twice daily for 3 days. **Pyrantel** is also an effective broad-spectrum anthelmintic and a single dose of 10 mg/kg (max. 1 g) is usually sufficient to eradicate ascaris; it may occasionally produce mild nausea but experience shows it to be a very safe drug. **Piperazine** may also be given in a single dose equivalent to 4 g of piperazine hydrate.

PYRANTEL

Indications: roundworm, threadworm, and hook-worm infections
Cautions: liver disease
Side-effects: see notes above
Dose: ADULT and CHILD over 6 months, *Ascaris lumbricoides* alone, a single dose of 5 mg/kg; mixed infections involving *Ascaris lumbricoides*, single dose of 10 mg/kg
Hookworm—section 5.5.4
Threadworms—section 5.5.1

PoM **Combantrin®** (Pfizer)
Tablets, orange, pyrantel 125 mg (as embonate). Net price 6-tab pack = 64p

5.5.3 Taenicides

(tapeworms)

Niclosamide is the most widely used drug for tapeworm infections and side-effects are limited to occasional gastro-intestinal upset, light-headedness, and pruritus. Fears of developing cysticercosis in *Taenia solium* infections have proved unfounded. All the same, it is wise to anticipate this possibility by using an anti-emetic on wakening.

Praziquantel (not on UK market) is as effective as niclosamide and is given as a single dose of 10–20 mg/kg after a light breakfast.

NICLOSAMIDE

Indications: tapeworm infections—see notes above and under Dose
Side-effects: gastro-intestinal discomfort
Dose: *Taenia solium*, 2 g as a single dose after a light breakfast, followed by a purgative after 2 hours; CHILD up to 2 years, 500 mg, 2–6 years, 1 g
T. saginata and *Diphyllobothrium latum*, as for *T. solium* but half the dose may be taken after breakfast and the remainder one hour later followed by a purgative after a further 2 hours
Hymenolepsis nana, 2 g on first day, then 1 g daily for next 6 days; CHILD up to 2 years, quarter adult dose; 2–6 years, half adult dose
COUNSELLING. To be chewed thoroughly and washed down with water or taken crushed in water

Yomesan® (Bayer)
Tablets, yellow, chewable, niclosamide 500 mg. Net price 4-tab pack = £1.41. Label: 4, 24, 27, counselling, administration

5.5.4 Drugs for hookworms

(ancylostomiasis, necatoriasis)

Hookworms live in the upper small intestine and draw blood from the point of their attachment to their host. An iron-deficiency anaemia may thereby be produced and, if present, effective treatment of the infection requires not only expulsion of the worms but treatment of the anaemia.

Bephenium is still widely used and its side-effects are limited to occasional nausea and vomiting. A single dose of 2.5 g is given and repeated after 1–2 days. It is unpleasant to take and activity against *Necator americanus* is unreliable. **Pyrantel** (section 5.5.2) is very effective against hookworms and, like bephenium, has side-effects limited to occasional nausea and vomiting. The usual dose is 10 mg/kg (max. 1 g) given as a single dose.

Mebendazole (section 5.5.1) has a useful broad-spectrum activity, and is effective against hookworms; the usual dose is 100 mg twice daily for 3 days.

BEPHENIUM

Indications: roundworm and hookworm infections
Side-effects: nausea, vomiting, diarrhoea, headache, vertigo
Dose: see notes above

Alcopar® (Wellcome)
Granules, yellow/green, bephenium 2.5 g (as hydroxynaphthoate)/sachet. Net price per sachet = 73p. Label: 13

5.5.5 Schistosomicides
(bilharziasis)

Adult *Schistosoma haematobium* worms live in the genito-urinary veins and adult *S. mansoni* in those of the colon and mesentery. *S. japonicum* is more widely distributed in veins of the alimentary tract and portal system.

Praziquantel (Biltricide®, not on UK market) is effective against all human schistosomes. The dose is 40 mg/kg as a single oral dose (60 mg/kg in 3 divided doses on one day for *S. japonicum* infections). No serious toxic effects have been reported. Of all the available schistosomicides, it has the most attractive combination of effectiveness, broad-spectrum activity, and low toxicity.

Oxamniquine (Vansil®, *Pfizer*) is effective against *S. mansoni* infections only. It is a quinoline compound given by mouth; the dosage ranges from 15 mg/kg as a single dose to a total of 60 mg/kg over 2 to 3 days according to the geographical region. It can occasionally cause epileptic fits.

Metriphonate (Bilarcil®, not on UK market) is an organophosphorus compound which is only effective against *S. haematobium* infections. It is given by mouth in 3 doses of 7.5 mg/kg at intervals of 2 weeks. As it reduces plasma-cholinesterase concentrations it should be used with caution in patients likely to be frequently exposed to organophosphorus insecticides.

Hycanthone, lucanthone, niridazole, and stibocaptate have now been superseded.

5.5.6 Filaricides

Diethylcarbamazine is effective against microfilariae and adults of *Loa loa*, *Wuchereria bancrofti*, and *Brugia Malayi*. To minimise reactions treatment is commenced with a dose of 1 mg/kg and increased gradually over 3 days to 6 mg/kg daily in divided doses; this dosage is maintained for 21 days and usually gives a radical cure for these infections. Close medical supervision is necessary particularly in the early phase of treatment.

In heavy infections there may be a febrile reaction, and in heavy *Loa loa* infection there is a small risk of encephalopathy. In such cases treatment must be given under careful in-patient supervision and stopped at the first sign of cerebral involvement (and specialist advice sought).

Diethylcarbamazine can cause such serious reactions in onchocerciasis, that it should no longer be used for this infection. Suramin has also been used for onchocerciasis but is now obsolete because of its toxicity.

Ivermectin (Mectizan®, *MSD*, not on UK market) is very effective in *onchocerciasis* and it is now the drug of choice. A single dose of 200 micrograms/kg by mouth produces a prolonged reduction in microfilarial levels; annual retreatment must be given until the adult worms die out. Reactions are usually slight and most commonly take the form of temporary aggravation of itching and rash.

DIETHYLCARBAMAZINE CITRATE

Indications: filariasis
Cautions; Side-effects: see notes above
Dose: see notes above

Banocide® (Wellcome)
Tablets, scored, diethylcarbamazine citrate 50 mg. Net price 100 = £4.55. Label: 9

5.5.7 Drugs for guinea worms
(dracontiasis)

Guinea worms, *Dracunculus medinensis*, may be killed and their removal from the tissues facilitated by a course of **niridazole** (Ambilhar®, not on UK market). Use of niridazole does not obviate the concomitant need for sterile dressing of the ulcer caused by a guinea worm and for its extraction, wherever possible, under sterile conditions. In India, mebendazole has been reported as effective at a dosage of 200 mg twice daily for 7 days. **Metronidazole** has also been reported to be effective in a dose of 400 mg three times daily for 5 days.

5.5.8 Drugs for strongyloidiasis

Adult *Strongyloides stercoralis* live in the gut and produce larvae which penetrate the gut wall and invade the tissues, setting up a cycle of autoinfection. **Thiabendazole** is the drug of choice, at a dosage of 25 mg/kg every 12 hours for 3 days. **Mebendazole** is only moderately effective; it is given in 3 courses of 100 mg twice daily for 3 days at intervals of 2 weeks.

THIABENDAZOLE

Indications: strongyloidiasis, cutaneous and visceral larva migrans, dracontiasis, symptoms of trichinosis; secondary treatment for threadworm when mixed with above infestations; adjunct in hookworm, whipworm, or roundworm
Cautions: hepatic or renal impairment, if drowsiness occurs warn patients not to drive, discontinue if hypersensitivity reactions occur; **interactions**: Appendix 1 (thiabendazole)
Contra-indications: pregnancy (teratogenesis in *animal* studies)
Side-effects: anorexia, nausea, vomiting, dizziness, diarrhoea, headache, pruritus, drowsiness; hypersensitivity reactions including fever, chills, angioedema, rashes, erythema multiforme; rarely tinnitus, collapse, parenchymal liver damage
Dose: see notes above

PoM **Mintezol®** (MSD)
Tablets, orange, chewable, thiabendazole 500 mg. Net price 6-tab pack = 52p. Label: 3, 21, 24

6: Drugs used in the treatment of disorders of the ENDOCRINE SYSTEM

In this chapter, drug treatment is discussed under the following headings:

6.1 Drugs used in diabetes
6.2 Thyroid and antithyroid drugs
6.3 Corticosteroids
6.4 Sex hormones
6.5 Hypothalamic and pituitary hormones
6.6 Drugs affecting bone metabolism
6.7 Other endocrine drugs

6.1 Drugs used in diabetes

Two groups of drugs are used in the treatment of diabetes, insulin (section 6.1.1) and oral antidiabetic drugs (section 6.1.2).

The treatment of diabetic ketoacidosis or hyperosmolar non-ketotic 'coma' (section 6.1.3), hypoglycaemia (section 6.1.4), and diabetic neuropathy (section 6.1.5) are also discussed.

6.1.1 Insulin

6.1.1.1 Short-acting insulin
6.1.1.2 Intermediate- and long-acting insulins

Insulin plays a key role in the body's regulation of carbohydrate, fat, and protein metabolism. Diabetes mellitus is due to a deficiency in insulin synthesis and secretion. Patients are generally described as insulin-dependent diabetics (type 1) or non-insulin-dependent diabetics (type 2), although many of the latter need insulin to maintain satisfactory control.

Insulin is a polypeptide hormone of complex structure. It is extracted mainly from pork pancreas and purified by crystallisation; it can also be made biosynthetically by recombinant DNA technology using *Escherichia coli* or semisynthetically by enzymatic modification of porcine material (see under Human Insulins, below). All insulin preparations are to a greater or lesser extent immunogenic in man but immunological resistance to insulin action is uncommon.

Insulin is inactivated by gastro-intestinal enzymes, and must therefore be given by injection; the subcutaneous route is ideal for most circumstances. It is usually injected into the upper arms, thighs, buttocks, or abdomen; there may be increased absorption from a limb site if the limb is used in strenuous exercise. Insulin is usually administered using a syringe and needle but portable injection devices (e.g. NovoPen®, Penject®) which hold soluble insulin in cartridge form and meter the required dose are rapidly growing in popularity; they permit greater freedom even though injections may be needed 3 or 4 times daily.

Insulin can also be given by continuous subcutaneous infusion using soluble insulin in an infusion pump. This technique now has an established though limited place in the treatment of diabetes, and provides continuous basal insulin infusion with preprandial boosts. Its chief benefit is the considerable improvement in quality of life enjoyed by some patients, and, at times, the elimination of troublesome hypoglycaemia. It is unsuitable for emotionally or psychiatrically disturbed patients, and thus does not provide a general solution for 'brittle' diabetics. There are many disadvantages to this technique. Patients using it must be well-motivated, reliable, and able to monitor their own blood glucose, and must have access to expert advice both day and night.

When treating diabetic ketoacidosis (section 6.1.3), insulin should be given by intravenous or intramuscular injection, since absorption from subcutaneous depots may be slow and erratic.

Minor allergic reactions at the sites of injections during the first few weeks of treatment are uncommon, usually transient and require no treatment. Fat hypertrophy sometimes develops at sites of insulin injection and can to some extent be avoided by rotation of injection sites.

CHOICE OF TREATMENT. About 25% of diabetics require insulin treatment; apart from those presenting in ketoacidosis, insulin is needed by most of those with a rapid onset of symptoms, weight loss, weakness, and sometimes vomiting, often associated with ketonuria. The majority of those who are obese can be managed by restriction of carbohydrate or energy intake alone or with the subsequent administration of oral hypoglycaemic drugs. Most children require insulin from the outset.

MANAGEMENT OF DIABETIC PATIENTS. The aim of treatment is to achieve the best possible control of plasma glucose without making the patient obsessional, and avoiding disabling hypoglycaemia; close co-operation is needed between the patient and the medical team. Mixtures of available insulin preparations may be required and these combinations have to be worked out for the individual patient. Insulin requirements may be affected by variations in lifestyle, infection, and corticosteroids, and sometimes by a very small amount when the oral contraceptive pill is taken. In pregnancy insulin requirements should be assessed frequently by an experienced diabetic physician.

The energy and carbohydrate intake must be adequate to allow normal growth and development but obesity must be avoided. The carbohydrate intake must be regulated in those patients on insulin and should be distributed throughout the day. Fine control of plasma glucose can be achieved by moving portions of carbohydrate from one meal to another without altering the total intake.

Insulin doses are determined on an individual

basis, by gradually increasing the dose but avoiding troublesome hypoglycaemic reactions.

There are 3 main types of insulin preparations:

1. those of **short** duration which have a relatively rapid onset of action, namely soluble forms of insulin;
2. those with an **intermediate** action, e.g. Isophane Insulin Injection and Insulin Zinc Suspension; and
3. those whose action is slower in onset and lasts for **long** periods, e.g. Human Ultratard®.

The *duration of action* of different insulin preparations varies considerably from one patient to another, and needs to be assessed for every individual; those indicated below are only approximations. The type of insulin used and its dose and frequency of administration depend on the particular needs of the patient. Most patients are best started on insulins of intermediate action twice daily and a short-acting insulin can later be added to cover any hyperglycaemia which may follow breakfast or evening meal.

Some recommended insulin regimens

Insulin	Regimen
1. Short-acting insulin mixed with Intermediate-acting insulin	twice daily (before meals)
2. Short-acting insulin mixed with Intermediate-acting insulin	before breakfast
Short-acting insulin	before evening meal
Intermediate-acting insulin	bedtime
3. Short-acting insulin	three times daily (before breakfast, mid-day and evening meal)
Intermediate-acting insulin	bedtime
4. Short-acting insulin mixed with Intermediate-acting insulin	before breakfast (sufficient in some cases)

HUMAN INSULINS. There are differences in the amino-acid sequence in animal and human insulins; most available insulins are either porcine in origin or of human sequence prepared by modification of porcine material (emp) or biosynthetically (crb, prb, or pyr). Preparations of human sequence insulin should theoretically be less immunogenic, but in trials no real advantage has been shown.

HYPOGLYCAEMIA. This is a potential hazard when the type of insulin is changed, especially when converting from beef to human insulin. The conversion from beef to human sequence insulin should always be undertaken with specialist advice; it is usual to reduce the total dose by about 10%, with careful monitoring for the first few days. When changing from porcine to human sequence insulin, a dose change is not usually needed, but careful monitoring is advised. Loss of warning of hypoglycaemia is a common problem among insulin-treated diabetics and can be a serious hazard, especially for drivers. The cause is not known, but very tight control of diabetes appears to lower the blood glucose concentration needed to trigger hypoglycaemic symptoms. Beta-blockers can also blunt hypoglycaemic awareness (and can delay recovery). Some patients have reported loss of warning after transfer to human insulin; patients should be warned of this possibility and if they believe that human insulin is responsible for their loss of warning it is reasonable to transfer them back to porcine insulin.

DRIVING. Car drivers need to be particularly careful to avoid hypoglycaemia (see above) and should be warned of the problems. They should normally check their blood glucose concentration before driving and, on long journeys, at intervals of approximately two hours. If hypoglycaemia occurs a car driver should switch off the ignition until recovery is complete, which may take up to 15 minutes or longer. Driving is not permitted when hypoglycaemic awareness has been lost.

UNITS. The word 'unit' should **not** be abbreviated.

6.1.1.1 SHORT-ACTING INSULIN

Soluble Insulin is a short-acting form of insulin. For maintenance regimens it is usual to inject it 15 to 30 minutes before meals.

Soluble insulin is the only appropriate form of insulin for use in diabetic emergencies and at the time of surgical operations. It has the great advantage that it can be given intravenously and intramuscularly, as well as subcutaneously.

When injected subcutaneously, soluble insulin has a rapid onset of action (after 30 to 60 minutes), a peak action between 2 and 4 hours, and a duration of action of up to 8 hours. Human sequence preparations tend to have a more rapid onset and a shorter overall duration.

When injected intravenously, soluble insulin has a very short half-life of only about 5 minutes and its effect disappears within 30 minutes.

SOLUBLE INSULIN

(Insulin Injection; Neutral Insulin)

A sterile solution of insulin (i.e. bovine or porcine) or of human insulin; pH 6.6–8.0

Indications: diabetes mellitus; diabetic ketoacidosis (section 6.1.3)

Cautions: see notes above; reduce dose in renal impairment; **interactions:** Appendix 1 (antidiabetics)

Side-effects: see notes above; local reactions and fat hypertrophy at injection site; overdose causes hypoglycaemia

Dose: by subcutaneous, intramuscular, or intravenous injection or intravenous infusion, according to patient's requirements

Highly purified animal

Neutral Insulin Injection (Evans)

Injection, soluble insulin (bovine, highly purified), 100 units/mL. Net price 10-mL vial = £6.80

 Prices are **net**, see p. 1

Hypurin Neutral® (CP)
Injection, soluble insulin (bovine, highly purified) 100 units/mL. Net price 10-mL vial = £8.95
Velosulin® (Novo Nordisk Wellcome)
Injection, soluble insulin (porcine, highly purified) 100 units/mL. Net price 10-mL vial = £7.85
Velosulin Cartridge® (Novo Nordisk Wellcome)
Injection (subcutaneous infusion only), soluble insulin (porcine, highly purified) 100 units/mL. Net price 5.7-mL cartridge vial (for use only in Nordisk Wellcome Infuser®) = £5.14

Human sequence
Human Actrapid® (Novo Nordisk)
Injection, soluble insulin (human, pyr) 100 units/mL. Net price 10-mL vial = £8.45
Human Actrapid Penfill® (Novo Nordisk)
Injection, soluble insulin (human, pyr) 100 units/mL. Net price 5 × 1.5-mL cartridge (for use only in NovoPen® devices) = £7.69
Human Velosulin® (Novo Nordisk Wellcome)
Injection, soluble insulin (human, emp) 100 units/mL. Net price 10-mL vial = £8.45
Humulin S® (Lilly)
Injection, soluble insulin (human, prb) 100 units/mL. Net price 10-mL vial = £8.81

Injection devices
NHS **Autopen®** (Owen Mumford)
Injection device, for use with multidose insulin cartridges. Price = £22.95
NHS **NovoPen II®** (Novo Nordisk)
Injection device, for use with Human Actrapid Penfill®
NHS **Penject®** (Hypoguard)
Injection device, for use with a Becton Dickinson U100 1-mL syringe. Price = £16.00

Subcutaneous infusion pumps
NHS **MS36®** (Graseby Medical)
Infusion pump, for use with any brand of U-100 soluble insulin. Net price = £782.00

Mixed preparations, see Biphasic Insulin and Biphasic Isophane Insulin (section 6.1.1.2)

6.1.1.2 INTERMEDIATE- AND LONG-ACTING INSULINS

When given by subcutaneous injection intermediate- and long-acting insulins have an onset of action of approximately 1–2 hours, a maximal effect at 4–12 hours, and a duration of 16–35 hours. Some are given twice daily in conjunction with short-acting (soluble) insulin, and others are given once daily, particularly in elderly patients. They can be mixed with soluble insulin in the syringe, essentially retaining the properties of the two components, although there may be some blunting of the initial effect of the soluble insulin component (especially on mixing with protamine zinc insulin, see below).

Isophane Insulin is a suspension of insulin with protamine which is of particular value for initiation of twice-daily insulin regimens. Patients usually mix isophane with soluble insulin but ready-mixed preparations may be appropriate (**Biphasic Isophane Insulin**).

Biphasic Insulin is another ready-mixed insulin suitable for twice-daily injection.

Insulin Zinc Suspension (Amorphous) has an intermediate duration of action and **Insulin Zinc Suspension (Crystalline)** a more prolonged duration of action. These preparations may be used independently or in **Insulin Zinc Suspension** (30% amorphous, 70% crystalline).

Protamine Zinc Insulin is usually given once-daily in conjunction with short-acting (soluble) insulin. It has the drawback of binding with the soluble insulin when mixed in the same syringe, and is now rarely used.

INSULIN ZINC SUSPENSION

(Insulin Zinc Suspension (Mixed); I.Z.S.)
A sterile neutral suspension of bovine and/or porcine insulin or of human insulin in the form of a complex obtained by the addition of a suitable zinc salt; consists of rhombohedral crystals (10–40 microns) and of particles of no uniform shape (not exceeding 2 microns)
Indications: diabetes mellitus (long acting)
Cautions; Side-effects: see under Soluble Insulin (section 6.1.1.1)
Dose: by subcutaneous injection, according to patient's requirements

Highly purified animal
Insulin Zinc Suspension Lente (Evans)
Injection, insulin zinc suspension (bovine, highly purified) 100 units/mL. Net price 10-mL vial = £6.89
Hypurin Lente® (CP)
Injection, insulin zinc suspension (bovine, highly purified) 100 units/mL. Net price 10-mL vial = £8.95
Lentard MC® (Novo Nordisk)
Injection, insulin zinc suspension (bovine and porcine, highly purified) 100 units/mL. Net price 10-mL vial = £6.89

Human sequence
Human Monotard® (Novo Nordisk)
Injection, insulin zinc suspension (human, pyr) 100 units/mL. Net price 10-mL vial = £8.45
Humulin Lente® (Lilly)
Injection, insulin zinc suspension (human, prb) 100 units/mL. Net price 10-mL vial = £8.81

INSULIN ZINC SUSPENSION (AMORPHOUS)

(Amorph. I.Z.S.)
A sterile neutral suspension of bovine or porcine insulin in the form of a complex obtained by the addition of a suitable zinc salt; consists of particles of no uniform shape (not exceeding 2 microns)
Indications: diabetes mellitus (intermediate acting)

Cautions; Side-effects: see under Soluble Insulin (section 6.1.1.1)
Dose: by subcutaneous injection, according to patient's requirements

Semitard MC® (Novo Nordisk)
Injection, insulin zinc suspension (amorphous) (porcine, highly purified) 100 units/mL. Net price 10-mL vial = £7.49

INSULIN ZINC SUSPENSION (CRYSTALLINE)

(Cryst. I.Z.S.)
A sterile neutral suspension of bovine insulin or of human insulin in the form of a complex obtained by the addition of a suitable zinc salt; consists of rhombohedral crystals (10–40 microns)
Indications: diabetes mellitus (duration of action, see below)
Cautions; Side-effects: see under Soluble Insulin (section 6.1.1.1)
Dose: by subcutaneous injection, according to patient's requirements

Human sequence
Human Ultratard® (Novo Nordisk) (long acting)
Injection, insulin zinc suspension, crystalline (human, pyr) 100 units/mL. Net price 10-mL vial = £8.45
Humulin Zn® (Lilly) (intermediate acting)
Injection, insulin zinc suspension, crystalline (human, prb) 100 units/mL. Net price 10-mL vial = £8.81

ISOPHANE INSULIN

(Isophane Insulin Injection; Isophane Protamine Insulin Injection; Isophane Insulin (NPH))
A sterile suspension of bovine or porcine insulin or of human insulin in the form of a complex obtained by the addition of protamine sulphate or another suitable protamine
Indications: diabetes mellitus (intermediate acting)
Cautions; Side-effects: see under Soluble Insulin (section 6.1.1.1); protamine may cause allergic reactions
Dose: by subcutaneous injection, according to patient's requirements

Highly purified animal
Isophane Insulin Injection (Evans)
Injection, isophane insulin (bovine, highly purified) 100 units/mL. Net price 10-mL vial = £6.89
Hypurin Isophane® (CP)
Injection, isophane insulin (bovine, highly purified) 100 units/mL. Net price 10-mL vial = £8.95
Insulatard® (Novo Nordisk Wellcome)
Injection, isophane insulin (porcine, highly purified) 100 units/mL. Net price 10-mL vial = £7.85

Human sequence
Human Insulatard® (Novo Nordisk Wellcome)
Injection, isophane insulin (human, emp) 100 units/mL. Net price 10-mL vial = £8.45
Human Protaphane® (Novo Nordisk)
Injection, isophane insulin (human, pyr) 100 units/mL. Net price 10-mL vial = £8.45
Human Protaphane Penfill® (Novo Nordisk)
Injection, isophane insulin (human, pyr) 100 units/mL. Net price 5 × 1.5-mL cartridge (for use only in Novopen® devices) = £8.10
Humulin I® (Lilly)
Injection, isophane insulin (human, prb) 100 units/mL. Net price 10-mL vial = £8.81

Mixed preparations, see Biphasic Isophane Insulin (below)

PROTAMINE ZINC INSULIN

(Protamine Zinc Insulin Injection)
A sterile suspension of insulin in the form of a complex obtained by the addition of a suitable protamine and zinc chloride; this preparation was included in BP 1980 but is not included in BP 1988
Indications: diabetes mellitus (long acting)
Cautions; Side-effects: see under Soluble Insulin (section 6.1.1.1); protamine may cause allergic reactions; see also notes above
Dose: by subcutaneous injection, according to patient's requirements

Hypurin Protamine Zinc® (CP)
Injection, protamine zinc insulin (bovine, highly purified) 100 units/mL. Net price 10-mL vial = £9.60

BIPHASIC INSULINS

BIPHASIC INSULIN

(Biphasic Insulin Injection)
A sterile suspension of crystals containing bovine insulin in a solution of porcine insulin
Indications: diabetes mellitus (intermediate acting)
Cautions; Side-effects: see under Soluble Insulin (section 6.1.1.1)
Dose: by subcutaneous injection, according to patient's requirements

Rapitard MC® (Novo Nordisk)
Injection, biphasic insulin (highly purified) 100 units/mL. Net price 10-mL vial = £6.89

BIPHASIC ISOPHANE INSULIN

(Biphasic Isophane Insulin Injection)
A sterile buffered suspension of porcine insulin complexed with protamine sulphate (or another suitable protamine) in a solution of porcine insulin *or* a sterile buffered suspension of human insulin complexed with protamine sulphate (or another suitable protamine) in a solution of human insulin
Indications: diabetes mellitus (intermediate acting)
Cautions; Side-effects: see under Soluble Insulin (section 6.1.1.1); protamine may cause allergic reactions
Dose: by subcutaneous injection, according to the patient's requirements

Highly purified animal

Initard 50/50® (Novo Nordisk Wellcome)
Injection, biphasic isophane insulin (porcine, highly purified), 50% soluble, 50% isophane. 100 units/mL. Net price 10-mL vial = £7.85

Mixtard 30/70® (Novo Nordisk Wellcome)
Injection, biphasic isophane insulin (porcine, highly purified), 30% soluble, 70% isophane, 100 units/mL. Net price 10-mL vial = £7.85

Human sequence

Human Actraphane 30/70® (Novo Nordisk)
Injection, biphasic isophane insulin (human, pyr), 30% soluble, 70% isophane, 100 units/mL. Net price 10-mL vial = £8.45

Human Initard 50/50® (Novo Nordisk Wellcome)
Injection, biphasic isophane insulin (human, emp), 50% soluble, 50% isophane, 100 units/mL. Net price 10-mL vial = £8.45

Human Mixtard 30/70® (Novo Nordisk Wellcome)
Injection, biphasic isophane insulin (human, emp), 30% soluble, 70% isophane, 100 units/mL. Net price 10-mL vial = £8.45

Humulin M1® (Lilly)
Injection, biphasic isophane insulin (human, prb), 10% soluble, 90% isophane, 100 units/mL. Net price 10-mL vial = £8.81

Humulin M2® (Lilly)
Injection, biphasic isophane insulin (human, prb), 20% soluble, 80% isophane, 100 units/mL. Net price 10-mL vial = £8.81

Humulin M3® (Lilly)
Injection, biphasic isophane insulin (human, prb), 30% soluble, 70% isophane, 100 units/mL. Net price 10-mL vial = £8.81

Humulin M4® (Lilly)
Injection, biphasic isophane insulin (human, prb), 40% soluble, 60% isophane, 100 units/mL. Net price 10-mL vial = £8.81

PenMix 30/70® (Novo Nordisk)
Injection, biphasic isophane insulin (human, pyr), 30% soluble, 70% isophane, 100 units/mL. Net price 5 × 1.5-mL cartridge (for use only in Novopen® devices) = £8.10

6.1.2 Oral antidiabetic drugs

6.1.2.1 Sulphonylureas
6.1.2.2 Biguanides
6.1.2.3 Guar gum

Oral antidiabetic drugs are used for non-insulin-dependent (type 2) diabetes; they should not be prescribed until patients have been shown not to respond adequately to at least one month's restriction of energy and carbohydrate intake. They should be used to augment the effect of diet, and not to replace it.

6.1.2.1 SULPHONYLUREAS

The sulphonylureas act mainly by augmenting insulin secretion and consequently are effective only when some residual pancreatic beta-cell activity is present; during long-term administration they also have an extrapancreatic action. All may lead to hypoglycaemia 4 hours or more after food but this is usually an indication of overdose, and is relatively uncommon.

There are several sulphonylureas but there is no evidence for any difference in their effectiveness. Only **chlorpropamide** has appreciably more side-effects, mainly because of its very prolonged duration of action and the consequent hazard of hypoglycaemia, but also as a result of the common and unpleasant chlorpropamide-alcohol flush phenomenon. Selection of an individual sulphonylurea depends otherwise on the age of the patient and renal function (see below), or more generally just on personal preference.

Elderly patients are particularly prone to the dangers of hypoglycaemia when long-acting sulphonylureas are used; chlorpropamide, and also preferably **glibenclamide**, should be avoided in these patients and replaced by others, such as **gliclazide** or **tolbutamide**.

Sulphonylureas include those usually given once daily, such as glibenclamide and chlorpropamide, and those given more frequently, especially if higher doses are required, including gliclazide, glipizide, gliquidone and tolbutamide. **Acetohexamide** is rarely used.

CAUTIONS AND CONTRA-INDICATIONS. These drugs tend to encourage weight gain and should only be prescribed if poor control and symptoms persist despite adequate attempts at dieting. They should not be used during breast-feeding, and caution is needed in the elderly and those with hepatic and renal insufficiency because of the hazard of hypoglycaemia. The short-acting tolbutamide may be used in renal impairment, as may gliquidone and gliclazide which are principally metabolised and inactivated in the liver. Sulphonylureas should be avoided in porphyria but glipizide has been used.

Insulin therapy should be instituted temporarily during intercurrent illness (such as myocardial infarction, coma, infection, and trauma) and during surgery since control of diabetes with the sulphonylureas is often inadequate in such circumstances. Insulin therapy is also usually substituted during pregnancy. Sulphonylureas are contra-indicated in the presence of ketoacidosis.

SIDE-EFFECTS. These are generally mild and infrequent and include gastro-intestinal disturbances and headache.

Chlorpropamide may cause facial flushing after drinking alcohol; this effect is not normally witnessed with other sulphonylureas. Chlorpropamide may also enhance the effect of antidiuretic hormone and very rarely may cause hyponatraemia.

Sensitivity reactions (usually in first 6–8 weeks of therapy) include transient rashes which rarely progress to erythema multiforme and exfoliative dermatitis, fever, and jaundice; photosensitivity has also rarely been reported with chlorpropamide. Blood disorders are rare too but include thrombocytopenia, agranulocytosis, and aplastic anaemia. All these phenomena are very rare.

ACETOHEXAMIDE

Indications: diabetes mellitus (rarely used)
Cautions; Contra-indications; Side-effects: see notes above; **interactions:** Appendix 1 (antidiabetics)
Dose: 0.25–1.5 g daily, adjusted according to response; up to 1 g given as a single daily dose before breakfast, higher doses divided

PoM **Dimelor**® (Lilly)
Tablets, yellow, scored, acetohexamide 500 mg. Net price 20 = £1.30

CHLORPROPAMIDE

Indications: diabetes mellitus (for use in diabetes insipidus, see section 6.5.2)
Cautions; Contra-indications; Side-effects: see notes above; **interactions:** Appendix 1 (antidiabetics)
Dose: initially 250 mg daily (elderly patients 100–125 mg but avoid—see notes above), adjusted according to response; max. 500 mg daily; taken with breakfast

PoM **Chlorpropamide** (Non-proprietary)
Tablets, chlorpropamide 100 mg, net price 20 = 18p; 250 mg, 20 = 27p. Label: 4

PoM **Diabinese**® (Pfizer)
Tablets, scored, chlorpropamide 100 mg, net price 28-tab pack = 56p; 250 mg, 28-tab pack = £1.23. Label: 4

GLIBENCLAMIDE

Indications: diabetes mellitus
Cautions; Contra-indications; Side-effects: see notes above; **interactions:** Appendix 1 (antidiabetics)
Dose: initially 5 mg daily (elderly patients 2.5 mg (but see also notes above)), adjusted according to response; max. 15 mg daily; taken with breakfast

PoM **Glibenclamide** (Non-proprietary)
Tablets, glibenclamide 2.5 mg, net price 20 = 64p; 5 mg, 20 = 68p
Available from APS (Libanil®), Berk (Calabren®), Cox, Evans, Generics, Kerfoot, Lagap (Malix®)

PoM **Daonil**® (Hoechst)
Tablets, scored, glibenclamide 5 mg. Net price 28-tab pack = £2.70

PoM **Semi-Daonil**® (Hoechst)
Tablets, scored, glibenclamide 2.5 mg. Net price 28-tab pack = £1.62

PoM **Euglucon**® (Roussel)
Tablets, glibenclamide 2.5 mg, net price 28-tab = £1.62; 5 mg (scored), 28-tab = £2.70

GLICLAZIDE

Indications: diabetes mellitus
Cautions; Contra-indications; Side-effects: see notes above; **interactions:** Appendix 1 (antidiabetics)
Dose: initially, 40–80 mg daily, adjusted according to response; up to 160 mg as a single dose, with breakfast; higher doses divided; max. 320 mg daily

PoM **Diamicron**® (Servier)
Tablets, scored, gliclazide 80 mg. Net price 60 = £6.48

GLIPIZIDE

Indications: diabetes mellitus
Cautions; Contra-indications; Side-effects: see notes above; **interactions:** Appendix 1 (antidiabetics)
Dose: initially 2.5–5 mg daily, adjusted according to response; max. 40 mg daily; up to 15 mg may be given as a single dose before breakfast; higher doses divided

PoM **Glibenese**® (Pfizer)
Tablets, scored, glipizide 5 mg. Net price 56-tab pack = £3.30

PoM **Minodiab**® (Farmitalia Carlo Erba)
Tablets, glipizide 2.5 mg, net price 60 = £3.39; 5 mg (scored), 60 = £4.74

GLIQUIDONE

Indications: diabetes mellitus
Cautions; Contra-indications; Side-effects: see notes above; **interactions:** Appendix 1 (antidiabetics)
Dose: initially 15 mg daily before breakfast, adjusted to 45–60 mg daily in 2 or 3 divided doses; max. single dose 60 mg, max. daily dose 180 mg

PoM **Glurenorm**® (Sterling-Winthrop)
Tablets, scored, gliquidone 30 mg. Net price 100 = £15.21

TOLAZAMIDE

Indications: diabetes mellitus
Cautions; Contra-indications; Side-effects: see notes above; **interactions:** Appendix 1 (antidiabetics)
Dose: initially 100–250 mg daily with breakfast adjusted according to response; max. 1 g daily; higher doses divided

PoM **Tolanase**® (Upjohn)
Tablets, both scored, tolazamide 100 mg, net price 20 = £1.13; 250 mg, 20 = £2.46

TOLBUTAMIDE

Indications: diabetes mellitus
Cautions; Contra-indications; Side-effects: see notes above; **interactions:** Appendix 1 (antidiabetics)
Dose: 0.5–1.5 g (max. 2 g) daily in divided doses (see notes above)

PoM **Tolbutamide** (Non-proprietary)
Tablets, tolbutamide 500 mg. Net price 20 = 29p

PoM **Rastinon**® (Hoechst)
Tablets, scored, tolbutamide 500 mg. Net price 20 = 68p

Prices are **net**, see p. 1

6.1.2.2 BIGUANIDES

Metformin, the only available biguanide, has a different mode of action from the sulphonylureas, and is not interchangeable with them. It exerts its effect mainly by decreasing gluconeogenesis and by increasing peripheral utilisation of glucose; since it only acts in the presence of endogenous insulin it is only effective in diabetics with some residual functioning pancreatic islet cells. Metformin is used in the treatment of non-insulin-dependent diabetics when strict dieting and sulphonylurea treatment have failed to control diabetes, especially in overweight patients, in whom it may, if necessary, be used first. It can be used alone or with a sulphonylurea. It does not exert a hypoglycaemic action in non-diabetic subjects unless given in overdose. Gastro-intestinal side-effects are initially common, and may persist in some patients, particularly when very high doses such as 3 g daily are given.

Metformin is not free from the hazard of lactic acidosis but this occurs almost exclusively in renal failure patients, in whom it should not be used.

METFORMIN HYDROCHLORIDE

Indications: diabetes mellitus (see notes above)
Cautions: see notes above; **interactions:** Appendix 1 (antidiabetics)
Contra-indications: hepatic or renal impairment (withdraw if renal impairment suspected), predisposition to lactic acidosis, heart failure, severe infection or trauma, dehydration, alcoholism; pregnancy, breast-feeding
Side-effects: anorexia, nausea, vomiting, diarrhoea (usually transient), lactic acidosis (withdraw treatment), decreased vitamin-B_{12} absorption
Dose: 500 mg every 8 hours *or* 850 mg every 12 hours with or after food; max. 3 g daily in divided doses though most physicians limit this to 2 g daily (see notes above)

PoM **Metformin** (Non-proprietary)
Tablets, coated, metformin hydrochloride 500 mg, net price 21-tab pack = 50p, 84-tab pack = £2.02; 850 mg, 20 = 80p. Label: 21

PoM **Glucophage®** (Lipha)
Tablets, f/c, metformin hydrochloride 500 mg, net price 84 = £2.11; 850 mg, 56 = £2.34. Label: 21

PoM **Orabet®** (Lagap)
Tablets, f/c, metformin hydrochloride 500 mg, net price 20 = 48p; 850 mg, 20 = 80p. Label: 21

6.1.2.3 GUAR GUM

Guar gum, if taken in adequate quantities, results in some reduction of postprandial plasma-glucose concentrations in diabetes mellitus, probably by retarding carbohydrate absorption. It is also used to relieve symptoms of the dumping syndrome. Flatulence limits its use.

GUAR GUM

Indications: see notes above
Cautions: maintain adequate fluid intake; **interactions:** Appendix 1 (guar gum)
COUNSELLING. Preparations that swell in contact with liquid should always be carefully swallowed with water and should not be taken imediately before going to bed.
Contra-indications: gastro-intestinal obstruction
Side-effects: flatulence, abdominal distension, intestinal obstruction

Guarem® (Rybar)
Granules, ivory, sugar-free, guar gum 5 g/sachet. Net price 100 sachets = £15.31. Label: 13, counselling, food (see below), administration (see above)
Dose: 5 g stirred into 200 mL fluid 3 times daily immediately before main meals (or sprinkled on food and eaten accompanied by 200 mL fluid)

Guarina® (Norgine)
Granules, dispersible, guar gum 5 g/sachet. Net price 60 sachets = £8.95. Label: 13, counselling, food (see below), administration (see above)
Dose: 5 g stirred into 150 mL fluid immediately before main meals up to 3 times daily (or sprinkled on food and eaten accompanied by 150 mL of fluid)

6.1.3 Diabetic ketoacidosis

Soluble insulin is the only form of insulin that may be given intravenously and it should be used in the management of diabetic ketoacidotic and hyperosmolar nonketotic coma. It is preferable to use the type of insulin (highly purified or human sequence) that the patient has been using previously. It is necessary to achieve and to maintain an adequate plasma-insulin concentration until the metabolic disturbance is brought under control.

If a slow infusion pump is available, insulin is best given by the intravenous route; a single bolus (however large) will only achieve an adequate concentration for a short period of time. Adequate plasma concentrations are usually maintained with infusion rates of 6 units/hour for adults and 0.1 units/kg/hour for children. Insulin is diluted to 1 unit/mL (care in mixing: see Appendix 6).

If the response is judged inadequate the infusion rate may be doubled or quadrupled. When plasma glucose has fallen to 10 mmol/litre the rate of infusion can be dropped to about 0.02 units/kg/hour (1 to 2 units/hour for adults) and continued until the patient is ready to take food by mouth. The insulin infusion should not be stopped before subcutaneous insulin has been started.

If facilities for administering insulin by continuous infusion are inadequate it may be given by intramuscular injection. Absorption of insulin after intramuscular administration is usually rapid but may be impaired in patients who are hypotensive or who have poor peripheral circulation. An initial loading dose of 20 units is followed by 6 units given every hour until the plasma glucose concentration is less than 10 mmol/litre. Doses are then given by intramuscular injection every 2 hours.

In the presence of hypotension and poor tissue perfusion the intravenous route of insulin administration is preferable. Depots of insulin may build up during treatment therefore late hypoglycaemia should be watched for and treated appropriately.

Intravenous replacement of fluid and electrolytes with sodium chloride intravenous infusion is an essential part of the management of ketoacidosis; potassium chloride is included in the infusion as appropriate to prevent the hypokalaemia induced by the insulin. Sodium bicarbonate infusion (1.26% or 2.74%) is only used in cases of extreme acidosis and shock since the acid-base disturbance is normally corrected by the insulin. Glucose solution (10%) is infused once the blood glucose has decreased below 10 mmol/litre but insulin infusion must continue.

For reference to the role of glucose, see section 9.2.2.

6.1.4 Treatment of hypoglycaemia

Initially, glucose or 3 or 4 lumps of sugar should be taken with a little water. If necessary, this may be repeated in 10 to 15 minutes.

If hypoglycaemia causes unconsciousness, up to 50 mL of **50% glucose intravenous infusion** should be given intravenously (see section 9.2.2).

Glucagon can be given as an alternative to parenteral glucose in hypoglycaemia. It is a polypeptide hormone produced by the alpha cells of the islets of Langerhans. Its action is to increase plasma glucose concentration by mobilising glycogen stored in the liver.

Glucagon is used to treat acute hypoglycaemic reactions and it has the advantage that it can be injected by any route (intramuscular, subcutaneous, or intravenous) in a dose of 1 mg (1 unit) in circumstances when an intravenous injection of glucose would be difficult or impossible to administer.

It may be issued to close relatives of insulin-treated patients for emergency use in hypoglycaemic attacks. It is often advisable to prescribe on an 'if necessary' basis to all hospitalised insulin-treated patients, so that it may be given rapidly by the nurses during an hypoglycaemic emergency. If not effective in 20 minutes intravenous glucose should be given.

GLUCAGON

Indications: acute hypoglycaemia

Cautions: see notes above. Ineffective in chronic hypoglycaemia, starvation, and adrenal insufficiency

Contra-indications: insulinoma, phaeochromocytoma, glucagonoma

Side-effects: nausea, vomiting, rarely hypersensitivity reactions

Dose: by subcutaneous, intramuscular, or intravenous injection, adults and children 0.5–1 unit repeated after 20 minutes if necessary

Note. 1 unit of glucagon = 1 mg of glucagon or glucagon hydrochloride

PoM **Glucagon Injection,** powder for reconstitution, glucagon (as hydrochloride, with lactose). Net price 1-unit vial (Lilly) = £5.16; (Novo Nordisk) = £4.62; 10-unit vial (Novo Nordisk) = £27.06 (all with diluent)

CHRONIC HYPOGLYCAEMIA

Diazoxide, administered by mouth, is useful in the management of patients with chronic hypoglycaemia from excess endogenous insulin secretion, either from an islet cell tumour or islet cell hyperplasia. It has no place in the management of acute hypoglycaemia.

DIAZOXIDE

Indications: chronic intractable hypoglycaemia (for use in hypertensive crisis see section 2.5.1)

Cautions: ischaemic heart disease, pregnancy, labour, impaired renal function; haematological examinations and blood pressure monitoring required during prolonged treatment; growth, bone, and developmental checks in children; **interactions:** Appendix 1 (diazoxide)

Side-effects: anorexia, nausea, vomiting, hyperuricaemia, hypotension, oedema, tachycardia, arrhythmias, extrapyramidal effects; hypertrichosis on prolonged treatment

Dose: by mouth, adults and children, initially 5 mg/kg daily in 2–3 divided doses

PoM **Eudemine®** (A&H)

Tablets, s/c, diazoxide 50 mg. Net price 100 = £8.10

6.1.5 Treatment of diabetic neuropathy

Optimal diabetic control is beneficial for the management of *painful neuropathy*. Most patients should be treated with insulin, and relief can probably be accelerated by continuous insulin infusion. **Non-opioid analgesics** such as aspirin and paracetamol (see section 4.7.1) are indicated. Relief may also be obtained with the **tricyclic antidepressants**, amitriptyline, imipramine, and nortriptyline (see section 4.3.1) with or without a low dose of a **phenothiazine** (see section 4.2). **Carbamazepine** (see section 4.8.1) or mexiletine may be useful; lignocaine has also been used but needs further evaluation.

In *autonomic neuropathy* diabetic diarrhoea can often be aborted by two or three doses of **tetracycline** 250 mg (see section 5.1.3). Otherwise

codeine phosphate (see section 1.4.2) is the best drug, but all other antidiarrhoeal preparations can be tried.

In *neuropathic postural hypotension* an increased salt intake and the use of the **mineralocorticoid** fludrocortisone 100 to 400 micrograms daily (see section 6.3.1) help by increasing plasma volume but uncomfortable oedema is a common side-effect. Fludrocortisone can also be combined with **flurbiprofen** (see section 10.1.1) and **ephedrine hydrochloride** (see section 3.1.1.2).

Gustatory sweating can be treated with **antimuscarinics** (see section 1.2), poldine methylsulphate is the best but propantheline bromide may also be used; side-effects are common. In some patients with *neuropathic oedema*, **ephedrine hydrochloride** 30 to 60 mg three times daily offers impressive relief.

6.2 Thyroid and antithyroid drugs

6.2.1 Thyroid hormones

Thyroid hormones are used in hypothyroidism (myxoedema), and also in diffuse non-toxic goitre, Hashimoto's thyroiditis (lymphadenoid goitre), and thyroid carcinoma. Neonatal hypothyroidism requires prompt treatment for normal development.

Thyroxine sodium is the treatment of choice for *maintenance* therapy. The initial dose should not exceed 100 micrograms daily, preferably before breakfast, or 25 to 50 micrograms in elderly patients or those with cardiac disease, increased by 25 to 50 micrograms at intervals of 2 to 4 weeks. The usual maintenance dose to relieve hypothyroidism is 100 to 200 micrograms daily which can be administered as a single dose.

In infants a daily dose of 10 micrograms/kg up to a maximum of 50 micrograms daily should be given; subsequent therapy should reach 100 micrograms daily by 5 years and adult doses by 12 years, guided by clinical response, growth assessment, and measurements of plasma thyroxine and thyroid-stimulating hormone.

Liothyronine sodium has a similar action to thyroxine but is more rapidly metabolised; 20 micrograms is equivalent to 100 micrograms of thyroxine. Its effects develop after a few hours and disappear within 24 to 48 hours of discontinuing treatment. It may be used in *severe hypothyroid states* when a rapid response is desired.

Liothyronine by intravenous injection is the treatment of choice in *hypothyroid coma*. Adjunctive therapy includes intravenous fluids, hydrocortisone, and antibiotics; assisted ventilation is often required.

Dried **thyroid** should **not** be used as its effects are unpredictable.

THYROXINE SODIUM

Indications: hypothyroidism
Cautions: cardiovascular disorders, prolonged myxoedema, adrenal insufficiency; **interactions:** Appendix 1 (thyroxine)
Side-effects: arrhythmias, anginal pain, tachycardia, cramps in skeletal muscles, headache, restlessness, excitability, flushing, sweating, diarrhoea, excessive weight loss
Dose: see notes above

PoM **Thyroxine** (Non-proprietary)
Tablets, thyroxine sodium 25 micrograms, net price 20 = 7p; 50 micrograms, 20 = 4p; 100 micrograms, 20 = 5p

PoM **Eltroxin®** (Glaxo)
Tablets, scored, thyroxine sodium 50 micrograms, net price 20 = 5p; 100 micrograms, 20 = 6p

LIOTHYRONINE SODIUM

(L-Tri-iodothyronine sodium)
Indications: see notes above
Cautions; Contra-indications; Side-effects: see under Thyroxine Sodium; has a more rapid effect
Dose: by mouth, initially 10–20 micrograms daily in 2–3 divided doses gradually increased to 20 micrograms 3 times daily; elderly patients should receive smaller initial doses, gradually increased; CHILD, adult dose reduced in proportion to body-weight
By slow intravenous injection, hypothyroid coma, 5-20 micrograms repeated every 12 hours or more frequently (every 4 hours if necessary); alternatively 50 micrograms initially then 25 micrograms every 8 hours reducing to 25 micrograms twice daily

PoM **Tertroxin®** (Glaxo)
Tablets, scored, liothyronine sodium 20 micrograms. Net price 100-tab pack = 90p

PoM **Triiodothyronine** (Glaxo)
Injection, powder for reconstitution, liothyronine sodium (with dextran). Net price 20-microgram amp = £3.60

6.2.2 Antithyroid drugs

Antithyroid drugs are used to prepare patients for thyroidectomy. They are also used for prolonged periods in the hope of inducing life-long remission. In the UK carbimazole is the most commonly used drug. Propylthiouracil may be used in patients who suffer sensitivity reactions to carbimazole; sensitivity is not necessarily displayed to both drugs. Both drugs act primarily by interfering with the synthesis of thyroid hormones.

Carbimazole should be given in a daily dose of 30 to 60 mg and maintained at this dose until the patient becomes euthyroid, usually 4 to 8 weeks; the dose may then be progressively reduced to a maintenance dose of between 5 and 15 mg daily; therapy is usually given for 18 months. Children may be given 15 mg daily, adjusted according to

Prices are **net**, see p. 1

response. Rashes are common, and **propylthiouracil** may then be substituted. Pruritus and rashes can also be treated with antihistamines without discontinuing therapy, however patients should be advised to report any sore throat immediately because of the rare complication of agranulocytosis.

Antithyroid drugs may be given once daily although divided doses are still commonly used. Over-treatment with the rapid development of hypothyroidism is not uncommon and should be avoided particularly during pregnancy since it can cause fetal goitre.

A combination of carbimazole, 20 to 60 mg daily with thyroxine, 50 to 150 micrograms daily, may be used in a *blocking-replacement regimen*; therapy is again usually given for 18 months. The blocking-replacement regimen is not suitable during pregnancy.

Unless operation or use of radioactive iodine is planned, treatment should be for at least a year.

Before partial thyroidectomy **iodine** may be given for 10 to 14 days in addition to carbimazole or propylthiouracil to assist control and reduce vascularity of the thyroid. Iodine should not be used for long-term treatment since its antithyroid action tends to diminish.

Radioactive sodium iodide (^{131}I) solution is used increasingly for the treatment of thyrotoxicosis at all ages, particularly where medical therapy or compliance is a problem, in patients with cardiac disease, and in patients who relapse after thyroidectomy.

Propranolol is useful for rapid relief of thyrotoxic symptoms and may be used in conjunction with antithyroid drugs or as an adjunct to radioactive iodine. Beta-blockers are also useful in neonatal thyrotoxicosis and in supra-ventricular arrhythmias due to hyperthyroidism. Propranolol may be used in conjunction with iodine to prepare mildly thyrotoxic patients for surgery but it is still preferable to make the patient euthyroid with carbimazole before surgery. Laboratory tests of thyroid function are not altered by beta-blockers. Most experience in treating thyrotoxicosis has been gained with propranolol but **nadolol** and **sotalol** are also used. For doses and preparations see section 2.4.

Thyrotoxic crisis ('thyroid storm') requires emergency treatment with intravenous administration of fluids, propranolol (5 mg) and hydrocortisone (100 mg every 6 hours, as sodium succinate), as well as oral iodine solution and carbimazole or propylthiouracil which may need to be administered by nasogastric tube.

PREGNANCY AND BREAST-FEEDING. Radioactive iodine therapy is contra-indicated during pregnancy. Propylthiouracil and carbimazole can be given. Both drugs cross the placenta and in high doses may cause fetal goitre and hypothyroidism. Rarely, carbimazole has been associated with aplasia cutis of the neonate.

Carbimazole and propylthiouracil transfer to breast milk but this does not preclude breast-feeding as long as neonatal development is closely monitored.

CARBIMAZOLE

Indications: hyperthyroidism
Cautions: large goitre; pregnancy, breast-feeding (see notes)
Side-effects: nausea, headache, rashes and pruritus, arthralgia; rarely alopecia, agranulocytosis, jaundice
Dose: see notes above

PoM **Neo-Mercazole 5**® (Nicholas)
Tablets, pink, scored, carbimazole 5 mg. Net price 20 = 45p

PoM **Neo-Mercazole 20**® (Nicholas)
Tablets, pink, carbimazole 20 mg. Net price 20 = £1.84

IODINE AND IODIDE

Indications: thyrotoxicosis (pre-operative)
Cautions: pregnancy, children; not for long-term treatment
Contra-indications: breast-feeding
Side-effects: hypersensitivity reactions including coryza-like symptoms, headache, lachrymation, conjunctivitis, pain in salivary glands, laryngitis, bronchitis, rashes; on prolonged treatment depression, insomnia, impotence; goitre in infants of mothers taking iodides

Aqueous Iodine Oral Solution (Lugol's Solution), iodine 5%, potassium iodide 10% in purified water, freshly boiled and cooled, total iodine 130 mg/mL. Net price 100 mL = £1.43. Label: 27
Dose: 0.1–0.3 mL 3 times daily well diluted with milk or water

PROPYLTHIOURACIL

Indications: hyperthyroidism
Cautions; Side-effects: see under Carbimazole; also rarely tendency to haemorrhage; reduce dose in renal impairment; systemic lupus erythematosus reported
Dose: 300–450 mg daily in divided doses

PoM **Propylthiouracil Tablets,** propylthiouracil 50 mg. Net price 20 = £1.50

6.3 Corticosteroids

6.3.1 Replacement therapy
6.3.2 Comparisons of corticosteroids
6.3.3 Disadvantages of corticosteroids
6.3.4 Clinical management

6.3.1 Replacement therapy

The adrenal cortex normally secretes hydrocortisone (cortisol) which has glucocorticoid activity and weak mineralocorticoid activity. It also secretes the mineralocorticoid aldosterone.

In deficiency states, physiological replacement

is best achieved with a combination of **hydrocortisone**[1] and the mineralocorticoid **fludrocortisone**; hydrocortisone alone does not usually provide sufficient mineralocorticoid activity for complete replacement.

In *Addison's disease* or following adrenalectomy, **hydrocortisone** 20 to 30 mg daily by mouth is usually required. This is given in 2 doses, the larger in the morning and the smaller in the evening, mimicking the normal diurnal rhythm of cortisol secretion. The optimum daily dose is determined on the basis of clinical response. Glucocorticoid therapy is supplemented by fludrocortisone 50 to 300 micrograms daily.

In *acute adrenocortical insufficiency*, **hydrocortisone** is given intravenously (preferably as sodium succinate) in doses of 100 mg every 6 to 8 hours in sodium chloride intravenous infusion 0.9%.

In *hypopituitarism* glucocorticoids should be given as in adrenocortical insufficiency, but since the production of aldosterone is also regulated by the renin-angiotensin system a mineralocorticoid is not usually required. Additional replacement therapy with thyroxine (section 6.2.1) and sex hormones (section 6.4) should be given as indicated by the pattern of hormone deficiency.

Corticosteroid cover for *adrenalectomy*, for *hypophysectomy* or for operations on patients on long-term treatment with corticosteroids is determined logically from the knowledge that in a normal person major stress will not lead to the secretion of more than 300 mg of cortisol in 24 hours; once the stress is over, cortisol production rapidly returns to its usual level of approximately 20 mg per 24 hours. A simple way of mimicking this is to administer hydrocortisone. On the day of operation hydrocortisone 100 mg (usually as the succinate) is given by intramuscular or intravenous injection with the premedication, and repeated every 8 hours. In the absence of complications, the dose can be halved every 24 hours until a normal maintenance dose of 20 to 30 mg per 24 hours is reached on the 5th postoperative day.

FLUDROCORTISONE ACETATE

Indications: mineralocorticoid replacement in adrenocortical insufficiency

Cautions; Contra-indications; Side-effects: section 6.3.3

Dose: adrenocortical insufficiency, 50–300 micrograms daily; CHILD 5 micrograms/kg daily

PoM **Florinef**® (Squibb)

Tablets, pink, scored, fludrocortisone acetate 100 micrograms. Net price 20 = 96p. Label: 10 steroid card

1. Cortisone has generally been superseded by hydrocortisone; management with the more potent synthetic glucocorticoids such as prednisolone (with fludrocortisone) though practicable, offers no advantage. They tend to have less mineralocorticoid activity than hydrocortisone and their greater glucocorticoid activity is only of advantage in the treatment of inflammatory and neoplastic disease.

CORTISONE ACETATE

Section 6.3.4

HYDROCORTISONE

Section 6.3.4

6.3.2 Comparisons of corticosteroids

Betamethasone, dexamethasone, hydrocortisone, prednisolone, and prednisone are used for their anti-inflammatory effect; the following table shows equivalent anti-inflammatory doses.

Equivalent Anti-inflammatory Doses of Glucocorticoids

Drug	Equivalent anti-inflammatory dose (mg)
Betamethasone	0.75
Cortisone acetate	25
Dexamethasone	0.75
Hydrocortisone	20
Methylprednisolone	4
Prednisolone	5
Prednisone	5
Triamcinolone	4

Note. This table takes no account of mineralocorticoid effects (see text below), nor does it take account of variations in duration of action.

In comparing the relative potencies of corticosteroids in terms of their anti-inflammatory (glucocorticoid) effects it should be borne in mind that high anti-inflammatory (glucocorticoid) activity in itself is of no advantage unless it occurs in conjunction with relatively low mineralocorticoid activity so that the mineralocorticoid effect on water and electrolytes is not also increased.

The mineralocorticoid activity of **fludrocortisone** is so high that its anti-inflammatory activity is of no clinical relevance.

The mineralocorticoid effects of **cortisone** and **hydrocortisone** are too high for them to be used on a long-term basis for inflammatory disease suppression since fluid retention would be too great, but they are suitable for adrenal replacement therapy (section 6.3.1); hydrocortisone is preferred because cortisone is only active after conversion in the liver to hydrocortisone. Hydrocortisone is also used by intravenous injection for the emergency management of some conditions (section 6.3.4). The relatively moderate anti-inflammatory potency of hydrocortisone makes it a first-choice corticosteroid for the management of inflammatory skin conditions because side-effects (both topical and caused by absorption) are less marked (see section 13.4); cortisone is not active topically.

Prednisolone has predominantly glucocorticoid activity and is the corticosteroid most commonly used by mouth for long-term administration. **Prednisone** has a similar level of glucocorticoid activity but is only active after conversion in the liver to prednisolone; it is therefore not recommended.

Betamethasone and **dexamethasone** have very high glucocorticoid activity in conjunction with insignificant mineralocorticoid activity. This makes them particularly suitable for high-dose therapy in conditions where water retention would be a disadvantage (see *cerebral oedema*, section 6.3.4).

They also have a long duration of action and this, coupled with their lack of mineralocorticoid action makes them particularly suitable for conditions which require suppression of corticotrophin secretion (see *congenital adrenal hyperplasia*, section 6.3.4). Some esters of betamethasone and of **beclomethasone** exert a considerably more marked topical effect (e.g. on the skin or the lungs) than when given by mouth; use is made of this to obtain topical effects without corresponding systemic activity (e.g. for skin applications and asthma inhalations).

Stimulation of the adrenal cortex by **corticotrophin** or **tetracosactrin** has been used as an alternative to corticosteroids to control certain diseases; there is no close relationship between the dose producing satisfactory clinical improvement and the equivalent dose of oral corticosteroid producing the same degree of improvement.

6.3.3 Disadvantages of corticosteroids

Overdosage or prolonged use may exaggerate some of the normal physiological actions of corticosteroids.

Mineralocorticoid effects include *hypertension*, *sodium and water retention*, *potassium loss*, and *muscle weakness*. They are most marked with fludrocortisone, but are significant with cortisone, hydrocortisone, corticotrophin, and tetracosactrin. Mineralocorticoid actions are negligible with the high potency glucocorticoids, betamethasone and dexamethasone, and occur only slightly with methylprednisolone, prednisolone, prednisone, and triamcinolone.

Glucocorticoid effects include *diabetes* and *osteoporosis* which is a danger, particularly in the elderly, as it may result in osteoporotic fractures for example of the hip or vertebrae; in addition administration of high doses is associated with *avascular necrosis* of the femoral head. *Mental disturbances* may occur; a serious paranoid state or depression with risk of suicide may be induced, particularly in patients with a history of mental disorder. *Euphoria* is frequently observed.

Corticosteroid therapy is weakly linked with *peptic ulceration*; the use of soluble or enteric-coated preparations to reduce the risk is speculative only. Modification of tissue reactions may result in spread of *infection*; suppression of clinical signs may allow septicaemia or tuberculosis to reach an advanced stage before being recognised.

High doses of corticosteroids may cause *Cushing's syndrome*, with moon face, striae, and acne; it is usually reversible on withdrawal of treatment, but this must always be gradually tapered to avoid symptoms of acute adrenal insufficiency (see Adrenal Suppression).

In children, administration of corticosteroids may result in *suppression of growth*. Corticosteroids given in high dosage during *pregnancy* may affect adrenal development in the child.

For details of the adverse effects of topical and of systemic corticosteroid therapy on the *skin*, see sections 13.4 and 13.5.

For details of the adverse effects of topical and of systemic corticosteroid therapy on the *eye*, see section 11.4.

ADRENAL SUPPRESSION. Administration of corticosteroids suppresses the secretion of corticotrophin and may lead to adrenal atrophy; withdrawal of treatment must therefore be gradual to avoid symptoms of *acute adrenal insufficiency*. When long-term treatment is to be discontinued, the dose should be reduced gradually over a period of several weeks or months depending on the dosage and duration of the therapy. Too rapid a reduction of corticosteroid dosage can lead to *acute adrenal insufficiency*, *hypotension*, and *death*. A number of minor withdrawal symptoms may also result such as *rhinitis*, *conjunctivitis*, *loss of weight*, *arthralgia*, and *painful itchy skin nodules*.

Adrenal atrophy can persist for years after stopping prolonged corticosteroid therapy, therefore any illness or surgical emergency may require temporary reintroduction of corticosteroid therapy to compensate for lack of sufficient adrenocortical response. Anaesthetists **must** therefore know whether a patient is taking or has been taking corticosteroids to avoid a precipitous fall in blood pressure during anaesthesia or in the immediate postoperative period. Patients should therefore carry cards giving details of their dosage and possible complications. These 'steroid cards' can be obtained from local Family Practitioner Committees or

DHSS Printing and Stationery Unit,
Room 110, North Fylde Central Office,
Norcross, Blackpool FY5 3TA

In Scotland 'steroid cards' are available from Health Boards.

Pharmacists may obtain 'steroid cards' from the Royal Pharmaceutical Society of Great Britain.

Interactions: see Appendix 1 (corticosteroids and corticotrophin).

6.3.4 Clinical management

Corticosteroids should not be used unless the benefits justify the hazards; the lowest dose that will produce an acceptable response should be used (see also under Administration, below). Dosage varies widely in different diseases and in different patients.

If the use of a corticosteroid can save or prolong life, as in *exfoliative dermatitis*, *pemphigus*, or *acute leukaemia*, high doses may need to be given, as the complications of therapy are likely to be less serious than the effects of the disease itself.

When long-term corticosteroid therapy is used in relatively benign chronic diseases such as *rheumatoid arthritis* the danger of treatment may become greater than the disabilities produced by the disease. To minimise side-effects the maintenance dose should be kept as low as possible (see also section 10.1.2.1).

When potentially less harmful measures are ineffective corticosteroids are used topically for the treatment of *inflammatory conditions of the skin* (see section 13.4). Corticosteroids should be avoided or used only under specialist supervision in *psoriasis* (see section 13.5).

Corticosteroids are used both topically (by rectum) and systemically (by mouth or intravenously) in the management of *ulcerative colitis* and *Crohn's disease* (see sections 1.5 and 1.7.2).

Use can be made of the mineralocorticoid activity of fludrocortisone to treat *postural hypotension* in autonomic neuropathy (see section 6.1.5).

Very high doses of corticosteroids have been given by intravenous injection in *septic shock*. However a recent study (using methylprednisolone sodium succinate) did not demonstrate efficacy and, moreover, suggested a higher mortality in some subsets of patients given the high-dose corticosteroid therapy.

Dexamethasone and betamethasone have little if any mineralocorticoid action and their long duration of action makes them particularly suitable for suppressing corticotrophin secretion in *congenital adrenal hyperplasia* where the dose should be tailored to the individual on clinical grounds and by measurement of adrenal androgens and 17-hydroxyprogesterone. In common with all glucocorticoids their suppressive action on the hypothalamic-pituitary-adrenal axis is greatest and most prolonged when they are given at night. In most normal subjects a single dose of 1 mg of dexamethasone at night, depending on weight, is sufficient to inhibit corticotrophin secretion for 24 hours. This is the basis of the 'overnight dexamethasone suppression test' for diagnosing Cushing's syndrome.

Betamethasone and dexamethasone are also appropriate for conditions where water retention would be a disadvantage, as for example in treating traumatic *cerebral oedema* with doses of 12 to 20 mg daily.

In acute hypersensitivity reactions such as *angioedema* of the upper respiratory tract and *anaphylactic shock*, corticosteroids are indicated as an adjunct to emergency treatment with adrenaline (see section 3.4.3). In such cases hydrocortisone (as sodium succinate) by intravenous injection in a dose of 100 to 300 mg may be required.

Corticosteroids are preferably used by inhalation in the management of *asthma* (see section 3.2) but systemic therapy in association with bronchodilators is required for the emergency treatment of severe acute asthma (see section 3.1.1).

Corticosteroids may also be useful in conditions such as *rheumatic fever*, *chronic active hepatitis*, and *sarcoidosis*; they may also lead to remissions

---

I am a patient on—

STEROID TREATMENT

which must not be stopped abruptly

and in the case of intercurrent illness may have to be increased

full details are available from the hospital or general practitioners shown overleaf →

STC1

INSTRUCTIONS

1. *DO NOT STOP taking the steroid drug except on medical advice. Always have a supply in reserve.*
2. *In case of feverish illness, accident, operation (emergency or otherwise), diarrhoea or vomiting the steroid treatment MUST be continued. Your doctor may wish you to have a LARGER DOSE or an INJECTION at such times.*
3. *If the tablets cause indigestion consult your doctor AT ONCE.*
4. *Always carry this card while receiving steroid treatment and show it to any doctor, dentist, nurse or midwife or anyone else who is giving you treatment.*
5. *After your treatment has finished you must still tell any doctor, dentist, nurse or midwife or anyone else who is giving you treatment that you have had steroid treatment.*

of acquired *haemolytic anaemia*, and some cases of the *nephrotic syndrome* and *thrombocytopenic purpura*.

Corticosteroids can improve the prognosis of serious conditions such as *systemic lupus erythematosus*, *temporal arteritis*, and *polyarteritis nodosa*; the effects of the disease process may be suppressed and symptoms relieved, but the underlying condition is not cured, although it may ultimately burn itself out. It is usual to begin therapy in these conditions at fairly high dose, such as 40 to 60 mg prednisolone daily, and then to reduce the dose to the lowest commensurate with disease control.

For other reference to the use of corticosteroids see section 11.4 (eye), 12.1.1 (otitis externa), 12.2.1 (allergic rhinitis), and 12.3.1 (aphthous ulcers).

ADMINISTRATION. Whenever possible *local treatment* with creams, intra-articular injections, inhalations, eye-drops, or enemas should be used in preference to *systemic treatment*. The suppressive action of a corticosteroid on cortisol secretion is least when it is given in the morning, therefore in an attempt to reduce pituitary-adrenal suppression a corticosteroid (usually prednisolone) should normally be taken as a single dose in the morning. In an attempt to reduce pituitary-adrenal suppression further, the total dose for two days can sometimes be taken as a single dose on alternate days; alternate-day administration has not been very successful in the management of asthma (see section 3.2) but it can be suitable for rheumatoid arthritis (see section 10.1.2). Pituitary-adrenal suppression can also be reduced by means of intermittent therapy with short courses. In some conditions it may be possible to reduce the dose of corticosteroid by adding a small dose of an immunosuppressive drug (see section 8.2.1).

CHILDREN. In children the indications for corticosteroids are the same as for adults but risks are greater. The implications of starting these drugs are serious, and they should be used only when specifically indicated, in a minimal dosage, and for the shortest possible time. Prolonged or continuous treatment is rarely justified.

PREDNISOLONE

Indications: suppression of inflammatory and allergic disorders

Cautions; Contra-indications; Side-effects: section 6.3.3

Dose: *by mouth*, initially, up to 10–20 mg daily (severe disease, up to 60 mg daily), preferably taken in the morning after breakfast; can often be reduced within a few days but may need to be continued for several weeks or months

Maintenance, usual range, 2.5–15 mg daily, but higher doses may be needed; cushingoid side-effects increasingly likely with doses above 7.5 mg daily

See also section 3.2 (asthma), section 8.2.2 (immunosuppression), and section 10.1.2 (rheumatic diseases)

By intramuscular injection, prednisolone acetate, 25–100 mg once or twice weekly (for preparation see section 10.1.2.2)

PoM **Prednisolone** (Non-proprietary)
Tablets, prednisolone 1 mg, net price 20 = 7p; 5 mg, 20 = 15p. Label: 10 steroid card, 21

PoM **Deltacortril Enteric®** (Pfizer)
Tablets, both e/c, prednisolone 2.5 mg (brown), net price 56-tab pack = 62p; 5 mg (red), 56-tab pack = £1.18. Label: 5, 10 steroid card, 25

PoM **Deltastab®** (Boots)
Tablets, scored, prednisolone 1 mg, net price 20 = 5p; 5 mg, 20 = 12p. Label: 10 steroid card, 21
Injection, see section 10.1.2.2

PoM **Precortisyl®** (Roussel)
Tablets, prednisolone 1 mg, net price 20 = 7p; 5 mg (scored), 20 = 15p. Label: 10 steroid card, 21

PoM **Precortisyl Forte®** (Roussel)
Tablets, scored, prednisolone 25 mg. Net price 20 = £1.56. Label: 10 steroid card, 21

PoM **Prednesol®** (Glaxo)
Tablets, pink, scored, soluble, prednisolone 5 mg (as sodium phosphate). Net price 20 = £1.15. Label: 10 steroid card, 13, 21

PoM **Sintisone®** (Farmitalia Carlo Erba)
Tablets, scored, prednisolone steaglate 6.65 mg (≡ prednisolone 5 mg). Net price 20 = £1.29. Label: 10 steroid card, 21

BETAMETHASONE

Indications: suppression of inflammatory and allergic disorders; congenital adrenal hyperplasia (section 6.3.1); cerebral oedema (section 6.3.2)

Cautions; Contra-indications; Side-effects: section 6.3.4

Dose: *by mouth*, usual range 0.5–5 mg daily. See also Administration (above)

By intramuscular injection or slow intravenous injection or infusion, 4–20 mg, repeated up to 4 times in 24 hours; CHILD, *by slow intravenous injection*, up to 1 year 1 mg, 1–5 years 2 mg, 6–12 years 4 mg

PoM **Betnelan®** (Glaxo)
Tablets, scored, betamethasone 500 micrograms. Net price 20 = 73p. Label: 10 steroid card, 21

PoM **Betnesol®** (Glaxo)
Tablets, pink, scored, soluble, betamethasone 500 micrograms (as sodium phosphate). Net price 20 = 64p. Label: 10 steroid card, 13, 21
Injection, betamethasone 4 mg (as sodium phosphate)/mL. Net price 1-mL amp = 65p. Label: 10 steroid card

CORTISONE ACETATE

Indications: section 6.3.1

Cautions; Contra-indications; Side-effects: section 6.3.3

Dose: *by mouth*, replacement therapy, 25–37.5 mg daily in divided doses

PoM **Cortisone Acetate** (Non-proprietary)
Tablets, cortisone acetate 5 mg, net price 20 = 13p; 25 mg, 20 = 63p. Label: 10 steroid card, 21

PoM **Cortistab®** (Boots)
Tablets, both scored, cortisone acetate 5 mg, net price 20 = 13p; 25 mg, 20 = 52p. Label: 10 steroid card, 21

PoM **Cortisyl®** (Roussel)
Tablets, scored, cortisone acetate 25 mg. Net price 20 = £1.19. Label: 10 steroid card, 21

DEXAMETHASONE

Indications: suppression of inflammatory and allergic disorders; shock; diagnosis of Cushing's disease, congenital adrenal hyperplasia (both section 6.3.1); cerebral oedema (section 6.3.4)

Cautions; Contra-indications; Side-effects: section 6.3.3; perineal irritation may follow intravenous administration of the phosphate ester

Dose: *by mouth*, usual range 0.5–9 mg daily. See also Administration (above)

By intramuscular injection or slow intravenous injection or infusion (as dexamethasone phosphate), initially 0.5–20 mg; CHILD 200–500 micrograms/kg daily

Cerebral oedema (as dexamethasone phosphate), *by intravenous injection*, 10 mg initially, then 4 mg *by intramuscular injection* every 6 hours as required for 2–10 days

PoM **Dexamethasone** (Organon)
Tablets, dexamethasone 500 micrograms, net price 20 = 64p; 2 mg, 20 = £1.73. Label: 10 steroid card, 21
Injection, dexamethasone sodium phosphate 5 mg/mL (≡ dexamethasone 4 mg/mL, dexamethasone phosphate 4.8 mg/mL). Net price 1-mL amp = 83p; 2-mL vial = £1.27. Label: 10 steroid card

PoM **Decadron®** (MSD)
Tablets, scored, dexamethasone 500 micrograms. Net price 20 = 91p. Label: 10 steroid card, 21
Injection, dexamethasone phosphate 4 mg/mL (≡ dexamethasone 3.33 mg/mL, dexamethasone sodium phosphate 4.17 mg/mL). Net price 2-mL vial = £1.76. Label: 10 steroid card

PoM **Decadron Shock-Pak®** (MSD)
Injection, dexamethasone 20 mg/mL (≡ dexamethasone sodium phosphate 25 mg/mL). Net price 5-mL vial = £15.13. Label: 10 steroid card
Dose: shock, *by intravenous injection or infusion*, 2–6 mg/kg, repeated if necessary after 2–6 hours (but see section 6.3.2)

FLUDROCORTISONE

See section 6.3.1

HYDROCORTISONE

Indications: adrenocortical insufficiency (section 6.3.1); suppression of inflammatory and allergic disorders; shock (section 6.3.4)

Cautions; Contra-indications; Side-effects: section 6.3.3; perineal irritation may follow intravenous administration of the phosphate ester

Dose: *by mouth*, replacement therapy, 20–30 mg daily in divided doses—see section 6.3.1

By intramuscular injection or slow intravenous injection or infusion, 100–500 mg, 3–4 times in 24 hours or as required; CHILD *by slow intravenous injection* up to 1 year 25 mg, 1–5 years 50 mg, 6–12 years 100 mg

Anaphylactic shock—see section 6.3.2

Oral preparations

PoM **Hydrocortistab®** (Boots)
Tablets, scored, hydrocortisone 20 mg. Net price 20 = 56p. Label: 10 steroid card, 21

PoM **Hydrocortone®** (MSD)
Tablets, scored, hydrocortisone 10 mg, net price 20 = 46p; 20 mg, 20 = 71p. Label: 10 steroid card, 21

Parenteral preparations

PoM **Hydrocortisone Sodium Succinate** (Organon)
Injection, powder for reconstitution, hydrocortisone (as sodium succinate). Net price 100-mg vial = 67p; 500-mg vial = £3.39. Label: 10 steroid card

PoM **Efcortelan Soluble®** (Glaxo)
Injection, powder for reconstitution, hydrocortisone (as sodium succinate). Net price 100-mg vial (with 2-mL amp water for injections) = 67p. Label: 10 steroid card

PoM **Efcortesol®** (Glaxo)
Injection, hydrocortisone 100 mg (as sodium phosphate)/mL. Net price 1-mL amp = 75p; 5-mL amp = £3.40. Label: 10 steroid card

PoM **Solu-Cortef®** (Upjohn)
Injection, powder for reconstitution, hydrocortisone (as sodium succinate). Net price 100-mg vial (with 2-mL amp water for injections) = £1.02; without water for injections = 96p. Label: 10 steroid card

METHYLPREDNISOLONE

Indications: suppression of inflammatory and allergic disorders; cerebral oedema

Cautions; Contra-indications; Side-effects: section 6.3.3; rapid intravenous administration of large doses has been associated with cardiovascular collapse

Dose: *by mouth*, usual range 2–40 mg daily. See also Administration (above)

By intramuscular injection or slow intravenous injection or infusion, initially 10–500 mg; graft rejection, up to 1 g daily *by intravenous infusion* for up to 3 days

Oral preparations

PoM **Medrone®** (Upjohn)
Tablets, scored, methylprednisolone 2 mg (pink), net price 20 = £1.79; 4 mg, 30 = £2.69; 16 mg, 14-tab pack = £6.68. Label: 10 steroid card, 21

Parenteral preparations

PoM **Min-I-Mix Methylprednisolone®** (IMS)
Injection, powder for reconstitution, methylprednisolone sodium succinate. Net price 0.5-g vial = £10.97; 1-g vial = £18.06. Label: 10 steroid card

PoM **Solu-Medrone®** (Upjohn)
Injection, powder for reconstitution, methylprednisolone (as sodium succinate) (all with solvent). Net price 40-mg vial = £1.32; 125-mg vial = £3.96; 500-mg vial = £11.77; 1-g vial = £21.21; 2-g vial = £40.27. Label: 10 steroid card

Intramuscular depot
PoM **Depo-Medrone®** (Upjohn)
Injection (aqueous suspension), methylprednisolone acetate 40 mg/mL. Net price 1-mL vial = £2.59; 2-mL vial = £4.65; 3-mL vial = £6.75. Label: 10 steroid card
Dose: by deep intramuscular injection, 40–120 mg, repeated every 2–3 weeks if required

PREDNISONE

Indications: suppression of inflammatory and allergic disorders
Cautions; Contra-indications; Side-effects: section 6.3.3. Avoid in liver disease
Dose: see Prednisolone

PoM **Prednisone** (Non-proprietary)
Tablets, prednisone 1 mg, net price 20 = 10p; 5 mg, 20 = 15p. Label: 10 steroid card, 21
PoM **Decortisyl®** (Roussel)
Tablets, scored, prednisone 5 mg. Net price 20 = 15p. Label: 10 steroid card, 21

TRIAMCINOLONE

Indications: suppression of inflammatory and allergic disorders
Cautions; Contra-indications; Side-effects: section 6.3.3. Triamcinolone in high dosage has a tendency to cause proximal myopathy and should be avoided in chronic therapy
Dose: *by mouth*, 2–24 mg daily. See also Administration (above)
By deep intramuscular injection, 40 mg of acetonide for depot effect, repeated at intervals according to the patient's response; max. single dose 100 mg

PoM **Kenalog®** (Squibb)
Injection (aqueous suspension), triamcinolone acetonide 40 mg/mL. Net price 1-mL vial = £1.70; 1-mL syringe = £2.11; 2-mL syringe = £3.66. Label: 10 steroid card
PoM **Ledercort®** (Lederle)
Tablets, triamcinolone 2 mg (blue), net price 20 = £1.94; 4 mg, 20 = £3.87. Label: 10 steroid card, 21

6.4 Sex hormones

Sex hormones are described under the following section headings:

6.4.1 Female sex hormones
6.4.2 Male sex hormones and antagonists
6.4.3 Anabolic steroids

6.4.1 Female sex hormones

6.4.1.1 Oestrogens and HRT
6.4.1.2 Progestogens

6.4.1.1 OESTROGENS AND HRT

Oestrogens are necessary for the development of female secondary sexual characteristics; they also stimulate myometrial hypertrophy with endometrial hyperplasia.

Oestrogen therapy is given cyclically or continuously for a number of gynaecological conditions. If long-term therapy is required a progestogen should be added cyclically to prevent cystic hyperplasia of the endometrium and possible transformation to cancer. This cyclical addition of a progestogen is not necessary if the patient has had a hysterectomy.

PRIMARY AMENORRHOEA. After assessment by a specialist an oestrogen such as ethinyloestradiol is administered continuously together with cyclical progestogen, or a low-dose combined oral contraceptive is given (see section 7.3.1).

HORMONE REPLACEMENT THERAPY (HRT). Menopausal *vasomotor symptoms* and menopausal *vaginitis* are alleviated by administration of small doses of oestrogen. There is also good evidence that small doses of oestrogen given for several years starting in the perimenopausal period will diminish postmenopausal *osteoporosis* and reduce the incidence of *stroke and myocardial infarction*. There is an increased risk of *endometrial cancer* (countered by cyclical progestogen, see below) and, after some years of use, possibly a slightly increased risk of *breast cancer*.

Hormone replacement therapy (HRT) is indicated for menopausal women whose lives are inconvenienced by *vaginal atrophy* or *vasomotor instability*. Vaginal atrophy may respond to a short course of oestrogen cream given for a few weeks and repeated if necessary. Oral therapy is needed for vasomotor symptoms and should be given for at least a year; in a woman with a uterus cyclical progestogen should be added to reduce the risk of endometrial cancer (see above). Hormone replacement therapy is also indicated for women with *early natural or surgical menopause (before age 45)*, since they are at high risk of osteoporosis; in a woman with a uterus cyclical progestogen should again be added to reduce the risk of endometrial cancer (see above); hormone replacement therapy should be given to the age of at least 50 and possibly for a further 10 years.

Long-term hormone replacement therapy in general is almost certainly favourable in risk benefit terms for menopausal women *without a uterus* because they do not require cyclical progestogen therapy; it should probably be continued for about 10 years. The picture is less clear for menopausal women *with a uterus* because the need for cyclical administration of progestogen may blunt the protective effect of low-dose oestrogen against myocardial infarction and stroke; any effect of the progestogen (favourable or otherwise) on breast cancer is not yet known. Nevertheless, risk factors for osteoporosis should be borne in mind and, if there are several, consideration given to hormone replacement therapy. Risk factors include *recent corticosteroid therapy or any disease predisposing to osteoporosis, thinness, lack of exercise, alcoholism or smoking, and fracture of a hip or forearm before the age of 65; women of Afro-Caribbean origin appear to be less susceptible than those who are white or Asian.*

Choice. The choice of oestrogen for hormone replacement therapy is not straightforward and depends on an overall balance of indication, risk, and convenience. Vaginitis in a woman with a uterus can only be treated for a few weeks with an oestrogen, without addition of cyclical progestogen; the constraint includes topical cream since a significant amount is absorbed through the vaginal mucosa. Ethinyloestradiol is suitable for long-term continuous oral therapy in a woman without a uterus but conjugated oestrogens may be preferred. A woman with a uterus requires a regimen of continuous or cyclical oestrogen with cyclical progestogen for the last 10 to 13 days of the cycle; for this purpose combined oral preparations may be suitable. All oral preparations of oestrogen are subject to first-pass metabolism in the liver and intestine, therefore subcutaneous or transdermal administration reflects more closely endogenous hormone activity. In the case of subcutaneous implants, problems have been encountered with the recurrence of vasomotor symptoms at supraphysiological plasma concentrations; moreover, there is evidence of prolonged endometrial stimulation after discontinuation (calling for continued cyclical progestogen). Transdermal applications are convenient for vasomotor symptoms but oral progestogen is still needed on a cyclical basis if the woman has a uterus; they have not yet been fully assessed for protection against osteoporosis.

Providing calcium intake is adequate calcium supplements do not confer additional benefit on hormone replacement therapy (see section 9.5.1).

SUPPRESSION OF LACTATION. Oestrogens are no longer used to suppress lactation because of their association with thrombo-embolism. **Bromocriptine** (section 6.7.1) is used where necessary.

NEOPLASIA. Stilboestrol is used mainly in neoplastic conditions (see section 8.3.1)

ETHINYLOESTRADIOL

Indications: see notes above

Cautions: prolonged exposure to unopposed oestrogens may increase risk of development of endometrial cancer (see notes above); breast-feeding, diabetes, epilepsy, asthma, hypertension, migraine, cardiac or renal disease, history of jaundice, contact lenses (may irritate); may interfere with results of thyroid-function tests and cortisol estimations by increasing concentrations of hormone-binding protein; **interactions:** Appendix 1 (oestrogens)

SURGERY. For a warning on oestrogens and elective surgery, see Combined Oral Contraceptives, section 7.3.1

Contra-indications: pregnancy; oestrogen-dependent cancer, history of thrombo-embolism, hepatic impairment, Dubin-Johnson and Rotor syndromes, endometriosis, porphyria, sickle-cell anaemia (but see also Oral Contraceptives), undiagnosed vaginal bleeding, history of herpes gestationis; deterioration of otosclerosis

Side-effects: nausea and vomiting, weight gain, breast enlargement and tenderness, withdrawal bleeding, sodium retention with oedema and hypertension (minimal for HRT), changes in liver function, jaundice, thrombosis (but for HRT see notes above), rashes and chloasma, depression, headache, endometrial carcinoma in postmenopausal women

Dose: menopausal symptoms 10–20 micrograms daily continuously *or* for 21 days, repeated after 7 days, with progestogen from day 17 to day 26 of cycle if uterus intact

Primary amenorrhoea, 10 micrograms on alternate days increasing to a max. of 50 micrograms daily continuously with a progestogen for the last 5 days of month

Hereditary haemorrhagic telangiectasia, 0.5–1 mg daily (specialist use only)

Oestrogen-only

Note. Unsuitable for long-term use alone in women with an intact uterus (who require addition of cyclical progestogen)

PoM **Ethinyloestradiol Tablets,** ethinyloestradiol 10 micrograms, net price 20 = 58p; 20 micrograms, 20 = 60p; 50 micrograms, 20 = 70p; 1 mg, 20 = £1.97

MESTRANOL

Indications: see notes above and under preparations

Cautions; Contra-indications; Side-effects: see under Ethinyloestradiol

Dose: see below

With progestogen

Note. Unsuitable for use as or with an oral contraceptive; not necessary for women who have had a hysterectomy (who can receive oestrogen alone)

PoM **Menophase**® (Syntex)

Tablets, 5 pink, mestranol 12.5 micrograms; 8 orange, mestranol 25 micrograms; 2 yellow, mestranol 50 micrograms; 3 green, mestranol 25 micrograms and norethisterone 1 mg; 6 blue, mestranol 30 micrograms and norethisterone 1.5 mg; 4 lavender, mestranol 20 micrograms and norethisterone 750 micrograms. Net price per calendar pack = £3.33

Dose: menopausal symptoms (including osteoporosis prophylaxis), if uterus intact 1 tablet daily, starting with a pink tablet on Sunday, then in sequence (without interruption)

OESTRADIOL

Indications: see notes above and under preparations

Cautions; Contra-indications; Side-effects: see under Ethinyloestradiol; transdermal delivery systems may cause erythema and itching

Dose: see below

Oestrogen-only

Note. Unsuitable for long-term use alone in women with an intact uterus (who require addition of cyclical progestogen)

PoM **Oestradiol Implants** (Organon)

Implant, oestradiol 25 mg, net price each = £6.00; 50 mg, each = £12.00; 100 mg, each = £23.50

Dose: by implantation, oestrogen replacement (with cyclical progestogen on 10–13 days of each cycle if uterus intact, see notes above), 25–100 mg as required (usually every 4–8 months)

PoM **Estraderm TTS**® (Ciba)

25 Dressing (TTS 25), self-adhesive, releasing oestradiol approx. 25 micrograms/24 hours when in contact with skin. Net price 8 dressings = £6.75. Counselling, see below

50 Dressing (TTS 50), self-adhesive, releasing oestradiol approx. 50 micrograms/24 hours when in contact with skin. Net price 8 dressings = £7.45. Counselling, see below

100 Dressing (TTS 100), self-adhesive, releasing oestradiol approx. 100 micrograms/24 hours when in contact with skin. Net price 8 dressings = £8.20. Counselling, see below

Dose: for menopausal symptoms, 1 patch to be applied twice weekly on continuous basis; give progestogen on 12 days a month (unless patient has had hysterectomy); therapy should be initiated with TTS 50 for first month, subsequently adjusted to lowest effective dose; max. one TTS 100 daily

COUNSELLING. Patch should be removed after 3–4 days and replaced with fresh patch on slightly different site; recommended sites: clean, dry, unbroken areas of skin on trunk below waistline; not to be applied on or near breasts

PoM **Hormonin**® (Shire)

Tablets, pink, scored, oestradiol 600 micrograms, oestriol 270 micrograms, oestrone 1.4 mg. Net price 20 = £1.34

Dose: menopausal symptoms (with cyclical progestogen if uterus intact), ½–1 tablet daily for 21 days repeated after 7 days; up to 2 tablets may be given daily in first 21 days then gradually reduced

PoM **Progynova**® (Schering Health Care)

Tablets, both s/c, oestradiol valerate 1 mg (beige), net price 21-tab pack = £1.98; 2 mg (blue), 21-tab pack = £1.98

Dose: menopausal symptoms (short-term), 1 mg daily for 21 days, interval of at least 7 days before next course; increased to 2 mg daily if required

With progestogen

Note. Unsuitable for use as or with an oral contraceptive; not necessary for women who have had a hysterectomy (who can receive oestrogen alone)

PoM **Cyclo-Progynova**® (Schering Health Care)

1-mg Tablets, all s/c, 11 beige, oestradiol valerate 1 mg; 10 brown, oestradiol valerate 1 mg and norgestrel 500 micrograms (≡levonorgestrel 250 micrograms). Net price per calendar pack = £3.50

Dose: menopausal symptoms (including osteoporosis prophylaxis), if uterus intact, 1 beige tablet daily for 11 days, starting on 5th day of menstruation (or at any time if cycles have ceased or are infrequent), then 1 brown tablet daily for 10 days, followed by a 7-day interval

2-mg Tablets, all s/c, 11 white, oestradiol valerate 2 mg; 10 brown, oestradiol valerate 2 mg and norgestrel 500 micrograms (≡levonorgestrel 250 micrograms). Net price per calendar pack = £3.50

Dose: see above, but starting with 1 white tablet daily (instead of 1 beige tablet) if symptoms not fully controlled with lower strength

PoM **Estrapak 50**® (Ciba)

Calendar pack, 8 self-adhesive dressings, releasing oestradiol approx. 50 micrograms/24 hours when in contact with skin, and 12 tablets, red, norethisterone acetate 1 mg. Net price per pack = £8.45. Counselling, see below

Dose: menopausal symptoms (if uterus intact), starting within 5 days of onset of menstruation (or at any time if cycles have ceased or are infrequent), apply 1 dressing twice weekly on continuous basis, and take 1 tablet daily on days 15–26 of each 28-day treatment cycle

COUNSELLING. Patch should be removed after 3–4 days and replaced with fresh patch on slightly different site; recommended sites: clean, dry, unbroken areas of skin on trunk below waistline; not to be applied on or near breasts

PoM **Trisequens**® (Novo Nordisk)

Trisequens® *tablets*, 12 blue, oestradiol 2 mg, oestriol 1 mg; 10 white, oestradiol 2 mg, oestriol 1 mg, norethisterone acetate 1 mg; 6 red, oestradiol 1 mg, oestriol 500 micrograms. Net price per calendar pack = £3.74

Dose: menopausal symptoms (including osteoporosis prophylaxis), if uterus intact, 1 blue tablet daily, starting on 5th day of menstruation (or at any time if cycles have ceased or are infrequent), then 1 tablet daily in sequence (without interruption)

Trisequens Forte® *tablets*, 12 yellow, oestradiol 4 mg, oestriol 2 mg; 10 white, oestradiol 4 mg, oestriol 2 mg, norethisterone acetate 1 mg; 6 red, oestradiol 1 mg, oestriol 500 micrograms. Net price per calendar pack = £3.74

Dose: menopausal symptoms (but not osteoporosis prophylaxis), see under Trisequens®, starting with 1 yellow tablet daily (instead of 1 blue tablet) if symptoms not fully controlled with lower strength

OESTRIOL

Indications: see notes above and preparations
Cautions; Contra-indications; Side-effects: see under Ethinyloestradiol
Dose: see below

PoM **Ovestin®** (Organon)
Tablets, oestriol 250 micrograms. Net price 20 = 60p. Label: 25
Dose: genito-urinary symptoms associated with oestrogen-deficiency states, 0.5–3 mg daily, as single dose, for up to 1 month, then 0.5–1 mg daily until restoration of epithelial integrity (short-term use)
Infertility associated with poor cervical penetration, 0.25–1 mg daily, as single dose, on days 6–15 of cycle (with regular monitoring)
Ingredient of Hormonin® and (with progestogen) of Trisequens®, see Oestradiol

OESTROGENS, CONJUGATED

Indications: see notes above and preparations
Cautions; Contra-indications; Side-effects: see under Ethinyloestradiol
Dose: see below

Oestrogen-only preparations
Note. Unsuitable for long-term use alone in women with an intact uterus (who require addition of cyclical progestogen)

PoM **Premarin®** (Wyeth)
Tablets, all s/c, conjugated oestrogens 625 micrograms (maroon), net price 21-tab pack = £1.03; 1.25 mg (yellow), 21-tab pack = £1.69; 2.5 mg (purple), 20 = £2.09
Dose: menopausal symptoms (with progestogen for 10–12 days per cycle if uterus intact), 0.625–1.25 mg daily for 21 days from 5th day of cycle, repeated after 7 days if necessary

With progestogen
Note. Unsuitable for use as or with an oral contraceptive; not necessary for women who have had a hysterectomy (who can receive oestrogen alone)

PoM **Prempak-C®** (Wyeth)
0.625 Calendar pack, all s/c, 28 maroon tablets, conjugated oestrogens 625 micrograms; 12 light brown tablets, norgestrel 150 micrograms (≡levonorgestrel 75 micrograms). Net price per pack = £3.98
Dose: menopausal symptoms (including osteoporosis prophylaxis), if uterus intact, 1 maroon tablet daily on continuous basis, starting on 1st day of menstruation (or at any time if cycles have ceased or are infrequent), and 1 brown tablet daily on days 17–28 of each 28-day treatment cycle; subsequent courses are repeated without interval
1.25 Calendar pack, all s/c, 28 yellow tablets, conjugated oestrogens 1.25 mg; 12 light brown tablets, norgestrel 150 micrograms (≡levonorgestrel 75 micrograms). Net price per pack = £3.98
Dose: see above, but taking 1 yellow tablet daily on continuous basis (instead of 1 maroon tablet) if symptoms not fully controlled with lower strength

PIPERAZINE OESTRONE SULPHATE

(Estropipate)
Indications: see notes above and preparations
Cautions; Contra-indications; Side-effects: see under Ethinyloestradiol
Dose: see below
Note. Unsuitable for long-term use alone in women with an intact uterus (who require addition of cyclical progestogen)

PoM **Harmogen®** (Abbott)
Tablets, peach, scored, piperazine oestrone sulphate 1.5 mg. Net price 20 = £1.58
Dose: menopausal symptoms (short-term), 1.5–4.5 mg daily in single or divided doses for 21–28 days, repeated after 5–7 days if necessary

6.4.1.2 PROGESTOGENS

Progestogens modify some of the effects of, and act mainly on tissues sensitised by, oestrogens; their effects are inhibited by oestrogen excess. There are two main groups of progestogen, the naturally occurring hormone *progesterone* and its analogues (allyloestrenol, dydrogesterone, hydroxyprogesterone, and medroxyprogesterone) and the *testosterone* analogues e.g. norethisterone. Progesterone and its analogues are less androgenic than the testosterone derivatives and neither progesterone nor dydrogesterone causes virilisation. Other synthetic derivatives are variably metabolised into testosterone and oestrogen; thus side-effects vary with the preparation and the dose.

Progestogens are used in many menstrual disorders, including *severe dysmenorrhoea*, and *menorrhagia*. **Norethisterone** and **dydrogesterone** may be given alone on a cyclical basis during part of the menstrual cycle or in conjunction with an oestrogen. Where contraception is also required in younger women, however, the best choice is a combined oral contraceptive (see section 7.3.1).

Where *endometriosis* requires drug treatment, it may respond to a progestogen, e.g. norethisterone, administered on a continuous basis. Alternatively, danazol (section 6.7.3) may be given.

Progestogens have been widely advocated for the alleviation of *premenstrual symptoms* but no convincing physiological basis for such treatment has been shown.

The progestogens desogestrel, ethynodiol, levonorgestrel[1], lynoestrenol, and norethisterone are used in combined oral and in progestogen-only *contraceptives* (see sections 7.3.1 and 7.3.2).

Progestogens are also used in conjunction with oestrogens in *hormone replacement therapy* in menopausal women with an intact uterus (see section 6.4.1.1). See section 8.3.2 for use in *neoplastic disease*.

Progestogens have been used in *habitual abortion* but there is no evidence of benefit. If they are used for this purpose they should be of the true progesterone-derivative type, e.g. **hydroxyprogesterone hexanoate** to avoid any masculinisation of a female fetus.

1. Levonorgestrel is the active isomer and has twice the potency of racemic norgestrel.

PROGESTERONE

Indications: see under Dose and notes above
Cautions: diabetes, breast-feeding, hypertension; liver, cardiac, or renal disease; **interactions:** Appendix 1 (progestogens)
Contra-indications: undiagnosed vaginal bleeding, missed or incomplete abortion, past severe arterial disease or current high risk (e.g. family history, together with cholesterol above 6.5 mmol/L), mammary carcinoma
Side-effects: acne, urticaria, oedema, weight gain, gastro-intestinal disturbances, changes in libido, breast discomfort, premenstrual symptoms, irregular menstrual cycles; rarely jaundice. Injection may be painful
Dose: *by vagina or rectum*, premenstrual syndrome, 200 mg daily to 400 mg twice daily starting at day 12–14 and continued until onset of menstruation (but not recommended, see notes above); rectally if barrier methods of contraception are used, or if vaginal infection
By deep intramuscular injection into buttock, dysfunctional uterine bleeding, 5–10 mg daily for 5–10 days until 2 days before anticipated onset of menstruation
Embryo transfer, consult manufacturer's literature

PoM **Cyclogest®** (Hoechst)
Suppositories, progesterone 200 mg, net price 15 = £5.40; 400 mg, 15 = £7.83

PoM **Gestone®** (Paines & Byrne)
Injection, progesterone 25 mg/mL, 1-mL amp = 34p; 50 mg/mL, 1-mL amp = 44p, 2-mL amp = 58p

ALLYLOESTRENOL

Indications: habitual abortion, but see notes above
Cautions; Contra-indications; Side-effects: see under Progesterone and notes above
Dose: habitual abortion, 5–10 mg daily for at least 16 weeks (but see notes above)

PoM **Gestanin®** (Organon)
Tablets, allyloestrenol 5 mg. Net price 20 = £1.99

DESOGESTREL

See section 7.3.1

DYDROGESTERONE

Indications: see under Dose and notes above
Cautions; Contra-indications; Side-effects: see under Progesterone and notes above; break-through bleeding may occur (increase dose)
Dose: endometriosis, 10 mg 2–3 times daily from 5th to 25th day of cycle or continuously
Infertility, irregular cycles, 10 mg twice daily from 11th to 25th day for at least 6 cycles
Habitual abortion, 10 mg twice daily from day 11 to day 25 of cycle until conception, then continuously until 20th week of pregnancy and gradually reduced (but see notes above)
Dysfunctional uterine bleeding, 10 mg twice daily (together with an oestrogen) for 5–7 days to arrest bleeding; 10 mg twice daily (together with an oestrogen) from 11th to 25th day of cycle to prevent bleeding
Dysmenorrhoea, 10 mg twice daily from 5th to 25th day of cycle
Amenorrhoea, 10 mg twice daily from 11th to 25th day of cycle with oestrogen therapy from 1st to 25th day of cycle
Premenstrual syndrome, 10 mg twice daily from 12th to 26th day of cycle increased if necessary (but not recommended, see notes above)
Hormone replacement therapy, with continuous oestrogen therapy, 10 mg twice daily, for the first 12–14 days of each calendar month; with cyclical oestrogen, 10 mg twice daily for the last 12–14 days of each treatment cycle

PoM **Duphaston®** (Duphar)
Tablets, scored, dydrogesterone 10 mg. Net price 60-tab pack = £10.05

ETHYNODIOL

See section 7.3.1 and 7.3.2

GESTODENE

See section 7.3.1

HYDROXYPROGESTERONE HEXANOATE

Indications: habitual abortion but see notes above
Cautions; Contra-indications; Side-effects: see under Progesterone and notes above
Dose: *by intramuscular injection*, 250–500 mg weekly during first half of pregnancy

PoM **Proluton* Depot®** (Schering Health Care)
Injection (oily), hydroxyprogesterone hexanoate 250 mg/mL. Net price 1-mL amp = £2.35; 2-mL amp = £3.69
*formerly Primolut Depot®

LEVONORGESTREL

Ingredient of combined and progestogen-only oral contraceptives (sections 7.3.1 and 7.3.2)

MEDROXYPROGESTERONE ACETATE

Indications: see under Dose; for use as a contraceptive, see section 7.3.2; for use in malignant disease, see section 8.3.2
Cautions; Contra-indications; Side-effects: see under Progesterone and notes above; disturbances of normal menstrual cycle and irregular bleeding may occur; contra-indicated in pregnancy
Dose: *by mouth*, 2.5–10 mg daily for 5–10 days beginning on 16th–21st day of cycle, repeated for 2 cycles in dysfunctional uterine bleeding and 3 cycles in secondary amenorrhoea
Mild to moderate endometriosis, 10 mg 3 times daily for 90 consecutive days, beginning on 1st day of cycle
By deep intramuscular injection, endometriosis, 50 mg weekly or 100 mg every 2 weeks

PoM **Depo-Provera® 50mg/mL** (Upjohn)
Injection (aqueous suspension), medroxyprogesterone acetate 50 mg/mL. Net price 1-mL vial = £1.55; 3-mL vial = £4.17; 5-mL vial = £6.85

PoM **Provera®** (Upjohn)
Tablets, scored, medroxyprogesterone acetate 5 mg. Net price 20-tab pack = £2.58; 100-tab pack = £12.87

NORETHISTERONE

Indications: see under Dose; for use as a contraceptive see sections 7.3.1 and 7.3.2

Cautions; Contra-indications; Side-effects: see under Progesterone but more virilising and greater incidence of liver disturbances and jaundice; avoid in pregnancy; exacerbation of epilepsy and migraine

Dose: endometriosis 10 mg daily starting on 5th day of cycle (increased if spotting occurs to 25 mg daily in divided doses to prevent breakthrough bleeding)
Menorrhagia, 5 mg 3 times daily for 10 days to arrest bleeding; to prevent bleeding 5 mg twice daily from 19th to 26th day
Dysmenorrhoea, 5 mg 3 times daily from 5th to 24th day for 3–4 cycles
Premenstrual syndrome, 5 mg 2–3 times daily from 19th to 26th day for several cycles (but not recommended, see notes above)
Postponement of menstruation, 5 mg 3 times daily starting 3 days before anticipated onset

PoM **Menzol®** (Kabi)
Tablets, scored, norethisterone 5 mg. Net price 3 × 24-tab (8-day) 'Planapak' = £7.70; 3 × 60-tab (20-day) 'Planapak' = £19.35

PoM **Primolut N®** (Schering Health Care)
Tablets, norethisterone 5 mg. Net price 20 = £1.63

PoM **Utovlan®** (Syntex)
Tablets, scored, norethisterone 5 mg. Net price 20 = £1.70

NORGESTREL

Ingredient of combined and progestogen-only oral contraceptives (section 7.3.1) and of combined preparations for menopausal symptoms (section 6.4.1.1)

6.4.2 Male sex hormones and antagonists

Androgens cause masculinisation; they may be used as replacement therapy in castrated adults and in those who are hypogonadal due to either pituitary or testicular disease. In the normal male they depress spermatogenesis and inhibit pituitary gonadotrophin secretion. Androgens also have an anabolic action which led to the development of anabolic steroids (section 6.4.3).

Androgens are useless as a treatment of impotence and impaired spermatogenesis unless there is associated hypogonadism; they should not be given until the hypogonadism has been properly investigated. Treatment should be under expert supervision.

When given to patients with hypopituitarism they can lead to normal sexual development and potency but not to fertility. If fertility is desired, the usual treatment is with gonadotrophins (section 6.5.1) which will stimulate spermatogenesis as well as androgen production.

Caution should be used when androgens or chorionic gonadotrophin are used in treating boys with delayed puberty since the fusion of epiphyses is hastened and may result in short stature.

Androgens are still quite useful in occasional women with disseminated cancer of the breast despite their masculinising effects.

Intramuscular depot preparations of **testosterone esters** are preferred for replacement therapy. Testosterone enanthate or propionate or alternatively Sustanon®, which consists of a mixture of testosterone esters and has a longer duration of action, may be used. Satisfactory replacement therapy can sometimes be obtained with 1 mL of Sustanon 250®, given by intramuscular injection once a month, although more frequent dose intervals are often necessary. Implants of testosterone have been superseded.

Of the orally active preparations, methyltestosterone is no longer on the UK market; like other 17α-alkyl derivatives of testosterone it could sometimes cause dose-related but reversible cholestatic jaundice. **Mesterolone** is not a 17α-alkyl derivative and is less toxic to the liver.

TESTOSTERONE AND ESTERS

Indications: see under preparations

Cautions: cardiac, renal, or hepatic impairment (see Appendix 2), ischaemic heart disease, hypertension, epilepsy, migraine, thyroid disease, diabetes mellitus, skeletal metastases (risk of hypercalcaemia)

Contra-indications: breast cancer in men, prostatic cancer, pregnancy, breast-feeding, nephrosis

Side-effects: sodium retention with oedema, increase in weight, hypercalcaemia, increased bone growth, priapism, precocious sexual development and premature closure of epiphyses in pre-pubertal males, prostatism in elderly patients, high doses cause virilism in women, and suppress spermatogenesis in men

PoM **Primoteston Depot®** (Schering Health Care)
Injection (oily), testosterone enanthate 250 mg/mL. Net price 1-mL amp = £4.13
Dose: by intramuscular injection, hypogonadism, initially 250 mg every 2–3 weeks; maintenance 250 mg every 3–6 weeks
Breast cancer, 250 mg every 2 weeks

PoM **Restandol®** (Organon)
Capsules, red-brown, testosterone undecanoate 40 mg in oily solution. Net price 60 = £15.78. Label: 21, 25
Dose: androgen deficiency, 120–160 mg daily for 2–3 weeks; maintenance 40–120 mg daily

PoM **Sustanon 100®** (Organon)
Injection (oily), testosterone propionate 20 mg, testosterone phenylpropionate 40 mg, and testosterone isocaproate 40 mg/mL. Net price 1-mL amp = £1.11
Dose: by deep intramuscular injection, androgen deficiency, 1 mL every 2 weeks

PoM **Sustanon 250®** (Organon)
Injection (oily), testosterone propionate 30 mg, testosterone phenylpropionate 60 mg, testosterone isocaproate 60 mg, and testosterone decanoate 100 mg/mL. Net price 1-mL amp = £2.61
Dose: by deep intramuscular injection, androgen deficiency, 1 mL usually every 3 weeks

PoM **Virormone®** (Paines & Byrne)
Injection, testosterone propionate 50 mg/mL. Net price 2-mL amp = 46p
Dose: by intramuscular injection, androgen deficiency, 50 mg 2–3 times weekly
Delayed puberty, 50 mg weekly. Breast cancer, 100 mg 2–3 times weekly

Testosterone

PoM **Testosterone** (Organon)
Implant, testosterone 100 mg, net price = £5.10; 200 mg = £9.50
Dose: by implantation, male hypogonadism, 600 mg every 6 months

MESTEROLONE

Indications: see under Dose
Cautions; Contra-indications; Side-effects: see under Testosterone Esters; spermatogenesis unimpaired
Dose: androgen deficiency, 25 mg 3–4 times daily for several months, reduced to 50–75 mg daily in divided doses for maintenance

PoM **Pro-Viron®** (Schering Health Care)
Tablets, scored, mesterolone 25 mg. Net price 50 = £7.91

ANTI-ANDROGENS

Cyproterone acetate is an anti-androgen used in the treatment of severe hypersexuality and sexual deviation in the male; it inhibits spermatogenesis and produces reversible infertility. Abnormal sperm forms are produced. Cyproterone acetate is also used in the treatment of acne and hirsutism in women (see section 13.6) and in prostatic cancer (see section 8.3.4). As hepatic tumours have been produced in *animal* studies, careful consideration should be given to the risk/benefit ratio before treatment.

CYPROTERONE ACETATE

Indications: see notes above; prostate cancer, see section 8.3.4
Cautions: impaired ability to drive and operate machinery; ineffective for male hypersexuality in chronic alcoholism (relevance to prostate cancer not known); blood counts and monitor hepatic function, adrenocortical function and blood glucose regularly; diabetes mellitus, adrenocortical insufficiency
Contra-indications: (do not apply in prostate cancer) hepatic disease, malignant or wasting disease, severe depression, history of thrombo-embolic disorders; youths under 18 years (may arrest bone maturation and testicular development)
Side-effects: fatigue and lassitude, weight changes, changes in hair pattern, gynaecomastia (rarely leading to galactorrhoea and benign breast nodules); rarely osteoporosis; inhibition of spermatogenesis (see notes above); liver abnormalities reported in *animals*
Dose: male hypersexuality, 50 mg twice daily after food

PoM **Androcur®** (Schering Health Care)
Tablets, scored, cyproterone acetate 50 mg. Net price 56-tab pack = £32.23. Label: 2, 21

6.4.3 Anabolic steroids

All the anabolic steroids have some androgenic activity but they cause less virilisation than androgens in women. Their protein-building property led to the hope that they might be widely useful in medicine but this hope has not been realised. They have, for example, been given for osteoporosis in women and in cases of wasting. Their use as body builders or tonics is quite unjustified; they are abused by some athletes.

Anabolic steroids are also used in the treatment of some *aplastic anaemias* (see section 9.1.3) and to reduce the itching of *chronic biliary obstruction* (see Prescribing in Terminal Care).

NANDROLONE

Indications: osteoporosis in postmenopausal women; aplastic anaemia, see section 9.1.3
Cautions: cardiac and renal impairment, hepatic impairment (see Appendix 2), hypertension, diabetes mellitus, epilepsy, migraine; monitor skeletal maturation in young patients; skeletal metastases (risk of hypercalcaemia); **interactions:** Appendix 1 (anabolic steroids)
Contra-indications: hepatic impairment, prostatic cancer, male breast cancer, pregnancy, porphyria
Side-effects: acne, sodium retention with oedema, virilisation with high doses including voice changes (sometimes irreversible), amenorrhoea, inhibition of spermatogenesis, premature epiphyseal closure; abnormal liver-function tests reported with high doses; liver tumours reported occasionally on prolonged treatment with anabolic steroids
Dose: see below

PoM **Deca-Durabolin®** (Organon)
Injection (oily), nandrolone decanoate 25 mg/mL, net price 1-mL amp = £1.75, 1-mL syringe = £1.88; 50 mg/mL, 1-mL amp = £3.37, 1-mL syringe = £3.57
Dose: by deep intramuscular injection, 50 mg every 3 weeks

PoM **Deca-Durabolin 100®**, see section 9.1.3

PoM **Durabolin®** (Organon)
Injection (oily), nandrolone phenylpropionate 25 mg/mL, net price 1-mL amp = 86p, 1-mL syringe = 91p; 50 mg/mL, 1-mL syringe = £1.70
Dose: by deep intramuscular injection, 50 mg weekly

STANOZOLOL

Indications: see under Dose
Cautions; Contra-indications; Side-effects: see under Nandrolone. Headache, dyspepsia, euphoria, depression, cramp, and occasionally hair loss, also reported; cholestatic jaundice occasionally reported
Dose: by mouth, vascular manifestations of Behcet's disease, 10 mg daily
Hereditary angioedema, 2.5–10 mg daily to control attacks, reduced for maintenance (2.5 mg 3 times weekly may be sufficient); CHILD 1–6 years initially 2.5 mg daily, 6–12 years initially 2.5–5 mg daily, reduced for maintenance
Note: Restricted to well-established cases who have experienced serious attacks; not for premenopausal women except in life-threatening situations

PoM **Stromba®** (Sterling-Winthrop)
Tablets, scored, stanozolol 5 mg. Net price 56-tab pack = £22.25

6.5 Hypothalamic and pituitary hormones and anti-oestrogens

Hypothalamic and pituitary hormones are described under the following section headings:

6.5.1 Hypothalamic and anterior pituitary hormones and anti-oestrogens
6.5.2 Posterior pituitary hormones and antagonists

Use of preparations in these sections requires detailed prior investigation of the patient and *should be reserved for specialist centres.*

6.5.1 Hypothalamic and anterior pituitary hormones and anti-oestrogens

ANTI-OESTROGENS

The anti-oestrogens **clomiphene**, **cyclofenil**, and **tamoxifen** are used in the treatment of female infertility due to secondary amenorrhoea (e.g. polycystic ovarian disease). They induce gonadotrophin release by occupying oestrogen receptors in the hypothalamus, thereby interfering with feedback mechanisms; chorionic gonadotrophin is sometimes used as an adjunct. Care is taken to avoid hyperstimulation and multiple pregnancies.

CLOMIPHENE CITRATE

Indications: anovulatory infertility—see notes above
Cautions: see notes above; polycystic ovary syndrome (cysts may enlarge during treatment), incidence of multiple births increased
Contra-indications: hepatic disease, ovarian cysts, endometrial carcinoma, pregnancy, abnormal uterine bleeding
Side-effects: visual disturbances (withdraw), ovarian hyperstimulation (withdraw), hot flushes, abdominal discomfort, occasionally nausea, vomiting, depression, insomnia, breast tenderness, weight gain, rashes, dizziness, hair loss
Dose: 50 mg daily for 5 days starting on 2nd to 5th day of menstrual cycle or at any time if cycles have ceased; in absence of ovulation second course of 100 mg daily for 5 days may be given; most patients who are going to respond will do so to first course; 3 courses should constitute adequate therapeutic trial; long-term cyclical therapy not recommended

PoM **Clomid®** (Merrell)
Tablets, yellow, scored, clomiphene citrate 50 mg. Net price 20 = £6.73

PoM **Serophene®** (Serono)
Tablets, scored, clomiphene citrate 50 mg. Net price 20 = £6.73

CYCLOFENIL

Indications: anovulatory infertility—see notes above
Contra-indications: see under Clomiphene Citrate
Side-effects: hot flushes, abdominal discomfort, nausea; rarely cholestatic jaundice
Dose: 200 mg twice daily for 10 days starting on 3rd day of natural or progesterone-induced bleeding, followed by 20 treatment-free days, repeated for at least 3 months

PoM **Rehibin®** (Serono)
Tablets, scored, cyclofenil 100 mg. Net price 20 = £3.70

TAMOXIFEN

See section 8.3.4

ANTERIOR PITUITARY HORMONES

CORTICOTROPHINS

Corticotrophin and tetracosactrin are used mainly as diagnostic agents (see section 6.7.2). The long-acting depot forms (Synacthen Depot® etc.) were formerly used as alternatives to corticosteroids in conditions such as Crohn's disease or rheumatoid arthritis; their value was limited by the variable and unpredictable therapeutic response and by the waning of their effect with time.

CORTICOTROPHIN

(ACTH)

Indications: see notes above

Cautions; Contra-indications; Side-effects: see section 6.3.3; also caution in hypertension; important risk of anaphylaxis—see data sheet; **interactions:** Appendix 1 (corticosteroids and corticotrophin)

Dose: by subcutaneous or intramuscular injection, depot preparations, initially 40–80 units daily, reduced according to response

PoM **Acthar Gel®** (Rorer)

Injection, corticotrophin (with gelatin) 20 units/mL, net price 5-mL vial = £4.73; 40 units/mL, 2-mL vial = £3.39, 5-mL vial = £8.57; 80 units/mL, 5-mL vial = £16.68

TETRACOSACTRIN

Indications: see notes above

Cautions; Contra-indications; Side-effects: see section 6.3.3 and Corticotrophin; important risk of anaphylaxis (medical supervision; see data sheet)

PoM **Synacthen®** (Ciba)

Injection, tetracosactrin 250 micrograms (as acetate)/mL. Net price 1-mL amp = 93p

Dose: diagnostic, *by intramuscular or intravenous injection*, 250 micrograms as a single dose

PoM **Synacthen Depot®** (Ciba)

Injection (aqueous suspension), tetracosactrin 1 mg (as acetate)/mL, with zinc phosphate complex; also contains benzyl alcohol. Net price 1-mL amp = £1.05; 2-mL vial = £1.92

Dose: by intramuscular injection, initially 1 mg daily (or every 12 hours in acute cases); subsequently reduced to 1 mg every 2–3 days, then 1 mg weekly (or 500 micrograms every 2–3 days)

GONADOTROPHINS

Follicle-stimulating hormone (FSH) is used in the treatment of infertile women with proven hypopituitarism or who have not responded to clomiphene; it is used in conjunction with luteinising hormone (LH). Follicle-stimulating hormone is contained in **menotrophin** (which also contains luteinising hormone) and **urofollitrophin**; luteinising hormone is contained in **chorionic gonadotrophin**. Treatment requires careful monitoring to avoid the ovarian hyperstimulation syndrome and multiple pregnancy.

The gonadotrophins are also occasionally used in the treatment of oligospermia associated with hypopituitarism. There is no justification for their use in primary gonadal failure.

Chorionic gonadotrophin has also been used in delayed puberty in the male to stimulate endogenous testosterone production, but has little advantage over testosterone (section 6.4.2).

CHORIONIC GONADOTROPHIN

(Human Chorionic Gonadotrophin; HCG)

A preparation of a glycoprotein fraction secreted by the placenta and obtained from the urine of pregnant women having the action of the pituitary luteinising hormone

Indications: see notes above

Cautions: see notes above; cardiac or renal impairment, asthma, epilepsy, migraine

Side-effects: oedema (particularly in males—reduce dose), headache, tiredness, mood changes, gynaecomastia, local reactions; sexual precocity with high doses; may aggravate ovarian hyperstimulation

Dose: by intramuscular injection, according to patient's requirements

PoM **Gonadotraphon LH®** (Paines & Byrne)

Injection, powder for reconstitution, chorionic gonadotrophin. Net price 500-unit amp = 98p; 1000-unit amp = £1.25; 5000-unit amp = £3.71 (all with solvent)

PoM **Pregnyl®** (Organon)

Injection, powder for reconstitution, chorionic gonadotrophin. Net price 500-unit amp = 69p; 1500-unit amp = £2.07; 5000-unit amp = £3.08 (all with solvent)

PoM **Profasi®** (Serono)

Injection, powder for reconstitution, chorionic gonadotrophin. Net price 500-unit amp = 69p; 1000-unit amp = 95p; 2000-unit amp = £1.75; 5000-unit amp = £3.08 (all with solvent)

MENOTROPHIN

Extract of the urine of postmenopausal women containing primarily follicle-stimulating hormone (with luteinising hormone)

Indications: see notes above

Cautions: ovarian cysts, adrenal or thyroid disorders, hyperprolactinoma or pituitary tumour

Side-effects: ovarian hyperstimulation, multiple pregnancy; local reactions

Dose: by deep intramuscular injection, according to patient's response

PoM **Humegon®** (Organon)

Injection, powder for reconstitution, menotrophin as follicle-stimulating hormone 75 units, luteinising hormone 75 units. Net price per amp = £8.80; follicle-stimulating hormone 150 units, luteinising hormone 150 units, 1 amp = £16.00 (both with solvent)

PoM **Pergonal®** (Serono)

Injection, powder for reconstitution, menotrophin as follicle-stimulating hormone 75 units, luteinising hormone 75 units. Net price per amp (with solvent) = £9.79

UROFOLLITROPHIN

Extract of the urine of postmenopausal women containing follicle-stimulating hormone

Indications: see notes above

Cautions; Side-effects: see under Menotrophin

Dose: by deep intramuscular injection, according to patient's response

PoM **Metrodin®** (Serono)
Injection, powder for reconstitution, urofollitrophin as follicle-stimulating hormone 75 units. Net price per amp (with solvent) = £9.79

GROWTH HORMONE
Growth hormone is used in the treatment of short stature due to growth hormone deficiency (including short stature in Turner syndrome); only the human type is effective as growth hormone is species specific. Growth hormone of human origin (HGH; somatotrophin) has been replaced by a growth hormone of human sequence, **somatropin**, produced using recombinant DNA technology.

SOMATROPIN
(Biosynthetic Human Growth Hormone)
Indications: see notes above
Cautions: only patients with open epiphyses; relative deficiencies of other pituitary hormones (notably hypothyroidism); diabetes mellitus (adjustment of antidiabetic therapy may be necessary); avoid in pregnancy (theoretical risk)
Side-effects: antibody formation; local reactions (rotate subcutaneous injection sites to prevent lipo-atrophy); in Turner syndrome temporary exacerbation of lymphoedema reported
Dose: 0.5–0.7 units/kg (Turner syndrome, 1 unit/kg) weekly divided into 6 or 7 doses for *subcutaneous injection* (alternatively divided into 2 or 3 doses for *intramuscular injection*, but more painful)

▼ PoM **Genotropin®** (Kabi)
Injection, powder for preparing injections, somatropin (rbe), net price 4-unit vial (with diluent) = £30.50; 12-unit vial (with diluent) = £91.50
▼ PoM **Humatrope®** (Lilly)
Injection, powder for reconstitution, somatropin (rbe), net price 4-unit vial (with diluent) = £30.50
▼ PoM **Norditropin®** (Novo Nordisk)
Injection, powder for reconstitution, somatropin (epr), net price 12-unit vial (with diluent) = £91.50
▼ PoM **Saizen®** (Serono)
Injection, powder for reconstitution, somatropin (rmc), net price 4-unit vial (with diluent) = £30.50

HYPOTHALAMIC HORMONES

Gonadorelin (gonadotrophin-releasing hormone, LH-RH) and **protirelin** (thyrotrophin-releasing hormone, TRH) are used mainly as diagnostic agents (section 6.7.2). Gonadorelin is also used for treatment of infertility, particularly in the female. Buserelin and goserelin, gonadotrophin-releasing hormone analogues, are indicated in metastatic prostate cancer (see section 8.3.4).

6.5.2 Posterior pituitary hormones and antagonists

POSTERIOR PITUITARY HORMONES

DIABETES INSIPIDUS. Vasopressin (antidiuretic hormone, ADH) is used in the treatment of *pituitary* ('cranial') *diabetes insipidus* as its analogues **lypressin** or **desmopressin.** Dosage is tailored to produce a slight diuresis every 24 hours to avoid water intoxication. Treatment may be required for a limited period only in diabetes insipidus following trauma or pituitary surgery.

Desmopressin has a longer duration of action than vasopressin or lypressin; unlike vasopressin and lypressin it has no vasoconstrictor effect. It is given intranasally for maintenance therapy, and by injection in the postoperative period or in unconscious patients; the injection is also used for the diagnosis of diabetes insipidus (section 6.7.2).

In *nephrogenic* and *partial pituitary diabetes insipidus* benefit may be gained from the paradoxical antidiuretic effect of thiazides (see section 2.2.1) e.g. chlorthalidone 100 mg twice daily reduced to maintenance dose of 50 mg daily.

Chlorpropamide (section 6.1.2.1) is also useful in partial pituitary diabetes insipidus, and probably acts by sensitising the renal tubules to the action of remaining endogenous vasopressin; it is given in doses of up to 350 mg daily in adults and 200 mg daily in children, care being taken to avoid hypoglycaemia. Carbamazepine (see section 4.8.1) is also sometimes useful (in a dose of 200 mg once or twice daily); its mode of action may be similar to that of chlorpropamide.

OTHER USES. Desmopressin injection is also used to boost factor VIII concentrations in mild to moderate haemophilia.

Vasopressin infusion is used to control variceal bleeding in portal hypertension, prior to more definitive treatment and with variable results. Terlipressin, a new derivative of vasopressin, is used similarly.

Oxytocin, another posterior pituitary hormone, is indicated in obstetrics (see section 7.1.1).

VASOPRESSIN
Indications: pituitary diabetes insipidus; bleeding from oesophageal varices
Cautions: heart failure, asthma, epilepsy, migraine; adjust fluid intake to avoid hyponatraemia and water intoxication
Contra-indications: vascular disease, chronic nephritis (until reasonable blood nitrogen concentrations attained)
Side-effects: pallor, nausea, belching, cramp, desire to defaecate, uterine cramps, hypersensitivity reactions, constriction of coronary arteries (may cause anginal attacks and myocardial ischaemia)

Dose: by subcutaneous or intramuscular injection, diabetes insipidus, 5–20 units every four hours
By intravenous infusion, initial control of variceal bleeding, 20 units over 15 minutes

Synthetic vasopressin
PoM **Pitressin**® (P-D)
Injection, argipressin (synthetic vasopressin) 20 units/mL. Net price 1-mL amp = £1.18 (hosp. only)

DESMOPRESSIN

Indications: see under Dose; diagnostic procedures (section 6.7.2)
Cautions: see under Vasopressin; almost devoid of pressor activity and well tolerated; cystic fibrosis
Dose: *intranasally*, pituitary diabetes insipidus (diagnosis), adults and children, 20 micrograms
Pituitary diabetes insipidus (treatment), adults and children, 10–20 micrograms once or twice daily (young children, 5 micrograms)
Primary nocturnal enuresis, adults and children over 7 years, 20 micrograms at bedtime, increased to 40 micrograms if necessary; after 3 months withdraw for reassessment for at least 1 week
By intramuscular or intravenous injection, pituitary diabetes insipidus, 1–4 micrograms daily; CHILD 400 nanograms
Mild to moderate haemophilia and von Willebrand's disease, consult literature

PoM **DDAVP**® (Ferring)
Intranasal solution, desmopressin 100 micrograms/mL. Net price 2.5-mL dropper bottle and catheter = £9.50
Injection, desmopressin 4 micrograms/mL. Net price 1-mL amp = £1.07
PoM **Desmospray**® (Ferring)
Nasal spray, desmopressin 10 micrograms/metered spray. Net price 5-mL unit = £19.92

LYPRESSIN

Indications: pituitary diabetes insipidus
Cautions; Contra-indications; Side-effects: see under Vasopressin; less hypersensitivity; also nasal congestion with ulceration of mucosa
Dose: *intranasally*, 2.5–10 units 3–7 times daily

PoM **Syntopressin**® (Sandoz)
Nasal spray, lypressin 50 units/mL, 2.5 units/squeeze. Net price 5-mL bottle = £3.49

TERLIPRESSIN

Indications: bleeding from oesophageal varices
Cautions; Contra-indications; Side-effects: see under Vasopressin, but effects are milder
Dose: *by intravenous injection*, 2 mg followed by 1 or 2 mg every 4 to 6 hours until bleeding is controlled, for up to 72 hours

PoM **Glypressin**® (Ferring)
Injection, terlipressin, powder for reconstitution. Net price 1-mg vial with 5 mL diluent = £19.00 (hosp. only)

ANTIDIURETIC HORMONE ANTAGONISTS

Demeclocycline (see section 5.1.3) may be used in the treatment of hyponatraemia resulting from inappropriate secretion of antidiuretic hormone. It is thought to act by directly blocking the renal tubular effect of antidiuretic hormone. Initially 0.9 to 1.2 g is given daily in divided doses, reduced to 600–900 mg daily for maintenance.

6.6 Drugs affecting bone metabolism

6.6.1 Calcitonin
6.6.2 Biphosphonates

See also plicamycin (section 8.1.2), calcium and phosphorus compounds (sections 9.5.1.1 and 9.5.2), vitamin D preparations (section 9.6.4), and oestrogens in postmenopausal osteoporosis (section 6.4.1.1).

6.6.1 Calcitonin

Calcitonin is involved with parathyroid hormone in the regulation of bone turnover and hence in the maintenance of calcium balance and homoeostasis. It is used to lower the plasma-calcium concentration in some patients with hypercalcaemia (notably when associated with malignant disease). In the treatment of severe Paget's disease of bone it is used mainly for relief of pain but it is also effective in relieving some of the neurological complications, for example deafness. The prolonged use of **porcine calcitonin** can lead to the production of neutralising antibodies. **Salcatonin** (synthetic salmon calcitonin) is less immunogenic and thus more suitable for long-term therapy. When changing treatment in Paget's disease, calcitonin (pork) 80 units is equivalent to salcatonin 50 units.

CALCITONIN (PORK)

Indications: Paget's disease of bone; hypercalcaemia
Cautions: see notes above; porcine calcitonin may contain trace amounts of thyroid. Skin test advisable in patients with history of allergy; pregnancy and breast-feeding (avoid—inhibits lactation in *animals*)
Side-effects: nausea, vomiting, flushing, tingling of hands, unpleasant taste, inflammatory reactions at injection site
Dose: hypercalcaemia, *by subcutaneous or intramuscular injection*, initially 4 units/kg daily adjusted according to clinical and biochemical response (higher doses more conveniently given as salcatonin, see below)

Paget's disease of bone, *by subcutaneous or intramuscular injection*, dose range 80 units 3 times weekly to 160 units daily in single or divided doses; in patients with bone pain or nerve compression syndromes, 80–160 units daily for 3–6 months

PoM **Calcitare®** (Rhône-Poulenc Rorer)
Injection, powder for reconstitution, porcine calcitonin. Net price 160-unit vial (with gelatin diluent) = £11.36

SALCATONIN

Indications: Paget's disease of bone; hypercalcaemia; bone pain in neoplastic disease; postmenopausal osteoporosis

Cautions; Side-effects: see under Calcitonin (pork) and notes above

Dose: hypercalcaemia, *by subcutaneous or intramuscular injection*, range from 5–10 units/kg daily *to* 400 units every 6–8 hours adjusted according to clinical and biochemical response (no additional benefit with over 8 units/kg every 6 hours); *by slow intravenous infusion* (Miacalcic® only), 5–10 units/kg over at least 6 hours

Paget's disease of bone, *by subcutaneous or intramuscular injection*, dose range 50 units 3 times weekly to 100 units daily, in single or divided doses; in patients with bone pain or nerve compression syndromes, 50–100 units daily for 3–6 months

Bone pain in neoplastic disease, *by subcutaneous or intramuscular injection*, 200 units every 6 hours *or* 400 units every 12 hours for 48 hours; may be repeated at discretion of physician

Postmenopausal osteoporosis, *by subcutaneous or intramuscular injection*, 100 units daily with dietary calcium and vitamin D supplements (sections 9.5.1.1 and 9.6.4)

PoM **Calsynar®** (Rhône-Poulenc Rorer)
Injection, salcatonin 100 units/mL in saline/acetate, net price 1-mL amp = £8.12; 200 units/mL in saline/acetate, 2-mL vial = £29.20
For subcutaneous or intramuscular injection only

PoM **Miacalcic®** (Sandoz)
Injection, salcatonin 50 units/mL, net price 1-mL amp = £3.65; 100 units/mL, 1-mL amp = £7.31; 200 units/mL, 2-mL vial = £26.28
For subcutaneous or intramuscular injection and for dilution and use as an intravenous infusion

6.6.2 Biphosphonates

Disodium etidronate is used mainly in the treatment of Paget's disease of bone. It is adsorbed onto hydroxyapatite crystals, so slowing both their rate of growth and dissolution, and reduces the increased rate of bone turnover associated with the disease. Disodium etidronate is also highly effective in the treatment of hypercalcaemia of malignancy; more recently **disodium pamidronate** and **sodium clodronate** have been introduced for this purpose as well.

DISODIUM ETIDRONATE

Indications: see under Dose

Cautions: enterocolitis; discontinue use if fractures occur; reduce dose in renal impairment (avoid if severe); **interactions:** Appendix 1 (biphosphonates)

Side-effects: nausea, diarrhoea, increase in bone pain, increased risk of fractures with high doses; transient taste loss reported

Dose: Paget's disease of bone, *by mouth*, 5 mg/kg as a single daily dose for up to 6 months; doses above 10 mg/kg daily for up to 3 months may be used with caution but doses above 20 mg/kg daily are not recommended

Hypercalcaemia of malignancy, *by intravenous infusion*, 7.5 mg/kg daily for 3 days; repeat once if necessary after at least 7 days; *by mouth*, on day after last intravenous dose, 20 mg/kg as a single daily dose for 30 days; max. recommended treatment period 90 days

COUNSELLING. Avoid food for at least 2 hours before and after oral treatment, particularly calcium-containing products

PoM **Didronel®** (Norwich Eaton)
Tablets, disodium etidronate 200 mg. Net price 60-tab pack = £37.62. Counselling, food and calcium (see above)

PoM **Didronel IV®** (Norwich Eaton)
Injection, disodium etidronate 50 mg/mL. Net price 6-mL amp = £16.43

DISODIUM PAMIDRONATE

Note. Disodium pamidronate was formerly called aminohydroxypropylidenediphosphonate disodium (APD)

Indications: hypercalcaemia of malignancy

Cautions: severe renal impairment; possibility of convulsions due to electrolyte disturbances; transient rise in body temperature; **interactions:** Appendix 1 (biphosphonates)

Dose: *by slow intravenous infusion*, according to plasma calcium concentration 15–60 mg in single infusion or in divided doses over 2–4 days; max. 90 mg per treatment course (see Appendix 6)

▼ PoM **Aredia®** (Ciba)
Intravenous solution, disodium pamidronate (anhydrous) 3 mg/mL. For dilution and use as infusion. Net price 5-mL amp = £24.16

SODIUM CLODRONATE

Indications: hypercalcaemia of malignancy

Cautions: monitor renal and hepatic function and white cell count; **interactions:** Appendix I (biphosphonates)

Contra-indications: pregnancy, breast-feeding, renal impairment; avoid oral administration in severe inflammatory conditions of the gastro-intestinal tract

Side-effects: nausea, diarrhoea, hypocalcaemia; rarely skin reactions

Dose: *by mouth*, 1.6 g daily in single or 2 divided doses increased if necessary to a max. of 3.2 g daily; max. recommended treatment period 6 months

COUNSELLING. Avoid food for at least 1 hour before and after treatment, particularly calcium-containing products e.g. milk

By slow intravenous infusion, 300 mg daily for max. 10 days

▼ PoM **Loron**® (Boehringer Mannheim)
Capsules, sodium clodronate 400 mg. Net price 120-cap pack = £210.43. Counselling, food and calcium
Intravenous solution, sodium clodronate 30 mg/mL, for dilution and use as infusion. Net price 10-mL amp = £14.88

6.7 Other endocrine drugs

6.7.1 Bromocriptine

Bromocriptine is a stimulant of dopamine receptors in the brain; it also inhibits release of prolactin by the pituitary. Bromocriptine is used for the suppression of lactation when simpler measures fail, for the treatment of galactorrhoea and cyclical benign breast disease, and for the treatment of prolactinomas (when it reduces both plasma-prolactin concentration and tumour size). Bromocriptine also inhibits the release of growth hormone and is sometimes used in the treatment of acromegaly, the success rate is much lower than with prolactinomas.

For the use of bromocriptine in parkinsonism, see section 4.9.1.

BROMOCRIPTINE

Indications: see notes above

Cautions: monitor for pituitary enlargement, particularly during pregnancy, annual gynaecological assessment (post-menopausal, every 6 months), monitor for peptic ulceration in acromegalic patients; contraceptive advice if appropriate (oral contraceptives may increase prolactin concentrations); at high dosage caution in patients with history of psychotic disorders or with severe cardiovascular disease and monitor for retroperitoneal fibrosis; alcohol may reduce tolerance; avoid in porphyria; **interactions:** Appendix 1 (bromocriptine)

HYPOTENSIVE REACTIONS. Hypotensive reactions may be disturbing in some patients during the first few days of treatment and particular care should be exercised when driving or operating machinery

Side-effects: nausea, vomiting, constipation, headache, dizziness, postural hypotension, drowsiness, reversible pallor of fingers and toes particularly in patients with Raynaud's syndrome; *high doses*, confusion, psychomotor excitation, hallucinations, dyskinesia, dry mouth, leg cramps, pleural effusions (may necessitate withdrawal of treatment), retroperitoneal fibrosis reported (monitoring required)

Dose: prevention/suppression of lactation for medical reasons, 2.5 mg on 1st day (prevention) or daily for 2–3 days (suppression); then 2.5 mg twice daily for 14 days

Hypogonadism/galactorrhoea, infertility, initially 1–1.25 mg at bedtime, increased gradually; usual dose 7.5 mg daily in divided doses, increased if necessary to a max. of 30 mg daily. Usual dose in infertility without hyperprolactinaemia, 2.5 mg twice daily

Cyclical benign breast disease and cyclical menstrual disorders (particularly breast pain), 1–1.25 mg at bedtime, increased gradually; usual dose 2.5 mg twice daily

Acromegaly, initially 1–1.25 mg at bedtime, increase gradually to 5 mg every 6 hours

Prolactinoma, initially 1–1.25 mg at bedtime; increased gradually to 5 mg every 6 hours (occasional patients may require up to 30 mg daily)

Doses should be taken with food

PoM **Bromocriptine** (Non-proprietary)
Tablets, bromocriptine (as mesylate), 2.5 mg, net price 20 = £5.13. Label: 21, counselling, hypotensive reactions

PoM **Parlodel**® (Sandoz)
Tablets, both scored, bromocriptine (as mesylate) 1 mg, net price 20 = £1.86; 2.5 mg, 20 = £3.61. Label: 21, counselling, see above
Capsules, bromocriptine (as mesylate) 5 mg (blue/white), net price 20 = £7.04; 10 mg, 20 = £13.03. Label: 21, counselling, hypotensive reactions

6.7.2 Diagnostic agents for endocrine disorders

Tetracosactrin injection (section 6.5.1) is used to test adrenocortical function. Failure of the plasma cortisol concentration to rise after intramuscular administration indicates adrenocortical insufficiency.

Metyrapone is a competitive inhibitor of 11β-hydroxylation in the adrenal cortex; the resulting inhibition of cortisol production leads to an increase in ACTH production which, in turn, leads to increased synthesis and release of cortisol precursors. It may be used as a test of anterior pituitary function.

Although most types of *Cushing's syndrome* are treated surgically, that which occasionally accompanies carcinoma of the bronchus is not usually amenable to surgery. Metyrapone has been found helpful in controlling the symptoms of the disease; it is also used in other forms of Cushing's syndrome to prepare the patient for surgery. The dosages used are either low, and tailored to cortisol production, or high, in which case corticosteroid replacement therapy is also needed. Metyrapone should only be used under specialist advice.

See also trilostane (section 6.7.4) and aminoglutethimide (see section 8.3.4).

Thyrotrophin-releasing hormone (TRH, **protirelin**) may be of value in difficult cases of hyperthyroidism. Failure of plasma thyrotrophin (TSH) concentration to rise after intravenous injection indicates excess circulating thyroid hormones. Impaired or absent responses also occur in some euthyroid patients with single adenoma, multinodular goitre, or endocrine exophthalmos; patients with hypopituitarism show a reduced or delayed rise.

Gonadotrophin-releasing hormone (LH-RH, **gonadorelin**) when injected intravenously in normal subjects leads to a rapid rise in plasma concentrations of both luteinising hormone (LH) and follicle-stimulating hormone (FSH). It has not proved to be very helpful, however, in distinguishing hypothalamic from pituitary lesions.

Desmopressin (section 6.5.2) is used in the differential diagnosis of diabetes insipidus. Following a dose of 2 micrograms intramuscularly or 20 micrograms intranasally, restoration of the ability to concentrate urine after water deprivation confirms a diagnosis of cranial diabetes insipidus. Failure to respond occurs in nephrogenic diabetes insipidus.

The **glucose** tolerance test is used in the diagnosis of diabetes mellitus. In the UK this generally involves giving 75 g of glucose BP (= dextrose monohydrate) by mouth to the fasting patient, and measuring plasma concentrations at intervals. At an international level, however, confusion has arisen because in different pharmacopoeias the title 'glucose' can mean the anhydrous form or the monohydrate. Sources at the World Health Organisation have therefore suggested that the form of dextrose should be standardised as anhydrous, and that the standard amount should be 75 g. The equivalent value (and titles) in the UK are:

Anhydrous glucose BP (anhydrous dextrose) 75 g = Glucose BP (dextrose monohydrate) 82.5 g

GONADORELIN

(LH–RH)

Indications: see preparations below

Side-effects: rarely, nausea, headache, abdominal pain, increased menstrual bleeding; rarely, hypersensitivity reaction on repeated administration of large doses; irritation at injection site

Dose: see below

PoM **Fertiral®** (Hoechst)

Injection, gonadorelin 500 micrograms/mL. Net price 2-mL amp = £34.30

For amenorrhoea and infertility due to abnormal release of LH–RH (endogenous gonadorelin), *by pulsatile subcutaneous infusion*, initially 10–20 micrograms over 1 minute, repeated every 90 minutes for max. of 6 months; pulsatile intravenous infusion (in association with heparin) may be required

PoM **HRF®** (Wyeth)

Injection, powder for reconstitution, gonadorelin. Net price 100-microgram vial = £8.12; 500-microgram vial = £17.73 (both with diluent)

For assessment of pituitary function (adults), *by subcutaneous or intravenous injection*, 100 micrograms

PoM **Relefact LH-RH®** (Hoechst)

Injection, gonadorelin 100 micrograms/mL. Net price 1-mL amp = £9.68

For assessment of pituitary function, *by intravenous injection*, 100 micrograms

PoM **Relefact LH-RH/TRH®** (Hoechst)

Injection, gonadorelin 100 micrograms, protirelin 200 micrograms/mL. Net price 1-mL amp = £11.18

For assessment of anterior pituitary reserve by intravenous injection, 1 mL

METYRAPONE

Indications: see under Dose

Cautions: gross hypopituitarism (risk of precipitating acute adrenal failure); many drugs interfere with estimation of steroids

Contra-indications: pregnancy, breast-feeding

Side-effects: occasional nausea, vomiting, dizziness, headache, hypotension

Dose: in the assessment of pituitary function 750 mg every 4 hours for 6 doses; CHILD 15 mg/kg (minimum 250 mg)

Management of Cushing's syndrome, range 0.25–6 g daily, tailored to cortisol production; see also section 6.3.1

Resistant oedema due to increased aldosterone secretion in cirrhosis, nephrosis, and congestive heart failure, 2.5–4.5 g daily in divided doses (with glucocorticoids)

Note. Metyrapone should only be used under specialist advice; corticosteroid replacement therapy needed with high doses

PoM **Metopirone®** (Ciba)

Capsules, metyrapone 250 mg. Net price 20 = £4.18. Label: 21

PROTIRELIN

Indications: assessment of thyroid function and thyroid stimulating hormone reserve

Cautions: severe hypopituitarism, myocardial ischaemia, bronchial asthma and obstructive airways disease, pregnancy

Side-effects: after rapid intravenous administration desire to micturate, flushing, dizziness, nausea, strange taste; transient increase in pulse rate and blood pressure; rarely bronchospasm

Dose: by intravenous injection, 200 micrograms; CHILD 1 microgram/kg

PoM **TRH** (Roche)

Injection, protirelin 100 micrograms/mL. Net price 2-mL amp = £1.50 (hosp. only)

6.7.3 Danazol

Danazol inhibits pituitary gonadotrophin secretion, and is used in the treatment of endometriosis. It has also been used for menorrhagia and other menstrual disorders, mammary dysplasia, and gynaecomastia where other measures proved unsatisfactory. It may also be effective in the long-term management of hereditary angioedema.

DANAZOL

Indications: see notes above

Cautions: cardiac, hepatic, or renal impairment, epilepsy, diabetes mellitus, migraine, history of thrombosis; non-hormonal contraceptive methods should be used, if appropriate; **interactions:** Appendix 1 (danazol)

Contra-indications: porphyria; pregnancy, ensure that patients with amenorrhoea are not pregnant; breast-feeding

Side-effects: nausea, dizziness, rashes, backache, nervousness, headache, weight gain; flushing and reduction in breast size also reported; skeletal muscle spasm, hair loss; mild androgenic effects including acne, oily skin, oedema, mild hirsutism, voice changes and rarely clitoral hypertrophy, hyperglucagonaemia; thrombocytopenia reported; rarely cholestatic jaundice

Dose: usual range 200–800 mg daily in up to 4 divided doses; in adult females all doses should start during menstruation, preferably on the first day

Endometriosis, initially 400 mg daily in up to 4 divided doses, adjusted according to response, usually for 6 months

Menorrhagia, 100–400 mg daily in up to 4 divided doses, adjusted according to response (usual dose 200 mg daily), review after 3 months

Benign breast disorders, initially 300 mg daily in divided doses, adjusted according to response, usually for 3–6 months

CHILD, precocious puberty, 100–400 mg daily according to age and response

PoM **Danazol** (Non-proprietary)

Capsules, danazol 100 mg, net price 20 = £5.54; 200 mg, 20 = £10.98

PoM **Danol®** (Sterling-Winthrop)

Capsules, pink/white, danazol 200 mg. Net price 56-cap pack = £30.75

PoM **Danol-½®** (Sterling-Winthrop)

Capsules, grey/white, danazol 100 mg. Net price 20 = £5.55

6.7.4 Trilostane

Trilostane inhibits the synthesis of mineralocorticoids and glucocorticoids by the adrenal cortex, and may be useful in Cushing's syndrome and primary hyperaldosteronism. It appears to be less effective than metyrapone (section 6.7.2) for the treatment of Cushing's syndrome.

TRILOSTANE

Indications: see notes above

Cautions: impaired liver and kidney function, monitor circulating corticosteroids and blood-electrolyte concentrations; non-hormonal contraceptive methods should be used, if appropriate; **interactions:** Appendix 1 (trilostane)

Contra-indications: pregnancy

Side-effects: rarely flushing, nausea, rhinorrhoea with high doses

Dose: 60 mg 4 times daily for at least 3 days, then adjusted according to patient's response; usual dose range 120–480 mg daily in divided doses

PoM **Modrenal®** (Farillon)

Capsules, pink/black, trilostane 60 mg. Net price 20 = £7.92

7: Drugs used in OBSTETRICS, GYNAECOLOGY, and URINARY-TRACT DISORDERS

In this chapter, drugs are discussed under the following headings:

For hormonal therapy of gynaecological disorders see sections 6.4.1 and 6.5.1.

7.1 Drugs acting on smooth muscle

This section includes prostaglandins and oxytocics (section 7.1.1) and myometrial relaxants (section 7.1.2).

> *Note*. Because of the complexity of dosage regimens in obstetrics, in all cases detailed specialist literature should be consulted.

7.1.1 Prostaglandins and oxytocics

Myometrial stimulants are used to induce abortion or induce or augment labour and to minimise blood loss from the placental site. They include oxytocin, ergometrine, and the prostaglandins. All induce uterine contractions with varying degrees of pain according to the strength of contractions induced.

INDUCTION OF ABORTION. The prostaglandins **dinoprost** and **dinoprostone** can be used for the induction of abortion; dinoprostone is now preferred. They are contra-indicated in conditions where prolonged uterine contractions would be inappropriate.

The *intravenous route* is associated with a high incidence of side-effects and is rarely used.

Extra- or *intra-amniotic* administration of a prostaglandin is preferable for the induction of late therapeutic abortion. Extra-amniotic dinoprostone is also of value as an adjunct in 'priming' the cervix prior to suction termination but is less commonly used nowadays. The intra-amniotic route can only be used after about 14–16 weeks gestation.

Prior to induction of abortion, ripening or softening of the cervix with prostaglandin *pessaries* or *gel* is favoured by many nowadays, particularly in primigravida or in the presence of an unfavourable cervix, to avoid damage to the cervix. Dinoprostone is available in the form of pessaries or gel and gemeprost in the form of pessaries.

INDUCTION AND AUGMENTATION OF LABOUR. **Oxytocin** (Syntocinon®) is administered by slow intravenous infusion, preferably using an infusion pump, to induce or augment labour, often in conjunction with amniotomy. Uterine activity must be monitored carefully and hyperstimulation avoided. Large doses of oxytocin may result in excessive fluid retention.

Prostaglandins have now been developed as vaginal tablets and vaginal gels for the induction of labour at term. The intravenous and oral routes are rarely used.

PREVENTION AND TREATMENT OF HAEMORRHAGE. Bleeding due to *incomplete abortion* can be controlled with **ergometrine** and **oxytocin** (Syntometrine®) given intravenously or intramuscularly, the dose being adjusted according to the patient's condition and blood loss. This is commonly used prior to surgical evacuation of the uterus, particularly when surgery is delayed. Oxytocin and ergometrine combined are more effective in early pregnancy than either drug alone.

For the routine management of the *third stage of labour* ergometrine 500 micrograms with oxytocin 5 units (Syntometrine® 1 mL) is given by intramuscular injection with or after delivery of the shoulders. Intravenous injection is recommended for the prevention of postpartum haemorrhage in *high-risk cases*, giving either ergometrine 125–250 micrograms alone *or* oxytocin 5–10 units alone, after delivery of the shoulders (repeated if necessary); alternatively intravenous infusion of oxytocin 10–20 units/ 500 mL can be given after delivery of the shoulders, particularly when the uterus is *atonic*. If these measures are ineffective the use of **carboprost** is considered.

In domiciliary obstetric practice small secondary postpartum haemorrhage may be treated with ergometrine by mouth in a dose of 500 micrograms three times daily for 3 days.

CARBOPROST

Indications: postpartum haemorrhage due to uterine atony in patients unresponsive to ergometrine and oxytocin

Cautions: history of glaucoma or raised intraocular pressure, asthma, hypertension, hypotension, anaemia, jaundice, diabetes, history of epilepsy, uterine scars; not indicated for induction of labour

Contra-indications: acute pelvic inflammatory disease, cardiac renal, pulmonary, or hepatic disease

Side-effects: nausea, vomiting, diarrhoea, hyperthermia, flushing, asthma, chills, headache, diaphoresis, dizziness, erythema and pain at injection site; less frequent effects are elevated blood pressure, dyspnoea, pulmonary oedema

Dose: *by deep intramuscular injection*, 250 micrograms repeated if necessary at intervals of 1½ hours (in severe cases the interval may be reduced but should not be less than 15 minutes); total dose should not exceed 12 mg (48 doses)

▼ PoM **Hemabate®** (Upjohn)
Injection, carboprost trometamol (tromethamine) 250 micrograms/mL, net price 1-mL amp = £16.50 (hosp. only)

DINOPROSTONE

Indications: see notes above
Cautions: asthma, glaucoma and raised intra-ocular pressure; excessive dosage may cause uterine rupture; continuous administration for more than 2 days not recommended; see also notes above
Contra-indications: hypertonic uterine inertia, mechanical obstruction of delivery, placenta praevia, predisposition to uterine rupture, severe toxaemia, untreated pelvic infection, fetal distress, grand multiparas and multiple pregnancy, prior history of difficult or traumatic delivery; avoid extra-amniotic route in cervicitis or vaginitis
Side-effects: nausea, vomiting, diarrhoea, flushing, shivering, headache, dizziness, temporary pyrexia and raised white blood cell count, uterine hypertonus, unduly severe uterine contractions; all dose-related and more common after intravenous administration; also local tissue reaction and erythema after intravenous administration
Dose: see under Preparations, below
IMPORTANT. Do not confuse dose of **Prostin E2®** vaginal **gel** with that of **Prostin E2®** vaginal **tablets**—not bioequivalent. In addition, do not confuse **Prostin E2®** vaginal gel with **Prepidil®** cervical gel—different site of administration and different indication—see under Preparations, below.

PoM **Prepidil®** (Upjohn)
Cervical gel, dinoprostone 200 micrograms/mL in disposable syringe. Net price 2.5-mL syringe (500 micrograms) = £14.12
Dose: by cervix, pre-induction cervical softening and dilation, inserted into cervical canal (just below level of internal cervical os), 500 micrograms [single dose gel]

PoM **Prostin E2®** (Upjohn)
Tablets, dinoprostone 500 micrograms. Net price 10-tab pack = £14.93 (hosp. only)
Dose: by mouth, induction of labour, 500 micrograms, followed by 0.5–1 mg (max. 1.5 mg) at hourly intervals
Intravenous solution, for dilution and use as an infusion, dinoprostone 1 mg/mL, net price 0.75-mL amp = £6.91; 10 mg/mL, 0.5-mL amp = £14.93 (both hosp. only; rarely used, see data sheet for dose and indications)
Extra-amniotic solution, dinoprostone 10 mg/mL. Net price 0.5-mL amp (with diluent) = £16.05 (hosp. only; less commonly used nowadays, see data sheet for dose and indications)
Vaginal gel, dinoprostone 400 micrograms/mL, net price 2.5 mL (1 mg) = £14.52; 800 micrograms/mL, 2.5 mL (2 mg) = £16.00
Dose: by vagina, induction of labour, inserted high into posterior fornix (avoid administration into cervical canal), 1 mg, followed after 6 hours by 1–2 mg if required; max. 3 mg [gel]
Vaginal tablets, dinoprostone 3 mg. Net price 8-vaginal tab pack = £65.04
Dose: by vagina, induction of labour, inserted high into posterior fornix, 3 mg, followed after 6–8 hours by 3 mg if labour is not established; max. 6 mg [vaginal tablets]
Note. Prostin E2 Vaginal Gel and Vaginal Tablets are **not** bioequivalent

DINOPROST

Indications: see notes above
Cautions; Contra-indications; Side-effects: see under Dinoprostone and notes above

PoM **Prostin F2 alpha®** (Upjohn)
Intra-amniotic injection, dinoprost 5 mg (as trometamol salt)/mL. Net price 4-mL amp = £19.71 (hosp. only; rarely used, see data sheet for dose and indications)

ERGOMETRINE MALEATE

Indications: active management of third stage of labour, postpartum haemorrhage
Cautions: toxaemia, cardiac disease, hypertension, sepsis, multiple pregnancy; porphyria (see section 9.8.2)
Contra-indications: 1st and 2nd stages of labour, vascular disease, impaired pulmonary, hepatic, and renal function
Side-effects: nausea, vomiting, transient hypertension, vasoconstriction
Dose: *by mouth*, 0.5–1 mg (onset about 8 minutes, duration about 1 hour); see also notes above
By intramuscular injection, 200–500 micrograms (onset about 5–7 minutes, duration about 45 minutes)
By intravenous injection for emergency control of haemorrhage, 100–500 micrograms (onset about 1 minute)
See also notes above

PoM **Ergometrine Tablets,** ergometrine maleate 250 micrograms, net price 20 = £1.21; 500 micrograms, 20 = £1.74
PoM **Ergometrine Injection,** ergometrine maleate 500 micrograms/mL. Net price 1-mL amp = 18p

Combined preparation
PoM **Syntometrine®** (Sandoz)
Injection, ergometrine maleate 500 micrograms, oxytocin 5 units/mL. Net price 1-mL amp = 19p
Dose: by intramuscular injection, 1 mL; by intravenous injection, 0.5–1 mL

GEMEPROST

Indications: see under Dose
Cautions: obstructive airways disease, cardiovascular insufficiency, raised intra-ocular pressure, cervicitis or vaginitis

Side-effects: vaginal bleeding and uterine pain; nausea, vomiting, or diarrhoea; headache, muscle weakness, dizziness, flushing, chills, backache, dyspnoea, chest pain, palpitations and mild pyrexia; uterine rupture reported rarely

Dose: by vagina in pessaries, softening and dilation of the cervix to facilitate transcervical operative procedures in first trimester, 1 mg 3 hours before surgery

Second trimester abortion, 1 mg every 3 hours for max. of 5 administrations; second course may begin 24 hours after start of treatment

Second trimester intra-uterine death, 1 mg every 3 hours for max. of 5 administrations only; monitor for coagulopathy

PoM **Cervagem®** (Rhône-Poulenc Rorer)
Pessaries, gemeprost 1 mg. Net price 1 pessary = £20.96

OXYTOCIN

Indications: see under Dose

Cautions: hypertension, pressor drugs (may precipitate severe hypertension), multiple pregnancy, high parity, previous Caesarean section

Contra-indications: hypertonic uterine action, mechanical obstruction to delivery, failed trial labour, severe toxaemia, predisposition to amniotic fluid embolism, fetal distress, and placenta praevia

Side-effects: high doses cause violent uterine contractions leading to rupture and fetal asphyxiation, arrhythmias, maternal hypertension and subarachnoid haemorrhage, water intoxication

Dose: by slow intravenous infusion, induction of labour and augmentation of labour in hypotonic uterine inertia, as a solution containing 1 unit per litre, 1–3 milliunits per minute, adjusted according to response

Missed abortion, as a solution containing 10–20 units/500 mL given at a rate of 10–30 drops/minute, increased in strength by 10–20 units/500 mL every hour to a max. strength of 100 units/500 mL

Postpartum haemorrhage, see notes above

PoM **Syntocinon®** (Sandoz)
Injection, oxytocin 1 unit/mL, net price 2-mL amp = 18p; 5 units/mL, 1-mL amp = 20p; 10 units/mL, 1-mL amp = 23p, 5-mL amp = 84p

Combined preparation—see Syntometrine

DUCTUS ARTERIOSUS

MAINTENANCE OF PATENCY

Alprostadil (prostaglandin E_1) is used to maintain patency of the ductus arteriosus in neonates with congenital heart defects, prior to corrective surgery in centres where intensive care is immediately available.

ALPROSTADIL

Indications: congenital heart defects in neonates prior to corrective surgery

Cautions: see notes above; history of haemorrhage, avoid in hyaline membrane disease, monitor arterial pressure

Side-effects: apnoea (particularly in infants under 2 kg), flushing, bradycardia, hypotension, tachycardia, cardiac arrest, oedema, diarrhoea, fever, convulsions, disseminated intravascular coagulation, hypokalaemia; cortical proliferation of long bones, weakening of the wall of the ductus arteriosus and pulmonary artery may follow prolonged use

Dose: by intravenous infusion, initially 50–100 nanograms/kg/minute, then decreased to lowest effective dose

PoM **Prostin VR®** (Upjohn)
Intravenous solution, alprostadil 500 micrograms/mL in alcohol. For dilution and use as an infusion. Net price 1-mL amp = £56.96 (hosp. only)

CLOSURE OF DUCTUS ARTERIOSUS

Prostaglandin E_1 has the role of dilating the ductus arteriosus; indomethacin is believed to close it by inhibiting prostaglandin synthesis.

INDOMETHACIN

Indications: patent ductus arteriosus in premature infants (under specialist supervision)

Cautions: may mask symptoms of infection; may reduce renal function by 50% or more and precipitate renal insufficiency especially in infants with heart failure, sepsis, or hepatic impairment, or who are receiving nephrotoxic drugs; if urine volume reduced, discontinue until output returns to normal; may induce hyponatraemia; monitor renal function and electrolytes

Contra-indications: untreated infection, bleeding, congenital heart disease where patency of ductus arteriosus necessary for satisfactory pulmonary or systemic blood flow; thrombocytopenia, coagulation defects, necrotising enterocolitis, renal impairment

Side-effects: include haemorrhagic, renal, gastro-intestinal, metabolic, and coagulation disorders; fluid retention, and exacerbation of infection

Dose: by intravenous injection, over 5–10 seconds, 3 doses at intervals of 12–24 hours, age less than 48 hours, 200 micrograms/kg then 100 micrograms/kg then 100 micrograms/kg; age 2–7 days, 200 micrograms/kg then 200 micrograms/kg then 200 micrograms/kg; age over 7 days, 200 micrograms/kg then 250 micrograms/kg then 250 micrograms/kg; solution prepared with 1–2 mL sodium chloride 0.9% or water for injections (not glucose and no preservatives)

If ductus arteriosus reopens a second course of 3 injections may be given

PoM **Indocid PDA®** (Morson)
Injection, powder for reconstitution, indomethacin (as sodium trihydrate). Net price 3 × 1-mg vials = £22.50 (hosp. only)

7.1.2 Myometrial relaxants

Beta$_2$-adrenoceptor stimulants (sympathomimetics) relax uterine muscle and are used in selected cases in an attempt to inhibit *premature labour*.

They should not be used unless a clear benefit is likely. Tachycardia is the commonest side-effect and may be extreme if atropine is also administered.

Drugs used in the treatment of *spasmodic dysmenorrhoea* include prostaglandin-synthetase inhibitors such as aspirin, mefenamic acid and naproxen sodium (see section 4.7.1). See section 6.4.1.1 for hormone treatment.

ISOXSUPRINE HYDROCHLORIDE

Indications: uncomplicated premature labour
Cautions: may cause hypotension in the newborn; see notes above
Contra-indications: recent arterial haemorrhage, heart disease, premature detachment of placenta, severe anaemia, infection
Side-effects: hypotension, tachycardia, flushing, nausea, vomiting
Dose: *by intravenous infusion*, initially 200–300 micrograms/minute gradually increased to 500 micrograms/minute until labour is arrested; subsequently *by intramuscular injection*, 10 mg every 3 hours for 24 hours, then every 4–6 hours for 48 hours

PoM **Duvadilan®** (Duphar)
Injection, isoxsuprine hydrochloride 5 mg/mL. Net price 2-mL amp = 35p

RITODRINE HYDROCHLORIDE

Indications: uncomplicated premature labour; fetal asphyxia due to hypertonic uterine action
Cautions: diabetes mellitus (monitor blood sugar during intravenous treatment), cardiac disorders, thyrotoxicosis, treatment with corticosteroids, anaesthetics, potassium-depleting diuretics (depresses potassium plasma concentrations); monitor blood pressure and pulse; **interactions:** Appendix 1 (sympathomimetics)
Contra-indications: haemorrhage, hypertension, pre-eclampsia, cord compression, infection
Side-effects: nausea, vomiting, flushing, sweating, tremor; hypokalaemia, tachycardia and hypotension with high doses
Dose: *by intravenous infusion*, premature labour, initially 50 micrograms/minute, gradually increased to 150–350 micrograms/minute and continued for 12–48 hours after contractions have ceased; or *by intramuscular injection*, 10 mg every 3–8 hours continued for 12–48 hours after contractions have ceased; then *by mouth*, 10 mg 30 minutes before termination of intravenous infusion, repeated every 2 hours for 24 hours, followed by 10–20 mg every 4–6 hours, max. 120 mg daily
Fetal asphyxia due to hypertonic uterine action, *by intravenous infusion*, 50 micrograms/minute increased as necessary to a max. of 350 micrograms/minute, while preparations are made for delivery

PoM **Yutopar®** (Duphar)
Tablets, buff, scored, ritodrine hydrochloride 10 mg. Net price 90-tab pack = £19.80
Injection, ritodrine hydrochloride 10 mg/mL. Net price 5-mL amp = £2.15

SALBUTAMOL

Indications: uncomplicated premature labour
Cautions; Contra-indications; Side-effects: see under Ritodrine Hydrochloride
Dose: *by intravenous infusion*, 10 micrograms/minute gradually increased to max. of 45 micrograms/minute until contractions have ceased, then gradually reduced; or *by intravenous or intramuscular injection*, 100–250 micrograms repeated according to patient's response; subsequently *by mouth* 4 mg every 6–8 hours

Preparations
See section 3.1.1.1

TERBUTALINE SULPHATE

Indications: uncomplicated premature labour
Cautions; Contra-indications; Side-effects: see under Ritodrine Hydrochloride
Dose: *by intravenous infusion*, 10 micrograms/minute (as a 0.0005% solution) for 1 hour, gradually increased to a max. of 25 micrograms/minute until contractions have ceased, then reduced; subsequently *by subcutaneous injection*, 250 micrograms every 6 hours for 3 days, and *by mouth*, 5 mg every 8 hours until 37th week of pregnancy

Preparations
See section 3.1.1.1

7.2 Treatment of vaginal and vulval conditions

Preparations for topical application to the vulva and vagina include pessaries, creams, and medicated tampons.

Symptoms are primarily referable to the vulva, but infections almost invariably involve the vagina which should also be treated. Applications to the vulva alone are likely to give only symptomatic relief without cure.

Aqueous medicated douches may disturb normal vaginal acidity and bacterial flora.

Topical anaesthetic agents give only symptomatic relief and may cause sensitivity reactions. They are indicated only in cases of pruritus where specific local causes have been excluded.

Systemic drugs are required in the treatment of infections such as gonorrhoea and syphilis (see section 5.1).

7.2.1 Topical hormones

When there is a lack of endogenous oestrogens (as in postmenopausal women) application of cream containing an oestrogen may be used on a short-term basis to improve the quality of the vaginal epithelium in conditions such as menopausal atrophic vaginitis. For further comment see section 6.4.1.1.

Topical oestrogens are also used prior to vaginal surgery for prolapse when there is epithelial atrophy.

> Topical oestrogens should be used in the minimum effective amount and treatment discontinued as soon as possible to minimise absorption of the oestrogen.

OESTROGENS, TOPICAL

Indications: see notes above

Cautions; Contra-indications; Side-effects: see Ethinyloestradiol (section 6.4.1.1); contra-indicated in pregnancy and lactation; discontinue treatment and examine patients periodically to assess need for further treatment

PoM **Ortho® Dienoestrol** (Cilag)
Cream, dienoestrol 0.01%. Net price 78 g with applicator = £2.44
Insert 1–2 applicatorfuls daily for 1–2 weeks, then gradually reduced to 1 applicatorful 1–3 times weekly if necessary; attempts to reduce or discontinue should be made at 3–6 month intervals with re-examination

PoM **Ortho-Gynest®** (Cilag)
Intravaginal cream, oestriol 0.01%. Net price 78 g with applicator = £5.40
For postmenopausal atrophic vaginitis and kraurosis vulvae, insert 1 applicatorful daily, preferably in evening; reduced to 1 applicatorful twice a week; attempts to reduce or discontinue should be made at 3–6 month intervals with re-examination
Pessaries, oestriol 500 micrograms. Net price 15 pessaries = £5.29
Insert 1 pessary daily, preferably in the evening, until improvement occurs; maintenance 1 pessary twice a week; attempts to reduce or discontinue should be made at 3–6 month intervals with re-examination

PoM **Ovestin®** (Organon)
Intravaginal cream, oestriol 0.1%. Net price 15 g with applicator = £3.95
Insert 1 applicator-dose daily for 2–3 weeks, then reduce to twice a week (discontinue every 2–3 months for 4 weeks to assess need for further treatment); post-menopausal surgery, 1 applicatorful daily for 2 weeks, resuming 2 weeks after surgery

PoM **Premarin®** (Wyeth)
Vaginal cream, conjugated oestrogens 625 micrograms/g. Net price 42.5 g with calibrated applicator = £2.19
Insert 1–2 g daily, starting on 5th day of cycle, for 3 weeks, followed by 1-week interval; if therapy long term, oral progestogen for 10–12 days at end of each cycle essential

PoM **Tampovagan® Stilboestrol and Lactic Acid** (Norgine)
Pessaries, stilboestrol 500 micrograms, lactic acid 5%. Net price 10 pessaries = £7.46
Insert 2 pessaries at night for 1–2 weeks then reduce (short-term only, see notes above)

7.2.2 Anti-infective drugs

Effective specific treatments are available for the common vaginal infections, therefore the causal organism should be identified before starting treatment.

Vaginal candidiasis is treated primarily with antifungal pessaries or cream inserted high into the vagina (including the time of menstruation). *Candidal vulvitis* can be treated locally with cream but is almost invariably associated with vaginal infection which should be treated as well.

Nystatin is a well established treatment. One or two pessaries are inserted for 14 to 28 nights; they may be supplemented with cream for vulvitis and to treat other superficial sites of infection.

Imidazole drugs (clotrimazole, econazole, isoconazole, and miconazole) appear to be equally effective in shorter courses of 3 to 14 days according to the preparation used; single dose preparations are also available, which is an advantage when compliance is a problem. Vaginal applications may be supplemented with cream for vulvitis and to treat other superficial sites of infection.

Recurrence is common if the full course of treatment is not completed and is also particularly likely if there are predisposing factors such as antibiotic therapy, oral contraceptive use, pregnancy, or diabetes mellitus. Possible reservoirs of infection may also lead to recontamination and should be treated. These include other skin sites such as the digits, nail beds, and umbilicus as well as the gut and the bladder. The partner may also be the source of re-infection and should be treated with cream at the same time.

Oral treatment with fluconazole or itraconazole may be necessary in resistant or recurrent infection (see section 5.2); oral ketoconazole has been associated with fatal hepatotoxicity (see section 5.2 for CSM warning).

GENITAL ANTIFUNGAL PREPARATIONS

Indications: vaginal and vulval candidiasis

Side-effects: local irritation, possibly including burning, oedema, erythema

Administration: insert pessaries or cream high into the vagina and complete the course regardless of intervening menstruation

Canesten® (Baypharm)
Cream (topical), clotrimazole 1%. Net price 20 g= £1.82; 50 g = £4.26
Apply to anogenital area 2–3 times daily
PoM *Vaginal cream*, clotrimazole 2%. Net price 35 g (with 5-g applicators) = £5.22
Insert 5 g twice daily for 3 days or once nightly for 6 nights
PoM *Vaginal cream (10% VC®)*, clotrimazole 10%. Net price 5-g applicator pack = £3.43
Insert 5 g at night as a single dose
PoM *Vaginal tablets*, clotrimazole 100 mg. Net price 6 tabs with applicator = £2.64
PoM *Vaginal tablets*, clotrimazole 200 mg. Net price 3 tabs with applicator = £2.58
Insert 200 mg for 3 nights *or* 100 mg for 6 nights
PoM *Vaginal tablets (Canesten 1®)*, clotrimazole 500 mg. Net price 1 with applicator = £2.58
Insert 1 at night as a single dose
PoM *Duopak*, clotrimazole 100-mg vaginal tablets and cream (topical) 1%. Net price 6 tabs and 20 g cream = £4.35

Prices are **net**, see p. 1

Ecostatin® (Squibb)
Cream (topical), econazole nitrate 1%. Net price 15 g = £1.49; 30 g = £2.75
Apply to anogenital area twice daily
PoM *Pessaries*, econazole nitrate 150 mg. Net price 3 with applicator = £3.96
Insert 1 pessary for 3 nights
PoM *Twinpack*, econazole nitrate 150-mg pessaries and cream 1%. Net price 3 pessaries and 15 g cream = £4.98

PoM **Ecostatin-1**® (Squibb)
Pessary, econazole nitrate 150 mg. Net price 1 pessary with applicator = £4.40
Insert 1 pessary at night as a single dose

PoM **Flagyl Compak**®, see section 5.1.11

PoM **Fungilin**® (Squibb)
Cream, amphotericin 3%. Net price 15 g = £1.30
Apply to anogenital area 2–4 times daily

PoM **Gyno-Daktarin**® (Janssen)
Intravaginal cream, miconazole nitrate 2%. Net price 78 g with applicators = £4.95
Insert two 5-g applicatorfuls at night for 7 nights; *topical*, apply to anogenital area twice daily
Pessaries, miconazole nitrate 100 mg. Net price 14 = £4.04
Insert 2 pessaries for 7 nights
Tampons, coated with miconazole nitrate 100 mg. Net price 10 = £3.83
Insert 1 tampon night and morning for 5 days
Combipack, miconazole nitrate 100-mg pessaries and cream (topical) 2%. Net price 14 pessaries and 15 g cream = £5.94

PoM **Gyno-Daktarin 1**® (Janssen)
Ovule (= vaginal capsule), miconazole nitrate 1.2 g in a fatty basis. Net price 1 ovule (with finger stall) = £3.95
Insert 1 ovule at night as a single dose

PoM **Gyno-Pevaryl**® (Cilag)
Cream, econazole nitrate 1%. Net price 15 g = £1.74; 30 g = £3.45
Apply to anogenital area 2–3 times daily for 14 days
Pessaries, econazole nitrate 150 mg with applicator. Net price 3 = £3.17
Insert 1 pessary for 3 nights
Combipack, econazole nitrate 150-mg pessaries, econazole nitrate 1% cream (to be applied to anogenital area). Net price 3 pessaries and 15 g cream = £4.98

PoM **Gyno-Pevaryl 1**® (Cilag)
Pessary, econazole nitrate 150 mg (formulated for single-dose therapy). Net price 1 = £4.40
Insert 1 pessary at night as a single dose
Cream and Pessary CP pack, econazole nitrate 150-mg pessary, econazole nitrate 1% cream (to be applied to anogenital area). Net price 1 pessary and 15 g cream = £5.84

PoM **Monistat**® (Cilag)
Vaginal cream, miconazole nitrate 2%. Net price 78 g with applicator = £3.07
Insert 1 applicatorful (approx. 5 g) at night for 14 nights; also apply to anogenital area

PoM **Nizoral**® (Janssen)
Cream (topical), ketoconazole 2%. Net price 30 g = £3.81
Apply to anogenital area once or twice daily

PoM **Nystan**® (Squibb)
Cream and *Ointment*, see section 13.10.2
Gel (topical), nystatin 100000 units/g. Net price 30 g = £2.66
Apply to anogenital area 2–4 times daily
Vaginal cream, nystatin 100000 units/4-g application. Net price 60 g with applicator = £3.26
Pessaries, yellow, nystatin 100000 units. Net price 28-pessary pack = £1.96
Insert 1–2 applicatorfuls of cream or 1–2 pessaries at night for at least 14 nights

Pevaryl® (Cilag)
Cream, econazole nitrate 1%. Net price 30 g = £2.65
Apply to anogenital area 2–3 times daily
Lotion and *Dusting-powder*, see section 13.10.2

PoM **Pimafucin**® (Brocades)
Cream, natamycin 2%. Net price 30 g = £1.75
Apply to anogenital area 2–3 times daily

PoM **Travogyn**® (Schering Health Care)
Cream (topical), isoconazole nitrate 1%. Net price 20 g = £1.88
Apply to anogenital area twice daily
Vaginal tablets (=pessaries), isoconazole nitrate 300 mg. Net price 2 = £3.90
Insert 2 pessaries as a single dose preferably at night

OTHER INFECTIONS

Vaginal preparations intended to restore normal acidity (Aci-Jel®) may prevent recurrence of vaginal infections and permit the re-establishment of the normal vaginal flora.

Trichomonal infections commonly involve the lower urinary tract as well as the genital system and need systemic treatment with metronidazole, nimorazole, or tinidazole (see section 5.1.11).

Bacterial infections with Gram-negative organisms are particularly common in association with gynaecological operations and trauma. Metronidazole is effective against certain Gram-negative organisms, especially *Bacteroides* spp. and may be used as a prophylactic measure in gynaecological surgery.

Antibacterial creams such as Sultrin® are used in the treatment of mixed bacterial infections but are of unproven value; they are ineffective against *Candida* spp. and *Trichomonas vaginalis*.

Acyclovir may be used in the treatment of genital infection due to *herpes simplex virus*, the HSV type 2 being a major cause of genital ulceration. It has a beneficial effect on virus shedding and healing, generally giving relief from pain and other symptoms. See section 5.3 for systemic preparations, and section 13.10.3 for cream.

PREPARATIONS FOR OTHER VAGINAL INFECTIONS

Aci-Jel® (Cilag)
Vaginal jelly, acetic acid 0.92% in a buffered (pH 4) basis. Net price 85 g with applicator = £3.37
Non-specific infections, insert 1 applicatorful twice daily to restore vaginal acidity

Betadine® (Napp)
Caution: avoid in pregnancy (and if planned) and in breast-feeding
Side-effects: rarely sensitivity; may interfere with thyroid function
Antiseptic Vaginal Cleansing Kit, solution, povidone-iodine 10%. Net price 250 mL with measuring bottle and applicator = £2.78
To be diluted and used once daily, preferably in the morning; may be used with Betadine® pessaries or vaginal gel
Pessaries, brown, povidone-iodine 200 mg. Net price 28 pessaries with applicator = £5.11
Vaginal gel, brown, povidone-iodine 10%. Net price 80 g with applicator = £2.33
Vaginal infections or pre-operatively, insert 1 moistened pessary night and morning for up to 14 days *or* use morning pessary with 5-g gel at night *or* morning douche with pessary (or 5-g gel) at night

PoM **Gynatren®** (Solco Basle)
Vaccine prepared from inactivated *Lactobacillus acidophilus*. Net price 3 × 0.5-mL amp = £16.00
Dose: for recurrent trichomoniasis, by intramuscular injection, 3 doses each of 0.5 mL separated by intervals of 2 weeks

PoM **Sultrin®** (Cilag)
Indications: bacterial vaginitis and cervicitis
Contra-indications: pregnancy
Side-effects: sensitivity
Cream, sulphathiazole 3.42%, sulphacetamide 2.86%, sulphabenzamide 3.7%. Net price 78 g with applicator = £3.48
Vaginal tablets, sulphathiazole 172.5 mg, sulphacetamide 143.75 mg, sulphabenzamide 184 mg. Net price 20 with applicator = £2.94
Insert 1 pessary or applicatorful of cream twice daily for 10 days, then once daily if necessary

7.3 Contraceptives

The criteria by which contraceptive methods should be judged are effectiveness, acceptability, and freedom from side-effects.

Hormonal contraception is the most effective method of fertility control, short of sterilisation, but has unwanted major and minor side-effects, especially for certain groups of women.

Intra-uterine devices have a high use-effectiveness but may produce undesirable side-effects, especially menorrhagia, or be otherwise unsuitable in a significant proportion of women; their use is generally inadvisable in nulliparous women because of the increased risk of pelvic sepsis and infertility.

Barrier methods alone (condoms, diaphragms, and caps) are less effective but can be very reliable for well-motivated couples if used in conjunction with a **spermicide**. Occasionally sensitivity reactions occur.

The health departments of the UK have recently issued a revised edition of the booklet, *Handbook of Contraceptive Practice*, 1990. Copies can be obtained from:

DOH Store, Health Publications Unit,
Central Store, Manchester Road,
Heywood, Lancs OL10 2PZ

7.3.1 Combined oral contraceptives

Oral contraceptives containing an oestrogen and a progestogen are the most effective preparations for general use. The oestrogen content ranges from 20 to 50 micrograms and generally a preparation with the lowest oestrogen and progestogen content which gives good cycle control and minimal side-effects in the individual patient is chosen.

DOSAGE. The dosage regimen for *combined oral contraceptives* is usually 1 tablet daily for 21 days, followed by a 7-day interval during which menstrual bleeding occurs. If the first course is started on the 5th day of the cycle ovulation may not be inhibited during that cycle and additional contraceptive precautions should therefore be taken during the first 7 days[1] or when changing from a high to a low oestrogen preparation. Additional contraceptive precautions are unnecessary in the first cycle if the tablets are started on the first day of the cycle as is now usually recommended.

Phased formulations more closely mimic normal endogenous cyclical hormonal activity. They are generally recommended for a day 1 start.

The tablet should be taken at approximately the same time each day. If it is delayed by longer than 12 hours, contraceptive protection may be lost.

MISSED PILL. It is important to bear in mind that the critical time for loss of protection is when a pill is forgotten at the *beginning* or *end* of a cycle. The following advice is now recommended by family planning organisations:

'If you forget a pill, take it as soon as you remember, and the next one at your normal time. If you are 12 or more hours late with any pill (especially the first or last in the packet) the pill may not work. As soon as you remember, continue normal pill taking. However, you will not be protected for the next seven days and must either not have sex or use another method such as the sheath. If these seven days run beyond the end of your packet, start the next packet at once when you have finished the present one, i.e. do not have a gap between packets. This will mean you may not have a period until the end of two packets but this does you no harm. Nor does it matter if you see some bleeding on tablet-taking days. If you are using everyday (ED) pills—miss out the seven inactive pills. If you are not sure which these are, ask your doctor.'

1. Formerly 14 days but family planning organisations now consider 7 days to be enough.

SIDE-EFFECTS. Combined oral contraceptives carry a small risk of thrombo-embolic and cardiovascular complications. This increases with age, obesity, and cigarette smoking, and with predisposing conditions such as diabetes, hypertension, and familial hyperlipidaemia.

Hypertension may develop as the result of therapy but when it is due to contraceptive usage reversion to normotension occurs on cessation of treatment.

Critical factors which limit effectiveness are vomiting and diarrhoea and some antibiotics, for example ampicillin, which interfere with oestrogen absorption. Drugs which induce hepatic enzyme activity (e.g. barbiturates, griseofulvin, phenytoin, rifampicin) also increase the risk of failure.

CSM advice.
It is important to balance the uncertainties in relation to carcinoma of the breast against the evidence available that combined oral contraceptives protect against ovarian and endometrial carcinoma. Taking into account both the benefits and potential risks of oral contraceptive use, the CSM recommends that there is no need for a change in oral contraceptive prescribing practice on the evidence presently available.

CHILDBIRTH. Following childbirth oral contraception can be started at any time after 3 to 4 weeks postpartum (not earlier because of the increased risk of thrombosis in relation to the combined pill, and of breakthrough bleeding in relation to the progestogen-only pill). If they are started later than 4 weeks postpartum extra contraceptive precautions should be taken for 7 days. Lactation may be affected by combined oral contraceptives as described in Appendix 5.

SURGERY. Oestrogen-containing oral contraceptives should be discontinued (and adequate alternative contraceptive arrangements made) 4 weeks before major elective surgery and all surgery to the legs; they should normally be recommenced at the first menses occurring at least 2 weeks after the procedure. When discontinuation is not possible, e.g. after trauma or if, by oversight, a patient admitted for an elective procedure is still on an oestrogen-containing oral contraceptive, some consideration should be given to subcutaneous heparin prophylaxis. These recommendations do not apply to minor surgery with short duration of anaesthesia, e.g. laparoscopic sterilisation or tooth extraction, or to women taking oestrogen-free hormonal contraceptives.

For hormone replacement therapy the same policy as for oestrogen-containing oral contraceptives may be appropriate, although the evidence of an increased risk is questionable. For reference to supraphysiological concentrations of oestradiol implants see section 6.4.1.

ORAL CONTRACEPTIVES (Combined)

Indications: contraception; menstrual symptoms, see section 6.4.1.1

Cautions: see notes above; diabetes, hypertension, cardiac or renal disease, migraine, epilepsy, depression, asthma, immobilisation, contact lenses (may irritate), varicose veins; cigarette-smokers, patients over 35 years, obesity, breast-feeding, sickle-cell anaemia (safety not established); **interactions:** Appendix 1 (contraceptives, oral)

Contra-indications: pregnancy; thrombosis and history of any thrombo-embolic disease, after evacuation of hydatidiform mole (until return to normal of urine and plasma gonadotrophin values); recurrent jaundice, acute and chronic liver disease, porphyria, Dubin-Johnson and Rotor syndromes, hyperlipidaemia, mammary or endometrial carcinoma, oestrogen-dependent tumours, severe or focal migraine, undiagnosed vaginal bleeding, history of pruritus of pregnancy or herpes gestationis, deterioration of otosclerosis

Side-effects: nausea, vomiting, headache, breast tenderness, changes in body weight, thrombosis (more common in blood groups A, B, and AB than O), changes in libido, depression, chloasma, hypertension, impairment of liver function, hepatic tumours, reduced menstrual loss, 'spotting' in early cycles, amenorrhoea; rarely photosensitivity

Dose: see notes above

Ethinyloestradiol 20 micrograms

Mercilon® has been reported to give much better cycle control than Loestrin 20®. Regularity of pill-taking is critical; appropriate for obese patients (provided oral contraceptive use otherwise suitable).

PoM **Loestrin 20®** (P-D)
Tablets, blue-grey, f/c, norethisterone acetate 1 mg, ethinyloestradiol 20 micrograms. Net price 21-tab calendar pack = 86p

PoM **Mercilon®** (Organon)
Tablets, desogestrel 150 micrograms, ethinyloestradiol 20 micrograms. Net price 21-tab pack = £1.93

Ethinyloestradiol 30 micrograms

Standard strength from which the initial choice is usually selected. Highly effective if the pill-free interval is not lengthened by dose omissions. Of these, Conova 30®, Eugynon 30®, and Ovran 30® are not good first choices since the others have less of the apparently unfavourable effects on plasma lipids.

PoM **Conova 30®** (Gold Cross)
Tablets, f/c, ethynodiol diacetate 2 mg, ethinyloestradiol 30 micrograms. Net price 21-tab pack = 80p

PoM **Eugynon 30**® (Schering Health Care)
Tablets, s/c, levonorgestrel 250 micrograms, ethinyloestradiol 30 micrograms. Net price 21-tab pack = 69p

▼ PoM **Femodene**® (Schering Health Care)
Tablets, s/c, gestodene 75 micrograms, ethinyloestradiol 30 micrograms. Net price 21-tab pack = £1.90

▼ PoM **Femodene ED**® (Schering Health Care)
As for Femodene and in addition 7 white placebo tablets. Net price 28-tab calendar pack = £1.90
Dose: 1 tablet daily starting in red sector on 1st day of cycle continuing in sequence without interruption

PoM **Loestrin 30**® (P-D)
Tablets, green, f/c, norethisterone acetate 1.5 mg, ethinyloestradiol 30 micrograms. Net price 21-tab pack = £1.26

PoM **Marvelon**® (Organon)
Tablets, desogestrel 150 micrograms, ethinyloestradiol 30 micrograms. Net price 21-tab pack = £1.48

PoM **Microgynon 30**® (Schering Health Care)
Tablets, beige, s/c, levonorgestrel 150 micrograms, ethinyloestradiol 30 micrograms. Net price 21-tab pack = 60p

▼ PoM **Minulet**® (Wyeth)
Tablets, s/c, gestodene 75 micrograms, ethinyloestradiol 30 micrograms. Net price 21-tab pack = £1.90

PoM **Ovran 30**® (Wyeth)
Tablets, levonorgestrel 250 micrograms, ethinyloestradiol 30 micrograms. Net price 21-tab pack = 57p

PoM **Ovranette**® (Wyeth)
Tablets, levonorgestrel 150 micrograms, ethinyloestradiol 30 micrograms. Net price 21-tab pack = 62p
Dose: see above and under Ovran below

Ethinyloestradiol 35 micrograms

In common with the 30-microgram strength (above), standard strength from which the initial choice is usually selected. Highly effective if the pill-free interval is not lengthened by dose omissions.

PoM **Brevinor**® (Syntex)
Tablets, norethisterone 500 micrograms, ethinyloestradiol 35 micrograms. Net price 21-tab pack = 52p

PoM **Neocon 1/35**® (Ortho)
Tablets, peach, norethisterone 1 mg, ethinyloestradiol 35 micrograms. Net price 21-tab calendar pack = 76p

PoM **Norimin**® (Syntex)
Tablets, yellow, norethisterone 1 mg, ethinyloestradiol 35 micrograms. Net price 21-tab calendar pack = 59p

PoM **Ovysmen**® (Ortho)
Tablets, norethisterone 500 micrograms, ethinyloestradiol 35 micrograms. Net price 21-tab pack = 53p

Ethinyloestradiol 50 micrograms

Increased security but possibility of increased side-effects. Used mainly in circumstances of reduced bioavailability (e.g. during long-term use of enzyme-inducing antiepileptics).

PoM **Ovran**® (Wyeth)
Tablets, levonorgestrel 250 micrograms, ethinyloestradiol 50 micrograms. Net price 21-tab pack = 37p
Dose: contraception, spasmodic dysmenorrhoea, see above; endometriosis 1–2 tablets daily without interruption; postponement of menstruation 1 tablet daily, preferably beginning before last 5 days of cycle, increased if spotting occurs to 2 tablets daily

Mestranol 50 micrograms

In common with the ethinyloestradiol 50-microgram strength (above), increased security but possibility of increased side-effects. Used mainly in circumstances of reduced bioavailability (e.g. during long-term use of enzyme-inducing antiepileptics).

PoM **Norinyl-1**® (Syntex)
Tablets, norethisterone 1 mg, mestranol 50 micrograms. Net price 21-tab pack = 57p

PoM **Ortho-Novin 1/50**® (Ortho)
Tablets, norethisterone 1 mg, mestranol 50 micrograms. Net price 21-tab pack = 78p

Phased formulations

A little more complex for the user to take, but provide better cycle control (with low metabolic effect) than equivalent fixed-dose levonorgestrel or norethisterone formulations.

PoM **BiNovum**® (Ortho)
Calendar pack, 7 white tablets, norethisterone 500 micrograms, ethinyloestradiol 35 micrograms; 14 peach tablets, norethisterone 1 mg, ethinyloestradiol 35 micrograms. Net price 21-tab pack = 70p
Dose: 1 tablet daily for 21 days, starting with a white tablet on 1st day of cycle, and repeated after a 7-day interval

PoM **Logynon**® (Schering Health Care)
Calendar pack, all s/c, 6 light brown tablets, levonorgestrel 50 micrograms, ethinyloestradiol 30 micrograms; 5 white tablets, levonorgestrel 75 micrograms, ethinyloestradiol 40 micrograms; 10 ochre tablets, levonorgestrel 125 micrograms, ethinyloestradiol 30 micrograms. Net price 21-tab pack = 95p
Dose: 1 tablet daily for 21 days, starting with tablet marked 1 on 1st day of cycle, and repeated after a 7-day interval

PoM **Logynon ED**® (Schering Health Care)
As for Logynon and in addition 7 white placebo tablets. Net price 28-tab calendar pack = 95p
Dose: 1 tablet daily starting in red sector on 1st day of cycle continuing in sequence without interruption

PoM **Synphase**® (Syntex)
Calendar pack, 7 white tablets, norethisterone 500 micrograms, ethinyloestradiol 35 micrograms; 9 yellow tablets, norethisterone 1 mg, ethinyloestradiol 35 micrograms; 5 white tablets, norethisterone 500 micrograms, ethinyloestradiol 35 micrograms. Net price 21-tab pack = £1.01
Dose: 1 tablet daily for 21 days, starting with tablet marked 1 on the 5th day of the cycle, and repeated after a 7-day interval

PoM **Trinordiol**® (Wyeth)
Calendar pack, all s/c, 6 light brown tablets, levonorgestrel 50 micrograms, ethinyloestradiol 30 micrograms; 5 white tablets, levonorgestrel 75 micrograms, ethinyloestradiol 40 micrograms; 10 ochre tablets, levonorgestrel 125 micrograms, ethinyloestradiol 30 micrograms. Net price 21-tab pack = £1.09
Dose: 1 tablet daily for 21 days, starting with tablet marked 1 on 1st day of cycle, and repeated after a 7-day interval

PoM **TriNovum**® (Ortho)
Calendar pack, 7 white tablets, norethisterone 500 micrograms, ethinyloestradiol 35 micrograms; 7 light peach tablets, norethisterone 750 micrograms, ethinyloestradiol 35 micrograms; 7 peach tablets, norethisterone 1 mg, ethinyloestradiol 35 micrograms. Net price 21-tab pack = 88p
Dose: 1 tablet daily for 21 days, starting with a white tablet on 1st day of cycle, and repeated after a 7-day interval

PoM **TriNovum ED**® (Ortho)
As for TriNovum and in addition 7 green placebo tablets. Net price 28-tab calendar pack = 99p
Dose: 1 tablet daily starting in the white sector on 1st day of cycle continuing in sequence without interruption

Emergency contraception

Combined oral contraceptives may also be given for occasional emergency use after unprotected intercourse. Two tablets of a preparation containing levonorgestrel 250 micrograms and ethinyloestradiol 50 micrograms ([1]Schering PC4®) are taken within 72 hours, and a further 2 tablets 12 hours later. The patient should be counselled on administration and should always consult her doctor approximately 3 weeks after using this treatment.

PoM **Schering PC4**® (Schering Health Care)
Tablets, s/c, levonorgestrel 250 micrograms, ethinyloestradiol 50 micrograms. Net price 4 = £1.40. For postcoital contraception as an occasional emergency measure; should not be administered if menstrual bleeding overdue or if unprotected intercourse occurred more than 72 hours previously
Dose: 2 tablets as soon as possible after coitus (up to 72 hours) then 2 tablets after 12 hours

1. **Ovran**® (see p. 268) also contains levonorgestrel 250 micrograms and ethinyloestradiol 50 micrograms but is not licensed or packed for post-coital contraception.

7.3.2 Progestogen-only contraceptives

When oestrogens are contra-indicated, progestogen-only preparations may offer a suitable alternative but the oral preparations have a higher failure rate than combined preparations. They are suitable for older patients who may be at risk from oestrogen, heavy smokers, and those in whom oestrogens cause severe side-effects. Menstrual irregularities (oligomenorrhoea, menorrhagia) are more common but patients tend to revert to a more regular cyclical menstrual pattern on long treatment. Oral preparations are started on the 1st day of the cycle and taken every day at the same time without a break. Additional contraceptive precautions are unnecessary when initiating treatment with progestogen-only contraceptives. When changing from a combined oral contraceptive to a progestogen-only preparation treatment should start on the day following completion of the combined oral contraceptive course so that there is no break in tablet taking.

The tablet should be taken at the same time each day. If it is delayed by longer than 3 hours, contraceptive protection may be lost.

Missed pill. The following advice is now recommended by family planning organisations:

'If you forget a pill, take it as soon as you remember and carry on with the next pill at the right time. If the pill was more than three hours overdue you are not protected. Continue normal pill-taking but you must also use another method, such as the sheath, for the next 48 hours. If you have vomiting or very severe diarrhoea the pill may not work. Continue to take it, but you may not be protected from the first day of vomiting or diarrhoea. Use another method, such as the sheath, for any intercourse during the stomach upset and for the next 48 hours.'

Medroxyprogesterone acetate (Depo-Provera®) is a long-acting progestogen given by intramuscular injection; it is as effective as the combined oral preparations but should never be given without full counselling backed by the manufacturer's approved leaflet. It is useful for short-term interim contraception, for example, before vasectomy becomes effective or after rubella vaccination. It may also be used as a long-term contraceptive for women who are unable to use any other method, after counselling on the long and short-term effects. Transient infertility and irregular cycles may occur after discontinuation of treatment. Heavy bleeding has been reported in patients given medroxyprogesterone acetate in the immediate puerperium (the first dose is best delayed until 6 to 7 weeks postpartum). **Nor-**

ethisterone enanthate (Noristerat®) is a long-acting progestogen given as an oily injection which provides contraception for 8 weeks.

Progestogen-only preparations can be administered in the early puerperium without adverse effects (except increased bleeding); established lactation is not affected.

PROGESTOGEN-ONLY CONTRACEPTIVES

Indications: contraception

Cautions: diabetes, hypertension, heart disease, past ectopic pregnancy (oral preparations only), functional ovarian cysts, malabsorption syndromes; migraine which is severe or focal or has begun for first time on a combined oral contraceptive; active liver disease, recurrent cholestatic jaundice, and history of jaundice in pregnancy; **interactions:** Appendix 1 (contraceptives)

Contra-indications: pregnancy, undiagnosed vaginal bleeding, past severe arterial disease or current high risk (e.g. family history, together with cholesterol above 6.5 mmol/L); liver adenoma; after evacuation of hydatidiform mole (until return to normal of urine and plasma gonadotrophin values); carcinoma of the breast and other sex hormone dependent cancers

Side-effects: menstrual irregularities (see also notes above); nausea and vomiting, headache, breast discomfort, depression, skin disorders, weight changes. For other critical factors affecting contraceptive efficacy such as vomiting, diarrhoea, enzyme induction, and for comment on progestogen-only contraceptives and surgical operations, see under Combined Oral Contraceptives (section 7.3.1)

Dose: by mouth, 1 tablet daily at the same time, preferably early in the evening, starting on 1st day of cycle then continuously

Oral preparations

PoM **Femulen®** (Gold Cross)
Tablets, ethynodiol diacetate 500 micrograms. Net price 28-tab calendar pack = 94p

PoM **Micronor®** (Ortho)
Tablets, norethisterone 350 micrograms. Net price 28-tab calendar pack = 63p

PoM **Microval®** (Wyeth)
Tablets, levonorgestrel 30 micrograms. Net price 35-tab calendar pack = £1.00

PoM **Neogest®** (Schering Health Care)
Tablets, brown, s/c, norgestrel 75 micrograms (≡ levonorgestrel 37.5 micrograms). Net price 35-tab calendar pack = 78p

PoM **Norgeston®** (Schering Health Care)
Tablets, s/c, levonorgestrel 30 micrograms. Net price 35-tab calendar pack = 78p

PoM **Noriday®** (Syntex)
Tablets, norethisterone 350 micrograms. Net price 28-tab calendar pack = 59p

Parenteral preparations

PoM **Depo-Provera®** (Upjohn)
Injection (aqueous suspension), medroxyprogesterone acetate 150 mg/mL, net price 1-mL vial = £4.17

Note. The 150 mg/mL strength of Depo-Provera is also available in a 3.3-mL vial for use in cancer (see section 8.3.2), and a 50 mg/mL strength is available in 1-, 3-, and 5-mL vials for endometriosis.

Dose: by deep intramuscular injection, 150 mg in first 5 days of cycle or first 6 weeks after parturition (delay until 6 weeks after parturition if breast-feeding); for long-term contraception, repeated every 3 months

PoM **Noristerat®** (Schering Health Care)
Injection (oily), norethisterone enanthate 200 mg/mL. Net price 1-mL amp = £3.00

Dose: by deep intramuscular injection, short-term contraception, 200 mg in first 5 days of cycle or immediately after parturition (duration 8 weeks); may be repeated once after 8 weeks (withhold breast-feeding for neonates with severe or persistent jaundice requiring medical treatment)

7.3.3 Spermicidal contraceptives

Spermicidal contraceptives are useful additional safeguards but do **not** give adequate protection if used alone; they are suitable for use in conjunction with barrier methods. They have two components: a spermicide and a vehicle which itself may have some inhibiting effect on sperm migration.

CSM Advice.
Oil-based vaginal and rectal preparations are likely to damage condoms and contraceptive diaphragms made from latex rubber, and may render them less effective as a barrier method of contraception and as a protection from sexually transmitted diseases (including AIDS).

C-Film® (Arun)
Film, nonoxinol '9' 67 mg in a water-soluble basis. Net price 10 films = £1.03

Delfen® (Ortho)
Foam, nonoxinol '9' 12.5%, pressurised aerosol unit in a water-miscible basis. Net price 20 g (with applicator) = £4.65

Double Check® (FP)
Pessaries, nonoxinol '9' 6% in a water-soluble basis. Net price 10 pessaries = 99p

Note. A pack including 10 condoms, called Two's Company®, costs £2.14 (not prescribable on NHS)

Duracreme® (LRC)
Cream, nonoxinol '11' 2% in a water-soluble basis. Net price 100-g tube = £2.60; applicator = 75p

Duragel® (LRC)
Gel, nonoxinol '11' 2% in a water-soluble basis. Net price 100-g tube = £2.60; applicator = 75p

Gynol II® (Ortho)
Jelly, nonoxinol '9' 2% in a water-soluble basis. Net price 81 g = £2.61; applicator = 75p

Ortho-Creme® (Ortho)
Cream, nonoxinol '9' 2% in a water-miscible basis. Net price 70 g = £2.44; applicator = 75p

Orthoforms® (Ortho)
Pessaries, nonoxinol '9' 5% in a water-soluble basis. Net price 15 pessaries = £2.40

Ortho-Gynol® (Ortho)
Jelly, *p*-di-isobutylphenoxypolyethoxyethanol 1% in a water-soluble basis. Net price 81 g = £2.44; applicator = 75p

Staycept® (Syntex)
Jelly, octoxinol 1% in a water-soluble basis. Net price 80 g = £1.80
Pessaries, nonoxinol '9' 6% in a water-soluble basis. Net price 10 pessaries = £1.30

7.3.4 Intra-uterine contraceptive devices

The intra-uterine device (IUD) is suitable for older parous women but should be a last-resort contraceptive for young nulliparous women because of the increased risk of pelvic inflammatory disease and infertility. Inert intra-uterine devices are no longer on the UK market but may still be worn by some women.

Smaller devices have now been introduced in order to minimise side-effects; these consist of a plastic carrier wound with copper wire; some also have a central core of silver with the aim of preventing fragmentation of the copper. Family planning organisations now recommend that the replacement time for these devices should be 5 years; any copper intrauterine device licensed currently in the UK, which is fitted in a woman over the age of 40, may remain in the uterus until menopause.

The timing and technique of fitting an intra-uterine device play a critical part in its subsequent performance and call for proper training and experience. Devices should not be fitted during the heavy days of the period; they are best fitted after the end of menstruation and before the calculated time of implantation.

An intra-uterine device should not be removed in mid-cycle unless an additional contraceptive was used for the previous 7 days. If removal is essential (e.g. to treat severe pelvic infection) post-coital contraception should be considered.

If an intra-uterine device fails and the woman wishes to continue to full-term the device should be removed in the first trimester if possible.

INTRA-UTERINE CONTRACEPTIVE DEVICES

Indications: see notes above

Cautions: anaemia, heavy menses, history of pelvic inflammatory disease, diabetes, valvular heart disease (antibiotic cover needed), epilepsy, increased risk of expulsion if inserted before uterine involution; gynaecological examination before insertion, 3 months after, and yearly; remove if pregnancy occurs; anticoagulant therapy (avoid if possible); if pregnancy occurs, increased likelihood that it may be tubal

Contra-indications: pregnancy, severe anaemia, very heavy menses, history of ectopic pregnancy or tubal surgery, distorted or small uterine cavity, genital malignancy, pelvic inflammatory disease, immunosuppressive therapy, *copper devices:* copper allergy, Wilson's disease, medical diathermy

Side-effects: uterine or cervical perforation, displacement, pelvic infection, heavy menses, dysmenorrhoea, allergy; *on insertion:* some pain and bleeding (helped by giving an NSAID, such as ibuprofen half-an-hour before insertion); occasionally, epileptic seizure, vasovagal attack

PoM **Multiload® Cu250** (Organon)
Intra-uterine device, copper wire, surface area approx. 250 mm² wound on vertical stem of plastic carrier, 3.6 cm length, with 2 down-curving flexible arms, monofilament thread attached to base of vertical stem; preloaded in inserter. Net price, each = £6.75
For uterine length over 7 cm; replacement every 3 years (but see notes above)

PoM **Multiload® Cu250 Short** (Organon)
Intra-uterine device, as above, with vertical stem length 2.5 cm. Net price, each = £6.75
For uterine length 5–7 cm; replacement every 3 years (but see notes above)

PoM **Multiload® Cu375** (Organon)
Intra-uterine device, as above, with copper surface area approx. 375 mm². Net price, each = £8.75
For uterine length over 7 cm; replacement every 5 years (see notes above)

PoM **Novagard®** (Kabi)
Intra-uterine device, copper wire with silver core, surface area approx. 200 mm² wound on vertical stem of T-shaped plastic carrier, impregnated with barium sulphate for radio-opacity, monofilament thread attached to base of vertical stem; partially preloaded in inserter. Dimensions: transverse arms, vertical stem, both 3.2 cm. Net price, each = £9.90
For uterine length over 5.5 cm; replacement every 5 years (see notes above)

PoM **Nova-T®** (Schering Health Care)
Intra-uterine device, copper wire with silver core, surface area approx. 200 mm² wound on vertical stem of T-shaped plastic carrier, impregnated with barium sulphate for radio-opacity, threads attached to base of vertical stem. Net price, each = £9.90
For uterine length over 6.5 cm; replacement every 5 years (see notes above)

PoM **Ortho Gyne-T®** (Ortho)
Intra-uterine device, copper wire, surface area 200 mm², wound on vertical stem of T-shaped plastic carrier, impregnated with barium sulphate for radio-opacity, 2-tail plastic thread attached to base of vertical stem. Net price each = £8.99
For uterine length over 6.5 cm; replacement every 3 years (but see notes above)

PoM **Ortho Gyne-T® 380 Slimline** (Ortho)
Intra-uterine device, as above, with copper wire surface area 320 mm² and copper collar surface 30 mm² on distal portion of each arm. Net price = £9.40. For uterine length over 6.5 cm; replacement every 4 years (but see notes above)

7.4 Drugs for genito-urinary disorders

For drugs used in the treatment of urinary-tract infections see section 5.1.13.

7.4.1 Drugs for urinary retention

Acute retention is painful and is initially treated by catheterisation. Thereafter, provided an obstructive cause is excluded, further episodes may be treated medically.

Chronic retention is painless and often long-standing. Catheterisation is unnecessary unless there is deterioration of renal function. After the cause has initially been established and treated, drugs may be required to increase detrusor muscle tone.

Parasympathomimetics produce the effects of parasympathetic nerve stimulation; they possess the muscarinic rather than the nicotinic effects of acetylcholine and improve voiding efficiency by increasing detrusor muscle contraction. In the absence of obstruction to the bladder outlet they have a limited role in the relief of urinary retention (e.g. in neurological disease or post-operatively). Generalised parasympathomimetic side-effects such as sweating, bradycardia, and intestinal colic may occur, particularly in the elderly.

Carbachol and **bethanechol** are choline esters whose actions are more prolonged than those of acetylcholine; both may relieve acute or chronic urinary retention.

Distigmine produces a similar effect by inhibiting the breakdown of acetylcholine. It may help patients with an upper motor neurone neurogenic bladder.

The selective alpha-blockers **indoramin** and **prazosin** relax smooth muscle in benign prostatic hyperplasia producing an increase in urinary flow-rate and an improvement in obstructive symptoms. Both have a low incidence of side-effects, although sedation, dizziness, and hypotension may occur. Hospital supervision is preferable.

ALPHA-BLOCKERS

INDORAMIN

See section 2.5.4

PRAZOSIN

See section 2.5.4

PARASYMPATHOMIMETICS

BETHANECHOL CHLORIDE

Indications: urinary retention (see section 1.6.2 for use in gastro-intestinal disease)

Cautions: elderly patients, asthma, cardiovascular disease, epilepsy, parkinsonism, vagotonia, hyperthyroidism; **interactions:** Appendix 1 (cholinergics)

Contra-indications: intestinal or urinary obstruction, recent myocardial infarction, recent intestinal anastomosis

Side-effects: parasympathomimetic effects such as nausea, vomiting, sweating, blurred vision, bradycardia, and intestinal colic

Dose: 10–30 mg 3–4 times daily half an hour before food

PoM **Myotonine**® (Glenwood)
Tablets, both pale blue, scored, bethanechol chloride 10 mg, net price 20 = 82p; 25 mg, 20 = £1.04. Label: 22

CARBACHOL

Indications: urinary retention

Cautions; Contra-indications; Side-effects: see under Bethanechol Chloride but side-effects are more frequent

Dose: by mouth, 2 mg 3 times daily half an hour before food

By subcutaneous injection (acute symptoms, postoperative urinary retention) 250 micrograms, repeated twice if necessary at 30-minute intervals

PoM **Carbachol** (Non-proprietary)
Tablets, carbachol 2 mg. Net price 20 = £1.06. Label: 22
Injection, carbachol 250 micrograms/mL.

DISTIGMINE BROMIDE

Indications: urinary retention due to upper motor lesions (see section 1.6.2 for use in gastro-intestinal disease)

Cautions; Contra-indications; Side-effects: see under Bethanechol Chloride; side-effects are mild but more prolonged

Dose: by mouth, 5 mg daily or on alternate days, half an hour before breakfast

By intramuscular injection, 500 micrograms 12 hours after surgery to prevent urinary retention; may be repeated every 24 hours

PoM **Ubretid**® (Rorer)
Tablets, scored, distigmine bromide 5 mg. Net price 20 = £10.86. Label: 22
Injection, distigmine bromide 500 micrograms/mL. Net price 1-mL amp = 54p

7.4.2 Drugs for urinary frequency, enuresis, and incontinence

Antimuscarinic drugs such as **terodiline** and **propantheline** are used to treat *urinary frequency*; they increase bladder capacity by diminishing unstable detrusor contractions. All these drugs may cause dry mouth and blurred vision and may precipitate glaucoma. Terodiline, possessing antimuscarinic and calcium antagonist properties, relaxes the detrusor muscle of the bladder and is useful in patients with urge incontinence and detrusor instability. The **tricyclic antidepressants** imipramine, amitriptyline, and nortriptyline (see section 4.3.1) are sometimes effective in the management of the unstable bladder because of their antimuscarinic properties.

Nocturnal enuresis is a normal occurrence in young children but persists in as many as 5% by 10 years of age. In the absence of urinary-tract infection simple measures such as bladder training or the use of an alarm system may be successful. Drug therapy is not appropriate for children under 7 years of age and should be reserved for when alternative measures have failed. The possible side-effects and potential toxicity of these agents if taken in overdose should be borne in mind when they are prescribed.

The most widely used treatment is with tricyclics such as **amitriptyline**, **imipramine**, and less often **nortriptyline** (see section 4.3.1). They are effective, but behaviour disturbances may occur and relapse is common after withdrawal. Treatment should not normally exceed 3 months unless a full physical examination (including ECG) is given.

Desmopressin, an analogue of vasopressin, is also used for nocturnal enuresis (see section 6.5.2)

The sympathomimetic drug **ephedrine** may also be useful.

AMITRIPTYLINE HYDROCHLORIDE
See section 4.3.1

DESMOPRESSIN
See section 6.5.2

EPHEDRINE HYDROCHLORIDE
Indications: nocturnal enuresis
Cautions; Contra-indications; Side-effects: see under Ephedrine Hydrochloride (section 3.1.1.2)
Dose: CHILD 7–8 years 30 mg, 9–12 years 45 mg, 13–15 years 60 mg at bedtime

Preparations
See section 3.1.1.2

FLAVOXATE HYDROCHLORIDE
Indications: urinary frequency and incontinence, dysuria
Cautions; Contra-indications: see Terodiline Hydrochloride
Side-effects: antimuscarinic side-effects (see Atropine Sulphate, section 1.2); see also notes above
Dose: 200 mg 3 times daily

PoM **Urispas®** (Syntex)
Tablets, s/c, flavoxate hydrochloride 100 mg. Net price 20 = 86p

IMIPRAMINE HYDROCHLORIDE
See section 4.3.1

NORTRIPTYLINE HYDROCHLORIDE
See section 4.3.1

PROPANTHELINE BROMIDE
Indications: urinary frequency and incontinence
Cautions; Contra-indications: see Terodiline Hydrochloride
Side-effects: antimuscarinic side-effects (see Atropine Sulphate, section 1.2); see also notes above
Dose: 15–30 mg 2–3 times daily one hour before meals

Preparations
See section 1.2

TERODILINE HYDROCHLORIDE
Indications: urinary frequency and incontinence
Cautions: gastric retention, fever, thyrotoxicosis, cardiac disease where increase in rate is undesirable, hepatic impairment; frail elderly; **interactions:** Appendix 1 (antimuscarinics)
Contra-indications: urinary obstruction, bladder outflow obstruction, flaccid bladder or high residual urine, severe hepatic or biliary tract disease, obstructive lesions (particularly of gastro-intestinal tract), glaucoma
Side-effects: antimuscarinic side-effects (see under Atropine Sulphate, section 1.2); also see notes above
Dose: 12.5–25 mg twice daily (frail elderly patients, 12.5 mg twice daily)

PoM [1]**Micturin®** (Kabi)
Tablets, f/c, terodiline hydrochloride 12.5 mg (Micturin®-12.5), net price 56-tab pack = £12.04; 25 mg (Micturin®-25), 56-tab pack = £24.08

1. Formerly Terolin®

7.4.3 Drugs used in urological pain

Alkalinisation of urine may be undertaken with **sodium bicarbonate**, or alternatively sodium or potassium citrate. By their alkalinising action they may relieve the discomfort of *cystitis* caused by lower urinary tract infections. Sodium bicarbonate, in particular, is also used as a urinary alkalinising agent in some metabolic and renal disorders (see section 9.2.2).

The acute pain of *ureteric colic* may be relieved with **pethidine**; **diclofenac** is also effective and compares favourably with pethidine.

Lignocaine gel is a useful topical application in *urethral pain* or to relieve the discomfort of catheterisation (see section 15.2).

ALKALINISATION OF URINE

POTASSIUM CITRATE
Indications: relief of discomfort in mild urinary-tract infections; alkalinisation of urine

Cautions: renal impairment, cardiac disease; elderly; **interactions:** Appendix 1 (potassium salts)
Side-effects: hyperkalaemia on prolonged high dosage, mild diuresis
Dose: cystitis, adults and children over 6 years, 3 g, well diluted with water, 3 times daily; CHILD 1–6 years 1.5 g
Alkalinisation of urine, 3–6 g with water every 6 hours

Potassium Citrate Mixture, BP (Potassium Citrate Oral Solution)
Oral solution, potassium citrate 30%, citric acid monohydrate 5% in a suitable vehicle with a lemon flavour. Contains about 28 mmol K^+/10 mL. Label: 27
Dose: 10 mL 3 times daily well diluted with water

Effercitrate® (Typharm)
Tablets, effervescent, the equivalent of potassium citrate 1.5 g (13.9 mmol K^+), citric acid 250 mg (1 tablet ≡ 5 mL potassium citrate mixture). Net price 12 = £1.50. Label: 13

SODIUM BICARBONATE

Indications: relief of discomfort in mild urinary-tract infections; alkalinisation of urine
Cautions; Side-effects: see section 1.1.2; also caution in elderly
Dose: 3 g in water every 2 hours until urinary pH exceeds 7; maintenance of alkaline urine 5-10 g daily

Sodium Bicarbonate Powder. Net price 50 g = 5p. Label: 13

SODIUM CITRATE

Indications: relief of discomfort in mild urinary-tract infections
Cautions: renal impairment, cardiac disease, pregnancy, patients on a sodium-restricted diet; elderly
Side-effects: mild diuresis
Dose: see below

Urisal® (Sterling-Winthrop)
Granules, yellow and white, effervescent, the equivalent of sodium citrate 4.4 g/sachet. Contains 41 mmol Na^+/sachet. Net price 9 sachets = £2.68. Label: 13
Dose: 1 sachet in a glass of water 3 times daily for max. of 3 days
Note. Although Urisal® is legally on the General Sale List it is restricted by product licence to prescription only

ACIDIFICATION OF URINE

Acidification of urine has been undertaken with **ascorbic acid** but it is not always reliable.

For pH-modifying solutions for the maintenance of indwelling urinary catheters, see section 7.4.4.

ASCORBIC ACID

Indications: acidification of urine but see notes above
Dose: by mouth, 4 g daily in divided doses

Preparations
See section 9.6.3

OTHER PREPARATIONS FOR URINARY DISORDERS

A terpene mixture (Rowatinex®) is claimed to be of benefit in *urolithiasis* for the expulsion of calculi.

Rowatinex® (Monmouth)
Capsules, yellow, e/c, 0.1 mL of liquid of composition below. Net price 50 = £7.54. Label: 25
Dose: 1 capsule 3–4 times daily
Liquid, yellow, anethole 400 mg, borneol 1 g, camphene 1.5 g, cineole 300 mg, fenchone 400 mg, pinene 3.1 g, olive oil to 10 g. Net price 10 mL = £6.60. Label: 22, counselling, use of dropper
Dose: 3–5 drops 4–5 times daily before food

7.4.4 Bladder instillations and urological surgery

INFECTED BLADDERS. Various solutions are available as irrigations or washouts for the infected bladder.

Initial treatment is with **sterile sodium chloride solution 0.9%** (physiological saline).

Aqueous **chlorhexidine** (see section 13.11.2) is effective against a wide range of common urinary-tract pathogens but not against most *Pseudomonas* spp. Solutions containing 1 in 5000 (0.02%) are used but they may irritate the mucosa and cause burning and haematuria (in which case they should be discontinued); solutions containing 1 in 10000 (0.01%) are usually preferred post-operatively. **Polymyxin B sulphate with neomycin** (Polybactrin®) and **colistin** (both section 5.1.7) are bactericidal to most pathogens and emergence of resistance is slow.

Noxythiolin is also bactericidal to most pathogens with slow emergence of resistance, but initial use in the purulent infected bladder is often accompanied by an intense reaction including the passage of large clumps of fibrin. Other indications for noxythiolin include intraperitoneal use during colonic surgery.

Bladder irrigations of **amphotericin** 100 micrograms/mL (see section 5.2) may be of value in mycotic infections.

DISSOLUTION OF BLOOD CLOTS. Clot retention is usually treated by irrigation with sterile **sodium chloride solution 0.9%** but sterile **sodium citrate** solution for bladder irrigation (3%) may also be helpful. **Streptokinase-streptodornase** (Varidase Topical®, see section 13.11.7) is an alternative.

LOCALLY ACTING CYTOTOXIC DRUGS. **Doxorubicin** (see section 8.1.2) is used to treat recurrent superficial bladder tumours, carcinoma-in-situ, and some papillary tumours. An instillation (50 mg in 50 mL of sterile sodium chloride solution 0.9%) is retained in the bladder for one hour and treatment repeated monthly. Although systemic side-effects are few, it may cause frequency, urgency, dysuria, and occasionally reduction in bladder capacity.

Mitomycin is used for recurrent bladder tumours. A solution containing 20 to 40 mg in 40 mL of sterile water is instilled weekly for 4 weeks then monthly for at least 11 months.

Thiotepa (see section 8.1.1) is used for bladder tumours of low to medium grade malignancy. A solution containing 30–60 mg in 60 mL of sterile water is retained in the bladder for 2 hours. It is given weekly for 4 weeks. The concentration should be reduced if there is evidence of bone-marrow suppression.

INTERSTITIAL CYSTITIS. Dimethyl sulphoxide may be used for symptomatic relief in patients with interstitial cystitis (Hunner's ulcer). 50 mL of a 50% solution (Rimso-50®) is instilled into the bladder, retained for 15 minutes, and voided by the patient. Treatment is repeated at intervals of 2 weeks. Bladder spasm and hypersensitivity reactions may occur and long-term use requires ophthalmic, renal, and hepatic assessment at 6-monthly intervals.

CHLORHEXIDINE

Indications: bladder washouts, see notes above and section 13.11.2

See also catheter patency solutions

DIMETHYL SULPHOXIDE

Indications: bladder washouts, see notes above

PoM **Rimso-50®** (Britannia)
Bladder instillation, sterile, dimethyl sulphoxide 50%, in aqueous solution. Net price 50 mL = £19.80

NOXYTHIOLIN

Indications: see notes above
Side-effects: burning sensation on application to bladder (relieved by addition of amethocaine)
Dose: bladder instillation, 100 mL of a 2.5% solution instilled 1–2 times daily
Intraperitoneal use, 100 mL of a 2.5% solution instilled prior to closure

PoM **Noxyflex S®** (Geistlich)
Solution, powder for reconstitution, noxythiolin. Net price 2.5 g in 20 mL vial = £5.32; 2.5 g in 100-mL vial with transfer needle = £6.65

SODIUM CHLORIDE

Indications: bladder washouts, see notes above

Available from Baxter, Kendall
See also catheter patency solutions

SODIUM CITRATE

Indications: bladder washouts, see notes above

Sterile Sodium Citrate Solution for Bladder Irrigation, sodium citrate 3%, dilute hydrochloric acid 0.2%, in purified water, freshly boiled and cooled, and sterilised

UROLOGICAL SURGERY

Endoscopic surgery within the urinary tract requires an isotonic irrigant as there is a high risk of fluid absorption; if this occurs in excess, hypervolaemia, haemolysis, and renal failure may result. **Glycine irrigation solution 1.5%** is the irrigant of choice for transurethral resection of the prostate gland and bladder tumours; **sterile sodium chloride solution 0.9%** (physiological saline) is used for percutaneous renal surgery.

GLYCINE

Indications: bladder irrigation during urological surgery; see notes above
Cautions; Side-effects: see notes above

Glycine Irrigation Solution (Non-proprietary)
Irrigation solution, glycine 1.5% in water for injections
Available from Baxter, Kendall

MAINTENANCE OF INDWELLING URINARY CATHETERS

The deposition which occurs in catheterised patients is usually chiefly composed of phosphate and to minimise this the catheter (if latex) should be changed at least as often as every 6 weeks. If the catheter is to be left for longer periods a silicone catheter should be used. If bladder washouts are required at frequent intervals this usually indicates that the catheter needs to be changed.

CATHETER PATENCY SOLUTIONS

Chlorhexidine 0.02%. Available from CliniMed (Uro-Tainer Chlorhexidine®, 100-mL sachet = £1.89), Galen (Uriflex C®, 100-mL sachet = £1.56)

Mandelic acid 1%. Available from CliniMed (Uro-Tainer Mandelic Acid®, 100-mL sachet = £1.89)

Sodium chloride 0.9%. Available from CliniMed (Uro-Tainer Sodium Chloride®, 100-mL sachet = £1.79, Uro-Tainer M®, with integral drug additive port, 50- and 100-mL sachets = £2.12), Galen (Uriflex S®, 100-mL sachet = £1.47, Uriflex SP® with integral drug additive port, 100-mL sachet = £1.75)

Solution G, citric acid 3.23%, magnesium oxide 0.38%, sodium bicarbonate 0.7%, disodium edetate 0.01%. Available from CliniMed (Uro-Tainer Suby G®, 100-mL sachet = £1.89), Galen (Uriflex G®, 100-mL sachet = £1.56)

Solution R, citric acid 6%, gluconolactone 0.6%, magnesium carbonate 2.8%, disodium edetate 0.01%. Available from CliniMed (Uro-Tainer Solution R®, 100-mL sachet = £1.89), Galen (Uriflex R®, 100-mL sachet = £1.56)

7.4.5 Drugs for impotence

Reasons for failure to produce a satisfactory erection include psychogenic, vascular, neurogenic, and endocrine abnormalities. Intracavernosal injection of vasoactive drugs under careful medical supervision is used for both diagnostic and therapeutic purposes.

Direct injection of the smooth muscle relaxant, **papaverine** (available from Boots and Penn on a named patient basis only), into the corpus cavernosum, in a dose of 12 to 40 mg, has been shown to be the most effective treatment; patients with spinal injuries are the most sensitive. Persistence of the erection for longer than 4 hours is an emergency requiring aspiration of the corpora; if aspiration fails, 1 mg of metaraminol can be diluted to 5 mL with sodium choride injection 0.9% and given by careful slow injection into the corpora.

8: Drugs used in the treatment of MALIGNANT DISEASE and for IMMUNOSUPPRESSION

In this chapter, drug treatment is discussed under the following headings:

Malignant disease may be treated by surgery, radiotherapy, and/or chemotherapy. Certain tumours are highly sensitive to chemotherapy but many are not, and inappropriate drug administration in these circumstances can only increase morbidity or mortality.

8.1 Cytotoxic drugs

Great care is needed when prescribing these drugs as damage to normal tissue, which may be irreversible, is an almost invariable consequence of their use. These drugs should rarely, if ever, be used empirically in a patient with cancer, and administration should always be regarded as a clinical trial with clear objectives in mind.

CRM guidelines on cytotoxic drug handling:

1. Trained personnel should reconstitute cytotoxics;
2. Reconstitution should be carried out in designated areas;
3. Protective clothing (including gloves) should be worn;
4. The eyes should be protected and means of first aid should be specified;
5. Pregnant staff should not handle cytotoxics;
6. Adequate care should be taken in the disposal of waste material, including syringes, containers, and absorbent material.

In a minority of cancers, chemotherapy may result in cure, or marked prolongation of survival. Here short-term drug-related toxicity, which may be severe, is acceptable. However, for the majority of patients, modest survival prolongation or palliation of symptoms will be the aim, and an attempt should be made to use relatively non-toxic treatments, or to consider the use of other effective modalities, e.g. radiotherapy.

Cytotoxics may be used either singly, or in combination. In the latter case, the initial letters of the drug names, or proprietary names, identify the regimen used. Drug combinations are frequently more toxic than single drugs but may have the advantage in certain tumours of enhanced response and increased survival. However for some tumours, single-agent chemotherapy remains the treatment of choice.

Most cytotoxic drugs are teratogenic, and all may cause life-threatening toxicity; administration should, where possible, be confined to those experienced in their use.

Because of the complexity of dosage regimens in the treatment of malignant disease, dose statements have been omitted from some of the drug entries in this chapter. *In all cases detailed specialist literature should be consulted.*

Prescriptions should **not** be repeated except on the instructions of a specialist.

Cytotoxic drugs fall naturally into a number of classes, each with characteristic antitumour activity, sites of action, and toxicity. A knowledge of sites of metabolism and excretion is important, as impaired drug handling as a result of disease is not uncommon and may result in enhanced toxic effects. A number of side-effects are characteristic of particular agents or groups of drugs, e.g. neurotoxicity of vinca alkaloids, and details will be provided in the appropriate sections. Most toxic effects are, however, common to many of these drugs and will be briefly outlined here.

EXTRAVASATION OF INTRAVENOUS DRUGS. A number of drugs will cause severe local tissue necrosis if leakage into the extravascular compartment occurs. Recommended modes of administration must be adhered to. Infusion of vesicant drugs should be stopped immediately if local pain is experienced. Where doubt exists as to whether significant leakage has occurred, the infusion should be discontinued and the cannula resited in another vein. There are no proven antidotes for extravasation, but general recommendations include elevation of the limb and application of ice packs three or four times daily until pain and swelling settle; if ulceration occurs plastic surgery may be required.

HYPERCALCAEMIA. Hypercalcaemia is a common complication of malignant disease. Treatment of the underlying malignancy may resolve it, but drugs which specifically lower serum calcium are often also required (see section 9.5.1.2).

HYPERURICAEMIA. Hyperuricaemia, which can result in uric acid crystal formation in the urinary tract with associated renal dysfunction is a complication of the treatment of non-Hodgkin's lymphoma and leukemia. Allopurinol (see section 10.1.4) should be started 24 hours before treating such tumours, and should be continued for 7 to 10 days; patients should be adequately hydrated.

The dose of mercaptopurine or azathioprine should be reduced if allopurinol needs to be given concomitantly (see Appendix 1).

NAUSEA AND VOMITING. Nausea and vomiting is a source of considerable distress to many patients receiving chemotherapy. It should be anticipated and, where possible, prevented with anti-emetic treatment tailored to the chemotherapy regimen and the response of the patient.

If first-line anti-emetics are ineffective treatment should be escalated as below. Hospital admission may be necessary.

Group 1: severe emesis unlikely
Drugs in this group include alkylating drugs by mouth, intravenous fluorouracil, vinca alkaloids, and methotrexate.

Phenothiazines (e.g. prochlorperazine) or domperidone, given by mouth, when necessary, will often suffice. Premedication with these drugs is often useful before intravenous chemotherapy, treatment being continued for up to 24 hours afterwards. Both prochlorperazine and domperidone are also available as suppositories which is useful for patients who develop vomiting despite oral therapy.

Group 2: moderate emesis
Drugs in this group include intravenous cyclophosphamide and doxorubicin; premedication is essential for all drugs in this group. Most patients can be treated on an out-patient basis therefore, if possible, the anti-emetics should be given by mouth.

Anti-emetics in group 1 are sufficient for some patients but it is probably preferable to start with dexamethasone 10 mg by mouth before and 6 hours after chemotherapy, or lorazepam 1 to 2 mg by mouth given similarly. Lorazepam has the advantage of causing drowsiness and amnesia, but patients cannot drive after it. Nabilone is also suitable, but may cause dysphoria. Ondansetron may also have a valuable role.

Patients in group 1 with an unsatisfactory response can be transferred to drugs in this group.

Group 3: severe emesis
Drugs in this group include mustine, dacarbazine, and cisplatin. They commonly cause severe emesis, particularly if used in combination.

A simple well-tolerated anti-emetic regimen is dexamethasone 10 mg by mouth with lorazepam 1 to 2 mg by mouth, given before and 6 hours after chemotherapy. Out-patients should be warned not to drive. Dexamethasone and lorazepam can also be given intravenously to inpatients; the dose of lorazepam is titrated according to the patient's level of consciousness (drowsiness should be obtained with 2 to 4 mg). This regimen should be avoided in patients with chronic chest disease and care is necessary in the elderly.

Alternatively, high-dose metoclopramide can be given by intravenous infusion but it may cause dystonic reactions in younger patients (see section 4.6).

Ondansetron may be useful for controlling vomiting in the short term.

Patients in group 2 with an unsatisfactory response can be transferred to drugs in this group.

BONE-MARROW SUPPRESSION. All cytotoxic drugs except vincristine and bleomycin cause marrow depression. This commonly occurs 7 to 10 days after administration, but is delayed for certain drugs, such as carmustine, lomustine, and melphalan. Peripheral blood counts must be checked prior to each treatment, and doses should be reduced or therapy delayed if marrow recovery has not occurred. Fever occurring in a neutropenic patient (neutrophil count less than 800×10^9/litre) is an indication for immediate parenteral broad-spectrum antibiotic therapy (see section 5.1, Table 1), once appropriate bacteriological investigations have taken place.

ALOPECIA. Reversible hair loss is a common complication, although it varies in degree between drugs and individual patients. No pharmacological methods of preventing this are available.

REPRODUCTIVE FUNCTION. Most cytotoxic drugs are teratogenic and should not be administered during pregnancy, especially during the first trimester (but for transplant therapy, see below).

Contraceptive advice should be offered where appropriate before cytotoxic therapy begins. Regimens that do not contain an alkylating drug may have less effect on fertility, but those with an alkylating drug will render almost all males permanently sterile early in a treatment course (there is no effect on potency). Pre-treatment counselling and consideration of sperm storage may be appropriate. Females are less severely affected, though the span of reproductive life may be shortened by the onset of a premature menopause. No increase in fetal abnormalities or abortion-rate has been recorded in patients who remain fertile after cytotoxic chemotherapy.

Transplant therapy. Female transplanted patients immunosuppressed with azathioprine should not discontinue it on becoming pregnant; although spontaneous abortion may be more common, congenital fetal abnormalities are not increased in successful pregnancies. There is less experience of cyclosporin in pregnancy; although compatible with normal pregnancy, retardation of fetal growth has been reported. Any risk to the offspring of azathioprine-treated men is small.

8.1.1 Alkylating drugs

Extensive experience is available with these drugs, which are among the most widely used in cancer chemotherapy. They act by damaging DNA, thus interfering with cell replication. In addition to the side-effects common to many cytotoxic drugs (section 8.1), there are two problems associated with prolonged usage. Firstly, gametogenesis is often severely affected (see above). Secondly, prolonged use of these drugs, particularly when combined with extensive irradiation, is associated with a marked increase in the incidence of acute non-lymphocytic leukaemia.

Cyclophosphamide is widely used in the treatment of chronic lymphocytic leukaemia, the lymphomas, and solid tumours. It may be given orally or intravenously and is inactive until metabolised by the liver. A urinary metabolite of cyclophosphamide, acrolein, may cause haemorrhagic cystitis; this is a serious complication and if it occurs cyclophosphamide is not normally used again. An increased fluid intake, for example 3 to 4 litres per day after intravenous injection, will help avoid this complication. When high-dose therapy is used mesna will also help prevent this complication.

Ifosfamide is related to cyclophosphamide and is also given with mesna to reduce urothelial toxicity.

Chlorambucil is commonly used to treat chronic lymphocytic leukaemia, the indolent non-Hodgkin's lymphomas, Hodgkin's disease, and ovarian cancer. Side-effects, apart from marrow suppression, are uncommon, although rashes may occur.

Melphalan is used to treat myeloma and occasionally solid tumours and lymphomas. Marrow toxicity is delayed and it is usually given at intervals of 4–6 weeks.

Busulphan is used almost exclusively to treat chronic myeloid leukaemia. Frequent blood counts are necessary as excessive myelosuppression may result in irreversible bone-marrow aplasia. Hyperpigmentation of the skin is a common side-effect and, rarely, progressive pulmonary fibrosis may occur.

Lomustine (CCNU) is a lipid-soluble nitrosourea and may be given orally. It is mainly used to treat Hodgkin's disease and certain solid tumours. Marrow toxicity is delayed, and the drug is therefore given at intervals of 4 to 6 weeks. Permanent marrow damage may occur with prolonged use. Nausea and vomiting are common and moderately severe.

Carmustine is given intravenously. It has similar activity and toxicities to lomustine. Cumulative renal damage and delayed pulmonary fibrosis may occur.

Mustine is now much less commonly used. It is a very toxic drug which causes severe vomiting. The freshly prepared injection must be given into a fast-running intravenous infusion. Local extravasation causes severe tissue necrosis.

Estramustine is a stable combination of an oestrogen and mustine, designed to deliver mustine to the oestrogen receptor site of a tumour, for example prostate cancer. It has both a local cytotoxic effect and (by reducing testosterone concentrations) a hormonal effect.

Treosulfan is used to treat ovarian cancer.

Thiotepa is usually used as an intracavitary drug for the treatment of malignant effusions or bladder cancer. It is also occasionally used to treat breast cancer, but requires parenteral administration.

Mitobronitol is occasionally used to treat chronic myeloid leukaemia; it is available on a named-patient basis only (as *Myelobromol*®, Sinclair).

BUSULPHAN

Indications: chronic myeloid leukaemia

Cautions; Side-effects: see section 8.1 and notes above; avoid in porphyria

Dose: induction of remission, 60 micrograms/kg to max. 4 mg daily; maintenance, 0.5–2 mg daily

PoM **Myleran**® (Calmic)

Tablets, busulphan 500 micrograms, net price 25 = £2.79; 2 mg, 25 = £4.21

CARMUSTINE

Indications: see notes above

Cautions; Side-effects: see section 8.1 and notes above; irritant to tissues

PoM **BiCNU**® (Bristol-Myers)

Injection, powder for reconstitution, carmustine. Net price 100-mg vial (with diluent) = £12.50

CHLORAMBUCIL

Indications: see notes above (for use as an immunosuppressant see section 8.2.1)

Cautions; Side-effects: see section 8.1 and notes above; caution in renal impairment; avoid in porphyria

Dose: used alone, usually 100–200 micrograms/kg daily for 4–8 weeks

PoM **Leukeran**® (Calmic)

Tablets, both yellow, chlorambucil 2 mg, net price 25 = £6.76; 5 mg, 25 = £10.30

CYCLOPHOSPHAMIDE

Indications: see notes above

Cautions; Side-effects: see section 8.1 and notes above; reduce dose in renal impairment; avoid in porphyria; **interactions:** Appendix 1 (cyclophosphamide)

PoM **Cyclophosphamide** (Farmitalia Carlo Erba)

Tablets, pink, s/c, cyclophosphamide (anhydrous) 50 mg. Net price 20 = 96p. Label: 27

Injection, powder for preparing injections, cyclophosphamide. Net price 107-mg vial = 78p; 214-mg vial = £1.11; 535-mg vial = £1.93; 1.07-g vial = £3.38

PoM **Endoxana**® (Degussa)

Tablets, compression-coated, cyclophosphamide 50 mg, net price 100-tab pack = £7.94. Label: 27

Injection, powder for reconstitution, cyclophosphamide. Net price 107-mg vial = 79p; 214-mg vial = £1.13; 535-mg vial = £1.97; 1.069-g vial = £3.44

ESTRAMUSTINE PHOSPHATE

Indications: prostate cancer

Cautions: see section 8.1

Contra-indications: peptic ulceration, severe liver or cardiac disease

Side-effects: see section 8.1; also gynaecomastia, altered liver function, cardiovascular disorders (angina and rare reports of myocardial infarction)
Dose: 0.14–1.4 g daily in divided doses (usual range 0.56–1.12 g daily)

PoM **Estracyt**® (Pharmacia)
Capsules, estramustine phosphate 140 mg (as disodium salt). Net price 20 = £20.90. Label: 21, counselling, should not be taken with dairy products

IFOSFAMIDE

Indications: see notes above
Cautions; Side-effects: see section 8.1 and notes under Cyclophosphamide; reduce dose in renal impairment

PoM **Mitoxana**® (Degussa)
Injection, powder for reconstitution, ifosfamide. Net price 500-mg vial = £6.10; 1-g vial = £10.64; 2-g vial = £19.59 (hosp. only)

LOMUSTINE

Indications: see notes above
Cautions; Side-effects: see section 8.1 and notes above
Dose: used alone, 120–130 mg/m² body-surface every 6–8 weeks

PoM **CCNU**® (Lundbeck)
Capsules, lomustine 10 mg (blue/white), net price 20 = £9.42; 40 mg (blue), 20 = £23.69

MELPHALAN

Indications: myelomatosis; see also notes above
Cautions; Side-effects: see section 8.1 and notes above; reduce dose in renal impairment
Dose: by mouth, 150–300 micrograms/kg daily for 4–6 days, repeated after 4–8 weeks

PoM **Alkeran**® (Calmic)
Tablets, melphalan 2 mg, net price 25 = £9.27; 5 mg, 25 = £16.40
Injection, powder for reconstitution, melphalan. Net price 100-mg vial (with solvent and diluent) = £44.68

MUSTINE HYDROCHLORIDE

Indications: Hodgkin's disease—see notes above
Cautions; Side-effects: see section 8.1 and notes above; also caution in handling—vesicant and a nasal irritant

PoM **Mustine Hydrochloride** (Boots)
Injection, powder for reconstitution, mustine hydrochloride. Net price 10-mg vial = £1.48

THIOTEPA

Indications: see notes above and section 7.4.4
Cautions; Side-effects: see section 8.1; **interactions:** Appendix 1 (thiotepa)

PoM **Thiotepa** (Lederle)
Injection, powder for reconstitution, thiotepa, net price 15-mg vial = £4.85

TREOSULFAN

Indications: see notes above
Cautions; Side-effects: see section 8.1
Dose: by mouth, courses of 1–2 g daily in 4 divided doses to provide total dose of 21–28 g over initial 8 weeks

PoM **Treosulfan** (Leo)
Capsules, treosulfan 250 mg. Net price 20 = £7.53. Label: 25
Injection, powder for reconstitution, treosulfan. Net price 5 g in infusion bottle with transfer needle = £13.75

UROTHELIAL TOXICITY

Urothelial toxicity, commonly manifest by haemorrhagic cystitis, is a problem peculiar to the use of cyclophosphamide or ifosfamide and is caused by a metabolite (acrolein). **Mesna** reacts specifically with this metabolite in the urinary tract, preventing toxicity. Mesna is given simultaneously with cyclophosphamide or ifosfamide, and further doses are given orally or intravenously 4 and 8 hours after treatment.

MESNA

Indications: see notes above
Side-effects: above max. therapeutic doses, gastro-intestinal disturbances, fatigue, headache, limb pains, depression, irritability, lack of energy, rash

PoM **Uromitexan**® (Degussa)
Injection, mesna 100 mg/mL. Net price 4-mL amp = £1.27; 10-mL amp = £2.76

Note. For oral administration contents of ampoule are taken in fruit juice

8.1.2 Cytotoxic antibiotics

Drugs within this group are widely used. Many cytotoxic antibiotics act as radiomimetics and simultaneous use of radiotherapy should be **avoided** as it may result in markedly enhanced normal tissue toxicity.

Doxorubicin is one of the most successful and widely used antitumour drugs, and is used to treat the acute leukaemias, lymphomas, and a variety of solid tumours. It is given by fast running infusion, commonly at 21-day intervals. Local extravasation will cause severe tissue necrosis. Common toxic effects include nausea and vomiting, myelosuppression, alopecia, and mucositis. This drug is largely excreted by the biliary tract, and an elevated bilirubin concentration is an indication for reducing the dose. Supraventricular tachycardia related to drug administration is an uncommon complication. Higher cumulative doses are associated with development of a cardiomyopathy. It is customary to limit total cumulative doses to 450–550 mg/m² body-surface area as symptomatic and potentially fatal heart failure is increasingly common above this level. Patients with pre-existing cardiac disease, the elderly, and those who have received myocardial irradiation should be treated cautiously. Cardiac monitoring, for example by sequential radionuclide ejection fraction measurement, may assist in safely limiting total dosage. Evidence is available to suggest that weekly low dose administration may be associated with less cardiac damage.

Epirubicin is structurally related to doxorubicin and clinical trials suggest that it is as effective in the treatment of breast cancer. A maximum cumulative dose of 0.9–1 g/m^2 is recommended to help avoid cardiotoxicity (but cardiotoxicity may be less than with doxorubicin).

Aclarubicin and **idarubicin** are newly introduced anthracyclines with general properties similar to those of doxorubicin.

Mitozantrone is structurally related to doxorubicin and preliminary work suggests that it has equal activity in breast cancer; it is well tolerated apart from myelosuppression and probable dose-related cardiotoxicity; cardiac examinations are recommended after a cumulative dose of 160 mg/m^2 if this complication is to be avoided.

Bleomycin is used to treat the lymphomas, certain solid tumours and, by the intracavitary route, malignant effusions. It is unusual in that it causes no marrow suppression. Dermatological toxicity is common; increased pigmentation particularly affecting the flexures and subcutaneous sclerotic plaques may occur. Mucositis is also relatively common and an association with Raynaud's phenomenon is reported. Hypersensitivity reactions manifest by chills and fevers commonly occur a few hours after drug administration and may be prevented by simultaneous administration of a corticosteroid, for example hydrocortisone intravenously. The principal problem associated with the use of bleomycin is progressive pulmonary fibrosis. This is dose related, occurring more commonly at cumulative doses greater than 300 units and in the elderly. Basal lung crepitations or suspicious chest X-ray changes are an indication to stop therapy with this drug. Patients who have received extensive treatment with bleomycin (e.g. cumulative dose more than 100 units) may be at risk of developing respiratory failure if a general anaesthetic is given with high inspired oxygen concentrations. Anaesthetists should be warned of this.

Actinomycin D is principally used to treat paediatric cancers. Its side-effects are similar to those of doxorubicin, except that cardiac toxicity is not a problem.

Plicamycin (mithramycin) is no longer used as a cytotoxic, but has found a useful role in low dose in the emergency therapy of hypercalcaemia due to malignant disease (for general management of hypercalcaemia, see section 9.5.1.2).

Mitomycin is used to treat upper gastro-intestinal and breast cancers. It causes delayed marrow toxicity and is usually administered at 6-weekly intervals. Prolonged use may result in permanent marrow damage. It is a relatively toxic drug and may cause lung fibrosis and renal damage.

ACLARUBICIN

Indications: acute non-lymphocytic leukaemia in patients who have relapsed or are resistant or refractory to first-line chemotherapy

Cautions; Side-effects: see section 8.1 and notes above; caution in hepatic and renal impairment; irritant to tissues

▼ PoM **Aclacin**® (Lundbeck)

Injection, powder for reconstitution, aclarubicin 20 mg (as hydrochloride). Net price 20-mg vial = £29.20

ACTINOMYCIN D

(Dactinomycin)

Indications: see notes above

Cautions; Side-effects: see section 8.1 and notes above; irritant to tissues

PoM **Cosmegen Lyovac**® (MSD)

Injection, powder for reconstitution, actinomycin D, net price 500-microgram vial = £1.25

BLEOMYCIN

Indications: squamous cell carcinoma; see also notes above

Cautions; Side-effects: see section 8.1 and notes above; reduce dose in renal impairment; also caution in handling—irritant to skin

PoM **Bleomycin** (Lundbeck)

Injection, powder for reconstitution, bleomycin (as sulphate). Net price 15-unit amp = £13.89

Note. 1 mg of bleomycin was formerly equivalent to 1 unit; due to improved production methods 1 mg of bleomycin is now equivalent to approximately 2 units. To avoid confusion potency is now expressed **only** in units.

DOXORUBICIN HYDROCHLORIDE

Indications: see notes above and section 7.4.4

Cautions; Side-effects: see section 8.1 and notes above; reduce dose in hepatic impairment; also caution in handling—irritant to skin and tissues

PoM **Doxorubicin Rapid Dissolution** (Farmitalia Carlo Erba)

Injection, powder for reconstitution, doxorubicin hydrochloride, net price 10-mg vial = £16.35; 50-mg vial = £81.73

Note. This preparation has replaced Adriamycin®

PoM **Doxorubicin Solution for Injection** (Farmitalia Carlo Erba)

Injection, doxorubicin hydrochloride 2 mg/mL, net price 5-ml vial = £17.98; 25-mL vial = £89.90

EPIRUBICIN HYDROCHLORIDE

Indications: see notes above

Cautions; Side-effects: see section 8.1 and notes above; reduce dose in hepatic impairment; irritant to tissues

PoM **Pharmorubicin® Rapid Dissolution** (Farmitalia Carlo Erba)
Injection, powder for reconstitution, epirubicin hydrochloride. Net price 10-mg vial = £16.35; 20-mg vial = £32.69; 50-mg vial = £81.73

IDARUBICIN HYDROCHLORIDE

Indications: acute leukaemias—see notes above
Cautions; Side-effects: see section 8.1 and notes above; caution in hepatic and renal impairment; also caution in handling—irritant to skin and tissues

▼ PoM **Zavedos®** (Farmitalia Carlo Erba)
Injection, powder for reconstitution, idarubicin hydrochloride, net price 5-mg vial = £63.30; 10-mg vial = £126.60

MITOMYCIN

Indications: see notes above
Cautions; Side-effects: see section 8.1 and notes above; irritant to tissues

PoM **Mitomycin C Kyowa®** (Martindale)
Injection, powder for reconstitution, mitomycin. Net price 2-mg vial = £5.46; 10-mg vial = £17.97; 20-mg vial = £34.27 (hosp. only)

MITOZANTRONE

Indications: see notes above
Cautions; Side-effects: see section 8.1 and notes above; intrathecal administration not recommended

PoM **Novantrone®** (Lederle)
Intravenous infusion, mitozantrone 2 mg (as hydrochloride)/mL, net price 20-mg vial = £141.92; 25-mg vial = £177.40; 30-mg vial = £212.87

PLICAMYCIN

(Mithramycin)
Indications: hypercalcaemia—see notes above
Cautions; Side-effects: see section 8.1 and notes above; caution in renal impairment; irritant to tissues

PoM **Mithracin®** (Pfizer)
Injection, powder for reconstitution, plicamycin, net price 2.5-mg vial = £7.51 (hosp. only)

8.1.3 Antimetabolites

Antimetabolites are incorporated into new nuclear material or combine irreversibly with vital cellular enzymes, preventing normal cellular division.

Methotrexate inhibits the enzyme dihydrofolate reductase, essential for the synthesis of purines and pyrimidines. It may be given orally, intravenously, intramuscularly, or intrathecally. High-dose methotrexate cannot generally be recommended except in clinical trials.

Methotrexate is used as maintenance therapy for childhood acute lymphoblastic leukaemia. Other uses include choriocarcinoma, non-Hodgkin lymphomas, and a number of solid tumours. Intrathecal methotrexate is used in the CNS prophylaxis of childhood acute lymphoblastic leukaemia, and as a therapy for established meningeal cancer or lymphoma.

Methotrexate causes myelosuppression, mucositis, and rarely pneumonitis. It is **contra-indicated** if significant renal impairment is present, as the kidney is its route of excretion. It should also be **avoided** if a significant pleural effusion or ascites are present as it tends to accumulate at these sites, and its subsequent return to the circulation will be associated with myelosuppression. For similar reasons blood counts should be carefully monitored when intrathecal methotrexate is given.

Oral or parenteral folinic acid (see below) will speed recovery from methotrexate mucositis or myelosuppression.

Cytarabine acts by interfering with pyrimidine synthesis. It may be given subcutaneously, intravenously, or intrathecally. Its predominant use is in the induction of remission and maintenance therapy of acute myeloblastic leukaemia. It is a potent myelosuppressant and requires careful haematological monitoring.

Fluorouracil may be given orally but is usually given intravenously. It is used to treat a number of solid tumours, including colon and breast cancer. It may also be used topically for certain malignant skin lesions. Toxicity is unusual, but may include myelosuppression, mucositis, and rarely a cerebellar syndrome.

Mercaptopurine is used almost exclusively as maintenance therapy for the acute leukaemias. The dose should be reduced if the patient is receiving concurrent allopurinol as this drug interferes with the metabolism of mercaptopurine.

Thioguanine is used orally to induce remission and for maintenance in acute myeloid leukaemia.

Azathioprine, a derivative of the antimetabolite mercaptopurine, is commonly used as an immunosuppressant (section 8.2.1).

CYTARABINE

Indications: acute leukaemias
Cautions; Side-effects: see section 8.1 and notes above

PoM **Cytarabine** (Non-proprietary)
Injection, powder for reconstitution, cytarabine. Net price 100-mg vial = £2.75; 500-mg vial = £14.95; 1-g vial = £25.86

PoM **Alexan®** (Pfizer)
Injection, cytarabine 20 mg/mL. Net price 2-mL amp = £1.06; 5-mL amp = £2.65

PoM **Alexan® 100** (Pfizer)
Injection, cytarabine 100 mg/mL. Net price 1-mL amp = £2.65; 10-mL amp = £26.46. For intravenous infusion only

PoM **Cytosar®** (Upjohn)
Injection, powder for reconstitution, cytarabine. Net price 100-mg vial = £3.01; 500-mg vial = £15.45. For intravenous injection or infusion and subcutaneous injection only

FLUOROURACIL

Indications: see notes above

Cautions; Side-effects: see section 8.1; also caution in handling—irritant; **interactions:** Appendix 1 (fluorouracil)

Dose: by mouth, maintenance 15 mg/kg weekly; max. in one day 1 g

PoM **Fluorouracil** (Non-proprietary)

Injection, fluorouracil 25 mg/mL (as sodium salt). Net price 10-mL vial = £1.42; 20-mL vial = £2.60; 100-mL vial = £12.60

PoM **Fluoro-uracil** (Roche)

Capsules, blue/orange, fluorouracil 250 mg. Net price 30-cap pack = £35.38. Label: 21

Injection, fluorouracil 25 mg (as sodium salt)/mL. Net price 10-mL amp = £1.42

Note. The injection solution can also be given by mouth in fruit juice.

PoM **Efudix®** (Roche)

Cream, fluorouracil 5%. Net price 20 g = £3.75

MERCAPTOPURINE

Indications: acute leukaemias

Cautions; Side-effects: see section 8.1 and notes above; reduce dose in renal impairment; avoid in porphyria; **interactions:** Appendix 1 (mercaptopurine)

Dose: initially 2.5 mg/kg daily

PoM **Puri-Nethol®** (Calmic)

Tablets, fawn, scored, mercaptopurine 50 mg. Net price 25 = £15.19

METHOTREXATE

Indications: see notes above

Cautions; Side-effects: see section 8.1 and notes above; reduce dose in renal impairment; dose-related toxicity in hepatic impairment (avoid in non-malignant conditions, e.g. psoriasis); avoid in porphyria; **interactions:** Appendix 1 (methotrexate)

Dose: by mouth, leukaemia in children (maintenance), 15 mg/m^2 weekly in combination with other drugs; psoriasis, 10–25 mg weekly

PoM **Methotrexate** (Lederle)

Tablets, both yellow, scored, methotrexate 2.5 mg, net price 20 = £2.17.

Injection, methotrexate 2.5 mg (as sodium salt)/mL. Net price 1-mL amp = 83p; 2-mL vial = 91p

Injection, methotrexate 25 mg (as sodium salt)/mL. Net price 1-mL vial = £1.94; 2-mL vial = £2.69; 4-mL vial = £5.14; 8-mL vial = £10.28; 20-mL vial = £25.71; 40-mL vial = £45.71; 200-mL vial = £205.71

Injection, powder for reconstitution, methotrexate (as sodium salt). Net price 500-mg vial = £32.00

THIOGUANINE

Indications: acute leukaemias

Cautions; Side-effects: see section 8.1 and notes above; reduce dose in renal impairment

Dose: initially 2–2.5 mg/kg daily

PoM **Lanvis®** (Calmic)

Tablets, yellow, scored, thioguanine 40 mg. Net price 25-tab pack = £36.74

FOLINIC ACID RESCUE

Folinic acid (leucovorin) is used to counteract the folate-antagonist action of methotrexate and thus speed recovery from methotrexate-induced mucositis or myelosuppression. It does not counteract the antibacterial activity of folate antagonists such as trimethoprim.

FOLINIC ACID

Indications: see notes above

Cautions: avoid simultaneous administration of methotrexate; as for Folic Acid (section 9.1.2) **not** indicated for pernicious anaemia or other megaloblastic anaemias where vitamin B_{12} deficient

Side-effects: rarely, pyrexia after parenteral adminstration

Dose: as an antidote to methotrexate (started 8–24 hours after the beginning of methotrexate infusion), in general up to 120 mg in divided doses over 12–24 hours *by intramuscular or intravenous injection or infusion*, followed by 12–15 mg *intramuscularly or* 15 mg *by mouth* every 6 hours for the next 48 hours

Suspected methotrexate overdosage, immediate administration of an equal or higher dose of folinic acid

PoM **Calcium Folinate** (Non-proprietary)

Tablets, scored, folinic acid (as calcium salt) 15 mg. Net price 10-tab pack = £42.28

PoM **Calcium Leucovorin** (Lederle)

Tablets, scored, folinic acid 15 mg (as calcium salt). Net price 10-tab pack = £42.28

Injection, folinic acid 3 mg (as calcium salt)/mL. Net price 1-mL amp = £1.09

Injection, powder for reconstitution, folinic acid (as calcium salt). Net price 15-mg vial = £4.57; 30-mg vial = £8.57

PoM **Refolinon®** (Farmitalia Carlo Erba)

Tablets, yellow, scored, folinic acid 15 mg (as calcium salt). Net price 30 = £105.00

Injection, folinic acid 3 mg (as calcium salt)/mL. Net price 2-mL amp = £1·60; 10-mL amp = £6.70

8.1.4 Vinca alkaloids and etoposide

These interfere with microtubule assembly, causing metaphase arrest. All vinca alkaloids have similar activity but vary in the predominant site of toxicity.

The vinca alkaloids are used to treat the acute leukaemias, lymphomas, and some solid tumours (e.g. breast and lung cancer). They commonly cause peripheral and autonomic neuropathy. This side-effect is most obvious with vincristine, and is manifest by peripheral paraesthesia, loss of deep tendon reflexes, and abdominal bloating and constipation. If these symptoms are severe, doses should be reduced. Significant new motor weakness is a **contra indication** to further use of these drugs. Recovery of the nervous system is generally slow but complete. Intrathecal administration of **all** vinca alkaloids is **contra-indicated** (usually fatal).

Vincristine causes virtually no myelosuppression. Its use may be associated with alopecia; hyponatraemia, as a result of inappropriate ADH secretion, has been described.

Vinblastine is a more myelosuppressive drug than vincristine, but causes less neurotoxicity.

Vindesine is the most recent addition to the vinca alkaloid group. It has a similar range of clinical activity, and side-effects intermediate between those of the above two drugs.

Etoposide may be given orally or intravenously, the dose when used orally being double that when given intravenously. There is limited clinical evidence to suggest that administration in divided doses over 3–5 days may be beneficial; courses may not be repeated more frequently than at intervals of 21 days. It has useful activity in small cell carcinoma of the bronchus, the lymphomas, and testicular teratoma. Common toxic effects include alopecia, myelosuppression, nausea, and vomiting.

ETOPOSIDE

Indications: see notes above

Cautions; Contra-indications; Side-effects: see section 8.1 and notes above; irritant to tissues

PoM **Vepesid**® (Bristol-Myers)

Capsules, etoposide 50 mg, net price 20 = £113.95; 100 mg, 10-tab pack = £99.57

Injection, etoposide 20 mg/mL. To be diluted. Net price 5-mL amp = £14.58

Caution: may dissolve certain types of filter

VINBLASTINE SULPHATE

Indications: see notes above

Cautions; Contra-indications; Side-effects: see section 8.1 and notes above; caution in handling—avoid contact with eyes; irritant to tissues

PoM **Vinblastine** (Non-proprietary)

Injection, powder for reconstitution, vinblastine sulphate. Net price 10-mg vial (with diluent) = £6.86

PoM **Velbe**® (Lilly)

Injection, powder for reconstitution, vinblastine sulphate. Net price 10-mg amp (with diluent) = £10.29

VINCRISTINE SULPHATE

Indications: see notes above

Cautions; Contra-indications; Side-effects: see section 8.1 and notes above; caution in handling—avoid contact with eyes; irritant to tissues

PoM **Vincristine** (Non-proprietary)

Injection, vincristine sulphate 1 mg/mL. Net price 1-mL syringe = £10·49; 2-mL syringe = £19.00

Injection, powder for reconstitution, vincristine sulphate, net price, 1-mg vial = £3.42; 2-mg vial = £6.86; 5-mg vial = £17.14 (all with diluent)

PoM **Oncovin**® (Lilly)

Injection, vincristine sulphate 1 mg/mL, net price 1-mL vial = £10.31; 2-mL vial = £20.40

Injection, powder for reconstitution, vincristine sulphate. Net price 1-mg vial = £9.36 (with diluent)

VINDESINE SULPHATE

Indications: see notes above

Cautions; Contra-indications; Side-effects: see section 8.1 and notes above; caution in handling—avoid contact with eyes; irritant to tissues

PoM **Eldisine**® (Lilly)

Injection, powder for reconstitution, vindesine sulphate, net price 5-mg vial (with diluent) = £51.77 (hosp. only)

8.1.5 Other antineoplastic drugs

Amsacrine has an action and toxic effects similar to those of doxorubicin. It is used as second-line treatment in refractory acute myeloid leukaemia. Side-effects include myelosuppression and mucositis; electrolytes should be monitored as fatal arrhythmias have occurred in association with hypokalaemia.

AMSACRINE

Indications: see notes above

Cautions; Side-effects: see section 8.1 and notes above; reduce dose in renal or hepatic impairment; also caution in handling—irritant to skin and tissues

PoM **Amsidine**® (P-D)

Concentrate for intravenous infusion, amsacrine 5 mg (as lactate)/mL, when reconstituted by mixing two solutions. Net price 1.5-mL amp with 13.5-mL vial = £32.60 (hosp. only)

Note. Use glass apparatus for reconstitution

Carboplatin is a derivative of cisplatin which has probably equivalent activity in ovarian cancer. It is at present under trial in a variety of other malignancies. Carboplatin is better tolerated than cisplatin; nausea and vomiting are reduced in severity and nephrotoxicity, neurotoxicity, and ototoxicity are much less of a problem than with cisplatin. It is, however, more myelosuppressive than cisplatin, and for this reason should not be repeated at intervals of less than 4 weeks.

 Prices are **net**, see p. 1

CARBOPLATIN

Indications: see notes above
Cautions; Side-effects: see section 8.1 and notes above; reduce dose in renal impairment

PoM **Paraplatin®** (Bristol-Myers)
Injection, powder for reconstitution, carboplatin. Net price 50-mg vial = £22.85; 150-mg vial = £68.57; 450-mg vial = £205.71

Cisplatin has an alkylating action. It has useful antitumour activity in certain solid tumours including ovarian cancer and testicular teratoma. It is, however, a toxic drug. Common problems include severe nausea and vomiting, nephrotoxicity (pretreatment hydration recommended and renal function should be closely monitored), myelotoxicity, ototoxicity (high tone hearing loss and tinnitus), peripheral neuropathy, and hypomagnesaemia. These toxic effects commonly necessitate dose reduction or drug withdrawal. It is preferable that treatment with this drug be supervised by specialists familiar with its use.

CISPLATIN

Indications: see notes above
Cautions; Side-effects: see section 8.1 and notes above; reduce dose in renal impairment; **interactions:** Appendix 1 (cisplatin)

PoM **Cisplatin** (Non-proprietary)
Injection, cisplatin 1 mg/mL. Net price 10-mL vial = £2.90; 50-mL vial = £14.00; 100-mL vial = £27.00
Injection, powder for reconstitution, cisplatin 10-mg vial, net price = £2.50; 50-mg vial = £12.10; 150-mg vial = £68.57; 450-mg vial = £205.71

Crisantaspase is the enzyme asparaginase produced by *Erwinia chrysanthemi*. It is used almost exclusively in acute lymphoblastic leukaemia. Facilities for the management of anaphylaxis should be available. Side-effects also include nausea, vomiting, CNS depression, and liver function and blood lipid changes therefore careful monitoring is necessary and the urine is tested for glucose to exclude hyperglycaemia.

CRISANTASPASE

Indications; Cautions; Side-effects: see notes above

PoM **Erwinase®** (Porton)
Injection, powder for reconstitution, crisantaspase. Net price 20 × 10000-unit vial = £650.00

Dacarbazine is not commonly used on account of its toxicity. It has been used to treat melanoma and, in combination therapy, the soft tissue sarcomas. It is also a component of a commonly used second-line combination for Hodgkin's disease (ABVD—doxorubicin [Adriamycin®], bleomycin, vinblastine, and dacarbazine). The predominant side-effects are myelosuppression and intense nausea and vomiting.

DACARBAZINE

Indications: see notes above
Cautions; Side-effects: see section 8.1; also caution in handling—irritant to skin and tissues

PoM **DTIC-Dome** (Bayer)
Injection, powder for reconstitution, dacarbazine. Net price 100-mg vial = £4.83; 200-mg vial = £7.40

Hydroxyurea is an orally active drug used mainly in the treatment of chronic myeloid leukaemia. Myelosuppression, nausea, and skin reactions are the commonest toxic effects.

HYDROXYUREA

Indications: see notes above
Cautions; Side-effects: see section 8.1 and notes above
Dose: 20–30 mg/kg daily *or* 80 mg/kg every 3rd day

PoM **Hydrea®** (Squibb)
Capsules, pink/green, hydroxyurea 500 mg. Net price 20 = £2.39

Procarbazine is a first-line drug in Hodgkin's disease, for example in MOPP (mustine, vincristine [Oncovin®], procarbazine, and prednisolone) chemotherapy. It is also used to treat non-Hodgkin lymphomas and small cell carcinoma of the bronchus. It is given orally. Toxic effects include nausea, myelosuppression, and a hypersensitivity rash preventing further use of this drug. It is a mild monoamine-oxidase inhibitor and appropriate dietary advice is recommended (see section 4.3.2). Alcohol ingestion may cause a disulfiram-like reaction.

PROCARBAZINE

Indications: see notes above
Cautions; Side-effects: see section 8.1 and notes above; reduce dose in renal impairment; **interactions:** Appendix 1 (procarbazine)
Dose: initially 50 mg daily, increased by 50 mg daily to 250–300 mg daily in divided doses; maintenance (on remission) 50–150 mg daily to cumulative total of at least 6 g

PoM **Natulan®** (Roche)
Capsules, ivory, procarbazine 50 mg (as hydrochloride). Net price 50-cap pack = £3.44. Label: 4

Razoxane has limited activity in the leukaemias, and is little used.

RAZOXANE

Indications: see notes above
Cautions; Side-effects: see section 8.1
Dose: acute leukaemias, 150–500 mg/m^2 daily for 3–5 days

PoM **Razoxin®** (ICI)
Tablets, scored, razoxane 125 mg. Net price 30-tab pack = £27.56

8.2 Drugs affecting the immune response

8.2.1 Cytotoxic immunosuppressants

These drugs are used to suppress rejection in organ transplant recipients and are also used to treat a variety of auto-immune and collagen diseases (see section 10.1.3). They are non-specific in their action and careful monitoring of peripheral blood counts is required, with dose adjustments for marrow toxicity. Patients receiving these drugs will be prone to atypical infections, e.g. fungal infections.

Azathioprine is widely used for transplant recipients and is also used to treat a number of auto-immune conditions, usually when corticosteroid therapy alone has provided inadequate control. This drug is metabolised to mercaptopurine, and doses should be reduced when concurrent therapy with allopurinol is given. The predominant toxic effect is myelosuppression, although hepatic toxicity is also well recognised.

Cyclophosphamide and chlorambucil (section 8.1.1) are less commonly prescribed as immunosuppressants.

AZATHIOPRINE

Indications: see notes above

Cautions; Side-effects: see section 8.1 and notes above; also rashes; reduce dose in severe hepatic or renal impairment; **interactions:** Appendix 1 (azathioprine)

Dose: by mouth, 2–2.5 mg/kg daily.

Chronic active hepatitis, 1–1.5 mg/kg daily

Suppression of transplant rejection, loading dose, up to 5 mg/kg; maintenance 1–4 mg/kg daily

By intravenous injection, suppression of transplant rejection, loading dose, up to 5 mg/kg; maintenance dose (if oral route not possible), 1–2.5 mg/kg daily

PoM **Azathioprine** (Non-proprietary)

Tablets, azathioprine 50 mg. Net price 20 = £5.80

Available from APS, Berk (Berkaprine®), Cox, Evans, Kerfoot, Penn (Azamune®)

PoM **Imuran®** (Calmic)

Tablets, both f/c, azathioprine 25 mg (orange), net price 100-tab pack = £39.35; 50 mg (yellow), 100-tab pack = £65.61

Injection, powder for reconstitution, azathioprine (as sodium salt). Net price 50-mg vial = £16.54

8.2.2 Corticosteroids and other immunosuppressants

Prednisolone is widely used in oncology. It has a marked antitumour effect in acute lymphoblastic leukaemia, Hodgkin's disease, and the non-Hodgkin lymphomas. It is also active in hormone-sensitive breast cancer and may cause useful disease regression. Finally, it has a role in the palliation of symptomatic end-stage malignant disease when it may produce a sense of well-being.

The corticosteroids are also powerful immunosuppressants. They are used to prevent organ transplant rejection, and in high dose to treat rejection episodes. For notes on corticosteroids see section 6.3.

Cyclosporin is a fungal metabolite and potent immunosuppressant which is virtually non-myelotoxic but markedly nephrotoxic. It has found particular use in the field of organ and tissue transplantation, for prevention of graft rejection following bone marrow, kidney, liver, pancreas, heart, and heart-lung transplantation, and for prophylaxis of graft-versus-host disease.

Antilymphocyte immunoglobulin is obtained from immunised horses. It has mainly been used to prevent transplant rejection. It is available on a restricted basis only (as *Pressimmune®*, Hoechst).

CYCLOSPORIN

Indications: see notes above

Cautions: monitor liver and kidney function; other immunosuppressants; over-suppression may increase susceptibility to infection and lymphoma; avoid during pregnancy, breast-feeding; **interactions:** Appendix 1 (cyclosporin)

Side-effects: hepatic and renal impairment; tremor, gastro-intestinal disturbances, hypertrichosis; gum hyperplasia; hyperkalaemia; *occasionally* facial oedema, hypertension, fluid retention, and convulsions; serum creatinine, urea, bilirubin, and liver enzymes may be increased; burning sensation in hands and feet during first week of oral administration

Dose: organ transplantation, used alone, 14–17.5 mg/kg as a single dose *by mouth* 4–12 hours before transplantation followed by 14–17.5 mg/kg daily for 1–2 weeks post-operatively then reduced in steps of about 2 mg/kg daily at intervals of 1 month to 6–8 mg/kg daily for maintenance (dose may be adjusted by monitoring blood concentrations); maintenance dose lower and reached sooner with concomitant corticosteroid therapy; if necessary one-third oral dose can be given *by intravenous infusion* over 2–6 hours (3–5 mg/kg daily if initiating therapy)

Bone-marrow transplantation, prevention of graft-versus-host disease, 3–5 mg/kg daily *by intravenous infusion* over 2–6 hours from day before transplantation to 2 weeks post-operatively (or 12.5–25 mg/kg daily *by mouth* for about 5 days) then 12.5 mg/kg daily *by mouth* for 3–6 months (up to 25 mg/kg daily and 1 year recorded) then tailed off or maintained at low dosage for mild chronic graft-versus-host disease; if necessary one-third oral dose can be given *by intravenous infusion* over 2–6 hours

COUNSELLING. Total daily dose may be taken as a single dose or in 2 divided doses. To mask taste, mix with milk, chocolate drink, or fruit juice immediately before taking

PoM **Sandimmun®** (Sandoz)
Capsules, cyclosporin 25 mg (pale pink), net price 30-cap pack = £21.07; 100 mg (dusky pink), 30-cap pack = £78.29
Oral solution, oily, yellow, sugar-free, cyclosporin 100 mg/mL. Net price 50 mL = £117.31. Counselling, administration
Concentrate for intravenous infusion (oily), cyclosporin 50 mg/mL. To be diluted before use. Net price 1-mL amp = £1.82; 5-mL amp = £8.60
Note. Contains polyethoxylated castor oil which has been associated with anaphylaxis

PREDNISOLONE
See section 6.3.4

8.2.3 Immunostimulants
A suspension of inactivated *Corynebacterium parvum* organisms may be used by the intracavitary route to treat malignant effusions.

CORYNEBACTERIUM PARVUM VACCINE
Indications: see notes above
Cautions: avoid within 10 days of thoracotomy
Side-effects: pyrexia common; abdominal pain, nausea and vomiting
Dose: *by intrapleural or intraperitoneal injection*, 7–14 mg

PoM **Coparvax®** (Calmic)
Injection, powder for reconstitution, *Corynebacterium parvum* (inactivated). Net price 7-mg vial = £54.86

8.2.4 Interferons
The interferons (alfa, beta, and gamma) are naturally occurring proteins with complex effects on immunity and cell function. Recently alfa interferon (formerly called lymphoblastoid interferon) has shown some antitumour effect in certain lymphomas and solid tumours. Side-effects are dose-related, but commonly include influenza-like symptoms, lethargy, and depression. Myelosuppression may also occur, particularly affecting granulocyte counts. Finally, cardiovascular problems (hypotension, hypertension, and arrhythmias) have been reported; **interactions:** Appendix 1 (interferons)

PoM **Intron A®** (Schering-Plough)
Injection, powder for reconstitution, interferon alfa-2b (rbe). Net price 3-million unit vial = £16.96; 5-million unit vial = £28.26; 10-million unit vial = £56.52; 30-million unit vial = £169.56
For use in AIDS-related Kaposi's sarcoma, hairy cell leukaemia, chronic myelogenous leukaemia, condyloma acuminata

PoM **Roferon-A®** (Roche)
Injection, powder for reconstitution, interferon alfa-2a (rbe). Net price 3 million-unit vial = £16.96; 9 million-unit vial = £50.88; 18 million-unit vial = £101.77; all with syringe, needles, and water for injection
For use in AIDS-related Kaposi's sarcoma, hairy cell leukaemia, and recurrent or metastatic renal cell carcinoma

PoM **Wellferon®** (Wellcome)
Injection, interferon alfa-N1 (lns) 3 million units/mL, net price 1-mL vial = £19.93; 10 million units/mL, net price 1-mL vial = £64.55
For hairy cell leukaemia

8.3 Sex hormones and antagonists in malignant disease

Hormonal manipulation has an important role in the treatment of metastatic breast, prostate, and endometrial cancer, and a more marginal role in the treatment of hypernephroma. These treatments are not curative, but may provide excellent palliation of symptoms in selected patients, sometimes for a period of years. Tumour response, and treatment toxicity should be carefully monitored and treatment changed if progression occurs or side-effects exceed benefit.

BREAST CANCER. Overall, approximately 30% of patients with metastatic breast cancer respond to tamoxifen. This figure is increased to 60% in patients with oestrogen receptor positive tumours; receptor negative tumours responding in less than 10%. Tamoxifen is equivalent in effect to oophorectomy in pre-menopausal patients and it is so well tolerated that it is probably the treatment of choice in suitable patients of all ages. Whilst oophorectomy still has a therapeutic role, adrenalectomy has largely been replaced by aminoglutethimide, given together with prednisolone. Hypophysectomy is rarely used.

Patients with non-threatening metastases unresponsive to tamoxifen may still respond to a secondary hormonal treatment. Certainly, patients who initially respond to tamoxifen should receive second-line hormone treatment. No clear guidelines are available; for pre-menopausal patients oophorectomy or a progestogen may be used; for post-menopausal patients a progestogen or aminoglutethimide with corticosteroid cover may be used. Responding patients can receive further hormones at relapse, refractory patients are better treated with chemotherapy or palliative therapy.

Adjuvant hormonal treatment with tamoxifen has been used after treatment of the primary in postmenopausal patients with high-risk breast cancer. Such treatment has consistently prolonged

Prices are **net**, see p. 1

the period between diagnosis and the development of metastases; a modest increase in survival has now been reported in some studies.

PROSTATE CANCER. Metastatic cancer of the prostate is commonly responsive to hormonal treatment designed to deprive the cancer of androgen. Treatment is probably best reserved for patients with symptomatic metastatic disease. The most simple treatment is bilateral subcapsular orchidectomy, which commonly results in responses lasting 12–18 months. Alternatively, a gonadotrophin-releasing hormone analogue (e.g. buserelin) may be given; these require parenteral administration, at least initially, and are expensive. A number of patients develop an initial tumour 'flare' after treatment (with increased bone pain); it can usually be treated with analgesics, but the addition of an anti-androgen (such as flutamide) may be necessary for the first few weeks. Cyproterone acetate has also been used as first-line therapy; it has a number of theoretical advantages, but is expensive. Stilboestrol is still used; the dose should be restricted to 1–3 mg daily by mouth as higher doses are associated with unacceptable cardiovascular morbidity. Second-line treatment may palliate symptoms, but rarely results in appreciable disease regression. Alternatives after orchidectomy include cyproterone acetate or aminoglutethimide with prednisolone.

8.3.1 Oestrogens

Stilboestrol may be used in low dosage to treat symptomatic metastases from prostate cancer. It is now less commonly used in postmenopausal women with breast cancer. Toxicity is common and dose-related side-effects include nausea, fluid retention, and venous and arterial thrombosis. Impotence and gynaecomastia always occur in men, and withdrawal bleeding may be a problem in women. Hypercalcaemia and bone pain may also occur in breast cancer.

Fosfestrol is activated by the enzyme acid phosphatase to produce stilboestrol. Side-effects are as for stilboestrol and, in addition, perineal pain may complicate intravenous use in prostate cancer.

Ethinyloestradiol is the most potent oestrogen available. Unlike other oestrogens it is only slowly metabolised in the liver. It is used in breast cancer and may be better tolerated than stilboestrol in patients suffering from nausea.

Polyestradiol is a long-acting oestrogen preparation.

STILBOESTROL

Indications: see notes above
Cautions; Side-effects: cardiovascular disease (sodium retention with oedema, thromboembolism), hepatic impairment (jaundice), feminising effects in men; see also notes above
Dose: breast cancer, 10–20 mg daily
Prostate cancer, 1–3 mg daily

PoM **Stilboestrol Tablets,** stilboestrol 1 mg, net price 20 = 87p; 5 mg, 20 = £1.63

ETHINYLOESTRADIOL

Indications: see notes above; other indications, see section 6.4.1.1
Cautions; Side-effects: see under Stilboestrol and notes above
Dose: breast cancer, 1–3 mg daily

Preparations
See section 6.4.1.1

FOSFESTROL TETRASODIUM

Indications: prostate cancer
Cautions; Contra-indications; Side-effects: see under Stilboestrol and notes above; nausea and vomiting; after intravenous injection, perineal irritation and pain in bony metastases
Dose: by slow intravenous injection, 552–1104 mg daily for at least 5 days; maintenance 276 mg 1–4 times weekly
By mouth, maintenance 100–200 mg 3 times daily, reducing to 100–300 mg daily in divided doses

PoM **Honvan**® (Boehringer Ingelheim)
Tablets, fosfestrol tetrasodium 100 mg. Net price 20 = £1.87
Injection, fosfestrol tetrasodium 55.2 mg/mL. Net price 5-mL amp = 92p

POLYESTRADIOL PHOSPHATE

Indications: prostate cancer
Cautions; Side-effects: see under Stilboestrol and notes above
Dose: by deep intramuscular injection, 80–160 mg every 4 weeks; maintenance 40–80 mg

PoM **Estradurin**® (Pharmacia)
Injection, powder for reconstitution, polyestradiol phosphate (with mepivacaine and nicotinamide). Net price 40-mg vial = £2.18; 80-mg vial = £3.51 (both with diluent)

8.3.2 Progestogens

These drugs are used largely as second- or third-line therapy in breast cancer. They are also used to treat endometrial cancer and hypernephroma, but are little used for prostate cancer. **Medroxyprogesterone** or **megestrol** are usually used and can be given orally. High-dose or parenteral treatment cannot be recommended. Side-effects are mild but may include nausea, fluid retention, and weight gain.

GESTRONOL HEXANOATE

Indications: see notes above; benign prostatic hypertrophy
Cautions; Contra-indications; Side-effects: see under Progesterone (section 6.4.1.2) and notes above
Dose: endometrial cancer, *by intramuscular injection*, 200–400 mg every 5–7 days
Benign prostatic hypertrophy, *by intramuscular injection*, 200 mg every week, increased to 300–400 mg every week if necessary

PoM **Depostat®** (Schering Health Care)
Injection (oily), gestronol hexanoate 100 mg/mL. Net price 2-mL amp = £4.28

MEDROXYPROGESTERONE ACETATE

Indications: see notes above; other indications, see section 6.4.1.2
Cautions; Contra-indications; Side-effects: see under Progesterone (section 6.4.1.2) and notes above; Cushingoid side-effects at high doses reported
Dose: by mouth, endometrial, prostate, and renal cancer, 100–500 mg daily; breast cancer, various doses in range 0.4–1.5 g daily
By deep intramuscular injection, various doses in range 1 g daily down to 250 mg weekly

PoM **Depo-Provera®** (Upjohn)
Injection, medroxyprogesterone acetate 150 mg/mL. Net price 3.3-mL (500-mg) vial = £12.49
PoM **Farlutal®** (Farmitalia Carlo Erba)
Tablets, both scored, medroxyprogesterone acetate 100 mg, net price 20 = £8.32; 250 mg, 50 = £52.03
Tablets, scored, medroxyprogesterone acetate 500 mg. Net price 56 = £116.54. Label: 27
Injection, medroxyprogesterone acetate 200 mg/mL. Net price 2.5-mL vial = £14.24; 5-mL vial = £23.73
PoM **Provera®** (Upjohn)
Tablets, medroxyprogesterone acetate 100 mg (scored), net price 20 = £8.32; 200 mg (scored), 20 = £16.47; 400 mg, 30 = £48.89
Suspension, sugar-free, medroxyprogesterone 400 mg/5 mL. Diluent purified water, freshly boiled and cooled, life of diluted suspension 28 days. Net price 100 mL = £32.59

MEGESTROL ACETATE

Indications: see notes above
Cautions; Contra-indications; Side-effects: see under Progesterone (section 6.4.1.2) and notes above
Dose: breast cancer, 160 mg daily in single or divided doses; endometrial cancer, 40–320 mg daily in divided doses

PoM **Megace®** (Bristol-Myers)
Tablets, both scored, megestrol acetate 40 mg, net price 20 = £5.08; 160 mg (off-white), 30-tab pack = £29.30

NORETHISTERONE

Indications: see notes above; other indications, see section 6.4.1.2
Cautions; Contra-indications; Side-effects: see section 6.4.1.2 and notes above
Dose: breast cancer, 40 mg daily, increased to 60 mg daily if required

Preparations
See section 6.4.1.2

NORETHISTERONE ACETATE

Indications: see notes above
Cautions; Contra-indications; Side-effects: see under Norethisterone (section 6.4.1.2) and notes above
Dose: breast cancer, 10 mg 3 times daily, increased to 60 mg daily if required

PoM **SH 420®** (Schering Health Care)
Tablets, scored, norethisterone acetate 10 mg. Net price 20 = £4.95

8.3.3 Androgens

The androgens are given parenterally and are predominantly used as second- or third-line therapy for metastatic breast cancer.

TESTOSTERONE ESTERS

Indications: see notes above; other indications, see section 6.4.2
Cautions; Contra-indications; Side-effects: see under Testosterone (section 6.4.2)
Dose: see under Preparations

PoM **Primoteston Depot®** : see section 6.4.2
PoM **Virormone®** : see section 6.4.2

8.3.4 Hormone antagonists

Tamoxifen acts as an oestrogen antagonist and blocks receptor sites in target organs. This drug, at a dose of 20 mg daily, is the hormonal treatment of choice for breast cancer in postmenopausal women with metastatic disease and is also increasingly commonly used as a first-line treatment for premenopausal women. Side-effects are unusual, but patients with bony metastases may experience an exacerbation of their pain, sometimes associated with hypercalcaemia. This reaction commonly precedes tumour response. Amenorrhoea commonly develops in premenopausal women.

Aminoglutethimide is used in postmenopausal women with breast cancer. It acts predominantly by inhibiting the conversion of androgens to oestrogens in the peripheral tissues. Corticosteroid replacement therapy is necessary (see section 6.3.1). Early toxicity is common and may include drowsiness, drug fever, and a morbilliform eruption. These side-effects generally settle spontaneously. The dose is usually increased to 500 mg daily over 2 to 4 weeks. Hepatic enzyme induction occurs, and may require modification of the doses of other drugs, e.g. oral anticoagulants.

Cyproterone acetate is an anti-androgen used in metastatic prostate cancer.

Flutamide is an anti-androgen which is being studied alone and in combination for prostate cancer. It may have a role in preventing and treating the 'flare' which can occur in patients treated with gonadotrophin-releasing hormone analogues.

Buserelin and **goserelin** are gonadotrophin-releasing hormone analogues used to treat metastatic prostate cancer. They cause an initial stimulation of luteinising hormone (LH) release by the pituitary, which in turn causes testosterone secretion by the testis; subsequently inhibition of LH release occurs, with achievement of an anorchic state.

Drugs of this type are as effective as orchidectomy or stilboestrol. Buserelin requires parenteral administration initially, then intranasal administration; goserelin is given subcutaneously every 28 days into the anterior abdominal wall. During the first 1 to 2 weeks of treatment increased tumour growth may occur causing, for example, spinal cord compression. When such problems are anticipated alternative treatments (e.g. orchidectomy) or simultaneous use of an anti-androgen (e.g. cyproterone acetate) are recommended. Other side-effects are similar to those of orchidectomy.

Octreotide is a long-acting analogue of the hypothalamic release-inhibiting hormone somatostatin; it is indicated for the relief of symptoms associated with gastro-enteropancreatic endocrine tumours.

AMINOGLUTETHIMIDE

Indications: see notes above and under Dose

Cautions: see notes above; contra-indicated in porphyria; **interactions:** Appendix 1 (aminoglutethimide)

Side-effects: see notes above; dizziness, somnolence, lethargy; unsteadiness at higher doses; less frequently nausea, vomiting, diarrhoea; rash (sometimes with fever) reported; allergic alveolitis and blood disorders (regular blood counts) also reported; altered thyroid function

Dose: breast or prostate cancer, 250 mg daily, increased once a week to max. 250 mg 4 times daily (lower doses may be adequate, see notes above); given with a glucocorticoid (and sometimes with a mineralocorticoid as well)

Cushing's syndrome due to malignant disease, 250 mg daily, increased gradually to 1 g daily in divided doses (occasionally 1.5–2 g daily); glucocorticoid given only if necessary

PoM **Orimeten®** (Ciba)

Tablets, scored, aminoglutethimide 250 mg. Net price 20 = £6.57

BUSERELIN

Indications: prostate cancer

Cautions: during first month monitor patients at risk of ureteric obstruction or spinal cord compression, see notes above

Side-effects: initial increase in bone pain (due to transient increases in plasma testosterone); hot flushes, decreased libido, infrequent gynaecomastia, urticaria

Dose: see below

PoM **Suprefact®** (Hoechst)

Injection, buserelin 1 mg (as acetate)/mL. Net price treatment pack of 2 × 5.5-mL vial = £30.37

Dose: by subcutaneous injection, 500 micrograms every 8 hours for 7 days

Nasal spray, buserelin 100 micrograms (as acetate)/metered spray. Net price treatment pack of 4 × 10-g bottle with spray pump = £99.92

Dose: apply 1 spray into each nostril 6 times daily

CYPROTERONE ACETATE

Indications: prostate cancer, see notes above; other indications, see section 6.4.2

Cautions: hepatic disease; risk of recurrence of thrombo-embolic disease; severe depression; see also section 6.4.2

Contra-indications: none in prostate cancer; for contra-indications relating to other indications see section 6.4.2

Side-effects: see section 6.4.2

Dose: prostate cancer, 300 mg daily in 2–3 divided doses after food

PoM **Cyprostat®** (Schering Health Care)

Tablets, scored, cyproterone acetate 50 mg. Net price 84-tab pack = £48.35 (hosp. only); 168-tab pack = £96.70. Label: 3, 21

FLUTAMIDE

Indications: prostate cancer, see notes above

Cautions: cardiac disease (sodium retention with oedema); monitor hepatic function; **interactions:** Appendix 1 (flutamide)

Side-effects: gynaecomastia (sometimes with galactorrhoea); nausea, vomiting, diarrhoea, increased appetite, insomnia, tiredness; other side-effects reported include decreased libido, inhibition of spermatogenesis, gastric and chest pain, headache, dizziness, cholestatic jaundice, oedema, blurred vision, thirst, rashes, pruritus, haemolytic anaemia, systemic lupus erythematosus-like syndrome, and lymphoedema

Dose: 250 mg 3 times daily; started 3 days before gonadotrophin-releasing hormone analogue if combination given

▼ PoM **Drogenil®** (Schering-Plough)

Tablets, yellow, scored, flutamide 250 mg, net price 100-tab pack = £107.00

GOSERELIN

Indications: prostate cancer

Cautions; Side-effects: see under Buserelin; also rashes (reversible without stopping therapy); bruising at injection site

Dose: see below

PoM **Zoladex®** (ICI)

Implant, goserelin 3.6 mg (as acetate) in syringe applicator. Net price each = £125.40

Dose: by subcutaneous injection into anterior abdominal wall, 3.6 mg every 28 days (local anaesthetic if desired)

OCTREOTIDE

Indications: symptoms associated with carcinoid tumours with features of carcinoid syndrome, VIPomas, glucagonomas

Cautions: occasional sudden escape from symptomatic control with rapid recurrence of severe symptoms; in insulinoma may increase depth and duration of hypoglycaemia (close observation initially and with dose changes; marked fluctuations may be reduced by increasing administration frequency); in diabetes mellitus may reduce insulin or oral antidiabetic requirements; monitor thyroid function on long-term therapy; **interactions:** Appendix 1 (octreotide)

Contra-indications: pregnancy (unless compelling reasons) and breast-feeding

Side-effects: gastro-intestinal disturbances including anorexia, nausea, vomiting, abdominal pain and bloating, flatulence, diarrhoea, and steatorrhoea; symptoms may be reduced by injecting between meals or at bedtime; impairment of postprandial glucose tolerance (rarely persistent hyperglycaemia on chronic administration); hepatic disturbance reported; gall stone formation reported after long-term treatment; pain and irritation at injection site (rotate sites)

Dose: by subcutaneous injection, initially 50 micrograms once or twice daily, gradually increased according to response to 200 micrograms 3 times daily (higher doses required exceptionally); maintenance doses variable; in carcinoid tumours discontinue after 1 week if no effect

▼ PoM **Sandostatin®** (Sandoz)

Injection, octreotide (as acetate) 50 micrograms/mL, net price 1-mL amp = £2.98; 100 micrograms/mL, 1-mL amp = £5.60; 500 micrograms/mL, 1-mL amp = £27.13

TAMOXIFEN

Indications: breast cancer, see notes above

Cautions: **interactions:** Appendix 1 (tamoxifen)

Contra-indications: pregnancy; porphyria

Side-effects: hot flushes, vaginal bleeding (but suppression of menstruation in some pre-menopausal women), gastro-intestinal disturbances, dizziness; rarely fluid retention, visual disturbances; see also notes above

Dose: breast cancer, 20–40 mg daily as a single dose or in 2 divided doses

Anovulatory infertility, 20 mg daily on second to fifth days of cycle inclusive; if necessary increased to 40 mg daily then 80 mg daily for subsequent courses; if cycles irregular, start initial course on any day, with subsequent course starting 45 days later *or* on second day of cycle if menstruation occurs

PoM **Tamoxifen** (Non-proprietary)

Tablets, tamoxifen (as citrate) 10 mg, net price 30-tab pack = £6.60; 20 mg, 30-tab pack = £9.60; 40 mg, 30-tab pack = £22.00

Various strengths available from APS, Berk (Emblon®), Cox, CP, Evans, Farmitalia Carlo Erba, Kerfoot, Lederle (Noltam®), Tillotts (Tamofen®)

PoM **Nolvadex®** (ICI)

Tablets, tamoxifen (as citrate) 10 mg, net price 30-tab pack = £6.20; 20 mg (Nolvadex-D®), 30-tab pack = £9.35; 40 mg (scored, Nolvadex-Forte®), 30-tab pack = £22.20

9: Drugs affecting NUTRITION and BLOOD

In this chapter drugs and preparations are discussed under the following headings:

9.1 Anaemias and some other blood disorders

Before initiating treatment it is essential to determine which type of anaemia is present. Iron salts may be harmful and result in iron overload if given alone to patients with anaemias other than those due to iron deficiency.

9.1.1 Iron-deficiency anaemias

Treatment is only justified in the presence of a demonstrable iron-deficiency state.

Prophylaxis is justifiable in pregnancy, menorrhagia, after subtotal or total gastrectomy, and in the management of low birth-weight infants such as premature babies, twins, and in infants delivered by Caesarean section.

9.1.1.1 ORAL IRON

Iron salts should be given by mouth unless there are good reasons for using another route.

Ferrous salts show only marginal differences in efficiency of absorption of iron, but ferric salts are much less well absorbed. Haemoglobin regeneration rate is little affected by the type of salt used provided sufficient iron is given, and in most patients the time factor is not critical. Choice of preparation is thus usually decided by incidence of side-effects and cost.

The oral dose of elemental iron should be 100 to 200 mg daily; it is customary to give this as dried **ferrous sulphate**, 200 mg three times daily. If side-effects arise, dosage can be reduced or a change made to an alternative iron salt. It should be remembered, however, that an apparent improvement in tolerance on changing to another salt may be due to its lower content of elemental iron. The incidence of side-effects due to ferrous sulphate is no greater than with other iron salts when compared on the basis of equivalent amounts of elemental iron.

Iron content of different iron salts

Iron salt	Amount	Content of ferrous iron
Ferrous fumarate	200 mg	65 mg
Ferrous gluconate	300 mg	35 mg
Ferrous glycine sulphate	225 mg	40 mg
Ferrous succinate	100 mg	35 mg
Ferrous sulphate	300 mg	60 mg
Ferrous sulphate, dried	200 mg	60 mg[1]

1. Good quality dried ferrous sulphate 200 mg may now contain approximately 65 mg ferrous iron

THERAPEUTIC RESPONSE. The haemoglobin concentration should rise by about 100–200 mg per 100 mL (1–2 g per litre) per day. After the haemoglobin has risen to normal, treatment should be continued for a further three months in an attempt to replenish the iron stores. Epithelial tissue changes such as atrophic glossitis and koilonychia are usually improved although the response is often slow.

COMPOUND PREPARATIONS. Some oral preparations contain ascorbic acid to aid absorption, or the iron is in the form of a chelate, which can be shown experimentally to produce a modest increase in absorption of iron. However, the therapeutic advantage is minimal and cost may be increased.

There is neither theoretical nor clinical justification for the inclusion of other therapeutically active ingredients, such as the B group of vitamins (except folic acid for pregnant women, see Iron and Folic Acid below).

SLOW-RELEASE CAPSULES AND TABLETS. These are designed to release iron gradually as the capsule or tablet passes along the gut so that a smaller amount of iron is present in the lumen at any one time. It is claimed that each dose unit contains enough iron for 24 hours, thus permitting once daily dosage.

These preparations are likely to carry the iron past the first part of the duodenum into an area of the gut where conditions for iron absorption are poor. The low incidence of side-effects may well be because of the small amounts of iron available under these conditions and so the preparations have no therapeutic advantage and should not be used.

SIDE-EFFECTS. Because iron salts are astringent, gastro-intestinal irritation may occur. Nausea and epigastric pain are dose-related but the relationship between dose and altered bowel habit (constipation or diarrhoea) is less clear.

Iron preparations taken orally may have a constipating effect particularly in older patients, occasionally leading to faecal impaction.

FERROUS SULPHATE

Indications: iron-deficiency anaemia
Cautions: **interactions:** Appendix 1 (iron)
Side-effects: large doses may produce gastro-intestinal irritation, vomiting, diarrhoea; continued administration may result in constipation
Dose: ferrous iron, therapeutic, 120–180 mg daily in divided doses; prophylactic, 60 mg daily; CHILD, therapeutic, daily in divided doses, up to 1 year 36 mg, 1–5 years 72 mg, 6–12 years 120 mg
See also under Preparations
COUNSELLING. Although iron preparations are best absorbed on an empty stomach they may be taken after food to reduce gastro-intestinal side-effects

Ferrous Sulphate (Non-proprietary)
Tablets, coated, dried ferrous sulphate 200 mg (60 mg[1] iron), net price 20 = 7p
Dose: prophylactic, 1 tablet daily; therapeutic, 1 tablet 2–3 times daily
1. Good quality dried ferrous sulphate 200 mg may now contain approximately 65 mg iron

Ferrous Sulphate Oral Solution, Paediatric, BP
(Paediatric Ferrous Sulphate Mixture)
Mixture, ferrous sulphate 1.2% and a suitable antoxidant in a suitable vehicle with an orange flavour. Extemporaneous preparations should be recently prepared according to the following formula: ferrous sulphate 60 mg, ascorbic acid 10 mg, orange syrup 0.5 mL, double-strength chloroform water 2.5 mL, water to 5 mL
Dose: therapeutic, CHILD up to 1 year, 5 mL 3 times daily; 1–5 years, 10 mL 3 times daily; 6–12 years, 15 mL 3 times daily *or* 25 mL twice daily. To be taken well diluted with water

Sustained-release preparations
Feospan® (SK&F)
Spansule® (= capsules s/r), clear/red, enclosing green and red pellets, dried ferrous sulphate 150 mg (47 mg iron). Net price 30-cap pack = 90p. Label: 25
Dose: 1–2 capsules daily; CHILD over 1 year 1 capsule daily; can be opened and sprinkled on food
Ferrograd® (Abbott)
Filmtabs® (= tablets f/c), s/r, red, dried ferrous sulphate 325 mg (105 mg iron). Net price 5 × 30-tab pack = £3.94. Label: 25
Dose: 1 tablet daily before food
Slow-Fe® (Ciba)
Tablets, s/r, dried ferrous sulphate 160 mg (50 mg iron). Net price 150-tab pack = £2.30. Label: 25
Dose: prophylactic, 1 tablet daily; therapeutic, 2 tablets daily; CHILD over 6 years, 1 tablet daily

FERROUS FUMARATE

Indications; Cautions; Side-effects: see under Ferrous Sulphate
Dose: see under preparations below

Fersaday® (DF)
Tablets, orange, f/c, ferrous fumarate 304 mg (100 mg iron). Net price 28-tab pack = 45p
Dose: prophylactic, 1 tablet daily; therapeutic, 1 tablet twice daily

Fersamal® (DF)
Tablets, brown, ferrous fumarate 200 mg (65 mg iron). Net price 20 = 14p
Dose: 1–2 tablets 3 times daily
Syrup, brown, ferrous fumarate 140 mg (45 mg iron)/5 mL. Diluent syrup, life of diluted preparation 14 days. Net price 200 mL = £1.47
Dose: 10–20 mL twice daily; PREMATURE INFANT 0.6–2.4 mL/kg daily; CHILD up to 6 years 2.5–5 mL twice daily
Galfer® (Galen)
Capsules, red/green, ferrous fumarate 290 mg (100 mg iron). Net price 20 = 50p
Dose: 1 capsule 1–2 times daily before food
Syrup, brown, ferrous fumarate 140 mg (45 mg iron)/5 mL. Net price 100 mL = £2.54
Dose: 10 mL 1–2 times daily before food; CHILD (full-term infant and young child) 2.5–5 mL 1–2 times daily

Sustained-release preparations
Ferrocap® (Consolidated)
Capsules, s/r, green/orange, enclosing brown and white granules, ferrous fumarate 330 mg (110 mg iron). Net price 20 = 54p. Label: 25
Dose: 1 capsule daily

FERROUS GLUCONATE

Indications; Cautions; Side-effects: see under Ferrous Sulphate
Dose: see under preparations below

Ferrous Gluconate (Non-proprietary)
Tablets, red, coated, ferrous gluconate 300 mg (35 mg iron). Net price 20 = 12p
Dose: prophylactic, 2 tablets daily before food; therapeutic, 4–6 tablets daily in divided doses before food; CHILD 6–12 years, prophylactic and therapeutic, 1–3 tablets daily
Fergon® (Sterling-Winthrop)
Tablets, red, s/c, ferrous gluconate 300 mg (35 mg iron). Net price 20 = 44p
Dose: see above

FERROUS GLYCINE SULPHATE

Indications; Cautions; Side-effects: see under Ferrous Sulphate
Dose: see under preparations below

Plesmet® (Napp)
Syrup, ferrous glycine sulphate 141 mg (25 mg iron)/5 mL. Diluent syrup, life of diluted preparation 14 days. Net price 100 mL = 74p
Dose: 5–10 mL 3 times daily; CHILD 2–5 mL 2–3 times daily, according to age

Sustained-release preparations
Ferrocontin Continus® (Degussa)
Tablets, s/r, red, f/c, ferrous glycine sulphate 562.5 mg (100 mg iron). Net price 30-tab pack = 69p. Label: 25
Dose: 1 tablet daily

FERROUS SUCCINATE

Indications; Cautions; Side-effects: see under Ferrous Sulphate
Dose: see under preparations below

Ferromyn® (Calmic)
Elixir, brown, ferrous succinate 106 mg (37 mg iron)/5 mL. Diluent syrup, life of diluted elixir 14 days. Net price 100 mL = £3.19
Dose: 5 mL 3 times daily; CHILD up to 2 years max. 1 mL twice daily, 2–5 years 2.5 mL 3 times daily, 5–10 years 5 mL twice daily

POLYSACCHARIDE-IRON COMPLEX

Indications; Cautions; Side-effects: see under Ferrous Sulphate
Dose: see under preparations below

Niferex® (Tillotts)
Tablets, brown, polysaccharide-iron complex equivalent to 50 mg of iron. Net price 100 = £3.00
Dose: prophylactic, 1 tablet daily; therapeutic, 2 tablets 1–2 times daily
Elixir, brown, polysaccharide-iron complex equivalent to 100 mg of iron/5 mL. Diluent purified water, freshly boiled and cooled, or sorbitol solution, life of diluted elixir 14 days. Net price 100 mL = £2.10; 30-mL dropper bottle for paediatric use = £1.80. Counselling, use of dropper
Dose: prophylactic, 2.5 mL daily; therapeutic, 5 mL daily; INFANT, 1 drop (from dropper bottle) per pound body-weight 3 times daily; CHILD 2–6 years, 2.5 mL daily, 6–12 years 5 mL daily

Niferex-150® (Tillotts)
Capsules, brown/orange, polysaccharide-iron complex equivalent to 150 mg of iron. Net price 20 = £1.80
Dose: 1–2 capsules daily

SODIUM IRONEDETATE

Indications; Cautions; Side-effects: see under Ferrous Sulphate
Dose: see under preparation below

Sytron® (P-D)
Elixir, sugar-free, sodium ironedetate 190 mg equivalent to 27.5 mg of iron/5 mL. Diluent water, life of diluted elixir 14 days. Net price 100 mL = 28p
Dose: 5 mL increasing gradually to 10 mL 3 times daily; INFANT and PREMATURE INFANT 2.5 mL twice daily (smaller doses should be used initially); CHILD 1–5 years 2.5 mL 3 times daily, 6–12 years 5 mL 3 times daily

IRON AND FOLIC ACID

These preparations are used for the prevention of iron and folic acid deficiences in pregnancy. The prophylactic dose in pregnancy is the equivalent of approximately 100 mg of iron with folic acid 200–500 micrograms daily.

It is important to note that the small doses of folic acid contained in these preparations are inadequate for the treatment of megaloblastic anaemias.

Fefol® (SK&F)
Spansule® (=capsules s/r), clear/green, enclosing red, yellow, and white pellets, dried ferrous sulphate 150 mg (47 mg iron), folic acid 500 micrograms. Net price 30-cap pack = £1.00. Label: 25
Dose: 1 capsule daily

Ferrocap-F 350® (Consolidated)
Capsules, s/r, pink, enclosing brown, white, and yellow granules, ferrous fumarate 330 mg (110 mg iron), folic acid 350 micrograms. Net price 20 = 67p. Label: 25
Dose: 1 capsule daily

Ferrocontin Folic Continus® (Degussa)
Tablets, orange, f/c, ferrous glycine sulphate 562.5 mg (100 mg iron) for sustained release, folic acid 500 micrograms. Net price 30-tab pack = 69p. Label: 25
Dose: 1 tablet daily

Ferrograd Folic® (Abbott)
Filmtabs® (= tablets f/c), red/yellow, dried ferrous sulphate 325 mg (105 mg iron) for sustained release, folic acid 350 micrograms. Net price 150-tab pack = £4.03. Label: 25
Dose: 1 tablet daily before food

Folex-350® (Rybar)
Tablets, pink, s/c, ferrous fumarate 308 mg (100 mg iron), folic acid 350 micrograms. Net price 20 = 42p
Dose: 1 tablet daily

Galfer FA® (Galen)
Capsules, red/yellow, ferrous fumarate 290 mg (100 mg iron), folic acid 350 micrograms. Net price 20 = 51p
Dose: 1 capsule daily before food

PoM **Lexpec with Iron-M®** (RP Drugs)
Syrup, brown, sugar-free, ferric ammonium citrate equivalent to 80 mg iron, folic acid 500 micrograms/5 mL. Net price 125 mL = £4.10
Dose: 5–10 mL daily before food
Note. Lexpec with Iron-M® contains five times less folic acid than Lexpec with Iron®

PoM **Meterfolic®** (Sinclair)
Tablets, grey, f/c, ferrous fumarate equivalent to 100 mg iron, folic acid 350 micrograms. Net price 20 = 43p
Dose: 1 tablet 1–2 times daily

PoM **Pregaday®** (DF)
Tablets, brown, f/c, ferrous fumarate 304 mg (100 mg iron), folic acid 350 micrograms. Net price 28-tab pack = 51p
Dose: 1 tablet daily

Pregnavite Forte F, see compound iron preparations

PoM **Slow-Fe Folic®** (Ciba)
Tablets, s/r, ivory, f/c, dried ferrous sulphate 160 mg (50 mg iron), folic acid 400 micrograms. Net price 30-tab pack = 46p. Label: 25
Dose: 1–2 tablets daily

HIGHER FOLIC ACID CONTENT

The daily dose of folic acid in these preparations is unnecessarily high for the prevention of folate deficiency; it also has the theoretical disadvantage of masking anaemia due to vitamin-B_{12} deficiency (which could allow vitamin-B_{12} neuropathy to develop).

PoM **Ferfolic SV®** (Sinclair)
Tablets, pink, s/c, ferrous gluconate 250 mg (30 mg iron), folic acid 5 mg. Net price 20 = 66p
Dose: 1 tablet 3 times daily

PoM **Lexpec with Iron®** (RP Drugs)
Syrup, brown, sugar-free, ferric ammonium citrate equivalent to 80 mg iron, folic acid 2.5 mg/5 mL. Net price 125 mL = £4.30
Dose: 5–10 mL daily before food
Note. Lexpec with Iron® contains five times as much folic acid as Lexpec with Iron-M®

COMPOUND IRON PREPARATIONS

There is no justification for prescribing compound iron preparations, except for preparations of iron and folic acid for prophylactic use in pregnancy (see above).

Ferrous Sulphate Tablets, Compound, green, s/c, dried ferrous sulphate equivalent to 170 mg of $FeSO_4$, copper sulphate 2.5 mg, manganese sulphate 2.5 mg. Net price 20 tabs = 9p
Dose: 1–2 tablets daily

NHS **BC 500 with Iron®** (Whitehall)
Tablets, red, f/c, ferrous fumarate 200 mg (65 mg iron) with vitamins B group and C. Net price 30-tab pack = £1.69
Dose: 1 tablet daily

NHS **Fefol-Vit®** (SK&F)
Spansule® (= capsules s/r), clear/white, enclosing red, orange, yellow, and white pellets, dried ferrous sulphate 150 mg (47 mg iron) with vitamins B group (including folic acid 500 micrograms) and C. Net price 30-cap pack = £1.40. Label: 25
Dose: 1 capsule daily during pregnancy

Fefol Z® (SK&F)
Spansule® (= capsules s/r), blue/clear, enclosing red, yellow, and white pellets, dried ferrous sulphate 150 mg (47 mg iron), folic acid 500 micrograms, zinc sulphate monohydrate 61.8 mg (22.5 mg zinc). Net price 30-cap pack = £1.79. Label: 25
Dose: 1 capsule daily during pregnancy

NHS **Ferrograd C®** (Abbott)
Filmtabs® (= tablets f/c), red, dried ferrous sulphate 325 mg (105 mg iron) for sustained release, ascorbic acid 500 mg (as sodium salt). Net price 30-tab pack = £1.40. Label: 25
Dose: 1 tablet daily before food

NHS **Fesovit®** (SK&F)
Spansule® (= capsules s/r), colourless/yellow, enclosing red, orange, and white pellets, dried ferrous sulphate 150 mg (47 mg iron) with vitamins B group and C. Net price 30-cap pack = £1.62. Label: 25
Dose: 1–2 capsules daily; CHILD over 1 year 1 capsule daily

NHS **Fesovit Z®** (SK&F)
Spansule® (= capsules s/r), orange/clear, enclosing red, orange, and white pellets, dried ferrous sulphate 150 mg (47 mg iron), zinc sulphate monohydrate 61.8 mg (22.5 mg zinc) with vitamins B group and C. Net price 30-cap pack = £2.15. Label: 25
Dose: 1–2 capsules daily; CHILD over 1 year 1 capsule daily

PoM **Folicin®** (Paines & Byrne)
Tablets, s/c, dried ferrous sulphate 200 mg (60 mg iron), folic acid 2.5 mg with minerals. Net price 20 = 20p
Dose: 1–2 tablets daily during pregnancy

NHS **Forceval®** (Unigreg)
Capsules, ferrous fumarate 30.8 mg (10 mg iron) with vitamins A, B group, C, D, E, and minerals. Net price 15-cap pack = £1.76; 30 = £3.50; 90 = £8.91
Dose: 1 capsule daily
Junior capsules, red, ferrous fumarate 15.4 mg (5 mg iron) with vitamins A, B group, C, D, E, and minerals. Net price 10-cap pack = 91p; 30 = £2.54
Dose: CHILD over 5 years, 1 capsule daily

NHS **Galfer-Vit®** (Galen)
Capsules, maroon/orange, ferrous fumarate 305 mg (100 mg iron) with vitamins B group and C. Net price 20 = 58p
Dose: 1 capsule 1–2 times daily before food

NHS **Givitol®** (Galen)
Capsules, red/maroon, ferrous fumarate 305 mg (100 mg iron) with vitamins B group and C. Net price 20 = 82p
Dose: 1 capsule daily before food

NHS **Glykola®** (Sinclair)
Elixir, red, ferric chloride solution 0.01 mL (500 micrograms iron), caffeine 20 mg, calcium glycerophosphate 30 mg, kola liquid extract 0.12 mL/5 mL. Net price 100 mL = 70p
Dose: 5–10 mL 3 times daily after food

NHS **Octovit®** (SK&F)
Tablets, maroon, f/c, dried ferrous sulphate (10 mg iron) with vitamins A, B group, C, D, E, and minerals. Net price 14-tab pack = £1.56
Dose: 1 tablet daily

NHS ***Pregnavite Forte F®** (Bencard)
Tablets, lilac, s/c, dried ferrous sulphate 84 mg (25.2 mg iron), folic acid 120 micrograms, vitamin A 1333 units, thiamine hydrochloride 500 micrograms, riboflavine 500 micrograms, nicotinamide 5 mg, pyridoxine hydrochloride 330 micrograms, ascorbic acid 13.3 mg, vitamin D 133 units, calcium phosphate 160 mg. Net price 84-tab pack = £1.96
* except to reduce the risk of spina bifida or anencephaly in babies born to women who have previously given birth to one or more babies (or aborted a fetus) with a neural tube defect and endorsed 'S3B' ('S2B' in Scotland)
Dose: 1 tablet 3 times daily during or after food
Note. For prophylaxis of neural tube defects in pregnancy, dosage should be started not less than 28 days prior to conception and continue uninterrupted at least until the date of the second missed period

9.1.1.2 PARENTERAL IRON

The only valid reason for administering iron **parenterally** is failure of oral therapy. Such failure may be due to lack of patient co-operation with oral treatment, gastro-intestinal side-effects, continuing severe blood loss or malabsorption. Provided that the oral iron preparation is taken reliably and is absorbed, then with equivalent doses of iron the rate of haemoglobin response is not significantly faster when the intramuscular or intravenous instead of the oral route is used. The need for a rapid cure of the anaemia is therefore not met by intramuscular administration of iron.

It is customary to give a course of *deep intramuscular* injections. The manufacturer's dosage schedules should be consulted; these usually include a supplement for reconstitution of iron stores.

Iron dextran (Imferon®) may also be administered as a single dose by *slow intravenous infusion* over 6 to 8 hours provided that there is no reaction to administration of a test dose. Although the incidence of side-effects is low, disquieting adverse reactions may occur, especially in allergic subjects, and intravenous infusion is contra-indicated in asthmatic patients. Iron dextran should only be administered *intravenously* in selected cases where proper indications exist for its use, that is, when continuing blood loss is likely to be permanent and oral prophylaxis cannot keep pace, when a patient requiring parenteral iron has a small muscle mass or a haemostatic defect contra-indicating intramuscular injection, or when psychological or social pressures make iron treatment by other means impracticable.

Preparations suitable for parenteral use contain iron either in the form of **Iron Dextran Injection**, containing a complex of ferric hydroxide with dextrans of high molecular weight, or as **Iron Sorbitol Injection** (Jectofer®), containing a complex of iron, sorbitol and citric acid. The latter preparation is **not** suitable for intravenous injection and, although the low mean molecular weight allows rapid absorption from the injection site, excretion in the saliva and substantial urinary losses from each dose also occur.

To prevent leakage along the needle track with subsequent staining of the skin, intramuscular injections should be deep for both preparations.

IRON DEXTRAN INJECTION

Contains 5% (50 mg/mL) of iron

Indications: iron deficiency anaemia (see notes above)

Cautions: risk of anaphylaxis especially in patients with history of allergy; test dose essential when given by intravenous infusion; patient should be under observation for entire period of infusion and 1 hour after; facilities to control allergic reactions including adrenaline should be available (see section 3.4.3)

Contra-indications: cardiac abnormalities (e.g. angina or arrhythmia), severe liver disease, acute kidney infections; intravenous infusion in asthmatic patients

Side-effects: staining of the skin if leakage along needle track occurs, transient nausea, vomiting, flushing; occasionally severe dyspnoea; rarely severe anaphylaxis (see Cautions)

Dose: see notes above and manufacturer's literature

PoM **Imferon®** (Fisons)

Injection, iron dextran injection. Net price 2-mL amp = 67p; 5-mL amp = £1.35

Intravenous infusion, iron dextran injection. Net price 20-mL amp = £4.48 (hosp. only)

IRON SORBITOL INJECTION

Contains 5% (50 mg/mL) of iron

Indications: iron-deficiency anaemia

Cautions: oral administration of iron should be stopped at least 24 hours before giving iron sorbitol injection; administration of other injectable iron preparations should be stopped a week beforehand; urine may darken on standing

Contra-indications: cardiac abnormalities (e.g. angina or arrhythmia), liver disease, kidney disease (particularly pyelonephritis), untreated urinary-tract infections

Side-effects: occasionally severe arrhythmias

Dose: by intramuscular injection, see notes above and manufacturer's literature

PoM **Jectofer®** (Astra)

Injection, iron sorbitol injection. Net price 2-mL amp = 47p

9.1.2 Drugs used in megaloblastic anaemias

Most megaloblastic anaemias are due to lack of either vitamin B_{12} or folate and it is essential to establish in every case which deficiency is present and the underlying cause. In emergencies, where delay might be dangerous, it is sometimes necessary to administer both substances after the bone marrow test while plasma assay results are awaited. Normally, however, appropriate treatment should be instituted only when the results of tests are available.

The most common cause of megaloblastic anaemia in the UK is *pernicious anaemia* in which lack of gastric intrinsic factor due to an auto-immune gastritis causes malabsorption of vitamin B_{12}.

Vitamin B_{12} is also needed in the treatment of megaloblastosis due to *prolonged nitrous oxide anaesthesia*, which inactivates the vitamin, and in the rare syndrome of *congenital transcobalamin II deficiency*.

Vitamin B_{12} should be given prophylactically after *total gastrectomy* or *total ileal resection* (or after *partial gastrectomy* if a vitamin B_{12} absorption test shows vitamin B_{12} malabsorption).

Apart from dietary deficiency, all other causes of vitamin-B_{12} deficiency are attributable to *malabsorption* so there is little place for the use of vitamin B_{12} orally and none for vitamin B_{12} intrinsic factor complexes given by mouth.

Hydroxocobalamin has completely replaced cyanocobalamin as the form of vitamin B_{12} of choice for therapy; when vitamin B_{12} injection is prescribed hydroxocobalamin injection should be given. It is retained in the body longer than cyanocobalamin and thus for maintenance therapy need only be given at intervals of 3 months. Although a haematological response in vitamin-B_{12} deficiency may be obtained by small doses, it is customary to start treatment with 1 mg by intramuscular injection repeated 5 times at intervals of 2 to 3 days to replenish the depleted body stores. Thereafter, maintenance treatment, which is usually for life, can be instituted. There is no evidence that larger doses provide any additional benefit in vitamin-B_{12} neuropathy.

Folic acid has few indications for long-term therapy since most causes of folate deficiency are self-limiting or will yield to a short course of treatment. It should not be used in undiagnosed megaloblastic anaemia unless vitamin B_{12} is administered concurrently otherwise neuropathy may be precipitated (see above).

In *folate-deficient megaloblastic anaemia* (e.g. due to poor nutrition, pregnancy, or antiepileptics), standard treatment to bring about a haematological remission and replenish body stores, is oral administration of folic acid 5 mg daily for 4 months; up to 15 mg daily may be necessary in malabsorption states.

For *prophylaxis in chronic haemolytic states or in renal dialysis*, it is sufficient to give folic acid 5 mg daily or even weekly, depending on the diet and the rate of haemolysis.

For *prophylaxis in pregnancy* the dose of folic

acid is 200–500 micrograms daily (see Iron and Folic Acid, section 9.1.1.1).

> There is **no** justification for prescribing multiple-ingredient vitamin preparations containing vitamin B_{12} or folic acid.

HYDROXOCOBALAMIN

Indications: Pernicious anaemia, other causes of vitamin-B_{12} deficiency, subacute combined degeneration of the spinal cord

Cautions: should not be given before diagnosis fully established but see also notes above

Dose: *by intramuscular injection*, initially 1 mg repeated 5 times at intervals of 2–3 days; maintenance dose 1 mg every 3 months; CHILD, dosage as for adult

PoM **Hydroxocobalamin Injection,** hydroxocobalamin 1 mg/mL. Net price 1-mL amp = 36p

Note. The BP directs that when vitamin B_{12} injection is prescribed or demanded hydroxocobalamin injection shall be dispensed or supplied

The brand names NHS Cobalin-H® (Paines & Byrne) and NHS Neo-Cytamen® (DF) are used for hydroxocobalamin injection

CYANOCOBALAMIN

Indications: see notes above

Dose: *by intramuscular injection*, initially 1 mg repeated 10 times at intervals of 2–3 days, maintenance 1 mg every month, but see notes above

PoM **Cyanocobalamin Injection,** cyanocobalamin 1 mg/mL. Net price 1 mL amp = 34p

Note. The BP directs that when vitamin B_{12} injection is prescribed or demanded hydroxocobalamin injection shall be dispensed or supplied

The brand name NHS Cytamen® (DF) is used for cyanocobalamin injection

NHS **Cytacon®** (DF)

Tablets, f/c, cyanocobalamin 50 micrograms. Net price 50-tab pack = £1·59

Liquid, red, cyanocobalamin 35 micrograms/5 mL. Net price 200 mL = £1.59

FOLIC ACID

Indications: see notes above

Cautions: should never be given alone in the treatment of Addisonian pernicious anaemia and other vitamin B_{12}-deficiency states because it may precipitate the onset of subacute combined degeneration of the spinal cord. Do not use in malignant disease unless megaloblastic anaemia due to folate deficiency is an important complication (some malignant tumours are folate-dependent); **interactions:** Appendix 1 (vitamins)

Dose: initially, 5 mg daily for 4 months (see notes above); maintenance, 5 mg every 1–7 days depending on underlying disease; CHILD up to 1 year, 500 micrograms/kg daily; over 1 year, as adult dose

PoM [1]**Folic Acid Tablets,** folic acid 5 mg, net price 20 = 6p; 100-microgram tablets also available

1. *Note.* Can be sold to the public provided daily doses do not exceed 500 micrograms

PoM **Lexpec®** (RP Drugs)

Syrup, sugar-free, folic acid 2.5 mg/5 mL. Diluent sorbitol solution, life of syrup diluted to 75% up to 21 days. Net price 125 mL = £3.80

9.1.3 Drugs used in hypoplastic, haemolytic, and renal anaemias

Anabolic steroids, pyridoxine, antilymphocyte immunoglobulin, and various corticosteroids are used in hypoplastic and haemolytic anaemias.

The place of non-androgenic **anabolic steroids** in the therapy of *aplastic anaemia* remains somewhat controversial and their effectiveness is unclear. There is a wide variation in the reported successful responses. Occasional patients, however, do seem to derive benefit. Since nandrolone decanoate requires intramuscular injection it is unsuitable in aplastic anaemia or cytotoxic aplasia because of the low platelet count; it is customary to prescribe oxymetholone in doses of the order of 2–3 mg/kg daily, and to continue therapy for at least 3 to 6 months. At these dose levels, virilising side-effects may be expected in female patients and in children. Controlled trials have shown that antilymphocyte immunoglobulin produces a response in 50% of acquired cases.

It is unlikely that dietary deprivation of **pyridoxine** (section 9.6.2) produces haematological effects in man. However, certain forms of *sideroblastic anaemia* respond to pharmacological doses, possibly reflecting its role as a co-enzyme during haemoglobin synthesis. Pyridoxine is indicated in both *idiopathic acquired* and *hereditary sideroblastic anaemias*. Although complete cures have not been reported, some increase in haemoglobin may occur; the dose required is usually high, up to 400 mg daily. *Reversible sideroblastic anaemias* respond to treatment of the underlying cause but in pregnancy, haemolytic anaemias, and alcoholism, or during isoniazid treatment, pyridoxine is also indicated.

Corticosteroids (see section 6.3) have an important place in the management of a wide variety of haematological disorders. They include conditions with an immune basis such as *autoimmune haemolytic anaemia, immune thrombocytopenias* and *neutropenias*, and *major transfusion reactions*. They are also used in chemotherapy schedules for all forms of *lymphoreticular malignancy, lymphoid leukaemias*, and *paraproteinaemias*, including *myelomatosis*. Corticosteroids are used in *aplastic anaemias*, where their usefulness is more debatable.

It is possible that corticosteroids in low doses may also reduce the capillary fragility which occurs in the *purpuric diseases*, thus lessening bleeding.

NANDROLONE

Indications: aplastic anaemia but see notes above; postmenopausal osteoporosis, see section 6.4.3

Contra-indications; Side-effects: see section 6.4.3

Dose: by deep intramuscular injection, aplastic anaemia (but not recommended, see notes above), nandrolone decanoate 50–100 mg weekly

PoM **Deca-Durabolin 100®** (Organon)
Injection (oily), nandrolone decanoate 100 mg/mL. Net price 1-mL amp = £6.68

OXYMETHOLONE

Indications: aplastic anaemia; see notes above
Cautions: cardiac and renal impairment, circulatory failure, hypertension, diabetes mellitus, epilepsy, migraine; monitor skeletal maturation in children for 6 months after treatment; **interactions:** Appendix 1 (anabolic steroids;
Contra-indications: hepatic impairment, prostatic carcinoma, pregnancy, breast-feeding, porphyria
Side-effects: acne, oedema, jaundice and liver dysfunction, virilism with high doses, hypercalcaemia, menstrual irregularities; hyperglucagonaemia has also been reported with oxymetholone
Dose: aplastic anaemia, 2–3 mg/kg daily in divided doses; CHILD 2–3 mg/kg daily (less in Fanconi's anaemia)
See also notes above

PoM **Anapolon 50®** (Syntex)
Tablets, scored, oxymetholone 50 mg. Net price 20 = £12.36

ERYTHROPOIETIN

Epoetin (recombinant human erythropoietin) is used for the anaemia associated with chronic renal failure in patients on dialysis. The clinical efficacy of epoetin alfa and epoetin beta is similar and they can be used interchangeably.

Other factors which contribute to the anaemia of chronic renal failure such as iron or folate deficiency should be corrected; aluminium toxicity, concurrent infection or other inflammatory disease, or renal osteodystrophy may also impair the response to epoetin.

EPOETIN

Recombinant human erythropoietin
Indications: anaemia associated with erythropoietin deficiency in chronic renal failure patients on dialysis
Cautions: uncontrolled hypertension (monitor closely for changes in haemoglobin, blood pressure and electrolytes—hypertensive episodes may be more likely with rapid haemoglobin response), history of convulsions, chronic hepatic failure, malignant disease, ischaemic vascular disease (monitor platelets for first 8 weeks); exclude other causes of anaemia and give iron supplements if needed; increase in dialysis heparin may be required (monitor dialyser)
Side-effects: increased blood pressure (treat as appropriate), moderately increased platelet count (rarely significant), influenza-like symptoms, convulsions, skin reactions and palpebral oedema (possibly allergic); shunt thrombosis, isolated side-effects reported include increased creatinine, urea and phosphate serum concentrations, acne-like symptoms, myocardial infarction, and anaphylaxis
Dose: (aimed at increasing haemoglobin concentration at rate not exceeding 2 g/100 mL/month to stable level of 10–12 g/100 mL): *by intravenous injection* over 2 minutes, initially 40–50 units/kg 3 times weekly, increased as necessary in steps of 20–25 units/kg at intervals of 4 weeks (usual max. 600–720 units/kg weekly in 2–3 divided doses); maintenance: 90–300 units/kg weekly in 2–3 divided doses

▼ PoM **Eprex®** (Cilag)
Injection, epoetin alfa 2000 units/mL, net price 1-mL amp = £18.00; 4000 units/mL, 1-mL amp = £36.00; 10 000 units/mL, 1-mL amp = £90.00

▼ PoM **Recormon®** (Boehringer Mannheim)
Injection, powder for reconstitution, epoetin beta. Net price 1000-unit vial = £9.00; 2000-unit vial = £18.00; 5000-unit vial = £45.00 (all with water for injection)

IRON OVERLOAD

Severe tissue iron overload may occur in aplastic and other refractory anaemias, mainly as the result of repeated blood transfusions. It is a particular problem in refractory anaemias with hyperplastic bone marrow, especially *thalassaemia major*, where excessive iron absorption from the gut and inappropriate iron therapy may add to the tissue siderosis.

Venesection therapy is contra-indicated, but the long-term administration of the iron chelating compound desferrioxamine mesylate is useful. Subcutaneous infusions of desferrioxamine (20–40 mg/kg over 12 hours) are given on 5 to 7 nights each week. Desferrioxamine (up to 2 g per unit of blood) may also be given through the infusion line at the time of blood transfusion.

Iron excretion induced by desferrioxamine is enhanced by administration of vitamin C (section 9.6.3) in a dose of 100 to 200 mg daily; it should be given separately from food since it also enhances iron absorption.

Infusion of desferrioxamine may be used to treat *aluminium overload* in dialysis patients; theoretically 100 mg of desferrioxamine binds with 4.1 mg of aluminium.

Orally active iron chelators are under clinical study but are not available for general use.

DESFERRIOXAMINE MESYLATE

Indications: see notes above; iron poisoning, see Emergency Treatment of Poisoning
Cautions: renal impairment, eye and ear examinations; avoid prochlorperazine; **interactions:** Appendix 1 (desferrioxamine)

Side-effects: pain on intramuscular injection, anaphylaxis, and hypotension when given too rapidly by intravenous injection; Yersinia infection more frequent
Dose: see notes above; iron poisoning, see Emergency Treatment of Poisoning
Note. For full details and warnings relating to administration, consult data sheet

Preparations
Emergency Treatment of Poisoning

9.1.4 Drugs used in autoimmune thrombocytopenic purpura

It is usual to commence the treatment of autoimmune (idiopathic) thrombocytopenic purpura with corticosteroids, e.g. prednisolone of the order of 1 mg/kg daily, gradually reducing the dosage over the subsequent weeks. In patients who fail to achieve a satisfactory platelet count or relapse when corticosteroid dosage is reduced or withdrawn, splenectomy is considered.

Other therapy that has been tried in refractory cases includes azathioprine (see section 8.2.1), vincristine or vinblastine (see section 8.1.4) (or vinblastine-loaded platelets), and danazol (section 6.7.3). Intravenous immunoglobulins, e.g. Sandoglobulin® (see section 14.5), have also been used in refractory cases or where a temporary rapid rise in platelets is needed, as in pregnancy or pre-operatively. For patients with chronic severe thrombocytopenia refractory to other therapy, tranexamic acid (see section 2.11) may be given to reduce the severity of haemorrhage.

9.1.5 G6PD deficiency

Glucose 6-phosphate dehydrogenase (G6PD) deficiency is highly prevalent in populations originating from most parts of Africa, from most parts of Asia, from Oceania, and from Southern Europe; it can also be encountered, rarely, in any other population.

When prescribing drugs for patients who are G6PD deficient, the following three points should be kept in mind:

1. G6PD deficiency is genetically heterogeneous; different genetic variants entail different susceptibility to the haemolytic risk from drugs; thus, a drug found to be safe in some G6PD-deficient subjects may not be equally safe in others;
2. no test specifically designed to identify potential risk in G6PD-deficient subjects is currently carried out by manufacturers;
3. the risk and severity of haemolysis is almost always dose-related.

The table below should be read with these points in mind. Whenever possible, a test for G6PD deficiency should be done before prescribing a drug in the list, especially if the patient belongs to a population group in which G6PD deficiency is common.

A very small group of G6PD-deficient individuals, with chronic non-spherocytic haemolytic anaemia, have haemolysis even in the absence of an exogeneous trigger. These patients must be regarded as being at high risk of severe exacerbation of haemolysis following administration of any of the drugs listed below.

Drugs with definite risk of haemolysis in most G6PD-deficient subjects

Dapsone and other sulphones (higher doses for dermatitis herpetiformis more likely to cause problems)
Methylene blue
Niridazole [not on UK market]
Nitrofurantoin
Pamaquin [not on UK market]
Primaquine (30 mg weekly for 8 weeks has been found to be without undue harmful effects in Afro and Asian people, see section 5.4.1)
4-Quinolones (including ciprofloxacin and nalidixic acid)
Sulphonamides (including co-trimoxazole; some sulphonamides, e.g. sulphadiazine, have been tested and found not to be haemolytic in many G6PD-deficient subjects)

Drugs with possible risk of haemolysis in some G6PD-deficient subjects

Aspirin (acceptable in a dose of at least 1 g daily in most G6PD-deficient subjects)
Chloroquine (acceptable in acute malaria)
Menadione, water-soluble derivatives (e.g. menadiol sodium phosphate)
Probenecid
Quinidine (acceptable in acute malaria)
Quinine (acceptable in acute malaria)

Note. Mothballs may contain naphthalene which also causes haemolysis in subjects with G6PD-deficiency.

9.2 Fluids and electrolytes

The following tables give a selection of useful electrolyte values:

Electrolyte concentrations—intravenous fluids

	Millimoles per litre				
Intravenous infusion	Na^+	K^+	HCO_3^-	Cl^-	Ca^{2+}
Normal Plasma Values	142	4.5	26	103	2.5
Sodium Chloride 0.9%	150	—	—	150	—
Compound Sodium Lactate (Hartmann's)	131	5	29	111	2
Sodium Chloride 0.18% and Glucose 4%	30	—	—	30	—
Potassium Chloride 0.3% and Glucose 5%	—	40	—	40	—
Potassium Chloride 0.3% and Sodium Chloride 0.9%	150	40	—	190	—
To correct metabolic acidosis					
Sodium Bicarbonate 1.26%	150	—	150	—	—
Sodium Bicarbonate 8.4% for cardiac arrest	1000	—	1000	—	—
Sodium Lactate (M/6)	167	—	167	—	—

Millimoles of each ion in 1 gram of salt

Electrolyte	mmol/g approx.
Ammonium chloride	18.7
Calcium chloride ($CaCl_2,2H_2O$)	Ca 6.8 Cl 13.6
Potassium bicarbonate	10
Potassium chloride	13.4
Sodium bicarbonate	11.9
Sodium chloride	17.1
Sodium lactate	8.9

Electrolyte content—gastro-intestinal secretions

Type of fluid	Millimoles per litre H^+	Na^+	K^+	HCO_3^-	Cl^-
Gastric	40–60	20–80	5–20	—	100–150
Biliary	—	120–140	5–15	30–50	80–120
Pancreatic	—	120–140	5–15	70–110	40–80
Small bowel	—	120–140	5–15	20–40	90–130

Faeces, vomit, or aspiration should be saved and analysed where possible if abnormal losses are suspected; where this is impracticable the approximations above may be helpful in planning replacement therapy.

9.2.1 Oral administration

9.2.1.1 Oral potassium
9.2.1.2 Oral sodium and water
9.2.1.3 Oral bicarbonate

Sodium and potassium salts, which may be given by mouth to prevent deficiencies or to treat established deficiencies of mild or moderate degree, are discussed in this section. Oral preparations for removing excess potassium and preparations for oral rehydration therapy are also included here. Oral bicarbonate, for metabolic acidosis, is also described in this section.

For reference to calcium, magnesium, and phosphate, see section 9.5.

9.2.1.1 ORAL POTASSIUM

Compensation for potassium loss is especially necessary:

1. in elderly patients, since they frequently take inadequate amounts of potassium in the diet (but see below for warning on renal insufficiency);
2. in those taking digoxin or anti-arrhythmic drugs, where potassium depletion may induce arrhythmias;
3. in patients in whom secondary hyperaldosteronism occurs, e.g. renal artery stenosis, cirrhosis of the liver, the nephrotic syndrome, and severe heart failure;
4. in patients with excessive losses of potassium in the faeces, e.g. chronic diarrhoea associated with intestinal malabsorption or laxative abuse.

Measures to compensate for potassium loss may also be required during long-term administration of drugs known to induce potassium loss (e.g. corticosteroids). Potassium supplements are seldom required with the small doses of diuretics given to treat hypertension; potassium-sparing diuretics (rather than potassium supplements) are recommended for prevention of hypokalaemia due to diuretics such as frusemide or the thiazides when these are given to eliminate oedema.

DOSAGE. If potassium salts are used for the *prevention of hypokalaemia*, then doses of potassium chloride 2 to 4 g (approx. 25 to 50 mmol) daily by mouth are suitable in patients taking a normal diet. Smaller doses must be used if there is renal insufficiency (common in the elderly) otherwise there is danger of hyperkalaemia. Potassium salts cause nausea and vomiting therefore poor compliance is a major limitation to their effectiveness; where appropriate, potassium-sparing diuretics are preferable.

When there is *established potassium depletion* or when the plasma-potassium concentration is less than 3.5mmol/litre, larger doses of 10 to 15 g (approx. 135 to 200 mmol) daily of potassium chloride may be required over periods of days or weeks. Potassium depletion is frequently associated with chloride depletion and with metabolic alkalosis, and these disorders require correction.

ADMINISTRATION. Potassium salts are preferably given as a liquid preparation, rather than sustained-release tablets; the use of potassium bicarbonate should be restricted to *hyperchloraemic states* (section 9.2.1.3).

Salt substitutes. A number of salt substitutes which contain significant amounts of potassium chloride are readily available as health food products (e.g. Losalt and Ruthmol). These should not be used by patients with renal failure as potassium intoxication may result.

POTASSIUM BICARBONATE

Section 9.2.1.3

POTASSIUM CHLORIDE

Indications: potassium depletion (see notes above)

Cautions: intestinal stricture, history of peptic ulcer, hiatus hernia (for sustained-release preparations); **interactions:** Appendix 1 (potassium salts)

Contra-indications: renal failure, plasma potassium concentrations above 5 mmol/litre

Side-effects: nausea and vomiting (severe symptoms may indicate obstruction), oesophageal or small bowel ulceration

Dose: see notes above

Kay-Cee-L® (Geistlich)
Syrup, red, sugar-free, potassium chloride 7.5% (1 mmol/mL each of K^+ and Cl^-). Net price 200 mL = £1.95; 500 mL = £2.74. Label: 21

Kloref® (Cox Pharmaceuticals)
Tablets, effervescent, betaine hydrochloride, potassium benzoate, bicarbonate, and chloride, equivalent to potassium chloride 500 mg (6.7 mmol each of K^+ and Cl^-). Net price 50 = £1.45. Label: 13, 21

Kloref-S® (Cox Pharmaceuticals)
Granules, effervescent, sugar-free, betaine hydrochloride, potassium bicarbonate and chloride equivalent to potassium chloride 1.5 g (20 mmol each of K^+ and Cl^-)/sachet. Net price 30 sachets = £2.58. Label: 13, 21

Sando-K® (Sandoz)
Tablets, effervescent, potassium bicarbonate and chloride equivalent to potassium 470 mg (12 mmol of K^+) and chloride 285 mg (8 mmol of Cl^-). Net price 20 = 35p. Label: 13, 21

Sustained-release preparations
Avoid unless effervescent tablets or liquid preparations inappropriate

Leo K® (Leo)
Tablets, s/r, f/c, potassium chloride 600 mg (8 mmol each of K^+ and Cl^-). Net price 20 = 20p. Label: 25, 27, counselling, swallow whole with fluid during meals while sitting or standing

Nu-K® (Consolidated)
Capsules, s/r, blue, potassium chloride 600 mg (8 mmol each of K^+ and Cl^-). Net price 20 = 35p. Label: 25, 27, counselling, swallow whole with fluid during meals while sitting or standing *or* open capsule and swallow enclosed granules with fluid or soft food

Slow-K® (Ciba)
Tablets, s/r, orange, s/c, potassium chloride 600 mg (8 mmol each of K^+ and Cl^-). Net price 20 = 10p. Label: 25, 27, counselling, swallow whole with fluid during meals while sitting or standing

POTASSIUM CITRATE

See section 7.4.3

POTASSIUM REMOVAL

Ion-exchange resins may be used to remove excess potassium in mild hyperkalaemia or in moderate hyperkalaemia when there are not ECG changes; intravenous therapy is required in emergencies (section 9.2.2).

POLYSTYRENE SULPHONATE RESINS

Indications: hyperkalaemia associated with anuria or severe oliguria, and in dialysis patients
Cautions: children (impaction of resin with excessive dosage or inadequate dilution)
Contra-indications: avoid calcium-containing resin in hyperparathyroidism, multiple myeloma, sarcoidosis, or metastatic carcinoma; avoid sodium-containing resin in congestive heart failure and severe renal impairment
Side-effects: rectal ulceration following rectal administration
Dose: *by mouth*, 15 g 3–4 times daily in water (not fruit juice which has a high K^+ content)
By rectum, as an enema, 30 g in methylcellulose solution, retained for 9 hours
CHILD, either route, 0.5–1 g/kg daily

Calcium Resonium® (Sterling-Winthrop)
Powder, brown, calcium polystyrene sulphonate. Net price 300 g = £40.31. Label: 13

Resonium A® (Sterling-Winthrop)
Powder, buff, sodium polystyrene sulphonate. Net price 454 g = £54.57. Label: 13

9.2.1.2 ORAL SODIUM AND WATER

Sodium chloride is indicated in states of sodium depletion and usually needs to be given intravenously (section 9.2.2). In chronic conditions associated with mild or moderate degrees of sodium depletion, e.g. in salt-losing bowel or renal disease, oral supplements of sodium chloride or bicarbonate (section 9.2.1.3), according to the acid-base status of the patient, may be sufficient.

SODIUM BICARBONATE

Section 9.2.1.3

SODIUM CHLORIDE

Indications: sodium depletion; see also section 9.2.2.

Sodium Chloride Tablets, sodium chloride 300 mg (approx 5 mmol each of Na^+ and Cl^-). Net price 20 = 20p. Label: 13

Slow Sodium® (Ciba)
Tablets, s/r, sodium chloride 600 mg (approx. 10 mmol each of Na^+ and Cl^-). Net price 20 = 11p. Label: 25

SODIUM CITRATE

See section 7.4.3

ORAL REHYDRATION THERAPY (ORT)

As a worldwide problem diarrhoea is by far the most important indication for fluid and electrolyte replacement. Intestinal absorption of sodium and water is enhanced by glucose, therefore replacement of fluid and electrolytes lost through diarrhoea can be achieved by giving solutions containing sodium, potassium, and glucose.

Oral rehydration solutions should:
enhance optimally the absorption of water and electrolytes;
replace the electrolyte deficit adequately and safely;
contain an alkalising agent to counter acidosis;
be simple to use in hospital and at home;
be palatable and acceptable, especially to children;
be readily available.

It is the policy of the World Health Organization (WHO) to promote a single oral rehydration solution but use it flexibly (e.g. by giving extra water between drinks of oral rehydration solution to moderately dehydrated infants).

Compared with the WHO formulation oral rehydration solutions used in the UK are low in sodium (30–50 mmol/litre) and high in glucose (approx. 200 mmol/litre). They are of benefit for mild to moderate diarrhoea, when the body's homoeostatic mechanisms are still working and will not be harmful, but they may be suboptimal in correction of fluid loss and electrolyte imbalance. In the more severe diarrhoeas the WHO formulation is marginally more effective in correcting dehydration; it carries no danger of hypernatraemia if used correctly.

For intravenous rehydration see section 9.2.2

ORAL REHYDRATION SALTS (ORS)

Indications: fluid and electrolyte loss in diarrhoea, see notes above

Dose: according to fluid loss, usually 200–400 mL solution after every loose motion; INFANT 1–1½ times usual feed volume; CHILD 200 mL after every loose motion

WHO formulations

WHO Oral Rehydration Salts

Oral powder, sodium chloride 3.5 g, potassium chloride 1.5 g, sodium citrate 2.9 g, anhydrous glucose 20 g. To be dissolved in sufficient water to produce 1 litre (providing Na^+ 90 mmol, K^+ 20 mmol, Cl^- 80 mmol, citrate 10 mmol, glucose 111 mmol/litre)

Note. Recommended by the WHO and the United Nations Childrens Fund but not commonly used in the UK. Corresponds to Oral Rehydration Salts—Citrate (Formula C) BP; the alternative WHO formulation corresponds to Oral Rehydration Salts—Bicarbonate (Formula B) BP and is less stable

UK formulations

Note. After reconstitution any unused solution should be discarded no later than 1 hour after preparation unless stored in a refrigerator when it may be kept for up to 24 hours.

Dextrolyte® (Cow & Gate)

Oral solution, glucose, potassium chloride, sodium chloride, sodium lactate, providing Na^+ 35 mmol, K^+ 13.4 mmol, Cl^- 30.5 mmol, lactate 17.7 mmol, and glucose 200 mmol/litre. 100 mL (hosp. only)

Dioralyte® (Rorer) [new formulation]

Effervescent tablets, sodium chloride 117 mg, sodium bicarbonate 336 mg, potassium chloride 186 mg, citric acid anhydrous 384 mg, anhydrous glucose 1.62 g. Net price 10-tab pack (blackcurrant- or citrus-flavoured) = £1.20. Label: 13

Reconstitute 2 tablets with 200 mL of water (only for adults and for children over 1 year)

Note. Ten tablets when reconstituted with 1 litre of water provide Na^+ 60 mmol, K^+ 25 mmol, Cl^- 45 mmol, citrate 20 mmol, and glucose 90 mmol

Oral powder, sodium chloride 470 mg, potassium chloride 300 mg, disodium hydrogen citrate 530 mg, glucose 3.56 g/sachet. Net price 20 sachets (blackcurrant- or citrus-flavoured or plain) = £4.17. Label: 13

Reconstitute one sachet with 200 mL of water (freshly boiled and cooled for infants).

Note. Five sachets reconstituted with 1 litre of water provide Na^+ 60 mmol, K^+ 20 mmol, Cl^- 60 mmol, citrate 10 mmol, and glucose 90 mmol

Electrolade® (Nicholas)

Oral powder, sodium chloride 236 mg, potassium chloride 300 mg, sodium bicarbonate 500 mg, anhydrous glucose 4 g/sachet (banana- and melon-flavoured). Net price 4-sachet pack = 80p; 20-sachet pack = £3.99. Label: 13

Reconstitute one sachet with 200 mL of water (freshly boiled and cooled for infants)

Note. Five sachets when reconstituted with 1 litre of water provide Na^+ 50 mmol, K^+ 20 mmol, Cl^- 40 mmol, HCO_3^- 30 mmol, and glucose 111 mmol

Gluco-lyte® (Cupal)

Oral powder, sodium chloride 200 mg, potassium chloride 300 mg, sodium bicarbonate 300 mg, glucose 8 g/sachet. Net price 6 sachets = £1.29. Label: 13

Reconstitute one sachet with 200 mL of water (freshly boiled and cooled for infants)

Note. Five sachets when reconstituted with 1 litre of water provide Na^+ 35 mmol, K^+ 20 mmol, Cl^- 37 mmol, HCO_3^- 18 mmol, and glucose 200 mmol (corresponds to Oral Rehydration Salts—Formula A, BP)

Rehidrat® (Searle)

Oral powder, sodium chloride 440 mg, potassium chloride 380 mg, sodium bicarbonate 420 mg, citric acid 440 mg, glucose 4.09 g, sucrose 8.07 g, fructose 70 mg/sachet. Net price 24-sachet pack (orange, blackcurrant or lemon and lime flavour) = £5.85; 16-sachet pack (mixed flavours) = £3.90. Label: 13

Note. Lemon and lime version stains vomit green

Reconstitute one sachet with 250 mL of water (freshly boiled and cooled for infants)

Note. Four sachets when reconstituted with one litre of water provide Na^+ 50 mmol, K^+ 20 mmol, Cl^- 50 mmol, HCO_3^- 20 mmol, citrate 9 mmol, glucose 91 mmol, sucrose 94 mmol, and fructose 2 mmol

9.2.1.3 ORAL BICARBONATE

Sodium bicarbonate is given by mouth for chronic acidotic states such as uraemic acidosis or renal tubular acidosis. The dose for correction of metabolic acidosis is not predictable and the response must be assessed; 4.8 g daily (57 mmol each of Na^+ and HCO_3^-) or more may be required. For severe metabolic acidosis, sodium bicarbonate can be given intravenously (section 9.2.2).

Sodium bicarbonate may also be used to make the pH of the urine alkaline (see section 7.4.3); for use in dyspepsia see section 1.1.2.

Sodium supplements may increase blood pressure or cause fluid retention and pulmonary oedema in those at risk; hypokalaemia may be exacerbated.

Where hyperchloraemic acidosis is associated with potassium deficiency, as in some renal tubular and gastro-intestinal disorders it may be appropriate to give oral **potassium bicarbonate**, although acute or severe deficiency should be managed by intravenous therapy.

SODIUM BICARBONATE

Indications: see notes above

Cautions: see notes above; avoid in respiratory acidosis; **interactions:** Appendix 1 (antacids and adsorbents)

Dose: see notes above

Sodium Bicarbonate (Non-proprietary)

Capsules, sodium bicarbonate usual strengths 300 mg (approx. 3.6 mmol each of Na^+ and

HCO_3^-), 500 mg (approx. 6 mmol each of Na^+ and HCO_3^-), 600 mg (approx. 7.1 mmol each of Na^+ and HCO_3^-)
Available from Macarthys, Penn, etc (special order)
Tablets, sodium bicarbonate 300 mg, net price 20 tabs = 24p; 600 mg, 20 = 30p

POTASSIUM BICARBONATE

Indications: see notes above
Cautions: cardiac disease, renal impairment; **interactions:** Appendix 1 (potassium salts)
Contra-indications: hypochloraemia; plasma potassium concentration above 5 mmol/litre
Side-effects: nausea and vomiting
Dose: see notes above

Potassium Tablets, Effervescent, potassium bicarbonate 500 mg, potassium acid tartrate 300 mg, each tablet providing 6.5 mmol of K^+. To be dissolved in water before administration. Net price 100 = £2.71. Label: 13, 21
Note. These tablets do not contain chloride; for effervescent tablets containing potassium and chloride, see under Potassium Chloride, section 9.2.1.1

WATER

The term water used without qualification means either potable water freshly drawn direct from the public supply and suitable for drinking or freshly boiled and cooled purified water. The latter should be used if the public supply is from a local storage tank or if the potable water is unsuitable for a particular preparation. (Water for injections, section 9.2.2.)

9.2.2 Intravenous administration

Solutions of electrolytes are given intravenously, to meet normal fluid and electrolyte requirements or to replenish substantial deficits or continuing losses, when the patient is nauseated or vomiting and is unable to take adequate amounts by mouth.

In an individual patient the nature and severity of the electrolyte imbalance must be assessed from the history and clinical and biochemical examination. Sodium, potassium, chloride, magnesium, phosphate, and water depletion can occur singly and in combination with or without disturbances of acid-base balance; for reference to the use of magnesium and phosphates, see section 9.5.

Isotonic solutions may be infused safely into a peripheral vein. Solutions more concentrated than plasma, for example 20% glucose are best given through an indwelling catheter positioned in a large vein.

INTRAVENOUS SODIUM

Sodium chloride in isotonic solution provides the most important extracellular ions in near physiological concentration and is indicated in *sodium depletion* which may arise from such conditions as gastro-enteritis, diabetic ketoacidosis, ileus, and ascites. In a severe deficit of from 4 to 8 litres, 2 to 3 litres of isotonic sodium chloride may be given over 2 to 3 hours; thereafter infusion can usually be at a slower rate.

Excessive administration should be avoided; the jugular venous pressure should be assessed, the bases of the lungs should be examined for crepitations, and in elderly or seriously ill patients it is often helpful to monitor the right atrial (central) venous pressure.

Sodium chloride and glucose solutions are indicated when there is combined *water and sodium depletion*. A 1:1 mixture of isotonic sodium chloride and 5% glucose allows some of the water (free of sodium) to enter body cells which suffer most from dehydration while the sodium salt with a volume of water determined by the normal plasma Na^+ remains extracellular. An example of combined sodium chloride and water depletion occurs in persistent vomiting.

SODIUM CHLORIDE

Indications: electrolyte imbalance, also section 9.2.1.2
Cautions: restrict intake in impaired renal function, cardiac failure, hypertension, peripheral and pulmonary oedema, toxaemia of pregnancy
Side-effects: administration of large doses may give rise to sodium accumulation and oedema
Dose: see notes above

PoM **Sodium Chloride Intravenous Infusion,** usual strength sodium chloride 0.9% (9 g, 150 mmol each of Na^+ and Cl^-/litre), this strength being supplied when normal saline for injection is requested. Net price 2-mL amp = 23p; 5-mL amp = 30p; 10-mL amp = 34p; 20-mL amp = 62p; 50-mL amp = £1.52
In hospitals, 500- and 1000-mL packs, and sometimes other sizes, are available
Note. The term 'normal saline' should **not** be used to describe sodium chloride intravenous infusion 0.9%; the term 'physiological saline' is acceptable but it is preferable to give the composition (i.e. sodium chloride intravenous infusion 0.9%).

PoM **Sodium Chloride and Glucose Intravenous Infusion,** usual strength sodium chloride 0.18% (1.8 g, 30 mmol each of Na^+ and Cl^-/litre) and 4% of anhydrous glucose
In hospitals, 500- and 1000-mL packs, and sometimes other sizes are available

PoM **Ringer's Solution for Injection,** calcium chloride (dihydrate) 322 micrograms, potassium chloride 300 micrograms, sodium chloride 8.6 mg/mL, providing the following ions (in mmol/litre), Ca^{2+} 2.2, K^+ 4, Na^+ 147, Cl^- 156
In hospitals, 500- and 1000-mL packs, and sometimes other sizes, are available

INTRAVENOUS GLUCOSE

Glucose solutions (5%) are mainly used to replace water deficits and should be given alone when there is no significant loss of electrolytes. Average water requirements in a healthy adult are 1.5 to 2.5 litres daily and this is needed to balance unavoidable losses of water through the skin and lungs and to provide sufficient for urinary excretion. Water depletion (dehydration) tends to occur when these losses are not matched by a comparable intake, as for example may occur in coma or dysphagia or in the aged or apathetic who may not drink water in sufficient amount on their own initiative.

Excessive loss of water without loss of electrolytes is uncommon, occurring in fevers, hyperthyroidism, and in uncommon water-losing renal states such as diabetes insipidus or hypercalcaemia. The volume of glucose solution needed to replenish deficits varies with the severity of the disorder, but usually lies within the range of 2 to 10 litres.

Glucose solutions are also given in regimens with calcium, bicarbonate, and insulin for the emergency management of *hyperkalaemia*. They are also given, after correction of hyperglycaemia, during treatment of diabetic ketoacidosis, when they must be accompanied by continuing insulin infusion.

GLUCOSE

(Dextrose Monohydrate)

Indications: fluid replacement (see notes above), provision of energy (section 9.3)

Side-effects: glucose injections especially if hypertonic may have a low pH and may cause venous irritation and thrombophlebitis

Dose: water replacement, see notes above; energy source, 1–3 litres daily of 20–50% solution

PoM **Glucose Intravenous Infusion,** glucose, usual strength 5% (50 mg/mL). 20% solution, net price 20-mL amp = £1.30; 25% solution, 25-mL amp = £2.01; 50% solution, price 20-mL amp = 65p; 25-mL amp = £2.82; 50-mL amp = £2.66

In hospitals, 500- and 1000-mL packs, and sometimes other sizes, are available.

INTRAVENOUS POTASSIUM

Potassium chloride and sodium chloride intravenous infusion and **potassium chloride and glucose** intravenous infusion are used to correct severe *hypokalaemia* and depletion and when sufficient potassium cannot be taken by mouth. Potassium chloride, as ampoules containing 1.5 g (20 mmol K^+) in 10 mL[1], may be added to 500 mL of sodium chloride or glucose intravenous infusion; the solution then contains 40mmol/litre and may be given slowly over 2 to 3 hours with ECG monitoring in difficult cases[2]. Repeated measurements of plasma potassium are necessary to determine whether further infusions are required and to avoid the development of hyperkalaemia; this is especially liable to occur in renal failure.

1. **Important**: mix infusion solution thoroughly after adding potassium chloride; use ready-prepared solutions when possible
2. Higher concentrations may be given in severe cases but require infusion pump control

POTASSIUM CHLORIDE

Indications: electrolyte imbalance; see also oral potassium supplements, section 9.2.1.1

Cautions: for intravenous infusion the concentration of solution should not usually exceed 3.2 g (43 mmol)/litre

Side-effects: rapid injection may be toxic to heart

Dose: *by slow intravenous infusion*, depending on the deficit or the daily maintenance requirements, see also notes above

PoM **Potassium Chloride and Glucose Intravenous Infusion,** usual strength potassium chloride 0.3% (3 g, 40 mmol each of K^+ and Cl^-/litre) with 5% of anhydrous glucose

In hospitals, 500- and 1000-mL packs, and sometimes other sizes, are available

PoM **Potassium Chloride and Sodium Chloride Intravenous Infusion,** usual strength potassium chloride 0.3% (3 g/litre) and sodium chloride 0.9% (9 g/litre), containing 40 mmol of K^+, 150 mmol of Na^+, and 190 mmol of Cl^-/litre

In hospitals, 500- and 1000-mL packs, and sometimes other sizes, are available

PoM **Potassium Chloride, Sodium Chloride, and Glucose Intravenous Infusion,** sodium chloride 0.18% (1.8 g, 30 mmol of Na^+/litre) with 4% of anhydrous glucose and usually sufficient potassium chloride to provide 10–40 mmol of K^+/litre (to be specified by the prescriber)

In hospitals, 500- and 1000-mL packs, and sometimes other sizes, are available

PoM **Potassium Chloride Solution, Strong** (sterile), potassium chloride 15% (150 mg, approximately 2 mmol each of K^+ and Cl^-/mL). Net price 10-mL amp = 74p

IMPORTANT. Must be diluted with not less than 50 times its volume of sodium chloride intravenous infusion 0.9% or other suitable diluent and mixed well

Solutions containing 10 and 20% of potassium chloride are also available in both 5- and 10-mL ampoules.

BICARBONATE AND LACTATE

Sodium bicarbonate is used to control severe *metabolic acidosis* (as in renal failure or diabetic ketoacidosis). Since this condition is usually attended by sodium depletion, it is reasonable to correct this first by the administration of isotonic sodium chloride intravenous infusion, provided the kidneys are not primarily affected and the degree of acidosis is not so severe as to impair renal function. In these circumstances, isotonic sodium chloride alone is usually effective as it restores the ability of the kidneys to generate bicarbonate. In renal acidosis or in severe acidosis of any origin (for example blood pH<7.1) sodium bicarbonate (1.26%) should be infused with isotonic sodium chloride; a total volume of up to 6 litres (4 litres of sodium chloride and 2 litres of sodium bicarbonate) may be necessary in the adult. In severe shock due for example to cardiac arrest, metabolic acidosis may develop without sodium depletion; in these circumstances sodium bicarbonate is best given in a small volume of hypertonic solution, such as 50 mL of 8.4% solution intravenously; plasma pH should be monitored.

Sodium bicarbonate infusion is used in the emergency management of *hyperkalaemia* (see also under Glucose).

Sodium lactate intravenous infusion is obsolete in metabolic acidosis, and carries the risk of producing lactic acidosis, particularly in seriously ill patients with poor tissue perfusion or impaired hepatic function.

SODIUM BICARBONATE

Indications: metabolic acidosis

Dose: *by slow intravenous injection*, a strong solution (up to 8.4%), or *by continuous intravenous infusion*, a weaker solution (usually 1.26%), an amount appropriate to the body base deficit (see notes above)

PoM **Sodium Bicarbonate Intravenous Infusion,** usual strength sodium bicarbonate 1.26% (12.6 g, 150 mmol each of Na^+ and HCO_3^-/litre); various other strengths available

In hospitals, 500- and 1000-mL packs, and sometimes other sizes, are available

PoM **Min-I-Jet® Sodium Bicarbonate** (IMS)

Intravenous Infusion, sodium bicarbonate in disposable syringe, net price 4.2%, 10 mL = £3.46; 8.4%, 10 mL = £3.62, 50 mL = £5.37

SODIUM LACTATE

Indications: diabetic coma, diminished alkali reserve (but see notes above)

PoM **Sodium Lactate Intravenous Infusion,** sodium lactate M/6, contains the following ions (in mmol/litre), Na^+ 167, HCO_3^- (as lactate) 167

PoM **Sodium Lactate Intravenous Infusion, Compound,** (Hartmann's Solution for Injection; Ringer-Lactate Solution for Injection), contains the following ions (in mmol/litre), Na^+ 131, K^+ 5, Ca^{2+} 2, HCO_3^- (as lactate) 29, Cl^- 111

In hospitals, 500- and 1000-mL packs, and sometimes other sizes, are available

WATER

PoM **Water for Injections.** Net price 1-mL amp = 12p; 2-mL amp = 11p; 5-mL amp = 17p; 20-mL amp = 49p; 50-mL amp = £1·03

9.2.3 Plasma and plasma substitutes

Plasma and albumin solutions, prepared from whole blood, contain soluble proteins and electrolytes but no clotting factors, blood group antibodies, or pseudocholinesterases; they may be given without regard to the recipient's blood group.

Plasma protein and albumin solutions are used for the treatment of hypoproteinaemia and the low plasma volume associated with conditions such as burns, the complications of surgery, and pancreatitis. Plasma substitutes are more appropriate for acute blood loss (e.g. haematemesis).

ALBUMIN SOLUTION

(Human Albumin Solution)

A solution containing protein derived from plasma, serum, or normal placentas; at least 95% of the protein is albumin. The solution may be isotonic (containing 4–5% protein) or concentrated (containing 15–25% protein).

Indications: see under preparations, below

Cautions: history of cardiac or circulatory disease (administer slowly to avoid rapid rise in blood pressure and cardiac failure); risk of further haemorrhage or shock due to rise in blood pressure; correct dehydration when administering concentrated solution

Contra-indications: cardiac failure; severe anaemia

Side-effects: nausea, fever, and chills particularly with rapid infusion

Isotonic solutions

Indications: acute or sub-acute loss of plasma volume e.g. in burns, pancreatitis, trauma, and complications of surgery; plasma exchange

Available as: *Human Albumin Solution 4.5%* (100-, 250-, and 500-mL bottles—BPL; 50-, 100-, 250-, and 400-mL bottles—Immuno); *Albuminar-5®* (250-mL, 500-mL, and 1-litre vials—Armour); *Albutein® 5%* (250- and 500-mL vials—Alpha); *Buminate® 5.0%* (250- and 500-mL bottles—Baxter)

Concentrated solutions (20–25%)

Indications: severe hypoalbuminaemia associated with low plasma volume and generalised oedema where salt and water restriction with plasma volume expansion are required; adjunct in the treatment of hyperbilirubinaemia by exchange transfusion in the newborn

Available as: *Albumin Solution 20%* (5- and 100-mL vials—SNBTS); *Human Albumin Solution 20%* (5- and 200-mL bottles—BPL; 10-, 50- and 100-mL vials—Immuno); *Albuminar-20®* (50- and 100-mL vials—Armour); *Albuminar-25®* (20-, 50-, and 100-mL vials—Armour); *Albutein® 20%* (50- and 100-mL vials—Alpha); *Albutein® 25%* (20-, 50-, and 100-mL vials—Alpha); *Buminate® 20%* (50- and 100-mL vials—Baxter)

PLASMA PROTEIN SOLUTION

(Plasma Protein Fraction, PPF)

An isotonic solution containing 4–5% protein derived from plasma or serum; at least 85% of the protein is albumin.

Indications: see notes above

Cautions; Contra-indications; Side-effects: see under Albumin Solution

Available as: *Plasma Protein Solution 4.5%* (100- and 500-mL bottles—SNBTS); *Plasmatein® 5%* (250- and 500-mL vials—Alpha)

PLASMA SUBSTITUTES

Dextrans, **gelatin**, and **hetastarch** are macromolecular substances which are slowly metabolised; they may be used at the outset to expand and maintain blood volume in shock arising from conditions such as burns or septicaemia. They are rarely needed when shock is due to sodium and water depletion as, in these circumstances, the shock responds to water and electrolyte repletion. They should not be used to maintain plasma volume in conditions such as burns or peritonitis where there is loss of plasma protein, water and electrolytes over periods of several days or weeks. In these situations, plasma or plasma protein fractions containing large amounts of albumin should be given. Plasma substitutes should be used in haemorrhage if blood is not available as an immediate short-term measure until it is.

Dextrans may interfere with blood group cross-matching or biochemical measurements and these should be carried out before infusion is begun. Dextran 70 by intravenous infusion is used predominantly for volume expansion. Dextran 40 intravenous infusion is used in an attempt to improve peripheral blood flow in ischaemic disease of the limbs and peripheral thrombo-embolism.

Gelatin and **hetastarch** are also used for short-term volume expansion.

> **Dosage**. Because of the complex requirements relating to blood volume expansion and the primary significance of blood, plasma protein, and electrolyte replacement, detailed dose statements have been omitted. *In all cases specialist literature should be consulted*.

DEXTRAN 40 INTRAVENOUS INFUSION

Dextrans of weight average molecular weight about '40000' 10% in glucose intravenous infusion 5% or in sodium chloride intravenous infusion 0.9%

Indications: conditions associated with peripheral local slowing of the blood flow; prophylaxis of post-surgical thrombo-embolic disease

Cautions; Contra-indications; Side-effects: see under Dextran 70 Intravenous Infusion; correct dehydration before infusion and give adequate fluids during therapy; very special care in those at risk of vascular overloading

Dose: *by intravenous infusion*, initially 500–1000 mL; further doses are given according to the patient's condition (see notes above)

PoM **Gentran 40®** (Baxter)
Intravenous infusion, dextran 40 intravenous infusion in glucose intravenous infusion 5% or in sodium chloride intravenous infusion 0.9%. 500-mL bottle (both)

PoM **Lomodex 40®** (CP)
Intravenous infusion, dextran 40 intravenous infusion in glucose intravenous infusion 5% or in sodium chloride intravenous infusion 0.9%. Net price 500-mL bottle (both) = £5.77

PoM **Rheomacrodex®** (Pharmacia)
Intravenous infusion, dextran 40 intravenous infusion in glucose intravenous infusion 5% or in sodium chloride intravenous infusion 0.9%. Net price 500-mL bottle (both) = £6.51

DEXTRAN 70 INTRAVENOUS INFUSION

Dextrans of weight average molecular weight about '70000' 6% in glucose intravenous infusion 5% or in sodium chloride intravenous infusion 0.9%

Indications: short-term blood volume expansion; prophylaxis of post-surgical thrombo-embolic disease

Cautions: congestive heart failure, renal impairment; blood samples for cross-matching should ideally be taken before infusion

Contra-indications: severe congestive heart failure; renal failure; bleeding disorders such as thrombocytopenia and hypofibrinogenaemia

Side-effects: rarely anaphylactoid reactions

Dose: *by intravenous infusion*, after moderate to severe haemorrhage, 500–1000 mL rapidly initially followed by 500 mL later if necessary; severe burns, up to 3000 mL in the first few days with electrolytes (see also notes above)

PoM **Gentran 70®** (Baxter)
Intravenous infusion, dextran 70 intravenous infusion in glucose intravenous infusion 5% or in sodium chloride intravenous infusion 0.9%. 500-mL bottle (both)

PoM **Lomodex 70®** (CP)
Intravenous infusion, dextran 70 intravenous infusion in glucose intravenous infusion 5% or in sodium chloride intravenous infusion 0.9%. Net price 500-mL bottle (both) = £3.66

PoM **Macrodex®** (Pharmacia)
Intravenous infusion, dextran 70 intravenous infusion in glucose intravenous infusion 5% or in sodium chloride intravenous infusion 0.9%. Net price 500-mL bottle (both) = £4.11

DEXTRAN 110 INTRAVENOUS INFUSION

Dextrans of weight average molecular weight about '110000' 6% in glucose intravenous infusion 5% or in sodium chloride intravenous infusion 0.9%

Indications: see under Dextran 70 Intravenous Infusion

Cautions; Contra-indications; Side-effects: see under Dextran 70 Intravenous Infusion; blood samples for cross-matching should be taken before infusion

Dose: *by intravenous infusion*, see under Dextran 70 Intravenous Infusion

PoM **Dextraven 110®** (CP)
Intravenous infusion, dextran 110 intravenous infusion in sodium chloride intravenous infusion 0.9%. Net price 500-mL bottle = £5.77

GELATIN

Note. The gelatin is partially degraded

Indications: low blood volume

Cautions; Contra-indications; Side-effects: see under Dextran 70 Intravenous Infusion

Dose: *by intravenous infusion*, initially 500–1000 mL of a 3.5–4% solution (see notes above)

PoM **Gelofusine®** (Consolidated)
Intravenous infusion, succinylated gelatin (modified fluid gelatin, average molecular weight 30000) 4%, sodium chloride 0.9%. Net price 500-mL bottle = £3.56

PoM **Haemaccel®** (Hoechst)
Intravenous infusion, polygeline (degraded and modified gelatin, average molecular weight 35 000) 35 g, Na^+ 145 mmol, K^+ 5.1 mmol, Ca^{2+} 6.25 mmol, Cl^- 145 mmol/litre. Net price 500-mL bottle = £3.81

HETASTARCH

Indications: low blood volume (expansion)
Cautions; Contra-indications; Side-effects: see under Dextran 70 Intravenous Infusion
Dose: *by intravenous infusion*, 500–1000 mL; usual max. 1500 mL daily (see notes above)

PoM **Elohes® 6%** (Oxford Nutrition)
Intravenous infusion, hetastarch (weight average molecular weight 200 000) 6% in sodium chloride intravenous infusion 0.9%. Net price 500-mL bottle = £9.75

PoM **Hespan®** (Du Pont)
Intravenous infusion, hetastarch (weight average molecular weight 450 000) 6% in sodium chloride intravenous infusion 0.9%. Net price 500-mL Steriflex® bag = £16.72

9.3 Intravenous nutrition

When adequate feeding via the alimentary tract is not possible, nutrients may be given by intravenous infusion. This may be in addition to ordinary oral or tube feeding—**supplemental parenteral nutrition**, or may be the sole source of nutrition—**total parenteral nutrition** (TPN). Indications for this method include preparation of undernourished patients for surgery, chemotherapy, or radiation therapy; severe or prolonged disorders of the gastro-intestinal tract; major surgery, trauma, or burns; prolonged coma or refusal to eat; and some patients with renal or hepatic failure. The composition of proprietary preparations available is in the table below.

Protein is given as mixtures of essential and non-essential synthetic L-amino acids. Ideally, all essential amino acids should be included with a wide variety of non-essential ones to provide sufficient nitrogen together with electrolytes (see also section 9.2.2). Available solutions vary in their composition of amino acids; they often contain an energy source (usually glucose) and electrolytes.

Energy is provided in a ratio of 0.6 to 1.1 megajoules (150–250 kcals) per gram of protein nitrogen. Energy requirements must be met if amino acids are to be utilised for tissue maintenance. Although it has long been held that carbohydrate has a greater nitrogen-sparing effect than fat, recent studies have shown that a mixture of both energy sources, usually 30 to 50% as fat, gives better utilisation of amino acid solutions than glucose alone.

Glucose is the preferred source of carbohydrate, but if more than 180 g is given per day frequent monitoring of blood glucose is required, and insulin may be necessary. Glucose in various strengths from 10 to 50% must be infused through a central venous catheter to avoid thrombosis. Preparations are available with useful added ions and trace elements, e.g. Glucoplex®.

Fructose and sorbitol have been used in an attempt to avoid the problem of hyperosmolar hyperglycaemic non-ketotic acidosis but other metabolic problems may occur, as with xylitol and ethanol which are now rarely used.

Fat emulsions have the advantages of a high energy to fluid volume ratio, neutral pH, and iso-osmolarity with plasma, and provide essential fatty acids. Available preparations are soya bean oil emulsions (Intralipid®). Several days of adaptation may be required to attain maximal utilisation. Reactions include occasional febrile episodes (usually only with 20% emulsions) and rare anaphylactic responses. Interference with biochemical measurements such as those for blood gases and calcium may occur if samples are taken before fat has been cleared. Daily checks are necessary to ensure complete clearance from the plasma in conditions where fat metabolism may be disturbed. **Additives may only be mixed with fat emulsions where compatibility is known.**

Total parenteral nutrition (TPN) requires the use of a solution containing amino acids, glucose, fat, electrolytes, trace elements, and vitamins. This is now commonly provided by the pharmacy in the form of the 3-litre bag. The solution is infused through a central venous catheter inserted under full surgical precautions. Only nutritional fluids should be given by this line. Loading doses of vitamin B_{12} and folic acid are advised and other vitamins are given parenterally twice weekly.

Before starting, the patient should be well oxygenated with a near normal circulating blood volume, renal function, and acid-base status. Appropriate biochemical tests should have been carried out beforehand and serious deficits corrected. Nutritional and electrolyte status must be monitored throughout treatment.

SUPPLEMENTARY PREPARATIONS

PoM **Addamel®** (Kabi)
Solution, electrolytes and trace elements for addition to Vamin® solutions except Vamin 18®, Ca^{2+} 5 mmol, Mg^{2+} 1.5 mmol, Cl^- 13.3 mmol/10 mL; traces of Fe^{3+}, Zn^{2+}, Mn^{2+}, Cu^{2+}, F^-, I^-. For adult use. Net price 10-mL amp = £1.59

PoM **Addiphos®** (Kabi)
Solution, sterile, phosphate 40 mmol, K^+ 30 mmol, Na^+ 30 mmol/20 mL. For addition to Vamin® solutions and glucose intravenous infusions. Net price 20-mL vial = £1.18

PoM **Additrace®** (Kabi)
Solution, trace elements for addition to Vamin® solutions traces of Fe^{3+}, Zn^{2+}, Mn^{2+}, Cu^{2+}, Cr^{3+}, Se^{4+}, Mo^{6+}, F^-, I^-. For adult use. Net price 10-mL amp = £1.79

PoM **Multibionta®** (Merck)
Solution, ascorbic acid 500 mg, dexpanthenol 25 mg, nicotinamide 100 mg, pyridoxine hydrochloride 15 mg, riboflavine sodium phosphate 10 mg, thiamine hydrochloride 50 mg, tocopheryl acetate 5 mg, vitamin A 10 000 units. For addition to infusion solutions. Net price 10-mL amp = £1.47

PoM **Ped-El®** (Kabi)
Solution, sterile, Ca^{2+}, Cu^{2+}, Fe^{3+}, Mg^{2+}, Mn^{2+}, Zn^{2+}, Cl^-, F^-, I^-, P. For addition to Vamin® solutions. For paediatric use. Net price 20-mL vial = £1.59

PoM **Solivito N®** (Kabi)
Solution, powder for reconstitution, biotin 60 micrograms, cyanocobalamin 5 micrograms, folic acid 400 micrograms, glycine 100 mg, nicotinamide 40 mg, pyridoxine hydrochloride 4.9 mg, riboflavine sodium phosphate 4.9 mg, sodium ascorbate 113 mg, sodium pantothenate 16.5 mg, thiamine mononitrate 3.1 mg. Dissolve in water for injections or glucose intravenous infusion for adding to glucose intravenous infusion or Intralipid®; dissolve in Vitlipid N® or Intralipid® for adding to Intralipid® only. Net price per vial = £1.80

PoM **Vitlipid N®** (Kabi)
Emulsion, adult, vitamin A 330 units, ergocalciferol 20 units, dl-alpha tocopherol 1 unit, phytomenadione 15 micrograms/mL. For addition to Intralipid®. Net price 10-mL amp = £1.75
Emulsion, infant, vitamin A 230 units, ergocalciferol 40 units, dl-alpha tocopherol 0.7 unit, phytomenadione 20 micrograms/mL. For addition to Intralipid®. Net price 10-mL amp = £1.75

Proprietary Infusion Fluids for Parenteral Feeding

Preparation	Nitrogen g/litre	Total energy kJ/litre	Electrolytes mmol/litre K^+	Mg^{2+}	Na^+	$Acet^-$	Cl^-	Other components/litre
Aminoplasmal L5 (Braun) Net price 500 mL = £7.50	8.03	850	25	2.5	48	59	31	acid phosphate 9 mmol, malate 7.5 mmol
Aminoplasmal L10 (Braun) Net price 500 mL = £14.20	16.06	1700	25	2.5	48	59	62	acid phosphate 9 mmol, malate 7.5 mmol
Aminoplasmal Ped (Braun) Net price 100 mL = £3.80; 250 mL = £6.45	7.4	850	25	2.5	50	27	15	
Aminoplex 5 (Geistlich) Net price 1000 mL = £10.71	5.0	4200	28	4	35	28	43	ethanol 5%, sorbitol 125 g, malic acid 1.85 g
Aminoplex 12 (Geistlich) Net price 500 mL = £10.36; 1000 mL = £17.48	12.44	1300	30	2.5	35	5	67	malic acid 4.6 g
Aminoplex 14 (Geistlich) Net price 500 mL = £10.36	13.4	1400	30		35		79	vitamins, malic acid 5.36 g
Aminoplex 24 (Geistlich) Net price 250 mL = £10.20; 500 mL = £15.85	24.9	2600	30	2.5	35	5	67	malic acid 4.5 g
Branched Chain Amino Acids (Clintec) 500-mL Viaflex® pack	4.4							
FreAmine III 8.5% (Kendall) Net price 500 mL = £10.20; 1000 mL = £18.95	13.0	1400			10	72	<3	phosphate 10 mmol
FreAmine III 10% (Kendall) 1000 mL	15.3	1650			10	88	<2	phosphate 20 mmol
Glucoplex 1000 (Geistlich) Net price 500 mL = £2.54; 1000 mL = £2.83		4200	30	2.5	50		67	acid phosphate 18 mmol, Zn^{2+} 0.046 mmol, anhydrous glucose 240 g
Glucoplex 1600 (Geistlich) Net price 500 mL = £2.66; 1000 mL = £3.07		6700	30	2.5	50		67	acid phosphate 18 mmol, Zn^{2+} 0.046 mmol, anhydrous glucose 400 g
Hepanutrin (Geistlich) Net price 500 mL = £13.96	15.6	1700						
Intralipid 10% (Kabi) Net price 100 mL = £4.35; 500 mL = £9.65		4600						fractionated soya oil 100 g, glycerol 22.5 g
Intralipid 20% (Kabi) Net price 100 mL = £6.55; 500 mL = £14.40		8400						fractionated soya oil 200 g, glycerol 22.5 g
[1]Lipofundin MCT/LCT 10% (Braun) Net price 100 mL = £6.40; 500 mL = £10.50		4430						soya oil 50 g, medium chain triglycerides 50 g
[1]Lipofundin MCT/LCT 20% (Braun) Net price 100 mL = £7.30; 500 mL = £16.00		8000						soya oil 100 g, medium chain triglycerides 100 g
Lipofundin S 10% (Braun) Net price 100 mL = £6.00; 500 mL = £9.80		4470						soya oil 100 g
Lipofundin S 20% (Braun) Net price 100 mL = £7.00; 500 mL = £15.30		8520						soya oil 200 g
Nephramine 5.4% (Kendall) 250 mL = £24.99	6.4	840			5	44	<3	essential amino acids only
Nutracel 400 (Clintec) Net price 500 mL = £2.60		3400		18		0.16	66	Ca^{2+} 15 mmol, Mn^{2+} 0.08 mmol, Zn^{2+} 0.08 mmol, anhydrous glucose 200 g
Nutracel 800 (Clintec) Net price 1000 mL = £4.50		3400		9		0.08	33	Ca^{2+} 7.5 mmol, Mn^{2+} 0.04 mmol, Zn^{2+} 0.04 mmol, anhydrous glucose 200 g
Perifusin (Kabi) Net price 1000 mL = £7.20	5.0	550	30	5	40	10	9	malate 22.5 mmol

1. Treatment with Lipofundin MCT/LCT should be limited to up to 10 days

Note. 1000 kcal = 4.1868 MJ; 1 MJ (1000 kJ) = 238.8 kcal. All entries are PoM

 Prices are **net**, see p. 1

Proprietary Infusion Fluids for Parenteral Feeding (*continued*)

Preparation	Nitrogen g/litre	Total energy kJ/litre	Electrolytes mmol/litre K^+	Mg^{2+}	Na^+	$Acet^-$	Cl^-	Other components/litre
Plasma-Lyte 148 (water) (Baxter) 1000 mL		80	5	1.5	140	27	98	gluconate 23 mmol
Plasma-Lyte 148 (dextrose 5%) (Baxter) 500 mL and 1000 mL		880	5	1.5	140	27	98	gluconate 23 mmol, anhydrous glucose 50 g
Plasma-Lyte M (dextrose 5%) (Baxter) 1000 mL		800	16	1.5	40	12	40	Ca^{2+} 2.5 mmol, lactate 12 mmol, anhydrous glucose 50 g
Synthamin 9 (Clintec) Net price 500 mL = £7.15; 1000 mL = £13.25	9.1	1000	60	5	70	100	70	acid phosphate 30 mmol
Synthamin 14 (Clintec) Net price 500 mL = £10.35; 1000 mL = £18.40	14.0	1600	60	5	70	140	70	acid phosphate 30 mmol
Synthamin 14 without electrolytes (Clintec) Net price 500 mL = £10.60; 1000 mL = £18.80	14.0	1600				68	34	
Synthamin 17 (Clintec) Net price 500 mL = £13.60; 1000 mL = £24.70	16.5	1900	60	5	70	150	70	acid phosphate 30 mmol
Synthamin 17 without electrolytes (Clintec) Net price 500 mL = £13.60	16.5	1900				82	40	
Synthamix 9/800X (Clintec) Net price 2000 mL = £35.00	4.55	2175	30	7	35	50	51.5	acid phosphate 15 mmol, Zn^{2+} 0.02 mmol, Ca^{2+} 3.75 mmol, Mn^{2+} 0.02 mmol, anhydrous glucose 100 g
Synthamix 9/1800X (Clintec) Net price 2500 mL = £36.50	3.64	3414	24	5.6	28	40	41.2	acid phosphate 12 mmol, Zn^{2+} 0.016 mmol, Ca^{2+} 3 mmol, Mn^{2+} 0.016 mmol, anhydrous glucose 180 g
Synthamix 14/1200X (Clintec) Net price 2000 mL = £38.50	7	3312	30	7	35	70	51.5	acid phosphate 15 mmol, Zn^{2+} 0.02 mmol, Ca^{2+} 3.75 mmol, Mn^{2+} 0.02 mmol, anhydrous glucose 150 g
Synthamix 14/2200X (Clintec) Net price 2500 mL = £40.00	5.6	4324	24	5.6	28	56	41.2	acid phosphate 12 mmol, Zn^{2+} 0.016 mmol, Ca^{2+} 3 mmol, Mn^{2+} 0.016 mmol, anhydrous glucose 220 g
Vamin 9 (Kabi) Net price 500 mL = £6.60; 1000 mL = £11.90	9.4	1000	20	1.5	50		55	Ca^{2+} 2.5 mmol
Vamin 9 glucose (Kabi) Net price 100 mL = £3.40; 500 mL = £7.10; 1000 mL = £12.80	9.4	2700	20	1.5	50		55	Ca^{2+} 2.5 mmol, anhydrous glucose 100 g
Vamin 14 (Kabi) Net price 500 mL = £9.55; 1000 mL = £16.95	13.5	1400	50	8	100	135	100	Ca^{2+} 5 mmol, SO_4^{2-} 8 mmol
Vamin 14 (electrolyte-free) (Kabi) Net price 500 mL = £9.55; 1000 mL = £16.95	13.5	1400						
Vamin 18 (electrolyte-free) (Kabi) Net price 500 mL = £12.70; 1000 mL = £22.80	18.0	1900						
Vamin Infant (Kabi) Net price 100 mL = £3.80; 500 mL = £8.70	9.3	1000						
Vitrimix KV (Kabi) Net price (combined pack of Intralipid 20% 250 mL and Vamin 9 glucose 750 mL) = £19.90	7.0	4180	15	1.1	38		38	Ca^{2+} 1.9 mmol, anhydrous glucose 75 g

Note. 1000 kcal = 4.1868 MJ; 1 MJ (1000 kJ) = 238.8 kcal. All entries are PoM

9.4 Oral nutrition

9.4.1 Foods for special diets

These are preparations that have been modified to eliminate a particular constituent from a food or are nutrient mixtures formulated as substitutes for the food. They are for patients who either cannot tolerate or cannot metabolise certain common constituents of food. An example is the coeliac patient who cannot tolerate gluten which is present in wheat (and to a lesser extent other cereals). In other cases, for example, in patients with phenylketonuria who cannot metabolise phenylalanine, a small amount, sufficient for tissue building and repair, must be incorporated in the formulation.

Prices are **net**, see p. 1

ACBS. In certain clinical conditions some foods may have the characteristics of drugs and the Advisory Committee on Borderline Substances advises as to the circumstances in which such foods may be regarded as drugs and so can be prescribed in the NHS. Prescriptions for these foods issued in accordance with the advice of this committee and endorsed 'ACBS' will normally not be investigated.

See Appendix 7 for details of these foods and a listing by clinical condition (consult Drug Tariff for late amendments).

Preparations

See Appendix 7

9.4.2 Enteral nutrition

The body's reserves of protein rapidly become exhausted in severely ill patients, especially during chronic illness or in those with severe burns, extensive trauma, pancreatitis, or intestinal fistula. Much can be achieved by frequent meals and by persuading the patient to take supplementary snacks of ordinary food between the meals.

However, extra calories, protein, other nutrients, and vitamins are often best given by supplementing ordinary meals with sip or tube feeds of one of the nutritionally complete foods.

When patients cannot feed normally at all, for example patients with severe facial injury, oesophageal obstruction, or coma, a diet composed solely of nutritionally complete foods must be given. This is planned by a dietitian who will take into account the protein and total energy requirement of the patient and decide on the form and relative contribution of carbohydrate and fat to the energy requirements.

There are a number of nutritionally complete foods available and their use reduces an otherwise heavy workload in hospital or in the home. Most contain protein derived from milk or soya. Some contain protein hydrolysates or free amino acids and are only appropriate for patients who have diminished ability to break down protein, as may be the case in inflammatory bowel disease or pancreatic insufficiency.

Even when nutritionally complete feeds are being given it may be important to monitor water and electrolyte balance. Extra minerals (e.g. magnesium and zinc) may be needed in patients where gastro-intestinal secretions are being lost. Additional vitamins may also be needed. Regular haematological and biochemical tests may be needed particularly in the unstable patient.

Some feeds are supplemented with vitamin K; for drug interactions of vitamin K see Appendix 1 (vitamins).

CHILDREN. Infants and young children have special requirements and in most situations liquid feeds prepared for adults are totally unsuitable and should not be given. Expert advice should be sought.

Preparations

See Appendix 7

9.5 Minerals

See section 9.1.1 for iron salts.

9.5.1 Calcium and magnesium

9.5.1.1 CALCIUM SUPPLEMENTS

Calcium supplements are usually only required where dietary calcium intake is deficient. This dietary requirement varies with age and is relatively greater in childhood, pregnancy, and lactation, due to an increased demand, and in old age, due to impaired absorption. In osteoporosis a daily supplement of 800 mg (20 mmol) calcium may reduce the rate of bone loss, but larger doses have not been shown to be more effective. Patients with hypoparathyroidism rarely require calcium supplements after the early stages of stabilisation on vitamin D (section 9.6.4).

In hypocalcaemic tetany an initial intravenous injection of 10 mL (2.25 mmol) of calcium gluconate injection 10% may be followed by the continuous infusion of about 40 mL (9 mmol) daily, but plasma calcium should be monitored. This regimen can also be used, immediately but temporarily, to reduce the toxic effects of hyperkalaemia.

Calcium may also be used in cardiac resuscitation (see section 2.7).

CALCIUM SALTS

Indications: see notes above; calcium deficiency
Cautions: **interactions:** Appendix 1 (calcium salts)
Side-effects: bradycardia, arrhythmias, and irritation after intravenous injection
Dose: by mouth, daily in divided doses, as calcium gluconate or lactate, see notes above
By intramuscular or slow intravenous injection, acute hypocalcaemia, calcium gluconate 1–2 g (2.25–4.5 mmol of Ca^{2+}); avoid intramuscular route in children

Oral preparations

Calcium Gluconate Tablets, calcium gluconate 600 mg (1.35 mmol Ca^{2+}). To be chewed before swallowing. Net price 20 = 44p. Label: 24

Calcium Gluconate Tablets, Effervescent, calcium gluconate 1 g (2.25 mmol Ca^{2+}). Net price 100 = £4.83. Label: 13
Note. Each tablet usually contains sodium 102.6 mg (4.46 mmol Na^{+})

Calcium Lactate Tablets, calcium lactate 300 mg (1 mmol Ca^{2+}), net price 20 = 22p; 600 mg (2 mmol Ca^{2+}), 20 = 40p

Cacit® (Norwich Eaton)
Tablets, effervescent, pink, calcium carbonate

1.25 g, providing calcium citrate when dispersed in water (500 mg calcium or 12.6 mmol Ca^{2+}). Net price 76-tab pack = £19.64. Label: 13

Calcichew® (Shire)
Tablets (chewable), calcium carbonate 1.26 g (500 mg calcium or 12.6 mmol Ca^{2+}). Net price 100 = £9.78. Label: 24

Calcium-500 (Macarthys)
Tablets, pink, f/c, calcium carbonate 1.25 g (500 mg calcium or 12.5 mmol Ca^{2+}). Net price 100-tab pack = £3.49. Label: 25

Calcium-Sandoz® (Sandoz)
Syrup, calcium glubionate 1.09 g, calcium lactobionate 723 mg (108.3 mg calcium or 2.7 mmol Ca^{2+})/5 mL. Diluent syrup, life of diluted syrup 14 days. Net price 100 mL = 49p

Citrical® (Shire)
Granules, calcium carbonate 1.26 g (500 mg or 12.6 mmol Ca^{2+})/sachet. Net price 90-sachet pack = £20.88. Label: 13

Ossopan® (Sanofi)
Tablets, buff, f/c, hydroxyapatite 830 mg (4.4mmol Ca^{2+}). Net price 50 = £10.35
Granules, brown, hydroxyapatite 3.32 g (17.8 mmol Ca^{2+}). Net price 28-sachet pack = £18.50

Sandocal® (Sandoz)
Sandocal-400 tablets, effervescent, calcium lactate gluconate 930 mg, calcium carbonate 700 mg, anhydrous citric acid 1.189 g, providing calcium 400 mg (10 mmol Ca^{2+}). Net price 5 × 20-tab pack = £7.37. Label: 13
Sandocal-1000 tablets, effervescent, calcium lactate gluconate 2.327 g, calcium carbonate 1.75 g, anhydrous citric acid 2.973 g providing 1 g calcium (25 mmol Ca^{2+}). Net price 3 × 10-tab pack = £6.63. Label: 13

Titralac®: section 9.5.2.2

Parenteral preparations

PoM **Calcium Gluconate Injection,** calcium gluconate 10%. Net price 5-mL amp = 43p; 10-mL amp = 50p

Calcium Sandoz® (Sandoz)
PoM *Injection*, calcium glubionate equivalent to 10% of calcium gluconate (93 mg calcium or 2.32 mmol Ca^{2+}/10 mL). Net price 10-mL amp = 27p

PoM **Min-I-Jet® Calcium Chloride 10%** (IMS)
Injection, calcium chloride 100 mg/mL. Net price 10-mL disposable syringe = £2.74

9.5.1.2 HYPERCALCAEMIA

Severe hypercalcaemia calls for urgent treatment before detailed investigation of the cause. After rehydration (if necessary with intravenous infusion of **sodium chloride 0.9%**) a **loop diuretic** may be given to increase urinary calcium excretion. Drugs (such as thiazides and vitamin D compounds) which promote hypercalcaemia, should be discontinued and dietary calcium should be restricted.

If *severe hypercalcaemia persists* drugs which inhibit mobilisation of calcium from the skeleton may be required. The **biphosphonates** are useful and disodium pamidronate (see section 6.6.2) is probably the most effective; it is probably as effective as plicamycin, yet is less toxic and has a much longer effect. **Plicamycin** (see section 8.1.2) is probably the most rapidly effective drug but cannot be given continuously for more than a few days because of marrow toxicity; the duration of its hypocalcaemic effect is unpredictable but can last several days.

Corticosteroids (see section 6.3) are widely given, but may only be useful where hypercalcaemia is due to sarcoidosis, or vitamin D intoxication; they often take several days to achieve the desired effect.

Calcitonin (see section 6.6.1) is relatively non-toxic but is expensive and its effect can wear off after a few days despite continued use; it is rarely effective where biphosphonates have failed to reduce serum calcium adequately.

Intravenous chelating drugs such as **trisodium edetate** are rarely used; they usually cause pain in the limb receiving the infusion and may cause renal damage.

After treatment of severe hypercalcaemia the underlying cause must be established. *Further treatment* is governed by the same principles as for initial therapy. Salt and water depletion and drugs promoting hypercalcaemia should be avoided; oral administration of a biphosphonate may be useful. **Sodium cellulose phosphate**, which binds calcium in the gut, is rarely helpful, and any associated increase in serum phosphate may be harmful. Similarly, oral and intravenous phosphate may only achieve a reduction in serum calcium by precipitating calcium phosphate in the tissues, resulting in nephrocalcinosis and impairment of renal function. Parathyroidectomy may be indicated for hyperparathyroidism.

SODIUM CELLULOSE PHOSPHATE

Indications: hypercalcaemia (but see notes above), reduction of calcium absorption from food (in conjunction with low-calcium diet)
Contra-indications: congestive heart failure, renal impairment
Side-effects: occasional diarrhoea
Dose: 5 g 3 times daily with meals; CHILD 10 g daily in 3 divided doses with meals

Calcisorb® (3M)
Sachets, sodium cellulose phosphate 5 g. Net price 90-sachet pack = £19.71. Label: 13, 21, counselling, may be sprinkled on food

TRISODIUM EDETATE

Indications: hypercalcaemia (but see notes above); removal of lime burns in the eye (see under Preparations)
Cautions: plasma-calcium determinations required; caution in tuberculosis
Contra-indications: impaired renal function
Side-effects: nausea, diarrhoea, cramp; in overdosage renal damage
Dose: hypercalcaemia, *by slow intravenous infusion*, up to 70 mg/kg daily over 2–3 hours

PoM **Limclair®** (Sinclair)
Injection, trisodium edetate 200 mg/mL. Net price 5-mL amp = £3.43
For topical use in the eye, dilute 1 mL to 50 mL with sterile purified water

9.5.1.3 MAGNESIUM

Magnesium is an essential constituent of a vast number of enzyme systems, in particular those involved in energy generation. Most of it is found in the skeleton in the calcium apatite crystal lattice.

Magnesium salts are not well absorbed from the gastro-intestinal tract which explains the use of magnesium sulphate (section 1.6.4) as an osmotic laxative.

Magnesium is mainly excreted by the kidneys and is therefore retained in renal failure.

The effects of hypermagnesaemia and of hypomagnesaemia are similar to those of hyperkalaemia and hypokalaemia; hypocalcaemia is usually associated with hypomagnesaemia.

Oral magnesium salts are occasionally required on a long-term basis in patients with malabsorption.

Parenteral magnesium chloride or sulphate is occasionally needed to correct magnesium deficiency in alcoholism or that has arisen from prolonged diarrhoea or vomiting which has been treated with parenteral fluid and nutrition without magnesium supplements; 35–50 mmol of magnesium chloride (or sulphate) may be added to 1 litre of 5% glucose or other isotonic solution and given over a period of 12 to 24 hours. Repeated measurements of plasma magnesium are advisable to determine the rate and duration of the infusion. The dose should be reduced in renal failure. For maintenance (e.g. for intravenous nutrition) parenteral doses of magnesium are of the order of 10–20 mmol daily (often about 12 mmol daily).

9.5.2 Phosphorus

9.5.2.1 PHOSPHATE SUPPLEMENTS

Oral phosphate supplements may be required in addition to vitamin D in a small minority of patients with hypophosphataemic vitamin D-resistant rickets. Diarrhoea is a common side-effect and should prompt a reduction in dosage.

Phosphate infusion is occasionally needed in alcoholism or phosphate deficiency arising from parenteral fluid and nutrition deficient in phosphate supplements; phosphate depletion also occurs in severe diabetic ketoacidosis. A solution containing up to 50 mmol/litre can be infused in sodium chloride or glucose over 12 to 24 hours. Since potassium depletion is also commonly present the phosphate may be given as a mixture of the sodium and potassium salts.

Phosphate-Sandoz® (Sandoz)
Tablets, effervescent, anhydrous sodium acid phosphate 1.936 g, sodium bicarbonate 350 mg, potassium bicarbonate 315 mg, equivalent to phosphorus 500 mg (16.1 mmol phosphate), sodium 468.8 mg (20.4 mmol Na^+), potassium 123 mg (3.1 mmol K^+). Net price 20 = 75p. Label: 13

9.5.2.2 PHOSPHATE-BINDING AGENTS

Aluminium-containing and calcium-containing antacids are used as phosphate-binding agents in the management of hyperphosphataemia complicating renal failure. Calcium-containing phosphate-binding agents are contra-indicated in hypercalcaemia or hypercalciuria. Phosphate-binding agents which contain aluminium may increase plasma aluminium in dialysis patients.

ALUMINIUM HYDROXIDE

Indications: hyperphosphataemia
Cautions: hyperaluminaemia; see also notes above; **interactions:** Appendix 1 (antacids and adsorbents)

Aluminium Hydroxide (Non-proprietary)
Mixture (gel), about 4% w/w Al_2O_3 in water. Net price 200 mL = 37p
Dose: hyperphosphataemia, 20–100 mL according to requirements of patient; antacid, see section 1.1.1
Note: The brand name NHS Aludrox® (Charwell) is used for aluminium hydroxide mixture, net price 200 mL = 58p. For NHS Aludrox® tablets see preparations with magnesium, section 1.1.1

Alu-Cap® (3M)
Capsules, green/red, dried aluminium hydroxide 475 mg (low Na^+). Net price 120-cap pack = £3.84
Dose: phosphate-binding agent in renal failure, 4–20 capsules daily in divided doses with meals; antacid, see section 1.1.1

CALCIUM CARBONATE

Indications: hyperphosphataemia
Cautions: see notes above; **interactions:** Appendix 1 (calcium salts)
Side-effects: hypercalcaemia

Calcichew®, section 9.5.1.1
Calcium-500, section 9.5.1.1
Titralac® (3M)
Tablets, calcium carbonate 420 mg, glycine 180 mg. Net price 180-tab pack = £2.23
Dose: calcium supplement, or phosphate-binding agent (with meals) in renal failure, according to the requirements of the patient

9.5.3 Fluoride

Availability of adequate fluoride confers significant resistance to dental caries. It is now considered that the topical action of fluoride on enamel and plaque is more important than the systemic effect.

Where the natural fluoride content of the drinking water is significantly less than 1 mg per litre (one part per million) artificial fluoridation is the most economical method of supplementing fluoride intake.

Daily administration of tablets or drops is a suitable alternative, but systemic fluoride supplements should not be prescribed without prior reference to the fluoride content of the local water supply; they are not advisable when the water contains more than 700 micrograms per litre (0.7 parts per million). In addition, the British Association for the Study of Community Dentistry now recommends that infants need not receive fluoride supplements until the age of 6 months.

Use of dentifrices which incorporate sodium fluoride and/or monofluorophosphate is also a convenient source of fluoride.

Individuals who are either particularly caries prone or medically compromised may be given additional protection by use of fluoride rinses or by application of fluoride gels. Rinses may be used daily or weekly; daily use of a less concentrated rinse is more effective than weekly use of a more concentrated one. Gels must be applied on a regular basis under professional supervision; extreme caution is necessary to prevent the child from swallowing any excess. Less concentrated gels have recently become available for home use. Varnishes are also available and are particularly valuable for young or handicapped children since they adhere to the teeth and set in the presence of moisture.

> There are arrangements for health authorities to supply fluoride tablets in the course of pre-school dental schemes, and they may also be supplied in school dental schemes.

SODIUM FLUORIDE

Note. Sodium fluoride 2.2 mg provides approx. 1 mg fluoride ion

Indications: prophylaxis of dental caries—see notes above

Contra-indications: not for areas where drinking water is fluoridated

Side-effects: occasional white flecks on teeth with recommended doses; rarely yellowish-brown discoloration if recommended doses are exceeded

Dose: CHILD, as fluoride ion:

Water content less than 300 micrograms/litre, up to 6 months, none; 6 months–2 years, 250 micrograms daily; 2–4 years, 500 micrograms daily; over 4 years, 1 mg daily

Water content between 300 and 700 micrograms/litre, up to 2 years, none; 2–4 years, 250 micrograms daily; over 4 years, 500 micrograms daily

Tablets

COUNSELLING. Tablets should be sucked or dissolved in the mouth and taken preferably in the evening

En-De-Kay® (Stafford-Miller)

Fluotabs 2–4 years, natural orange-flavoured, scored, sodium fluoride 1.1 mg (500 micrograms F^-). Net price 200-tab pack = £1.61

Fluotabs 4+ years, natural orange-flavoured, scored, sodium fluoride 2.2 mg (1 mg F^-). Net price 200-tab pack = £1.61

Fluor-a-day® (Dental Health)

Tablets, buff, scored, sodium fluoride 2.2 mg (1 mg F^-). Net price 200-tab pack = £1·22

Fluorigard® (RMT)

Tablets 0.5, purple, sodium fluoride 1.1 mg (500 micrograms F^-). Net price 120-tab pack = £1.08

Tablets 1.0, sodium fluoride 2.2 mg (1 mg F^-). Net price 120-tab pack = £1.08 (available in 4 colours and flavours)

Oral-B Fluoride® (Oral-B Labs)

Tablets, sodium fluoride 1.1 mg (500 micrograms F^-), net price 200-tab pack = £1.62; 2.2 mg (1 mg F^-) (pink), 12-tab pack = £1.62

Zymafluor® (Zyma)

Tablets, sodium fluoride 550 micrograms (250 micrograms F^-), net price 400-tab pack = 75p; 2.2 mg (1 mg F^-) (yellow-grey), 100-tab pack = 55p

Oral drops

Note. Fluoride supplements no longer considered necessary below 6 months of age (see notes above)

En-De-Kay® (Stafford-Miller)

Fluodrops® (= paediatric drops), sugar-free, sodium fluoride 500 micrograms (250 micrograms F^-)/0.15 mL. Net price 60 mL = £1.21

Fluorigard® (RMT)

Paediatric drops, sodium fluoride 275 micrograms (125 micrograms F^-)/drop. Net price 30 mL = £1.16

Oral-B Fluoride® (Oral-B Labs)

Drops, sodium fluoride 0.15% (250 micrograms F^-/8 drops). Net price 48.7 mL = £1.30

Mouthwashes

Rinse mouth for 1 minute and spit out

COUNSELLING. Avoid eating, drinking, or rinsing mouth for 15 minutes after use

PoM **En-De-Kay®** (Stafford-Miller)

Fluorinse (= mouthwash), red, sodium fluoride 2%. Net price 100 mL = £2.31. Counselling, see above

CHILD 8 years and over, for *daily* use, dilute 5 drops to 10 mL of water; for *weekly* use, dilute 20 drops to 10 mL

Fluorigard® (RMT)

Daily dental rinse (= mouthwash), blue, sodium fluoride 0.05%. Net price 500 mL = £2.31. Counselling, see above

CHILD 6 years and over, for *daily* use, rinse with 5–10 mL

Weekly dental rinse (= mouthwash), blue, sodium fluoride 0.2%. Net price 150 mL = £1.54. Counselling, see above

CHILD 6 years and over, for *weekly* use, rinse with 5–10 mL

9.5.4 Zinc

Oral zinc therapy should only be given when there is good evidence of deficiency (hypoproteinaemia spuriously lowers plasma-zinc concentrations). Zinc deficiency can occur in individuals on inadequate diets, in malabsorption, with increased body loss due to trauma, burns and protein-losing conditions, and during intravenous feeding. Therapy should continue until clinical improvement occurs and be replaced by dietary measures unless there is severe malabsorption, metabolic disease, or continuing zinc loss. Side-effects of zinc salts are abdominal pain and dyspepsia.

ZINC SALTS

Indications; Cautions; Side-effects: see notes above; **interactions:** Appendix 1 (zinc)

Solvazinc® (Thames)
Effervescent tablets, yellow-white, zinc sulphate 200 mg (45 mg zinc). Net price 30 = £3.00. Label: 13, 21
Dose: 1 tablet in water 1–3 times daily after food

Zincomed® (Medo)
Capsules, blue/white, zinc sulphate 220 mg. Net price 30-cap pack = 99p. Label: 21
Dose: 1 capsule 3 times daily after food

Z Span® (SK&F)
Spansule® (= capsules s/r), blue/clear, enclosing white and grey pellets, zinc sulphate monohydrate 61.8 mg (22.5 mg zinc). Net price 30-cap pack = £1.38. Label: 25
Dose: adults and children over 1 year, 1–3 capsules daily as required; can be opened and sprinkled on food

9.6 Vitamins

9.6.1 Vitamin A
9.6.2 Vitamin B group
9.6.3 Vitamin C
9.6.4 Vitamin D
9.6.5 Vitamin E
9.6.6 Vitamin K
9.6.7 Multivitamin preparations

Vitamins are used for the prevention and treatment of specific deficiency states or where the diet is known to be inadequate; they may be prescribed in the NHS to prevent or treat deficiency but not as dietary supplements.

Their use as general 'pick-me-ups' is of unproven value and, in the case of preparations containing vitamin A or D, may actually be harmful if patients take more than the prescribed dose. The 'fad' for mega-vitamin therapy with water-soluble vitamins, such as ascorbic acid and pyridoxine, is unscientific and can be harmful.

9.6.1 Vitamin A

Deficiency of vitamin A (retinol) is rare in Britain even in disorders of fat absorption.

Massive overdose can cause rough skin, dry hair, an enlarged liver, and a raised erythrocyte sedimentation rate and raised serum calcium and serum alkaline phosphatase concentrations. Use of excessive doses should be **avoided** in pregnancy (see below).

The Department of Health has advised that:
1. The recommended daily amount of vitamin A in the UK is 2250 units daily, increased to 4000 units daily for nursing mothers;
2. Several national and international organisations have proposed a maximum intake of vitamin A during pregnancy of 8000 to 10000 units daily;
3. Reports in the USA suggest that birth defects may follow an intake of vitamin A of 24000 to 30000 units daily;
4. Supplements of vitamin A of 1200 to 4000 units daily given to pregnant women under medical supervision are safe.

In view of evidence suggesting that high levels of vitamin A may cause birth defects, the Chief Medical Officer has cautioned women who are (or may become) pregnant against taking any dietary supplements (including tablets and fish-liver oil drops) containing vitamin A, except on the advice of a doctor or an antenatal clinic; nor should they eat liver or products such as liver paté or liver sausage.

VITAMIN A
(Retinol)

Indications; Cautions; Side-effects: see notes above
Dose: see notes above and under preparations

PoM **Ro-A-Vit®** (Roche)
Injection, vitamin A (retinol) 50000 units (as palmitate)/mL. Net price 2-mL amp = 88p
Dose: by deep intramuscular injection, deficiency, 100000 units monthly, increased to weekly in acute deficiency states; courses no longer than 6 weeks with 2-week interval; Liver disease, 100000 units every 2–4 months; INFANT under 1 year and CHILD 50000 units monthly
Note. Contains polyethoxylated castor oil which has been associated with anaphylaxis; do **not** mix or dilute
Cautions: children, liver disease (specialist use); considerably enhanced bioavailability compared with previous formulation (dosage adjustment may be needed)

Vitamins A and D
Halibut-liver Oil Capsules, vitamin A 4000 units [also contains vitamin D]. Net price 20 = 18p
Vitamins A and D Capsules, vitamin A 4000 units, vitamin D 400 units. Net price 20 = 26p
NHS **Halycitrol®** (LAB)
Emulsion, vitamin A 4600 units, vitamin D 380 units/5 mL. Net price 114 mL = £1.03
Dose: 5 mL daily but see notes above

Vitamins A, D, and C for children
Children's Vitamin Drops (Hough)
Oral drops, ascorbic acid (as sodium ascorbate) 20 mg, vitamin A 700 units, vitamin D 300 units/5 drops.
Recommended by Department of Health for routine supplementation in young children. Available direct to

public under the Welfare Food Scheme from maternity and child health clinics and welfare food distribution centres; not available on prescription
Dose: CHILD 1 month–5 years, 5 drops daily
Note. The Department of Health recommends these drops for children aged 6 months to 2 years (preferably 5 years particularly in winter and early spring); some infants from 1 month of age may also benefit (for details see *Present Day Practice in Infant Feeding* 3rd Report)

9.6.2 Vitamin B group

Deficiency of the B vitamins, other than deficiency of vitamin B_{12} (section 9.1.2) is rare in Britain and is usually treated by preparations containing thiamine (B_1), riboflavine (B_2), and nicotinamide, which is used in preference to nicotinic acid, as it does not cause vasodilatation. Other members (or substances traditionally classified as members) of the vitamin B complex such as aminobenzoic acid, biotin, choline, inositol, and pantothenic acid or panthenol may be included in vitamin B preparations but there is no evidence of their value.

Severe deficiency states and encephalopathy, especially as seen in chronic alcoholism, are best treated by the parenteral administration of B vitamins (Pabrinex®, Parentrovite®); anaphylaxis has been reported with these preparations (see CSM advice, below).

As with other vitamins of the B group, pyridoxine (B_6) deficiency is rare, but it may occur during isoniazid therapy and is characterised by peripheral neuritis. High doses of pyridoxine are given in some metabolic disorders, such as hyperoxaluria, and it is also used in sideroblastic anaemia (section 9.1.3). Pyridoxine has been tried in a wide variety of other disorders, including the premenstrual syndrome, but there is little sound evidence to support the claims, and overdosage induces toxic effects.

THIAMINE

(Vitamin B_1)
Indications: see notes above
Cautions: anaphylactic shock may occasionally follow injection (see CSM advice below)
Dose: mild chronic deficiency, 10–25 mg daily; severe deficiency, 200–300 mg daily

Thiamine Hydrochloride Tablets, thiamine hydrochloride 25 mg, net price 20 = 12p; 50 mg, 20 = 20p; 100 mg, 20 = 35p; 300 mg, 20 = 57p

NHS **Benerva®** (Roche)
Tablets, thiamine hydrochloride 25 mg, net price 20 = 12p; 50 mg, 20 = 20p; 100 mg, 20 = 35p; 300 mg, 20 = 57p

CSM advice
Since potentially serious allergic adverse reactions may occur during, or shortly after, administration, the CSM has recommended that:
1. Use be restricted to patients in whom parenteral treatment is essential;
2. Intravenous injections should be administered slowly (over 10 minutes);
3. Facilities for treating anaphylaxis should be available when administered.

PoM **Vitamins B and C Injection**
Weak, for intramuscular use, ascorbic acid 500 mg, nicotinamide 160 mg, pyridoxine hydrochloride 50 mg, riboflavine 4 mg, thiamine hydrochloride 100 mg/4 mL
Strong, for intramuscular use, ascorbic acid 500 mg, nicotinamide 160 mg, pyridoxine hydrochloride 50 mg, riboflavine 4 mg, thiamine hydrochloride 250 mg/7 mL
Strong, for intravenous use, ascorbic acid 500 mg, anhydrous glucose 1 g, nicotinamide 160 mg, pyridoxine hydrochloride 50 mg, riboflavine 4 mg, thiamine hydrochloride 250 mg/10 mL

Available as:
PoM **Pabrinex®** (Paines & Byrne)
Intramuscular maintenance injection, vitamins B and C injection, weak, for intramuscular use. Net price 4 mL (in 2 amps) = 42p
Intramuscular high potency injection, vitamins B and C injection, strong, for intramuscular use. Net price 7 mL (in 2 amps) = 45p
Intravenous high potency injection, vitamins B and C injection, strong, for intravenous use. Net price 10 mL (in 2 amps) = 45p

PoM **Parentrovite®** (Bencard)
IMM Injection, vitamins B and C injection, weak, for intramuscular use. Net price 4 mL (in 2 amps) = 40p
IMHP Injection, vitamins B and C injection, strong, for intramuscular use. Net price 7 mL (in 2 amps) = 43p
IVHP Injection, vitamins B and C injection, strong, for intravenous use. Net price 10 mL (in 2 amps) = 43p

Oral vitamin B complex preparations, see below

RIBOFLAVINE

(Vitamin B_2)
Indications: see notes above

Preparations

Injections of vitamins B and C, see under Thiamine
Oral vitamin B complex preparations, see below

PYRIDOXINE HYDROCHLORIDE

(Vitamin B_6)
Indications: see under Dose
Cautions: **interactions:** Appendix 1 (vitamins)
Dose: deficiency states, 20–50 mg up to 3 times daily
Isoniazid neuropathy, prophylaxis 10 mg daily; therapeutic, 50 mg three times daily
Idiopathic sideroblastic anaemia, 100–400 mg daily in divided doses
Premenstrual syndrome, 50–100 mg daily (but see notes above)

Pyridoxine Tablets, pyridoxine hydrochloride 10 mg, net price 20 = 32p; 20 mg, 20 = 28p; 50 mg, 20 = 51p

NHS **Benadon®** (Roche)
Tablets, pyridoxine hydrochloride 20 mg. Net price 20 = 28p
Tablets, scored, pyridoxine hydrochloride 50 mg. Net price 20 = 28p

NHS **Comploment Continus®** (Napp)
Tablets, s/r, yellow, pyridoxine hydrochloride 100 mg. Net price 28-tab pack = £1.55. Label: 25

NHS **Paxadon®** (Mercury)
Tablets, scored, pyridoxine hydrochloride 50 mg. Net price 20 = 46p

Injections of vitamins B and C, see under Thiamine

NICOTINAMIDE

Indications: see notes above

Nicotinamide Tablets, nicotinamide 50 mg. Net price 20 = 18p

Injections of vitamins B and C, see under Thiamine

Oral vitamin B complex preparations, see below

NICOTINIC ACID

See section 2.12

FOLIC ACID

See section 9.1.2

FOLINIC ACID

See section 8.1.3

VITAMIN B_{12}

See section 9.1.2

ORAL VITAMIN B COMPLEX PREPARATIONS

Note. Other multivitamin preparations are in section 9.6.7.

Vitamin B Tablets, Compound, nicotinamide 15 mg, riboflavine 1 mg, thiamine hydrochloride 1 mg. Net price 20 = 7p
Dose: prophylactic, 1–2 tablets daily

Vitamin B Tablets, Compound, Strong, brown, f/c or s/c, nicotinamide 20 mg, pyridoxine hydrochloride 2 mg, riboflavine 2 mg, thiamine hydrochloride 5 mg. Net price 20 = 13p
Dose: treatment of vitamin-B deficiency, 1–2 tablets 3 times daily

NHS **Becosym®** (Roche)
Tablets, brown, f/c, vitamin B tablets, compound, strong. Net price 20 = 13p
Forte tablets, brown, f/c, thiamine hydrochloride 15 mg, riboflavine 15 mg, nicotinamide 50 mg, pyridoxine hydrochloride 10 mg. Net price 20 = 49p
Syrup, orange, thiamine hydrochloride 5 mg, riboflavine 2 mg, nicotinamide 20 mg, pyridoxine hydrochloride 2 mg/5 mL. Diluent syrup, life of diluted syrup 14 days. Net price 100 mL = 91p

NHS **Benerva Compound®** (Roche)
Tablets, yellow, vitamin B tablets, compound. Net price 20 = 9p

NHS **Vigranon B®** (Wallace Mfg)
Syrup, thiamine hydrochloride 5 mg, riboflavine 2 mg, nicotinamide 20 mg, pyridoxine hydrochloride 2 mg, panthenol 3 mg/5 mL. Net price 150 mL = £1.18

OTHER COMPOUNDS

Potassium aminobenzoate has been used in the treatment of various disorders associated with excessive fibrosis such as scleroderma but its therapeutic value is **doubtful**.

Potaba® (Glenwood)
Capsules, red/white, potassium aminobenzoate 500 mg. Net price 20 = 83p. Label: 21
Tablets, potassium aminobenzoate 500 mg. Net price 20 = 65p. Label: 21
Dose: Peyronie's disease, scleroderma, 12 g daily in divided doses after food
Envules® (= powder in sachets), potassium aminobenzoate 3 g. Net price 40 sachets = £10.01. Label: 13, 21

9.6.3 Vitamin C

(Ascorbic acid)

Vitamin C therapy is essential in scurvy, but less florid manifestations of vitamin C deficiency are commonly found, especially in the elderly. It is rarely necessary to prescribe more than 100 mg daily except early in the treatment of scurvy.

Claims that vitamin C ameliorates colds or promotes wound healing have not been proved.

ASCORBIC ACID

Indications: prevention and treatment of scurvy
Dose: prophylactic, 25–75 mg daily; therapeutic, not less than 250 mg daily in divided doses

Ascorbic Acid Tablets, ascorbic acid 25 mg, net price 20 = 6p; 50 mg, 20 = 6p; 100 mg, 20 = 23p; 200 mg, 20 = 24p; 500 mg (label: 24), 20 = 58p

PoM **Ascorbic Acid Injection,** ascorbic acid 100 mg/mL. Net price 5-mL amp = 65p

NHS **Redoxon®** (Roche)
Tablets, ascorbic acid 25 mg, net price 20 = 6p; 50 mg, 20 = 6p; 200 mg, 20 = 24p; 500 mg (label: 24), 50 = £1.45
Tablets, effervescent, ascorbic acid 1 g. Net price 10-tab pack = 75p. Label: 13

For children's welfare vitamin drops containing vitamin C with A and D, see vitamin A

9.6.4 Vitamin D

Note. The term Vitamin D is used for a range of compounds which possess the property of preventing or curing rickets. They include ergocalciferol (calciferol, vitamin D_2), cholecalciferol (vitamin D_3), dihydrotachysterol, alfacalcidol (1α-hydroxycholecalciferol), and calcitriol (1,25-dihydroxycholecalciferol). Calcitriol is considered to be the most active form of vitamin D, but ergocalciferol is suitable for most purposes.

Simple vitamin D *deficiency*, which is not uncommon in Asians consuming unleavened bread and in the elderly living alone, can be prevented by taking an oral supplement of only 10 micrograms (400 units) **calciferol** daily. Unfortunately there is no plain vitamin D tablet of this strength available. Some sources therefore use calcium and vitamin D tablets although the calcium in such preparations is unnecessary and better avoided.

Vitamin D deficiency caused by *intestinal malabsorption* or *chronic liver disease* usually requires pharmacological doses of up to 1 mg (40 000 units) daily. The hypocalcaemia of *hypoparathyroidism* often requires doses of up to 5 mg (200 000 units) daily in order to achieve normocalcaemia and **dihydrotachysterol** may be used as an alternative.

Alfacalcidol or **calcitriol** should be prescribed for functionally *anephric* patients; these preparations offer no advantages over calciferol in the treatment of simple vitamin D deficiency and offer few advantages in most other patients where pharmacological doses of vitamin D are required.

Important. All patients receiving pharmacological doses of vitamin D should have the plasma calcium concentration checked at intervals (initially weekly) and whenever nausea or vomiting are present. Breast milk from women taking pharmacological doses of vitamin D may cause hypercalcaemia if given to an infant.

ERGOCALCIFEROL

(Calciferol, Vitamin D_2)

Indications: see notes above

Cautions: take care to ensure correct dose in infants; monitor plasma calcium in patients receiving high doses

Contra-indications: hypercalcaemia

Side-effects: symptoms of overdosage include anorexia, lassitude, nausea and vomiting, diarrhoea, weight loss, polyuria, sweating, headache, thirst, vertigo, and raised concentrations of calcium and phosphate in plasma and urine

Daily supplements

Note. There is no vitamin D tablet available of the strength suitable for treating simple deficiency (see notes above). Alternatives include vitamins capsules (see 9.6.7), preparations of vitamins A and D (see 9.6.1), and calcium and ergocalciferol tablets (see below).

Calcium and Ergocalciferol Tablets[1] (Non-proprietary)

(Calcium and Vitamin D Tablets)

Tablets, calcium lactate 300 mg, calcium phosphate 150 mg (97 mg calcium or 2.4 mmol Ca^{2+}), ergocalciferol 10 micrograms (400 units). Net price 20 = 23p. Counselling, crush before administration or may be chewed

1. Calcium with Vitamin D Tablets (BPC) which contained ergocalciferol 12.5 micrograms (500 units) are being replaced by Calcium and Ergocalciferol Tablets

NHS **Chocovite**® (Torbet)

Tablets, brown, ergocalciferol 15 micrograms (600 units), calcium gluconate 500 mg. Net price 20 = 46p

Pharmacological strengths (see notes above)

Calciferol Tablets, BP

Important: it is essential to distinguish between the two strengths available which have different indications, see notes above

Tablets, cholecalciferol or ergocalciferol 250 micrograms (10 000 units), net price 20 = 45p; 1.25 mg (50 000 units), 20 = 59p

Note. The BP directs that when high-strength calciferol tablets are prescribed or demanded, tablets containing 250 micrograms shall be dispensed or supplied, and when strong calciferol tablets are prescribed or demanded it should be **confirmed** that tablets containing 1.25 mg are intended.

PoM **Calciferol Injection,** cholecalciferol or ergocalciferol, 7.5 mg (300 000 units)/mL in oil. Net price 1-mL amp = £2.58; 2-mL amp = £3.07

ALFACALCIDOL

(1α-Hydroxycholecalciferol)

Indications: see notes above

Cautions; Contra-indications; Side-effects: see under Ergocalciferol

Dose: see notes above and under preparations

PoM **One-alpha**® (Leo)

Capsules, alfacalcidol 250 nanograms, net price 20 = £2.42; 1 microgram (brown), 20 = £7.20

Solution, sugar-free, alfacalcidol 200 nanograms/mL. Net price 60 mL = £15.58 (with oral syringe)

Dose: ADULTS and CHILDREN over 20 kg, initially 1 microgram daily (elderly 500 nanograms), adjusted to avoid hypercalcaemia; maintenance 0.25–1 microgram daily; CHILD under 20 kg, initially 50 nanograms/kg daily; NEONATES and premature infants 50–100 nanograms/kg daily.

Note. This solution replaces the drops which were more concentrated and required dilution

CALCITRIOL

(1,25-Dihydroxycholecalciferol)

Indications: see notes above

Cautions; Contra-indications; Side-effects: see under Ergocalciferol

Dose: see notes above and under preparations

PoM **Rocaltrol**® (Roche)

Capsules, red/white, calcitriol 250 nanograms. Net price 20 = £3.92

Capsules, red, calcitriol 500 nanograms. Net price 20 = £7.01

Dose: initially 1–2 micrograms daily, gradually increased to 2–3 micrograms daily

CHOLECALCIFEROL

(Vitamin D_3)

Indications: see notes above

Cautions; Contra-indications; Side-effects: see under Ergocalciferol

Preparations

See under Ergocalciferol

DIHYDROTACHYSTEROL

Indications: see notes above

Cautions; Contra-indications; Side-effects: see under Ergocalciferol

Dose: see notes above and under preparations

AT 10® (Sterling-Winthrop)

Oral solution, dihydrotachysterol 250 micrograms/mL. Net price 15-mL dropper bottle = £19.84

Tachyrol® (Duphar)

Tablets, scored, dihydrotachysterol 200 micrograms. Net price 75 = £10.90

Dose: initially 200 micrograms daily, adjusted according to response

9.6.5 Vitamin E

(Tocopherols)

The daily requirement of vitamin E has not been well defined but is probably about 3 to 15 mg daily. There is little evidence that oral supplements of vitamin E are essential in adults, even where there is fat malabsorption secondary to cholestasis. In young children with congenital cholestasis, abnormally low vitamin E concentrations may be found in association with neuromuscular abnormalities, which usually respond only to the parenteral administration of vitamin E.

Vitamin E has been tried for various other conditions but there is no scientific evidence of its value. High doses have been associated with adverse effects.

ALPHA TOCOPHERYL ACETATE

Indications: see notes above

Ephynal® (Roche)

Suspension, alpha tocopheryl acetate 500 mg/5 mL. Net price 100 mL = £3.35

Dose: cystic fibrosis, 100–200 mg daily; CHILD under 1 year 50 mg daily; 1 year and over 100 mg daily

Abetalipoproteinaemia, ADULT and CHILD 50–100 mg/kg daily

Vita-E® (Bioglan)

Gels (= capsules), *d-α*-tocopheryl acetate 75 units (yellow), net price 20 = 55p; 200 units (yellow), 20 = £1.32; 400 units (red), 20 = £2.09

Gelucaps® (= tablets), chewable, yellow, *d-α*-tocopheryl acetate 75 units. Net price 20 = 67p. Label: 24

Succinate tablets, yellow, *d-α*-tocopheryl succinate 50 units, net price 20 = 46p; 200 units, 20 = £1.37

9.6.6 Vitamin K

Vitamin K is necessary for the production of blood clotting factors and proteins necessary for the normal calcification of bone.

Because vitamin K is fat soluble, patients with *fat malabsorption*, especially if due to biliary obstruction or hepatic disease, may become deficient. For oral administration to prevent vitamin-K deficiency in malabsorption syndromes, a water-soluble preparation, **menadiol sodium phosphate** must be used; the usual dose is about 10 mg daily.

In *neonates* deficiency of vitamin K may occur because the gut is sterile and there is no synthesis of the vitamin by *Escherichia coli*. It may be treated with **phytomenadione** (vitamin K_1), 1 mg by intramuscular injection.

Oral coumarin *anticoagulants* act by interfering with vitamin K metabolism in the hepatic cells and their effects can be antagonised by giving vitamin K; for British Society for Haematology Guidelines, see section 2.8.2.

MENADIOL SODIUM PHOSPHATE

Indications: Dose: see notes above

Cautions: pregnancy; **interactions:** Appendix 1 (vitamins)

Synkavit® (Roche)

Tablets, scored, menadiol sodium phosphate equivalent to 10 mg of menadiol phosphate. Net price 20 = 41p

PHYTOMENADIONE

(Vitamin K_1)

Indications; Dose: see notes above

Cautions: intravenous injections should be given very slowly; **interactions:** Appendix 1 (vitamins)

Konakion® (Roche)

Tablets, s/c, phytomenadione 10 mg. Net price 25 = £4.20. Label: 24

PoM *Injection*, phytomenadione 2 mg/mL, net price 0.5-mL amp = 22p; 10 mg/mL, 1-mL amp = 41p

Note. Contains polyethoxylated castor oil which has been associated with anaphylaxis

9.6.7 Multivitamin preparations

There are many preparations available. The proprietary preparations have no advantage over the non-proprietary preparations given separately and many are expensive. For children's vitamin drops available under the Welfare Food Scheme, see section 9.6.1

Vitamins Capsules, ascorbic acid 15 mg, nicotinamide 7.5 mg, riboflavine 500 micrograms, thiamine hydrochloride 1 mg, vitamin A 2500 units, vitamin D 300 units. Net price 20 = 18p

Abidec® (W-L)

NHS *Capsules*, vitamins A, B group, C, and D. Net price 20 = 30p

Drops, vitamins A, B group, C, and D. Net price 2 × 25 mL (with dropper) = £2.06

NHS **Allbee with C®** (Robins)

Capsules, yellow/green, vitamins B group and C. Net price 20 = £1.19

NHS **BC 500®** (Whitehall)

Tablets, orange, f/c, vitamins B group and C. Net price 30 = £1.27

NHS **Calcimax®** (Wallace Mfg)

Syrup, brown, vitamins B group, C, and D. Net price 150 mL = £1.41

NHS **Concavit®** (Wallace Mfg)

Capsules, vitamins A, B group, C, D, and E. Net price 20 = 93p

Drops and *syrup*, vitamins A, B group, C, and D. Net price drops 15 mL = £1.36; syrup 150 mL = £1.58

Dalivit® (Paines & Byrne)

NHS *Capsules*, red, vitamins A, B group, C, and D. Net price 20 = 31p

Oral drops, vitamins A, B group, C, and D. Net price 2 × 15 mL = £1.26

NHS **Minamino®** (Consolidated)

Syrup, vitamins B group, with amino acids, extracts of liver, spleen, and gastric mucosa, and minerals. Net price 100 mL = 56p

NHS **Orovite®** (Bencard)

Tablets, maroon, s/c, vitamins B group and C. Net price 25-tab pack = £1.33

Syrup, vitamins B group and C. Net price 200 mL = £1.48

NHS **Orovite 7®** (Bencard)
Granules, orange, vitamins A, B group, C, and D. Net price 30 × 5-g sachet = £3.11. Label: 13

NHS **Surbex T®** (Abbott)
Tablets, orange, vitamins B group and C. Net price 20 = 58p

VITAMIN SUPPLEMENTS FOR SYNTHETIC DIETS

Ketovite® (Paines & Byrne)
PoM *Tablets*, yellow, ascorbic acid 16.6 mg, riboflavine 1 mg, thiamine hydrochloride 1 mg, pyridoxine hydrochloride 330 micrograms, nicotinamide 3.3 mg, calcium pantothenate 1.16 mg, alpha tocopheryl acetate 5 mg, inositol 50 mg, biotin 170 micrograms, folic acid 250 micrograms, acetomenaphthone 500 micrograms. Net price 20 = 57p
Dose: prevention of deficiency in disorders of carbohydrate or amino acid metabolism, 1 tablet 3 times daily; with Ketovite® Liquid as vitamin supplement with synthetic diets
Liquid, pink, sugar-free, vitamin A 2500 units, ergocalciferol 400 units, choline chloride 150 mg, cyanocobalamin 12.5 micrograms/5 mL. Net price 100 mL = £1.78
Dose: prevention of deficiency in disorders of carbohydrate or amino acid metabolism, 5 mL daily; with Ketovite® Tablets as vitamin supplement with synthetic diets

Supplementary Vitamin Tablets for Infants (Cow & Gate)
Tablets, ferrous sulphate 4.21 mg (850 micrograms iron), folic acid 63 micrograms, thiamine hydrochloride 250 micrograms, nicotinamide 830 micrograms, riboflavine 250 micrograms, pyridoxine hydrochloride 83 micrograms, cyanocobalamin 1 microgram, ascorbic acid 10 mg, d-α-tocopheryl acetate 1.24 mg, acetomenaphthone 125 micrograms, biotin 8 micrograms, calcium pantothenate 500 micrograms, copper 34 micrograms (as sulphate), iodine 12 micrograms (as potassium iodate), manganese 5 micrograms (as sulphate), molybdenum 6 micrograms (as ammonium molybdate), zinc 620 micrograms (as sulphate). Contains sucrose. Net price 100 = £3.44
Note. For infants on nutritionally incomplete synthetic foods
Dose: consult manufacturer's literature

9.7 Bitters and tonics

Mixtures containing simple and aromatic bitters, such as alkaline gentian mixture, are traditional remedies for loss of appetite. All depend on suggestion.

Gentian Mixture, Acid, BP
Mixture, concentrated compound gentian infusion 10%, dilute hydrochloric acid 5% in a suitable vehicle. Extemporaneous preparations should be recently prepared according to the following formula: concentrated compound gentian infusion 1 mL, dilute hydrochloric acid 0.5 mL, double-strength chloroform water 5 mL, water to 10 mL

Gentian Mixture, Alkaline, BP
(Alkaline Gentian Oral Solution)
Mixture, concentrated compound gentian infusion 10%, sodium bicarbonate 5% in a suitable vehicle. Extemporaneous preparations should be recently prepared according to the following formula: concentrated compound gentian infusion 1 mL, sodium bicarbonate 500 mg, double-strength chloroform water 5 mL, water to 10 mL

NHS **Effico®** (Pharmax)
Tonic, green, thiamine hydrochloride 180 micrograms, nicotinamide 2.1 mg, caffeine 20.2 mg, compound gentian infusion 0.31 mL/5 mL. Net price 300 mL pack = £1.35

NHS **Fosfor®** (Consolidated)
Syrup, pink, phosphorylcolamine 5%. Net price 100 mL = 26p

NHS **Labiton®** (LAB)
Tonic, brown, thiamine hydrochloride 375 micrograms, caffeine 3.5 mg, kola nut dried extract 3.025 mg, alcohol 1.4 mL/5 mL. Net price 200 mL = £1.06

NHS **Metatone ®** (W-L)
Tonic, thiamine hydrochloride 500 micrograms, calcium glycerophosphate 45.6 mg, manganese glycerophosphate 5.7 mg, potassium glycerophosphate 45.6 mg, sodium glycerophosphate 22.8 mg/5 mL. Net price 300 mL = £1.29

9.8 Metabolic disorders

This section covers drugs used in metabolic disorders and not readily classified elsewhere.

9.8.1 Wilson's disease

Penicillamine (see also section 10.1.3) is used in Wilson's disease (hepatolenticular degeneration) to aid the elimination of copper ions. For use in copper and lead poisoning, see p. 21.

Trientine is used for the treatment of Wilson's disease only, in patients intolerant of penicillamine; it is **not** an alternative to penicillamine for rheumatoid arthritis or cystinuria.

PENICILLAMINE

Indications: see Dose below
Cautions; Contra-indications; Side-effects: see section 10.1.3
Dose: Wilson's disease, 1.5–2 g daily in divided doses before food; max. 2 g daily for 1 year; maintenance 0.75–1 g daily; ELDERLY, 20 mg/kg daily in divided doses; CHILD, up to 20 mg/kg daily in divided doses, min. 500 mg daily
Chronic active hepatitis (after disease is controlled), 500 mg daily in divided doses slowly increased over 3 months; usual maintenance dose 1.25 g daily
Cystinuria, therapeutic, 1–3 g daily in divided doses before food, adjusted to maintain urinary cystine below 200 mg/litre. Prophylactic (maintain urinary cystine below 300 mg/litre) 0.5–1 g at bedtime; maintain adequate fluid intake (at least 3 litres daily); CHILD minimum dose to maintain urinary cystine below 200 mg/litre

Preparations: see section 10.1.3

TRIENTINE DIHYDROCHLORIDE

Indications: Wilson's disease in patients intolerant of penicillamine

Cautions: see notes above; pregnancy; **interactions:** Appendix 1 (trientine)

Side-effects: nausea; penicillamine-induced systemic lupus erythematosus may not resolve on transfer to trientine

Dose: 1.2–2.4 g daily in 2–4 divided doses before food

▼ PoM **Trientine Dihydrochloride Capsules,** trientine dihydrochloride 300 mg. Label: 6, 22
Available from K & K Greeff

Note. The CSM has requested that in addition to the usual CSM reporting request special records should also be kept by the pharmacist

9.8.2 Acute porphyrias

The acute porphyrias (acute intermittent porphyria, variegate porphyria, hereditary coproporphyria and plumboporphyria) are hereditary disorders of haem biosynthesis; they have a prevalence of about 1 in 10 000 of the population.

Great care must be taken when prescribing for patients with acute porphyria since many drugs can induce acute porphyric crises. Since acute porphyrias are hereditary, relatives of affected individuals should be screened and advised about the potential danger of certain drugs.

The following list contains drugs on the UK market that have been classified as 'unsafe' in porphyria because they have been shown to be porphyrinogenic in animals or *in vitro*, or have been associated with acute attacks in patients.

Further information may be obtained from:

Porphyria Research Unit
Western Infirmary
Glasgow G11 6NT
Telephone 041-339 8822 Extn 4150

Drugs unsafe for use in acute porphyrias

Note. Quite modest changes in chemical structure can lead to changes in porphyrinogenicity but where possible general statements have been made about groups of drugs; these appear in bold print

Alcohol
Alcuronium
Aluminium-containing Antacids[1]
Aminoglutethimide
Amiodarone
Amphetamines
Anabolic Steroids
Antidepressants[2]
Antihistamines[3]
Azapropazone
Baclofen
Barbiturates[4]
Benzodiazepines[5]
Bromocriptine
Busulphan
Captopril
Carbamazepine
Carisoprodol
Cephalosporins
Chlorambucil
Chloramphenicol
Chlormezanone
Chloroform[6]
Clonidine
Cocaine
Colistin
Contraceptives, Steroid[7]
Danazol
Dapsone
Dextropropoxyphene[8]
Diclofenac
Diethylpropion
Diltiazem
Diuretics[9]
Doxycycline
Econazole
Enalapril
Enflurane
Ergot Derivatives[10]
Erythromycin
Ethamsylate
Ethionamide
Ethosuximide
Etomidate
Flucloxacillin
Flupenthixol
Gold salts
Griseofulvin
Guaiphenesin
Halothane
Hydralazine
Hyoscine Butylbromide
Isometheptene Mucate
Isoniazid
Ketoconazole
Lignocaine
Loxapine
Mebeverine
Mefenamic Acid
Menopausal steroids[7]
Meprobamate
Mercaptopurine
Mercury Compounds
Methotrexate
Methyldopa
Metoclopramide
Metronidazole
Metyrapone
Miconazole
Minoxidil
Nalidixic Acid
Natamycin
Nifedipine
Nikethamide
Nitrofurantoin
Orphenadrine
Oxycodone
Oxymetazoline
Oxyphenbutazone
Oxytetracycline
Pentazocine[8]
Phenoxybenzamine
Phenylbutazone
Phenytoin
Piroxicam
Pivampicillin[11]
Prilocaine
Probenecid
Progestogens
Pyrazinamide
Rifampicin
Simvastatin
Sulphinpyrazone
Sulphonamides[12]
Sulphonylureas[13]
Sulpiride
Tamoxifen
Theophylline
Thioridazine
Tinidazole
Trimethoprim
Valproate[5]
Verapamil
Viloxazine
Zuclopenthixol

1. Absorption limited but magnesium-containing antacids preferable.
2. Includes tricyclic (and related) and MAOIs.
3. Most antihistamines should be avoided but chlorpheniramine and cyclizine thought to be safe.
4. Includes methohexitone, primidone, and thiopentone.
5. Status epilepticus has been treated successfully with intravenous diazepam; where essential, seizure prophylaxis has been undertaken with clonazepam or valproate.
6. Small amounts in medicines probably safe.
7. Includes both progestogen-only and combined (progestogen content probably more hazardous than oestrogen).
8. Morphine, diamorphine, codeine, dihydrocodeine, and pethidine are thought to be safe.
9. Acetazolamide, amiloride, bumetanide, and triamterene have been used.
10. Includes ergometrine (oxytocin probably safe) and lysuride.
11. Ampicillin and amoxycillin probably safe.
12. Includes co-trimoxazole and sulphasalazine.
13. Glipizide has been used.

10: Drugs used in the treatment of MUSCULOSKELETAL and JOINT DISEASES

In this chapter, drug treatment is discussed under the following headings:

10.1 Drugs used in rheumatic diseases and gout
10.2 Drugs used in neuromuscular disorders
10.3 Drugs for the relief of soft-tissue inflammation

For treatment of septic arthritis see section 5.1, Table 1.

10.1 Drugs used in rheumatic diseases and gout

10.1.1 Non-steroidal anti-inflammatory drugs (NSAIDs)
10.1.2 Corticosteroids
10.1.3 Drugs which suppress the disease process
10.1.4 Drugs used in the treatment of gout

Most rheumatic diseases require symptomatic treatment to relieve pain and stiffness. This applies to inflammatory diseases both in the adult and in the juvenile age group (juvenile arthritis—Still's disease). Suitable non-steroidal anti-inflammatory drugs (NSAIDs) are described in section 10.1.1; reference should also be made to section 10.1.4 for the treatment of acute gout.

In certain circumstances corticosteroids (section 10.1.2) may be used to suppress inflammation.

Drugs are also available which may affect the disease process itself and favourably influence the outcome. For *rheumatoid arthritis* these include penicillamine, gold salts, antimalarials (chloroquine and hydroxychloroquine), immunosuppressants (azathioprine, chlorambucil, cyclophosphamide, and methotrexate), and sulphasalazine; they are sometimes known as second-line or disease-modifying antirheumatic drugs. For *psoriatic arthritis* they include gold salts, azathioprine, and methotrexate, and for *gout* they include uricosuric drugs and allopurinol.

10.1.1 Non-steroidal anti-inflammatory drugs (NSAIDs)

Non-steroidal anti-inflammatory drugs (NSAIDs) have two separate actions.

In *single doses* they have analgesic activity comparable to that of paracetamol (see section 4.7.1) and can therefore be taken on demand for mild or intermittent pain or as a supplement to regular treatment.

In regular *full dosage* they have both a lasting analgesic and an anti-inflammatory effect. This combination makes them particularly useful for the treatment of continuous or regular pain associated with inflammation. NSAIDs are, therefore, more appropriate than paracetamol or the opioid analgesics in the inflammatory arthritides (e.g. rheumatoid arthritis) and in advanced osteoarthrosis (also termed osteoarthritis). They may also be of benefit in the less well defined conditions of back pain and soft-tissue disorders.

Paracetamol, nefopam, and the opioid analgesics have no demonstrable anti-inflammatory activity and are therefore not included in this section (see instead 4.7.1).

CAUTIONS. NSAIDs should be used with caution in the *elderly*, in *allergic disorders* (particularly salicylate hypersensitivity and asthma, see **CSM warning** below), and during *pregnancy*.

In patients with *renal, cardiac, or hepatic impairment* caution is required since the use of NSAIDs may result in deterioration of renal function (see also under Side-effects, below); the dose should be kept as **low as possible** and renal function should be **monitored**.

NSAIDs should not be given to patients with *active peptic ulceration*, see also **CSM advice** below. While it is preferable to avoid them in patients with current or previous peptic ulceration, and to withdraw them if gastro-intestinal lesions develop, nevertheless patients with serious rheumatic diseases (e.g. rheumatoid arthritis) are usually dependent on NSAIDs for effective relief of pain and stiffness. Administration of histamine H_2-receptor blocking drugs or misoprostol (see section 1.3.4) may permit recommencement of a NSAID without further gastro-intestinal problems.

See also **interactions:** Appendix 1 (aspirin, NSAIDs) and under individual entries. Dosage of anticoagulants may need to be adjusted when anti-inflammatory analgesics are used; the risk of haemorrhage is greatest with aspirin or other salicylates.

CSM advice (peptic ulceration).
1. NSAIDs should not be given to patients with active peptic ulceration.
2. In patients with a history of peptic ulcer disease and in the elderly they should be given only after other forms of treatment have been carefully considered.
3. In all patients it is prudent to start at the bottom end of the dose range.

CSM warning (asthma).
Any degree of worsening of asthma may be related to the ingestion of NSAIDs, either prescribed or (in the case of ibuprofen and others) purchased over the counter.

SIDE-EFFECTS. Side-effects are variable in severity and frequency. Gastro-intestinal discomfort, nausea, diarrhoea, and occasionally bleeding and ulceration occur; dyspepsia may be minimised by taking these drugs with food or milk. Other side-effects include hypersensitivity reactions (particularly angioedema, asthma, and rashes), headache, dizziness, vertigo, and hearing disturbances such as tinnitus. Blood disorders have also occurred. Fluid retention may occur (rarely precipitating congestive heart failure in elderly patients). Reversible acute renal failure may be provoked by NSAIDs especially in patients with pre-existing renal impairment (**important**, see also under Cautions above). Rarely, papillary necrosis or interstitial fibrosis associated with NSAIDs may lead to chronic renal failure (analgesic nephropathy).

CHOICE. Differences in anti-inflammatory activity between different NSAIDs are small, but there is considerable variation in individual patient response. About 60% of patients will respond to any NSAID. Among the rest, those who do not respond to one may well respond to another. Therefore it is often necessary to try several drugs before finding one to suit a particular patient. Most NSAIDs should produce an effect within a few days. If used for analgesia alone they should be changed if no response is obtained after a week; if an anti-inflammatory action is also required they should be changed if no response is obtained after three weeks.

The main differences between NSAIDs are in the incidence and type of side-effects. Before treatment is started the prescriber should weigh efficacy against possible side-effects.

Aspirin[1] was the traditional first choice but most physicians now prefer to start treatment with other NSAIDs because they may be better tolerated and more convenient for the patient.

In regular high dosage aspirin has about the same anti-inflammatory effect as other NSAIDs. The required dose for active inflammatory joint disease is 3.6 g or more daily. There is little anti-inflammatory effect with less than 3 g daily. Gastro-intestinal side-effects such as nausea, dyspepsia, and gastro-intestinal bleeding may occur with any dosage of aspirin but anti-inflammatory doses are associated with a much higher incidence of side-effects. Gastro-intestinal side-effects may be minimised by taking the dose after food. Numerous formulations are available which improve gastric tolerance and minimise occult bleeding, including buffered, dispersible, and enteric-coated preparations.

Anti-inflammatory doses of aspirin may also cause mild chronic salicylate intoxication (salicylism) characterised by dizziness, tinnitus, and deafness; these symptoms may be controlled by reducing the dosage.

Benorylate[1], an aspirin-paracetamol ester, is broken down after absorption from the gastro-intestinal tract. It need only be given twice daily and gastric tolerance is slightly better than with aspirin. As it is more slowly absorbed than paracetamol, hepatotoxicity in overdosage may be reduced. Anti-inflammatory doses are achieved with 4 to 8 g daily.

Ibuprofen is a propionic acid derivative with anti-inflammatory, analgesic, and antipyretic properties. It has fewer side-effects than other NSAIDs but its anti-inflammatory properties are weaker. Doses of 1.6 to 2.4 g daily are needed for rheumatoid arthritis and it is unsuitable for conditions where inflammation is prominent such as acute gout.

Other propionic acid derivatives:

Naproxen has emerged as one of the first choices as it combines good efficacy with a low incidence of side-effects and administration is only twice daily.

Fenbufen is claimed to be associated with less gastro-intestinal bleeding, but there is a high risk of rashes (see p. 325).

Fenoprofen is as effective as naproxen, and **flurbiprofen** may be slightly more effective. Both are associated with slightly more gastro-intestinal side-effects than ibuprofen.

Ketoprofen has anti-inflammatory properties similar to ibuprofen and has more side-effects. A slow-release preparation is claimed to cause less gastro-intestinal irritation.

Tiaprofenic acid is as effective as naproxen; it has more side-effects than ibuprofen.

Drugs with properties similar to those of propionic acid derivatives:

Azapropazone is similar in effect to naproxen; it has a tendency to cause rashes.

Diclofenac has an action similar to that of naproxen; its side-effects are also similar. Diclofenac is also available as suppositories and as a sustained-release preparation.

Diflunisal is an aspirin derivative but its clinical effect more closely resembles that of the propionic acid derivatives than that of its parent compound. Its long duration of action allows twice-daily administration.

Etodolac is comparable in effect to naproxen; side-effects appear to be comparable to those of ibuprofen but long-term data are awaited.

Indomethacin has an action equal to or superior to that of naproxen, but with a high incidence of side-effects including headaches, dizziness, and gastro-intestinal disturbances. It can also be used for acute gout.

Mefenamic acid is a related analgesic but its anti-inflammatory properties are minor and side-effects differ in that diarrhoea and occasionally haemolytic anaemia may occur which necessitate discontinuation of treatment.

Nabumetone is comparable in effect to naproxen; side-effects appear to be comparable to those of ibuprofen but long-term data are awaited.

Phenylbutazone is a potent anti-inflammatory drug but because of occasional serious side-effects

1. Owing to an association with Reye's syndrome the CSM has recommended that aspirin-containing preparations should no longer be given to children under the age of 12 years, unless specifically indicated, e.g. for juvenile arthritis (Still's disease).

its use is limited to the hospital treatment of ankylosing spondylitis. In addition to its gastric side-effects it has two rare but dangerous side-effects. It causes fluid retention and, in predisposed patients, may precipitate cardiac failure. It also causes agranulocytosis (which may occur within the first few days of treatment) and aplastic anaemia. In ankylosing spondylitis prolonged administration may be necessary but it should not be used unless other drugs have been tried and have failed.

Piroxicam is as effective as naproxen and has a prolonged duration of action which permits once-daily administration. It has more gastro-intestinal side-effects than ibuprofen, especially in the elderly; suppositories or dispersible tablets are available.

Sulindac is similar in tolerance to naproxen.

Tenoxicam is similar in effectiveness and tolerance to naproxen. Its long half-life allows once-daily administration.

Tolmetin is comparable to ibuprofen.

ASPIRIN AND THE SALICYLATES

ASPIRIN

Indications: pain and inflammation in rheumatic disease and other musculoskeletal disorders (including juvenile arthritis); see also section 4.7.1; antiplatelet, see section 2.9

Cautions: asthma, allergic disease, hepatic or renal impairment (avoid if severe), dehydration, pregnancy (particularly at term), elderly, concurrent anticoagulant therapy; **interactions:** Appendix 1 (aspirin)

Contra-indications: gastro-intestinal ulceration; gout; children under 12 years (except for juvenile arthritis) and breast-feeding (association with Reye's syndrome, see section 4.7.1)

Side-effects: common with anti-inflammatory doses; gastro-intestinal discomfort, ulceration, bleeding, or nausea, hearing disturbances such as tinnitus (leading rarely to deafness), vertigo, mental confusion, hypersensitivity reactions (angioedema, bronchospasm and rashes); increased bleeding time; rarely oedema, myocarditis, blood disorders, particularly thrombocytopenia

Dose: 0.3–1 g every 4 hours; max. in acute conditions 8 g daily; CHILD, juvenile arthritis, up to 80 mg/kg daily in 5–6 divided doses, increased in acute exacerbations to 130 mg/kg. Doses should be taken after food

Aspirin (Non-proprietary)

Tablets, aspirin 300 mg. Net price 20 = 9p. Label: 21

Tablets, Dispersible, aspirin 300 mg. Net price 20 = 9p. Label: 13, 21

Note. Addendum 1989 to BP 1988 directs that when soluble aspirin tablets are prescribed, dispersible aspirin tablets will be dispensed.

Proprietary preparations

See section 4.7.1

BENORYLATE

(Aspirin-paracetamol ester; 2 g benorylate is equivalent to approximately 1.15 g aspirin and 970 mg paracetamol)

Indications: pain and inflammation in rheumatic disease and other musculoskeletal disorders; see also section 4.7.1

Cautions; Contra-indications; Side-effects: see under Aspirin (above) and Paracetamol (section 4.7.1). Patients should be advised against taking analgesics containing aspirin or paracetamol

Dose: 4–8 g daily divided into 2–3 doses

Benorylate (Non-proprietary)

Tablets, benorylate 750 mg. Net price 100 = £8.10. Label: 21, counselling, avoid aspirin, paracetamol

Suspension, benorylate 2 g/5 mL. Net price 100 mL = £3.80. Label: 21, counselling, avoid aspirin, paracetamol

Benoral® (Sterling-Winthrop)

Tablets, benorylate 750 mg. Net price 20 = £1.62. Label: 21, counselling, avoid aspirin, paracetamol

Granules, benorylate 2 g/sachet. Net price 60 sachet-pack = £14.12. Label: 13, 21, counselling, avoid aspirin, paracetamol

Suspension, sugar-free, benorylate 2 g/5 mL. Net price 150 mL = £5.73. Label: 21, counselling, avoid aspirin, paracetamol

---

SALICYLATE COMPOUNDS

Indications: pain and inflammation in rheumatic disease and other musculoskeletal disorders

Cautions; Contra-indications; Side-effects: see under Aspirin (above)

PoM **Disalcid®** (3M)

Capsules, orange/grey, salsalate 500 mg, net price 120-cap pack = £6.88. Label: 12, 21

Dose: 2–4 g daily in 3–4 divided doses

Trilisate® (Napp)

Tablets, orange, scored, choline magnesium trisalicylate ≡ salicylate 500 mg, net price 60-tab pack = £4.95. Label: 12, 21

Dose: 0.5–1.5 g of salicylate twice daily; for maintenance, total daily dose may be taken once daily

---

OTHER NSAIDs

IBUPROFEN

Indications: pain and inflammation in rheumatic disease (including juvenile arthritis) and other musculoskeletal disorders; see also section 4.7.1

Cautions; Side-effects: see notes above; **interactions:** Appendix 1 (NSAIDs)

Dose: initially 1.2–1.8 g daily in 3–4 divided doses preferably after food; increased if necessary to max. of 2.4 g daily; maintenance dose of 0.6–1.2 g daily may be adequate; CHILD 20 mg/kg daily in divided doses (juvenile arthritis, up to 40 mg/kg daily), children under 30 kg max. in 24 hours 500 mg

PoM **Ibuprofen** (Non-proprietary)
Tablets, coated, ibuprofen 200 mg, net price 20 = 26p; 400 mg, 20 = 51p; 600 mg, 20 = £1.36. Label: 21
Various strengths available from APS (Apsifen®), Berk (Lidifen®), Cox, DDSA (Ebufac®), Evans, Kerfoot, Lagap (Ibular®), Mercury (Paxofen®), Upjohn (Motrin®)
Note. Proprietary brands of ibuprofen tablets are on sale to the public; brand names include Contrapain Femafen®, Cuprofen®, Ibrufhalal®, Inoven®, Migrafen®, Nurofen®, Pacifene®, Proflex®, Relcofen®, Seclodin®

PoM **Brufen®** (Boots)
Tablets, both magenta, s/c, ibuprofen 200 mg, net price 20 = 61p; 400 mg, 20 = £1.21. Label: 21
Tablets, magenta, f/c, ibuprofen 600 mg. Net price 20 = £1.93. Label: 21
Syrup, orange, ibuprofen 100 mg/5 mL. Diluent syrup, life of diluted syrup 14 days. Net price 200 mL = £1.54. Label: 21

PoM **Fenbid®** (SK&F)
Spansule® (= capsule s/r), maroon/pink, enclosing off-white pellets, ibuprofen 300 mg. Net price 120-cap pack = £7.14. Label: 25
Dose: 1–3 capsules every 12 hours

PoM **Junifen®** : see section 4.7.1

AZAPROPAZONE

Indications: pain and inflammation in rheumatic disease and other musculoskeletal disorders; gout
Cautions; Side-effects: see notes above; photosensitivity may occur. Avoid in porphyria; **interactions:** Appendix 1 (NSAIDs)
Dose: 1.2 g daily in 2 or 4 divided doses (elderly 300 mg twice daily, max. 900 mg daily)
Acute gout, initially 2.4 g in divided doses over 24 hours, then 1.8 g reducing to 1.2 g daily in divided doses
Chronic gout, 600 mg twice daily (elderly 300 mg twice daily, max. 900 mg daily)

PoM **Rheumox®** (Wyeth)
Capsules, orange, azapropazone 300 mg. Net price 20 = £3.06. Label: 21, counselling: in some patients direct sunlight may lead to a rash
Tablets, orange, f/c, scored, azapropazone 600 mg. Net price 20 = £5.85. Label: 21, counselling: in some patients direct sunlight may lead to a rash

DICLOFENAC SODIUM

Indications: pain and inflammation in rheumatic disease (including juvenile arthritis) and other musculoskeletal disorders; acute gout
Cautions; Side-effects: see notes above. Avoid in porphyria; pain may occur at the injection site; suppositories may cause irritation; **interactions:** Appendix 1 (NSAIDs)
Dose: by mouth, 75–150 mg daily in 2–3 divided doses, preferably after food
By deep intramuscular injection acute exacerbations and post-operative, 75 mg once daily (twice daily in severe cases) for max. of 2 days
Ureteric colic, 75 mg then a further 75 mg after 30 minutes if necessary
By rectum in suppositories, 100 mg, usually at night
Max. total daily dose by any route 150 mg
CHILD 1 year or over, juvenile arthritis, *by mouth or by rectum*, 1–3 mg/kg daily in divided doses

PoM **Diclofenac Sodium** (Non-proprietary)
Tablets, both e/c, diclofenac sodium 25 mg, net price 20 = £1.88; 50 mg, 20 = £3.65. Label: 5, 25
Available from APS, Cox, Kerfoot, Lagap, (Rhumalgan®), Shire (Valenac®), Eastern (Volraman®)

PoM **Voltarol®** (Geigy)
Tablets, both e/c, diclofenac sodium 25 mg (yellow), net price 20 = £1.88; 50 mg (brown), 20 = £3.65. Label: 5, 25
Dispersible tablets, pink, diclofenac, equivalent to diclofenac sodium 50 mg, net price 21-tab pack = £4.68. Label: 13, 21
Injection, diclofenac sodium 25 mg/mL. Net price 3-mL amp = 79p
Suppositories, diclofenac sodium 100 mg. Net price 10 = £3.11
Paediatric suppositories, diclofenac sodium 12.5 mg. Net price 10 = 59p

PoM **Voltarol Retard®** (Geigy)
Tablets, s/r, red, diclofenac sodium 100 mg. Net price 28-tab pack = £12.49. Label: 21, 25
Dose: 100 mg once daily preferably with food

DIFLUNISAL

Indications: pain and inflammation in rheumatic disease and other musculoskeletal disorders; see also section 4.7.1
Cautions; Side-effects: see notes above; breast-feeding; **interactions:** Appendix 1 (NSAIDs)
Dose: initially 1 g daily in 2 divided doses, then 0.5–1 g daily; max. 1.5 g daily
Osteoarthrosis, rheumatoid arthritis, 0.5–1 g daily as a single daily dose *or* in 2 divided doses

PoM **Dolobid®** (Morson)
Tablets, both f/c, diflunisal 250 mg (peach), net price 20 = £1.80; 500 mg (orange), 20 = £3.61. Label: 21, 25, counselling, avoid aluminium hydroxide

ETODOLAC

Indications: pain and inflammation in rheumatoid arthritis and osteoarthrosis
Cautions; Side-effects: see notes above; **interactions:** Appendix 1 (NSAIDs)
Dose: 200 mg or 300 mg twice daily *or* 400 mg or 600 mg once daily; max. 600 mg daily

PoM **Lodine®** (Wyeth)
Capsules, etodolac 200 mg (light- and dark-grey), net price 20 = £4.78; 300 mg (light-grey), 60-cap pack = £19.87. Label: 21
Tablets, brown, f/c, etodolac 200 mg. Net price 20 = £4.78. Label: 21

FENBUFEN

Indications: pain and inflammation in rheumatic disease and other musculoskeletal disorders
Cautions; Side-effects: see notes above, but high risk of rashes (discontinue immediately); erythema multiforme and Stevens-Johnson syndrome reported; also allergic interstitial lung disorders (may follow rashes); **interactions:** Appendix 1 (NSAIDs)
Dose: 300 mg in the morning and 600 mg at bedtime *or* 450 mg twice daily

PoM **Lederfen®** (Lederle)
Capsules, dark blue, fenbufen 300 mg. Net price 84-cap pack = £17.67. Label: 21
Tablets, both light blue, f/c, fenbufen 300 mg, net price 84-tab pack = £17.67; 450 mg, 56-tab pack = £17.67. Label: 21
PoM **Lederfen F®** (Lederle)
Effervescent tablets, fenbufen 450 mg. Net price 14-tab pack = £5.60. Label: 13, 21

FENOPROFEN

Indications: pain and inflammation in rheumatic disease and other musculoskeletal disorders; see also section 4.7.1
Cautions; Side-effects: see notes above; **interactions:** Appendix 1 (NSAIDs)
Dose: 300–600 mg 3–4 times daily with food; max. 3 g daily

PoM **Fenopron 300®** (Dista)
Tablets, orange, fenoprofen 300 mg (as calcium salt). Net price 20 = £2.30. Label: 21
PoM **Fenopron 600®** (Dista)
Tablets, orange, scored, fenoprofen 600 mg (as calcium salt). Net price 20 = £4.46. Label: 21
PoM **Progesic®**: see section 4.7.1

FLURBIPROFEN

Indications: pain and inflammation in rheumatoid arthritis, osteoarthrosis, and ankylosing spondylitis
Cautions; Side-effects: see notes above; local irritation on rectal administration; **interactions:** Appendix 1 (NSAIDs)
Dose: *by mouth or rectum* 150–200 mg, daily in divided doses, increased in acute conditions to 300 mg daily

PoM **Froben®** (Boots)
Tablets, both yellow, s/c, flurbiprofen 50 mg, net price 20 = £1.77; 100 mg, 20 = £3.54. Label: 21
Suppositories, flurbiprofen 100 mg. Net price 12 = £2.90
PoM **Froben SR®** (Boots)
Capsules, s/r, yellow, enclosing white, off-white beads, flurbiprofen 200 mg. Net price 30-cap pack = £12.80. Label: 21, 25
Dose: 1 capsule daily, preferably in the evening

INDOMETHACIN

Indications: pain and moderate to severe inflammation in rheumatic disease and other acute musculoskeletal disorders; acute gout; dysmenorrhoea
Cautions: see notes above; breast-feeding, epilepsy, parkinsonism, psychiatric disturbances; during prolonged therapy ophthalmic and blood examinations are particularly advisable; avoid rectal administration in proctitis and haemorrhoids; **interactions:** Appendix 1 (NSAIDs)

DRIVING. Dizziness may affect performance of skilled tasks (e.g. driving)

Side-effects: see notes above; frequently gastro-intestinal disturbances (including diarrhoea), headache, dizziness, and light-headedness; gastro-intestinal ulceration and bleeding; rarely, drowsiness, confusion, insomnia, convulsions, psychiatric disturbances, depression, syncope, blood disorders (particularly thrombocytopenia), hypertension, hyperglycaemia, blurred vision, corneal deposits, peripheral neuropathy. On rectal administration pruritus, discomfort, bleeding
Dose: *by mouth*, 50–200 mg daily in divided doses, with food
Dysmenorrhoea, up to 75 mg daily
By rectum in suppositories, 100 mg at night and in the morning if required
Combined oral and rectal treatment, max. total daily dose 150–200 mg

PoM **Indomethacin** (Non-proprietary)
Capsules, indomethacin 25 mg, net price 20 = 18p; 50 mg, 20 = 55p. Label: 21, counselling, driving, see above
Available from APS, Berk (Imbrilon®), Cox, DDSA (Artracin®), Evans, Galen (Mobilan®), Kerfoot
Suppositories, indomethacin 100 mg. Net price 10 = £1.83. Counselling, driving, see above
Available from Berk (Imbrilon®), Cox, Evans
PoM **Flexin Continus®** (Napp)
Tablets, s/r yellow, scored, indomethacin 75 mg. Net price 28-tab pack = £10.47. Label: 21, 25, counselling, driving, see above
Dose: 1 tablet once or twice daily
PoM **Indocid®** (Morson)
Capsules, indomethacin 25 mg, net price 20 = 99p; 50 mg, 20 = £1.78. Label: 21, counselling, driving, see above
Suspension, sugar-free, indomethacin 25 mg/5 mL. Net price 200 mL = £3.12. Label: 21, counselling, driving, see above
Suppositories, indomethacin 100 mg. Net price 10 = £2.43. Counselling, driving, see above
PoM **Indocid-R®** (Morson)
Capsules, s/r, ivory/clear, enclosing white and blue pellets, indomethacin 75 mg. Net price 20 = £5.71. Label: 21, 25, counselling, driving, see above
Dose: 1–2 capsules daily

PoM **Indolar SR®** (Lagap)
Capsules, s/r, blue/clear, enclosing white pellets, indomethacin 75 mg. Net price 20 = £4.02. Label: 21, 25, counselling, driving, see above
Dose: 1 capsule 1–2 times daily

PoM **Indomod®** (Pharmacia)
Capsules, both s/r, enclosing e/c pellets, indomethacin 25 mg (orange), net price 20 = £2.24; 75 mg (brown), 20 = £7.00. Label: 25, counselling, driving, see above

PoM **Rheumacin LA®** (CP)
Capsules, s/r, yellow/blue, enclosing off-white pellets, indomethacin 75 mg. Net price 20 = £2.85. Label: 21, 25, counselling, driving, see above
Dose: 1–2 capsules daily

PoM **Slo-Indo®** (Generics)
Capsules, s/r, red/yellow enclosing off-white pellets, indomethacin 75 mg. Net price 20 = £4.47. Label: 21, 25, counselling, driving, see above
Dose: 1–2 capsules daily

PoM **Indocid PDA®** : see section 7.1.1

KETOPROFEN

Indications: pain and mild inflammation in rheumatic disease and other musculoskeletal disorders; acute gout; dysmenorrhoea
Cautions; Side-effects: see notes above; suppositories may cause rectal irritation; **interactions:** Appendix 1 (NSAIDs)
Dose: *by mouth*, 100–200 mg daily in 2–4 divided doses with food
By rectum in suppositories, 100 mg at bedtime
Combined oral and rectal treatment, max. total daily dose 200 mg
By deep intramuscular injection, 50–100 mg every 4 hours (max. 200 mg in 24 hours) for up to 3 days

PoM **Ketoprofen** (Non-proprietary)
Capsules, ketoprofen 50 mg, net price 20 = £1.05; 100 mg, 20 = £2.89. Label: 21

PoM **Alrheumat®** (Bayer)
Capsules, off-white, ketoprofen 50 mg. Net price 20 = £1.22. Label: 21

PoM **Orudis®** (Rhône-Poulenc Rorer)
Capsules, ketoprofen 50 mg (green/purple), net price 112-cap pack = £8.07; 100 mg (pink), 56-cap pack = £8.09. Label: 21
Suppositories, ketoprofen 100 mg. Net price 10 = £3.54

PoM **Oruvail®** (Rhône-Poulenc Rorer)
Capsules, both s/r, enclosing white pellets, ketoprofen 100 mg (pink/purple), net price 56-cap pack = £16.14; 200 mg (pink/white), 28-cap pack = £16.14. Label: 21, 25
Dose: 100–200 mg once daily with food
Injection, ketoprofen 50 mg/mL. Net price 2-mL amp = 75p

MEFENAMIC ACID

Indications: mild to moderate pain in rheumatoid arthritis (including juvenile arthritis), osteoarthrosis, and related conditions; see also section 4.7.1
Cautions: see notes above; blood tests required during long-term treatment; **interactions:** Appendix 1 (NSAIDs)
Side-effects: see notes above; drowsiness; diarrhoea or rashes (withdraw treatment); thrombocytopenia, haemolytic anaemia; convulsions in overdosage
Dose: 500 mg 3 times daily preferably after food; CHILD over 6 months, 25 mg/kg daily in divided doses for not longer than 7 days, except in juvenile arthritis

PoM **Mefenamic Acid** (Non-proprietary)
Capsules, mefenamic acid 250 mg. Net price 20 = £1.32. Label: 21
Available from APS, Cox, Kerfoot
Tablets, mefenamic acid 500 mg, net price 20 = £2.44. Label: 21
Available from Ashbourne (Dysman Forte®), Cox, Kerfoot

PoM **Ponstan®** (P-D)
Capsules, ivory/blue, mefenamic acid 250 mg. Net price 20 = £1.51. Label: 21
Tablets forte, yellow, f/c, mefenamic acid 500 mg. Net price 20 = £2.76. Label: 21
Paediatric suspension, mefenamic acid 50 mg/5 mL. Diluent syrup, life of diluted suspension 14 days. Net price 125 mL = £3.37. Label: 21

PoM **Ponstan Dispersible®** (P-D)
Dispersible tablets, blue, mefenamic acid 250 mg. Net price 20 = £1.71. Label: 13, 21

NABUMETONE

Indications: pain and inflammation in osteoarthrosis and rheumatoid arthritis
Cautions; Side-effects: see notes above; **interactions:** Appendix 1 (NSAIDs)
Dose: 1 g at night, in severe conditions 0.5–1 g in morning as well; elderly 0.5–1 g daily

PoM **Relifex®** (Bencard)
Tablets, red, f/c, nabumetone 500 mg. Net price 56-tab pack = £15.68. Label: 21, 25
Suspension, nabumetone 500 mg/5 mL. Net price 300 mL = £21.84. Label: 21

NAPROXEN

Indications: pain and inflammation in rheumatic disease (including juvenile arthritis) and other musculoskeletal disorders; acute gout; see also Naproxen Sodium, section 4.7.1
Cautions; Side-effects: see notes above; **interactions:** Appendix 1 (NSAIDs)
Dose: *by mouth*, 0.5–1 g daily in 2 divided doses *or* 1 g once daily; CHILD (over 5 years), juvenile arthritis, 10 mg/kg daily in 2 divided doses
Acute musculoskeletal disorders, 500 mg initially, then 250 mg every 6–8 hours as required; max. dose after first day 1.25 g daily
Acute gout, 750 mg initially, then 250 mg every 8 hours until attack has passed
By rectum in suppositories, 500 mg at bedtime; if necessary 500 mg in morning as well

PoM **Naproxen** (Non-proprietary)
Tablets, naproxen 250 mg, net price 20 = £1.65; 500 mg, 20 = £3.30. Label: 21
Available from Cox, CP (Arthroxen®), Evans, Kerfoot, Lagap (Laraflex®), Shire (Valrox®)

PoM **Naprosyn®** (Syntex)
Tablets, all scored, naproxen 250 mg (buff), net price 20 = £2.50; 375 mg (pink), 60-tab pack = £11.25; 500 mg (buff), 60-tab pack = £14.98. Label: 21
Suspension, orange, naproxen 125 mg/5 mL. Diluent water or equal quantities of syrup and water, life of diluted suspension 14 days. Net price 100 mL = £1.65. Label: 21
Granules, naproxen 500 mg/sachet. Net price 60 sachets = £19.47. Label: 13, 21
Suppositories, naproxen 500 mg. Net price 10 = £2.96

PoM **Nycopren®** (Lundbeck)
Tablets, both e/c, naproxen 250 mg (scored), net price 20 = £2.07; 500 mg, 60-tab pack = £12.41. Label: 5, 25

PoM **Synflex®** : see section 4.7.1

PHENYLBUTAZONE

Indications: ankylosing spondylitis (in hospital)
Cautions: blood counts before and during treatment if for more than 7 days; elderly (reduce dose); breast-feeding; withdraw treatment if acute pulmonary syndrome including fever and dyspnoea occurs; see also notes above; **interactions:** Appendix 1 (NSAIDs)
Contra-indications: cardiovascular disease, renal and hepatic impairment; pregnancy; history of peptic ulceration, gastro-intestinal haemorrhage, or blood disorders; porphyria; thyroid disease; children under 14
Side-effects: see notes above; parotitis, stomatitis, goitre, pancreatitis, hepatitis, nephritis, visual disturbances; rarely leucopenia, thrombocytopenia, agranulocytosis, aplastic anaemia, erythema multiforme, toxic epidermal necrolysis
Dose: initially 200 mg 2–3 times daily for 2 days, with or after food, then reduced to minimum effective, usually 100 mg 2–3 times daily
Not for children under 14 years

PoM **Butacote®** (Geigy)
Tablets, violet, e/c, s/c, phenylbutazone 100 mg, net price 20 = 40p. Label: 5, 21, 25

PIROXICAM

Indications: pain and inflammation in rheumatic disease (including juvenile arthritis) and other musculoskeletal disorders; acute gout
Cautions: see notes above; **interactions:** Appendix 1 (NSAIDs)
Side-effects: see notes above
Dose: initially 20 mg daily, maintenance 10–30 mg daily, in single or divided doses
CHILD (over 6 years), juvenile arthritis, less than 15 kg, 5 mg daily; 16–25 kg, 10 mg; 26–45 kg, 15 mg; over 46 kg, 20 mg
Acute musculoskeletal disorders, 40 mg daily in single or divided doses for 2 days, then 20 mg daily for 7–14 days
Acute gout, 40 mg initially, then 40 mg daily in single or divided doses for 4–6 days

PoM **Piroxicam** (Non-proprietary)
Capsules, piroxicam 10 mg, net price 20 = £2.90; 20 mg, 20 = £5.80. Label: 21
Available from APS, Cox, Evans, Kerfoot, Lagap (Larapam®)

PoM **Feldene®** (Pfizer)
Capsules, piroxicam 10 mg (maroon/blue), net price 56-cap pack = £8.87; 20 mg (maroon), 28-cap pack = £8.87. Label: 21
Dispersible tablets, piroxicam 10 mg (scored), net price 56-tab pack = £9.75; 20 mg, 28-tab pack = £9.75. Label: 13, 21
Suppositories, piroxicam 20 mg. Net price 10 = £5.20
Gel, section 10.3.2

SULINDAC

Indications: pain and inflammation in rheumatic disease and other musculoskeletal disorders; acute gout
Cautions; Side-effects: see notes above; caution if history of renal stones; ensure adequate hydration; **interactions:** Appendix 1 (NSAIDs)
Dose: 200 mg twice daily with food (may be reduced according to response); max. 400 mg daily; acute gout should respond within 7 days; limit treatment of peri-articular disorders to 7–10 days

PoM **Sulindac** (Non-proprietary)
Tablets, sulindac 100 mg, net price 20 = £2.24; 200 mg, 20 = £4.11. Label: 21

PoM **Clinoril®** (MSD)
Tablets, both yellow, scored, sulindac 100 mg, net price 20 = £2.24; 200 mg, 20 = £4.11. Label: 21

TENOXICAM

Indications: pain and inflammation in rheumatoid arthritis and osteoarthrosis
Cautions; Side-effects: see notes above; **interactions:** Appendix 1 (NSAIDs)
Dose: 20 mg daily

PoM **Mobiflex®** (Roche)
Tablets, red-brown, f/c, tenoxicam 20 mg. Net price 28-tab pack = £16.52. Label: 21

TIAPROFENIC ACID

Indications: pain and inflammation in rheumatic disease and other musculoskeletal disorders
Cautions; Side-effects: see notes above; bladder irritation and haematuria reported; **interactions:** Appendix 1 (NSAIDs)
Dose: 600 mg daily in 2–3 divided doses

PoM **Surgam®** (Roussel)
Tablets, tiaprofenic acid 200 mg, net price 84-tab pack = £13.77; 300mg, 56-tab pack = £15.13. Label: 21
Granules, off-white, tiaprofenic acid 300 mg/sachet. Net price 60 = £15.44. Label: 13, 21

PoM **Surgam SA®** (Roussel)
Capsules, s/r, maroon/pink enclosing white pellets, tiaprofenic acid 300 mg. Net price 56-cap pack = £15.13. Label: 21, 25
Dose: 2 capsules once daily

TOLMETIN

Indications: pain and inflammation in rheumatic disease (including juvenile arthritis) and other musculoskeletal disorders

Cautions; Side-effects: see notes above; **interactions:** Appendix 1 (NSAIDs)

Dose: 0.6–1.8 g daily in 2–4 divided doses; max. 30 mg/kg daily up to 1.8 g

CHILD, juvenile arthritis, 20–25 mg/kg daily in 3–4 divided doses; max. 30 mg/kg daily up to 1.8 g

PoM **Tolectin®** (Cilag)

Capsules, tolmetin (as sodium salt) 200 mg (ivory/orange), net price 90-cap pack = £14.95; 400 mg (orange), 90-cap pack = £22.44. Label: 21

10.1.2 Corticosteroids

10.1.2.1 Systemic corticosteroids
10.1.2.2 Local corticosteroid injections

10.1.2.1 SYSTEMIC CORTICOSTEROIDS

The general actions and uses of the corticosteroids are described in section 6.3. Treatment with corticosteroids in rheumatic diseases should be reserved for specific indications, e.g. when other anti-inflammatory drugs unsuccessful.

In severe, possibly life-threatening, situations a high initial dose of corticosteroid is given to induce remission and the dose then gradually reduced to the lowest maintenance dose that will control the disease or, if possible, discontinued altogether. A major problem is that relapse may occur as dosage reduction is made, particularly if this is carried out too rapidly. The tendency is therefore to increase and maintain dosage and consequently the patient becomes dependent on corticosteroids. For this reason pulse doses of corticosteroids (e.g. methylprednisolone up to 1 g intravenously on three consecutive days) is in current use to suppress highly active inflammatory disease while longer term and slower acting medication is being commenced.

Prednisolone is used for most purposes; it has the advantage over the more potent corticosteroids (see section 6.3.2) of permitting finer dosage adjustments. To minimise side-effects the maintenance dose of prednisolone should be kept as low as possible, usually 7.5 mg daily and seldom exceeding 10 mg daily.

Polymyalgia rheumatica and *temporal (giant cell) arteritis* are always treated with corticosteroids. The usual initial dose of prednisolone in polymyalgia rheumatica is 10 to 15 mg daily and in temporal arteritis 40 to 60 mg daily (the higher dose being used if visual symptoms occur). Treatment should be continued until remission occurs and doses then gradually reduced. Relapse is common if therapy is stopped within 3 years but most patients can discontinue treatment after approximately 3 to 6 years after which recurrences become rare.

Polyarteritis nodosa and *polymyositis* are usually treated with corticosteroids. An initial dose of 60 mg of prednisolone daily is often used and reduced to a maintenance dose of 10 to 15 mg daily.

Systemic lupus erythematosus is treated with corticosteroids when necessary using a similar dosage regimen to that for polyarteritis nodosa and polymyositis (above). Patients with pleurisy, pericarditis, or other systemic manifestations will respond to corticosteroids. It may then be possible to reduce the dosage; alternate-day treatment is sometimes adequate, and the drug may be gradually withdrawn. In some mild cases corticosteroid treatment may be stopped after a few months. Many mild cases of systemic lupus erythematosus do not require corticosteroid treatment. Alternative treatment with anti-inflammatory analgesics, and possibly chloroquine, should be considered.

Since effective doses of systemic corticosteroids may cause Cushing's syndrome these drugs should **not** be used to suppress symptoms of *rheumatoid arthritis* unless alternative anti-inflammatory drugs and drugs which may affect the disease process (section 10.1.3) have proved unsuccessful, with increasing disability due to the inflammatory process. The smallest effective dose should be used and increased if necessary, but should not exceed the equivalent of prednisolone 7.5 to 10 mg daily. Attempts should always be made gradually to reduce the dose. Corticosteroids in low dosage may be useful in the elderly patient, and similar nocturnal doses may relieve morning stiffness.

Ankylosing spondylitis should not be treated with long-term corticosteroids; rarely, pulse doses may be needed and may be useful in extremely active disease that does not respond to conventional treatment.

10.1.2.2 LOCAL CORTICOSTEROID INJECTIONS

Corticosteroids are injected locally for an anti-inflammatory effect. In inflammatory conditions of the joints, particularly in rheumatoid arthritis, they are given by *intra-articular injection* to relieve pain, increase mobility, and reduce deformity in one or a few joints. Full aseptic precautions are essential. Infected areas should be avoided. An almost insoluble, long-acting compound such as triamcinolone hexacetonide is preferred for intra-articular injection.

Smaller amounts of corticosteroids may also be injected directly into soft tissues for the relief of inflammation in conditions such as *tennis* or *golfer's elbow* or *compression neuropathies*. In *tendinitis*, injections should be made into the tendon sheath and not directly into the tendon. A soluble, short-acting compound such as betamethasone is preferred for injection into the carpal tunnel.

Cortisone acetate is **not** effective for local injection and hydrocortisone acetate or one of the synthetic analogues such as triamcinolone hexacetonide is generally used. The risk of necrosis and muscle wasting may be slightly increased with triamcinolone; flushing has been reported with intra-articular corticosteroid injections.

Corticosteroid injections are also injected into soft tissues for the treatment of skin lesions (see section 13.4).

DEXAMETHASONE SODIUM PHOSPHATE

Indications: local inflammation of joints and soft tissues

Cautions; Contra-indications; Side-effects: see notes above and section 6.3.3

Dose: by intra-articular, intralesional, or soft-tissue injection, dexamethasone 0.4–4 mg, according to size of joint or amount of soft-tissue, at intervals of 3–21 days according to response

Note. 1.3 mg dexamethasone sodium phosphate ≡ 1.2 mg dexamethasone phosphate ≡ 1 mg dexamethasone

PoM **Dexamethasone** (Organon)
Injection, dexamethasone sodium phosphate 5 mg/mL (= 4 mg dexamethasone/mL). Net price 1-mL amp = 83p; 2-mL vial = £1.27

PoM **Decadron®** (MSD)
Injection, dexamethasone phosphate 4 mg/mL (as sodium salt) (≡ 3.33 mg/mL dexamethasone). Net price 2-mL vial = £1.76

HYDROCORTISONE ACETATE

Indications: local inflammation of joints and soft tissues

Cautions; Contra-indications; Side-effects: see notes above and section 6.3.3

Dose: by intra-articular, intrasynovial, or soft-tissue injection, 5–50 mg, according to joint size or amount of soft tissue; not more than 3 joints should be treated on any one day; CHILD, 5–30 mg daily (divided)

PoM **Hydrocortisone Acetate Injection** (aqueous suspension), hydrocortisone acetate 25 mg/mL. Net price 1-mL amp = 80p

PoM **Hydrocortistab®** (Boots)
Injection (aqueous suspension), hydrocortisone acetate 25 mg/mL. Net price 1-mL amp = 80p

METHYLPREDNISOLONE ACETATE

Indications: local inflammation of joints and soft-tissues

Cautions; Contra-indications; Side-effects: see notes above and section 6.3.3

Dose: by intra-articular, intrasynovial, intralesional, or soft-tissue injection, 4–80 mg, according to joint size or amount of soft tissue, repeated every 1–5 weeks according to response

PoM **Depo-Medrone®** (Upjohn)
Injection (aqueous suspension), methylprednisolone acetate 40 mg/mL. Net price 1-mL vial = £2.59; 2-mL vial = £4.65; 3-mL vial = £6.75

PoM **Depo-Medrone® with Lidocaine** (Upjohn)
Injection (aqueous suspension), methylprednisolone acetate 40 mg, lignocaine hydrochloride 10 mg/mL. For injection into joints, bursae, or tendon sheaths. Net price 1-mL vial = £2.56; 2-mL vial = £4.65

PREDNISOLONE ACETATE

Indications: local inflammation of joints and soft tissues

Cautions; Contra-indications; Side-effects: see notes above and section 6.3.3

Dose: by intra-articular, intrasynovial, or soft-tissue injection, 5–25 mg according to joint size or amount of soft tissue; not more than 3 joints should be treated on any one day

PoM **Deltastab®** (Boots)
Injection (aqueous suspension), prednisolone acetate 25 mg/mL. Net price 1-mL amp = 80p

TRIAMCINOLONE ACETONIDE

Indications: local inflammation of joints and soft tissues

Cautions; Contra-indications; Side-effects: see notes above and section 6.3.3; not recommended for children under 6 years

Dose: by intra-articular injection, 2.5–40 mg according to joint size, to a max. of 80 mg in multiple injections

By intralesional injection, 2–3 mg; max. 30 mg (5 mg at any one site). Doses are repeated every 1–2 weeks according to response

PoM **Adcortyl®** **Intra-articular / Intradermal** (Squibb)
Injection (aqueous suspension), triamcinolone acetonide 10 mg/mL. Net price 1-mL amp = £1.02; 5-mL vial = £4.14

PoM **Kenalog®** **Intra-articular / Intramuscular** (Squibb)
Injection (aqueous suspension), triamcinolone acetonide 40 mg/mL. Net price 1-mL vial = £1.70

TRIAMCINOLONE HEXACETONIDE

Indications: local inflammation of joints and soft tissues

Cautions; Contra-indications; Side-effects: see notes above and section 6.3.3

Dose: by intra-articular, intrasynovial, or soft-tissue injection, 2–30 mg, according to joint size or amount of soft tissue, repeated at intervals of not less than 3–4 weeks according to the response

By intracutaneous injection of a suspension containing not more than 5 mg/mL, up to 500 micrograms/square inch of affected skin

PoM **Lederspan®** (Lederle)
Injection (aqueous suspension), triamcinolone hexacetonide 5 mg/mL. For intralesional or sublesional injection. Net price 5-mL vial = £2.54
Injection (aqueous suspension), triamcinolone hexacetonide 20 mg/mL. For intra-articular or intrasynovial injection. Net price 1-mL vial = £2.21; 5-mL vial = £8.61

10.1.3 Drugs which may affect the rheumatic disease process

Certain drugs such as gold, penicillamine, hydroxychloroquine, chloroquine, immunosuppressants, and sulphasalazine may affect the disease process in *rheumatoid arthritis*, as may gold and immunosuppressants in *psoriatic arthritis*. Unlike NSAIDs they do not produce an immediate therapeutic effect but require 4 to 6 months of treatment for a full response. If one of these drugs does not lead to objective benefit within 6 months, it should be discontinued.

These drugs may improve not only the symptoms and signs of inflammatory joint disease but also extra-articular manifestations such as vasculitis. They reduce the erythrocyte sedimentation rate and sometimes the titre of rheumatoid factor. Some (e.g. the immunosuppressants) may retard erosive damage as judged radiologically.

These drugs are used in rheumatoid arthritis where treatment with NSAIDs has been unsuccessful, so that there is evidence of disease progression including continuing active joint inflammation and worsening radiological changes. Since, in the first few months, the course of rheumatoid arthritis is unpredictable, it is usual to delay treatment for about 6 months depending on the progress of the disease, but treatment should be initiated before joint damage becomes irreversible.

Penicillamine and immunosuppressants are also sometimes used in rheumatoid arthritis where there are troublesome extra-articular features such as vasculitis, and in patients who are taking excessive doses of corticosteroids. Where the response is satisfactory there is often a striking reduction in requirements of both corticosteroids and other drugs. Gold, penicillamine, and related drugs may also be used to treat *juvenile arthritis* (Still's disease) when indications are similar.

Gold and penicillamine are effective in *palindromic rheumatism* and chloroquine is sometimes used to treat *systemic* and *discoid lupus erythematosus*.

GOLD

Gold may be given by intramuscular injection as sodium aurothiomalate or by mouth as auranofin.

Sodium aurothiomalate must be given by deep intramuscular injection and the area gently massaged. A test dose of 10 mg must be given followed by doses of 50 mg at weekly intervals until there is definite evidence of remission. Benefit is not to be expected until about 300 to 500 mg has been given; if there is no remission after 1 g has been given it should be discontinued. In patients who do respond, the interval between injections is then gradually increased to 4 weeks and treatment is continued for up to 5 years after complete remission. If relapse occurs dosage may be immediately increased to 50 mg weekly and only once control has been obtained again should the dosage be reduced. It is important to avoid complete relapse since second courses of gold are not usually effective. Children may be given 1 mg/kg weekly to a maximum of 50 mg weekly, the intervals being gradually increased to 4 weeks according to response; an initial test dose is given corresponding to one-tenth to one-fifth of the calculated dose.

Auranofin is given by mouth. If there is no response after 9 months treatment should be discontinued.

Gold therapy should be discontinued in the presence of blood disorders or proteinuria (associated with immune complex nephritis) which is repeatedly above 300 mg/litre without other cause (such as urinary-tract infection). Urine tests and full blood counts (including total and differential white cell and platelet counts) must therefore be performed before each intramuscular injection; in the case of oral treatment the urine and blood tests should be carried out monthly. Rashes with pruritus often occur after 2 to 6 months of intramuscular treatment and may necessitate discontinuation of treatment; the most common side-effect of oral therapy, diarrhoea with or without nausea or abdominal pain, may respond to bulking agents (such as bran) or temporary reduction in dosage.

SODIUM AUROTHIOMALATE

Indications: active progressive rheumatoid arthritis, juvenile arthritis

Cautions: see notes above; patients should report pruritus, metallic taste, fever, sore throat or tongue, buccal ulceration, purpura, epistaxis, bleeding gums, bruising, menorrhagia, diarrhoea; renal and hepatic impairment, elderly, breast-feeding, history of urticaria, eczema, colitis, drugs which cause blood disorders; annual chest x-ray

Contra-indications: severe renal and hepatic disease (see notes above); history of blood disorders or bone marrow aplasia, exfoliative dermatitis, systemic lupus erythematosus, necrotising enterocolitis, pulmonary fibrosis; pregnancy (see Appendix 4); porphyria

Side-effects: severe reactions (occasionally fatal) in up to 5% of patients; mouth ulcers, skin reactions, proteinuria, blood disorders (sometimes sudden and fatal); rarely colitis, peripheral neuritis, pulmonary fibrosis, hepatotoxicity with cholestatic jaundice, alopecia

Dose: *by deep intramuscular injection*, administered on expert advice, see notes above

PoM **Myocrisin®** (Rorer)

Injection 10 mg, sodium aurothiomalate 20 mg/mL. Net price 0.5-mL amp = £1.34

Injection 20 mg, sodium aurothiomalate 40 mg/mL. Net price 0.5-mL amp = £1.95

Injection 50 mg, sodium aurothiomalate 100 mg/mL. Net price 0.5-mL amp = £3.97

AURANOFIN

Indications: active progressive rheumatoid arthritis when NSAIDs inadequate alone

Cautions; Contra-indications: see under Sodium Aurothiomalate

Side-effects: diarrhoea most common (reduced by bulking agents such as bran); see also under Sodium Aurothiomalate
Dose: 6 mg daily (initially in 2 divided doses then if tolerated as single dose), if response inadequate after 6 months, increase to 9 mg daily (in 3 divided doses), discontinue if no response after a further 3 months

PoM **Ridaura®** (Bridge)
Tablets, pale yellow, f/c, auranofin 3 mg. Net price 60-tab pack = £28.00. Label: 21

PENICILLAMINE

Penicillamine has a similar action to gold, and more patients are able to continue treatment than with gold but side-effects occur frequently. An initial dose of 125 to 250 mg daily before food is given for 1 month, increased by this amount every 4 to 12 weeks until remission occurs. Penicillamine should be discontinued if there is no improvement within 1 year. The usual maintenance dose is 500 to 750 mg daily, but up to 1.5 g may rarely be required.

Patients should be warned not to expect improvement for at least 6 to 12 weeks after treatment is initiated. If remission has been sustained for 6 months, reduction of dosage by 125 to 250 mg every 12 weeks may be attempted.

Blood counts, including platelets, and urine examinations should be carried out every 1 or 2 weeks for the first 2 months then every 4 weeks to detect blood disorders and proteinuria. A reduction in platelet count indicates that treatment with penicillamine should be stopped, subsequently re-introduced at a lower dosage level and then, if possible, gradually increased. Proteinuria, associated with immune complex nephritis, occurs in up to 30% of patients, but may resolve despite continuation of treatment; treatment may be continued provided that renal function tests remain normal, oedema is absent, and the 24-hour urinary excretion of protein does not exceed 2 g.

Nausea may occur but is not usually a problem provided that penicillamine is taken before food or on retiring and that low initial doses are used and only gradually increased. Loss of taste may occur about 6 weeks after treatment is started but usually returns 6 weeks later irrespective of whether or not treatment is discontinued; mineral supplements are not recommended. Rashes are a common side-effect. Those which occur in the first few months of treatment disappear when the drug is stopped and treatment may then be re-introduced at a lower dose level and gradually increased. Late rashes are more resistant and often necessitate discontinuation of treatment.

PENICILLAMINE

Indications: severe active or progressive rheumatoid arthritis, juvenile arthritis. For use in Wilson's disease, see section 9.8
For use in copper and lead poisoning, see Emergency Treatment of Poisoning
Cautions: see notes above; renal impairment, pregnancy, and portal hypertension; avoid concurrent gold, chloroquine, hydroxychloroquine, or immunosuppressive treatment; **interactions:** Appendix 1 (penicillamine)
Contra-indications: lupus erythematosus
Side-effects: hypersensitivity reactions (may necessitate discontinuation of treatment); nausea, anorexia, taste loss, mouth ulcers, skin reactions (see notes above), oedema, proteinuria, agranulocytosis or severe thrombocytopenia (sometimes fatal); rarely myasthenia, febrile reactions, lupus erythematosus
Dose: rheumatoid arthritis, administered on expert advice, ADULT, see notes above; CHILD initial dose, 50 mg daily before food for 1 month, increased at 4-week intervals to a maintenance dose of 15–20 mg/kg daily

PoM **Penicillamine** (Non-proprietary)
Tablets, coated, penicillamine 125 mg, net price 20 = £2.88; 250 mg, 20 = £4.97. Label: 6, 22
Available from Cox
PoM **Distamine®** (Dista)
Tablets, all f/c, penicillamine 50 mg (scored), net price 20 = £1.45; 125 mg, 20 = £2.90; 250 mg, 20 = £4.99. Label: 6, 22
PoM **Pendramine®** (Degussa)
Tablets, both scored, f/c, penicillamine 125 mg, net price 20 = £2.66; 250 mg, 20 = £4.58. Label: 6, 22

ANTIMALARIALS

Chloroquine and **hydroxychloroquine** have a similar action to, and are better tolerated than, gold or penicillamine but their use is limited by their ocular toxicity. However, retinopathy is rare provided the doses given below are not exceeded. Nevertheless, all patients should have a full ophthalmic examination before starting treatment and then subsequently at intervals of 3 to 6 months. Ocular toxicity is also reduced if the drug is not given continuously for longer than 2 years and some physicians advise their patients to stop treatment for 2 months of each year.

These drugs should not be used for psoriatic arthritis and are best **avoided** in elderly patients as it is difficult to distinguish ageing changes from drug-induced retinopathy.

They are also used in systemic lupus erythematosus (section 10.1.2.1).

Mepacrine (see section 5.4.4) is sometimes used in discoid lupus erythematosus.

CHLOROQUINE

Indications: active rheumatoid arthritis (including juvenile arthritis), systemic and discoid lupus erythematosus; malaria, see section 5.4.1
Cautions: hepatic and renal impairment, pregnancy (but for malaria benefit outweighs risk, see Appendix 4, Antimalarials), porphyria, may exacerbate psoriasis, neurological disorders (especially history of epilepsy), severe gastro-intestinal disorders, G6PD deficiency

(see section 9.1.5); elderly (see notes above); regular ophthalmic examinations required (see notes above); avoid concurrent therapy with hepatotoxic drugs—other **interactions:** Appendix 1 (chloroquine)

Side-effects: gastro-intestinal disturbances, headache, visual disturbances, irreversible retinal damage, corneal opacities, depigmentation or loss of hair, skin reactions; rarely blood disorders (thrombocytopenia, agranulocytosis and aplastic anaemia)

Dose: administered on expert advice, chloroquine 150 mg daily preferably after food; CHILD, 3 mg/kg daily

Note. Chloroquine base 150 mg ≡ chloroquine sulphate 200 mg ≡ chloroquine phosphate 250 mg (approx.).

Preparations

See section 5.4.1

HYDROXYCHLOROQUINE SULPHATE

Indications: active rheumatoid arthritis (including juvenile arthritis), systemic and discoid lupus erythematosus

Cautions; Side-effects: see under Chloroquine and notes (above)

Dose: administered on expert advice, initially 400 mg daily in divided doses; maintenance 200–400 mg daily; max. 6.5 mg/kg daily; CHILD, up to 6.5 mg/kg daily (dosage form not suitable for children who weigh less than 33 kg)

PoM **Plaquenil®** (Sterling-Winthrop)

Tablets, orange, s/c, hydroxychloroquine sulphate 200 mg. Net price 56-tab pack = £17.60. Label: 5

IMMUNOSUPPRESSANTS

When used in *rheumatoid arthritis* **immunosuppressants** have a similar action to gold and are useful alternatives in cases that have failed to respond to gold, penicillamine, chloroquine, or hydroxychloroquine.

Azathioprine (see section 8.2.1) is usually chosen and is given in a dose of 1.5 to 2.5 mg/kg daily in divided doses. Blood counts should be carried out every 4 weeks to detect possible neutropenia and/or thrombocytopenia which is usually resolved by reducing the dose. Nausea, vomiting, and diarrhoea may occur, usually starting early during the course of treatment, and may necessitate withdrawal of the drug; herpes zoster infection may also occur.

Methotrexate (see section 8.1.3) has also been shown to be effective. It is usually given in an initial dose of 2.5 mg by mouth once a week, increased to a maximum of 15 mg once a week, subject to regular full blood counts (including differential white cell count and platelet count) and liver-function tests initially weekly and monthly thereafter.

Chlorambucil (see section 8.1.1) is another immunosuppressant which is used in rheumatoid arthritis; a dose of 100 to 200 micrograms/kg daily is usually given initially; most patients require between 2.5 and 7.5 mg daily. Regular blood counts including platelets should be carried out. **Cyclophosphamide** is more toxic but may be used at a dose of 1 to 1.5 mg/kg daily for rheumatoid arthritis with severe systemic manifestations.

Immunosuppressants are also used in the management of severe cases of *systemic lupus erythematosus* and other connective tissue disorders. They are often given in conjunction with corticosteroids for patients with severe or progressive renal disease though the evidence for their benefit is doubtful. They may be used in cases of *polymyositis* which are resistant to corticosteroids. They are used for their corticosteroid-sparing effect in patients whose corticosteroid requirements are excessive. **Azathioprine** is usually used but **chlorambucil** is an alternative.

Azathioprine and methotrexate are used in the treatment of *psoriatic arthropathy* for severe or progressive cases which are not controlled with anti-inflammatory drugs. There is an impression that **azathioprine** is the more effective for psoriatic arthritis and that **methotrexate** is the more effective for skin manifestations. Methotrexate is usually given in a dose of 10–25 mg once a week by mouth. Regular full blood counts and liver-function tests should be carried out initially weekly and monthly thereafter.

SULPHASALAZINE

Sulphasalazine was initially introduced for the treatment of rheumatoid arthritis. Recent re-evaluation has confirmed that it has a beneficial effect in suppressing the inflammatory activity of rheumatoid arthritis. Side-effects include rashes, gastro-intestinal intolerance and, especially in patients with rheumatoid arthritis, occasional leucopenia, neutropenia, and thrombocytopenia. These haematological abnormalities occur usually in the first 3 to 6 months of treatment and are reversible on cessation of treatment. Close monitoring of full blood counts (including differential white cell count and platelet count) is necessary throughout treatment of rheumatoid arthritis, monthly during the first 6 months and 3-monthly thereafter, liver function tests being performed at the same time.

SULPHASALAZINE

Indications: active rheumatoid arthritis; ulcerative colitis, see section 1.5

Cautions; Contra-indications; Side-effects: see section 1.5

Dose: by mouth, administered on expert advice, as enteric-coated tablets, initially 500 mg daily, increased by 500 mg at intervals of 1 week to a max. of 2–3 g daily in divided doses

PoM **Salazopyrin EN-tabs®** (Pharmacia)

Tablets, e/c, yellow, f/c, sulphasalazine 500 mg. Net price 125-tab pack = £12.75. Label: 5, 14, 25, counselling, see lenses section 1.5

10.1.4 Drugs used in the treatment of gout

It is important to distinguish drugs used for the treatment of acute attacks of gout from those used in the long-term control of the disease. The latter exacerbate and prolong the acute manifestations if started during an attack.

ACUTE ATTACKS

Acute attacks of gout are usually treated with high doses of **NSAIDs** such as azapropazone, diclofenac, indomethacin, ketoprofen, naproxen, piroxicam, and sulindac (section 10.1.1). Colchicine is an alternative. Aspirin is **contra-indicated** in gout. Allopurinol and uricosurics are not effective in treating an acute attack and may prolong it indefinitely if started during the acute episode.

Indomethacin is often chosen in acute attacks. High doses are usually well tolerated for short periods (50 to 100 mg repeated after a few hours if necessary and followed by reducing doses every 6 hours as the patient improves). If courses of treatment last for less than one week side-effects are unusual despite the high doses used.

Colchicine is probably as effective as indomethacin. Its use is limited by the development of toxicity at higher doses, but it is of value in patients with heart failure since, unlike NSAIDs, it does not induce fluid retention; moreover it can be given to patients receiving anticoagulants.

COLCHICINE

Indications: acute gout, short-term prophylaxis during initial therapy with allopurinol and uricosuric drugs

Cautions: gastro-intestinal disease, renal impairment, pregnancy and breast-feeding

Side-effects: most common are nausea, vomiting, and abdominal pain; excessive doses may also cause profuse diarrhoea, gastro-intestinal haemorrhage, rashes, and renal damage. Rarely peripheral neuritis, alopecia, and with prolonged treatment blood disorders

Dose: 1 mg initially, followed by 500 micrograms every 2–3 hours until relief of pain is obtained or vomiting or diarrhoea occurs, or until a total dose of 10 mg has been reached. The course should not be repeated within 3 days

Prevention of attacks during initial treatment with allopurinol or uricosuric drugs, 500 micrograms 2–3 times daily

PoM **Colchicine** (Non-proprietary)

Tablets, colchicine 500 micrograms, net price 20 = 66p

INTERVAL TREATMENT

For long-term ('interval') control of gout the formation of uric acid from purines may be reduced with the **xanthine-oxidase inhibitor** allopurinol, or the **uricosuric drugs** probenecid or sulphinpyrazone may be used to increase the excretion of uric acid in the urine. Treatment should be continued indefinitely once the decision has been made to prevent further attacks of gout by correcting the hyperuricaemia. These drugs should never be started during an acute attack. The initiation of treatment may precipitate an acute attack therefore colchicine or an anti-inflammatory analgesic should be used as a prophylactic and continued for at least one month after the hyperuricaemia has been corrected (usually about 3 months of prophylaxis).

Allopurinol is a convenient well tolerated drug which is now widely used. It is especially useful in patients with renal impairment or urate stones where uricosuric drugs cannot be used. It is usually given once daily, as the active metabolite of allopurinol has a long half-life, but doses over 300 mg daily should be divided. Allopurinol treatment should not be started until an acute attack of gout has completely subsided, as further attacks may be precipitated. It is well tolerated in most patients but may occasionally cause rashes.

The uricosuric drugs include **probenecid** and **sulphinpyrazone**. They can be used instead of allopurinol, or in conjunction with it in cases that are resistant to treatment.

If an acute attack develops in a patient taking allopurinol or a uricosuric the treatment should continue at the same dosage while the acute attack is treated in its own right.

Azapropazone (section 10.1.1) also has a uricosuric effect and may be useful in the long-term treatment of chronic gout.

Aspirin and salicylates antagonise the uricosuric drugs; they do not antagonise allopurinol but are nevertheless **contra-indicated** in gout.

Crystallisation of urate in the urine may occur with the uricosuric drugs and it is important to ensure that there is an adequate urine output especially in the first few weeks of treatment. As an additional precaution the urine may be rendered alkaline.

The NSAIDs are described in section 10.1.1.

ALLOPURINOL

Indications: gout prophylaxis, hyperuricaemia

Cautions: administer prophylactic colchicine or NSAID (*not* aspirin or salicylates) until at least 1 month after hyperuricaemia corrected; ensure adequate fluid intake (2 litres/day); hepatic and renal impairment. In neoplastic conditions treatment with allopurinol (if required) should be commenced before cytotoxic drugs are given; **interactions:** Appendix 1 (allopurinol)

Contra-indications: as a treatment for acute gout (but continue if attack develops when already receiving allopurinol, and treat attack separately, see notes above)

Side-effects: rashes, sometimes with fever (withdraw therapy; if rash mild re-introduce cautiously but discontinue immediately if recurrence); gastro-intestinal disorders. Rarely malaise, headache, vertigo, drowsiness, taste disturbances, hypertension, symptomless xanthine deposits in muscle, alopecia, hepatotoxicity

Dose: initially 100 mg daily as a single dose, after food, gradually increased over 1–3 weeks according to the plasma or urinary uric acid concentration, to about 300 mg daily; usual maintenance dose 200–600 mg, rarely 900 mg daily, divided into doses of not more than 300 mg; CHILD (in neoplastic conditions, enzyme disorders) 10–20 mg/kg daily

PoM **Allopurinol** (Non-proprietary)
Tablets, allopurinol 100 mg, net price 20 = 50p; 300 mg, 20 = £1.74. Label: 8, 21, 27
Available from APS, Berk (Caplenal®), Cox, DDSA (Cosuric®), Evans, Kerfoot, Lagap (Aloral®), Nicholas (Hamarin®), Steinhard (Aluline®)

PoM **Zyloric®** (Calmic)
Tablets, allopurinol 100 mg, net price 20 = £4.06; 300 mg, 28-tab pack = £14.56. Label: 8, 21, 27

PROBENECID

Indications: gout prophylaxis, hyperuricaemia; reduction of tubular excretion of penicillins and certain cephalosporins, see section 5.1
Cautions: during initial gout therapy administer prophylactic colchicine or NSAID (*not* aspirin or salicylates), ensure adequate fluid intake (about 2 litres daily), render urine alkaline if uric acid overload is high; peptic ulceration, renal impairment (avoid if severe); transient false-positive Benedict's test; **interactions:** Appendix 1 (probenecid)
Contra-indications: history of blood disorders, nephrolithiasis, porphyria, acute gout attack and 3 weeks after; avoid aspirin and salicylates
Side-effects: infrequent; occasionally nausea and vomiting, urinary frequency, headache, flushing, dizziness, rashes; rarely hypersensitivity, nephrotic syndrome, hepatic necrosis, aplastic anaemia
Dose: uricosuric therapy, initially 250 mg twice daily after food, increased after a week to 500 mg twice daily then up to 2 g daily in 2–4 divided doses according to plasma-uric acid concentration and reduced for maintenance

PoM **Benemid®** (MSD)
Tablets, scored, probenecid 500 mg. Net price 20 = 55p. Label: 12, 21, 27

SULPHINPYRAZONE

Indications: gout prophylaxis, hyperuricaemia
Cautions; Contra-indications: see under Probenecid; regular blood counts advisable; avoid in hypersensitivity to NSAIDs; **interactions:** Appendix 1 (sulphinpyrazone)
Side-effects: gastro-intestinal disorders, occasionally hypersensitivity reactions; rarely blood disorders
Dose: initially 100–200 mg daily with food (or milk) increasing over 2–3 weeks to 600 mg daily, continued until serum uric acid concentration normal then reduced for maintenance

PoM **Anturan®** (Geigy)
Tablets, both yellow, s/c, sulphinpyrazone 100 mg, net price 20 = 94p; 200 mg, 112-tab pack = £10.42. Label: 12, 21

10.2 Drugs used in neuromuscular disorders

10.2.1 Drugs which enhance neuromuscular transmission

Anticholinesterases are used as first-line treatment in *myasthenia gravis*.

Corticosteroids are only given concomitantly if anticholinesterase treatment is failing.

Plasmapheresis may produce temporary remission in otherwise unresponsive patients.

ANTICHOLINESTERASES

Anticholinesterase drugs are used to enhance neuromuscular transmission in voluntary and involuntary muscle in myasthenia gravis. They prolong the action of acetylcholine by inhibiting the action of the enzyme acetylcholinesterase. Excessive dosage of these drugs may impair neuromuscular transmission and precipitate 'cholinergic crises' by causing a depolarising block. This may be difficult to distinguish from a worsening myasthenic state.

Side-effects of anticholinesterases are due to their parasympathomimetic action. Muscarinic effects include increased sweating, salivary, and gastric secretion, also increased gastro intestinal and uterine motility, and bradycardia. These effects are antagonised by atropine.

Edrophonium has a very brief action and is therefore used mainly for the diagnosis of myasthenia gravis. A single test-dose usually causes substantial improvement in muscle power (lasting about 5 minutes) in patients with the disease (if respiration already impaired, *only* in conjunction with someone skilled at intubation).

It can also be used to determine whether a patient with myasthenia is receiving inadequate or excessive treatment with cholinergic drugs. If treatment is excessive an injection of edrophonium will either have no effect or will intensify symptoms (if respiration already impaired, *only* in conjunction with someone skilled at intubation). Conversely, transient improvement may be seen if the patient is being inadequately treated. The test is best performed just before the next dose of anticholinesterase.

Neostigmine produces a therapeutic effect for up to 4 hours. Its pronounced muscarinic action is a disadvantage, and simultaneous administration of an antimuscarinic drug such as atropine or propantheline may be required to prevent colic, excessive salivation, or diarrhoea. In severe disease neostigmine may be given every 2 hours. The maximum that most patients can tolerate is 180 mg daily.

Pyridostigmine is less powerful and slower in action than neostigmine but it has a longer duration of action. It is preferable to neostigmine because of its smoother action and the need for less frequent dosage. It is particularly preferred in patients whose muscles are weak on wakening. It has a comparatively mild gastro-intestinal effect but an antimuscarinic drug may still be required. It is inadvisable to exceed a daily dose of 720 mg.

Distigmine has the most protracted action but the danger of a 'cholinergic crisis' caused by accumulation of the drug is greater than with shorter-acting drugs.

Neostigmine and edrophonium are also used to reverse the actions of the non-depolarising muscle relaxants (see section 15.1.6).

NEOSTIGMINE

Indications: myasthenia gravis; other indications, see section 15.1.6

Cautions: asthma, bradycardia, recent myocardial infarction, epilepsy, hypotension, parkinsonism, vagotonia, peptic ulceration, pregnancy. Atropine or other antidote to muscarinic effects may be necessary (particularly when neostigmine is given by injection), but it should not be given routinely as it may mask signs of overdosage; **interactions:** Appendix 1 (cholinergics)

Contra-indications: intestinal or urinary obstruction

Side-effects: nausea, vomiting, increased salivation, diarrhoea, abdominal cramps (more marked with higher doses). Signs of overdosage are increased gastro-intestinal discomfort, bronchial secretions, and sweating, involuntary defaecation and micturition, miosis, nystagmus, bradycardia, hypotension, agitation, excessive dreaming, and weakness eventually leading to fasciculation and paralysis

Dose: by mouth, neostigmine bromide 15–30 mg at suitable intervals throughout day, total daily dose 75–300 mg (but see also notes above); NEONATE 1–5 mg every 4 hours, half an hour before feeds; CHILD up to 6 years initially 7.5 mg, 6–12 years initially 15 mg, usual total daily dose 15–90 mg

By subcutaneous or intramuscular injection, neostigmine methylsulphate 1–2.5 mg at suitable intervals throughout day (usual total daily dose 5–20 mg); NEONATE 50–250 micrograms every 4 hours; CHILD 200–500 micrograms as required

PoM **Prostigmin®** (Roche)

Tablets, scored, neostigmine bromide 15 mg. Net price 20 = 53p

Injection, neostigmine methylsulphate 500 micrograms/mL, net price 1-mL amp = 16p; 2.5 mg/mL, 1-mL amp = 16p

DISTIGMINE BROMIDE

Indications: myasthenia gravis; urinary retention and other indications, see section 7.4.1

Cautions; Contra-indications; Side-effects: see under Neostigmine

Dose: initially 5 mg daily half an hour before breakfast, increased at intervals of 3–4 days if necessary to a max. of 20 mg daily; CHILD up to 10 mg daily according to age

Preparations

See section 7.4.1

EDROPHONIUM CHLORIDE

Indications: see under Dose and notes above; surgery, see section 15.1.6

Cautions; Contra-indications; Side-effects: see under Neostigmine; *great* caution in respiratory distress (see notes above)

Dose: diagnosis of myasthenia gravis, *by intravenous injection*, 2 mg followed after 30 seconds (if no adverse reaction has occurred) by 8 mg; in adults without suitable veins, *by intramuscular injection*, 10 mg

Detection of overdosage or underdosage of cholinergic drugs, *by intravenous injection*, 2 mg one hour after the last dose of cholinergic drug

CHILD *by intravenous injection* 20 micrograms/kg followed after 30 seconds (if no adverse reaction has occurred) by 80 micrograms/kg

PoM **Tensilon®** (Roche)

Injection, edrophonium chloride 10 mg/mL. Net price 1-mL amp = 27p

PYRIDOSTIGMINE BROMIDE

Indications: myasthenia gravis

Cautions; Contra-indications; Side-effects: see under Neostigmine; weaker muscarinic action

Dose: by mouth, 30–120 mg at suitable intervals throughout day, total daily dose 0.3–1.2 g (but see also notes above); NEONATE 5–10 mg every 4 hours, ½–1 hour before feeds; CHILD up to 6 years initially 30 mg, 6–12 years initially 60 mg, usual total daily dose 30–360 mg

PoM **Mestinon®** (Roche)

Tablets, scored, pyridostigmine bromide 60 mg. Net price 20 = £1.01

IMMUNOSUPPRESSANT THERAPY

Corticosteroids (see section 6.3) are established as treatment for myasthenia gravis where *thymectomy* is inadvisable or to reduce the risk of surgery beforehand. The initial dose may be high (up to 100 mg **prednisolone** daily) but most advise starting with a smaller dose (20 mg prednisolone daily) and gradually increasing it. There is grave risk of exacerbation of the myasthenia during the initial stages of therapy, particularly in the first 2–3 weeks, therefore inpatient supervision is essential. Improvement usually begins after about 2 weeks on the high-dose regimen. In some patients a prolonged remission may be induced, but often patients need a maintenance dose of 10–40 mg of prednisolone daily; alternate-day therapy is popular. Patients who need a corticosteroid may benefit from the addition of **azathioprine** (see section 8.2.1) in a dose of 2 mg/kg daily which may allow a reduction in corticosteroid dosage.

AZATHIOPRINE

See section 8.2.1

PREDNISOLONE
See section 6.3.4

10.2.2 Skeletal muscle relaxants

Drugs described below are used for the relief of chronic muscle spasm or spasticity; they are not indicated for spasm associated with minor injuries. They act principally on the central nervous system with the exception of dantrolene which has a peripheral site of action. They differ in action from the muscle relaxants used in anaesthesia (see section 15.1.5) which block transmission of impulses at the neuromuscular junction.

The underlying cause of spasticity should be treated and any aggravating factors (e.g. pressure sores, infection) remedied. Skeletal muscle relaxants are effective in most forms of spasticity except the rare alpha variety. The major disadvantage of treatment with these drugs is that reduction in muscle tone can cause a loss of splinting action of the spastic leg and trunk muscles and sometimes lead to an increase in disability.

Dantrolene acts directly on skeletal muscle and produces fewer central adverse effects making it a drug of choice. The dose should be increased slowly.

Baclofen inhibits transmission at spinal level and also depresses the central nervous system. The dose should be increased slowly to avoid sedation and hypotonia.

Diazepam may also be used. Sedation and, occasionally, extensor hypotonus are disadvantages. Other benzodiazepines also have muscle-relaxant properties. Muscle-relaxant doses of benzodiazepines are similar to anxiolytic doses (see section 4.1.2).

Clonazepam (see section 4.8) may sometimes help in myoclonus.

Quinine salts (see section 5.4.1) 200 to 300 mg at bedtime are effective in relieving nocturnal leg cramps. They are toxic in overdosage and accidental fatalities have occurred in children.

BACLOFEN

Indications: chronic severe spasticity of voluntary muscle

Cautions: psychiatric illness, cerebrovascular disease, elderly; respiratory, hepatic, or renal impairment, epilepsy; hypertonic bladder sphincter; pregnancy; avoid abrupt withdrawal; avoid in peptic ulceration and in porphyria; **interactions:** Appendix 1 (baclofen)

DRIVING. Drowsiness may affect performance of skilled tasks (e.g. driving); effects of alcohol enhanced

Side-effects: frequently sedation, drowsiness, nausea; occasionally lightheadedness, lassitude, confusion, dizziness, ataxia, hallucinations, headache, euphoria, insomnia, depression, tremor, nystagmus, paraesthesias, convulsions, muscular pain and weakness, respiratory or cardiovascular depression, hypotension, gastro-intestinal and urinary disturbances; rarely visual disorders, taste alterations, increased sweating, rash, altered liver function, and paradoxical increase in spasticity

Dose: 5 mg 3 times daily, preferably after food, gradually increased; max. 100 mg daily; CHILD 0.75–2 mg/kg daily (over 10 years, max. 2.5 mg/kg daily) *or* 2.5 mg 4 times daily increased gradually according to age to maintenance: 1–2 years 10–20 mg daily, 2–6 years 20–30 mg daily, 6–10 years 30–60 mg daily

PoM **Baclofen** (Non-proprietary)
Tablets, baclofen 10 mg. Net price 20 = £2.46. Label: 2, 8

PoM **Lioresal®** (Geigy)
Tablets, scored, baclofen 10 mg. Net price 20 = £2.34. Label: 2, 8
Additives: include gluten
Liquid, sugar-free, baclofen 5 mg/5 mL. Diluent purified water, freshly boiled and cooled, life of diluted liquid 14 days. Net price 300 mL = £6.16. Label: 2, 8

DANTROLENE SODIUM

Indications: chronic severe spasticity of voluntary muscle

Cautions: impaired cardiac, pulmonary, and liver function; test liver function before and at intervals during therapy. Therapeutic effect may take a few weeks to develop but if treatment is ineffective it should be discontinued after 4–6 weeks. Avoid in children or when spasticity is useful, for example, locomotion.

DRIVING. Drowsiness may affect performance of skilled tasks (e.g. driving); effects of alcohol enhanced

Side-effects: transient drowsiness, dizziness, weakness, malaise, fatigue, diarrhoea (withdraw if severe, discontinue treatment if recurs on re-introduction), anorexia, nausea, headache, rash; less frequently constipation, dysphagia, speech and visual disturbances, confusion, nervousness, insomnia, depression, seizures, chills, fever, increased urinary frequency; rarely, tachycardia, erratic blood pressure, dyspnoea, haematuria, possible crystalluria, urinary incontinence or retention, pleural effusion, pericarditis, dose-related hepatotoxicity (occasionally fatal) may be more common in women over 30 especially those taking oestrogens

Dose: initially 25 mg daily, may be increased at weekly intervals to max. of 100 mg 4 times daily; usual dose 75 mg 3 times daily

PoM **Dantrium®** (Norwich Eaton)
Capsules, both orange/brown, dantrolene sodium 25 mg, net price 20 = £3.11; 100 mg, 20 = £10.88. Label: 2
Injection—see section 15.1.8

DIAZEPAM

Indications: muscle spasm of varied aetiology, including tetanus; other indications, see sections 4.1.2, 4.8, 15.1.4.2

Cautions; Contra-indications; Side-effects: see section 4.1.2; also hypotonia; special precautions for intravenous injection (see section 4.8.2)

Dose: by mouth, 2–15 mg daily in divided doses, increased if necessary in spastic conditions to 60 mg daily according to response

Cerebral spasticity in selected cases, CHILD 2–40 mg daily in divided doses

By intramuscular or slow intravenous injection, in acute muscle spasm, 10 mg repeated if necessary after 4 hours; CHILD, 100–200 micrograms/kg, repeated if necessary

Tetanus, *by intravenous injection*, 100–300 micrograms/kg repeated every 1–4 hours; *by intravenous infusion* (*or by nasoduodenal tube*), 3–10 mg/kg over 24 hours, adjusted according to response

Preparations: see section 4.1.2

OTHER MUSCLE RELAXANTS

The clinical efficacy of carisoprodol, chlormezanone and meprobamate (see section 4.1.2), methocarbamol, and orphenadrine as muscle relaxants is **not** well established although they have been included in compound analgesic preparations.

CARISOPRODOL

Indications: short-term symptomatic relief of muscle spasm (but see notes above)

Cautions; Contra-indications; Side-effects: see under Meprobamate, section 4.1.2. Drowsiness is common; avoid in porphyria

Dose: 350 mg 3 times daily; elderly half adult dose or less

PoM **Carisoma**® (Pharmax)

Tablets, carisoprodol 125 mg, net price 20 = 38p; 350 mg, 20 = 42p. Label: 2

METHOCARBAMOL

Indications: short-term symptomatic relief of muscle spasm (but see notes above)

Cautions: may cause drowsiness; hepatic and renal impairment (avoid injection in renal impairment)

DRIVING. Drowsiness may affect performance of skilled tasks (e.g. driving); effects of alcohol enhanced

Contra-indications: coma or pre-coma, brain damage, epilepsy, myasthenia gravis

Side-effects: lassitude, light-headedness, dizziness, restlessness, anxiety, confusion, drowsiness, nausea, allergic rash or angioedema, convulsions

Dose: by mouth, 1.5 g 4 times daily (elderly 750 mg or less); may be reduced to 750 mg 3 times daily

By slow intravenous injection or by infusion, 1–3 g (max. rate 300 mg/min.); max. dose 3 g (elderly, 1.5 g) daily for 3 days

PoM **Robaxin**® (Wyeth)

750 Tablets, scored, methocarbamol 750 mg. Net price 20 = £2.36. Label: 2

Injection, methocarbamol 100 mg/mL in aqueous macrogol '300'. Net price 10-mL amp = £1.39

PoM **Robaxisal Forte**®: see section 4.7.1.1

ORPHENADRINE CITRATE

Indications: short-term symptomatic relief of muscle spasm (but see notes above)

Cautions: see under Benzhexol, section 4.9.2. Avoid in children and in porphyria; reduce dose in elderly

Side-effects: dry mouth and other antimuscarinic side-effects; see also Orphenadrine Hydrochloride, section 4.9.2

Dose: by intramuscular or by slow intravenous injection (over 5 minutes), 60 mg repeated after 12 hours if necessary

PoM **Norflex**® (3M)

Injection, orphenadrine citrate 30 mg/mL. Net price 2-mL amp = 60p

10.3 Drugs for the relief of soft-tissue inflammation

10.3.1 Enzymes

Hyaluronidase is used to render the tissues more easily permeable to injected fluids, e.g. for introduction of fluids by subcutaneous infusion (termed hypodermoclysis).

HYALURONIDASE

Indications: enhance permeation of subcutaneous or intramuscular injections; promote resorption of excess fluids and blood

Contra-indications: intravenous route, bites or stings, infection or malignancy at site

Dose: to enhance tissue permeability, *by subcutaneous or intramuscular injection*, usually 1500 units, either mixed with the injection fluid or injected into the site before injection is administered

By subcutaneous infusion, 1500 units administered before 500–1000 mL infusion fluid

PoM **Hyalase**® (CP)

Injection, powder for reconstitution, hyaluronidase (ovine). Net price 1500-unit amp = £1.98

10.3.2 Rubefacients and other topical antirheumatics

Rubefacients act by counter-irritation. Pain, whether superficial or deep-seated, is relieved by any method which itself produces irritation of the skin. Counter-irritation is comforting in painful lesions of the muscles, tendons, and joints, and in non-articular rheumatism. Rubefacients probably all act through the same essential mechanism and differ mainly in intensity and duration of action.

Topical **NSAIDs** (e.g. benzydamine, felbinac, ibuprofen, salicylamide) have a transient effect. **Adrenaline** is inactive when applied topically.

CAUTIONS. Apply with gentle massage. Avoid contact with eyes, mucous membranes, and inflamed or broken skin. Not generally suitable for children. Liniments are very toxic if taken by mouth.

COUNTER-IRRITANTS

Algesal® (Duphar)
Cream, diethylamine salicylate 10%. Net price 50 g = 75p. Apply 3 times daily

Algipan® (Whitehall)
Cream, methyl nicotinate 1%, capsicum oleoresin 0.1%, glycol salicylate 10%. Net price 40 g = 70p; 80 g = £1.13

Spray application, methyl nicotinate 1.5%, glycol salicylate 10%. Net price 120-mL aerosol spray = £1.03

Aradolene® (Fisons)
Cream, diethylamine salicylate 5%, 'capsicin water-soluble' 0.4%, menthol 2.5%, rectified camphor oil 1.4% in a lanolin basis. Net price 40 g = 76p

Aspellin® (Fisons)
Liniment, ammonium salicylate 1%, camphor 0.6%, menthol 1.4%, ethyl and methyl salicylate 0.54%. Net price 100 mL = 71p; 500 mL = £3.06; 150-mL spray can = 96p
Additives: include tartrazine

Balmosa® (Pharmax)
Cream, camphor 4%, capsicum oleoresin 0.035%, menthol 2%, methyl salicylate 4%. Net price 20 g = 36p; 40 g = 47p

Bayolin® (Bayer)
Cream, benzyl nicotinate 2.5%, glycol salicylate 10%, heparinoid 50 units/g. Net price 35 g = 70p. Apply 2–3 times daily

Bengué's Balsam® (Bengué)
Ointment, menthol 20%, methyl salicylate 20% in a lanolin basis. Net price 25 g = 68p

Bengué's Balsam SG® (Bengué)
Cream, menthol 10%, methyl salicylate 15% in a vanishing cream basis. Net price 25 g = 68p

Cremalgin® (Rhône-Poulenc Rorer)
Balm (= cream), capsicin 0.1%, glycol salicylate 10%, methyl nicotinate 1%. Net price 30 g = 52p. Apply 2–3 times daily

Dubam® (Norma)
Spray application, glycol salicylate 5%, methyl nicotinate 1.6%, methyl salicylate 1%, ethyl salicylate 4%. Net price 50-g aerosol spray = £1.75; 113 g = £2.68

Finalgon® (Boehringer Ingelheim)
Ointment, butoxyethyl nicotinate 2.5%, vanillylnonanamide 0.4%. Net price 20 g (with applicator) = 27p

Transvasin® (R&C)
Cream, benzocaine 2%, ethyl nicotinate 2%, hexyl nicotinate 2%, tetrahydrofurfuryl salicylate 14%. Net price 30 g = 41p. Apply at least twice daily

POULTICES

Kaolin Poultice, heavy kaolin 52.7%, thymol 0.05%, boric acid 4.5%, peppermint oil 0.05%, methyl salicylate 0.2%, glycerol 42.5%. Net price 200 g = £1.27
Warm and apply directly or between layers of muslin; avoid application of overheated poultice

Kaolin Poultice K/L Pack® (K/L)
Kaolin poultice. Net price 4 × 100-g pouches = £3.15

TOPICAL NSAIDs

Note. For NSAID asthma warning, see p. 321.

Difflam® (3M)
Cream, benzydamine hydrochloride 3%. Net price 50 g = £4.56; 100 g = £8.62. Apply 3–6 times daily for up to 10 days

PoM **Feldene® Gel** (Invicta)
Gel, piroxicam 0.5%. Net price 60 g = £7.77
Apply 1 g (3 cm) 3–4 times daily; therapy should be reviewed after 4 weeks; 30-g tube for short-term use, net price £3.89

Intralgin® (3M)
Gel, benzocaine 2%, salicylamide 5% in an alcoholic vehicle. Net price 50 g = 51p

PoM **Movelat®** (Panpharma)
Cream, corticosteroids 0.02% (as adrenocortical extract), heparinoid 0.2%, salicylic acid 2%. Net price 100 g = £3.90. Apply up to 4 times daily
Gel, ingredients as for cream but in a colourless alcoholic basis. Net price 100 g = £3.90. Apply up to 4 times daily

Proflex® (Zyma)
Cream, ibuprofen 5%. Net price 100 g = £8.70. Apply 4–10 cm 3–4 times daily

PoM **Traxam®** (Lederle)
Gel, felbinac 3%. Net price 50 g = £8.72.
Apply 2–4 times daily for up to 14 days; max. 25 g daily
Note. Felbinac is an active metabolite of the NSAID fenbufen

PoM **Voltarol® Emulgel** (Geigy)
Gel, diclofenac diethylammonium salt 1.16% (equivalent to diclofenac sodium 1%). Net price 100 g = £7.75. Apply 2–4 g 3–4 times daily for up to 14 days

11: Drugs acting on the EYE

In this chapter, drug treatment is discussed under the following headings:

The entries in this chapter generally relate only to local eye treatment. Systemic indications and side-effects of many of the drugs are given elsewhere (see index).

11.1 Administration of drugs to the eye

EYE-DROPS AND EYE OINTMENTS. When administered in the form of eye-drops, drugs penetrate the eyeball, probably through the cornea. However, systemic effects, which are usually undesirable, may well arise from absorption of drugs into the general circulation via conjunctival vessels or from the nasal mucosa after the excess of the preparation has drained down through the tear ducts. For example, timolol (a beta-blocker), administered as eye-drops may induce bronchospasm or bradycardia in susceptible individuals.

Eye ointments are often applied to lid margins for blepharitis. They may also be used in the conjunctival sac for other conditions especially where a prolonged action is required.

When two different preparations in the form of eye-drops are required at the same time of day, for example pilocarpine and timolol in glaucoma, dilution and overflow may occur when one immediately follows the other. The patient should therefore leave an interval of a few minutes. At night, an eye ointment for the second drug will reduce the problem.

Generally it is inadvisable for patients to continue to wear hydrophilic (soft) contact lenses when receiving eye-drops. For warnings relating to eye-drops and contact lenses, see section 11.9.

EYE LOTIONS. These are solutions for the irrigation of the conjuctival sac. They act mechanically to flush out irritants or foreign bodies as a first-aid treatment. **Sodium Chloride Eye Lotion** (section 11.8.2) is usually used. However, the lotion, which is sterile, should be used once only from a previously unopened container for first aid, while for treatment it should be used for no longer than 24 hours after the container is first opened. Single-application containers of the lotion are available. In emergency, tap water drawn freshly from the main (not stored water) will suffice.

OTHER PREPARATIONS. Subconjunctival injection may be used to administer anti-infective drugs, mydriatics, or corticosteroids for conditions not responding to topical therapy. The drug diffuses through the sclera to the anterior and posterior chambers and vitreous humour in higher concentration than can be achieved by absorption from eye-drops. However, because the dose-volume is limited (usually not more than 1 mL), this route is suitable only for drugs which are readily soluble.

Drugs such as antibiotics and corticosteroids may be administered systemically to treat an eye condition.

Suitable plastic devices which gradually release a specified amount of drug over a period of, say, 1 week are also used (e.g. Ocuserts®).

11.2 Control of microbial contamination

Preparations for the eye should be sterile when issued. For routine domiciliary use they are supplied in multiple-application containers for individual use. They contain a suitable preservative and provided that contamination is avoided they may be used for about one month after which a new container should be opened (if treatment is to be continued) and the old one discarded.

In eye surgery it is wise to use single-application containers. Preparations used during intra-ocular procedures and others that may penetrate into the anterior chamber must be isotonic and without preservatives and buffered if necessary to a neutral pH. Large volume intravenous infusion preparations are not suitable for this purpose. For all surgical procedures, a previously unopened container is used for each patient.

11.3 Anti-infective preparations

Most acute eye infections can be treated topically. Ideally, eye-drops should be instilled very frequently (at least every 2 hours).

A useful addition for night-time use is an eye ointment because of its longer action. It will also soften crusts which cause the lids and eye lashes to adhere together when the patient is asleep. A small quantity of eye ointment is applied to the eye or within the lower lid.

In severe infections, *subconjunctival injection* of a suitable drug may help to achieve a high intraocular concentration. *Systemic* treatment may also help as, for example, in gonococcal conjunctivitis in the newborn and infective endophthalmitis. The blood-aqueous barrier usually breaks down in the latter case allowing intraocular penetration of systemically administered drugs.

11.3.1 Antibacterials

When prescribing antibiotics, in general, it is preferable to use topically in the eye antibiotics that are seldom or never used for systemic infections. However, the possibility of systemic absorption (section 11.1) must be taken into consideration. Examples of antibiotics with a wide spectrum of activity are **chloramphenicol, framycetin**, **gentamicin**, and **neomycin**. **Gentamicin** and **tobramycin** are effective for treating infections due to *Pseudomonas aeruginosa*; **fusidic acid** is useful for staphylococcal infections. **Sulphacetamide** should no longer be used topically to treat eye infections, since it is rarely of any value.

Propamidine isethionate eye-drops are suitable for the treatment of *blepharitis* and acute and chronic *conjunctivitis*. The use of **mercuric oxide** eye ointment, even for short periods, is **not** recommended.

WITH CORTICOSTEROIDS. Many antibiotic preparations also incorporate a corticosteroid but such mixtures should **not** be used unless a patient is under close specialist supervision. In particular they should not be prescribed for undiagnosed 'red eye' which is sometimes caused by the herpes simplex virus and may be difficult to diagnose (section 11.4).

ADMINISTRATION.
Eye-drops. Apply at least every 2 hours then reduce frequency as infection is controlled and continue for 48 hours after healing.
Eye ointment. Apply *either* at night (if eye-drops used during the day) *or* 3–4 times daily (if eye ointment used alone).

CHLORAMPHENICOL

Indications; Administration: see notes above
Side-effects: transient stinging; rare reports of aplastic anaemia

PoM **Chloramphenicol** (Non-proprietary)
Eye-drops, chloramphenicol 0.5%. Net price 10 mL = 67p
Eye ointment, chloramphenicol 1%. Net price 4 g = 68p

PoM **Chloromycetin®** (P-D)
Ophthalmic ointment (= eye ointment), chloramphenicol 1%. Net price 4 g = 67p
Redidrops (= eye-drops), chloramphenicol 0.5%. Net price 5 mL = £1.10; 10 mL = £1.18
Additives: include phenylmercuric acetate

PoM **Sno Phenicol®** (S&N Pharm.)
Eye-drops, chloramphenicol 0.5%, in a viscous vehicle. Net price 10 mL = £1.00
Additives: include chlorhexidine acetate

Single use
PoM **Minims® Chloramphenicol** (S&N Pharm.)
Eye-drops, chloramphenicol 0.5%. Net price 20 × 0.5 mL = £4.57

PoM **Opulets® Chloramphenicol** (Alcon)
Eye-drops, chloramphenicol 0.5%. Net price 20 × 0.5 mL = £3.54

CHLORTETRACYCLINE

Indications: local treatment of infections, including trachoma (see notes above and under Tetracycline)
Administration: see notes above

PoM **Aureomycin®** (Lederle)
Ophthalmic ointment (= eye ointment), chlortetracycline hydrochloride 1%. Net price 3.5 g = 94p

FRAMYCETIN SULPHATE

Indications; Administration: see notes above

PoM **Framygen®** (Fisons)
Drops (for ear or eye), framycetin sulphate 0.5%. Net price 5 mL = £1.27
Additives: include benzalkonium chloride, benzyl alcohol
Eye ointment, framycetin sulphate 0.5%. Net price 3.5 g = 61p

PoM **Soframycin®** (Roussel)
Eye-drops, framycetin sulphate 0.5%. Net price 8 mL = £2.97
Additives: include phenylmercuric nitrate
Eye ointment, framycetin sulphate 0.5%. Net price 5 g = £1.20
Ophthalmic powder, framycetin sulphate (sterile) for preparing subconjunctival injections. Net price 500-mg vial = £3.85

FUSIDIC ACID

Indications: see notes above

PoM **Fucithalmic®** (Leo)
Eye-drops, s/r, fusidic acid 1% in gel basis (liquifies on contact with eye). Net price 5 g = £2.25
Additives: include benzalkonium chloride
Apply twice daily

GENTAMICIN

Indications; Administration: see notes above

PoM **Cidomycin®** (Roussel)
Drops (for ear or eye), gentamicin 0.3% (as sulphate). Net price 8 mL = £1.34
Additives: include benzalkonium chloride, disodium edetate
Eye ointment, gentamicin 0.3% (as sulphate). Net price 3 g = £1.21

PoM **Garamycin®** (Schering-Plough)
Drops (for ear or eye), gentamicin 0.3% (as sulphate). Net price 10 mL = £1.79
Additives: include benzalkonium chloride

PoM **Genticin®** (Nicholas)
Eye-drops, gentamicin 0.3% (as sulphate). Net price 10 mL = £1.94
Additives: include benzalkonium chloride
Eye ointment, gentamicin 0.3% (as sulphate). Net price 3 g = £1.30
Additives: include hydroxybenzoates

Single use
PoM **Minims® Gentamicin** (S&N Pharm.)
Eye-drops, gentamicin 0.3% (as sulphate). Net price 20 × 0.5 mL = £5.57

NEOMYCIN SULPHATE

Indications; Administration: see notes above

PoM **Neomycin** (Non-proprietary)
Eye-drops, neomycin sulphate 0.5% (3500 units/mL). Net price 10 mL = £1.53
Eye-ointment, neomycin sulphate 0.5% (3500 units/g). Net price 3 g = 64p

PoM **Graneodin®** (Squibb)
Ophthalmic ointment (= eye ointment), gramicidin 0.025%, neomycin sulphate 0.25%. Net price 3.6 g = 61p
Apply 2–4 times daily

PoM **Neosporin®** (Calmic)
Eye-drops, gramicidin 25 units, neomycin sulphate 1700 units, polymyxin B sulphate 5000 units/mL. Net price 5 mL = £4.11
Additives: include thiomersal
Apply 2–4 times daily or more frequently if required

Single use
PoM **Minims® Neomycin Sulphate** (S&N Pharm.)
Eye-drops, neomycin sulphate 0.5%. Net price 20 × 0.5 mL = £5.57

POLYMYXIN B SULPHATE

Indications; Administration: see notes above

PoM **Polyfax®** (Calmic)
Eye ointment, polymyxin B sulphate 10 000 units, bacitracin zinc 500 units/g. Net price 4 g = £2.50

PoM **Polytrim®** (Wellcome)
Eye-drops, trimethoprim 0.1%, polymyxin B sulphate 10000 units/mL. Net price 5 mL = £2.77
Additives: include thiomersal
Eye ointment, trimethoprim 0.5%, polymyxin B sulphate 10000 units/g. Net price 4 g = £2.77

PROPAMIDINE ISETHIONATE

Indications: local treatment of infections

Brolene® (M&B)
Eye-drops, propamidine isethionate 0.1%. Net price 10 mL = £1.33
Apply 4 times daily

SULPHACETAMIDE SODIUM

Indications: not recommended, see notes above
Administration: apply eye-drops every 2–6 hours

PoM **Albucid®** (Nicholas)
Eye-drops, sulphacetamide sodium 10%, net price 10 mL = 85p
Additives: include cetrimide

Single use
PoM **Minims® Sulphacetamide Sodium** (S&N Pharm.)
Eye-drops, sulphacetamide sodium 10%. Net price 20 × 0.5 mL = £5.57

TETRACYCLINE HYDROCHLORIDE

Indications; Administration: see notes above

TRACHOMA. For mass antitrachoma treatment, the World Health Organization recommends **tetracycline hydrochloride** eye ointment applied to both eyes twice daily for 5 days in each month for 6 months. Chlortetracycline eye ointment may also be used but chloramphenicol is not as effective.

For active trachoma in the individual, one or both of the following are effective. (i) For adults, orally administered sulphonamides for 2 weeks or the long-acting sulphadimethoxine (no longer on UK market) 1 g initially followed by 500 mg daily for 10 days (see section 5.1.8). For children, erythromycin should be used (see section 5.1.5). (ii) Tetracycline eye ointment three times daily for 6 weeks.

PoM **Achromycin®** (Lederle)
Ophthalmic oil suspension (= eye-drops), tetracycline hydrochloride 1%, in sesame oil vehicle. Net price 6 mL = £1.85
Ointment (for ear or eye), tetracycline hydrochloride 1%. Net price 3.5 g = 70p

TOBRAMYCIN

Indications; Administration: see notes above

PoM **Tobralex®** (Alcon)
Eye-drops, tobramycin 0.3%. Net price 5 mL = £1.43
Additives: include benzalkonium chloride

11.3.2 Antifungals

Fungal infections of the cornea are rare but tend to occur after agricultural injuries, especially in hot and humid climates. Orbital mycosis is rare, and when it occurs is usually due to direct spread of infection from the paranasal sinuses. Increasing age, debility, or immunosuppression by drugs, for example, following renal transplantation, may encourage fungal proliferation in many parts of the body. The spread of infection via the blood-stream occasionally produces a metastatic endophthalmitis.

A wide range of fungi are capable of producing ocular mycosis and may be identified by appropriate laboratory procedures.

Antifungal preparations for the eye are not generally available. Treatment will normally be carried out at specialist centres, but requests for information about supplies of preparations not available commercially should be addressed to the District Pharmaceutical Officer (or equivalent in

Scotland or Northern Ireland) or to Moorfields Eye Hospital, City Road, London EC1V 2PD (071-253 3411).

11.3.3 Antivirals

Herpes simplex infections producing, for example, dendritic corneal ulcer can be treated with **acyclovir**; alternatively **idoxuridine** may be used.

ACYCLOVIR

Indications: local treatment of herpes simplex infections

Administration: apply 5 times daily (continue for at least 3 days after complete healing)

PoM **Zovirax®** (Wellcome)

Eye ointment, acyclovir 3%. Net price 4.5 g = £9.28

IDOXURIDINE

Indications: local treatment of herpes simplex infections

Contra-indications: pregnancy (toxicity in *animal* studies)

Administration: apply eye-drops every hour during the day and every 2 hours at night; eye ointment every 4 hours

Max. period of treatment 21 days

PoM **Idoxene®** (Spodefell)

Eye ointment, idoxuridine 0.5%. Net price 3 g = £1·10

PoM **Kerecid®** (Allergan)

Eye-drops, idoxuridine 0.1%, polyvinyl alcohol (Liquifilm®) 1.4%. Net price 15 mL = £3.35

Additives: include benzalkonium chloride, disodium edetate

Dose, as above *or* 1 drop every minute for 5 minutes, schedule repeated every 4 hours day and night for max. 21 days

11.4 Corticosteroids and other anti-inflammatory preparations

Corticosteroids administered topically, by subconjunctival injection, and systemically have an important place in treating uveitis and scleritis; they are also used to reduce post-operative inflammation following eye operations.

Topical corticosteroids should normally only be used under expert supervision; they should not be prescribed for undiagnosed 'red eye'. There are two main dangers from topical corticosteroids. First the 'red eye' may be caused by herpes simplex virus which produces a dendritic ulcer; corticosteroids aggravate the condition which may lead to loss of vision or even loss of the eye. Second, again arising from the use of eye-drop formulations, a 'steroid glaucoma' may be produced, after a few weeks treatment, in patients predisposed to chronic simple glaucoma, especially with dexamethasone and prednisolone. Use of a combination product containing a corticosteroid with an anti-infective is rarely justified.

Systemic corticosteroids can usefully be given on an alternate-day basis to minimise side-effects. The risk of producing glaucoma is not great, but 'steroid cataract' is a very high risk (75%) if more than 15 mg of prednisolone or equivalent is given daily for several years. The longer the duration, the greater is the risk. A dose of less then 10 mg per day is usually safe.

Oxyphenbutazone eye ointment does not have the disadvantages of corticosteroids and has been used in the treatment of episcleritis.

Topical preparations of **antihistamines** such as eye-drops containing antazoline sulphate (with xylometazoline hydrochloride as Otrivine-Antistin®) may be used for short-term treatment of allergic conjunctivitis.

Sodium cromoglycate eye-drops may be useful for vernal catarrh and other allergic forms of conjunctivitis.

ANTAZOLINE

Indications: allergic conjunctivitis

Otrivine-Antistin® (Zyma)

Eye-drops, antazoline sulphate 0.5%, xylometazoline hydrochloride 0.05%. Net price 10 mL = £1.25

Additives: include benzalkonium chloride, disodium edetate

Apply 2–3 times daily

PoM **Vasocon A®** (Iolab)

Eye-drops, antazoline phosphate 0.5%, naphazoline hydrochloride 0.05%. Net price 10 mL = £2.41

Additives: include benzalkonium chloride, disodium edetate

Apply every 3–4 hours

BETAMETHASONE

Indications: local treatment of inflammation (short-term)

Cautions; Side-effects: see notes above

Administration: apply eye-drops every 1–2 hours until controlled then reduce frequency, eye ointment 2–4 times daily or at night when used with eye-drops

PoM **Betnesol®** (Glaxo)

Drops (for ear, eye, or nose), betamethasone sodium phosphate 0.1%. Net price 10 mL = £1.31

Additives: include benzalkonium chloride

Eye ointment, betamethasone sodium phosphate 0.1%. Net price 3 g = 56p

PoM **Betnesol-N®** (Glaxo)

Drops (for ear, eye, or nose), see section 12.1.1

Eye ointment, betamethasone sodium phosphate 0.1%, neomycin sulphate 0.5%. Net price 3 g = 64p

PoM **Vista-Methasone®** (Daniel)

Drops (for ear, eye, or nose), betamethasone sodium phosphate 0.1%. Net price 5 mL = 68p; 10 mL = £1.05

Additives: include benzalkonium chloride

PoM **Vista-Methasone N®** (Daniel)

Drops (for ear, eye, or nose), see section 12.1.1

CLOBETASONE BUTYRATE

Indications: local treatment of inflammation (short-term)

Cautions; Side-effects: see notes above; reduced tendency to raise intra-ocular pressure
Administration: apply eye-drops 4 times daily; severe conditions every 1–2 hours until controlled then reduce frequency

PoM **Eumovate®** (Glaxo)
Eye-drops, clobetasone butyrate 0.1%. Net price 10 mL = £3.04
Additives: include benzalkonium chloride

PoM **Eumovate-N®** (Glaxo)
Eye-drops, clobetasone butyrate 0.1%, neomycin sulphate 0.5%. Net price 10 mL = £2.70
Additives: include benzalkonium chloride

DEXAMETHASONE

Indications: local treatment of inflammation (short-term)
Cautions; Side-effects: see notes above
Administration: apply eye-drops 4–6 times daily; severe conditions every hour until controlled then reduce frequency

PoM **Maxidex®** (Alcon)
Eye-drops, dexamethasone 0.1%, hypromellose 0.5%. Net price 5 mL = £1.53; 10 mL = £3.03
Additives: include benzalkonium chloride

PoM **Maxitrol®** (Alcon)
Eye-drops, dexamethasone 0.1%, hypromellose 0.5%, neomycin 0.35% (as sulphate), polymyxin B sulphate 6000 units/mL. Net price 5 mL = £1.81
Additives: include benzalkonium chloride
Eye ointment, dexamethasone 0.1%, neomycin 0.35% (as sulphate), polymyxin B sulphate 6000 units/g. Net price 3.5 g = £1.56
Additives: include hydroxybenzoates

PoM **Sofradex®** (Roussel)
Drops and ointment (for ear or eye), see section 12.1.1

FLUOROMETHOLONE

Indications: local treatment of inflammation (short-term)
Cautions; Side-effects: see notes above; reduced tendency to raise intra-ocular pressure
Administration: apply eye-drops 2–4 times daily (initially every hour for 24–48 hours then reduce frequency)

PoM **FML®** (Allergan)
Ophthalmic suspension (= eye-drops), fluorometholone 0.1%, polyvinyl alcohol (Liquifilm®) 1.4%. Net price 5 mL = £1.78; 10 mL = £2.83
Additives: include benzalkonium chloride, disodium edetate, polysorbate 80

PoM **FML-Neo®** (Allergan)
Eye-drops, fluorometholone 0.1%, neomycin sulphate 0.5%, polyvinyl alcohol (Liquifilm®) 1.4%. Net price 5 mL = £1.90
Additives: include benzalkonium chloride, disodium edetate, polysorbate 80

HYDROCORTISONE ACETATE

Indications: local treatment of inflammation (short-term)
Cautions; Side-effects: see notes above

PoM **Hydrocortisone** (Non-proprietary)
Eye-drops, hydrocortisone acetate 1%. Net price 10 mL = £1.20
Eye ointment, hydrocortisone acetate 0.5%, net price 3 g = 85p; 1%, 3 g = £1.00; 2.5%, 3 g = 75p

PoM **Chloromycetin Hydrocortisone®** (P-D)
Eye ointment, chloramphenicol 1%, hydrocortisone acetate 0.5%. Net price 4 g = 70p

PoM **Framycort®** (Fisons)
Drops (for ear or eye), framycetin sulphate 0.5%, hydrocortisone acetate 0.5%. Net price 5 mL = £2.21
Additives: include benzalkonium chloride, benzyl alcohol
Eye ointment, framycetin sulphate 0.5%, hydrocortisone acetate 0.5%. Net price 3.5 g = £1.17

PoM **Neo-Cortef®** (Upjohn)
Drops and *ointment* (for ear or eye), see section 12.1.1

OXYPHENBUTAZONE

Indications: local treatment of inflammation
Administration: apply eye ointment 2–5 times daily (discontinue if no improvement after 8 days)

PoM **Tanderil®** (Zyma)
Eye ointment, oxyphenbutazone 10%. Net price 5 g = 63p
Additives: include wool fat

PoM **Tanderil Chloramphenicol®** (Zyma)
Eye ointment, chloramphenicol 1%, oxyphenbutazone 10%. Net price 5 g = £1.02
Additives: include wool fat

PREDNISOLONE

Indications: local treatment of inflammation (short-term)
Cautions; Side-effects: see notes above
Administration: apply eye-drops every 1–2 hours until controlled then reduce frequency

PoM **Pred Forte®** (Allergan)
Eye-drops, prednisolone acetate 1%. Net price 5 mL = £1.55; 10 mL = £3.09
Additives: include benzalkonium chloride, disodium edetate, polysorbate 80
Apply 2–4 times daily

PoM **Predsol®** (Glaxo)
Drops (for ear or eye), prednisolone sodium phosphate 0.5%. Net price 10 mL = £1.31
Additives: include benzalkonium chloride

PoM **Predsol-N®** (Glaxo)
Drops (for ear or eye), see section 12.1.1

Single use
PoM **Minims® Prednisolone** (S&N Pharm.)
Eye-drops, prednisolone sodium phosphate 0.5%. Net price 20 × 0.5 mL = £5.57

SODIUM CROMOGLYCATE

Indications: allergic conjunctivitis
Administration: apply eye-drops 4 times daily, eye ointment 2–3 times daily

PoM **Opticrom®** (Fisons)
[1]*Aqueous eye-drops*, sodium cromoglycate 2%. Net price 13.5 mL = £5.59
Additives: include benzalkonium chloride, disodium edetate
1. Formerly called *Opticrom® Eye-drops*
Eye ointment, sodium cromoglycate 4%. Net price 5 g = £5.99
Additives: include wool fat

11.5 Mydriatics and cycloplegics

Antimuscarinics dilate the pupil and paralyse the ciliary muscle; they vary in potency and duration of action. The relative potencies and durations of action of the principal drugs, in ascending order, are:

tropicamide (3 hours)
cyclopentolate, hyoscine, homatropine (all up to 24 hours)
atropine (7 days or longer)

Short-acting, relatively weak mydriatics, such as **tropicamide 0.5%**, facilitate the examination of the fundus of the eye.

Cyclopentolate 1% or **atropine** are preferable for producing cycloplegia for refraction in young children. Atropine 1% (in ointment form) is preferred for children under 5 years of age. Atropine is also used for the treatment of iridocyclitis mainly to prevent posterior synechiae, often with phenylephrine 10% eye-drops (2.5% in children and those with cardiac disease).

CAUTIONS AND SIDE-EFFECTS. Contact dermatitis is not uncommon with the antimuscarinic mydriatic drugs, especially atropine. In addition, toxic systemic reactions to atropine (and hyoscine) may occur in the very young and the very old.

Darkly pigmented iris is more resistant to pupillary dilatation and caution should be exercised to avoid overdosage.

Mydriasis may precipitate acute closed-angle ('congestive') glaucoma in a few patients, usually aged over 60 years, who are predisposed to the condition because of a shallow anterior chamber and small diameter cornea.

Interactions. Phenylephrine may interact with systemically administered monoamine-oxidase inhibitors; see also Appendix 1 (sympathomimetics).

DRIVING. Patients should be warned not to drive for 1 to 2 hours after mydriasis.

ANTIMUSCARINICS

ATROPINE SULPHATE

Indications: refraction procedures in young children; see also notes above
Cautions: action persistent, may precipitate glaucoma; see also notes above

PoM **Atropine Eye-drops,** atropine sulphate 1%. Net price 10 mL = 68p
PoM **Atropine Eye Ointment,** atropine sulphate 1%. Net price 3 g = £1.01
PoM **Isopto Atropine®** (Alcon)
Eye-drops, atropine sulphate 1%, hypromellose 0.5%. Net price 5 mL = £1.02
Additives: include benzalkonium chloride

Single use
PoM **Minims® Atropine Sulphate** (S&N Pharm.)
Eye-drops, atropine sulphate 1%. Net price 20 × 0.5 mL = £4.57

PoM **Opulets® Atropine Sulphate** (Alcon)
Eye-drops, atropine 1%. Net price 20 × 0.5 mL = £3.54

CYCLOPENTOLATE HYDROCHLORIDE

Indications: see notes above
Cautions: patients with raised intra-ocular pressure; see notes above

PoM **Mydrilate®** (Boehringer Ingelheim)
Eye-drops, cyclopentolate hydrochloride 0.5%, net price 5 mL = 67p; 1%, 5 mL = 90p
Additives: include benzalkonium chloride
PoM **Opulets® Cyclopentolate** (Alcon)
Eye-drops, cyclopentolate hydrochloride 1%. Net price 20 × 0.5 mL = £3.54

Single use
PoM **Minims® Cyclopentolate** (S&N Pharm.)
Eye-drops, cyclopentolate hydrochloride 0.5 and 1%. Net price 20 × 0.5 mL (both) = £4.57

HOMATROPINE HYDROBROMIDE

Indications; Cautions: see notes above

PoM **Homatropine Eye-drops,** homatropine hydrobromide 1%, net price 10 mL = £1.68; 2%, 10 mL = £1.79

Single use
PoM **Minims® Homatropine Hydrobromide** (S&N Pharm.)
Eye-drops, homatropine hydrobromide 2%. Net price 20 × 0.5 mL = £5.57

HYOSCINE HYDROBROMIDE

Indications; Cautions: see notes above

PoM **Hyoscine Eye-drops,** usual strength hyoscine hydrobromide 0.25%. Net price 10 mL = 84p

LACHESINE CHLORIDE

Indications: see notes above; useful in patients hypersensitive to other mydriatics
Cautions: see notes above

Lachesine Eye-drops, lachesine chloride 1%. Net price 10 mL = £3.60

TROPICAMIDE

Indications; Cautions: see notes above

PoM **Mydriacyl®** (Alcon)
Eye-drops, tropicamide 0.5%, net price 5 mL = £1.39; 1%, 5 mL = £1.72
Additives: include benzalkonium chloride

Single use
PoM **Minims® Tropicamide** (S&N Pharm.)
Eye-drops, tropicamide 0.5 and 1%. Net price 20 × 0.5 mL (both) = £5.57

SYMPATHOMIMETICS

ADRENALINE
See section 11.6

PHENYLEPHRINE HYDROCHLORIDE
Indications; Cautions: see notes above

Phenylephrine Eye-drops, phenylephrine hydrochloride 10%. Net price 10 mL = £1.75
See also under Hypromellose (section 11.8.1)

Single use
Minims® Phenylephrine Hydrochloride (S&N Pharm.)
Eye-drops, phenylephrine hydrochloride 2.5%, net price 20 × 0.5 mL = £5.57; 10%, 20 × 0.5 mL = £5.57

11.6 Treatment of glaucoma

An abnormally high intra-ocular pressure, glaucoma, may result in blindness. In virtually all cases, rise in pressure is due to reduced outflow of aqueous humour, the inflow remaining constant.

Glaucoma is treated by the application of eye-drops containing beta-blockers, miotics, or adrenaline (and guanethidine). Acetazolamide and dichlorphenamide are given by mouth and, in emergency or before surgery, mannitol may be given by intravenous infusion.

Probably the commonest condition is *chronic simple glaucoma* where the obstruction is in the trabecular meshwork. It is commonly first treated with a topical beta-blocker and other drugs added as necessary to control the intra-ocular pressure e.g. adrenaline or pilocarpine.

If supplementary topical treatment is required after *iridectomy* or a drainage operation in either open-angle or closed-angle glaucoma, a beta-blocker is preferred to pilocarpine. This is because of the risk that posterior synechiae will be formed as a result of the miotic effect of pilocarpine, especially in closed-angle glaucoma. It is then also advantageous to utilise the mydriatic side-effect of adrenaline.

MIOTICS

The small pupil is an unfortunate side-effect of these drugs (except when pilocarpine is used temporarily prior to operation for *closed-angle glaucoma*). The key factor is the opening up of the inefficient drainage channels in the trabecular meshwork resulting from contraction or spasm of the ciliary muscle. This also produces accommodation spasm that may result in blurring of vision and browache (a particular disadvantage in patients under 40 years of age).

Pilocarpine has a duration of action of 3 to 4 hours. **Physostigmine** is more potent; it is still used with pilocarpine but is not usually used alone. **Carbachol** is sometimes used to lower intra-ocular pressure, usually in conjunction with other miotics such as physostigmine.

Demecarium bromide (as *Tosmilen®*, Sinclair) and **ecothiopate iodide** (as *Phospholine Iodide®*, Cusi) are no longer on the UK market but are still available on a named-patient basis for use under expert supervision.

CARBACHOL
Indications: see notes above
Administration: apply eye-drops up to 4 times daily

PoM **Isopto Carbachol®** (Alcon)
Eye-drops, carbachol 3%, hypromellose 1%. Net price 10 mL = £1.80
Additives: include benzalkonium chloride

PHYSOSTIGMINE SULPHATE
(Eserine)
Indications; Side-effects: see notes above
Administration: apply eye-drops 2–6 times daily

PoM **Physostigmine** (Non-proprietary)
Eye-drops, physostigmine sulphate 0.25 and 0.5%. Net price 10 mL (both) = £1.90

PoM **Physostigmine and Pilocarpine** (Non-proprietary)
Eye-drops, physostigmine sulphate 0.25%, pilocarpine hydrochloride 2%. Net price 10 mL = £1.59
Eye-drops, physostigmine sulphate 0.25%, pilocarpine hydrochloride 4%. Net price 10 mL = £2.75
Eye-drops, physostigmine sulphate 0.5%, pilocarpine hydrochloride 4%. Net price 10 mL = £3.10

PILOCARPINE
Indications; Side-effects: see notes above
Administration: apply eye-drops 3–6 times daily

PoM **Pilocarpine** (Non-proprietary)
Eye-drops, pilocarpine hydrochloride 0.5 and 1%, net price 10 mL = £1.11; 2%, 10 mL = £1.20; 3%, 10 mL = £1.36; 4%, 10 mL = £1.51

PoM **Isopto Carpine®** (Alcon)
Eye-drops, all with hypromellose 0.5%; pilocarpine hydrochloride 0.5%, net price 10 mL = 75p; 1%, 10 mL = 83p; 2%, 10 mL = 92p; 3%, 10 mL = 99p; 4%, 10 mL = £1.07
Additives: include benzalkonium chloride

PoM **Sno Pilo®** (S&N Pharm.)
Eye-drops, in a viscous vehicle, pilocarpine hydrochloride 1%, net price 10 mL = 96p; 2%, 10 mL = £1.05; 4%, 10 mL = £1.25
Additives: include benzalkonium chloride

Single use
PoM **Minims® Pilocarpine Nitrate** (S&N Pharm.)
Eye-drops, pilocarpine nitrate 1, 2, and 4%. Net price 20 × 0.5 mL (all) = £4.57

PoM **Opulets® Pilocarpine** (Alcon)
Eye-drops, pilocarpine hydrochloride 1, 2, and 4%. Net price 20 × 0.5 mL (all) = £3.54

Sustained-release

PoM **Ocusert®** (M&B)

Pilo-20 ocular insert, s/r, pilocarpine 20 micrograms released per hour for 1 week. Net price per insert = £3.37. Counselling, method of use

Pilo-40 ocular insert, s/r, pilocarpine 40 micrograms released per hour for 1 week. Net price per insert = £3.87. Counselling, method of use

ADRENALINE/GUANETHIDINE

Adrenaline probably acts both by reducing the rate of production of aqueous humour and by increasing the outflow through the trabecular meshwork. It is contra-indicated in closed-angle glaucoma because it is a mydriatic, unless an iridectomy has been carried out. Side-effects include severe smarting and redness of the eye; adrenaline should be used with caution in patients with hypertension and heart disease.

Dipivefrine is a prodrug of adrenaline. It is stated to pass more rapidly through the cornea and is then converted to the active form.

Guanethidine enhances and prolongs the effects of adrenaline. It is also used alone and produces initial mydriasis with increased aqueous outflow followed by miosis with reduced aqueous secretion. Prolonged use, particularly of the higher strengths may result in conjunctival fibrosis with secondary corneal changes; the conjunctiva and cornea should be examined at least every six months.

ADRENALINE

Indications; Contra-indications: see notes above
Administration: apply eye-drops 1–2 times daily

PoM **Epifrin®** (Allergan)

Eye-drops, adrenaline 1% (as hydrochloride). Net price 10 mL = £2.24

Additives: include benzalkonium chloride, disodium edetate

Eppy® (S&N Pharm.)

Eye-drops, adrenaline 1%. Net price 7.5 mL = £3.75

Additives: include phenylmercuric acetate

Isopto Epinal® (Alcon)

Eye-drops, adrenaline 1% (as borate complex) and hypromellose 0.5%. Net price 7.5 mL = £1.62

Additives: include benzalkonium chloride

PoM **Simplene®** (S&N Pharm.)

Eye-drops, adrenaline, in a viscous vehicle, 0.5%, net price 7.5 mL = £3.19; 1%, 7.5 mL = £3.50

DIPIVEFRINE HYDROCHLORIDE

Indications; Contra-indications: as for Adrenaline, see notes above
Administration: apply 1 drop twice daily

PoM **Propine®** (Allergan)

Eye-drops, dipivefrine hydrochloride 0.1%. Net price 10 mL = £4.89

Additives: include benzalkonium chloride, disodium edetate

GUANETHIDINE MONOSULPHATE

Indications; Cautions: see notes above
Administration: apply eye-drops 1–2 times daily

PoM **Ganda®** (S&N Pharm.)

Eye-drops '1 + 0.2', guanethidine monosulphate 1%, adrenaline 0.2% in a viscous vehicle. Net price 7.5 mL = £4.14

Additives: include benzalkonium chloride

Eye-drops '3 + 0.5', guanethidine monosulphate 3%, adrenaline 0.5% in a viscous vehicle. Net price 7.5 mL = £5.41

Additives: include benzalkonium chloride

PoM **Ismelin®** (Zyma)

Eye-drops, guanethidine monosulphate 5%. Net price 5 mL = £1.87

Additives: include benzalkonium chloride

BETA-BLOCKERS

Topical application of a beta-blocker to the eye reduces intra-ocular pressure effectively in *chronic simple glaucoma*, probably by reducing the rate of production of aqueous humour. Administration by mouth also reduces intra-ocular pressure but this route is not used (see comment under Systemic Drugs).

Beta-blockers used as eye-drops include **timolol** and, more recently, **betaxolol**, **carteolol**, **levobunolol**, and **metipranolol**.

SIDE-EFFECTS. Systemic absorption may follow topical application, therefore beta-blocker eye-drops are contra-indicated in patients with asthma or a history of obstructive airways disease; the CSM has advised that both cardioselective *and* non-cardioselective beta-blocker eye-drops should be avoided.

> **CSM advice.** The CSM has advised that beta-blockers, even those with apparent cardioselectivity, should not be used in patients with asthma or a history of obstructive airways disease, unless no alternative treatment is available. In such cases the risk of inducing bronchospasm should be appreciated and appropriate precautions taken.

Eye-drops containing a beta-blocker are also contra-indicated in patients with bradycardia, heart block, or heart failure.

Local side-effects of eye-drops containing a beta-blocker include transitory dry eyes and allergic blepharoconjunctivitis.

DRUG INTERACTIONS. Administration may give rise notably to an interaction with drugs such as verapamil. See also section 2.3.2 and Appendix 1 (beta-blockers).

BETAXOLOL HYDROCHLORIDE

Indications; Cautions; Contra-indications; Side-effects: see notes above
Administration: apply eye-drops twice daily

PoM **Betoptic®** (Alcon)
Eye-drops, betaxolol 0.5% (as hydrochloride). Net price 5 mL = £5.30
Additives: include benzalkonium chloride

CARTEOLOL HYDROCHLORIDE

Indications; Cautions; Contra-indications; Side-effects: see notes above
Administration: apply eye-drops twice daily

PoM **Teoptic®** (Dispersa)
Eye-drops, carteolol hydrochloride 1%, net price 5 mL = £5.05; 2%, 5 mL = £5.67
Additives: include benzalkonium chloride

LEVOBUNOLOL HYDROCHLORIDE

Indications; Cautions; Contra-indications; Side-effects: see notes above
Administration: apply eye-drops once or twice daily

▼ PoM **Betagan®** (Allergan)
Eye-drops, levobunolol hydrochloride 0.5%, polyvinyl alcohol (Liquifilm®) 1.4%. Net price 5 mL = £5.05
Additives: include benzalkonium chloride, disodium edetate

METIPRANOLOL

Indications; Cautions; Contra-indications; Side-effects: see notes above; granulomatous anterior uveitis reported
Administration: apply eye-drops twice daily

PoM **Glauline®** (S&N Pharm.)
Sales suspended following reports of anterior uveitis

Single use
PoM **Minims® Metipranolol** (S&N Pharm.)
Eye-drops, metipranolol 0.1%, net price 20 × 0.5 mL = £9.21; 0.3%, 20 × 0.5 mL = £10.73; 0.6%, 20 × 0.5 mL = £11.81

TIMOLOL MALEATE

Indications; Cautions; Contra-indications; Side-effects: see notes above
Administration: apply eye-drops twice daily

PoM **Timoptol®** (MSD)
Eye-drops, in Ocumeter® metered-dose unit, timolol (as maleate) 0.25%, net price 5 mL = £5.18; 0.5%, 5 mL = £5.82
Additives: include benzalkonium chloride

SYSTEMIC DRUGS

The side-effects of beta-blockers are probably sufficient to prevent their being prescribed by the ophthalmologist for administration by mouth. Hence **acetazolamide** will retain a significant place in treatment. It inhibits carbonic anhydrase, thus reducing the bicarbonate in aqueous humour and the water secreted with it, resulting in a fall in the intra-ocular pressure. **Dichlorphenamide** has a similar but more prolonged action. Both these drugs have a diuretic action and a moderate incidence of side-effects, giving rise, especially in the elderly, to paraesthesia, hypokalaemia, lack of appetite, drowsiness and depression; rashes and blood disorders occur rarely. Intravenous hypertonic **mannitol**, or **glycerol** by mouth, are useful short-term ocular hypotensive drugs. Acetazolamide by intramuscular or preferably intravenous injection is also useful in the pre-operative treatment of closed-angle glaucoma.

ACETAZOLAMIDE

Indications; Side-effects: see notes above
Cautions: avoid in severe renal impairment; pregnancy; not generally recommended for prolonged administration but if given blood counts needed; **interactions:** Appendix 1 (acetazolamide)
Dose: *by mouth or by intravenous injection*, 0.25–1 g daily in divided doses
By intramuscular injection, as for intravenous injection but preferably avoided because of alkaline pH

PoM **Acetazolamide** (Non-proprietary)
Tablets, acetazolamide 250 mg. Net price 20 = 25p. Label: 3

PoM **Diamox®** (Lederle)
Tablets, acetazolamide 250 mg. Net price 20 = £1.96. Label: 3
Sustets® (= capsules s/r), orange, acetazolamide 500 mg. Net price 20 = £5.49. Label: 3, 25
Dose: 1 capsule twice daily
Sodium Parenteral (= injection), powder for reconstitution, acetazolamide (as sodium salt). Net price 500-mg vial = £15.14

DICHLORPHENAMIDE

Indications; Cautions; Side-effects: see under Acetazolamide and notes above
Dose: initially 100–200 mg, then 100 mg every 12 hours, adjusted according to the patient's response

PoM **Daranide®** (MSD)
Tablets, yellow, scored, dichlorphenamide 50 mg. Net price 20 = 79p

11.7 Local anaesthetics

Oxybuprocaine and amethocaine are probably the most widely used topical local anaesthetics. Proxymetacaine causes less initial stinging and is useful for children. Cocaine, by potentiating noradrenaline, produces useful vasoconstriction, but is now much less used in surgery. Oxybuprocaine or a combined preparation of lignocaine and fluorescein is used for tonometry. Lignocaine, with or without adrenaline, is injected into the eyelids for minor surgery, while a retrobulbar injection may be used for major eye surgery.

AMETHOCAINE HYDROCHLORIDE
Indications: local anaesthetic

PoM **Amethocaine Eye-drops,** amethocaine hydrochloride 0.5%, net price, 10 mL = £1.65; 1%, 10 mL = £1.46

Single use
PoM **Minims® Amethocaine Hydrochloride** (S&N Pharm.)
Eye-drops, amethocaine hydrochloride 0.5 and 1%. Net price 20 × 0.5 mL (both) = £5.57

COCAINE HYDROCHLORIDE
Indications: local anaesthetic

CD **Cocaine Eye-drops,** cocaine hydrochloride 4%. Net price 10 mL = £3.20
CD **Cocaine and Homatropine Eye-drops,** cocaine hydrochloride 2%, homatropine hydrobromide 2%.

LIGNOCAINE HYDROCHLORIDE
Indications: local anaesthetic

PoM **Minims® Lignocaine and Fluorescein** (S&N Pharm.)
Eye-drops, lignocaine hydrochloride 4%, fluorescein sodium 0.25%. Net price 20 × 0.5 mL = £6.71

OXYBUPROCAINE HYDROCHLORIDE
Indications: local anaesthetic

PoM **Minims® Benoxinate (Oxybuprocaine) Hydrochloride** (S&N Pharm.)
Eye-drops, oxybuprocaine hydrochloride 0.4%. Net price 20 × 0.5 mL = £4.57
PoM **Opulets® Benoxinate (Oxybuprocaine) Hydrochloride** (Alcon)
Eye-drops, oxybuprocaine hydrochloride 0.4%. Net price 20 × 0.5 mL = £3.54

PROXYMETACAINE HYDROCHLORIDE
Indications: local anaesthetic

PoM **Ophthaine®** (Squibb)
Eye-drops, proxymetacaine hydrochloride 0.5%. Net price 15 mL = £4.49
Additives: include benzalkonium chloride, chlorbutol

11.8 Miscellaneous ophthalmic preparations

11.8.1 Preparations for tear deficiency

Chronically sore eyes associated with reduced tear secretion, usually in cases of rheumatoid arthritis (Sjögren's syndrome), often respond to hypromellose eye-drops and mucolytic agents.

ACETYLCYSTEINE
Indications: tear deficiency, impaired mucus production
Administration: apply eye-drops 3–4 times daily

PoM **Ilube®** (DF)
Eye-drops, acetylcysteine 5%, hypromellose 0.35%. Net price 15 mL = £4.96
Additives: include benzalkonium chloride

HYDROXYETHYLCELLULOSE
Indications: tear deficiency

Minims® Artifical Tears (S&N Pharm.)
Eye-drops, hydroxyethylcellulose 0.44%. Net price 20 × 0.5 mL = £5.57

HYPROMELLOSE
Indications: tear deficiency

Hypromellose Eye-drops, hypromellose '4000' (or '4500' or '5000') 0.3%. Net price 10 mL = 75p
BJ6 (Macarthys; Thornton & Ross)
Eye-drops, hypromellose 0.25%. Net price 10 mL = 90p and 85p, respectively
Additives: include chlorhexidine (as acetate or gluconate), polysorbate 80
Isopto Alkaline® (Alcon)
Eye-drops, hypromellose 1%. Net price 10 mL = £1.02
Additives: include benzalkonium chloride
Isopto Plain® (Alcon)
Eye-drops, hypromellose 0.5%. Net price 10 mL = 87p
Additives: include benzalkonium chloride
Tears Naturale® (Alcon)
Eye-drops, dextran '70' 0.1%, hypromellose 0.3%. Net price 15 mL = £1.72
Additives: include benzalkonium chloride, disodium edetate

With phenylephrine
Isopto Frin® (Alcon)
Eye-drops, phenylephrine hydrochloride 0.12%, hypromellose 0.5%. Net price 10 mL = £1.17
Additives: include benzethonium chloride

LIQUID PARAFFIN
Indications: tear deficiency

Lacri-Lube® (Allergan)
Eye ointment, liquid paraffin. Net price 3.5 g = £1.97
Additives: include chlorbutol, wool fat derivatives

POLYVINYL ALCOHOL
Indications: tear deficiency

Hypotears® (Iolab)
Eye-drops, macrogol '8000' 2%, polyvinyl alcohol 1%. Net price 10 mL = £1.85
Additives: include benzalkonium chloride, disodium edetate
Liquifilm Tears® (Allergan)
Eye-drops, polyvinyl alcohol 1.4%. Net price 15 mL = £1.72
Additives: include benzalkonium chloride, disodium edetate

Sno Tears® (S&N Pharm.)
Eye-drops, polyvinyl alcohol 1.4%. Net price 10 mL = £1.02
Additives: include benzalkonium chloride, disodium edetate

11.8.2 Other preparations

Zinc sulphate is a traditional astringent which has been used in eye-drops for treatment of excessive lachrymation.

Simple eye ointment is a bland sterile preparation which may be used to soften crusts in blepharitis or as a bland lubricant at night.

Thymoxamine is used to reverse the mydriasis produced by phenylephrine.

Fluorescein sodium and **rose bengal** are used in diagnostic procedures and for locating damaged areas of the cornea due to injury or disease. Rose bengal is much more efficient for the diagnosis of conjunctival epithelial damage.

Certain eye-drops, e.g. benzylpenicillin, colistin, desferrioxamine, and trisodium edetate (see also section 9.5.1.2), may be prepared aseptically from material supplied for injection.

ACETYLCHOLINE CHLORIDE

Indications: cataract surgery, penetrating keratoplasty, iridectomy, and other anterior segment surgery requiring rapid miosis

PoM **Miochol®** (Iolab)
Solution for intra-ocular irrigation, acetylcholine chloride 1%, mannitol 3% when reconstituted. Net price 2 mL-vial = £7.78

CASTOR OIL

Indications: emollient and lubricant used in removal of foreign bodies

Minims® Castor Oil (S&N Pharm.)
Eye-drops, castor oil. Net price 20 × 0.5 mL = £5.57

CHYMOTRYPSIN

Indications: zonulolysis in intracapsular cataract extraction

PoM **Zonulysin®** (Henleys)
Injection, powder for reconstitution, alphachymotrypsin 300 USP units (≡ 1.5 microkatals). Net price per vial (with diluent) = £3.42

PARAFFIN, YELLOW, SOFT

Indications: see notes above

Simple Eye Ointment, liquid paraffin 10%, wool fat 10%, in yellow soft paraffin. Net price 4 g = 68p

SODIUM CHLORIDE

Indications: irrigation, including first-aid removal of harmful substances

Sodium Chloride Eye Lotion, sodium chloride 0.9%. Net price 200 mL = £1.36
Note. The BP directs that any Eye Lotion not used within 24 hours of opening the container should be discarded.

Balanced Salt Solution
Solution (sterile), sodium chloride 0.64%, sodium acetate 0.39%, sodium citrate 0.17%, calcium chloride 0.048%, magnesium chloride 0.03%, potassium chloride 0.075%.
Available from Alcon (15 mL and 30 mL) and from Iolab (15 mL)

Normasol® (Seton Prebbles)
Solution (sterile), sodium chloride 0.9%. Net price 25 mL sachet = 13p

Single use

Minims® Sodium Chloride (S&N Pharm.)
Eye-drops, sodium chloride 0.9%. Net price 20 × 0.5 mL = £4.57

Opulets® Sodium Chloride (Alcon)
Eye-drops, sodium chloride 0.9%. Net price 20 × 0.5 mL = £3.54

SODIUM HYALURONATE

(a visco-elastic polymer normally present in the aqueous and vitreous humour)

Indications: used during surgical procedures on the eye
Side-effects: occasional hypersensitivity (avian origin); occasional transient rise in intra-ocular pressure

PoM **Healonid®** (Pharmacia)
Injection, sodium hyaluronate 10 mg/mL in disposable syringes, net price 0.5 mL = £41.10, 0.75 mL = £61.62

THYMOXAMINE HYDROCHLORIDE

Indications: see notes above
Side-effects: minimal conjunctival hyperaemia for a few hours; rarely transient ptosis
Administration: apply one drop as required

PoM **Minims® Thymoxamine Hydrochloride** (S&N Pharm.)
Eye-drops, thymoxamine hydrochloride 0.5%. Net price 20 × 0.5 mL = £5.57

ZINC SULPHATE

Indications; Cautions: see notes above

Zinc Sulphate Eye-drops, zinc sulphate 0.25%. Net price 10 mL = £1.64

DIAGNOSTIC PREPARATIONS

FLUORESCEIN SODIUM

Indications: detection of lesions and foreign bodies, but see notes above

Minims® Fluorescein Sodium (S&N Pharm.)
Eye-drops, fluorescein sodium 1 or 2%. Net price 20 × 0.5 mL (both) = £4.57

Opulets® Fluorescein Sodium (Alcon)
Eye-drops, fluorescein sodium 1%. Net price 20 × 0.5 mL = £3.54

ROSE BENGAL
Indications: detection of lesions and foreign bodies

Minims® Rose Bengal (S&N Pharm.)
Eye-drops, rose bengal 1%. Net price 20 × 0.5 mL = £5.57

11.9 Contact lenses

Many patients wear these lenses and special care is required in prescribing eye preparations for them. Unless medically indicated the lenses should not be worn during treatment. If the patient is wearing hard lenses the use of eye-drops containing anti-inflammatory drugs over long periods of time is to be deprecated. Some drugs can spoil hydrophilic soft lenses. Therefore unless eye-drops are specifically indicated as safe to use with hydrophilic contact lenses, the lenses should be removed before instillation and not worn during the period of treatment.

Hydrophilic plastic used for many soft contact lenses will selectively bind certain preservatives and could then be a source of irritation. Thiomersal is usually satisfactory. Chlorhexidine acetate is satisfactory in some cases, while phenylmercuric acetate or nitrate is usually satisfactory but is not recommended for long-term treatment. Benzalkonium chloride is unsuitable in all cases.

Sodium chloride solution 0.9% (sterile) can be used to store soft hydrophilic lenses provided that the case, lenses, and solution are regularly subjected to a heat treatment to reduce microbial contamination (such as 80°C for 40 minutes).

12: Drugs used in the treatment of diseases of the EAR, NOSE, and OROPHARYNX

In this chapter, drug treatment is discussed under the following headings:

12.1 Drugs acting on the ear
12.2 Drugs acting on the nose
12.3 Drugs acting on the oropharynx

12.1 Drugs acting on the ear

12.1.1 Otitis externa
12.1.2 Otitis media
12.1.3 Removal of ear wax

For treatment of labyrinthine disorders see section 4.6.

12.1.1 Otitis externa

Otitis externa is an eczematous reaction of the meatal skin. It is important to exclude an underlying chronic otitis media before treatment is commenced. Many cases recover after thorough cleansing of the external ear canal by suction, dry mopping, or gentle syringing. A frequent problem in resistant cases is the difficulty in applying lotions and ointments satisfactorily to the relatively inaccessible affected skin. The most effective method is to introduce a ribbon gauze dressing soaked with **corticosteroid** ear drops or with an astringent such as **aluminium acetate** solution. When this is not practical, the ear should be gently cleaned with a probe covered in cotton wool and the patient encouraged to lie with the affected ear uppermost for ten minutes after the canal has been filled with a liberal quantity of the appropriate solution.

If infection is present, a topical anti-infective which is not used systemically (such as **framycetin, neomycin**, or **clioquinol**) may be used, but for only about a week as excessive use may result in fungal infections; these may be difficult to treat and require expert advice. Sensitivity to the anti-infective or solvent may occur and resistance to antibacterials is a possibility with prolonged use. **Chloramphenicol** may also be used but the ear drops contain propylene glycol and cause sensitivity in about 10% of patients (the eye ointment can be used instead). Solutions containing an anti-infective and a corticosteroid (such as Locorten-Vioform®) are used for treating cases where infection is present with inflammation and eczema. The CSM has warned that when otitis externa is treated topically with preparations containing chlorhexidine, aminoglycosides (e.g. neomycin, framycetin), or polymyxins in patients who have a perforation of the tympanic membrane, there is an increased risk of drug-induced deafness. It is therefore important to ensure that there is no perforation in such patients before prescription of these preparations. In the presence of a perforation many specialists, however, do use these drops cautiously in patients with *otitis media*, see section 12.1.2.

An acute infection may cause severe pain and a systemic antibiotic is required with a simple analgesic such as paracetamol. When a resistant staphylococcal infection (a boil) is present in the external auditory meatus, **flucloxacillin** is the drug of choice (see section 5.1.1.2). Amoxycillin or phenoxymethylpenicillin are used for other infections (see section 5.1, Table 1).

The skin of the pinna adjacent to the ear canal is often affected by eczema, and topical corticosteroid creams and ointments (see section 13.4) are then required and should be applied five or six times daily. Prolonged use should be avoided.

Ear drops or **ointment** should be applied using 3–4 drops of a liquid preparation or a similar quantity of ointment, warmed if necessary, inserted into the affected ear. If discharge is profuse, ear drops applied directly may be washed away; in these circumstances the ear canal should be carefully cleaned and a quarter-inch gauze wick impregnated with the ear drops should be introduced into it.

ASTRINGENT PREPARATIONS

ALUMINIUM ACETATE

Indications: inflammation in otitis externa

Aluminium Acetate Ear drops (13%) consists of aluminium acetate solution, BP.
Insert into the meatus or apply on a gauze wick which should be kept saturated with the ear-drops
Available from Macarthys and Penn (special order)

Aluminium Acetate Ear drops (8%), prepared by diluting 8 parts of aluminium acetate solution, BP, with 5 parts of purified water, freshly boiled and cooled. It must be freshly prepared.
Directions as above

ANTI-INFLAMMATORY PREPARATIONS

BETAMETHASONE SODIUM PHOSPHATE

Indications: eczematous inflammation in otitis externa
Cautions: avoid prolonged use
Contra-indications: untreated infection

PoM **Betnesol®** (Glaxo)
Drops (for ear, eye, or nose), betamethasone sodium phosphate 0.1%. Net price 10 mL = £1.31
Additives: include benzalkonium chloride
Apply every 2–3 hours; reduce frequency of application when relief is obtained

PoM **Vista-Methasone®** (Daniel)
Drops (for ear, eye, or nose), betamethasone sodium phosphate 0.1%. Net price 5 mL = 68p; 10 mL = £1.05
Additives: include benzalkonium chloride
Apply every 3–4 hours; reduce frequency of application when relief is obtained

PREDNISOLONE SODIUM PHOSPHATE

Indications: eczematous inflammation in otitis externa
Cautions: avoid prolonged use
Contra-indications: untreated infection

PoM **Predsol®** (Glaxo)
Drops (for ear or eye), prednisolone sodium phosphate 0.5%. Net price 10 mL = £1.31
Additives: include benzalkonium chloride
Apply every 2–3 hours; reduce frequency of application when relief is obtained

ANTI-INFECTIVE PREPARATIONS

CHLORAMPHENICOL

Indications: bacterial infection in otitis externa
Cautions: avoid prolonged use (see notes above)
Side-effects: high incidence of sensitivity reactions to vehicle
Administration: Apply 2–3 times daily

PoM **Chloramphenicol Ear drops 5%** and **10%,** chloramphenicol in propylene glycol. Net price 10 mL (5%) = £1.48; 10 mL (10%) = 95p

CLIOQUINOL

Indications: mild bacterial or fungal infections in otitis externa
Cautions: avoid prolonged use (see notes above)
Side-effects: local sensitivity; stains skin and clothing

PoM **Locorten-Vioform®** (Zyma)
Ear drops, clioquinol 1%, flumethasone pivalate 0.02%. Net price 7.5 mL = £1.05
Apply 2–3 drops twice daily

CLOTRIMAZOLE

Indications: fungal infection in otitis externa
Side-effects: occasional skin irritation or sensitivity

Canesten® (Baypharm)
Solution, clotrimazole 1% in polyethylene glycol. Net price 20 mL = £2.38
Apply 2–3 times daily continuing for at least 14 days after disappearance of infection

FRAMYCETIN SULPHATE

Indications: bacterial infection in otitis externa
Cautions: avoid prolonged use; slight risk of ototoxicity increased if perforated ear-drum (see notes above)
Side-effects: local sensitivity
Administration: Apply 3–4 times daily

PoM **Framygen®** (Fisons)
Drops (for ear or eye), framycetin sulphate 0.5%. Net price 5 mL = £1.27
Additives: include benzalkonium chloride, benzyl alcohol

PoM **Framycort®** (Fisons)
Drops (for ear or eye), framycetin sulphate 0.5%, hydrocortisone acetate 0.5%. Net price 5 mL = £2.21
Additives: include benzalkonium chloride, benzyl alcohol

GENTAMICIN

Indications: bacterial infection in otitis externa
Cautions: avoid prolonged use; slight risk of ototoxicity increased if perforated eardrum (see notes above)
Side-effects: local sensitivity
Administration: Apply 3–4 times daily and at night

PoM **Cidomycin®** (Roussel)
Drops (for ear or eye), gentamicin 0.3% (as sulphate). Net price 8 mL = £1.34
Additives: include benzalkonium chloride, disodium edetate

PoM **Garamycin®** (Schering-Plough)
Drops (for ear or eye), gentamicin 0.3% (as sulphate). Net price 10 mL = £1.79
Additives: include benzalkonium chloride

PoM **Genticin®** (Nicholas)
Drops (for ear or eye), gentamicin 0.3% (as sulphate). Net price 10 mL = £1.94
Additives: include benzalkonium chloride

PoM **Gentisone HC®** (Nicholas)
Ear drops, gentamicin 0.3% (as sulphate), hydrocortisone acetate 1%. Net price 10 mL = £3.99

NEOMYCIN SULPHATE

Indications: bacterial infection in otitis externa
Cautions: avoid prolonged use; slight risk of ototoxicity increased if perforated eardrum (see notes above)
Side-effects: local sensitivity
Administration: Apply ear drops every 2–3 hours; ear ointment 2–4 times daily. Reduce frequency of application when relief is obtained

PoM **Audicort®** (Lederle)
Ear drops, neomycin (as neomycin undecenoate) 0.35%, triamcinolone acetonide 0.1%. Net price 10 mL = £5.85
Apply 3–4 times daily

PoM **Betnesol-N®** (Glaxo)
Drops (for ear, eye, or nose), betamethasone sodium phosphate 0.1%, neomycin sulphate 0.5%. Net price 10 mL = £1.31
Additives: include thiomersal

PoM **Neo-Cortef®** (Upjohn)
Drops (for ear or eye), hydrocortisone acetate 1.5%, neomycin sulphate 0.5%. Net price 5 mL = £3.07
Ointment (for ear or eye), hydrocortisone acetate 1.5%, neomycin sulphate 0.5%. Net price 3.9 g = £2.21

PoM **Otomize®** (Stafford-Miller)
Ear spray, dexamethasone 0.1%, neomycin

sulphate 3250 units/mL. Net price 5-mL pump-action aerosol unit = £3.95
Apply 1 metered spray 3 times daily

PoM **Predsol-N®** (Glaxo)
Drops (for ear or eye), neomycin sulphate 0.5%, prednisolone sodium phosphate 0.5%. Net price 10 mL = £1.20
Additives: include thiomersal

PoM **Vista-Methasone N®** (Daniel)
Drops (for ear, eye, or nose), betamethasone sodium phosphate 0.1%, neomycin sulphate 0.5%. Net price 5 mL = 75p; 10 mL = £1.11

TETRACYCLINE HYDROCHLORIDE

Indications: susceptible bacterial infection in otitis externa
Cautions: avoid prolonged use
Side-effects: local sensitivity; stains skin and clothing
Administration: Apply every 2 hours

PoM **Achromycin®** (Lederle)
Ointment (for ear or eye), tetracycline hydrochloride 1%. Net price 3.5 g = 70p

COMPOUND ANTI-INFECTIVE PREPARATIONS

PoM **Otosporin®** (Calmic)
Ear drops, hydrocortisone 1%, neomycin sulphate 0.439%, polymyxin B sulphate 0.119%. Net price 5 mL = £4.58; 10 mL = £7.83
Apply 3–4 times daily

PoM **Sofradex®** (Roussel)
Drops (for ear or eye), dexamethasone (as sodium metasulphobenzoate) 0.05%, framycetin sulphate 0.5%, gramicidin 0.005%. Net price 10 mL = £5.50
Apply 3–4 times daily
Ointment (for ear or eye), dexamethasone 0.05%, framycetin sulphate 0.5%, gramicidin 0.005%. Net price 5 g = £3.64
Apply 2–3 times daily and at bedtime

PoM **Soframycin®** (Roussel)
Cream, framycetin sulphate 1.5%, gramicidin 0.005% in a water-miscible basis. Net price 15 g = £1.72
Ointment, ingredients as for cream, but in a greasy basis. Net price 15 g = £1.72
Apply 1–3 times daily

PoM **Terra-Cortril®** (Pfizer)
Ear suspension (= ear drops), hydrocortisone acetate 1.5%, oxytetracycline 0.5% (as hydrochloride), polymyxin B sulphate 0.119%. Net price 5 mL = £2.06
Apply 3 times daily

PoM **Tri-Adcortyl Otic®** (Squibb)
Ear ointment, gramicidin 0.025%, neomycin 0.25% (as sulphate), nystatin 3.33%, triamcinolone acetonide 0.1% in Plastibase®. Net price 10 g = £1.58
Apply 2–4 times daily

OTHER AURAL PREPARATIONS

Choline salicylate is a mild analgesic but it is of doubtful value when applied topically. There is no place for the use of local anaesthetics in ear drops.

Audax® (Napp)
Ear drops, choline salicylate 20%, glycerol 10%. Net price 8 mL = £1.33

12.1.2 Otitis media

Acute otitis media is the commonest cause of severe pain in small children and recurrent attacks, especially in infants, are particularly distressing. *Sero-mucinous otitis media* ('glue ear') is present in about 10% of the child population and in 90% of children with cleft palates; this condition should be referred to hospital because of the risk of permanent damage to middle ear function and impaired language development. Chronic otitis media is thought to be a legacy from untreated or resistant cases of sero-mucinous otitis media.

Local treatment of *acute otitis media* is ineffective and there is no place for drops containing a local anaesthetic. Many attacks are viral in origin and need only treatment with a **simple analgesic** such as paracetamol for pain. Severe attacks of bacterial origin should be treated with **systemic antibiotics**; bacterial examination of any discharge is helpful in selecting the appropriate treatment (see section 5.1, Table 1). Again, simple analgesics such as paracetamol are used to relieve pain. In *recurrent acute otitis media* a daily dose of a prophylactic antibiotic (trimethoprim or erythromycin) during the winter months can be tried.

The organisms recovered from patients with *chronic otitis media* are often opportunists living in the debris, keratin, and necrotic bone present in the middle ear and mastoid. Thorough cleansing with an aural suction tube may completely control infection of many years duration. Acute exacerbations of chronic infection may require systemic antibiotics (see section 5.1, Table 1). A swab should be taken to determine the organism present and its antibiotic sensitivity. Unfortunately the culture often produces *Pseudomonas aeruginosa* and *Proteus* spp, sensitive only to parenteral antibiotics. Local debridement of the meatal and middle ear contents may then be followed by topical treatment with ribbon gauze dressings as for otitis externa (section 12.1.1). This is particularly true with infections in mastoid cavities when dusting powders can also be tried.

In the presence of a perforation, however, many specialists use ear drops containing **aminoglycosides** (e.g. neomycin, framycetin) or **polymyxins**, if the otitis media has failed to settle with systemic antibiotics; it is considered that the pus in the middle ear associated with otitis media carries a higher risk of ototoxicity than the drops themselves.

12.1.3 Removal of ear wax

Wax is a normal bodily secretion which provides a protective film on the meatal skin and need only be removed if it causes deafness or interferes with a proper view of the eardrum. It may be removed by syringing with warm water. If necessary, wax can be softened before syringing with topical solutions, the most effective of which is **sodium bicarbonate ear drops**. Other simple remedies are **olive oil** and **almond oil**. The patient should lie with the affected ear uppermost for 5 to 10 minutes after a generous amount of the solution has been introduced into the ear. Some proprietary preparations containing organic solvents can cause irritation of the meatal skin, and in most cases the simple remedies which are indicated above are just as effective and less likely to cause irritation. **Docusate sodium** is an ingredient in a number of proprietary preparations.

Almond Oil (warm before use)
Olive Oil (warm before use)
Sodium Bicarbonate Ear Drops, BP
Ear drops, sodium bicarbonate 5%. Extemporaneous preparations should be recently prepared according to the following formula: sodium bicarbonate 500 mg, glycerol 3 mL, freshly boiled and cooled purified water to 10 mL

Audinorm® (Carlton)
Ear drops, docusate sodium 5%, glycerol 10%. Net price 12 mL = 30p

Cerumol® (LAB)
Ear drops, chlorbutol 5%, paradichlorobenzene 2%, arachis oil 57%. Net price 11 mL = 92p

Dioctyl® (Medo)
Ear drops, docusate sodium 5% in macrogol. Net price 10 mL = 79p

Exterol® (Dermal)
Ear drops, urea-hydrogen peroxide complex 5% in glycerol. Net price 12 mL = £2.51

Molcer® (Wallace Mfg)
Ear drops, docusate sodium 5%. Net price 15 mL = 90p

Soliwax® (Martindale)
Ear capsules (= ear drops), docusate sodium 5% in oil, red, single-application capsules. Net price 10 = 73p

Waxsol® (Norgine)
Ear drops, docusate sodium 0.5%. Net price 10 mL = 90p

12.2 Drugs acting on the nose

12.2.1 Drugs used in nasal allergy
12.2.2 Topical nasal decongestants
12.2.3 Anti-infective nasal preparations

Rhinitis is often self-limiting and sinusitis is best treated with antibiotics (see section 5.1, Table 1). There are few indications for the use of sprays and drops except in allergic rhinitis where topical preparations of corticosteroids or sodium cromoglycate have much to offer. Most other preparations contain sympathomimetic drugs which may damage the nasal cilia and their prolonged use causes mucosal oedema and severe nasal obstruction (rhinitis medicamentosa). Symptomatic relief in chronic nasal obstruction may be obtained with **systemic nasal decongestants** (see section 3.10). Douching the nose with salt and water is **not** recommended.

12.2.1 Drugs used in nasal allergy

Mild cases are controlled by **oral antihistamines** and **systemic nasal decongestants** (see sections 3.4.1 and 3.10). Many patients with severe symptoms can now expect relief from topical preparations of **corticosteroids** or **sodium cromoglycate**. Treatment should begin 2 to 3 weeks before the hay fever season commences and may have to be continued for months or even years in some patients. No significant side-effects have been reported. Very disabling symptoms occasionally justify the use of **systemic corticosteroids** for short periods (see section 6.3), for example in students taking important examinations. They may also be used at the beginning of a course of treatment with a corticosteroid spray to relieve severe mucosal oedema and allow the spray to penetrate the nasal cavity.

For reference to injections of **allergen extracts** see section 3.4.2.

BECLOMETHASONE DIPROPIONATE

Indications: allergic and vasomotor rhinitis
Cautions: untreated nasal infection, prolonged use in children, previous treatment with corticosteroids by mouth
Side-effects: sneezing after administration
Administration: Adults and children over 6 years, apply 100 micrograms (2 puffs) into each nostril twice daily or 50 micrograms (1 puff) 3–4 times daily; max. 8 puffs daily

PoM **Beconase®** (A&H)
Beconase® nasal spray (aerosol), beclomethasone dipropionate 50 micrograms/metered inhalation. Net price 200-dose unit with nasal adaptor = £5.01
Beconase® aqueous nasal spray (aqueous suspension), beclomethasone dipropionate 50 micrograms/metered spray. Net price 200-dose unit with nasal applicator = £5.01

BETAMETHASONE SODIUM PHOSPHATE

Indications; Cautions; Side-effects: see under Beclomethasone Dipropionate
Administration: Apply 2–3 drops into each nostril 2–3 times daily

PoM **Betnesol®** (Glaxo)
Drops (for ear, eye, or nose), betamethasone sodium phosphate 0.1%. Net price 10 mL = £1.31
Additives: include benzalkonium chloride

PoM **Vista-Methasone®** (Daniel)
Drops (for ear, eye, or nose), betamethasone sodium phosphate 0.1%. Net price 5 mL = 68p; 10 mL = £1.05
Additives: include benzalkonium chloride

BUDESONIDE

Indications: allergic and vasomotor rhinitis
Cautions: see under Beclomethasone Dipropionate; also patients with pulmonary tuberculosis
Side-effects: see under Beclomethasone Dipropionate
Administration: Apply 100 micrograms (2 puffs) into each nostril twice daily, reducing to 50 micrograms (1 puff) twice daily

PoM **Rhinocort®** (Astra)
Nasal aerosol, budesonide 50 micrograms/metered inhalation, 200-dose unit with nasal adaptor. Net price complete unit = £5.66

FLUNISOLIDE

Indications; Cautions; Side-effects: see under Beclomethasone Dipropionate
Administration: Apply 50 micrograms (2 sprays) into each nostril 2–3 times daily; CHILD over 5 years 25 micrograms (1 spray) into each nostril 3 times daily, reduced for maintenance

PoM **Syntaris®** (Syntex)
Nasal spray, flunisolide 25 micrograms/0.1 mL metered spray. Net price 24 mL with pump and applicator = £5.47

SODIUM CROMOGLYCATE

Indications: prophylaxis of allergic rhinitis (see notes above)
Side-effects: local irritation, particularly during initial treatment with insufflations; rarely transient bronchospasm

Rynacrom® (Fisons)
Nasal insufflation, cartridges, pink, sodium cromoglycate 10 mg for use with insufflator. Net price 20 cartridges = 78p; insufflator = £1.66
Adults and children, insufflate 10 mg into each nostril up to 4 times daily
Nasal drops, sodium cromoglycate 2%. Net price 15 mL = £4.31
Adults and children, instil 2 drops into each nostril 6 times daily
Nasal spray, sodium cromoglycate 2% (2.6 mg/squeeze). Net price 26 mL with pump = £5.36
Adults and children, apply 1 squeeze into each nostril 4–6 times daily

Rynacrom Compound® (Fisons)
Nasal spray, sodium cromoglycate 2% (2.6 mg/metered spray) and xylometazoline hydrochloride 0.025% (32.5 micrograms/metered spray). Net price 26 mL with pump = £5.94
Apply 1 spray into each nostril 4 times daily

12.2.2 Topical nasal decongestants

The nasal mucosa is sensitive to changes in the atmospheric temperature and humidity and these alone may cause slight nasal congestion. The nose and nasal sinuses produce a litre of mucus in 24 hours and much of this finds its way silently into the stomach via the nasopharynx. Slight changes in the nasal airway, accompanied by an awareness of mucus passing along the nasopharynx causes some patients to be inaccurately diagnosed as suffering from chronic sinusitis. These symptoms are particularly noticeable in the later stages of the common cold for which there is no effective treatment at the moment; the temptation to use nasal drops should be resisted. **Sodium chloride** 0.9% given as nasal drops may relieve nasal congestion by helping to liquefy mucous secretions.

Symptomatic relief from the nasal congestion associated with vasomotor rhinitis, nasal polypi, and the common cold can be obtained by the short-term use of decongestant nasal drops and sprays. These all contain sympathomimetic drugs which exert their effect by vasoconstriction of the mucosal blood vessels which in turn reduces the thickness of the nasal mucosa. They are of limited value as they can give rise to a rebound phenomenon as their effects wear off, due to a secondary vasodilatation with a subsequent temporary increase in nasal congestion. This in turn tempts the further use of the decongestant, leading to a vicious circle of events. **Ephedrine nasal drops** is the safest sympathomimetic preparation and can give relief for several hours. The more potent sympathomimetic drugs oxymetazoline, phenylephrine, and xylometazoline are more likely to cause a rebound effect. **All** of these preparations may cause a hypertensive crisis if used during treatment with a monoamine-oxidase inhibitor.

Non-allergic watery rhinorrhoea often responds well to treatment with **ipratropium bromide**.

Inhalations of **warm moist air** are useful in the treatment of symptoms of acute infective conditions, and the use of compounds containing volatile substances such as menthol and eucalyptus may encourage their use (see section 3.8). There is no evidence that nasal preparations containing antihistamines and anti-infective agents have any therapeutic effect.

Systemic nasal decongestants—see section 3.10.

SYMPATHOMIMETICS

EPHEDRINE HYDROCHLORIDE

Indications: nasal congestion
Cautions: avoid excessive use; caution in infants under 3 months (no good evidence of value—if irritation occurs might narrow nasal passage); **interactions:** Appendix 1 (sympathomimetics)
Side-effects: local irritation; after excessive use tolerance with diminished effect, rebound congestion
Administration: Instil 1–2 drops (see below) into each nostril when required

Ephedrine Nasal Drops, BPC
Nasal drops 0.5%, ephedrine hydrochloride 50 mg, chlorbutol 50 mg, sodium chloride 50 mg, water to 10 mL
Note. When Ephedrine Nasal Drops 1% is prescribed, nasal drops containing ephedrine hydrochloride 100 mg/10 mL in the same vehicle is supplied; if no strength is specified 0.5% drops should be supplied

OXYMETAZOLINE HYDROCHLORIDE

Indications: nasal congestion
Cautions; Side-effects: see under Ephedrine Hydrochloride; avoid in porphyria

Prices are **net**, see p. 1

NHS **Afrazine®** (Schering-Plough)
Nasal drops, oxymetazoline hydrochloride 0.05%. Net price 15 mL = 81p
Instil 2–3 drops into each nostril every 12 hours when required
Nasal spray, oxymetazoline hydrochloride 0.05%. Net price 15 mL = 81p
Apply 2–3 times to each nostril every 12 hours when required

PHENYLEPHRINE HYDROCHLORIDE

Indications: nasal congestion
Cautions; Side-effects: see under Ephedrine Hydrochloride

Compound preparations
Section 12.2.3

XYLOMETAZOLINE HYDROCHLORIDE

Indications: nasal congestion
Cautions; Side-effects: see under Ephedrine Hydrochloride; not recommended for infants under 3 months

Xylometazoline Nasal Drops, xylometazoline hydrochloride 0.1%, net price 10 mL = 85p
Instil 2–3 drops into each nostril 2–3 times daily when required
Xylometazoline Nasal Drops, Paediatric xylometazoline hydrochloride 0.05%, net price 10 mL = 85p
CHILD over 3 months instil 1–2 drops into each nostril 1–2 times daily when required (not recommended for infants under 3 months of age)
Note. The brand name NHS Otrivine® (Ciba Consumer) is used for xylometazoline nasal drops 0.1%, paediatric nasal drops 0.05%, and nasal spray 0.1%.

ANTIMUSCARINIC

IPRATROPIUM BROMIDE

Indications: watery rhinorrhoea associated with perennial rhinitis
Cautions; Side-effects: see section 3.1.2; avoid spraying near eyes
Administration: Apply 20–40 micrograms (1–2 puffs) into affected nostril up to 4 times daily; not recommended for children under 12 years

PoM **Rinatec®** (Boehringer Ingelheim)
Nasal spray, ipratropium bromide 20 micrograms/metered spray. Net price 200-dose unit = £4.21

12.2.3 Anti-infective nasal preparations

There is **no** evidence that topical anti-infective nasal preparations have any therapeutic value; for elimination of nasal staphylococci, see below.

Systemic treatment of sinusitis—see section 5.1, Table 1.

PoM **Betnesol-N®** (Glaxo)
Drops (for ear, eye, or nose), section 12.1.1
PoM **Dexa-Rhinaspray®** (Boehringer Ingelheim)
Nasal inhalation, dexamethasone 21-isonicotinate 20 micrograms, neomycin sulphate 100 micrograms, tramazoline hydrochloride 120 micrograms/metered inhalation. Net price 125-dose unit = £1.79
PoM **Locabiotal®** (Servier)
Nasal inhalation, fusafungine 125 micrograms/metered inhalation. Net price 200-dose unit = £1.59
PoM **Vibrocil®** (Zyma)
Nasal drops, dimethindene maleate 0.025%, neomycin sulphate 0.35%, phenylephrine 0.25%. Net price 15 mL = 52p
Nasal gel, dimethindene maleate 0.025%, neomycin sulphate 0.35%, phenylephrine 0.25%. Net price 12 g = 52p
Nasal spray, dimethindene maleate 0.025%, neomycin sulphate 0.35%, phenylephrine 0.25%. Net price 10 mL = 52p
PoM **Vista-Methasone N®** (Daniel)
Drops (for ear, eye, or nose), section 12.1.1

NASAL STAPHYLOCOCCI

Elimination of organisms such as staphylococci from the nasal vestibule can be achieved by the use of a cream containing **chlorhexidine and neomycin** (Naseptin®), but re-colonisation frequently occurs. Coagulase-positive staphylococci can be obtained from the noses of 40% of the population.

A nasal ointment containing **mupirocin** is also available.

PoM **Bactroban® Nasal** (Beecham)
Nasal ointment, mupirocin 2% in white soft paraffin basis. Net price 3 g = £5.15
Apply 2–3 times daily to the inner surface of each nostril
PoM **Naseptin®** (ICI)
Cream, chlorhexidine hydrochloride 0.1%, neomycin sulphate 0.5%. Do not dilute. Net price 15 g = £1.02
For treatment of staphylococcal infections apply to nostrils 4 times daily for 10 days; for preventing nasal carriage of staphylococci apply to nostrils twice daily

12.3 Drugs acting on the oropharynx

12.3.1 Drugs for oral ulceration and inflammation

Ulceration of the oral mucosa may be caused by trauma (physical or chemical), recurrent aphthae, infections, carcinoma, dermatological disorders, nutritional deficiencies, gastro-intestinal disease, haematopoietic disorders, and drug therapy. It is important to establish the diagnosis in each case as the majority of these lesions require specific management in addition to local treatment. Local treatment aims at protecting the ulcerated area, or at relieving pain or reducing inflammation.

SIMPLE MOUTHWASHES. A **saline** or **compound thymol glycerin** mouthwash may relieve the pain of traumatic ulceration. The mouthwash is made up with warm water and used at frequent intervals until the discomfort and swelling subsides.

ANTISEPTIC MOUTHWASHES. Secondary bacterial infection may be a feature of any mucosal ulceration; it can increase discomfort and delay healing. Use of a **chlorhexidine** or **povidone-iodine** mouthwash is often beneficial and may accelerate healing of recurrent aphthae.

MECHANICAL PROTECTION. **Carmellose gelatin paste** may relieve some discomfort arising from ulceration by protecting the ulcer site. The paste adheres to the mucosa, but is difficult to apply effectively to some parts of the mouth.

ZINC SULPHATE. Zinc sulphate mouthwash (see section 13.11.6) is an astringent. Some patients find it beneficial in recurrent aphthae.

CORTICOSTEROIDS. Topical corticosteroid therapy may be used for different forms of oral ulceration. In the case of aphthous ulcers it is most effective if applied in the 'prodromal' phase.

Thrush or other types of candidiasis are recognised complications of corticosteroid treatment.

Hydrocortisone lozenges are allowed to dissolve next to an ulcer and are useful in recurrent aphthae, erosive lichen planus, discoid lupus erythematosus, and benign mucous membrane pemphigoid.

Triamcinolone dental paste is designed to keep the corticosteroid in contact with the mucosa for long enough to permit penetration of the lesion, but is difficult for patients to apply properly.

Systemic corticosteroid therapy is reserved for severe conditions such as pemphigus vulgaris (see section 6.3.4).

LOCAL ANALGESICS. Local analgesics have a limited role in the management of oral ulceration. When applied topically their action is of a relatively short duration so that analgesia cannot be maintained continuously throughout the day. The main indication for a topical local analgesic is to relieve the pain of otherwise intractable oral ulceration particularly when it is due to major aphthae. For this purpose lignocaine 5% ointment or lozenges containing a local anaesthetic are applied to the ulcer. When local anaesthetics are used in the mouth care must be taken not to produce anaesthesia of the pharynx before meals as this might lead to choking.

Benzydamine mouthwash or spray may be useful in palliating the discomfort associated with a variety of ulcerative conditions. It has also been found to be effective in reducing the discomfort of post-irradiation mucositis. Some patients find the full-strength mouthwash causes some stinging and, for them, it should be diluted with an equal volume of water.

Choline salicylate dental gel has some analgesic action and may provide relief for recurrent aphthae, but excessive application or confinement under a denture irritates the mucosa and can itself cause ulceration. Benefit in teething may merely be due to pressure of application (comparable with biting a teething ring); excessive use can lead to salicylate poisoning.

OTHER PREPARATIONS. **Carbenoxolone** gel or mouthwash may be of some value. **Tetracycline** rinsed in the mouth may also be of value.

BENZYDAMINE HYDROCHLORIDE

Indications: painful inflammatory conditions of oropharynx

Side-effects: occasional numbness or stinging

Difflam® (3M)

Oral rinse, green, benzydamine hydrochloride 0.15%. Net price 200 mL = £2.70

Rinse or gargle, using 15 mL (diluted if stinging occurs) every 1½–3 hours as required, usually for not more than 7 days; not suitable for children under 12 years

Spray, benzydamine hydrochloride 0.15%. Net price 30-mL unit = £3.23

4–8 puffs onto affected area every 1½–3 hours; CHILD 6–12 years 4 puffs every 1½–3 hours

CARBENOXOLONE SODIUM

Indications: mild oral and perioral lesions

Bioral Gel® (Sterling-Winthrop)

Gel, carbenoxolone sodium 2% in adhesive basis. Net price 5 g = £1.83

Apply after meals and at bedtime

PoM **Bioplex®** (Thames)

Mouthwash granules, carbenoxolone sodium 1%. Net price 24 × 2-g sachets = £9.60

For mouth ulcers, rinse with 2 g in 30–50 mL of warm water 3 times daily and at bedtime

CARMELLOSE SODIUM

Indications: mechanical protection of oral and perioral lesions

Orabase® (Squibb)

Oral paste, carmellose sodium 16.58%, pectin 16.58%, gelatin 16.58%, in Plastibase®. Net price 30 g = £1.30; 100 g = £3.10

Apply a thin layer when necessary after meals

Orahesive® (Squibb)

Powder, carmellose sodium, pectin, gelatin, equal parts. Net price 25 g = £1.50

Sprinkle on the affected area

CORTICOSTEROIDS

Indications: oral and perioral lesions

Contra-indications: untreated oral infection

PoM **Adcortyl in Orabase®** (Squibb)
Oral paste, triamcinolone acetonide 0.1% in adhesive basis. Net price 10 g = £1.27
Apply a thin layer 2–4 times daily

PoM **Corlan®** (Glaxo)
Pellets (= lozenges), hydrocortisone 2.5 mg (as sodium succinate). Net price 20 = £1.40
One lozenge 4 times daily, allowed to dissolve slowly in the mouth in contact with the ulcer; if ulcers recur rapidly treatment may be continued for a period at reduced dosage

LOCAL ANAESTHETICS

Indications: relief of pain in oral lesions
Cautions: avoid prolonged use; hypersensitivity may occur

Standard strength lozenges
Available with antiseptics, section 12.3.3

High strength lozenges
Benzocaine Lozenges, Compound, benzocaine 100 mg, menthol 3 mg
Note. It is **essential** not to confuse these with benzocaine lozenges which contained one-tenth the amount of benzocaine and are no longer available
Available from Penn (**special order**, bulk quantities only)

SALICYLATES

Indications: mild oral and perioral lesions
Cautions: frequent application, especially in children, may give rise to salicylate poisoning
Note. CSM warning on aspirin and Reye's syndrome does not apply to non-aspirin salicylates or to topical preparations such as teething gels

Choline salicylate
Bonjela® (R&C)
Oral gel, sugar-free, choline salicylate dental gel containing choline salicylate 8.7%. Net price 15 g = £1.04

Teejel® (Napp)
Oral gel, choline salicylate dental gel containing choline salicylate 8.7%. Net price 10 g = 58p

Salicylic acid
Pyralvex® (Norgine)
Oral paint, brown, anthraquinone glycosides 5%, salicylic acid 1%. Net price 10 mL with brush = £1.15. Apply 3–4 times daily

TETRACYCLINE

Indications: severe recurrent aphthous ulceration; oral herpes (section 12.3.2)
Side-effects: fungal superinfection

PoM **Tetracycline Mixture[1],** tetracycline hydrochloride 125 mg (as tetracycline)/5 mL
Administration: 10 mL to be held in the mouth for 2–3 minutes 3 times daily for not longer than 3 days followed by a break of at least 3 days before treatment is recommenced (to avoid oral thrush); it should preferably not be swallowed
Note. Tetracycline stains teeth; avoid in children under 12 years of age
1. Available as Achromycin® Syrup (see section 5.1.3); alternatively the contents of a 250-mg capsule can be stirred in a small amount of water and used in the same way as the mixture—this ensures a sugar-free version

12.3.2 Oropharyngeal anti-infective drugs

The most common cause of a sore throat is a viral infection which does not benefit from anti-infective treatment. Streptococcal sore throats require systemic **penicillin** therapy (see section 5.1.1). Acute ulcerative gingivitis (Vincent's infection) responds to systemic **metronidazole** 200 mg 3 times daily for 3 days (see section 5.1.11) or **nimorazole** 500 mg twice daily for 2 days (see section 5.4.3).

FUNGAL INFECTIONS

Candida albicans may cause thrush and other forms of stomatitis which are sometimes a sequel to the use of broad-spectrum antibiotics or cytotoxics; withdrawing the causative drug may lead to rapid resolution. Otherwise, **nystatin, amphotericin**, or **miconazole** may be effective.

AMPHOTERICIN

Indications: oral and perioral fungal infections

PoM **Fungilin®** (Squibb)
Lozenges, yellow, amphotericin 10 mg. Net price 6 × 10 lozenge-pack = £3.95. Label: 9, 24, counselling, after food
Dissolve 1 lozenge slowly in the mouth 4 times daily, may require 10–15 days' treatment; increase to 8 daily if infection severe
Suspension, yellow, sugar-free, amphotericin 100 mg/mL. Net price 12 mL with pipette = £2.31. Label: 9, counselling, use of pipette, hold in mouth, after food
Place 1 mL in the mouth after food and retain near lesions 4 times daily for 14 days

MICONAZOLE

Indications: oral fungal infections
Cautions: pregnancy; **interactions:** Appendix 1 (miconazole)

PoM[1] **Daktarin** (Janssen)
Oral gel, sugar-free, miconazole 25 mg/mL. Net price 40 g = £2.50. Label: 9, counselling, hold in mouth, after food
Place 5–10 mL in the mouth after food and retain near lesions before swallowing, 4 times daily; CHILD under 2 years 2.5 mL twice daily, 2–6 years 5 mL twice daily, over 6 years 5 mL 4 times daily
Localised lesions, smear affected area with clean finger; a 15-g tube (net price £1.27) also available
1. 15-g tube can be sold to the public
Tablets—see section 5.2

NYSTATIN

Indications: oral and perioral fungal infections

Dose: (as pastilles or as suspension) 100000 units 4 times daily after food, continued for 48 hours after lesions have resolved

Note. Immunosuppressed patients may require higher doses (e.g. 500000 units 4 times daily)

PoM **Nystan®** (Squibb)

Pastilles, yellow/brown, nystatin 100000 units. Net price 28 pastille-pack = £3.95. Label: 9, 24, counselling, after food

Suspension, yellow, nystatin 100000 units/mL. Net price 30 mL with pipette = £2.50. Label: 9, counselling, use of pipette, hold in mouth, after food

Suspension, gluten-, lactose-, and sugar-free, nystatin 100000 units/mL when reconstituted with water. Measure with pipette. Net price 24 mL with pipette = £1.67. Label: 9, counselling, use of pipette

PoM **Nystatin-Dome®** (Lagap)

Suspension, yellow, nystatin 100000 units/mL. Net price 30 mL with 1-mL spoon = £2.86. Label: 9, counselling, use of 1-mL spoon, hold in mouth, after food

VIRAL INFECTIONS

The management of herpes infections of the mouth is a soft diet, adequate fluid intake, analgesics as required, and the use of **chlorhexidine** mouthwash (Corsodyl®, section 12.3.4) to control plaque accumulation if toothbrushing is painful. In the case of severe herpetic stomatitis, systemic **acyclovir** is required (see section 5.3).

Herpes infections of the mouth may also respond to **tetracycline** (section 12.3.1) rinsed in the mouth.

Idoxuridine 0.1% paint has been superseded by more effective preparations.

ACYCLOVIR

See section 5.3

TETRACYCLINE

Section 12.3.1

12.3.3 Antiseptic lozenges, sprays and gels

There is no convincing evidence that antiseptic lozenges and sprays have a beneficial action and they sometimes irritate and cause sore tongue and sore lips. Some of these preparations also contain local anaesthetics which relieve pain but may cause sensitisation.

In particular preparations containing clioquinol are not recommended.

Benzalkonium Lozenges, benzalkonium chloride 500 micrograms. Net price 20 lozenges = 48p

Bradosol® (Ciba Consumer)

Lozenges, domiphen bromide 500 micrograms. Net price 24 lozenges = 64p

Dequadin® (Crookes)

Lozenges, orange, dequalinium chloride 250 micrograms. Net price 20 lozenges = 46p

Dissolve 1 lozenge slowly in the mouth when required

Labosept® (LAB)

Pastilles, red, dequalinium chloride 250 micrograms. Net price 20 pastilles = 58p

Suck 1 pastille slowly when required

PoM **Locabiotal®** (Servier)

Aerosol spray, fusafungine 125 micrograms/metered inhalation. Net price 200-dose unit with nasal and oral adaptor = £1.59

Merocets® (Merrell)

Lozenges, yellow, cetylpyridinium chloride 0.066%. Net price 24 lozenges = 72p

Clioquinol

Oralcer® (Vitabiotics)

Lozenges, green, ascorbic acid 6 mg, clioquinol 35 mg. Net price 20 lozenges = 75p

With local anaesthetic

AAA® (Rhône-Poulenc Rorer)

Mouth and throat spray, benzocaine 1.5%, cetalkonium chloride 0.0413%. Net price 60-dose unit = £2.46

Bradosol Plus® (Ciba Consumer)

Lozenges, pink, lignocaine hydrochloride 5 mg, domiphen bromide 500 micrograms. Net price 24 = 84p

Dequacaine® (Crookes)

Lozenges, amber, benzocaine 10 mg, dequalinium chloride 250 micrograms. Net price 24 lozenges = 85p

Eludril® (Fabre)

Aerosol spray, amethocaine hydrochloride 0.015%, chlorhexidine gluconate 0.05%. Net price 55 mL = £1.37

Medilave® (Martindale)

Gel, benzocaine 1%, cetylpyridinium chloride 0.01%. Net price 10 g = 61p

Adults, apply a thin layer 3–4 times daily; no longer recommended for children

Merocaine® (Merrell)

Lozenges, green, benzocaine 10 mg, cetylpyridinium chloride 1.4 mg. Net price 24 lozenges = 79p

Tyrozets® (MSD)

Lozenges, pink, benzocaine 5 mg, tyrothricin 1 mg. Net price 24 lozenges = 66p

12.3.4 Mouthwashes, gargles, and dentifrices

Mouthwashes have a mechanical cleansing action and freshen the mouth. Warm **compound sodium chloride mouthwash** or **compound thymol glycerin** is as useful as any.

Hydrogen peroxide mouthwash has a mechanical cleansing effect due to frothing when in contact with oral debris. **Sodium perborate** is similar in effect to hydrogen peroxide.

There is evidence that **chlorhexidine** has a specific effect in inhibiting the formation of plaque on teeth. A chlorhexidine mouthwash may be useful as an adjunct to other oral hygiene measures in cases of oral infection or when toothbrushing is not possible.

There is no convincing evidence that gargles are effective.

CETYLPYRIDINIUM CHLORIDE

Indications: oral hygiene

Merocet® (Merrell)
Solution (= mouthwash or gargle), yellow, cetylpyridinium chloride 0.05%. Net price 200 mL = £1·01
To be used undiluted or diluted with an equal volume of warm water

CHLORHEXIDINE GLUCONATE

Indications: oral hygiene; inhibition of plaque formation
Side-effects: idiosyncratic mucosal irritation; reversible brown staining of teeth

Corsodyl® (ICI)
Dental gel, chlorhexidine gluconate 1%. Net price 50 g = 83p
Brush on the teeth once or twice daily
Mouthwash, chlorhexidine gluconate 0.2% (original or mint-flavoured). Net price 300 mL = £1.25
Rinse the mouth with 10 mL for about 1 minute twice daily

Eludril® (Fabre)
Mouthwash, red, chlorhexidine gluconate 0.1%, chlorbutol 0.5%. Net price 90 mL = 67p; 250 mL = £1.46; 500 mL = £2.74
Use 10–15 mL in a third of a tumblerful of warm water 2–3 times daily

HEXETIDINE

Indications: oral hygiene

Oraldene® (W-L)
Mouthwash or *gargle*, red, hexetidine 0.1%. Net price 100 mL = 75p; 200 mL = £1.19
Use 15 mL undiluted 2–3 times daily

OXIDISING AGENTS

Indications: oral hygiene, see notes above

Hydrogen Peroxide Mouthwash, consists of hydrogen peroxide solution (6% ≡ approx. 20 volume)
Rinse the mouth for 2–3 minutes with 15 mL in half a tumblerful of warm water 2–3 times daily

Bocasan® (Oral-B Labs)
Mouthwash, sodium perborate 70% (buffered). Net price 20 × 1.7-g sachet-pack = £1.22
Use 1 sachet in 30 mL of water
Cautions: Do not use for longer than 7 days because of possible absorption of borate; not recommended in renal impairment or for children under 5 years

PHENOL

Indications: oral hygiene

Chloraseptic® (Richardson Vicks)
Throat spray or *gargle*, green, phenol and sodium phenolate (total phenol 1.4%), menthol, thymol, and glycerol. Net price 100 mL with spray = £1.75; 150 mL = £1.85
Use every 2 hours if necessary, undiluted as a throat spray, undiluted or diluted with an equal volume of water as a mouthwash or gargle
CSM Warning. Following 4 reports of epiglottitis or laryngeal oedema (1 fatality) CSM has advised that Chloraseptic® should **not** be used by patients who may have epiglottitis, is **contra-indicated** in children under 6 years, and should **only** be used by children aged 6-12 years on doctor's advice.

POVIDONE-IODINE

Indications: oral hygiene
Cautions: pregnancy; breast-feeding
Side-effects: idiosyncratic mucosal irritation and hypersensitivity reactions

Betadine® (Napp)
Mouthwash or *gargle*, amber, povidone-iodine 1%. Net price 250 mL = 82p
To be used undiluted or diluted with an equal volume of warm water every 2–4 hours if necessary

SODIUM CHLORIDE

Indications: oral hygiene, see notes above

Sodium Chloride Mouthwash, Compound, BP
Mouthwash, sodium bicarbonate 1%, sodium chloride 1.5% in a suitable vehicle with a peppermint flavour.
Extemporaneous preparations should be prepared according to the following formula: sodium chloride 1.5 g, sodium bicarbonate 1 g, concentrated peppermint emulsion 2.5 mL, double-strength chloroform water 50 mL, water to 100 mL
To be diluted with an equal volume of warm water

THYMOL

Indications: oral hygiene, see notes above

Compound Thymol Glycerin, glycerol 10%, thymol 0.05% with colouring and flavouring
To be used undiluted or diluted with 3 volumes of warm water

Mouthwash Solution-tablets, consist of tablets which may contain antimicrobial, colouring, and flavouring agents in a suitable soluble effervescent basis to make a mouthwash suitable for dental purposes. Net price 20 solution-tablets = 29p
Dissolve 1 tablet in a tumblerful of warm water

OTHER PREPARATIONS FOR OROPHARYNGEAL USE

Artificial saliva may be indicated for dry mouth. Proprietary preparations are available.

Artificial Saliva, DPF
A suitable inert, slightly viscous, aqueous liquid; it may contain an antimicrobial preservative, normal salivary constituents, small amounts of fluoride, and colouring and flavouring agents.
Extemporaneous preparations may be prepared accord-

ing to the following formula: sodium chloride 100 mg, hypromellose '4500' 1.3 g, benzalkonium chloride solution 0.02 mL, saccharin sodium 10 mg, thymol 10 mg, peppermint oil 0.02 mL, spearmint oil 0.03 mL, amaranth solution 0.1 mL, water to 100 mL

Dose: up to 5 mL as required; max. 20 mL daily

Glandosane® (Fresenius)

Aerosol spray, carmellose sodium 500 mg, sorbitol 1.5 g, potassium chloride 60 mg, sodium chloride 42.2 mg, magnesium chloride 2.6 mg, calcium chloride 7.3 mg, and dipotassium hydrogen phosphate 17.1 mg/50 g. Net price 50-mL unit (neutral or flavoured) = £3.30

Spray onto oral and pharyngeal mucosa as required to provide artificial saliva

Saliva Orthana® (Nycomed)

Aerosol spray, gastric mucin (porcine) 3.5%, with preservatives and flavouring agents. Net price 50-mL spray bottle = £3.75 (hosp. only)

Dry mouth, spray 2–3 times onto oral and pharyngeal mucosa, when required

13: Drugs acting on the SKIN

In this chapter, drug treatment is discussed under the following headings:

Suitable quantities of dermatological preparations to be prescribed for specific areas of the body are:

	Creams and Ointments	Lotions
Face	5 to 15 g	100 mL
Both hands	25 to 50 g	200 mL
Scalp	50 to 100 g	200 mL
Both arms or both legs	100 to 200 g	200 mL
Body	200 g	500 mL
Groins and genitalia	15 to 25 g	100 mL
Dusting powders	50 to 100 g	
Paints	10 to 25 mL	

These amounts are usually suitable for 2 to 4 weeks. The recommendations do not apply to corticosteroid preparations which should be applied thinly. Corticosteroid creams and ointments are available in various pack sizes, commonly 15 g or 30 g, while corticosteroid lotions are usually packed in 20- or 100-mL sizes.

13.1 Vehicles and diluents

Both vehicle and active ingredients are important in the treatment of skin conditions; it is being increasingly recognised that the vehicle alone may have more than a mere placebo effect. The vehicle affects the degree of hydration of the skin, has a mild anti-inflammatory effect, and aids the penetration of active drug in the preparation.

DILUTION. The BP directs that creams and ointments should **not** normally be diluted but that should dilution be necessary care should be taken, in particular, to prevent microbial contamination. The appropriate diluent should be used and heating should be avoided during mixing; excessive dilution may affect the stability of some creams. Diluted creams should normally be used within 2 weeks of their preparation.

ADDITIVES. The following additives in topical preparations may be associated with sensitisation, particularly of eczematous skin. Details of whether they are contained in preparations listed in the BNF are given after the preparation entry.

Most commonly	Less commonly	Rarely[1]
Wool fat and related substances	Benzyl alcohol	Beeswax
Chlorocresol	Butylated hydroxyanisole	Edetic acid (EDTA)
Ethylenediamine	Butylated hydroxytoluene	Isopropyl palmitate
Fragrances	Hydroxybenzoates (parabens)	
	Polysorbates	
	Propylene glycol	
	Sorbic acid	

1. Non-dermatologists can reasonably disregard the substances in this category

CHOICE OF VEHICLE

The vehicle may take the form of a cream, ointment, lotion, paste, dusting-powder, application, collodion, or paint basis.

CREAMS are essentially miscible with the skin secretion. They may contain an antimicrobial preservative unless the active ingredient or basis has sufficient intrinsic bactericidal or fungicidal activity. Generally, creams are cosmetically more acceptable than ointments as they are less greasy and easier to apply.

Aqueous Cream, BP, emulsifying ointment 30%, phenoxyethanol 1%, in freshly boiled and cooled purified water. Net price 100 g = 28p

Buffered Cream, BP, emulsifying ointment 30%, citric acid monohydrate 0.5%, sodium phosphate 2.5%, chlorocresol 0.1%, in freshly boiled and cooled purified water. Net price 100 g = 42p

Cetomacrogol Cream, BP, *Formula B*, cetomacrogol emulsifying ointment 30%, propyl hydroxybenzoate 0.08%, methyl hydroxybenzoate 0.15%, benzyl alcohol 1.5%, in freshly boiled and cooled purified water. Net price 100 g = £1.70

Diprobase® (Schering-Plough)
Cream, cetomacrogol 2.25%, cetostearyl alcohol 7.2%, liquid paraffin 6%, white soft paraffin 15%, water-miscible basis used for Diprosone® cream. Net price 50 g = £1.60; 500-g dispenser = £6.93
Additives: chlorocresol

Lipobase® (Brocades)
Cream, fatty cream basis used for Locoid Lipocream®. Net price 50 g = £2.05
Additives: hydroxybenzoates (parabens)

Ultrabase® (Schering Health Care)
Cream, water-miscible, containing liquid paraffin and white soft paraffin. Net price 50 g = £1.05; 500 g = £5.70
Additives: hydroxybenzoates (parabens), disodium edetate, fragrance

OINTMENTS are greasy preparations which are normally anhydrous and insoluble in water, and are more occlusive than creams. The most commonly used ointment bases consist of soft paraffin or a combination of soft paraffin with liquid paraffin and hard paraffin. Some modern ointment bases have both hydrophilic and lipophilic properties; they may have occlusive properties on the skin surface, encourage hydration, and be miscible with water; they often have a mild anti-inflammatory effect. Water-soluble ointments contain macrogols which are freely soluble in water and are therefore readily washed off; they have a limited but useful application in circumstances where ready removal is desirable. Ointments are particularly suitable for chronic, dry lesions.

Cetomacrogol Emulsifying Ointment, BP, cetomacrogol emulsifying wax 30%, liquid paraffin 20%, white soft paraffin 50%. Net price 100 g = 39p
Emulsifying Ointment, BP, emulsifying wax 30%, white soft paraffin 50%, liquid paraffin 20%. Net price 100 g = 30p
Hydrous Ointment, BP (oily cream), dried magnesium sulphate 0.5%, phenoxyethanol 1%, wool alcohols ointment 50%, in freshly boiled and cooled purified water. Net price 100 g = 35p
Hydrous Wool Fat, BP, wool fat 75% in freshly boiled and cooled purified water. Net price 100 g = 69p
Hydrous Wool Fat Ointment, BPC, hydrous wool fat 50%, yellow soft paraffin 50%. Net price 100 g = 65p
Macrogol Ointment, BP, macrogol '4000' 35%, macrogol '300' 65%
Paraffin, White Soft, BP (white petroleum jelly). Net price 100 g = 33p
Paraffin, Yellow Soft, BP (yellow petroleum jelly). Net price 100 g = 37p
Paraffin Ointment, BP, white beeswax 2%, cetostearyl alcohol 5%, hard paraffin 3%, in white soft paraffin. Net price 100 g = 40p
Simple Ointment, BP, cetostearyl alcohol 5%, hard paraffin 5%, wool fat 5%, in yellow or white soft paraffin. Net price 100 g = 34p
Wool Alcohols Ointment, BP, wool alcohols 6%, yellow or white soft paraffin 10%, hard paraffin 24%, in liquid paraffin. Net price 100 g = 97p
Diprobase® (Schering-Plough)
Ointment, liquid paraffin 5%, white soft paraffin 95%, basis used for Diprosone® ointment. Net price 50 g = £1.60
Additives: none as listed in table above
Locobase® (Brocades)
Ointment, basis used for Locoid® ointment. Net price 100 g = £2.70
Additives: none as listed in table above

Unguentum Merck® (Merck)
Cream (hydrophilic and lipophilic), cetostearyl alcohol 9%, glyceryl monostearate 3%, saturated neutral oil 2%, liquid paraffin 3%, white soft paraffin 32%, propylene glycol 5%, polysorbate '40' 8%, silicic acid 0.1%, sorbic acid 0.2%. Net price 50 g = £1.63; 100 g = £3.21; 200 mL = £6.35; 500 g = £9.80

LOTIONS are usually aqueous solutions or suspensions which cool diffusely inflamed unbroken skin. They cool by evaporation and should be reapplied frequently. Volatile solvents increase the cooling effect but are liable to cause stinging. Lotions are also used to apply drugs to the skin and may be preferred to ointments or creams when it is intended to apply a thin layer of the preparation over a large or hairy area. *Shake lotions* (such as calamine lotion) containing insoluble powders are applied to less acute, scabbed, dry lesions. In addition to cooling they leave a deposit of inert powder on the skin surface.

PASTES are stiff preparations containing a high proportion of finely powdered solids such as zinc oxide and starch. They are used for circumscribed lesions such as those which occur in lichen simplex, chronic eczema, or psoriasis. They are less occlusive than ointments and can be used to protect sub-acute, lichenified, or excoriated skin.

Zinc Paste, Compound, BP, zinc oxide 25%, starch 25%, white soft paraffin 50%. Net price 25 g = 9p

APPLICATIONS are usually viscous solutions, emulsions, or suspensions for application to the skin.

COLLODIONS are painted on the skin and allowed to dry to leave a flexible film over the site of application. Flexible collodion may be used to seal minor cuts and wounds. Collodions may also be used to provide a means of holding a dissolved drug in contact with the skin for a long period, e.g. salicylic acid collodion (section 13.7).

Collodion, Flexible, BP, castor oil 2.5%, colophony 2.5% in a collodion basis, prepared by dissolving pyroxylin (10%) in a mixture of 3 volumes of ether and 1 volume of alcohol (90%). Net price 10 mL = 12p. Label: 15
Caution: highly flammable

LINIMENTS are liquid preparations for external application and may contain analgesics and rubefacients, see section 10.3.2.

PAINTS are liquid preparations intended for application with a brush to the skin or mucous surfaces.

13.2 Emollient and barrier preparations

13.2.1 Emollients and barrier creams
13.2.2 Emollient bath additives
13.2.3 Dusting powders

13.2.1 Emollients and barrier creams

Emollients soothe, smooth and hydrate the skin and are indicated for all dry scaling disorders (such as ichthyosis). Their effects are short-lived and they should be applied frequently even after improvement occurs. They are useful in dry eczematous disorders, and to a lesser extent in psoriasis (section 13.5). Simple preparations such as **aqueous cream** are often as effective as the more complex proprietary formulations; sprays offer little advantage but, in general, the choice depends on patient preference. Some ingredients may cause sensitisation, notably hydrous wool fat (lanolin) or antibacterials and this should be suspected if an eczematous reaction occurs.

Camphor, menthol, and phenol have a mild antipruritic effect when used in emollient preparations. Calamine and zinc oxide may also be included as they slightly enhance therapeutic efficacy; they are particularly useful in dry eczema. Zinc and titanium preparations have mild astringent properties. Thickening agents such as talc and kaolin may also be included. Preparations containing an antibacterial should be avoided unless infection is present (section 13.10).

Urea is employed as a hydrating agent. It is used in scaling conditions and may be useful in elderly patients and infantile eczemas. It is often used with other topical agents such as corticosteroids to enhance penetration.

Barrier creams often contain water-repellent substances such as **dimethicone** or other silicones. They are used to give protection against irritation or repeated hydration (napkin rash, areas around stomata, sore areas in the elderly, bedsores, etc.). They are no substitute for adequate nursing care, and it is doubtful if they are any more effective than the traditional compound zinc ointments.

Napkin rash is usually a local dermatitis. The first line of treatment is to ensure that napkins are changed frequently, and that tightly fitting rubber pants are avoided. The rash may clear when left exposed to the air and an emollient, or preparations containing calamine and emollients, may be helpful. See also section 13.4.

For stoma care preparations, see section 1.8.1.

Aqueous Cream—section 13.1

Dimethicone Cream, BPC, dimethicone '350' 10%, cetostearyl alcohol 5%, cetrimide 0.5%, chlorocresol 0.1%, liquid paraffin 40%, in freshly boiled and cooled purified water. Net price 50 g = 27p

Hydrous Ointment—section 13.1

Titanium Dioxide Paste, BP, titanium dioxide 20%, chlorocresol 0.1%, red ferric oxide 2%, glycerol 15%, light kaolin 10%, zinc oxide 25%, in water. For urinary rash and as a sunscreen

Zinc Cream, BP, zinc oxide 32%, arachis oil 32%, calcium hydroxide 0.045%, oleic acid 0.5%, wool fat 8%, in freshly boiled and cooled purified water. Net price 50 g = 44p. For napkin and urinary rash and eczematous conditions

Zinc Ointment, BP, zinc oxide 15%, in simple ointment. Net price 25 g = 20p. For napkin and urinary rash and eczematous conditions

Zinc and Castor Oil Ointment, BP, zinc oxide 7.5%, castor oil 50%, arachis oil 30.5%, white beeswax 10%, cetostearyl alcohol 2%. Net price 25 g = 13p. For napkin and urinary rash

Alcoderm® (Alcon)

Cream, water-miscible, containing carbomer, cetyl alcohol, liquid paraffin, polysorbate 60, sodium lauryl sulphate, stearyl alcohol, triethanolamine. Net price 60 g = £2.40. For dry skin conditions
Additives: isopropyl palmitate, hydroxybenzoates (parabens)

Lotion, water-miscible, ingredients as above. Net price 120 mL = £2.86
Additives: hydroxybenzoates (parabens)

Conotrane® (Boehringer Ingelheim)

Cream, benzalkonium chloride 0.1%, dimethicone '350' 22%. Net price 50 g = 59p; 100 g = 96p; 500 g = £3.66. For napkin and urinary rash and pressure sores
Additives: fragrance

Dermalex®—section 13.10.5

Diprobase®—section 13.1

Drapolene®—section 13.10.5

E45® (Crookes)

Cream, light liquid paraffin 11.6%, white soft paraffin 14.5%, wool fat 1%, with methyl hydroxybenzoate, self-emulsifying monostearin, stearic acid, triethanolamine. Net price 50 g = 86p; 125 g = £1.76; 500 g = £4.08

Eczederm® (Quinoderm Ltd)

Cream, calamine 20.88%, arachis oil 12.5%, in an emollient basis. Net price 30 g = £1.04; 60 g = £1.79; 500 g = £9.57. For mild dermatoses including eczema
Additives: fragrance

Emulsiderm®—section 13.2.2

Hewletts Cream® (Astra)

Cream, hydrous wool fat 4%, zinc oxide 8%. Net price 35 g = 56p; 400 g = £3.14. For nursing hygiene and care of skin
Additives: fragrance

Humiderm® (BritCair)

Cream, pyrrolidone carboxylic acid 5% (as sodium salt). Net price 60 g = £3.20. For dry skin conditions
Additives: hydroxybenzoates (parabens), propylene glycol

Hydromol® (Quinoderm Ltd)

Cream, arachis oil 10%, isopropyl myristate 5%, liquid paraffin 10%, sodium pyrrolidone carboxylate 2.5%, sodium lactate 1%. Net price 50 g = £1.96; 100 g = £3.24; 500 g = £10.43. For dry skin conditions
Additives: benzyl alcohol, propylene glycol

Kamillosan® (Norgine)

Ointment, chamomile extracts 10.5%. Net price 5 g = 57p (hosp. only); 24 g = £1.43. For napkin rash, cracked nipples and chapped hands
Additives: beeswax, hydroxybenzoates (parabens), wool fat

Keri® (Bristol-Myers)

Lotion, mineral oil 16%, with lanolin oil. Net price 190-mL pump pack = £3.65; 380-mL pump pack = £5.96. For dry skin conditions and napkin rash
Additives: hydroxybenzoates (parabens), propylene glycol, fragrance

Lacticare® (Stiefel)
Lotion, lactic acid 5%, sodium pyrrolidone carboxylate 2.5%, in an emulsion basis. Net price 150 mL = £3.19. For dry skin conditions
Additives: isopropyl palmitate, fragrance

Locobase®—section 13.1

Massé Breast Cream® (Cilag)
Cream (water-miscible), containing arachis oil, cetyl alcohol, glycerol, glyceryl monostearate, wool fat, polysorbate 60, potassium hydroxide, sorbitan monostearate, stearic acid. Net price 28 g = £1.40. For pre- and post-natal nipple care
Additives: hydroxybenzoates (parabens)

Metanium® (Bengué)
Ointment, titanium dioxide 20%, titanium peroxide 5%, titanium salicylate 3%, titanium tannate 0.1%, in a silicone basis. Net price 25 g = 57p. For napkin rash and related disorders
Additives: none as listed in section 13.1

Morhulin® (Napp)
Ointment, cod-liver oil 11.4%, zinc oxide 38%, in a basis containing wool fat and paraffin. Net price 50 g = 67p; 350 g = £3.86. For minor wounds, varicose ulcers, and pressure sores

Morsep® (Napp)
Cream, cetrimide 0.5%, ergocalciferol 10 units/g, vitamin A 70 units/g. Net price 40 g = 64p; 300 g = £3.13. For urinary rash
Additives: wool fat derivative, fragrance

Natuderm® (Burgess)
Cream (hydrophilic and lipophilic), free fatty acids 5%, glycerides 15.5%, glycerol 3.7%, phospholipids 0.2%, polysorbate '60' 1.1%, sorbitan monostearate 1%, squalane 0.5%, squalene 3.3%, free sterols 0.8%, sterol esters 1.3%, α-tocopherol 0.003%, waxes 7%, butylated hydroxyanisole 0.003%. Net price 100 g = £2.08; 450 g = £8.19

Noratex® (Norton)
Cream, cod-liver oil 2.15%, light kaolin 3.5%, talc 7.4%, wool fat 1.075%, zinc oxide 21.8%. Net price 40 g = 38p; 500 g = £2.52. For napkin and urinary rash and pressure sores

Oilatum® (Stiefel)
Cream, arachis oil 21%, povidone (polyvinylpyrrolidone) 1%, in a water-miscible basis. Net price 40 g = £1.79; 80 g = £2.78
Additives: fragrance

Rikospray Balsam® (3M)
Spray application, soluble solids of benzoin equivalent to Sumatra benzoin 12.5%, prepared storax 2.5% (pressurised aerosol pack). Net price 50-g unit = £2.31. For application to skin under adhesive plasters, in ileostomy and colostomy care
Additives: none as listed in section 13.1

Rikospray Silicone® (3M)
Spray application, aldioxa 0.5%, cetylpyridinium chloride 0.02%, in a water-repellent basis containing dimethicone 1000. Net price 200-g pressurised aerosol pack = £2.45. For urinary rash, pressure sores, and colostomy care
Additives: none as listed in section 13.1

Siopel® (ICI)
Barrier cream, dimethicone '1000' 10%, cetrimide 0.3%. Net price 50 g = 57p; 250 g = £1.82. For dermatoses, colostomy and ileostomy care, urinary rash, and related conditions
Additives: butylated hydroxytoluene, hydroxybenzoates (parabens)

Sprilon® (Pharmacia)
Spray application, dimethicone 0.6%, zinc oxide 7.2%, in a basis containing wool fat, wool alcohols, cetyl alcohol, dextran, white soft paraffin, liquid paraffin, propellants. Net price 200-g pressurised aerosol unit = £2.82. For urinary rash, pressure sores, and colostomy and ileostomy

Sudocrem® (Tosara)
Cream, benzyl alcohol 0.39%, benzyl benzoate 1.01%, benzyl cinnamate 0.15%, wool fat 4%, zinc oxide 15.25%. Net price 30 g = 56p; 60 g = 64p; 125 g = £1.07; 250 g = £1.94; 400 g = £2.79. For napkin rash and pressure sores
Additives: beeswax (synthetic), butylated hydroxyanisole, propylene glycol, fragrance

Thovaline® (Ilon)
Ointment, cod-liver oil 1.5%, light kaolin 2.5%, talc 3.3%, wool fat 2.5%, zinc oxide 19.8%. Net price 15 g = 36p; 40 g = 39p; 50 g = 46p; 90 g = 75p; 125 g = 90p; 500 g = £2.78. For napkin and urinary rash and pressure sores
Additives: fragrance
Spray application, ingredients as for ointment in pressurised aerosol pack. Net price 142 g = £1.73

Ultrabase®—section 13.1

Unguentum Merck®—section 13.1

Vasogen® (Pharmax)
Barrier cream, dimethicone 20%, calamine 1.5%, zinc oxide 7.5%. Net price 50 g= 64p; 100 g = £1.08. For napkin and urinary rash, pressure sores, and pruritus ani
Additives: hydroxybenzoates (parabens), wool fat

Vita-E® (Bioglan)
Ointment, *d*-α-tocopheryl acetate 30 units/g in yellow soft paraffin. Net price 50 g = £1.74. For pressure sores and related conditions
Additives: none as listed in section 13.1

Preparations containing urea

Aquadrate® (Norwich Eaton)
Cream, urea 10% in a powder-in-cream basis. Net price 30 g = £1.63; 100 g = £4.91
Additives: none as listed in section 13.1
Apply thinly and rub into area when required

Calmurid® (Pharmacia)
Cream, urea 10%, lactic acid 5%, in a water-miscible basis. Diluent aqueous cream, life of diluted cream 14 days. Net price 100 g = £3.49; 400-g dispenser = £12.50
Additives: none as listed in section 13.1
Apply a thick layer for 3–5 minutes, massage into area, and remove excess, usually twice daily. Use half-strength cream for 1 week if stinging occurs with undiluted preparation

Nutraplus® (Alcon)
Cream, urea 10% in a water-miscible basis. Net price 60 g = £2.62
Additives: hydroxybenzoates (parabens), propylene glycol
Apply 2–3 times daily

PoM **Sential E®** (Pharmacia)
Cream, urea 4%, sodium chloride 4%. Net price 100 g = £2.97
Additives: hydroxybenzoates (parabens)
For dry, scaling and itching skin, apply twice daily after washing

13.2.2 Emollient bath additives

For bath additives containing tar, see section 13.5 and for antiseptic bath additives, see section 13.11.

Alpha Keri Bath® (Bristol-Myers)
Bath oil, liquid paraffin 91.7%, oil-soluble fraction of wool fat 3%. Net price 240 mL = £3.54; 480 mL = £6.59
Additives: fragrance

Aveeno Oilated® (Dendron)
Bath additive, oat (protein fraction) 41%, liquid paraffin 35%. Net price 10 × 30-g sachets = £4.60. ACBS: for endogenous and exogenous eczema, xeroderma, icthyosis, and senile pruritus associated with dry skin
Additives: none as listed in section 13.1
Add 1 sachet/bath

[1]**Aveeno Regular®** (Dendron)
Bath additive, oat (protein fraction). Net price 6 × 50-g sachets = £2.76. ACBS: as for Aveeno Oilated
Additives: none as listed in section 13.1
Add 1 sachet/bath

1. Formerly Aveeno Colloidal

Balneum® (Merck)
Bath oil, soya oil 84.75%. Net price 225 mL = £3.14; 500 mL = £6.22; 1 litre = £12.00
Additives: butylated hydroxytoluene, propylene glycol, fragrance
Add 20 mL/bath

Balneum with Tar®—section 13.5

Emulsiderm® (Dermal)
Liquid emulsion, liquid paraffin 25%, isopropyl myristate 25%, benzalkonium chloride 0.5%. Net price 250 mL (with 10-mL measure) = £4.44; 1 litre (with 30-mL measure) = £11.87
Additives: polysorbate 60
Add 30 mL/bath (infants 15 mL) and soak for 5–10 minutes

Hydromol Emollient® (Quinoderm Ltd)
Bath additive, isopropyl myristate 13%, light liquid paraffin 37.8%. Net price 150 mL = £1.54; 350 mL = £2.89; 1 litre = £6.74

Oilatum Emollient® (Stiefel)
Bath additive (emulsion), acetylated wool alcohols 5%, liquid paraffin 63.7%. Net price 150 mL = £1.65; 350 mL = £3.20
Additives: isopropyl palmitate, fragrance
Add 5–15 mL/bath and soak for 10–20 minutes

13.2.3 Dusting powders

Dusting powders are used in folds where friction may occur between opposing skin surfaces. They should not be applied in areas that are very moist as they tend to cake and abrade the skin. **Talc** acts as a lubricant powder but does not absorb moisture whereas **starch** is less lubricant but absorbs water. Other inert powders such as kaolin or zinc oxide may also be used in the formulation of dusting powders.

See also section 13.11 for antiseptic dusting powders.

Talc Dusting Powder, BP, starch 10% in sterilised purified talc. Net price 100 g = 27p

Zinc, Starch and Talc Dusting-powder, BPC, zinc oxide 25%, starch 25%, sterilised purified talc 50%. Net price 50 g = 16p

ZeaSORB® (Stiefel)
Dusting powder, aldioxa 0.2%, chloroxylenol 0.5%, pulverised maize core 45%. Net price 50 g = £2.15
Additives: fragrance

13.3 Local anaesthetics and antipruritics

Pruritus may be caused by systemic disease (such as drug hypersensitivity, obstructive jaundice, endocrine disease, and certain malignant diseases) as well as by skin disease (e.g. psoriasis, eczema, urticaria, and scabies). Where possible the underlying causes should be treated.

There is no really effective antipruritic. **Calamine** preparations are widely prescribed. **Emollient** preparations (section 13.2.1) may also be of value. **Oral antihistamines** (section 3.4.1) should be used in allergic rashes.

Some topical antihistamines and local anaesthetics may cause sensitisation. Topical antihistamines are only marginally effective. Insect bites and stings, though often treated with such preparations, are best treated with calamine preparations or emollients.

Crotamiton shows little evidence of greater effectiveness than calamine in the relief of pruritus.

For preparations used in pruritus ani, see section 1.7.1.

CALAMINE

Indications: pruritus

Calamine Cream, Aqueous, BP, calamine 4%, zinc oxide 3%, liquid paraffin 20%, self-emulsifying glyceryl monostearate 5%, cetomacrogol emulsifying wax 5%, phenoxyethanol 0.5%, freshly boiled and cooled purified water 62.5%. Net price 50 g = 28p

Calamine Lotion, BP, calamine 15%, zinc oxide 5%, glycerol 5%, bentonite 3%, sodium citrate 0.5%, liquefied phenol 0.5%, in freshly boiled and cooled purified water. Net price 200 mL = £1.16

Calamine Lotion, Oily, BP1980, calamine 5%, arachis oil 50%, oleic acid 0.5%, wool fat 1%, in calcium hydroxide solution. Net price 200 mL = £2.55

Calamine Ointment, BP, calamine 15%, in white soft paraffin

Eczederm®—section 13.2.1

CROTAMITON

Indications: pruritus
Cautions: avoid use near eyes
Contra-indications: acute exudative dermatoses

Eurax® (Ciba Consumer)
Lotion, crotamiton 10%. Net price 100 mL = £1.71
Additives: propylene glycol
Cream, crotamiton 10%. Net price 30 g = £1.27; 100 g = £2.20
Additives: beeswax, hydroxybenzoates (parabens)

LOCAL ANAESTHETICS

Indications: relief of local pain, see notes above. See section 15.2 for use in surface anaesthesia
Cautions: may cause hypersensitivity
Note. Topical local anaesthetic preparations may be absorbed, especially through mucosal surfaces, therefore excessive application should be avoided, particularly in infants and children.

Anethaine® (Crookes)
Cream, amethocaine hydrochloride 1%, in a water-miscible basis. Net price 25 g = 81p
Additives: fragrance
Solarcaine® (Schering-Plough)
Cream, benzocaine 1%, triclosan 0.2%. Net price 25 mL = £1.13
Additives: benzyl alcohol, disodium edetate
Lotion, benzocaine 0.5%, triclosan 0.2%. Net price 75 mL = £1.58
Additives: disodium edetate, hydroxybenzoates (parabens)
Spray (= application), benzocaine 5%, triclosan 0.1%, pressurised aerosol unit. Net price 100 g = £2.05
Additives: propylene glycol
Xylocaine® (Astra)
Ointment, see section 15.2

TOPICAL ANTIHISTAMINES

Indications: pruritus, urticaria, see notes above
Cautions: may cause hypersensitivity; avoid in eczema; photosensitivity (diphenhydramine)

Anthisan® (Rhône-Poulenc Rorer)
Cream, mepyramine maleate 2%. Net price 25 g = £1.05
Additives: hydroxybenzoates (parabens), fragrance
Apply 2–3 times daily for up to 3 days
Caladryl® (W-L)
Cream, diphenhydramine hydrochloride 1%, calamine 8%, camphor 0.1%, in a water-miscible basis. Net price 42 g = £1.21
Additives: hydroxybenzoates (parabens), polysorbate 60, propylene glycol
Lotion, ingredients as for cream. Net price 125 mL = £1.21
Additives: fragrance
Apply 3–4 times daily for up to 3 days
R.B.C.® (Rybar)
Cream, antazoline hydrochloride 1.8%, calamine 8%, camphor 0.1%, cetrimide 0.5%. Net price 25 g = £1.03
Additives: propylene glycol
Apply when required for up to 3 days

13.4 Topical corticosteroids

Topical corticosteroids are used for the treatment of inflammatory conditions of the skin other than those due to an infection, in particular the eczematous disorders. Corticosteroids suppress various components of the inflammatory reaction while in use; they are in no sense curative, and when treatment is discontinued a rebound exacerbation of the condition may occur. They are indicated for the relief of symptoms and for the suppression of signs of the disorder when potentially less harmful measures are ineffective.

Corticosteroids are of no value in the treatment of urticaria and are **contra-indicated** in rosacea and in ulcerative conditions as they worsen the condition. They should not be used indiscriminately in pruritus.

CHOICE OF PREPARATION. The preparation containing the **least potent** drug at the **lowest strength** which is effective is the one of choice, but extemporaneous dilution should be avoided whenever possible.

There is no good evidence that it is of any benefit to prescribe a potent corticosteroid for initial treatment; it is probably just as useful to "ascend" in potency as it is to "descend". It should be noted that if a patient ceases to respond to a particular corticosteroid another of similar potency ought to be prescribed, not a more potent one. In general, the most potent corticosteroids should be reserved for recalcitrant dermatoses such as *chronic discoid lupus erythematosus, lichen simplex chronicus, hypertrophic lichen planus*, and *palmar plantar pustulosis*. With rare exceptions, potent corticosteroids should not be used on the face as they may precipitate a rosacea-like disorder and aggravate pre-existing rosacea.

Considerable caution must be exercised in the use of potent corticosteroids in children (see below).

Topical corticosteroid preparations are divided into four groups in respect of potency. In ascending order these are:

	Potency	Examples
IV	Mild	Hydrocortisone 1%
III	Moderately potent	Clobetasone butyrate 0.05% (Eumovate®)
II	Potent	Betamethasone 0.1% (as valerate) (Betnovate®); hydrocortisone butyrate (Locoid®)
I	Very potent	Clobetasol propionate 0.05% (Dermovate®)

Intradermal corticosteroid injections (see section 10.1.2.2) are more effective than the very potent topical corticosteroid preparations and they should be reserved for severe cases where there are localised lesions and topical treatment has failed. Their effects last for several weeks.

SIDE-EFFECTS. Unlike groups I and II, groups III and IV are rarely associated with side-effects. The more potent the preparation the more care is required, as absorption through the skin can cause severe pituitary-adrenal-axis suppression and hypercorticism (see section 6.3.3), both of which depend on the area of the body treated and the duration of the treatment. It must also be remembered that absorption is greatest from areas of thin skin, raw surfaces, and intertriginous areas, and is increased by occlusion.

Local side-effects from the use of corticosteroids topically include:
(a) spread and worsening of untreated infection;
(b) thinning of the skin which may be restored over a period of time although the original structure may never return;
(c) irreversible striae atrophicae;
(d) increased hair growth;
(e) perioral dermatitis, an inflammatory papular disorder on the face of young women;
(f) acne at the site of application in some patients;
(g) mild depigmentation and vellus hair.

CHOICE OF FORMULATION. Water-miscible creams are suitable for moist or weeping lesions whereas ointments are generally chosen for dry, lichenified or scaly lesions or where a more occlusive effect is required. Lotions may be useful when minimal application to a large area is required. Occlusive polythene dressings have been used to increase the effect, but also increase the risk of side-effects. The inclusion of urea increases the penetration of the corticosteroid.

USE IN CHILDREN. Children, especially babies, are particularly susceptible to side-effects. The more potent corticosteroids should be **avoided** in paediatric treatment or if necessary used with great care for short periods; a mild corticosteroid such as hydrocortisone is useful for treating napkin rash and infantile eczemas (but see caution below). Napkins and plastic pants may however act as an occlusive dressing and increase absorption.

COMPOUND PREPARATIONS. The advantages of including other substances with corticosteroids in topical preparations are debatable. The commonest ones are the **antibacterials**.

LABELS. The application of excessive quantities of external corticosteroid preparations can result in undesirable local and systemic side-effects (see above). Accordingly, label 28 (To be applied sparingly) should be used with all external corticosteroid preparations.

HYDROCORTISONE

Indications: mild inflammatory skin disorders
Cautions: see notes above and in section 13.5 (psoriasis); also avoid prolonged use in infants and children (extreme caution in dermatoses of infancy including napkin rash—where possible treatment should be limited to 5–7 days), and on the face; more potent corticosteroids contra-indicated in infants and young children
Contra-indications: untreated bacterial, fungal, or viral skin lesions
Side-effects: see notes above
Administration: apply thinly 2–3 times daily, reducing strength and frequency as condition responds

Over-the-counter sales. Proprietary brands of hydrocortisone cream (0.1 and 1%) and ointment (1%) are on sale to the public for treatment of allergic contact dermatitis, irritant dermatitis, and insect bite reactions only
Cautions: not for children under 10 years or in pregnancy, without medical advice
Contra-indications: eyes/face, anogenital region, broken or infected skin (including cold sores, acne, and athlete's foot)
Administration: apply sparingly over small area 1–2 times daily for max. of 1 week
Labelling must state. If the condition is not improved, consult your doctor.

Creams

PoM **Hydrocortisone** (Non-proprietary)
Cream, hydrocortisone in a suitable basis. Net price 0.5%, 15 g = 38p; 30 g = 60p; 1%, 15 g = 47p. Label: 28. Potency IV
When hydrocortisone cream is prescribed and no strength is stated, the 1% strength should be supplied

PoM **Cobadex®** (Cox Pharmaceuticals)
Cream, hydrocortisone 0.5 or 1%, dimethicone '350' 20%, in a water-miscible basis, net price 20 g (0.5%) = £1.17; 20 g (1%) = £1.68. Label: 28. Potency IV
Additives: hydroxybenzoates (parabens), polysorbate 80, propylene glycol

PoM **Dioderm®** (Dermal)
Cream, hydrocortisone 0.1%, in a water-miscible basis. Net price 30 g = £2.42. Label: 28. Potency IV
Additives: propylene glycol

PoM **Efcortelan®** (Glaxo)
Cream, hydrocortisone in a water-miscible basis. Net price 0.5%, 30 g = 60p; 1%, 30 g = 74p; 2.5%, 30 g = £1.66. Label: 28. Potency IV
Additives: chlorocresol

PoM **Hydrocortistab®** (Boots)
Cream, hydrocortisone acetate 1%, in a water-miscible basis. Net price 15 g = 30p. Label: 28. Potency IV
Additives: chlorocresol

PoM **Hydrocortisyl®** (Roussel)
Cream, hydrocortisone 1%, in a water-miscible basis. Net price 15 g = 28p. Label: 28. Potency IV
Additives: chlorocresol

PoM **Mildison®** (Brocades)
Lipocream, hydrocortisone 1% in a fatty cream basis. Net price 30 g = £2.19. Label: 28. Potency IV
Additives: hydroxybenzoates (parabens)

Ointments

PoM **Hydrocortisone** (Non-proprietary)
Ointment, hydrocortisone in a suitable basis. Net price 0.5%, 15 g = 39p; 30 g = 60p; 1%, 15 g = 49p. Label: 28. Potency IV
When hydrocortisone ointment is prescribed and no strength is stated, the 1% strength should be supplied

PoM **Efcortelan®** (Glaxo)
Ointment, hydrocortisone in a paraffin basis. Net price 0.5%, 30 g = 60p; 1%, 30 g = 74p; 2.5%, 30 g = £1.66. Label: 28. Potency IV
Additives: none as listed in section 13.1

PoM **Hydrocortistab**® (Boots)
Ointment, hydrocortisone 1%, in an anhydrous greasy basis. Net price 15 g = 30p. Label: 28. Potency IV
Additives: none as listed in section 13.1

PoM **Hydrocortisyl**® (Roussel)
Ointment, hydrocortisone 1%, in an anhydrous greasy basis. Net price 15 g = 28p. Label: 28. Potency IV
Additives: wool fat

Compound preparations
Note. Compound preparations with coal tar, section 13.5

PoM **Alphaderm**® (Norwich Eaton)
Cream, hydrocortisone 1%, urea 10%, in a powder-in-cream basis. Net price 30 g = £2.42; 100 g = £7.51. Label: 28. Potency III
Additives: none as listed in section 13.1
Apply thinly twice daily

PoM **Calmurid HC**® (Pharmacia)
Cream, hydrocortisone 1%, urea 10%, lactic acid 5%, in a water-miscible basis. Diluent aqueous cream, life of diluted cream 14 days. Net price 30 g = £2.33; 100 g = £6.75. Label: 28. Potency III
Additives: none as listed in section 13.1
Apply thinly twice daily.
Note. Dilute to half-strength with aqueous cream for 1 week if stinging occurs then transfer to undiluted preparation

PoM **Epifoam**® (Stafford-Miller)
Foam (= application), hydrocortisone acetate 1%, pramoxine hydrochloride 1%, in a muco-adherent basis (pressurised aerosol pack). Net price 12-g unit (approx. 20 applications of 5 mL) = £2.81. Label: 28. Potency IV
Additives: information not disclosed for BNF
For perineal trauma including post-episiotomy pain and dermatoses
Apply on a pad 3–4 times daily

PoM **Eurax-Hydrocortisone**® (Zyma)
Cream, hydrocortisone 0.25%, crotamiton 10%. Net price 30 g = 93p. Label: 28. Potency IV
Additives: hydroxybenzoates (parabens), propylene glycol
Apply thinly 2–3 times daily

PoM **Hydrocal**® (Bioglan)
Cream, hydrocortisone acetate 1%, in a basis containing calamine. Net price 25 g = £2.41. Label: 28. Potency IV
Additives: hydroxybenzoates (parabens), polysorbates
Apply thinly 2–3 times daily

PoM **Sential**® (Pharmacia)
Cream, hydrocortisone 0.5%, urea 4%, sodium chloride 4%, in a water-miscible basis. Net price 30 g = £2.40; 100 g = £7.25. Label: 28. Potency IV
Additives: sorbic acid
Apply thinly twice daily

With antimicrobials

PoM **Barquinol HC**® (Fisons)
Cream, hydrocortisone acetate 0.5%, clioquinol 3%. Net price 15 g = 58p. Label: 28. Potency IV
Additives: hydroxybenzoates (parabens), wool fat
Apply thinly 2–3 times daily
Caution: stains clothing

PoM **Canesten HC**® (Baypharm)
Cream, hydrocortisone 1%, clotrimazole 1%. Net price 30 g = £3.18. Label: 28. Potency IV
Additives: benzyl alcohol
Apply thinly twice daily

PoM **Daktacort**® (Janssen)
Cream, hydrocortisone 1%, miconazole nitrate 2%, in a water-miscible basis. Net price 30 g = £2.24. Label: 28. Potency IV
Additives: butylated hydroxyanisole, disodium edetate
Ointment, hydrocortisone 1%, miconazole nitrate 2%, in a greasy basis. Net price 30 g = £3.10. Label: 28. Potency IV
Additives: none as listed in section 13.1
Apply thinly 2–3 times daily

PoM **Econacort**® (Squibb)
Cream, hydrocortisone 1%, econazole nitrate 1%. Net price 30 g = £2.85. Label: 28. Potency IV
Additives: butylated hydroxyanisole
Apply thinly twice daily

PoM **Framycort**® (Fisons)
Ointment, hydrocortisone acetate 0.5%, framycetin sulphate 0.5%. Net price 15 g = £1.82. Label: 28. Potency IV
Additives: none as listed in section 13.1
Apply thinly 2–3 times daily

PoM **Fucidin H**® (Leo)
Cream, hydrocortisone acetate 1%, fusidic acid 2%. Net price 15 g = £3.30; 30 g = £5.69. Label: 28. Potency IV
Additives: butylated hydroxyanisole, potassium sorbate
Gel, hydrocortisone acetate 1%, fusidic acid 2%, in a water-miscible basis. Net price 15 g = £2.91; 30 g = £5.06. Label: 28. Potency IV
Additives: hydroxybenzoates (parabens), polysorbate 80
Ointment, hydrocortisone acetate 1%, sodium fusidate 2%. Net price 15 g = £2.70; 30 g = £4.68. Label: 28. Potency IV
Additives: wool fat
Apply thinly 3–4 times daily

PoM **Genticin HC**® (Nicholas)
Cream, hydrocortisone acetate 1%, gentamicin 0.3% (as sulphate), in a water-miscible basis. Net price 15 g = £1.86. Label: 28. Potency IV
Additives: hydroxybenzoates (parabens), polysorbates, propylene glycol
Ointment, ingredients as for cream but greasy basis. Net price 15 g = £1.86. Label: 28. Potency IV
Additives: hydroxybenzoates (parabens), polysorbates, propylene glycol
Apply thinly 3–4 times daily

PoM **Gregoderm**® (Unigreg)
Ointment, hydrocortisone 1%, neomycin sulphate 0.4%, nystatin 100 000 units/g, polymyxin B sulphate 7250 units/g. Net price 15 g = £2.04. Label: 28. Potency IV
Additives: none as listed in section 13.1
Apply thinly 2–3 times daily

PoM **Nystaform-HC**® (Bayer)
Cream, hydrocortisone 0.5%, nystatin 100 000 units/g, chlorhexidine hydrochloride 1%, in a water-miscible basis. Net price 30 g = £2.73. Label: 28. Potency IV
Additives: benzyl alcohol, polysorbate 60
Ointment, hydrocortisone 1%, nystatin 100 000 units/g, chlorhexidine acetate 1%, in a water-

Prices are **net**, see p. 1

repellent basis. Net price 30 g = £2.73. Label: 28. Potency IV
Additives: none as listed in section 13.1
Apply thinly 2–3 times daily

PoM **Quinocort®** (Quinoderm Ltd)
Cream, hydrocortisone 1%, potassium hydroxyquinoline sulphate 0.5% in a vanishing cream basis. Net price 30 g = £2.59. Label: 28. Potency IV
Additives: edetic acid (EDTA)
Apply thinly 2–3 times daily

PoM **Terra-Cortril®** (Pfizer)
Topical ointment, hydrocortisone 1%, oxytetracycline 3% (as hydrochloride), in a paraffin basis. Net price 15 g = £1.01; 30 g = £1.82. Label: 28. Potency IV
Additives: none as listed in section 13.1
Apply thinly 2–4 times daily
Spray application, hydrocortisone 50 mg, oxytetracycline 150 mg (as hydrochloride), 30-mL pressurised aerosol unit, net price = £1.44; double these amounts in 60-mL unit, net price = £2.50. Label: 28. Potency IV
Additives: none as listed in section 13.1
Spray area thinly 2–4 times daily

PoM **Terra-Cortril Nystatin®** (Pfizer)
Cream, hydrocortisone 1%, nystatin 100 000 units/g, oxytetracycline 3% (as calcium salt). Net price 30 g = £2.01. Label: 28. Potency IV
Additives: hydroxybenzoates (parabens), polysorbate, propylene glycol, fragrance
Apply thinly 2–4 times daily

PoM **Timodine®** (R&C)
Cream, hydrocortisone 0.5%, nystatin 100 000 units/g, benzalkonium chloride solution 0.2%, dimethicone '350' 10%. Net price 30 g = £2.38. Label: 28. Potency IV
Additives: butylated hydroxyanisole, hydroxybenzoates (parabens), sorbic acid
Apply thinly 3 times daily (napkin rash, after each change)

PoM **Tri-Cicatrin®** (Calmic)
Ointment, hydrocortisone 1%, bacitracin zinc 250 units/g, neomycin sulphate 3400 units/g, nystatin 100000 units/g. Net price 15 g = £4.75; 30 g = £8.64. Label: 28. Potency IV
Additives: none as listed in section 13.1
Apply thinly 1–3 times daily

PoM **Vioform-Hydrocortisone®** (Zyma)
Cream, hydrocortisone 1%, clioquinol 3%. Net price 30 g = £1.57. Label: 28. Potency IV
Ointment, hydrocortisone 1%, clioquinol 3%. Net price 30 g = £1.57. Label: 28. Potency IV
Apply thinly 1–3 times daily
Caution: stains clothing

HYDROCORTISONE BUTYRATE

Indications: severe inflammatory skin disorders such as eczema unresponsive to less potent corticosteroids
Cautions; Contra-indications; Side-effects: see under Hydrocortisone and notes above
Administration: apply thinly 2–4 times daily, reducing frequency as condition responds

PoM **Locoid®** (Brocades)
Cream, hydrocortisone butyrate 0.1%, in a water-miscible basis. Net price 30 g = £2.27; 100 g = £6.95. Label: 28. Potency II
Additives: hydroxybenzoates (parabens)
Note. For bland cream basis see Locobase®, section 13.1
Lipocream, hydrocortisone butyrate 0.1% in a fatty cream basis. Net price 30 g = £2.38; 100 g = £7.29. Label: 28. Potency II
Additives: hydroxybenzoates (parabens)
Note. For bland cream basis see Lipobase®, section 13.1
Ointment, hydrocortisone butyrate 0.1%, in an anhydrous greasy basis. Net price 30 g = £2.27; 100 g = £6.95. Label: 28. Potency II
Additives: none as listed in section 13.1
Note. For bland ointment basis see Locobase®, section 13.1
Scalp lotion, hydrocortisone butyrate 0.1%, in an aqueous isopropyl alcohol basis. Net price 30 mL = £3.20; 100 mL = £9.81. Label: 28. Potency II
Additives: none as listed in section 13.1
Apply 1–2 times daily, reducing frequency as condition responds
Caution: flammable

With antimicrobials

PoM **Locoid C®** (Brocades)
Cream, hydrocortisone butyrate 0.1%, chlorquinaldol 3%. Net price 30 g = £2.97. Label: 28. Potency II
Additives: none as listed in section 13.1
Ointment, ingredients as for cream, in a greasy basis. Net price 30 g = £2.97. Label: 28. Potency II
Additives: none as listed in section 13.1
Apply thinly 2–4 times daily. Max. 60 g for up to 14 days

ALCLOMETASONE DIPROPIONATE

Indications: inflammatory skin disorders such as eczema
Cautions; Contra-indications; Side-effects: see under Hydrocortisone and notes above
Administration: apply thinly 2–3 times daily, reducing frequency as condition responds

PoM **Modrasone®** (Schering-Plough)
Cream, alclometasone dipropionate 0.05%. Net price 15 g = £1.70; 50 g = £4.80. Label: 28. Potency III
Additives: chlorocresol, propylene glycol
Ointment, alclometasone dipropionate 0.05%. Net price 15 g = £1.70; 50 g = £4.80. Label: 28. Potency III
Additives: beeswax, propylene glycol

BECLÓMETHASONE DIPROPIONATE

Indications: severe inflammatory skin disorders such as eczema unresponsive to less potent corticosteroids
Cautions; Contra-indications; Side-effects: see under Hydrocortisone and notes above
Administration: apply thinly twice daily, reducing strength and frequency as condition responds

PoM **Propaderm®** (Glaxo)
Cream, beclomethasone dipropionate 0.025%. Net price 30 g = £1.58. Label: 28. Potency II
Additives: chlorocresol
Ointment, beclomethasone dipropionate 0.025%. Net price 30 g = £1.58. Label: 28. Potency II
Additives: propylene glycol

With antibacterials
PoM **Propaderm-A®** (Glaxo)
Ointment, beclomethasone dipropionate 0.025%, chlortetracycline hydrochloride 3%. Net price 30 g = £1.78. Label: 28. Potency II
Additives: none as listed in section 13.1
Initially apply thinly twice daily, reducing frequency as condition responds
Caution: stains clothing

BETAMETHASONE ESTERS

Indications: severe inflammatory skin disorders such as eczema unresponsive to less potent corticosteroids

Cautions; Contra-indications; Side-effects: see under Hydrocortisone and notes above. Application of more than 100 g per week of 0.1% preparation is likely to cause adrenal suppression

Administration: apply thinly 2–3 times daily, reducing strength and frequency as condition responds

PoM **Betamethasone Valerate** (Non-proprietary)
Cream, betamethasone 0.1% (as valerate). Net price 15 g = £1.40; 30 g = £3.95. Label: 28. Potency II
Ointment, betamethasone 0.1% (as valerate). Net price 15 g = £1.40; 30 g = £3.95. Label: 28. Potency II

PoM **Betnovate®** (Glaxo)
Cream, betamethasone 0.1% (as valerate), in a water-miscible basis. Net price 30 g = £1.40; 100 g = £3.95. Label: 28. Potency II
Additives: chlorocresol
Ointment, betamethasone 0.1% (as valerate), in an anhydrous paraffin basis. Net price 30 g = £1.40; 100 g = £3.95. Label: 28. Potency II
Additives: none as listed in section 13.1
Lotion, betamethasone 0.1% (as valerate). Net price 100 mL = £4.75. Label: 28. Potency II
Additives: hydroxybenzoates (parabens)
Scalp application, betamethasone 0.1% (as valerate), in a thickened alcoholic basis. Net price 100 mL = £5.18. Label: 28. Potency II
Additives: none as listed in section 13.1
Apply thinly 1–2 times daily, then reduce
Caution: flammable

PoM **Betnovate-RD®** (Glaxo)
Cream, betamethasone 0.025% (as valerate) in a water-miscible basis (1 in 4 dilution of Betnovate cream). Net price 100 g = £3.26. Label: 28. Potency III
Additives: chlorocresol
Ointment, betamethasone 0.025% (as valerate) in an anhydrous paraffin basis (1 in 4 dilution of Betnovate ointment). Net price 100 g = £3.26. Label: 28. Potency III
Additives: none as listed in section 13.1

PoM **Diprosalic®** (Schering-Plough)
Ointment, betamethasone 0.05% (as dipropionate), salicylic acid 3%. Net price 30 g = £3.20; 100 g = £9.30. Label: 28. Potency II
Additives: none as listed in section 13.1
[1]*Scalp application*, betamethasone 0.05% (as dipropionate), salicylic acid 2%, in an alcoholic basis. Net price 30 mL = £4.10; 100 mL = £10.32. Label: 28. Potency II
Additives: disodium edetate
Apply thinly 1–2 times daily; max. 60 g per week
1. formerly Diprosalic lotion

PoM **Diprosone®** (Schering-Plough)
Cream, betamethasone 0.05% (as dipropionate), in a water-miscible basis. Net price 30 g = £2.57; 100 g = £7.30. Label: 28. Potency II
Additives: chlorocresol
Note. For bland cream basis see Diprobase®, section 13.1
Ointment, betamethasone 0.05% (as dipropionate). Net price 30 g = £2.57; 100 g = £7.30. Label: 28. Potency II
Additives: none as listed in section 13.1
Note. For bland ointment basis see Diprobase®, section 13.1
Apply thinly once or twice daily
[2]*Lotion*, betamethasone 0.05% (as dipropionate), in a thickened alcoholic basis. Net price 30 mL = £3.25; 100 mL = £9.30. Label: 28. Potency II
Additives: none as listed in section 13.1
Apply twice daily, then reduce
2. formerly Diprosone scalp application

With antimicrobials
PoM **Betnovate-C®** (Glaxo)
Cream, betamethasone 0.1% (as valerate), clioquinol 3%, in a water-miscible basis. Net price 30 g = £1.72. Label: 28. Potency II
Additives: chlorocresol
Ointment, betamethasone 0.1% (as valerate), clioquinol 3%, in a paraffin basis. Net price 30 g = £1.72. Label: 28. Potency II
Additives: none as listed in section 13.1
Apply thinly 2–3 times daily
Caution: stains clothing

PoM **Betnovate-N®** (Glaxo)
Cream, betamethasone 0.1% (as valerate), neomycin sulphate 0.5%, in a water-miscible basis. Net price 30 g = £1.72; 100 g = £4.77. Label: 28. Potency II
Additives: chlorocresol
Ointment, betamethasone 0.1% (as valerate), neomycin sulphate 0.5%, in a paraffin basis. Net price 30 g = £1.72; 100 g = £4.77. Label: 28. Potency II
Additives: none as listed in section 13.1
Apply thinly 2–3 times daily

PoM **Fucibet®** (Leo)
Cream, betamethasone 0.1% (as valerate), fusidic acid 2%, in a water-miscible basis. Net price 15 g = £3.84; 30 g = £6.48. Label: 28. Potency II
Additives: chlorocresol
Apply thinly 2–3 times daily

PoM **Lotriderm®** (Schering-Plough)
Cream, betamethasone 0.05% (as dipropionate), clotrimazole 1%. Net price 15 g = £3.49. Label: 28. Potency II
Additives: benzyl alcohol, propylene glycol
Apply thinly twice daily

BUDESONIDE

Indications: severe inflammatory skin disorders such as eczema
Cautions; Contra-indications; Side-effects: see under Hydrocortisone and notes above
Administration: apply thinly 2–3 times daily

▼ PoM **Preferid®** (Brocades)
Cream, budesonide 0.025% in a water-miscible basis. Net price 30 g = £2.96; 100 g = £9.06. Label: 28. Potency II
Additives: sorbic acid
Ointment, budesonide 0.025% in a paraffin basis. Net price 30 g = £2.96; 100 g = £9.06. Label: 28. Potency II
Additives: white beeswax, propylene glycol

CLOBETASOL PROPIONATE

Indications: short-term treatment only of severe resistant inflammatory skin disorders such as psoriasis (excluding widespread plaque psoriasis), recalcitrant eczemas, lichen planus, discoid lupus erythematosus unresponsive to less potent corticosteroids
Cautions; Contra-indications; Side-effects: see under Hydrocortisone and notes above. Not more than 50 g of 0.05% preparation should be applied per week
Administration: apply thinly 1–2 times daily for up to 4 weeks, reducing frequency as condition responds

PoM **Dermovate®** (Glaxo)
Cream, clobetasol propionate 0.05%, in a water-miscible basis. Net price 30 g = £2.56; 100 g = £7.52. Label: 28. Potency I
Additives: beeswax (or beeswax substitute), chlorocresol, propylene glycol
Ointment, clobetasol propionate 0.05%, in an anhydrous paraffin basis. Net price 30 g = £2.56; 100 g = £7.52. Label: 28. Potency I
Additives: propylene glycol
Scalp application, clobetasol propionate 0.05%, in a thickened alcoholic basis. Net price 30 mL = £2.93; 100 mL = £9.91. Label: 28. Potency I
Caution: flammable
Additives: none as listed in section 13.1

With antimicrobials
PoM **Dermovate-NN®** (Glaxo)
Cream, clobetasol propionate 0.05%, neomycin sulphate 0.5%, nystatin 100 000 units/g. Net price 30 g = £3.50. Label: 28. Potency I
Additives: beeswax substitute
Ointment, ingredients as for cream, in a paraffin basis. Net price 30 g = £3.50. Label: 28. Potency I
Additives: none as listed in section 13.1
Apply thinly once or twice daily, for up to 4 weeks reducing as condition responds

CLOBETASONE BUTYRATE

Indications: eczema and dermatitis of all types; maintenance between courses of more potent corticosteroids
Cautions; Contra-indications; Side-effects: see under Hydrocortisone and notes above
Administration: apply thinly up to 4 times daily, reducing frequency as condition responds

PoM **Eumovate®** (Glaxo)
Cream, clobetasone butyrate 0.05%, in a water-miscible basis. Net price 30 g = £1.76; 100 g = £5.16. Label: 28. Potency III
Additives: beeswax substitute, chlorocresol
Ointment, clobetasone butyrate 0.05%, in an anhydrous paraffin basis. Net price 30 g = £1.76; 100 g = £5.16. Label: 28. Potency III
Additives: none as listed in section 13.1

With antimicrobials
PoM **Trimovate®** (Glaxo)
Cream, clobetasone butyrate 0.05%, oxytetracycline 3% (as calcium salt), nystatin 100 000 units/g, in a water-miscible basis. Net price 30 g = £3.13. Label: 28. Potency III
Additives: chlorocresol
Ointment, clobetasone butyrate 0.05%, chlortetracycline hydrochloride 3%, nystatin 100 000 units/g, in a paraffin basis. Net price 30 g = £3.13. Label: 28. Potency III
Additives: none as listed in section 13.1
Apply thinly up to 4 times daily
Caution: stains clothing

DESONIDE

Indications: severe inflammatory skin disorders such as eczema unresponsive to less potent corticosteroids
Cautions; Contra-indications; Side-effects: see under Hydrocortisone and notes above
Administration: apply thinly 2–3 times daily reducing frequency as condition responds

PoM **Tridesilon®** (Lagap)
Cream, desonide 0.05%, in a water-miscible basis. Net price 30 g = £3.44. Label: 28. Potency II
Additives: beeswax, hydroxybenzoates (parabens)
Note. May temporarily be unavailable

DESOXYMETHASONE

Indications: severe acute inflammatory, allergic, and chronic skin disorders
Cautions; Contra-indications; Side-effects: see under Hydrocortisone and notes above
Administration: apply thinly 2–3 times daily reducing frequency as condition responds

PoM **Stiedex®** (Stiefel)
Oily cream, desoxymethasone 0.25%, in an oily basis. Net price 30 g = £3.43. Label: 28. Potency II
Additives: wool fat
LP Oily cream, desoxymethasone 0.05%, in an oily basis. Net price 30 g = £2.86. Label: 28. Potency III
Additives: edetic acid (EDTA), wool fat
Lotion, desoxymethasone 0.25%, salicylic acid 1%. Net price 50 mL = £8.05. Label: 28. Potency II
Additives: disodium edetate, propylene glycol

With antibacterials
PoM **Stiedex LPN®** (Stiefel)
Oily cream, desoxymethasone 0.05%, neomycin (as sulphate) 0.5%, in an oily basis. Net price 15 g = £2.17. Label: 28. Potency III
Additives: edetic acid (EDTA), wool fat
Apply thinly 2–3 times daily

DIFLUCORTOLONE VALERATE

Indications: severe inflammatory skin disorders such as eczema unresponsive to less potent corticosteroids; high strength (0.3%), short-term treatment of severe exacerbations
Cautions; Contra-indications; Side-effects: see under Hydrocortisone and notes above; not more than 50 g of 0.3% applied per week
Administration: apply thinly 2–3 times daily for up to 4 weeks (0.1% preparations) or 2 weeks (0.3% preparations), reducing strength and frequency as condition responds

PoM **Nerisone®** (Schering Health Care)
Cream, diflucortolone valerate 0.1%, in a water-miscible basis. Net price 30 g = £2.56. Label: 28. Potency II
Additives: disodium edetate, hydroxybenzoates (parabens)
Note. For bland cream basis see Ultrabase®, section 13.1
Oily cream, diflucortolone valerate 0.1%, in a water-in-oil basis. Net price 30 g = £2.56. Label: 28. Potency II
Additives: none as listed in section 13.1
Ointment, diflucortolone valerate 0.1%, in an anhydrous basis. Net price 30 g = £2.56. Label: 28. Potency II
Additives: none as listed in section 13.1
PoM **Nerisone Forte®** (Schering Health Care)
Oily cream, diflucortolone valerate 0.3%, in a water-in-oil basis. Net price 15 g = £2.09. Label: 28. Potency I
Additives: none as listed in section 13.1
Ointment, diflucortolone valerate 0.3% in an anhydrous fatty basis. Net price 15 g = £2.09. Label: 28. Potency I
Additives: none as listed in section 13.1

FLUCLOROLONE ACETONIDE

Indications: severe inflammatory skin disorders such as eczema unresponsive to less potent corticosteroids
Cautions; Contra-indications; Side-effects: see under Hydrocortisone and notes above
Administration: apply thinly twice daily, reducing frequency as condition responds

PoM **Topilar®** (Syntex)
Cream, fluclorolone acetonide 0.025%, in a non-aqueous, water-miscible basis. Net price 30 g = £1.70; 100 g = £4.62. Label: 28. Potency II
Additives: propylene glycol
Ointment, fluclorolone acetonide 0.025%, in an ointment basis. Net price 30 g = £1.70; 100 g = £4.62. Label: 28. Potency II
Additives: propylene glycol, wool fat

FLUOCINOLONE ACETONIDE

Indications: inflammatory skin disorders such as eczema, 0.0025–0.01% in milder conditions, 0.025% in severe conditions
Cautions; Contra-indications; Side-effects: see under Hydrocortisone and notes above
Administration: apply thinly 2–3 times daily, reducing strength and frequency as condition responds

PoM **Synalar®** (ICI)
Cream, fluocinolone acetonide 0.025%, in a water-miscible basis. Net price 15 g = 78p; 30 g = £1.40; 50 g = £2.10; Label: 28. Potency II
Additives: benzyl alcohol, polysorbates, propylene glycol
Gel, fluocinolone acetonide 0.025%, in a water-miscible basis. Net price 30 g = £1.49. For use on scalp and other hairy areas. Label: 28. Potency II
Additives: hydroxybenzoates (parabens), propylene glycol
Ointment, fluocinolone acetonide 0.025%, in a greasy basis. Net price 15 g = 78p; 30 g = £1.40; 50 g = £2.10. Label: 28. Potency II
Additives: propylene glycol, wool fat
PoM **Synalar 1 in 4 Dilution®** (ICI)
Cream, fluocinolone acetonide 0.00625% in a water-miscible basis. Net price 50 g = £1.60. Label: 28. Potency III
Additives: benzyl alcohol, polysorbates, propylene glycol
Ointment, fluocinolone acetonide 0.00625% in a greasy basis. Net price 50 g = £1.88. Label: 28. Potency III
Additives: propylene glycol, wool fat
PoM **Synalar 1 in 10 Dilution®** (ICI)
Cream, fluocinolone acetonide 0.0025% in a water-miscible basis. Net price 50 g = £1.52. Label: 28. Potency IV
Additives: benzyl alcohol, polysorbates, propylene glycol

With antibacterials
PoM **Synalar C®** (ICI)
Cream, fluocinolone acetonide 0.025%, clioquinol 3%, in a water-miscible basis. Net price 15 g = 96p. Label: 28. Potency II
Additives: disodium edetate, hydroxybenzoates (parabens), polysorbates, propylene glycol
Ointment, ingredients as for cream, in a greasy basis. Net price 15 g = 96p. Label: 28. Potency II
Additives: propylene glycol, wool fat
Apply thinly 2–3 times daily
Caution: stains clothing

PoM **Synalar N®** (ICI)
Cream, fluocinolone acetonide 0.025%, neomycin sulphate 0.5%, in a water-miscible basis. Net price 15 g = 83p; 30 g = £1.45. Label: 28. Potency II
Additives: hydroxybenzoates (parabens), polysorbates, propylene glycol
Ointment, ingredients as for cream, in a greasy basis. Net price 15 g = 83p; 30 g = £1.45. Label: 28. Potency II
Additives: propylene glycol, wool fat
Apply thinly 2–3 times daily

FLUOCINONIDE

Indications: severe inflammatory skin disorders such as eczema unresponsive to less potent corticosteroids
Cautions; Contra-indications; Side-effects: see under Hydrocortisone and notes above
Administration: apply thinly 3–4 times daily, reducing frequency as condition responds

PoM **Metosyn®** (Stuart)
FAPG cream, fluocinonide 0.05%, in a non-aqueous water-miscible basis. Net price 25 g = £1.25; 100 g = £4.71. Label: 28. Potency II
Additives: propylene glycol
Ointment, fluocinonide 0.05%, in a paraffin basis. Net price 25 g = £1.25; 100 g = £4.71. Label: 28. Potency II
Additives: propylene glycol, wool fat
Scalp lotion, fluocinonide 0.05% in a propylene glycol-alcohol basis. Net price 30 mL (with applicator) = £2.59. Label: 28. Potency II
Additives: propylene glycol
Apply 1–2 times daily, reducing frequency as condition responds
Caution: flammable

FLUOCORTOLONE

Indications: 0.25%—severe inflammatory skin disorders such as eczema unresponsive to less potent corticosteroids; 0.1%—milder inflammatory skin disorders
Cautions; Contra-indications; Side-effects: see under Hydrocortisone and notes above
Administration: apply thinly 2–3 times daily, reducing strength and frequency as condition responds

PoM **Ultradil Plain®** (Schering Health Care)
Cream, fluocortolone hexanoate 0.1%, fluocortolone pivalate 0.1%, in a water-miscible basis. Net price 50 g = £2.86. Label: 28. Potency III
Additives: disodium edetate, hydroxybenzoates (parabens), fragrance
Note. For bland cream basis see Ultrabase®, section 13.1
Ointment, fluocortolone hexanoate 0.1%, fluocortolone pivalate 0.1%, in a water-in-oil emulsion basis. Net price 50 g = £2.86. Label: 28. Potency III
Additives: wool fat, fragrance

PoM **Ultralanum Plain®** (Schering Health Care)
Cream, fluocortolone hexanoate 0.25%, fluocortolone pivalate 0.25%, in a water-miscible basis. Net price 50 g = £4.65. Label: 28. Potency III
Additives: disodium edetate, hydroxybenzoates (parabens), fragrance
Note. For bland cream basis see Ultrabase®, section 13.1
Ointment, fluocortolone 0.25%, fluocortolone pivalate 0.25%, in a water-in-oil emulsion basis. Net price 50 g = £4.65. Label: 28. Potency III
Additives: wool fat, fragrance

FLURANDRENOLONE

Indications: eczema and dermatitis of all types
Cautions; Contra-indications; Side-effects: see under Hydrocortisone and notes above
Administration: apply thinly 2–3 times daily, reducing strength and frequency as condition responds

PoM **Haelan®** (Dista)
Cream, flurandrenolone 0.0125%, in a water-miscible basis. Net price 60 g = £3.96. Label: 28. Potency III
Additives: propylene glycol
Ointment, flurandrenolone 0.0125%, in an anhydrous greasy basis. Net price 60 g = £3.96. Label: 28. Potency III
Additives: beeswax, polysorbate

With antibacterials
PoM **Haelan-C®** (Dista)
Cream, flurandrenolone 0.0125%, clioquinol 3%. Net price 30 g = £2.69. Label: 28. Potency III
Additives: hydroxybenzoates (parabens), sodium edetate
Ointment, flurandrenolone 0.0125%, clioquinol 3%. Net price 30 g = £2.69. Label: 28. Potency III
Additives: none as listed in section 13.1
Apply thinly 2–3 times daily
Caution: stains clothing

HALCINONIDE

Indications: severe inflammatory skin disorders such as eczema unresponsive to less potent corticosteroids
Cautions; Contra-indications; Side-effects: see under Hydrocortisone and notes above
Administration: apply thinly 2–3 times daily, reducing frequency as condition responds

PoM **Halciderm Topical®** (Squibb)
Cream, halcinonide 0.1%, in a water-miscible basis. Net price 30 g = £3.40. Label: 28. Potency I
Additives: propylene glycol

METHYLPREDNISOLONE ACETATE

Indications: see notes above
Cautions; Contra-indications; Side-effects: see under Hydrocortisone

PoM **Neo-Medrone®** (Upjohn)
Cream, methylprednisolone acetate 0.25%, neomycin sulphate 0.5%. Net price 15 g = £1.44. Label: 28. Potency IV
Additives: information not disclosed for BNF
Apply thinly 1–3 times daily

TRIAMCINOLONE ACETONIDE

Indications: severe inflammatory skin disorders such as eczema unresponsive to less potent corticosteroids

Cautions; Contra-indications; Side-effects: see under Hydrocortisone and notes above

Administration: apply thinly 2–4 times daily, reducing frequency as condition responds

PoM **Adcortyl®** (Squibb)
Cream, triamcinolone acetonide 0.1%, in a water-miscible basis. Net price 30 g = £1.98. Label: 28. Potency II
Additives: benzyl alcohol, propylene glycol
Ointment, triamcinolone acetonide 0.1%, in an anhydrous greasy basis. Net price 30 g = £1.98. Label: 28. Potency II
Additives: none as listed in section 13.1

PoM **Ledercort®** (Lederle)
Cream, triamcinolone acetonide 0.1%, in water-miscible basis. Net price 15 g = £1.72; 250 g = £25.90. Label: 28. Potency II
Additives: hydroxybenzoates (parabens), polysorbate 80
Ointment, triamcinolone acetonide 0.1%, in an anhydrous greasy basis. Net price 15 g = £1.72; 250 g = £25.90. Label: 28. Potency II
Additives: hydroxybenzoates (parabens), wool fat

With antimicrobials

PoM **Adcortyl with Graneodin®** (Squibb)
Cream, triamcinolone acetonide 0.1%, gramicidin 0.025%, neomycin 0.25% (as sulphate), in a vanishing-cream basis. Net price 25 g = £3.00. Label: 28. Potency II
Additives: benzyl alcohol, propylene glycol
Ointment, ingredients as for cream, in an ointment basis. Net price 15 g = £1.80. Label: 28. Potency II
Additives: none as listed in section 13.1
Apply thinly 2–4 times daily

PoM **Aureocort®** (Lederle)
Cream, triamcinolone acetonide 0.1%, chlortetracycline hydrochloride 3% (as chlortetracycline), in a water-miscible basis. Net price 15 g = £2.77. Label: 28. Potency II
Additives: chlorocresol
Ointment, triamcinolone acetonide 0.1%, chlortetracycline hydrochloride 3%, in an anhydrous greasy basis containing wool fat and white soft paraffin. Net price 15 g = £2.77. Label: 28. Potency II
Additives: hydroxybenzoates (parabens), wool fat
Caution: stains clothing
Apply thinly 2–3 times daily

PoM **Nystadermal®** (Squibb)
Cream, triamcinolone acetonide 0.1%, nystatin 100 000 units/g. Net price 15 g = £2.27. Label: 28. Potency II
Additives: benzyl alcohol, propylene glycol, fragrance
Apply thinly 2–4 times daily on moist weeping lesions

PoM **Pevaryl TC®** (Cilag)
Cream, triamcinolone 0.1%, econazole nitrate 1%. Net price 15 g = £4.00. Label: 28. Potency II
Apply thinly twice daily for 14 days

PoM **Tri-Adcortyl®** (Squibb)
Cream, triamcinolone acetonide 0.1%, gramicidin 0.025%, neomycin 0.25% (as sulphate), nystatin 100 000 units/g. Net price 30 g = £3.23. Label: 28. Potency II
Additives: benzyl alcohol, ethylenediamine, propylene glycol, fragrance
Ointment, ingredients as for cream, in an ointment basis. Net price 30 g = £3.23. Label: 28. Potency II
Additives: none as listed in section 13.1
Apply thinly 2–4 times daily

13.5 Preparations for psoriasis and eczema

ECZEMA

Eczema ('dermatitis') is due to a particular type of epidermal inflammation and is caused by a wide variety of factors; where possible the causative factors should be established and removed. In many cases no underlying factor can be identified (atopic eczema).

Dry, fissured, scaly lesions are treated with bland **emollients** (section 13.2.1) which are often all that is necessary to allay irritation and permit healing. Preparations containing zinc oxide and calamine are sometimes useful; zinc may have a weak anti-eczematous action. Preparations such as **emulsifying ointment** are used as soap substitutes and in the bath. **Keratolytics** such as salicylic acid, followed by coal tar (see p. 377) are used in chronic eczematous conditions where there is marked thickening of the skin and pronounced scaling.

Weeping eczemas may be treated with corticosteroids; they are, however, commonly secondarily infected. Wet dressings of **potassium permanganate** (0.01%) (section 13.11) are applied; if a large area is involved, potassium permanganate baths are taken. When necessary **topical antibacterials** are used (section 13.10.1) but those which are not given systemically should be chosen.

Coal tar is more active than salicylic acid and has anti-inflammatory, antipruritic and keratolytic properties. It is used in psoriasis and eczema. Coal tar has superseded wood tar as it is more active. The formulation and strength chosen depends on patient acceptability and severity of the condition; the 'thicker' the patch of eczema or psoriasis the stronger the concentration of coal tar required. **Coal tar paste** or **zinc and coal tar**

paste are generally suitable for most cases but are limited by their unpleasant appearance and smell and they may not be used on the face. Some of the newer preparations are less unsightly and may be preferred. Preparations such as Carbo-Dome® are suitable for treating the face. **Zinc paste and coal tar bandage** (section 13.13.1) is useful for treating the limbs. **Tar** shampoos are described in section 13.9. When lesions are extensive coal tar baths are useful. Combinations of coal tar with zinc or salicylic acid have no advantage over the simpler preparations. Preparations containing hydrocortisone and coal tar are useful in eczemas.

Ichthammol has a milder action than coal tar and has been used in the less acute forms of eczema. It can be applied conveniently to flexures of the limbs as **zinc paste and ichthammol bandage** (section 13.13.1).

Gamolenic acid has been claimed to improve patients with eczema and in particular atopic dermatitis. However, the evidence in favour of a useful therapeutic effect is slim.

PSORIASIS

Psoriasis is characterised by epidermal thickening and scaling. It has less tendency to heal spontaneously than eczema. For mild conditions, treatment, other than reassurance and an emollient, may be unnecessary. In more troublesome cases, local application of **salicylic acid**, **coal tar**, or **dithranol** may have a beneficial effect. Topical and systemic corticosteroids should be avoided or given under specialist supervision because, although they may be effective, subsequent treatment becomes more difficult, as tachyphylaxis may occur and they may induce or precipitate severe pustular psoriasis. In resistant cases an antimetabolite, usually methotrexate (see section 8.1.3), may be used for its antimitotic activity but this must always be done under hospital supervision and the dose adjusted according to severity of the condition and in accordance with haematological and biochemical measurements; the usual dose is 15 to 25 mg of methotrexate weekly, usually by mouth.

Salicylic acid may be used in all hyperkeratotic and scaling conditions to enhance the rate of loss of surface scale. Preparations containing salicylic acid 2% are used initially and then gradually increased to concentrations of 3 to 6%. Side-effects are few but include allergic contact sensitivity, or, when large areas are treated, salicylism (see section 10.1.1).

Dithranol is used in psoriasis and is the most potent topical preparation available for this condition. The preparation is applied carefully to the lesion, covered with a dressing, and left for one hour. Traditionally applications have been left on the skin overnight but this has now been shown to be unnecessary as short contact applications of one hour are equally effective. Usual concentrations are 0.1–2% although in individual patients 5% or more may be used. Dithranol must be used with caution as it can cause quite severe skin irritation. For this reason it must be applied only to the lesions and it is customary to start with low concentrations and gradually build up to the maximum concentration which produces a therapeutic effect without irritation. Hands should be washed thoroughly after use. Some patients are intolerant to dithranol even in low concentrations; it is important to recognise them early in treatment. Fair skin is more sensitive than dark skin. Proprietary preparations such as Dithrocream® are most commonly used as they may cause less staining and irritation than dithranol paste. Dithranol and urea combinations (Psoradrate®) may improve skin texture by rehydration. **Dithranol triacetate** has no advantage over traditional preparations.

Ingram's method of applying dithranol is a frequent method used in hospitals. The patient soaks in a warm bath containing coal tar solution 1 in 800 and after drying is exposed to ultraviolet radiation B (UVB) to produce a slight erythema. **Dithranol paste** is applied to the lesions and the normal skin protected by applying talc and stockinette dressings. The procedure is repeated daily.

PUVA, photochemotherapy using psoralens with long-wave ultraviolet irradiation (UVA), is an effective method of treating some patients with psoriasis. Special lamps are required, and a psoralen, generally methoxsalen (available on named-patient basis only) is given by mouth about 2 hours beforehand, to sensitise the skin to the effects of irradiation. A course of PUVA may last 4 to 6 weeks and requires a variable number of treatments. Treatment is only available in specialist centres; it has to be carefully regulated, owing to the short-term hazard of severe burning and the long-term hazards of cataract formation, accelerated ageing, and the development of skin cancer.

Etretinate is given by mouth for the treatment of severe resistant or complicated psoriasis and some of the congenital disorders of keratinisation including Darier's disease (keratosis follicularis). It should be prescribed **only** by, or under the supervision of, a consultant dermatologist and is available to hospitals **only**. It is a retinoid compound with marked effects on keratinising epithelia. A therapeutic effect occurs after 2 to 4 weeks with maximum benefit after 4 to 6 weeks. Etretinate treats only manifestations not the ultimate causes of these diseases, but treatment should be limited to a period of 6 to 9 months with a 3- to 4-month rest period before repeating treatment, as experience with this drug is limited. Most patients suffer from dryness and cracking of the lips. Other side-effects include a mild transient increase in the rate of hair fall (reversible on withdrawal), occasional generalised pruritus, paronychia, and nose bleeds. There is a tendency for the plasma lipids to rise in some patients. Etretinate is **teratogenic** and must be **avoided** in pregnancy. Contraceptive measures must be taken at least 1 month before and during treatment by women who may become pregnant and for at least two years after a course of the drug.

TOPICAL PREPARATIONS FOR PSORIASIS OR ECZEMA

COAL TAR

Indications: chronic eczema and psoriasis
Cautions: avoid broken or inflamed skin
Side-effects: skin irritation and acne-like eruptions, photosensitivity; stains skin, hair, and fabric
Administration: apply 1–3 times daily starting with low-strength preparations

Ointments and similar preparations

Calamine and Coal Tar Ointment, BP, calamine 12.5 g, strong coal tar solution 2.5 g, zinc oxide 12.5 g, hydrous wool fat 25 g, white soft paraffin 47.5 g

Coal Tar and Salicylic Acid Ointment, BP, coal tar 2 g, salicylic acid 2 g, emulsifying wax 11.4 g, white soft paraffin 19 g, coconut oil 54 g, polysorbate '80' 4 g, liquid paraffin 7.6 g

Coal Tar Paste, BP, strong coal tar solution 7.5%, in compound zinc paste

Zinc and Coal Tar Paste, BP, zinc oxide 6%, coal tar 6%, emulsifying wax 5%, starch 38%, yellow soft paraffin 45%

Alphosyl® (Stafford-Miller)
Cream, coal tar extract 5%, allantoin 2%, in a vanishing-cream basis. Net price 75 g = £1.56.
Additives: information not disclosed for BNF
For application to skin particularly intertriginous areas
Lotion, coal tar extract 5%, allantoin 2%. Net price 250 mL = £2.27. For application to skin or scalp
Additives: information not disclosed for BNF
Apply liberally 2–4 times daily

Carbo-Dome® (Lagap)
Cream, coal tar solution 10%, in a water-miscible basis. Net price 30 g = £1.79; 100 g = £5.41
Additives: beeswax, hydroxybenzoates (parabens)
Apply 2–3 times daily

Clinitar® (S&N Pharm.)
Cream, coal tar extract 1%. Net price 60 g = £3.31
Additives: isopropyl palmitate, propylene glycol
Apply 1–2 times daily

Cocois® (Bioglan)
Ointment, coal tar solution 12%, salicylic acid 2%, precipitated sulphur 4%, and coconut oil. Net price 40 g (with applicator nozzle) = £2.89
For dry and scaly scalp conditions, apply at night and remove by washing in the morning

Gelcosal® (Quinoderm Ltd)
Gel, strong coal tar solution 5%, pine tar 5%, salicylic acid 2% in a water-miscible basis. Net price 50 g = £2.89
Additives: none as listed in section 13.1
Apply twice daily

Gelcotar® (Quinoderm Ltd)
Gel, strong coal tar solution 5%, pine tar 5%, in a water-miscible basis. Net price 50 g = £2.66; 500 g = £13.90
Additives: none as listed in section 13.1
Apply twice daily
Liquid, see section 13.9

Pragmatar® (Bioglan)
Cream, cetyl alcohol-coal tar distillate 4%, salicylic acid 3%, sulphur (precipitated) 3%, in a water-miscible basis. Net price 25 g = £1.76; 100 g = £5.90
Additives: fragrance
Apply thinly daily; for scalp apply weekly to clean hair or in severe cases daily. Dilute with a few drops of water before application to infants

Psoriderm® (Dermal)
Cream, coal tar 6%, lecithin 0.4%. Net price 225 mL = £3.08
Additives: hydroxybenzoates (parabens), isopropyl palmitate, propylene glycol
Apply 1–2 times daily

PsoriGel® (Alcon)
Gel, coal tar solution USP 7.5% in an alcoholic emollient basis. Net price 90 g = £3.81
Additives: propylene glycol
Apply 1–2 times daily

Impregnated dressings

Zinc Paste and Coal Tar Bandage, BP, (Coltapaste®, Tarband®), see section 13.13.1

Bath preparations

Coal Tar Solution, BP, coal tar 20%, polysorbate '80' 5%, in alcohol (96%). Net price 100 mL = 66p
Use 100 mL in a bath
Note. Strong Coal Tar Solution BP contains coal tar 40%

Balneum with Tar® (Merck)
Bath oil, coal tar distillate 30%, soya oil 55%. Net price 225 mL = £3.72. For psoriasis and eczema
Additives, none as listed in section 13.1
Use 1 measure (20 mL) in bath

Polytar Emollient® (Stiefel)
Bath additive, coal tar solution 2.5%, arachis oil extract of coal tar 7.5%, tar 7.5%, cade oil 7.5%, liquid paraffin 35%. Net price 350 mL = £4.87; 1 litre = £12.00. ACBS: for psoriasis, eczema, atopic and pruritic dermatoses
Additives: isopropyl palmitate
Use 2–4 capfuls in bath and soak for 20 minutes

Psoriderm® (Dermal)
Bath emulsion, coal tar 40%. Net price 200 mL = £2.73. For psoriasis
Additives: polysorbate 20
Use 30 mL in a bath and soak for 5 minutes

Shampoo preparations
Section 13.9

Coal tar and corticosteroid preparations

PoM **Alphosyl HC®** (Stafford-Miller)
Cream, coal tar extract 5%, hydrocortisone 0.5%, allantoin 2%, in a vanishing-cream basis. Net price 30 g = £1.70; 45 g = £2.41; 100 g = £4.85. Label: 28. Potency IV
Additives: information not disclosed for BNF
Apply thinly 2–4 times daily

PoM **Carbo-Cort®** (Lagap)
Cream, coal tar solution 3%, hydrocortisone 0.25%, in a water-miscible basis. Price 30 g = £3.28. Label: 28. Potency IV
Additives: beeswax, hydroxybenzoates (parabens)
Apply thinly 2–3 times daily

PoM **Tarcortin**® (Stafford-Miller)
Cream, coal tar extract 5%, hydrocortisone 0.5%, in a vanishing-cream basis. Net price 45 g = £1.55. Label: 28. Potency IV
Additives: information not disclosed for BNF
Apply thinly 2–4 times daily

BUFEXAMAC

Indications: mild inflammatory skin disorders
Cautions: avoid broken skin
Side-effects: skin irritation

PoM **Parfenac**® (Lederle)
Cream, bufexamac 5%, in a water-miscible basis. Do not dilute. Net price 30 g = £2.16
Additives: hydroxybenzoates (parabens)
Apply thinly 2–3 times daily (not indicated for infants)

DITHRANOL

Indications: subacute and chronic psoriasis, see notes above
Cautions: avoid use near eyes; see also notes above
Contra-indications: hypersensitivity; acute psoriasis
Side-effects: local burning sensation and irritation; stains skin, hair, and fabrics
Administration: see notes above

*PoM **Dithranol Ointment, BP,** dithranol, in yellow soft paraffin; usual strengths 0.1–2%. Part of basis may be replaced by hard paraffin if a stiffer preparation is required. Label: 28
*PoM if dithranol content more than 1%, otherwise P

Dithranol Paste, BP, dithranol in zinc and salicylic acid (Lassar's) paste. Usual strengths 0.1% ('weak dithranol paste') and 1% ('strong dithranol paste') of dithranol. Label: 28

PoM **Anthranol**® (Stiefel)
'0.4%' Ointment, dithranol 0.4%. Net price 50 g = £3.50. Label: 28. For application to skin or scalp
Additives: none as listed in section 13.1; contains salicylic acid 0.4% as an antoxidant
'1%' Ointment, dithranol 1%. Net price 50 g = £4.25. Label: 28. For short contact application to skin or scalp
Additives: none as listed in section 13.1; contains salicylic acid 0.5% as an antoxidant
'2%' Ointment, dithranol 2%. Net price 50 g = £6.00. Label: 28. For short contact application to skin or scalp
Additives: none as listed in section 13.1; contains salicylic acid 0.5% as an antoxidant

Antraderm® (Brocades)
Mild application, dithranol 0.5% in a wax stick. Net price 20 mL = £5.48. Label: 28. For sensitive skins
Additives: beeswax, butylated hydroxytoluene
PoM *Application*, dithranol 1% in a wax stick. Net price 20 mL = £6.13. Label: 28
Additives: beeswax, butylated hydroxytoluene
PoM *Forte application*, dithranol 2% in a wax stick. Net price 20 mL = £6.78. Label: 28
Additives: beeswax, butylated hydroxytoluene

Dithrocream® (Dermal)
Cream, dithranol in a water-miscible basis, 0.1%, net price 50 g = £3.62; 0.25%, 50 g = £3.89; 0.5% (Forte), 50 g = £4.49; 1% (HP); 50 g = £5.19; PoM 2%, 50 g = £6.49. Label: 28. For application to skin or scalp
Additives: chlorocresol

Dithrolan® (Dermal)
Ointment, dithranol 0.5%, salicylic acid 0.5%. Diluent yellow soft paraffin, life of diluted ointment 14 days. Net price 90 g = £5.13. Label: 28
Additives: none as listed in section 13.1

Psoradrate® (Norwich Eaton)
Cream, dithranol in a powder-in-cream basis containing urea. 0.1%, net price 30 g = £2.54, 100 g = £7.59; 0.2%, 30 g = £2.81, 100 g = £8.72; 0.4%, 100 g = £10.03. Label: 28
Additives: polysorbate 40

Psorin® (Thames)
Ointment, dithranol 0.11%, crude coal tar 1%, salicylic acid 1.6%, in an emollient basis. Net price 25 g = £2.79; 50 g = £5.30; 100 g = £10.50. Label: 28
Additives: beeswax, wool fat

DITHRANOL TRIACETATE

Indications; Cautions; Contra-indications; Side-effects; Administration: see under Dithranol and notes above

Exolan® (Dermal)
Cream, dithranol triacetate 1% in a water-miscible basis. Net price 50 g = £3.00. Label: 28
Additives: chlorocresol
Apply daily to skin and scalp

ICHTHAMMOL

Indications: chronic eczema
Side-effects: skin irritation and sensitisation
Administration: apply 1–3 times daily

Ichthammol Ointment, BP1980, ichthammol 10%, yellow soft paraffin 45%, wool fat 45%. Net price 25 g = 17p

Zinc and Ichthammol Cream, BP, ichthammol 5%, cetostearyl alcohol 3%, wool fat 10%, in zinc cream. Net price 100 g = 57p

Zinc Paste and Ichthammol Bandage, BP (Ichthopaste®, Icthaband®), see section 13.13.1

SALICYLIC ACID

Indications: hyperkeratoses
Cautions: see notes above; avoid broken or inflamed skin
Side-effects: sensitivity, excessive drying, irritation, systemic effects after prolonged use (see section 10.1.1)

Salicylic Acid Collodion, BP—section 13.7

Salicylic Acid Ointment, BP, salicylic acid 2%, in wool alcohols ointment. Net price 25 g = 18p
Apply twice daily

Zinc and Salicylic Acid Paste, BP (Lassar's Paste), zinc oxide 24%, salicylic acid 2%, starch 24%, white soft paraffin 50%. Net price 25 g = 15p
Apply twice daily

ORAL PREPARATIONS FOR PSORIASIS OR ECZEMA

ETRETINATE

Indications: severe extensive psoriasis resistant to other forms of therapy; palmo-plantar pustular psoriasis; severe congenital ichthyosis; severe Darier's disease (keratosis follicularis)

Cautions: exclude pregnancy before starting; patients should avoid pregnancy at least 1 month before, during, and for at least 2 years after treatment, should avoid concomitant high doses of vitamin A and use of keratolytics, and should not donate blood during or for 2 years after stopping therapy (teratogenic risk); monitor hepatic function and plasma lipids (especially in hypertriglyceridaemia) at start, 1 month after initiating treatment, and then at intervals of 3 months; diabetes (can alter glucose tolerance); radiographic assessment on long-term treatment; investigate atypical musculoskeletal symptoms; avoid long-term use in children (skeletal hyperostosis and extra-osseous calcification); **interactions:** Appendix 1 (etretinate)

Contra-indications: hepatic and renal impairment; pregnancy (**important teratogenic risk:** see Cautions and Appendix 4); breast-feeding

Side-effects: (mainly dose-related) dryness of mucous membranes (sometimes erosion), of skin (sometimes scaling, thinning, erythema, and pruritus), and of conjunctiva (sometimes conjunctivitis); palmar and plantar exfoliation, epistaxis, and epidermal fragility reported, also paronychia; granulomatous lesions reported; reversible alopecia; myalgia and arthralgia; occasional nausea, headache, malaise, drowsiness and sweating; benign intracranial hypertension reported (avoid concomitant tetracyclines); raised liver enzymes, rarely jaundice and hepatitis (avoid concomitant methotrexate); raised triglycerides; decreased night vision reported

Dose: administered in accordance with expert advice, adults and children, initially up to 750 micrograms/kg daily in divided doses for 2–4 weeks, increased to 1 mg/kg daily if necessary (max. daily dose 75 mg), then reduced to 500 micrograms/kg daily for a further 6–8 weeks, then intermittently as necessary; usual maintenance dose 250–500 micrograms/kg daily (**important:** see Cautions and notes above)

PoM **Tigason®** (Roche)

Capsules, etretinate 10 mg (yellow), net price 56-cap pack = £20.40; 25 mg (orange/yellow), 56-cap pack = £44.05 (**hosp. only**, specialist dermatological supervision). Label: 10, patient information card, 21

GAMOLENIC ACID

Indications: symptomatic relief of atopic eczema

Cautions: history of epilepsy, concomitant treatment with epileptogenic drugs e.g. phenothiazines

Side-effects: occasional nausea, indigestion, headache

Dose: see below

PoM **Epogam®** (Scotia)

Capsules, gamolenic acid 40 mg in evening primrose oil. Net price 240-cap pack = £25.04. Counselling, see below

Additives: include vitamin E 10 mg as *in vivo* antoxidant

Dose: 4–6 capsules twice daily; CHILD 1–12 years 2–4 capsules twice daily

Note. Gamolenic acid 40 mg in evening primrose oil is also available as Efamast® for the symptomatic relief of cyclical and non-cyclical mastalgia in a dose of 3–4 capsules twice daily, net price 224-cap pack = £24.33

Paediatric capsules, gamolenic acid 80 mg in evening primrose oil. Net price 60-cap pack = £15.80. Councelling, see below

Additives: include vitamin E 20 mg as *in vivo* antoxidant

Dose: CHILD over 1 year, 1–2 capsules twice daily

COUNSELLING. Capsules may be cut open and contents swallowed or taken on bread; paediatric capsules have 'snip-off' neck for convenience of administration

13.6 Preparations for acne

TOPICAL TREATMENT. Most topical preparations are intended for removing follicular plugs and reducing skin flora. The skin is cleansed regularly with detergent solutions, for example cetrimide solution (section 13.11.3). Abrasive agents may also be used but their effectiveness is uncertain.

Cleansing is followed by application of **antiseptics** and **keratolytics**; thick greasy preparations should not be used. Preparations usually contain benzoyl peroxide, hydroxyquinoline, sulphur, salicylic acid, or tretinoin. Many of these irritate the skin but it is doubtful if a therapeutic effect can be obtained without some degree of irritation (which subsides with continued treatment). Topical application of **tretinoin** (Retin-A®) a vitamin A derivative has been shown to be useful in treating acne but patients should be warned that some redness and skin peeling may occur after application for several days.

Topical antibiotics are also used for mild to moderately severe acne. Topical preparations of erythromycin, tetracycline, and clindamycin seem to be quite useful for many patients with the milder forms of acne; they can produce mild irritation of the skin but rarely sensitise. It has been suggested that percutaneous absorption of clindamycin can cause pseudomembranous colitis. Chloramphenicol is included in some preparations but can sensitise the skin; topical neomycin is not suitable owing to sensitisation. Antibiotics cause resistant strains of micro-organisms to appear but as yet no adverse clinical effects have resulted.

Topical **corticosteroids** should **not** be used in acne.

SYSTEMIC TREATMENT. Systemic antibacterial treatment is useful. **Tetracycline** (see section 5.1.3), **erythromycin** (see section 5.1.5), and occasionally other antibacterials are used. The usual dosage regimen for tetracycline and erythromycin, taken before meals, is 250 mg 3 times daily for 1–4 weeks and then reduced to twice daily until improvement occurs. Higher doses are sometimes indicated when there is a poor response to the usual regimen; in general the dose of the antibiotic used should be matched to the patient's condition. Maximum improvement usually occurs after three or four months but in resistant cases treatment may need to be continued for two or more years. As there have been some reports of pseudomembranous colitis with tetracycline, caution is necessary in long-term administration.

Cyproterone acetate with **ethinyloestradiol** (Dianette®) contains an anti-androgen and is used to treat women with severe acne refractory to prolonged oral antibacterial therapy. Improvement of acne probably occurs because of decreased sebum secretion which is under androgen control. Some women with mild to moderate idiopathic hirsutism may also benefit as hair growth is also androgen-dependent (see also section 6.4.2). Dianette® may also be used as an oral contraceptive but should be reserved for women who are being treated for androgen-dependent skin conditions. It is contra-indicated in pregnancy and in a predisposition to thrombosis.

Isotretinoin (Roaccutane®) has recently been introduced for the systemic treatment of cystic and conglobate acne and severe acne which has failed to respond to an adequate course of a systemic antimicrobial agent. It should be prescribed **only** by, or under the supervision of, a consultant dermatologist, and is available to hospitals **only**. It is given in doses of 500 micrograms/kg/day for 12–16 weeks but doses may be adjusted if necessary after 4 weeks. Repeat courses should not normally be given. An exacerbation is common some 2–4 weeks after starting treatment but usually subsides after a few weeks.

Side-effects include dry lips, sore eyes, nose bleeds, mild transient hair loss, and joint pains. Plasma lipids and liver function should be checked by investigation monthly as there is a tendency for the plasma lipids to rise in some patients. The drug is **teratogenic** and must **not** be given to women who are pregnant or those who may become pregnant unless there is concomitant effective contraception and then only after detailed explanation by the physician. The contraceptive measures must continue for at least one month after ceasing treatment with the drug.

TOPICAL ACNE PREPARATIONS

ABRASIVE AGENTS

Indications: cleansing in acne vulgaris
Cautions: avoid contact with eyes; discontinue use temporarily if skin becomes irritated
Contra-indications: superficial venules, telangiectasia

Brasivol® (Stiefel)
Paste No. 1, aluminium oxide 38.09% in fine particles, in a soap-detergent basis. Net price 75 g = £2.49
Additives: fragrance
Paste No. 2, aluminium oxide 52.2% in medium particles, in a soap-detergent basis. Net price 75 g = £2.49
Additives: fragrance
Use instead of soap 1–3 times daily, starting with fine grade

Ionax Scrub® (Alcon)
Gel, polyethylene granules 21.9%, benzalkonium chloride 0.25% in a foaming aqueous alcoholic basis. Net price 60 g = £3.13. ACBS: for control and hygiene of acne and cleansing of the skin prior to acne treatment
Additives: propylene glycol
Use instead of soap 1–2 times daily

ANTIBIOTICS

Indications: acne vulgaris

PoM **Dalacin T®** (Upjohn)
Topical solution, clindamycin (as phosphate) 1%, in an aqueous alcoholic basis. Net price 30 mL (with applicator) = £6.05
Additives: propylene glycol
Apply to clean skin twice daily

PoM **Stiemycin®** (Stiefel)
Solution, erythromycin 2% in an alcoholic basis. Net price 2 × 25 mL applicator bottles = £9.00
Additives: propylene glycol
Apply to clean skin twice daily

PoM **Topicycline®** (Norwich Eaton)
Solution, powder for reconstitution, tetracycline hydrochloride, 4-epitetracycline hydrochloride, providing tetracycline hydrochloride 2.2 mg/mL when reconstituted with solvent containing n-decyl methyl sulphoxide and citric acid in 40% alcohol. Net price per pack of powder and solvent to provide 70 mL = £7.90
Additives: none as listed in section 13.1
Apply to clean skin twice daily

PoM **Zineryt®** (Brocades)
Topical solution, powder for reconstitution, erythromycin 40 mg, zinc acetate 12 mg/mL when reconstituted with solvent containing ethanol. Net price per pack of powder and solvent to provide 30 mL = £8.04
Additives: none as listed in section 13.1.
Apply to clean skin twice daily for 10–12 weeks

BENZOYL PEROXIDE

Indications: acne vulgaris
Cautions: avoid contact with eyes, mouth, and mucous membranes; may bleach fabrics
Contra-indications: acne rosacea
Side-effects: skin irritation
Administration: apply 1–2 times daily to clean skin, starting treatment with lower-strength preparations

Acetoxyl® (Stiefel)
'2.5' Gel, benzoyl peroxide 2.5%, in an aqueous-acetone-gel basis. Net price 40 g = £1.59
Additives: propylene glycol
'5' Gel, benzoyl peroxide 5%, in an aqueous-acetone-gel basis. Net price 40 g = £1.76
Additives: propylene glycol

Acnegel® (Stiefel)
Gel, benzoyl peroxide 5%, in an aqueous alcoholic basis. Net price 50 g = £2.17
Additives: none as listed in section 13.1
Forte gel, benzoyl peroxide 10%, in an aqueous alcoholic basis. Net price 50 g = £2.38
Additives: none as listed in section 13.1

Acnidazil® (Janssen)
Cream, benzoyl peroxide 5%, miconazole nitrate 2%. Net price 15 g = £1.91; 20 g = £2.31; 30 g = £3.40
Additives: polysorbate 20, propylene glycol

Benoxyl® (Stiefel)
'5' Cream, benzoyl peroxide 5%, in a non-greasy basis. Net price 40 g = £1.29
Additives: isopropyl palmitate, propylene glycol
'5' Lotion, benzoyl peroxide 5%, in a non-greasy basis. Net price 30 mL = £1.03
Additives: isopropyl palmitate, propylene glycol
'10' Lotion, benzoyl peroxide 10%, in a water-miscible basis. Net price 30 mL = £1.09
Additives: isopropyl palmitate, propylene glycol

Benzagel® (Bioglan)
'5' Gel, benzoyl peroxide 5%. Net price 40 g = £2.40
Additives: fragrance
'10' Gel, benzoyl peroxide 10%. Net price 40 g = £2.74
Additives: fragrance

Nericur® (Schering Health Care)
Gel 5, benzoyl peroxide 5%, in an aqueous gel basis. Net price 30 g = £1.45
Additives: propylene glycol
Gel 10, benzoyl peroxide 10%, in an aqueous gel basis. Net price 30 g = £1.60
Additives: propylene glycol

Panoxyl® (Stiefel)
'2.5' Aquagel (= aqueous gel), benzoyl peroxide 2.5%. Net price 40 g = £1.72
Additives: propylene glycol
'5' Gel, benzoyl peroxide 5%, in an aqueous alcoholic basis. Net price 40 g = £1.44
Additives: fragrance
'5' Aquagel (= aqueous gel), benzoyl peroxide 5%. Net price 40 g = £1.92
Additives: propylene glycol
'10' Gel, benzoyl peroxide 10%, in an aqueous alcoholic basis. Net price 40 g = £1.63
Additives: fragrance
'10' Aquagel (= aqueous gel), benzoyl peroxide 10%. Net price 40 g = £2.12
Additives: propylene glycol
'10' Wash, benzoyl peroxide 10%, in a detergent basis. Net price 150 mL = £3.50
Additives: none as listed in section 13.1

Quinoderm® (Quinoderm Ltd)
Cream, benzoyl peroxide 10%, potassium hydroxyquinoline sulphate 0.5%, in an astringent vanishing-cream basis. Net price 25 g = £1.15; 50 g = £1.73
Additives: edetic acid (EDTA)
Cream 5, benzoyl peroxide 5%, potassium hydroxyquinoline sulphate 0.5%, in an astringent vanishing-cream basis. Net price 50 g = £1.61
Additives: edetic acid (EDTA)
Lotio-gel 5%, benzoyl peroxide 5%, potassium hydroxyquinoline sulphate 0.5%, in an astringent creamy basis. Net price 30 mL = £1.38
Additives: edetic acid (EDTA)
Apply 1–3 times daily

CORTICOSTEROIDS

Indications: not recommended (see notes above)
Cautions; Contra-indications; Side-effects: section 13.4 and notes above

PoM **Actinac®** (Roussel)
Lotion (powder for reconstitution), chloramphenicol 1.25%, hydrocortisone acetate 1.25%, allantoin 0.75%, butoxyethyl nicotinate 0.75%, precipitated sulphur 10%, when reconstituted with solvent. Discard after 21 days. Net price 2 × 6.25 g bottles powder with 2 × 20-mL bottles solvent = £9.54. Label: 28. Potency IV
Additives: fragrance

PoM **Quinoderm with Hydrocortisone®** (Quinoderm Ltd)
Cream, hydrocortisone 1%, benzoyl peroxide 10%, potassium hydroxyquinoline sulphate 0.5%, in an astringent vanishing-cream basis. Net price 30 g = £1.77. Label: 28. Potency IV
Additives: edetic acid (EDTA)

SULPHUR

Cautions: avoid contact with eyes, mouth, and mucous membranes; causes skin irritation

With resorcinol
Prolonged application of resorcinol may interfere with thyroid function therefore not recommended

Eskamel® (SK&F)
Cream, resorcinol 2%, sulphur 8%, in a non-greasy flesh-coloured basis. Net price 25 g = £1.26
Additives: propylene glycol, fragrance

With salicylic acid
Salicylic Acid and Sulphur Cream, BP 1980, salicylic acid 2%, precipitated sulphur 2%, in aqueous cream
Salicylic Acid and Sulphur Ointment, BPC, salicylic acid 3%, precipitated sulphur 3%, in hydrous ointment (oily cream). Net price 25 g = 21p

TRETINOIN

Indications: acne vulgaris
Cautions: avoid contact with eyes, mouth, and mucous membranes; do not use simultaneously with other peeling agents (can be alternated every 12 hours with benzoyl peroxide); do not use with ultra-violet lamps
Contra-indications: eczema, broken skin
Side-effects: irritation, erythema, peeling, with excessive use; changes in pigmentation, photosensitivity
Administration: apply to clean skin 1–2 times daily

PoM **Retin-A**® (Cilag)
Cream, tretinoin 0.025%, net price 60 g = £5.65; 0.05% (cream forte), 60 g = £5.65. For dry or fair skin
Additives: butylated hydroxytoluene, sorbic acid
Gel, tretinoin 0.01%, net price 60 g = £5.65; 0.025% (gel forte), 60 g = £5.65. For severe acne, initial treatment, or dark and oily skins
Additives: butylated hydroxytoluene
Lotion, tretinoin 0.025%. Net price 100 mL = £6.50. For application to large areas such as the back
Additives: butylated hydroxytoluene

ORAL PREPARATIONS

CYPROTERONE ACETATE

Indications: see notes above
Cautions; Contra-indications; Side-effects: see under Combined Oral Contraceptives (section 7.3.1)

PoM **Dianette**® (Schering Health Care)
Tablets, beige, s/c, cyproterone acetate 2 mg, ethinyloestradiol 35 micrograms. Net price 21-tab pack = £4.40
Dose: 1 tablet daily for 21 days starting on 5th day of menstrual cycle and repeated after a 7-day interval, usually for several months

ISOTRETINOIN

Indications: see notes above
Cautions: exclude pregnancy before starting; pregnancy must be avoided at least 1 month before, during, and for at least 1 month after treatment; avoid donating blood during and for at least 1 month after treatment; monitor hepatic function and plasma lipids at start, 1 month after initiating treatment, then at intervals; avoid high doses of vitamin A and use of keratolytics during treatment; monitor blood glucose in diabetic patients
Contra-indications: pregnancy (**important teratogenic risk:** see Cautions and Appendix 4); breast-feeding; renal or hepatic impairment
Side-effects: (mainly dose-related) dryness of skin (with scaling, thinning, erythema, pruritus), epidermal fragility (trauma may cause blistering); dryness of nasal mucosa (with mild epistaxis), dryness of conjunctiva (sometimes conjunctivitis), decreased tolerance to contact lenses; visual disturbances (papilloedema, optic neuritis, corneal opacities, decreased night vision, blurred vision); hair thinning (reversible on withdrawal); nausea, headache, malaise, drowsiness, sweating; benign intracranial hypertension (avoid concomitant tetracyclines); myalgia and arthralgia; raised liver enzymes; raised plasma triglycerides and cholesterol; allergic vasculitis and granulomatous lesions reported
Dose: initially 500 micrograms/kg daily in 1–2 divided doses with food for 4 weeks; if good response continue for further 8–12 weeks; if little response, up to 1 mg/kg daily for 8–12 weeks; if intolerant, reduce dose to 100–200 micrograms/kg daily

PoM **Roaccutane**® (Roche)
Capsules, isotretinoin 5 mg (red-violet/white), net price 56-cap pack = £19.08; 20 mg (red-violet/white), 56-cap pack = £54.98 (**hosp. only**, specialist dermatological supervision). Label: 10, patient information card, 21

13.7 Preparations for warts and calluses

The least destructive method possible should be chosen to treat these lesions as they are self-limiting and all viral warts including those on the soles of the feet (verrucas) eventually disappear spontaneously. The preparations used are keratolytics which slowly remove the hyperkeratotic layers and destroy the underlying epidermis. Salicylic acid and podophyllin preparations are useful but can cause considerable irritation of the treated area, and podophyllin treatment may be painful. **Salicylic acid** collodion is suitable for removal of warts and calluses.

Podophyllin preparations may also be useful. Podophyllum resin made into a paint, in concentrations of between 5 and 20% is employed for the treatment of anogenital warts. The paint should be allowed to stay on the treated area for not longer than 6 hours and then washed off. Care should be taken to avoid splashing the surrounding skin during application; it must be covered with soft paraffin as a protection. Where there are a large number of warts only a few should be treated at any one time as severe toxicity caused by absorption of podophyllin has been reported. It should also be avoided in pregnancy. Posalfilin® is suitable for treating plantar warts.

Preparations containing formaldehyde, glutaraldehyde, and bromine are also available but their effects are unpredictable. Formaldehyde and glutaraldehyde preparations may irritate and sensitise the skin.

Ointments and liquid preparations are applied to the wart or callus, avoiding contact with surrounding skin, and covered with a plaster. Dead skin may be removed at intervals by rubbing with a pumice stone.

SALICYLIC ACID

Indications: removal of warts and hard skin
Cautions: avoid normal skin and application to large areas; not indicated for application to face or anogenital region
Contra-indications: diabetes or if peripheral blood circulation impaired

Salicylic Acid Collodion, BP, salicylic acid 12%, in flexible collodion. Label: 15. Apply daily or on alternate days
Caution: flammable

Cuplex® (S&N Pharm.)
Gel, salicylic acid 11%, lactic acid 4%, copper acetate (= Cu^{2+} 0.0011%), in a collodion basis. Net price 5 g = £2.26. For plantar and mosaic warts, corns, and calluses
Additives: none as listed in section 13.1
Apply twice daily
Caution: flammable

Duofilm® (Stiefel)
Paint, salicylic acid 16.7%, lactic acid 16.7%, in flexible collodion. Net price 15 mL (with applicator) = £1.95. For plantar and mosaic warts, apply daily

Salactol® (Dermal)
Paint, salicylic acid 16.7%, lactic acid 16.7%, in flexible collodion. Net price 10 mL (with applicator) = £1.92. For warts, particularly plantar warts, apply daily

Salatac® (Dermal)
Gel, salicylic acid 12%, lactic acid 4% in a collodion basis. Net price 8 g (with applicator) = £3.45. For warts, corns, and calluses, apply daily

Verrugon® (Pickles)
Ointment, salicylic acid 50% in a paraffin basis. Net price 6 g = £1.16, apply daily

BROMINE COMPLEXES

Indications: warts, particularly plantar warts
Cautions: avoid normal skin

Callusolve® (Dermal)
Paint, benzalkonium chloride-bromine adduct 25%. Net price 10 mL (with applicator) = £2.22. For warts, particularly plantar and mosaic warts, apply daily

FORMALDEHYDE

Indications: warts, particularly plantar warts
Cautions: avoid normal skin

Formaldehyde Lotion, formaldehyde solution, BP, 3 mL, water to 100 mL

Veracur® (Typharm)
Gel, formaldehyde solution 1.5% in a water-miscible gel basis. Net price 15 g = £1.01
Apply twice daily

GLUTARALDEHYDE

Indications: warts, particularly plantar warts
Cautions: avoid normal skin; stains skin brown

Glutarol® (Dermal)
Solution (= application), glutaraldehyde 10%. Net price 10 mL (with applicator) = £2.11
Apply twice daily

Novaruca® (Bioglan)
Gel, glutaraldehyde 10%. Net price 15 g = £1.95
Warts (except warts on face and in anal and perineal regions), apply twice daily

Verucasep® (Galen)
Gel, glutaraldehyde 10%. Net price 15 g = £1.95
Additives: none as listed in section 13.1
Apply twice daily

PODOPHYLLUM RESIN

Indications: anogenital and plantar warts
Cautions: avoid normal skin; very irritant to eyes
Contra-indications: pregnancy; facial warts
Side-effects: may cause pain on application
Administration: see notes above

PoM **Podophyllin Paint, Compound, BP,** (podophyllum resin 15% in compound benzoin tincture), podophyllum resin 1.5 g, compound benzoin tincture to 10 mL; 5 mL to be dispensed unless otherwise directed. Label: 15, counselling, application, see notes above. For warts, including anogenital warts
Apply daily to plantar warts, weekly to anogenital warts

Posalfilin® (Norgine)
Ointment, podophyllum resin 20%, salicylic acid 25%. Net price 10 g = £2.85. For plantar warts
Apply 2–3 times weekly

Podophyllotoxin

PoM **Condyline®** (Brocades)
Solution, podophyllotoxin 0.5% in alcoholic basis. Net price 3.5 mL (with applicators) = £16.00
Penile warts (in preputial space), apply twice daily for 3 days; treatment may be repeated after 7 days if necessary; max. 5 treatment courses

PoM **Warticon®** (Kabi)
Solution, podophyllotoxin 0.5% in alcoholic basis. Net price 3 mL (with applicators) = £16.00
Penile warts (in preputial space), apply twice daily for 3 days; treatment may be repeated after 7 days if necessary

13.8 Sunscreens and camouflagers

BORDERLINE SUBSTANCES. The preparations marked 'ACBS' are regarded as drugs when prescribed for skin protection against ultraviolet radiation in photodermatoses, including those resulting from radiotherapy. Prescriptions issued in accordance with this advice and endorsed 'ACBS' will normally not be investigated. See Appendix 7 for listing by clinical condition.

13.8.1 Sunscreening preparations

Solar ultraviolet irradiation is harmful to the skin. It is responsible for disorders such as polymorphic light eruption, Hutchinson's summer prurigo, and the various cutaneous porphyrias. It also provokes (or at least aggravates) disorders such as rosacea and lupus erythematosus. It may also contribute to serious skin disorders in patients sensitised by drugs such as demeclocycline, phenothiazines, or amiodarone. All these conditions (as well as sunburn) may occur after relatively short periods of exposure to the sun. Exposure over longer periods may cause more serious problems. Both melanoma and non-melanoma skin cancer are now thought to be caused in many instances by solar ultraviolet irradiation. It is now also believed that exposure to the sun causes the skin to wrinkle and develop other signs associated with aging.

Solar ultraviolet radiation is approximately 200–400 nm in wavelength. The medium wavelengths (280–310 nm, known as UVB) cause sunburn and contribute to the long-term changes responsible for skin cancer and aging. The long wavelengths (310–400 nm, known as UVA) do not cause sunburn but are responsible for many photosensitivity reactions and photodermatoses; they also seem to contribute to long-term damage and to be involved in the pathogenesis of skin cancer and aging.

Sunscreen preparations that contain substances such as aminobenzoic acid protect the skin against UVB and hence against sunburn. The sun protection factor (SPF, usually indicated in the preparation title) provides guidance on the degree of protection offered against UVB; it indicates the multiples of protection provided against burning, compared with unprotected skin; for example, an SPF of 8 should enable a person to remain 8 times longer in the sun without burning. Such preparations, however, do not prevent long-term damage associated with UVA, which might not become apparent for 10 to 20 years. Preparations that also contain reflective substances, such as titanium dioxide, provide the most effective protection against UVA.

Some sunscreens, particularly aminobenzoates, may rarely cause photosensitivity reactions. Bergamot oil (which contains 5-methoxypsoralen) occasionally causes photosensitisation with subsequent pigmentation; it is suspected of increasing the incidence of skin cancers, but this has not been established.

Almay Total Sunbloc® (Nicholas Cosmetics)
Cream, (SPF 15), padimate-O 7%, oxybenzone 3%, titanium dioxide. Net price 50 mL = £2.41. ACBS
Lip protector, (SPF 15), padimate-O 7%, oxybenzone 3%. Net price 10 mL = £1.42. ACBS

Coppertone® (Scholl)
Sunstick 15, titanium dioxide 17.6% in wax-based stick. Net price 6 g = £2.25. ACBS
Supershade 15 lotion, padimate-O 7%, oxybenzone 3%. Net price 125 mL = £3.88. ACBS
Ultrashade 23 lotion, ethylhexyl *p*-methoxycinnamate 7.5%, oxybenzone 3%, padimate-O 2.5%. Net price 150 mL = £4.24. ACBS

Piz Buin® (Ciba Consumer)
Cream No. 12, ethylhexyl *p*-methoxycinnamate 7%, butyl methoxydibenzoylmethane 1.5%, titanium dioxide 1.5%. Net price 30 mL = £3.01. ACBS
Lotion, (SPF 12), ethylhexyl *p*-methoxycinnamate 7.5%, butyl methoxydibenzoylmethane 1.5%, titanium dioxide 1.5%. Net price 125 mL = £5.03. ACBS
Sun allergy lotion, (SPF 12), ethylhexyl *p*-methoxycinnamate 7.5%, butyl methoxydibenzoylmethane 2.5%, titanium dioxide 2%. Net price 125 mL = £5.91. ACBS
Sunblock lotion, (SPF 24), ethylhexyl *p*-methoxycinnamate 7.5%, butyl methoxydibenzoylmethane 2%, titanium dioxide 3%. Net price 125 mL = £5.91. ACBS

RoC Total Sunblock® (RoC)
Cream, (SPF over 15), colourless or tinted, ethylhexyl *p*-methoxycinnamate 5%, oxybenzone 4%, dibenzoylmethane 2%, titanium dioxide 4%. Net price 50 mL = £3.57. ACBS
Apply every 2 hours or more frequently

Spectraban® (Stiefel)
15 Lotion, aminobenzoic acid 5%, padimate-O 3.2%, in an alcoholic basis. Net price 150 mL = £2.49. ACBS
Apply once daily; renew after bathing or excessive sweating
Caution: flammable; stains clothing

Uvistat® (Windsor)
Cream, (SPF 8), water-resistant, mexenone 4%, ethylhexyl *p*-methoxycinnamate 7.5%. Net price 100 g = £3.30. ACBS
Cream, (SPF 10), mexenone 2%, ethylhexyl *p*-methoxycinnamate 7%, butyl methoxydibenzoylmethane 2%, titanium dioxide 2%. Net price 100 g = £3.70. ACBS
Cream (SPF 15), water-resistant, mexenone 4%, ethylhexyl *p*-methoxycinnamate 7.5%, butyl methoxydibenzoylmethane 2%. Net price 100 g = £3.88. ACBS
Lipscreen, (SPF 15), mexenone 2%, ethylhexyl *p*-methoxycinnamate 6%, butyl methoxydibenzoylmethane 2%. Net price 5-g stick = £1.15. ACBS (also sunlight-provoked chronic or recurrent herpes labialis)
Cream (SPF 20), water-resistant, ethylhexyl *p*-methoxycinnamate 7%, mexenone 2%, butyl methoxydibenzoylmethane 2%, titanium dioxide 4.5%. Net price 50 g = £2.89, 100 g = £4.34. ACBS
Ultrablock cream, (SPF 30), mexenone 2%, ethylhexyl *p*-methoxycinnamate 7.5%, butyl methoxydibenzoylmethane 4%, titanium dioxide 6%. Net price 50 g = £3.47. ACBS

13.8.2 Camouflagers

BORDERLINE SUBSTANCES. The preparations marked 'ACBS' are regarded as drugs when prescribed in accordance with the advice of the Advisory Committee on Borderline Substances for the clinical conditions listed. Prescriptions issued in accordance with this advice and endorsed 'ACBS' will normally not be investigated. See Appendix 7 for listing by clinical condition.

Disfigurement of the skin can be very distressing to patients and have a marked psychological effect. In skilled hands, or with experience, these preparations can be very effective in concealing scars, areas of discoloration, and birthmarks.

Boots Covering Cream® (Boots)
Cream (4 shades). 20 g. ACBS
Additives: hydroxybenzoates (parabens)

Covermark® (Stiefel)
Additives: beeswax, hydroxybenzoates (parabens), fragrance
Cream rouge (3 shades). Net price 4.5 g = £2.96. ACBS
Grey toner (= cream). Net price 8 g = £2.96. ACBS
Masking cream (covering cream, 10 shades). Net price 25 g = £4.35. ACBS
Shading cream. Net price 4.5 g = £2.96. ACBS
Finishing powder. Net price 50 g = £2.62; 250 g = £9.37. ACBS

Dermacolor® (Fox)
Camouflage creme, 30 shades. Net price 30 g = £5.43. ACBS
Additives: information not disclosed for BNF
Fixing powder, 5 shades. Net price 75 g = £4.35. ACBS
Additives: information not disclosed for BNF

Keromask® (Innoxa)
Masking cream, 2 shades. Net price 15 mL = £3.20. ACBS
Additives: butylated hydroxyanisole, hydroxybenzoates (parabens), wool fat
Finishing powder. Net price 25 g = £3.20. ACBS
Additives: none as listed in section 13.1

Veil® (Blake)
Cover cream, 18 shades. Net price 19 g = £2.90; 44 g = £4.06; 70 g = £5.51. ACBS
Additives: hydroxybenzoates (parabens), wool fat derivative

13.9 Shampoos and some other scalp preparations

BORDERLINE SUBSTANCES. The preparations marked 'ACBS' are regarded as drugs when prescribed in accordance with the advice of the Advisory Committee on Borderline Substances for the clinical conditions listed. Prescriptions issued in accordance with this advice and endorsed 'ACBS' will normally not be investigated. See Appendix 7 for listing by clinical condition.

Dandruff (*pityriasis capitis*) is excessive non-inflammatory scaling of the scalp, and often increases at puberty. The treatment of choice is the frequent use of a mild detergent shampoo generally once or twice weekly; this rids the scalp of scale but does not have a therapeutic effect in itself. Shampoos containing antimicrobial agents such as **pyrithione zinc** have beneficial effects but are not prescribable in the general medical service. Shampoos containing **tar** extracts may be useful and they are also used in *psoriasis*, both as adjunctive treatment and for the removal of pastes etc. Shampoos containing **selenium sulphide** are of no more value than the other shampoos and should not be used within 48 hours of applying hair colouring or permanent waving preparations.

For more severe conditions, weak **corticosteroid** gels and lotions (section 13.4), applied to the scalp may be helpful.

Cradle cap in infants may be treated with **olive oil** or **arachis oil** applications before shampooing.

See also sections 13.5 (psoriasis and eczema), 13.10.4 (lice), and 13.10.2 (ringworm).

ADMINISTRATION. Shampoos should be used once or twice weekly

Alphosyl® (Stafford-Miller)
Shampoo[1], allantoin 0.2%, refined coal tar extract 5%. Net price 125 mL = £1.30; 250 mL = £2.41. ACBS: for psoriasis and other scaly disorders of the scalp
Additives: information not disclosed for BNF
1. Formerly called *Application PC*

Baltar® (Merck)
Shampoo, coal tar distillate 1.5% in soap-free basis. Net price 225 mL = £2.63; 500 mL = £4.60
Additives: fragrance

Betadine® (Napp)
Scalp and skin cleanser—section 13.11.4
Shampoo solution, povidone-iodine 4%, in a surfactant solution. Net price 250 mL = £1.74. ACBS: for seborrhoeic scalp conditions associated with excessive dandruff, pruritic scaling, seborrhoeic dermatitis, pityriasis capitis, infected lesions of the scalp, pyodermas (recurrent furunculosis, infective folliculitis, impetigo)
Additives: wool fat, fragrance

Calmurid® (Pharmacia)
Solution, urea 20%, lactic acid 5%, in an aqueous vehicle. Net price 125 mL = £4.10
Additives: polysorbate 20
Apply twice daily to scalp

Capitol® (Dermal)
Gel, benzalkonium chloride 0.5%. Net price 120 g = £2.86. ACBS: for pityriasis capitis and seborrhoeic dermatitis of the scalp
Additives: none as listed in section 13.1

Ceanel Concentrate® (Quinoderm Ltd)
Shampoo, cetrimide 10%, undecenoic acid 1%, phenethyl alcohol 7.5%. Net price 50 mL = 98p; 150 mL = £2.60; 500 mL = £7.70. ACBS: for psoriasis or seborrhoeic conditions
Additives: fragrance

Clinitar® (S&N Pharm.)
Shampoo solution, coal tar extract 2%. Net price 60 g = £2.47
Additives: polysorbate, fragrance

PoM **Efalith®** (Scotia)
Ointment, lithium succinate 8%, zinc sulphate 0.05%. Net price 20 g = £12.50
Additives: wool fat derivative
Cautions: psoriasis
Seborrhoeic dermatitis, apply thinly twice daily initially, then reduce

Gelcotar® (Quinoderm Ltd)
Liquid, strong coal tar solution 1.25%, cade oil 0.5%, in a shampoo basis. Net price 150 mL = £1.33; 350 mL = £2.66. ACBS: for psoriasis of the scalp, seborrhoeic dermatitis, and dandruff
Additives: fragrance
Gel, see section 13.5

Genisol® (Fisons)
Liquid, prepared coal tar 2% (as purified coal tar fractions), sodium sulphosuccinated undecylenic monoalkylolamide 1%. Net price 58 mL = £1.11; 250 mL = £3.69; 600 mL = £7.67. ACBS: for psoriasis, eczema, and scaling of the scalp (psoriasis, dandruff, or eczema)
Additives: fragrance

Ionil T® (Alcon)
Shampoo application, benzalkonium chloride 0.2%, coal tar solution 5%, salicylic acid 2% in an alcoholic basis. Net price 200 mL = £2.56. ACBS: for seborrhoeic dermatitis of the scalp
Additives: tetrasodium edetate

Lenium® (Janssen)
Cream, selenium sulphide 2.5%. Net price 9 g sachet = 15p; 42 g = 72p; 100 g = £1.49
Additives: fragrance

PoM **Nizoral®** shampoo—section 13.10.2

Polytar® (Stiefel)
Liquid, arachis oil extract of crude coal tar 0.3%, cade oil 0.3%, coal tar solution 0.1%, oleyl alcohol 1%, tar 0.3%. Net price 65 mL = 91p; 150 mL = £1.34; 350 mL = £2.37. ACBS: for psoriasis, eczema, and scaling of the scalp (psoriasis, dandruff, and eczema)
Additives: polysorbate 80, fragrance

Polytar Plus® (Stiefel)
Liquid, ingredients as above with hydrolysed animal protein 3%. Net price 350 mL = £3.29. ACBS: for scalp disorders such as scaling (psoriasis, dandruff, eczema), pruritus, and in the removal of pastes and pomades used in psoriasis
Additives: fragrance

Pragmatar®—section 13.5

Psoriderm® (Dermal)
Scalp lotion (= shampoo), coal tar 2.5%, lecithin 0.3%. Net price 250 mL = £4.97
Additives: disodium edetate

Selsun® (Abbott)
Shampoo application, selenium sulphide 2.5%. Net price 50 mL = 75p; 100 mL = £1.28; 150 mL = £1.73
Additives: fragrance

Synogist® (Townendale)
Shampoo solution, sodium sulphosuccinated undecylenic monoalkylolamide 2%. Net price 200 mL = £12.98
Additives: hydroxybenzoates (parabens)

T/Gel® (Neutrogena)
Shampoo, coal tar extract 2%. Net price 125 mL = £1.98. ACBS: for psoriasis, eczema, and scaling of the scalp (psoriasis, dandruff, and eczema)
Additives: hydroxybenzoates (parabens), tetrasodium edetate, fragrance

---

MALE-PATTERN BALDNESS

MINOXIDIL

Indications: male-pattern baldness (men and women)

Cautions; Contra-indications; Side-effects: see section 2.5.1 (about 1.4% absorbed); local side-effects: itching, dermatitis

NHS ▼ PoM **Regaine®** (Upjohn)
Topical solution, minoxidil 2% in an aqueous alcoholic basis. Net price 60-mL bottle = £20.00
Additives: propylene glycol
Cautions: flammable; wash hands after application
Note. The Royal Pharmaceutical Society's Law Department has reminded pharmacists that neither the safety nor the stability of mixtures of Minoxidil lotion with other products has been established, and that this fact should be drawn to the prescriber's attention before any such mixture is dispensed.

13.10 Anti-infective skin preparations

13.10.1 Antibacterial preparations

For many skin infections such as *erysipelas* and *cellulitis* systemic antibacterial treatment is the method of choice because the infection is too deeply sited for adequate penetration of topical preparations. For details of suitable treatment see section 5.1, Table 1.

Impetigo may be treated by local application with **chlortetracycline** or, if there is systemic toxicity, with oral **flucloxacillin** (see section 5.1, Table 1). Mild antiseptics such as **povidone-iodine** (section 13.11.4) are used to remove crusts and exudate.

Although there are a great many antibacterial drugs presented in topical preparations they are potentially hazardous and frequently their use is not necessary if adequate hygienic measures can be taken. Moreover not all skin conditions that are oozing, crusted, or characterised by pustules are actually infected.

To minimise the development of resistant organisms it is advisable to limit the choice of drugs applied topically to those not used systemically. Unfortunately some of these drugs, for example neomycin, may cause sensitisation and, if large areas of skin are being treated, ototoxicity may be a hazard, particularly in children and the elderly. Resistant organisms are more common in hospitals, and whenever possible swabs for examination should be taken before beginning treatment.

Mupirocin is not related to any other antibiotic in use.

Silver sulphadiazine is used in the treatment of infected burns.

13.10.1.1 ANTIBACTERIAL PREPARATIONS ONLY USED TOPICALLY

FRAMYCETIN SULPHATE

Indications; Cautions; Side-effects: see under Neomycin Sulphate

Administration: apply 3 times daily

PoM **Framygen®** (Fisons)
Cream, framycetin sulphate 0.5%, in a water-miscible basis. Net price 15 g = £1.65
Additives: hydroxybenzoates (parabens)

PoM **Soframycin®** (Roussel)

Cream, framycetin sulphate 1.5%, gramicidin 0.005%, in a vanishing-cream basis. Net price 15 g = £1.72

Additives: hydroxybenzoates (parabens)

Ointment, ingredients as for cream, in a wool fat and paraffin basis. Net price 15 g = £1.72

Additives: wool fat

Sterile powder for preparing topical solutions, framycetin sulphate. Net price 500-mg vial = £3.85

Sofra-Tulle® *see* Framycetin Gauze Dressing, section 13.13.6

MUPIROCIN

(Pseudomonic Acid)

Indications: bacterial skin infections

Cautions: see below

Administration: apply up to 3 times daily for up to 10 days

PoM **Bactroban®** (Beecham)

Ointment, mupirocin 2%, in a water-miscible macrogol basis. Net price 15 g = £3.55

Additives: none as listed in section 13.1

Note. Contains macrogol therefore caution in renal impairment; may sting

Nasal ointment, see section 12.2.3

NEOMYCIN SULPHATE

Indications: skin infections

Cautions: see notes above; large open wounds, sensitivity to other aminoglycosides

Side-effects: local hypersensitivity reactions

Administration: apply up to 3 times daily

Creams and ointments

PoM **Neomycin Cream, BPC,** neomycin sulphate 0.5%, cetomacrogol emulsifying ointment 30%, chlorocresol 0.1%, disodium edetate 0.01%, in freshly boiled and cooled purified water. Net price 15 g = 52p

PoM **Cicatrin®** (Calmic)

Cream, neomycin sulphate 3300 units, bacitracin zinc 250 units, cysteine 2 mg, glycine 10 mg, threonine 1 mg/g. Net price 15 g = £4.52; 30 g = £8.22

Additives: wool fat derivative

Apply 3 times daily; max. 60 g daily for 3 weeks; do not repeat for at least 3 months

PoM **Graneodin®** (Squibb)

Ointment, neomycin sulphate 0.25%, gramicidin 0.025%. Net price 25 g = £1.47

Additives: none as listed in section 13.1

Apply 3 times daily

Powders and sprays

PoM **Cicatrin®** (Calmic)

Dusting powder, neomycin sulphate 3300 units, bacitracin zinc 250 units, cysteine 2 mg, glycine 10 mg, threonine 1 mg/g. Net price 15 g = £4.87; 50 g = £12.31. Max. 50 g daily for 4 weeks; do not repeat for at least 3 months

Powder spray, neomycin sulphate 16500 units, bacitracin zinc 1250 units, cysteine 12 mg, glycine 60 mg/g; pressurised aerosol unit. Net price 3 g = £11.74. Max. 3 g daily for 12 weeks; do not repeat for at least 3 months

PoM **Polybactrin®** (Calmic)

Powder spray, neomycin sulphate 495000 units, bacitracin zinc 37500 units, polymyxin B sulphate 150000 units/pressurised aerosol unit. Net price per unit (115 mL) = £18.70. Max. 1 unit daily for 7 days; do not repeat for at least 3 months

Additives: none as listed in section 13.1

PoM **Tribiotic®** (3M)

Spray application, neomycin sulphate 500000 units, bacitracin zinc 10000 units, polymyxin B sulphate 150000 units/pressurised aerosol unit. Net price per unit (110 g) = £5.72. Max. 1 unit daily for 7 days; do not repeat for at least 3 months

Additives: information not disclosed for BNF

POLYMYXINS

(Includes colistin sulphate and polymyxin B sulphate)

Indications: skin infections

Cautions: see notes above; large open wounds

Side-effects: transient irritation; local hypersensitivity reactions

PoM **Polyfax®** (Calmic)

Ointment, polymyxin B sulphate 10 000 units, bacitracin zinc 500 units/g, in a paraffin basis. Net price 20 g = £6.49

Additives: none as listed in section 13.1

Apply 3 times daily

PoM **Colomycin®** (Pharmax)

Powder, sterile, for making topical preparations (usually 1%), colistin sulphate. Net price 1 g vial = £18.79

Other preparations

Ingredient of Polybactrin® and Tribiotic®

SILVER SULPHADIAZINE

Indications: skin infection, particularly Gram-negative infections such as pseudomonal infections in second- and third-degree burns, infected leg ulcers, and pressure sores

Cautions: hepatic and renal impairment

Contra-indications: sensitivity to sulphonamides

Side-effects: rarely allergic reactions including rashes

PoM **Flamazine®** (S&N Pharm.)

Cream, silver sulphadiazine 1%, in a water-soluble basis. Net price 50 g = £4.09; 250 g = £10.84; 500 g = £19.19

Additives: polysorbates, propylene glycol

In burns apply daily with sterile applicator; in leg ulcers apply at least 3 times a week

13.10.1.2 ANTIBACTERIAL PREPARATIONS ALSO USED SYSTEMICALLY

CHLORTETRACYCLINE

Indications: susceptible skin infections; impetigo, see section 5.1, Table 1

Cautions: see notes above; overgrowth with non-susceptible organisms; stains clothing

Side-effects: rarely local hypersensitivity reactions
Administration: apply 1 to 3 times daily

PoM **Aureomycin®** (Lederle)
Cream, chlortetracycline hydrochloride 3% (as chlortetracycline), in a water-miscible basis. Net price 30 g = £1.82
Additives: chlorocresol
Ointment, chlortetracycline hydrochloride 3%, in a greasy basis. Net price 30 g = £1.82
Additives: hydroxybenzoates (parabens), wool fat

FUSIDIC ACID

Indications: staphylococcal skin infections and abscesses
Cautions: see notes above; avoid contact with eyes
Side-effects: rarely local hypersensitivity reactions
Administration: apply 3 times daily

PoM **Fucidin®** (Leo)
Cream, fusidic acid 2%. Net price 15 g = £2.94; 30 g = £4.96
Additives: butylated hydroxyanisole, polysorbates, potassium sorbate
Gel, fusidic acid 2%, in a water-miscible basis. Net price 15 g = £2.54; 30 g = £4.40
Additives: hydroxybenzoates (parabens), polysorbate 80
Caviject gel, fusidic acid 2%, in a single-dose unit (7 g) fitted with elongated nozzle. For treatment of abscesses. Net price 1 unit = £1.49
Inject once only into curetted abscess and apply dressing
Ointment, sodium fusidate 2%, in an anhydrous greasy basis. Net price 15 g = £2.40; 30 g = £4.07
Additives: wool fat

PoM **Fucidin Intertulle®** *see* Sodium Fusidate Gauze Dressing, section 13.13.6

GENTAMICIN

Indications: skin infections
Cautions: see notes above; large open wounds, sensitivity to other aminoglycosides
Administration: apply 3 times daily

PoM **Cidomycin Topical®** (Roussel)
Cream, gentamicin 0.3% (as sulphate), in a water-miscible basis. Do not dilute. Net price 15 g = £1.75; 30 g = £3.40
Additives: hydroxybenzoates (parabens), propylene glycol
Ointment, gentamicin 0.3% (as sulphate), in a paraffin basis. Do not dilute. Net price 15 g = £1.75; 30 g = £3.40
Additives: none as listed in section 13.1

PoM **Genticin®** (Nicholas)
Cream, gentamicin 0.3% (as sulphate), in a water-miscible basis. Net price 15 g = £1.37; 100 g = £9.15
Additives: hydroxybenzoates (parabens)
Ointment, gentamicin 0.3% (as sulphate), in an anhydrous greasy basis. Net price 15 g = £1.37; 100 g = £9.15
Additives: hydroxybenzoates (parabens)

TETRACYCLINE HYDROCHLORIDE

Indications; Cautions; Side-effects: see under Chlortetracycline Hydrochloride

PoM **Achromycin Topical®** (Lederle)
Ointment, tetracycline hydrochloride 3%, in a wool fat and paraffin basis. Net price 30 g = £1.48
Additives: hydroxybenzoates (parabens), wool fat
Apply 1–3 times daily

13.10.2 Antifungal preparations

Ideally skin scrapings should be examined to confirm diagnosis before treatment is begun. Widespread or intractable fungal infections are treated systemically (see section 5.2). Most localised infections are treated with the topical preparations described below.

Nail ringworm (tinea unguium) and scalp ringworm (*T. capitis*) are best treated systemically (see section 5.2). Most other ringworm infections, including tinea pedis, may be adequately treated with topical preparations. The imidazoles **clotrimazole**, **econazole**, and **miconazole** are all effective and commonly used. **Sulconazole** is a recently introduced imidazole with similar properties. Combinations of imidazoles and weak corticosteroids may be of use in the treatment of some eczematous disorders and, in the first few days only, of a severely inflamed patch of ringworm. **Compound benzoic acid ointment** (Whitfield's ointment) is also quite effective but cosmetically less acceptable than the proprietary preparations. It is generally used to treat patches of ringworm (tinea) on the trunk, limbs, palms, or soles. The **undecenoates** and **tolnaftate** are less effective in treating ringworm infections.

Candidal skin infections may also be treated by topical application with the broad-spectrum antifungals, clotrimazole, econazole, and miconazole. **Amphotericin** and **nystatin** preparations are also equally as effective in candidiasis although they are ineffective against infections due to dermatophyte fungi (tinea).

Lotions are generally chosen for application to large and hairy areas. Ointments are best avoided on moist surfaces because of their occlusive properties. Dusting-powders have no place in the treatment of fungal infections, except for toiletry or cosmetic purposes, as they are therapeutically ineffective and may cause skin irritation.

AMPHOTERICIN

Indications: skin infections due to *Candida* spp.
Administration: apply 2–4 times daily

PoM **Fungilin®** (Squibb)
Ointment, amphotericin 3%, in Plastibase®. Do not dilute. Net price 15 g = £1.30
Additives: none as listed in section 13.1

BENZOIC ACID

Indications: ringworm (tinea)

Benzoic Acid Ointment, Compound, BP (Whitfield's ointment), benzoic acid 6%, salicylic acid 3%, in emulsifying ointment. Net price 25 g = 14p
Apply twice daily

BENZOYL PEROXIDE

Indications: fungal skin infections, particularly tinea pedis

Quinoped® (Quinoderm Ltd)
Cream, benzoyl peroxide 5%, potassium hydroxyquinoline sulphate 0.5%, in an astringent basis. Net price 25 g = 92p
Additives: edetic acid (EDTA)
Apply twice daily

CLOTRIMAZOLE

Indications: fungal skin infections
Side-effects: occasional skin irritation or sensitivity
Administration: apply 2–3 times daily continuing for 14 days after lesions have healed

Canesten® (Baypharm)
Cream, clotrimazole 1%, in a water-miscible basis. Net price 20 g = £1.82; 50 g = £4.26
Additives: benzyl alcohol, polysorbate 60
Solution, clotrimazole 1% in macrogol 400. Net price 20 mL = £2.38. For hairy areas
Additives: none as listed in section 13.1
Spray, clotrimazole 1%, in 30% isopropyl alcohol. Net price 40-mL atomiser = £5.12. For large or hairy areas
Additives: propylene glycol
Caution: flammable
Dusting-powder, clotrimazole 1%. Net price 30 g = £1.56
Additives: none as listed in section 13.1

ECONAZOLE NITRATE

Indications; Side-effects: see under Clotrimazole
Administration: apply 2–3 times daily continuing for 14 days after lesions have healed; nail infections, apply daily under occlusive dressing

Ecostatin® (Squibb)
Cream, econazole nitrate 1%, in a water-miscible basis. Net price 15 g = £1.49; 30 g = £2.75
Additives: butylated hydroxyanisole, fragrance
Lotion, econazole nitrate 1%. Net price 30 mL = £2.75
Additives: butylated hydroxyanisole, fragrance
Spray solution, econazole nitrate 1% in an alcoholic solution. Net price 150 g = £3.48
Additives: propylene glycol, fragrance
Dusting-powder, econazole nitrate 1% in a talc basis. Net price 30 g = £2.90
Additives: fragrance
Spray-powder, econazole nitrate 1% in a talc basis. Net price 200-g unit = £2.64
Additives: fragrance

Pevaryl® (Cilag)
Cream, econazole nitrate 1% in a water-miscible basis. Net price 30 g = £2.65
Additives: butylated hydroxyanisole, fragrance
Lotion, econazole nitrate 1% in a water-miscible basis. Net price 30 mL = £3.33
Additives: butylated hydroxyanisole, fragrance
Spray-powder, econazole nitrate 1%. Net price 200-g pressurised aerosol unit (20 g powder) = £3.33
Additives: fragrance

KETOCONAZOLE

Indications; Side-effects: see under Clotrimazole

PoM **Nizoral®** (Janssen)
Cream, ketoconazole 2% in a water-miscible basis. Net price 30 g = £3.81
Additives: polysorbates, propylene glycol
Apply 1–2 times daily, continuing for a few days after lesions have healed
Shampoo, ketoconazole 2%. Net price 100 mL = £8.75
Additives: fragrance
For seborrhoeic dermatitis and dandruff apply twice weekly for 2–4 weeks, for pityriasis versicolor once daily for max. 5 days; avoid for 2 weeks following topical corticosteroid treatment

MICONAZOLE NITRATE

Indications; Side-effects: see under Clotrimazole
Administration: apply twice daily continuing for 10 days after lesions have healed; nail infections, apply daily under occlusive dressing

Daktarin® (Janssen)
Cream, miconazole nitrate 2%, in a water-miscible basis. Net price 30 g = £2.07
Additives: butylated hydroxyanisole
Dusting-powder, miconazole nitrate 2%. Net price 20 g = £1.39
Spray powder, miconazole nitrate 0.16%, in an aerosol basis. Net price 100 g = £1.39
Additives: none as listed in section 13.1
Twin pack, 1 × 30 g pack of cream miconazole nitrate 2%, with 1 × 30 g dusting-powder miconazole nitrate 2%. Net price (complete pack) = £3.80

NATAMYCIN

Indications: skin infections due to *Candida* spp. (includes candidal infections of oral mucosa)
Administration: apply 2–3 times daily

PoM **Pimafucin®** (Brocades)
Cream, natamycin 2%, in a water-miscible basis. Net price 30 g = £1.75
Additives: hydroxybenzoates (parabens)

NYSTATIN

Indications: skin infections due to *Candida* spp.
Administration: apply 2–4 times daily, continuing for 7 days after lesions have healed

PoM **Multilind®** (Squibb)
Ointment, nystatin 100000 units/g, zinc oxide 20% in an emollient basis. Net price 50 g = £3.45. For superinfection, particularly in napkin rash
Additives: fragrance

PoM **Nystaform®** (Bayer)
Cream, nystatin 100000 units/g, chlorhexidine hydrochloride 1%. Net price 30 g = £2.69
Additives: benzyl alcohol, polysorbate 60
Ointment, nystatin 100000 units/g, chlorhexidine acetate 1%, in a water-repellent basis. Net price 30 g = £2.69
Additives: none as listed in section 13.1

PoM **Nystan®** (Squibb)
Cream, nystatin 100 000 units/g, in a water-miscible basis. Net price 30 g = £2.66
Additives: benzyl alcohol, propylene glycol, fragrance
Gel, nystatin 100 000 units/g. Net price 30 g = £2.66
Additives: chlorocresol, fragrance
Ointment, nystatin 100 000 units/g, in Plastibase®. Net price 30 g = £2.14
Additives: none as listed in section 13.1

PoM **Tinaderm-M®** (Schering-Plough)
Cream, nystatin 100000 units/g, tolnaftate 1%, in a water-miscible basis. Net price 20 g = £1.83. For *Candida* infections and tinea
Additives: butylated hydroxytoluene, hydroxybenzoates (parabens), fragrance
Apply 2–3 times daily

SALICYLIC ACID

Indications: fungal skin infections, particularly tinea
Side-effects: hypersensitivity reactions

Phytex® (Pharmax)
Paint, salicylic acid 1.46% (total combined), tannic acid 4.89% and boric acid 3.12% (as borotannic complex), in a vehicle containing alcohol and ethyl acetate. Net price 25 mL (with brush) = £1.33. For fungal nail infections (onychomycosis)
Additives: none as listed in section 13.1
Apply twice daily
Caution: flammable; avoid in pregnancy and children under 5 years

Phytocil® (Fisons)
Cream, salicylic acid 1.5%, 2-*p*-chlorophenoxyethanol 1%, menthol 1%, 1-phenoxypropan-2-ol 2%. Net price 25 g = 61p. For tinea pedis, tinea cruris, and tinea circinata
Additives: none as listed in section 13.1
Apply 2–3 times daily

SULCONAZOLE NITRATE

Indications; Side-effects: see under Clotrimazole
Cautions: avoid contact with eyes (lens changes in *animals* after high oral doses)
Administration: apply 1–2 times daily continuing for 2–3 weeks after lesions have healed

PoM **Exelderm®** (ICI)
Cream, sulconazole nitrate 1%, in a water-miscible basis. Net price 30 g = £3.90
Additives: polysorbates, propylene glycol

TIOCONAZOLE

Indications: fungal nail infections
Side-effects: local irritation, usually during first week of treatment; discontinue if sensitivity reaction develops
Administration: apply to nails and surrounding skin twice daily for up to 6 months (may be extended to 12 months)

PoM **Trosyl®** (Pfizer)
Nail solution, tioconazole 28%. Net price 12 mL (with applicator brush) = £25.00
Additives: none as listed in section 13.1

TOLNAFTATE

Indications: skin infections, particularly tinea pedis
Side-effects: rarely hypersensitivity

Timoped® (R&C)
Cream, tolnaftate 1%, triclosan 0.25%. Net price 30 g = £3.10
Additives: none as listed in section 13.1
Apply twice daily

UNDECENOATES

Indications: skin infections, particularly tinea pedis

Monphytol® (LAB)
Paint, methyl undecenoate 5%, propyl undecenoate 0.7%, salicylic acid 3%, methyl salicylate 25%, propyl salicylate 5%, chlorbutol 3%. Net price 18 mL (with brush) = £1.01. For fungal (particularly nail) infections
Additives: none as listed in section 13.1
Apply 4 times daily

Mycota® (Crookes)
Cream, zinc undecenoate 20%, undecenoic acid 5%. Net price 25 g = 67p
Additives: fragrance
Dusting-powder, zinc undecenoate 20%, undecenoic acid 2%. Net price 70 g = £1.10
Additives: fragrance
Spray application, undecenoic acid 2.5%, dichlorophen 0.25% (pressurised aerosol pack). Net price 113 g = £1.10
Additives: fragrance
Apply 1–2 times daily

Phytocil® (Fisons)
Dusting-powder, zinc undecenoate 5.8%, 2-*p*-chlorophenoxyethanol 1%, 1-phenoxypropan-2-ol 2%. Net price 50 g = 84p. For use with cream
Additives: none as listed in section 13.1

13.10.3 Antiviral preparations

Acyclovir cream is indicated for the treatment of initial and recurrent labial and genital herpes simplex infections; treatment should begin as early as possible. Systemic treatment is necessary for buccal or vaginal infections; herpes zoster (shingles) also requires systemic treatment (for details of systemic use see section 5.3).

Idoxuridine solution (5% in dimethyl sulphoxide) is used less frequently for herpetic infections of the skin since acyclovir is more effective. Herpes simplex seems to respond to frequent applications if started early and continued for 3 to 4 days, but may be less successful if delayed after 7 days. Evidence of its value in herpes zoster infections is conflicting.

ACYCLOVIR

Indications: see notes above

Side-effects: transient stinging or burning on application; occasionally erythema or drying of the skin

Application: apply to lesions every 4 hours (5 times daily) for 5 days

PoM **Zovirax®** (Wellcome)

Cream, acyclovir 5% in an aqueous cream basis. Net price 2 g = £7.28; 10 g = £21.93

Additives: propylene glycol

Eye ointment, see section 11.3.1

IDOXURIDINE IN DIMETHYL SULPHOXIDE

Indications: see notes above

Cautions: avoid contact with the eyes, mucous membranes, and textiles; breast-feeding

Contra-indications: pregnancy (toxicity in *animal* studies)

Side-effects: stinging on application, changes in taste; overuse may cause maceration

Administration: apply 5% solution to lesions 4 times daily for 3–4 days; in severe zoster (shingles) apply 40% solution over affected area daily for 4 days

Note. Not to be used in mouth

PoM **Herpid®** (Boehringer Ingelheim)

Application, idoxuridine 5% in dimethyl sulphoxide. Net price 5 mL (with brush) = £7.04

Additives: none as listed in section 13.1

PoM **Iduridin®** (Ferring)

Application, idoxuridine 5% in dimethyl sulphoxide. Net price 5 mL (with applicator) = £4.90

Additives: none as listed in section 13.1

Application, idoxuridine 40% in dimethyl sulphoxide. Net price 5 mL (with applicator) = £19.00; 20 mL with dropper = £39.00. For severe herpes zoster

Additives: none as listed in section 13.1

PoM **Virudox®** (Bioglan)

Application, idoxuridine 5% in dimethyl sulphoxide. Net price 5 mL (with brush) = £5.95

Additives: none as listed in section 13.1

13.10.4 Parasiticidal preparations

SCABIES (*Sarcoptes scabiei*). **Lindane** and **malathion** are the treatments of choice for scabies, but lindane should be avoided during pregnancy or breast-feeding, in young children, and in patients with low body-weight or a history of epilepsy.

Older preparations include benzyl benzoate, which is an irritant and should be avoided in children, and monosulfiram, which may induce disulfiram-like reactions with alcohol. Evidence that monosulfiram is particularly suitable for children is inconclusive; it is not appropriate for self treatment.

Aqueous lotions are preferable to creams as they give better coverage; alcoholic lotions are not recommended owing to irritation of excoriated skin and the genitalia. Although the preparations have traditionally been applied after a hot bath there is evidence that this may increase absorption of the acaricide into the bloodstream.

All members of the affected household should be treated. Treatment should be applied to the whole body paying particular attention to the webs of the fingers and toes and brushing lotion under the ends of the nails. In the case of infants and young children (up to the age of about 2 years) the lotion (preferably malathion, see notes above) should also be applied on the scalp, neck, face, and ears. Providing the application is done properly lindane and malathion need only be applied once; in the case of benzyl benzoate up to three applications on consecutive days may be needed.

The itch of scabies persists for some days after the infestation has been eliminated and antipruritic treatment may be required. Application of **crotamiton** can be used to control itching after treatment with more effective acaricides, but caution is necessary if the skin is excoriated. **Calamine** is probably more suitable.

HEAD LICE (*Pediculus humanis capitis*). **Malathion** and **carbaryl** are the treatments of choice for *head lice*. **Lindane** is no longer recommended because of resistant strains. Lotions should be used in preference to shampoos, which are not in contact with the hair long enough and are normally diluted too much in use to be effective; aqueous lotions are preferred for asthmatic patients and small children, to avoid alcoholic fumes. A contact time of 12 hours or overnight treatment is recommended, with a second treatment after one week in order to kill lice emerging from eggs that survived the first application. A 2-hour treatment is no longer regarded as sufficient to ensure death of eggs. **Permethrin** and **phenothrin** are two recently introduced pyrethroids, both of which are very effective at killing lice, but less effective at killing eggs. They need to be formulated in a good carrier basis to glue them to the hair.

Rotational policies. Most health districts operate a rotating policy for head lice treatment. Details of the drugs which are currently recommended for use in the different health districts can be obtained from District Pharmaceutical Officers.

CRAB (PUBIC) LICE (*Pthirus pubis*). **Malathion** and **lindane** are effective for *crab lice*. Aqueous lotions should be applied to all hairy parts of the body for 12 hours or overnight; a second treatment is necessary after one week to kill lice emerging from surviving eggs. **Carbaryl** is also effective but no suitable aqueous preparation is available and alcoholic lotions are not recommended (owing to irritation of excoriated skin and the genitalia). Aqueous malathion lotion should be used for *crab lice of the eye lashes*.

BENZYL BENZOATE

Indications: scabies, pediculosis (but see notes above)

Cautions: children (see notes above), avoid contact with eyes and mucous membranes
Side-effects: skin irritation, burning sensation especially on genitalia and excoriations, occasionally rashes

Ascabiol® (Rhône-Poulenc Rorer)
Application, benzyl benzoate 25% in an emulsion basis. Net price 100 mL = £1.17
Additives: fragrance
Administration: scabies—apply 25% application over the whole body, omitting the head and neck; repeat without bathing on the following day and wash off 24 hours later; a third application may be required in some cases
Note. Not recommended for children—dilution to reduce irritant effect also reduces efficacy (see notes above)

CARBARYL

Indications: pediculosis
Cautions: avoid contact with eyes; alcoholic lotions **not** recommended for pediculosis in asthmatics or small children, or for crab lice (see notes above); do not use more than once a week for 3 weeks at a time
Side-effects: skin irritation
Administration: lotion—apply to dry hair and rub into the hair and scalp or affected areas, allow to dry, comb, and remove by washing 12 hours later (see also notes above); repeat procedure after 7 days; shampoo—shampoo in, leave on hair for 5 minutes, rinse, repeat, rinse, allow to dry, comb, repeat twice at intervals of 3 days

Carylderm® (Napp)
Lotion, carbaryl 0.5%, in an alcoholic basis. Net price 55 mL = £1.10; 110 mL = £2.05
Additives: none as listed in section 13.1
Caution: flammable
Shampoo, carbaryl 1%. Net price 100 mL = £1.70
Additives: wool fat derivative, fragrance

Clinicide® (De Witt)
Lotion, carbaryl 0.5% in an aqueous basis containing 10% alcohol. Net price 50 mL = 95p
Additives: none as listed in section 13.1

Derbac® (International Labs)
Shampoo solution, carbaryl 0.5% in an aqueous basis. Net price 75 mL = £1.06
Additives: hydroxybenzoates (parabens), fragrance

Suleo-C® (International Labs)
Lotion, carbaryl 0.5%, in an alcoholic basis. Net price 55 mL = £1.05; 210 mL = £2.39
Additives: fragrance
Caution: flammable
Shampoo solution, carbaryl 0.5% in a shampoo basis. Net price 75 mL = £1.05
Additives: fragrance

CROTAMITON

Indications: pruritus after scabies, see notes above
Cautions; Contra-indications: section 13.3
Administration: apply as required to control itch after scabies, see notes above

Preparations: section 13.3

LINDANE

Indications: scabies, pediculosis (but see notes above)
Cautions: avoid contact with eyes and mucous membranes; do not use more than twice for one course of treatment; see also above (under Scabies)
Side-effects: skin irritation
Administration: see preparations

Quellada® (Stafford-Miller)
Lotion, lindane 1%, in a lotion basis. Net price 100 mL = 63p; 500 mL = £2.08. For scabies
Additives. information not disclosed for BNF
Administration: scabies, apply thinly over whole body, omitting head and neck, wash off using cool water after 24 hours; repeat if necessary after 7–10 days
Application PC, lindane 1%, in a shampoo basis. Net price 100 mL = 71p; 500 mL = £2.54. For pediculosis (but see notes above)
Additives: information not disclosed for BNF
Administration: pediculosis, apply to dry hair, leave for 4 minutes, add water to produce lather, rinse, towel dry, comb; repeat after 7 days (but see notes above)

MALATHION

Indications: pediculosis, scabies
Cautions: avoid contact with eyes; alcoholic lotions **not** recommended for pediculosis in asthmatics or small children, or for scabies or crab lice (see notes above); do not use more than once a week for 3 weeks at a time
Side-effects: skin irritation
Administration: pediculosis—rub 0.5% lotion into dry hair, scalp, and affected area, comb, allow to dry naturally, remove by washing after 12 hours (see also notes above), repeat after 7 days; apply 1% shampoo to hair for 5 minutes, rinse, repeat, rinse again, comb, repeat twice at intervals of 3 days
Scabies—apply 0.5% preparation over whole body, omitting the head and neck, and wash off after 24 hours, but see also notes above

Derbac-M® (International Labs)
Liquid, malathion 0.5% in an aqueous basis. Net price 55 mL = £1.08; 200 mL = £2.56
Additives: hydroxybenzoates (parabens), fragrance

Prioderm® (Napp)
Lotion, malathion 0.5%, in an alcoholic basis. Net price 55 mL = £1.10; 110 mL = £2.05
Additives: fragrance
Caution: flammable
Cream shampoo, malathion 1%. Net price 40 g = £1.10
Additives: disodium edetate, hydroxybenzoates (parabens), propylene glycol, wool fat derivative, fragrance

Suleo-M® (International Labs)
Lotion, malathion 0.5%, in an alcoholic basis. Net price 55 mL = £1.04; 210 mL = £2.39
Additives: fragrance
Caution: flammable

MONOSULFIRAM

Indications: scabies, but see notes above
Cautions: avoid contact with eyes; avoid alcohol; not appropriate for self-treatment; **interactions:** Appendix 1 (monosulfiram)
Side-effects: hypersensitivity, rashes
Administration: apply diluted solution over whole body omitting head and neck; repeat if necessary for 2–3 consecutive days

Tetmosol® (ICI)
Solution, monosulfiram 25%, in industrial methylated spirit. Dilute with 2–3 parts of water before use. Net price 100 mL = £1.20. Label: 4. ACBS: for control of scabies (clinic use)
Additives: none as listed in section 13.1
Caution: flammable

PERMETHRIN

Indications: pediculosis
Cautions: avoid contact with eyes; use in children under 2 years only under medical supervision
Side-effects: pruritus, erythema, and stinging of scalp; rarely scalp rashes and oedema

Lyclear® (Wellcome)
Cream rinse, permethrin 1% in a basis containing 20% isopropyl alcohol. Net price 59 mL = £1.68
Additives: hydroxybenzoates (parabens), propylene glycol, fragrance
Administration: apply to clean damp hair, leave on for 10 minutes, rinse and dry

PHENOTHRIN

Indications: pediculosis
Cautions: avoid contact with eyes; children under 6 months (medical supervision required)
Side-effects: skin irritation

Full Marks® (Napp)
Shampoo, phenothrin 0.2%. Net price 125 mL = £2.38
Additives: fragrance
Administration: shampoo hair, leave on for at least 5 minutes, rinse, repeat once, comb

13.10.5 Preparations for minor skin infections

Some of the preparations listed are used in minor burns, and abrasions. They are applied as necessary. Preparations containing camphor, hydrargaphen, and sulphonamides should be **avoided**. Preparations such as magnesium sulphate paste are also listed but are now rarely used to treat carbuncles and boils as these are best treated with antibiotics (see section 5.1.1.2).

Flexible collodion (section 13.1) may be used to seal minor cuts and wounds that have partially healed.

Cetrimide Cream, BP, cetrimide 0.5% in a suitable water-miscible basis such as cetostearyl alcohol 5%, liquid paraffin 50% in freshly boiled and cooled purified water. Net price 50 g = 16p

Chlorhexidine Cream, BP, chlorhexidine gluconate solution usually 5% (≡ chlorhexidine gluconate 1%), cetomacrogol emulsifying wax 25%, liquid paraffin 10%, in purified water, freshly boiled and cooled

Proflavine Cream, BPC, proflavine hemisulphate 0.1%, yellow beeswax 2.5%, chlorocresol 0.1%, liquid paraffin 67.3%, freshly boiled and cooled purified water 25%, wool fat 5%. Net price 100 mL = 33p
Caution: stains clothing

Anaflex® (Geistlich)
Cream, polynoxylin 10%, in a water-miscible basis. Net price 50 g = £2.59
Additives: fragrance

Bactrian® (Loveridge)
Cream, cetrimide 1%. Net price 45 g = 43p
Additives: information not disclosed for BNF

Betadine® (Napp)
Ointment, povidone-iodine 10%, in a water-miscible basis. Net price 80 g = £2.03
Additives: none as listed in section 13.1

Brulidine® (Rhône-Poulenc Rorer)
Cream, dibromopropamidine isethionate 0.15%, in a water-miscible basis. Net price 25 g = 68p
Additives: hydroxybenzoates (parabens), fragrance

Cetavlex® (ICI)
Cream, cetrimide 0.5%, in a water-miscible basis. Net price 50 g = 50p
Additives: hydroxybenzoates (parabens)

Dermalex® (Sanofi)
Skin lotion, allantoin 0.25%, hexachlorophane 0.5%, squalane 3% in an emulsion basis. Net price 100 mL = £2.05; 250 mL = £5.35. For prevention of pressure sores and prevention and treatment of urinary rash. Avoid in children under 2 years
Additives: information not disclosed for BNF

Drapolene® (Calmic)
Cream, benzalkonium chloride 0.01%, cetrimide 0.2% in a water-miscible basis. Net price 55 g = 64p; 100 g = 99p. For urinary rash and minor wounds
Additives: chlorocresol, wool fat

Miol (Formula M1)® (BritCair)
Cream, alcloxa 1%, calcium chloride 0.2%, camphor 4%, chlorphenesin 0.1%, magnesium chloride 1.5%, sodium chloride 2.1% in a water-miscible basis. Net price 30 g = £2.08
Additives: none as listed in section 13.1
Lotion, alcloxa 1%, calcium chloride 0.17%, camphor 1%, magnesium chloride 1.42%, sodium chloride 1.98%. Net price 100 mL = £2.40
Additives: none as listed in section 13.1

Vesagex® (Rybar)
Cream, cetrimide 1%. Net price 500 g = £4.57
Additives: chlorocresol

Preparations for boils

Magnesium Sulphate Paste, BP, dried magnesium sulphate 45 g, glycerol 55 g, phenol 500 mg
Should be stirred before use
Apply under dressing

Secaderm®—section 13.14

13.11 Disinfectants and cleansers

The choice of *cleanser* is an important factor in treating skin conditions. For example, scaling disorders are best treated with **emulsifying ointment** (section 13.1) or other cleansers that do not irritate the skin.

Sodium chloride solution 0.9% is suitable for general cleansing of skin and wounds.

Useful *disinfectants* for skin cleansing include **cetrimide** (which has useful detergent properties), **chlorhexidine** and **potassium permanganate solution** 1 in 8000. **Povidone-iodine** is preferred to chlorinated solutions (such as dilute sodium hypochlorite solution) which are too irritant and are no longer recommended. Topical preparations of **hexachlorophane** should be used with caution in neonates and should **not** be used on large raw surfaces.

Astringent preparations, such as **potassium permanganate** solution are useful for treating eczematous reactions (section 13.5). Silver nitrate lotion is now rarely used as it stains the skin black and may cause toxic effects if used for prolonged periods.

BORDERLINE SUBSTANCES. The preparations marked 'ACBS' are regarded as drugs when prescribed in accordance with the advice of the Advisory Committee on Borderline Substances for the clinical conditions listed. Prescriptions issued in accordance with this advice and endorsed 'ACBS' will normally not be investigated. See Appendix 7 for listing by clinical condition.

13.11.1 Alcohols and saline

ALCOHOL

Indications: skin preparation before injection

Cautions: flammable; avoid broken skin; patients have suffered severe burns when diathermy has been preceded by application of alcoholic skin disinfectants.

Industrial Methylated Spirit, BP

Mixture of 19 volumes of ethanol (absolute alcohol) of an appropriate strength with 1 volume of approved wood naphtha and is Industrial Methylated Spirit of the quality known either as '66 OP' or as '74 OP'

Net price 100 mL = 14p. Label: 15

Surgical Spirit, BP, methyl salicylate 0.5 mL, diethyl phthalate 2%, castor oil 2.5%, in industrial methylated spirit. Net price 100 mL = 17p. Label: 15

SODIUM CHLORIDE

Indications: see notes above

Normasol® (Seton Prebbles)

Solution (sterile), sodium chloride 0.9%. Net price 25 × 25-mL sachet = £3.24; 6 × 100-mL sachet = £2.38. To be used undiluted for topical irrigation of burns, wounds, and eyes

Additives: none as listed in section 13.1

See also section 11.8.2

Topiclens® (S&N)

Solution (sterile), sodium chloride 0.9%. Net price 50 × 25-mL sachet = £4.86; 25 × 100-mL sachet = £7.75. To be used undiluted for irrigating eyes and wounds

Additives: none as listed in section 13.1

13.11.2 Chlorhexidine salts

CHLORHEXIDINE

Indications: skin disinfection such as pre-operative skin preparation, obstetrics and wound cleansing; bladder irrigation (see also section 7.4.4)

Cautions: avoid contact with eyes; bladder irrigations of concentrated solutions may cause haematuria

Side-effects: sensitivity may occur, avoid contact with mucous membranes and meninges

Administration: chlorhexidine acetate or gluconate, body cavity and bladder irrigation 0.01–0.02%[1], urethral disinfection and catheter lubrication 0.05% (in glycerol), pre-operative skin preparation 0.5% (in alcohol 70%); chlorhexidine hydrochloride 1% as a dusting-powder or cream

1. See section 7.4.4 for a comment that solutions containing chlorhexidine 0.01% are usually preferred for postoperative bladder instillation

Bacticlens® (S&N)

Solution (sterile), pink, chlorhexidine gluconate 0.05%. Net price 50 × 25-mL sachet = £4.69; 25 × 100-mL sachet = £5.61. To be used undiluted for skin disinfection

Additives: none as listed in section 13.1

Cetriclens® (S&N)

Solution (sterile), yellow, chlorhexidine gluconate 0.015%, cetrimide 0.15%. Net price 50 × 25-mL sachet = £3.03; 25 × 100-mL sachet = £4.30. To be used undiluted for skin disinfection and wound cleansing

Additives: none as listed in section 13.1

Forte solution (sterile), yellow, chlorhexidine gluconate 0.05%, cetrimide 0.5%. Net price 25 × 100-mL sachet = £5.27. To be used undiluted for cleansing physically contaminated wounds

Additives: none as listed in section 13.1

Chlorasept® (Baxter)

2000 Solution (sterile), pink, chlorhexidine acetate 0.05%. Net price 20 × 25-mL sachet = £1.50; 10 × 100-mL sachet = £1.70; 250, 500, and 1000 mL packs also available. For general disinfection and wound cleansing

Additives: none as listed in section 13.1

CX Antiseptic Dusting Powder® (Seton)

Dusting powder, sterile, chlorhexidine acetate 1%. Net price 15 g = £2.00

Note. Chlorhexidine Dusting Powder BP contains chlorhexidine hydrochloride 0.5% but no preparation is available commercially

Hibidil® (ICI)

Solution (sterile), pink, chlorhexidine gluconate solution 0.25% (≡ chlorhexidine gluconate 0.05%) in sterile aqueous solution. Net price

25 × 25-mL sachets = £2.00; 6 × 100-mL sachets = £1.15; 1000 mL also available. To be used undiluted for skin disinfection in wounds, burns and obstetrics

Hibiscrub® (ICI)
Cleansing solution, red, chlorhexidine gluconate solution 20% (≡4% chlorhexidine gluconate), perfumed, in a surfactant solution. Net price 12 × 100-mL sachets = £11.16; 250 mL = £1.13; 500 mL = £1.65. Use instead of soap as pre-operative scrub or disinfectant wash for hands and skin

Hibisol® (ICI)
Solution, chlorhexidine gluconate solution 2.5% (≡0.5% chlorhexidine gluconate), in isopropyl alcohol 70% with emollients. Net price 250 mL = £1.04; 500 mL = £1.72. To be used undiluted for hand and skin disinfection

Hibitane 5% Concentrate® (ICI)
Solution, red, chlorhexidine gluconate solution 25% (≡ 5% chlorhexidine gluconate), in a perfumed aqueous solution. Net price 5 litres = £11.75. To be used diluted 1 in 10 (0.5%) with alcohol 70% for pre-operative skin preparation, or 1 in 100 (0.05%) with water for general skin disinfection
Note. Alcoholic solutions not suitable before diathermy (see Alcohol, above)

Hibitane Gluconate 20%® (ICI)
Solution, chlorhexidine gluconate 20% in an aqueous solution. Net price 500 mL = £4.25. To be used diluted as above in body cavity and bladder irrigation, urethral disinfection and catheter lubrication

Hibitane Obstetric® (ICI)
Cream, chlorhexidine gluconate solution 5% (≡1% chlorhexidine gluconate), in a pourable water-miscible basis. Net price 250 mL = 91p. For use in obstetrics as a vaginal lubricant and for application to the vulva and perineum during labour

Phiso-med® (Sterling-Winthrop)
Solution, chlorhexidine gluconate 4% in an emulsion basis. Net price 150 mL = £4.76. For use as a soap substitute in acne and seborrhoeic conditions; for bathing mothers and babies in maternity units (as 1 in 10 dilution) to prevent cross-infection and for pre-operative hand and skin preparation
Additives: benzyl alcohol, wool fat derivative

Rotersept® (Roterpharma)
Spray application, chlorhexidine gluconate 0.2% in a pressurised aerosol unit. Net price 284-g unit = £1.99. For prevention and treatment of sore cracked nipples

Savloclens® (ICI)
Solution (sterile), yellow, chlorhexidine gluconate solution 0.25% (≡ chlorhexidine gluconate 0.05%), cetrimide 0.5% ≡ a dilution of 1 in 30 of Savlon Hospital Concentrate. Net price 100-mL sachet = 20p. To be used undiluted in general skin disinfection and wound cleansing

Savlodil® (ICI)
Solution (sterile), yellow, chlorhexidine gluconate solution 0.075% (≡ chlorhexidine gluconate 0.015%), cetrimide 0.15% (sterile). Net price 25 × 25-mL sachets = £1.29; 6 × 100-mL sachets = 88p. To be used undiluted for general skin disinfection and wound cleansing

Savlon Hospital Concentrate® (ICI)
Solution, orange, chlorhexidine gluconate solution 7.5% (≡ chlorhexidine gluconate 1.5%), cetrimide 15%. Net price 1 litre = £1.59. To be used diluted 1 in 100 (1%) to 1 in 30 with water for skin disinfection and wound cleansing, and diluted 1 in 30 in alcohol 70% for pre-operative skin preparation
Note. Alcoholic solutions not suitable before diathermy (see Alcohol, above)

Tisept® (Seton Prebbles)
Solution (sterile), yellow, chlorhexidine gluconate 0.015%, cetrimide 0.15%. Net price 25 × 25-mL sachet = £1.35; 6 × 100-mL sachet = 92p. To be used undiluted for general skin disinfection and wound cleansing
Additives: none as listed in section 13.1

Travasept 30® (Baxter)
Solution (sterile), yellow, chlorhexidine acetate 0.05%, cetrimide 0.5%. Net price 500 mL = 70p, 1000 mL = 75p; 25- and 100-mL sachets also available. To be used undiluted for skin cleansing and disinfection of wounds
Additives: none as listed in section 13.1

Travasept 100® (Baxter)
Solution (sterile), yellow, chlorhexidine acetate 0.015%, cetrimide 0.15%. Net price 20 × 25-mL sachet = £1.04; 10 × 100-mL sachet = £1.45; 250 mL = 69p; 500 mL = 70p; 1000 mL = 75p. To be used undiluted in skin disinfection such as wound cleansing and obstetrics
Additives: none as listed in section 13.1

Unisept® (Seton Prebbles)
Solution (sterile), pink, chlorhexidine gluconate 0.05%. Net price 25 × 25-mL sachet = £2.09; 6 × 100-mL sachet = £1.20. To be used undiluted for general skin disinfection and wound cleansing
Additives: none as listed in section 13.1

13.11.3 Cationic surfactants and soaps

BENZALKONIUM CHLORIDE

Indications: skin disinfection such as pre-operative skin preparation, obstetrics, wound cleansing and bladder irrigation
Cautions: avoid contact with eyes

Roccal® (Sterling-Winthrop)
Solution, blue, benzalkonium chloride 1%. Net price 250 mL = 78p; 500 mL = £1.55. To be used diluted 1 in 10 to 1 in 200
Additives: fragrance

Roccal Concentrate 10X® (Sterling-Winthrop)
Concentrate, blue, benzalkonium chloride 10%. Net price 2.25 litres = £30.06. For preparation of Roccal Solution with freshly boiled and cooled purified water
Additives: fragrance

CETRIMIDE

Indications: skin disinfection
Cautions: avoid contact with eyes; avoid use in body cavities
Side-effects: skin irritation and occasionally sensitisation

Preparations
Ingredient of Cetriclens®, Savloclens®, Savlodil®, Savlon Hospital Concentrate®, Tisept®, and Travasept® 30 and 100, see above

SOFT SOAP

Indications: removal of adherent crusts

Soap Spirit, BP, soft soap 65% in alcohol (90%). Net price 100 mL = 54p

SUBSTITUTE SOAPS

See section 13.1 (emulsifying ointment); section 13.2.2 (emollient bath additives)

13.11.4 Chlorine and iodine

CHLORINATED SOLUTIONS

Cautions: bleaches fabric; irritant (protect surrounding tissues with soft paraffin)

Chlorinated Lime and Boric Acid Solution, BP, (Eusol), chlorinated lime 1.25%, boric acid 1.25%, in purified water, freshly boiled and cooled. Contains not less than 0.25% available chlorine. It must be freshly prepared. Has been used undiluted for skin disinfection, particularly in wound and ulcer cleansing but no longer recommended (too irritant)

Chlorinated Soda Solution, Surgical, BPC, (Dakin's Solution), boric acid, chlorinated lime, sodium carbonate, sufficient of each to provide a solution containing 0.5% of available chlorine in purified water, freshly boiled and cooled. Net price 500 mL = 63p. Has been used undiluted for cleansing wounds and ulcers but no longer recommended (too irritant)

Chlorasol® (Seton Prebbles)
Solution (sterile), sodium hypochlorite, containing 0.3–0.4% available chlorine. Net price 25 × 25-mL sachets = £5.75
Additives: none as listed in section 13.1
Irritant therefore no longer recommended

IODINE COMPOUNDS

Indications: skin disinfection
Cautions: pregnancy, breast-feeding; broken skin
Side-effects: rarely sensitivity; may interfere with thyroid function tests

Betadine® (Napp)
Antiseptic paint, povidone-iodine 10% in an alcoholic solution. Net price 8 mL (with applicator brush) = 69p. Apply undiluted to minor wounds and infections, twice daily
Additives: none as listed in section 13.1
Alcoholic solution, povidone-iodine 10%. Net price 500 mL = £1.24. To be applied undiluted in pre- and post-operative skin disinfection
Additives: none as listed in section 13.1
Antiseptic solution, povidone-iodine 10% in aqueous solution. Net price 500 mL = £1.09. To be applied undiluted in pre- and post-operative skin disinfection
Additives: none as listed in section 13.1
Dry powder spray, povidone-iodine 2.5% in a pressurised aerosol unit. Net price 150-g unit = £2.36. For skin disinfection, particularly minor wounds and infections
Scalp and skin cleanser solution, povidone-iodine 7.5%, in a surfactant basis. Net price 250 mL = £2.06. ACBS: for infective conditions of the skin. Retain on scalp for 5 minutes before rinsing
Skin cleanser solution, povidone-iodine 4%, in a surfactant basis. Net price 250 mL = £1.74. ACBS: for infective conditions of the skin. Retain on skin for 3–5 minutes before rinsing; repeat twice daily
Surgical scrub, povidone-iodine 7.5%, in a non-ionic surfactant basis. Net price 500 mL = 96p. To be used as a pre-operative scrub for hands and skin
Additives: wool fat derivative

Disadine DP® (Stuart)
Dry powder spray (= application), povidone-iodine 0.5%, in a pressurised aerosol unit. Net price 150-g unit = £1.99. For skin disinfection, including wounds, varicose ulcers, and bedsores
Additives: none as listed in section 13.1

Videne® (3M)
Disinfectant solution, red-brown, povidone-iodine 10% (≡ 1% available iodine), in an aqueous solution. Net price 500 mL = £1.35. (hosp. only)
Additives: none as listed in section 13.1
Apply undiluted in skin disinfection and pre-operative skin preparation
Disinfectant tincture, red-brown, povidone-iodine 10% (≡ 1% available iodine), in industrial methylated spirit. Net price 500 mL = £1.50 (hosp. only). Apply undiluted in pre-operative skin disinfection, particularly orthopaedic surgery
Additives: none as listed in section 13.1
Caution: flammable
Dusting-powder, povidone-iodine 5%. Net price 15 g = £2.60. For minor wounds and infections
Surgical scrub, red-brown, povidone-iodine 7.5% (≡ 0.75% available iodine), in a detergent basis. Net price 500 mL = £1.25. To be used as a pre-operative scrub for hands and skin and disinfecting site of incision before surgery
Additives: none as listed in section 13.1

13.11.5 Phenolics

CHLOROXYLENOL

Indications: skin disinfection
Cautions: may irritate skin and cause sensitisation

Chloroxylenol Solution, BP, chloroxylenol 5%, alcohol about 20%, terpineol 10% in a detergent solution. Net price 100 mL = 30p. To be used as 1 in 20 dilution (5%)

HEXACHLOROPHANE

Indications: see under preparations (below)
Contra-indications: avoid use on badly burned or excoriated skin; pregnancy; children under 2 years except on medical advice
Side-effects: sensitivity; rarely photosensitivity

PoM **Ster-Zac DC Skin Cleanser®** (Hough)
Cream, hexachlorophane 3%. Net price 100 mL = 69p. Use 3–5 mL instead of soap as pre-operative scrub for hands
Additives: information not disclosed for BNF

Ster-Zac Powder® (Hough)
Dusting-powder, hexachlorophane 0.33%, zinc oxide 3%, talc 88.67%, starch 8% (sterile). Net price 30 g = 62p
Additives: information not disclosed for BNF
Prevention of neonatal staphylococcal sepsis, after ligature of cord sprinkle on perineum, groin, front of abdomen, and axillas; after cutting cord and spraying with plastic dressing, powder stump and adjacent skin; after every napkin change powder stump, adjacent skin, perineum, groin, axillas, buttocks, and front of abdomen; continue until stump drops away and wound healed
Adjunct for treatment of recurrent furunculosis, powder daily area of skin normally subject to furunculosis

TRICLOSAN

Indications: skin disinfection
Cautions: avoid contact with eyes

Manusept® (Hough)
Antibacterial hand rub, blue, triclosan 0.5%, isopropyl alcohol 70%. Net price 250 mL = 96p; 500 mL = £1.47. For disinfection and pre-operative hand preparation
Additives: information not disclosed for BNF

Ster-Zac Bath Concentrate® (Hough)
Solution, triclosan 2%. Net price 28.5 mL = 38p; 500 mL = £3.64. ACBS: for staphylococcal skin infections. For prevention of cross-infection use 1 sachet/bath
Additives: information not disclosed for BNF

13.11.6 Astringents, oxidisers, and dyes

ALUMINIUM ACETATE

Indications: suppurating and exudative eczematous reactions and wounds

Aluminium Acetate Lotion, aluminium acetate solution 5 mL, purified water, freshly boiled and cooled, to 100 mL. It should be freshly prepared. To be used undiluted as a wet dressing
Note. Aluminium acetate solution (13%) for the preparation of aluminium acetate lotion (0.65%) is available from Macarthys, Penn, etc. on special order

CRYSTAL VIOLET

(Gentian violet)
Indications: see below
Cautions: stains clothes and skin
Side-effects: mucosal ulcerations

Crystal Violet Paint, BP1980, crystal violet 0.5%, in purified water, freshly boiled and cooled. To be used undiluted
Note. Licensed for topical application on unbroken skin only; no longer recommended for application to mucous membranes or open wounds; restrictions do not apply to use for skin marking prior to surgery

HYDROGEN PEROXIDE

Indications: skin disinfection, particularly cleansing and deodorising wounds and ulcers
Cautions: large or deep wounds; bleaches fabric

Hydrogen Peroxide Solution, BP
Solution 6% (20 vols). Net price 100 mL = 20p
Solution 3% (10 vols). Net price 100 mL = 15p
Note. The BP directs that when hydrogen peroxide is prescribed, hydrogen peroxide solution 6% (20 vols) should be dispensed.
IMPORTANT. Strong solutions of hydrogen peroxide which contain 27% (90 vols) and 30% (100 vols) are only for the preparation of weaker solutions

Hioxyl® see Desloughing Agents (below)

POTASSIUM PERMANGANATE

Indications: cleansing and deodorising suppurating eczematous reactions and wounds
Cautions: irritant to mucous membranes; stains skin and clothing
Administration: wet dressings or baths, approx. 0.01% solution (10 g/bath)

Potassium Permanganate Solution, potassium permanganate 100 mg, water to 100 mL.
To be diluted 1 in 10 to provide a 0.01% solution

Permitabs® (Bioglan)
Solution tablets, for preparation of topical solution, potassium permanganate 400 mg. Net price 30-tab pack = £1.98
1 tablet dissolved in 4 litres of water provides a 0.01% solution

ZINC SULPHATE

Indications: indolent ulcers

Zinc Sulphate Lotion, BP (Lotio Rubra), zinc sulphate 1 g, amaranth solution 1 mL, water to 100 mL. It must be freshly prepared. Apply undiluted as a wet dressing
Note. Zinc Sulphate Mouthwash DPF consists of zinc sulphate lotion BP; 1 part is diluted with 4 parts of warm water before use

13.11.7 Desloughing agents

Desloughing agents for ulcers are second-line treatment and the underlying causes should be treated. The main beneficial effect is removal of slough and clot and the ablation of local infection. Preparations which absorb or help promote the removal of exudate may also help (section 13.13.8). It should be noted that substances applied to an open area are easily absorbed and perilesional skin is easily sensitised. Gravitational dermatitis may be due to neomycin or lanolin sensitivity. Enzyme preparations such as streptokinase-streptodornase or alternatively dextranomer (section 13.13.8) are designed for sloughing ulcers and may help.

Aserbine® (Bencard)
Cream, benzoic acid 0.024%, malic acid 0.36%, propylene glycol 1.7%, salicylic acid 0.006%. Net price 100 g = 96p
Additives: chlorocresol, hydroxybenzoates (parabens), propylene glycol
Solution, benzoic acid 0.15%, malic acid 2.25%, propylene glycol 40%, salicylic acid 0.0375%. Net price 500 mL = £1.45
Additives: propylene glycol, fragrance

Hioxyl® (Quinoderm Ltd)
Cream, hydrogen peroxide (stabilised) 1.5%. Net price 25 g = £1.68; 100 g = £5.29; 10 × 10-g sachets = £5.49. For leg ulcers and pressure sores
Additives: none as listed in section 13.1
Apply when necessary and if necessary cover with a dressing

Malatex® (Norton)
Solution, benzoic acid 0.15%, malic acid 2.25%, propylene glycol 40%, salicylic acid 0.0375%. Net price 500 mL = £1.26

Variclene® (Dermal)
Gel, brilliant green 0.5%, lactic acid 0.5%, in an aqueous basis. Net price 50 g = £4.58. For venous and other skin ulcers
Additives: none as listed in section 13.1
Apply to cleaned and dried lesion with a sterile applicator avoiding surrounding skin; in severe ulceration apply on dressing and repeat as required at intervals of not more than 7 days

PoM **Varidase Topical®** (Lederle)
Powder, streptokinase 100 000 units, streptodornase 25 000 units. For preparing solutions for topical use. Net price per vial = £7.09
Additives: none as listed in section 13.1
Apply as wet dressing usually 1–2 times daily
Also used to dissolve clots in the bladder or urinary catheters

13.12 Antiperspirants

Aluminium chloride and hydroxychloride are potent antiperspirants used in the treatment of severe hyperhidrosis.

Dusting-powders are described in section 13.2.3.

ALUMINIUM CHLORIDE

Indications: hyperhidrosis
Cautions: avoid contact with eyes; do not shave axilla or use depilatories within 12 hours of use
Side-effects: skin irritation—may be less with hydroxychloride
Administration: apply at night to dry skin, wash off on following morning, initially daily then reduce frequency as condition improves—do not bathe immediately before use

PoM **Anhydrol Forte®** (Dermal)
Solution (= application), aluminium chloride hexahydrate 20%. Net price 10-mL bottle with roll-on applicator = £2.75
Additives: none as listed in section 13.1
Caution: flammable

PoM **Driclor®** (Stiefel)
Application, aluminium chloride hexahydrate 20% in an alcoholic basis. Net price 60-mL bottle with roll-on applicator = £2.82
Additives: none as listed in section 13.1
Caution: flammable

Hyperdrol® (BritCair)
Cream, aluminium hydroxychloride 19%. Net price 60 g = £3.50
Additives: hydroxybenzoates (parabens), propylene glycol
Gel, aluminium hydroxychloride 19%. Net price 60-g roll-on applicator = £4.50
Additives: none as listed in section 13.1

13.13 Wound management products

13.13.1 Bandages
13.13.2 Surgical adhesive tapes
13.13.3 Adhesive dressings
13.13.4 Surgical absorbents
13.13.5 Wound dressing pads
13.13.6 Tulle dressings
13.13.7 Semipermeable adhesive film
13.13.8 Gel and colloid dressings
13.13.9 Foam dressings

13.13.1 Bandages

RETENTION BANDAGES

Non-stretch fabric retention bandages

Open-wove Bandage, BP (types 1, 2 and 3). Cotton cloth, plain weave, warp of cotton, weft of cotton, viscose, or combination, one continuous length. Type 1, 5 m (all): 2.5 cm, net price = 22p; 5 cm = 37p; 7.5 cm = 53p; 10 cm = 68p (most suppliers) 5 m × 5 cm supplied when size not stated
Uses: protection and retention of absorbent dressings; support for minor strains, sprains; securing splints
Note. Type 1 bandage formerly described as Open-Wove Bandage BPC 1973; Type 2 formerly described as 'medium quality'; Type 3 formerly described as 'hospital quality'

Triangular Calico Bandage, BP. Unbleached calico rt. angle triangle. 90 cm × 90 cm × 1.27 m, net price = 83p (most suppliers)
Uses: sling

NHS **Domette Bandage,** BP. Fabric, plain weave, cotton warp and wool weft (hospital quality also available, all cotton). 5 m (all): 5 cm, net price = 54p; 7.5 cm = 81p; 10 cm = £1.08; 15 cm = £1.61 (Robert Bailey, Vernon-Carus)
Uses: protection and support where warmth required

Multiple Pack Dressing No. 1 (Drug Tariff). Contains absorbent cotton, absorbent cotton gauze type 13 light (sterile), open-wove bandages (banded). Net price per pack = £2.53

Multiple Pack Dressing No. 2 (Drug Tariff). As for No. 1 (above) but with larger quantities of cotton and cotton gauze and two sizes of bandages. Net price per pack = £4.26

Stretch fabric retention bandages

Cotton Conforming Bandage, BP. Cotton fabric, plain weave, treated to impart some elasticity to warp and weft. 3.5 m (all):

type A, 5 cm, net price = 42p, 7.5 cm = 54p, 10 cm = 66p, 15 cm = 90p (S&N—*Crinx*®)
type B, 5 cm = 42p, 7.5 cm = 54p, 10 cm = 66p, 15 cm = 88p (J&J—*Kling*®)
Uses: retention of dressings in difficult positions (e.g. over joints)

Polyamide and Cellulose Contour Bandage, BP (formerly Nylon and Viscose Stretch Bandage). Fabric, plain weave, warp of polyamide filament, weft of cotton or viscose, fast edges, one continuous length. 4 m stretched (all): Robinsons—*Stayform*® (5 cm = 25p, 7.5 cm = 32p, 10 cm = 36p, 15 cm = 62p); Seton—*Slinky*® (net price 5 cm = 31p, 7.5 cm = 43p, 10 cm = 52p, 15 cm = 73p); S&N—*Easifix*® (5 cm = 23p, 7.5 cm = 29p, 10 cm = 33p, 15 cm = 55p)
Uses: retention of dressings

NHS **Tubular Gauze Bandage, Seamless.** Unbleached cotton yarn, positioned with applicators. 20 m roll (all): 00, net price = £1.70; 01 = £1.74; 12 = £2.33; 34 = £3.42; 56 = £4.73; 78 = £5.54; T1 = £7.98; T2 = £10.29 (Seton—*Tubegauz*®)
Uses: retention of dressings on limbs, abdomen, trunk

Elasticated Tubular Bandage, BP (formerly Elasticated Surgical Tubular Stockinette). Knitted fabric, elasticated threads of rubber-cored polyamide or polyester with cotton or cotton and viscose yarn, tubular. Lengths 50 cm and 1 m, various widths 6.25 cm–12 cm, net price 45p–£1.43 (Kendall-Lastonet—*Lastogrip*®; Salt—*Rediform*®; S&N—*Tensogrip*®; Seton—*Tubigrip*®; Texlastic—*Texagrip*®). Where no brand stated by prescriber, net price of stockinette supplied not to exceed: length 50 cm, 6.25 cm = 39p, 6.75 cm = 41p, 7.5 cm = 41p, 8.75 cm = 43p, 10 cm = 43p, 12 cm = 50p; length 1 m, 6.25 cm = 76p, 6.75 cm = 78p, 7.5 cm = 78p, 8.75 cm = 83p, 10 cm = 83p, 12 cm = 94p
Uses: retention of dressings on limbs, abdomen, trunk

Foam Padded Elasticated Surgical Tubular Stockinette (Drug Tariff). Fabric as for Elasticated Tubular Bandage with polyurethane foam lining. Heel, elbow, knee, small, net price = £1.81, medium = £1.95, large = £2.10; sacral, small, medium, and large (all) =£9.29 (Seton—*Tubipad*®)
Uses: relief of pressure and elimination of friction in relevant area; porosity of foam lining allows normal water loss from skin surface

Elasticated Viscose Stockinette (Drug Tariff). Lightweight plain-knitted elasticated tubular bandage. Length 1 m (all): net price 5 cm (medium limb) = 59p; 7.5 cm (large limb) = 77p; 10.75 cm (OS limb, head, child trunk) = £1.24; 17.5 cm (adult trunk) = £1.56 (Seton—*Tubifast*®)
Uses: retention of dressings

Elastic Net Surgical Tubular Stockinette (Drug Tariff). Lightweight elastic open-work net tubular fabric.
type A: arm/leg, 40 cm × 1.8 cm (size C), net price = 32p; thigh/head, 60 cm × 2.5 cm (size E) = 58p; trunk (adult), 60 cm × 4.5 cm (size F) = 85p; trunk (OS adult) 60 cm × 5.4 cm (size G) = £1.14 (Lenton—*Netelast*®)
type B: withdrawn
type C: arm/leg, 40 cm × 1.8 cm (size C) = 25p; thigh/head, 60 cm × 2.7 cm (size E) = 48p; trunk (adult), 60 cm × 5.5 cm (size F) = 67p; trunk (OS adult) 60 cm × 6 cm (size G) = 85p (Macarthys—*Macrofix*®)
Drug Tariff requires size and type to be specified by prescriber
Uses: retention of dressings, particularly on awkward sites

Cotton Stockinette, BP (formerly Cotton Surgical Tubular Stockinette). Knitted fabric, cotton yarn, tubular. 1 m × 2.5 cm, net price = 18p; 5 cm = 28p; 7.5 cm = 35p; 6 m × 10 cm = £2.40 (J&J, Seton)
Uses: 1 m lengths, basis (with wadding) for Plaster of Paris bandages etc.; 6 m length, compression bandage

Ribbed Cotton and Viscose Surgical Tubular Stockinette, BP. Knitted fabric of 1:1 ribbed structure, singles yarn spun from blend of two-thirds cotton and one third viscose fibres, tubular. Length 5 m (all):
type A (lightweight): arm/leg (child), arm (adult) 5 cm, net price = £1.58; arm (OS adult), leg (adult) 7.5 cm = £2.05; leg (OS adult) 10 cm = £2.72; trunk (child) 15 cm = £3.92; trunk (adult) 20 cm = £4.52; trunk (OS adult) 25 cm = £5.42 (Seton)
type B (heavyweight): sizes as for type A, net price £1.47–£5.04 (Sallis—*Eesiban*®)
Drug Tariff specifies various combinations of sizes to provide sufficient material for part or full body coverage
Uses: protective dressings with tar-based and other non-steroid ointments

SUPPORT AND COMPRESSION BANDAGES

Non-adhesive woven extensible bandages

Crepe Bandage, BP. Fabric, plain weave, warp of wool threads and crepe-twisted cotton threads, weft of cotton threads; stretch bandage. 4.5 m stretched (all): 5 cm, net price = 64p; 7.5 cm = 88p; 10 cm = £1.16; 15 cm = £1.66 (most suppliers)
Uses: light support system for strains, sprains, compression over paste bandages for varicose veins

Cotton Crepe Bandage, BP. Fabric, plain weave, warp of crepe-twisted cotton threads, weft of cotton and/or viscose threads; stretch bandage. 4.5 m stretched (both): 7.5 cm, net price = £1.89; 10 cm = £2.44; other sizes NHS (most suppliers)
Uses: light support system for strains, sprains, compression over paste bandages for varicose ulcers

NHS **Cotton Stretch Bandage,** BP. Fabric, plain weave, warp of crepe-twisted cotton threads, weft of cotton threads; stretch bandage, lighter than cotton crepe. 4.5 m stretched (all): 5 cm, net price = 30p; 7.5 cm = 41p; 10 cm = 54p; 15 cm = 76p (most suppliers)
Uses: light support system for strains, sprains, compression over paste bandages for varicose veins

Cotton Suspensory Bandage (Drug Tariff). Type 1: cotton net bag with draw tapes and webbing waistband; net price small, medium, and large (all) = £1.07, extra large = £1.11. Type 2: cotton net bag with elastic edge and webbing waistband; small = £1.17, medium = £1.21, large = £1.25, extra large = £1.31. Type 3: cotton net bag with elastic edge and webbing waistband with elastic insertion; small, medium, and large (all) = £1.27; extra large = £1.31
Type supplied to be endorsed
Uses: support of scrotum

NHS **Cotton and Rubber Elastic Bandage,** BP. Fabric, plain weave, warp of combined cotton and rubber threads, weft of cotton threads (S&N)
Uses: provision of high compression and medium support

Heavy Cotton and Rubber Elastic Bandage, BP. Heavy version of above with one end folded as foot loop; fastener also supplied. 1.8 m unstretched × 7.5 cm, net price = £8.12 (Marlow, Seton, S&N—*Elastoweb*®).
Uses: provision of high even compression over large surface

Elastic Web Bandage, BP. (also termed Blue Line Webbing). Characteristic fabric woven ribbon fashion, warp threads of cotton and rubber with mid-line threads coloured blue, weft threads of cotton or combined cotton and viscose; may be dyed skin colour; with or without foot loop. Per m (both): 7.5 cm, net price = 61p; 10 cm = 85p; with foot loop 7.5 cm each = £3.21 (Marlow, Seton)
Uses: provision of support and high compression over large surface

Elastic Web Bandage without Foot Loop (also termed Red Line Webbing) (Scott-Curwen). Characteristic fabric woven ribbon fashion, warp threads of cotton and rubber with mid-line threads coloured red, weft threads of cotton or combined cotton and viscose.

7.5 cm × 2.75 m (2.5 m approx. unstretched), net price = £2.85; 7.5 cm × 3.75 m (3.5 m approx. unstretched) = £3.45
Uses: provision of support and high compression over large surfaces

Adhesive woven extensible bandages

Titanium Dioxide Elastic Adhesive Bandage, BP. (Drug Tariff title: Porous Flexible Adhesive Bandage). Woven fabric, elastic in warp (crepe-twisted cotton threads), weft of cotton and/or viscose threads, spread with adhesive mass containing titanium dioxide but free from rubber and zinc oxide. 4.5 m stretched × 7.5 cm, net price = £2.99 (Scholl—*Poroplast*®)
Uses: compression for chronic leg ulcers; continuous pressure and support in patients hypersensitive to rubber and zinc oxide.

Elastic Adhesive Bandage, BP. Woven fabric, elastic in warp (crepe-twisted cotton threads), weft of cotton and/ or viscose threads spread with adhesive mass containing zinc oxide. 4.5 m stretched (all): 5 cm, net price = £2.21; 7.5 cm = £3.23; 10 cm = £4.30 (Robinsons—*Flexoplast*®; S&N—*Elastoplast*® Bandage). 7.5 cm width supplied when size not stated
Uses: compression for chronic leg ulcers; compression and support for fractured ribs, clavicles, swollen or sprained joints

NHS **Half-spread Elastic Adhesive Bandage,** BP. Fabric as for elastic adhesive bandage but only partially spread with adhesive. (S&N)
Uses: compression for leg ulcers; compression and support for fractured ribs, clavicles, swollen/sprained joints

NHS **Ventilated Elastic Adhesive Bandage,** BP. Fabric as for elastic adhesive bandage but adhesive spread such that there are regular strips of unspread fabric along length. (S&N)
Uses: compression for leg ulcers; compression and support for fractured ribs, clavicles, swollen/sprained joints

NHS **Extension Plaster,** BP. Woven fabric, elastic in weft, spread with adhesive mass containing zinc oxide, warp threads cotton and/or viscose, weft threads crepe-twisted cotton. (S&N)
Uses: support of light strains, joints and limbs removed from plaster casts, fractured ribs; traction bandaging

NHS Cohesive extensible bandages.

These elastic bandages adhere to themselves and not to the patient's skin, which prevents slipping during use. 2.25 m (both): 5 cm, 10 cm; 4.5 m (all): 5 cm, 7.5 cm, 10 cm, 15 cm (Boots, 3M—*Coban*®, J&J—*Secure*®, Seton, Steriseal—*Cohepress*®)
Uses: support of sprained joints

MEDICATED BANDAGES

Zinc Paste Bandage, BP. Cotton fabric, plain weave, impregnated with suitable paste containing zinc oxide; requires additional bandaging. Net price 6m × 7.5 cm = £1.99 (Seton—*Zincaband*®); £2.11 (S&N—*Viscopaste PB7*®, *additives:*hydroxybenzoates)

Zinc Paste and Calamine Bandage (Drug Tariff). Cotton fabric, plain weave, impregnated with suitable paste containing calamine and zinc oxide; requires additional bandaging. Net price 6 m × 7.5 cm = £2.23 (Seton—*Calaband*®)

Zinc Paste, Calamine, and Clioquinol Bandage, BP. Cotton fabric, plain weave, impregnated with suitable paste containing calamine, clioquinol, and zinc oxide; requires additional bandaging. Net price 6 m × 7.5 cm = £2.23 (Seton—*Quinaband*®, *additives:* hydroxybenzoates)

Zinc Paste and Coal Tar Bandage, BP. Cotton fabric, plain weave, impregnated with a suitable paste containing coal tar and zinc oxide; requires additional bandaging. Net price 6 m × 7.5 cm = £2.15 (Seton—*Tarband*®, *additives:* hydroxybenzoates; S&N—*Coltapaste*®, *additives:* wool fat)
Uses: see section 13.5

Zinc Paste and Ichthammol Bandage, BP. Cotton fabric, plain weave, impregnated with suitable paste containing ichthammol and zinc oxide; requires additional bandaging. Net price 6 m × 7.5 cm = £2.12 (Seton—*Icthaband*®, *additives:* hydroxybenzoates; S&N—*Ichthopaste*®, *additives:* none as listed in section 13.1)
Uses: see section 13.5

13.13.2 Surgical adhesive tapes

PERMEABLE SURGICAL ADHESIVE TAPES

Zinc Oxide Surgical Adhesive Tape, BP. (Zinc Oxide Plaster). Fabric, plain weave, warp and weft of cotton and/or viscose, spread with an adhesive containing zinc oxide. 1.25 cm, net price 1 m = 20p, 3 m = 41p, 5 m = 57p; 2.5 cm, 1 m = 27p, 3 m = 62p, 5 m = 84p; 5 cm × 5 m = £1.42; 7.5 cm × 5 m = £2.01 (most suppliers)
Drug Tariff specifies 1 m × 2.5 cm supplied when size not stated
Uses: securing dressings and immobilising small areas

Permeable Woven Surgical Synthetic Adhesive Tape, BP. Non-extensible closely woven fabric, spread with a polymeric adhesive. 5 m (all): 1.25 cm, net price = 63p; 2.5 cm = 91p; 5 cm = £1.60 (Beiersdorf—*Leukosilk*®; J&J—*Dermicel*®)
Uses: securing dressings
For patients with skin reaction to other plasters and strapping, requiring use for long periods

Elastic Surgical Adhesive Tape, BP (Elastic Adhesive Plaster). Woven fabric, elastic in warp (crepe-twisted cotton threads), weft of cotton and/or viscose threads, spread with adhesive mass containing zinc oxide. 1.5 m stretched × 2.5 cm, net price = 55p; 4.5 m stretched × 2.5 cm = £1.04 (Robinsons—*Flexoplast*®; S&N—*Elastoplast* ®)
Uses: securing dressings
For 5 cm width, see Elastic Adhesive Bandage, section 13.13.1

Permeable Non-woven Surgical Synthetic Adhesive Tape, BP. Backing of paper-based or non-woven textile material spread with a polymeric adhesive mass. 5 m (all): Associated Hospital Supply—*Scanpor*® (net price 1.25 cm = 34p, 2.5 cm = 54p, 5 cm = 96p); Beiersdorf—*Leukopor*® (1.25 cm = 39p, 2.5 cm = 61p, 5 cm = £1.07); J&J—*Dermilite*® (1.25 cm = 46p, 2.5 cm = 72p, 5 cm = £1.28); 3M—*Micropore*® (1.25 cm = 43p, 2.5 cm = 67p, 5 cm = £1.19); S&N—*Hypal 2*® (1.25 cm = 46p, 2.5 cm = 71p, 5 cm = £1.29)
Where no brand stated by prescriber, net price of tape supplied not to exceed 34p (1.25 cm), 54p (2.5 cm), 96p (5 cm)
Uses: securing dressings; skin closures for small incisions
For patients with skin reaction to other plasters and strapping, requiring use for long periods

NHS **Permeable Plastic Surgical Adhesive Tape,** BP. Extensible perforated plastic film spread with an adhesive mass; permeable to air and water (most suppliers)
Uses: securing dressings and appliances; covering sites of infection; allows immersion in water without loss of adhesion

SEMIPERMEABLE SURGICAL ADHESIVE TAPES

NHS **Semipermeable Waterproof Plastic Surgical Adhesive Tape,** BP. Extensible water-impermeable, air and water-vapour permeable plastic film spread with an adhesive mass. (3M; J&J; S&N)

Uses: covering dressings and appliances where free passage of air and water-vapour but exclusion of water required; covering possible sites of infection; preparation of waterproof, microporous plastic wound dressings

OCCLUSIVE SURGICAL ADHESIVE TAPES

Impermeable Plastic Surgical Adhesive Tape, BP. Extensible water-impermeable plastic film spread with an adhesive mass. 2.5 cm × 1 m, net price = 36p; 3 m = 79p; 5 m = £1.18; 5 cm × 5 m = £1.52; 7.5 cm × 5 m = £2.19 (Robinsons; Seton; S&N)
Uses: securing dressings; covering site of infection where exclusion of air, water, and water vapour is required

Impermeable Plastic Surgical Synthetic Adhesive Tape, BP. Extensible water-impermeable plastic film spread with a polymeric adhesive mass. 5 m (both): net price, 2.5 cm = £1.09; 5 cm = £2.07 (3M—*Blenderm*®)
Uses: isolating wounds from external environment; covering sites where total exclusion of water and water vapour required; securing dressings and appliances

13.13.3 Adhesive dressings

(also termed Island dressings)

PERMEABLE ADHESIVE DRESSINGS

NHS **Elastic Adhesive Dressing,** BP. Wound dressing or dressing strip, pad attached to piece of extension plaster, leaving suitable adhesive margin; both pad and margin covered with suitable protector; pad may be dyed yellow and may be impregnated with suitable antiseptic (see below); extension plaster may be perforated or ventilated (most suppliers)
Uses: general purpose wound dressing
Note. Permitted antiseptics are aminacrine hydrochloride, chlorhexidine hydrochloride (both 0.07–0.13%), chlorhexidine gluconate (0.11–0.20%); domiphen bromide (0.05–0.25%)

NHS **Permeable Plastic Wound Dressing,** BP. Consisting of an absorbent pad, which may be dyed and impregnated with a suitable antiseptic (see under Elastic Adhesive Dressing), attached to a piece of permeable plastic surgical adhesive tape, to leave a suitable adhesive margin; both pad and margin covered with suitable protector (most suppliers)
Uses: general purpose wound dressing, permeable to air and water

SEMIPERMEABLE ADHESIVE DRESSINGS

Semipermeable Waterproof Plastic Wound Dressing, BP. Consists of absorbent pad, may be dyed and impregnated with suitable antiseptic (see under Elastic Adhesive Dressing), attached to piece of semipermeable waterproof surgical adhesive tape, to leave suitable adhesive margin; both pad and margin covered with suitable protector. 8.5 cm × 6 cm, net price = 23p (S&N—*Airstrip*®)
Uses: general purpose waterproof wound dressing, permeable to air and water vapour

OCCLUSIVE ADHESIVE DRESSINGS

NHS **Impermeable Plastic Wound Dressing,** BP. Consists of absorbent pad, may be dyed and impregnated with suitable antiseptic (see under Elastic Adhesive Dressing), attached to piece of impermeable plastic surgical adhesive tape, to leave suitable adhesive margin; both pad and margin covered with suitable protector (most suppliers)
Uses: protective covering for wounds requiring an occlusive dressing

13.13.4 Surgical absorbents

Absorbent Cotton, BP. Carded cotton fibres of not less than 10 mm average staple length, available in rolls and balls. 25 g, net price = 43p; 100 g = 99p; 500 g = £3.43 (most suppliers). 25-g pack to be supplied when weight not stated
Uses: cleansing and swabbing wounds, pre-operative skin preparation, application of medicaments; supplementary absorbent pad to absorb excess wound exudate

Absorbent Cotton, Hospital Quality. As for absorbent cotton but lower quality materials, shorter staple length etc. 100 g, net price = 69p; 500 g = £2.31 (most suppliers)
Drug Tariff specifies to be supplied only where specifically ordered
Uses: suitable only as general purpose absorbent, for swabbing, and routine cleansing of incontinent patients; not for wound cleansing

Gauze and Cotton Tissue, BP. Consists of absorbent cotton enclosed in absorbent cotton gauze type 12 or absorbent cotton and viscose gauze type 2. 500 g, net price = £4.57 (most suppliers)
Uses: absorbent and protective pad, as burns dressing on non-adherent layer

Gauze and Cotton Tissue (Drug Tariff). Similar to above. 500 g, net price = £3.42 (most suppliers)
Drug Tariff specifies to be supplied only where specifically ordered
Uses: absorbent and protective pad, as burns dressing on non-adherent layer

Absorbent Lint, BPC. Cotton cloth of plain weave with nap raised on one side from warp yarns. 25 g, net price = 56p; 100 g = £1.75; 500 g = £7.37 (most suppliers). 25-g pack supplied where no quantity stated
Uses: external absorbent protective dressing

Absorbent Cotton Gauze, BP. Cotton fabric of plain weave, in rolls and as swabs (see below), usually Type 13 light, sterile. 90 cm (all) × 1 m, net price = 70p; 3 m = £1.46; 5 m = £2.28; 10 m = £4.41 (most suppliers). 1-m packet supplied when no size stated
Uses: pre-operative preparation, for cleansing and swabbing
Note. Drug Tariff also includes unsterilised absorbent cotton gauze, 25 m roll, net price = £9.77

Cellulose Wadding, BP. Delignified wood pulp bleached white, in multiple laminate form. 500 g, net price = £1.79 (most suppliers, including Robinsons—*Cellosene*®)
Uses: absorbing large volumes of fluid

Gauze and Cellulose Wadding Tissue, BP. Consists of thick layer of cellulose wadding enclosed in absorbent cotton gauze type 12 or absorbent cotton and viscose gauze type 2. 500 g, net price = £2.19 (most suppliers)
Uses: absorbing large volumes of fluid

NHS **Absorbent Muslin,** BP. Fabric of plain weave, warp threads of cotton, weft threads of cotton and/or viscose (most suppliers)
Uses: wet dressing, soaked in 0.9% sterile sodium chloride solution

NHS **Absorbent Cotton Ribbon Gauze,** BP. Cotton fabric of plain weave in ribbon form with fast selvedge edges (most suppliers)
Uses: post-surgery cavity packing for sinus, dental, throat cavities etc.

Absorbent Cotton and Viscose Ribbon Gauze, BP. Woven fabric in ribbon form with fast selvedge edges, warp threads of cotton, weft threads of viscose or combined cotton and viscose yarn, sterile. 5 m (both) × 1.25 cm, net price = 49p; 2.5 cm = 56p (most suppliers)
Uses: post-surgery cavity packing for sinus, dental, throat cavities etc.

Gauze Swab, BP. Consists of absorbent cotton gauze type 13 light or absorbent cotton and viscose gauze type 1 folded into squares or rectangles of 8-ply with no cut edges exposed. Sterile, 7.5 cm square, net price 5-pad packet = 25p; non-sterile, 10 cm square 100-pad packet = £4.25 (most suppliers)

Filmated Gauze Swab, BP. As for Gauze Swab, but with thin layer of Absorbent Cotton enclosed within. Non-sterile, 10 cm × 10 cm, net price 100-pad packet = £5.25 (Vernon-Carus—*Cotfil*®)
Uses: general swabbing and cleansing

Non-woven Swab (Drug Tariff). Consists of non-woven viscose fabric folded 4-ply; alternative to gauze swabs, type 13 light. Sterile, 7.5 cm square, net price 5-pad packet = 21p; non-sterile, 10 cm square, 100-pad packet = £2.69 (J&J—*Topper 8*®)
Uses: general purpose swabbing and cleansing; absorbs more quickly than gauze

Non-woven Filmated Swab (Drug Tariff). Film of viscose fibres enclosed within non-woven viscose fabric folded 8-ply. Non-sterile, 10 cm square, net price 100-pad packet = £3.67 (J&J—*Regal*®)
Uses: general purpose swabbing and cleansing

13.13.5 Wound dressing pads

Perforated Film Absorbent Dressing, BP. Low-adherence dressing consisting of 3 layers; wound-facing layer, film of poly-(ethylene terephthalate) perforated in regular pattern; absorbent middle layer of type 1 consists of non-woven bleached cotton and viscose fibres or mixture of these with polyacrylonitrile fibres; in type 2 (NHS) middle layer consists of bleached cotton fibres; backing layer of type 1 is apertured non-woven cellulose material; in type 2, the backing layer is identical with wound-facing layer. Type 1, 5 cm × 5 cm, net price, each = 8p; 10 cm × 10 cm = 17p; 20 × 10 cm = 31p (S&N—*Melolin*® (type 1); Kendall—*Telfa*® (type 2)). 5 cm size supplied where size not stated
Uses: dressing for post-operative and low exudate wounds; low adherence property and low absorption capacity

Knitted Viscose Primary Dressing, BP. (Drug Tariff title: Sterile Knitted Viscose Dressing). Warp knitted fabric manufactured from a bright viscose monofilament. 9.5 cm × 9.5 cm (both): net price = 23p (J&J—*N-A Dressing*®); net price = 18p (S&N—*Tricotex*®)
Uses: low adherence wound contact layer for use on ulcerative and other granulating wounds with superimposed absorbent pad

Sterile Dressing Pack (Drug Tariff specification 10). Contains gauze and cotton tissue pad, gauze swabs, absorbent cotton balls, absorbent paper towel, water repellent inner wrapper. Net price per pack = 55p

Sterile Dressing Pack with Non-woven Pads (Drug Tariff specification 35). Contains non-woven fabric covered dressing pad (*Surgipad*®), non-woven fabric swabs (*Topper 8*®), absorbent cotton wool balls, absorbent paper towel, water repellent inner wrapper. Net price per pack = 54p

NHS* **Surgipad**®. Absorbent pad of absorbent cotton and viscose in sleeve of non-woven viscose fabric (J&J)
Uses: for heavily exuding wounds requiring frequent dressing changes
* Except in Sterile Dressing Pack with Non-woven Pads (see above)

NHS **Perfron**®. Absorbent pad consisting of alternate layers of absorbent cotton and crepe cellulose tissue, in sleeve of non-woven viscose fabric with coating of polypropylene (J&J)
Uses: low adherence pad for heavily exuding wounds; laminate structure delays strike through

NHS **Melolite**®. Absorbent fabric pad covered on both sides by polyethylene net (S&N)
Uses: primary dressing over clean sutured wounds, lacerations, and abrasions

NHS **Mesorb**®. Cellulose wadding pad with gauze wound contact layer and non-woven water repellent backing (Molnlycke)
Uses: post-operative dressing for heavily exuding wounds

NHS **Ete**®. Wound pad of rayon wadding with rayon silk wound contact layer stitched in chequered pattern (Molnlycke)
Uses: leg wounds, decubitus ulcers, minor burns, donor sites

NHS **Release II**®. Two layered knitted construction of bright viscose in non-woven, non-adherent sleeve. Pack of 100 (all): 5 cm × 5 cm, net price = £5.23; 10 cm × 10 cm = £11.50; 10 cm × 20 cm = £18.93 (J&J)
Uses: high absorbency, low adherence wound contact dressing

Charcoal cloth dressings

Uses: to deodorise discharging, infected, malodorous wounds and ulcers

NHS **Actisorb Plus**®. Knitted fabric of activated charcoal, with one-way stretch, with silver residues, within spun-bonded nylon sleeve. Net price (each) 10.5 cm × 10.5 cm = £1.37; 19 cm × 10.5 cm = £2.66 (J&J)

NHS **Carbonet**®. Activated charcoal dressing. 10 cm × 10 cm, net price, each = £1.56; 10 cm × 20 cm = £3.05 (S&N)

NHS **Carbosorb**®. Outer cover of non-woven polyester-nylon fabric, activated charcoal cloth layer bonded to outer cover and semipermeable polyurethane film contact layer (Seton)

NHS **CliniFlex**® **Odour Control Dressings**. Layer of activated charcoal cloth between viscose rayon with outer polyamide coating. Net price 10 cm × 10 cm, 10 = £12.00; 10 cm × 20 cm, 10 = £16.00; 15 cm × 25 cm, 10 = £26.00 (CliniMed)

NHS **Lyofoam C**®. Lyofoam sheet with layer of activated charcoal cloth and additional outer envelope of polyurethane foam. 10 cm × 10 cm, net price, each = £1.26; 15 cm × 20 cm = £2.80 (Ultra)

13.13.6 Tulle dressings

Non-medicated tulle dressings

Paraffin Gauze Dressing, BP. Fabric of leno weave, weft and warp threads of cotton and/or viscose yarn, impregnated with white or yellow soft paraffin; sterile. 10 cm × 10 cm, net price, each = 23p; pack of 10 pieces = £1.62 (most suppliers including Seton—*Paratulle*®; Roussel—*Unitulle*®; S&N—*Jelonet*®)
Uses: treatment of abrasions, burns, and other injuries of skin, and ulcerative conditions; post-operatively as penial and vaginal dressing and for sinus packing; heavier loading for skin graft transfer

Medicated tulle dressings

Chlorhexidine Gauze Dressing, BP. Fabric of leno weave, weft and warp threads of cotton and/or viscose yarn, impregnated with ointment containing chlorhexidine acetate; sterile. 5 cm × 5 cm, net price = 17p; 10 cm × 10 cm = 35p (Seton—*Serotulle*®; Roussel—*Clorhexitulle*®; S&N—*Bactigras*®)

PoM **Framycetin Gauze Dressing**, BP. Fabric of leno weave, weft and warp threads of cotton, impregnated with ointment containing framycetin sulphate 1% in white soft paraffin containing 10% wool fat; sterile. 10 cm × 10 cm, net price = 24p; NHS 10 cm × 30 cm, 10 = £8.45 (Roussel—*Sofra-Tulle*®)

PoM **Sodium Fusidate Gauze Dressing**, BP. Leno weave cotton gauze impregnated with ointment containing sodium fusidate 2% in white soft paraffin and wool fat. 10 cm × 10 cm, net price = 22p (Leo—*Fucidin Intertulle*®)

Povidone-Iodine Fabric Dressing. Knitted viscose primary dressing impregnated with povidone-iodine oint-

ment 10%. 5 cm × 5 cm, net price, each = 17p; 9.5 cm × 9.5 cm = 31p (J&J—*Inadine*®)
Uses: wound contact layer for abrasions and superficial burns; max. 4 dressings at same time

13.13.7 Semipermeable adhesive film

Semipermeable Adhesive Film, BP. Sterile, extensible, waterproof, water vapour-permeable polyurethane film coated with synthetic adhesive mass; transparent. Supplied in single-use pieces. Type 1: 10 cm × 10 cm, net price = 99p (S&N—*Opsite*® Flexigrid), Type 2: 10 cm × 12 cm, net price = 94p (3M—*Tegaderm*®). Type 3: 10.2 cm × 12.7 cm, net price = 93p (J&J—*Bioclusive*®)
Uses: post-operative dressing, donor sites, IV sites, superficial decubitus ulcers, amputation stumps, stoma care; protective cover to prevent skin breakdown

NHS **Dermoclude**®. Sterile, water-vapour permeable, transparent copolymer film. Supplied in single-use pieces. Pack of 25 (both): 10 cm × 10 cm, net price per pack = £19.75; 15 cm × 20 cm, £56.25 (BritCair).
Uses: cuts, grazes, minor burns and scalds, pressure sores, superficial leg ulcers

NHS **Flexipore 6000**®. Sterile, water-vapour permeable polyurethane film. Net price 10 cm × 10 cm, 50 = £92.50; 10 cm × 30 cm, 20 = £99.00; 15 cm × 20 cm, 20 = £99.00; 20 cm × 30 cm, 10 = £99.00 (CliniMed)
Uses: donor sites, superficial burns, cuts, grazes, orthopaedic surgery

NHS **Omiderm**®. Sterile, adherent, water-vapour permeable polyurethane film. Net price 5 cm × 7 cm, net price 20 = £23.00; 8 cm × 10 cm, 20 = £49.00; 18 cm × 10 cm, 25 = £121.25; 60 cm × 10 cm, 10 = £138.00; 21 cm × 31 cm, 5 = £72.50 (Perstorp)
Uses: donor sites; superficial and partial thickness burns

NHS **Transite Film Dressing**®. Primary exudate transfer film composed of two layers which allow excess exudate to pass to secondary absorbent dressing through fine slits which narrow again when exudation decreases. Pack of 10 (all): 10 cm × 10 cm, net price = 79p; 15 cm × 20 cm = £1.24; 30 cm × 40 cm = £2.36 (S&N)
Uses: donor sites; partial and full thickness burns

13.13.8 Gel and colloid dressings

Occlusive or semi-occlusive dressings which adhere to dry skin and interact with moisture in the wound to form a gel; may remain on a wound for up to 7 days.

Hydrogels

NHS **Bard Absorption Dressing**®. A dry polysaccharide derivative in flake form which is mixed with water and applied directly into the wound. 60-g pack
Uses: treatment of wounds and ulcers.

Debrisan®. Spherical beads of dextranomer packed in plastic castors, single-use sachets, paste or pads. Beads sprinkled onto cleansed wound and covered with a suitable non-woven, adhesive, semi-occlusive covering, or sterile dressing. Alternatively paste or pad is applied and covered in similar manner. Beads, net price 4-g sachet = £1.99, 60 g = £29.75; paste in sachets, 4 × 10 g = £20.40; pads, 3 g sachet = £2.36 (Pharmacia)
Uses: debriding agent to remove necrotic tissue

NHS **Geliperm**®. Gel sheets, dry and wet forms; tubed granulated gel. Dry, 11 cm × 25 cm, net price, 6 sheets = £51.23; granulate, 20 g, 6 tubes = £20.82, 50 g, 6 tubes = £52.04. Wet, 10 cm × 10 cm, net price, 20 sheets = £44.85, 12 cm × 13 cm, 6 sheets = £25.62; 12 cm × 26 cm, 6 sheets = £51.23 (Geistlich)
Uses: wound and ulcer dressing, burns, donor sites

PoM **Iodosorb**® Microbeads of cadexomer iodine (modified starch gel containing iodine 0.9%). Net price 3-g sachet = £2.07; also Iodosorb® Ointment, 4 × 10 g = £17.40 (Perstorp)
Uses: for venous leg ulcers and pressure sores apply 3 mm layer to wound surface and renew daily or when saturated with exudate

NHS **Kaltocarb**®. Dressing in 3 layers: wound-facing layer of calcium alginate fibre; absorbent middle layer of activated charcoal cloth; backing layer of bonded polyester and viscose non-woven material. Net price 7.5 cm × 12 cm each = £1.50 (BritCair)
Uses: discharging infected malodorous wounds and ulcers

NHS **Kaltoclude**®. Calcium alginate fibre bonded to semipermeable copolymer adhesive film. Pack of 25 (both); 10 cm × 10 cm, net price per pack = £32.00; 15 cm × 20 cm = £87.50 (BritCair)
Uses: light to moderately exuding wounds such as leg ulcers and pressure sores

Kaltostat®. (Drug Tariff title: Calcium Alginate Dressing, type 2). Calcium alginate fibre, flat non-woven pads, 5 cm × 5 cm, net price, each = 50p; 7.5 cm × 12 cm = £1.22; other sizes (NHS) 10 cm × 20 cm, 25 = £49.75; 15 cm × 25 cm, 25 = £91.50; wound packing, 2 g, 25 = £29.75 (BritCair)
Uses: haemostatic

Scherisorb® **Gel.** A ready-mixed hydrogel containing Graft T® starch copolymer applied directly into the wound. 15-g sachet, net price = £1.40 (S&N)

Sorbsan® (Drug Tariff title: Calcium Alginate Dressing, type 1). Calcium alginate fibre, highly absorbent, flat non-woven pads, 5 cm × 5 cm, net price, each = 77p; 10 cm × 10 cm = £1.22; other sizes (NHS) 10 cm × 20 cm, 5 = £18.00; surgical packing 30 cm, 5 = £19.50; ribbon, 40 cm (+12.5-cm probe), 5 = £12.50; also (bonded to a secondary absorbent viscose pad) Sorbsan® + (NHS), 7.5 cm × 10 cm, 5 = £9.95; 10 cm × 15 cm, 5 = £18.25 (Steriseal)
Uses: heavily to moderately exudating wounds

NHS **Sorbsan**® **SA** Calcium alginate fibre, highly absorbent flat non-woven pads for wound contact bonded to adhesive semipermeable polyurethane foam. Net price 9 cm × 11 cm, 5 = £9.50 (Steriseal)
Uses: moderately to lightly exudating shallow wounds

NHS **Vigilon**®. Semi-permeable hydrogel sheets on a polyethylene mesh support. Sterile, 3 in × 6 in, net price 10 = £35.50, 4 in × 4 in, 10 = £35.50; non-sterile, 4 in × 4 in, 10 = £24.75, 13 in × 24 in, 2 = £43.00 (Seton)

Hydrocolloids

NHS **Biofilm**®. Hydrocolloid dressing with non-woven fibre backing; also in powder form for direct application into wound: 10 cm × 10 cm, net price 10 = £16.50; 20 cm × 20 cm, 5 = £28.50; powder, 10 sachets = £18.20 (CliniMed)

Comfeel®. Soft elastic pad consisting of carmellose sodium particles embedded in adhesive mass; smooth outer layer and polyurethane film backing; available as sheets, powder in plastic blister units and paste for direct application into the wound: ulcer dressing, 10 cm × 10 cm, net price each = £1.64; other sizes (NHS) 4 cm × 6 cm, 30 = £22.20; 15 cm × 15 cm, 5 = £20.05; 20 cm × 20 cm, 5 = £32.45; transparent dressing, 5 cm × 7 cm, 10 = £9.70; 9 cm × 14 cm, 10 = £28.60; 15 cm × 20 cm, 5 = £32.15; powder 6 g, 10 = £24.80; paste 12-g sachet, 10 = £9.50, 50-g tube, 10 = £36.60 (Coloplast)

NHS **Dermiflex**®. Hydrocolloid dressing bonded to PVC foam 10.2 cm × 10.2 cm, net price, each = £1.95 (J&J)

Granuflex®. Hydrocolloid wound contact layer bonded to plastic foam layer, with outer impermeable plastic film. 10 cm × 10 cm, net price each = £1.77; other sizes (NHS), 15 cm × 20 cm, 3 = £14.64, 20 cm × 20 cm, 3 = £18.11, 15 cm × 15 cm with adhesive foam border, 5 = £19.47; also Granuflex® Extra Thin (NHS), 7.5 cm × 7.5 cm, 5 = £5.05; 10 cm × 10 cm, 5 = £6.91; 15 cm × 15 cm, 5 = £15.58; 5 cm × 10 cm, 10 = £6.92; 5 cm × 20

cm, 10 = £13.82; also Granuflex® Transparent, 5 cm × 7.5 cm, 10 = £4.05; 10 cm × 10 cm, 10 = £10.71; 15 cm × 20 cm, 10 = £30.24; also Granuflex® Compression Bandage (NHS), 10 cm × 6.5 m, 6 = £32.62; also Granuflex Paste (NHS), net price 30 g = £2.61 (Convatec)
Uses: chronic ulcers, pressure sores, open wounds, debridement of wounds; powders and pastes used with sheet dressings to fill deep or heavily exudating wounds

Varihesive®. Wafers containing gelatin 20%, pectin 20%, polyisobutylene 40%, carmellose sodium 20%. 10 cm × 10 cm, net price 5 dressings = £7.40 (Convatec)
Uses: wound dressing for leg ulcers

13.13.9 Foam dressings

Polyurethane Foam Dressing, BP. Absorbent foam dressing of low adherence; sterile. 7.5 cm × 7.5 cm, net price, each = 63p; 10 cm × 10 cm, each = 75p; other sizes (NHS) 10 cm × 17.5 cm, 25 = £31.68; 15 cm × 20 cm, 20 = £34.46; 10 cm × 25 cm, 35 = £58.05; 25 cm × 30 cm, each = £3.91 (Ultra—*Lyofoam®*)
Uses: treatment of burns, decubitus ulcers, donor sites, granulating wounds

NHS **Allevyn®**. Hydrophilic polyurethane dressing; foam sheets with trilaminate structure, non-adherent wound contact layer, foam based central layer, bacteria and waterproof outer layer. 10 cm × 10 cm, each = £2.95 (S&N)
Uses: treatment of heavily exuding wounds, specifically venous leg ulcers

NHS **Silicone Foam Cavity Wound Dressing**, BP. Soft slightly absorbent wound dressing of low adherence prepared from fluid silicone elastomer base and tin (II) 2-ethylhexanoate by mixing thoroughly for 15 seconds immediately before use and allowing to expand to about 4 times its volume within the wound. Foam dressing, 20 g, net price = £5.10; 500 g = £83.43; gel sheeting, 12 cm × 15 cm, 10 = £77.50 (Dow Corning—*Silastic®*)
Uses: in the managment of open granulating wounds such as pressure sores, abdominal wall breakdown, pilonidal sinus excision

13.14 Topical circulatory preparations

These preparations are used to improve circulation in conditions such as bruising, superficial thrombophlebitis, chilblains and varicose veins but are of little value. Chilblains are best managed by avoidance of exposure to cold; neither systemic nor topical vasodilator therapy is recommended. Sclerotherapy of varicose veins is described in section 2.13.

Rubefacients are described in section 10.3.2.

Hirudoid® (Panpharma)
Cream, heparinoid 0.3% in a vanishing-cream basis. Net price 40 g = £1.90
Additives: hydroxybenzoates (parabens)
Gel, heparinoid 0.3%. Net price 40 g = £1.90
Additives: propylene glycol, fragrance
Apply up to 4 times daily in superficial soft-tissue injuries and varicose conditions

Lasonil® (Bayer)
Ointment, heparinoid 50 units, hyaluronidase 150 units/g. Net price 14 g = 38p; 40 g = £1.08
Additives: wool fat derivative
Apply 2–5 times daily in superficial tissue injuries and varicose conditions

Secaderm® (Fisons)
Salve (= ointment), colophony 26%, melaleuca oil 5.6%, phenol 2.4%, terebene 5.25%, turpentine oil 6%. For boils and chilblains. Net price 15 g = 78p
Additives: beeswax
Apply 1–2 times daily and cover with dressing

14: Immunological products and VACCINES

In this chapter, immunisation is discussed under the following headings:

14.1 Active immunity

Vaccines produce specific protection against a given disease. They may consist of:

1. an attenuated form of an infective agent, as in the vaccines which are used against virus diseases such as rubella and measles, or BCG used against tuberculosis,
2. inactivated preparations of the virus (e.g. influenza vaccine) or bacteria (e.g. typhoid vaccine), or
3. extracts of or detoxified exotoxins produced by a micro-organism (e.g. tetanus vaccine).

Vaccines stimulate the production of protective antibodies and other components of the immune mechanism.

For **live** vaccines, immunisation is generally achieved with a single dose, but 3 doses are required with oral poliomyelitis vaccine. Live virus multiplies in the body and usually produces a durable immunity but not always as long as that of the natural infection. When two live virus vaccines are required (and are not available as a combined preparation) they should be given either simultaneously at different sites or with an interval of at least 3 weeks.

Inactivated vaccines usually require a primary series of doses of vaccine to produce an adequate antibody response and in most cases reinforcing or 'booster' injections are required. The duration of immunity following the use of inactivated vaccines varies from months to many years.

The health departments of the UK have issued a memorandum, *Immunisation against Infectious Disease 1990* which describes the vaccines, immunoglobulins, and antisera in routine use in the UK; recommended schemes for immunisation in childhood are included and advice is given on storage, technique, and record keeping.

Immunisation against Infectious Disease can be obtained from:
HMSO Publications Centre, PO Box 276, London SW8 5DT, (Telephone orders, 071-873 9090) *or* from HMSO bookshops and through all good booksellers.

SIDE-EFFECTS. Some vaccines (e.g. poliomyelitis vaccines) produce very few reactions, while others (e.g. measles and rubella vaccines) may produce a very mild form of the disease. Some vaccines may produce discomfort at the site of injection and mild fever and malaise. Occasionally there are more serious untoward reactions and these should always be reported in the usual way to the CSM. Anaphylactic reactions are very rare but can be fatal (see section 3.4.3 for the management of allergic emergencies).

CONTRA-INDICATIONS. Most vaccines have some basic contra-indication to their use, and the manufacturer's leaflet should always be consulted. In general, vaccination should be postponed if the subject is suffering from an *acute illness*. Minor infections without fever or systemic upset are not contra-indications.

Some viral vaccines contain small quantities of antibiotics such as neomycin or polymyxin (or both); such vaccines may need to be withheld from individuals who are *sensitive to the antibiotic*. *Hypersensitivity to egg* contra-indicates influenza vaccine (residual egg protein present) and, if evidence of previous anaphylactic reaction, also measles, mumps, rubella and yellow fever vaccines.

Live vaccines should not be routinely administered to *pregnant women* because of possible harm to the fetus but where there is a significant risk of exposure (e.g. to poliomyelitis or yellow fever), the need for vaccination outweighs any possible risk to the fetus. Live vaccines should not be given to individuals with *impaired immune responsiveness*, whether occurring naturally (for special reference to *AIDS*, see below) or as a result of radiotherapy or treatment with high doses of corticosteroids or other immunosuppressive drugs[1,2]. They should not be given to those suffering from *malignant conditions* or other tumours of the reticulo-endothelial system[2].

VACCINES AND AIDS. The Department of Health has advised that HIV-positive subjects with or without symptoms can receive the following live vaccines as appropriate:

measles[2] (or MMR), mumps, poliomyelitis[3], rubella;

and the following inactivated vaccines:

cholera, diphtheria, hepatitis B, pertussis, poliomyelitis[3], tetanus, typhoid.

HIV-positive subjects should **not** receive:

BCG, yellow fever[4]

Note. The above advice differs from that for other immunocompromised patients.

1. Live vaccines should be postponed until at least 3 months after stopping corticosteroids and 6 months after stopping chemotherapy.
2. Consideration should be given to use of normal immunoglobulin after exposure to measles and to varicella-zoster immunoglobulin after exposure to varicella.
3. Virus may be excreted for longer periods than in normal subjects; contacts should be warned of this and of need for washing hands after changing a vaccinated infant's nappies; HIV-positive contacts are at greater risk than normal contacts. For HIV-positive symptomatic subjects inactivated poliomyelitis vaccine can be used at discretion of clinician.
4. Because insufficient evidence of safety.

Vaccination programmes

The principal points are as follows:

1. The *basic course* is as set out below.

2. There is no contra-indication to administration of pertussis vaccine to unimmunised older children in order to protect infants and siblings. Since a course of 3 injections is required to protect against whooping cough, vaccine cannot be used to control an outbreak.

If the pertussis component has been omitted from earlier vaccinations 3 doses of pertussis vaccine can be given at monthly intervals to provide protection.

Where the basic course against diphtheria and tetanus is incomplete triple vaccine may be used to begin or complete the course against whooping-cough so that the infant is not given more injections than necessary.

3. Measles/mumps/rubella vaccine can be given at the time of the reinforcing dose of diphtheria/tetanus vaccine and poliomyelitis vaccine; because the diphtheria/tetanus vaccine can be more painful, measles/mumps/rubella vaccine should be injected first; the diphtheria/tetanus should then be given with a separate syringe and needle in the opposite limb (or a second appointment can be made).

Age	Vaccine	Interval	Notes
During the first year of life	DTPer/Vac/Ads *and* Pol/Vac (Oral)	3 doses at intervals of 4 weeks	The first doses should be given at 2 months of age
During the second year of life	Meas/Mump/Rub (MMR) Vac (Live)		
At school entry or entry to nursery school	DT/Vac/Ads *and* Pol/Vac (Oral)	Preferable to allow an interval of at least 3 years after completing basic course	
	Meas/Mump/Rub (MMR) Vac (Live)		Unless documented history of measles/mumps/rubella vaccination *or* valid contra-indication *or* laboratory evidence of immunity to measles, mumps, and rubella
Between 10th and 14th birthdays	BCG	Leave an interval of not less than 3 weeks between BCG and rubella vaccination	For tuberculin-negative children. For tuberculin-negative contacts at any age
Between 10th and 14th birthdays (girls only)	Rub/Vac (Live)		All girls of this age should be offered rubella vaccine regardless of a past history of an attack of rubella (unless documented history of Meas/Mump/Rub Vac)
On leaving school or before employment or further education	Pol/Vac (Oral) *and* Tet/Vac/Ads		
Adult life	Pol/Vac (Oral) if previously unvaccinated	3 doses at intervals of 4 weeks	No adult should remain unimmunised; reinforcing doses for travellers to countries where polio endemic and for health care workers in possible contact with polio
	Rub/Vac (Live) for susceptible women of child-bearing age		Women of child-bearing age should be tested for rubella antibodies and if sero-negative offered rubella vaccination. Pregnancy must be excluded and patient warned not to become pregnant for 1 month after
	Tet/Vac/Ads if previously unvaccinated	For previously unvaccinated adults: 2 doses at an interval of 4 weeks followed by a third dose 4 weeks later	A reinforcing dose 10 years after primary course and again 10 years later maintains a satisfactory level of protection
	Hepatitis B		Individuals in high-risk groups
	Influenza		Individuals in high-risk groups

Post-immunisation pyrexia—Joint Committee on Vaccination and Immunisation recommendation. The doctor should advise the parent that if pyrexia develops after immunisation the child can be given a dose of paracetamol followed, if necessary, by a second dose 4 to 6 hours later. The dose of paracetamol for post-immunisation pyrexia in an infant aged 2–3 months is 60 mg; an oral syringe can be purchased from any pharmacy to give the small dose-volume required. The doctor should warn the parent that if the pyrexia persists after the second dose medical advice should be sought.

For full range of doses of paracetamol, see p. 158.

14.2 Passive immunity

Immunity with immediate protection against certain infective organisms can be obtained by injecting preparations made from the plasma of immune individuals with adequate levels of antibody to the disease for which protection is sought. This passive immunity lasts only a few weeks; where necessary passive immunisation can be repeated.

Antibodies of human origin are usually termed *immunoglobulins*. The term *antiserum* is applied to material prepared in animals. Because of serum sickness and other allergic-type reactions that may follow injections of antisera, this therapy has been replaced wherever possible by the use of immunoglobulins. Reactions are theoretically possible after injection of human immunoglobulins but reports of such reactions are very rare.

14.3 Storage and use

Care must be taken to store all vaccines and other immunological products under the conditions recommended in the manufacturer's leaflet, otherwise the preparation may become denatured and totally ineffective. **Refrigerated storage** is usually necessary; many vaccines need to be stored at 2–8°C and not allowed to freeze. Opened multidose vials which have not been fully used should be discarded within one hour if no preservative is present (most live virus vaccines) or within 3 hours or at the end of a session (when vaccines containing a preservative are used but also including oral poliomyelitis vaccine).

Particular attention must be paid to the instructions on the use of diluents and ampoules of vaccine should always be adequately shaken before use to ensure uniformity of the material to be injected.

Note. The Department of Health has advised against the use of jet guns for vaccination owing to the risk of transmitting blood-borne infections, such as HIV.

14.4 Vaccines and antisera

AVAILABILITY. Anthrax, rabies, smallpox, and yellow fever vaccines, botulism antitoxin, and snake and scorpion venom antitoxins are available from local designated holding centres. Details of current arrangements with names, addresses, and telephone numbers of holding centres are given in:
The Health Service Supply Purchasing Guide, section D pp. 1101–1199
and
The Pharmaceutical Supplies Bulletin, volume 8, no. 5, Oct. 1985, 63/85

Enquiries for vaccines not available commercially can also be made to
Department of Health
Room 220
14 Russell Square
London WC1B 5EP
telephone 071-636 6811 extn 3117/3236.

In Scotland information about availability of vaccines can be obtained from the Chief Administrative Pharmaceutical Officer of the local Health Board. In Wales enquiries should be directed to the Welsh Office, Cathays Park, Cardiff CF1 3NQ, telephone 0222 825111, extn 4658 and in Northern Ireland to the Department of Health and Social Services. Dundonald House, Belfast BT4 3FS, telephone 0232 63939 extn 2841.

For further details of availability, see under individual vaccines.

ANTHRAX VACCINE

Anthrax vaccine is available for anyone subject to heavy exposure to anthrax, such as those exposed to infected hides and carcasses and to imported bonemeal, fishmeal, and feeding stuffs. The vaccine is the alum precipitate of an antigen from *Bacillus anthracis* and, following the primary course of injections, reinforcing doses should be given at about yearly intervals.

PoM **Anthrax Vaccine**
Dose: initial course 3 doses of 0.5 mL by intramuscular injection at intervals of 3 weeks followed by a 4th dose after an interval of 6 months
Reinforcing doses: 0.5 mL annually
Available from local designated centres

BCG VACCINES

BCG (Bacillus Calmette-Guérin) is a live attenuated strain derived from bovine *Mycobacterium tuberculosis* which stimulates the development of hypersensitivity to *M. tuberculosis*. BCG vaccine should be given intradermally by operators skilled in the technique (see below); the percutaneous vaccine is **not** recommended.

Within 2–6 weeks a small swelling appears at the injection site which progresses to a papule or to a benign ulcer about 10 mm in diameter after 3 weeks and heals in 6–12 weeks. A dry dressing may be used if the ulcer discharges, but the air should **not** be excluded. The CSM has reported that serious reactions with BCG are uncommon and most often consist of prolonged ulceration or subcutaneous abscess formation due to faulty injection technique.

BCG is recommended for the following groups if they are negative for tuberculoprotein hypersensitivity:

contacts of those with active respiratory tuberculosis (immigrants in whose communities there is a high incidence of tuberculosis may be regarded as contacts—newborn infants need not be tested for sensitivity but should be vaccinated without delay);

health service staff (including medical students, hospital medical staff, nurses, and anybody who comes into contact with patients, including physiotherapists and radiographers, technical staff in pathology departments and any others considered to be at special risk because of the likelihood of contact with infective patients or their sputum; particularly important to test staff in maternity and paediatric departments);

children between their tenth and fourteenth birthdays (see schedule, section 14.1);

students (including those in teacher training colleges);

veterinary and other staff who handle animal species known to be susceptible to tuberculosis;

those travelling to countries with a high incidence of tuberculosis (section 14.6)

Apart from newborn infants any person being considered for BCG vaccination must first be given a skin test for hypersensitivity to tuberculoprotein.

It is recommended that an interval of at least 3 weeks should be allowed between the administration of a live virus vaccine and BCG. However, when BCG is given to infants, there is no need to delay the primary immunisations, including poliomyelitis.

See section 14.1 for general contra-indications. BCG is also contra-indicated in subjects with generalised septic skin conditions (in the case of eczema, a vaccination site free from lesions should be chosen).

PoM **Bacillus Calmette-Guérin Vaccine.** BCG Vaccine, Dried Tub/Vac/BCG. A freeze-dried preparation of live bacteria of a strain derived from the bacillus of Calmette and Guérin.

Dose: 0.1 mL (INFANTS under 3 months 0.05 mL) by intradermal injection

Available from District Health Authorities (also from Evans)

INTRADERMAL INJECTION TECHNIQUE. After swabbing with spirit and allowing to dry, skin is stretched between thumb and forefinger and needle (size 25G) inserted (bevel upwards) for about 2 mm into superficial layers of dermis (almost parallel with surface). Needle should be short with short bevel (can usually be seen through epidermis during insertion). Raised blanched bleb showing tips of hair follicles is sign of correct injection; 7 mm bleb ≡ 0.1 mL injection; if considerable resistance not felt, needle is removed and reinserted before giving more vaccine.

Injection site is at insertion of deltoid muscle onto humerus (sites higher on arm more likely to lead to keloid formation); tip of shoulder should be **avoided**; in girls, for cosmetic reasons, upper and lateral surface of thigh may be preferred.

PoM **Bacillus Calmette-Guérin Vaccine, Isoniazid-Resistant.** A freeze-dried preparation of live bacteria of an isoniazid-resistant strain derived from the bacillus of Calmette and Guérin.

Dose: 0.1 mL (INFANT under 3 months 0.05 mL) by intradermal injection; for active immunisation of tuberculosis contacts receiving prophylactic treatment with isoniazid.

Available from Evans

PoM **Bacillus Calmette-Guérin Vaccine, Percutaneous** Tub/Vac/BCG(Perc). A preparation of live bacteria of a strain derived from the bacillus of Calmette and Guérin.

Dose: 0.02 mL by percutaneous administration but not recommended, see notes above.

Available from Evans

DIAGNOSTIC AGENTS. In the *Mantoux test* the initial diagnostic dose in patients in whom tuberculosis is suspected (or who are known to be hypersensitive to tuberculin) is 1 unit of tuberculin PPD in 0.1 mL by intradermal injection and in subsequent tests 10 and finally 100 units in 0.1 mL may be given. For routine pre-BCG skin-testing the 10-unit dose of tuberculin PPD is used. In the *Heaf test* (multiple puncture) a solution containing 100 000 units in 1 mL is used.

PoM **Tuberculin PPD.** Prepared from the heat-treated products of growth and lysis of the appropriate species of mycobacterium, and containing 100 000 units/mL. Net price 1-mL amp = £5.51. Also available diluted 1 in 100 (1000 units/mL), 1 in 1000 (100 units/mL), and 1 in 10 000 (10 units/mL). Net price 1 mL (all) = £2.04

Available from District Health Authorities

BOTULISM ANTITOXIN

A trivalent botulism antitoxin is available for the post-exposure prophylaxis of botulism and for the treatment of persons thought to be suffering from botulism. It specifically neutralises the toxins produced by *Clostridium botulinum* types A, B, and E. It is not effective against infantile botulism as the toxin (type A) is seldom, if ever, found in the blood in this type of infection.

Hypersensitivity reactions are a problem. It is essential to read the contra-indications, warnings, and details of sensitivity tests on the package insert. Prior to treatment checks should be made regarding previous administration of any antitoxin and history of any allergic condition, e.g. asthma, hay fever, etc. All patients should be tested for sensitivity (diluting the antitoxin if history of allergy).

PoM **Botulism Antitoxin.** A preparation containing the specific antitoxic globulins that have the power of neutralising the toxins formed by types A, B, and E of *Clostridium botulinum*.

Note. The BP title Botulinum Antitoxin is not used because the preparation currently available has a higher phenol content (0.45% against 0.25%).

Dose: prophylaxis, 20 mL by intramuscular injection as soon as possible after exposure; treatment, 20 mL by slow intravenous infusion followed by 10 mL 2–4 hours later if necessary, and further doses at intervals of 12–24 hours.

Available from local designated centres

CHOLERA VACCINE

Cholera vaccine contains heat-killed Inaba and Ogawa sub-types of *Vibrio cholerae*, Serovar O1. Although a certificate of vaccination (section 14.6) is still required for entry to some countries, it is now recognised that while cholera vaccine may provide some individual protection for about 6 months it cannot control the spread of the disease. Reinforcing injections are recommended every 6 months for those living in endemic areas.

Patients who travel to a country where cholera exists should be warned that attention to the hygiene of food and water is still essential, even after vaccination.

See section 14.1 for general contra-indications.

PoM **Cholera Vaccine** Cho/Vac. Net price 1.5-mL amp = £4.51; 10-mL vial = £7.18
Dose: first dose 0.5 mL by deep subcutaneous or by intramuscular injection; second dose, after at least a week and preferably 4 weeks, 1 mL; CHILD under 1 year, not recommended, 1–5 years 0.1 mL, second dose 0.3 mL; 5–10 years 0.3 mL, second dose 0.5 mL
Available from Wellcome

DIPHTHERIA VACCINES

Protection against diphtheria is essentially due to the presence in the blood stream of antitoxin, the production of which is stimulated by vaccines prepared from the toxin of *Corynebacterium diphtheriae*. These are more effective and cause fewer reactions if adsorbed onto a mineral carrier, and adsorbed diphtheria vaccines are recommended for the routine immunisation of babies and given in the form of a triple vaccine, **adsorbed diphtheria, tetanus, and pertussis vaccine**. A dose of poliomyelitis vaccine, live (oral) is generally given at the time of each of the doses of the triple vaccine (see schedule, section 14.1). Adsorbed diphtheria and tetanus vaccine is used in place of the triple vaccine when immunisation against whooping-cough is contra-indicated.

A reinforcing dose of adsorbed diphtheria and tetanus vaccine is recommended at school entry (4–5 years of age). This should preferably be given after an interval of at least 3 years from the last dose of the basic course.

Further reinforcing doses of diphtheria vaccine are not recommended as a routine except in the case of those who work in units where there is a potentially high risk of infection such as those employed in infectious disease units or microbiology laboratories. A dilute vaccine, adsorbed diphtheria vaccine for adults, is available for this purpose; the small quantity of diphtheria toxoid present in the preparation is sufficient to recall immunity in individuals previously immunised against diphtheria but whose immunity may have diminished with time. It is insufficient to cause the serious reactions that may occur when diphtheria vaccine of conventional formulation is used in an individual who is already immune and must be used when immunising adults and children over 10 years; it may be given without prior Schick testing.

Diphtheria antitoxin is used for passive immunisation; it is prepared in horses therefore reactions are common after administration.

It is now only used in suspected cases of diphtheria (without waiting for bacteriological confirmation); tests for hypersensitivity should be first carried out.

It is no longer used for prophylaxis because of the risk of hypersensitivity; unimmunised contacts should be promptly investigated and given erythromycin prophylaxis (see section 5.1, table 2) and vaccine (see below).

Combined vaccines
With tetanus and pertussis (triple vaccine)

PoM **Adsorbed Diphtheria, Tetanus, and Pertussis Vaccine** DTPer/Vac/Ads. Prepared from diphtheria formol toxoid, tetanus formol toxoid, and pertussis vaccine with a mineral carrier (aluminium hydroxide).
Dose: primary immunisation of children, 0.5 mL by intramuscular or deep subcutaneous injection at 2 months followed by second dose after 4 weeks and third dose after another 4 weeks (see schedule, section 14.1)
Available as **Trivax-AD**® (Wellcome). Net price 0.5-mL amp = £1.15; 5-mL vial = £6.10

PoM **Diphtheria, Tetanus, and Pertussis Vaccine** DTPer/Vac. A mixture of diphtheria formol toxoid, tetanus formol toxoid, and pertussis vaccine. The adsorbed vaccine is preferred
Available as **Trivax**® (Wellcome). Net price 0.5-mL amp = £1.15; 5-mL vial = £6.10

With tetanus only

PoM **Adsorbed Diphtheria and Tetanus Vaccine** DT/Vac/Ads. Prepared from diphtheria formol toxoid and tetanus formol toxoid with a mineral carrier (aluminium hydroxide).
Dose: primary immunisation of children omitting pertussis component, 0.5 mL by intramuscular or deep subcutaneous injection at 2 months followed by second dose after 4 weeks and third dose after another 4 weeks (see schedule, section 14.1); reinforcement at school entry, 0.5 mL (see schedule, section 14.1)
Available from Wellcome (net price 0.5-mL amp = 99p; 5-mL vial = £4.30) and from Evans (net price 0.5-mL amp = 86p; 5-mL vial = £3.61)

PoM **Diphtheria and Tetanus Vaccine** DT/Vac/FT. A mixture of diphtheria formol toxoid and tetanus formol toxoid. The adsorbed vaccine is preferred
Available from Wellcome. Net price 5-mL vial = £4.30

Single antigen vaccines
For children

PoM **Diphtheria Vaccine, Adsorbed** Dip/Vac/Ads. Prepared from diphtheria formol toxoid with a mineral carrier (aluminium hydroxide). Net price 0.5-mL amp = 97p
Note. Used only for contacts of a diphtheria case or carrier; immunised children under 10 years are given one dose of 0.5 mL by intramuscular or by deep subcutaneous injection, unimmunised children under 10 years are given three doses of 0.5 mL with an interval of 4 weeks between first and second doses and another 4 weeks between

second and third; adults and children over 10 years must be given diphtheria vaccine for adults, adsorbed (see below).

Available from Wellcome

Low dose vaccine for adults

PoM **Diphtheria Vaccine for Adults, Adsorbed.** Dip/Vac/Ads for Adults. Net price 0.5-mL amp = £3.00

Dose: primary immunisation in patients over 10 years without prior Schick testing, three doses each of 0.5 mL by intramuscular or deep subcutaneous injection separated by intervals of 1 month; reinforcement, 0.5 mL

Note. Unimmunised adults and children over 10 years who are contacts of a diphtheria case or carrier are given the primary immunisation course; immunised adults and children over 10 years are given the reinforcement dose.

Available from distributor (Regent)

Antisera

PoM **Diphtheria Antitoxin** Dip/Ser.

Dose: prophylactic 500 to 2000 units by intramuscular injection (but **not** used, see notes above); therapeutic 10 000 to 30 000 units increased to 40 000 to 100 000 units in severe cases; doses of up to 30 000 units should be given intramuscularly but for those over 40 000 units a portion is given intramuscularly followed by the bulk of the dose intravenously after an interval of ½–2 hours

Note. Children require the same dose as adults, depending on the severity of the case.

Available from distributor (Regent) or stocks may be held by hospital pharmacies

HEPATITIS B VACCINE

Hepatitis B vaccine is an alum-adsorbed, inactivated hepatitis B virus surface antigen (HBsAg) vaccine. It is made biosynthetically using recombinant DNA technology. The vaccine is used in individuals at high risk of contracting hepatitis B.

In the UK, high-risk groups include health care personnel and patients in units where there is a high incidence of hepatitis B or a direct risk of contact with contaminated human blood, and also certain family contacts of carriers. Similar persons in indirect contact with a source of infection and at a lower risk would be considered a lower priority group. Another group for whom vaccination is recommended is infants born to mothers who are hepatitis B carriers or HBsAg-positive (particularly if they are e antigen-positive or are without anti-e antibody). Active immunisation combined with hepatitis B immunoglobulin is started immediately after delivery.

It should be borne in mind that immunisation takes up to 6 months to confer adequate protection; the duration of immunity is thought to last for 3 to 5 years.

More detailed guidance is given in the memorandum *Immunisation against Infectious Disease 1990* (for availability see section 14.1). Vaccination does not eliminate the need for commonsense precautions for avoiding the risk of infection from known carriers by the routes of infection which have been clearly established, see *Guidance for Clinical Health Care Workers: Protection against Infection with HIV and Hepatitis Viruses*. Accidental inoculation of hepatitis B virus-infected blood into a wound, incision, needle-prick, or abrasion may lead to infection, whereas it is unlikely that indirect exposure to a carrier will do so.

Specific hepatitis B virus immunoglobulin ('HBIG') is available for use with the vaccine in those accidentally infected and in infants (section 14.5).

See section 14.1 for general contra-indications.

PoM **Engerix B®** (SK&F)

A suspension of hepatitis B surface antigen (prepared from yeast cells by recombinant DNA technique) 20 micrograms/mL adsorbed onto aluminium hydroxide. Net price 1-mL vial = £10.50

Dose: by intramuscular injection (see note below), 3 doses of 1 mL, the second 1 month and the third 6 months after the first dose; more rapid (e.g. for travellers), third dose 2 months after first dose with booster at 12 months; CHILD birth to 12 years 3 doses of 0.5 mL; INFANTS born to HBsAg-positive mothers, 3 doses of 0.5 mL, first dose at birth with hepatitis B immunoglobulin injection (separate site)

Note. The deltoid muscle is the preferred site of injection in adults; the anterolateral thigh is the preferred site in infants and children; the buttock must not be used because vaccine efficacy may be reduced.

PoM **H-B-Vax** (MSD)

Product discontinued

INFLUENZA VACCINES

While most viruses are antigenically stable, the influenza viruses A and B (especially A) are constantly altering their antigenic structure as indicated by changes in the haemagglutinins (H) and neuraminidases (N) on the surface of the viruses. It is essential that influenza vaccines in use contain the H and N components of the prevalent strain or strains. Every year the World Health Organization recommends which strains should be included; the number of doses depends on the differences between the H and N components of the prevalent strains.

The recommended strains are grown in the allantoic cavity of chick embryos (therefore **contra-indicated** in those hypersensitive to eggs.

Since influenza vaccines will not control epidemics they are recommended *only for persons at high risk*, including those, especially the elderly, with the following conditions:

chronic pulmonary disease;
chronic heart disease;
chronic renal disease;
diabetes, and other less common endocrine disorders;
conditions involving immunosuppressive therapy.

In non-pandemic years immunisation is not recommended for Health Service staff, except for those at high risk (owing to medical disorders).

For children aged 4–13 years two doses (at an interval of 4–6 weeks) are recommended for primary vaccination.

Interactions: Appendix 1 (influenza vaccine).

See section 14.1 for general contra-indications.

PoM **Fluvirin®** (Servier)
Inactivated influenza vaccine, surface antigen. Net price 0.5-mL syringe = £5.09
Dose: 0.5 mL by deep subcutaneous or intramuscular injection; CHILD see notes above

PoM **Influvac Sub-unit®** (Duphar)
Inactivated influenza vaccine, surface antigen. Net price 0.5-mL disposable syringe = £5.08; 5-mL vial = £46.20
Dose: 0.5 mL by deep subcutaneous or intramuscular injection; CHILD see notes above

PoM **MFV-Ject®** (Merieux)
Inactivated influenza vaccine (split virion vaccine). Net price 0.5-mL syringe = £5.10
Dose: 0.5 mL by deep subcutaneous or intramuscular injection; CHILD see notes above

MEASLES VACCINE

Measles vaccine consists of a live attenuated strain of measles virus grown in chick-embryo fibroblast-tissue cultures. The single vaccine has been replaced by a combined measles/mumps/rubella vaccine (MMR vaccine) for all eligible children.

Administration of measles vaccine to children may be associated with a mild measles-like syndrome with a measles-like rash and pyrexia which come on about a week after the injection of the vaccine. Much less commonly, convulsions and, very rarely, encephalitis have been reported as being associated with measles vaccines. Convulsions in infants are relatively common and may occur by chance following any immunisation procedure; they are certainly much less frequently associated with measles vaccine than with other conditions leading to febrile episodes.

Serious neurological complications following measles vaccine are extremely rare, perhaps of the order of 1 in 87 000 vaccinees and probably about 12–20 times less common than such complications associated with natural infections of measles. Subacute sclerosing panencephalitis follows natural measles infection at a rate of approximately 5 to 10 cases for every million children who have developed measles. This condition may be associated with live measles vaccine at a rate of 0.5–1.0 case per million doses of vaccine distributed, and so it appears that measles vaccination to some extent protects against subacute sclerosing panencephalitis.

Measles or MMR vaccine may also be used in the control of outbreaks and should be offered to susceptible children within 3 days of exposure to infection (**important:** MMR vaccine is not suitable for prophylaxis following exposure to mumps or rubella since the antibody response to the mumps and rubella components is too slow for effective prophylaxis).

Children with a personal history of convulsions, or whose parents or siblings (first-degree relatives) have a history of idiopathic epilepsy should be given suitable prophylactic treatment against febrile convulsions, but simultaneous administration of specially diluted normal immunoglobulin is no longer recommended (for full advice see under MMR vaccine).

Children with partially or totally impaired immune responsiveness should not receive live vaccines (for advice on AIDS see section 14.1). If they have been exposed to measles infection they should be given immunoglobulin (section 14.5). Measles vaccine is contra-indicated if there has been a previous anaphylactic reaction to egg.

For further contra-indications to live vaccines, see section 14.1; see also MMR vaccine.

PoM **Attenuvax®** (Morson)
Product discontinued

PoM **Mevilin-L®** (Evans)
Measles vaccine, live, Schwarz strain. Net price single-dose vial (with diluent) = £1.42
Dose: 0.5 mL by deep subcutaneous or intramuscular injection

Combined vaccines
With mumps and rubella
See below

MMR VACCINE

A combined measles/mumps/rubella vaccine (MMR vaccine) has been introduced with the aim of eliminating rubella (and congenital rubella syndrome), measles, and mumps. Health authorities have an obligation to ensure that every child has received MMR vaccine by entry to primary school, unless there is a valid contra-indication, parental refusal, or laboratory evidence of previous infection. Vaccination records should be checked; where there is no record of MMR vaccination or where the child has received single-antigen measles vaccine, parents should be advised that their children should receive MMR.

MMR vaccine has replaced measles vaccine for children of both sexes aged 1 to 2 years (or after this age if appointments have been missed).

MMR vaccine should be given to children of both sexes aged 4 to 5 years before starting primary school (irrespective of previous measles vaccine or of a history of measles, mumps, or rubella) unless there is:

a documented history of MMR vaccination;
a valid contra-indication (see below);
laboratory evidence of immunity to measles, mumps, and rubella.

As with measles vaccine, malaise, fever and/or a rash may occur with MMR vaccine, most commonly about a week after vaccination and lasting about 2 to 3 days. Parents should be given written information and advice for reducing fever (including the use of paracetamol). Parotid swelling occasionally occurs, usually in the third week. Post-vaccination meningoencephalitis has been reported very rarely (with complete recovery). Children with post-vaccination symptoms are not infectious.

Contra-indications to MMR include:

children with untreated malignant disease or altered immunity, and those receiving immunosuppressive drugs or radiotherapy, or high-dose corticosteroids;
children who have received another live vaccine by injection within 3 weeks;
children with allergies to neomycin or kanamycin, or a history of anaphylaxis due to any cause;
children with acute febrile illness (vaccination should be deferred);
if given to adult women, pregnancy should be avoided for 1 month (as for rubella vaccine);
should not be given within 3 months of an immunoglobulin injection.

It should be noted that:

children with a personal or close family history of convulsions should be given MMR vaccine, provided the parents understand that there may be a febrile response;
immunoglobulin must not be given with MMR vaccine since the immune response to rubella and mumps may be inhibited; doctors should seek specialist paediatric advice rather than refuse vaccination;
allergy to egg is only a contra-indication if the child has had an anaphylactic reaction to food containing egg (dislike of egg or refusal to eat is not a contra-indication).

For general contra-indications, see section 14.1

PoM **MMR Vaccine**
Live, measles, mumps, and rubella vaccine
Dose: 0.5 mL by deep subcutaneous or by intramuscular injection

Available from District Health Authorities as *Immravax*® (Merieux), *MMR II*® (Wellcome), *Pluserix MMR*® (SK&F)

MENINGOCOCCAL POLYSACCHARIDE VACCINE

Meningococcal polysaccharide vaccine is indicated for areas of the world where the risk of acquiring meningococcal infection is much higher than in the UK, particularly for travellers proposing to travel 'rough'.

These areas include New Delhi, Nepal, Mecca (see below), and the meningitis belt of Africa, which encompasses southern sub-Saharan parts of Senegal, Mali, Niger, Chad, and Sudan; all of Gambia, Guinea, Togo, and Benin; South-west Ethiopia; northern parts of Sierra Leone, Liberia, Ivory Coast, Nigeria, Cameroon, Central African Republic, Uganda, and Kenya.

Saudi Arabia requires vaccination of pilgrims to Mecca during the Haj annual pilgrimage; this may apply to others visiting Saudi Arabia in the months leading up to August.

See section 14.1 for general contra-indications.

PoM **AC Vax**® (SK&F)
Meningococcal polysaccharide vaccine prepared from *Neisseria meningitidis* (meningococcus) groups A and C. Net price single-dose vial (with diluent) = £6.86; 10-dose vial = £61.74
Dose: ADULT and CHILD aged 2 months and over, 0.5 mL by deep subcutaneous or intramuscular injection

PoM **Mengivac (A+C)**® (Merieux)
Meningococcal polysaccharide vaccine prepared from *Neisseria meningitidis* (meningococcus) groups A and C. Net price single-dose vial (with syringe containing diluent) = £6.86
Dose: ADULT and CHILD aged over 18 months, 0.5 mL by deep subcutaneous or intramuscular injection
Note. The lower age range for AC Vax® and Mengivac (A+C)® differ; in the case of Mengivac (A+C)® the manufacturer's literature states that clinical data has confirmed efficacy of the serogroup A component over 3 months of age, that although the response to the serogroup C component is transitory it can be of limited value during a severe epidemic, and that transient side-effects are more common below the age of 18 months

MUMPS VACCINE

Mumps vaccine consists of a live attenuated strain of virus grown in chick-embryo tissue culture.

See under MMR vaccine and section 14.1 for contra-indications.

PoM **Mumpsvax**® (Morson)
Mumps vaccine (Jeryl Lynn strain). Net price single-dose vial (with diluent) = £4.00
Dose: ADULT and CHILD over 1 year, 0.5 mL by subcutaneous injection

Combined vaccines
With measles and rubella
See MMR Vaccine

PERTUSSIS VACCINE

(Whooping-cough vaccine)

Pertussis vaccine is usually given combined with diphtheria and tetanus vaccine (in triple vaccine) starting at 2 months of age (see schedule, section 14.1) but may also be given as a single antigen vaccine.

With some vaccines available in the early 1960s persistent screaming and collapse were reported but these reactions are rarely observed with the vaccines now available.

Convulsions and encephalopathy have been reported as rare complications, but such conditions may arise from other causes and be falsely attributed to the vaccine. Neurological complications after whooping cough itself are considerably more common than after the vaccine.

As with any other elective immunisation procedure it is advisable to postpone vaccination if the child is suffering from any acute illness, until fully recovered. Minor infections without fever or systemic upset are not reasons to delay immunisation. Vaccination should not be carried out in children who have a history of severe local or general reaction to a preceding dose; the following reactions should be regarded as severe:

Local—an extensive area of redness and swelling which becomes indurated and involves most of the antero-lateral surface of the thigh or a major part of the circumference of the upper arm; this reaction may increase in severity with each subsequent injection.

General—fever equal to or more than 39.5°C within 48 hours of vaccine, anaphylaxis, bronchospasm, laryngeal oedema, generalised collapse, prolonged unresponsiveness, prolonged inconsolable screaming, and convulsions occurring within 72 hours.

A personal or family history of allergy is **not** a contra-indication to immunisation against whooping cough; nor are stable neurological conditions such as cerebral palsy or spina bifida.

There are certain groups of children in whom the advisability of whooping cough immunisation requires special consideration because of their own or their family histories. For these, the likelihood of febrile convulsions following vaccine may be higher, but the effects of whooping cough could be more severe. The balance of risk and benefit should be assessed in each case. Where there is doubt, appropriate advice should be sought from a consultant paediatrician, a consultant in public health medicine, or a district immunisation coordinator before a decision is made to withhold vaccine. When pertussis vaccine is give to such children, parents should be given advice on the management of pyrexia and the prevention of febrile convulsions (see also p. 407).

Groups requiring special consideration are:

children with a documented history of cerebral damage in the neonatal period;
children with a personal history of convulsions;
children whose parents or siblings have a history of idiopathic epilepsy; in such children there may be a risk of developing a similar condition irrespective of vaccine.

PoM **Pertussis Vaccine** Per/Vac. A sterile suspension of killed *Bordetella pertussis*. Net price 0.5-mL amp = £1.14

Dose: primary immunisation if pertussis component has been omitted from earlier vaccinations, three doses each of 0.5 mL by intramuscular or deep subcutaneous injection, separated by intervals of 1 month (see section 14.1)

Available from Wellcome

Combined vaccines, see under Diphtheria Vaccines

PNEUMOCOCCAL VACCINE

A polyvalent pneumococcal vaccine is available for the immunisation of persons for whom the risk of contracting pneumococcal pneumonia is unusually high, for example patients who have had a splenectomy. It is effective in a single dose if the types of pneumonia in the community are reflected in the polysaccharides contained in the vaccine. Studies with other pneumococcal vaccines suggest that protection may last for 5 years. Revaccination should not be carried out because of the risk of adverse reactions. The vaccine should not be given to children under 2 years, in pregnancy, or when there is infection. It should be used with caution in cardiovascular or respiratory disease. Hypersensitivity reactions may occur.

See section 14.1 for general contra-indications.

PoM **Pneumovax® II** (Morson)

Polysaccharide from each of 23 capsular types of pneumococcus

Dose: 0.5 mL by subcutaneous or intramuscular injection

POLIOMYELITIS VACCINES

There are two types of poliomyelitis vaccine, namely poliomyelitis vaccine, inactivated (Salk), and poliomyelitis vaccine, live (oral) (Sabin). The oral vaccine, consisting of a mixture of attenuated strains of virus types 1, 2, and 3 is at present generally used in the UK.

INITIAL COURSE. **Poliomyelitis vaccine, live (oral)** is given on 3 occasions, usually at the same time as routine immunisation against diphtheria, tetanus, and pertussis (see schedule, section 14.1).

The initial course of 3 doses should also be given to all unimmunised adults.

REINFORCEMENT. A reinforcing dose of oral poliomyelitis vaccine is recommended at school entry at which time children should also receive a reinforcing dose of diphtheria and tetanus vaccine, and a dose of MMR vaccine if this has not already been given. Oral poliomyelitis vaccine is also recommended at school leaving.

Vaccine-associated poliomyelitis and poliomyelitis in contacts of vaccinees are both rare. In England and Wales there is an annual average of 1 recipient and 1 contact case in relation to over 2 million doses of oral vaccine. The need for strict personal hygiene must be stressed; the contacts of a recently vaccinated baby should be advised of the necessity for personal hygiene, particularly of the need to wash their hands after changing the baby's napkins.

Contra-indications to the use of oral poliomyelitis vaccine include vomiting and diarrhoea, and immunodeficiency disorders (or household contacts of patients with immunodeficiency disorders). See section 14.1 for further contra-indications.

Poliomyelitis vaccine (inactivated) may be used for those in whom poliomyelitis vaccine (oral) is contra-indicated because of immunosuppressive disorders (for advice on AIDS see section 14.1).

TRAVELLERS. Travellers to areas other than Australia, New Zealand, Europe, and North America should be given a full course of oral poliomyelitis vaccine if they have not been immunised in the past. Those who have not received immunisation within the last 10 years should be given a booster dose of oral poliomyelitis vaccine.

Live (oral) (Sabin)

PoM **Poliomyelitis Vaccine, Live (Oral)** Pol/Vac (Oral)[1]. A suspension of suitable live attenuated strains of poliomyelitis virus, types 1, 2, and 3. Available in single-dose and 10-dose containers

Dose: 3 drops from a multidose container or the total contents of a single-dose container; for primary immunisation 3 doses are required (see schedule, section 14.1)

Available from District Health Authorities (private purchases available from SK&F and Wellcome)

1. BP permits code OPV for vaccine in single doses provided it also appears on pack.

Note. Poliomyelitis vaccine loses potency once the container has been opened, therefore any vaccine remaining at the end of an immunisation session should be discarded; whenever possible sessions should be arranged to avoid undue wastage.

Inactivated (Salk)

PoM **Poliomyelitis Vaccine, Inactivated** Pol/Vac (Inact). An inactivated suspension of suitable strains of poliomyelitis virus, types 1, 2, and 3.

Dose: 0.5 mL or as stated on the label by deep subcutaneous or intramuscular injection; for primary immunisation 3 doses are required (see schedule, section 14.1)

Available from Department of Health, Room 220, 14 Russell Square, London WC1B 5EP, telephone 071-636 6811, extn 3117/3236 *and* Scottish Home and Health Department, telephone 031-552 6255, extn 2162 *and* Welsh Health Common Services Authority, Heron House, 35–43 Newport Road, Cardiff CF2 1SB, telephone 0222 471234

Note. Should be ordered one dose at a time and only when required for use.

RABIES VACCINE

A human diploid cell **rabies vaccine** is now in use. It should be offered prophylactically to those at high risk—those working in quarantine stations, animal handlers, veterinary surgeons, and field workers who may be exposed to bites of wild animals. A detailed list is given in Health Circular HC(77)29. For *prophylactic* use the vaccine produces a good antibody response when given in a 2-dose schedule with an interval of one month between doses and a reinforcing dose after an interval of 6–12 months with further reinforcing doses every 1–3 years depending on the risk of exposure, and also following exposure to possible rabies.

For *post-exposure treatment* of previously unvaccinated patients a course of injections should be started as soon as possible after exposure (days 0, 3, 7, 14, 30, and 90). The course may be discontinued if it is proved that the patient was not at risk. There are no specific contra-indications to this diploid cell vaccine and its use should be considered whenever a patient has been attacked by an animal in a country where rabies is endemic, even if there is no direct evidence of rabies in the attacking animal. Rabies immunoglobulin (section 14.5) should also be given.

Staff in attendance on a patient who is highly suspected of, or known to be suffering from, rabies should be offered vaccination. Four intradermal doses of 0.1 mL of human diploid cell vaccine (Merieux) given on the same day at different sites has been suggested for this purpose.

Advice on post-exposure vaccination and treatment of rabies is available from the Virus Reference Laboratory, Central Public Health Laboratory, Colindale Avenue, Colindale, London NW9 5HT, telephone 081-200 4400.

PoM **Merieux Inactivated Rabies Vaccine** (Merieux)

Freeze-dried human diploid cell rabies vaccine prepared from Wistar strain PM/WI 38 1503-3M. Single-dose vial with syringe containing diluent

Note. Studies have shown that when this vaccine is injected into the gluteal region there is a poor response.

Dose: prophylactic, 1 mL by deep subcutaneous or intramuscular injection in the deltoid region, followed by a second dose after 1 month and a third after 6–12 months; also further reinforcing doses every 1–3 years depending on the risk of infection

Post-exposure, 1 mL on the first, third, seventh and fourteenth day and after 1 and 3 months

Staff in attendance, see notes above

Also available from local designated centres (special workers and post-exposure treatment)

RUBELLA VACCINE

The selective policy of protecting women of child-bearing age from the risks of rubella (German measles) in pregnancy has been extended to a policy of eliminating the circulation of rubella among young children. The existing rubella vaccination policy will therefore be reinforced by the mass vaccination of children of both sexes, using a combined measles, mumps, and rubella vaccine (see under MMR Vaccine).

Rubella vaccine is still recommended for prepubertal girls between their tenth and fourteenth birthdays (unless there is documented evidence that they have received MMR) and for seronegative women of child-bearing age (see schedule, section 14.1) as well as those who might put pregnant women at risk of infection (e.g. nurses and doctors in obstetric units).

Rubella vaccination should be avoided in early pregnancy, and women of child-bearing age should be advised not to become pregnant within 1 month of vaccination. However, despite active surveillance in the UK, the USA, and Germany, no case of congenital rubella syndrome has been reported following inadvertent vaccination shortly before or during pregnancy. There is thus no evidence that the vaccine is teratogenic, and termination of pregnancy following inadvertent vaccination should not be routinely recommended; potential parents should be given this information before making a decision about termination.

Vaccine may conveniently be offered to previously unvaccinated and seronegative post-partum women. Again they must avoid pregnancy for 1 month. Immunising susceptible post-partum women a few days after delivery is important as far as the overall reduction of congenital abnormalities in the UK is concerned, for about 60% of these abnormalities occur in the babies of multiparous women.

Susceptible pregnant women who are exposed to rubella and who do not want therapeutic abortion may be offered normal immunoglobulin injection (section 14.5).

See section 14.1 for further contra-indications.

PoM **Rubella Vaccine, Live** Rub/Vac (Live). A freeze-dried suspension of a suitable live attenuated strain of rubella virus grown in suitable cell cultures.
Dose: 0.5 mL by deep subcutaneous or by intramuscular injection (see schedule, section 14.1 and notes above)

Available as

PoM **Almevax®** (Wellcome)
Rubella vaccine, live, prepared from Wistar RA 27/3 strain propagated in human diploid cells. Net price single-dose amp with diluent = £2.61; 10-dose vial with diluent = £21.64

PoM **Ervevax®** (SK&F)
Rubella vaccine, live, prepared from Wistar RA 27/3 strain propagated in human diploid cells. Net price single-dose vial = £2.30; 10-dose vial = £19.10 (both with diluent)

PoM **Meruvax II®** (Morson)
Product discontinued

PoM **Rubavax®** (Merieux)
Rubella vaccine, live, prepared from Wistar RA27/3 strain propagated in human diploid cells. Single-dose vial with syringe containing diluent

Combined vaccines
With measles and mumps
See MMR Vaccine

SMALLPOX VACCINE

Smallpox vaccination is no longer required routinely in the UK and other countries because global eradication of smallpox has now been achieved. Workers in laboratories where pox viruses (such as vaccinia) are handled, and others whose work involves an identifiable risk of exposure to pox virus, should be advised of the possible risk and vaccination should be considered. Detailed guidance for laboratory staff has been prepared by the Advisory Committee on Dangerous Pathogens and the Advisory Committee on Genetic Manipulation. There is no requirement for smallpox vaccination of travellers.

PoM **Smallpox Vaccine** Var/Vac. Consists of a suspension of live vaccinia virus grown in the skin of living animals, supplied in freeze-dried form with diluent
Advice on the need for vaccination and on contra-indications should be obtained from the Virus Reference Laboratory, Central Public Health Laboratory, Colindale (081-200 4400) who will also supply the vaccine (free of charge)

TETANUS VACCINES

(Tetanus toxoids)

Tetanus vaccines stimulate the production of the protective antitoxin. In general, adsorption on aluminium hydroxide, aluminium phosphate, or calcium phosphate improves antigenicity. Adsorbed tetanus vaccine is offered routinely to babies in combination with adsorbed diphtheria vaccine (DT/Vac/Ads) and more usually also combined with killed *Bordetella pertussis* organisms as a triple vaccine, adsorbed diphtheria, tetanus, and pertussis vaccine (DT Per/Vac/Ads), see schedule, section 14.1.

Of the single antigen tetanus vaccines adsorbed tetanus vaccine is again preferred to the plain vaccine. Adsorbed vaccine must not be given intradermally.

In children, the triple vaccine not only gives protection against tetanus in childhood but also gives the basic immunity for subsequent reinforcing doses of tetanus vaccine at school entry and at school leaving and also when a potentially tetanus-contaminated injury has been received. Normally, tetanus vaccine should not be given unless more than 10 years have elapsed since the last reinforcing dose because of the possibility that hypersensitivity reactions may develop.

Active immunisation is important for persons in older age groups who may never have had a routine or complete course of immunisation when younger. In these persons a course of adsorbed tetanus vaccine may be given. Very rarely, tetanus has developed after abdominal surgery; patients awaiting elective surgery should be asked about tetanus immunisation and immunised if necessary.

See section 14.1 for general contra-indications.

For serious, potentially contaminated wounds tetanus immunoglobulin injection (section 14.5) should be selectively used in addition to wound toilet, adsorbed tetanus vaccine, and benzylpenicillin or another appropriate antibiotic.

Single antigen vaccines
The BP directs that when Tetanus Vaccine is prescribed or demanded and the form is not stated, Adsorbed Tetanus Vaccine may be dispensed or supplied.

PoM **Adsorbed Tetanus Vaccine** Tet/Vac/Ads. Prepared from tetanus formol toxoid with a mineral carrier (aluminium hydroxide).
Dose: 0.5 mL or as stated on the label, by intramuscular or deep subcutaneous injection followed after 4 weeks by a second dose and after a further 4 weeks by a third
Available from Servier (net price 0.5-mL amp = 64p; 5-mL vial = £2.89) and from Wellcome (0.5-mL amp = 71p; 5-mL vial = £3.86), and from Merieux (as **Tetavax®**). Net price 0.5-mL amp = 55p; 0.5-mL single-dose syringe = £1.20; 5-mL vial = £2.80

PoM **Tetanus Vaccine** Tet/Vac/FT. Tetanus formol

toxoid. 0.5-mL amp and 5-mL vial
Dose: as for Adsorbed Tetanus Vaccine which is preferred (see notes above)
Available from Wellcome

Combined vaccines, see Diphtheria Vaccines

TUBERCULOSIS VACCINES

See BCG Vaccines

TYPHOID VACCINE

Typhoid vaccine consists of single antigen typhoid vaccine; it is no substitute for personal hygiene (see section 14.6). Normally, 2 doses should be given at 4–6 weeks interval for primary immunisation, with reinforcing doses about every 3 years on continued exposure.
Local reactions, which consist of swelling, pain, and tenderness, appear about 2–3 hours after the deep subcutaneous or intramuscular injection of the vaccine. Systemic reactions which consist of fever, malaise, and headache may also occur and usually last for about 36 hours after injection.

See section 14.1 for general contra-indications.

PoM **Typhoid Vaccine** Typhoid/Vac. A suspension of killed *Salmonella typhi* organisms. Net price 1.5-mL vial = £4.11
Dose: 0.5 mL by deep subcutaneous or intramuscular injection; CHILD 1–10 years 0.25 mL
Second dose after 4–6 weeks, 0.5 mL; CHILD 1–10 years 0.25 mL
Note. It is no longer recommended that the second dose of typhoid vaccine can be given intradermally to reduce reactions; this is due to lack of established evidence of efficacy by the intradermal route
Available from Wellcome

WHOOPING-COUGH VACCINES

See Pertussis Vaccines

YELLOW FEVER VACCINE

Yellow fever vaccine consists of a live attenuated yellow fever virus (17D strain) grown in developing chick embryos. Infants under 9 months of age should only be vaccinated if the risk of yellow fever is unavoidable since there is a small risk of encephalitis. The vaccine should not be given to those with impaired immune responsiveness, or who have had an anaphylactic reaction to egg; it should not be given during pregnancy (but where there is a significant risk of exposure the need for vaccination outweighs any risk to the fetus). See section 14.1 for further contra-indications. Reactions are few. The immunity which probably lasts for life is officially accepted for 10 years starting from 10 days after primary vaccination and for a further 10 years immediately after revaccination.

PoM **Yellow Fever Vaccine, Live** Yel/Vac. A suspension of chick embryo proteins containing attenuated 17D strain virus
Dose: 0.5 mL by subcutaneous injection
Available (only to designated Yellow Fever Vaccination centres) as
PoM **Arilvax**® (Wellcome)
Freeze-dried yellow fever vaccine, live. 1-, 5-, and 10-dose vials (with diluent)

14.5 Immunoglobulins

Injection of immunoglobulins produces immediate protection lasting a few weeks. Immunoglobulins of animal origin (antisera) were frequently associated with hypersensitivity which led to their virtual abandonment; human immunoglobulins took their place.

The two types of human immunoglobulin preparation are **normal immunoglobulin** and **specific immunoglobulins**.

AVAILABILITY. Normal immunoglobulin and the specific immunoglobulins are available from the Public Health Laboratory Service laboratories and Regional Blood Transfusion Centres in England and Wales with the exception of tetanus immunoglobulin which is distributed through Regional Blood Transfusion Centres to hospital pharmacies or blood transfusion departments and is also available to general medical practitioners. Rabies immunoglobulin is available from the Central Public Health Laboratory, London.

In Scotland all immunoglobulins are available from the Blood Transfusion Service. Tetanus immunoglobulin is distributed by the Blood Transfusion Service to hospitals and general medical practitioners on demand.

Normal immunoglobulin injection and tetanus immunoglobulin injection are also available commercially.

For further details of availability see under individual immunoglobulins.

NORMAL IMMUNOGLOBULIN

(Gamma Globulin)

Human **normal immunoglobulin** ('HNIG') is prepared from pools of at least 1000 donations of human plasma; it contains antibody to measles, mumps, varicella, hepatitis A, and other viruses that are currently prevalent in the general population. It is administered by intramuscular injection for the protection of susceptible contacts against hepatitis A virus (infective hepatitis), measles and, to a lesser extent, rubella. Injection of human immunoglobulin produces immediate passive immunity lasting a few weeks. Intravenous administration is used for replacement therapy (see below).

HEPATITIS A. **Hepatitis A** viral vaccines are undergoing clinical trials but are not yet generally available. Control depends on good hygiene and many studies have also shown the value of normal immunoglobulin in the prevention and control of outbreaks of this disease. It is recommended for controlling infection in contacts in closed institutions and also, under certain conditions, in school and home contacts and for travellers going to areas where the disease is highly endemic (all countries excluding Northern Europe, North America, Australia, and New Zealand).

MEASLES. Normal immunoglobulin may be given for prophylaxis in children with compromised immunity (and in adults with compromised immunity who have no measles antibodies); it should be given as soon as possible after contact with measles. It should also be given to children under 12 months with recent severe illness for whom measles should be avoided; MMR vaccine should then be given (after an interval of **at least** 3 months) at around the usual age.

RUBELLA. Immunoglobulin after exposure does **not** prevent infection in non-immune contacts and is **not** recommended for protection of pregnant women exposed to rubella. It may however reduce the likelihood of a clinical attack which may possibly reduce the risk to the fetus. It should only be used when termination of pregnancy would be unacceptable when it should be given as soon as possible after exposure. Serological follow-up of recipients is essential.

For routine prophylaxis, see Rubella Vaccine.

> Normal immunoglobulin may interfere with the immune response to live virus vaccines which should therefore only be given at least 3 weeks before or 3 months after an injection of normal immunoglobulin. This does not apply to yellow fever vaccine since normal immunoglobulin does not contain antibody to this virus. For travellers, if there is insufficient time, the recommended interval may have to be ignored.

For intramuscular use

PoM **Human Normal Immunoglobulin**

Human normal immunoglobulin injection. 250-mg amp; 750-mg amp

Available from BPL and SNBTS (250-mg vial)

Dose: by intramuscular injection, Hepatitis A travel prophylaxis (2 months or less abroad), 250 mg; CHILD under 10 years 125 mg; longer travel prophylaxis (3–5 months abroad) and to control outbreaks, 500 mg; CHILD under 10 years 250 mg

Measles prophylaxis, CHILD under 1 year 250 mg, 1–2 years 500 mg, 3 years and over 750 mg; to allow attenuated attack, CHILD under 1 year 100 mg, 1 year and over 250 mg

Rubella in pregnancy, prevention of clinical attack, 750 mg

[1]PoM **Gammabulin®** (Immuno)

Human normal immunoglobulin injection. Net price 2-mL vial = £3.20; 5-mL vial = £6.50; 10-mL vial = £11.00; 320-mg vial with 2 mL water for injections = £3.50

[1]PoM **Kabiglobulin®** (Kabi)

Human normal immunoglobulin injection 16%. Net price 2-mL amp = £3.40; 5-mL amp = £8.20

1. Doses for these preparations are expressed in terms of volume:
Dose: by intramuscular injection,
Hepatitis A prophylaxis, ADULT and CHILD 0.02–0.04 mL/kg; greater exposure risk, 0.06–0.12 mL/kg
Measles prophylaxis, 0.2 mL/kg; to allow attenuated attack, 0.04 mL/kg
Rubella in pregnancy, prevention of clinical attack, 20 mL

REPLACEMENT THERAPY

Special forms for intravenous administration are available for replacement therapy for patients with congenital agammaglobulinaemia and hypogammaglobulinaemia and for the treatment of idiopathic thrombocytopenic purpura.

For intravenous use

Available as: *Endobulin®* (500 mg, 1 g, 2.5 g, 5 g, 7.5 g, 10 g—Immuno); *Gamimune-N®* (500 mg, 2.5 g, 5 g—Cutter); Human Immunoglobulin (3 g—SNBTS); *Sandoglobulin®* (1 g, 3 g, 6 g—Sandoz); *Venoglobulin®* (500 mg, 2.5 g, 5g—Alpha)

SPECIFIC IMMUNOGLOBULINS

Specific immunoglobulins are prepared by pooling the blood of convalescent patients or of immunised donors who have recently been specifically boosted.

Although a hepatitis B vaccine is now available for those at high risk of infection, specific **hepatitis B immunoglobulin** ('HBIG') is available for use in association with the vaccine for the prevention of infection in laboratory and other personnel who have accidentally become contaminated with hepatitis B virus, and in infants born to mothers who have become infected with this virus in pregnancy or who are high-risk carriers.

Following exposure to a rabid animal, specific **rabies immunoglobulin**, if possible of human origin, should be injected at the site of the bite and also given intramuscularly. Rabies vaccine should also be given.

Tetanus immunoglobulin of human origin ('HTIG') should be used selectively in addition to wound toilet, vaccine, and benzylpenicillin (or another appropriate antibiotic) for the more seriously contaminated wounds; it is rarely required for those with an established immunity in whom protection may be achieved by a reinforcing dose of vaccine if considered advisable. The administration of tetanus immunoglobulin should be considered for patients not known to have received active immunisation (a) whose wound was sustained more than 6 hours before treatment was received and (b) with puncture wounds or wounds potentially heavily contaminated with tetanus spores, septic, or with much devitalised tissue. A dose of adsorbed tetanus vaccine should be given at the same time as the tetanus immunoglobulin and the course of vaccine subsequently completed.

Other specific immunoglobulins include varicella-zoster immunoglobulin ('ZIG') and are in limited supply. Others are under study, but their availability and evaluation requires the cooperation of general practitioners to provide blood from patients who are convalescent from these and other specific viral infections in order to prepare specific immunoglobulin preparations.

PoM **Hepatitis B Immunoglobulin** (Antihepatitis B Immunoglobulin). See notes above
Available from Public Health Laboratory Service (also from BPL and SNBTS)

PoM **Rabies Immunoglobulin** (Antirabies Immunoglobulin Injection). Used for protection of persons who have been bitten by rabid animals or otherwise exposed to infection (see notes above)
Dose: 20 units/kg, half by intramuscular injection and half by infiltration around wound
Available from the Public Health Laboratory Service (also from BPL and SNBTS)

PoM **Tetanus Immunoglobulin** (Antitetanus Immunoglobulin Injection). Used for the protection of unimmunised persons when there is a specific risk of tetanus
Dose: by intramuscular injection, prophylactic 250 units, increased to 500 units if more than 24 hours have elapsed or there is risk of heavy contamination
Therapeutic, 30–300 units/kg (multiple sites)
Available from BPL, SNBTS, and Wellcome (as *Humotet*®; net price 1-mL vial = £18.94)

PoM **Varicella-Zoster Immunoglobulin** (Antivaricella-zoster Immunoglobulin). Used for protection of immunosuppressed persons and neonates at risk.
Available from Public Health Laboratory Service (also from BPL and SNBTS)

ANTI-D (Rh_0) IMMUNOGLOBULIN

Anti-D immunoglobulin is available to prevent a rhesus-negative mother from forming antibodies to fetal rhesus-positive cells which may pass into the maternal circulation during childbirth or abortion. It must be injected within 72 hours of the birth or abortion. The objective is to protect any further child from the hazard of haemolytic disease.

PoM **Anti-D (Rh_0) Immunoglobulin Injection.** See notes above
Dose: for rhesus-negative women, 500 units by intramuscular injection following birth of rhesus-positive infant; 250 units if before 20 weeks gestation; after transfusion, consult literature (5000 units capable of neutralising 40–50 mL packed red cells)
Note. Rubella vaccine may be administered in the post-partum period simultaneously with anti-D (Rh_0) immunoglobulin injection providing separate syringes are used and the products are administered into contralateral limbs. A blood test should be done not sooner than 8 weeks later to ensure that rubella antibodies have been produced. If blood transfusion was necessary vaccination should be delayed for 3 months.
Available from Regional Blood Transfusion Centres (also from BPL, Immuno (*Partobulin*®), and SNBTS)

14.6 International travel

Note. For advice on malaria chemoprophylaxis, see section 5.4.1.

No particular immunisation is required for travellers to the United States, Europe, Australia, or New Zealand. In Non-European areas surrounding the Mediterranean, in Africa, the Middle East, Asia, and South America, certain special precautions are required.

Typhoid vaccine is indicated for travellers to those countries where typhoid is endemic but is no substitute for personal precautions. Green salads and uncooked vegetables should be avoided and only fruits which can be peeled should be eaten. Only suitable bottled water, or water that has been boiled, or treated with sterilising tablets should be used for drinking purposes. This advice also applies to cholera and other diarrhoeal diseases (including travellers' diarrhoea).

Long-term travellers to areas that have a high incidence of **poliomyelitis** or **tuberculosis** should be immunised with the appropriate vaccine; in the case of poliomyelitis previously vaccinated adults may be given a reinforcing dose of oral poliomyelitis vaccine. BCG vaccination is recommended for travellers proposing to stay for longer than one month in Asia, Africa, or Central and South America; it should preferably be given three months or more before departure.

Overland travellers to Asia and Africa and others at high risk may be given **normal immunoglobulin injection** (section 14.5) for protection against hepatitis A. It is preferable to complete active immunisation and wait 4 weeks before administering the immunoglobulin. An interval of 2 weeks is acceptable provided the immunoglobulin is given just before departure. If time is short, it can be given with any vaccine (including polio).

Although **cholera vaccine** is no substitute for personal hygiene it has some protective value for about 6 months in preventing individual infections. Some countries require evidence of vaccination, which can be provided in the form of a Certificate of Cholera Vaccination available from the Department of Health. Stamped certificates supplied to general medical practitioners by Family Health Services Authorities (in Scotland by Health Boards) do not require to be authenticated by health authorities.

International Certificates of vaccination against **yellow fever** (section 14.4) are still required for travel to much of Africa and South America.

Vaccination against **meningococcal meningitis** is required for a number of areas of the world (for details, see p. 412).

The Department of Health has issued a booklet, *The Traveller's Guide To Health* (code: T1) which can be obtained from travel agents or by telephoning 0800 555 777 (24-hour service); bulk copies may be ordered from:

DHSS Leaflets Unit
PO Box 21
Stanmore
Middx HA7 1AY

It provides details of vaccination requirements or recommendations country-by-country; further advice (including details of a **rapid schedule** for travellers required to go abroad at short notice) may be obtained from the Department of Health memorandum, *Immunisation against Infectious Disease* (for details, section 14.1).

Travel Information for Medical Practitioners is a Department of Health booklet supplementing the guidance provided by the publications mentioned above. It is not available to the public, but medical practitioners may obtain copies from:

DOH Store
Health Publications Unit
No. 2 Site
Manchester Road
Heywood
Lancs OL10 2PZ

Vaccination requirements change from time to time, and information on the current requirements for any particular country may be obtained from:

Department of Health
Hannibal House
London SE1 6TE
telephone 071-972 2000

Scottish Home and Health Department
St. Andrew's House
Edinburgh EH1 3DE
telephone 031-556 8400

Welsh Office
Cathays Park,
Cardiff CF1 3NQ
telephone Cardiff 825111

Department of Health and Social Services
Dundonald House
Upper Newtownards Road
Belfast BT4 3FS
telephone 0232 63939;

or from the embassy or legation of the appropriate country.

15: Drugs used in ANAESTHESIA

This chapter describes briefly drugs used in anaesthesia; the reader is referred to other sources for more detailed information. The chapter is divided into two sections:

15.1 General anaesthesia

Note. The drugs in section 15.1 should be used only by experienced personnel and where adequate resuscitative equipment is available.

ANAESTHESIA AND DRIVING. Patients given sedatives and analgesics during minor outpatient procedures should be very carefully warned about the risk of driving afterwards. For intravenous benzodiazepines and for a short general anaesthetic the risk extends to **at least 24 hours** after administration. Responsible persons should be available to take patients home. The dangers of taking **alcohol** should also be emphasised.

MODERN ANAESTHETIC TECHNIQUE. It is now common practice to administer several drugs with different actions to produce a state of surgical anaesthesia with minimal risk of toxic effects. An intravenous anaesthetic is frequently used for induction, followed by maintenance with inhalational anaesthetics, perhaps supplemented by other drugs administered intravenously. Specific drugs are often used to produce muscular relaxation. Many of the drugs used interfere with the reflex maintenance of spontaneous respiration and intermittent positive pressure ventilation by manual or mechanical means is commonly employed.

For certain procedures controlled hypotension may be required. Labetalol (see section 2.4), sodium nitroprusside (see section 2.5.1), and trimetaphan camsylate (see section 2.5.6) are used.

Beta-blockers (see section 2.4) may be used to control arrhythmias during anaesthesia.

SURGERY AND LONG-TERM MEDICATION. The risk of stopping long-term medication before surgery is often greater than the risk of continuing it during surgery. This applies particularly to corticosteroids, since patients with adrenal atrophy (see section 6.3.3) may experience a precipitous fall

GAS CYLINDERS

Each gas cylinder bears a label with the name of the gas contained in the cylinder. The name or chemical symbol of the gas is stencilled in paint on the shoulder of the cylinder; the letters are not less than 9 mm high on cylinders up to and including 80 mm diameter, not less than 12 mm high on cylinders over 80 mm and up to and including 105 mm diameter, and 19 mm high on cylinders above 105 mm diameter. The name or chemical symbol of the gas is also clearly and indelibly stamped on the cylinder valve. The colours applied to the valve end of the cylinder extend down the cylinder to the shoulder; in the case of mixed gases the colours for the individual gases are applied in four segments, two for each colour. See table below.

Gas cylinders should be stored in a cool well-ventilated room, free from materials of a flammable nature.

No lubricant of any description should be used.

Name of gas	Symbol	Colour of cylinder body	Colour of valve end where different from body
Oxygen	O_2	Black	White
Nitrous oxide	N_2O	Blue	—
Cyclopropane	C_3H_6	Orange	—
Carbon dioxide	CO_2	Grey	—
Ethylene	C_2H_4	Violet	—
Helium	He	Brown	—
Nitrogen	N_2	Grey	Black
Oxygen and carbon dioxide mixture	$O_2 + CO_2$	Black	White and Grey
Oxygen and helium mixture	O_2 + He	Black	White and Brown
Oxygen and nitrous oxide mixture	$O_2 + N_2O$	Blue	Blue and White
Air (medical)	AIR	Grey	White and Black

British Standard 1319:1976; Medical gas cylinders, valves and yoke connections. The colours used for gas cylinders comply with specifications in British Standards 4800 and 5252.

in blood pressure unless corticosteroid cover is provided during anaesthesia or in the immediate postoperative period. Anaesthetists must therefore know whether a patient is, or has been, taking corticosteroids. Other drugs that should not normally be stopped before surgery include analgesics, antiepileptics, antiparkinsonian drugs, bronchodilators, cardiovascular drugs, glaucoma drugs, and thyroid or antithyroid drugs. Although it is preferable to discontinue oral anticoagulants electively before operation, this is not possible in patients requiring long-term treatment (e.g. for valve prostheses). The haematologist or physician should be consulted for further advice.

Drugs that should be stopped before surgery include oestrogens and combined oral contraceptives, which should be discontinued (and adequate alternative contraceptive arrangements made) 4 weeks before major elective surgery (for details see Surgery, section 7.3.1). In view of their hazardous interactions MAOIs should normally be stopped 2 weeks before surgery. Tricyclic antidepressants need not be stopped, but there may be an increased risk of arrhythmias and hypotension, therefore the anaesthetist should be informed if they are not. Lithium should be stopped 2 days before major surgery but the normal dose can be continued for minor surgery (with careful monitoring of fluids and electrolytes). To avoid withdrawal symptoms antidepressants need to be withdrawn gradually (see section 4.3.1).

In all cases it is vital that the anaesthetist should know of all drugs that a patient is, or has been, taking.

15.1.1 Intravenous anaesthetics

Intravenous anaesthesics may be used alone to produce anaesthesia for short surgical procedures but are more commonly used for induction only. Intravenous anaesthetics are potent drugs which nearly all produce their effect in one arm-brain circulation time and can cause apnoea and hypotension, and so adequate resuscitative facilities **must** be available. Large doses should be avoided in obstetrics, as the drug may cross the placental barrier. The drugs are **contra-indicated** in any dose in patients in whom the anaesthetist is not confident to maintain the airway, for example if there are tumours in the pharynx or larynx. Extreme care is required in surgery of the mouth, pharynx, or larynx and patients with acute cardiovascular failure (shock) or fixed cardiac output. Patients with a full stomach present a hazard during induction since there is a danger of silent regurgitation.

Individual requirements vary considerably and the recommended dosage is only a guide. Smaller dosage is indicated in ill, shocked, or debilitated patients, while robust individuals may require more. The estimated dosage should be injected over 20 seconds and a further 20 to 30 seconds allowed to assess the effect before a supplementary dose is given. For tracheal intubation, induction should be followed by inhalational anaesthesia or by a neuromuscular blocking drug.

TOTAL INTRAVENOUS ANAESTHESIA. This is a technique in which major surgery is carried out with all anaesthetic drugs being given intravenously. Respiration is controlled, the lungs being inflated with oxygen-enriched air. Muscle relaxant drugs are used to provide relaxation and prevent reflex muscle movements. The main problem to be overcome is the assessment of depth of anaesthesia in the paralysed ventilated patient.

DRIVING. For advice on anaesthesia and driving, see previous page.

BARBITURATES

Thiopentone sodium is the most widely used intravenous anaesthetic, but has no analgesic properties. Induction is generally smooth and rapid, but owing to the potency of the drug, overdosage with cardiorespiratory depression may occur. Aqueous solutions are unstable, particularly when exposed to air. The solution is alkaline and therefore irritant on misplaced injection outside the vein, while arterial injection is particularly dangerous. The usual strength used is a 2.5% solution in water for injections.

Awakening from a moderate dose of thiopentone is rapid due to redistribution of the drug in the whole body tissues. Metabolism is, however, slow and some sedative effects may persist for up to 24 hours during which time the subject is particularly susceptible to the effects of alcohol. Repeated doses have a cumulative effect.

Methohexitone sodium is less irritant to tissues than thiopentone; it is usually used in 1% solution. Recovery is marginally more rapid than in the case of thiopentone. Induction is less smooth with an incidence of hiccup, tremor, involuntary movements, and pain on injection.

Both thiopentone and methohexitone are **contra-indicated** in porphyria.

OTHER INTRAVENOUS ANAESTHETICS

Etomidate is an induction agent associated with rapid recovery without hangover effect. It causes less hypotension than other drugs used for induction. There is a high incidence of extraneous muscle movement and pain on injection. These effects can be minimised by premedication with an opioid analgesic and use of larger veins. There is evidence that repeated doses of etomidate have an undesirable suppressant effect on adrenocortical function.

Propofol is associated with rapid recovery without hangover effect. There is sometimes pain on intravenous injection, but significant extraneous muscle movements do not occur. The CSM have received reports of convulsions, anaphylaxis, and delayed recovery from anaesthesia after propofol administration.

Ketamine can be given by the intravenous or the intramuscular route, and has good analgesic properties when used in sub-anaesthetic dosage. The maximum effect occurs in more than one arm-brain circulation time. Muscle tone is increased and the airway is usually well maintained. There is cardiovascular stimulation and arterial pressure may rise with tachycardia. The main disadvantage is the high incidence of hallucinations and other transient psychotic sequelae, though it is believed that these are much less significant in children. The incidence can be reduced when drugs such as diazepam are also used. Ketamine is **contra-indicated** in patients with hypertension and is best avoided in those prone to hallucinations. It is used mainly for paediatric anaesthesia, particularly when repeated administrations are required. Recovery is relatively slow.

THIOPENTONE SODIUM

Indications: induction of general anaesthesia; anaesthesia of short duration in minor surgical procedures

Cautions; Contra-indications; Side-effects: see notes above; reduce induction dose in severe liver disease; avoid in porphyria; **interactions:** Appendix 1 (anaesthetics)

Dose: *by intravenous injection*, in fit premedicated adults, initially 100–150 mg (4–6 mL of 2.5% solution) over 10–15 seconds, repeated if necessary according to response after 20–30 seconds; *or* up to 4 mg/kg; CHILD induction 4–8 mg/kg

PoM **Thiopentone Sodium** (Non-proprietary)
Injection, powder for reconstitution, thiopentone sodium. Net price 500-mg vial = £1.10

PoM **Add-A-Med® Thiopentone Sodium** (IMS)
Injection, thiopentone sodium 2.5 g with 100 mL diluent to provide a 2.5% solution, net price per unit = £7.75; 5 g with 200 mL diluent to provide a 2.5% solution, net price per unit = £13.25

PoM **Intraval Sodium®** (Rhône-Poulenc Rorer)
Injection 2.5%, powder for reconstitution, thiopentone sodium. Net price 500-mg amp = £1.49; 2.5-g vial = £4.80
Injection 5%, powder for reconstitution, thiopentone sodium. Net price 1-g amp = £1.79

PoM **Min-I-Mix® Thiopentone Sodium** (IMS)
Injection, thiopentone sodium 500 mg with diluent to provide a 2.5% solution on reconstitution. Net price per unit = £4.34

ETOMIDATE

Indications: induction of anaesthesia

Cautions; Contra-indications; Side-effects: see notes above; **interactions:** Appendix 1 (anaesthetics)

Dose: *by slow intravenous injection*, 300 micrograms/kg; high-risk patients, 100 micrograms/kg/minute until anaesthetised (about 3 minutes)

PoM **Hypnomidate®** (Janssen)
Injection, etomidate 2 mg/mL in propylene glycol 35%. Net price 10-mL amp = £1.62
Concentrate injection, etomidate 125 mg (as hydrochloride)/mL. To be diluted before use. Net price 1-mL amp = £5.47
Note. With the concentrate use only glass syringes, avoid contact with plastics

KETAMINE

Indications: induction and maintenance of anaesthesia

Cautions; Contra-indications; Side-effects: see notes above; **interactions:** Appendix 1 (anaesthetics)

Dose: *By intramuscular injection*, short procedures, initially 6.5–13 mg/kg (10 mg/kg usually produces 12–25 minutes of surgical anaesthesia)
Diagnostic manoeuvres and procedures not involving intense pain, initially 4 mg/kg
By intravenous injection over at least 60 seconds, short procedures, initially 1–4.5 mg/kg (2 mg/kg usually produces 5–10 minutes of surgical anaesthesia)
By intravenous infusion of a solution containing 1 mg/mL, longer procedures, induction, total dose of 0.5–2 mg/kg; maintenance (using microdrip infusion), 10–45 micrograms/kg/minute, rate adjusted according to response

PoM **Ketalar®** (P-D)
Injection, ketamine (as hydrochloride) 10 mg/mL, net price 20-mL vial = £3.52; 50 mg/mL, 10-mL vial = £7.31; 100 mg/mL, 5-mL vial = £6.71

METHOHEXITONE SODIUM

Indications: induction and maintenance of anaesthesia for short procedures; with other agents for more prolonged anaesthesia

Cautions; Contra-indications; Side-effects: see under Thiopentone Sodium and notes above

Dose: *by intravenous injection*, usually as a 1% solution, 50–120 mg according to response at rate of 10 mg in 5 seconds; maintenance, 20–40 mg (2–4 mL of 1% solution) every 4–7 minutes; CHILD induction approx. 1 mg/kg

PoM **Brietal Sodium®** (Lilly)
Injection, powder for reconstitution, methohexitone sodium, net price 100 mg in 10-mL vial = 83p; 500 mg in 50-mL vial = £2.14; 2.5 g in 250-mL vial = £7.98

PROPOFOL

Indications: induction and maintenance of general anaesthesia

Cautions; Contra-indications; Side-effects: see notes above; contra-indicated if history of propofol allergy (see CSM warning above); **interactions:** Appendix 1 (anaesthetics)

Dose: induction, *by intravenous injection*, 2–2.5 mg/kg at a rate of 20–40 mg every 10 seconds; maintenance, *by intravenous infusion*, 100–200 micrograms/kg/minute

▼ PoM **Diprivan®** (ICI)
Injection (emulsion), propofol 10 mg/mL, net price 20-mL amp = £3.98; 50-mL vial = £9.95

15.1.2 Inhalational anaesthetics

Inhalational anaesthetics may be gases or volatile liquids. They can be used both for induction and maintenance of anaesthesia and may be used following induction with an intravenous agent (section 15.1.1).

Gaseous anaesthetics require suitable equipment for storage and administration. They may be supplied via hospital pipelines or from metal cylinders. In clinical use it is necessary to monitor flow rate. Volatile agents are usually administered using calibrated vaporisers, using air, oxygen, or nitrous oxide–oxygen mixtures as the carrier gas.

To prevent hypoxia gaseous anaesthetics must be given with adequate concentrations of oxygen.

DRIVING. For advice on outpatient anaesthesia and driving, see section 15.1.

HALOGENATED ANAESTHETICS

Halothane is a widely used volatile anaesthetic. Its advantages are that it is potent, induction is smooth, the vapour is non-irritant, pleasant to inhale, and seldom induces coughing or breath-holding. The incidence of postoperative vomiting is low.

It is used for induction and maintenance of anaesthesia in major surgery with oxygen or nitrous oxide–oxygen mixtures.

Halothane causes cardiorespiratory depression and because of its potency is administered from calibrated vaporisers. Respiratory depression results in elevation of arterial carbon dioxide tension and perhaps ventricular dysrhythmias. Intermittent positive-pressure ventilation must be carried out with care as myocardial depression may follow increase in blood concentrations. Halothane depresses the cardiac muscle fibres and may cause bradycardia. The result is diminished cardiac output and fall of arterial pressure. There is also peripheral vasodilatation. Adrenaline infiltrations should be used with care as ventricular dysrhythmias may result.

Halothane produces moderate muscle relaxation, but this may be inadequate for major abdominal surgery and specific muscle relaxants are then used.

In a publication on findings confirming that *severe hepatotoxicity* can follow halothane anaesthesia the CSM has reported that this occurs more frequently after repeated exposures to halothane and has a high mortality. The risk of severe hepatotoxicity appears to be increased by repeated exposures within a short time interval, but even after a long interval (sometimes of several years) susceptible patients have been reported to develop jaundice. Since there is no reliable way of identifying susceptible patients the CSM recommends the following precautions prior to use of halothane:

1. a careful anaesthetic history should be taken to determine previous exposure and previous reactions to halothane;
2. repeated exposure to halothane within a period of at least 3 months should be avoided unless there are overriding clinical circumstances;
3. a history of unexplained jaundice or pyrexia in a patient following exposure to halothane is an absolute **contra-indication** to its future use in that patient.

Enflurane is a volatile anaesthetic similar to halothane, but it is less potent, about twice the concentration being necessary for induction and maintenance. Administration from a calibrated vaporiser is recommended.

Enflurane is a powerful cardiorespiratory depressant. Shallow respiration is likely to result in a rise of arterial carbon dioxide tension, but ventricular dysrhythmias are uncommon and it is probably safe to use adrenaline infiltrations. Myocardial depression may result in a fall in cardiac output and arterial hypotension.

Enflurane is usually given to supplement nitrous oxide–oxygen mixtures in concentrations of 1 to 3%. The drug is often used in preference to halothane when repeated anaesthesia is required.

Isoflurane is an isomer of enflurane. It has a potency intermediate between that of halothane and enflurane, and even less of an inhaled dose is metabolised than with enflurane. Heart rhythm is generally stable during isoflurane anaesthesia, but heart-rate may rise, particularly in younger patients. Systemic arterial pressure may fall, due to a decrease in systemic vascular resistance and with less decrease in cardiac output than occurs with halothane. Respiration is depressed. Muscle relaxation is produced and muscle relaxant drugs potentiated.

NITROUS OXIDE

Nitrous oxide is used for induction and maintenance of anaesthesia and, in sub-anaesthetic concentrations, for analgesia in a variety of situations. For anaesthesia it is commonly used in a concentration of 50 to 70% in oxygen as part of a balanced technique in association with other inhalational or intravenous agents. Nitrous oxide is unsatisfactory as a sole anaesthetic owing to lack of potency, but is useful as part of a sequence of drugs since it allows a significant reduction in dosage.

A mixture of nitrous oxide and oxygen containing 50% of each gas (Entonox®) is used to produce analgesia without loss of consciousness. Self-administration using a demand valve is popular and may be appropriate in obstetric practice, for changing painful dressings, as an aid to post-operative physiotherapy, and in emergency ambulances.

Nitrous oxide may have a deleterious effect if used in patients with an air-containing closed space since nitrous oxide diffuses into such a space with a resulting build up of pressure. This effect may be dangerous in the presence of a pneumothorax which may enlarge to compromise respiration. Exposure of patients to nitrous oxide for prolonged periods, either by continuous or intermittent administration, may result in megaloblastic anaemia due to interference with the action of vitamin B_{12}. For the same reason, exposure of anaesthetists and theatre staff to nitrous oxide should be minimised. Depression of white cell formation may also occur.

OTHER INHALATIONAL ANAESTHETICS

Cyclopropane is a potent gas which may be used for induction and maintenance. It forms explosive mixtures with air and oxygen and is used in a closed-circuit system. Muscle relaxation is produced and muscle relaxant drugs are potentiated. Respiration is depressed but arterial blood pressure is usually well maintained. It is useful for induction in paediatric and obstetric practice but has lost popularity for maintenance in major surgery because of its explosive properties. For major surgery it is best used in association with intermittent positive-pressure ventilation or the respiratory depressant action may result in elevation of arterial carbon dioxide tension with resultant ventricular dysrhythmias. Adrenaline infiltration should be avoided because of the danger of dysrhythmias. Recovery is rapid, though associated with postoperative vomiting and restlessness.

Anaesthetic ether (diethyl ether) is a potent anaesthetic, but is only available in the UK on a named-patient basis. The vapour forms flammable and explosive mixtures with oxygen. Both induction and recovery from anaesthesia are slow, and there is a high incidence of nausea and vomiting. Cardiac rhythm is stable and adrenaline infiltration may be allowed. Arterial blood pressure is well maintained.

CYCLOPROPANE

Indications; Cautions; Side-effects: see notes above; **interactions:** Appendix 1 (anaesthetics)

Dose: using a suitable closed-circuit anaesthetic apparatus, for light *anaesthesia* 7–10% in oxygen, for moderate to deep anaesthesia 20–30%

ENFLURANE

Indications; Cautions; Side-effects: see notes above; **interactions:** Appendix 1 (anaesthetics)

Dose: using a specifically calibrated vaporiser, *induction*, increased gradually from 0.4% to max. of 4.5% in air, oxygen, or nitrous oxide–oxygen, according to response

Maintenance, 0.5–3%

Enflurane (Abbott)
Enflurane. 250 mL

HALOTHANE

Indications; Cautions; Contra-indications; Side-effects: see notes above; **interactions:** Appendix 1 (anaesthetics)

Dose: using a suitable vaporiser, *induction*, increased gradually to 2–4% in oxygen or nitrous oxide–oxygen; CHILD 1.5–2%

Maintenance, 0.5–2%

Halothane (Rhône-Poulenc Rorer)
Net price 250 mL = £10.49

Fluothane® (ICI)
Halothane. Net price 250 mL = £10.49

ISOFLURANE

Indications; Cautions; Side-effects: see notes above; **interactions:** Appendix 1 (anaesthetics)

Dose: using a specifically calibrated vaporiser, *induction*, increased gradually from 0.5% to 3%, in oxygen or nitrous oxide–oxygen

Maintenance, 1–2.5% in nitrous oxide–oxygen; Caesarian section, 0.5–0.75% in nitrous oxide–oxygen

Isoflurane (Abbott)
Isoflurane. Net price 100 mL = £35.95

NITROUS OXIDE

Indications; Cautions; Side-effects: see notes above; **interactions:** Appendix 1 (anaesthetics)

Dose: using a suitable anaesthetic apparatus, a mixture with 20–30% oxygen for *induction* and *maintenance* of light anaesthesia

Analgesic, as a mixture with 50% oxygen, according to the patient's needs

15.1.3 Antimuscarinic premedication drugs

Antimuscarinic premedication drugs, usually atropine, hyoscine (scopolamine), or glycopyrronium are used to dry bronchial and salivary secretions which are increased by intubation and the inhalational anaesthetics. They are also used to prevent excessive bradycardia and hypotension caused by halothane, cyclopropane, suxamethonium, and neostigmine.

Atropine is the most commonly used. Intravenous administration immediately before anaesthesia or intramuscular injection (which should be given 30–60 minutes before the operation) is satisfactory.

Hyoscine effectively reduces secretions and also provides a degree of amnesia. It produces less tachycardia than atropine. In some patients, especially the elderly, hyoscine may cause the central anticholinergic syndrome (excitement, ataxia, hallucinations, behavioural abnormalities, and drowsiness).

Glycopyrronium bromide produces good drying of salivary secretions. When given intravenously it produces less tachycardia than atropine.

Phenothiazines have too little activity to be effective drying agents when used alone.

ATROPINE SULPHATE

Indications: drying secretions, reversal of excessive bradycardia; with neostigmine for reversal of competitive neuromuscular block; other indications, see sections 1.2, 11.5

Cautions: cardiovascular disease; **interactions:** Appendix 1 (antimuscarinics)

Side-effects: tachycardia; see also section 1.2

Dose: premedication, *by intravenous injection*, 300–600 micrograms immediately before induction of anaesthesia, and in incremental doses of 100 micrograms for the treatment of bradycardia

By intramuscular injection, 300–600 micrograms 30–60 minutes before induction; CHILD 20 micrograms/kg

For control of muscarinic side-effects of neostigmine in reversal of competitive neuromuscular block, *by intravenous injection*, 0.6–1.2 mg

PoM **Atropine** (Non-proprietary)

Tablets, atropine sulphate 600 micrograms. Net price 20 = £1.56

Injection, atropine sulphate 600 micrograms. Net price 1-mL amp = 31p

Note. Other strengths also available

CD **Morphine and Atropine Injection** see under Morphine Salts (section 15.1.4.1)

GLYCOPYRRONIUM BROMIDE

Indications; Cautions; Side-effects: see under Atropine Sulphate

Dose: premedication, *by intramuscular or intravenous injection*, 200–400 micrograms, *or* 4–5 micrograms/kg to a max. of 400 micrograms; CHILD, *by intramuscular or intravenous injection*, 4–8 micrograms/kg to a max. of 200 micrograms; intra-operative use, *by intravenous injection*, as for premedication

For control of muscarinic side-effects of neostigmine in reversal of competitive neuromuscular block, *by intravenous injection*, 10–15 micrograms/kg with 50 micrograms/kg neostigmine; CHILD, 10 micrograms/kg with 50 micrograms/kg neostigmine

PoM **Robinul®** (Wyeth)

Injection, glycopyrronium bromide 200 micrograms/mL. Net price 1-mL amp = 63p; 3-mL amp = £1.06

PoM **Robinul-Neostigmine®**: section 15.1.6

HYOSCINE HYDROBROMIDE

(Scopolamine Hydrobromide)

Indications: drying secretions, amnesia; other indications, see sections 4.6, 11.5

Cautions; Side-effects: see under Atropine Sulphate; may slow heart; avoid in the elderly (see notes above)

Dose: premedication, *by subcutaneous or intramuscular injection*, 200–600 micrograms 30–60 minutes before induction of anaesthesia, usually with papaveretum; CHILD 15 micrograms/kg

PoM **Hyoscine** (Non-proprietary)

Injection, hyoscine hydrobromide 400 micrograms/mL, net price 1-mL amp = £1.11; 600 micrograms/mL, 1-mL amp = 90p

CD **Papaveretum and Hyoscine Injection,** see under Papaveretum (section 15.1.4.1)

15.1.4 Sedative and analgesic peri-operative drugs

15.1.4.1 Opioid analgesics

15.1.4.2 Anxiolytics and neuroleptics

These drugs are given to allay the apprehension of the patient in the pre-operative period (including the night before operation), to relieve pain and discomfort when present, and to augment the action of subsequent anaesthetic agents. A number of the drugs used also provide some degree of pre-operative amnesia. The choice will vary with the individual patient, the nature of the operative procedure, the anaesthetic to be used and other prevailing circumstances such as outpatients, obstetrics, recovery facilities etc. The choice would also vary in elective and emergency operations.

For many procedures, particularly minor operations, premedication is omitted completely and in these circumstances antisialogogues will usually be given intravenously, either with or just before the induction agent.

PREMEDICATION IN CHILDREN. Oral or rectal administration is preferred to injections where possible but is not altogether satisfactory. Oral **trimeprazine** is still used but when given alone it may cause postoperative restlessness when pain is present. An alternative is **diazepam**. Some anaesthetists prefer the use of adult regimens, with dosage on a weight basis. (For guidelines on dose calculation in children, see Prescribing for Children.)

Atropine or hyoscine is often given orally to children, but may be given intravenously immediately before induction.

DRIVING. For advice on outpatient anaesthesia and driving, see section 15.1.

15.1.4.1 OPIOID ANALGESICS

The most common premedicants are still the opioid analgesics, e.g. morphine, papaveretum, and pethidine given intramuscularly about an hour before operation, usually combined with an antisialogogue. Sometimes they are combined with a phenothiazine or droperidol. The main side-effects are respiratory depression, cardiovascular depression, and nausea and vomiting. The principal advantages are that opioid analgesics provide analgesia persisting into the operative period giving a reduced chance of awareness during anaesthesia with full doses of muscle relaxants.

INTRA-OPERATIVE ANALGESIA. Many of the conventional opioid analgesics are used to supplement general anaesthesia, usually in combination with nitrous oxide–oxygen and a muscle relaxant. Pethidine was the first to be used for this purpose but other drugs now available include alfentanil, fentanyl, meptazinol, nalbuphine, and phenoperidine. The longer-acting drugs morphine and papaveretum, although equally effective for this purpose, are not commonly used because of the problems of respiratory depression in the postoperative period.

Small doses of opioids given immediately before or with thiopentone will reduce the induction dose of the barbiturate and this is a popular technique in poor-risk patients. **Alfentanil** and **fentanyl** are particularly useful in this respect because of their short duration of action although there may be some cumulation with large doses. Alfentanil may be preferable for short operations because of its very brief duration of action; for long procedures it can be given as a continuous infusion.

Repeated doses of intra-operative analgesics should be given with care, since not only may the respiratory depression persist into the postoperative period but it may become apparent for the first time postoperatively when the patient is away from immediate nursing attention. The specific opioid antagonist, naloxone, will immediately reverse this respiratory depression but the dose may have to be repeated. In clinical doses it will also reverse most of the analgesia. An alternative and equally acceptable approach is to use the specific respiratory stimulant, doxapram (see section 3.5), which can be given in an infusion and which will not affect the opioid analgesia. The use of intra-operative opioids should be borne in mind when prescribing postoperative analgesics. In many instances they will delay the need for the first dose but caution is necessary since there may be some residual respiratory depression potentiated by the postoperative analgesic.

Fentanyl may produce severe respiratory depression, especially in patients with decreased respiratory function or when other respiratory depressant drugs have been given. Respiratory depression may be treated by artificial ventilation or be reversed by naloxone or doxapram. Alfentanil may also cause severe respiratory depression, especially when other respiratory depressant drugs have already been given; this may be reversed with naloxone.

Meptazinol can be used for analgesia during or after operation. It is associated with nausea and vomiting, but is claimed to have a reduced incidence of respiratory depression.

For further notes on analgesics see section 4.7.

ALFENTANIL

Indications: analgesia especially during short operative procedure and outpatient surgery; enhancement of anaesthesia; analgesic and respiratory depressant in assisted respiration

Cautions; Contra-indications; Side-effects: see under Fentanyl and notes above

Dose: *by intravenous injection*, spontaneous respiration, adults, initially up to 500 micrograms over 30 seconds; supplemental, 250 micrograms

With assisted ventilation, adults and children, initially 30–50 micrograms/kg; supplemental, 15 micrograms/kg

By intravenous infusion, with assisted ventilation, adults and children, initially 50–100 micrograms/kg over 10 minutes *or* as a bolus, followed by maintenance of 0.5–1 micrograms/kg/minute

CD Rapifen® (Janssen)

Injection, alfentanil 500 micrograms (as hydrochloride)/mL. Net price 2-mL amp = 74p; 10-mL amp = £3.39

Dilute injection[1], alfentanil 100 micrograms (as hydrochloride)/mL. Net price 5-mL amp = 46p

1. Formerly Rapifen® Paediatric

Intensive care[2] *injection*, alfentanil 5 mg (as hydrochloride)/mL. To be diluted before use. Net price 1-mL amp = £2.72

2. Formerly Rapifen® Concentrate injection

FENTANYL

Indications: analgesia during operation, neuroleptanalgesia, enhancement of anaesthesia; respiratory depressant in assisted respiration

Cautions: chronic respiratory disease, myasthenia gravis; reduce dose in elderly, hypothyroidism, chronic liver disease; obstetric use may cause respiratory depression in neonate; see also notes above; **interactions:** Appendix 1 (opioid analgesics)

Contra-indications: respiratory depression or obstructive airways disease unless patient ventilated

Side-effects: respiratory depression, transient hypotension, bradycardia, nausea and vomiting

Dose: *by intravenous injection*, with spontaneous respiration, 50–200 micrograms, then 50 micrograms as required; CHILD 3–5 micrograms/kg, then 1 microgram/kg as required

With assisted ventilation, 0.3–3.5 mg, then 100–200 micrograms as required; CHILD 15 micrograms/kg, then 1–3 micrograms/kg as required

CD Fentanyl Citrate (Non-proprietary)

Injection, fentanyl 50 micrograms (as citrate)/mL, net price 2-mL amp = 25p; 10-mL amp = £1.20

CD Sublimaze® (Janssen)

Injection, fentanyl 50 micrograms (as citrate)/mL. Net price 2-mL amp = 25p; 10-mL amp = £1.20

CD Thalamonal® (Janssen)

Injection, fentanyl 50 micrograms (as citrate), droperidol 2.5 mg/mL. Net price 2-mL amp = 95p

Dose: premedication, by intramuscular injection 1–2 mL; induction, by intravenous injection 6–8 mL followed by assisted ventilation; maintenance, by intravenous injection, 1–2 mL as required; CHILD premedication, by intramuscular injection 0.4–1.5 mL

MEPTAZINOL

Indications: analgesia during and after operation

Cautions; Contra-indications; Side-effects: see section 4.7.2 and notes above

Dose: by mouth, 200 mg every 3–6 hours as required
By intramuscular injection, 75–100 mg, repeated every 2–4 hours as required
By slow intravenous injection, 50–100 mg, repeated every 2–4 hours as required

PoM **Meptid**® (Wyeth)
Tablets, orange, f/c, meptazinol 200 mg. Net price 20 = £1.80. Label: 2
Injection, meptazinol 100 mg (as hydrochloride)/mL. Net price 1-mL amp = 79p

MORPHINE SALTS

Indications: analgesia during and after operation; enhancement of anaesthesia; pre-operative sedation; analgesia in other situations, see section 4.7.2
Cautions; Contra-indications; Side-effects: see section 4.7.2 and notes above
Dose: *by subcutaneous or intramuscular injection*, up to 10 mg 1–1½ hours before operation; CHILD, *by intramuscular injection*, 150 micrograms/kg. See also section 4.7.2 for analgesia

CD **Morphine Sulphate Injection,** morphine sulphate, 10, 15 and 30 mg/mL. Net price 1- and 2-mL amp (all) = 37–41p
CD **Morphine and Atropine Injection,** morphine sulphate 10 mg, atropine sulphate 600 micrograms/mL. Net price 1-mL amp = 49p
Dose: by subcutaneous injection, 0.5–1 mL

NALBUPHINE HYDROCHLORIDE

Indications: peri-operative analgesia; premedication
Cautions; Contra-indications; Side-effects: see section 4.7.2 and notes above; also caution in ambulant patients (impairment of mental and physical ability)
Dose: acute pain, *by subcutaneous, intramuscular, or intravenous injection*, 10–20 mg, adjusted according to response; CHILD up to 300 micrograms/kg repeated once or twice as necessary
Premedication, *by subcutaneous, intramuscular, or intravenous injection*, 100–200 micrograms/kg
Induction, *by intravenous injection*, 0.3–1 mg/kg over 10–15 minutes
Intra-operative analgesia, *by intravenous injection*, 250–500 micrograms/kg at 30-minute intervals

PoM **Nubain**® (Du Pont)
Injection, nalbuphine hydrochloride 10 mg/mL. Net price 1-mL amp = 75p; 2-mL amp = £1.16

PAPAVERETUM

The hydrochlorides of alkaloids of opium, containing the equivalent of anhydrous morphine 47.5–52.5%, anhydrous codeine 2.5–5%, noscapine 16–22%, and papaverine 2.5–7%
Indications: analgesia during and after operation; enhancement of anaesthetics; pre-operative sedation
Cautions; Contra-indications; Side-effects: see section 4.7.2 and notes above
Dose: acute pain, *by subcutaneous or intramuscular injection*, 20 mg repeated every 4 hours if necessary (10 mg for elderly or lighter patients); CHILD up to 1 month 150 micrograms/kg, 1–12 months 200 micrograms/kg, 1–12 years 200–300 micrograms/kg
By slow intravenous injection, Quarter to half corresponding subcutaneous or intramuscular dose
Pre-operative sedation, *by subcutaneous or intramuscular injection*, 10–20 mg 45–60 minutes before anaesthesia; CHILD single doses as above
Note. Papaveretum 20 mg is approximately equivalent to morphine 12.5 mg
IMPORTANT. Do **not** confuse with papaverine (see section 7.4.5)

CD **Papaveretum Injection,** papaveretum 10 mg/mL, net price 1-mL amp = 13p; 20 mg/mL, 1-mL amp = 13p
CD **Papaveretum and Hyoscine Injection,** papaveretum 20 mg, hyoscine hydrobromide 400 micrograms/mL. Net price 1-mL amp = 14p
Dose: by subcutaneous or intramuscular injection, 1 mL
CD **Omnopon**® (Roche)
Injection, papaveretum 20 mg/mL. Net price 1-mL amp = 13p
Paediatric injection, papaveretum 10 mg/mL. Net price 1-mL amp = 13p
CD **Omnopon-Scopolamine**® (Roche)
Injection, papaveretum 20 mg, hyoscine hydrobromide 400 micrograms/mL. Net price 1-mL amp = 14p
Dose: by subcutaneous or intramuscular injection, 1 mL

PETHIDINE HYDROCHLORIDE

Indications: peri-operative analgesia, enhancement of anaesthesia, for basal narcosis with phenothiazines
Cautions; Contra-indications; Side-effects: see section 4.7.2 and notes above
Dose: premedication, *by intramuscular injection*, 50–100 mg 1 hour before operation; CHILD 1–2 mg/kg
Adjunct to nitrous oxide–oxygen, *by slow intravenous injection*, 10–25 mg repeated when required

CD **Pethidine** (Roche)
Injection, pethidine hydrochloride 50 mg/mL, net price 1-mL amp = 11p; 2-mL amp = 14p; 10 mg/mL, 5-mL amp = 60p; 10-mL amp = 65p
CD **Pethidine Tablets,** see section 4.7.2
CD **Pamergan P100**® (Martindale)
Injection, pethidine hydrochloride 50 mg, promethazine hydrochloride 25 mg/mL. Net price 2-mL amp = 45p
Dose: 2 mL by intramuscular injection or, diluted to 10 mL, by intravenous injection, 1–1½ hours before operation; CHILD, by intramuscular injection, 8–12 years 0.75 mL, 13–16 years 1 mL

PHENOPERIDINE HYDROCHLORIDE

Indications: analgesia during operation, neuroleptanalgesia, enhancement of anaesthetics; respiratory depressant in prolonged assisted respiration

Cautions; Contra-indications; Side-effects: see under Pethidine Hydrochloride and Fentanyl. Doses above 1 mg cause respiratory depression and require assisted ventilation (effects may be terminated with naloxone)

Dose: by intravenous injection, with spontaneous respiration, up to 1 mg, then 500 micrograms every 40–60 minutes as required; CHILD 30–50 micrograms/kg

With assisted ventilation, 2–5 mg, then 1 mg as required; CHILD 100–150 micrograms/kg

CD **Operidine**® (Janssen)

Injection, phenoperidine hydrochloride 1 mg/mL. Net price 2-mL amp = 77p; 10-mL amp = £4.05

15.1.4.2 ANXIOLYTICS AND NEUROLEPTICS

Oral premedication is increasing in popularity using benzodiazepines such as diazepam, lorazepam, and temazepam.

Diazepam is used to produce light sedation with amnesia. The 'sleep' dose shows too great an individual variation to recommend it for induction of anaesthesia, and while this variation exists with regard to its sedative effect, it is probably less marked with lower doses and of little clinical significance. It is particularly valuable in sub-anaesthetic doses to produce light sedation for unpleasant procedures or for operations under local anaesthesia, including dentistry; sub-anaesthetic doses allow retention of the pharyngeal reflexes while a local block is performed, and the resultant amnesia is such that the patient is unlikely to have any unpleasant memories of the procedure (however, benzodiazepines, particularly when used for deep sedation, can sometimes induce sexual fantasies). Diazepam can also be used in a similar manner for endoscopy, with or without an opioid analgesic.

Preparations of diazepam in organic solvents are painful on intravenous injection and followed by a high incidence of venous thrombosis which may not be noticed until a week after the injection. They are also painful on intramuscular injection, and absorption from the injection site is erratic. An emulsion preparation of diazepam (Diazemuls®) is less irritant on intravenous injection and is followed by a negligible incidence of venous thrombosis, but it should not be given intramuscularly. Diazepam is also available as a rectal solution.

Diazepam and related drugs are of particular value for sedation of patients in an intensive care unit, particularly those on ventilators. It can be given 4–6 hourly but dosage should be gradually reduced after some days to prevent delay in recovery, which can be caused by a build up of its metabolite. Since it has no analgesic action it is often given in conjunction with small doses of opioid analgesics.

Diazepam may on occasions cause marked respiratory depression and facilities for treatment of this are essential. Dental patients who are sitting in one position for a long time may develop hypotonia after diazepam and they should be warned about this possibility. Outpatients should be advised that this is a long-acting drug, and that a second period of drowsiness can occur 4–6 hours after its administration.

By virtue of its physical characteristics, diazepam can accumulate in the fetus and, particularly after the mother has been given large doses, babies can be born in a depressed state, with hypotonia and a tendency to develop hypothermia.

Temazepam has a shorter action and relatively more rapid onset than diazepam. Used orally as a premedicant, anxiolytic and sedative effects are produced which continue for one and a half hours. After this period patients are usually fully alert but there may be residual drowsiness. It has proved useful as a premedicant in inpatient and day-case surgery.

Lorazepam produces more prolonged sedation than temazepam. In addition amnesia is commonplace. It is particularly useful when used as a premedicant the night prior to major surgery; sound sleep is assured when an oral dose of 1 to 5 mg is given. A further, smaller, dose the following morning will be required if any delay in the commencement of surgery is anticipated. Alternatively the first dose may be given in the early morning of the day of operation.

Midazolam is a water-soluble benzodiazepine which is often used in preference to diazepam. Recovery is faster than with diazepam. The incidence of side-effects is low but the CSM has received reports of respiratory depression (sometimes associated with severe hypotension) following intravenous administration. A preparation containing 2 mg/mL is available to ensure easier titration of dosage.

Chlormethiazole has been used as an intravenous infusion to maintain sleep during surgery carried out under regional analgesia, including extradural block. It has no analgesic effect, little cardiac and respiratory depression, and may be used in elderly patients.

CHLORMETHIAZOLE EDISYLATE

Indications: sedative during regional anaesthesia; other indications, see sections 4.1.1, 4.8.2

Cautions; Side-effects: see section 4.8.2

Contra-indications: acute pulmonary insufficiency

Dose: by intravenous infusion, as a 0.8% solution, induction 25 mL (200 mg)/minute for 1–2 minutes; maintenance 1–4 mL (8–32 mg)/minute

Note. Special care on prolonged intravenous administration since accumulation may occur; also, contains no electrolytes

PoM **Heminevrin®** (Astra)
Intravenous infusion 0.8%, chlormethiazole edisylate 8 mg/mL. Net price 500-mL bottle = £5.25

CHLORPROMAZINE HYDROCHLORIDE

Indications: see under Dose; other indications, see section 4.2
Cautions; Contra-indications; Side-effects: see section 4.2.1
Dose: induction of hypothermia (to prevent shivering), *by deep intramuscular injection*, 25–50 mg every 6–8 hours; CHILD 1–12 years, initially 0.5–1 mg/kg, maintenance 500 micrograms/kg every 4–6 hours

PoM **Largactil®** (Rhône-Poulenc Rorer)
Injection, chlorpromazine hydrochloride 25 mg/mL. Net price 2-mL amp = 28p

DIAZEPAM

Indications: premedication; sedation with amnesia, and in conjunction with local anaesthesia; other indications, see sections 4.1.2, 4.8, 10.2.2
Cautions; Contra-indications; Side-effects: see notes above and sections 4.1.2, 4.8.2
Dose: *by mouth*, 5 mg at night, 5 mg on waking, and 5 mg 2 hours before minor or dental surgery
By intravenous injection, 10–20 mg over 2–4 minutes as sedative cover for minor surgical and medical procedures; premedication 100–200 micrograms/kg
By rectum in solution, ADULT and CHILD over 3 years 10 mg; CHILD 1–3 years and elderly 5 mg

Oral and rectal preparations: see section 4.1.2

Parenteral preparations
PoM **Diazepam** (Non-proprietary)
Injection (solution), diazepam 5 mg/mL. See Appendix 6. Net price 2-mL amp = 25p
Available from CP
PoM **Diazemuls®** (Dumex)
Injection (emulsion), diazepam 5 mg/mL. For intravenous injection or infusion. See Appendix 6. Net price 2-mL amp = 63p
PoM **Valium®** (Roche)
Injection (solution), diazepam 5 mg/mL. See Appendix 6. Net price 2-mL amp = 28p

DROPERIDOL

Indications: anti-emetic, pre-operative sedation; neuroleptanalgesia; other indications, see section 4.2.1
Cautions; Contra-indications; Side-effects: see section 4.2.1
Dose: premedication, *by intramuscular injection*, up to 10 mg 60 minutes before operation; CHILD 200–500 micrograms/kg
Neuroleptanalgesia, *by intravenous injection*, 5–15 mg at induction with an opioid analgesic; CHILD 200–300 micrograms/kg

PoM **Droleptan®** (Janssen)
Injection, droperidol 5 mg/mL. Net price 2-mL amp = 92p
CD Thalamonal® — see under Fentanyl (section 15.1.4.1)

LORAZEPAM

Indications: sedation with amnesia; as premedication; other indications, see sections 4.1.2, 4.8.2
Cautions; Contra-indications; Side-effects: see under Diazepam
Dose: *by mouth*, 1–3 mg at night *or* 1–5 mg 2–6 hours before surgery
By slow intravenous injection, preferably diluted with an equal volume of sodium chloride intravenous infusion 0.9% or water for injections, 50 micrograms/kg 30–45 minutes before operation
By intramuscular injection, diluted as above, 50 micrograms/kg 1–1½ hours before operation

PoM **Ativan®** (Wyeth)
Injection, lorazepam 4 mg/mL in solvent. Net price 1-mL amp = 40p
Tablets, see section 4.1.2

MIDAZOLAM

Indications: sedation with amnesia, and in conjunction with local anaesthesia; premedication, induction
Cautions; Contra-indications; Side-effects: see under Diazepam; see notes above for CSM warning
Dose: sedation, *by intravenous injection* over 30 seconds, 2 mg (elderly 1–1.5 mg) followed after 2 minutes by increments of 0.5–1 mg if sedation not adequate; usual range 2.5–7.5 mg (about 70 micrograms/kg), elderly 1–2 mg
Premedication, *by intramuscular injection*, 70–100 micrograms/kg 30–60 minutes before surgery; usual dose 5 mg (2.5 mg in elderly)
Induction, *by slow intravenous injection*, 200–300 micrograms/kg (elderly 100–200 micrograms/kg)

PoM **Hypnovel®** (Roche)
Injection, midazolam (as hydrochloride) 2 mg/mL, net price 5-mL amp = 92p; 5 mg/mL, 2-mL amp = 77p

PROMETHAZINE HYDROCHLORIDE

Indications: anti-emetic, pre-operative sedative and antimuscarinic agent; other indications, see sections 3.4.1, 3.4.3
Cautions; Side-effects: see section 4.6
Dose: premedication, *by mouth*, CHILD 1–5 years 15–20 mg, 6–10 years 20–25 mg
By deep intramuscular injection, 25–50 mg 1 hour before operation; CHILD 5–10 years, 6.25–12.5 mg

Preparations
See section 3.4.1

TEMAZEPAM

Indications: premedication before minor surgery; anxiety before investigatory procedures; hypnotic, see section 4.1.1

Cautions; Contra-indications; Side-effects: see under Diazepam

Dose: premedication, 20–40 mg (elderly, 10–20 mg) 1 hour before operation; CHILD 1 mg/kg (max. 30 mg)

Preparations See section 4.1.1

TRIMEPRAZINE TARTRATE

Indications: pre-operative sedation, anti-emetic; other indications, see section 3.4.1

Cautions; Side-effects: see notes above and section 3.4.1

Dose: premedication, 3 mg/kg 1–2 hours before operation; CHILD 2–7 years up to 2 mg/kg

Preparations: See section 3.4.1

15.1.5 Muscle relaxants

Muscle relaxants used in anaesthesia are also known as **neuromuscular blocking drugs** or **myoneural blocking drugs**. By specific blockade of the neuromuscular junction they enable light levels of anaesthesia to be employed with adequate relaxation of the muscles of the abdomen and diaphragm. They also relax the vocal cords and allow the passage of a tracheal tube. Their action differs from the muscle relaxants acting on the spinal cord or brain which are used in musculoskeletal disorders (see section 10.2.2).

Patients who have received a muscle relaxant should **always** have their respiration assisted or controlled until the drug has been inactivated or antagonised (section 15.1.6).

NON-DEPOLARISING MUSCLE RELAXANTS

Drugs of this group (also known as competitive muscle relaxants) cause blockade by competing with acetylcholine at the receptor site at the neuromuscular junction. These drugs are best suited to the production of paralysis of long duration. They have a slower, less complete action than the depolarising muscle relaxants and should be avoided in myasthenia gravis.

These drugs may be used during surgical operations and for patients receiving long-term ventilation in intensive care units, when larger total doses will be appropriate.

The action of the competitive muscle relaxants may be reversed with anticholinesterases such as neostigmine (section 15.1.6).

Atracurium and **vecuronium** are much more widely employed than the other muscle relaxants, atracurium because of its non-enzymatic elimination and vecuronium because it has the fewest side-effects.

Atracurium has a duration of action of 15 to 35 minutes. Histamine release may occur. The drug is without vagolytic or sympatholytic properties. It has an advantage over other non-depolarising muscle relaxants in patients with renal or hepatic impairment, as it is degraded by non-enzymatic Hofmann elimination, which is independent of liver and kidney function. It is non-cumulative on repeated dosage. Its action is reversed by neostigmine. Duration of action may be prolonged in hypothermia.

Vecuronium has a duration of action of 20 to 30 minutes. Large doses may have a cumulative effect. The drug does not cause histamine release, sympathetic blockade, or vagolytic effects.

Pancuronium does not cause ganglionic blockade or significant changes in blood pressure and may therefore be favoured when it is important to maintain cardiac output.

Tubocurarine starts to act between 3–5 minutes and lasts for about 30 minutes after injection. It may cause an erythematous rash on the chest and neck and this is probably due to histamine release. Onset of blockade may be associated with hypotension and this, though transient, may be important in poor-risk patients.

Gallamine has a more rapid onset of action and recovery than tubocurarine or pancuronium. It causes undesirable tachycardia by its vagolytic action. It should be avoided in patients with severe renal disease.

Alcuronium appears to have no significant advantages over other muscle relaxants. Its duration of action is similar to that of tubocurarine.

ALCURONIUM CHLORIDE

Indications: non-depolarising muscle relaxant of medium duration

Cautions; Contra-indications; Side-effects: see notes above. Reduce dose in renal impairment; **interactions:** Appendix 1 (muscle relaxants)

Dose: by intravenous injection, initially 200–250 micrograms/kg, then incremental doses of one-sixth to one-quarter of the initial dose, as required; CHILD over 1 month, 125–200 micrograms/kg

PoM **Alloferin®** (Roche)

Injection, alcuronium chloride 5 mg/mL. Net price 2-mL amp = 58p

ATRACURIUM BESYLATE

Indications: non-depolarising muscle relaxant of medium duration

Cautions; Contra-indications; Side-effects: see notes above; **interactions:** Appendix 1 (muscle relaxants)

Dose: by intravenous injection, ADULT and CHILD over 1 month initially 300–600 micrograms/kg, then 100–200 micrograms/kg as required

By intravenous infusion, 5–10 micrograms/kg/minute (300–600 micrograms/kg/hour)

PoM **Tracrium®** (Wellcome)

Injection, atracurium besylate 10 mg/mL. Net price 2.5-mL amp = £1.69; 5-mL amp = £3.25; 25-mL amp = £13.91

GALLAMINE TRIETHIODIDE

Indications: non-depolarising muscle relaxant of medium duration
Cautions; Contra-indications; Side-effects: see notes above; reduce dose in renal impairment (avoid if severe); **interactions:** Appendix 1 (muscle relaxants)
Dose: by intravenous injection, 80–120 mg, then 20–40 mg as required; CHILD, 1.5 mg/kg

PoM **Flaxedil**® (Rhône–Poulenc Rorer)
Injection, gallamine triethiodide 40 mg/mL. Net price 2-mL amp = 74p

PANCURONIUM BROMIDE

Indications: non-depolarising muscle relaxant of medium duration
Cautions; Contra-indications; Side-effects: see notes above; caution in hepatic impairment; reduce dose in renal impairment; **interactions:** Appendix 1 (muscle relaxants)
Dose: by intravenous injection, initially for intubation 50–100 micrograms/kg then 10–20 micrograms/kg as required; CHILD initially 60–100 micrograms/kg, then 10–20 micrograms/kg, NEONATE 30–40 micrograms/kg initially then 10–20 micrograms/kg
Intensive care, *by intravenous injection*, 60 micrograms/kg every 1–1½ hours

PoM **Pavulon**® (Organon-Teknika)
Injection, pancuronium bromide 2 mg/mL. Net price 2-mL amp = 67p

TUBOCURARINE CHLORIDE

Indications: non-depolarising muscle relaxant of medium to long duration
Cautions; Contra-indications; Side-effects: see notes above. Reduce dose in renal impairment; **interactions:** Appendix 1 (muscle relaxants)
Dose: by intravenous injection, initially 15–30 mg according to circumstances then 5–10 mg as required; CHILD, initially 300–500 micrograms/kg then 60–100 micrograms/kg as required; NEONATE initially 200–250 micrograms/kg then 40–50 micrograms/kg as required

PoM **Jexin**® (DF)
Injection, tubocurarine chloride 10 mg/mL. Net price 1.5-mL amp = 71p
PoM **Tubarine Miscible**® (Calmic)
Injection, tubocurarine chloride 10 mg/mL. Net price 1.5-mL amp = £1.62

VECURONIUM BROMIDE

Indications: non-depolarising muscle relaxant of short to medium duration
Cautions; Contra-indications; Side-effects: see notes above; reduce dose in renal impairment; **interactions:** Appendix 1 (muscle relaxants)
Dose: by intravenous injection, initially 80–100 micrograms/kg (max. 250 micrograms/kg), then 30–50 micrograms/kg as required; CHILD, as adult dose (onset more rapid)
By intravenous infusion, 50–80 micrograms/kg/hour

PoM **Norcuron**® (Organon-Teknika)
Injection, powder for reconstitution, vecuronium bromide. Net price 10-mg vial = £3.29 (with water for injections)

DEPOLARISING MUSCLE RELAXANTS

Suxamethonium is the only commonly used drug of this group. With a 5-minute duration of action it is ideal for passage of a tracheal tube but may be used in repeated dosage for longer procedures.

It acts by mimicking acetylcholine at the neuromuscular junction but disengagement from the receptor site and subsequent breakdown is slower than for acetylcholine; depolarisation is therefore prolonged and neuromuscular blockade results.

It produces rapid, complete, and predictable paralysis, and recovery is spontaneous. Unlike the non-depolarising muscle relaxants its action cannot be reversed and clinical application is therefore limited.

Suxamethonium should be given after induction of anaesthesia because paralysis is usually preceded by painful muscle fasciculation. There is a transient rise in plasma potassium and creatine phosphokinase and there may be muscle pains postoperatively. Suxamethonium is **contra-indicated** in severe liver disease and in burned patients. Premedication with atropine is desirable.

Prolonged muscle paralysis may occur in patients with low or atypical plasma pseudocholinesterase enzymes. Prolonged paralysis may also occur in **dual block**, which occurs after repeated doses of suxamethonium have been used and is caused by the development of a non-depolarising block following the primary depolarising block. Artificial ventilation should be continued until muscle function is restored. Dual block is diagnosed by giving a short-acting anticholinesterase such as edrophonium; if an improvement occurs the block is treated with neostigmine (section 15.1.6).

SUXAMETHONIUM CHLORIDE

Indications: depolarising muscle relaxant of short duration
Cautions; Contra-indications; Side-effects: see notes above; **interactions:** Appendix 1 (muscle relaxants)
Dose: by intravenous injection, 600 micrograms/kg (range 0.3–1.1 mg/kg depending on degree of relaxation required); usual range 20–100 mg
By intravenous infusion, as a 0.1% solution, 2–5 mg/minute (2–5 mL/minute)
By intramuscular injection, ADULT and CHILD, up to 2.5 mg/kg (max. 150 mg)

PoM **Anectine®** (Calmic)
Injection, suxamethonium chloride 50 mg/mL. Net price 2-mL amp = 63p

PoM **Min-I-Mix® Suxamethonium Chloride** (IMS)
Injection, suxamethonium chloride 100 mg with diluent to provide a 2% solution on reconstitution. Net price per unit = £3.55

PoM **Scoline®** (DF)
Injection, suxamethonium chloride 50 mg/mL. Net price 2-mL amp = 31p

15.1.6 Anticholinesterases used in surgery

Anticholinesterase drugs reverse the effects of the non-depolarising (competitive) muscle relaxant drugs such as tubocurarine but they prolong the action of the depolarising muscle relaxant drug suxamethonium.

Edrophonium has a transient action and is used to diagnose dual block caused by suxamethonium (section 15.1.5).

Neostigmine has a longer duration of action than edrophonium. It is the specific drug for reversal of non-depolarising (competitive) blockade. It acts within one minute of intravenous injection and lasts for 20 to 30 minutes; a second dose may then be necessary. It is also used in the treatment of dual block.

Atropine or **glycopyrronium** (section 15.1.3) should be given before or with neostigmine in order to prevent bradycardia, excessive salivation, or other muscarinic actions of neostigmine.

For drugs used in myasthenia gravis see section 10.2.1.

EDROPHONIUM CHLORIDE

Indications: see under Dose
Cautions; Contra-indications; Side-effects: see section 10.2.1 and notes above. Atropine should also be given
Dose: brief reversal of non-depolarising neuromuscular blockade, *by intravenous injection* over several minutes, 500–700 micrograms/kg (after or with atropine sulphate 0.6–1.2 mg)
Diagnosis of dual block, *by intravenous injection*, 10 mg (with atropine)
Diagnosis of myasthenia gravis, see section 10.2.1

PoM **Tensilon®** (Roche)
Injection, edrophonium chloride 10 mg/mL. Net price 1-mL amp = 27p

NEOSTIGMINE METHYLSULPHATE

Indications: see under Dose
Cautions; Contra-indications; Side-effects: see section 10.2.1 and notes above. Atropine should also be given
Dose: reversal of non-depolarising neuromuscular blockade, *by intravenous injection* over 1 minute, 50–70 micrograms/kg (max. 5 mg), after or with atropine sulphate 0.6–1.2 mg
Myasthenia gravis, see section 10.2.1

PoM **Prostigmin®** (Roche)
Injection, neostigmine methylsulphate 500 micrograms/mL, net price 1-mL amp = 16p; 2.5 mg/mL, 1-mL amp = 16p

PoM **Robinul-Neostigmine®** (Wyeth)
Injection, neostigmine methylsulphate 2.5 mg, glycopyrronium bromide 500 micrograms/mL. Net price 1-mL amp = £1.06
Dose: by intravenous injection over 10–30 seconds, 1–2 mL *or* 0.02 mL/kg; CHILD 0.02 mL/kg (*or* 0.2 mL/kg of a 1 in 10 dilution using water for injections or sodium chloride injection 0.9%)

15.1.7 Antagonists for central and respiratory depression

The opioid antagonist **naloxone**, can be used at the end of an operation to reverse respiratory depression caused by opioid analgesics. Unless the dosage is carefully adjusted, analgesia may also be reversed. For respiratory stimulants see section 3.5. **Doxapram** is a respiratory stimulant which does not reverse the other effects of opioid analgesics.

Flumazenil is a benzodiazepine antagonist for the reversal of the central sedative effects of benzodiazepines in anaesthetic and similar procedures. It is important to recognize that the half-life of flumazenil is shorter than those of diazepam and midazolam, in order to avoid the risk of patients becoming resedated.

DOXAPRAM HYDROCHLORIDE

Indications: see under Dose
Cautions; Contra-indications; Side-effects: see section 3.5
Dose: postoperative respiratory depression, *by intravenous injection* over at least 30 seconds, 1–1.5 mg/kg repeated if necessary after intervals of 1 hour
By intravenous infusion, 2–3 mg/minute
Ventilatory failure, see section 3.5

PoM **Dopram®** (Wyeth)
Injection, doxapram hydrochloride 20 mg/mL. Net price 5-mL amp = £2.14
Intravenous infusion: see section 3.5

FLUMAZENIL

Indications: reversal of sedative effects of benzodiazepines in anaesthetic, intensive care, and diagnostic procedures
Cautions: short-acting (repeat doses may be necessary); benzodiazepine effects may persist for at least 24 hours; benzodiazepine dependence; ensure neuromuscular blockade cleared before giving; avoid rapid injection in high-risk or anxious patients and following major surgery; hepatic impairment

 Prices are **net**, see p. 1

Contra-indications: epileptics who have received prolonged benzodiazepine therapy
Side-effects: nausea, vomiting, and flushing; if wakening too rapid, agitation, anxiety, and fear; transient increase in blood pressure and heart-rate in intensive care patients; very rarely convulsions (particularly in epileptics)
Dose: *by intravenous injection*, 200 micrograms over 15 seconds, then 100 micrograms at 60-second intervals if required; usual dose range, 300–600 micrograms; max. total dose 1 mg (2 mg in intensive care); question aetiology if no response to repeated doses
By intravenous infusion, if drowsiness recurs after injection, 100–400 micrograms/hour, adjusted according to level of arousal

PoM **Anexate**® (Roche)
Injection, flumazenil 100 micrograms/mL. Net price 5-mL amp = £16.32

NALOXONE HYDROCHLORIDE

Indications: reversal of opioid-induced respiratory depression
Cautions: see under Emergency Treatment of Poisoning
Dose: *by intravenous injection*, 100–200 micrograms (1.5–3 micrograms/kg); if response inadequate, increments of 100 micrograms every 2 minutes; further doses *by intramuscular injection* after 1–2 hours if required
CHILD, *by intravenous injection*, 10 micrograms/kg; subsequent dose of 100 micrograms/kg if no response; if intravenous route not possible, may be given in divided doses by *intramuscular or subcutaneous injection*
NEONATE, *by subcutaneous, intramuscular, or intravenous injection*, 10 micrograms/kg, repeated every 2 to 3 minutes *or* 200 micrograms (60 micrograms/kg) *by intramuscular injection* as a single dose at birth (onset of action slower)

PoM **Naloxone Hydrochloride** (Non-proprietary)
Injection, naloxone hydrochloride 20 micrograms/mL. Net price 2-mL amp = £3.57
Injection, naloxone hydrochloride 400 micrograms/mL—see under Emergency Treatment of Poisoning
PoM **Narcan**®—see under Emergency Treatment of Poisoning
PoM **Narcan Neonatal**® (Du Pont)
Injection, naloxone hydrochloride 20 micrograms/mL. Net price 2-mL amp = £3.57

15.1.8 Antagonists for malignant hyperthermia

Dantrolene is used in the prophylaxis and treatment of malignant hyperthermia which is a rare but lethal complication of anaesthesia. It is characterised by a rapid rise in temperature, increasing muscle rigidity, tachycardia, and acidosis and can be triggered off by volatile anaesthetics, especially halothane, and suxamethonium. Dantrolene acts on skeletal muscle by interfering with calcium efflux in the muscle cell and stopping the contractile process. The oral preparation (see section 10.2.2) has been advocated for prophylactic use in malignant hyperthermia in susceptible individuals. The recommended dose is 5 mg/kg given in the 24 hours prior to surgery. Known trigger agents should be avoided during anaesthesia.

DANTROLENE SODIUM

Indications: malignant hyperthermia
Cautions: avoid extravasation; **interactions:** Appendix 1 (dantrolene)
Dose: *by rapid intravenous injection*, 1 mg/kg, repeated as required to a cumulative max. of 10 mg/kg

PoM **Dantrium Intravenous**® (Norwich Eaton)
Injection, powder for reconstitution, dantrolene sodium, with mannitol. Net price 20-mg vial = £22.52 (hosp. only)

15.2 Local anaesthesia

The use of local anaesthetics by injection or by application to mucous membranes to produce local analgesia is discussed in this section.

The following sections also include information on local anaesthetics acting on the sites shown:
1.7 Colon and rectum
11.7 Eye
12.3 Oropharynx
13.3 Skin

USE OF LOCAL ANAESTHETICS. Local anaesthetic drugs act by causing a reversible block to conduction along nerve fibres. The smaller the nerve fibre the more sensitive it is so that a differential block may occur where the smaller fibres carrying pain sensation and automatic impulses are blocked, sparing coarse touch and movement. The drugs used vary widely in their potency, toxicity, duration of action, stability, solubility in water, and ability to penetrate mucous membranes. These variations determine their suitability for use by various routes, e.g. topical (surface), infiltration, plexus, epidural or spinal block.

ADMINISTRATION. In estimating the safe dosage of these drugs it is important to take account of the rate at which they are absorbed and excreted as well as their potency. The patient's age, weight, physique, and clinical condition, the degree of vascularity of the area to which the drug is to be applied, and the duration of administration are other factors which must be taken into account.

Local anaesthetics do not rely on the circulation to transport them to their sites of action, but uptake into the general circulation is important in terminating their action. Following most regional anaesthetic procedures, maximum arterial plasma concentrations of anaesthetic develop within about 10 to 25 minutes, so careful surveillance for toxic effects is necessary during the first 30 minutes after injection.

TOXICITY. Toxic effects associated with the local anaesthetics are usually a result of excessively high plasma concentrations. The main effects are excitation of the central nervous system (nervousness, nausea, and convulsions) followed by depression. Less commonly the cardiovascular system is depressed. Hypersensitivity reactions occur mainly with the ester-type local anaesthetics such as amethocaine, benzocaine, cocaine, and procaine; reactions are less frequent with the amide types such as lignocaine, bupivacaine, and prilocaine.

USE OF VASOCONSTRICTORS. Toxicity may occur with repeated dosages due to accumulation of the drug, and reducing doses should therefore be given. Toxic effects may also occur if the injection is too rapid. Local anaesthetics should **not** be injected into inflamed or infected tissues nor should they be applied to the traumatised urethra. Under these conditions the drug may be so rapidly absorbed that a systemic rather than a local reaction is produced.

Most local anaesthetics, with the exception of cocaine, cause dilatation of blood vessels. The addition of a vasoconstrictor such as **adrenaline** diminishes local blood flow, slows the rate of absorption of the local anaesthetic, and prolongs its local effect. Care is necessary when using adrenaline for this purpose because, in excess, it may produce ischaemic necrosis.

Adrenaline should **not** be added to injections used in digits and appendages. When adrenaline is included in an injection of lignocaine or procaine the final concentration should be 1 in 200000. In dental surgery, up to 1 in 80000 of adrenaline is used with local anaesthetics. There is no justification for using higher concentrations.

The total dose of adrenaline should **not** exceed 500 micrograms and it is essential not to exceed a concentration of 1 in 200000 if more than 50 mL of the mixture is to be injected. For cautions associated with the use of adrenaline, see section 2.7. For drug interactions, see Appendix 1 (sympathomimetics).

LIGNOCAINE

Lignocaine is the most widely used local anaesthetic drug. It acts more rapidly and is more stable than most other local anaesthetics. It is effectively absorbed from mucous membranes and is a useful surface anaesthetic in concentrations of 2 to 4%. Except for surface anaesthesia, solutions should not usually exceed 1% in strength. The duration of the block (with adrenaline) is about 1½ hours. Concentrations of 1.5% are used for epidural (extradural) block, and for spinal anaesthesia a 5% solution in glucose intravenous infusion is used as a hyperbaric solution.

LIGNOCAINE HYDROCHLORIDE

Indications: see under Dose; also dental anaesthesia; ventricular arrhythmias (section 2.3.2)

Cautions: epilepsy, hepatic or respiratory impairment, impaired cardiac conduction, bradycardia; reduce dose in elderly or debilitated; resuscitative equipment should be available; see section 2.3.2 for effects on heart

Contra-indications: hypovolaemia, complete heart block; avoid in porphyria; do not use solutions containing adrenaline for anaesthesia in appendages

Side-effects: hypotension, bradycardia, cardiac arrest. CNS effects include agitation, euphoria, respiratory depression, convulsions. See also notes above

Dose: adjusted according to the site of operation and response of the patient

By injection, max. dose 200 mg, or 500 mg with solutions which also contain adrenaline. Max. dose of adrenaline 500 micrograms (see also notes above)

Infiltration anaesthesia, 0.25–0.5%, with adrenaline 1 in 200000, using 2–50 mL of a 0.5% solution in minor surgery and up to 60 mL in more extensive surgery

Nerve blocks, with adrenaline 1 in 200000, 1% to a max. of 50 mL, 2% to a max. of 25 mL

Epidural and caudal block, with adrenaline 1 in 200000, 1% to a max. of 50 mL, 2% to a max. of 25 mL

Surface anaesthesia, usual strengths 2–4%. Mouth, throat, and upper gastro-intestinal tract, max. 200 mg

Lignocaine hydrochloride injections

PoM **Lignocaine** (Non-proprietary)

Injection 0.5%, lignocaine hydrochloride 5 mg/mL, net price 10-mL amp = 17p

Injection 1%, lignocaine hydrochloride 10 mg/mL, net price 2-mL amp = 11p; 5-mL amp = 16p; 10-mL amp = 31p; 20-mL amp = 32p

Injection 2%, lignocaine hydrochloride 20 mg/mL, net price 2-mL amp = 17p; 5-mL amp = 19p

PoM **Min-I-Jet® Lignocaine Hydrochloride with Adrenaline** (IMS)

Injection, lignocaine hydrochloride 5 mg/mL, adrenaline 1 in 200000 (500 micrograms/100 mL). Net price 5-mL disposable syringe = £2.74

PoM **Xylocaine®** (Astra)

Injection 0.5%, anhydrous lignocaine hydrochloride 5 mg/mL. Net price 20-mL vial = 67p

Injection 0.5% with adrenaline 1 in 200000, anhydrous lignocaine hydrochloride 5 mg/mL, adrenaline 1 in 200000. Net price 20-mL vial = 69p

Injection 1%, anhydrous lignocaine hydrochloride 10 mg/mL. Net price 20-mL vial = 69p

Injection 1% with adrenaline 1 in 200000, anhydrous lignocaine hydrochloride 10 mg/mL, adrenaline 1 in 200000. Net price 20-mL vial = 71p

Injection 1.5%, for epidural use, anhydrous lignocaine hydrochloride 15 mg/mL. Net price 25-mL amp = £1.21

Injection 2%, anhydrous lignocaine hydrochloride 20 mg/mL. Net price 20-mL vial = 73p

Injection 2% with adrenaline 1 in 200000, anhydrous lignocaine hydrochloride 20 mg/mL, adrenaline 1 in 200000. Net price 20-mL vial = 75p

Lignocaine injections for dental use

A large variety of lignocaine injections, plain or with adrenaline or noradrenaline, is also available in dental cartridges under the names **Lidocaton, Lignostab, Neo-Lidocaton, Pensacaine, Xylocaine**, and **Xylotox.**

Lignocaine for surface anaesthesia

Note. Local anaesthetic ointments can be absorbed through the rectal mucosa therefore excessive application should be avoided, particularly in infants and children

PoM **Emla®** (Astra)

Drug Tariff cream, lignocaine 2.5%, prilocaine 2.5%. Net price 10 × 5-g tube = £17.00

Surgical pack cream, lignocaine 2.5%, prilocaine 2.5%. Net price 30-g tube (with spatula) = £10.25

NHS *Hospital pack cream*, lignocaine 2.5%, prilocaine 2.5%. Net price 10 × 5-g tube with 25 occlusive dressings = £19.50

Anaesthesia before venepuncture, apply a thick layer for 1–2 hours under an occlusive dressing; split skin grafting, apply a thick layer for at least 2 hours; genital warts, apply up to 10 g 5–10 minutes before removal

Instillagel® (CliniMed)

Gel, lignocaine hydrochloride 2%, chlorhexidine gluconate solution 0.25%, in a sterile lubricant basis in disposable syringe. Net price 6-mL syringe = 96p; 11-mL syringe = £1.07

Dose: 6–11 mL into urethra

Xylocaine® (Astra)

Antiseptic gel, lignocaine hydrochloride 2%, chlorhexidine gluconate solution 0.25% in a sterile lubricant water-miscible basis. Net price 20 g = £1.09

Dose: into urethra, men 10 mL followed by 3–5 mL; women 3–5 mL

Gel, anhydrous lignocaine hydrochloride 2%, in a sterile lubricant water-miscible basis. Net price 20 g = 78p; 20-g single-use syringe (Accordion®) = £1.00

Dose: into urethra, men 10 mL followed by 3–5 mL; women 3–5 mL

Ointment, lignocaine 5% in a water-miscible basis. Net price 15 g = 83p

Dose: max. 35 g in 24 hours

Spray (= aerosol spray), lignocaine 10% (100 mg/g) with cetylpyridinium chloride 0.01% in a metered spray container supplying 10 mg lignocaine/dose; 800 spray doses per container. With sterilisable spray nozzles. Net price 80-g bottle = £4.67

Dose: dental practice, 1–5 doses; maxillary sinus puncture, 3 doses; during delivery in obstetrics, up to 20 doses; procedures in pharynx, larynx, and trachea, up to 20 doses

Topical 4%, anhydrous lignocaine hydrochloride 40 mg/mL. Net price 30-mL bottle = £1.24

Dose: bronchoscopy, 2–3 mL with suitable spray; biopsy in mouth, 3–4 mL with suitable spray *or* swab (with adrenaline if necessary); max. 7.5 mL

BUPIVACAINE

The great advantage of bupivacaine over other local anaesthetics is its duration of action of up to 8 hours when used for nerve blocks. It has a slow onset of action, taking up to 30 minutes for full effect. It is often used in lumbar epidural blockade and is particularly suitable for continuous epidural analgesia in labour; it then has a 2- to 3-hour duration of action. It is **contra-indicated** in intravenous regional anaesthesia (Bier's block). It is the principal drug for spinal anaesthesia in the UK.

BUPIVACAINE HYDROCHLORIDE

Indications: see under Dose

Cautions; Contra-indications; Side-effects: see under Lignocaine Hydrochloride and notes above; myocardial depression may be more severe and more resistant to treatment; contra-indicated in intravenous regional anaesthesia (Bier's block)

Dose: adjusted according to the site of operation and response of the patient

Local infiltration, 0.25% (up to 60 mL)

Peripheral nerve block, 0.25% (max. 60 mL), 0.5% (max. 30 mL)

Epidural block,

Surgery, *lumbar*, 0.5–0.75% (max. 20 mL of either)
caudal, 0.5% (max. 30 mL)

Labour, *lumbar*, 0.25–0.5% (max. 12 mL of either)
caudal, 0.25% (max. 30 mL), 0.5% (max. 20 mL)

Note. 0.75% **contra-indicated** for epidural use in obstetrics.

PoM **Marcain Heavy®** (Astra)

Injection, bupivacaine hydrochloride 5 mg, glucose 80 mg/mL. Net price 4-ml amp = £1.00

Dose: spinal anaesthesia, 2–4 mL

PoM **Marcain®** (Astra)

Injection 0.25%, bupivacaine hydrochloride 2.5 mg/mL. Net price 10-mL amp = £1.13

Injection 0.5%, bupivacaine hydrochloride 5 mg/mL. Net price 10-mL amp = £1.30

Injection 0.75%, bupivacaine hydrochloride 7.5 mg/mL. Net price 10-mL amp = £1.95

PoM **Marcain with Adrenaline®** (Astra)

Injection 0.25%, bupivacaine hydrochloride 2.5 mg/mL, adrenaline 1 in 200000. Net price 10-mL amp = £1.27

Injection 0.5%, bupivacaine hydrochloride 5 mg/mL, adrenaline 1 in 200000. Net price 10-mL amp = £1.43

PRILOCAINE

Prilocaine is a local anaesthetic of low toxicity which is similar to lignocaine. It can be used for infiltration, regional nerve block, and spinal anaesthesia and regional intravenous analgesia. If used in high doses, methaemoglobinaemia may occur which can be treated with intravenous injection of methylene blue 1% using a dose of 75–100 mg.

PRILOCAINE HYDROCHLORIDE

Indications: see under Dose; also dental anaesthesia

Cautions; Contra-indications; Side-effects: see under Lignocaine Hydrochloride and notes above; avoid in patients with anaemia or congenital or acquired methaemoglobinaemia

Dose: adjusted according to the site of operation and response of patient, to a max. of 400 mg used alone, or 600 mg if used with adrenaline or felypressin

PoM **Citanest®** (Astra)

Injection 0.5%, prilocaine hydrochloride 5 mg/mL. Net price 20-mL multidose vial = 73p; 50-mL multidose vial = £1.02; 50-mL single dose vial = £1.30

Injection 1%, prilocaine hydrochloride 10 mg/mL. Net price 20-mL vial = 75p; 50-mL vial = £1.06

Injection 2%, prilocaine hydrochloride 20 mg/mL. Net price 10-mL single dose vial = 75p

Injection 4%, prilocaine hydrochloride 40 mg/mL. Net price 2-mL cartridge = 11p

PoM **Citanest with Octapressin®** (Astra)

Injection 3%, prilocaine hydrochloride 30 mg/mL, felypressin 0.03 unit/mL. Net price 2-mL cartridge and self-aspirating cartridge (both) = 11p

PROCAINE

Procaine is now seldom used. It is as potent an anaesthetic as lignocaine but has a shorter duration of action. It provides less intense analgesia because it has less tendency to spread through the tissues. It is poorly absorbed from mucous membranes and is of no value as a surface anaesthetic. When used for infiltration or regional anaesthesia, adrenaline 1 in 200000 is generally added. Its metabolite para-aminobenzoic acid inhibits the action of the sulphonamides.

PROCAINE HYDROCHLORIDE

Indications: local anaesthesia by infiltration and regional routes

Cautions; Side-effects: see notes above

Dose: adjusted according to the site of operation and the patient's response

By injection, up to 1 g (200 mL of 0.5% solution or 100 mL of 1%) with adrenaline 1 in 200000

PoM **Procaine Injection,** procaine hydrochloride 2% (20 mg/mL) in sodium chloride intravenous infusion. Net price 2-mL amp = 52p; 1% in 2-mL amp also available

OTHER LOCAL ANAESTHETICS

Amethocaine is an effective local anaesthetic for topical application. It is rapidly absorbed from mucous membranes and should **never** be applied to inflamed, traumatised, or highly vascular surfaces. It should **never** be used to provide anaesthesia for bronchoscopy or cystoscopy, as lignocaine is a safer alternative. It is used in ophthalmology (see section 11.7) and in skin preparations (see section 13.3). Hypersensitivity to amethocaine has been reported.

Benzocaine is a local anaesthetic of low potency and toxicity. Its only use is in surface anaesthesia for the relief of pain and irritation in the oropharynx (see section 12.3.1).

Cocaine readily penetrates mucous membranes and is an effective surface anaesthetic but it has now been replaced by less toxic alternatives. It potentiates the action of adrenaline and possesses vasoconstrictor and mydriatic properties and should therefore **not** be used with adrenaline. It should **never** be given by injection because of its toxicity and doses not exceeding 3 mg/kg should be applied to mucous membranes. It stimulates the central nervous system and is a drug of addiction. Concentrations of 4 to 20% (50–200 mg/mL) are applied to the nose, throat, and larynx. For the use of cocaine in ophthalmology see section 11.7.

Appendix 1: Interactions

Two or more drugs given at the same time may exert their effects independently or may interact. The interaction may be potentiation or antagonism of one drug by another, or occasionally some other effect. Adverse drug interactions should be reported to the CSM as for other adverse drug reactions.

Drug interactions may be **pharmacodynamic** or **pharmacokinetic.**

PHARMACODYNAMIC INTERACTIONS

These are interactions between drugs which have similar or antagonistic pharmacological effects or side-effects. They may be due to competition at receptor sites, or occur between drugs acting on the same physiological system. They are usually predictable from a knowledge of the pharmacology of the interacting drugs; in general, those demonstrated with one drug are likely to occur with related drugs. They occur to a greater or lesser extent in most patients who receive the interacting drugs.

PHARMACOKINETIC INTERACTIONS

These occur when one drug alters the absorption, distribution, metabolism, or excretion of another, thus increasing or reducing the amount of drug available to produce its pharmacological effects. They are not easily predicted and many of them affect only a small proportion of patients taking the combination of drugs. Pharmacokinetic interactions occurring with one drug cannot be assumed to occur with related drugs unless their pharmacokinetic properties are known to be similar.

Pharmacokinetic interactions are of several types:

AFFECTING ABSORPTION. The rate of absorption or the total amount absorbed can both be altered by drug interactions. Delayed absorption is rarely of clinical importance unless high peak plasma concentrations are required (e.g. when giving an analgesic). Reduction in the total amount absorbed, however, may result in ineffective therapy.

DUE TO CHANGES IN PROTEIN BINDING. To a variable extent most drugs are loosely bound to plasma proteins. Protein-binding sites are non-specific and one drug can displace another thereby increasing its proportion free to diffuse from plasma to its site of action. This only produces a detectable increase in effect if it is an extensively bound drug (more than 90%) that is not widely distributed throughout the body. Even so displacement rarely produces more than transient potentiation because this increased concentration of free drug results in an increased rate of elimination.

Displacement from protein binding plays a part in the potentiation of warfarin by phenylbutazone, sulphonamides, and tolbutamide but the importance of these interactions is due mainly to the fact that warfarin metabolism is also inhibited.

AFFECTING METABOLISM. Many drugs are metabolised in the liver. Induction of the hepatic microsomal enzyme system by one drug can gradually increase the rate of metabolism of another, resulting in lower plasma concentrations and a reduced effect. On withdrawal of the inducer plasma concentrations increase and toxicity may occur. Barbiturates, griseofulvin, most antiepileptics, and rifampicin are the most important enzyme inducers in man. Drugs affected include warfarin and the oral contraceptives.

Conversely when one drug inhibits the metabolism of another higher plasma concentrations are produced, rapidly resulting in an increased effect with risk of toxicity. Some drugs which potentiate warfarin and phenytoin do so by this mechanism.

AFFECTING RENAL EXCRETION. Drugs are eliminated through the kidney both by glomerular filtration and by active tubular secretion. Competition occurs between those which share active transport mechanisms in the proximal tubule. Thus probenecid delays the excretion of many drugs including penicillins, some cephalosporins, indomethacin, and dapsone; aspirin may increase the toxicity of methotrexate by a similar mechanism.

RELATIVE IMPORTANCE OF INTERACTIONS

Many drug interactions are harmless and many of those which are potentially harmful only occur in a small proportion of patients; moreover, the severity of an interaction varies from one patient to another. Drugs with a small therapeutic ratio (e.g. phenytoin) and those which require careful control of dosage (e.g. anticoagulants, antihypertensives, and antidiabetics) are most often involved.

Patients at increased risk from drug interactions include the elderly and those with impaired renal or liver function.

HAZARDOUS INTERACTIONS. The symbol • has been placed against interactions that are potentially hazardous and where combined administration of the drugs involved should be avoided (or only undertaken with caution and appropriate monitoring).

Interactions that have no symbol do not usually have serious consequences.

List of drug interactions

The following is an alphabetical list of drugs and their interactions; to avoid excessive cross-referencing each drug or group is listed twice: in the alphabetical list and also against the drug or group with which it interacts; changes in the interactions lists since BNF No. 20 (September 1990) are in **bold** print

For explanation of symbol • see previous page

ACE Inhibitors
Alcohol: enhanced hypotensive effect
• Anaesthetics: enhanced hypotensive effect
Analgesics: antagonism of hypotensive effect and increased risk of renal failure with *NSAIDs*; hyperkalaemia with *indomethacin and possibly other NSAIDs*
Antibacterials: absorption of *tetracyclines* reduced by *quinapril* (tablets contain magnesium carbonate excipient)
Antidepressants: enhanced hypotensive effect
other Antihypertensives: enhanced hypotensive effect
Antipsychotics: severe postural hypotension with *chlorpromazine and possibly other phenothiazines*
Anxiolytics and Hypnotics: enhanced hypotensive effect
Beta-blockers: enhanced hypotensive effect
Calcium-channel Blockers: enhanced hypotensive effect
Corticosteroids: antagonism of hypotensive effect
Cyclosporin: increased risk of hyperkalaemia
• **Diuretics:** enhanced hypotensive effect (can be extreme); hyperkalaemia with *potassium-sparing diuretics*
Dopaminergics: *levodopa* enhances hypotensive effect
• **Lithium:** *ACE inhibitors* reduce excretion of *lithium* (increased plasma-lithium concentration)
Nitrates: enhance hypotensive effect
• Potassium Salts: hyperkalaemia
Sex Hormones: *oestrogens and combined oral contraceptives* antagonise hypotensive effect
Sympathomimetics: *see* Sympathomimetics (main list)
Ulcer-healing Drugs: *carbenoxolone* antagonises hypotensive effect
Uricosurics: *probenecid* reduces excretion of *captopril*

Acebutolol *see* Beta-blockers

Acetazolamide (general hypokalaemic interactions *as for* Diuretics)
Analgesics: *aspirin* reduces excretion of *acetazolamide* (risk of toxicity)
Anti-arrhythmics: excretion of *flecainide, mexiletine, and quinidine* reduced in alkaline urine (occasionally increased plasma-concentrations)
Lithium: *lithium* excretion increased

Acetohexamide *see* Antidiabetics (sulphonylurea)

Acrivastine *see* Antihistamines

Acrosoxacin *see* 4-Quinolones

Acyclovir
other Antivirals: extreme lethargy reported on administration of *zidovudine* with *intravenous acyclovir*
Uricosurics: *probenecid* reduces *acyclovir* excretion (increased plasma concentrations)

Adrenaline *see* Sympathomimetics

Adrenergic Neurone Blockers (*see also* Bretylium)
Alcohol: enhanced hypotensive effect
• Anaesthetics: enhanced hypotensive effect
Analgesics: *NSAIDs* antagonise hypotensive effect
Antidepressants: *tricyclics* antagonise hypotensive effect

Adrenergic Neurone Blockers (*continued*)
other Antihypertensives: enhanced hypotensive effect
Antipsychotics: *phenothiazines* enhance hypotensive effect
Anxiolytics and Hypnotics: enhanced hypotensive effect
Beta-blockers: enhanced hypotensive effect
Calcium-channel Blockers: enhanced hypotensive effect
Corticosteroids: antagonism of hypotensive effect
Diuretics: enhanced hypotensive effect
Dopaminergics: *levodopa* enhances hypotensive effect
Nitrates: enhance hypotensive effect
Pizotifen: antagonism of hypotensive effect
Sex Hormones: *oestrogens and combined oral contraceptives* antagonise hypotensive effect
• Sympathomimetics: *some anorectics (e.g. mazindol) and some cough and cold remedies (e.g. ephedrine)* antagonise hypotensive effect
Ulcer-healing Drugs: *carbenoxolone* antagonises hypotensive effect

Alcohol
Antibacterials: disulfiram-like reaction with *cephamandole, metronidazole, nimorazole and tinidazole*
• Anticoagulants: anticoagulant effects of *warfarin and nicoumalone* enhanced
• Antidepressants: sedative effect of *tricyclics* enhanced; *tyramine contained in some alcoholic and dealcoholised beverages* interacts with *MAOIs* (hypertensive crisis)
Antidiabetics: enhanced hypoglycaemic effect; flushing with *chlorpropamide* (in susceptible persons); increased risk of lactic acidosis with *metformin*
Antihistamines: enhanced sedative effect
Antihypertensives: enhanced hypotensive effect
Antipsychotics: enhanced sedative effect
Anxiolytics and Hypnotics: enhanced sedative effect
Beta-blockers: enhanced hypotensive effect
Cytotoxics: disulfiram-like reaction with *procarbazine*
Monosulfiram: disulfiram-like reaction
Muscle Relaxants: *baclofen* enhances sedative effect
Nitrates: enhanced hypotensive effect

Alcuronium *see* Muscle Relaxants (non-depolarising)

Alfentanil *see* Opioid Analgesics

Allopurinol
Anticoagulants: effects of *nicoumalone and warfarin* may be enhanced
• Cytotoxics: effects of *azathioprine, cyclophosphamide, and mercaptopurine* enhanced with increased toxicity

Allyloestrenol *see* Progestogens

Alpha-blockers (general hypotensive interactions *as for* Hydralazine)
Alcohol: sedative effect of *indoramin* enhanced
Anxiolytics and Hypnotics: enhanced sedative effect
• Beta-blockers: increased risk of first-dose hypotensive effect of *post-synaptic alpha-blockers such as prazosin and terazosin*

Alpha-blockers (*continued*)
• Diuretics: increased risk of first-dose hypotensive effect of *post-synaptic alpha-blockers such as prazosin and terazosin*

Alprazolam *see* Benzodiazepines and other Anxiolytics and Hypnotics

Aluminium Hydroxide *see* Antacids and Adsorbents

Amantadine
Antihypertensives: *methyldopa, metirosine, and reserpine* have extrapyramidal side-effects
Antimuscarinics: increased antimuscarinic side-effects
Antipsychotics: all have extrapyramidal side-effects
Domperidone and Metoclopramide: have extrapyramidal side-effects
Tetrabenazine: has extrapyramidal side-effects

Ambutonium *see* Antimuscarinics

Amikacin *see* Aminoglycosides

Amiloride *see* Diuretics (potassium-sparing)

Aminoglutethimide
• Anticoagulants: metabolism of *nicoumalone and warfarin* accelerated (reduced anticoagulant effect)
Cardiac glycosides: metabolism of *digitoxin only* accelerated (reduced effect)
Corticosteroids: metabolism of *dexamethasone* accelerated (reduced effect)
Theophylline: metabolism of *theophylline* accelerated (reduced effect)

Aminoglycosides
other Antibacterials: increased risk of nephrotoxicity with *cephalosporins notably cephalothin*; increased risk of ototoxicity and nephrotoxicity with *vancomycin*
Anticoagulants: *see* Phenindione and Warfarin
Antifungals: increased risk of nephrotoxicity with *amphotericin*
• Cholinergics: antagonism of effect of *neostigmine and pyridostigmine*
• Cyclosporin: increased risk of nephrotoxicity
• Cytotoxics: increased risk of nephrotoxicity and possibly of ototoxicity with *cisplatin*
Diuretics: increased risk of ototoxicity with *loop diuretics*
• Muscle Relaxants: effect of *non-depolarising muscle relaxants such as tubocurarine* enhanced

Aminophylline *see* Theophylline

Amiodarone
• *other* Anti-arrhythmics: additive effect with *disopyramide, flecainide, procainamide, and quinidine* (increased risk of ventricular arrhythmias); increased plasma concentrations of *flecainide and procainamide*; increased myocardial depression with any anti-arrhythmic
• Anticoagulants: metabolism of *nicoumalone and warfarin* inhibited (enhanced anticoagulant effect)
• Antiepileptics: metabolism of *phenytoin* inhibited (increased plasma concentration)
• Beta-blockers: increased risk of bradycardia, AV block, and myocardial depression
• Calcium-channel Blockers: *diltiazem and verapamil* increase risk of bradycardia, AV block, and myocardial depression
• Cardiac Glycosides: increased plasma concentration of *digoxin* (halve digoxin maintenance dose)
Diuretics: toxicity increased if hypokalaemia occurs with *acetazolamide, loop diuretics, and thiazides*
Ulcer-healing Drugs: *cimetidine* increases plasma concentrations of *amiodarone*

Amitriptyline *see* Antidepressants, Tricyclic

Amlodipine *see* Calcium-channel Blockers

Amoxapine *see* Antidepressants, Tricyclic

Amoxycillin *see* Penicillins

Amphetamines *see* Sympathomimetics

Amphotericin
Antibacterials: increased risk of nephrotoxicity with *aminoglycosides and cephalothin*
other Antifungals: antagonises *miconazole*
• Cyclosporin: increased risk of nephrotoxicity

Ampicillin *see* Penicillins

Amylobarbitone *see* Barbiturates and Primidone

Anabolic Steroids
• Anticoagulants: anticoagulant effect of *nicoumalone, phenindione, and warfarin* enhanced

Anaesthetics
Antibacterials: effect of *thiopentone* enhanced by *sulphonamides*
• Antihypertensives: enhanced hypotensive effect
• Antipsychotics: enhanced hypotensive effect
Anxiolytics and Hypnotics: enhanced sedative effect
• Beta-blockers: enhanced hypotensive effect
• Calcium-channel Blockers: enhanced hypotensive effect and AV delay with *verapamil*
• Dopaminergics: risk of arrhythmias if *volatile anaesthetics such as cyclopropane or halothane* given with *levodopa*
• Sympathomimetics: risk of arrhythmias if *adrenaline or isoprenaline* given with *volatile anaesthetics such as cyclopropane or halothane*

Analgesics *see* Aspirin, NSAIDs, Opioid Analgesics, and Paracetamol

Anion-exchange Resins *see* Cholestyramine

Antacids and Adsorbents
Analgesics: excretion of *aspirin* increased in alkaline urine; *antacids* reduce absorption of *diflunisal*
Anti-arrhythmics: excretion of *flecainide, mexiletine, and quinidine* reduced in alkaline urine (may occasionally increase plasma concentrations)
Antibacterials: *antacids* reduce absorption of *ciprofloxacin, norfloxacin, ofloxacin, pivampicillin, rifampicin, and most tetracyclines; kaolin* reduces absorption of *lincomycin*
Antiepileptics: *antacids* reduce *phenytoin* absorption
Antifungals: *antacids* reduce absorption of *itraconazole* and *ketoconazole*
Antiplatelet Drugs: *dipyridamole* patient information leaflet advises avoidance of *antacids*
Antimalarials: *antacids* reduce absorption of *chloroquine and hydroxychloroquine*
Antipsychotics: *antacids* reduce absorption of *phenothiazines*
Biphosphonates: *antacids* reduce absorption
Iron: *magnesium trisilicate* reduces absorption of *oral iron*
Lithium: *sodium bicarbonate* increases excretion (reduced plasma-lithium concentration)
Penicillamine: *antacids* reduce absorption

Antazoline *see* Antihistamines

Anti-arrhythmics *see* individual drugs

Anticholinergics *see* Antimuscarinics

Anticoagulants *see* Heparin, Phenindione, and Warfarin

Antidepressants *see* individual entries for fluoxetine, fluvoxamine, MAOIs, mianserin, trazodone, and viloxazine

Antidepressants, Tricyclic
• Alcohol: enhanced sedative effect
• *other* Antidepressants: CNS excitation and hypertension with *MAOIs* (avoid for at least 2 weeks after stopping MAOIs); *fluoxetine* increases plasma concentrations of some *tricyclics*

Antidepressants, Tricyclic (*continued*)

• Antiepileptics: antagonism (convulsive threshold lowered); plasma concentrations of *tricyclics* reduced (reduced antidepressant effect)

Antihypertensives: in general, hypotensive effect enhanced, but antagonism of effect of *adrenergic neurone blockers* and of *clonidine* (and increased risk of hypertension on clonidine withdrawal)

Antihistamines: increased antimuscarinic and sedative effects

Antimuscarinics: increased antimuscarinic side-effects

Antipsychotics: increased antimuscarinic side-effects with *phenothiazines*

Anxiolytics and Hypnotics: enhanced sedative effect

Barbiturates: *see under* Antiepileptics, above

Disulfiram: inhibition of metabolism of *tricyclics* (increased plasma concentrations and increased disulfiram reaction reported with *alcohol with amitriptyline*)

Nitrates: reduced effect of *sublingual nitrates* (owing to dry mouth)

Sex Hormones: *oral contraceptives* antagonise antidepressant effect (but side-effects may be increased due to increased plasma concentrations of *tricyclics*)

• Sympathomimetics: hypertension and arrhythmias with *adrenaline* (but local anaesthetics with adrenaline appear to be safe); hypertension with *noradrenaline*

Ulcer-healing Drugs: plasma concentrations of *amitriptyline, desipramine, doxepin, imipramine, nortriptyline, and probably other tricyclics* increased by *cimetidine* (inhibition of metabolism)

Antidiabetics (includes Insulin, Metformin, and Sulphonylureas)

Alcohol: enhanced hypoglycaemic effect; flushing with *chlorpropamide* (in susceptible subjects); risk of lactic acidosis with *metformin*

• Analgesics: *azapropazone and phenylbutazone* enhance effect of *sulphonylureas*

• **Antibacterials:** *chloramphenicol, co-trimoxazole, sulphonamides,* and *trimethoprim* enhance effect of *sulphonylureas*; *rifampicin* reduces effect of *sulphonylureas* (accelerates metabolism)

Antidepressants: *MAOIs* enhance hypoglycaemic effect

• **Antifungals:** *miconazole* and possibly *fluconazole* enhance effect of *sulphonylureas*

Antihypertensives: hypoglycaemic effect antagonised by *diazoxide*

Beta-blockers: enhanced hypoglycaemic effect (and masking of warning signs such as tremor)

Calcium-channel Blockers: *nifedipine* may occasionally impair glucose tolerance

Clofibrate Group: may improve glucose tolerance and have an additive effect

Corticosteroids: antagonism of hypoglycaemic effect

Diuretics: hypoglycaemic effect antagonised by *loop and thiazide diuretics*; *chlorpropamide* increases risk of hyponatraemia with *thiazides in combination with potassium-sparing diuretics*

Hormone Antagonists: *octreotide* may reduce *insulin and antidiabetic drug* requirements in diabetes mellitus

Lithium: may occasionally impair glucose tolerance

Sex Hormones: *oral contraceptives* antagonise hypoglycaemic effect

Antidiabetics (*continued*)

Ulcer-healing Drugs: *cimetidine* inhibits renal excretion of *metformin* (increased plasma-metformin concentrations)

• Uricosurics: *sulphinpyrazone* enhances effect of *sulphonylureas*

Antiepileptics *see* individual drugs

Antifungals *see* individual drugs

Antihistamines

Note. The following drug interactions apply to a lesser extent to the non-sedative antihistamines, and they do not appear to potentiate the effects of alcohol

Alcohol: enhanced sedative effect

Antidepressants: *tricyclics* increase antimuscarinic and sedative effects

Antifungals: *ketoconazole* inhibits *terfenadine* metabolism (cardiac toxicity reported)

Antimuscarinics: increased antimuscarinic side-effects

Anxiolytics and Hypnotics: enhanced sedative effect

Betahistine: antagonism (theoretical)

Antihypertensives *see* individual drugs or groups

Antimalarials *see* individual drugs

Antimuscarinics

Note. Many drugs have antimuscarinic effects; concomitant use of two or three such drugs can increase side-effects such as dry mouth, urine retention, and constipation; concomitant use can also lead to confusion in the elderly

Anti-arrhythmics: increased antimuscarinic effects with *disopyramide; atropine* delays absorption of *mexiletine*

Antidepressants: increased antimuscarinic side-effects with *tricyclics and MAOIs*

Antifungals: reduced absorption of *ketoconazole*

Antihistamines: increased antimuscarinic side-effects

Antipsychotics: increased antimuscarinic side-effects of *phenothiazines* (but reduced plasma concentrations)

Cisapride: antagonism of gastro-intestinal effect

Domperidone and Metoclopramide: *antimuscarinics such as propantheline* antagonise gastro-intestinal effects

Dopaminergics: increased antimuscarinic side-effects with *amantadine*

Nitrates: reduced effect of *sublingual nitrates* (failure to dissolve under tongue owing to dry mouth)

Antiplatelet Drugs *see* Aspirin and Dipyridamole

Antipsychotics *see* Phenothiazines and other Antipsychotics

Antivirals *see* individual drugs

Anxiolytics *see* Benzodiazepines and other Anxiolytics and Hypnotics

Appetite Suppressants *see* Sympathomimetics

Aspirin

Antacids and Adsorbents: excretion of *aspirin* increased in alkaline urine

• Anticoagulants: increased risk of bleeding due to antiplatelet effect

Antiepileptics: enhancement of effect of *phenytoin and sodium valproate*

• Cytotoxics: reduced excretion of *methotrexate* (increased toxicity)

Diuretics: antagonism of diuretic effect of *spironolactone;* reduced excretion of *acetazolamide* (risk of toxicity)

Domperidone and Metoclopramide: *metoclopramide* enhances effect of *aspirin* (increased rate of absorption)

Aspirin (*continued*)
Uricosurics: effect of *probenecid and sulphinpyrazone* reduced
Astemizole *see* Antihistamines
Atenolol *see* Beta-blockers
Atracurium *see* Muscle Relaxants (non-depolarising)
Atropine *see* Antimuscarinics
Azapropazone *see* NSAIDs
Azatadine *see* Antihistamines
Azathioprine
• Allopurinol: enhancement of effect with increased toxicity
Azlocillin *see* Penicillins
Aztreonam
• Anticoagulants: anticoagulant effect of *nicoumalone and warfarin* enhanced
Baclofen
Alcohol: enhanced sedative effect
Antihypertensives: enhanced hypotensive effect
Anxiolytics and Hypnotics: enhanced sedative effect
Barbiturates and Primidone
Anti-arrhythmics: metabolism of *disopyramide and quinidine* increased (reduced plasma concentrations)
Antibacterials: metabolism of *chloramphenicol, doxycycline, and metronidazole* accelerated (reduced effect); *sulphonamides* enhance effect of *thiopentone*
• Anticoagulants: metabolism of *nicoumalone and warfarin* accelerated (reduced anticoagulant effect)
• Antidepressants: antagonism of anticonvulsant effect (convulsive threshold lowered); metabolism of *tricyclics* accelerated (reduced plasma concentrations)
• Antiepileptics: concomitant administration of *phenobarbitone or primidone* with other antiepileptics may enhance toxicity without a corresponding increase in antiepileptic effect; moreover interactions can complicate monitoring of treatment; interactions include enhanced effects, increased sedation, and reductions in plasma concentrations
Antifungals: *phenobarbitone* accelerates metabolism of *griseofulvin* (reduced effect)
• Antipsychotics: antagonism of anticonvulsant effect (convulsive threshold lowered)
Calcium-channel Blockers: effect of *isradipine* and probably *nicardipine* and *nifedipine* reduced
Cardiac Glycosides: metabolism of *digitoxin only* accelerated (reduced effect)
• Corticosteroids: metabolism of *corticosteroids* accelerated (reduced effect)
• Cyclosporin: metabolism of *cyclosporin* accelerated (reduced effect)
• Sex Hormones: metabolism of *oral contraceptives* accelerated (reduced effect)
Theophylline: metabolism of *theophylline* accelerated (reduced effect)
Thyroxine: metabolism of thyroxine accelerated (may increase thyroxine requirements in hypothyroidism)
Beclomethasone *see* Corticosteroids
Bendrofluazide *see* Diuretics (thiazide)
Benorylate *see* Aspirin *and* Paracetamol
Benperidol *see* Phenothiazines and other Antipsychotics
Benzhexol *see* Antimuscarinics

Benzodiazepines and other Anxiolytics and Hypnotics
Alcohol: enhanced sedative effect
Anaesthetics: enhanced sedative effect
Analgesics: *opioid analgesics* enhance sedative effect
Antibacterials: *erythromycin* inhibits metabolism of *triazolam* (increased plasma concentration)
Anticoagulants: *chloral hydrate* may transiently enhance effect of *nicoumalone and warfarin*
Antidepressants: enhanced sedative effect
Antiepileptics: metabolism of *clonazepam* accelerated (reduced effect)
Antihistamines: enhanced sedative effect
Antihypertensives: enhanced hypotensive effect; enhanced sedative effect with *alpha-blockers*
Antipsychotics: enhanced sedative effect
Disulfiram: metabolism of *diazepam and chlordiazepoxide* inhibited (enhanced sedative effect)
Dopaminergics: *benzodiazepines* occasionally antagonise effect of *levodopa*
Muscle Relaxants: *baclofen* enhances sedative effect
Ulcer-healing Drugs: *cimetidine* inhibits metabolism of *benzodiazepines and chlormethiazole* (increased plasma concentrations)
Benzthiazide *see* Diuretics (thiazide)
Benztropine *see* Antimuscarinics
Beta-blockers
Alcohol: enhanced hypotensive effect
• Anaesthetics: enhanced hypotensive effect
Analgesics: *NSAIDs* antagonise hypotensive effect
• Anti-arrhythmics: increased risk of myocardial depression and bradycardia; with *amiodarone* increased risk of bradycardia and AV block; increased risk of *lignocaine* toxicity with *propranolol*
Antibacterials: *rifampicin* accelerates metabolism of *propranolol* (reduced plasma concentration)
Antidepressants: *fluvoxamine* increases plasma concentration of *propranolol*
Antidiabetics: enhanced hypoglycaemic effect (and masking of warning signs such as tremor)
• Antihypertensives: enhanced hypotensive effect; increased risk of withdrawal hypertension with *clonidine*; increased risk of first-dose hypotensive effect with *post-synaptic alpha-blockers such as prazosin and terazosin*; increased bradycardia with *reserpine*
Antimalarials: increased risk of bradycardia with *mefloquine*
Antipsychotics: plasma concentration of *chlorpromazine* increased by *propranolol*
Anxiolytics and Hypnotics: enhanced hypotensive effect
• Calcium-channel Blockers: increased risk of bradycardia and AV block with *diltiazem*; severe hypotension and heart failure occasionally with *nifedipine*; asystole, severe hypotension, and heart failure with *verapamil* (see section 2.3.2)
Cardiac Glycosides: increased AV block and bradycardia
Cholinergics: *propranolol* antagonises effect of *neostigmine and pyridostigmine*
Corticosteroids: antagonism of hypotensive effect
Diuretics: enhanced hypotensive effect; risk of ventricular arrhythmias associated with *sotalol* increased by hypokalaemia
Ergotamine: increased peripheral vasconstriction
Muscle Relaxants: *propranolol* enhances effect
Sex Hormones: *oestrogens* and *combined oral contraceptives* antagonise hypotensive effect

Beta-blockers (*continued*)
- • Sympathomimetics: severe hypertension with *adrenaline and noradrenaline* (especially with *non-selective beta-blockers*); severe hypertension also possible with *sympathomimetics in anorectics and cough and cold remedies*

Theophylline: *beta-blockers* should be avoided on pharmacological grounds (bronchospasm)
Thyroxine: metabolism of *propranolol* accelerated (reduced effect)
Ulcer-healing Drugs: plasma concentrations of *labetalol and propranolol* increased by *cimetidine;* hypotensive effect antagonised by *carbenoxolone*
Xamoterol: antagonism of effect of xamoterol and reduction in beta-blockade

Betahistine
Antihistamines: antagonism (theoretical)

Betamethasone *see* Corticosteroids
Betaxolol *see* Beta-blockers
Bethanechol *see* Cholinergics
Bethanidine *see* Adrenergic Neurone Blockers
Bezafibrate *see* Clofibrate Group
Biperiden *see* Antimuscarinics

Biphosphonates
Antacids: absorption reduced
Calcium Salts: reduced absorption (give at least 2 hours apart)

Bismuth Chelates
Antibacterials: reduced absorption of *tetracyclines*

Bisoprolol *see* Beta-blockers

Bretylium *(see also* Adrenergic Neurone Blockers)
other Antiarrhythmics: increased myocardial depression with any combination of two or more anti-arrhythmics

Bromazepam *see* Benzodiazepines and other Anxiolytics and Hypnotics

Bromocriptine
Antibacterials: *erythromycin* increases plasma concentration
Antipsychotics: antagonism of hypoprolactinaemic and antiparkinsonian effects
Domperidone and Metoclopramide: antagonise hypoprolactinaemic effect

Budesonide *see* Corticosteroids
Bumetanide *see* Diuretics (loop)
Buprenorphine *see* Opioid Analgesics

Buspirone
Antidepressants: *MAOIs* contra-indicated by manufacturer

Butobarbitone *see* Barbiturates
Butriptyline *see* Antidepressants, Tricyclic

Calcium Salts
Antibacterials: reduced absorption of *tetracyclines*
Biphosphonates: reduce absorption
Cardiac glycosides: large intravenous doses of *calcium* can precipitate arrhythmias
Diuretics: increased risk of hypercalcaemia with *thiazides*

Calcium-channel Blockers
- • Anaesthetics: *verapamil* increases hypotensive effect of *general anaesthetics* and risk of AV delay
- • Anti-arrhythmics: *amiodarone-induced risk* of bradycardia, AV block, and myocardial depression increased by *diltiazem and verapamil*; with *verapamil* raised plasma concentration of *quinidine* (extreme hypotension may occur)

Antibacterials: *rifampicin* increases metabolism of *verapamil and possibly isradipine* (reduced plasma concentrations)
Antidiabetics: *nifedipine* may occasionally impair glucose tolerance

Calcium-channel Blockers (*continued*)
Antiepileptics: effect of *carbamazepine* enhanced by *diltiazem and verapamil;* effect of *isradipine* and probably *nicardipine and nifedipine* reduced by *carbamazepine, phenobarbitone, phenytoin, and primidone*
Antihypertensives: enhanced hypotensive effect
Antimalarials: possible increased risk of bradycardia with some *calcium-channel blockers* and *mefloquine*
Antipsychotics: enhanced hypotensive effect
- • Beta-blockers: increased risk of bradycardia and AV block with *diltiazem;* occasionally severe hypotension and heart failure with *nifedipine;* asystole, severe hypotension, and heart failure with *verapamil* (see section 2.3.2)
- • **Cardiac Glycosides:** plasma concentration of *digoxin* increased by *diltiazem, nicardipine,* and *verapamil*; increased AV block and bradycardia with *verapamil*

Cyclosporin: plasma-cyclosporin concentrations increased by *diltiazem, nicardipine, and verapamil;* possibly increases plasma concentration of *nifedipine*
Lithium: neurotoxicity may occur without increased plasma-lithium concentrations in patients given *diltiazem and verapamil*
Muscle Relaxants: *nifedipine* and *verapamil* enhance effect of *non-depolarising muscle relaxants such as tubocurarine*; hypotension, myocardial depression, and hyperkalaemia with *verapamil* and intravenous *dantrolene*
Sympathomimetics: *see* Sympathomimetics (main list)
- • Theophylline: *diltiazem and verapamil* enhance effect

Ulcer-healing Drugs: *cimetidine* inhibits metabolism of *some calcium-channel blockers* (increased plasma concentrations)

Canrenoate *see* Diuretics (*as for* spironolactone)
Captopril *see* ACE Inhibitors
Carbachol *see* Cholinergics

Carbamazepine
- • Analgesics: *dextropropoxyphene* enhances effect of *carbamazepine*
- • Antibacterials: metabolism of *doxycycline* accelerated (reduced effect); plasma-*carbamazepine* concentration increased by *erythromycin and isoniazid*
- • Anticoagulants: metabolism of *nicoumalone and warfarin* accelerated (reduced anticoagulant effect)
- • **Antidepressants:** antagonism of anticonvulsant effect (convulsive threshold lowered); plasma concentration of *carbamazepine* increased by *fluoxetine* and *viloxazine*; metabolism of *tricyclics* accelerated (reduced plasma concentrations); manufacturer advises avoid with *MAOIs* or within 2 weeks of *MAOIs*
- • *other* Antiepileptics: concomitant administration of *two or more antiepileptics* may enhance toxicity without a corresponding increase in antiepileptic effect; moreover interactions between individual antiepileptics can complicate monitoring of treatment; interactions include enhanced effects, increased sedation, and reductions in plasma concentrations
- • Antipsychotics: antagonism of anticonvulsant effect (convulsive threshold lowered); metabolism of *haloperidol* accelerated (reduced plasma-haloperidol concentration)

Carbamazepine (*continued*)
- **Calcium-channel Blockers:** *diltiazem and verapamil* enhance effect of *carbamazepine*; effect of *isradipine* and probably *nicardipine* and *nifedipine* reduced

Cardiac Glycosides: metabolism of *digitoxin only* accelerated (reduced effect)
- Corticosteroids: metabolism accelerated (reduced effect)
- Cyclosporin: metabolism accelerated (reduced plasma-cyclosporin concentration)
- Hormone Antagonists: *danazol* inhibits metabolism of *carbamazepine* (enhanced effect)

Lithium: neurotoxicity may occur without increased plasma-lithium concentration
- Sex Hormones: *carbamazepine* accelerates metabolism of *oral contraceptives* (reduced contraceptive effect)

Theophylline: metabolism of *theophylline* accelerated (reduced effect)

Thyroxine: metabolism accelerated (may increase thyroxine requirements in hypothyroidism)
- Ulcer-healing Drugs: metabolism inhibited by *cimetidine* (increased plasma-carbamazepine concentration)

Carbenicillin *see* Penicillins

Carbenoxolone

Note. Do not apply to small amounts used topically on oral mucosa

Antihypertensives: antagonism of hypotensive effect

Cardiac glycosides: toxicity increased if hypokalaemia occurs

Corticosteroids: increased risk of hypokalaemia

Diuretics: antagonism of diuretic effect; increased risk of hypokalaemia with *acetazolamide, thiazides, and loop diuretics*; inhibition of ulcer healing with *amiloride and spironolactone*

Cardiac Glycosides

Analgesics: *NSAIDs* may exacerbate heart failure, reduce GFR and increase plasma-cardiac glycoside concentrations

Anion-exchange Resins: absorption reduced by *cholestyramine and colestipol*
- Anti-arrhythmics: plasma concentration of *digoxin* increased by *amiodarone, propafenone, and quinidine* (halve maintenance dose of digoxin)

Antibacterials: *erythromycin* enhances effect of *digoxin*; *rifampicin* accelerates metabolism of *digitoxin only* (reduced effect)

Antiepileptics: metabolism of *digitoxin only* accelerated (reduced effect)
- **Antimalarials:** *quinine* and possibly *chloroquine* raises plasma concentration of *digoxin* (halve maintenance dose of digoxin); includes use of *quinine* for cramp; possible increased risk of bradycardia with *mefloquine*

Barbiturates: *see under* Antiepileptics, above

Beta-blockers: increased AV block and bradycardia

Calcium Salts: large intravenous doses of *calcium* can precipitate arrhythmias
- **Calcium-channel Blockers:** plasma concentration of *digoxin* increased by *diltiazem, nicardipine,* and *verapamil*; increased AV block and bradycardia with *verapamil*
- Diuretics: increased toxicity if hypokalaemia occurs with *acetazolamide, loop diuretics, and thiazides*; effects of *digoxin* enhanced by *spironolactone*

Hormone Antagonists: *aminoglutethimide* accelerates metabolism of *digitoxin only* (reduced effect)

Cardiac Glycosides (*continued*)

Muscle Relaxants: arrhythmias with *suxamethonium*

Ulcer-healing Drugs: increased toxicity if hypokalaemia occurs with *carbenoxolone*

Carfecillin *see* Penicillins

Carteolol *see* Beta-blockers

Cephalosporins

Alcohol: disulfiram-like reaction with *cephamandole*

other Antibacterials: *cephalothin* increases risk of nephrotoxicity with *aminoglycosides and vancomycin*
- Anticoagulants: anticoagulant effect of *warfarin and nicoumalone* enhanced by *cephamandole*

Antifungals: *cephalothin* increases risk of nephrotoxicity with *amphotericin*

Diuretics: *loop diuretics* increase nephrotoxicity of *cephalothin*

Probenecid: reduced excretion of *cephalosporins* (increased plasma concentrations)

Cetirizine *see* Antihistamines

Chloral (general sedative interactions *as for* Benzodiazepines and other Anxiolytics and Hypnotics)

Anticoagulants: may transiently enhance anticoagulant effect of *nicoumalone and warfarin*

Chloramphenicol

other Antibacterials: *rifampicin* accelerates metabolism (reduced chloramphenicol-plasma concentration)
- Anticoagulants: anticoagulant effect of *nicoumalone and warfarin* enhanced
- Antidiabetics: effect of *sulphonylureas* enhanced
- Antiepileptics: metabolism accelerated by *phenobarbitone* (reduced chloramphenicol-plasma concentration); increased plasma concentration of *phenytoin* (risk of toxicity)

Barbiturates: *see under* Antiepileptics, above

Chlordiazepoxide *see* Benzodiazepines and other Anxiolytics and Hypnotics

Chlormethiazole (for general sedative interactions *see also* Benzodiazepines and other Anxiolytics and Hypnotics)

Ulcer-healing Drugs: *cimetidine* inhibits metabolism (increased plasma-chlormethiazole concentration)

Chlormezanone *see* Benzodiazepines and other Anxiolytics and Hypnotics

Chloroquine and Hydroxychloroquine

Antacids: reduced absorption
- **Cardiac Glycosides:** *chloroquine* possibly increases plasma concentration of *digoxin*

Cholinergics: antagonism of effect of *neostigmine and pyridostigmine*

Ulcer-healing Drugs: *cimetidine* inhibits metabolism of *chloroquine* (increased plasma concentration)

Chlorothiazide *see* Diuretics (thiazide)

Chlorpheniramine *see* Antihistamines

Chlorpromazine *see* Phenothiazines and other Antipsychotics

Chlorpropamide *see* Antidiabetics (sulphonylurea)

Chlorprothixene *see* Phenothiazines and other Antipsychotics

Chlortetracycline *see* Tetracyclines

Chlorthalidone *see* Diuretics (thiazide-related)

Cholestyramine and Colestipol

Analgesics: reduced absorption of *paracetamol* and *phenylbutazone*

Antibacterials: antagonism of effect of oral *vancomycin*

Cholestyramine and Colestipol (*continued*)
• Anticoagulants: anticoagulant effect of *nicoumalone, phenindione, and warfarin* may be enhanced or reduced
Cardiac Glycosides: reduced absorption
Diuretics: reduced absorption of *thiazides* (give at least 2 hours apart)
Thyroxine: reduced absorption

Cholinergics
Anti-arrhythmics: *quinidine* and possibly *propafenone* antagonise effect of *neostigmine and pyridostigmine*
• Antibacterials: *aminoglycosides, clindamycin, lincomycin, and polymyxins* antagonise effect of *neostigmine and pyridostigmine*
Antimalarials: *chloroquine* antagonises effect of *neostigmine and pyridostigmine*
Beta-blockers: *propranolol* antagonises effect of *neostigmine and pyridostigmine*
Lithium: antagonism of effect of *neostigmine and pyridostigmine*
Muscle Relaxants: *demecarium and ecothiopate eye-drops, and neostigmine and pyridostigmine* enhance effect of *suxamethonium,* but antagonise effect of *non-depolarising muscle relaxants such as tubocurarine*

Cimetidine *see* Histamine H2-antagonists
Cinnarizine *see* Antihistamines
Cinoxacin *see* 4-Quinolones
Ciprofloxacin *see* 4-Quinolones

Cisapride
Analgesics: *opioid analgesics* possible antagonism of effect on gastro-intestinal motility
Antimuscarinics: antagonism of effect on gastro-intestinal motility

Cisplatin
• Antibacterials: *aminoglycosides* increase risk of nephrotoxicity and possibly of ototoxicity

Clemastine *see* Antihistamines

Clindamycin
Cholinergics: antagonism of effect of *neostigmine and pyridostigmine*
Muscle relaxants: enhancement of effect of *non-depolarising muscle relaxants such as tubocurarine*

Clobazam *see* Benzodiazepines and other Anxiolytics and Hypnotics
Clodronate Sodium *see* Biphosphonates

Clofibrate Group
• Anticoagulants: enhancement of effect of *nicoumalone, phenindione, and warfarin*
Antidiabetics: may improve glucose tolerance and have additive effect

Clomipramine *see* Antidepressants, Tricyclic
Clomocycline *see* Tetracyclines

Clonazepam (general sedative interactions *as for* Benzodiazepines and other Anxiolytics and Hypnotics)
other Antiepileptics: metabolism of *clonazepam* accelerated by *carbamazepine, phenobarbitone and phenytoin*

Clonidine (for general hypotensive interactions *see also* Hydralazine)
• Antidepressants: *tricyclics* antagonise hypotensive effect and also increase risk of rebound hypertension on *clonidine* withdrawal
• Beta-blockers: increased risk of hypertension on *clonidine withdrawal*

Clopamide *see* Diuretics (thiazide)
Clorazepate *see* Benzodiazepines and other Anxiolytics and Hypnotics
Cloxacillin *see* Penicillins

Clozapine
Note. Clozapine should not be used concurrently with drugs associated with a substantial potential for causing agranulocytosis, such as co-trimoxazole, chloramphenicol, sulphonamides, penicillamine, or cytotoxics
see also Phenothiazines and other Antipsychotics

Codeine *see* Opioid Analgesics
Cold and Cough Remedies *see* Antihistamines and Sympathomimetics
Colestipol *see* Cholestyramine and Colestipol
Colistin *see* Polymyxins

Contraceptives, Oral
Note. Also covers oestrogens taken alone; in case of hormone replacement therapy low dose unlikely to induce interactions
• Antibacterials: *rifampicin* accelerates metabolism of both *combined and progestogen-only oral contraceptives* (possibility of reduced contraceptive effect); when *broad-spectrum antibiotics such as ampicillin and tetracycline* given with *combined oral contraceptives* possibility of reduced contraceptive effect (risk probably small)
• Anticoagulants: antagonism of anticoagulant effect of *nicoumalone, phenindione, and warfarin*
Antidepressants: antagonism of antidepressant effect has been reported, but side-effects of *tricyclics* may be increased due to higher plasma concentrations
Antidiabetics: antagonism of hypoglycaemic effect
• Antiepileptics: *carbamazepine, phenobarbitone, phenytoin, and primidone* accelerate metabolism (reduced contraceptive effect)
• Antifungals: *griseofulvin* accelerates metabolism (reduced contraceptive effect)
Antihypertensives: *combined oral contraceptives* antagonise hypotensive effect
Barbiturates: *see under* Antiepileptics, above
Beta-blockers: *oestrogens* and *combined oral contraceptives* antagonise hypotensive effect
• Cyclosporin: increased plasma-cyclosporin concentration
Diuretics: *combined oral contraceptives* antagonise diuretic effect
Theophylline: *combined oral contraceptives* delay excretion (increased plasma-theophylline concentration)

Corticosteroids and Corticotrophin
Note. Do not generally apply to corticosteroids with potent topical action such as beclomethasone
• Antibacterials: *rifampicin* accelerates metabolism of *corticosteroids* (reduced effect)
Antidiabetics: antagonism of hypoglycaemic effect
• Antiepileptics: *carbamazepine, phenobarbitone, phenytoin, and primidone* accelerate metabolism of *corticosteroids* (reduced effect)
Antihypertensives: antagonism of hypotensive effect
Barbiturates: *see under* Antiepileptics, above
Diuretics: antagonism of diuretic effect; *acetazolamide, loop diuretics, and thiazides* increase risk of hypokalaemia
Hormone Antagonists: *aminoglutethimide* accelerates metabolism of *dexamethasone* (reduced effect)
Sympathomimetics *see* Sympathomimetics, $Beta_2$ (main list)
Ulcer-healing Drugs: *carbenoxolone* increases risk of hypokalaemia

Corticotrophin *see* Corticosteroids

Co-trimoxazole and Sulphonamides
Anaesthetics: effect of *thiopentone* enhanced
• Anticoagulants: effect of *nicoumalone and warfarin* enhanced
• Antidiabetics: effect of *sulphonylureas* enhanced
• Antiepileptics: antifolate effect and plasma concentration of *phenytoin* increased by *co-trimoxazole*
Antimalarials: increased risk of antifolate effect with *pyrimethamine* (includes *Fansidar®* and *Maloprim®*)
Cyclosporin: increased risk of nephrotoxicity
Cytotoxics: antifolate effect of *methotrexate* increased by *co-trimoxazole*
Cyclizine *see* Antihistamines
Cyclobarbitone *see* Barbiturates
Cyclopenthiazide *see* Diuretics (thiazide)
Cyclopentolate *see* Antimuscarinics
Cyclophosphamide
• Allopurinol: toxicity of *cyclophosphamide* increased
Muscle Relaxants: *cyclophosphamide* enhances effect of *suxamethonium*
Cyclopropane *see* Anaesthetics
Cyclosporin
• **Antibacterials:** *aminoglycosides, co-trimoxazole,* and *4-quinolones* increase risk of nephrotoxicity; *erythromycin* increases plasma-cyclosporin concentration; *rifampicin* reduces plasma-cyclosporin concentration
• **Antiepileptics:** *carbamazepine, phenobarbitone, phenytoin, and primidone* accelerate metabolism (reduced plasma-cyclosporin concentration)
• **Antifungals:** *amphotericin* increases risk of nephrotoxicity; *itraconazole, ketoconazole* and possibly *fluconazole* inhibit metabolism (increased plasma-cyclosporin concentration)
Antihypertensives: increased risk of hyperkalaemia with *ACE inhibitors*
Barbiturates: *see under* Antiepileptics, above
• **Calcium-channel Blockers:** *diltiazem, nicardipine, and verapamil* increase plasma-cyclosporin concentration; *cyclosporin* possibly increases plasma concentration of *nifedipine*
• Diuretics: *potassium-sparing diuretics* increase risk of hyperkalaemia
• Hormone Antagonists: *danazol* inhibits metabolism (increased plasma-cyclosporin concentration)
• Potassium Salts: increased risk of hyperkalaemia
• Sex Hormones: *progestogens* inhibit metabolism (increased plasma-cyclosporin concentration)
Cyproheptadine *see* Antihistamines
Cytotoxics *see under* individual drugs
Danazol
• Anticoagulants: effect of *nicoumalone and warfarin* enhanced (inhibits metabolism)
• Antiepileptics: inhibits metabolism of *carbamazepine* (increased plasma-carbamazepine concentration)
• Cyclosporin: inhibits metabolism (increased plasma-cyclosporin concentration)
Dantrolene *see* Muscle Relaxants
Dapsone
Probenecid: *dapsone* excretion reduced (increased risk of side-effects)
Debrisoquine *see* Adrenergic Neurone Blockers
Demecarium *see* Cholinergics
Demeclocycline *see* Tetracyclines
Desferrioxamine
Antipsychotics: manufacturer advises avoid *prochlorperazine*
Desipramine *see* Antidepressants, Tricyclic
Dexamethasone *see* Corticosteroids
Dexamphetamine *see* Sympathomimetics
Dexfenfluramine *see* Sympathomimetics
Dextromoramide *see* Opioid Analgesics
Dextropropoxyphene *see* Opioid Analgesics
Dextrothyroxine
Anticoagulants: effect of *nicoumalone and warfarin* enhanced
Diamorphine *see* Opioid Analgesics
Diazepam *see* Benzodiazepines and other Anxiolytics and Hypnotics
Diazoxide (general hypotensive interactions *as for* Hydralazine)
Antidiabetics: antagonism of hypoglycaemic effect
Dichlorphenamide *see* Acetazolamide
Diclofenac *see* NSAIDs
Dicyclomine *see* Antimuscarinics
Diethylpropion *see* Sympathomimetics
Diflunisal *see* NSAIDs
Digitoxin *see* Cardiac Glycosides
Digoxin *see* Cardiac Glycosides
Dihydroergotamine *see* Ergotamine
Diltiazem *see* Calcium-channel Blockers
Dimenhydrinate *see* Antihistamines
Dimethindene *see* Antihistamines
Diphenhydramine *see* Antihistamines
Diphenylpyraline *see* Antihistamines
Diphenoxylate *see* Opioid Analgesics
Dipipanone *see* Opioid Analgesics
Dipivefrine *see* Sympathomimetics (*as for* adrenaline)
Dipyridamole
Antacids: patient information leaflet advises avoidance of *antacids*
• Anticoagulants: enhanced effect due to antiplatelet action of *dipyridamole*
Disopyramide
• *other* Anti-arrhythmics: *amiodarone* increases risk of ventricular arrhythmias; increased myocardial depression with any *anti-arrhythmic*
• Antibacterials: plasma concentration of *disopyramide* reduced by *rifampicin* but increased by *erythromycin* (risk of toxicity)
Antiepileptics: plasma concentration of *disopyramide* reduced by *phenobarbitone, phenytoin, and primidone*
Antimuscarinics: increased antimuscarinic side-effects
Barbiturates: *see under* Antiepileptics, above
• Diuretics: toxicity of *disopyramide* increased if hypokalaemia occurs with *acetazolamide, loop diuretics, and thiazides*
Nitrates: reduced effect of *sublingual nitrates* (failure to dissolve under tongue owing to dry mouth)
Distigmine *see* Cholinergics
Disulfiram
Alcohol: disulfiram reaction (*see* section 4.10)
Antibacterials: psychotic reaction with *metronidazole* reported
• Anticoagulants: effect of *nicoumalone and warfarin* enhanced
Antidepressants: inhibition of metabolism of *tricyclic antidepressants* (increased plasma concentrations); increased disulfiram reaction with alcohol reported if *amitriptyline* also taken
• Antiepileptics: inhibition of metabolism of *phenytoin* (increased risk of toxicity)
Anxiolytics and Hypnotics: inhibition of metabolism of *chlordiazepoxide and diazepam* (enhanced sedative effect)
Theophylline: inhibition of metabolism (increased risk of toxicity)

Diuretics
Analgesics: *diuretics* increase risk of nephrotoxicity of *NSAIDs*; *NSAIDs notably indomethacin* antagonise diuretic effect; *indomethacin and possibly other NSAIDs* increase risk of hyperkalaemia with *potassium-sparing diuretics*; diuretic effect of *spironolactone* antagonised by *aspirin*; *aspirin* reduces excretion of *acetazolamide* (risk of toxicity)
Anion-exchange Resins: *cholestyramine* reduces absorption of *thiazides* (give at least 2 hours apart)
• Anti-arrhythmics: toxicity of *amiodarone, disopyramide, flecainide, and quinidine* increased if hypokalaemia occurs; action of *lignocaine, mexiletine, and tocainide* antagonised by hypokalaemia; *acetazolamide* reduces excretion of *quinidine* (increased plasma concentration)
Antibacterials: *loop diuretics* increase ototoxicity of *aminoglycosides, polymyxins, and vancomycin; loop diuretics* increase nephrotoxicity of *cephalothin*
Antidiabetics: hypoglycaemic effect antagonised by *loop and thiazide diuretics; chlorpropamide* increases risk of hyponatraemia associated with *thiazides in combination with potassium-sparing diuretics*
• Antihypertensives: enhanced hypotensive effect; enhancement of effect of *ACE inhibitors* (risk of extreme hypotension, also risk of hyperkalaemia with *potassium-sparing diuretics); increased* risk of first-dose hypotensive effect of post-synaptic *alpha-blockers such as prazosin and terazosin;* increased risk of hypokalaemia with *indapamide*
Beta-blockers: in hypokalaemia increased risk of ventricular arrhythmias with *sotalol*
Calcium Salts: risk of hypercalcaemia with *thiazides*
• Cardiac Glycosides: increased toxicity if hypokalaemia occurs with *acetazolamide, loop diuretics, and thiazides;* effect enhanced by *spironolactone*
Corticosteroids and Corticotrophin: increased risk of hypokalaemia with *acetazolamide, loop diuretics, and thiazides;* antagonism of diuretic effect
• Cyclosporin: increased risk of hyperkalaemia with *potassium-sparing* diuretics
other Diuretics: increased risk of hypokalaemia if *acetazolamide, loop diuretics or thiazides* given together; profound diuresis possible if *metolazone* given with *frusemide* (section 2.2.1)
Hormone Antagonists: *trilostane* increases risk of hyperkalaemia with *potassium-sparing diuretics*
• Lithium: lithium excretion reduced by *loop diuretics and thiazides* (increased plasma-lithium concentration and risk of toxicity—*loop diuretics* safer than *thiazides);* lithium excretion increased by *acetazolamide*
• Potassium Salts: hyperkalaemia with *potassium-sparing diuretics*
Sex Hormones: *oestrogens and combined oral contraceptives* antagonise diuretic effect
Ulcer-healing Drugs: increased risk of hypokalaemia if *acetazolamide, loop diuretics, and thiazides* given with *carbenoxolone; carbenoxolone* antagonises diuretic effect; *amiloride and spironolactone* antagonise ulcer-healing effect of *carbenoxolone*

Domperidone
Analgesics: *opioid analgesics* antagonise effect on gastro-intestinal activity
Antimuscarinics: antagonism of effect on gastro-intestinal activity
Dopaminergics: antagonism of hypoprolactinaemic effect of *bromocriptine*

Dopamine *see* Sympathomimetics
Dopaminergics *see* Bromocriptine, Levodopa, and Lysuride
Dopexamine *see* Sympathomimetics
Dothiepin *see* Antidepressants, Tricyclic
Doxapram
Sympathomimetics: risk of hypertension
Theophylline: increased CNS stimulation

Doxazosin *see* Alpha-blockers (post-synaptic)
Doxepin *see* Antidepressants, Tricyclic
Doxycycline *see* Tetracyclines
Droperidol *see* Phenothiazines and other Antipsychotics
Ecothiopate *see* Cholinergics
Edrophonium *see* Cholinergics
Enalapril *see* ACE Inhibitors
Enoxacin *see* 4-Quinolines
Ephedrine *see* Sympathomimetics
Ergotamine
Antibacterials: ergotism reported with *erythromycin*
Beta-blockers: increased peripheral vasconstriction

Erythromycin
Analgesics: plasma concentration of *alfentanil* increased
• Anti-arrhythmics: plasma concentration of *disopyramide* increased (risk of toxicity)
• Anticoagulants: effect of *nicoumalone and warfarin* enhanced
• Antiepileptics: inhibition of metabolism of *carbamazepine* (increased plasma-carbamazepine concentration)
Anxiolytics and Hypnotics: inhibition of metabolism of *triazolam* (increased plasma-triazolam concentration)
Cardiac Glycosides: effect of *digoxin* enhanced
• Cyclosporin: inhibition of metabolism (increased plasma-cyclosporin concentration)
Dopaminergics: plasma concentration of *bromocriptine* increased
Ergotamine: ergotism reported
• Theophylline: inhibition of metabolism (increased plasma-theophylline concentration)

Ethacrynic Acid *see* Diuretics (loop)
Ethosuximide
• Antibacterials: *isoniazid* increases plasma concentrations (increased risk of toxicity)
• Antidepressants: antagonism (convulsive threshold lowered)
• *other* Antiepileptics: concomitant administration of two or more antiepileptics may enhance toxicity without a corresponding increase in antiepileptic effect; moreover interactions between individual antiepileptics can complicate monitoring of treatment; interactions include enhanced effects, increased sedation, and reductions in plasma concentrations
• Antipsychotics: antagonism (convulsive threshold lowered)

Etidronate Disodium *see* Biphosphonates
Etodolac *see* NSAIDs
Etretinate
Cytotoxics: increased plasma concentration of *methotrexate*

Famotidine *see* Histamine H2-antagonists
Fansidar® *contains* Sulfadoxine and Pyrimethamine
Fenbufen *see* NSAIDs
Fenfluramine *see* Sympathomimetics
Fenofibrate *see* Clofibrate Group
Fenoprofen *see* NSAIDs
Fenoterol *see* Sympathomimetics, Beta$_2$
Ferrous Salts *see* Iron
Flavoxate *see* Antimuscarinics
Flecainide
Antacids and Adsorbents: reduced excretion in alkaline urine (plasma-flecainide concentration occasionally increased)
• *other* Anti-arrhythmics: *amiodarone* increases plasma-flecainide concentration (and increases risk of ventricular arrhythmias); increased myocardial depression with any *anti-arrhythmic*
• Diuretics: toxicity increased if hypokalaemia occurs; excretion reduced by *acetazolamide* (occasionally increased plasma concentration)
Ulcer-healing Drugs: *cimetidine* inhibits metabolism of *flecainide* (increased plasma-flecainide concentration)
Flucloxacillin *see* Penicillins
Fluconazole
Antibacterials: *rifampicin* reduces plasma concentration
• Anticoagulants: effect of *nicoumalone and warfarin* enhanced
Antidiabetics: plasma concentrations of *sulphonylureas* possibly increased
• Antiepileptics: effect of *phenytoin* enhanced
Cyclosporin: possible inhibition of metabolism and increased plasma-cyclosporin concentration
Fludrocortisone *see* Corticosteroids
Flunitrazepam *see* Benzodiazepines and other Anxiolytics and Hypnotics
Fluorouracil
Ulcer-healing Drugs: *cimetidine* inhibits metabolism (increased plasma-fluorouracil concentration)
Fluoxetine
• *other* Antidepressants: CNS effects of *MAOIs* increased; manufacturer advises avoidance of *MAOIs* for at least 2 weeks before *fluoxetine* and avoidance of *fluoxetine* for at least 5 weeks before *MAOIs;* increased plasma concentrations of some *tricyclics*; agitation and nausea with *tryptophan*
Antiepileptics: increased plasma concentration of *carbamazepine*
• Lithium: increased risk of CNS toxicity
Flupenthixol *see* Phenothiazines and other Antipsychotics
Fluphenazine *see* Phenothiazines and other Antipsychotics
Flurazepam *see* Benzodiazepines and other Anxiolytics and Hypnotics
Flurbiprofen *see* NSAIDs
Fluspirilene *see* Phenothiazines and other Antipsychotics
Flutamide
• Anticoagulants: effect of *warfarin* enhanced
Fluvoxamine
• Anticoagulants: effect of *nicoumalone and warfarin* may be enhanced
• *other* Antidepressants: CNS effects of *MAOIs* increased (risk of toxicity); manufacturer advises avoid *MAOIs* for at least 2 weeks before *fluvoxamine*; agitation and nausea with *tryptophan*
Beta-blockers: increased plasma concentration of *propranolol*
• Lithium: increased risk of CNS toxicity

Folic Acid *see* Vitamins
Framycetin *see* Aminoglycosides
Frusemide *see* Diuretics (loop)
Gallamine *see* Muscle Relaxants (non-depolarising)
Ganciclovir
Note: increased risk of myelosuppression with other *myelosuppressive drugs*
other Antivirals: profound myelosuppression with *zidovudine*
Gemfibrozil *see* Clofibrate Group
Gentamicin *see* Aminoglycosides
Glibenclamide *see* Antidiabetics (sulphonylurea)
Gliclazide *see* Antidiabetics (sulphonylurea)
Glipizide *see* Antidiabetics (sulphonylurea)
Gliquidone *see* Antidiabetics (sulphonylurea)
Glyceryl Trinitrate (general hypotensive interactions *as for* Hydralazine)
Anti-arrhythmics: *disopyramide* may reduce effect of *sublingual nitrates* (owing to dry mouth)
Antidepressants: *tricyclics* may reduce effect of *sublingual nitrates* (owing to dry mouth)
Antimuscarinics: *antimuscarinics such as atropine and propantheline* may reduce effect of *sublingual nitrates* (owing to dry mouth)
Griseofulvin
• Anticoagulants: metabolism of *nicoumalone and warfarin* accelerated (reduced anticoagulant effect)
Antiepileptics: metabolism accelerated by *phenobarbitone* (reduced effect)
• Sex Hormones: metabolism of *oral contraceptives* accelerated (reduced effect)
Guanethidine *see* Adrenergic Neurone Blockers
Guar Gum
Antibacterials: absorption of *phenoxymethylpenicillin* reduced
Haloperidol *see* Phenothiazines and other Antipsychotics
Halothane *see* Anaesthetics (volatile)
Heparin
Analgesics: *aspirin* enhances anticoagulant effect
Antiplatelet Drugs: *aspirin, dipyridamole and sulphinpyrazone* enhance anticoagulant effect
Hexamine
Potassium Citrate: urine should be acid
Histamine H1-antagonists *see* Antihistamines
Histamine H2-antagonists
Analgesics: *cimetidine* inhibits metabolism of *opioid analgesics notably pethidine* (increased plasma concentrations)
• Anti-arrhythmics: *cimetidine* increases plasma concentrations of *amiodarone, flecainide, lignocaine, procainamide, propafenone, and quinidine*
Antibacterials: *rifampicin* accelerates metabolism of *cimetidine* (reduced plasma-cimetidine concentration); *cimetidine* inhibits metabolism of *metronidazole* (increased plasma-metronidazole concentration)
• Anticoagulants: *cimetidine* enhances anticoagulant effect of *nicoumalone and warfarin* (inhibits metabolism)
Antidepressants: *cimetidine* inhibits metabolism of *amitriptyline, desipramine, doxepin, imipramine, and nortriptyline* (increased plasma concentrations)
Antidiabetics: *cimetidine* inhibits renal excretion of *metformin* (increased plasma concentration)
• Antiepileptics: *cimetidine* inhibits metabolism of *carbamazepine and phenytoin* (increased plasma concentrations)
Antifungals: absorption of *itraconazole and ketoconazole* reduced

Histamine H2-antagonists (*continued*)
Antimalarials: *cimetidine* inhibits metabolism of *chloroquine and quinine* (increased plasma concentrations)
Antipsychotics: *cimetidine* may enhance effect of *chlorpromazine*
Anxiolytics and Hypnotics: *cimetidine* inhibits metabolism of *benzodiazepines and chlormethiazole* (increased plasma concentrations)
Beta-blockers: *cimetidine* inhibits metabolism of *beta-blockers such as labetalol and propranolol* (increased plasma concentrations)
Calcium-channel Blockers: *cimetidine* inhibits metabolism of *some calcium-channel blockers* (increased plasma concentrations)
Cytotoxics: *cimetidine* increases plasma concentration of *fluorouracil*
• Theophylline: *cimetidine* inhibits metabolism (increased plasma-theophylline concentration)

Homatropine *see* Antimuscarinics

Hydralazine
Alcohol: enhanced hypotensive effect
• Anaesthetics: enhanced hypotensive effect
Analgesics: *NSAIDs* antagonise hypotensive effect
Antidepressants: enhanced hypotensive effect
other Antihypertensives: additive hypotensive effect
Antipsychotics: enhanced hypotensive effect
Anxiolytics and Hypnotics: enhanced hypotensive effect
Beta-blockers: enhanced hypotensive effect
Calcium-channel Blockers: enhanced hypotensive effect
Corticosteroids: antagonism of hypotensive effect
Diuretics: enhanced hypotensive effect
Dopaminergics: *levodopa* enhances hypotensive effect
Muscle Relaxants: *baclofen* enhances hypotensive effect
Nitrates: enhance hypotensive effect
Sex Hormones: *oestrogens and combined oral contraceptives* antagonise hypotensive effect
Ulcer-healing Drugs: *carbenoxolone* antagonises hypotensive effect

Hydrochlorothiazide *see* Diuretics (thiazide)

Hydrocortisone *see* Corticosteroids

Hydroflumethiazide *see* Diuretics (thiazide)

Hydroxychloroquine *see* Chloroquine and Hydroxychloroquine

Hydroxyzine *see* Antihistamines

Hyoscine *see* Antimuscarinics

Hypnotics *see* Benzodiazepines and other Anxiolytics and Hypnotics

Ibuprofen *see* NSAIDs

Imipramine *see* Antidepressants, Tricyclic

Indapamide *see* Diuretics (thiazide-related)

Indomethacin *see* NSAIDs

Indoramin *see* Alpha-blockers

Influenza Vaccine
Antiepileptics: effect of *phenytoin* enhanced

Insulin *see* Antidiabetics

Interferons
Theophylline: metabolism of *theophylline* inhibited (enhanced effect)

Iprindole *see* Antidepressants, Tricyclic

Iron
Antacids: *magnesium trisilicate* reduces absorption of *oral iron*
Antibacterials: *tetracyclines* reduce absorption of *oral iron* (and *vice versa*); absorption of *ciprofloxacin, norfloxacin,* and *ofloxacin* reduced by *oral iron*

Iron (*continued*)
Dopaminergics: absorption of *levodopa* may be reduced
Penicillamine: reduced absorption of *penicillamine*
Trientine: reduced absorption of *oral iron*
Zinc: reduced absorption of *oral iron* (and *vice versa*)

Isocarboxazid *see* MAOIs

Isometheptene *see* Sympathomimetics

Isoniazid
• Antiepileptics: metabolism of *carbamazepine, ethosuximide, and phenytoin* inhibited (enhanced effect)

Isoprenaline *see* Sympathomimetics

Isosorbide Dinitrate *see* Glyceryl Trinitrate

Isosorbide Mononitrate *see* Glyceryl Trinitrate

Isradipine *see* Calcium-channel Blockers

Itraconazole
Antacids and Adsorbents: *antacids* reduce absorption
Antibacterials: metabolism accelerated by *rifampicin* (reduced plasma-itraconazole concentration)
• **Anticoagulants:** effect of *warfarin* enhanced
• **Cyclosporin:** metabolism inhibited (increased plasma-cyclosporin concentration)
Ulcer-healing Drugs: *histamine H2-antagonists* reduce absorption

Kanamycin *see* Aminoglycosides

Kaolin *see* Antacids and Adsorbents

Ketoconazole
Antacids and Adsorbents: *antacids* reduce absorption
Antibacterials: metabolism accelerated by *rifampicin* (reduced plasma-ketoconazole concentration)
• Anticoagulants: effect of *nicoumalone and warfarin* enhanced
• Antiepileptics: plasma-ketoconazole concentration reduced by *phenytoin* and effect of *phenytoin* enhanced
Antihistamines: *terfenadine* metabolism inhibited (risk of cardiac toxicity)
Antimuscarinics: reduced absorption
• Cyclosporin: metabolism inhibited (increased plasma-cyclosporin concentration)
Ulcer-healing Drugs: *histamine H2-antagonists* reduce absorption

Ketoprofen *see* NSAIDs

Ketotifen *see* Antihistamines

Labetalol *see* Beta-blockers

Lanatoside C *see* Cardiac Glycosides

Levodopa
• Anaesthetics: risk of arrhythmias with *volatile anaesthetics such as cyclopropane and halothane*
• Antidepressants: hypertensive crisis with *MAOIs*
Antihypertensives: enhanced hypotensive effect; effect of *levodopa* antagonised by *reserpine*
Antipsychotics: antagonism of effect
Anxiolytics: occasional antagonism of effect by *chlordiazepoxide, diazepam, lorazepam and possibly other benzodiazepines*
Domperidone and Metoclopramide: levodopa-plasma concentrations increased by *metoclopramide*
Iron: absorption of *levodopa* may be reduced
Vitamins: effect of *levodopa* antagonised by *pyridoxine* unless a *dopa decarboxylase inhibitor* also given

Lignocaine
other Anti-arrhythmics: increased myocardial depression
Beta-blockers: increased risk of myocardial depression; increased risk of *lignocaine* toxicity with *propranolol*
Diuretics: effect of *lignocaine* antagonised by hypokalaemia with *acetazolamide, loop diuretics, and thiazides*
Ulcer-healing Drugs: *cimetidine* inhibits metabolism of *lignocaine* (increased risk of toxicity)

Lincomycin
Antacids and Adsorbents: *kaolin* reduces absorption
Cholinergics: antagonism of effect of *neostigmine and pyridostigmine*
• Muscle Relaxants: enhancement of effect of *non-depolarising muscle relaxants such as tubocurarine*

Lisinopril *see* ACE Inhibitors

Lithium
• Analgesics: *NSAIDs* reduce excretion of *lithium* (possibility of toxicity)
Antacids and Adsorbents: *sodium bicarbonate* increases excretion of *lithium* (reduced plasma-lithium concentrations)
Antibacterials: *lithium* toxicity reported with *metronidazole*
• Antidepressants: *fluoxetine* and *fluvoxamine* increase risk of CNS toxicity
Antidiabetics: *lithium* may occasionally impair glucose tolerance
Antiepileptics: neurotoxicity may occur with *carbamazepine and phenytoin* without increased plasma-lithium concentration
• **Antihypertensives:** *ACE inhibitors* reduce excretion of *lithium* (increased plasma-lithium concentration); neurotoxicity may occur with *methyldopa* without increased plasma-lithium concentration
Antipsychotics: increased risk of extrapyramidal effects and possibility of neurotoxicity (notably with *haloperidol)*
Calcium-channel Blockers: neurotoxicity may occur with *diltiazem and verapamil* without increased plasma-lithium concentration
Cholinergics: *lithium* antagonises effect of *neostigmine and pyridostigmine*
• Diuretics: *lithium* excretion reduced by *loop diuretics and thiazides* (increased plasma-lithium concentration and risk of toxicity—*loop diuretics* safer than *thiazides); lithium* excretion increased by *acetazolamide*
Domperidone and Metoclopramide: increased risk of extrapyramidal effects and possibility of neurotoxicity with *metoclopramide*
Muscle Relaxants: muscle relaxant effect enhanced
Theophylline: *lithium* excretion increased (reduced plasma-lithium concentration)

Lofepramine *see* Antidepressants, Tricyclic

Loprazolam *see* Benzodiazepines and other Anxiolytics and Hypnotics

Loratadine *see* Antihistamines

Lorazepam *see* Benzodiazepines and other Anxiolytics and Hypnotics

Lormetazepam *see* Benzodiazepines and other Anxiolytics and Hypnotics

Loxapine *see* Phenothiazines and other Antipsychotics

Lymecycline *see* Tetracyclines

Lysuride
Antipsychotics: antagonism of effect

Magnesium Salts (*see also* Antacids and Adsorbents)
Muscle Relaxants: effect of *non-depolarising muscle relaxants such as tubocurarine* enhanced by *parenteral magnesium salts*

Magnesium Trisilicate *see* Antacids and Adsorbents

Maloprim® *contains* Dapsone and Pyrimethamine

MAOIs
• Alcohol: some *alcoholic and dealcoholised beverages contain tyramine* which interacts with *MAOIs* (hypertensive crisis); foods, *see* MAOI card, section 4.3.2
• Analgesics: CNS excitation or depression (hypertension or hypotension) with *pethidine and possibly other opioid analgesics;* manufacturer advises avoid *nefopam*
Anorectics: *see* Sympathomimetics, below
• *other* Antidepressants: enhancement of CNS effects and toxicity with *other MAOIs* (avoid for at least a week after stopping *previous MAOIs* then start with reduced dose); CNS excitation and hypertension with most *tricyclics* (avoid for at least 2 weeks after stopping MAOIs); enhancement of CNS effects and toxicity possible with *fluvoxamine and fluoxetine* (manufacturer advises avoidance of *MAOIs* for at least 2 weeks before *fluoxetine and fluvoxamine* and avoidance of *fluoxetine* for at least 5 weeks before *MAOIs);* CNS excitation and confusion with *tryptophan* (reduce tryptophan dose)
Antidiabetics: effect of *insulin, metformin, and sulphonylureas* enhanced
• Antiepileptics: antagonism of anticonvulsant effect; manufacturer advises avoid *carbamazepine* with or within 2 weeks of *MAOIs*
• Antihypertensives: hypotensive effect enhanced; CNS excitation and hypertension with *reserpine*
Antimuscarinics: increased side-effects
• Antipsychotics: CNS excitation and hypertension with *oxypertine*
Anxiolytics and Hypnotics: manufacturer advises avoidance of *buspirone*
• Dopaminergics: hypertensive crisis with *levodopa*
• Sympathomimetics: hypertensive crisis with *sympathomimetics such as dexamphetamine and other amphetamines, dexfenfluramine, diethylpropion, dopamine, dopexamine, ephedrine, fenfluramine, isometheptene, mazindol, pemoline, phentermine, phenylephrine, phenylpropanolamine, and pseudoephedrine*
• Tetrabenazine: CNS excitation and hypertension

Maprotiline *see* Antidepressants, Tricyclic

Mazindol *see* Sympathomimetics

Mebhydrolin *see* Antihistamines

Medazepam *see* Benzodiazepines and other Anxiolytics and Hypnotics

Mefenamic Acid *see* NSAIDs

Mefloquine
other Antimalarials: increased risk of side-effects with *quinine*, but should not prevent use of intravenous quinine in severe cases; for full precautions see p. 224 (also applies to *quinidine*)
Cardioactive drugs: possible increased risk of bradycardia with *beta-blockers*, *digoxin*, and *some calcium-channel blockers*

Mefruside *see* Diuretics (thiazide)

Menadiol *see* Vitamins (Vitamin K)

Mepacrine
other Antimalarials: increased plasma concentration of *primaquine* (risk of toxicity)

Mepenzolate *see* Antimuscarinics

Meprobamate *see* Benzodiazepines and other Anxiolytics and Hypnotics

Meptazinol *see* Opioid Analgesics
Mequitazine *see* Antihistamines
Mercaptopurine
Allopurinol: enhancement of effect (increased toxicity)
Metaraminol *see* Sympathomimetics (*as* noradrenaline)
Metformin *see* Antidiabetics
Methadone *see* Opioid Analgesics
Methixene *see* Antimuscarinics
Methocarbamol *see* Muscle Relaxants
Methotrexate
• Analgesics: excretion reduced by *aspirin, azapropazone, diclofenac, indomethacin, ketoprofen, naproxen, phenylbutazone, and probably other NSAIDs* (increased risk of toxicity)
Antibacterials: antifolate effect increased by *co-trimoxazole and trimethoprim*
Antiepileptics: *phenytoin* increases antifolate effect
Antimalarials: antifolate effect increased by *pyrimethamine* (ingredient of *Fansidar®* and *Maloprim®*)
Etretinate: increased plasma concentration of *methotrexate*
• Uricosurics: excretion reduced by *probenecid* (increased risk of toxicity)
Methotrimeprazine *see* Phenothiazines and other Antipsychotics
Methoxamine *see* Sympathomimetics (*as* noradrenaline)
Methyclothiazide *see* Diuretics (thiazide)
Methyldopa
Alcohol: enhanced hypotensive effect
• Anaesthetics: enhanced hypotensive effect
Analgesics: *NSAIDs* antagonise hypotensive effect
Antidepressants: enhanced hypotensive effect
other Antihypertensives: enhanced hypotensive effect
Antipsychotics: increased risk of extrapyramidal effects; enhanced hypotensive effect
Anxiolytics and Hypnotics: enhanced hypotensive effect
Beta-blockers: enhanced hypotensive effect
Calcium-channel Blockers: enhanced hypotensive effect
Corticosteroids: antagonism of hypotensive effect
Diuretics: enhanced hypotensive effect
Dopaminergics: antagonism of antiparkinsonian effect; *levodopa* enhances hypotensive effect
Lithium: neurotoxicity may occur without increased plasma-lithium concentration
Nitrates: enhance hypotensive effect
Sex Hormones: *oestrogens and combined oral contraceptives* antagonise hypotensive effect
Sympathomimetics: *see* Sympathomimetics (main list)
Ulcer-healing Drugs: *carbenoxolone* antagonises hypotensive effect
Methylphenobarbitone *see* Barbiturates
Methylprednisolone *see* Corticosteroids
Metipranolol *see* Beta-blockers
Metirosine
Antipsychotics: increased risk of extrapyramidal effects
Dopaminergics: antagonism
Metoclopramide
Analgesics: increased absorption of *aspirin and paracetamol* (enhanced effect); *opioid analgesics* antagonise effect on gastro-intestinal activity
Antihypertensives: increased risk of extrapyramidal effects with *reserpine*

Metoclopramide (*continued*)
Antimuscarinics: antagonism of effect on gastro-intestinal activity
Antipsychotics: increased risk of extrapyramidal effects
Dopaminergics: antagonism of hypoprolactinaemic effect of *bromocriptine*; increased plasma concentration of *levodopa*
Lithium: increased risk of extrapyramidal effects and possibility of neurotoxicity
Tetrabenazine: increased risk of extrapyramidal effects
Metolazone *see* Diuretics (thiazide-related)
Metoprolol *see* Beta-blockers
Metronidazole
Alcohol: disulfiram-like reaction
• Anticoagulants: effect of *nicoumalone and warfarin* enhanced
• Antiepileptics: *metronidazole* inhibits metabolism of *phenytoin* (increased plasma-phenytoin concentration); *phenobarbitone* accelerates metabolism of *metronidazole* (reduced plasma-metronidazole concentration)
Disulfiram: psychotic reactions reported
Lithium: increased toxicity reported
Ulcer-healing Drugs: *cimetidine* inhibits metabolism (increased plasma-metronidazole concentration)
Mexiletine
Analgesics: *opioid analgesics* delay absorption
Antacids and Adsorbents: excretion of *mexiletine* reduced in alkaline urine (plasma-mexiletine concentrations occasionally increased)
• *other* Anti-arrhythmics: increased myocardial depression with any combination of *anti-arrhythmics*
Antibacterials: *rifampicin* accelerates metabolism (reduced plasma-mexiletine concentration)
Anti-epileptics: *phenytoin* accelerates metabolism (reduced plasma-mexiletine concentration)
Antimuscarinics: *atropine* delays absorption
Diuretics: action of *mexiletine* antagonised by hypokalaemia due to *acetazolamide, loop diuretics, and thiazides;* excretion of mexiletine reduced by *acetazolamide* (plasma-mexiletine concentrations occasionally increased)
Mianserin
Alcohol: enhanced effect
Anxiolytics and Hypnotics: enhanced effect
Miconazole
• Anticoagulants: effect of *nicoumalone and warfarin* enhanced
• Antidiabetics: effect of *sulphonylureas* enhanced
• Antiepileptics: effect of *phenytoin* enhanced
other Antifungals: *amphotericin* antagonises effect
Minocycline *see* Tetracyclines
Minoxidil *see* Hydralazine for general hypotensive interactions
Monoamine-oxidase Inhibitors *see* MAOIs
Monosulfiram
Alcohol: disulfiram-like reaction
Morphine *see* Opioid Analgesics
Muscle Relaxants
• Anti-arrhythmics: *quinidine* enhances muscle relaxant effect
• Antibacterials: effect of *non-depolarising muscle relaxants such as tubocurarine* enhanced by *aminoglycosides, clindamycin, lincomycin, and polymyxins*
Beta-blockers: *propranolol* enhances muscle relaxant effect

Muscle Relaxants (*continued*)
Calcium-channel Blockers: *nifedipine* and *verapamil* enhance effect of *non-depolarising muscle relaxants such as tubocurarine*; hypotension, myocardial depression, and hyperkalaemia reported with intravenous *dantrolene* and *verapamil*
Cardiac Glycosides: arrhythmias if *suxamethonium* given with *digoxin*
Cholinergics: *demecarium* and *ecothiopate* eye-drops, and *neostigmine, and pyridostigmine* enhance effect of *suxamethonium* but antagonise effect of *non-depolarising muscle relaxants such as tubocurarine*
Cytotoxics: *cyclophosphamide and thiotepa* enhance effect of *suxamethonium*
Lithium: *lithium* enhances muscle relaxant effect
Magnesium Salts: *parenteral magnesium* enhances effect of *non-depolarising muscle relaxants such as tubocurarine*
Nabumetone *see* NSAIDs
Nadolol *see* Beta-blockers
Nalbuphine *see* Opioid Analgesics
Nalidixic Acid *see* 4-Quinolones
Nandrolone *see* Anabolic Steroids
Naproxen *see* NSAIDs
Nefopam
• Antidepressants: manufacturer recommends avoid *MAOIs*
Antimuscarinics: increased side-effects
Neomycin *see* Aminoglycosides
Neostigmine *see* Cholinergics
Netilmicin *see* Aminoglycosides
Nicardipine *see* Calcium-channel Blockers
Nicoumalone *see* Warfarin
Nifedipine *see* Calcium-channel Blockers
Nimodipine *see* Calcium-channel Blockers
Nimorazole alcohol interaction *as for* Metronidazole
Nitrates *see* Glyceryl Trinitrate
Nitrazepam *see* Benzodiazepines and other Anxiolytics and Hypnotics
Nitrofurantoin
Uricosurics: *probenecid* reduces excretion of *nitrofurantoin* (risk of toxicity)
Nitroprusside *as for* Hydralazine
Nizatidine *see* Histamine H2-antagonists
Noradrenaline *see* Sympathomimetics
Norfloxacin *see* 4-Quinolones
Nortriptyline *see* Antidepressants, Tricyclic
NSAIDs (*see also* Aspirin)
Anion-exchange Resins: *cholestyramine* reduces absorption of *phenylbutazone*
Antacids and Adsorbents: *antacids* reduce absorption of *diflunisal*
Anticoagulants: *see* Warfarin
• Antidiabetics: effect of *sulphonylureas* enhanced by *azapropazone and phenylbutazone*
• Antiepileptics: effect of *phenytoin* enhanced by *azapropazone and phenylbutazone*
Antihypertensives: antagonism of hypotensive effect; hyperkalaemia and increased risk of renal failure on administration of *ACE inhibitors* with *indomethacin and possibly other NSAIDs*
Cardiac Glycosides: *NSAIDs* may exacerbate heart failure, reduce GFR, and increase plasma cardiac glycoside concentration
• Cytotoxics: excretion of *methotrexate* reduced by *aspirin, azapropazone, diclofenac, indomethacin, ketoprofen, naproxen, phenylbutazone and probably other NSAIDs* (increased risk of toxicity)

NSAIDs (*continued*)
Diuretics: risk of nephrotoxicity of *NSAIDs* increased; *NSAIDs notably indomethacin* antagonise diuretic effect; *indomethacin and possibly other NSAIDs* increase risk of hyperkalaemia with *potassium-sparing diuretics*; occasional reports of decreased renal function when *indomethacin* given with *triamterene*
• Lithium: excretion of *lithium* reduced by *diclofenac, ibuprofen, indomethacin, mefenamic acid, naproxen, phenylbutazone, piroxicam, and probably other NSAIDs* (possibility of toxicity)
Thyroxine: false low total plasma-thyroxine concentration with *phenylbutazone*
Uricosurics: *probenecid* delays excretion of *indomethacin, ketoprofen, and naproxen* (raised plasma concentrations)
Octreotide
Antidiabetics: reduces *insulin and antidiabetic drug* requirements in diabetes mellitus
Oestrogens *see* Contraceptives, Oral
Ofloxacin *see* 4-Quinolones
Omeprazole
• Anticoagulants: effects of *warfarin* enhanced
• Antiepileptics: effects of *phenytoin* enhanced
Opioid Analgesics
Anti-arrhythmics: delayed absorption of *mexiletine*
Antibacterials: *rifampicin* accelerates metabolism of *methadone* (reduced effect); *erythromycin* increases plasma concentration of *alfentanil*
• Anticoagulants: *dextropropoxyphene* may enhance effect of *nicoumalone and warfarin*
• Antidepressants: CNS excitation or depression (hypertension or hypotension) if *pethidine and possibly other opioid analgesics* given to patients receiving *MAOIs*
• Antiepileptics: *dextropropoxyphene* enhances effect of *carbamazepine*
Anxiolytics and Hypnotics: enhanced sedative effect
Cisapride: possible antagonism of gastro-intestinal effect
Domperidone and Metoclopramide: antagonism of gastro-intestinal effects
Ulcer-healing Drugs: *cimetidine* inhibits metabolism of opioid analgesics notably *pethidine* (increased plasma concentration)
Orciprenaline *see* Sympathomimetics
Orphenadrine *see* Antimuscarinics
Oxatomide *see* Antihistamines
Oxazepam *see* Benzodiazepines and other Anxiolytics and Hypnotics
Oxprenolol *see* Beta-blockers
Oxymetazoline *see* Sympathomimetics
Oxymetholone *see* Anabolic Steroids
Oxypertine *see* Phenothiazines and other Antipsychotics
Oxytetracycline *see* Tetracyclines
Pamidronate Sodium *see* Biphosphonates
Pancuronium *see* Muscle Relaxants (non-depolarising)
Paracetamol
Anion-exchange Resins: *cholestyramine* reduces absorption of *paracetamol*
Domperidone and Metoclopramide: *metoclopramide* accelerates absorption of *paracetamol* (enhanced effect)
Pemoline *see* Sympathomimetics
Penbutolol *see* Beta-blockers

Penicillamine
Antacids and Adsorbents: *antacids* reduce absorption
Iron: reduced absorption of *penicillamine*
Zinc: reduced absorption of *penicillamine*
Penicillins
Antacids: reduced absorption of *pivampicillin*
Anticoagulants: *see* Phenindione and Warfarin
Guar Gum: reduced absorption of *phenoxymethylpenicillin*
Probenecid: reduced excretion of *penicillins*
Sex Hormones: *see* Contraceptives, Oral
Pentaerythritol Tetranitrate *see* Glyceryl Trinitrate
Pentazocine *see* Opioid Analgesics
Pericyazine *see* Phenothiazines and other Antipsychotics
Perindopril *see* ACE Inhibitors
Perphenazine *see* Phenothiazines and other Antipsychotics
Pethidine *see* Opioid Analgesics
Phenazocine *see* Opioid Analgesics
Phenelzine *see* MAOIs
Phenindamine *see* Antihistamines
Phenindione
• Anabolic Steroids: anticoagulant effect enhanced by *oxymetholone, stanozolol and others*
• Analgesics: anticoagulant effect enhanced by *aspirin*
Anion-exchange Resins: anticoagulant effect enhanced or reduced by *cholestyramine*
Antibacterials: although studies have failed to demonstrate interaction common experience in anticoagulant clinics is that prothrombin time can be prolonged by course of *oral broad-spectrum antibiotic such as ampicillin* (may also apply to antibiotics given for local action on gut such as *neomycin)*
• Antiplatelet Drugs: anticoagulant effect enhanced by *aspirin and dipyridamole*
• Clofibrate Group: enhanced anticoagulant effect
• Sex Hormones: anticoagulant effect antagonised by *oral contraceptives*
• Thyroxine: enhanced anticoagulant effect
• Vitamins: anticoagulant effect antagonised by vitamin K (present in some enteral feeds)
Pheniramine *see* Antihistamines
Phenobarbitone *see* Barbiturates
Phenothiazines and other Antipsychotics
Alcohol: enhanced sedative effect
• Anaesthetics: enhanced hypotensive effect
Antacids: reduced absorption of *phenothiazines*
Antibacterials: *rifampicin* accelerates metabolism of *haloperidol* (reduced plasma-haloperidol concentration)
• Antidepressants: increased antimuscarinic effects notably on administration of *tricyclics* with *phenothiazines; oxypertine* causes CNS excitation and hypertension with *MAOIs*
• Antiepileptics: antagonism (convulsive threshold lowered); *carbamazepine* accelerates metabolism of *haloperidol* (reduced plasma concentration)
Antihypertensives: enhanced hypotensive effect; severe postural hypotension on administration of *ACE inhibitors* with *chlorpromazine and possibly other antipsychotics*; increased risk of extrapyramidal effects on administration of *methyldopa, metirosine, and reserpine*
Antimuscarinics: antimuscarinic side-effects of *phenothiazines* increased (but reduced plasma concentrations)
Anxiolytics and Hypnotics: enhanced sedative effect

Phenothiazines and other Antipsychotics (*continued*)
Beta-blockers: *propranolol* increases plasma concentration of *chlorpromazine*
Calcium-channel Blockers: enhanced hypotensive effect
Desferrioxamine: manufacturer advises avoid *prochlorperazine*
Domperidone and Metoclopramide: increased risk of extrapyramidal effects with *metoclopramide*
Dopaminergics: antagonism of hypoprolactinaemic and antiparkinsonian effect of *bromocriptine*
Lithium: increased risk of extrapyramidal effects and possibility of neurotoxicity with *haloperidol and phenothiazines*
Tetrabenazine: increased risk of extrapyramidal effects
Ulcer-healing Drugs: *cimetidine* may enhance effects of *chlorpromazine*
Phenoxymethylpenicillin *see* Penicillins
Phentermine *see* Sympathomimetics
Phenylbutazone *see* NSAIDs
Phenylephrine *see* Sympathomimetics
Phenylpropanolamine *see* Sympathomimetics
Phenytoin
• Analgesics: plasma-phenytoin concentration increased by *aspirin, azapropazone, and phenylbutazone*
Antacids: possibility of reduced *phenytoin* absorption
• Anti-arrhythmics: *amiodarone* increases plasma-phenytoin concentration; *phenytoin* reduces plasma concentrations of *disopyramide, mexiletine, and quinidine*
• **Antibacterials:** plasma-phenytoin concentration increased by *chloramphenicol, isoniazid, and metronidazole*; plasma-phenytoin concentration and antifolate effect increased by *co-trimoxazole* and *trimethoprim*; plasma phenytoin concentration reduced by *rifampicin*; plasma concentration of *doxycycline* reduced by *phenytoin*
• Anticoagulants: metabolism of *nicoumalone and warfarin* accelerated (possibility of reduced anticoagulant effect, but enhancement also reported)
• Antidepressants: antagonism of anticonvulsant effect (convulsive threshold lowered); *viloxazine* increases plasma-phenytoin concentration; *phenytoin* reduces plasma concentrations of *tricyclics*
• *other* Antiepileptics: concomitant administration of *two or more antiepileptics* may enhance toxicity without a corresponding increase in antiepileptic effect; moreover interactions between individual antiepileptics can complicate monitoring of treatment; interactions include enhanced effects, increased sedation, and reductions in plasma concentrations
• Antifungals: plasma-phenytoin concentration increased by *fluconazole, ketoconazole, and miconazole*; plasma concentration of *ketoconazole and possibly others* reduced
Antimalarials: increased risk of antifolate effect with *pyrimethamine* (includes *Fansidar®* and *Maloprim®*)
Antiplatelet Drugs: plasma-phenytoin concentration increased by *aspirin*
• Antipsychotics: antagonism of anticonvulsant effect (convulsive threshold lowered)
Calcium-channel Blockers: effect of *isradipine* and probably *nicardipine* and *nifedipine* reduced
Cardiac Glycosides: metabolism of *digitoxin only* accelerated (reduced effect)

Phenytoin (*continued*)
• Corticosteroids: metabolism of *corticosteroids* accelerated (reduced effect)
• Cyclosporin: metabolism of *cyclosporin* accelerated (reduced plasma concentration)
Cytotoxics: reduced absorption of *phenytoin*; increased anti-folate effect with *methotrexate*
• Disulfiram: plasma-phenytoin concentration increased
Food: some *enteral foods* may interfere with absorption of *phenytoin*
Lithium: neurotoxicity may occur without increased plasma-lithium concentration
• Sex Hormones: metabolism of *oral contraceptives* accelerated (reduced contraceptive effect)
Theophylline: metabolism of *theophylline* accelerated (reduced plasma-theophylline concentration)
Thyroxine: metabolism of *thyroxine* accelerated (may increase thyroxine requirements in hypothyroidism)
• Ulcer-healing Drugs: *cimetidine* inhibits metabolism (increased plasma-phenytoin concentration); *sucralfate* reduces absorption; *omeprazole* enhances effect of *phenytoin*
• Uricosurics: plasma-phenytoin concentration increased by *sulphinpyrazone*
Vaccines: effect enhanced by *influenza vaccine*
Vitamins: plasma-phenytoin concentration occasionally reduced by *folic acid*

Physostigmine *see* Cholinergics
Phytomenadione *see* Vitamins (Vitamin K)
Pimozide *see* Phenothiazines and other Antipsychotics (**CSM**: *see also* p. 136)
Pindolol *see* Beta-blockers
Pipenzolate *see* Antimuscarinics
Pipothiazine *see* Phenothiazines and other Antipsychotics
Pirbuterol *see* Sympathomimetics, Beta$_2$
Piretanide *see* Diuretics (loop)
Piroxicam *see* NSAIDs
Pivampicillin *see* Penicillins

Pizotifen
Antihypertensives: hypotensive effect of *adrenergic neurone blockers* antagonised

Poldine *see* Antimuscarinics

Polymyxins (*see also* Aminoglycosides)
Muscle Relaxants: enhanced muscle relaxant effect

Polythiazide *see* Diuretics (thiazides)

Potassium Salts
• Antihypertensives: hyperkalaemia with *ACE inhibitors*
• Cyclosporin: increased risk of hyperkalaemia
• Diuretics: hyperkalaemia with *potassium-sparing diuretics*

Prazosin *see* Alpha-blockers (post-synaptic)
Prednisolone *see* Corticosteroids
Prednisone *see* Corticosteroids

Primaquine
other Antimalarials: *mepacrine* increases plasma concentration of *primaquine* (risk of toxicity)

Primidone *see* Barbiturates and Primidone

Probenecid
Analgesics: *aspirin* antagonises effect; excretion of *indomethacin, ketoprofen, and naproxen* delayed (increased plasma concentrations)
Antibacterials: reduced excretion of *cephalosporins, cinoxacin, dapsone, nalidixic acid, nitrofurantoin, and penicillins* (increased plasma-concentrations); antagonism by *pyrazinamide*

Probenecid (*continued*)
Antihypertensives: reduced excretion of *captopril*
Antivirals: reduced excretion of *acyclovir and zidovudine* (increased plasma concentrations and risk of toxicity)
• Cytotoxics: reduced excretion of *methotrexate* (increased risk of toxicity)

Procainamide
• *other* Anti-arrhythmics: *amiodarone* increases procainamide-plasma concentrations; increased myocardial depression with any anti-arrhythmic
• Ulcer-healing Drugs: *cimetidine* inhibits metabolism (increased plasma-procainamide concentration)

Procarbazine
Alcohol: disulfiram-like reaction

Prochlorperazine *see* Phenothiazines and other Antipsychotics
Procyclidine *see* Antimuscarinics

Progestogens (*see also* Contraceptives, Oral)
• Cyclosporin: increased plasma-cyclosporin concentration (inhibition of metabolism)

Promazine *see* Phenothiazines and other Antipsychotics
Promethazine *see* Antihistamines

Propafenone
other **Anti-arrhythmics:** *quinidine* increases plasma concentration of *propafenone*; increased myocardial depression with any *anti-arrhythmic*
Antibacterials: *rifampicin* reduces plasma concentration of *propafenone*
• Anticoagulants: increased plasma concentration of *warfarin and nicoumalone* (enhanced effect)
• Cardiac Glycosides: increased plasma concentrations of *digoxin* (halve maintenance dose of digoxin)
Cholinergics: possible antagonism of effect of *neostigmine* and *pyridostigmine*
• Ulcer-healing Drugs: *cimetidine* increases plasma-propafenone concentration

Propantheline *see* Antimuscarinics
Propranolol *see* Beta-Blockers
Protriptyline *see* Antidepressants, Tricyclic

Pyrazinamide
Uricosurics: antagonism of effect of *probenecid and sulphinpyrazone*

Pyridostigmine *see* Cholinergics
Pyridoxine *see* Vitamins

Pyrimethamine
Antibacterials: increased antifolate effect with *co-trimoxazole* and *trimethoprim*
Antiepileptics: increased antifolate effect with *phenytoin*
Cytotoxics: increased antifolate effect with *methotrexate*

Quinalbarbitone *see* Barbiturates and Primidone
Quinapril *see* ACE Inhibitors

Quinidine
Antacids: reduced excretion in alkaline urine (plasma-quinidine concentration occasionally increased)
• *other* Anti-arrhythmics: *amiodarone* increases plasma-quinidine concentrations (and increases risk of ventricular arrhythmias); plasma concentration of *propafenone* increased; increased myocardial depression with *any anti-arrhythmic*
Antibacterials: *rifampicin* accelerates metabolism (reduced plasma-quinidine concentration)
Anticoagulants: effect of *nicoumalone and warfarin* may be enhanced

Quinidine (*continued*)
Antiepileptics: *phenobarbitone, phenytoin, and primidone* accelerate metabolism (reduced plasma-quinidine concentration)
Barbiturates: *see under* Antiepileptics, above
• Calcium-channel Blockers: *verapamil* increases plasma-quinidine concentration (possibility of extreme hypotension)
• Cardiac Glycosides: plasma concentration of *digoxin* increased (halve digoxin maintenance dose)
Cholinergics: antagonism of effect of *neostigmine and pyridostigmine*
• Diuretics: *acetazolamide* reduces excretion (plasma-quinidine concentration occasionally increased); quinidine toxicity increased if hypokalaemia occurs with *acetazolamide, loop diuretics, and thiazides*
• Muscle Relaxants: muscle relaxant effect enhanced
• Ulcer-healing Drugs: *cimetidine* inhibits metabolism (increased plasma-quinidine concentration)

Quinine
other Antimalarials: see Mefloquine
• Cardiac Glycosides: plasma concentration of *digoxin* increased (halve digoxin maintenance dose)
Ulcer-healing Drugs: *cimetidine* inhibits metabolism (increased plasma-quinine concentration)

4-Quinolones
Antacids and Adsorbents: *antacids* reduce absorption of *ciprofloxacin, norfloxacin* and *ofloxacin*
• **Anticoagulants:** anticoagulant effect of *nicoumalone and warfarin* enhanced by *ciprofloxacin, enoxacin, nalidixic acid,* and *norfloxacin*
Cyclosporin: increased risk of nephrotoxicity
Iron: absorption of *ciprofloxacin, norfloxacin,* and *ofloxacin* reduced by *oral iron*
• **Theophylline:** *ciprofloxacin, enoxacin,* and *norfloxacin* increase plasma-theophylline concentration
Ulcer-healing Drugs: *sucralfate* reduces absorption of *ciprofloxacin, norfloxacin,* and *ofloxacin*
Uricosurics: *probenecid* reduces excretion of *cinoxacin* and *nalidixic acid* (increased side-effects)
Zinc Salts: *zinc* reduces absorption of *ciprofloxacin*

Ramipril *see* ACE Inhibitors
Ranitidine *see* Histamine H2-antagonists
Reproterol *see* Sympathomimetics, $Beta_2$

Reserpine and Rauwolfia Alkaloids
Alcohol: enhanced hypotensive effect
Anaesthetics: enhanced hypotensive effect
Analgesics: *NSAIDs* antagonise hypotensive effect
• Antidepressants: CNS excitation and hypertension with *MAOIs*
other Antihypertensives: additive hypotensive effect
Antipsychotics: increased risk of extrapyramidal effects
Anxiolytics and Hypnotics: enhanced hypotensive effect
Beta-blockers: increased bradycardia
Calcium-channel Blockers: enhanced hypotensive effect
Corticosteroids: antagonism of hypotensive effect
Diuretics: enhanced hypotensive effect
Domperidone and Metoclopramide: increased risk of extrapyramidal effects with *metoclopramide*
Dopaminergics: *levodopa* enhances hypotensive effect; antagonism of *amantadine* and *levodopa*
Nitrates: *nitrates* enhance hypotensive effect
Sex Hormones: *oestrogens and combined oral contraceptives* antagonise hypotensive effect

Reserpine and Rauwolfia Alkaloids (*continued*)
Sympathomimetics: *see* Sympathomimetics (main list)
Ulcer-healing Drugs: *carbenoxolone* antagonises hypotensive effect

Rifampicin
Analgesics: metabolism of *methadone* accelerated (reduced effect)
Antacids: reduced absorption of *rifampicin*
Anti-arrhythmics: metabolism accelerated—reduced plasma concentrations of *disopyramide, mexiletine, propafenone, and quinidine*
other Antibacterials: metabolism of *chloramphenicol* accelerated (reduced plasma concentration)
• Anticoagulants: metabolism of *nicoumalone and warfarin* accelerated (reduced anticoagulant effect)
• Antidiabetics: metabolism of *chlorpropamide, tolbutamide and possibly other sulphonylureas* accelerated (reduced effect)
• Antiepileptics: metabolism of *phenytoin* accelerated (reduced plasma concentration)
Antifungals: metabolism of *fluconazole, itraconazole and ketoconazole* accelerated (reduced plasma concentrations)
Antipsychotics: metabolism of *haloperidol* accelerated (reduced plasma concentration)
Beta-blockers: metabolism of *propranolol* accelerated (reduced plasma concentration)
Calcium-channel Blockers: metabolism of *verapamil and possibly isradipine* accelerated (reduced plasma concentration)
Cardiac glycosides: metabolism of *digitoxin only* accelerated (reduced effect)
• Corticosteroids: metabolism of *corticosteroids* accelerated (reduced effect)
• Cyclosporin: metabolism accelerated (reduced plasma-cyclosporin concentration)
• Sex Hormones: metabolism accelerated (contraceptive effect of *both combined and progestogen-only oral contraceptives* reduced)
Theophylline: metabolism accelerated (reduced plasma-theophylline concentration)
Thyroxine: metabolism of *thyroxine* accelerated (may increase requirements in hypothyroidism)
Ulcer-healing Drugs: metabolism of *cimetidine* accelerated (reduced plasma concentration)

Rimiterol *see* Sympathomimetics, $Beta_2$
Ritodrine *see* Sympathomimetics, $Beta_2$

Rowachol®
Anticoagulants: effect of *nicoumalone and warfarin* may be enhanced

Salbutamol *see* Sympathomimetics, $Beta_2$

Simvastatin
• Anticoagulants: effect of *nicoumalone and warfarin* may be enhanced

Sodium Bicarbonate *see* Antacids and Adsorbents
Sodium Valproate *see* Valproate
Sotalol *see* Beta-blockers
Spironolactone *see* Diuretics (potassium-sparing)
Stanozolol *see* Anabolic Steroids
Streptomycin *see* Aminoglycosides

Sucralfate
Antibacterials: reduced absorption of *ciprofloxacin, norfloxacin, ofloxacin,* and *tetracycline*
• Anticoagulants: reduced absorption of *warfarin*
• Antiepileptics: reduced absorption of *phenytoin*

Sulfadoxine *see* Co-trimoxazole and Sulphonamides
Sulfametopyrazine *see* Co-trimoxazole and Sulphonamides
Sulindac *see* NSAIDs
Sulphadiazine *see* Co-trimoxazole and Sulphonamides

Sulphadimidine *see* Co-trimoxazole and Sulphonamides

Sulphinpyrazone

Analgesics: *aspirin* antagonises uricosuric effect

Antibacterials: *pyrazinamide* antagonises effect

• Anticoagulants: anticoagulant effect of *nicoumalone and warfarin* enhanced

• Antidiabetics: effect of *sulphonylureas* enhanced

• Antiepileptics: plasma concentration of *phenytoin* increased

Theophylline: plasma-theophylline concentration reduced

Sulphonamides *see* Co-trimoxazole and Sulphonamides

Sulphonylureas *see* Antidiabetics

Sulpiride *see* Phenothiazines and other Antipsychotics

Suxamethonium *see* Muscle Relaxants

Sympathomimetics

• Anaesthetics: risk of arrhythmias if *adrenaline and isoprenaline* given with *volatile anaesthetics*

• Antidepressants: with *tricyclics* administration of *adrenaline and noradrenaline* may cause hypertension and arrhythmias (but local anaesthetics with adrenaline appear to be safe); with *MAOIs* administration of inotropics such as *dopamine* and *dopexamine* may cause hypertensive crisis; also with *MAOIs* administration of *dexamphetamine and other amphetamines, dexfenfluramine, diethylpropion, ephedrine, fenfluramine, isometheptene, mazindol, pemoline, phentermine, phenylephrine, phenylpropanolamine, and pseudoephedrine* may cause hypertensive crisis (these drugs are contained in anorectics or cold and cough remedies)

Antihypertensives: sympathomimetics in *anorectics and cold and cough remedies, (see* above) antagonise hypotensive effect of *adrenergic neurone blockers;* hypotensive effect of some other antihypertensives may be enhanced by *dexfenfluramine, and fenfluramine*

• Beta-blockers: severe hypertension with *adrenaline and noradrenaline* (especially with non-selective beta-blockers); severe hypertension also possible with sympathomimetics in *anorectics and cold and cough remedies, see* above

Respiratory Stimulants: risk of hypertension with *doxapram*

other **Sympathomimetics:** *dopexamine* possibly potentiates effect of *adrenaline* and *noradrenaline*

Sympathomimetics, Beta$_2$

Corticosteroids: increased risk of hypokalaemia if high doses of *corticosteroids* given with high doses of *fenoterol, pirbuterol, reproterol, rimiterol, ritodrine, salbutamol, and terbutaline*

Theophylline: increased risk of hypokalaemia if given with high doses of *fenoterol, pirbuterol, reproterol, rimiterol, ritodrine, salbutamol,* and *terbutaline*

Tamoxifen

• Anticoagulants: anticoagulant effect of *nicoumalone and warfarin* enhanced

Temazepam *see* Benzodiazepines and other Anxiolytics and Hypnotics

Tenoxicam *see* NSAIDs

Terazosin *see* Alpha-blockers (post-synaptic)

Terbutaline *see* Sympathomimetics, Beta$_2$

Terfenadine *see* Antihistamines

Terodiline *see* Antimuscarinics

Tetrabenazine (general extrapyramidal interactions *as for* phenothiazines)

• Antidepressants: CNS excitation and hypertension with *MAOIs*

Tetracyclines

Antacids: reduced absorption

Anticoagulants: *see* Phenindione and Warfarin

Antiepileptics: *carbamazepine, phenobarbitone, phenytoin, and primidone* increase metabolism of *doxycycline* (reduced plasma concentration)

Antihypertensives: *quinapril* reduces absorption (tablets contain magnesium carbonate excipient)

Barbiturates: *see under* Antiepileptics, above

Calcium Salts: reduced absorption of *tetracyclines*

Dairy products: reduced absorption (except *doxycycline* and *minocycline)*

Iron: absorption of *oral iron* reduced by *tetracyclines* and *vice versa*

Sex Hormones: *see* Contraceptives, Oral (main list)

Ulcer-healing Drugs: *bismuth chelates* and *sucralfate* reduce absorption

Zinc Salts: reduced absorption (and *vice versa)*

Theophylline

Anthelmintics: *thiabendazole* may increase plasma-theophylline concentration

• **Antibacterials:** plasma-theophylline concentration increased by *ciprofloxacin, enoxacin, erythromycin,* and *norfloxacin*; plasma-theophylline concentration reduced by *rifampicin*

Antidepressants: plasma-theophylline concentration increased by *viloxazine*

Antiepileptics: plasma-theophylline concentration reduced by *carbamazepine, phenobarbitone, phenytoin, and primidone*

Barbiturates: *see under* Antiepileptics, above

Beta-blockers: should be avoided on pharmacological grounds (bronchospasm)

• Calcium-channel Blockers: plasma-theophylline concentration increased by *diltiazem and verapamil*

Disulfiram: increases plasma-theophylline concentration

Hormone Antagonists: plasma-theophylline concentration reduced by *aminoglutethimide*

Interferons: plasma-theophylline concentration increased

Lithium: *lithium* excretion accelerated (reduced plasma-lithium concentration)

Respiratory Stimulants: increased CNS stimulation

Sex Hormones: plasma-theophylline concentration increased by *combined oral contraceptives*

Sympathomimetics: increased risk of hypokalaemia if *theophylline* given with high doses of *fenoterol, pirbuterol, reproterol, rimiterol, ritodrine, salbutamol, and terbutaline*

• Ulcer-healing Drugs: plasma-theophylline concentration increased by *cimetidine*

Uricosurics: plasma-theophylline concentration reduced by *sulphinpyrazone*

Thiabendazole

Theophylline: plasma concentration may be increased

Thiazides *see* Diuretics

Thiethylperazine *see* Phenothiazines and other Antipsychotics

Thiopentone *see* Barbiturates and Primidone

Thioridazine *see* Phenothiazines and other Antipsychotics

Thiotepa

Muscle Relaxants: effect of *suxamethonium* enhanced

Thyroxine

Analgesics: false low total plasma-thyroxine concentration with *phenylbutazone*

Anion-exchange Resins: absorption of *thyroxine* reduced by *cholestyramine*

Thyroxine (*continued*)
Antibacterials: *rifampicin* accelerates metabolism of thyroxine (may increase requirements in hypothyroidism)
• Anticoagulants: effect of *nicoumalone, phenindione, and warfarin* enhanced
Antiepileptics: *carbamazepine, phenobarbitone, phenytoin, and primidone* accelerate metabolism of *thyroxine* (may increase requirements in hypothyroidism)
Barbiturates: *see under* Antiepileptics, above
Beta-blockers: metabolism of propranolol accelerated (reduced effect)

Tiaprofenic Acid *see* NSAIDs
Timolol *see* Beta-blockers
Tinidazole alcohol interaction *as for* Metronidazole
Tobramycin *see* Aminoglycosides

Tocainide
other Anti-arrhythmics: increased myocardial depression with any anti-arrhythmic
Beta-blockers: increased risk of bradycardia and myocardial depression
Diuretics: effect of *tocainide* antagonised by hypokalaemia with *acetazolamide, loop diuretics, and thiazides*

Tolazamide *see* Antidiabetics (sulphonylurea)
Tolbutamide *see* Antidiabetics (sulphonylurea)
Tolmetin *see* NSAIDs
Tranylcypromine *see* MAOIs

Trazodone
Alcohol: enhanced sedative effect
Anxiolytics and Hypnotics: enhanced sedative effect

Triamcinolone *see* Corticosteroids
Triamterene *see* Diuretics (potassium-sparing)
Triazolam *see* Benzodiazepines and other Anxiolytics and Hypnotics
Triclofos *see* Chloral

Trientine
Iron: absorption of *oral iron* reduced

Trifluoperazine *see* Phenothiazines and other Antipsychotics
Trifluperidol *see* Phenothiazines and other Antipsychotics

Trilostane
Diuretics: increased risk of hyperkalaemia with *potassium-sparing diuretics*

Trimeprazine *see* Antihistamines

Trimethoprim
Anticoagulants: effect of *nicoumalone* and *warfarin* enhanced
Antidiabetics: effect of *sulphonylureas* enhanced
Antiepileptics: antifolate effect of *phenytoin* increased
Antimalarials: increased risk of antifolate effect with *pyrimethamine* (ingredient of *Fansidar*® and *Maloprim*®)
Cytotoxics: antifolate effect of *methotrexate* increased

Trimipramine *see* Antidepressants, Tricyclic
Triprolidine *see* Antihistamines
Tropicamide *see* Antimuscarinics

Tryptophan
• *other* Antidepressants: CNS excitation and confusion with *MAOIs* (reduce tryptophan dose); agitation and nausea with *fluoxetine* and *fluvoxamine*

Tubocurarine *see* Muscle Relaxants (non-depolarising)
Ulcer-healing Drugs *see* individual drugs
Uricosurics *see* individual drugs
Vaccines *see* Influenza Vaccine

Valproate
Analgesics: *aspirin* enhances effect
• Antidepressants: antagonism of anticonvulsant effect (convulsive threshold lowered)
• *other* Antiepileptics: concomitant administration of two or more antiepileptics may enhance toxicity without a corresponding increase in antiepileptic effect; moreover, interactions between individual antiepileptics can complicate monitoring of treatment; interactions include enhanced effects, increased sedation, and reductions in plasma concentrations
• Antipsychotics: antagonism of anticonvulsant effect (convulsive threshold lowered)

Vancomycin
Anion-exchange Resins: antagonism of *oral vancomycin* by *cholestyramine*
other Antibacterials: increased risk of ototoxicity with *aminoglycosides;* increased risk of nephrotoxicity with *aminoglycosides and cephalosporins notably cephalothin*
Diuretics: increased risk of ototoxicity with *loop diuretics*

Vecuronium *see* Muscle Relaxants (non-depolarising)
Verapamil *see* Calcium-channel blockers

Vigabatrin
other **Antiepileptics:** *vigabatrin* lowers plasma concentration of *phenytoin*

Viloxazine
• Antiepileptics: increased plasma concentrations of *carbamazepine* and *phenytoin*
Theophylline: increased plasma-theophylline concentration

Vitamins
• Anticoagulants: anticoagulant effect of *nicoumalone, phenindione, and warfarin* antagonised by *vitamin K* (present in some enteral feeds)
Antiepileptics: *folic acid* occasionally reduces plasma-phenytoin concentration
Dopaminergics: effect of *levodopa* antagonised by *pyridoxine* (unless a dopa decarboxylase inhibitor also given)

Warfarin
• Alcohol: enhanced anticoagulant effect
Allopurinol: anticoagulant effect may be enhanced
• Anabolic Steroids: *oxymetholone, stanozolol and others* enhance anticoagulant effect
• Analgesics: *aspirin* increases risk of bleeding due to antiplatelet effect; anticoagulant effect enhanced by *azapropazone and phenylbutazone,* and may be enhanced by *diflunisal, flurbiprofen, mefenamic acid, piroxicam, sulindac, and possibly other NSAIDs*; anticoagulant effect may also be enhanced by *dextropropoxyphene*
• Anion-exchange Resins: *cholestyramine* may enhance or reduce anticoagulant effect
• Anti-arrhythmics: *amiodarone and propafenone* enhance anticoagulant effect; *quinidine* may enhance anticoagulant effect
• **Antibacterials:** anticoagulant effect reduced by *rifampicin*; anticoagulant effect enhanced by *aztreonam, cephamandole, chloramphenicol, ciprofloxacin, co-trimoxazole, erythromycin, metronidazole, sulphonamides,* and *trimethoprim*; anticoagulant effect may also be enhanced by *enoxacin, nalidixic acid, neomycin, norfloxacin, and tetracyclines*; although studies have failed to demonstrate interaction, common experience in anticoagulant clinics is that prothrombin time can be prolonged by few seconds following course of *broad-spectrum antibiotic, such as ampicillin* (may also apply to antibiotics given for local action on gut such as neomycin)

Warfarin (*continued*)
- Antidepressants: *fluvoxamine* may enhance anticoagulant effect
- Antiepileptics: reduced anticoagulant effect with *carbamazepine, phenobarbitone, and primidone*; both reduced and enhanced effects reported with *phenytoin*
- **Antifungals:** anticoagulant effect reduced by *griseofulvin;* anticoagulant effect enhanced by *fluconazole, itraconazole, ketoconazole, and miconazole*
- Antiplatelet Drugs: *aspirin and dipyridamole* increase risk of bleeding due to antiplatelet effect

Anxiolytics and Hypnotics: *chloral* may transiently enhance anticoagulant effect
- Barbiturates: anticoagulant effect reduced
- Clofibrate Group: enhanced anticoagulant effect
- Disulfiram: enhanced anticoagulant effect
- Hormone Antagonists: *aminoglutethimide* reduces anticoagulant effect; *danazol, flutamide, and tamoxifen* enhance anticoagulant effect

Rowachol®: may enhance anticoagulant effect
- Sex Hormones: *oral contraceptives* reduce anticoagulant effect
- Simvastatin: may enhance anticoagulant effect
- Thyroxine and Dextrothyroxine: enhanced anticoagulant effect
- Ulcer-healing Drugs: *sucralfate* reduces anticoagulant effect (reduced absorption); *cimetidine and omeprazole* enhance anticoagulant effect

Warfarin (*continued*)
- Uricosurics: *sulphinpyrazone* enhances anticoagulant effect
- Vitamins: *vitamin K* reduces anticoagulant effect (present in some enteral feeds)

Xamoterol

Beta-blockers: antagonism of effect of *xamoterol* and reduction in beta-blockade

Xipamide *see* Diuretics (thiazide-related)

Xylometazoline *see* Sympathomimetics

Zidovudine

Note. Increased risk of toxicity with other nephrotoxic and myelosuppressive drugs

other Antivirals: extreme lethargy reported on administration of *intravenous acyclovir*; profound myelosuppression with *ganciclovir*

Uricosurics: *probenecid* increases plasma-zidovudine concentration and risk of toxicity

Zinc

Antibacterials: reduced absorption of *ciprofloxacin*; *tetracyclines* reduce absorption of *zinc* (and *vice versa)*

Iron: reduced absorption of *oral iron* (and *vice versa)*

Penicillamine: reduced absorption of *penicillamine*

Zopiclone (general sedative interactions *as for* Benzodiazepines and other Anxiolytics and Hypnotics)

Zuclopenthixol *see* Phenothiazines and other Antipsychotics

Appendix 2: Liver Disease

Liver disease may alter the response to drugs in several ways as indicated below, and drug prescribing should be kept to a minimum in all patients with severe liver disease. The main problems occur in patients with jaundice, ascites, or evidence of encephalopathy.

IMPAIRED DRUG METABOLISM. Metabolism by the liver is the main route of elimination for many drugs, but the hepatic reserve appears to be large and liver disease has to be severe before important changes in drug metabolism occur. Routine liver-function tests are a poor guide to the capacity of the liver to metabolise drugs, and in the individual patient it is not possible to predict the extent to which the metabolism of a particular drug may be impaired.

A few drugs, e.g. rifampicin and fusidic acid, are excreted in the bile unchanged and may accumulate in patients with intrahepatic or extrahepatic obstructive jaundice.

HYPOPROTEINAEMIA. The hypoalbuminaemia in severe liver disease is associated with reduced protein binding and increased toxicity of some highly protein-bound drugs such as phenytoin and prednisolone.

REDUCED CLOTTING. Reduced hepatic synthesis of blood-clotting factors, indicated by a prolonged prothrombin time, increases the sensitivity to oral anticoagulants such as warfarin and phenindione.

HEPATIC ENCEPHALOPATHY. In severe liver disease many drugs can further impair cerebral function and may precipitate hepatic encephalopathy. These include all sedative drugs, opioid analgesics, those diuretics that produce hypokalaemia, and drugs that cause constipation.

FLUID OVERLOAD. Oedema and ascites in chronic liver disease may be exacerbated by drugs that give rise to fluid retention, e.g. NSAIDs, corticosteroids, and carbenoxolone.

HEPATOTOXIC DRUGS. Hepatotoxicity is either dose-related or unpredictable (idiosyncratic). Drugs causing dose-related toxicity may do so at lower doses than in patients with normal liver function, and some drugs producing reactions of the idiosyncratic kind do so more frequently in patients with liver disease. These drugs should be avoided.

Table of drugs to be avoided or used with caution in liver disease

The list of drugs given below is not comprehensive and is based on current information concerning the use of these drugs in therapeutic dosage. Products introduced or amended since publication of BNF No. 20 (September 1990) are in **bold** print.

Drugs	Comment
Acrivastine *see* Antihistamines	
Alfentanil *see* Opioid Analgesics	
Alprazolam *see* Anxiolytics and Hypnotics	
Aminophylline *see* Theophylline	
Amitriptyline *see* Antidepressants	
Amlodipine	Reduce dose
Amoxapine *see* Antidepressants	
Anabolic Steroids	Preferably avoid—dose-related toxicity
Analgesics *see* NSAIDs and Opioid Analgesics	
Androgens	Preferably avoid—dose-related toxicity with some, and produce fluid retention
Antacids	In patients with fluid retention, avoid those containing large amounts of sodium, e.g. magnesium trisilicate mixture, *Gaviscon®*. Avoid those causing constipation—can precipitate coma
Anticoagulants, Oral	Avoid, especially if prothrombin time is already prolonged
Antidepressants	Tricyclics preferable to MAOIs but sedative effects increased; iprindole and MAOIs may cause idiosyncratic hepatotoxicity
Antihistamines	Avoid—may precipitate coma
Antipsychotics	All can precipitate coma; phenothiazines are hepatotoxic
Anxiolytics and Hypnotics	All can precipitate coma; small dose of lorazepam or oxazepam probably safest; reduce oral dose of chlormethiazole
Aspirin	Avoid—increased risk of gastro-intestinal bleeding
Astemizole *see* Antihistamines	
Auranofin *see* Gold	
Aurothiomalate *see* Gold	
Azapropazone *see* NSAIDs	
Azatadine *see* Antihistamines	
Azathioprine	May need dose reduction
Bendrofluazide *see* Thiazides	
Benorylate [aspirin-paracetamol ester] *see* Aspirin	
Benperidol *see* Antipsychotics	
Benzodiazepines *see* Anxiolytics and Hypnotics	
Beta-blockers *see* individual drugs	
Bezafibrate	Avoid in severe liver disease
Bromazepam *see* Anxiolytics and Hypnotics	
Brompheniramine *see* Antihistamines	
Bumetanide *see* Loop Diuretics	
Bupivacaine *see* Lignocaine	
Buprenorphine *see* Opioid Analgesics	
Butriptyline *see* Antidepressants	
Carbenoxolone	Produces sodium and water retention and hypokalaemia
Cetirizine *see* Antihistamines	

Table of drugs to be avoided or used with caution in liver disease (*continued*)

Drugs	Comment
Chenodeoxycholic Acid	Avoid in chronic liver disease; patients with non-functioning gall-bladder do not respond
Chloral Hydrate *see* Anxiolytics and Hypnotics	
Chloramphenicol	Avoid—increased risk of bone-marrow depression
Chlordiazepoxide *see* Anxiolytics and Hypnotics	
Chlormethiazole	Reduce oral dose; *see* Anxiolytics and Hypnotics
Chlormezanone *see* Anxiolytics and Hypnotics	
Chlorothiazide *see* Thiazides	
Chlorpheniramine *see* Antihistamines	
Chlorpromazine *see* Antipsychotics	
Chlorpropamide	Avoid—increased risk of hypoglycaemia and can produce jaundice
Chlorprothixene *see* Antipsychotics	
Chlorthalidone *see* Thiazides	
Cholestyramine	Interferes with absorption of fat-soluble vitamins and may aggravate malabsorption in primary biliary cirrhosis
Choline Magnesium Trisalicylate *see* Aspirin	
Choline Theophyllinate *see* Theophylline	
Cimetidine	Increased risk of confusion; reduce dose
Cinnarizine *see* Antihistamines	
Cisapride	Halve dose initially
Clemastine *see* Antihistamines	
Clindamycin	Reduce dose
Clobazam *see* Anxiolytics and Hypnotics	
Clofibrate	Avoid in severe liver disease
Clomiphene	Avoid in severe liver disease
Clomipramine *see* Antidepressants	
Clopamide *see* Thiazides	
Clorazepate *see* Anxiolytics and Hypnotics	
Codeine *see* Opioid Analgesics	
Contraceptives, Oral	Avoid in cholestatic liver disease and in patients with a history of pruritus or cholestasis during pregnancy
Cyclizine *see* Antihistamines	
Cyclofenil	Avoid in severe liver disease
Cyclopenthiazide *see* Thiazides	
Cyproheptadine *see* Antihistamines	
Cyproterone Acetate	Avoid—dose-related toxicity
Dantrolene	Avoid—may cause severe liver damage
Dehydrocholic Acid	Avoid in intra-hepatic cholestasis or complete biliary obstruction
Desipramine *see* Antidepressants	
Dextromethorphan *see* Opioid Analgesics	
Dextromoramide *see* Opioid Analgesics	
Dextropropoxyphene *see* Opioid Analgesics	
Diamorphine *see* Opioid Analgesics	
Diazepam *see* Anxiolytics and Hypnotics	
Diclofenac *see* NSAIDs	
Diflunisal *see* NSAIDs	
Dihydrocodeine *see* Opioid Analgesics	
Diltiazem	Reduce dose
Dimenhydrinate *see* Antihistamines	
Dimethindene *see* Antihistamines	
Diphenoxylate *see* Opioid Analgesics	
Diphenylpyraline *see* Antihistamines	
Dipipanone *see* Opioid Analgesics	
Dothiepin *see* Antidepressants	
Doxepin *see* Antidepressants	
Doxorubicin	Reduce dose according to bilirubin concentration
Droperidol *see* Antipsychotics	
Epirubicin	Reduce dose according to bilirubin concentration
Ergotamine	Avoid in severe liver disease—risk of toxicity increased
Erythromycin	May cause idiosyncratic hepatotoxicity
Ethacrynic acid *see* Loop Diuretics	
Etodolac *see* NSAIDs	
Etretinate	Avoid—further impairment of liver function may occur
Fenbufen *see* NSAIDs	
Fenofibrate *see* Clofibrate	
Fenoprofen *see* NSAIDs	
Flecainide	Avoid (or reduce dose) in severe liver disease
Flunitrazepam *see* Anxiolytics and Hypnotics	
Fluoxetine	Reduce dose in severe liver disease
Flupenthixol *see* Antipsychotics	
Fluphenazine *see* Antipsychotics	
Flurazepam *see* Anxiolytics and Hypnotics	
Flurbiprofen *see* NSAIDs	
Fluspirilene *see* Antipsychotics	
Fluvoxamine	Reduce dose in severe liver disease
Frusemide *see* Loop Diuretics	
Fusidic Acid	Impaired biliary excretion; may be increased risk of hepatotoxicity; avoid or reduce dose
Gemfibrozil	Avoid in severe liver disease
Gold (auranofin, aurothiomalate)	Avoid in severe liver disease—hepatotoxicity may occur
Haloperidol *see* Antipsychotics	
Hydrochlorothiazide *see* Thiazides	
Hydroflumethiazide *see* Thiazides	
Hydroxyzine *see* Antihistamines	
Hypnotics *see* Anxiolytics and Hypnotics	
Ibuprofen *see* NSAIDs	
Idarubicin	Reduce dose according to bilirubin concentration
Imipramine *see* Antidepressants	
Indapamide *see* Thiazides	
Indomethacin *see* NSAIDs	
Iprindole	May cause idiosyncratic hepatotoxicity; *see* Antidepressants
Isocarboxazid *see* Antidepressants	
Isoniazid	Avoid—idiosyncratic hepatotoxicity more common
Isotretinoin	Avoid—see Etretinate
Isradipine	Reduce dose
Itraconazole	Avoid—toxicity with related drugs
Ketoconazole	Induces hepatitis-like reaction; may accumulate in severe liver disease; contra-indicated unless no alternative
Ketoprofen *see* NSAIDs	
Ketotifen *see* Antihistamines	
Labetalol	Reduce oral dose

Table of drugs to be avoided or used with caution in liver disease (*continued*)

Drugs	Comment
Lignocaine	Avoid (or reduce dose) in severe liver disease
Lincomycin	Avoid if possible
Lofepramine *see* Antidepressants	
Loop diuretics	Hypokalaemia may precipitate coma; potassium-sparing diuretic should be used to prevent this; increased risk of hypomagnesaemia in alcoholic cirrhosis
Loprazolam *see* Anxiolytics and Hypnotics	
Lorazepam *see* Anxiolytics and Hypnotics	
Lormetazepam *see* Anxiolytics and Hypnotics	
Magnesium Sulphate	Avoid in hepatic coma if risk of renal failure
MAOIs *see* Antidepressants	
Maprotiline *see* Antidepressants	
Mebhydrolin *see* Antihistamines	
Medazepam *see* Anxiolytics and Hypnotics	
Mefenamic Acid *see* NSAIDs	
Mefruside *see* Thiazides	
Meprobamate *see* Anxiolytics and Hypnotics	
Meptazinol *see* Opioid Analgesics	
Mequitazine *see* Antihistamines	
Metformin	Avoid—increased risk of lactic acidosis
Methadone *see* Opioid Analgesics	
Methotrexate	Dose-related toxicity—avoid in non-malignant conditions (e.g. psoriasis)
Methotrimeprazine *see* Antipsychotics	
Methyclothiazide *see* Thiazides	
Methyldopa	Avoid—increased risk of hepatotoxicity
Metoprolol	Reduce oral dose
Metronidazole	Reduce dose in severe liver disease
Mexiletine	Avoid (or reduce dose) in severe liver disease
Mianserin *see* Antidepressants	
Monoamine-oxidase Inhibitors (MAOIs)	May cause idiosyncratic hepatotoxicity; *see* Antidepressants
Morphine *see* Opioid Analgesics	
Nabumetone *see* NSAIDs	
Nalbuphine *see* Opioid Analgesics	
Nalidixic Acid	Partially conjugated in liver
Nandrolone *see* Anabolic Steroids	
Naproxen *see* NSAIDs	
Narcotic Analgesics *see* Opioid Analgesics	
Nicardipine	Reduce dose
Nifedipine	Reduce dose
Niridazole	Increased CNS toxicity in patients with cirrhosis or portal-systemic shunts
Nitrazepam *see* Anxiolytics and Hypnotics	
Nitroprusside	Avoid in severe liver disease
Nortriptyline *see* Antidepressants	
NSAIDs	Increased risk of gastro-intestinal bleeding and can cause fluid retention
Oestrogens	Avoid; *see also* Contraceptives, oral
Omeprazole	In severe liver disease not more than 20 mg daily should be needed
Opioid Analgesics	Avoid—may precipitate coma
Oxatomide *see* Antihistamines	
Oxazepam *see* Anxiolytics and Hypnotics	
Oxprenolol	Reduce oral dose
Oxymetholone *see* Anabolic Steroids	
Oxypertine *see* Antipsychotics	
Papaveretum *see* Opioid Analgesics	
Paracetamol	Dose-related toxicity—avoid large doses
Pentazocine *see* Opioid Analgesics	
Pericyazine *see* Antipsychotics	
Perphenazine *see* Antipsychotics	
Pethidine *see* Opioid Analgesics	
Phenazocine *see* Opioid Analgesics	
Phenelzine *see* Antidepressants	
Phenindamine *see* Antihistamines	
Pheniramine *see* Antihistamines	
Phenobarbitone	May precipitate coma
Phenoperidine *see* Opioid Analgesics	
Phenothiazines *see* Antipsychotics	
Phenylbutazone *see* NSAIDs	
Phenytoin	Reduce dose to avoid toxicity
Pholcodine *see* Opioid Analgesics	
Pimozide *see* Antipsychotics	
Pipothiazine *see* Antipsychotics	
Piretanide *see* Loop Diuretics	
Piroxicam *see* NSAIDs	
Plicamycin	Avoid if possible (increased risk of toxicity)
Polythiazide *see* Thiazides	
Prednisolone	Side-effects more common
Prednisone	Prednisolone is preferable (prednisone needs conversion to prednisolone by liver before active)
Primidone	May precipitate coma
Procainamide	Avoid or reduce dose
Prochlorperazine *see* Antipsychotics	
Progestogens	Avoid; *see also* Contraceptives, Oral
Promazine *see* Antipsychotics	
Promethazine *see* Antihistamines	
Propafenone	Reduce dose
Propranolol	Reduce oral dose
Protriptyline *see* Antidepressants	
Pyrazinamide	Avoid—idiosyncratic hepatotoxicity more common
Ranitidine	Increased risk of confusion; reduce dose
Rifampicin	Impaired elimination; may be increased risk of hepatotoxicity; avoid or do not exceed 8 mg/kg daily
Salsalate *see* Aspirin	
Simvastatin	Avoid—hepatotoxic
Sodium Aurothiomalate *see* Gold	
Sodium Fusidate *see* Fusidic Acid	
Sodium Nitroprusside *see* Nitroprusside	
Sodium Valproate *see* Valproate	
Stanozolol *see* Anabolic Steroids	
Sulindac *see* NSAIDs	
Suxamethonium	Prolonged apnoea may occur in severe liver disease due to reduced hepatic synthesis of pseudocholinesterase
Temazepam *see* Anxiolytics and Hypnotics	
Tenoxicam *see* NSAIDs	
Terfenadine *see* Antihistamines	
Testosterone *see* Androgens	

Table of drugs to be avoided or used with caution in liver disease (*continued*)

Drugs	Comment
Tetracyclines	Avoid—dose-related toxicity by i/v route
Theophylline	Reduce dose
Thiazides	Hypokalaemia may precipitate coma (potassium-sparing diuretic can prevent); increased risk of hypomagnesaemia in alcoholic cirrhosis
Thiethylperazine *see* Antipsychotics	
Thiopentone	Reduce dose for induction in severe liver disease
Thioridazine *see* Antipsychotics	
Tiaprofenic acid *see* NSAIDs	
Tocainide	Avoid (or reduce dose) in severe liver disease
Tolbutamide	Avoid—increased risk of hypoglycaemia; can produce jaundice
Tolmetin *see* NSAIDs	
Tranylcypromine *see* Antidepressants	
Trazodone *see* Antidepressants	
Triazolam *see* Anxiolytics and Hypnotics	
Triclofos *see* Anxiolytics and Hypnotics	
Trifluoperazine *see* Antipsychotics	
Trifluperidol *see* Antipsychotics	
Trimeprazine *see* Antihistamines	
Trimipramine *see* Antidepressants	
Triprolidine *see* Antihistamines	
Valproate	Avoid if possible—hepatotoxicity and liver failure may occasionally occur (usually in first 6 months)
Verapamil	Reduce oral dose
Zidovudine	Accumulation may occur
Zopiclone	Reduce dose
Zuclopenthixol *see* Antipsychotics	

Appendix 3: Renal Impairment

The use of drugs in patients with reduced renal function can give rise to problems for several reasons:

- failure to excrete a drug or its metabolites may produce toxicity;
- sensitivity to some drugs is increased even if elimination is unimpaired;
- many side-effects are tolerated poorly by patients in renal failure;
- some drugs cease to be effective when renal function is reduced.

Many of these problems can be avoided by reducing the dose or by using alternative drugs.

Principles of dose adjustment in renal impairment

The level of renal function below which the dose of a drug must be reduced depends on whether the drug is eliminated entirely by renal excretion or is partly metabolised, and on how toxic it is.

For many drugs with only minor or no dose-related side-effects very precise modification of the dose regimen is unnecessary and a simple scheme for dose reduction is sufficient.

For more toxic drugs with a small safety margin dose regimens based on glomerular filtration rate should be used. For those where both efficacy and toxicity are closely related to plasma concentrations recommended regimens should be seen only as a guide to initial treatment; subsequent treatment must be adjusted according to clinical response and plasma concentration.

The total daily maintenance dose of a drug can be reduced either by reducing the size of the individual doses or by increasing the interval between doses. For some drugs, if the size of the maintenance dose is reduced it will be important to give a loading dose if an immediate effect is required. This is because when a patient is given a regular dose of any drug it takes more than five times the half-life to achieve steady-state plasma concentrations. As the plasma half-life of drugs excreted by the kidney is prolonged in renal failure it may take many days for the reduced dosage to achieve a therapeutic plasma concentration. The loading dose should usually be the same size as the initial dose for a patient with normal renal function.

Nephrotoxic drugs should, if possible, be avoided in patients with renal disease because the consequences of nephrotoxicity are likely to be more serious when the renal reserve is already reduced.

Use of dosage table

Dose recommendations are based on the severity of renal impairment. This is expressed in terms of glomerular filtration rate (GFR), usually measured by the **creatinine clearance**. The serum-creatinine concentration can be used instead as a measure of renal function but is only a rough guide unless corrected for age, weight, and sex. Nomograms are available for making the correction and should be used where accuracy is important.

Renal impairment is arbitrarily divided into 3 grades:

Grade	*GFR*	*Serum creatinine (approx.)*
Mild	20–50 mL/min	150–300 μmol/litre
Moderate	10–20 mL/min	300–700 μmol/litre
Severe	< 10 mL/min	> 700 μmol/litre

Renal function declines with age; many elderly patients have a glomerular filtration rate below 50 mL/minute which, because of reduced muscle mass, may not be indicated by a raised serum creatinine. It is wise to assume at least mild impairment of renal function when prescribing for the elderly.

The following table may be used as a guide to drugs which are known to require a reduction in dose in renal impairment, and to those which are potentially harmful or are ineffective. Drug prescribing should be kept to the minimum in all patients with severe renal disease.

If renal impairment is considered likely on clinical grounds renal function should be checked before prescribing **any** drug which requires dose modification even when renal impairment is mild.

Table of drugs to be avoided or used with caution in renal impairment

Products introduced or amended since publication of BNF No. 20 (September 1990) are in **bold** print.

Drugs	GFR mL/minute	Dosage recommendations	Comments
Acebutolol	<10	Start with small dose	Active metabolite accumulates
Acetazolamide	<10	Avoid	Metabolic acidosis
Acetohexamide	<50	Avoid	Tolbutamide and gliquidone suitable alternatives
Acrivastine	<20	Avoid	Excreted by kidney

Table of drugs to be avoided or used with caution in renal impairment (*continued*)

Drugs	GFR mL/minute	Dosage recommendations	Comments
Acyclovir	<50	Reduce dose	Possible transient increase in plasma urea
Alcuronium *see* Tubocurarine			
Alfentanil *see* Opioid Analgesics			
Allopurinol	10–20 <10	Max. 200 mg daily Max. 100 mg daily	Increased toxicity; rashes
Alprazolam *see* Anxiolytics and Hypnotics			
Alteplase	<20		Risk of hyperkalaemia
Amantadine	<50	Avoid	Excreted by kidney
Amikacin *see* Aminoglycosides			
Amiloride *see* Potassium-sparing Diuretics			
Aminoglycosides	<50	Reduce dose. Monitor plasma concentrations	Ototoxic; nephrotoxic
Amiodarone	<20		Accumulation of iodine may increase risk of thyroid dysfunction
Amoxycillin	<10	Reduce dose	Rashes more common
Amphotericin	<50	Use only if no alternative	Nephrotoxic
Ampicillin	<10	Reduce dose	Rashes more common
Amylobarbitone	<10	Reduce dose	Active metabolite accumulates
Analgesics *see* Opioid Analgesics and NSAIDs			
Antipsychotics	<10	Start with small doses	Increased cerebral sensitivity; *see also* Sulpiride
Anxiolytics and Hypnotics	<10	Start with small doses	Increased cerebral sensitivity
Aspirin	<10	Avoid	Fluid retention; deterioration in renal function; increased risk of gastro-intestinal bleeding
Atenolol	<20	Reduce dose	Excreted unchanged
Auranofin *see* Gold			
Aurothiomalate *see* Gold			
Azapropazone *see* NSAIDs (excreted by kidney)			
Azathioprine	<10	Reduce dose	
Azlocillin	<20	Reduce dose	
Aztreonam	<20	Reduce dose	
Bacampicillin	<10	Reduce dose	Rashes more common
Baclofen	<50	Use smaller doses	Excreted by kidney
Bendrofluazide *see* Thiazides			
Benorylate [aspirin-paracetamol ester] *see* Aspirin			
Benperidol *see* Antipsychotics			
Benzodiazepines *see* Anxiolytics and Hypnotics			
Benzylpenicillin	<10	Max. 6 g daily	Neurotoxicity—high doses may cause convulsions
Beta-blockers	<10	Start with small dose	
Betaxolol *see* Beta-blockers			
Bethanidine	<20	Avoid	Increased postural hypotension; decrease in renal blood flow
Bezafibrate	10–50 <10	Reduce dose Avoid	Further deterioration in renal function

Table of drugs to be avoided or used with caution in renal impairment (*continued*)

Drugs	GFR mL/minute	Dosage recommendations	Comments
Bicarbonate *see* Sodium Bicarbonate			
Bisoprolol *see* Beta-blockers			
Bleomycin	<20	Reduce dose	
Bromazepam *see* Anxiolytics and Hypnotics			
Bumetanide	<20	May need high doses	
Buprenorphine *see* Opioid Analgesics			
Capreomycin	<50	Reduce dose	Neurotoxic; ototoxic
Captopril	<50	Reduce dose and monitor response; avoid if possible	Excreted by kidney; hyperkalaemia and other side-effects more common
Carbenicillin	<20	Reduce dose	Neurotoxic; may produce bleeding diathesis; 1 g contains 5.4 mmol sodium
Carbenoxolone	<10	Avoid	Fluid retention
Carboplatin *see* Cisplatin			
Carteolol *see* Beta-blockers			
Cefadroxil	<20	Reduce dose	
Cefixime	<20	Reduce dose	
Cefotaxime	<5	Use half dose	
Cefoxitin	<50	Reduce dose	
Cefsulodin	<20	Reduce dose	
Ceftazidime	<50	Reduce dose	
Ceftizoxime	<50	Reduce dose	
Cefuroxime	<50	Reduce parenteral dose	
Cephalexin	<10	Max. 500 mg daily	
Cephalothin	<50	Avoid	Nephrotoxic
Cephamandole	<50	Reduce dose	
Cephazolin	<50	Reduce dose	
Cephradine	<50	Reduce dose	
Cetirizine	<20	Use half dose	
Chloral Hydrate *see* Anxiolytics and Hypnotics			
Chloramphenicol	<10	Avoid unless no alternative	Dose-related depression of haemopoiesis
Chlordiazepoxide *see* Anxiolytics and Hypnotics			
Chlormethiazole *see* Anxiolytics and Hypnotics			
Chlormezanone *see* Anxiolytics and Hypnotics			
Chloroquine	20–50 10–20 <10	Max. 75 mg daily Max. 50 mg daily Avoid	Only on prolonged use
Chlorothiazide *see* Thiazides			
Chlorpromazine *see* Antipsychotics			
Chlorpropamide	<50	Avoid	Tolbutamide and gliquidone suitable alternatives
Chlorprothixene *see* Antipsychotics			
Chlorthalidone *see* Thiazides			
Choline Magnesium Trisalicylate *see* Aspirin			
Cimetidine	10–20 <10	400–600 mg daily 400 mg daily	Occasional risk of confusion
Cinoxacin	<20	Avoid	Nausea, rashes
Ciprofloxacin	<20	Use half dose	
Cisapride	<20	Start with half dose	
Cisplatin	<50	Avoid if possible	Nephrotoxic
Clavulanic acid [ingredient] *see* Co-amoxiclav, *Timentin*®			
Clobazam *see* Anxiolytics and Hypnotics			

Table of drugs to be avoided or used with caution in renal impairment (*continued*)

Drugs	GFR mL/minute	Dosage recommendations	Comments
Clodronate sodium	<20	Avoid	
Clofibrate	10–50	Reduce dose	Further deterioration in renal function; myopathy
	<10	Avoid	
Clopamide *see* Thiazides			
Clorazepate *see* Anxiolytics and Hypnotics			
Co-amoxiclav	<20	Reduce dose	
Codeine	<20	Avoid	Increased and prolonged effect; *see also* Opioid Analgesics
Colchicine	<10	Avoid or reduce dose if no alternative	
Colistin Sulphomethate Sodium	<50	Reduce dose	Nephrotoxic; neurotoxic
Colven®	<10	Avoid	High sodium content
Co-trimoxazole	<20	Reduce dose	Rashes and blood disorders; may cause further deterioration in renal function
Cyclopenthiazide *see* Thiazides			
Cyclophosphamide	<20	Reduce dose	
Cycloserine	<50	Avoid	
Debrisoquine	<20	Avoid	Increased postural hypotension; decrease in renal blood flow
De-Nol®, *De-Noltab*®	<10	Avoid	
Dextromethorphan *see* Opioid Analgesics			
Dextromoramide *see* Opioid Analgesics			
Dextropropoxyphene	<10	Avoid	Increased CNS toxicity
Diamorphine *see* Opioid Analgesics			
Diazepam *see* Anxiolytics and Hypnotics			
Diazoxide	<10	75–150 mg i/v	Increased sensitivity to hypotensive effect
Dicapen®	<10	Reduce dose	
Diclofenac *see* NSAIDs			
Diflunisal *see* NSAIDs (excreted by kidney)			
Digitoxin	<10	Max. 100 micrograms daily	As Digoxin
Digoxin	20–50	250 micrograms daily	Toxicity increased by electrolyte disturbances in severe impairment
	10–20	125–250 micrograms daily	
	<10	Up to 125 micrograms daily	
Dihydrocodeine	<20	Avoid	Increased and prolonged effect; *see also* Opioid Analgesics
Diphenoxylate *see* Opioid Analgesics			
Dipipanone *see* Opioid Analgesics			
Disopyramide	20–50	100 mg every 8 hours *or* 150 mg every 12 hours	
	10–20	100 mg every 12 hours	
	<10	150 mg every 24 hours	
Domperidone	<10	Reduce dose by 30–50%	
Droperidol *see* Antipsychotics			
Enalapril	<50	Reduce dose and monitor response; avoid if possible	As for Captopril
Enoxacin	<20	Max. 400 mg daily	

Table of drugs to be avoided or used with caution in renal impairment (*continued*)

Drugs	GFR mL/minute	Dosage recommendations	Comments
Ergotamine	<20	Avoid	Nausea and vomiting; risk of renal vasoconstriction
Ethacrynic Acid	<10	Avoid	Ototoxic
Ethambutol	<50	Avoid	Optic nerve damage
Etidronate Disodium	20–50	Max. 5 mg/kg daily	Excreted by kidney
	<20	Avoid	
Etodolac *see* NSAIDs			
Etretinate	<50	Avoid	Increased risk of toxicity
Famotidine	<20	Reduce dose	
Fenbufen *see* NSAIDs			
Fenofibrate	20–50	200 mg daily	
	<20	100 mg daily	
Fenoprofen *see* NSAIDs			
Fentanyl *see* Opioid Analgesics			
Flecainide	<50	Reduce dose	
Fluconazole	<50		Reduce dose for multiple dose therapy
Flucytosine	<50	Reduce dose	
Flunitrazepam *see* Anxiolytics and Hypnotics			
Fluoxetine	<20	Start with smaller dose	
	<10	Avoid	
Flupenthixol *see* Antipsychotics			
Fluphenazine *see* Antipsychotics			
Flurazepam *see* Anxiolytics and Hypnotics			
Flurbiprofen *see* NSAIDs			
Fluspirilene *see* Antipsychotics			
Fluvoxamine	<20	Start with smaller dose	
Foscarnet	<50	Reduce dose	Consult data sheet
Frusemide	<20	May need high doses	Deafness may follow rapid i/v injection
Fybogel®	<10	Avoid	Contains 7 mmol potassium per sachet
Gallamine	<20	Avoid	Prolonged paralysis
Ganciclovir	<50	Reduce dose	Consult data sheet
Gaviscon®	<10	Avoid	High sodium content
Gemfibrozil	<10	Start with 900 mg daily	
Gentamicin *see* Aminoglycosides			
Glibenclamide	<10	Avoid	Increased risk of prolonged hypoglycaemia
Gliclazide	<10	Start with small dose	Increased risk of hypoglycaemia
Glipizide	<10	Start with small dose	Increased risk of hypoglycaemia
Gliquidone	<10	May need dose reduction	Increased risk of hypoglycaemia
Gold (auranofin, aurothiomalate)	<50	Avoid	Nephrotoxic
Guanethidine	<20	Avoid	Increased postural hypotension and decrease in renal blood flow
Haloperidol *see* Antipsychotics			
Hexamine	<50	Avoid	Ineffective
Hydralazine	<10	Start with small dose	Increased hypotensive effect
Hydrochlorothiazide *see* Thiazides			
Hydroflumethiazide *see* Thiazides			

Table of drugs to be avoided or used with caution in renal impairment (*continued*)

Drugs	GFR mL/minute	Dosage recommendations	Comments
Hydroxychloroquine	20–50	Max. 75 mg daily	Only on prolonged use
	10–20	Max. 50 mg daily	
	<10	Avoid	
Hypnotics *see* Anxiolytics and Hypnotics			
Ibuprofen *see* NSAIDs			
Idarubicin	<50	Reduce dose	
Ifosfamide	<20	Reduce dose	
Indapamide *see* Thiazides			
Indomethacin *see* NSAIDs			
Inosine Pranobex	<50	Avoid	Metabolised to uric acid
Insulin	<10	May need dose reduction	Insulin requirements fall; compensatory response to hypoglycaemia is impaired
Isoniazid	<10	Max. 200 mg daily	Peripheral neuropathy
Isotretinoin	<50	Avoid	Increased risk of toxicity
Kanamycin *see* Aminoglycosides			
Ketoprofen *see* NSAIDs			
Lincomycin	<20	Use clindamycin instead	
Lisinopril	<50	Reduce dose and monitor response	As for Captopril
Lithium	20–50	Avoid if possible or reduce dose and monitor plasma concentration carefully	
	<20	Avoid	
Loprazolam *see* Anxiolytics and Hypnotics			
Lorazepam *see* Anxiolytics and Hypnotics			
Lormetazepam *see* Anxiolytics and Hypnotics			
Magnesium salts	<20	Avoid or reduce dose	Increased risk of toxicity; magnesium carbonate mixture and magnesium trisilicate mixture also have high sodium content
Medazepam *see* Anxiolytics and Hypnotics			
Mefenamic Acid *see* NSAIDs			
Mefruside *see* Thiazides			
Melphalan	<20	Reduce dose	
Meprobamate *see* Anxiolytics and Hypnotics			
Meptazinol *see* Opioid Analgesics			
Mercaptopurine	<20	Reduce dose	
Mesalazine	<50	Avoid	Manufacturer recommends avoidance as metabolite excreted by kidney
Metformin	<50	Avoid	Increased risk of lactic acidosis
Methadone *see* Opioid Analgesics			
Methocarbamol	<50	Avoid	Increased plasma urea and acidosis due to solvent in injection
Methotrexate	20–50	Reduce dose	Accumulates; nephrotoxic
	<20	Avoid	
Methotrimeprazine *see* Antipsychotics			
Methyclothiazide *see* Thiazides			
Methyldopa	<10	Start with small dose	Increased sensitivity to hypotensive and sedative effect

Table of drugs to be avoided or used with caution in renal impairment (*continued*)

Drugs	GFR mL/minute	Dosage recommendations	Comments
Metoclopramide	<10	Avoid or use small dose	Increased risk of extrapyramidal reactions
Metolazone *see* Thiazides			
Metoprolol	<10	Start with small dose	Higher plasma concentrations after oral administration; may reduce renal blood flow and adversely affect renal function in severe impairment
Mezlocillin	<10	Reduce dose	
Milrinone	<50	Reduce dose and monitor response	
Morphine	<20	Avoid	Increased and prolonged effect; *see also* Opioid Analgesics
Nabumetone *see* NSAIDs			
Nadolol	<20	Reduce dose	Excreted unchanged
Nalbuphine *see* Opioid Analgesics			
Nalidixic Acid	<20	Avoid	Increased risk of nausea, vomiting, rashes, photosensitivity
Naproxen *see* NSAIDs			
Narcotic Analgesics *see* Opioid Analgesics			
Neomycin	<50	Avoid	Ototoxic; nephrotoxic
Netilmicin *see* Aminoglycosides			
Nicardipine	<20	Start with small dose	
Nifedipine	<20	Start with small dose	Reversible deterioration in renal function has been reported
Nitrazepam *see* Anxiolytics and Hypnotics			
Nitrofurantoin	<50	Avoid	Peripheral neuropathy
Nitroprusside	<20	Avoid prolonged use	
Nizatidine	20–50	150 mg daily	
	<20	150 mg on alternate days	
Norfloxacin	10–20	Use half dose	
	<10	Avoid	
NSAIDs	<50	Avoid if possible	Deterioration in renal function (**important**: see section 10.1.1); sodium and water retention
Ofloxacin	20–50	Use half dose	
	<20	100 mg every 48 hours	
Opioid Analgesics	<20	Use small doses—avoid codeine, dihydrocodeine, morphine	Increased cerebral sensitivity; *see also* individual entries
	<10	Avoid dextropropoxyphene, pethidine	
Oxazepam *see* Anxiolytics and Hypnotics			
Oxprenolol *see* Beta-blockers			
Oxypertine *see* Antipsychotics			
Pamidronate Disodium	<10	Divide daily dose	
Pancuronium *see* Tubocurarine			
Papaveretum *see* Opioid Analgesics			
Penbutolol *see* Beta-blockers			
Penicillamine	<50	Avoid if possible or reduce dose	Nephrotoxic

Table of drugs to be avoided or used with caution in renal impairment (*continued*)

Drugs	GFR mL/minute	Dosage recommendations	Comments
Pentamidine	<50	Reduce dose	Consult manufacturer's literature
Pentazocine *see* Opioid Analgesics			
Pericyazine *see* Antipsychotics			
Perindopril	<50	Reduce dose and monitor response	As for Captopril
Perphenazine *see* Antipsychotics			
Pethidine	<10	Avoid	Increased CNS toxicity; *see also* Opioid Analgesics
Phenazocine *see* Opioid Analgesics			
Phenobarbitone	<10	Avoid large doses	
Phenoperidine *see* Opioid Analgesics			
Phenothiazines *see* Antipsychotics			
Phenylbutazone *see* NSAIDs			
Pholcodine *see* Opioid Analgesics			
Pimozide *see* Antipsychotics			
Pindolol	<20	Reduce dose	Excreted unchanged
Piperacillin	<20	Reduce dose	
Piperazine	<10	Reduce dose	Neurotoxic
Pipothiazine *see* Antipsychotics			
Piroxicam *see* NSAIDs			
Pivampicillin	<10	Reduce dose	Rashes more common
Plicamycin	<20	Avoid if possible	
Polythiazide *see* Thiazides			
Potassium salts	<20	Avoid routine use	High risk of hyperkalaemia
Potassium-sparing Diuretics	20–50 <20	Monitor plasma K^+ Avoid	High risk of hyperkalaemia in renal impairment; amiloride excreted by kidney unchanged
Prazosin	<10	Start with small dose	Increased sensitivity to hypotensive effect and possible CNS toxicity
Primidone	<10	Avoid large doses	
Probenecid	<20	Avoid	Ineffective and toxicity increased
Procainamide	<50	Avoid or reduce dose	
Procarbazine	<20	Reduce dose	
Prochlorperazine *see* Antipsychotics			
Proguanil	<10	Avoid or reduce dose	Increased risk of haematological toxicity
Promazine *see* Antipsychotics			
Propranolol	<10	Start with small dose	Higher plasma concentrations after oral administration; may reduce renal blood flow and adversely affect renal function in severe impairment
Propylthiouracil	<50	Reduce dose	
Pseudoephedrine	<10	Avoid	Increased CNS toxicity
Quinapril	<50	Start with 2.5 mg daily	As for Captopril
Ramipril	<50	Start with 1.25 mg daily	As for Captopril
Ranitidine	<10	Use half normal dose	Occasional risk of confusion

Table of drugs to be avoided or used with caution in renal impairment (*continued*)

Drugs	GFR mL/minute	Dosage recommendations	Comments
Regulan®	<10	Avoid	Contains 6.4 mmol potassium per sachet
Salicylates *see* Aspirin			
Salsalate *see* Aspirin			
Salt substitutes	<20	Avoid routine use	High risk of hyperkalaemia
Sodium Aurothiomalate *see* Gold			
Sodium Bicarbonate	<10	Avoid	Specialised role in some forms of renal disease
Sodium Nitroprusside *see* Nitroprusside			
Sodium salts	<10	Avoid	
Solpadeine®	<10	Avoid	High sodium content
Sotalol	<20	Reduce dose	Excreted unchanged
Spironolactone *see* Potassium-sparing Diuretics			
Streptomycin *see* Aminoglycosides			
Sulfametopyrazine *see* Sulphonamides			
Sulindac *see* NSAIDs (excreted by kidney)			
Sulphadiazine	<10	Avoid	High risk of crystalluria
Sulphadimidine *see* Sulphonamides			
Sulphasalazine	<10	Ensure high fluid intake	Rashes and blood disorders; crystalluria a risk
Sulphinpyrazone	<20	Avoid	Ineffective as uricosuric
Sulphonamides	<20	Ensure high fluid intake	Rashes and blood disorders; crystalluria a risk
Sulphonylureas *see* under individual drugs			
Sulpiride	<20	Avoid if possible, or reduce dose	
Talampicillin	<10	Avoid	Rashes more common
Teicoplanin	<50	Reduce dose after 4 days	
Temazepam *see* Anxiolytics and Hypnotics			
Temocillin	<20	Reduce dose	
Tenoxicam *see* NSAIDs			
Tetracyclines (except doxycycline and minocycline)	<50	Avoid—use doxycycline or minocycline if necessary	Anti-anabolic effect, increased plasma urea, further deterioration in renal function
Thiazides and Related Diuretics (except metolazone)	<20	Avoid	Ineffective (metolazone remains effective but risk of excessive diuresis)
Thiethylperazine *see* Antipsychotics			
Thioguanine	<20	Reduce dose	
Thioridazine *see* Antipsychotics			
Tiaprofenic acid *see* NSAIDs			
Ticarcillin	<20	Reduce dose	1 g contains 5.3 mmol sodium
Timentin®	<20	Reduce dose	
Timolol *see* Beta-blockers			
Tobramycin *see* Aminoglycosides			
Tocainide	<50	Reduce dose	
Tolazamide	<10	May need dose reduction	Increased risk of hypoglycaemia
Tolbutamide	<10	May need dose reduction	Increased risk of hypoglycaemia
Tolmetin *see* NSAIDs (excreted by kidney)			

Table of drugs to be avoided or used with caution in renal impairment (*continued*)

Drugs	GFR mL/minute	Dosage recommendations	Comments
Triamterene *see* Potassium-sparing Diuretics			
Triazolam *see* Anxiolytics and Hypnotics			
Triclofos *see* Anxiolytics and Hypnotics			
Trifluoperazine *see* Antipsychotics			
Trifluperidol *see* Antipsychotics			
Trimethoprim	<20	Reduce dose	
Tubocurarine	<20	Reduce dose	Prolonged paralysis with large or repeated doses
Vancomycin	<50	Avoid parenteral use if possible	Ototoxic; nephrotoxic
Vecuronium *see* Tubocurarine			
Vigabatrin	<50	Reduce dose	Excreted by kidney
Xamoterol	<20	Reduce dose	Excreted by kidney
Xipamide *see* Thiazides			
Zidovudine	<50		Excreted by kidney; increased risk of toxicity
Zuclopenthixol *see* Antipsychotics			

Appendix 4: Pregnancy

Drugs can have harmful effects on the fetus at any time during pregnancy. Experience with many drugs in pregnancy is limited.

During the *first trimester* they may produce congenital malformations (teratogenesis), and the period of greatest risk is from the third to the eleventh week of pregnancy.

During the *second* and *third trimesters* drugs may affect the growth and functional development of the fetus or have toxic effects on fetal tissues; and drugs given shortly before term or during labour may have adverse effects on labour or on the neonate after delivery.

The following table lists drugs which may have harmful effects in pregnancy and indicates the trimester of risk.

The table is based on human data but information on *animal* studies has been included for some newer drugs when its omission might be misleading.

> Drugs should be prescribed in pregnancy only if the expected benefit to the mother is thought to be greater than the risk to the fetus, and all drugs should be avoided if possible during the first trimester. Drugs which have been extensively used in pregnancy and appear to be usually safe should be prescribed in preference to new or untried drugs; and the smallest effective dose should be used.
>
> Few drugs have been shown conclusively to be teratogenic in man but no drug is safe beyond all doubt in early pregnancy. Screening procedures are available where there is a known risk of certain defects.
>
> It should be noted that the BNF provides independent advice and may not always agree with the data sheets.
>
> Absence of a drug from the list does not imply safety.

Table of drugs to be avoided or used with caution in pregnancy

Products introduced or amended since publication of BNF No. 20 (September 1990) are in **bold** print.

Drug (Trimester of risk)	Comments
ACE Inhibitors (1, 2, 3)	Avoid; may adversely affect fetal and neonatal blood pressure control and renal function; also possible skull defects and oligohydramnios; toxicity in *animal* studies
Acebutolol *see* Beta-blockers	
Acetazolamide *see* Diuretics	
Acetohexamide *see* Sulphonylureas	
Acrivastine *see* Antihistamines	
Alclometasone *see* Corticosteroids	
Alcohol	
(1, 2)	Regular daily drinking is teratogenic ('fetal alcohol syndrome') and may cause growth retardation; occasional single drinks are probably safe
(3)	Withdrawal syndrome may occur in babies of alcoholic mothers
Alfentanil *see* Opioid Analgesics	
Allyloestrenol *see* Progestogens	
Alprazolam *see* Anxiolytics and Hypnotics	
Alteplase *see* Streptokinase	
Amikacin *see* Aminoglycosides	
Amiloride *see* Diuretics	
Aminoglycosides (2, 3)	Auditory or vestibular nerve damage; risk greatest with streptomycin and kanamycin; probably small with gentamicin and tobramycin
Aminophylline *see* Theophylline	
Amiodarone (2, 3)	Possible risk of neonatal goitre; use only if no alternative
Amitriptyline *see* Antidepressants, Tricyclic	
Amlodipine *see* Calcium-channel Blockers	
Amoxapine *see* Antidepressants, Tricyclic	
Amylobarbitone *see* Barbiturates	
Anabolic Steroids (1, 2, 3)	Virilisation of female fetus
Anaesthetics, General (3)	Depress neonatal respiration
Anaesthetics, Local (3)	With large doses, neonatal respiratory depression, hypotonia, and bradycardia after paracervical or epidural block
Analgesics *see* Opioid Analgesics and NSAIDs	
Androgens (1, 2, 3)	Virilisation of female fetus
Anistreplase *see* Streptokinase	
Anticoagulants, Oral (1, 2, 3)	Congenital malformations; fetal and neonatal haemorrhage; subcutaneous heparin should be substituted in the last few weeks of pregnancy in patients with prosthetic heart valve and can be substituted throughout for deep-vein thrombosis; *see also* section 2.8
Antidepressants	
Fluoxetine, Fluvoxamine, MAOIs (1, 2, 3)	No evidence of harm but manufacturers advise avoid unless compelling reasons
Tricyclic (and related) (3)	Tachycardia, irritability, muscle spasms, and convulsions in neonate reported occasionally

Table of drugs to be avoided or used with caution in pregnancy (*continued*)

Drug (Trimester of risk)	Comments
Antiepileptics	Benefit of treatment outweighs risk to fetus; risk of teratogenicity greater if more than one drug used; **important:** *see also* carbamazepine, ethosuximide, phenobarbitone, phenytoin, valproate, and section 4.8
Antihistamines	No evidence of teratogenicity; some packs of antihistamines sold to the public carry warning to avoid in pregnancy; manufacturer of astemizole advises toxicity at high doses in *animal* studies
Antimalarials (1, 3)	Benefit of prophylaxis and treatment in malaria outweighs risk; **important:** *see also* individual drugs
Antipsychotics (3)	Extrapyramidal effects in neonate occasionally reported
Anxiolytics and Hypnotics (3)	Depress neonatal respiration. Benzodiazepines cause neonatal drowsiness, hypotonia, and withdrawal symptoms; avoid large doses and regular use; short-acting benzodiazepines preferable to long-acting
Aspirin (3)	Impaired platelet function and risk of haemorrhage; delayed onset and increased duration of labour with increased blood loss; avoid if possible in last week; with high doses, closure of fetal ductus arteriosus *in utero* and possibly persistent pulmonary hypertension of newborn; kernicterus in jaundiced neonates
Astemizole *see* Antihistamines	
Atenolol *see* Beta-blockers	
Auranofin *see* Gold	
Aurothiomalate *see* Gold	
Azapropazone *see* NSAIDs	
Azatadine *see* Antihistamines	
Azathioprine (1)	Risk of teratogenicity appears to be small
Aztreonam	Manufacturer advises avoid (but no evidence of teratogenicity)
Barbiturates (3)	Withdrawal effects in neonate; *see also* Phenobarbitone
Beclomethasone *see* Corticosteroids	
Bendrofluazide *see* Diuretics	
Benorylate [aspirin-paracetamol ester] *see* Aspirin	
Benperidol *see* Antipsychotics	
Benserazide [ingredient] *see Madopar®*	
Benzodiazepines *see* Anxiolytics and Hypnotics	
Beta-blockers (3)	Neonatal hypoglycaemia and bradycardia; risk greater in severe hypertension; may possibly cause intra-uterine growth retardation
Betamethasone *see* Corticosteroids	
Betaxolol *see* Beta-blockers	
Bethanidine *see* Guanethidine	
Bezafibrate *see* Clofibrate	
Bisoprolol *see* Beta-blockers	
Bromazepam *see* Anxiolytics and Hypnotics	
Brompheniramine *see* Antihistamines	
Bumetanide *see* Diuretics	
Bupivacaine *see* Anaesthetics, Local	
Buprenorphine *see* Opioid Analgesics	
Butriptyline *see* Antidepressants, Tricyclic	
Calcium-channel Blockers	May inhibit labour and manufacturers advise that diltiazem and some dihydropyridines are teratogenic in *animals*
Captopril *see* ACE Inhibitors	
Carbamazepine (1)	May be small risk of teratogenesis; *see also* Antiepileptics
Carbenoxolone (3)	Avoid; causes sodium retention with oedema
Carbimazole (2, 3)	Has been associated with aplasia cutis of the neonate
Cetirizine *see* Antihistamines	
Chenodeoxycholic acid (1, 2, 3)	Theoretical risk of effects on fetal metabolism
Chloral hydrate *see* Anxiolytics and Hypnotics	
Chloramphenicol (3)	Neonatal 'grey syndrome'
Chlordiazepoxide *see* Anxiolytics and Hypnotics	
Chlormethiazole *see* Anxiolytics and Hypnotics	
Chlormezanone *see* Anxiolytics and Hypnotics	
Chloroquine *see* Antimalarials	
Chlorothiazide *see* Diuretics	
Chlorpheniramine *see* Antihistamines	
Chlorpromazine *see* Antipsychotics	
Chlorpropamide *see* Sulphonylureas	
Chlorprothixene *see* Antipsychotics	
Chlortetracycline *see* Tetracyclines	
Chlorthalidone *see* Diuretics	
Choline magnesium trisalicylate *see* Aspirin	
Cinnarizine *see* Antihistamines	
Ciprofloxacin *see* 4-Quinolones	
Cisapride	Manufacturer advises avoid (but no evidence of teratogenicity)
Clemastine *see* Antihistamines	
Clobazam *see* Anxiolytics and Hypnotics	
Clobetasol *see* Corticosteroids	
Clobetasone *see* Corticosteroids	
Clofibrate (1, 2, 3)	Avoid—theoretical possibility of interference with embryonic growth and development due to anticholesterol effect
Clomipramine *see* Antidepressants, Tricyclic	
Clomocycline *see* Tetracyclines	
Clonazepam *see* Antiepileptics	
Clorazepate *see* Anxiolytics and Hypnotics	
Codeine *see* Opioid Analgesics	

Table of drugs to be avoided or used with caution in pregnancy (*continued*)

Drug (Trimester of risk)	Comments
Contraceptives, Oral (1)	May possibly be a small risk of congenital malformations
Corticosteroids (2, 3)	Benefit of treatment, e.g. in asthma, outweighs risk; high doses (>10 mg prednisolone daily) may produce fetal and neonatal adrenal suppression; corticosteroid cover required by mother during labour
Co-trimoxazole (1)	Possible teratogenic risk (trimethoprim a folate antagonist)
(3)	Neonatal haemolysis and methaemoglobinaemia; increased risk of kernicterus in jaundiced neonates (due to sulphamethoxazole)
Cyclizine *see* Antihistamines	
Cyclopenthiazide *see* Diuretics	
Cyclopropane *see* Anaesthetics, General	
Cyclosporin	May cause fetal growth retardation
Cyproheptadine *see* Antihistamines	
Cyproterone [ingredient] *see Dianette*®	
Cytotoxic drugs	Most are teratogenic; *see* section 8.1
Danazol (1, 2, 3)	Has weak androgenic effects and virilisation of female fetus reported
Dapsone (3)	Neonatal haemolysis and methaemoglobinaemia; folate supplements should be given to mother
Debrisoquine *see* Guanethidine	
Demeclocycline *see* Tetracyclines	
Desferrioxamine	Manufacturer advises toxicity in *animal* studies
Desipramine *see* Antidepressants, Tricyclic	
Desonide *see* Corticosteroids	
Desoxymethasone *see* Corticosteroids	
Dexamethasone *see* Corticosteroids	
Dextromethorphan *see* Opioid Analgesics	
Dextromoramide *see* Opioid Analgesics	
Dextropropoxyphene *see* Opioid Analgesics	
Diamorphine *see* Opioid Analgesics	
Dianette® (1, 2, 3)	Feminisation of male fetus (due to cyproterone)
Diazepam *see* Anxiolytics and Hypnotics	
Diazoxide (2, 3)	Prolonged use may produce alopecia and impaired glucose tolerance in neonate; inhibits uterine activity during labour
Diclofenac *see* NSAIDs	
Diethylpropion	Avoid—congenital malformations reported to CSM
Diflucortolone *see* Corticosteroids	
Diflunisal *see* NSAIDs	
Dihydrocodeine *see* Opioid Analgesics	
Dihydroergotamine *see* Ergotamine	
Diltiazem *see* Calcium-channel Blockers	
Dimenhydrinate *see* Antihistamines	
Dimethindene *see* Antihistamines	
Diphenhydramine *see* Antihistamines	
Diphenoxylate *see* Opioid Analgesics	
Diphenylpyraline *see* Antihistamines	
Dipipanone *see* Opioid Analgesics	
Disopyramide (3)	May induce labour
Distigmine	Manufacturer advises avoid (may stimulate uterine contractions)
Disulfiram (1)	High concentrations of acetaldehyde which occur in presence of alcohol may be teratogenic
Diuretics (3)	Not used to treat hypertension in pregnancy; thiazides may cause neonatal thrombocytopenia
Dothiepin *see* Antidepressants, Tricyclic	
Doxepin *see* Antidepressants, Tricyclic	
Doxycycline *see* Tetracyclines	
Droperidol *see* Antipsychotics	
Dydrogesterone *see* Progestogens	
Enalapril *see* ACE Inhibitors	
Enflurane *see* Anaesthetics, General	
Enoxacin *see* 4-Quinolones	
Ergotamine (1, 2, 3)	Oxytocic effects on the pregnant uterus
Ethacrynic acid *see* Diuretics	
Ether *see* Anaesthetics, General	
Ethinyloestradiol *see* Contraceptives, Oral	
Ethosuximide (1)	May possibly be teratogenic; *see* Antiepileptics
Etodolac *see* NSAIDs	
Etomidate *see* Anaesthetics, General	
Etretinate (1, 2, 3)	Teratogenic; effective contraception must be used for at least 1 month before treatment, during treatment, and for at least two years after stopping
Fansidar® (1)	Possible teratogenic risk (pyrimethamine a folate antagonist)
(3)	Neonatal haemolysis and methaemoglobinaemia; increased risk of kernicterus in jaundiced neonates (due to sulfadoxine) *see also* Antimalarials
Fenbufen *see* NSAIDs	
Fenofibrate (1, 2, 3)	Manufacturer advises toxicity in *animal* studies; *see also* Clofibrate
Fenoprofen *see* NSAIDs	
Fentanyl *see* Opioid Analgesics	
Flecainide	Manufacturer advises toxicity in *animal* studies
Fluclorolone *see* Corticosteroids	
Fluconazole	Manufacturer advises toxicity at high doses in *animal* studies
Flucytosine (1)	Possible teratogenic risk
Flunitrazepam *see* Anxiolytics and Hypnotics	
Fluocinolone *see* Corticosteroids	

Table of drugs to be avoided or used with caution in pregnancy (*continued*)

Drug (Trimester of risk)	Comments
Fluocinonide *see* Corticosteroids	
Fluocortolone *see* Corticosteroids	
Fluoxetine *see* Antidepressants	
Flupenthixol *see* Antipsychotics	
Fluphenazine *see* Antipsychotics	
Flurandrenolone *see* Corticosteroids	
Flurazepam *see* Anxiolytics and Hypnotics	
Flurbiprofen *see* NSAIDs	
Fluspirilene *see* Antipsychotics	
Fluvoxamine *see* Antidepressants	
Foscarnet	Manufacturer advises avoid
Frusemide *see* Diuretics	
Ganciclovir	Avoid—teratogenic risk
Gemfibrozil *see* Clofibrate	
Gentamicin *see* Aminoglycosides	
Glibenclamide *see* Sulphonylureas	
Gliclazide *see* Sulphonylureas	
Glipizide *see* Sulphonylureas	
Gliquidone *see* Sulphonylureas	
Gold	
Auranofin	Manufacturer advises teratogenicity in *animal* studies; effective contraception should be used during and for at least 6 months after treatment
Aurothiomalate (1, 2, 3)	No good evidence of harm but avoid if possible
Griseofulvin	CRM advises avoid (fetotoxicity and teratogenicity in *animals*)
Growth Hormone	Avoid on theoretical grounds
Guanethidine (3)	Postural hypotension and reduced uteroplacental perfusion; should not be used to treat hypertension in pregnancy
Halcinonide *see* Corticosteroids	
Haloperidol *see* Antipsychotics	
Halothane *see* Anaesthetics, General	
Heparin (1, 2, 3)	Osteoporosis has been reported after prolonged use
Hydralazine (1)	Manufacturer advises toxicity in *animal* studies
Hydrochlorothiazide *see* Diuretics	
Hydrocortisone *see* Corticosteroids	
Hydroflumethiazide *see* Diuretics	
Hydroxychloroquine	Avoid for rheumatic disease (but for malaria *see* Antimalarials)
Hydroxyprogesterone *see* Progestogens	
Hydroxyzine *see* Antihistamines	
Hypnotics *see* Anxiolytics and Hypnotics	
Ibuprofen *see* NSAIDs	
Idoxuridine	Manufacturers advise toxicity in *animal* studies
Imipramine *see* Antidepressants, Tricyclic	
Immunosuppressants *see* section 8.1	
Indapamide *see* Diuretics	
Indomethacin *see* NSAIDs	
Iodine and Iodides (2, 3)	Neonatal goitre and hypothyroidism
Radioactive iodine (1, 2, 3)	Permanent hypothyroidism—avoid
Iprindole *see* Antidepressants, Tricyclic (and related)	
Isoflurane *see* Anaesthetics, General	
Isotretinoin (1, 2, 3)	Teratogenic; effective contraception must be used for at least 1 month before treatment, during treatment and for at least 1 month after stopping
Isradipine *see* Calcium-channel Blockers	
Itraconazole	Manufacturer advises toxicity in *animal* studies
Kanamycin *see* Aminoglycosides	
Ketamine *see* Anaesthetics, General	
Ketoconazole	Manufacturer advises teratogenicity in *animal* studies
Ketoprofen *see* NSAIDs	
Ketotifen *see* Antihistamines	
Labetalol *see* Beta-blockers	
Levodopa	Manufacturers advise toxicity in *animal* studies
Lignocaine *see* Anaesthetics, Local	
Lisinopril *see* ACE Inhibitors	
Lithium (1, 2, 3)	Dose requirements increased; congenital malformations; neonatal goitre reported; lithium toxicity (hypotonia and cyanosis) in neonate if maternal therapy poorly controlled
Lofepramine *see* Antidepressants, Tricyclic	
Loprazolam *see* Anxiolytics and Hypnotics	
Loratadine *see* Antihistamines	
Lorazepam *see* Anxiolytics and Hypnotics	
Lormetazepam *see* Anxiolytics and Hypnotics	
Lymecycline *see* Tetracyclines	
Madopar® *see* Levodopa	
Maloprim®	
(1)	Possible teratogenic risk (pyrimethamine a folate antagonist)
(3)	Neonatal haemolysis and methaemoglobinaemia (due to dapsone); folate supplements should be given to mother *see also* Antimalarials
Maprotiline *see* Antidepressants, Tricyclic (and related)	
Mebendazole	Manufacturer advises toxicity in *animal* studies
Mebhydrolin *see* Antihistamines	
Medazepam *see* Anxiolytics and Hypnotics	
Mefenamic Acid *see* NSAIDs	
Mefloquine (1)	Manufacturer advises teratogenicity in *animal* studies; avoid for prophylaxis, *see* p. 224
Mefruside *see* Diuretics	
Meprobamate *see* Anxiolytics and Hypnotics	
Meptazinol *see* Opioid Analgesics	
Mesterolone *see* Androgens	
Mestranol *see* Contraceptives, Oral	
Metaraminol (1, 2, 3)	Avoid—may reduce placental perfusion
Metformin (1, 2, 3)	Avoid

Table of drugs to be avoided or used with caution in pregnancy (*continued*)

Drug (Trimester of risk)	Comments
Methadone *see* Opioid Analgesics	
Methohexitone *see* Anaesthetics, General	
Methotrimeprazine *see* Antipsychotics	
Methyclothiazide *see* Diuretics	
Methylphenobarbitone *see* Antiepileptics	
Methylprednisolone *see* Corticosteroids	
Metolazone *see* Diuretics	
Metoprolol *see* Beta-blockers	
Metronidazole	Manufacturer advises avoidance of high-dose regimens
Metyrapone	Avoid (may impair biosynthesis of fetal-placental steroids)
Mianserin *see* Antidepressants, Tricyclic (and related)	
Minocycline *see* Tetracyclines	
Minoxidil (3)	Neonatal hirsutism reported
Misoprostol (1, 2, 3)	Avoid; increases uterine tone
Morphine *see* Opioid Analgesics	
Nabumetone *see* NSAIDs	
Nadolol *see* Beta-blockers	
Nalbuphine *see* Opioid Analgesics	
Nalidixic acid *see* 4-Quinolones	
Nandrolone *see* Anabolic Steroids	
Naproxen *see* NSAIDs	
Narcotic Analgesics *see* Opioid Analgesics	
Neomycin *see* Aminoglycosides	
Neostigmine (3)	Neonatal myasthenia with large doses
Netilmicin *see* Aminoglycosides	
Nicardipine *see* Calcium-channel Blockers	
Nicoumalone *see* Anticoagulants, Oral	
Nifedipine *see* Calcium-channel Blockers	
Nimodipine *see* Calcium-channel Blockers	
Nitrazepam *see* Anxiolytics and Hypnotics	
Nitrofurantoin (3)	May produce neonatal haemolysis if used at term
Nitrous oxide *see* Anaesthetics, General	
Noradrenaline (1, 2, 3)	Avoid—may reduce placental perfusion
Norfloxacin *see* 4-Quinolones	
Nortriptyline *see* Antidepressants, Tricyclic	
NSAIDs (3)	With regular use closure of fetal ductus arteriosus *in utero* and possibly persistent pulmonary hypertension of the newborn. Delayed onset and increased duration of labour
Octreotide (1, 2, 3)	Avoid; possible effect on fetal growth
Oestrogens *see* Contraceptives, Oral	
Ofloxacin *see* 4-Quinolones	
Omeprazole	Manufacturer advises toxicity in *animal* studies
Opioid Analgesics (3)	Depress neonatal respiration; withdrawal effects in neonates of dependent mothers; gastric stasis and risk of inhalation pneumonia in mother during labour
Oxatomide *see* Antihistamines	
Oxazepam *see* Anxiolytics and Hypnotics	
Oxprenolol *see* Beta-blockers	
Oxypertine *see* Antipsychotics	
Oxytetracycline *see* Tetracyclines	
Papaveretum *see* Opioid Analgesics	
Penbutolol *see* Beta-blockers	
Penicillamine (1, 2, 3)	Fetal abnormalities reported rarely; avoid if possible
Pentazocine *see* Opioid Analgesics	
Pericyazine *see* Antipsychotics	
Perindopril *see* ACE Inhibitors	
Perphenazine *see* Antipsychotics	
Pethidine *see* Opioid Analgesics	
Phenindamine *see* Antihistamines	
Phenindione *see* Anticoagulants, Oral	
Pheniramine *see* Antihistamines	
Phenobarbitone (1, 3)	Congenital malformations. Neonatal bleeding tendency—prophylactic vitamin K_1 should be given; *see also* Antiepileptics
Phenoperidine *see* Opioid Analgesics	
Phenothiazines *see* Antipsychotics	
Phenytoin (1, 3)	Congenital malformations. Neonatal bleeding tendency—prophylactic vitamin K_1 should be given. Caution in interpreting plasma concentrations—bound may be reduced but free (i.e. effective) unchanged; *see also* Antiepileptics
Pholcodine *see* Opioid Analgesics	
Pimozide *see* Antipsychotics	
Pindolol *see* Beta-blockers	
Piperazine	Packs sold to the general public carry a warning to avoid in pregnancy except on medical advice
Pipothiazine *see* Antipsychotics	
Piroxicam *see* NSAIDs	
Podophyllum resin (1, 2, 3)	Avoid—neonatal death and teratogenesis have been reported
Polythiazide *see* Diuretics	
Povidone-iodine (2, 3)	Sufficient iodine may be absorbed to affect the fetal thyroid
Pravastatin *see* Clofibrate	
Prednisolone *see* Corticosteroids	
Prednisone *see* Corticosteroids	
Prilocaine (3)	Neonatal methaemoglobinaemia; *see also* Anaesthetics, Local
Primaquine (3)	Neonatal haemolysis and methaemoglobinaemia; *see also* Antimalarials
Primidone *see* Antiepileptics	
Probucol *see* Clofibrate	
Procaine (3)	Neonatal methaemoglobinaemia; *see also* Anaesthetics, Local
Prochlorperazine *see* Antipsychotics	
Progestogens (1)	High doses may possibly be teratogenic

Table of drugs to be avoided or used with caution in pregnancy (*continued*)

Drug (Trimester of risk)	Comments
Proguanil	Folate supplements should be given to mother; *see also* Antimalarials
Promazine *see* Antipsychotics	
Promethazine *see* Antihistamines	
Propofol *see* Anaesthetics, General	
Propranolol *see* Beta-blockers	
Propylthiouracil (2, 3)	Neonatal goitre and hypothyroidism
Protriptyline *see* Antidepressants, Tricyclic	
Pyridostigmine (3)	Neonatal myasthenia with large doses
Pyrimethamine (1)	Possible teratogenic risk (folate antagonist); folate supplements should be given to mother; *see also* Antimalarials
Quinapril *see* ACE Inhibitors	
Quinine (1)	High doses are teratogenic; but in malaria benefit of treatment outweighs risk
4-Quinolones (1, 2, 3)	Arthropathy in *animal* studies
Ramipril *see* ACE inhibitors	
Reserpine (3)	Neonatal bradycardia, drowsiness, and nasal stuffiness
Rifampicin	
(1)	Manufacturers advise very high doses teratogenic in *animal* studies
(3)	Risk of neonatal bleeding may be increased
Salbutamol (3)	Large parenteral doses given at term for asthma could delay onset of labour
Salicylates *see* Aspirin	
Salsalate *see* Aspirin	
Simvastatin	Manufacturer advises toxicity in *animal* studies
Sodium Aurothiomalate *see* Gold	
Sodium Valproate *see* Valproate	
Sotalol *see* Beta-blockers	
Spironolactone	Potential human metabolic products carcinogenic in *rodents*
Stanozolol *see* Anabolic Steroids	
Stilboestrol (1)	High doses associated with vaginal carcinoma in female offspring
Streptokinase (1, 2, 3)	Possibility of premature separation of placenta in first 18 weeks; theoretical possibility of fetal haemorrhage throughout pregnancy; avoid postpartum use—maternal haemorrhage
Streptomycin *see* Aminoglycosides	
Sulfadoxine *see* Sulphonamides	
Sulfametopyrazine *see* Sulphonamides	
Sulindac *see* NSAIDs	
Sulphadiazine *see* Sulphonamides	
Sulphadimidine *see* Sulphonamides	
Sulphasalazine (3)	Theoretical risk of neonatal haemolysis; folate supplements should be given to mother

Drug (Trimester of risk)	Comments
Sulphaurea *see* Sulphonamides	
Sulphonamides (3)	Neonatal haemolysis and methaemoglobinaemia; increased risk of kernicterus in jaundiced neonates
Sulphonylureas (3)	Neonatal hypoglycaemia; insulin is normally substituted in all diabetics; if oral drugs are used therapy should be stopped at least 2 days before delivery
Sulpiride *see* Antipsychotics	
Temazepam *see* Anxiolytics and Hypnotics	
Tenoxicam *see* NSAIDS	
Terbutaline (3)	Large parenteral doses given at term for asthma could delay onset of labour
Terfenadine *see* Antihistamines	
Testosterone *see* Androgens	
Tetracyclines (2, 3)	Dental discoloration; maternal hepatotoxicity with large parenteral doses
Theophylline (3)	Neonatal irritability and apnoea have been reported
Thiabendazole (1)	Teratogenic in *animal* studies
Thiazides (3)	May cause neonatal thrombocytopenia; *see also* Diuretics
Thiethylperazine *see* Antipsychotics	
Thiopentone *see* Anaesthetics, General	
Thioridazine *see* Antipsychotics	
Tiaprofenic acid *see* NSAIDs	
Timolol *see* Beta-blockers	
Tinidazole	Manufacturer advises avoid in first trimester
Tobramycin *see* Aminoglycosides	
Tocainide	Manufacturer advises toxicity in *animal* studies
Tolbutamide *see* Sulphonylureas	
Tolmetin *see* NSAIDs	
Trazodone *see* Antidepressants, Tricyclic (and related)	
Triamcinolone *see* Corticosteroids	
Triamterene *see* Diuretics	
Triazolam *see* Anxiolytics and Hypnotics	
Tribavirin	Manufacturer advises avoid
Trichloroethylene *see* Anaesthetics, General	
Triclofos *see* Anxiolytics and Hypnotics	
Trifluoperazine *see* Antipsychotics	
Trifluperidol *see* Antipsychotics	
Trilostane (1, 2, 3)	Interferes with placental sex hormone production
Trimeprazine *see* Antihistamines	
Trimethoprim (1)	Possible teratogenic risk (folate antagonist)
Trimipramine *see* Antidepressants, Tricyclic	
Triprolidine *see* Antihistamines	
Urokinase (1, 2, 3)	Possibility of premature separation of placenta in first 18 weeks; theoretical possibility of fetal haemorrhage throughout pregnancy; avoid postpartum use—maternal haemorrhage

Table of drugs to be avoided or used with caution in pregnancy (*continued*)

Drug (Trimester of risk)	Comments
Vaccines (live) (1)	Theoretical risk of congenital malformations; see section 14.1
Valproate (1, 3)	Increased risk of neural tube defects (screening advised); neonatal bleeding and hepatotoxicity also reported
Verapamil *see* Calcium-channel Blockers	
Vigabatrin	Manufacturer advises toxicity in *animal* studies; *see also* Antiepileptics
Viloxazine *see* Antidepressants, Tricyclic (and related)	
Vitamin A (1)	Excessive doses may be teratogenic; *see also* p. 314
Warfarin *see* Anticoagulants, Oral	
Xamoterol	Manufacturer advises toxicity in *animal* studies
Xipamide *see* Diuretics	
Zuclopenthixol *see* Antipsychotics	

Appendix 5: Breast-feeding

Administration of some drugs to nursing mothers may cause toxicity in the infant (e.g. ergotamine), whereas administration of others (e.g. digoxin), has little effect on the neonate. Some drugs inhibit lactation (e.g. bromocriptine).

Toxicity to the infant can occur if the drug enters the milk in pharmacologically significant quantities. Milk concentrations of some drugs (e.g. iodides), may exceed those in the maternal plasma so that therapeutic doses in the mother may cause toxicity to the infant. Some drugs inhibit the infant's sucking reflex (e.g. phenobarbitone). Drugs in breast milk may, at least theoretically, cause hypersensitivity in the infant even when concentrations are too low for a pharmacological effect.

The following table lists drugs:

which should be used with caution or which are contra-indicated in breast-feeding for the reasons given above;

which, on present evidence, may be given to the mother during breast-feeding, because they are excreted in milk in amounts which are too small to be harmful to the infant;

which are not known to be harmful to the infant although they are present in milk in significant amounts.

For many drugs there is insufficient evidence available to provide guidance and it is advisable only to administer essential drugs to a mother during breast-feeding. Because of the inadequacy of currently available information on drugs in breast milk the following table should be used only as a guide; absence from the table does not imply safety.

Table of drugs excreted in breast milk

Products introduced or amended since publication of BNF No. 20 (September 1990) are in **bold** print.

Drug	Comments
Acebutolol *see* Beta-blockers	
Acetazolamide	Amount too small to be harmful
Acetohexamide *see* Sulphonylureas	
Acrivastine *see* Antihistamines	
Alcohol	Large amounts may affect infant
Alfacalcidol *see* Vitamin D	
Alprazolam *see* Benzodiazepines	
Aminophylline *see* Theophylline	
Amiodarone	Avoid; present in milk in significant amounts; theoretical risk from release of iodine; *see also* Iodine
Amitriptyline *see* Antidepressants, Tricyclic	
Amoxapine *see* Antidepressants, Tricyclic	
Amphetamines	Significant amount in milk. Avoid
Amylobarbitone *see* Barbiturates	
Androgens	Avoid; may cause masculinisation in the female infant or precocious development in the male infant; high doses suppress lactation
Anthraquinones	Avoid; large doses may cause increased gastric motility and diarrhoea (particularly cascara and danthron)
Anticoagulants, Oral	Risk of haemorrhage; increased by vitamin-K deficiency; warfarin appears safe but phenindione should be avoided
Antidepressants, Tricyclic (and related)	Amount of tricyclic antidepressants (including related drugs such as mianserin and trazodone) too small to be harmful; accumulation of doxepin metabolite may cause sedation and respiratory depression
Antihistamines	Significant amount of some but not known to be harmful; drowsiness in infant reported with clemastine
Antipsychotics	Although amount excreted in milk probably too small to be harmful, *animal* studies indicate possible adverse effects of these drugs on developing nervous system therefore avoid unless absolutely necessary; drowsiness in infant reported with chlorpromazine; significant amount of sulpiride excreted in milk (best avoided)
Aspirin	Avoid—possible risk of Reye's syndrome; regular use of high doses could impair platelet function and produce hypoprothrombinaemia in infant if neonatal vitamin K stores low
Astemizole *see* Antihistamines	
Atenolol *see* Beta-blockers	
Atropine	May possibly have antimuscarinic effects in infants
Auranofin *see* Gold	
Aurothiomalate *see* Gold	
Azatadine *see* Antihistamines	
Baclofen	Amount too small to be harmful
Barbiturates	Avoid if possible (*see also* phenobarbitone); large doses may produce drowsiness
Bendrofluazide *see* Thiazides	
Benperidol *see* Antipsychotics	
Benzodiazepines	Avoid repeated doses; lethargy and weight loss may occur in infant

Table of drugs excreted in breast milk (*continued*)

Drug	Comments
Beta-blockers and Labetalol	Monitor infant; possible toxicity due to beta-blockade but amount of most beta-blockers excreted in milk too small to affect infant; acebutolol, atenolol, nadolol, and sotalol are present in greater amounts than other beta-blockers
Betamethasone *see* Corticosteroids	
Betaxolol *see* Beta-blockers	
Bisoprolol *see* Beta-blockers	
Bromazepam *see* Benzodiazepines	
Bromide salts	Avoid; sedation and rash in infant
Bromocriptine	Suppresses lactation
Brompheniramine *see* Antihistamines	
Butobarbitone *see* Barbiturates	
Butriptyline *see* Antidepressants, Tricyclic	
Caffeine	Regular intake of large amounts can affect infant
Calciferol *see* Vitamin D	
Calcitonin	Avoid; inhibits lactation in *animals*
Calcitriol *see* Vitamin D	
Captopril	Amount too small to be harmful
Carbamazepine	Amount too small to be harmful
Carbimazole	Amounts in milk may be sufficient to affect neonatal thyroid function (but *see also* section 6.2.2)
Carisoprodol	Concentrated in milk; no adverse effects reported but best avoided
Cascara *see* Anthraquinones	
Cetirizine *see* Antihistamines	
Chloral Hydrate	Sedation in infant
Chloramphenicol	Stop breast-feeding; may cause bone-marrow toxicity in infant; concentration in milk usually insufficient to cause 'grey syndrome'
Chlordiazepoxide *see* Benzodiazepines	
Chlormethiazole	Amount too small to be harmful
Chloroquine	Amount too small to be harmful
Chlorothiazide *see* Thiazides	
Chlorpheniramine *see* Antihistamines	
Chlorpromazine	Drowsiness in infant reported; *see* Antipsychotics
Chlorpropamide *see* Sulphonylureas	
Chlortetracycline *see* Tetracyclines	
Chlorthalidone *see* Thiazides	
Cholecalciferol *see* Vitamin D	
Cimetidine	Significant amount but not known to be harmful
Ciprofloxacin	High concentrations in breast milk
Clavulanic acid (in *Augmentin®*, *Timentin®*)	Amount too small to be harmful
Clemastine *see* Antihistamines	
Clobazam *see* Benzodiazepines	
Clomipramine *see* Antidepressants, Tricyclic	
Clomocycline *see* Tetracyclines	
Clorazepate *see* Benzodiazepines	
Clozapine *see* Antipsychotics	
Codeine	Amount too small to be harmful
Colchicine	Caution because of its cytotoxicity
Contraceptives, Oral	Oestrogen/progestogen contraceptives usually have little effect on milk flow; in some women, usually when lactation not well established, suppression may occur; one report of neonatal folate deficiency; progestogen-only contraceptives do not appear to adversely affect established milk flow
Corticosteroids	Continuous therapy with high doses (>10 mg prednisolone daily) could possibly affect infant's adrenal function—monitor carefully
Corticotrophin	Amount too small to be harmful
Cortisone Acetate *see* Corticosteroids	
Co-trimoxazole	Small risk of kernicterus in jaundiced infants and of haemolysis in G6PD-deficient infants (due to sulphamethoxazole)
Cough mixtures containing iodides	Use alternative cough mixtures; *see* Iodine
Cyclopenthiazide *see* Thiazides	
Cycloserine	Amount too small to be harmful
Cyclosporin	Caution—excreted in milk
Cyproheptadine *see* Antihistamines	
Cyproterone Acetate	Caution; possibility of anti-androgen effects in neonate
Cytotoxics	Discontinue breast-feeding
Danazol	No data available but avoid because of possible androgenic effects in infant
Danthron *see* Anthraquinones	
Dapsone	Haemolytic anaemia; although significant amount in milk risk to infant very small
Demeclocycline *see* Tetracyclines	
Desipramine *see* Antidepressants, Tricyclic	
Dexamethasone *see* Corticosteroids	
Dexamphetamine *see* Amphetamines	
Dextropropoxyphene	Amount too small to be harmful
Diamorphine	Therapeutic doses unlikely to affect infant; withdrawal symptoms in infants of dependent mothers; breast-feeding no longer considered best method of treating dependence in offspring of dependent mothers and should be stopped
Diazepam *see* Benzodiazepines	
Diclofenac	Amount too small to be harmful

Table of drugs excreted in breast milk (*continued*)

Drug	Comments
Digoxin	Amount too small to be harmful
Dihydrotachysterol *see* Vitamin D	
Diltiazem	Significant amount but not known to be harmful
Dimethindene *see* Antihistamines	
Diphenylpyraline *see* Antihistamines	
Disopyramide	Amount too small to be harmful
Domperidone	Amount probably too small to be harmful
Dothiepin *see* Antidepressants, Tricyclic	
Doxepin *see* Antidepressants, Tricyclic	
Doxycycline *see* Tetracyclines	
Droperidol *see* Antipsychotics	
Enalapril	Amount too small to be harmful
Enoxacin	High concentrations in breast milk in *animals*
Ephedrine	Irritability and disturbed sleep reported
Ergocalciferol *see* Vitamin D	
Ergotamine	Avoid where possible; ergotism may occur in infant; repeated doses may inhibit lactation
Ethambutol	Amount too small to be harmful
Ethamsylate	Significant amount but not known to be harmful
Ethosuximide	Significant amount; hyperexcitability and poor suckling reported
Etretinate	Avoid
Famotidine	Amount too small to be harmful
Fansidar®	Small risk of kernicterus in jaundiced infants and of haemolysis in G6PD-deficient infants (due to sulfadoxine)
Fenbufen	Amount too small to be harmful
Fenoprofen	Amount too small to be harmful
Flunitrazepam *see* Benzodiazepines	
Fluoxetine	Only small amounts in milk but could accumulate in infant
Flupenthixol *see* Antipsychotics	
Fluphenazine *see* Antipsychotics	
Flurazepam *see* Benzodiazepines	
Flurbiprofen	Amount too small to be harmful
Frusemide	Amount too small to be harmful
Ganciclovir	Avoid
Glibenclamide *see* Sulphonylureas	
Gliclazide *see* Sulphonylureas	
Glipizide *see* Sulphonylureas	
Gliquidone *see* Sulphonylureas	
Glymidine *see* Sulphonylureas	
Gold (auranofin, aurothiomalate)	Caution—excreted in milk; theoretical possibility of rashes and idiosyncratic reactions
Haloperidol *see* Antipsychotics	

Drug	Comments
Heparin	Amount too small to be harmful
Hydrochlorothiazide *see* Thiazides	
Hydrocortisone *see* Corticosteroids	
Hydroflumethiazide *see* Thiazides	
Hydroxychloroquine	Amount too small to be harmful
Hydroxyzine *see* Antihistamines	
Hyoscine	Amount too small to be harmful
Ibuprofen	Amount too small to be harmful
Idoxuridine	May possibly make milk taste unpleasant
Imipramine *see* Antidepressants, Tricyclic	
Indapamide *see* Thiazides	
Indomethacin	Significant amounts are present in milk; convulsions reported in one infant
Insulin	Amount too small to be harmful
Iodine	Stop breast-feeding; danger of neonatal hypothyroidism or goitre; appears to be concentrated in milk
Radioactive iodine	Breast-feeding contra-indicated after therapeutic doses. With diagnostic doses withhold breast-feeding for at least 24 hours
Iprindole *see* Antidepressants, Tricyclic (and related)	
Isoniazid	Monitor infant for possible toxicity; theoretical risk of convulsions and neuropathy; prophylactic pyridoxine advisable in mother and infant
Isotretinoin	Avoid
Ketoprofen	Amount too small to be harmful
Ketotifen *see* Antihistamines	
Labetalol *see* Beta-blockers	
Liothyronine	May interfere with neonatal screening for hypothyroidism
Lithium salts	Monitor infant for possible intoxication; low incidence of adverse effects but increased by continuous ingestion; good control of maternal plasma concentrations minimises the risk
Lofepramine *see* Antidepressants, Tricyclic	
Loprazolam *see* Benzodiazepines	
Lorazepam *see* Benzodiazepines	
Lormetazepam *see* Benzodiazepines	
Lymecycline *see* Tetracyclines	
Maloprim®	Haemolytic anaemia (due to dapsone); risk to infant very small
Maprotiline *see* Antidepressants, Tricyclic (and related)	
Mebeverine	Amount too small to be harmful
Mebhydrolin *see* Antihistamines	
Medazepam *see* Benzodiazepines	

Table of drugs excreted in breast milk (*continued*)

Drug	Comments
Mefenamic Acid	Amount too small to be harmful
Mefruside *see* Thiazides	
Meprobamate	Avoid; concentration in milk may exceed maternal plasma concentrations fourfold and may cause drowsiness in infant
Mequitazine *see* Antihistamines	
Mesalazine	Diarrhoea has been reported
Methadone	Withdrawal symptoms in infant; breast-feeding permissible during maintenance dosage
Methotrimeprazine *see* Antipsychotics	
Methyclothiazide *see* Thiazides	
Methyldopa	Amount too small to be harmful
Methylprednisolone *see* Corticosteroids	
Metoclopramide	Amount probably too small to be harmful
Metolazone *see* Thiazides	
Metoprolol *see* Beta-blockers	
Metronidazole	Significant amount in milk; avoid for 24 hours after large single doses; may give a bitter taste to the milk
Mexiletine	Amount too small to be harmful
Mianserin *see* Antidepressants, Tricyclic (and related)	
Minocycline *see* Tetracyclines	
Minoxidil	Significant amount but not known to be harmful
Morphine	Therapeutic doses unlikely to affect infant; withdrawal symptoms in infants of dependent mothers; breast-feeding not best method of treating dependence in offspring and should be stopped
Nadolol *see* Beta-blockers	
Nalidixic Acid	Risk to infant very small but one case of haemolytic anaemia reported
Naproxen	Amount too small to be harmful
Nefopam	Amount too small to be harmful
Nicoumalone *see* Anticoagulants, Oral	
Nifedipine	Amount too small to be harmful
Nitrazepam *see* Benzodiazepines	
Nitrofurantoin	Only small amounts in milk but could be enough to produce haemolysis in G6PD-deficient infants
Nortriptyline *see* Antidepressants, Tricyclic	
NSAIDs *see* individual entries	
Octreotide	Avoid
Oestrogens	High doses suppress lactation but *see also* Contraceptives, Oral
Oxatomide *see* Antihistamines	
Oxazepam *see* Benzodiazepines	
Oxprenolol *see* Beta-blockers	
Oxypertine *see* Antipsychotics	

Drug	Comments
Oxytetracycline *see* Tetracyclines	
Paracetamol	Significant amount but not known to be harmful
Penbutolol *see* Beta-blockers	
Pericyazine *see* Antipsychotics	
Perphenazine *see* Antipsychotics	
Phenindamine *see* Antihistamines	
Phenindione *see* Anticoagulants, Oral	
Pheniramine *see* Antihistamines	
Phenobarbitone	Avoid when possible; drowsiness may occur but risk probably small; one report of methaemoglobinaemia with phenobarbitone and phenytoin
Phenolphthalein	Avoid; increased gastric motility, diarrhoea, and possibly rash
Phenytoin	Amount too small to be harmful
Pimozide *see* Antipsychotics	
Pindolol *see* Beta-blockers	
Pirenzepine	Amount too small to be harmful
Piroxicam	Amount too small to be harmful
Polythiazide *see* Thiazides	
Povidone-iodine	Avoid; iodine absorbed from vaginal preparations is concentrated in milk
Prednisolone *see* Corticosteroids	
Prednisone *see* Corticosteroids	
Primidone *see* Phenobarbitone	
Prochlorperazine *see* Antipsychotics	
Progestogens	High doses suppress lactation but *see also* Contraceptives, Oral
Promazine *see* Antipsychotics	
Promethazine *see* Antihistamines	
Propranolol *see* Beta-blockers	
Propylthiouracil	Monitor infant's thyroid status but amounts in milk probably too small to affect infant; high doses might affect neonatal thyroid function
Protriptyline *see* Antidepressants, Tricyclic	
Pseudoephedrine	Amount too small to be harmful
Pyrazinamide	Amount too small to be harmful
Pyridostigmine	Amount too small to be harmful
Pyrimethamine	Significant amount but not known to be harmful
Quinalbarbitone *see* Barbiturates	
Quinidine	Significant amount but not known to be harmful
Ranitidine	Significant amount but not known to be harmful
Rifampicin	Amount too small to be harmful
Senna *see* Anthraquinones	
Sodium Valproate *see* Valproate	
Sotalol *see* Beta-blockers	
Sulfametopyrazine *see* Sulphonamides	
Sulphadiazine *see* Sulphonamides	

Table of drugs excreted in breast milk (*continued*)

Drug	Comments
Sulphadimidine *see* Sulphonamides	
Sulphasalazine	Small amounts in milk but bloody diarrhoea has been reported; theoretical risk of neonatal haemolysis especially in G6PD-deficient infants
Sulphaurea *see* Sulphonamides	
Sulphonamides	Small risk of kernicterus in jaundiced infants particularly with long-acting sulphonamides, and of haemolysis in G6PD-deficient infants
Sulphonylureas	Caution; theoretical possibility of hypoglycaemia in infant
Sulpiride	Best avoided; significant amounts in milk; *see also* Antipsychotics
Temazepam *see* Benzodiazepines	
Terbutaline	Amount too small to be harmful
Terfenadine *see* Antihistamines	
Tetracyclines	Some authorities recommend avoidance but absorption and therefore discoloration of teeth in infant probably prevented by chelation with calcium in milk
Theophylline	Irritability in infant reported; sustained-release preparations probably safe
Thiamine	Severely thiamine-deficient mothers should avoid breast-feeding as toxic methylglyoxal excreted in milk
Thiazides	Amount too small to be harmful; large doses may suppress lactation
Thiethylperazine *see* Antipsychotics	
Thioridazine *see* Antipsychotics	
Thyroxine	May interfere with neonatal screening for hypothyroidism
Tiaprofenic acid	Amount too small to be harmful
Timolol *see* Beta-blockers	
Tolazamide *see* Sulphonylureas	
Tolbutamide *see* Sulphonylureas	
Tolmetin	Amount too small to be harmful
Trazodone	Amount too small to be harmful
Triamcinolone *see* Corticosteroids	
Triazolam *see* Benzodiazepines	
Trifluoperazine *see* Antipsychotics	
Trifluperidol *see* Antipsychotics	
Trimeprazine *see* Antihistamines	
Trimipramine *see* Antidepressants, Tricyclic	
Triprolidine *see* Antihistamines	
Valproate	Amount too small to be harmful
Verapamil	Amount too small to be harmful
Viloxazine *see* Antidepressants, Tricyclic (and related)	
Vitamin A	Theoretical risk of toxicity in infants of mothers taking large doses
Vitamin D (and related compounds)	Caution with high doses; may cause hypercalcaemia in infant
Warfarin *see* Anticoagulants, Oral	
Xipamide *see* Thiazides	
Zopiclone	Amount too small to be harmful
Zuclopenthixol *see* Antipsychotics	

Appendix 6: Intravenous Additives

INTRAVENOUS ADDITIVE POLICIES. A local policy on the addition of drugs to intravenous fluids should be drawn up by a multi-disciplinary team in each Health District and issued as a document to the members of staff concerned.

Centralised additive services are provided in a number of hospital pharmacy departments and should be used in preference to making additions on wards.

The information that follows should be read in conjunction with local policy documents.

Guidelines

1. Drugs should only be added to infusion containers when constant plasma concentrations are needed or when the administration of a more concentrated solution would be harmful.
2. In general, only one drug should be added to any infusion container and the components should be compatible (see Table). Ready-prepared solutions should be used whenever possible. Drugs should not normally be added to blood products, mannitol, or sodium bicarbonate. Only specially formulated additives should be used with fat emulsions or amino-acid solutions (see section 9.3).
3. Solutions should be thoroughly mixed by shaking and checked for absence of particulate matter before use.
4. Strict asepsis should be maintained throughout and in general the giving set should not be used for more than 24 hours.
5. The infusion container should be labelled with the patient's name, the name and quantity of additives, and the date and time of addition (and the new expiry date or time). Such additional labelling should not interfere with information on the manufacturer's label that is still valid. When possible, containers should be retained for a period after use in case they are needed for investigation.
6. It is good practice to examine intravenous infusions from time to time while they are running. If cloudiness, crystallisation, change of colour, or any other sign of interaction or contamination is observed the infusion should be discontinued.

Problems

MICROBIAL CONTAMINATION. The accidental entry and subsequent growth of micro-organisms converts the infusion fluid pathway into a potential vehicle for infection with micro-organisms, particularly species of *Candida, Enterobacter*, and *Klebsiella*. Ready-prepared infusions containing the additional drugs, or infusions prepared by an additive service (when available) should therefore be used in preference to making extemporaneous additions to infusion containers on wards etc. However, when this is necessary strict aseptic procedure should be followed.

INCOMPATIBILITY. Physical and chemical incompatibilities may occur with loss of potency, increase in toxicity, or other adverse effect. The solutions may become opalescent or precipitation may occur, but in many instances there is no visual indication of incompatibility. Interaction may take place at any point in the infusion fluid pathway, and the potential for incompatibility is increased when more than one substance is added to the infusion fluid.

Common incompatibilities. Precipitation reactions are numerous and varied and may occur as a result of pH, concentration changes, 'salting-out' effects, complexation or other chemical changes. Precipitation or other particle formation must be avoided since, apart from lack of control of dosage on administration, it may initiate or exacerbate adverse effects. This is particularly important in the case of drugs which have been implicated in either thrombophlebitis (e.g. diazepam) or in skin sloughing or necrosis caused by extravasation (e.g. sodium bicarbonate and certain cytotoxic drugs). It is also especially important to effect solution of colloidal drugs and to prevent their subsequent precipitation in order to avoid a pyrogenic reaction (e.g. amphotericin).

It is considered undesirable to mix beta-lactam antibiotics, such as semi-synthetic penicillins and cephalosporins, with proteinaceous materials on the grounds that immunogenic and allergenic conjugates could be formed.

A number of preparations undergo significant loss of potency when added singly or in combination to large volume infusions. Examples include ampicillin in infusions that contain glucose or lactates, mustine hydrochloride in isotonic saline and gentamicin/carbenicillin combinations. The breakdown products of dacarbazine have been implicated in adverse effects.

Blood. Because of the large number of incompatibilities, drugs should not normally be added to blood and blood products for infusion purposes. Examples of incompatibility with blood include hypertonic mannitol solutions (irreversible crenation of red cells), dextrans (rouleaux formation and interference with cross-matching), glucose (clumping of red cells), and oxytocin (inactivated).

If the giving set is not changed after the administration of blood, but used for other infusion fluids, a fibrin clot may form which, apart from blocking the set, increases the likelihood of microbial growth.

Intravenous fat emulsions may break down with coalescence of fat globules and separation of phases when additions such as antibiotics or electrolytes are made, thus increasing the possibility of embolism. Only specially formulated products such as Vitlipid N® (see section 9.3) may be added to appropriate intravenous fat emulsions.

Other infusions that frequently give rise to incompatibility include amino acids, mannitol, and sodium bicarbonate.

Bactericides such as chlorocresol 0.1% or phenylmercuric nitrate 0.001% are present in some injection solutions. The total volume of such solutions added to a container for infusion on one occasion should not exceed 15 mL.

Method

Ready-prepared infusions should be used whenever available. **Potassium chloride** is usually available in concentrations of 20, 27, and 40 mmol/litre in sodium chloride intravenous infusion (0.9%), glucose intravenous infusion (5%) or sodium chloride and glucose intravenous infusion. **Lignocaine hydrochloride** is usually available in concentrations of 0.1 or 0.2% in glucose intravenous infusion (5%).

When addition is required to be made extemporaneously, any product reconstitution instructions such as those relating to concentration, vehicle, mixing, and handling precautions should be strictly followed using an aseptic technique throughout. Once the product has been reconstituted, addition to the infusion fluid should be made immediately in order to minimise microbial contamination and, with certain products, to prevent degradation or other formulation change which may occur; e.g. reconstituted ampicillin injection degrades rapidly on standing, and also may form polymers which could cause sensitivity reactions.

It is also important in certain instances that an infusion fluid of specific pH be used. **Amphotericin** injection requires dilution in glucose injection of pH greater than 4.2 and **frusemide** injection should be added to infusions of pH greater than 5.5.

When drug additions are made it is important to mix thoroughly; additions should not be made to an infusion container that has been connected to a giving set, as mixing is hampered. If the solutions are not thoroughly mixed a concentrated layer of the additive may form owing to differences in density. **Potassium chloride** is particularly prone to this 'layering' effect when added without adequate mixing to infusions packed in non-rigid infusion containers; if such a mixture is administered it may have a serious effect on the heart.

A time limit between addition and completion of administration must be imposed for certain admixtures to guarantee satisfactory drug potency and compatibility. For admixtures in which degradation occurs without the formation of toxic substances, an acceptable limit is the time taken for 10% decomposition of the drug. When toxic substances are produced stricter limits may be imposed. Because of the risk of microbial contamination a maximum time limit of 12 hours should be imposed for additions made elsewhere than in hospital pharmacies offering central additive service.

Certain injections must be protected from light during continuous infusion to minimise oxidation, e.g. amphotericin, dacarbazine, and sodium nitroprusside.

Dilution with a small volume of an appropriate vehicle and administration using a motorised infusion pump is advocated for preparations such as heparin where strict control over administration is required. In this case the appropriate dose may be dissolved in a convenient volume (e.g. 24 to 48 mL) of sodium chloride intravenous infusion (0.9%).

Use of table

The Table lists preparations given by three methods:

continuous infusion,
intermittent infusion, and
addition via the drip tubing.

Drugs for **continuous infusion** must be diluted in a large volume infusion. Penicillins and cephalosporins are not usually given by continuous infusion because of stability problems and because adequate plasma and tissue concentrations are best obtained by intermittent infusion. Where it is necessary to administer them by continuous infusion, detailed literature should be consulted.

Drugs that are both compatible and clinically suitable may be given by **intermittent infusion** in a relatively small volume of infusion over a short period of time, e.g. 100 mL in 30 minutes. The method is used if the product is incompatible or unstable over the period necessary for continuous infusion; the limited stability of ampicillin or amoxycillin in large volume glucose or lactate infusions may be overcome in this way.

Intermittent infusion is also used if adequate plasma and tissue concentrations are not produced by continuous infusion as in the case of drugs such as carbenicillin, dacarbazine, gentamicin and ticarcillin.

An in-line burette may be used for intermittent infusion techniques in order to achieve strict control over the time and rate of administration, especially for infants and children and in intensive care units. Intermittent infusion may also make use of the 'piggy-back' technique provided that no additions are made to the primary infusion. In this method the drug is added to a small secondary container connected to a Y-type injection site on the primary infusion giving set; the secondary solution is usually infused within 30 minutes.

Addition via the drip tubing is indicated for a number of cytotoxic drugs in order to minimise extravasation. The preparation is added aseptically via the rubber septum of the injection site of a fast-running infusion. In general, drug preparations intended for a bolus effect should be given directly into a separate vein where possible. Failing this, administration may be made via the drip tubing provided that the preparation is compatible with the infusion fluid when given in this manner.

Table of drugs given by intravenous infusion

Covers addition to glucose 5 and 10%, Sodium chloride 0.9%, Compound sodium chloride (Ringer's solution), and Compound sodium lactate (Hartmann's solution). Compatibility with glucose 5% and with sodium chloride 0.9% indicates compatibility with any strength of sodium chloride and glucose infusion. If water for injection is used care should be taken to avoid hypotonic solution. The information in the Table relates to the proprietary preparations indicated; for other preparations suitability should be checked with the manufacturer

Drug	Infusion method	Notes
Acetylcysteine *Parvolex®*	Continuous *in* Glucose 5%	See Emergency Treatment of Poisoning
Aclarubicin hydrochloride *Aclacin®*	Intermittent *in* Glucose 5% *or* Sodium chloride 0.9%	Dissolve initially in 10 mL water for injections or sodium chloride 0.9% then dilute with 200–500 mL infusion fluid to a concentration of 200–500 micrograms/mL; give over 30–60 minutes and protect from light during administration; pH of glucose infusion should be between 5 and 6
Actinomycin D *Cosmegen Lyovac®*	Via drip tubing *in* Glucose 5% *or* Sodium chloride 0.9%	
Acyclovir sodium *Zovirax IV®*	Intermittent *in* Sodium chloride 0.9% *or* Sodium chloride and glucose *or* Compound sodium lactate	Initially reconstitute to 25 mg/mL in water for injections or sodium chloride 0.9% then dilute to not more than 5 mg/mL with the infusion fluid; minimum volume 50 mL; to be given over 1 hour
Alfentanil hydrochloride *Rapifen® preparations*	Continuous *or* Intermittent *in* Glucose 5% *or* Sodium chloride 0.9% *or* Compound sodium lactate	
Alprostadil *Prostin VR®*	Continuous *in* Glucose 5% *or* Sodium chloride 0.9%	
Amikacin sulphate *Amikin®*	Intermittent *in* Glucose 5% *or* Sodium chloride 0.9% *or* Compound sodium lactate	To be given over 30 minutes
Aminophylline	Continuous *in* Glucose 5% *or* Sodium chloride 0.9% *or* Compound sodium lactate	
Amiodarone hydrochloride *Cordarone X®*	Continuous *or* intermittent *in* Glucose 5%	Suggested initial infusion volume 250 mL given over 20–120 minutes; for repeat infusions up to 1.2 g in a maximum volume of 500 mL; incompatible with sodium chloride infusion
Amoxycillin sodium *Amoxil®*	[1]Intermittent *in* Glucose 5% *or* Sodium chloride 0.9%	Reconstituted solutions diluted and given without delay; suggested volume 100 mL given over 30–60 minutes
	Via drip tubing *in* Glucose 5% *or* Sodium chloride 0.9% *or* Ringer's solution *or* Compound sodium lactate	
Amphotericin sodium deoxycholate complex *Fungizone®*	Continuous *in* Glucose 5%	Dissolve thoroughly at reconstitution stage; preparation must be diluted in a large volume infusion; pH of the glucose must not be below 4.2 (check each container); protect from light; suggested infusion time 6 hours
Ampicillin sodium *Penbritin®*	[1]Intermittent *in* Glucose 5% *or* Sodium chloride 0.9%	Reconstituted solutions diluted and given without delay; suggested volume 100 mL given over 30–60 minutes
	Via drip tubing *in* Glucose 5% *or* Sodium chloride 0.9% *or* Ringer's solution *or* Compound sodium lactate	
Ampicillin/cloxacillin (sodium salts) *Ampiclox®*	Intermittent *in* Glucose 5% *or* Sodium chloride 0.9%	Reconstituted solutions diluted and given without delay; suggested volume 100 mL given over 30–60 minutes
	Via drip tubing *in* Glucose 5% *or* Sodium chloride 0.9% *or* Ringer's solution *or* Compound sodium lactate	
Ampicillin/sulbactam (sodium salts) *Dicapen®*	Intermittent *in* Glucose 5% *or* Sodium chloride 0.9% *or* Water for injections	Reconstituted solutions diluted and given without delay; give over 15–30 minutes
Amsacrine *Amsidine®*	Intermittent *in* Glucose 5%	Reconstitute with diluent provided and dilute to suggested volume 500 mL; give over 60–90 minutes; use glass syringes; incompatible with sodium chloride infusion

1. continuous infusion not usually recommended

Drug	Infusion method
Ancrod *Arvin®*	Continuous *in* Sodium chloride 0.9%
Suggested volume 50–500 mL given over 4–12 hours	
Aprotinin *Trasylol®*	Continuous *or* via drip tubing *in* Glucose 5% *or* Sodium chloride 0.9% *or* Ringer's solution
Atenolol *Tenormin®*	Intermittent *in* Glucose 5% *or* Sodium chloride 0.9%
Suggested infusion time 20 minutes	
Atracurium besylate *Tracrium®*	Continuous *in* Glucose 5% *or* Sodium chloride 0.9% *or* Compound sodium lactate
Stability varies with diluent	
Azathioprine *Imuran®*	Via drip tubing *in* Glucose 5% *or* Sodium chloride 0.9%
Reconstituted solutions should be administered without delay	
Azlocillin sodium *Securopen®* (5 g)	Intermittent *in* Glucose 5 and 10% *or* Sodium chloride 0.9% *or* Ringer's solution
Intermittent infusion suggested for doses over 2 g; to be given over 20–30 minutes	
Aztreonam *Azactam®*	Intermittent *in* Glucose 5% *or* Sodium chloride 0.9% *or* Ringer's solution *or* Compound sodium lactate
Dissolve initially in water for injections (1 g per 3 mL) then dilute to a concentration of less than 20 mg/mL; to be given over 20–60 minutes	
Benzylpenicillin sodium *Crystapen®*	[1]Intermittent *in* Glucose 5% *or* Sodium chloride 0.9%
Suggested volume 100 mL given over 30–60 minutes	
Betamethasone sodium phosphate *Betnesol®*	Continuous *or* Intermittent *or* Via drip tubing *in* Glucose 5%; *or* Sodium chloride 0.9%
Bleomycin sulphate	Intermittent *in* Sodium chloride 0.9%
To be given slowly; suggested volume 200 mL	
Bumetanide *Burinex®*	Intermittent *in* Glucose 5% *or* Sodium chloride 0.9%
Suggested volume 500 mL given over 30–60 minutes	
Calcium gluconate	Continuous *in* Glucose 5% *or* Sodium chloride 0.9%
Avoid bicarbonates, phosphates, or sulphates	
Carbenicillin sodium *Pyopen®*	Intermittent *in* Glucose 5% *or* Water for injections
Suggested volume 100 mL given over 30–40 minutes	
Carboplatin *Paraplatin®*	Continuous *in* Glucose 5% *or* Sodium chloride 0.9%
Short-term infusion; final concentration as low as 500 micrograms/mL	
Carmustine *BiCNU®*	Intermittent *in* Glucose 5% *or* Sodium chloride 0.9%
Reconstitute with diluent provided; give over 1–2 hours	
Cefotaxime sodium *Claforan®*	Intermittent *in* Glucose 5% *or* Sodium chloride 0.9% *or* Compound sodium lactate *or* Water for injections
Suggested volume 40–100 mL given over 20–60 minutes	
Cefoxitin sodium *Mefoxin®*	[1]Intermittent *or* Via drip tubing *in* Glucose 5 and 10% *or* Sodium chloride 0.9%
Cefsulodin sodium *Monaspor®*	[1]Intermittent *or* Via drip tubing *in* Glucose 5% *or* Sodium chloride 0.9%
Ceftazidime pentahydrate *Fortum®*	Intermittent *or* Via drip tubing *in* Glucose 5 and 10% *or* Sodium chloride 0.9% *or* Compound sodium lactate *or* Water for injections
Ceftizoxime sodium *Cefizox®*	Continuous *or* Intermittent *or* Via drip tubing *in* Glucose 5 and 10% *or* Sodium chloride 0.9% *or* Ringer's solution *or* Compound sodium lactate
Suggested volume 50–100 mL	
Cefuroxime sodium *Zinacef®*	Intermittent *or* Via drip tubing *in* Glucose 5% *or* Sodium chloride 0.9% *or* Compound sodium lactate
Suggested volume 50–100 mL given over 30 minutes	
Cephalothin sodium *Keflin®*	[1]Intermittent *or* Via drip tubing *in* Glucose 5% *or* Sodium chloride 0.9% *or* Compound sodium lactate
Cephamandole nafate *Kefadol®*	[1]Intermittent *or* Via drip tubing *in* Glucose 5 and 10% *or* Sodium chloride 0.9% *or* Water for injections

1. continuous infusion not usually recommended

Drug	Infusion method
Cephazolin sodium *Kefzol®*	[1]Intermittent *or* Via drip tubing *in* Glucose 5 and 10% *or* Sodium chloride 0.9% *or* Compound sodium lactate *or* Water for injections
Cephradine *Velosef®*	Continuous *or* Intermittent *in* Glucose 5 and 10% *or* Sodium chloride 0.9% *or* Ringer's solution *or* Compound sodium lactate *or* Water for injections
Reconstituted solutions diluted and given without delay; max. 8 hours between addition and completion of administration	
Chloramphenicol sodium succinate *Kemicetine®*	Intermittent *or* Via drip tubing *in* Glucose 5% *or* Sodium chloride 0.9%
Chloroquine sulphate *Nivaquine®* See also section 5.4.1	Continuous *in* Sodium chloride 0.9%
Cimetidine *Tagamet®*	Continuous *or* Intermittent *in* Glucose 5% *or* Sodium chloride 0.9%
For intermittent infusion; suggested volume 250 mL given over 2 hours	
Cisplatin	Continuous *in* Sodium chloride 0.9% *or* Sodium chloride and glucose
Suggested volume 1 litre given over 6–8 hours	
Clindamycin phosphate *Dalacin C®*	Continuous *or* Intermittent *in* Glucose 5% *or* Sodium chloride 0.9%
Clomipramine *Anafranil®*	Intermittent *in* Glucose 5% *or* Sodium chloride 0.9%
Suggested volume 125–500 mL given over 45–120 minutes	
Clonazepam *Rivotril®*	Intermittent *in* Glucose 5 and 10% *or* Sodium chloride 0.9%
Suggested volume 250 mL	
Cloxacillin sodium *Orbenin®*	[1]Intermittent *in* Glucose 5% *or* Sodium chloride 0.9%
Suggested volume 100 mL given over 30–60 minutes	
	Via drip tubing *in* Glucose 5% *or* Sodium chloride 0.9% *or* Ringer's solution *or* Compound sodium lactate

Drug	Infusion method
Co-amoxiclav *Augmentin®*	Intermittent *in* Sodium chloride 0.9% *or* Water for injections *or* see also package leaflet
Suggested volume 50–100 mL given over 30–40 minutes and completed within 2 hours of reconstitution	
	Via drip tubing *in* Glucose 5% *or* Sodium chloride 0.9%
Co-fluampicil (sodium salts) *Magnapen®*	Intermittent *in* Glucose 5% *or* Sodium chloride 0.9%
Reconstituted solutions diluted and given without delay; suggested volume 100 mL given over 30–60 minutes	
	Via drip tubing *in* Glucose 5% *or* Sodium chloride 0.9% *or* Ringer's solution *or* Compound sodium lactate
Colistin sulphomethate sodium *Colomycin®*	Continuous *or* Intermittent *in* Glucose 5% *or* Sodium chloride 0.9% *or* Ringer's solution
Max. 6 hours between addition and completion of administration	
Co-trimoxazole *Bactrim®* for infusion, *Septrin®* for infusion	Continuous *in* Glucose 5 and 10% *or* Sodium chloride 0.9% *or* Ringer's solution
Ampoule solution has a pH of about 10; suggested infusion time 90 minutes; *Bactrim®* can also be infused in Compound sodium lactate	
Cyclophosphamide *Endoxana®*	Intermittent *or* Via drip tubing *in* Water for injections
For intermittent infusion suggested volume 50–100 mL given over 5–15 minutes; max. 30 minutes between addition and completion of administration	
	Via drip tubing *in* Glucose 5%
Cyclosporin *Sandimmun®*	Continuous *in* Glucose 5% *or* Sodium chloride 0.9%
Dilute to a concentration of 50 mg in 20–100 mL; give over 2–6 hours.	
Cytarabine *Alexan®*, *Cytosar®*	Continuous *or* intermittent *or* via drip tubing *in* Glucose 5% *or* Sodium chloride 0.9%
Reconstitute *Cytosar®* with the diluent provided; check container for haze or precipitate during administration.	
Dacarbazine *DTIC-Dome®*	Intermittent *in* Glucose 5% *or* Sodium chloride 0.9%
Suggested volume 125–250 mL given over 15–30 minutes; protect infusion from light	

1. continuous infusion not usually recommended

Drug	Infusion method
Desferrioxamine mesylate *Desferal®*	Continuous *or* intermittent *in* Glucose 5% *or* Sodium chloride 0.9%
Dexamethasone sodium phosphate *Decadron®* *Dexamethasone* (Organon)	Continuous *or* intermittent *or* via drip tubing *in* Glucose 5% *or* Sodium chloride 0.9%
Dexamethasone (Organon) can also be infused in Glucose 10% *or* Ringer's solution *or* Compound sodium lactate	
Diazepam (solution) *Valium®*	Continuous *in* Glucose 5% *or* Sodium chloride 0.9%
Dilute to a concentration of not more than 40 mg in 500 mL; max. 6 hours between addition and completion of administration; adsorbed to some extent by the plastics of the infusion set	
Diazepam (emulsion) *Diazemuls®*	Continuous *in* Glucose 5 and 10%
May be diluted to a max. concentration of 200 mg in 500 mL; max. 6 hours between addition and completion of administration; adsorbed to some extent by the plastics of the infusion set	
	Via drip tubing *in* Glucose 5 and 10% *or* Sodium chloride 0.9%
Adsorbed to some extent by the plastics of the infusion set	
Digoxin *Lanoxin®*	Continuous *in* Glucose 5% *or* Sodium chloride 0.9%
To be given slowly; see also section 2.1.1.	
Digoxin-specific antibody fragments *Digibind®*	Intermittent *in* Sodium chloride 0.9%
Dissolve initially in water for injections (4 mL/vial) then dilute with the sodium chloride 0.9% and give through a 0.22 micron Millipore filter over 20 minutes	
Dinoprostone *Prostin E2®*	Continuous *or* intermittent *in* Glucose 5% *or* Sodium chloride 0.9%
Disodium etidronate *Didronel IV®*	Continuous *in* Sodium chloride 0.9%
Dilute in large-volume infusion, suggested minimum volume 250 mL; minimum period of infusion 2 hours	
Disodium pamidronate *Aredia®*	Continuous *in* Glucose 5% *or* Sodium chloride 0.9%
For doses of 15–60 mg dilute to a concentration of 15 mg in 125 mL and give each 15 mg over at least 2 hours; 90-mg dose to be dissolved in at least 1 litre and given over 24 hours; not to be given with infusion fluids containing calcium	
Disopyramide phosphate *Rythmodan®*	Continuous *or* intermittent *in* Glucose 5% *or* Sodium chloride 0.9% *or* Ringer's solution *or* Compound sodium lactate
Max. rate by continuous infusion 20–30 mg/hour (or 400 micrograms/kg/hour)	
Dobutamine hydrochloride *Dobutrex®* Solution	Continuous *in* Glucose 5% *or* Sodium chloride 0.9%
Dilute to a concentration of 0.5–1 mg/mL; give higher concentration (max. 5 mg/mL) with infusion pump; incompatible with bicarbonate	
Dopamine hydrochloride *Intropin®*	Continuous *in* Glucose 5% *or* Sodium chloride 0.9% *or* Compound sodium lactate
Dilute to a concentration of 1.6 mg/mL; incompatible with bicarbonate	
Dopexamine hydrochloride *Dopacard®*	Continuous *in* Glucose 5% *or* Sodium chloride 0.9%
Dilute to a concentration of 400 or 800 micrograms/mL; give via infusion pump or other device which provides accurate control of rate; contact with metal should be minimised; incompatible with bicarbonate	
Doxorubicin hydrochloride *Doxorubicin Rapid Dissolution*, *Doxorubicin Solution* (both Farmitalia Carlo Erba)	Via drip tubing *in* Glucose 5% *or* Sodium chloride 0.9%
Reconstitute *Doxorubicin Rapid Dissolution* with water for injections or sodium chloride 0.9%	
Electrolytes *Addiphos®*	Continuous *in* Glucose 5 and 10%
Suggested volume 500 mL	
Enoximone *Perfan®*	Continuous *or* intermittent *in* Sodium chloride 0.9% *or* Water for injections
Dilute to a concentration of 2.5 mg/mL; incompatible with glucose solutions; use only plastic containers or syringes	
Epirubicin hydrochloride *Pharmorubicin® Rapid Dissolution*	Via drip tubing *in* Sodium chloride 0.9%
Reconstitute with sodium chloride 0.9% or with water for injections (10 mg in 5 mL, 20 mg in 10 mL, 50 mg in 25 mL)	
Epoprostenol *Flolan®*	Intermittent *in* Sodium chloride 0.9%
Reconstitute with the diluent provided (pH 10.5) to make a concentrate; use this concentrate within 12 hours and store at 2°–8°C; dilute with not more than 6 times the volume of sodium chloride 0.9% before use	

1. continuous infusion not usually recommended

Drug	Infusion method
Erythromycin lactobionate *Erythrocin®*	Continuous *or* intermittent *in* Glucose 5% (neutralised with sodium bicarbonate) *or* Sodium chloride 0.9% *or* Compound sodium lactate
Dissolve initially in water for injections (1 g in 20 mL) then dilute to a concentration of 1 mg/mL for continuous infusion and 1–5 mg/mL for intermittent infusion	
Ethacrynic acid (sodium salt) *Edecrin®*	Via drip tubing *in* Glucose 5% *or* Sodium chloride 0.9%
pH of glucose infusion should be adjusted to above 5	
Ethanol	Continuous *in* Glucose 5% *or* Sodium chloride 0.9% *or* Ringer's solution *or* Compound sodium lactate
Dilute to a concentration of 5–10%	
Etoposide *Vepesid®*	Intermittent *in* Sodium chloride 0.9%
Dilute to a concentration of not more than 250 micrograms/mL and give over not less than 30 minutes and not more than 6 hours; check container for haze or precipitate during administration; may dissolve certain types of filter.	
Flecainide acetate *Tambocor®*	Continuous *or* intermittent *in* Glucose 5% *or* Sodium chloride 0.9% *or* Compound sodium lactate
Minimum volume in infusion fluids containing chlorides 500 mL	
Flucloxacillin sodium *Floxapen®*	[1]Intermittent *in* Glucose 5% *or* Sodium chloride 0.9%
Suggested volume 100 mL given over 30–60 minutes	
	Via drip tubing *in* Glucose 5% *or* Sodium chloride 0.9% *or* Ringer's solution *or* Compound sodium lactate
Flumazenil *Anexate®*	Continuous *in* Glucose 5% *or* Sodium chloride 0.9%
Fluorouracil sodium	Continuous *or* via drip tubing *in* Glucose 5%
For continuous infusion suggested volume 500 mL given over 4 hours	
Folinic acid (calcium salt) *Calcium Leucovorin®*, *Refolinon®*	Continuous *in* Sodium chloride 0.9%
Calcium Leucovorin® can also be infused in Glucose 5 and 10% *or* Compound sodium lactate	
Foscarnet trisodium *Foscavir®*	Continuous *in* Glucose 5%
Dilute to a concentration of 12 mg/mL or less for infusion into peripheral vein (undiluted solution via central venous line only)	
Frusemide (sodium salt) *Lasix®*	Continuous *in* Sodium chloride 0.9% *or* Ringer's solution
Infusion pH must be above 5.5; glucose solutions are unsuitable	
Fusidic acid (diethanolamine salt) *Fucidin®*	Continuous *in* Glucose 5% *or* Sodium chloride 0.9%
Reconstitute with the buffer solution provided and dilute to a maximum equivalent to 1 mg sodium fusidate/mL; to be given over not less than 6 hours	
Ganciclovir (sodium salt) *Cymevene®*	Intermittent *in* Glucose 5% *or* Sodium chloride 0.9% *or* Ringer's solution *or* Compound sodium lactate
Reconstitute initially in water for injections (500 mg/10 mL) then dilute to not more than 10 mg/mL with infusion fluid (usually 100 mL); infuse over 1 hour	
Gentamicin sulphate *Cidomycin®*	Intermittent *or* Via drip tubing *in* Glucose 5% *or* Sodium chloride 0.9%
Suggested volume for intermittent infusion 50–100 mL given over 20 minutes	
Glyceryl trinitrate *Nitrocine®*, *Nitronal®*, *Tridil®*	Continuous *in* Glucose 5% *or* Sodium chloride 0.9%
For *Tridil®* dilute to a concentration of not more than 400 micrograms/mL; for *Nitrocine®* suggested infusion concentration 100 micrograms/mL; incompatible with polyvinyl chloride infusion containers such as Viaflex® or Steriflex®; use glass or polyethylene containers or give via a syringe pump	
Heparin sodium	Continuous *in* Glucose 5% *or* Sodium chloride 0.9%
Administration with a motorised pump may be advisable	
Hydralazine hydrochloride *Apresoline®*	Continuous *in* Sodium chloride 0.9% *or* Ringer's solution
Suggested infusion volume 500 mL	
Hydrocortisone sodium phosphate *Efcortesol®*	Continuous *or* intermittent *or* via drip tubing *in* Glucose 5% *or* Sodium chloride 0.9%
Hydrocortisone sodium succinate *Efcortelan Soluble®*, *Solu-Cortef®*	Continuous *or* intermittent *or* via drip tubing *in* Glucose 5% *or* Sodium chloride 0.9%

1. continuous infusion not usually recommended

Drug	Infusion method
Idarubicin hydrochloride *Zavedos®*	Via drip tubing *in* Sodium chloride 0.9%
Reconstitute with water for injections; give over 5–10 minutes	
Ifosfamide *Mitoxana®*	Continuous *or* intermittent *or* via drip tubing *in* Sodium chloride 0.9% *or* Sodium chloride and glucose
For continuous infusion, suggested volume 3 litres given over 24 hours; for intermittent infusion, give over 30–120 minutes	
Imipenem/cilastatin (sodium salt) *Primaxin®*	[1]Intermittent *in* Glucose 5% *or* Sodium chloride 0.9% *or* Water for injections
Dilute to a concentration of 5 mg (as imipenem)/mL; infuse 250–500 mg (as imipenem) over 20–30 minutes, 1 g over 40–60 minutes	
Insulin	Continuous *in* Sodium chloride 0.9% *or* Compound sodium lactate
Adsorbed to some extent by plastics of infusion set; see also section 6.1.3; ensure insulin is not injected into 'dead space' of injection port of the infusion bag	
Iron dextran *Imferon®*	Intermittent *in* Glucose 5% *or* Sodium chloride 0.9%
Suggested volume 500 mL	
Isoprenaline hydrochloride *Saventrine IV®*	Continuous *in* Glucose 5% *or* Sodium chloride and glucose
Dilute in a large-volume infusion; suggested minimum volume 500 mL; pH of the infusion must be below 5.	
Isosorbide dinitrate *Cedocard IV®*, *Isoket 0.05%®*, *Isoket 0.1%®*	Continuous *in* Glucose 5% *or* Sodium chloride 0.9%
Adsorbed to some extent by polyvinyl chloride infusion containers; preferably use glass or polyethylene containers or give via a syringe pump; *Isoket 0.05%®* can alternatively be administered undiluted using a syringe pump with a glass or rigid plastic syringe	
Isoxsuprine hydrochloride *Duvadilan®*	Continuous *in* Glucose 5% *or* Sodium chloride 0.9%
Suggested infusion concentration 0.02%	
Kanamycin sulphate *Kannasyn®*	Intermittent *in* Glucose 5% *or* Sodium chloride 0.9%
Dilute to 2.5 mg/mL and give at a rate of 3–4 mL/minute	
Ketamine hydrochloride *Ketalar®*	Continuous *in* Glucose 5% *or* Sodium chloride 0.9%
Dilute to 1 mg/mL; microdrip infusion for maintenance of anaesthesia	
Labetalol hydrochloride *Trandate®*	Intermittent *in* Glucose 5% *or* Sodium chloride and glucose
Dilute to a concentration of 1 mg/mL. Suggested volume 200 mL. Adjust rate with in-line burette	
Lignocaine hydrochloride *Xylocard 20%®*	Continuous *in* Glucose 5% *or* Sodium chloride 0.9% *or* Ringer's solution
Suggested infusion concentration 0.2%; use ready-prepared solution when available	
Lincomycin hydrochloride *Lincocin®*	Continuous *in* Glucose 5% *or* Sodium chloride 0.9%
Suggested minimum volume 250 mL; minimum period of infusion 1 hour	
Mecillinam *Selexidin®*	Intermittent *in* Glucose 5% *or* Sodium chloride 0.9%
Reconstituted solutions diluted and given without delay; suggested infusion time 15–30 minutes	
Melphalan *Alkeran®*	Continuous *or* via drip tubing *in* Sodium chloride 0.9%
Reconstitute with the solvent and diluent provided then dilute with infusion fluid; max. 2 hours between addition and completion of administration	
Mesna *Uromitexan®*	Continuous *or* via drip tubing *in* Sodium chloride and glucose *or* Sodium chloride 0.9%
Max. 24 hours between addition and completion of administration	
Metaraminol tartrate *Aramine®*	Continuous *or* via drip tubing *in* Glucose 5% *or* Sodium chloride 0.9% *or* Ringer's solution *or* Compound sodium lactate
Suggested infusion volume 500 mL	
Methicillin sodium *Celbenin®*	[1]Intermittent *in* Glucose 5% *or* Sodium chloride 0.9%
Suggested volume 100 mL given over 30–60 minutes	
	Via drip tubing *in* Glucose 5% *or* Sodium chloride 0.9% *or* Ringer's solution *or* Compound sodium lactate
Methocarbamol *Robaxin®*	Intermittent *in* Glucose 5% *or* Sodium chloride 0.9%
Dilute to a concentration of not less than 1 g in 250 mL	

1. continuous infusion not usually recommended

Drug	Infusion method
Methotrexate sodium *Methotrexate* (Lederle)	Continuous *or* via drip tubing *in* Glucose 5% *or* Sodium chloride 0.9% *or* Compound sodium lactate *or* Ringer's solution
Dilute in a large-volume infusion; max. 24 hours between addition and completion of administration	
Methyldopate hydrochloride *Aldomet®*	Intermittent *in* Glucose 5%
Suggested volume 100 mL given over 30–60 minutes	
Methylprednisolone sodium succinate *Solu-Medrone®*	Continuous *or* intermittent *or* via drip tubing *in* Glucose 5% *or* Sodium chloride 0.9%
Metoclopramide hydrochloride *Maxolon High Dose®*	Continuous *or* intermittent *in* Glucose 5% *or* Sodium chloride 0.9% *or* Compound sodium lactate
Loading dose, dilute with 50–100 mL and give over 15–30 minutes; maintenance dose, dilute with 500 mL and give over 8–12 hours; for intermittent infusion dilute with at least 50 mL and give over at least 15 minutes	
Mexiletine hydrochloride *Mexitil®*	Continuous *in* Glucose 5% *or* Sodium chloride 0.9%
Mezlocillin sodium *Baypen®* (5 g)	Intermittent *in* Glucose 5 and 10% *or* Sodium chloride 0.9% *or* Ringer's solution *or* Water for injections
Suggested volume 50 mL given over 15–20 minutes	
Miconazole *Daktarin®*	Continuous *or* intermittent *in* Glucose 5% *or* Sodium chloride 0.9%
Minimum period of infusion 30 minutes; for intermittent infusion suggested volume 200–500 mL	
Milrinone *Primacor®*	Continuous *in* Glucose 5% *or* Sodium chloride 0.9%
Dilute to a suggested concentration of 200 micrograms/mL	
Mitozantrone hydrochloride *Novantrone®*	Via drip tubing *in* Glucose 5% *or* Sodium chloride 0.9%
Suggested volume at least 50 mL given over at least 3–5 minutes	
Mustine hydrochloride	Via drip tubing *in* Glucose 5% *or* Sodium chloride 0.9%
Naftidrofuryl oxalate *Praxilene Forte®*	Intermittent *in* Glucose 5 and 10% *or* Sodium chloride 0.9%
Suggested volume 250–500 mL given over 90–120 minutes	
Naloxone *Min-I-Jet Naloxone Hydrochloride®*, *Narcan®*	Continuous *in* Glucose 5% *or* Sodium chloride 0.9%
Dilute to a concentration of 4 micrograms/mL	
Netilmicin sulphate *Netillin®*	Intermittent *or* via drip tubing *in* Glucose 5 and 10% *or* Sodium chloride 0.9%
For intermittent infusion suggested volume 50–200 mL given over 30–120 minutes	
Nimodipine *Nimotop®*	Via drip tubing *in* Glucose 5% *or* Sodium chloride 0.9% *or* Ringer's solution
Not to be added to infusion container; administer via an infusion pump through a Y-piece into a central catheter; incompatible with polyvinyl chloride giving sets or containers	
Noradrenaline solution strong sterile *Levophed®*	Continuous *in* Glucose 5% *or* Sodium chloride and glucose
Dilute in a large-volume infusion; pH of the infusion solution must be below 6	
Ondansetron hydrochloride *Zofran®*	Continuous *or* intermittent *in* Glucose 5% *or* Sodium chloride 0.9% *or* Ringer's solution
Oxytocin *Syntocinon®*	Continuous *in* Glucose 5% *or* Sodium chloride 0.9% *or* Ringer's solution
Dilute in a large-volume infusion	
Pentamidine isethionate *Pentacarinat®*	Intermittent *in* Glucose 5% *or* Sodium chloride 0.9%
Dissolve initially in water for injections (300 mg in 3–5 mL) then dilute in 50–250 mL; give over at least 60 minutes	
Phenoxybenzamine hydrochloride *Dibenyline®*	Intermittent *in* Sodium chloride 0.9%
To be given over not less than 60 minutes	
Phentolamine mesylate *Rogitine®*	Intermittent *in* Glucose 5% *or* Sodium chloride 0.9%
Phenylephrine hydrochloride	Intermittent *in* Glucose 5% *or* Sodium chloride 0.9%
Piperacillin sodium *Pipril®*	Intermittent *in* Glucose 5% *or* Sodium chloride 0.9% *or* Compound sodium lactate *or* Water for injections
Minimum volume 50 mL given over 20–40 minutes	

1. continuous infusion not usually recommended

Drug	Infusion method
Plicamycin *Mithracin®*	Intermittent *in* Glucose 5% *or* Sodium chloride 0.9% Reconstitute 2.5 mg with 4.9 mL water for injections then dilute appropriate dose to suggested volume 1000 mL given over 4–6 hours
Polymyxin B sulphate *Aerosporin®*	Continuous *in* Glucose 5% Suggested volume 200–500 mL given over 60–90 minutes
Potassium canrenoate *Spiroctan-M®*	Intermittent *in* Glucose 5% *or* Sodium chloride 0.9% Suggested volume 250 mL
Potassium chloride	Continuous *in* Glucose 5% *or* Sodium chloride 0.9% Dilute in a large-volume infusion; mix thoroughly to avoid 'layering', especially in non-rigid infusion containers; use ready-prepared solutions when possible
Procainamide hydrochloride *Pronestyl®*	Continuous *or* intermittent *in* Glucose 5% For maintenance, dilute to a concentration of *either* 2 mg/mL and give at a rate of 1–3 mL/minute *or* 4 mg/mL and give at a rate of 0.5–1.5 mL/minute
Propofol *Diprivan®*	Via drip tubing *in* Glucose 5% *or* Sodium chloride 0.9% Not to be mixed with other therapeutic agents or infusion fluids; to be administered via a Y-piece close to injection site
	Continuous *in* Glucose 5% Dilute to a concentration not exceeding 2 mg/mL. Usual infusion rate 6–12 mg/kg/hour; propofol may alternatively be infused undiluted using a suitable infusion pump
Quinine dihydrochloride	Continuous *in* Sodium chloride 0.9% To be given over 4 hours; see also section 5.4.1
Ranitidine hydrochloride *Zantac®*	Intermittent *in* Glucose 5% *or* Sodium chloride 0.9% *or* Compound sodium lactate
Rifampicin *Rifadin®*, *Rimactane®* infusion	Intermittent *in* Glucose 5 and 10% *or* Sodium chloride 0.9% *or* Ringer's solution Reconstitute with solvent provided then dilute with 250 mL infusion fluid; give over 2–3 hours.
Ritodrine hydrochloride *Yutopar®*	Continuous *in* Glucose 5% *or* Sodium chloride 0.9% Dilute in a large-volume infusion
Salbutamol sulphate *Ventolin®* for intravenous infusion	Continuous *in* Glucose 5% *or* Sodium chloride 0.9% Suggested volume 500 mL as a solution containing 10 micrograms/mL
Salcatonin *Miacalcic®*	Continuous *in* Sodium chloride 0.9% Diluted solution given without delay; dilute in 500 mL and give over at least 6 hours; glass or hard plastic containers should not be used
Sodium calciumedetate *Ledclair®*	Continuous *in* Glucose 5% *or* Sodium chloride 0.9% Dilute to a concentration of not more than 3%; suggested volume 250–500 mL given over at least 1 hour
Sodium nitroprusside *Nipride®*	Continuous *in* Glucose 5% *or* Sodium chloride 0.9% *or* Ringer's solution *or* Compound sodium lactate Reconstitute with solvent provided then dilute immediately with 250–1000 mL infusion fluid; preferably infuse via infusion device to allow precise control; protect infusion from light
Sodium valproate *Epilim®*	Continuous *or* intermittent *in* Glucose 5% *or* Sodium chloride 0.9% Reconstitute with solvent provided then dilute with infusion fluid
Streptokinase *Kabikinase®*, *Streptase®*	Continuous *in* Sodium chloride 0.9% *Kabikinase®* can also be infused in Glucose 5%
Sulphadiazine sodium	Continuous *in* Sodium chloride 0.9% Suggested volume 500 mL; ampoule solution has a pH of over 10
Suxamethonium chloride *Anectine®*, *Scoline®*	Continuous *in* Glucose 5% *or* Sodium chloride 0.9%
Teicoplanin *Targocid®*	[1]Intermittent *in* Glucose 5% *or* Sodium chloride 0.9% *or* Compound sodium lactate Reconstitute initially with water for injections provided; infuse over 30 minutes
Temocillin sodium *Temopen®*	Intermittent *in* Glucose 5% *or* Sodium chloride 0.9% *or* Ringer's solution *or* Compound sodium lactate Dissolve initially in water for injections (500 mg in 10 mL; 1–2 g in 20 mL) then dilute with infusion fluid and give over 30–40 minutes
Terbutaline sulphate *Bricanyl®*	Continuous *in* Glucose 5% *or* Sodium chloride 0.9% Suggested volume 500 mL; to be given over 8–10 hours
Tetracosactrin *Synacthen®*	Continuous *in* Glucose 5% *or* Sodium chloride 0.9% Suggested volume 500 mL given over 6 hours

1. continuous infusion not usually recommended

Drug	Infusion method
Tetracycline hydrochloride *Achromycin Intravenous®*	Continuous *in* Glucose 5% *or* Sodium chloride 0.9% *or* Compound sodium lactate
Reconstitute initially with water for injections (250 mg in 5 mL, 500 mg in 10 mL) then dilute to at least 100 mL (max. 1 litre) and give at a rate not exceeding 100 mL in 5 minutes preferably through a 0.22 micron filter	
Theophylline (solubilised with lysine) *Labophylline®*	Continuous *in* Glucose 5% *or* Sodium chloride 0.9%
Ticarcillin sodium *Ticar®*	Intermittent *in* Glucose 5% *or* Water for injections
Suggested volume 100–150 mL given over 30–40 minutes	
Ticarcillin sodium/ clavulanic acid *Timentin®*	Intermittent *in* Glucose 5% *or* Water for injections
Suggested volume glucose 5%, 50–150 mL (depending on dose) or water, 25–100 mL; given over 30–40 minutes	
Tobramycin sulphate *Nebcin®*	Intermittent *or* via drip tubing *in* Glucose 5% *or* Sodium chloride 0.9%
For intermittent infusion suggested volume 100–150 mL given over 20–60 minutes	
Tocainide hydrochloride *Tonocard®*	Intermittent *in* Glucose 5% *or* Sodium chloride 0.9%
Suggested volume 50–100 mL given over 15–30 minutes	
Treosulfan *Treosulfan* (Leo)	Intermittent *in* Water for injections
Infusion suggested for doses above 5 g; use diluted to a concentration of 5 g in 100 mL	
Trimetaphan camsylate *Arfonad®*	Intermittent *in* Glucose 5% *or* Sodium chloride 0.9%
Suggested infusion concentration 0.05–0.1%; suggested volume 100–500 mL	
Trimethoprim lactate *Monotrim®* *Syraprim®*	Via drip tubing *in* Glucose 5%
Monotrim® can also be infused via drip tubing in Sodium chloride 0.9% *or* Compound sodium lactate; *Syraprim®* can also be given by intermittent infusion in Glucose 5%	
Trisodium edetate *Limclair®*	Continuous *in* Glucose 5% *or* Sodium chloride 0.9%
Suggested volume 500 mL given over 2–3 hours	
Urokinase *Urokinase* (Leo)	Continuous *in* Sodium chloride 0.9%
Vancomycin hydrochloride *Vancocin®*	[1]Intermittent *in* Glucose 5% *or* Sodium chloride 0.9%
Suggested volume 100–200 mL given over 60 minutes	
Vasopressin, synthetic *Pitressin®*	Intermittent *in* Glucose 5%
Suggested concentration 20 units/100 mL given over 15 minutes	
Vecuronium bromide *Norcuron®*	Continuous *in* Glucose 5% *or* Sodium chloride 0.9% *or* Ringer's solution
Reconstitute with the solvent provided	
Vinblastine sulphate *Velbe®*	Via drip tubing *in* Sodium chloride 0.9% *or* Water for injections
Reconstitute with the diluent provided	
Vincristine sulphate *Oncovin®*	Via drip tubing *in* Sodium chloride 0.9% *or* Water for injections
Reconstitute with the diluent provided	
Vindesine sulphate *Eldisine®*	Via drip tubing *in* Glucose 5% *or* Sodium chloride 0.9%
Reconstitute with the diluent provided	
Vitamins B & C *Pabrinex®*, *Parentrovite IVHP®*	Intermittent *or* via drip tubing *in* Glucose 5% *or* Sodium chloride 0.9%
Ampoule contents should be mixed, diluted, and administered without delay; give over 10 minutes (see CSM advice, section 9.6.2)	
Vitamins, multiple *Multibionta®*	Intermittent *in* Glucose 5% *or* Sodium chloride 0.9%
Dilute 10 mL in not less than 250 mL of infusion fluid (adults); see also section 9.3	
Solivito N®	Intermittent *in* Glucose 5 and 10%
Suggested volume 500–1000 mL given over 2–3 hours; see also section 9.3	

1. continuous infusion not usually recommended

Appendix 7: Borderline Substances

In certain conditions some foods (and toilet preparations) have characteristics of drugs and the Advisory Committee on Borderline Substances advises as to the circumstances in which such substances may be regarded as drugs. Prescriptions issued in accordance with the Committee's advice and endorsed 'ACBS' will normally not be investigated.

> General Practitioners are reminded that the ACBS recommends products on the basis that they may be regarded as drugs for the treatment of specified conditions. Doctors should satisfy themselves that the products can safely be prescribed, that patients are adequately monitored and that, where necessary, expert hospital supervision is available.

FOODS WHICH MAY BE PRESCRIBED ON FP10

Note. This is a list of food products which the ACBS has approved. The clinical condition for which the product has approval follows each entry.

Aglutella® (Nutricia)
Pasta, protein not more than 500 mg, carbohydrate 86.8 g, fat 500 mg/100 g, low Na^+ and K^+, gluten-free; macaroni, pasta spirals, semolina, spaghetti rings. Net price 250 g = £2.72; spaghetti, tagliatelle, 500 g = £4.66. For phenylketonuria; similar amino-acid abnormalities; renal failure; liver failure and liver cirrhosis; gluten-sensitive enteropathies including steatorrhoea due to gluten sensitivity, coeliac disease, and dermatitis herpetiformis

Aglutella Azeta® (Nutricia)
Wafers, cream-filled, gluten-free, low protein, low sodium, low potassium. Net price 150 g = £3.49. For phenylketonuria; similar amino-acid abnormalities; renal failure; liver failure and liver cirrhosis

AL 110® (Nestle)
Powder, protein 14.0 g, fat 25.0 g, carbohydrate 55.3 g, energy 2100 kJ (502 kcal)/100 g with vitamins and minerals. Net price 400 g = £7.27. For proven lactose intolerance in pre-school children, galactosaemia, and galactokinase deficiency

Albumaid® (Scientific Hospital Supplies)
Complete, powder, amino acids 89.4%, with vitamins, minerals, trace elements, free from carbohydrate and fat. Net price 200 g = £29.04. For malabsorption states where there is failure to hydrolyse and/or absorb protein
RVHB, powder, amino acid mixture, methionine-free. Net price 200 g = £28.23. For homocystinuria
RVHB complete, powder, amino acid mixture, methionine-free, with vitamins, minerals, and trace elements. Net price 200 g = £28.23. For homocystinuria
XP, powder, amino acids 40%, carbohydrate 50%, fat nil, phenylalanine not more than 10 mg per 100 g, with vitamins, minerals, and trace elements. Net price 200 g = £14.37. For phenylketonuria
XP Concentrate, powder, amino acids 85%, carbohydrate and fat nil, phenylalanine not more than 25 mg per 100 g, with vitamins, minerals, and trace elements. Net price 200 g = £27.45. For phenylketonuria

Alcoholic Beverages see under Rectified Spirit

Alembicol D® (Alembic Products)
Fractionated coconut oil. Net price 4 kg = £66.64. For steatorrhoea associated with cystic fibrosis of the pancreas, intestinal lymphangiectasia, surgery of the intestine, chronic liver disease, liver cirrhosis, other proven malabsorption syndromes; and in a ketogenic diet in the management of epilepsy

Alfare® (Nestle)
Powder, protein 16.5 g, fat 24.0 g, carbohydrate 51.7 g, energy 2010 kJ (480 kcal)/100 g with vitamins and minerals. Net price 400 g = £5.49. For proven whole protein sensitivity

Aminex® (Cow & Gate)
Biscuits, protein 0.9% (phenylalanine 0.021%), carbohydrate 80%, fat 8.4%, lactose- and sucrose-free. Net price 12 × 12.5-g biscuits = £1.60. For phenylketonuria; similar amino acid abnormalities; liver cirrhosis; chronic renal failure; lactose with sucrose intolerance

Aminogran® (UCB Pharma)
Food Supplement, powder, containing all essential amino acids except phenylalanine, for use with mineral mixture (see below). Net price 500 g = £43.87. For phenylketonuria
Mineral Mixture, powder, containing all appropriate minerals for use with the above food supplement and other synthetic diets. Net price 250 g = £7.43. For phenylketonuria and as a mineral supplement in synthetic diets

Analog MSUD® (Scientific Hospital Supplies)
Powder, essential and non-essential amino acids 15.5% except isoleucine, leucine and valine, with carbohydrate, fat, vitamins, minerals and trace elements. Net price 400 g = £17.25. For maple syrup urine disease

Analog RVHB® (Scientific Hospital Supplies)
Powder, essential and non-essential amino acids 15.5% except methionine, with carbohydrate, fat, vitamins, minerals and trace elements. Net price 40 g = £17.25. For hypermethioninaemia; homocystinuria

Analog XMet, Thre, Val, Isoleu® (Scientific Hospital Supplies)
Powder, essential and non-essential amino acids 15.5% except methionine, threonine, valine and low isoleucine, with carbohydrate, fat, vitamins, minerals and trace elements. Net price 400 g = £17.25. For methylmalonic or propionic acidaemia

Analog XP® (Scientific Hospital Supplies)
Powder, essential and non-essential amino acids 15.5% except phenylalanine, with carbohydrate, fat, vitamins, minerals and trace elements. Net price 400 g = £15.00. For phenylketonuria

Analog XPhen, Tyr® (Scientific Hospital Supplies)
Powder, essential and non-essential amino acids 15.5% except phenylalanine and tyrosine, with carbohydrate, fat, vitamins, minerals and trace elements. Net price 400 g = £17.25. For tyrosinaemia

Aproten® (Ultrapharm)
Various products, gluten-free, low protein, low Na^+ and K^+. Net prices: anellini 250 g = £2.10; biscuits 180 g (36) = £2.60; bread mix 250 g = £2.00; cake mix 300 g = £2.10; crispbread 240 g = £3.95; ditalini 250 g = £2.10; flour 500 g = £2.15; rigatini 250 g = £2.10; tagliatelle 250 g = £2.10. For phenylketonuria; similar amino acid abnormalities; renal failure; liver failure and liver cirrhosis; gluten-sensitive enteropathies including steatorrhoea due to gluten sensitivity, coeliac disease, and dermatitis herpetiformis

Bi-Aglut® (Ultrapharm)
Biscuits, gluten-free. Net price 180 g (36) = £2.50
Cracker toast, gluten-, lactose-, and milk-protein-free. Net price 240 g (40) = £3.25. For gluten-sensitive enteropathies including steatorrhoea due to gluten sensitivity, coeliac disease, and dermatitis herpetiformis

Calogen® (Scientific Hospital Supplies)
Emulsion, arachis oil 50% in water. Net price 1 litre = £8.28; 2 litres = £15.96. For renal failure and other conditions requiring a high-energy, low-fluid, low-electrolyte diet, disorders of amino acid metabolism or carbohydrate absorption; in a ketogenic diet in the management of epilepsy

Caloreen® (Roussel)

Powder, water-soluble dextrins, predominantly polysaccharides containing an average of 5 glucose molecules, with less than 1.8 mmol of Na^+ and 0.3 mmol of K^+/100 g. Net price 250 g = £1.38; 5 kg = £22.54.

For renal failure; liver cirrhosis; disaccharide intolerance (without isomaltose intolerance), disorders of amino acid metabolism (and other similar disorders) and/or whole protein intolerance; malabsorption states and other conditions (including proven hypoglycaemia) requiring a high energy, low fluid intake, whether or not sodium and/or potassium restriction is essential

Carobel, Instant® (Cow & Gate)

Powder, carob seed flour. Net price 45 g = £1.63. For thickening feeds in the treatment of vomiting

Casilan® (Farley)

Powder, whole protein, containing all essential amino acids, 90% with less than 0.1% Na^+. Net price 250 g = £3.61. For biochemically proven hypoproteinaemia

Clinifeed® (Roussel)

Complete gluten-free foods in 4 formulations. For short-bowel syndrome, intractable malabsorption, pre-operative preparation of patients who are undernourished, treatment for proven inflammatory bowel disease, treatment following total gastrectomy, dysphagia, bowel fistulas, anorexia nervosa; neoplasia-related (associated) cachexia (anorexia). Not to be prescribed for any child under one year, unsuitable as a sole source of nutrition for young children up to 5 years of age

Clinifeed 400, protein 15 g, carbohydrate 55 g, fat 13.4 g, energy 1674 kJ (400 kcal)/375 mL, with vitamins and minerals, vanilla flavour. Fructose-free. Net price 375-mL can = £1.10

Clinifeed Favour, protein 14.1 g, carbohydrate 49.9 g, fat 14.6 g, energy 1575 kJ (375 kcal)/375 mL, with vitamins and minerals, neutral flavour. Lactose-, fructose-, and sucrose-free. Net price 375-mL can = 88p

Clinifeed Iso, protein 10.5 g, carbohydrate 49.2 g, fat 15.4 g, energy 1575 kJ (375 kcal)/375 mL, with vitamins and minerals, vanilla flavour. Fructose- and sucrose-free, and low sodium. Net price 375-mL can = £1.24

Clinifeed Protein Rich, protein 30 g, carbohydrate 70 g, fat 11 g, energy 2092 kJ (500 kcal)/375 mL, with vitamins and minerals, vanilla flavour. Fructose- and lactose-free. Net price 375-mL can = £1.23

Comminuted Chicken Meat (Cow & Gate)

Suspension (aqueous). Net price 128 g = £1.00. For carbohydrate intolerance in association with possible or proven intolerance of milk; glucose and galactose intolerance

Corn flour and **corn starch.** For hypoglycaemia associated with glycogen-storage disease

Corn oil (maize oil). Net price 100 mL = 37p. For familial hypercholesterolaemia

Dialamine® (Scientific Hospital Supplies)

Powder, essential amino acids 30%, with carbohydrate 62%, energy 1500 kJ (360 kcal)/100 g, with ascorbic acid, minerals, and trace elements. Flavour: orange. Net price 100 g = £6.43. For oral feeding where essential amino acid supplements are required; e.g. chronic renal failure, hypoproteinaemia, wound fistula leakage with excessive protein loss, conditions requiring a controlled nitrogen intake, and haemodialysis

dp® (Nutricia)

Biscuits, low-protein, butterscotch- or chocolate-flavoured chip cookies. Net price 170 g = £4.66. For phenylketonuria; similar amino acid abnormalities; renal failure; liver failure and liver cirrhosis

Duocal® (Scientific Hospital Supplies)

Liquid, emulsion providing carbohydrate 23.4 g, fat 7.1 g, energy 628 kJ/100 mL. Low-electrolyte, gluten-, lactose-, and protein-free. Net price 250 mL = £1.35; 1 litre = £4.78

Super Soluble Powder, carbohydrate 72.7 g, fat 22.3 g, energy 1988 kJ/100 g. Low electrolyte, gluten-, protein-, and lactose-free. Net price 400 g = £8.72. For renal failure; liver cirrhosis; disaccharide intolerance (without isomaltose intolerance), disorders of amino acid metabolism (and other similar disorders), and/or whole protein intolerance; malabsorption states and other conditions requiring a high energy, low fluid intake, whether or not sodium and/or potassium restriction is essential

Elemental 028® (Scientific Hospital Supplies)

Powder, amino acids 12%, carbohydrate 70.5–72%, fat 6.64%, energy 1544–1568 kJ (364–370 kcal)/100 g with vitamins and minerals. For preparation with water before use. Net price 100-g box (orange flavoured or plain) = £3.28. For short-bowel syndrome, intractable malabsorption, pre-operative preparation of patients who are undernourished, treatment for proven inflammatory bowel disease, treatment following total gastrectomy, dysphagia, bowel fistulas; neoplasia-related (associated) cachexia (anorexia). Not to be prescribed for any child under one year, unsuitable as a sole source of nutrition for young children up to 5 years of age

Ener-G® (General Designs)

Rice bread (brown, sliced), gluten-free. Net price 400 g = £2.86.

Tapioca bread (sliced), gluten-free. Net price 200 g = £1.05. For gluten-sensitive enteropathies including steatorrhoea due to gluten sensitivity, coeliac disease, and dermatitis herpetiformis

Enrich® (Abbott)

Liquid with dietary fibre, providing protein 9.4 g, carbohydrate 38.3 g (including 5 g as dietary fibre), fat 8.8 g, energy 1090 kJ (260 kcal)/250 mL with vitamins and minerals. Lactose- and gluten-free. Vanilla and chocolate flavours. Net price 250-mL can = £1.45. For short-bowel syndrome, intractable malabsorption, pre-operative preparation of patients who are undernourished, treatment for proven inflammatory bowel disease, treatment following total gastrectomy, dysphagia, bowel fistulas, anorexia nervosa; neoplasia-related (associated) cachexia (anorexia). Not to be prescribed for any child under one year, unsuitable as a sole source of nutrition for young children up to 5 years of age

Ensure® (Abbott)

Liquid, protein 3.7%, fat 3.7%, carbohydrate 14.5%, with minerals and vitamins, lactose- and gluten-free, energy 1050 kJ (253 kcal)/250 mL. Vanilla flavour. Net price 237-mL bottle = £1.32; 250-mL can = £1.23; 946-mL can = £4.91. Chocolate, coffee, eggnog, and nut flavours. Net price 237-mL can = £1.23. Chicken, mushroom, and asparagus flavours. Net price 250-mL can = £1.23.

Powder, same composition as Ensure liquid when reconstituted. Net price 400 g = £5.18

For short-bowel syndrome, intractable malabsorption, pre-operative preparation of patients who are undernourished, treatment for proven inflammatory bowel disease, treatment following total gastrectomy, dysphagia, bowel fistulas, anorexia nervosa; neoplasia-related (associated) cachexia (anorexia). Neither to be prescribed for any child under one year, unsuitable as a sole source of nutrition for young children up to 5 years of age

Ensure Plus® (Abbott)

Liquid, protein 6.3%, fat 5%, carbohydrate 20%, with vitamins and minerals, lactose- and gluten-free, energy 1570 kJ (375 kcal)/250 mL. Vanilla flavour. Net price 250-mL can = £1.37; 500-mL bottle = £2.74. Caramel, chocolate, strawberry, and vanilla flavours. Net price 200-mL Tetrapak = £1.22. For indications, see Ensure

Farley's Gluten-free biscuits (Farley)

Biscuits. Net price 200 g = £1.03. For indications, see under Glutenex

Flexical® (Bristol-Myers)

Powder, protein 9.9%, carbohydrate 67%, fat 15% with vitamins and minerals. Gluten- and lactose-free. Net price 454 g = £9.36. For short-bowel syndrome, intractable malabsorption, pre-operative preparation of patients who are undernourished, and treatment following total gastrectomy, bowel fistulas; neoplasia-related (associated) cachexia (anorexia). Not to be prescribed for any child under one year, unsuitable as a sole source of nutrition for young children up to 5 years of age

Forceval Protein® (Unigreg)

Powder, calcium caseinate 60%, carbohydrate 30%, with vitamins and minerals, providing not less than 55% protein, not more than 1% of fat, not more than 0.12% of Na^+. Lactose- and gluten-free. Custard, strawberry, orange, and neutral flavours. Net price 300 g = £7.03. For biochemically proven hypoproteinaemia; dysphagia, short-bowel syndrome, intractable malabsorption, pre-operative preparation of patients who are undernourished, treatment for proven inflammatory bowel disease; treatment following total gastrectomy; bowel fistulas

Formula MCT(1) see under MCT(1)

Formula S® (Cow & Gate)

Powder, carbohydrate 7.1%, fat 3.6%, and protein 1.8% with vitamins and minerals when used as a 12.7% solution. Net price 450 g = £2.66. For proven lactose and associated sucrose intolerance in pre-school children, galactokinase deficiency, galactosaemia, and proven whole cow's milk sensitivity

Fortical® (Cow & Gate)

Liquid, glucose polymers providing carbohydrate 61.5 g/100 mL. Low-electrolyte, protein-free. Flavours: apple, apricot, black currant, lemon, orange, and neutral. Net price 200 mL = 86p. For renal failure; liver cirrhosis, or other conditions requiring a high-energy, low-fluid, low-electrolyte diet

[1]**Fortisip®** (Cow & Gate)

Liquid, protein 10 g, carbohydrate 35.8 g, fat 13 g, energy 1260 kJ (300 kcal)/200 mL, with vitamins and minerals. Gluten-free and low lactose. Vanilla, banana, orange, tropical fruits, mushroom, and neutral flavours. Net price 200 mL = 92p

For short-bowel syndrome, intractable malabsorption, pre-operative preparation of patients who are undernourished, treatment for proven inflammatory bowel disease, treatment following total gastrectomy, dysphagia, bowel fistulas, anorexia nervosa; neoplasia-related (associated) cachexia (anorexia). Not to be prescribed for any child under one year, unsuitable as a sole source of nutrition for young children up to 5 years of age

1. Formerly Fortisip® Energy-plus; Fortisip® Standard has been discontinued

Fortison® (Cow & Gate)

Energy-plus, same composition as Fortisip, providing 3150 kJ (750 kcal)/500 mL. Net price 500 mL = £1.98

Soya, liquid, protein 20 g, carbohydrate 60 g, fat 20 g, energy 2100 kJ (500 kcal)/500 mL, with vitamins and minerals. Gluten-free. Net price 500 mL = £1.60. For milk intolerance and lactose intolerance

Standard, liquid, protein 20 g, carbohydrate 60 g, fat 20 g, energy 2100 kJ (500 kcal)/500 mL, with vitamins and minerals. Net price 500 mL = £2.11. For indications, see under Fortisip

None to be prescribed for any child under one year, unsuitable as a sole source of nutrition for young children up to 5 years of age

Fresubin® (Fresenius)

Liquid, protein 7.6 g, carbohydrate 27.6 g, fat 6.8 g, energy 840 kJ (200 kcal)/200 mL with vitamins and minerals. Gluten-free, low lactose and cholesterol. Nut, peach, chocolate, mocha, and vanilla flavours. Net price 200-mL carton = 76p; 500-mL bottle = £1.63. For short-bowel syndrome, intractable malabsorption, pre-operative preparation of patients who are undernourished, treatment for proven inflammatory bowel disease, treatment following total gastrectomy, dysphagia, bowel fistulas, anorexia nervosa; neoplasia-related (associated) cachexia (anorexia). Not to be prescribed for any child under one year, unsuitable as a sole source of nutrition for young children up to 5 years of age

Fresubin Plus F® (Fresenius)

Liquid foods with dietary fibre in 2 formulations. For short-bowel syndrome, intractable malabsorption, pre-operative preparation of patients who are undernourished, treatment for proven inflammatory bowel disease, treatment following total gastrectomy, dysphagia, bowel fistulas, anorexia nervosa; neoplasia-related (associated) cachexia (anorexia). Not to be prescribed for any child under one year, unsuitable as a sole source of nutrition for young children up to 5 years of age

Muesli-flavour, milk protein, cereals, coconut, sunflower oil, vitamins and minerals providing protein 19.0 g, fat 17.0 g, carbohydrate 69.0 g, fibre 5.0 g, energy 2100 kJ (500 kcal)/500 mL. Low sodium, lactose, and cholesterol. Net price 200-mL carton = 89p; 500-mL bottle = £1.94

Vegetable soup-flavour, milk protein, beef fat and protein, sunflower oil, maize starch, vitamins and minerals providing protein 19.0 g, fat 17.0 g, carbohydrate 69.0 g, fibre 3.0 g, energy 2100 kJ (500 kcal)/500 mL. Gluten-free, low sodium, lactose, and cholesterol. Net price 500-mLbottle = £1.85

Fructose (laevulose). For proven glucose/galactose intolerance

Galactomin® (Cow & Gate)

Formula 17 (new formula), powder, protein 14.5 g, fat 25.9 g, carbohydrate 56.9 g, mineral salts 3.4 g/100 g. Used as a 13.1% solution with additional vitamins in place of milk. Net price 400 g = £6.97. For proven lactose intolerance in preschool children, galactosaemia and galactokinase deficiency

Formula 19, powder, modification of Formula 17 with reduced fat (14.4%) and fructose as carbohydrate source. Net price 400 g = £15.52. For glucose plus galactose intolerance

Generaid® (Scientific Hospital Supplies)

Powder, whey protein and additional branched-chain amino acids (protein equivalent 81%). Net price 200 g = £14.69. For patients with chronic liver disease and/or porto-hepatic encephalopathy

GF Dietary® (Nutricia)

Biscuits, gluten-free. Net price 150 g = 76p

Crackers, gluten-free. Net price 200 g = £1.94. For gluten-sensitive enteropathies including steatorrhoea due to gluten sensitivity, coeliac disease, and dermatitis herpetiformis

Glucose (dextrose monohydrate). Net price 100 g = 18p. For glycogen storage disease and sucrose/isomaltose intolerance

Glutafin® (Nutricia)

[2]*Biscuits*, gluten-free. Net price 200 g (38) = £2.65

Pasta, gluten-free; macaroni, pasta spirals, spaghetti shortcut. Net price 250 g = £1.96. For gluten-sensitive enteropathies, including steatorrhoea due to gluten sensitivity, coeliac disease, and dermatitis herpetiformis

2. Formerly Nutricia®

Glutenex® (Cow & Gate)

Biscuits, free from milk products, gluten-free. Net price 250 g (pack of 18) = £1.20. For gluten-sensitive enteropathies including steatorrhoea due to gluten sensitivity, coeliac disease, and dermatitis herpetiformis

Gluten-free biscuits and **crackers**, see under Farley and GF

Hepatic-Aid II® (Kendall)

Powder, amino acids 4.4%, carbohydrate 16.8%, fat 3.6% when reconstituted. Low sodium and electrolytes; mineral and vitamin supplementation is required. Flavours: chocolate, chocolate mint, custard, and eggnog. Net price per packet = £7.95. For patients with chronic liver disease and/or porto-hepatic encephalopathy

Hycal® (SmithKline Beecham Brands)

Liquid, protein-free, low-electrolyte, glucose syrup solids 49.5%. Flavours, blackcurrant, lemon, orange, and raspberry. Net price 171 mL = 64p. For renal failure; liver cirrhosis or other conditions requiring a high-energy, low-fluid, low-electrolyte diet

Isocal® (Bristol-Myers)
Liquid, protein 3.2%, carbohydrate 12.6%, fat 4.2% with vitamins and minerals. Gluten- and lactose-free. Vanilla flavour. Net price 250 mL =60p. For short-bowel syndrome, intractable malabsorption, pre-operative preparation of patients who are undernourished, treatment for proven inflammatory bowel disease, treatment following total gastrectomy, dysphagia, bowel fistulas, anorexia nervosa; neoplasia-related (associated) cachexia (anorexia). Not to be prescribed for any child under one year, unsuitable as a sole source of nutrition for young children up to 5 years of age

Isomil® (Abbott)
Powder, protein 1.8%, carbohydrate 6.9%, fat 4.69% with vitamins and minerals when reconstituted. Lactose-free. Net price 400 g = £2.67. For proven lactose intolerance in preschool children, galactokinase deficiency, galactosaemia, and proven whole cow's milk sensitivity

Juvela® (Nutricia)
Gluten-free. Bread/cake mix; net price 500 g = £3.88. Bread (sliced and unsliced); 400-g loaf = £1.85. High-fibre bread (sliced and unsliced); 400-g loaf = £1.85. Corn mix; 500 g = £3.88. Fibre mix; 500 g = £3.88. For gluten-sensitive enteropathies including steatorrhoea due to gluten sensitivity, coeliac disease, and dermatitis herpetiformis
Low Protein. Bread/cake mix; net price 500 g = £3.88. Bread (sliced and unsliced); 400-g loaf = £1.85. Biscuits, chocolate chip, orange, and cinnamon flavour; 150 g = £3.88. For phenylketonuria and similar amino-acid abnormalities; renal failure; liver failure and liver cirrhosis; gluten-sensitive enteropathies, see above

Liga® (Cow & Gate)
Rusks, egg- and gluten-free. Net price 24 = 70p. For gluten-sensitive enteropathies including steatorrhoea due to gluten sensitivity, coeliac disease, and dermatitis herpetiformis

Liquigen® (Scientific Hospital Supplies)
Emulsion, medium chain triglycerides 52%. Net price 1 litre = £13.46; 2 litres = £24.21. For steatorrhoea associated with cystic fibrosis of the pancreas; intestinal lymphangiectasia, surgery of the intestine; chronic liver disease and liver cirrhosis; other proven malabsorption syndromes; ketogenic diet in the management of epilepsy; type I hyperlipoproteinaemia

Liquisorb® (Merck)
Liquid, protein 20 g, carbohydrate 59 g, fat 20 g, energy 2095 kJ (500 kcal)/500 mL with vitamins and minerals. Gluten-free, low lactose. Banana, vanilla, chocolate, strawberry, and neutral flavours. Net price 500-mL bottle = £1.90. Strawberry and vanilla flavours only. Net price 200-mL Tetrapak = 78p. For short-bowel syndrome, intractable malabsorption, pre-operative preparation of patients who are undernourished, treatment for proven inflammatory bowel disease, treatment following total gastrectomy, dysphagia, bowel fistulas, anorexia nervosa; neoplasia-related (associated) cachexia (anorexia). Not to be prescribed for any child under one year, unsuitable as a sole source of nutrition for young children up to 5 years of age

Liquisorbon MCT® (Merck)
Liquid, protein 25 g, carbohydrate 61.5 g, fat 16.5 g, energy 2095 kJ (500 kcal)/500 mL with vitamins and minerals. Gluten- and fructose-free, low lactose. Chocolate, strawberry, vanilla, and neutral flavours. Net price 500 mL = £2.65. For indications see Liquisorb. Not to be prescribed for any child under one year, unsuitable as a sole source of nutrition for young children up to 5 years of age

Locasol New Formula® (Cow & Gate)
Powder, protein 14.6 g, carbohydrate 56.5 g, fat 26.1 g, mineral salts 1.9 g, not more than 55 mg of Ca^{2+}/100 g and vitamins. Used as a 13.1% solution in place of milk. Net price 400 g = £9.16. For calcium intolerance

Lofenalac® (Bristol-Myers)
Powder, protein 15%, carbohydrate 60%, fat 18%, phenylalanine not more than 0.1% with vitamins and minerals. Gluten-, sucrose-, and lactose-free. Net price 450 g = £8.00. For phenylketonuria

Lorenzo's Oil (Scientific Hospital Supplies)
Liquid, glycerol trioleate oil 4 parts, glycerol trierucate oil 1 part. Net price 710 mL = £53.25. For biochemically proven and/or clinically manifest adrenoleukodystrophy

Low Protein Drink[1] (Milupa)
Powder, protein 0.4%, carbohydrate 5.1%, fat 2% when reconstituted. Net price 400 g = £4.80. For inherited disorders of amino acid metabolism in childhood
1. Termed Milupa lpd by manufacturer

Maxamaid XP® (Scientific Hospital Supplies)
Powder, essential and non-essential amino acids 30% except phenylalanine, with carbohydrates, vitamins, minerals, and trace elements. Orange-flavoured or unflavoured. Net price 575 g = £32.35.
Bar. Net price 25-g bar = 76p. For phenylketonuria. Not to be prescribed for children under 2 years of age

Maxamum XP® (Scientific Hospital Supplies)
Powder, essential and non-essential amino acids 47% except phenylalanine, with carbohydrates, vitamins, minerals, and trace elements. Orange-flavoured or unflavoured. Net price 575 g = £51.83. For phenylketonuria. Not to be prescribed for children under 8 years

Maxijul® (Scientific Hospital Supplies)
Liquid, carbohydrate 50%, with potassium 0.004%, sodium 0.023%. Gluten-, lactose-, and fructose-free. Flavours: black currant, lemon and lime, orange, and natural. Net price 200 mL = 58p
Super Soluble Powder, glucose polymer, potassium 0.004%, sodium 0.046%. Gluten-, lactose-, and fructose-free. Net price 100 g = 55p, 2.5 kg = £9.98. For renal failure; liver cirrhosis; disaccharide intolerance (without isomaltose intolerance); disorders of amino acid metabolism (and other similar disorders) and/or whole protein intolerance; malabsorption states and other conditions, including proven hypoglycaemia, requiring a high-energy, low-fluid intake

Maxijul LE® (Scientific Hospital Supplies)
Powder, modification of Maxijul with lower concentrations of sodium and potassium. Net price 100 g = 84p, 2.5 kg = £13.98. For indications, see under Maxijul where sodium and/or potassium restriction is also essential

Maxipro HBV® Super Soluble[2] (Scientific Hospital Supplies)
Powder, whey protein and additional amino acids (protein equivalent 80%). Net price 200 g = £4.58; 1 kg = £18.30. For biochemically proven hypoproteinaemia
2. Termed 'instant' in ACBS list

MCT Oil
Triglycerides from medium chain fatty acids. For steatorrhoea associated with cystic fibrosis of the pancreas; intestinal lymphangiectasia; surgery of the intestine; chronic liver disease and liver cirrhosis; other proven malabsorption syndromes; in a ketogenic diet in the management of epilepsy; in type I hyperlipoproteinaemia
Available from Bristol-Myers (net price 950 mL = £7.80); Cow & Gate (net price 1 litre = £12.46); Scientific Hospital Supplies (net price 250 mL = £3.21)

MCT (1)® (Cow & Gate)
Powder, protein 25.6%, carbohydrate 40.6%, medium chain triglycerides 28%, when used as a 12.5% solution. Low in lactose and sucrose-free. Net price 400 g = £5.95. For steatorrhoea associated with cystic fibrosis of the pancreas; intestinal lymphangiectasia; chronic liver disease; surgery of the intestine in infants

Metabolic Mineral Mixture® (Scientific Hospital Supplies)
Powder, essential mineral salts. Net price 100 g = £5.11. For mineral supplementation in synthetic diets

Milupa® Low Protein Drink see under **Low Protein Drink**

Milupa® PKU2 and **PKU3** see under **PKU2** and **PKU3**

Minafen® (Cow & Gate)
Powder, equivalent of 12.5% protein, carbohydrate 48%, fat 31%, not more than 0.02% of phenylalanine. For use as 13.1% solution with additional vitamins. Net price 400 g = £11.65. For phenylketonuria

MSUD Aid® (Scientific Hospital Supplies)
Powder, containing full range of amino acids except isoleucine, leucine, and valine, with vitamins, minerals, and trace elements. Net price 200 g = £28.23. For maple syrup urine disease

Nestargel® (Nestlé)
Powder, carob seed flour 96.5%, calcium lactate 3.5%. Net price 125 g = £3.46. For thickening feeds in the treatment of vomiting

Nutramigen® (Bristol-Myers)
Powder, protein 13%, carbohydrate 62%, fat 18% with vitamins and minerals. Gluten-, sucrose-, and lactose-free. Net price 425 g = £7.00. For infants over 3 months and children with galactokinase deficiency; galactosaemia; proven lactose intolerance and/or sucrose intolerance in preschool children; proven sensitivity to whole protein

Nutranel® now called **Pepti-2000 LF®**

Nutricia® now called **Glutafin®**

Osmolite® (Abbott)
Liquid, protein 10.5 g, carbohydrate 33.4 g, fat 8.7 g, energy 1050 kJ (250 kcal)/250 mL with vitamins and minerals. Gluten- and lactose-free. Net price 250-mL can = £1.23; 500-mL bottle = £2.45. For short-bowel syndrome, intractable malabsorption, pre-operative preparation of patients who are undernourished, treatment for proven inflammatory bowel disease, treatment following total gastrectomy, dysphagia, bowel fistulas, anorexia nervosa; neoplasia-related (associated) cachexia (anorexia). Not to be prescribed for any child under one year, unsuitable as a sole source of nutrition for young children up to 5 years of age

OsterSoy® (Farley)
Powder, providing protein 2%, carbohydrate 7%, fat 3.8% with vitamins and minerals when reconstituted. Gluten-, sucrose-, and lactose-free. Net price 450 g = £2.62. For proven lactose and sucrose intolerance in preschool children, galactokinase deficiency, galactosaemia, and proven whole cow's milk protein sensitivity

Paediasure® (Abbott)
Liquid, protein 3%, fat 5%, carbohydrate 11%, with minerals and vitamins, gluten-free, energy 995 kJ (238 kcal)/237 mL. Vanilla flavour. Net price 237-mL can = £1.77. For short-bowel syndrome, intractable malabsorption, pre-operative preparation of patients who are undernourished, treatment for proven inflammatory bowl disease, dysphagia, bowel fistulas, cystic fibrosis; neoplasia related (associated) cachexia (anorexia). Not to be prescribed for any child under one year

Peptamen® (Clintec Nutrition)
Liquid, protein 4%, carbohydrate 12.7%, fat 3.9%, energy 420 kJ (100 kcal)/100 mL, with vitamins and minerals. Lactose- and gluten-free. Net price 500 mL = £4.50. For short bowel syndrome, intractable malabsorption, pre-operative preparation of patients who are undernourished, treatment for proven inflammatory bowel disease, treatment following total gastrectomy, dysphagia, bowel fistulas, anorexia nervosa; neoplasia-related (associated) cachexia (anorexia). Not to be prescribed for any child under one year, unsuitable as a sole source of nutrition for young children up to 5 years of age

Pepti-2000 LF® (Cow & Gate)
Liquid, protein 20 g, fat 5 g, carbohydrate 94 g, energy 2100 kJ (500 kcal)/500 mL with vitamins and minerals. Gluten-free. Net price 500 mL = £2.07.
Powder, same composition as Pepti-2000 LF liquid when reconstituted. Net price 126-g sachet = £3.12.
For intractable malabsorption; bowel fistulas; following total gastrectomy; neoplasia-related (associated) cachexia (anorexia). Not to be prescribed for any child under one year, unsuitable as a sole source of nutrition for young children up to 5 years of age

Pepti-Junior® (Cow & Gate)
Powder, protein 15.3 g, fat 28.3 g, carbohydrate 55.1 g, energy 2140 kJ (507 kcal)/100 g with vitamins and minerals. Used as a 13.1% solution in place of milk. Net price 400 g = £6.66. For proven lactose and associated sucrose intolerance in association with proven whole protein intolerance, steatorrhea associated with cystic fibrosis, and other proven malabsorption syndromes

Peptisorb® (Merck)
Liquid, amino acids and peptides 3.75%, carbohydrate 18.75%, fat 1.11%, with vitamins and minerals, low lactose, and fructose- and gluten-free, energy 2100 kJ (500 kcal)/500 mL. Net price 500 mL = £4.60. For intractable malabsorption; bowel fistulas; treatment following total gastrectomy; neoplasia-related (associated) cachexia (anorexia)
For adults only

Peptisorbon® (Merck)
Powder, amino acids and peptides 18%, carbohydrate 70%, fat 5.3%, with vitamins and minerals, low lactose, and fructose- and gluten-free, energy 1393 kJ (333 kcal)/sachet. Net price 83.3-g sachet = £2.07. For intractable malabsorption; bowel fistulas; treatment following total gastrectomy; neoplasia-related (associated) cachexia (anorexia)
For adults only

PK Aid 3® (Scientific Hospital Supplies)
Powder, containing essential and non-essential amino acids except phenylalanine. Net price 500 g = £76.86. For phenylketonuria

PKU 2® (Milupa)
Granules, containing essential and non-essential amino acids except phenylalanine; with vitamins, minerals, trace elements, 7.1% sucrose. Flavour: vanilla. Net price 500 g = £36.00. For phenylketonuria

PKU 3® (Milupa)
Granules, containing essential and non-essential amino acids except phenylalanine, vitamins, minerals, and trace elements, with 3.4% sucrose. Flavour vanilla. Net price 500 g = £36.00. For phenylketonuria, not recommended for child under 8 years

P.K.U. Drink® (Nutricia)
Liquid, protein 1 g (phenylalanine 30 mg), lactose 9.4 g, fat 4 g, energy 300kJ/200 mL. Net price 200 mL = 38p. For phenylketonuria

Polial® (Ultrapharm)
Biscuits. Free from egg, milk protein, wheat starch, gluten, and lactose. Net price 200-g pack = £2.85. For gluten-sensitive enteropathies including steatorrhea due to gluten sensitivity, coeliac disease, and dermatitis herpetiformis

Polycal® (Cow & Gate)
Powder, glucose, maltose, and polysaccharides, providing 1610kJ (380kcal)/100 g. Net price 400 g = £2.18; 900 g = £3.75. For renal failure; liver cirrhosis; disaccharide intolerance (without isomaltose intolerance); disorders of amino acid metabolism (and other similar disorders) and/or whole protein intolerance; malabsorption states and other conditions, including proven hypoglycaemia, requiring a high-energy, low-fluid intake, whether or not sodium and/or potassium restriction is essential

Polycose® (Abbott)
Powder, glucose polymers, providing carbohydrate 94 g, energy 1600 kJ (380 kcal)/100 g. Net price 350-g can = £2.60. For renal failure; liver cirrhosis; disaccharide intolerance (without isomaltose intolerance); disorders of amino acid metabolism (and other similar disorders) and/or whole protein intolerance; malabsorption states and other conditions, including proven hypoglycaemia, requiring a high-energy, low-fluid intake, whether or not sodium and/or potassium restriction is essential

Portagen® (Bristol-Myers)
Powder, protein 16.5%, carbohydrate 54%, fat 22% with vitamins and minerals. Gluten- and lactose-free. Net

price 454 g = £6.23. For lactose intolerance without sucrose intolerance but requiring medium chain triglycerides; malabsorption associated with cystic fibrosis of the pancreas; intestinal lymphangiectasia; surgery of the intestine; chronic liver disease and liver cirrhosis; other proven malabsorption syndromes; neoplasia-related (associated) cachexia (anorexia)

Pregestimil® (Bristol-Myers)

Powder, protein 12.8%, carbohydrate 61.6%, fat 18.3% with vitamins and minerals. Gluten-, sucrose-, and lactose-free. Net price 454 g = £8.01. For sucrose and/or lactose intolerance in association with whole protein intolerance, or where amino acids and peptides are indicated in conjunction with medium chain triglycerides. Also for proven malabsorption syndromes in which a reduced fat diet is indicated such as steatorrhoea associated with cystic fibrosis and surgery of the intestine; galactosaemia and galactokinase deficiency; neoplasia-related (associated) cachexia (anorexia)

Prejomin® (Milupa)

Granules, protein 13.3 g, carbohydrate 57 g, fat 24.2 g, energy 2090 kJ (499 kcal)/100 g, with vitamins and minerals. Gluten-free. For preparation with water before use. Net price 400 g = £7.00. For proven lactose and sucrose intolerance in pre-school children, fructose intolerance, galactosaemia, galactokinase deficiency, and proven sensitivity to whole protein

ProMod® (Abbott)

Powder, protein 75.8%, carbohydrate 10.2%, fat 9.1%. Gluten-free. Net price 275-g can = £6.88. For biochemically proven hypoproteinaemia

Prosobee® (Bristol-Myers)

Liquid concentrate, protein 4.1%, carbohydrate 13.7%, fat 7.2% with vitamins and minerals. Gluten-, sucrose-, and lactose-free. Net price 385 mL = £1.39

Powder, protein 15.6%, carbohydrate 51.4%, fat 27.9% with vitamins and minerals. Gluten-, sucrose-, and lactose-free. Net price 400 g = £3.56. For proven lactose and associated sucrose intolerance in pre-school children, galactokinase deficiency, galactosaemia, and proven whole cow's milk sensitivity

Protifar® (Cow & Gate)

Powder, protein 88.5%. Low lactose, gluten- and sucrose-free. Net price 225 g = £4.60. For biochemically proven hypoproteinaemia

Reabilan® (Roussel)

Liquid, protein 11.8 g, carbohydrate 49.3 g, fat 14.6 g, energy 1575 kJ (375 kcal)/375 mL with vitamins and minerals. Gluten- and lactose-free. Net price 375 mL = £4.58. For short bowel syndrome; intractable malabsorption; pre-operative preparation of patients who are undernourished; treatment for those with inflammatory bowel disease; treatment following total gastrectomy; dysphagia; bowel fistulas; neoplasia-related (associated) cachexia (anorexia). Not to be prescribed for any child under 1 year, unsuitable as a sole source of nutrition for young children up to 5 years of age

Rectified Spirit. Where the therapeutic qualities of alcohol are required rectified spirit (suitably flavoured and diluted) should be prescribed

Rite-Diet® (Nutricia)

Gluten-free. Sweet biscuits. Net price 150 g = £1.18. High-fibre crackers. 150 g = £1.62. Digestive biscuits. 150 g = £1.18. Savoury biscuits. 125 g = £1.18. Tea biscuits. 125 g = £1.18. Flour mix. 500 g = £2.30. Bread mix. 500 g (brown) = £2.30; white, 500 g = £2.30. Bread (white). 400 g = £1.85. High-fibre bread (with soya bran). 400 g = £1.85. For gluten-sensitive enteropathies including steatorrhoea due to gluten sensitivity, coeliac disease, and dermatitis herpetiformis

Low protein/gluten-free. Macaroni. Net price 250 g = £1.96. Spaghetti, shortcut. 250 g = £1.96. Rings. 250 g = £1.96. Baking mix. 500 g = £2.30. Flour mix. 400 g = £2.30p. Bread; 227 g = £1.25. Bread with soya bran; 280 g = £1.25. Bread (with or without salt). 227 g = £1.25. White bread (with added fibre). 400 g = £1.85. Crackers. 150 g = £1.62. Sweet biscuits. 150 g = £1.18. Vanilla cream wafers. 100 g = £1.16. Chocolate-flavoured cream wafers, 100 g = £1.16. Orange-flavoured cream wafers 100 g = £1.16. Cream-filled biscuits (chocolate flavour). 125 g = £1.18. For phenylketonuria and similar amino-acid abnormalities; renal failure; liver failure and liver cirrhosis; see also gluten-free foods above

Low sodium. Bread containing protein 8.5%, carbohydrate 53.8%, fat 5.5%, Na^+ 0.01%, K^+ 0.055%. Net price 227 g = £1·11. For conditions in which a low-sodium diet is indicated

Sunflower oil. Net price 100 mL = 40p. For familial hypercholesterolaemia

Super Soluble Maxijul®, see under Maxijul®

Triosorbon® (Merck)

Powder, protein 19%, carbohydrate 56%, fat 19%, with vitamins and minerals. Gluten-free. Net price 85-g sachet = £1.66. For short-bowel syndrome, intractable malabsorption, pre-operative preparation of patients who are undernourished, treatment for proven inflammatory bowel disease, treatment following total gastrectomy, dysphagia, bowel fistulas, anorexia nervosa; neoplasia-related (associated) cachexia (anorexia). Not to be prescribed for any child under one year, unsuitable as a sole source of nutrition for young children up to 5 years of age

Tritamyl® (Procea)

Flour, self-raising (starch-based), gluten- and lactose-free. Net price 2 kg = £5.86. For gluten-sensitive enteropathies including steatorrhoea due to gluten sensitivity, coeliac disease, and dermatitis herpetiformis

Tritamyl PK® (Procea)

Flour, self-raising (starch-based), gluten-, lactose-, and protein-free. Net price 2 kg = £5.86. For phenylketonuria and similar amino acid abnormalities; renal failure; liver failure and liver cirrhosis; gluten-sensitive enteropathies as above

Trufree® (Cantassium)

Gluten-free, wheat-free flours. For gluten-sensitive enteropathies including steatorrhoea due to gluten-sensitivity, coeliac disease, and dermatitis herpetiformis

No. 1 (formerly bread mix 420 g). Net price 1 kg = £3.19

No. 2 with rice bran (formerly bread mix with rice bran 410 g). Net price 1 kg = £4.01

No. 3 for Cantabread® (formerly Cantabread mix). Net price 1 kg = £4.09

No. 4 white. Net price 1 kg = £3.19

No. 5 brown. Net price 1 kg = £3.19

No. 6 plain (formerly Trufree plain flour). Net price 1 kg = £2.96

No. 7 self-raising (formerly Trufree self-raising flour). Net price 1 kg = £3.15

Wysoy® (Wyeth)

Powder, carbohydrate 6.9%, fat 3.6%, and protein 2.1% with vitamins and minerals when reconstituted. Net price 430 g = £2.72; 860 g = £5.26. For proven lactose intolerance in pre-school children, galactokinase deficiency, galactosaemia and proven whole cows milk sensitivity

CONDITIONS FOR WHICH FOODS MAY BE PRESCRIBED ON FP10

Note. This is a list of clinical conditions for which the ACBS has approved food products. It is essential to check the list of products (above) for availability.

Adrenoleukodystrophy: Lorenzo's Oil.

Amino acid metabolic disorders and similar protein disorders: low protein drink (Milupa); see also phenylketonuria; histidinaemia; homocystinuria; maple syrup urine disease; synthetic diets; low-protein products.

Anorexia nervosa: Clinifeed; Enrich; Ensure; Ensure Plus; Ensure Powder; Flexical; Fortisip; Fortison Energy-Plus and Standard; Fresubin Liquid, Sip Feeds and Plus F; Isocal; Liquisorb; Liquisorb (high fibre)

feed and drink; Liquisorbon MCT; Osmolite; Peptamen; Triosorbon.

Bowel fistulas: Clinifeed; Elemental 028; Enrich; Ensure; Ensure Plus; Ensure Powder; Flexical; Forceval Protein; Fortisip; Fortison Energy-Plus and Standard; Fresubin Liquid, Sip Feeds and Plus F; Isocal; Liquisorb; Liquisorb (high fibre) feed and drink; Liquisorbon MCT; Maxipro HBV; Osmolite; Paediasure; Peptamen; Pepti-2000 LF; Peptisorb; Peptisorbon; Reabilan; Triosorbon.

Calcium intolerance: Locasol New Formula.

Carbohydrate malabsorption: Calogen. See also synthetic diets; malabsorption states.

Disaccharide intolerance (without isomaltose intolerance): Caloreen; Duocal, Super Soluble and Duocal Liquid; Maxijul LE, Liquid, Super Soluble; Polycal; Polycose powder. See also lactose intolerance; lactose with sucrose intolerance.

Glucose and galactose intolerance: Comminuted chicken meat (Cow & Gate); Fructose; Galactomin Formula 19 (fructose formula).

Isomaltose intolerance: Glucose (dextrose).

Lactose intolerance[1]: AL110; Aminex; Comminuted chicken meat (Cow & Gate); Formula S (Cow & Gate); Fortison Soya; Galactomin Formula 17 (new formula); Isomil powder; Nutramigen; Ostersoy; Portagen; Pregestimil; Prejomin; Prosobee; Prosparol; Wysoy.

Lactose with sucrose intolerance[1]: Aminex; Comminuted Chicken Meat (Cow & Gate); Formula S (Cow & Gate); Galactomin Formula 17 (new formula); Nutramigen; Ostersoy; Pepti-Junior; Pregestimil; Prejomin; Prosobee.

Sucrose intolerance[1]: Glucose (dextrose) and see also synthetic diets; malabsorption states; lactose with sucrose intolerance.

Cirrhosis of the liver and chronic liver disease: see liver disease.

Coeliac disease: see gluten-sensitive enteropathies.

Cystic fibrosis: see malabsorption states.

Disaccharide intolerance: see carbohydrate malabsorption.

Dysphagia (associated with: intrinsic disease of the oesophagus, e.g. oesophagitis; neuromuscular disorders, e.g. multiple sclerosis and motor neurone disease; major surgery and/or radiotherapy for cancer of the upper digestive tract; protracted severe inflammatory disease of the upper digestive tract, e.g. Stevens-Johnson syndrome and epidermolysis bullosa): Clinifeed; Elemental 028; Enrich; Ensure; Ensure Plus; Ensure Powder; Forceval Protein; Fortisip; Fortison Energy-Plus and Standard; Fresubin Liquid, Sip Feeds and Plus F; Isocal; Liquisorb; Liquisorb (high fibre) feed and drink; Liquisorbon MCT; Maxipro HBV; Osmolite; Paediasure Peptamen; Reabilan; Triosorbon.

Epilepsy (ketogenic diet in): Alembicol D; Calogen; Liquigen; Medium-Chain Triglyceride Oil (MCT).

Galactokinase deficiency and galactosaemia: AL 110; Alfare; Formula S (Cow & Gate); Galactomin Formula 17 (new formula); Isomil powder; Nutramigen; Ostersoy; Pregestimil; Prejomin; Prosobee Liquid and Powder; Wysoy.

Gastrectomy (total): Clinifeed; Elemental 028; Enrich; Ensure; Ensure Plus; Ensure Powder; Flexical; Forceval protein; Fortisip; Fortison Energy-Plus and Standard; Fresubin Liquid, Sip Feeds and Plus F; Isocal; Liquisorb; Liquisorbon MCT; Maxipro HBV; Osmolite; Peptamen; Pepti-2000 LF; Peptisorb; Peptisorbon; Reabilan; Triosorbon.

---

1. Defined as a condition of intolerance to an intake of the relevant disaccharide confirmed by demonstrated clinical benefit of effectiveness of disaccharide free diet, and presence of reducing substances or excessive acid in stools, low concentration of corresponding disaccharidase enzyme on intestinal biopsy, or breath tests, or lactose tolerance tests.

Glucose/galactose intolerance: see carbohydrate malabsorption.

Gluten-sensitive enteropathies: Aglutella gluten-free low-protein macaroni, pasta spirals, semolina, spaghetti, spaghetti rings, tagliatelle; Aproten products (anellini, biscuits, breadmix, cake mix, crispbread, ditalini, flour, rigatini, tagliatelle); Bi-Aglut biscuits, flour, and gluten-free toast; Ener-G brown rice bread. gluten-free tapioca bread; Gluten-free biscuits (Farley); Gluten-free biscuits and crackers (Nutricia); Glutenex (Cow & Gate); Juvela gluten-free corn mix, gluten-free loaf and high-fibre loaf (sliced and unsliced), gluten-free mix and fibre mix; Juvela low-protein loaf (sliced and unsliced) and low-protein mix; Liga gluten-free rusks (Cow & Gate); Nutricia gluten-free tea biscuits, Polial gluten-free biscuits; Rite-Diet gluten-free high-fibre bread (with added soya-bran); Rite-Diet gluten-free white bread 400 g; Rite-Diet gluten-free white bread mix; Rite-Diet gluten-free brown bread mix; Rite-Diet gluten-free bread with soya bran (dispensed in tin); Rite-Diet gluten-free high-fibre crackers; Rite-Diet low-protein flour mix; Rite-Diet gluten-free flour mix; Rite-Diet gluten-free low-protein bread (dispensed in tin, with or without salt); Rite-Diet low-protein white bread (with added fibre); Rite-Diet gluten-free digestive biscuits, sweet (without chocolate or sultanas) biscuits, savoury biscuits, tea biscuits, and gluten-free crackers; Rite-Diet low-protein spaghetti (short cut), spaghetti rings, and macaroni; Tritamyl gluten-free flour; Tritamyl PK flour; Trufree special dietary flours No. 1, No. 2 with rice bran, No. 3 for Cantabread, No. 4 white, No. 5 brown, No. 6 plain, No. 7 self-raising.

Glycogen storage disease: Caloreen; Corn Flour or Corn Starch; Glucose (dextrose); Maxijul LE, Liquid, and Super Soluble; Polycal; Polycose.

Histidinaemia: HF(2), and see also low-protein products; synthetic diets.

Homocystinuria: Albumaid RVHB X Methionine; Albumaid RVHB Complete X Methionine, Analog RVHB, and see also low-protein products; synthetic diets.

Hypercholesterolaemia (familial): Corn oil; Sunflower oil.

Hyperlipoproteinaemia type 1: Liquigen; Medium Chain Triglyceride Oil.

Hypermethioninaemia: Analog RVHB.

Hypoglycaemia: Caloreen; Corn Flour or Corn Starch; Maxijul LE, Liquid, and Super Soluble; Polycal; Polycose, and see also glycogen storage disease.

Hypoproteinaemia: Casilan; Dialamine; Forceval Protein; Maxipro HBV Super Soluble; ProMod; Protifar.

Intestinal lymphangiectasia: see malabsorption states.

Intestinal surgery: see malabsorption states.

Isomaltose intolerance: see carbohydrate malabsorption.

Lactose intolerance: see carbohydrate malabsorption.

Liver disease (i.e. chronic liver disease, cirrhosis): Aglutella Azeta cream-filled wafers; Aglutella gluten-free low-protein macaroni, pasta spirals, semolina, spaghetti, spaghetti rings, tagliatelle; Alembicol D; Aminex; Aproten products (anellini, biscuits, bread mix, cake mix, crispbread, ditalini, flour, rigatini, tagliatelle); Caloreen; dp Low-Protein butterscotch-flavoured or chocolate-flavoured chip cookies; Duocal, Super Soluble, and Duocal Liquid; Fortical; Generaid; Hepatic Aid; Hycal; Juvela gluten-free low-protein (chocolate chip, orange, and cinnamon flavour) cookies; Juvela low-protein loaf (sliced and unsliced) and low-protein flour mix; Liquigen; Maxijul LE, Liquid, and Super Soluble; MCT (1) Powder; Medium Chain Triglyceride Oil; Polycal; Polycose; Portagen; Rite-Diet gluten-free low-protein bread (dispensed in tin with or without salt); Rite-Diet low-protein white bread (with added fibre); Rite-Diet gluten-free low-protein crackers; Rite-Diet low-protein baking mix; Rite-Diet low-protein flour mix; Rite-Diet low-protein cream-filled biscuits (chocolate flavour) and sweet biscuits; Rite-Diet low-protein macaroni, spaghetti (short cut), and spaghetti rings; Rite-Diet low-protein chocolate, orange, and vanilla cream wafers; Tritamyl PK flour.

Low-protein products: Aglutella Azeta cream-filled wafers*; Aglutella gluten-free low protein (macaroni, pasta spirals, semolina, spaghetti, spaghetti-rings, tagliatelle); Aminex*; Aproten products (anellini, biscuits, bread mix, cake mix, crispbread, ditalini, flour, rigatini, tagliatelle); dp Low-Protein butterscotch-flavoured or chocolate-flavoured chip cookies*; Juvela gluten-free low-protein (chocolate chip, orange, and cinnamon flavour) cookies*; Juvela low-protein loaf (sliced and unsliced); Juvela low-protein mix; Rite-Diet gluten-free low-protein bread (dispensed in tin, with or without salt); Rite-Diet low-protein white bread (with added fibre); Rite-Diet low-protein gluten-free crackers; Rite-Diet low-protein flour mix; Rite-Diet low-protein cream-filled biscuits (chocolate flavour)*; Rite-Diet low-protein sweet biscuits; Rite-Diet low-protein macaroni, spaghetti (short cut), and spaghetti rings; Rite-Diet low-protein chocolate, orange, and vanilla cream wafers*; Tritamyl PK flour.

*Not prescribable on ACBS for coeliac disease, dermatitis herpetiformis, steatorrhoea due to gluten sensitivity

Malabsorption states: (see also gluten-sensitive enteropathies; liver disease; carbohydrate malabsorption; intestinal lymphangiectasia; milk intolerance and synthetic diets).

(a) Protein sources: Albumaid Complete; Comminuted Chicken Meat (Cow & Gate); Duocal, Super Soluble, and Duocal Liquid; Forceval Protein; Maxipro HBV.

(b) Fat: Alembicol D; Calogen; Liquigen; Medium Chain Triglyceride Oil.

(c) Carbohydrate: Caloreen; Fortical; Hycal; Maxijul LE, Liquid, and Super Soluble; Polycal; Polycose.

(d) Complete Feeds: Clinifeed and Clinifeed Favour; Elemental 028; Enrich; Ensure; Ensure Plus; Ensure Powder; Flexical; Fortisip; Fortison Energy-Plus and Standard; Fresubin Liquid, Sip Feeds, and Plus F; Isocal; Liquisorb; Liquisorb (high fibre) feed and drink; Liquisorbon MCT; MCT (1) Powder (with appropriate vitamin and mineral supplements); Osmolite; Paediasure; Peptamen; Pepti-2000 LF; Pepti-Junior; Peptisorb; Peptisorbon; Portagen; Pregestimil; Reabilan; Triosorbon.

(e) Minerals: Aminogran Mineral Mixture; Metabolic Mineral Mixture.

(f) Vitamins: As appropriate, and see synthetic diets.

Maple syrup urine disease: Analog MSUD; MSUD Aid, and see also low-protein products; synthetic diets.

Methylmalonic or propionic acidaemia: Analog XMet, Thre, Val, Isoleu.

Milk protein sensitivity: Comminuted Chicken Meat (Cow & Gate); Formula S (Cow & Gate); Fortison Soya; Isomil powder; Nutramigen; Ostersoy; Pregestimil; Prosobee Liquid and powder; Wysoy, and see also synthetic diets.

Neoplasia-related (associated) cachexia (anorexia): Clinifeed and Clinifeed Favour; Elemental 028; Enrich; Ensure, Ensure Plus, Ensure Powder; Flexical; Fortisip; Fortison Energy-Plus and Standard; Fresubin Liquid, Sip Feeds, and Plus F; Isocal; Liquisorb; Liquisorb (high fibre); Liquisorbon MCT; Osmolite; Paediasure; Peptamen; Pepti-2000 LF; Peptisorb; Peptisorbon; Portagen; Pregestimil; Reabilan; Triosorbon

Nutritional support for adults (for precise conditions for which these products have ACBS approval, see products above):

A. (a) Nutritionally complete feeds (chemically defined diets, whole protein based), for oral, sip or tube feeding.

(i) Gluten-Free: Clinifeed and Clinifeed Favour; Fortisip; Fortison Energy-Plus and Standard; Fresubin Liquid, Sip Feeds, and Plus F (vegetable soup flavour only); Liquisorb; Liquisorb (high fibre) feed and drink; Liquisorbon MCT; Peptamen; Peptisorb; Peptisorbon; Triosorbon.

(ii) Lactose- and Gluten-Free: Enrich; Ensure, Ensure Plus, Ensure Powder; Isocal; MCT (1) Powder (with appropriate vitamin and mineral supplements); Osmolite; Portagen; Reabilan.

(b) Elemental and Low-lactose: Flexical; Pepti-2000 LF.

B. Nutritional source supplements; see synthetic diets; malabsorption states.

(a) Carbohydrates; lactose-free and gluten-free; Caloreen*; Super-Soluble Duocal, and Duocal Liquid*; Fortical*; Hycal*; Maxijul LE*, Liquid, and Super Soluble; Polycal; Polycose.

*Have low electrolyte content.

(b) Fat: Alembicol D; Calogen; MCT Oil; Liquigen.

C. Nitrogen sources: Albumaid Complete (hydrolysed protein based); Casilan (whole protein based, low-sodium); Forceval Protein (whole protein based, low-sodium); Maxipro HBV (whole protein based, low-sodium); Pro-Mod (whey protein based, low-sodium).

D. Minerals: Aminogran Mineral Mixture; Metabolic Mineral Mixture.

Phenylketonuria: Aglutella Azeta cream-filled wafers; Aglutella gluten-free low-protein macaroni, pasta spirals, semolina, spaghetti, spaghetti rings, tagliatelle; Albumaid XP and XP Concentrate; Aminex; Aminogran Food Supplement and Mineral Mixture; Analog XP; Aproten products (annellini, biscuits, bread mix, cake mix, crispbread, ditalini, flour, rigatini, tagliatelle); Calogen; Caloreen; dp Low-Protein butterscotch-flavoured or chocolate-flavoured chip cookies; Juvela low-protein loaf (sliced and unsliced); Juvela gluten-free low-protein (chocolate chip, orange, and cinnamon flavour) cookies; Juvela low-protein mix; Lofenalac; Maxamaid XP and orange; Maxamaid XP bar; Metabolic Mineral Mixture; Milupa PKU3; Minafen; PK Aid 3; PKU Drink; PKU 2; Polycal; Polycose powder; Rite-Diet gluten-free low-protein bread (dispensed in tin, with or without salt); Rite-Diet low-protein white bread (with added fibre); Rite-Diet low-protein baking mix; Rite-Diet low-protein flour mix; Rite-Diet low-protein cream-filled biscuits (chocolate flavour), sweet biscuits and gluten-free low-protein crackers; Rite-Diet low-protein macaroni, spaghetti (short cut), and spaghetti rings; Rite-Diet low-protein chocolate, orange, and vanilla cream wafers; Tritamyl PK flour, and see low-protein products and synthetic diets.

Protein intolerance: see milk protein sensitivity, whole protein sensitivity, low-protein products, synthetic diets, and amino acid metabolic disorders.

Renal failure: Aglutella Azeta cream-filled wafers; Aglutella gluten-free low-protein macaroni, pasta spirals, semolina, spaghetti, spaghetti rings, tagliatelle; Aminex; Aproten products (annellini, biscuits, bread mix, cake mix, crispbread, ditalini, flour, rigatini, tagliatelle); Calogen; Caloreen; Dialamine; dp Low-Protein butterscotch-flavoured or chocolate-flavoured chip cookies; Super-Soluble Duocal and Duocal Liquid; Fortical; Hycal; Juvela gluten-free low-protein (chocolate chip, orange, and cinnamon flavour) cookies; Juvela low-protein loaf (sliced and unsliced) and low-protein flour mix; Maxijul LE, Liquid, and Super Soluble; Polycal; Polycose; Rite-Diet gluten-free low-protein bread (dispensed in tin, with or without salt); Rite-Diet low-protein white bread (with added fibre); Rite-Diet low-protein gluten-free crackers; Rite-Diet low-protein flour mix; Rite-Diet low-protein baking mix; Rite-Diet low-protein cream-filled biscuits (chocolate flavour); Rite-Diet low-protein sweet biscuits; Rite-Diet low-protein macaroni, spaghetti (short cut), and spaghetti rings; Rite-Diet low-protein chocolate, orange, and vanilla cream wafers; Rite-Diet low-sodium bread; Tritamyl PK flour.

Short bowel syndrome: see malabsorption states.

Sodium dietary reduction: Rite-Diet low-sodium bread.

Sucrose intolerance: see carbohydrate malabsorption.

Synthetic diets:
(a) Fat: Alembicol D; Calogen; Liquigen; Medium Chain Triglyceride Oil.
(b) Carbohydrate: Caloreen; Fortical; Hycal; Maxijul LE, Liquid (and orange), Super Soluble; Polycal; Polycose powder.
(c) Minerals; Aminogran Mineral Mixture; Metabolic Mineral Mixture.
(d) Protein sources: see malabsorption states, complete feeds.
(e) Vitamins: as appropriate and see malabsorption states, nutritional support for adults.

Tyrosinaemia: Analog XPhen; Tyr.
Vomiting in infancy: Instant Carobel, Nestargel.
Whole protein sensitivity[1]: Alfare; Nutramigen; Pepti-Junior; Prejomin.
Xerostomia: Salivace.

CONDITIONS FOR WHICH TOILET PREPARATIONS MAY BE PRESCRIBED ON FP10

Note. This is a list of clinical conditions for which the ACBS has approved toilet preparations. For details of the preparations see Chapter 13.

Acne: Ionax scrub.
Birthmarks: see disfiguring skin lesions.

1. Defined as: intolerance to whole protein, proven by at least two withdrawal and challenge tests, as suggested by an accurate dietary history.

Dermatitis (includes contact, atopic and infective dermatoses, eczema and pruritic dermatoses): Betadine Skin Cleanser and Foam; Genisol; Polytar Emollient, Liquid, and Plus; Ster-Zac Bath Concentrate; T/Gel shampoo.
Dermatitis herpetiformis: see gluten-sensitive enteropathies.
Disfiguring skin lesions (birthmarks, mutilating lesions and scars): Boots Covering Cream; Covermark products; Dermacolor Camouflage System; Keromask masking cream and finishing powder; Veil Cover cream. (Cleansing Creams, Cleansing Milks, and Cleansing Lotions are excluded.)
Disinfectants (antiseptics): drugs only when ordered in such quantities and with such directions as are appropriate for the treatment of patients. Not to be regarded as drugs if ordered for general hygienic purposes.
Eczema: see dermatitis.
Photodermatoses (skin protection in): Almay Total Sunblock Cream and Lip protector; Coppertone Supershade, and Sunstick 15 and Ultrashade 23; Piz Buin Creme, SPF 12; Piz Buin Lotion 12; Piz Buin Sun Allergy Lotion 12; Piz Buin Sunblock Lotion 24; RoC Opaque Total Sunblock Cream SPF 15 A & B (Colourless and tinted); RoC Total Sunblock Cream 10 (colourless); Spectraban 15; Uvistat Sun Cream 10 and 15; Uvistat Lipscreen 15; Uvistat Water-resistant Cream 8; Uvistat Sun Block Cream 20; Uvistat Ultrablock Cream 30.
Pruritus: see dermatitis.
Psoriasis: see scaling of the scalp.
Scabies: Tetmosol.
Scaling of the scalp (psoriasis, dandruff, eczema): Alphosyl; Betadine; Capitol; Ceanel Concentrate; Cetavlon PC; Gelcotar; Genisol; Ionil T; Polytar Emollient, Liquid, and Plus; T/Gel shampoo.

Appendix 8: Cautionary and Advisory Labels for Dispensed Medicines

In recent years there has been a growing need for patients to be given better information on the medicines they have been prescribed so that they will be reminded to take the medicine correctly and most effectively. One aspect of this is the provision of more detailed cautionary and advisory labels than have been used in the past.

What a patient learns about a medicine will include whatever the prescriber says, what the labels on the dispensed medicines say, what any patient information leaflet may say, and whatever the pharmacist says by way of explanation and encouragement. Nevertheless, the label is what the patient will see when taking each dose. Leaflets may be discarded and verbal advice forgotten.

The BNF now shows under many preparations the numbers of any labels that pharmacists are recommended to apply to the containers of preparations when they are dispensed. The wordings chosen for the labels represent a carefully considered balance between the unintelligibly short and the inconveniently long. Since any fixed set of words cannot cover the language needs of all patients it is expected that pharmacists will counsel patients.

All counselling needs to be related to the age, experience, background, and understanding of the individual patient. The patient will then be able to obtain the maximum benefit from following the directions.

Compliance with the intentions of the prescriber should be encouraged. The pharmacist should ensure that the patient understands not only how to use the medicine but also how much and how often. Any effects of the medicine on driving or work, any foods or medicines to be avoided, and what to do if a dose is missed should also be explained. There may be other matters that are better dealt with by counselling than by a label, such as the possibility of staining of the clothes or skin by a medicine.

For some preparations there is a special need for counselling, such as an unusual method or time of administration or a potential interaction with a common food or domestic remedy, and this is indicated where necessary.

Manufacturers' instructions

Many preparations are now dispensed in unbroken original packs that bear complete instructions for the patient or provide a leaflet addressed to the patient. These labels or leaflets should not normally be obscured or removed. Where it is known that such instructions are provided with an original pack intended for the patient no label has been listed under the preparation. Label 10 may be used where appropriate. Leaflets are available from various sources advising on the administration of preparations such as eye-drops, eye ointments, inhalers, and suppositories.

Scope of the recommended labels

No label recommendations have been made for injections (except for selected systemic corticosteroids) on the assumption that they will be administered by a health professional or a well-trained patient. The labelling is not exhaustive and pharmacists are recommended to use their professional discretion in labelling new preparations and those for which no labels are shown.

Individual labelling advice is not given on the administration of the large variety of antacids. In the absence of instructions from the prescriber, and if on enquiry the patient has had no verbal instructions, the directions given under 'Dose' should be used on the label.

It is recognised that there may be occasions when pharmacists will use their knowledge and professional discretion and decide to omit one or more of the recommended labels for a particular patient. In this case counselling is of the utmost importance. There may also be an occasion when a prescriber does not wish additional cautionary labels to be used, in which case the prescription should be endorsed 'NCL' (no cautionary labels). The exact wording that is required instead should then be specified on the prescription.

Pharmacists have traditionally labelled medicines with various wordings in addition to those directions specified on the prescription. Such labels include 'Shake the bottle', 'For external use only', 'Not to be taken', and 'Store in a cool place', as well as 'Discard . . . . days after opening' and 'Do not use after . . . .', which apply particularly to antibiotic mixtures, diluted liquid and topical preparations, and to eye-drops. Although not listed in the BNF these labels should continue to be used when appropriate; indeed, 'For external use only' is a legal requirement on external liquid preparations, while 'Keep out of the reach of children' is a legal requirement on all dispensed medicines.

It is the usual practice for patients to take oral solid-dose preparations with water or other liquid and for this reason no separate label has been recommended.

The label or labels for each preparation are recommended after careful consideration of the information available. However, it is recognised that in some cases this information may be either incomplete or open to a different interpretation. The Executive Editor will therefore be grateful to receive any constructive comments on the labelling suggested for any preparation.

Recommended label wordings

The wordings which can be given as separate warnings are labels 1–19 and label 29. Wordings which can be incorporated in an appropriate position in the directions for dosage or administration are labels 21–28. A label has been omitted for number 20.

If separate labels are used it is recommended that the wordings be used without modification. If changes are made to suit computer requirements, care should be taken to retain the sense of the original.

(1) Warning. May cause drowsiness

To be used on children's preparations containing antihistamines, e.g., paediatric elixirs and linctuses, or other preparations given to children where the warnings of label 2 on driving or alcohol would not be appropriate.

(2) Warning. May cause drowsiness. If affected do not drive or operate machinery. Avoid alcoholic drink

To be used on preparations that can cause drowsiness, thereby affecting the ability to drive and operate hazardous machinery. The main preparations are most antihistamines; central nervous system depressants such as anxiolytics, antipsychotics, opioid analgesics, and tricyclic antidepressants; some antihypertensives; some analgesics; some antiepileptics; some antiemetics; and some muscle relaxants. Label 2 is now seen as unhelpful in relation to hypnotics, hence a new label (label 19) has been introduced to cover hypnotics, and also anxiolytics, taken at night. *It is an offence to drive while under the influence of drink or drugs.*

Label 1 is more appropriate for children.

Some of these preparations only cause drowsiness in the first few days of treatment and the patient then becomes tolerant; some only cause drowsiness in higher doses.

In such cases the patient should be told that the advice to avoid driving, etc., applies until the effects have worn off. Many of these preparations can produce a slowing of reaction time and a loss of mental concentration that can have the same effects as drowsiness on activities that require alertness to avoid hazard.

The avoidance of alcoholic drink is recommended, since the effects of CNS depressants are enhanced by alcohol, but it must be realised that a strict prohibition could lead to certain patients not taking the medicine at all. Pharmacists should explain the risk and encourage compliance, particularly in patients who may think they already tolerate the effects of alcohol (see also label 3).

Queries from patients with epilepsy regarding fitness to drive should be referred back to the patient's doctor.

There are other side-effects unrelated to drowsiness that may affect a patient's ability to drive or operate machinery safely, for example, blurred vision, dizziness, or nausea. In general, no label has been recommended to cover these cases, but the patient should be suitably counselled.

(3) Warning. May cause drowsiness. If affected do not drive or operate machinery

To be used on monoamine-oxidase inhibitors (because alcohol is covered by label 10 and the MAOI treatment card).

Some patients given CNS depressants may have been advised how much alcohol they may drink by their doctor and in such cases label 3 may be more appropriate than label 2.

(4) Warning. Avoid alcoholic drink

To be used on preparations where a reaction such as flushing may occur if alcohol is taken, e.g. metronidazole and chlorpropamide. Alcohol may also enhance the hypoglycaemia produced by some oral antidiabetic drugs but routine application of a warning label is not considered necessary.

For most interactions with alcohol label 2 is more appropriate.

(5) Do not take indigestion remedies at the same time of day as this medicine

To be used in conjunction with label 25 on preparations coated to resist gastric acid, such as enteric-coated tablets, capsules, and granules.

The coating may be ruptured prematurely in the presence of alkalis present in antacids.

Label 5 also applies to drugs such as ciprofloxacin and ketoconazole where the absorption is significantly affected by antacids; the usual period of avoidance recommended is 2 to 4 hours.

(6) Do not take iron preparations or indigestion remedies at the same time of day as this medicine

To be used on preparations of doxycycline, minocycline, and penicillamine. These drugs chelate iron and calcium ions and are less well absorbed when given with iron or calcium-containing antacids. If necessary these incompatible preparations may be given about two hours apart.

(7) Do not take milk, iron preparations or indigestion remedies at the same time of day as this medicine

To be used on preparations of tetracyclines (except doxycycline and minocycline). These drugs chelate iron, calcium, and magnesium ions and are then less well absorbed. If necessary these incompatible preparations may be given about two hours apart.

(8) Do not stop taking this medicine except on your doctor's advice

To be used on beta-blockers, certain antihypertensive drugs, drugs used in the treatment and prophylaxis of asthma, antituberculous drugs, and allopurinol.

This label is used to encourage compliance where the drug is to be taken over long periods without the patient necessarily perceiving any benefit. Patients should be told that this label does not override the need to consult the prescriber if side-effects occur.

For certain medicines the patient should be advised to ensure that the supply does not run out.

(9) Take at regular intervals. Complete the prescribed course unless otherwise directed

To be used on preparations where a course of treatment should be completed to reduce the incidence of relapse, the development of resistance, or failure of treatment. The preparations are antimicrobial drugs given by mouth.

Very occasionally, some of these antimicrobial agents may have severe side-effects and in such cases the patient may need to be advised of reasons for stopping treatment quickly and returning to the doctor. Examples are the development of diarrhoea in patients receiving clindamycin or lincomycin (see section 5.1.6), or sensitivity reactions with the penicillins.

(10) Warning. Follow the printed instructions you have been given with this medicine

To be used particularly on anticoagulants, lithium, monoamine-oxidase inhibitors, and oral corticosteroids. The appropriate treatment card should be given to the patient and any necessary explanations given.

This label may also be used on other preparations to remind the patient of the instructions that have been given.

(11) Avoid exposure of skin to direct sunlight or sun lamps

To be used on preparations that may cause phototoxic or photoallergic reactions if the patient is exposed to ultraviolet radiation. Many drugs other than those listed (e.g. phenothiazines and sulphonamides) may on rare occasions cause reactions in susceptible patients. Reactions have also been caused by external preparations (e.g. coal tar) and by various ingredients of perfumes and cosmetics. Exposure to high intensity ultraviolet radiation from sunray lamps and sunbeds is particularly likely to cause reactions and in advising patients this should be mentioned.

Drugs involved include amiodarone, demeclocycline, nalidixic acid, and protriptyline.

(12) Do not take anything containing aspirin while taking this medicine

To be used on preparations containing salicylate derivatives, where it may not be known to the patient that the medicine has a similar action to aspirin, and on preparations containing the uricosuric drugs probenecid and sulphinpyrazone whose activity is reduced by aspirin.

Label 12 should not be used for anticoagulants; label 10 is more appropriate.

(13) Dissolve or mix with water before taking

To be used on preparations that are intended to be dissolved in water (e.g. soluble tablets) or mixed with water (e.g. powders, granules) before use. In a few cases the manufacturer's literature indicates that other liquids such as fruit juice or milk may be used.

(14) This medicine may colour the urine

To be used on preparations that may cause the patient's urine to turn unusual colours. These include anthraquinones (alkaline urine red), phenolphthalein (alkaline urine pink), triamterene (blue under some lights), levodopa (dark reddish), and rifampicin (red).

(15) Caution flammable: keep away from fire or flames

To be applied to preparations containing sufficient alcohol, acetone, ether, or other flammable solvent to render them flammable if exposed to a naked flame. The term flammable is now used by the British Pharmacopoeia and in legislation in preference to inflammable. Since both terms are now liable to cause confusion, the pharmacist should make sure that the patient understands what is meant.

(16) Allow to dissolve under the tongue. Do not transfer from this container. Keep tightly closed. Discard eight weeks after opening

To be used on glyceryl trinitrate tablets to remind the patient not to transfer the tablets to plastic or less suitable containers. The manufacturer's original pack normally carries most of this wording and it may only be necessary to add 'Discard eight weeks after opening'.

(17) Do not take more than . . . . in 24 hours

To be used on preparations for the treatment of acute migraine except those containing ergotamine, for which label 18 is used.

It may also be used on preparations for which no dose has been specified by the prescriber.

It is recommended that the dose form should be specified, e.g. tablets or capsules.

(18) Do not take more than . . . in 24 hours or . . . in any one week

To be used on preparations of ergotamine tartrate.

It is recommended that the dose form should be specified, e.g. tablets or capsules.

(19) Warning. Causes drowsiness which may continue the next day. If affected do not drive or operate machinery. Avoid alcoholic drink

To be used on those preparations (e.g. nitrazepam) which are classified as hypnotics in the BNF when they are prescribed to be taken at night. On the rare occasions (e.g. nitrazepam in epilepsy) when hypnotics are prescribed for daytime administration this label would clearly not be appropriate. Also to be used as an alternative to the label 2 wording (the choice being at the discretion of the pharmacist) for anxiolytics (e.g. diazepam) prescribed to be taken at night. It is hoped that this wording will convey adequately the problem of residual morning sedation after taking 'sleeping tablets'.

(21) . . . with or after food

To be used on preparations that are liable to cause gastric irritation with nausea and vomiting, or those that are better absorbed with food.

The incidence of gastric irritation may be reduced when some preparations are given during or immediately after a meal. The presence of food in the upper gastro-intestinal tract may reduce the rate of absorption of certain drugs. Nausea and vomiting are liable to decrease compliance and possibly lead to loss of the drug from vomiting.

Patients may on occasions be advised to take their medicine with or after food in the interest of compliance when normally it should be taken before meals. There is a wide variation in the instructions given for iron salts and their preparations. They are usually best absorbed when given on an empty stomach but may then cause irritation. They are therefore often taken with a meal.

The prescriber's instructions should be followed.

A small number of preparations are better absorbed when given with food.

The word 'food' is used in preference to 'meal' on the label. Patients differ in their interpretation of the words and may decide not to take a dose if it has to be taken with a meal that they normally omit.

Patients should be advised when to take their doses, according to their particular circumstances, and that a small amount of food is sufficient.

(22) . . . half to one hour before food

To be used on some antimuscarinic or antacid preparations; some pancreatin and other enzyme preparations; most appetite suppressants; and certain other drugs whose absorption or local effect is thereby improved.

(23) . . . an hour before food or on an empty stomach

To be used on some oral antibiotics whose absorption may be reduced by the presence of food and acid in the stomach.

Many of the antibiotics introduced in recent years are less affected by acid and/or food in the stomach and may be given at any time relative to meals.

(24) . . . sucked or chewed

To be used on preparations that may be sucked or chewed. Certain preparations must be chewed before swallowing to improve their absorption or because of their size; others have been specially formulated to be chewed. All pastilles and lozenges should be sucked slowly to aid their local effect on the oropharynx. The pharmacist should use discretion as to which of these words is appropriate.

(25) . . . swallowed whole, not chewed

To be used on preparations designed for modified-release; on certain preparations that are very unpleasant or may damage the mouth or oesophagus if not swallowed whole; and with label 5 for enteric-coated preparations. Most modified-release preparations rely on the coating of pellets, granules, tablets, or capsules or compression in a matrix material to achieve their effect. Chewing can cause premature release of active ingredient.

(26) . . . dissolved under the tongue

To be used on preparations intended for sublingual use. Several drugs are absorbed into the circulation more effectively from the mucosa of the mouth, thereby avoiding the portal circulation into the liver. Patients should be advised to hold the tablet still under the tongue and avoid swallowing until the tablet is dissolved. The buccal mucosa between the gum and cheek is occasionally specified by the prescriber and specific directions should then be used.

(27) . . . with plenty of water

To be used on preparations that should be well diluted (e.g. chloral hydrate), where a high fluid intake is required (e.g. sulphonamides), or where water is required to aid the action of the preparation (e.g. methylcellulose). The patient should be advised that 'plenty' means at least 150 mL (about a tumblerful). In most cases a beverage such as fruit juice, tea, or coffee could be used. There have been reports of solid-dose preparations sticking in the oesophagus, particularly in the elderly, and all patients should be reminded of the necessity of taking capsules and tablets with water or other liquid. As much as 100 mL may be required and the patient should stand or sit while taking the dose.

(28) To be applied sparingly . . .

To be used with external corticosteroid preparations and dithranol preparations.

The application of excessive quantities to the skin can increase the incidence of local side-effects and give rise to undesirable systemic effects.

(29) Do not take more than 2 at any one time. Do not take more than 8 in 24 hours

To be used on containers of dispensed solid dose preparations containing paracetamol for adults[1]. This label has been introduced because of the serious consequences of overdosage with paracetamol.

It is recommended that the dose form should be specified, e.g. tablets or capsules.

1. **Important.** The amounts specified here are applicable to adults.

Products and their labels

Products introduced or amended since publication of BNF No. 20 September (1990) are in **bold**.
Proprietary names are in italic.
C = counselling advised; see BNF = consult product entry in BNF.

Acebutolol, 8
Acetazolamide, 3
Acetazolamide s/r, 3, 25
Acetylcysteine gran, 13
Achromycin, 7, 9, 23, C, posture
Achromycin V, 7, 9, 23, C, posture
Acipimox, 21
Acrivastine, C, driving, alcohol, see BNF
Acrosoxacin, 2, 23
Actidil, 2
Actifed, 2
Actifed Compound, 2
Actifed Expectorant, 2
Actinac, 28
Actonorm pdr, 13
Acupan, 14 (urine pink)
Acyclovir susp and tabs, 9
Adalat caps, 21, C, see BNF
Adalat Retard, 21, 25
Adcortyl external preps, 28
Adcortyl with Graneodin, 28
Adizem preps, 25
Agarol, 14
Akineton, 2
Alclometasone external preps, 28
Alcopar, 13
Aldomet, 3, 8
Algitec, C, chew thoroughly
Alimix, C, administration
Allegron, 2
Allopurinol, 8, 21, 27
Almazine, 2 or 19
Almodan, 9
Alophen, 14 (alkaline urine pink)
Alphosyl HC, 28
Aloral, 8, 21, 27
Aloxiprin, 12, 21
Alphaderm, 28
Alprazolam, 2
Alrheumat, 21
Aluline, 8, 21, 27
Alunex, 2
Alupram, 2 or 19
Alvercol, 25, 27, C, administration, see BNF
Amantadine, C, driving
Ambaxin, 9
Amfipen, 9, 23
Aminophylline s/r, see preps
Aminophylline tabs, 21
Amiodarone, 11
Amitriptyline, 2
Amitriptyline s/r, 2, 25
Amoxapine, 2
Amoxil, 9
Amoxil dispersible tabs and sachets, 9, 13
Amoxil paed susp, 9, C, use of pipette
Amoxycillin, 9
Amphotericin loz, 9, 24, C, after food
Amphotericin mixt (g.i.), 9, C, use of pipette
Amphotericin mixt (mouth), 9, C, use of pipette, hold in mouth, after food
Amphotericin tabs, 9
Ampicillin, 9, 23
Ampiclox Neonatal, 9, C, use of pipette
Amylobarbitone, 19
Amytal, 19
Anafranil, 2
Anafranil s/r, 2, 25
Androcur, 2, 21
Anquil, 2
Antabuse, 2
Antacids, see BNF dosage statements
Antepar tabs, 24
Antepsin, 5, C, administration, see BNF
Anthranol preps, 28
Anticoagulants, oral, 10 anticoagulant card
Antihistamines (see individual preparations)
Antipressan, 8
Antoin, 13, 21
Antraderm preps, 28
Anturan, 12, 21
Apisate, 25, C, driving
APP pdr, 13
Apsifen, 21
Apsin VK, 9, 23
Apsolol, 8
Apsolox, 8
Arelix, 21
Arpimycin, 9
***Arpicolin*, C, driving**
***Artane*, C, before or after food, driving, see BNF**
Artracin, 21
Arythmol, 21, 25
Asacol, 25
Ascorbic acid, effervescent, 13
Ascorbic acid tabs (500 mg), 24
Asendis, 2
Aspav, 2, 13, 21
Aspirin and papaveretum dispersible tabs, 2, 13, 21
Aspirin dispersible tabs, 13, 21
Aspirin effervescent, 13
Aspirin e/c, 5, 25
Aspirin s/r, 25
Aspirin tabs, 21
Aspirin, paracetamol, and codeine tabs, 21, 29
Astemizole, 23, C, driving, alcohol, see BNF
Atarax, 2
Atenolol, 8
Atensine, 2 or 19
Ativan, 2 or 19
Atromid-S, 21
Augmentin, 9
Augmentin dispersible tabs, 9, 13
Auranofin, 21
Aureocort, 28
Aureomycin, 7, 9, 23
Aventyl, 2
Avloclor, 5
Avomine, 2
Azapropazone, 21, C, see BNF
Azatadine, 2

Bacampicillin, 9
Baclofen, 2, 8
Bactrim, 9
Bactrim dispersible tabs, 9, 13
Banocide, 9
Baratol, 2
Barquinol HC, 28
Baxan, 9
Becloforte preps, 8, 10 steroid card, C, dose
Beclomethasone external preps, 28
Beclomethasone inhalations, 8, 10 steroid card (high-dose preparations only), C, dose
Becodisks, 8, C, dose
Becotide preps, 8, C, dose
Bedranol S.R., 8, 25
Bendogen, 21
Benemid, 12, 21, 27
Benoral susp and tabs, 21, C, avoid aspirin, paracetamol
Benoral gran, 13, 21, C, avoid aspirin, paracetamol
Benorylate, 21, C, avoid aspirin, paracetamol
Benorylate gran, 13, 21, C, avoid aspirin, paracetamol
Benperidol, 2
***Bentex*, C, before or after food, driving, see BNF**
Benylin adult preps, 2
Benylin paediatric preps, 1
Benzathine penicillin, 9
Benzhexol, C, before or after food, driving, see BNF
Benzoin tincture, cpd, 15
Benztropine, 2
Bephenium, 13
Berkfurin, 9, 14, 21
Berkolol, 8
Beta-Adalat, 8, 25
Beta-Cardone, 8
Betadren, 8
Betahistine, 21
Betaloc, 8
Betaloc-SA, 8, 25
Betamethasone inj, 10 steroid card
Betamethasone tab, 10 steroid card, 21
Betamethasone external preps, 28
Betaxolol tabs, 8
Bethanechol, 22
Bethanidine, 21
Betim, 8
Betnelan, 10 steroid card, 21
Betnesol injection, 10 steroid card
Betnesol tabs, 10 steroid card, 13, 21
Betnovate external preps, 28
Betnovate-RD, 28
Bezafibrate, 21
Bezalip, 21
Bezalip-Mono, 21, 25
Biogastrone, 21
Biophylline syr, 21
Biophylline s/r, 25
***Biorphen*, C, driving**
Biperiden, 2
Bisacodyl tabs, 5, 25
Bisoprolol, 8
Blocadren, 8
Bolvidon, 2, 25
Bradilan, 5, 25
Bricanyl SA, 25
***Britiazim*, 25**
Brocadopa, 14 (urine reddish), 21
***Broflex*, C, before or after food, driving, see BNF**
Bromazepam, 2
Bromocriptine, 21, C, hypotensive reactions
Brompheniramine, 2
Brufen, 21
Buccastem, 2, C, administration, see BNF
Budesonide external preps, 28
Budesonide inhalations, 8, 10 steroid card (high-dose preparations only), C, dose
Buprenorphine, 2, 26
Burinex K, 25, 27, C, posture, see BNF
Buspar, C, driving
Buspirone, C, driving
Butacote, 5, 21, 25
Butobarbitone, 19
Butriptyline, 2

Cacit, 13
Cafadol, 29
Cafergot, 18, C, dosage
Calcichew, 24
Calcisorb, 13, 21, C, may be sprinkled on food
Calcium-500, 25
Calcium carbonate tab, chewable, 24
Calcium carbonate tab effervescent, 13
Calcium gluconate tabs, 24
Calcium Resonium, 13

Diumide-K Continus, 25, 27, C, posture, see BNF
Dolmatil, 2
Dolobid, 21, 25, C, avoid aluminium hydroxide
Doloxene, 2
Doloxene Compound, 2, 21
Domical, 2
Dopamet, 3, 8
Doralese, 2
Dormonoct, 19
Dothiepin, 2
Doxepin, 2
Doxycycline caps and tabs, 6, 9, 27, C, posture, see BNF
Doxycycline syrup, 6, 9
Dozic, 2
Dramamine, 2
Droleptan, 2
Droperidol, 2
Dulcolax tabs, 5, 25
Duogastrone, 22, 25
Duromine, 25, C, driving
Dyazide, 14 (urine blue in some lights), 21
Dyspamet tab, C, administration
Dytac, 14 (urine blue in some lights), 21
Dytide, 14 (urine blue in some lights), 21

Econacort, 28
Edecrin, 21
Efcortelan external preps, 28
Efcortelan soluble, 10 steroid card
Efcortesol, 10 steroid card
Effercitrate, 13
Elantan preps, 25
Electrolade, 13
Electrolyte pdr (see individual preparations)
Emcor preps, 8
Emeside, 2
***En-De-kay* mouthwash, C, food and drink, see BNF**
Endoxana, 27
Enoxacin, 9
Entamizole, 4, 9, 21, 25
Epanutin caps, 27, C, administration, see BNF
Epanutin Infatabs, 24
Epanutin susp, C, administration, see BNF
Epifoam, 28
Epilim e/c tabs, 5, 25
Epogam, C, administration, see BNF
Equagesic, 2, 21
Equanil, 2
Eradacin, 2, 23
Ergotamine, 18, C, dosage
Erycen tabs, 5, 9, 25
Erymax, 5, 9, 25
Erythrocin, 9
Erythrolar susp, 9
Erythromid, 5, 9, 25
Erythromid DS, 5, 9, 25
Erythromycin estolate, 9
Erythromycin ethyl succinate, 9
Erythromycin ethyl succinate gran, 9, 13
Erythromycin stearate tabs, 9
Erythromycin tabs, 5, 9, 25
Erythroped, 9
Erythroped sachets, 9, 13
Erythroped A tabs, 9
Erythroped A sachets, 9, 13
Esbatal, 21
Eskornade Spansule, 2, 25
Eskornade syrup, 2
Estracyt, 21, C, dairy products, see BNF
Estraderm TTS, C, administration, see BNF
Estrapak-50, C, administration, see BNF
Estramustine, 21, C, dairy products, see BNF
Ethacrynic acid, 21
Ethambutol, 8
Ethosuximide, 2

Etidronate, C, food and calcium, see BNF
Etodolac, 21
Etretinate, 10 patient information card, 21
Eumovate external preps, 28
Eurax-Hydrocortisone, 28
Evadyne, 2
Exolan, 28
Expulin, 2
Expulin (paed), 1
Expurhin, 1

Fabahistin, 2
Fabrol, 13
Farlutal 500 mg tab, 27
Fasigyn, 4, 9, 21, 25
Faverin, 2, 5, 25, C, driving, see BNF
Fefol, 25
Fefol-Vit, 25
Fefol Z, 25
Feldene caps, 21
Feldene dispersible tabs, 13, 21
Fenbid, 25
Fenbufen, 21
Fenbufen effervescent tabs, 13, 21
Fenfluramine s/r, 2, 25
Fenofibrate, 21
Fenoprofen, 21
Fenopron, 21
Fenostil Retard, 2, 25
Fentazin, 2
Feospan, 25
Feospan Z, 25
Ferrocap, 25
Ferrocap-F 350, 25
Ferrocontin Continus, 25
Ferrocontin Folic Continus, 25
Ferrograd, 25
Ferrograd C, 25
Ferrograd Folic, 25
Ferrous salts s/r (see individual preparations)
Ferrous sulphate paed mixt, 27
Fesovit, 25
Fesovit Z, 25
Flagyl S, 4, 9, 23
Flagyl supps, 4, 9
Flagyl tabs, 4, 9, 21, 25, 27
Flexin Continus, 21, 25, C, driving
Florinef, 10 steroid card
Floxapen, 9, 23
Flu-Amp, 9, 23
Fluanxol, C, administration
Fluclorolone external preps, 28
Flucloxacillin, 9, 23
Fluconazole 50 and 200 mg, 9
Fludrocortisone, 10 steroid card
Flunitrazepam, 19
Fluocinolone external preps, 28
Fluocinonide external preps, 28
Fluocortolone external preps, 28
***Fluorigard* mouthwash, C, food and drink, see BNF**
Fluorouracil caps, 21
Fluoxetine, C, driving, see BNF
Flupenthixol, see preps
Fluphenazine, 2
Flurandrenolone external preps, 28
Flurazepam, 19
Flurbiprofen, 21
Flurbiprofen s/r, 21, 25
Fluvoxamine, 2, 5, 25, C, driving, see BNF
***Formulix*, 3**
Fortral caps and tabs, 2, 21
Fortral supps, 2
Fortunan, 2
Framycort oint, 28
Franol, 21
Franol Plus, 21
Frisium, 2 or 19
Froben, 21
Froben SR, 21, 25
Frusene, 14 (urine blue in some lights), 21
Fucibet, 28
Fucidin susp, 9, 21
Fucidin tabs, 9
Fucidin H, 28

Fulcin, 9, 21
Fungilin loz, 9, 24, C, after food
Fungilin susp (g.i.), 9, C, use of pipette
Fungilin susp (mouth), 9, C, use of pipette, hold in mouth, after food
Fungilin tabs, 9
Furadantin, 9, 14 (urine yellow or brown), 21
Furamide, 9
Fybogel, 13, C, administration, see BNF
Fybranta, 24, 27, C, administration, see BNF

Gamanil, 2
Gamolenic acid in evening primrose oil, C, administration, see BNF
Gastrobid Continus, 25
Gastromax, 22, 25
Gastrozepin, 22
Genticin HC, 28
Gluco-lyte, 13
Glucophage, 21
Glyceryl trinitrate patch, see preps
Glyceryl trinitrate s/r, 25
Glyceryl trinitrate tabs, 16
***Golytely*, 10, patient information leaflet, C, administration, see BNF**
Gregoderm, 28
Griseofulvin, 9, 21
Grisovin, 9, 21
GTN 300 mcg, 16
Guanor Expectorant, 2
Guar gum, see preps
Guarem, 13, C, food, administration, see BNF
Guarina, 13, C, food

Haelan, 28
Haelan-C, 28
Halciderm Topical, 28
Halcinonide external preps, 28
Halcion, 19
Haldol, 2
Half-Inderal LA, 8, 25
Haloperidol, 2
Hamarin, 8, 21, 27
Haymine, 2, 25
Heminevrin, 19
Hexamine, 9
Hiprex, 9
Hismanal, 23, C, driving, alcohol, see BNF
Histalix, 2
Histryl, 2, 25
Histryl (paed), 1, 25
Hydergine, 22
***Hydrea*, no longer 3**
Hydrocal, 28
Hydrocortisone inj, 10 steroid card
Hydrocortisone external preps, 28
Hydrocortisone tabs, 10 steroid card, 21
Hydrocortistab inj, 10 steroid card
Hydrocortistab external preps, 28
Hydrocortistab tabs, 10 steroid card, 21
Hydrocortisyl, 28
Hydrocortone, 10 steroid card, 21
Hydromet, 3, 8
Hydroxychloroquine, 5
Hydroxyurea caps, no longer 3
Hydroxyzine, 2
Hygroton-K, 25, 27, C, posture, see BNF
Hyoscine, 2
Hypercal, 3
Hypercal B, 2
Hypon, 21
Hypovase, 3, C, dose, see BNF
Hytrin, 3, C, dose, see BNF

Ibular, 21
Ibuprofen, 21
Ilosone, 9
Imbrilon caps, 21, C, driving
Imdur, 25
Imipramine, 2
Imperacin, 7, 9, 23
Imunovir, 9

Inderal, 8
Inderal-LA, 8, 25
Inderetic, 8
Inderex, 8, 25
Indocid caps and susp, 21, C, driving
Indocid-R, 21, 25, C, driving
Indolar SR, 21, 25, C, driving
Indomethacin caps and mixt, 21, C, driving
Indomethacin s/r, 21, 25, C, driving
Indomethacin supps, C, driving
Indomod, 25, C, driving
Indoramin, 2
Industrial methylated spirit, 15
Infacol, C, use of dropper
Inosine pranobex, 9
Intal Spincaps and inhalers, 8
Integrin, 2
Iodine Solution, Aqueous, 27
Ionamin, 25, C, driving
Ipral, 9
Iprindole, 2
Ismo Retard, 25
Ismo tabs, 25
Isocarboxazid, 3, 10 MAOI card
Isoetharine s/r, 25
Isogel, 13, C, administration, see BNF
Isoket Retard, 25
Isoniazid elixir and tabs, 8, 22
Isoprenaline sulphate tabs, 26
Isordil (sublingual), 26
Isordil Tembids, 25
Isosorbide dinitrate s/r, 25
Isosorbide mononitrate, 25
Isosorbide mononitrate s/r, 25
Isotrate, 25
Isotretinoin, 10 patient information card, 21
Ispaghula, 13, C, administration, see BNF
Itraconazole, 5, 9, 21, 25

***Junifen*, 21**

Kalspare, 14 (urine blue in some lights), 21
Kalten, 8
Kay-Cee-L, 21
Keflex, 9
Kelfizine W tabs, 9,13
***Kemadrin*, C, driving**
Kenalog (systemic), 10 steroid card
Kerlone, 8
Kest, 14 (alkaline urine pink)
Ketoconazole tabs and susp, 5, 9, 21
Ketoprofen caps, 21
Ketotifen, 2, 8, 21
Kiditard, 25
Kinidin Durules, 25
Klean-Prep, C, administration, see BNF
Kloref, 13, 21
Kloref-S, 13, 21
Konakion tabs, 24

Labetalol, 8, 21
Laboprin, 21
Labrocol, 8, 21
Ladropen, 9, 23
Lamprene, 8, 14 (urine red), 21
Lanoxin-PG elixir, C, use of pipette
Laraflex, 21
Larapam, 21
Laratrim, 9
Largactil, 2
Lariam, 21, 25, 27
Larodopa, 14 (urine reddish), 21
Lasikal, 25, 27, C, posture, see BNF
Lasipressin, 8
Lasix + K, 25, 27, C, posture, see BNF
Lasma, 25
Ledercort external preps, 28
Ledercort tabs, 10 steroid card, 21
Lederfen, 21
Lederfen F, 13
Lederkyn, 9, 27
Ledermycin caps and tabs, 7, 9, 11, 23
Ledermycin drops, 7, 9, 11, 23, C, use of pipette

Lentizol, 2, 25
Leo K, 25, 27, C, posture, see BNF
Lergoban, 2, 25
Levodopa, 14 (urine reddish), 21
Levodopa s/r, 5, 14 (urine reddish), 25
Lexotan, 2
Librium, 2
Lidifen, 21
Limbitrol, 2
Lincocin, 9, 23, C, diarrhoea
Lincomycin, 9, 23, C, diarrhoea
Lingraine, 18, 26, C, dosage
Lioresal, 2, 8
Lipantil, 21
Liquid paraffin/phenolphthalein mixt, 14 (alkaline urine pink)
Liskonum, 10 lithium card, 25, C, fluid and salt intake
Litarex, 10 lithium card, 25, C, fluid and salt intake
Lithium carbonate, 10 lithium card, C, fluid and salt intake
Lithium carbonate s/r, 10 lithium card, 25, C, fluid and salt intake
Lithium citrate liq, 10 lithium card, C, fluid and salt intake
Lithium citrate s/r, 10 lithium card, 25, C, fluid and salt intake
Lobak, 2, 29
Locoid, 28
Locoid C, 28
Lodine, 21
Lofepramine, 2
Loprazolam, 19
Lopresor, 8
Lopresor SR, 8, 25
Lopresoretic, 8
Loratadine, C, driving, alcohol, see BNF
Lorazepam, 2 or 19
Lormetazepam, 19
***Loron caps*, C, food and calcium, see BNF**
Losec, 25
Lotriderm, 28
Lotussin, 2
Loxapac, 2
Loxapine, 2
Ludiomil, 2
Lugol's solution, 27
Lurselle, 21
Lymecycline, 6, 9
Lysuride, 21, C, hypotensive reactions

Macrodantin, 9, 14 (urine yellow or brown), 21
Madopar, 14 (urine reddish), 21
Madopar dispersible tabs, 14 (urine reddish), 21, C, administration, see BNF
Madopar CR, 5, 14 (urine reddish), 25
Magnapen, 9, 23
Magnesium sulphate, 13, 23
Magnesium sulphate mixt, 23
Magnesium trisilicate oral pdr, cpd, 13
***Manevac*, 25, 27**
Mantadine, C, driving
Maprotiline, 2
Marevan, 10 anticoagulant card
Marplan, 3, 10 MAOI card
Maxepa, 21
Maxolon paed liquid, C, use of pipette
Maxolon SR, 25
Mazindol, C, driving
Mebeverine, 22
Mebhydrolin, 2
Medazepam, 2
Medihaler-ergotamine, 18, C, dosage
Medised susp, 1
Medocodene, 29
Medrone tabs, 10 steroid card, 21
Mefenamic acid caps, paed susp, and tabs, 21
Mefenamic acid dispersible tabs, 13, 21
Mefloquine, 21, 25, 27
Megaclor, 7, 9
Melleril, 2

Menthol and benzoin inhalation, 15
Mepacrine, 4, 9, 14, 21
Meprobamate, 2
Meptazinol, 2
Meptid, 2
Mequitazine, 2
Mesalazine, 25
Metamucil, 13, C, administration, see BNF
Metformin, 21
Methadone, 2
Methixene, 2
Methocarbamol, 2
Methotrimeprazine, 2
Methylcellulose (constip. or diarrhoea), C, administration, see BNF
Methylcellulose tabs (anorectic), C, administration, see BNF
Methylcysteine, 5, 22, 25
Methyldopa, 3, 8
Methylphenobarbitone, 2
Methylprednisolone external preps, 28
Methylprednisolone inj, 10 steroid card
Methylprednisolone tabs, 10 steroid card, 21
Methysergide, 2, 21
Metirosine, 2
Metoclopramide paed liquid, C, use of pipette
Metoclopramide s/r, see preps
Metopirone, 21
Metoprolol, 8
Metoprolol s/r, see preps
Metosyn, 28
Metrolyl supps, 4, 9
Metrolyl tabs, 4, 9, 21, 25, 27
Metronidazole mixt, 4, 9, 23
Metronidazole supps, 4, 9
Metronidazole tabs, 4, 9, 21, 25, 27
Metyrapone, 21
Mexiletine s/r, 25
Mexitil PL Perlongets, 25
Mianserin, 2, 25
Miconazole oral gel, 9, C, hold in mouth, after food
Miconazole tabs, 9, 21
Mictral, 9, 11, 13
Midrid, 17
Migraleve, 2, 17
Migravess, 13, 17
Migravess Forte, 13, 17
Migril, 2, 18, C, dosage
Mildison, 28
Min-I-Mix Methylprednisolone, 10 steroid card
Minocin, 6, 9
Minocycline, 6, 9
Mintec, 5, 22, 25
Mintezol, 3, 21, 24
Miraxid tabs, 9, 21, 27, C, posture, see BNF
Miraxid paed sachets, 9, 13, 21
Mobiflex, 21
Mobilan, 21, C, driving
Moditen, 2
Modrasone, 28
Moducren, 8
Mogadon, 19
Molipaxin, 2, 21
Monit, 25
Monit LS, 25
***Monit SR*, 25**
Mono-Cedocard, 25
Monocor, 8
Monosulfiram, 4
Monotrim, 9
Monovent SA, 25
Morphine preps, 2
Morphine s/r, 2, 25
Motipress, 2
Motival, 2
Motrin, 21
MST Continus, 2, 25
Muripsin, 21
Myambutol, 8
Mycardol, 22
Mynah, 8, 23

Myotonine Chloride, 22
Mysoline, 2
Mysteclin, 7, 9, 23, C, posture

Nabilone, 2
Nabumetone, 21, 25
Nabumetone susp, 21
Nadolol, 8
Nalcrom, 22, C, administration, see BNF
Nalidixic acid, 9, 11
Naprosyn granules, 13, 21
Naprosyn tabs and susp, 21
Naproxen e/c, 5, 25
Naproxen granules, 13, 21
Naproxen tabs and susp, 21
Nardil, 3, 10 MAOI card
Narphen, 2
Natulan, 4
Navidrex-K, 25, 27, C, posture, see BNF
Naxogin, 4, 21
Nedocromil sodium inhalation, 8
Nefopam, 14 (urine pink)
Negram, 9, 11
Neo-Medrone, 28
Neo-NaClex-K, 25, 27, C, posture, BNF
Nepenthe, 2
Nerisone, 28
Nerisone Forte, 28
Neulactil, 2
Niclosamide, 4, 24, 27, C, administration, see BNF
Nicofuranose, 5, 25
Nicotinic acid tabs, 21
Nicoumalone, 10 anticoagulant card
Nidazol, 4, 9, 21, 25, 27
Nifedipine caps, 21, C, see BNF
Nifedipine caps s/r, 25
Nifedipine tabs, 21, 25
Niferex elixir, C, infants, use of dropper
Nilstim, C, administration
Nimorazole, 4, 21
Nitoman, 2
Nitrazepam, 19
Nitrocontin Continus, 25
Nitrofurantoin tabs, 9, 14 (urine yellow or brown), 21
Nivaquine, 5
Nizoral, 5, 9, 21
Nobrium, 2
Noctec, 19, 27
Noradran, 2
Nordox, 6, 9, 27, C, posture, see BNF
Norfloxacin, 5, 9
Normacol preps, 25, 27, C, administration, see BNF
Normax, 14 (urine red)
Normison, 19
Nortriptyline, 2
Norval, 2, 25
Nozinan, 2
Nuelin, 21
Nuelin SA preps, 25
Nu-K, 25, 27, C, see BNF
Numotac, 25
Nu-Seals Aspirin, 5, 25
Nutrizym GR, C, administration, see BNF
***Nycopren*, 5, 25**
Nystadermal 28
Nystaform-HC, 28
Nystan pastilles, 9, 24, C, after food
Nystan susp (g.i.), 9, C, use of pipette
Nystan susp (mouth), 9, C, use of pipette, hold in mouth, after food
Nystan tabs, 9
Nystatin mixt (g.i.), 9, C, use of pipette
Nystatin mixt (mouth), 9, C, use of pipette, hold in mouth, after food
Nystatin pastilles, 9, 24, C, after food
Nystatin tabs, 9
Nystatin-Dome (g.i.), 9, C, use of 1-mL spoon
Nystatin-Dome (mouth), 9, C, use of 1-mL spoon, hold in mouth, after food

Ocusert Pilo, C, method of use
Oestriol, 25
Ofloxacin, 5, 9, C, driving
Olbetam, 21
Olsalazine, 21
Omeprazole, 25
Opilon, 21
Opium tincture, 2
Optimine, 2
Oramorph, 2
Orap, 2
Orbenin, 9, 23
Orovite-7 gran, 13
Orphenadrine, C, driving
Orudis caps, 21
Oruvail, 21, 25
Ovestin, 25
Oxanid, 2
Oxatomide, 2
Oxazepam, 2
Oxerutins, 21
Oxpentifylline s/r, 21, 25
Oxprenolol, 8
Oxprenolol s/r, 8, 25
Oxypertine, 2
Oxytetracycline, 7, 9, 23

Palaprin Forte, 12, 21
Paludrine, 21
Pameton, 29
Panadeine, 29
Panadol, 29
Panadol Soluble, 13, 29
Panasorb, 29
Pancrease caps, C, administration, see BNF
Pancreatin, see BNF
Pancrex gran, 25, C, dose, see BNF
Pancrex V Forte tabs, 5, 25, C, dose, see BNF
Pancrex V caps, 125 caps and pdr, C, administration, see BNF
Pancrex V tabs, 5, 25, C, dose, see BNF
Panmycin, 7, 9, 23, C, posture
Paracetamol tabs, 29
Paracetamol tabs, soluble, 13, 29
Paracodol, 13, 29
Parahypon, 29
Parake, 29
Paramax sachets, 13, 17
Paramax tabs, 17
Paramol, 21, 29
Pardale, 29
Parlodel, 21, C, hypotensive reactions
Parnate, 3, 10 MAOI card
Paroven, 21
Parstelin, 3, 10 MAOI card
Paxalgesic, 2, 29
Paxane, 19
Paxofen, 21
Pecram, 25
Penbritin caps and syrup, 9, 23
Penbritin paed syrup, 9, 23, C, use of pipette
Pendramine, 6, 22
Penicillamine, 6, 22
Penidural paed drops, 9, C, use of pipette
Penidural susp, 9
Pentaerythritol tetranitrate, 22
Pentaerythritol tetranitrate s/r, 22, 25
Pentasa tabs, 25
Pentazocine caps and tabs, 2, 21
Pentazocine supps, 2
Pentobarbitone, 19
Peppermint oil caps, 5, 22, 25
Percutol, C, administration, see BNF
Periactin, 2
Pericyazine, 2
Perindopril, 22
Perphenazine, 2
Persantin, 22
Pertofran, 2
Pethidine, 2
Pevaryl TC, 28
Phasal, 10 lithium card, 25, C, fluid and salt intake
Phenazocine, 2
Phenelzine, 3, 10 MAOI card
Phenergan, 2
Phenethicillin, 9, 23
Phenindamine, 2
Phenindione, 10 anticoagulant card, 14 (urine pink)
Pheniramine s/r, 2, 25
Phenobarbitone elixir and tabs, 2
Phenolphthalein, 14 (alkaline urine pink)
Phenoxymethylpenicillin, 9, 23
Phensedyl, 2
Phentermine s/r, 25, C, driving
Phenylbutazone, e/c, 5, 21, 25
Phenytoin caps and tabs, 27, C, administration, see BNF
Phenytoin chewable tabs, 24
Phenytoin susp, C, administration, see BNF
Phosphate-Sandoz, 13
Phyllocontin Continus, 25
Physeptone, 2
Phytomenadione, 24
Picolax, 13, C, see BNF
Pimozide, 2
Pindolol, 8
Piperazine tabs, 24
Pirenzepine, 22
Piretanide, 21
Piriton, 2
Piriton Spandets, 2, 25
Piroxicam caps, 21
Piroxicam dispersible tabs, 13, 21
Pivampicillin sachets, 5, 9, 13, 21
Pivampicillin susp and tabs, 5, 9, 21
Pivmecillinam susp, 9, 21
Pivmecillinam tabs, 9, 21, 27, C, posture, see BNF
Pizotifen, 2
Plaquenil, 5
Platet, 13
Podophyllin paint cpd, 15, C, application, see BNF
Polynoxylin loz, 9, 24, C, after food
Ponderax Pacaps, 2, 25
Pondocillin sachets, 5, 9, 13, 21
Pondocillin susp and tabs, 5, 9, 21
Pondocillin Plus, 9, 21, 27, C, posture, see BNF
Ponstan, 21
Ponstan Dispersible, 13, 21
Potaba caps and tabs, 21
Potaba Envules, 13, 21
Potassium chloride s/r, see preps
Potassium citrate mixt, 27
Potassium effervescent tabs, 13, 21
Prazosin, 3, C, dose, see BNF
Precortisyl, 10 steroid card, 21
Precortisyl Forte, 10 steroid card, 21
Prednesol, 10 steroid card, 13, 21
Prednisolone inj, 10 steroid card
Prednisolone tabs, steroid card, 21
Prednisolone e/c, 5, 10 steroid card, 25
Prednisone, 10 steroid card, 21
Preferid, 28
Prefil, 22, 27, C, administration
Prepulsid, C, administration
Prestim, 8
Prestim Forte, 8
***Priadel liq*, 10 lithium card, C, fluid and salt intake, see BNF**
Priadel tabs, 10 lithium card, 25, C, fluid and salt intake, see BNF
Primalan, 2
Primidone, 2
Pripsen, 13
Pro-Actidil, 2, 25
***Pro-Banthine*, 23**
Probenecid, 12, 21, 27
Probucol, 21
Procainamide Durules, 25
Procarbazine, 4
Prochlorperazine, 2
Prochlorperazine s/r, 2, 25
Prochlorperazine buccal tabs, 2, C, administration, see BNF
Prochlorperazine sachets, 2, 13
Proctofibe, C, administration, see BNF
Procyclidine, C, driving
Progesic, 21

Proguanil, 21
Promazine, 2
Promethazine, 2
Prominal, 2
Prondol, 2
Propaderm, 28
Propaderm-A, 28
Propafenone, 21, 25
Propain, 2, 29
Propantheline, 23
Propranolol, 8
Propranolol s/r, 8, 25
Prothiaden, 2
Prothionamide, 8, 21
Protriptyline, 2, 11
Pro-Vent, 25
Prozac, C, driving, see BNF
Psoradrate, 28
Psorin, 28
Pulmicort, 8, C, dose, 10 steroid card
Pulmicort LS, 8, C, dose
Pyrazinamide, 8
Pyrogastrone liquid, 21
Pyrogastrone tabs, 21, 24

Questran preps, 13, C, avoid other drugs at same time
Quinalbarbitone, 19
Quinidine s/r, 25
Quinocort, 28
Quinoderm with Hydrocortisone, 28

Rabro, 21, 24
Ranitidine dispersible tabs, 13
Redoxon effervescent, 13
Redoxon (500 mg), 24
Regulan, 13, C, administration, see BNF
Rehidrat, 13
Relifex, 21, 25
Relifex susp, 21
Remnos, 19
Reserpine, 3
Resonium A, 13
Restandol, 21, 25
Revanil, 21, C, hypotensive reactions
Rheumacin LA, 21, 25, C, driving
Rheumox, 21, C, see BNF
Rhumalgan, 5, 25
Ridaura, 21
Rifadin, 8, 14 (urine orange-red), 22, C, soft lenses
Rifampicin caps and mixt, 8, 14 (urine orange-red), 22, C, soft lenses
Rifater, 8, 14 (urine orange-red), 22, C, soft lenses
Rifinah, 8, 14 (urine orange-red), 22, C, scft lenses
Rimactane, 8, 14 (urine orange-red), 22, C, soft lenses
Rimactazid, 8, 14 (urine orange-red), 22, C, soft lenses
Rivotril, 2
Roaccutane, 10 patient information card, 21
Robaxin, 2
Robaxisal Forte, 2, 21
Rohypnol, 19
Ronicol Timespan, 25
Rowachol, 22
Rowatinex caps, 25
Rowatinex liquid, 22, C, use of dropper
Rythmodan Retard, 25

Sabidal SR, 25
Sabril, 3
Safapryn, 5, 25
Safapryn-Co, 5, 25
Salazopyrin, 14 (urine orange-yellow), C, soft lenses
Salazopyrin EN-tabs, 5, 14 (urine orange-yellow) 25, C, soft lenses
Salbutamol s/r, see preps
Salicylic acid collodion, 15
Salicylic acid lotion, 15
Salsalate, 12, 21
Sandimmun solution, C, administration
Sando-K, 13, 21
Sandocal, 13
Sanomigran, 2
Scopoderm TTS, 2, C, administration, see BNF
Secadrex, 8
Seconal, 19
Sectral, 8
Securon SR, 25
Selexid susp, 9, 13, 21
Selexid tabs, 9, 21, 27, C, posture, see BNF
Semprex, C, driving, alcohol, see BNF
Sential, 28
Septrin susp and tabs, 9
Septrin dispersible tabs, 9, 13
Serc, 21
Serenace, 2
Serpasil, 3
Serpasil-Esidrex, 3
***Sevredol*, 2**
Sinemet preps, 14 (urine reddish), 21
Sinequan, 2
Sinthrome, 10 anticoagulant card
Sintisone, 10 steroid card, 21
Slo-Indo, 21, 25, C, driving
Slo-Phyllin, 25 or C, administration, see BNF
Sloprolol, 8, 25
Slow Sodium, 25
Slow-Fe, 25
Slow-Fe Folic, 25
Slow-K, 25, 27, C, posture, see BNF
Slow-Pren, 8, 25
Slow-Trasicor, 8, 25
Sodium Amytal, 19
Sodium bicarbonate pdr, 13
Sodium cellulose phosphate, 13, 21, C, may be sprinkled on food
Sodium chloride s/r, 25
Sodium chloride tabs, 13
Sodium chloride and glucose oral pdr, cpd, 13
Sodium chloride solution-tabs, 13
Sodium clodronate, C, food and calcium, see BNF
Sodium cromoglycate (oral), 22, C, administration, see BNF
Sodium cromoglycate inhalations, 8
Sodium fusidate susp, 9, 21
Sodium fusidate tabs, 9
Sodium picosulphate pdr, 13, C, see BNF
Sodium valproate e/c, 5, 25
Solis, 2 or 19
Solpadeine caps, 29
Solpadeine effervescent tabs, 13, 29
***Solpadol*, 2, 13**
Solprin, 13, 21
Solu-Cortef, 10 steroid card
Solu-Medrone, 10 steroid card
Solvazinc, 13, 21
Somnite, 19
Soneryl, 19
Soni-Slo, 25
Sorbichew, 24
Sorbid-SA, 25
Sotacor, 8
Sotalol, 8
Sotazide, 8
Sparine, 2
Sporanox, 5, 9, 21, 25
Stabillin V-K, 9, 23
Stafoxil, 9, 23
Stelazine syrup and tabs, 2
Stelazine Spansule, 2, 25
Stemetil, 2
Stemetil Eff, 2, 13
Sterculia, C, administration, see BNF
Stiedex, 28
Stiedex LPN, 28
Stugeron, 2
Stugeron Forte, 2
Sucralfate, 5, C, administration, see BNF
Sudafed linct, 2
Sudafed Plus, 2
Sudafed SA, 25
Sulfametopyrazine, 9, 13
Sulindac, 21
Sulphadiazine, 9, 27
Sulphadimidine, 9, 27
Sulphasalazine e/c, 5, 14 (urine orange-yellow), 25, C, soft lenses
Sulphasalazine, 14 (urine orange-yellow), C, soft lenses
Sulphinpyrazone, 12, 21
Sulpiride, 2
Sulpitil, 2
***Suprax*, 9**
Surem, 19
Surgam tabs, 21
Surgam SA caps, 21, 25
Surgam 300 sachets, 13, 21
Surgical spirit, 15
Surmontil, 2
Suscard Buccal, C, administration, see BNF
Sustac, 25
Sustamycin, 7, 9, 23, 25
Symmetrel, C, driving
Synalar external preps, 28
Syndol, 2, 29
Synflex, 21
Syraprim, 9

Talampicillin, 9
Talpen, 9
Tarcortin, 28
Tarivid, 5, 9, C, driving
Tavegil, 2
Tegretol Chewtabs, 21, 24
Tegretol Retard, 25
Temazepam, 19
Temgesic, 2, 26
Tenif, 8, 25
Tenoret 50, 8
Tenoretic, 8
Tenormin, 8
Tenoxicam, 21
Tenuate Dospan, 25, C, driving
Terazosin, 3, C, dose, see BNF
Terbutaline s/r, 25
Terfenadine, C, driving, alcohol, see BNF
Teronac, C, driving
Terra-Cortril oint and spray, 28
Terra-Cortril Nystatin, 28
Terramycin, 7, 9, 23
Testosterone undecanoate caps, 21, 25
Tetmosol, 4
Tetrabenazine, 2
Tetrabid, 7, 9, 23, 25
Tetrachel, 7, 9, 23, C, posture
Tetracycline, 7, 9, 23, C, posture
Tetracycline mouthbath, see BNF
Tetralysal preps, 6, 9
Tetrex, 7, 9, 23, C, posture
Theodrox, 21
Theo-Dur, 25
Theophylline, 21
Theophylline s/r, see preps
Thephorin, 2
Thiabendazole, 3, 21, 24
Thiethylperazine, 2
Thioridazine, 2
Thymoxamine, 21
Tiaprofenic acid gran, 13, 21
Tiaprofenic acid tabs, 21
Tiaprofenic acid s/r, 21, 25
Tigason, 10 patient information card, 21
Tilade, 8
***Tildiem*, 25**
Timodine, 28
Timolol, 8
Tinidazole tabs, 4, 9, 21, 25
Tinset, 2, 21
Tixylix, 1 or 2
Tofranil, 2
Tolectin, 21
Tolerzide, 8
Tolmetin, 21
Topilar, 28
Torecan, 2
Trancopal, 2 or 19
Trandate, 8, 21
Transiderm-Nitro, C, administration, see BNF
Tranxene, 2 or 19

Dental Practitioners' Formulary

List of Dental Preparations

The following list has been approved by the appropriate Secretaries of State, and the preparations therein may be prescribed by dental practitioners on form FP14 (GP14 in Scotland).

Sugar-free versions, where available, are preferred.

Acyclovir Cream, DPF
Acyclovir Oral Suspension, DPF
Acyclovir Tablets 200 mg, DPF
Amoxycillin Capsules, BP
Amoxycillin Injection, DPF
Amoxycillin Oral Powder, DPF
Amoxycillin Oral Suspension, BP
Amoxycillin Tablets, Dispersible, DPF
Amphotericin Lozenges, BP
Amphotericin Ointment, DPF
Amphotericin Oral Suspension, DPF
Amphotericin Tablets, DPF
Ampicillin Capsules, BP
Ampicillin Oral Suspension, BP
Artificial Saliva, DPF
Ascorbic Acid Tablets, BP
Aspirin Tablets, Dispersible, BP[1]
Benzydamine Mouthwash, DPF
Benzydamine Oral Spray, DPF
Benzylpenicillin Injection, BP
Carbamazepine Tablets, BP
Carmellose Gelatin Paste, DPF
Cephalexin Capsules, BP
Cephalexin Oral Suspension, DPF
Cephalexin Tablets, BP
Cephradine Capsules, BP
Cephradine Injection, DPF
Cephradine Oral Solution, DPF
Chlorhexidine Gluconate gels containing at least 1 per cent
Chlorhexidine Mouthwash, DPF
Chlorpheniramine Tablets, BP
Choline Salicylate Dental Gel, BP
Clindamycin Capsules, BP
Clindamycin Injection, DPF
Clindamycin Oral Suspension, Paediatric, DPF
Co-trimoxazole Oral Suspension, BP
Co-trimoxazole Oral Suspension, Paediatric, BP
Co-trimoxazole Tablets, BP
Co-trimoxazole Tablets, Dispersible, BP
Co-trimoxazole Tablets, Paediatric, BP
Diazepam Capsules, BP
Diazepam Oral Solution, BP
Diazepam Tablets, BP
Diflunisal Tablets, BP
Dihydrocodeine Tablets, BP
Doxycycline Capsules 100 mg, BP
Ephedrine Nasal Drops, BPC
Erythromycin Ethyl Succinate Oral Powder, DPF[2]
Erythromycin Ethyl Succinate Oral Suspension, DPF
Erythromycin Ethyl Succinate Oral Suspension, Paediatric, DPF
Erythromycin Ethyl Succinate Tablets, DPF
Erythromycin Lactobionate Injection, DPF
Erythromycin Stearate Tablets, BP
Erythromycin Tablets, BP
Hydrocortisone Cream, BP
Hydrocortisone Lozenges, BPC
Hydrocortisone and Miconazole Cream, DPF
Hydrocortisone and Miconazole Ointment, DPF
Hydrogen Peroxide Mouthwash, DPF
Ibuprofen Tablets, BP
Idoxuridine 5% in Dimethyl Sulphoxide, DPF
Lignocaine 5% Ointment, DPF
Menthol and Eucalyptus Inhalation, BP 1980[3]
Metronidazole Oral Suspension, DPF
Metronidazole Tablets, BP
Miconazole Oral Gel, DPF
Mouthwash Solution-tablets, DPF
Nitrazepam Tablets, BP
Nystatin Ointment, BP
Nystatin Oral Suspension, BP
Nystatin Pastilles, DPF
Nystatin Tablets, BP
Oxytetracycline Capsules, BP
Oxytetracycline Tablets, BP
Paracetamol Oral Suspension, Paediatric, BP[4]
Paracetamol Tablets, BP
Paracetamol Tablets, Dispersible, DPF
Penicillin Triple Injection, BPC
Pethidine Tablets, BP
Phenoxymethylpenicillin Capsules, BP
Phenoxymethylpenicillin Oral Solution, BP
Phenoxymethylpenicillin Tablets, BP
Povidone-iodine Mouthwash, DPF
Procaine Penicillin Injection, BP
[not currently available]
Promethazine Hydrochloride Tablets, BP
Promethazine Oral Solution, BP
Sodium Chloride Mouthwash, Compound, BP
Sodium Fusidate Ointment, BP
(former title Fusidic Acid Ointment, DPF)
Sodium Perborate Mouthwash, DPF
Temazepam Capsules, DPF
Temazepam Oral Solution, DPF
Temazepam Tablets, DPF
Tetracycline Capsules, BP
Tetracycline Oral Suspension, BP
Tetracycline Tablets, BP
Thymol Glycerin, Compound, BP
Triamcinolone Dental Paste, BP
Vitamin B Tablets, Compound, Strong, BPC
Zinc Sulphate Mouthwash, DPF

1. Addendum 1989 to BP 1988 has directed that when soluble aspirin tablets are prescribed, dispersible aspirin tablets should be dispensed.
2. Includes only the sugar-free 250-mg strength.
3. This preparation does not appear in BP 1988
4. BP 1988 directs that when Paediatric Paracetamol Oral Suspension or Paediatric Paracetamol Mixture is prescribed and no strength stated Paracetamol Oral Suspension 120 mg/5 mL should be dispensed

Details of DPF preparations

Preparations on the List of Dental Preparations which are not included in the BP or BPC are described as follows in the DPF.

Although brand names have sometimes been included for identification purposes preparations on the list should be prescribed by non-proprietary name.

PoM **Acyclovir Cream,** (proprietary product: *Zovirax Cream*), acyclovir 5%

PoM **Acyclovir Oral Suspension,** (proprietary product: *Zovirax Suspension*), acyclovir 200 mg/5 mL

PoM **Acyclovir Tablets 200 mg,** (proprietary product: *Zovirax Tablets*), acyclovir 200 mg

PoM **Amoxycillin Injection,** sterile powder for reconstitution

PoM **Amoxycillin Oral Powder** (proprietary products: *Amoxil Sachets SF*), amoxycillin 750 mg and 3 g (as trihydrate)

PoM **Amoxycillin Tablets Dispersible,** (proprietary product: *Amoxil Dispersible Tablets*), amoxycillin 500 mg (as trihydrate)

PoM **Amphotericin Ointment** (proprietary product: *Fungilin Ointment*), amphotericin 3%, in a suitable basis

PoM **Amphotericin Oral Suspension** (proprietary product: *Fungilin Suspension*), amphotericin 100 mg/mL

PoM **Amphotericin Tablets** (proprietary product: *Fungilin Tablets*), amphotericin 100 mg

Artificial Saliva, consists of a suitable inert, slightly viscous, aqueous liquid; may contain a suitable antimicrobial preservative, normal salivary constituents, small amounts of fluoride, and colouring and flavouring agents (see section 12.3.4)

Benzydamine Mouthwash (proprietary product: *Difflam Oral Rinse*), benzydamine hydrochloride 0.15%

Benzydamine Oral Spray, (proprietary product: *Difflam Spray*), benzydamine hydrochloride 0.15%

Carmellose Gelatin Paste (proprietary product: *Orabase Paste*), gelatin, pectin, carmellose sodium, 16.58% of each in a suitable basis

PoM **Cephalexin Oral Suspension,** cephalexin 125 mg, 250 mg, or 500 mg/5 mL (may be powder for reconstitution or ready prepared)

PoM **Cephradine Injection** (proprietary product: *Velosef Injection*), sterile powder for reconstitution

PoM **Cephradine Oral Solution** (proprietary product: *Velosef Syrup*), cephradine 250 mg/5 mL when reconstituted with water

Chlorhexidine Gel (proprietary product: *Corsodyl Dental Gel*), chlorhexidine gluconate 1%

Chlorhexidine Mouthwash (proprietary product: *Corsodyl Mouth-wash*), chlorhexidine gluconate 0.2%

PoM **Clindamycin Injection** (proprietary product: *Dalacin C Phosphate Sterile Solution*), clindamycin 150 mg (as phosphate)/mL

PoM **Clindamycin Oral Suspension, Paediatric** (proprietary product: *Dalacin C Paediatric Suspension*), clindamycin 75 mg (as hydrochloride palmitate)/5 mL when reconstituted with purified water (freshly boiled and cooled)

PoM **Erythromycin Ethyl Succinate Oral Powder** (proprietary product: *Erythroped Sugar-free*), erythromycin 250 mg (as ethyl succinate)/sachet

PoM **Erythromycin Ethyl Succinate Oral Suspension** (proprietary product: *Erythroped Suspension*), erythromycin 250 mg and 500 mg (as ethyl succinate)/5 mL when reconstituted with water

PoM **Erythromycin Ethyl Succinate Oral Suspension, Paediatric** (proprietary product: *Erythroped PI*), erythromycin 125 mg (as ethyl succinate)/5 mL when reconstituted with water

PoM **Erythromycin Ethyl Succinate Tablets** (proprietary product: *Erythroped A*), erythromycin ethyl succinate 500 mg

PoM **Erythromycin Lactobionate Injection** (proprietary product: *Erythrocin IV Lactobionate*), sterile powder for reconstitution

PoM **Hydrocortisone and Miconazole Cream** (proprietary product: *Daktacort Cream*), hydrocortisone 1%, miconazole nitrate 2%

PoM **Hydrocortisone and Miconazole Ointment** (proprietary product: *Daktacort Ointment*), hydrocortisone 1%, miconazole nitrate 2%

Hydrogen Peroxide Mouthwash consists of hydrogen peroxide solution (6%), BP

PoM **Idoxuridine 5% in Dimethyl Sulphoxide,** idoxuridine 5% in dimethyl sulphoxide

Lignocaine 5% Ointment, lignocaine 5% in a suitable basis

PoM **Metronidazole Oral Suspension** (proprietary product: *Flagyl S*), metronidazole 200 mg (as benzoate)/5 mL

Miconazole Oral Gel (proprietary product: *Daktarin Oral Gel*), miconazole 25 mg/mL

Mouthwash Solution-tablets, DPF, consist of tablets which may contain antimicrobial, colouring and flavouring agents in a suitable soluble effervescent basis to make a mouthwash suitable for dental purposes

PoM **Nystatin Pastilles** (proprietary product: *Nystan Pastilles*), nystatin 100000 units

Paracetamol Tablets, Dispersible (proprietary product: *Panadol Soluble*), paracetamol 500 mg in an effervescent basis

Povidone-iodine Mouthwash (proprietary product: *Betadine Mouthwash*), povidone-iodine 1%

Sodium Perborate Mouthwash, (proprietary product: *Bocasan Mouthwash*), sodium perborate 70%

PoM **Temazepam Capsules,** DPF, temazepam 10, 15, 20 and 30 mg

Note. Temazepam Capsules DPF are hard or soft gelatin capsules

PoM **Temazepam Oral Solution,** temazepam 10 mg/5 mL

PoM **Temazepam Tablets,** temazepam 10 and 20 mg

Zinc Sulphate Mouthwash, consists of zinc sulphate lotion, BP (see section 13.11.6)

Directions for use: dilute 1 part with 4 parts of warm water

Index of Manufacturers

Abbott
Abbott Laboratories Ltd,
Abbott House, Moorbridge Rd,
Maidenhead, Berks SL6 8JG.
Maidenhead (0628) 773355

A&H
Allen & Hanburys Ltd,
Horsenden House, Oldfield Lane
North, Greenford, Middx
UB6 0HB.
081-422 4225

Alcon
Alcon Laboratories (UK) Ltd,
Imperial Way, Watford
WD2 4YR.
Watford (0923) 246133

Alembic Products
Alembic Products Ltd,
Unit 4, Brymau 2 Estate,
River Lane, Saltney,
Chester, Cheshire CH4 8RQ.
Chester (0244) 680147

Allergan
Allergan Ltd,
Coronation Rd, High Wycombe,
Bucks HP12 3SH.
High Wycombe (0494) 444722

Alpha
Alpha Therapeutic UK Ltd,
Howlett Way, Fison Way
Industrial Estate, Thetford,
Norfolk IP24 1HZ.
Thetford (0842) 764260

American Hospital Supply
Contact Du Pont.

APS
Approved Prescription Services
Ltd,
Water St, Towngate, Wyke,
Bradford, West Yorks
BD12 9AF.
Bradford (0274) 606974

Armour
Armour Pharmaceutical Co. Ltd,
St. Leonards House,
St. Leonards Rd, Eastbourne,
East Sussex BN21 3YG.
Eastbourne (0323) 410200

Arun
Arun Products Ltd,
Contact De Witt

Ashbourne
Ashbourne Pharmaceuticals Ltd,
Scaldwell Rd, Industrial
Estate (North), Brixworth,
Northampton NN6 9EN.
Northampton (0604) 881640

Ashe
Ashe Consumer Products Ltd,
Ashetree Works, Kingston Rd,
Leatherhead, Surrey KT22 7JZ.
Leatherhead (0372) 376151

Associated Hospital Supply,
Associated Hospital Supply,
PO Box 4, Pershore,
Worcestershire.
Pershore (0386) 554848

Astra
Astra Pharmaceuticals Ltd,
Home Park Estate,
Kings Langley,
Herts WD4 8DH.
Watford (0923) 266191

Bailey, Robert
Robert Bailey & Son PLC,
Dysart St, Great Moor,
Stockport, Cheshire
SK7 7PF.
061-483 1133

Bard
C.R. Bard International Ltd,
Forest House, Brighton Rd,
Crawley, West Sussex
RH11 1BP.
Crawley (0293) 27888

Baxter
Baxter Healthcare Ltd,
Caxton Way, Thetford, Norfolk
IP24 3SE.
Thetford (0842) 754581

Bayer
Bayer UK Ltd,
Pharmaceutical Business Group,
Bayer House, Strawberry Hill,
Newbury, Berks RG13 1JA.
Newbury (0635) 39000

Baypharm
Contact Bayer.

Beecham
Beecham Research Laboratories,
Contact SmithKline Beecham

Beecham Products
see SmithKline Beecham Brands

Bencard
Contact SmithKline Beecham

Bengué
Bengué & Co. Ltd,
Syntex House, St. Ives Rd,
Maidenhead, Berks SL6 1RD.
Maidenhead (0628) 33191

Berk
Berk Pharmaceuticals Ltd,
Water St, Towngate, Wyke,
Bradford, West Yorks
BD12 9AF.
Bradford (0274) 606974

Beiersdorf
Beiersdorf UK Ltd,
Yeomans Drive, Blakelands,
Milton Keynes,
Bucks MK14 5LS.
Milton Keynes (0908) 211444

Bioglan
Bioglan Laboratories Ltd,
1 The Cam Centre
Wilbury Way, Hitchin,
Herts SG4 0TW.
Hitchin (0462) 438444

Bio-Medical
Bio-Medical Services Ltd.
The White House, Bishopthorpe,
York YO2 1QF.
York (0904) 702704

Biorex
Biorex Laboratories Ltd,
2 Crossfield Chambers, Gladbeck
Way, Enfield, Middx EN2 7HT.
081-366 9301

Biotest
Biotest (UK) Ltd,
Unit 21A Monkspath Business
Park, Highlands Rd, Shirley,
Solihull, West Midlands
B90 4NZ.
021-733 3393

Blake
Thomas Blake & Co,
The Byre House, Fearby, near
Masham, North Yorkshire
HG4 4NF.
Ripon (0765) 89042

Boehringer Ingelheim
Boehringer Ingelheim Ltd,
Ellesfield Ave, Bracknell, Berks
RG12 4YS.
Bracknell (0344) 424600

Boehringer Mannheim
Boehringer Mannheim UK
(Pharmaceuticals) Ltd,
Simpson Parkway, Kirkton
Campus, Livingston, West
Lothian EH54 7BH.
Livingston (0506) 412512

Boots
The Boots Co. PLC,
1 Thane Rd West, Nottingham
NG2 3AA.
Nottingham (0602) 506255

BPL
Bio Products Laboratory,
Dagger Lane, Elstree, Herts
WD6 3BX.
081-905 1818

Braun
B. Braun (Medical) Ltd,
Braun House, 13–14 Farmbrough
Close, Aylesbury Vale Industrial
Park, Aylesbury, Bucks
HP20 1DQ.
Aylesbury (0296) 393900

Bridge
Bridge Pharmaceuticals,
Contact SmithKline Beecham

Bristol-Myers
Bristol-Myers Pharmaceuticals,
Swakeleys House, Milton Rd,
Ickenham, Uxbridge, Middx
UB10 8NS.
081-572 7422

Britannia
Britannia Pharmaceuticals Ltd,
Forum House, 41–75 Brighton
Rd, Redhill, Surrey RH1 6YS.
Redhill (0737) 773741

BritCair
BritCair Ltd,
Gordon House, Gordon Rd,
Aldershot, Hants GU11 1LD.
Aldershot (0252) 333314

Brocades
Brocades (Great Britain) Ltd, Brocades House, Pyrford Rd, West Byfleet, Weybridge, Surrey KT14 6RA.
Byfleet (0932) 345535

David Bull
David Bull Laboratories, Spartan Close, Tachbrook Park, Warwick CV34 6RS.
Warwick (0926) 451515

Bullen
C.S. Bullen Ltd, 7 Moss St, Liverpool L6 1EY.
051-207 6995

Burgess
Edwin Burgess Ltd, Contact Leo.

Cabot
see Solco Basle

Calmic
Calmic Medical Division, Contact Wellcome.

Cantassium
The Cantassium Company, Larkhall Laboratories, 225 Putney Bridge Rd, London SW15 2PY.
081-874 1130

Care
Contact ICI.

Carlton
Carlton Laboratories (UK) Ltd, 4 Manor Parade, Salvington Rd, Durrington, Worthing, West Sussex BN13 2JP.
Worthing (0903) 63235

Carnrick
Carnrick Laboratories, Acres Down, Furze Hill, London Rd, Shipston-on-Stour, Warwickshire.
Shipston-on-Stour (0608) 61610

Charwell
Charwell Pharmaceuticals Ltd, Charwell House, Wilsom Rd, Alton, Hants GU34 2TJ.
Alton (0420) 84801

Ciba
CIBA Laboratories, Wimblehurst Rd, Horsham, West Sussex RH12 4AB.
Horsham (0403) 50101

Cilag
Cilag Ltd, PO Box 79, Saunderton, High Wycombe, Bucks HP14 4HJ.
Naphill (024024) 3541

Clement Clarke
Clement Clarke International Ltd, Airmed House, Edinburgh Way, Harlow, Essex CM20 2ED.
Harlow (0279) 414969

CliniMed
CliniMed Ltd, Cavell House, Knaves Beech Way, Loudwater, High Wycombe, Bucks HP10 9QY.
Maidenhead (0628) 850100

Clintec
Clintec Nutrition Ltd, Thorpe Lea Manor, Thorpe Lea Rd, Egham, Surrey TW20 8HY.
Egham (0784) 434388

Coloplast
Coloplast Ltd, Peterborough Business Park, Peterborough PE2 0FX.
Peterborough (0733) 239898

Concept
Concept Pharmaceuticals Ltd see Fabre

ConvaTec
ConvaTec Ltd, Harrington House, Milton Rd, Ickenham, Uxbridge, Middx UB10 8PU.
Uxbridge (0895) 678888

Consolidated
Consolidated Chemicals Ltd, The Industrial Estate, Wrexham, Clwyd LL13 9PW.
Wrexham (0978) 661351

CooperVision
CooperVision Optics Ltd, Permalens House, 1 Botley Rd, Hedge End, Southampton SO3 3HB.
Botley (04892) 5155

Cow & Gate
Cow & Gate Ltd, Cow & Gate House, Trowbridge, Wilts BA14 8YX.
Trowbridge (0225) 768381

Cox Pharmaceuticals
A. H. Cox & Co Ltd, Whiddon Valley, Barnstaple, Devon EX32 8NS.
Barnstaple (0271) 75001

CP
CP Pharmaceuticals Ltd, Ash Rd North, Wrexham Industrial Estate, Wrexham, Clwyd LL13 9UF.
Wrexham (0978) 661261

Crookes
Crookes Healthcare Ltd, PO Box 94, 1 Thane Rd West, Nottingham NG2 3AA.
Nottingham (0602) 507431

Cupal
Cupal Ltd, Pharmaceutical Laboratories, Blackburn, Lancs BB2 2DX.
Blackburn (0254) 580321

Cusi
Cusi (UK) Ltd, 8A Liphook Rd, Haslemere, Surrey GU27 1NL.
Haslemere (0428) 61078

Cutter
Contact Bayer.

Cuxson
Cuxson, Gerrard & Co. (IMS) Ltd, Oldbury, Warley, West Midlands B69 3BB.
021-552 1355

Cyanamid
Division of Lederle Laboratories. Contact Lederle.

Daniel
Richard Daniel & Son Ltd, Mansfield Rd, Derby DE1 3RE.
Derby (0332) 40671

DDSA
DDSA Pharmaceuticals Ltd, 310 Old Brompton Rd, London SW5 9JQ.
071-373 7884

De Witt
De Witt International Ltd, 62–64 East Barnet Rd, New Barnet, Herts EN4 8RQ.
081-441 9310

Degussa
Degussa Pharmaceuticals Ltd, 168 Cowley Rd, Cambridge CB4 4DL.
Cambridge (0223) 423434

Delandale
Delandale Laboratories Ltd, Delandale House, 37 Old Dover Rd, Canterbury, Kent CT1 3JF.
Canterbury (0227) 766353

Delta
Delta Pharmaceuticals, Denbigh House, Denbigh Rd, Bletchley, Milton Keynes MK1 1YP.
Milton Keynes (0908) 368071

Dendron
Dendron Ltd, 94 Rickmansworth Rd, Watford, Herts WD1 7JJ.
Watford (0923) 229251

Dental Health
Dental Health Promotion Ltd, 51 Greencroft Gardens, London NW6 3II.
071-625 4389

Dermal
Dermal Laboratories Ltd, Tatmore Place, Gosmore, Hitchin, Herts SG4 7QR.
Hitchin (0462) 458866

Dermalex
Contact Sanofi.

DF
Duncan, Flockhart & Co. Ltd, 700 Oldfield Lane North, Greenford, Middx UB6 0HE.
081-422 2331

Dispersa
Dispersa (United Kingdom) Ltd, Lockwood Fold, Buxton Rd, Heaviley, Stockport, Cheshire SK2 6LS.
061-474 1526

Dista
Dista Products Ltd, Kingsclere Rd, Basingstoke, Hants RG21 2XA.
Basingstoke (0256) 52011

Dome/Hollister-Stier
Dome/Hollister-Stier, Strawberry Hill, Newbury, Berks RG13 1JA.
Newbury (0635) 39000

Dow Corning
Dow Corning Ltd, PO Box 22, Caledonian House, Knutsford, Cheshire WA16 6AQ.
Knutsford (0565) 50415

Downs
Contact Simcare

Du Pont
Du Pont (UK) Ltd., Wedgwood Way, Stevenage, Herts SG1 4QN.
Stevenage (0438) 734549

Dumex
Dumex Ltd, Longwick Rd, Princes Risborough, Aylesbury, Bucks HP17 9UZ.
Princes Risborough (0844) 274414

Duphar
Duphar Laboratories Ltd, Gaters Hill, West End, Southampton SO3 3JD.
Southampton (0703) 472281

Dylade
Contact Fresenius Ltd.

Eastern
Eastern Pharmaceuticals Ltd, Coomb House, St Johns Rd, Isleworth, Middx TW7 6NA.
081-569 8174

Evans
Evans Medical Ltd, Langhurst, Horsham, Sussex RH12 4QD.
Horsham (0403) 41400

Fabre
Pierre Fabre Ltd, The Old Coach House, Amersham Hill, High Wycombe, Bucks HP13 6NQ.
High Wycombe (0494) 451938

Farillon
Farillon Ltd, Ashton Rd, Harold Hill, Romford, Essex RM3 8UE.
Ingrebourne (04023) 71136

Farley
Farley Health Products Ltd, Torr Lane, Plymouth PL3 5UA.
Plymouth (0752) 24151

Farmitalia Carlo Erba
Farmitalia Carlo Erba Ltd, Italia House, 23 Grosvenor Rd, St. Albans, Herts AL1 3AW.
St. Albans (0727) 40041

Ferring
Ferring Pharmaceuticals Ltd, 11 Mount Road, Feltham, Middx TW13 6JG.
081-898 8396

Fisons
Fisons plc, Pharmaceutical Division, 12 Derby Rd, Loughborough, Leics LE11 0BB.
Loughborough (0509) 611001

Fournier
Fournier Pharmaceuticals Ltd, 116–120 London Rd, Oxford, OX3 9AT.
Oxford (0865) 741641

Fox
C. H. Fox Ltd, 22 Tavistock St, London WC2E 7PY
071-240 3111

FP
Family Planning Sales Ltd, 28 Kelburne Rd, Cowley, Oxford OX4 3SZ.
Oxford (0865) 772486

Francol
Francol Surgical Ltd, PO Box 2, High Wycombe HP14 4LJ.
Naphill (024024) 2504

Fresenius
Fresenius Ltd, 6 Christleton Court, Stuart Rd, Manor Park, Runcorn, Cheshire WA7 1ST.
Runcorn (0928) 580058

Galen
Galen Ltd, 19 Lower Seagoe Industrial Estate, Portadown, Craigavon, Armagh BT63 5UA.
Craigavon (0762) 334974

Geigy
Geigy Pharmaceuticals, Wimblehurst Rd, Horsham, West Sussex RH12 4AB.
Horsham (0403) 50101

Geistlich
Geistlich Sons Ltd, Newton Bank, Long Lane, Chester CH2 3QZ.
Chester (0244) 347534

General Designs
General Designs Ltd, PO Box 38E, Worcester Park, Surrey KT4 7LX.
081-337 9366

Generics
Generics (UK) Ltd, 12 Station Close, Potters Bar, Herts EN6 1TL.
Potters Bar (0707) 44556

GF Supplies
see Nutricia

Glaxo
Glaxo Laboratories Ltd, Greenford Rd, Greenford, Middx UB6 0HE.
081-422 3434

Glenwood
Glenwood Laboratories Ltd, Jenkins Dale, Chatham, Kent ME4 5RD.
Chatham (0634) 830535

Gold Cross
Gold Cross Pharmaceuticals, PO Box 53, Lane End Rd, High Wycombe, Bucks HP12 4HL.
High Wycombe (0494) 21124

Graseby Medical
Graseby Medical Ltd, Colonial Way, Watford, Herts WD2 4LG.
Watford (0923) 246434

Henleys
Henleys Medical Supplies Ltd, Brownfields, Welwyn Garden City, Herts AL7 1AN.
Welwyn Garden (0707) 333164

Hoechst
Hoechst UK Ltd, Pharmaceutical Division, Hoechst House, Salisbury Rd, Hounslow, Middx TW4 6JH.
081-570 7712

Hollister
Hollister Ltd, 43 Castle St, Reading, Berks RG1 7SN.
Reading (0734) 597211

Hough
Hough, Hoseason & Co. Ltd, 22 Chapel St, Levenshulme, Manchester M19 3PT.
061-224 3271

Hypoguard
Hypoguard Ltd, Dock Lane, Melton, Woodbridge, Suffolk IP12 1PE.
Woodbridge (03943) 7333

ICI
ICI Pharmaceuticals, Southbank, Alderley Park, Macclesfield, Cheshire SK10 4TF.
Alderley Edge (0625) 584848

Ilon
Ilon Laboratories (Hamilton) Ltd, Lorne St, Hamilton, Strathclyde ML3 9AB.
Hamilton (0698) 285129

Immuno
Immuno Ltd, Arctic House, Rye Lane, Dunton Green, Nr Sevenoaks, Kent TN14 5HB.
Sevenoaks (0732) 458101

IMS
International Medication Systems (UK) Ltd, 11 Royal Oak Way South, Daventry, Northants NN11 5PJ.
Daventry (0327) 703231

Innoxa
Innoxa (England) Ltd, 202 Terminus Rd, Eastbourne, East Sussex BN21 3DF.
Eastbourne (0323) 639671

Innovex
Innovex Medical Products Ltd, Innovex House, Reading Rd, Henley on Thames, Oxon RG9 1HG.
Henley on Thames (0491) 578171

International Labs
International Laboratories Ltd, Floats Rd, Wythenshawe, Manchester M23 9NF.
061-945 4161

Invicta
Contact Pfizer.

Iolab
Iolab, Enterprise House, Station Rd, Loudwater, High Wycombe, Bucks HP10 9UG.
High Wycombe (0494) 461096

J&J
Johnson & Johnson Patient Care Ltd, Coronation Rd, Ascot, Berks SL5 9EY.
Ascot (0990) 872626

Jackson
Ernest Jackson & Co. Ltd, Crediton, Devon EX17 3AP.
Crediton (03632) 2251

Janssen
Janssen Pharmaceutical Ltd, Grove, Wantage, Oxon OX12 0DQ.
Wantage (0235) 772966

K & K-Greeff
K & K-Greeff Ltd, Suffolk House, George St, Croydon CR9 3QL.
081-686 0544

K/L
K/L Pharmaceuticals Ltd, 25 Macadam Place, South Newmoor Industrial Estate, Irvine KA11 4HP.
Irvine (0294) 215951

Kabi
Kabi Pharmacia Ltd, Davy Ave, Knowlhill, Milton Keynes MK5 8PH.
Milton Keynes (0908) 661101

Kendall
The Kendall Company (UK) Ltd, Pool, Redruth, Cornwall TR15 3QN.
Redruth (0209) 215151

Kendall-Lastonet
Contact Kendall

Kerfoot
Thomas Kerfoot & Co. Ltd, Vale of Bardsley, Ashton-under-Lyne, Lancs OL7 9RR.
061-330 4531

Kirby-Warrick
see Schering-Plough

Knoll
Knoll Ltd, Fleming House, 71 King St, Maidenhead, Berks SL6 1DU.
Maidenhead (0628) 776360

LAB
Laboratories for Applied Biology Ltd, 91 Amhurst Park, London N16 5DR.
081-800 2252

Labaz
Contact Sanofi

Laerdal
Laerdal Medical Ltd, Laerdal House, Goodmead Rd, Orpington, Kent BR6 0HX.
Orpington (0689) 76634

Lagap
Lagap Pharmaceuticals Ltd, 37 Woolmer Way, Bordon, Hants GU35 9QE.
Bordon (0420) 478301

Lederle
Lederle Laboratories, Fareham Rd, Gosport, Hants PO13 0AS.
Fareham (0329) 224000

Lenton
Lenton Products Ltd, Radford Mill, Norton St, Nottingham NG7 3HN.
Nottingham (0602) 420047

Leo
Leo Laboratories Ltd, Longwick Rd, Princes Risborough, Aylesbury, Bucks HP17 9RR.
Princes Risborough (08444) 7333

Lilly
Eli Lilly & Co. Ltd, Kingsclere Rd, Basingstoke, Hants RG21 2SY.
Basingstoke (0256) 473241

Lipha
Lipha Pharmaceuticals Ltd, Harrier House, High St, West Drayton, Middx UB7 7QG.
West Drayton (0895) 449331

Lorex
Lorex Pharmaceuticals Ltd, PO Box 293, Lane End Rd, High Wycombe, Bucks HP12 4HL.
High Wycombe (0494) 26188

Loveridge
J. M. Loveridge PLC, Southbrook Rd, Southampton SO9 3LT.
Southampton (0703) 228411

Loxley
Loxley Medical, Unit 5D, Carnaby Industrial Estate, Bridlington, North Humberside YO15 3QY.
Bridlington (0262) 603979

LRC
LRC Products Ltd, North Circular Rd, London E4 8QA.
081-527 2377

Lundbeck
Lundbeck Ltd, Lundbeck House, Hastings St, Luton LU1 5BE.
Luton (0582) 416565

3M
3M Health Care Ltd, 3M House, Morley St, Loughborough, Leics LE11 1EP.
Loughborough (0509) 611611

Macarthys
see Martindale

Macfarlan Smith
Macfarlan Smith Ltd, Wheatfield Rd, Edinburgh EH11 2QA.
031-337 2434

Martindale
Martindale Pharmaceuticals Ltd, Chesham House, Chesham Close, Romford RM1 4JX.
Romford (0708) 46033

Medo
Medo Pharmaceuticals Ltd, East St, Chesham, Bucks HP5 1DG.
Chesham (0494) 772071

Merck
E. Merck Ltd, Winchester Rd, Four Marks, Alton, Hants GU34 5HG.
Alton (0420) 64011

Mercury
Mercury Trading Ltd, 29–31 Minerva Rd, London NW10 6HJ.
081-961 5806

Merieux
Merieux UK, Clivemont House, Clivemont Rd, Maidenhead, Berks SL6 7BU.
Maidenhead (0628) 785291

Merrell
Merrell Dow Pharmaceuticals Ltd, Lakeside House, Stockley Park, Uxbridge, Middx UB11 1BE.
081-848 3456

Milupa
Milupa Ltd, Milupa House, Uxbridge Rd, Hillingdon, Middx UB10 0NE.
081-573 9966

Molnlycke
Molnlycke Ltd, Southfields Rd, Dunstable, Beds LU6 3EJ.
Dunstable (0582) 600211

Monmouth
Monmouth Pharmaceuticals, 4 Chancellor Court, 20 Priestley Rd, The Surrey Research Park, Guildford, Surrey GU2 5YP.
Guildford (0483) 65299

Morson
Thomas Morson Pharmaceuticals, Contact MSD

MSD
Merck Sharp & Dohme Ltd, Hertford Rd, Hoddesdon, Herts EN11 9BU.
Hoddesdon (0992) 467272

Napp
Napp Laboratories Ltd, Cambridge Science Park, Milton Rd, Cambridge CB4 4GW.
Cambridge (0223) 424444

Nestlé
Nestlé Co. Ltd,
St. George's House, Croydon
CR9 1NR.
081-686 3333

Neutrogena
Neutrogena (UK) Ltd,
2 Mansfield Rd, South Croydon,
Surrey CR2 6HN.
081-680 5504

Nicholas
Nicholas Laboratories Ltd,
225 Bath Rd, Slough SL1 4AU.
Slough (0753) 23971

Nicholas Cosmetics
see Nicholas

Nordic
Nordic Pharmaceuticals Ltd,
Contact Ferring.
081-898 8665

Norgine
Norgine Ltd,
116 London Rd, Headington,
Oxford OX3 9BA.
Oxford (0865) 750717

Norma
Norma Chemicals Ltd,
Contact Wallace Mfg.

Norton
H. N. Norton & Co. Ltd,
Patman House, George Lane,
South Woodford, London
E18 2LY.
081-530 6421

Norwich Eaton
Norwich Eaton Ltd,
New Sandgate House, City Rd,
Newcastle-upon-Tyne
NE99 1YD.
091-222 1882

Novo Nordisk
Novo Nordisk Pharmaceutical
Ltd,
Novo Nordisk House, Broadfield
Park, Brighton Rd, Pease
Pottage, Crawley, West Sussex
RH11 9RT.
Crawley (0293) 613555

Nutricia
Nutricia Dietary Products Ltd,
494–496 Honeypot Lane,
Stanmore, Middx HA7 1JH.
081-951 5155

Nycomed
Nycomed (UK) Ltd,
Nycomed House, 2111 Coventry
Rd, Sheldon, Birmingham
B26 3EA.
021-742 2444

Oral B Labs
Oral B Laboratories Ltd,
Gatehouse Rd, Aylesbury, Bucks
HP19 3ED.
Aylesbury (0296) 32601

Organon
Organon Laboratories Ltd,
Cambridge Science Park,
Milton Rd, Cambridge,
CB4 4FL.
Cambridge (0223) 423445

Organon-Teknika
Organon-Teknika Ltd,
Cambridge Science Park,
Milton Rd, Cambridge,
CB4 4FL.
Cambridge (0223) 423650

Ortho
Ortho Pharmaceutical Ltd
Contact Cilag

Owen Mumford
Owen Mumford Ltd,
Brook Hill, Woodstock, Oxford
OX7 1TU.
Woodstock (0993) 812021

Oxford Nutrition
Oxford Nutrition Ltd,
PO Box 31, Oxford OX4 3UH.
Oxford (0865) 716323

Paines & Byrne
Paines & Byrne Ltd,
Pabyrn Laboratories, 177 Bilton
Rd, Perivale, Greenford, Middx
UB6 7HG.
081-997 1143

Panpharma
Panpharma Ltd,
Hayes Gate House, 27 Uxbridge
Rd, Hayes, Middx UB4 0JN.
081-561 8774

P-D
Parke-Davis Medical,
Lambert Court, Chestnut Ave,
Eastleigh, Hants SO5 3ZQ.
Eastleigh (0703) 620500

Penn
Penn Pharmaceuticals Ltd,
Buckingham House, Church Rd,
Penn, High Wycombe, Bucks
HP10 8LN.
Penn (049481) 3340

Perstorp
Perstorp Pharma Ltd,
Wound-Care Division,
Studio 1, Intec 2,
Wade Rd, Basingstoke,
Hants RG24 0NE.
Basingstoke (0256) 477868

Pfizer
Pfizer Ltd,
Sandwich, Kent CT13 9NJ.
Sandwich (0304) 616161

Pharmacia
Pharmacia Biosystems Ltd.
Contact Kabi.

Pharmax
Pharmax Ltd,
Bourne Rd, Bexley, Kent
DA5 1NX.
Dartford (0322) 91321

Philip Harris
Philip Harris Medical Ltd,
Hazelwell Lane, Birmingham
B30 2PS.
021-433 3030

Phillips Yeast
Phillips Yeast Products Ltd,
Park Royal Rd, London
NW10 7JX.
081-965 7533

Pickles
J. Pickles & Sons,
Beech House, 62 High St,
Knaresborough, N. Yorks
HG5 0EA.
Harrogate (0423) 867314

Porton
Porton Products Ltd,
Porton House, Vanwall Rd,
Maidenhead, Berks SL6 4UB.
Maidenhead (0628) 771417

Procea
Procea,
Alexandra Road, Dublin 1.
Dublin (0001) 741741

Quinoderm Ltd
Quinoderm Ltd,
Manchester Rd, Oldham, Lancs
OL8 4PB.
061-624 9307

Radiol
see Fisons.

R&C
Reckitt & Colman,
Pharmaceutical Division,
Dansom Lane, Hull HU8 7DS.
Hull (0482) 26151

Ransom
William Ransom & Son plc,
Hitchin, Herts SG5 1LY.
Hitchin (0462) 437615

Regent
Regent Laboratories Ltd,
Cunard Rd, London NW10 6PN.
081-965 3637

Rendell
W. J. Rendell Ltd,
Ickleford Manor, Hitchin,
Herts SG5 3XE.
Hitchin (0462) 32596

Rhône-Poulenc Rorer
Rhône-Poulenc Rorer UK Ltd,
Rainham Rd South, Dagenham,
Essex RM10 7XS.
081-592 3060

Richardson-Vicks
Richardson-Vicks Ltd,
Rusham Park, Whitehall Lane,
Egham, Surrey TW20 9NW.
0784-34422

Riker
see 3M

Rima
Rima Pharmaceuticals Ltd,
214–216 St James's Rd,
Croydon, Surrey CR0 2BW.
081-683 1266

RMT
RMT Products Ltd,
57A Soulbury Rd, Leighton
Buzzard, Beds LU7 7RW.
Leighton Buzzard (0525) 374523

Robinsons
Robinson Healthcare
Hipper House, Chesterfield,
Derbyshire S40 1YF.
Chesterfield (0246) 220022

RoC
Laboratoires RoC UK Ltd,
Silver City House, 62 Brompton
Rd, London SW3 1BW.
071-823 9223

Roche
Roche Products Ltd,
PO Box 8, Welwyn Garden City,
Herts AL7 3AY.
Welwyn Garden (0707) 328128

Rona
Contact: Lipha Pharmaceuticals
Ltd

Rorer
Rorer Pharmaceuticals,
Rhône-Poulenc Rorer UK Ltd,
St Leonards House, St Leonards
Road, Eastbourne,
East Sussex BN21 3YG
Eastbourne (0323) 21422

Roterpharma
Roterpharma Ltd,
Littleton House, Littleton Rd,
Ashford, Middx TW15 1UU.
Ashford (0784) 248279

Roussel
Roussel Laboratories Ltd,
Broadwater Park, North Orbital
Rd, Uxbridge, Middx UB9 5HP.
Uxbridge (0895) 834343

RP Drugs
RP Drugs Ltd,
RPD House, Yorkdale Industrial
Park, Braithwaite St, Leeds
LS11 9XE.
Leeds (0532) 441400

Rybar
Rybar Laboratories Ltd,
30 Sycamore Rd, Amersham,
Bucks HP6 5DR.
Amersham (0494) 722741

Sallis
E. Sallis Ltd,
Vernon Works, Waterford St,
Old Basford, Nottingham
NG6 0DH.
Nottingham (0602) 787841

Salt
Salt & Son Ltd,
Saltair House, Lord St,
Nechells, Birmingham
B7 4DS.
021-359 5123

Sandoz
Sandoz Pharmaceuticals,
Frimley Business Park, Frimley,
Camberley, Surrey GU16 5SG.
Camberley (0276) 692255

Sanofi
Sanofi Pharma,
Floats Rd, Wythenshawe,
Manchester M23 9NF.
061-945 4161

Schering Health Care
Schering Health Care Ltd,
The Brow, Burgess Hill, West
Sussex RH15 9NE.
Burgess Hill (0444) 232323

Schering-Plough
Schering-Plough Ltd,
Mildenhall, Bury St. Edmunds,
Suffolk IP28 7AX.
Mildenhall (0638) 716321

Scholl
Scholl Consumer Products Ltd,
475 Capability Green, Luton,
Beds LU1 3LU.
Luton (0582) 482929

Schwarz
Schwarz Pharma Ltd,
Schwarz House, East St,
Chesham, Bucks HP5 1DG.
Chesham (0494) 772071

Scientific Hospital Supplies
Scientific Hospital Supplies Ltd,
38 Queensland St, Liverpool
L7 3JG.
051-708 8008

Scotia
Scotia Pharmaceuticals Ltd,
Woodbridge Meadows,
Guildford, Surrey GU1 1BA.
Guildford (0483) 574949

Searle
Searle Pharmaceuticals,
PO Box 53, Lane End Rd, High
Wycombe, Bucks HP12 4HL.
High Wycombe (0494) 21124

Serono
Serono Laboratories (UK) Ltd,
99 Bridge Rd. East, Welwyn
Garden City, Herts AL7 1BG.
Welwyn Garden (0707) 331972

Servier
Servier Laboratories Ltd,
Fulmer Hall, Windmill Rd,
Fulmer, Slough SL3 6HH.

Seton
Seton Healthcare,
Seton Healthcare Group PLC,
Tubiton House, Medlock St,
Oldham, Lancs OL1 3HS.
061-652 2222

Seton-Prebbles
As Seton

Seward
Seward Medical,
131 Great Suffolk St, London
SE1 1PP.
071-357 6527

Shannon
T.J. Shannon Ltd,
59 Bradford St, Bolton
BL2 1HT.
Bolton (0204) 21789

Shaw
A.H. Shaw and Partners Ltd,
Manor Rd, Ossett, West
Yorkshire WF5 0LF.
Wakefield (0924) 273474

Shire
Shire Pharmaceuticals Ltd,
1 Viscount Court, South Way,
Andover, Hants SP10 5NW.
Andover (0264) 333455

Simcare
Simcare,
Peter Rd, Lancing,
West Sussex BN15 8TJ.
Lancing (0903) 761122

Simpla
Simpla Plastics Ltd,
Phoenix Estate, Caerphilly Rd,
Cardiff CF4 4XG.
Cardiff (0222) 62100

Sinclair
Sinclair Pharmaceuticals Ltd,
Borough Rd, Godalming, Surrey
GU7 2AB.
Guildford (0483) 426644

S&N
Smith & Nephew Medical Ltd,
PO Box 81, 101 Hessle Rd, Hull
HU3 2BN.
Hull (0482) 25181

S&N Pharm.
Smith & Nephew
Pharmaceuticals Ltd,
Bampton Rd, Harold Hill,
Romford, Essex RM3 8SL.
Ingrebourne (04023) 49333

SK&F
Smith Kline & French
Laboratories Ltd.
Contact SmithKline Beecham

SmithKline Beecham
SmithKline Beecham plc,
Mundells, Welwyn Garden City,
Herts AL7 1EY.
Welwyn Garden (0707) 325111

SmithKline Beecham Brands
SmithKline Beecham Consumer
Brands,
St Georges Ave, Weybridge,
Surrey KT13 0DE.
Weybridge (0932) 822000

SNBTS
Scottish National Blood
Transfusion Service,
Protein Fractionation Centre,
21 Ellen's Glen Rd,
Edinburgh EH17 7QT.
031-664 2317

Solco Basle
Solco Basle (UK) Ltd,
Copyground Lane, High
Wycombe, Bucks HP12 3HE.
High Wycombe (0494) 37775

Spodefell
Spodefell Ltd,
5 Inverness Mews, London
W2 3QJ.
071-229 9125

Squibb
E. R. Squibb & Sons Ltd,
Squibb House, 141 Staines Rd,
Hounslow, Middx TW3 3JA.
081-572 7422

Squibb Surgicare
As Squibb

Stafford-Miller
Stafford-Miller Ltd,
Broadwater Rd, Welwyn Garden
City, Herts AL7 3SP.
Welwyn Garden (0707) 331001

STD Pharmaceutical
STD Pharmaceutical Products
Ltd,
Fields Yard, Plough Lane,
Hereford HR4 0EL.
Hereford (0432) 53684

Steinhard
M. A. Steinhard Ltd,
32 Minerva Rd, London
NW10 6HJ.
081-965 0194

Steriseal
Steriseal Ltd,
Thornhill Rd, Redditch,
Worcs B98 9NL.
Redditch (0527) 64222

Sterling-Winthrop
Sterling-Winthrop Group Ltd,
Sterling-Winthrop House,
Onslow St, Guildford, Surrey
GU1 4YS.
Guildford (0483) 505515

Stiefel
Stiefel Laboratories (UK) Ltd,
Holtspur Lane, Wooburn Green,
High Wycombe,
Bucks HP10 0AU
High Wycombe (06285) 24966

Stuart
Stuart Pharmaceuticals,
Stuart House, 50 Alderley Rd,
Wilmslow, Cheshire SK9 1RE.
Wilmslow (0625) 535999
Also Medical Dept.
Alderley Edge (0625) 584848

Syntex
Syntex Pharmaceuticals Ltd,
Syntex House, St. Ives Rd,
Maidenhead, Berks SL6 1RD.
Maidenhead (0628) 33191

Texlastic
Texlastic Ltd,
Units 9–10, Abbey Business
Park, Friday St, Leicester
LE1 3BW.
Leicester (0533) 626682

Thackraycare
Thackraycare Ltd,
45–47 Great George St,
Leeds LS1 3BB.
Leeds (0532) 430028

Thames
Thames Laboratories Ltd,
The Old Blue School, 5 Lower
Square, Isleworth, Middx
TW7 6RL.
081-568 7071

Thornton & Ross
Thornton & Ross Ltd,
Linthwaite Laboratories,
Huddersfield HD7 5QH.
Huddersfield (0484) 842217

Tillotts
Tillotts Laboratories,
Contact Farmitalia Carlo Erba

Torbet
Torbet Laboratories Ltd,
Broughton House, 33 Earl St,
Maidstone, Kent ME14 1PF.
Maidstone (0622) 762269

Tosara
Tosara Products (UK) Ltd,
PO Box 5, 70 Picton Rd,
Liverpool L15 4NS.
051-733 4432

Townendale
Townendale Pharmaceuticals,
PO Box 53, Harrogate, North
Yorks HG1 5BD.
Harrogate (0423) 62593

Travenol
Contact Baxter

Typharm
Typharm Ltd,
14 Parkstone Rd, Poole,
Dorset BH15 2PG.
Ringwood (04254) 79711

UCB Pharma
UCB Pharma Ltd,
Star House, 60 Clarendon Rd,
Watford,
Herts WD1 1DJ.
Watford (0923) 248011

Ultra
Ultra Laboratories Ltd,
Trinity Trading Estate,
Tribune Drive, Sittingbourne,
Kent ME10 2PG.
Sittingbourne (0795) 70953

Ultrapharm
Ultrapharm Ltd,
PO Box 18, Henley-on-Thames,
Oxon RG9 2AW.
Henley-on-Thames (0491) 578016

Unigreg
Unigreg Ltd,
Enterprise House, 181 Garth Rd,
Morden, Surrey SM4 4LL.
081-330 1421

United Medical
United Medical,
Staines House, 158 High St,
Staines, Middx TW18 4AZ.
Staines (0784) 61533

Upjohn
Upjohn Ltd,
Fleming Way, Crawley, West
Sussex RH10 2NJ.
Crawley (0293) 31133

Vernon-Carus
Vernon-Carus Ltd,
Penwortham Mills, Preston,
Lancs PR1 9SN.
Preston (0772) 744493

Vestric
Vestric Ltd,
West Lane, Runcorn, Cheshire
WA7 2PE.
Runcorn (0928) 717070

Vitabiotics
Vitabiotics Ltd,
122 Mount Pleasant, Alperton,
Middx HA0 1UG.
081-903 5541

Vitalograph
Vitalograph Ltd,
Maids Moreton House,
Buckingham MK18 1SW.
Buckingham (0280) 816868

Wallace Mfg
Wallace Manufacturing Chemists
Ltd,
15 Cochrane Mews,
St John's Wood,
London NW8 6NY.
071-722 9166

Warne-Franklin
Warne-Franklin Ltd,
PO Box 138, Turnpike Rd, High
Wycombe, Bucks HP12 3NB.
High Wycombe (0494) 32761

WBP
WB Pharmaceuticals Ltd,
Contact Boehringer Ingelheim
Ltd.

Welfare Foods
see Nutricia.

Wellcome
Wellcome Medical Division,
The Wellcome Foundation Ltd,
Crewe Hall, Crewe, Cheshire
CW1 1UB.
Crewe (0270) 583151

Whitehall
Whitehall Laboratories,
11 Chenies St,
London WC1E 7ET.
071-636 8080

Windsor
Windsor Pharmaceuticals Ltd,
Contact Boehringer Ingelheim.

W-L
Warner Lambert UK Ltd,
Lambert Court, Chestnut Ave,
Eastleigh, Hants SO5 3ZQ.
Eastleigh (0703) 620500

Wyeth
Wyeth Laboratories,
Huntercombe Lane South,
Taplow, Maidenhead, Berks
SL6 0PH.
Burnham (06286) 4377

Zyma
Zyma (UK) Ltd,
Westhead, 10 West St, Alderley
Edge, Cheshire SK9 7XP.
Alderley Edge (0625) 584788

Index

Where an entry is followed by more than one page reference, the principal reference is printed in **bold** type. Proprietary (trade) names are printed in *italic* type.

G

M

N

U

V